Two Powerful Student Software Tools on One CD-ROM

Houghton Mifflin General Ledger Software for Windows provides the journals, ledgers, and reporting features students need to complete a variety of problems in the text (identified in the text by an icon). It also includes eight open problems for individual use.

The Accounting Transaction Tutor (ATT) reinforces understanding of financial accounting transactions in the first four chapters of the text* by helping students review important terms and accounting procedures. Specifically, students will be able to:

- Study more efficiently. Built-in diagnostic tests identify strengths and weaknesses and allow students to select exercises where they need the most help.

- Learn interactively. Interactive exercises prompt students to discover the correct answers on their own while working at their own study speed.

- Seek glossary help when needed. The Tutor provides access to key accounting terms and concepts.

- Get more out of this accounting text. The Accounting Transaction Tutor is linked to the text's learning objectives.

Also Available on the Student CD-ROM:

Selected Video Cases from the in-class video series can be viewed at home. The videos include Intel Corporation, Office Depot, Inc., Fermi National Accelerator Laboratory, Lotus Development Corporation, and UPS.

Web link to the Needles Accounting Resource Center Web Site.

*A full version of the software, including tutorials for all chapters of the text, is also available online.

Principles of Financial Accounting

Principles
of Financial
Accounting

2002©

Belverd E. Needles, Jr., Ph.D., C.P.A., C.M.A.
DePaul University

Marian Powers, Ph.D.
Northwestern University

Houghton Mifflin Company   Boston   New York

To Jennifer, Jeffrey, Annabelle, and Abigail

Senior Sponsoring Editor: Bonnie Binkert
Senior Development Editor: Margaret M. Kearney
Associate Project Editor: Claudine Bellanton
Senior Production/Design Coordinator: Sarah L. Ambrose
Senior Manufacturing Coordinator: Priscilla J. Bailey
Marketing Manager: Steven Mikels
Associate Editor: Damaris Curran

Cover Image: © Theo Rudnak

PHOTO CREDITS: page 3, © PhotoDisc, Inc.; page 4, Courtesy of Intel Corporation; page 47, © 2000 Corbis; page 91, © Vesey/Vanderburgh/International Stock; page 133, Courtesy of Dell Computer Corporation; page 173, © PhotoDisc, Inc.; page 174, Courtesy of Office Depot, Inc.; page 221, © 2000 Corbis; page 305, © PhotoDisc, Inc.; page 347, © PhotoDisc, Inc.; page 387, © PhotoDisc, Inc.; page 427, © PhotoDisc, Inc.; page 467, © PhotoDisc, Inc.; page 468, Courtesy of Fermi National Accelerator Laboratory; page 515, © Peter Christopher/Wonderfile; page 549, © Stockbyte/PictureQuest; page 587, © Andrew Sacks/ Tony Stone Images; page 588, Courtesy of Lotus Development Corporation; page 627, © Danny Lehman/Corbis; page 667, © PhotoDisc, Inc.; page 711, © PhotoDisc, Inc.; page 713, Courtesy of Goodyear Tire & Rubber Company; page 765, © 2000 Corbis.

The Toys "R" Us Annual Report for the year ended January 29, 2000, which appears at the end of Chapter 6 (pages 277–303) and in excerpts throughout the book, is reprinted by permission.

This book is written to provide accurate and authoritative information concerning the covered topics. It is not meant to take the place of professional advice.

Printed in the U.S.A.
Library of Congress Control Number: 2001089368
Student Text ISBN: 0-618-12423-3

23456789-VH-05 04 03 02 01

Brief Contents

Contents

Part One
Accounting as an Information System

Part Two
Extensions of the Basic Accounting Model

5 Merchandising Operations   172

6 Financial Reporting and Analysis   220

Part Three
Accounting Information Systems and Internal Control

7 Accounting Information Systems 304

8 Internal Control 346

Part Four
Measuring and Reporting Assets and Current Liabilities

9 Short-Term Liquid Assets 386

10 Inventories 426

11 Long-Term Assets 466

12 Current Liabilities 514

Part Five
Accounting for Partnerships and Corporations

13 Partnerships 548

14 Contributed Capital 586

15 The Corporate Income Statement and the Statement of Stockholders' Equity 626

Part Six
Special Reports and Analyses of Accounting Information

18   Financial Performance Evaluation   764

Preface

Principles of Financial Accounting, 2002©, is intended for the first course in accounting and as such is designed for students—both business and accounting majors—with no previous training in accounting or business. It is part of a well-integrated text and technology program that includes an array of print and electronic support materials for students and instructors.

We recognize that the majority of students taking the first accounting course are business and management majors rather than accounting majors; our goal therefore is to provide information for decision making throughout a student's career. We want our text to enable students to

- Recognize the value of accounting to their future careers regardless of their majors.
- Read and interpret internal and external financial reports and gain an understanding of their underlying concepts and techniques.
- Make intelligent decisions using internal and external accounting information.
- Analyze the effects of these decisions on the performance of a company.

A course that achieves these objectives will give students a valuable and realistic portrayal of accounting practices.

An Integrated Text and Technology Program

The business environment has changed, driven mostly by the trend toward globalization and the growing use of technology. We have therefore developed an integrated text and technology program dedicated to helping instructors stay on top of the change curve and to take advantage of the opportunities created by new instructional technologies. Whether an instructor wants to present a user or procedural orientation, incorporate new instructional strategies, develop students' core skills and competencies, or integrate technology into the classroom, the new 2002© text provides a total solution, making it the leading choice among instructors of first-year accounting courses.

Applying and Using Technology

The 2002© text incorporates a number of electronic teaching and learning solutions. Each student and instructor copy of the textbook comes with a CD containing a variety of resources. The HMClassPrep CD for instructors provides valuable support material, including the popular Course Manual of instructor resources and teaching strategies, PowerPoint slides, and other electronic tools. The Student CD, packaged with every text, includes the Accounting Transaction Tutor software for Chapters 1–4, the Houghton Mifflin General Ledger Software for Windows, and selected video cases. Both CDs include a web link to other valuable materials at the Needles Accounting Resource Center web site at http://college.hmco.com. In addition, the text includes a variety of Internet exercises with links to real company financial statements. ACE icons 🌑 in the end-of-chapter review sections of the text provide a visual link between the text and ACE, an interactive self-quizzing program available at our web site. Additional online tutoring help is available through the HM Web Tutor, powered by SmarThinking.

For faculty who want an online component to their accounting courses, we provide a rich array of resources, including text-specific content that is available either in Blackboard Course Cartridges or WebCT e-Packs. These customized course materials may be used to enhance a traditional classroom setting or as a complete distance learning solution.

Houghton Mifflin's Teaching Accounting Online course provides online support to faculty who want to thoughtfully integrate web-based technology into their classes. The course was designed by a group of accounting faculty led by Susan Crosson of Santa Fe Community College in Florida. She has also developed courses for WebCT and Blackboard learning platforms.

A Balanced Approach to Beginning Accounting

Because of changes in the business environment, the needs of today's students have changed. This change is reflected in the analysis by Robert Elliott, KPMG partner and recent chairman of the IACPA, who has identified the five stages of the "value chain" in accounting as shown below:*

I.	II.	III.	IV.	V.
Business Events >	Data >	Information >	Knowledge >	Decisions

Elliott argues that too much time is spent on low-value activities represented by the first three stages (I, II, III) as opposed to the high-value activities represented in stages IV and V. The first three stages focus on transactions and information processing, which in today's business environment are likely to be achieved through the use of technology. We agree that the focus of accounting education today should be on the higher-level activities (stages IV and V) that provide a foundation for decision making. We also believe that business majors, who make up the vast majority of beginning accounting students, will benefit from this approach in subsequent business courses and throughout their business careers. Although our text provides a basic knowledge of the more procedural activities associated with stages I to III, our primary focus is on high-value learning activities, providing a balance between the procedural or preparer side of accounting and a more user-oriented approach.

Our overall objective is to provide a flexible learning system. To achieve balance and flexibility, the 2002© text includes far less procedural detail and fewer "pencil pushing" assignments. Because our focus is on the application of concepts, we have substantially revised many chapters to reduce procedural detail. We have accomplished this by placing procedures that are not essential to conceptual understanding in supplemental objectives at the ends of the chapters. In the end-of-chapter assignments, we have scrutinized all exercises and problems with a view toward reducing the number of journal entries and the amount of posting required. In addition, we now employ T accounts more frequently as a form of analysis.

*W. Steve Albrecht and Robert J. Sack, *Accounting Education: Charting the Course Through a Perilous Future* (Sarasota, Fla.: American Accounting Association, 2000), p. 36.

A Strong Emphasis on Decision Making and Critical Thinking

The AICPA, IMA, and other business organizations have emphasized the importance of developing students' core competencies and basic skills in such areas as communication, critical thinking, analysis and decision making, ethics, the use of technology, and teamwork. The pedagogical system underlying *Principles of Financial Accounting, 2002©,* is based on a model that encompasses a growing group of instructional strategies designed to develop and strengthen a broad skill set in students. This model, which includes learning objectives, the teaching-learning cycle, cognitive levels of learning, and output skills, is described in the Course Manual, which is now available to instructors on the HMClassPrep CD. The Course Manual contains a Chapter Planning Matrix for each chapter to assist instructors in planning assignments to achieve learning objectives.

Just as accounting education has changed, today's students have changed also. Our new text edition is designed to accommodate a variety of learning styles to ensure student success. A few examples of the text's pedagogical features follow:

LEARNING OBJECTIVES Learning objectives are clearly stated at the beginning of each chapter. They are keyed to the chapter discussion and assignment material and are used throughout the text and ancillary package. They provide a valuable "road map" for students.

CHAPTER 1 "USER'S MANUAL" New, annotated Chapter 1 provides a built-in "user's manual" to help students understand the purpose and value of the pedagogical framework and how to use it to their advantage.

COLOR SCHEME A consistent color scheme throughout the text presents inputs to the accounting system (source documents) in gold, the processing of accounting data (working papers and accounting forms) in green, and outputs of the system (financial and management reports) in purple.

KEY RATIOS Key ratios are integrated throughout the text at appropriate points to emphasize the use of accounting information in decision making and the importance this information plays in performance evaluation. These ratios (identified by the Key Ratio icon %) are usually introduced in the "management issues" section at the beginning of most chapters. We bring all the ratios together in a comprehensive financial analysis of Sun Microsystems, Inc., in Chapter 18.

CASH FLOWS We emphasize the effect of business activities on cash flow throughout the text. After introducing the statement of cash flows in Chapter 1, we point out in various subsequent chapters the difference between income measurement and cash flow, and we reinforce understanding through a variety of end-of-chapter assignments. A Cash Flow icon highlights these discussions in the text.

Relevant Real-World Coverage

We have taken many steps to increase the real-world emphasis of the text in order to reflect current business practice in a way that is relevant and exciting for students.

REAL COMPANIES We use information from the annual reports of real companies and from business publications, such as *Business Week, Forbes,* and *The Wall Street Journal,* to enhance students' appreciation of the usefulness and relevance of accounting information. In addition, we use more than 100 publicly held companies as examples, and we have substantially increased the number of real companies appearing in the assignment materials. A Hot Links to Real Companies icon or a CD-ROM icon identifies these companies. Our Needles Accounting Resource Center Student web site provides direct links to the web pages of most of these companies.

ACTUAL FINANCIAL STATEMENTS We have incorporated examples from the annual reports of real companies in both the text and assignment material. Chapter 6 presents the financial statements of Dell Computer in graphic form using the Fingraph® Financial Analyst™ CD that accompanies this book. A supplement to Chapter 6 contains a section entitled "How to Read an Annual Report," as well as the actual annual report of Toys "R" Us. As noted earlier, the comprehensive financial analysis in Chapter 18 features the financial statements of Sun Microsystems, Inc. These are only a few examples of the scores of other well-known companies featured in the text.

DECISION POINTS Every chapter begins with a Decision Point. Based on excerpts from real companies' annual reports or from articles in the business press, Decision Points present a situation requiring a decision by managers or other accounting information users; they also demonstrate how the decision can be made using accounting information.

FOCUS ON BUSINESS These boxes appear throughout each chapter and emphasize business strategy as it relates to four key themes:

- Focus on Business Ethics
- Focus on Business Practice
- Focus on Business Technology
- Focus on International Business

INTERNATIONAL ACCOUNTING Among the many foreign companies mentioned in the text and assignments are Yamaha Motor Company, Ltd. (Japanese), Glaxo-Wellcome (British), Philips Electronics, N.V. and Heineken N.V. (Dutch), Roche Group (Swiss), Nokia (Finnish), and Goslar Corporation (German).

REAL-WORLD GRAPHIC ILLUSTRATIONS Graphs, tables, and exhibits illustrating the relationship of actual business practices to chapter topics are a regular feature of the book. Many of these illustrations are based on data from studies of 600 annual reports published in *Accounting Trends and Techniques.* Beginning with Chapter 6, most chapters include a graph that shows various ratios for selected industries based on Dun & Bradstreet data. Service industry examples include advertising and interstate trucking companies. Manufacturing industry examples include pharmaceutical and tableware companies.

GOVERNMENTAL AND NOT-FOR-PROFIT ORGANIZATIONS Acknowledging the importance of governmental and not-for-profit organizations in our society, we include discussions and examples of these organizations at appropriate points in the text.

Expanded Assignment Materials Geared to Flexibility

In answer to the demand for a more sophisticated skill set for students and greater pedagogical choice for faculty members, we have expanded the variety of assignments and accompanying materials as described in the following sections.

Video Cases

Five videos, each accompanied by an in-text case, work equally well as individual or group assignments, and all include a written critical thinking component. Each video case, indicated by a video icon ▣, serves as an introduction to the chapter in which it is found.

- *Intel Corporation* (Chapter 1) examines the business goals of liquidity and profitability and the business activities of financing, investing, and operating.
- *Office Depot, Inc.* (Chapter 5), discusses the merchandising company, the merchandising income statement, and the concept of the operating cycle.
- *Fermi National Accelerator Laboratory* (Chapter 11) demonstrates the importance of long-term assets to a unique scientific laboratory.
- *Lotus Development Corporation* (Chapter 14) tells the history of Lotus from its beginning as a small start-up company through its growth to one of America's most successful companies and finally to its sale to IBM. The case emphasizes Lotus's equity financing needs along the way.
- *Goodyear Tire & Rubber Company* (Chapter 17) describes the vision and objectives of the world's largest tire and rubber company and how Goodyear will need strong cash flows to carry out its objectives.

The Annual Report Project

Because real companies' annual reports are rapidly becoming the most popular topic of term projects in the introductory accounting course, the Supplement to Chapter 6 provides a suggested annual report project that we have used in our classes for several years. To allow for projects of varied comprehensiveness, we have developed four assignment options, including the use of Fingraph® Financial Analyst™ data-base software.

Building Your Knowledge Foundation

This end-of-chapter section consists of a variety of questions, exercises, and problems designed to develop basic knowledge, comprehension, and application of the concepts and techniques presented in the chapter.

Questions (Q) Fifteen to 24 review questions that cover the essential topics of the chapter.

Short Exercises (SE) Approximately ten very brief exercises suitable for classroom use.

Exercises (E) An average of 15 single-topic exercises that stress application.

Problems (P) At least five extensive applications of chapter topics, often covering more than one learning objective and often containing writing components. All problems can be worked on our Excel Templates CD; some can be solved using our General Ledger Software for Windows.

Alternate Problems (P) An alternative set of the most popular problems, based on our study of users' syllabi.

The assignments most suitable for computer applications are marked with the following icons:

 Ledger icons indicate problems that can be solved using our General Ledger Software for Windows.

Spreadsheet icons indicate problems that can be solved using our Excel Templates CD.

Expanding Your Critical Thinking, Communication, and Interpersonal Skills

Recognizing that students need to be better prepared to communicate clearly, both in written and oral formats, we have included ten or more cases that deal with skills development (SD) and financial reporting and analysis (FRA). These cases are usually based on real companies. All require critical thinking and communication skills in the form of writing. At least one assignment in each chapter requires students to practice good business communication skills by writing a memorandum reporting results and offering recommendations. In addition, all cases are suitable for development of interpersonal skills through group activities. We have designated selected cases as being especially appropriate for group activities and for these have provided specific instructions for applying a group methodology. We use icons to identify these cases, as well as to provide guidance in the best use of other assignments. A list of these icons follows.

 Cash Flow icons indicate assignments dealing with cash flow; they also indicate text discussions of cash flow.

 CD-ROM icons indicate assignments designed to be worked with the Fingraph® Financial Analyst™ CD.

 Communication icons identify assignments designed to help students develop their ability to understand and communicate accounting information successfully.

 Critical Thinking icons indicate assignments intended to strengthen students' critical thinking skills.

Ethics icons identify assignments that address ethical issues.

 General Ledger icons indicate problems that can be solved using the Houghton Mifflin General Ledger Software for Windows.

 Group Activity icons identify assignments appropriate for groups or teamwork.

Hot Links to Real Companies icons indicate companies whose annual reports can be accessed by direct link from the Needles Accounting Resource Center web site. These icons are used in text discussions as well as in assignments.

 International icons indicate international company cases.

Internet icons designate assignments featuring use of the Internet.

 Key Ratio icons indicate the presence of financial analysis ratios in both the text and assignments.

 Memorandum icons point to problems and cases that require students to write short business memorandums.

 Spreadsheet icons indicate problems that can be solved using the Excel Templates CD.

Each Skills Development (SD) assignment has a specific purpose:

CONCEPTUAL ANALYSIS   These short cases address conceptual accounting issues and are based on real companies and situations. They are designed so that a written solution is appropriate, but they may also be used in other communication modes.

ETHICAL DILEMMA   Recognizing the need for accounting and business students to be exposed in all their courses to ethical considerations, we have included in every chapter a short case, often based on a real company, in which students must address an ethical dilemma directly related to the chapter content.

RESEARCH ACTIVITY   These exercises enhance student learning and participation in the classroom by acquainting students with business periodicals, annual reports and business references, and resources in the library and on the Internet. Some exercises are designed to improve students' interviewing and observation skills through field activities at actual businesses. An icon in the margin indicates activities that can be researched on the Internet.

DECISION-MAKING PRACTICE   Acting as decision makers—managers, investors, analysts, or creditors—students are asked to extract relevant data from a case, make computations as necessary, and arrive at a decision.

Cases in financial reporting and analysis (FRA) sharpen students' ability to comprehend and analyze financial and nonfinancial data:

INTERPRETING FINANCIAL REPORTS   These short cases are abstracted from business articles and the annual reports of well-known corporations and organizations, such as Netscape Communications Corporation, Sun Microsystems, Cisco Systems, RJR Nabisco, Mellon Bank, Charles Schwab, and Amazon.com. They require students to extract relevant data, make computations, and interpret the results.

INTERNATIONAL COMPANY   These exercises include companies from around the world. The focus is on companies that have an accounting experience compatible with chapter content.

TOYS "R" US ANNUAL REPORT   The actual Toys "R" Us Annual Report, reproduced in the Supplement to Chapter 6, provides the basis for these analytical cases.

FINGRAPH® FINANCIAL ANALYST™   These cases may be worked in conjunction with the Fingraph® Financial Analyst™ data-base software. This CD includes web links to the annual reports of more than 20 well-known companies. Students utilize the software to analyze the financial statements of the companies.

INTERNET CASE   Each chapter of the text now features an Internet case, which asks students to research a topic on the Internet, answer critical and analytical thinking questions, and then prepare either a written or oral report of their findings.

FINANCIAL ANALYSIS CASES   Also accompanying the text are a series of comprehensive financial analysis cases that may be integrated throughout the course after Chapter 5, or they may be used as capstone cases for the entire course. The first, "General Mills, Inc., Annual Report: A Decision Case in Financial Analysis," uses the actual financial statements of General Mills Corporation. The other cases, "Heartland Airways, Inc.," and "Richard Home Centers, Inc.," present complete annual reports for an airline company and a home improvement retailing chain. They will guide students through a complete financial analysis. Although these cases may be assigned individually, they also make excellent group assignments.

Readable, Accessible Text

Growing numbers of students who take the financial accounting course are from foreign countries, and English is a second language for them. To meet their needs fully, we as instructors must be aware of how the complexities and nuances of English, particularly business English, may hinder these students' understanding.

Each chapter of *Principles of Financial Accounting*, 2002©, has been reviewed by business instructors who teach English as a Second Language (ESL) courses and English for Special Purposes courses, as well as by students taking these classes. With their assistance and advice, we have taken the following measures to ensure that the text is accessible.

- *Word Choice:* We replaced words and phrases that were unfamiliar to ESL students with ones they more readily recognize and understand. For instance, we substituted *raise* for *bolster*, *require* for *call for*, and *available* for *on hand*.
- *Length:* Because short, direct sentences are more easily comprehended than sentences containing multiple clauses, we paid strict attention to the length and grammatical complexity of our sentences.
- *Examples:* Examples reinforce concepts discussed and help make the abstract concrete. We have therefore added many simple, straightforward examples.

Supplementary Support Materials

Supplementary Learning Aids

Our goal is to provide a complete supplemental learning system, including manual and technology applications for computer, CD-ROM, videotape, and the Internet. Supplementary learning aids include the following:

NEW! Student CD
NEW! Needles Accounting Resource Center Student Web Site
Fingraph® Financial Analyst™ CD
NEW! HM Web Tutor, powered by SmarThinking
NEW! Peachtree 8.0 Educational Version
Working Papers for Exercises and Problems
NEW! Excel Templates CD
Study Guide
Houghton Mifflin Brief Accounting Dictionary

Financial Practice Cases

Collegiate Ts
College Words and Sounds Store, Fifth Edition
Micro-Tec, Fifth Edition

Instructor's Support Materials

Instructor's Annotated Edition
Instructor's Solutions Manual
NEW! HMClassPrep Instructor CD
NEW! Needles Accounting Resource Center Instructor Web Site
Test Bank with Achievement Test Masters and Answers
HMTesting
Solutions Transparencies
NEW! Video Cases
NEW! Blackboard Course Cartridges
NEW! WebCT e-Packs
NEW! Teaching Accounting Online

Acknowledgments

Preparing an accounting text is a long and demanding project that cannot really succeed without the help of one's colleagues. We are grateful to numerous professional colleagues and students for their many constructive comments on the text. Unfortunately, any attempt to list all who have helped means that some who have contributed might inadvertently be slighted by omission. Some attempt, however, must be made to mention those who have been closely involved.

We wish to express our deep appreciation to our colleagues at DePaul University who have been extremely supportive and encouraging. We also wish to thank our colleagues at Lake Forest Graduate School of Management for their input and support.

The thoughtful and meticulous work of Edward H. Julius (California Lutheran University) is reflected not only in the Study Guide and Test Bank but in many other ways as well. We also want to thank Debbie Luna (El Paso Community College) for her work on the Study Guide, and Marion Taube (University of Pittsburgh) and Mark Dawson (La Roche College) for their work on the Test Bank.

Also important to the quality of the book is the work of Mary Cavanagh and J. Sophie Buchanan, who helped prepare the manuscript, and Cynthia Fostle and Jacquie Commanday, who developed the manuscript. We greatly appreciate the supportive collaboration of our senior sponsoring editor, Bonnie Binkert. We benefited from the ideas and guidance of senior development editor Margaret Kearney, associate editor Damaris Curran, associate project editor Claudine Bellanton, and editorial assistant James Dimock. We also extend thanks to Sarah Evans for her careful oversight of the production of this text.

Others who have been supportive and have had an impact on this book through their reviews and class testing are:

Kym Anderson	
Gregory D. Barnes	Clarion University
Charles M. Betts	Delaware Technical & Community College
Michael C. Blue	Bloomsburg University
Cynthia Bolt-Lee	The Citadel
Gary R. Bower	Community College of Rhode Island
Lee Cannell	El Paso Community College
Lloyd Carroll	The Borough of Manhattan Community College
Naranjan Chipalkatti	Ohio Northern University
Stanley Chu	The Borough of Manhattan Community College
John D. Cunha	University of California—Berkeley
Mark W. Dawson	La Roche College
Patricia A. Doherty	Boston University
Lizabeth England	American Language Academy
David Fetyko	Kent State University
Roxanne Gooch	Cameron University
Christine Uber Grosse	The American Graduate School of International Management
Dennis A. Gutting	Orange County Community College
Edward H. Julius	California Lutheran University
Howard A. Kanter	DePaul University
Debbie Luna	El Paso Community College
Kevin McClure	ESL Language Center
George McGowan	
Anita R. McKie	University of South Carolina—Aiken
Gail A. Mestas	
Michael F. Monahan	
Janette Moody	The Citadel
Jenine Moscove	
Glenn Owen	Alan Hancock College
Debra Parker-Fleming	Ohio Dominican College
Beth Brooks Patel	University of California—Berkeley
Yvonne Phangi-Hatami	The Borough of Manhattan Community College
LaVonda Ramey	Schoolcraft College
Roberta Rettner	American Ways
Donald Shannon	DePaul University
S. Murray Simons	Northeastern University
Ellen L. Sweatt	DeKalb College—Dunwoody
Marion Taube	University of Pittsburgh
Rita Taylor	University of Cincinnati
Robert G. Unterman	Glendale Community College
Stan Weikert	College of the Canyons
Kay Westerfield	University of Oregon
Carol Yacht	
Glenn Allen Young	Tulsa Junior College

To the Student

How to Study Accounting Successfully

The introductory accounting course is fundamental to the business curriculum and to success in the business world beyond college. Whether you are majoring in accounting or in another business discipline, it is one of the most important classes you will take. The course has multiple purposes because its students have diverse interests, backgrounds, and purposes for taking it. What are your goals in studying accounting? Being clear about your goals can contribute to your success in this course.

Success in this class also depends on your desire to learn and your willingness to work hard. And it depends on your understanding of how the text complements the way your instructor teaches and the way you learn. A familiarity with how this text is structured will help you to study more efficiently, make better use of classroom time, and improve your performance on examinations and other assignments.

To be successful in the business world after you graduate, you will need a broad set of skills, which may be summarized as follows:

TECHNICAL/ANALYTICAL SKILLS   A major objective of your accounting course is to give you a firm grasp of the essential business and accounting terminology and techniques that you will need to succeed in a business environment. With this foundation, you then can begin to develop the higher-level perception skills that will help you acquire further knowledge on your own.

An even more crucial objective of this course is to help you develop analytical skills that will allow you to evaluate data. An important aspect of analytical skills is the ability to use technology effectively in making analyses. Well-developed analytical and decision-making skills are among the professional skills most highly valued by employers and will serve you well throughout your academic and professional careers.

COMMUNICATION SKILLS   Another skill highly prized by employers is the ability to express oneself in a manner that others correctly understand. This can include writing skills, speaking skills, and presentation skills. Communication skills are developed through particular tasks and assignments and are improved through constructive criticism. Reading skills and listening skills support the direct communication skills.

INTERPERSONAL SKILLS   Effective interaction between two people requires a solid foundation of interpersonal skills. The success of such interaction depends on empathy, or the ability to identify with and understand the problems, concerns, and motives of others. Leadership, supervision, and interviewing skills also facilitate a professional's interaction with others.

PERSONAL/SELF SKILLS   Personal/self skills form the foundation for growth in the use of all other skills. To succeed, a professional must take initiative, possess self-confidence, show independence, and be ethical in all areas of life. Personal/self skills can be enhanced significantly by the formal learning process and by peers and mentors who provide models upon which one can build. Accounting is just one course in your entire curriculum, but it can play an important role in your skill development. Your instructor is interested in helping you gain both a knowledge of accounting and the more general skills you will need to succeed in the business world. The following sections describe how you can get the most out of this course.

The Teaching/Learning Cycle™

Both teaching and learning have natural, parallel, and mutually compatible cycles. This teaching/learning cycle, as shown in Figure 1, interacts with the basic structure of learning objectives in this text.

THE TEACHING CYCLE   The inner (tan) circle in Figure 1 shows the steps an instructor takes in teaching a chapter. Your teacher *assigns* material, *presents* the subject in lecture, *explains* by going over assignments and answering questions, *reviews* the subject prior to an exam, and *assesses* your knowledge and understanding using examinations and other means of evaluation.

THE LEARNING CYCLE   Moving outward, the next circle (green) in Figure 1 shows the steps you should take in studying a chapter. You should *preview* the material, *read* the chapter, *apply* your understanding by working the assignments, *review* the chapter, and *recall* and *demonstrate* your knowledge and understanding of the material in examinations and other assessments.

INTEGRATED LEARNING OBJECTIVES   Your textbook supports the teaching/learning cycle through the use of integrated learning objectives. Learning objectives are simply statements of what you should be able to do after you have completed a chapter. In Figure 1, the outside (blue) circle shows how learning objectives are integrated into your text and other study aids and how they interact with the teaching/learning cycle.

1. Learning objectives listed at the beginning of each chapter aid your teacher in making assignments and help you preview the chapter.
2. Each learning objective is referenced in the margin of the text at the point where that subject is covered to assist your teacher in presenting the material and to help you organize your thoughts as you read the material.
3. Every exercise, problem, and case in the end-of-chapter assignments shows the applicable learning objective(s) so you can refer to the text if you need help.
4. A summary of the key points for each learning objective, a list of new concepts and terms referenced by learning objectives, and a review problem covering key learning objectives assist you in reviewing each chapter. The Study Guide, also organized by learning objectives, provides additional review.

WHY STUDENTS SUCCEED   Students succeed in their accounting course when they coordinate their personal learning cycle with their instructor's cycle. Students who do a good job of previewing their assignments, reading the chapters before the instructor is ready to present them, preparing homework assignments before they are discussed in class, and reviewing carefully will ultimately achieve their potential on exams. Those who get out of phase with their instructor, for whatever reason, will do poorly or fail. To ensure that your learning cycle is synchronized with your instructor's teaching cycle, check your study habits against the following suggestions.

Previewing the Chapter

1. Read the learning objectives at the beginning of the chapter. These learning objectives specifically describe what you should be able to do after completing the chapter.

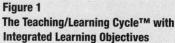

Figure 1
The Teaching/Learning Cycle™ with Integrated Learning Objectives

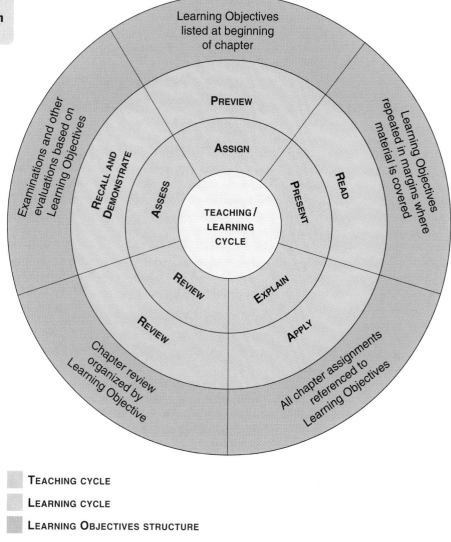

■ **TEACHING CYCLE**

■ **LEARNING CYCLE**

■ **LEARNING OBJECTIVES STRUCTURE**

2. Study your syllabus. Know where you are in the course and where you are going. Know the rules of the course.

3. Realize that in an accounting course, each assignment builds on previous ones. If you do poorly in Chapter 1, you may have difficulty in Chapter 2 and be lost in Chapter 3.

Reading the Chapter

1. As you read each chapter, be aware of the learning objectives in the margins. They will tell you why the material is relevant.

2. Allow yourself plenty of time to read the text. Accounting is a technical subject. Accounting books are so full of information that almost every sentence is important.

3. Strive to understand not only how each procedure is done, but also why it is done. Accounting is logical and requires reasoning. If you understand why something is done in accounting, there is little need to memorize.

4. Relate each new topic to its learning objective and be able to explain it in your own words.

5. Be aware of colors as you read. They are designed to help you understand the text. (For handy reference, the use of color is also explained on the back cover of the book.)
   Gold: All source documents and inputs are in gold.
   Green: All accounting forms, working papers, and accounting processes are shown in green.
   Purple: All financial statements, the output or final product of the accounting process, are shown in purple.

6. If there is something you do not understand, prepare specific questions for your instructor. Pinpoint the topic or concept that confuses you. Some students keep a notebook of points with which they have difficulty.

Applying the Chapter

1. In addition to understanding why each procedure is done, you must be able to do it yourself by working exercises, problems, and cases. Accounting is a "do-it-yourself" course.

2. Read assignments and instructions carefully. Each assignment has a specific purpose. The wording is precise, and a clear understanding of it will save time and improve your performance. Acquaint yourself with the end-of-chapter assignment materials by reading the description of them in the Preface.

3. Try to work exercises, problems, and cases without referring to their discussions in the chapter. If you cannot work an assignment without looking in the chapter, you will not be able to work a similar problem on an exam. After you have tried on your own, refer to the chapter (based on the learning objective reference) and check your answer. Try to understand any mistakes you may have made.

4. Be neat and orderly. Sloppy calculations, messy papers, and general carelessness cause most errors on accounting assignments.

5. Allow plenty of time to work the chapter assignments. You will find that assignments seem harder and that you make more errors when you are feeling pressed for time.

6. Keep up with your class. Check your work against the solutions presented in class. Find your mistakes. Be sure you understand the correct solutions.

7. Note the part of each exercise, problem, or case that causes you difficulty so you can ask for help.

8. Attend class. Most instructors design classes to help you and to answer your questions. Absence from even one class can hurt your performance.

Reviewing the Chapter

1. Read the summary of learning objectives in the chapter review. Be sure you know the definitions of all the words in the review of concepts and terminology.

2. Review all assigned exercises, problems, and cases. Know them cold. Be sure you can work the assignments without the aid of the book.

3. Determine the learning objectives for which most of the problems were assigned. They refer to topics that your instructor is most likely to emphasize on an exam. Scan the text for such learning objectives and pay particular attention to the examples and illustrations.

4. Look for and scan other similar assignments that cover the same learning objectives. They may be helpful on an exam.

5. Review quizzes. Similar material will often appear on longer exams.

6. Attend any labs or visit any tutors your school provides, or see your instructor during office hours to get assistance. Be sure to have specific questions ready.

Taking Examinations

1. Arrive at class early so you can get the feel of the room and make a last-minute review of your notes.

2. Have plenty of sharp pencils and your calculator (if allowed) ready.

3. Review the exam quickly when it is handed out to get an overview of your task. Start with a part you know. It will give you confidence and save time.

4. Allocate your time to the various parts of the exam, and stick to your schedule. Every exam has time constraints. You need to move ahead and make sure you attempt all parts of the exam.

5. Read the questions carefully. Some may not be exactly like your homework assignments. They may approach the material from a slightly different angle to test your understanding and ability to reason, rather than your ability to memorize.

6. To avoid unnecessary errors, be neat, use good form, and show calculations.

7. Relax. If you have followed the above guidelines, your effort will be rewarded.

Preparing Other Assignments

1. Understand the assignment. Written assignments, term papers, computer projects, oral presentations, case studies, group activities, individual field trips, video critiques, and other activities are designed to enhance skills beyond your technical knowledge. It is essential to know exactly what your instructor expects. Know the purpose, audience, scope, and expected end product.

2. Allow plenty of time. "Murphy's Law" applies to such assignments: If anything can go wrong, it will.

3. Prepare an outline of each report, paper, or presentation. A project that is done well always has a logical structure.

4. Write a rough draft of each paper and report, and practice each presentation. Professionals always try out their ideas in advance and thoroughly rehearse their presentations. Good results are not accomplished by accident.

5. Make sure that each paper, report, or presentation is of professional quality. Instructors appreciate attention to detail and polish. A good rule of thumb is to ask yourself: Would I give this work to my boss?

About the Authors

Central to the success of any accounting text is the expertise of its author team. This team has a wealth of classroom teaching experience, relevant business insight, and pedagogical expertise, as well as first-hand knowledge of today's students.

BELVERD E. NEEDLES, JR., PhD, CPA, CMA

Belverd Needles is the Andersen Distinguished Professor of Accounting at De Paul University. During his more than 30 years of teaching beginning accounting students, he has been an acknowledged innovator in accounting education. He has won teaching and education awards from DePaul University, the American Accounting Association, the Illinois CPA Society, the American Institute of CPAs, and the national honorary society Beta Alpha Psi. The Conference on Accounting Education, started by Dr. Needles and sponsored by Houghton Mifflin, is in its 17th year; it has helped more than 2,000 beginning accounting instructors improve their teaching. Dr. Needles is editor of the *Accounting Instructors' Report*, a newsletter now in its 18th year that thousands of accounting teachers rely on for new ideas in accounting education.

MARIAN POWERS, PhD

With more than 20 years of teaching experience, Marian Powers has taught beginning accounting at every level, from large lecture halls of 250 students to small classes of graduate students at the Kellogg Graduate School of Management at Northwestern University, the University of Illinois at Chicago, and the Lake Forest Graduate School of Management. She is a dynamic teacher who incorporates a variety of instructional strategies designed to broaden students' skills and experiences in critical thinking, group interaction, and communication. Consistently, Dr. Powers receives the highest ratings from students. She also brings practical experience to her students, including examples of how business managers at all levels use and evaluate financial information. In recent years, Dr. Powers has concentrated on executive education at the Allen Center at Northwestern University. She has taught thousands of executives from leading companies around the world how to read and analyze the financial statements of their own companies and those of their competitors.

A Special Tribute

HENRY "HANK" R. ANDERSON, PhD, CPA, CMA
Henry R. Anderson, co-author of earlier editions of this book and our dear friend, retired in 1999 after a long and highly successful career. We will always value the lasting contribution Hank made to this book and will miss his participation in author deliberations.

Hank Anderson is KPMG Peat Marwick Professor Emeritus of Accounting at the University of Central Florida. He has served as Director of UCF's School of Accounting; as Dean of the School of Business Administration & Economics at California State University, Fullerton; and as Assistant Director of the research staff of the Cost Accounting Standards Board, Washington, D.C. He was National President of Beta Alpha Psi in 1981–1982, and won the California CPA Society's 1981 Faculty Excellence Award and the 1987 Florida Excellence in Teaching Award from the College of Business at the University of Central Florida. He has been very active in the Institute of Management Accountants and has served on many committees of the American Accounting Association, the American Institute of Certified Public Accountants, and the Florida Institute of CPAs. Hank is a graduate of Augustana College and the University of Missouri at Columbia. He and his wife Sue have retired to California, where he owns and farms a successful vineyard.

JAMES C. CALDWELL, PhD, CPA   James C. Caldwell, our friend and co-author of previous editions of this book, passed away in 1999 after a battle with cancer. Jim never failed to challenge the status quo or to see methods of improving our series of accounting books. We will miss his intellectual contribution, but we will miss his friendship most of all.

Jim Caldwell was an accounting professor at Texas Tech University and held important positions on two national committees on accounting education with the National Association of Accountants and the Management Accounting Association. Most recently, he was the Office Managing Partner with Andersen Consulting (now Accenture) in Dallas/Fort Worth. He was also Change Management Leadership Partner of the Andersen Consulting National Energy Practice. Jim designed and implemented numerous training programs for major companies. He also served in a lead consultant role in managing major transformational change for clients. Jim received his Ph.D. from the University of Alabama. Andersen Consulting has established an award in his honor. This award, the Human Performance Award, is awarded annually to the individual in the global firm of Andersen Consulting who best exemplifies leadership, stewardship, and client values.

Check Figures

These check figures provide a key number in the solutions to the problems at the end of each chapter.

Chapter 1 Problems
P 1. Total Assets: $8,750
P 2. Total Assets: $11,530
P 3. Total Assets: $8,060
P 4. Total Assets: $57,500
P 5. Total Assets: $4,620
P 6. Total Assets: $10,420
P 7. Total Assets: $70,600
P 8. Total Assets: $48,750

Chapter 2 Problems
P 1. No check figure
P 2. Trial Balance: $21,100
P 3. Trial Balance: $22,780
P 4. Trial Balance: $10,540
P 5. Trial Balance: $56,960
P 6. No check figure
P 7. Trial Balance: $23,100
P 8. Trial Balance: $10,880

Chapter 3 Problems
P 1. No check figure
P 2. No check figure
P 3. Adjusted Trial Balance: $121,792
P 4. Adjusted Trial Balance: $16,436
P 5. Adjusted Trial Balance: $26,040
P 6. No check figure
P 7. No check figure
P 8. Adjusted Trial Balance: $106,167

Chapter 4 Problems
P 1. Total Assets: $96,929
P 2. Total Assets: $113,616
P 3. May Adjusted Trial Balance: $9,366; Total Assets: $8,151; Post-Closing Trial Balance: $8,186; June Adjusted Trial Balance: $9,580; Total Assets: $8,087; Post-Closing Trial Balance: $8,157
P 4. Total Assets: $9,897
P 5. Total Assets: $350,868
P 6. Total Assets: $1,255,600
P 7. Total Assets: $6,943
P 8. Total Assets: $247,148
Comprehensive Problem: Adjusted Trial Balance Totals: $30,990; Total Assets: $25,810; Net Income: $3,960

Chapter 5 Problems
P 1. Net Income: $15,435
P 2. No check figure

P 3. Net Income: $3,435
P 4. No check figure
P 5. Net Income: $30,105; Total Assets: $199,008
P 6. Net Income: $2,440; Total Assets: $533,590
P 7. No check figure
P 8. Net Income: $10,522
P 9. No check figure
P 10. Net Income: $23,941
P 11. No check figure

Chapter 6 Problems
P 1. No check figure
P 2. Net Income: $127,252
P 3. Total Assets: $794,286
P 4. Current Ratio: 20x4, 2.0; 20x3, 2.6; Return on Assets: 20x4, 14.8%; 20x3, 13.2%
P 5. Net Income: $29,130; Total Assets: $367,740
P 6. No check figure
P 7. Net Income (Loss): ($860)
P 8. Current Ratio: 20x4, 2.3; 20x3, 3.5; Return on Assets: 20x4, 12.5%; 20x3, 11.0%

Chapter 7 Problems
P 1. Lamb Company's Total Accounts Receivable: $3,020; Lamb Company's Total Accounts Payable: $2,600
P 2. Cash total in cash receipts journal: $66,968; Cash total in cash payments journal: $28,644
P 3. Accounts Payable total: $16,464
P 4. Trial Balance: $42,292
P 5. Trial Balance: $30,558
P 6. Dune Company's Total Accounts Receivable: $870; Dune Company's Total Accounts Payable: $2,100
P 7. Cash total in cash receipts journal: $23,340; Cash total in cash payments journal: $17,012
P 8. Trial Balance: $45,808

Chapter 8 Problems
P 1. Adjusted book balance: $27,242.80
P 2. Adjusted book balance: $21,608
P 3. No check figure
P 4. No check figure
P 5. Total Unpaid Vouchers: $3,159
P 6. No check figure
P 7. Adjusted book balance: $74,736.64
P 8. No check figure

Chapter 9 Problems
P 1. Short-Term Investments (at market): $903,875
P 2. No check figure
P 3. Amount of adjustment: $9,533

P 4. No check figure
P 5. Short-Term Investments (at market): $354,000
P 6. No check figure
P 7. Amount of adjustment: $73,413
P 8. No check figure

Chapter 10 Problems
P 1. 1. Cost of goods available for sale: $10,560,000
P 2. 1. Cost of goods sold: June, $19,320; July, $44,237
P 3. 1. Cost of goods sold: June, $19,160; July, $43,982
P 4. Estimated inventory shortage: at cost, $42,431; at retail, $56,200
P 5. Estimated destroyed inventory: $730,000
P 6. Cost of goods available for sale: $315,960
P 7. 1. Cost of goods sold: March, $4,578; April, $15,457
P 8. 1. Cost of goods sold: March, $4,560; April, $15,424

Chapter 11 Problems
P 1. Totals: Land: $426,212; Land Improvements: $166,560; Buildings: $833,940; Machinery: $1,262,640; Expense: $18,120
P 2. 1. Depreciation, Year 3: a. $54,250; b. $81,375; c. $53,407
P 3. Total Depreciation Expense: 20x1: $71,820; 20x2: $103,092; 20x3: $84,072
P 4. a. Gain on Sale of Computer: $6,000; b. Loss on Sale of Computer: $3,000; c. Gain on Exchange of Computer: $4,500; d. Loss on Exchange of Computer: $2,000; e. no gain recognized; f. Loss on Exchange of Computer: $2,000; g. Computer (new): $31,500; h. Computer (new): $38,000
P 5. Part A: d. Leasehold Amortization Expense: $6,000; e. Leasehold Improvements Amortization Expense: $13,500; Part B: c. Patent Amortization Expense: $148,000; d. Loss on Write-off of Patent: $1,184,000
P 6. Totals: Land: $723,900; Land Improvements: $142,000; Building: $1,383,600; Equipment: $210,800
P 7. 1. Depreciation, Year 3: a. $330,000; b. $264,000; c. $180,000
P 8. Total Depreciation Expense: 20x2: $26,560; 20x3: $37,520; 20x4: $31,456

Chapter 12 Problems
P 1. Total Current Liabilities: $36,988.20
P 2. No check figure
P 3. 1.b. Estimated Product Warranty Liability: $10,800
P 4. 3. Payroll Taxes Expense: $31,938.70
P 5. Net Pay, total: $8,176.32
P 6. No check figure
P 7. 1.b. Estimated Product Warranty Liability: $10,080
P 8. 3. Payroll Taxes Expense: $44,221.38

Chapter 13 Problems
P 1. 2.f. Chan's share of loss, 20x1: $11,000
P 2. 1. Gregory's share of income: $112,500
P 3. d. Luke, Capital: $94,000
P 4. 1. Cash distribution to Dawn: $208,800
P 5. Cash distribution to Stanford: $108,000
P 6. 3. Gloria's share of income: $16,080
P 7. d. Maureen, Capital: $96,000
P 8. Cash distribution to Nguyen: ($168,000)

Chapter 14 Problems
P 1. 2. Total Stockholders' Equity: $1,488,000
P 2. 1. 20x3 Total dividends: Preferred, $420,000; Common, $380,000
P 3. No check figure
P 4. 2. Total Stockholders' Equity: $1,446,900
P 5. 2. Total Stockholders' Equity: $330,375
P 6. 2. Total Stockholders' Equity: $351,400
P 7. 1. 20x3 Total dividends: Preferred, $120,000; Common, $68,000
P 8. 2. Total Stockholders' Equity: $475,040

Chapter 15 Problems
P 1. 2. Difference in net income: $97,600
P 2. Income Before Extraordinary Items and Cumulative Effect of Accounting Change: $410,000
P 3. Income from Continuing Operations, December 31, 20x3: $157,500
P 4. 2. Total Stockholders' Equity, December 31, 20x5: $2,964,000
P 5. 2. Retained Earnings: $250,000; Total Stockholders' Equity: $2,350,000
P 6. 2. Total Stockholders' Equity: $2,802,800
P 7. Income Before Extraordinary Items and Cumulative Effect of Accounting Change: $216,000
P 8. 2. Total Stockholders' Equity, December 31, 20x3: $518,500
P 9. 2. Retained Earnings: $397,000; Total Stockholders' Equity: $2,577,000

Chapter 16 Problems
P 1. 1. Bond Interest Expense: Nov. 30, $517,500
P 2. 1. Bond Interest Expense: Sept. 1, $377,200
P 3. Bond Interest Expense: June 30, 20x2, $289,332; Sept. 1, 20x2, $186,580
P 4. 2. Loss on early retirement: $2,261,504
P 5. Loss on Retirement of Bonds: Feb. 28, 20x5, $1,600,000

P 6.   1. Bond Interest Expense: Sept. 1, $374,400
P 7.   1. Bond Interest Expense: Nov. 30, $1,040,300
P 8.   1. Bond Interest Expense: June 30, 20x1,
       $93,195; Sept. 30, 20x1, $193,800

Chapter 17 Problems
P 1.   No check figure
P 2.   1. Net Cash Flows from: Operating Activities,
       $46,800; Investing Activities, ($14,400);
       Financing Activities, $102,000
P 3.   1. Net Cash Flows from: Operating Activities,
       ($106,000); Investing Activities, $34,000;
       Financing Activities, $44,000
P 4.   2. Net Cash Flows from: Operating Activities,
       ($106,000); Investing Activities, $34,000;
       Financing Activities, $44,000
P 5.   Net Cash Flows from Operating Activities:
       $47,600
P 6.   1. Net Cash Flows from: Operating Activities,
       $63,300; Investing Activities, ($12,900);
       Financing Activities, $7,000

P 7.   No check figure
P 8.   1. Net Cash Flows from: Operating Activities,
       $548,000; Investing Activities: $6,000; Financing
       Activities, ($260,000)
P 9.   2. Net Cash Flows from: Operating Activities,
       $63,300; Investing Activities, ($12,900);
       Financing Activities, $7,000

Chapter 18 Problems
P 1.   No check figure
P 2.   Increase: a, b, e, f, l, m
P 3.   1.c. Receivable turnover, 20x2: 14.1 times; 20x1:
       14.4 times
P 4.   1.b. Quick ratio, Lewis: 1.5 times; Ramsey: 1.2
       times; 2.d. Return on equity, Lewis: 8.8%;
       Ramsey, 4.9%
P 5.   Increase: d, h, i
P 6.   1.a. Current ratio, 20x2: 1.5 times; 20x1: 1.5
       times; 2.c. Return on assets, 20x2: 5.0%; 20x1:
       10.7%

Principles of Financial Accounting

1

Uses of Accounting Information and the Financial Statements

LEARNING OBJECTIVES

Look to the learning objectives (LOs) as a guide to help you master the material. You will see many references to LOs throughout each chapter.

1 Define *accounting*, identify business goals and activities, and describe the role of accounting in making informed decisions.

2 Identify the many users of accounting information in society.

3 Explain the importance of business transactions, money measure, and separate entity to accounting measurement.

4 Identify the three basic forms of business organization.

5 Define *financial position*, state the accounting equation, and show how they are affected by simple transactions.

6 Identify the four financial statements.

7 State the relationship of generally accepted accounting principles (GAAP) to financial statements and the independent CPA's report, and identify the organizations that influence GAAP.

8 Define *ethics* and describe the ethical responsibilities of accountants.

Microsoft Corporation

Microsoft Corporation, the giant software company, is considered one of the world's most successful companies. Why is Microsoft considered successful? An ordinary person sees the quality of the company's enormously successful products, such as Microsoft Windows, Microsoft Word, and Microsoft Excel; an investment company and others with a financial stake in the company evaluate Microsoft and its management in financial terms. Many Microsoft employees have become millionaires by owning a part of the company through stock ownership. This success is reflected in the Financial Highlights from the company's 2000 annual report, shown here.[1]

These Financial Highlights contain a number of terms for common financial measures of all companies, large or small. These measures are used to evaluate a company's management and to evaluate a company in comparison to other companies. It is easy to see the large increases at Microsoft over the years in such measures as revenue, net income, total assets, and stockholders' equity, but what do these terms mean? What financial knowledge do Microsoft's managers need in order to measure progress toward their financial goals? What financial knowledge does anyone who is evaluating Microsoft in relation to other companies need in order to understand these measures?

Microsoft's managers must have a thorough knowledge of accounting to understand how the operations for which they are responsible contribute to the firm's overall financial health.

A Decision Point introduces each chapter to show how leading businesses use accounting information reported in annual reports to make business decisions.

Financial Highlights

(In millions, except earnings per share)

			Year Ended June 30		
	1996	1997	1998	1999	2000
Revenue	$ 8,671	$11,358	$14,484	$19,747	$22,956
Net income	2,195	3,454	4,490	7,785	9,421
Earnings per share	0.86	1.32	1.67	1.42	1.70
Cash and short-term investments	6,940	8,966	13,927	17,236	23,798
Total assets	10,093	14,387	22,357	37,156	52,150
Stockholders' equity	6,908	10,777	16,627	28,438	41,368

People with a financial stake in the company, such as owners, investors, creditors, employees, attorneys, and governmental regulators, must also know accounting to evaluate the financial performance of a business. Anyone who aspires to any of these roles in a business requires mastery of accounting terminology and concepts, the process of producing financial information, and how that information is interpreted and analyzed. The purpose of this course and this textbook is to assist you in acquiring that mastery.

Video cases introduce key concepts and techniques presented in the chapter in the context of a real company.

VIDEO CASE

 ## Intel Corporation

Objectives

■ To examine the principal activities of a business enterprise: financing, investing, and operating.

■ To explore the principal performance goals of a business enterprise: liquidity and profitability.

■ To relate these activities and goals to the financial statements.

Background for the Case

You are probably familiar with the slogan "Intel Inside," from a marketing campaign for Intel Corporation, one of the

 most successful companies in the world. In 1971, Intel introduced the world's first microprocessor. The microprocessor made possible the personal computer (PC), which has changed the world. Today, Intel supplies the computing industry with chips, boards, systems, and software. Its principal products include:

■ **Microprocessors.** Also called central processing units (CPUs), these are frequently described as the "brains" of a computer because they act as the central control for the processing of data in PCs. This category includes the famous Pentium® processor.

■ **Networking and Communications Products.** These products enhance the capabilities and ease of use of PC systems by allowing users to talk to each other and to share information.

■ **Semiconductor Products.** Semiconductors facilitate flash memory, making possible easily reprogrammable

memory for computers, mobile phones, and many other products. Included in this category are embedded control chips that are programmed to regulate specific functions in products such as automobile engines, laser printers, disk drives, and home appliances.

In addition to PC users, Intel's customers include manufacturers of computers and computer systems, automobiles, and a wide range of other industrial and telecommunications equipment.

For more information about Intel Corporation, visit the company's web site through the Needles Accounting Resource Center at:

http://college.hmco.com

Required

View the video on Intel Corporation that accompanies this book. As you are watching the video, take notes related to the following:

1. All businesses engage in three basic activities—financing, investing, and operating—but how they engage in them differs from company to company. Describe in your own words the nature of each of these activities and give as many examples as you can of how Intel engages in each activity.

2. To be successful, all businesses must achieve two performance objectives—liquidity and profitability. Describe in your own words the nature of each of these goals and describe how each applies to Intel.

3. There are four financial statements that apply to business enterprises. Which statements are most closely associated with the goal of liquidity? Which statement is most closely associated with the goal of profitability? Which statement shows the financial position of the company?

Accounting as an Information System

OBJECTIVE

1 Define *accounting*, identify business goals and activities, and describe the role of accounting in making informed decisions

Each LO is stated in the margin to introduce the related text material.

Today's accountant focuses on the ultimate needs of decision makers who use accounting information, whether those decision makers are inside or outside the business. **Accounting** "is not an end in itself,"[2] but is *an information system that measures, processes, and communicates financial information about an identifiable economic entity.* An economic entity is a unit that exists independently—for example, a business, a hospital, or a governmental body. The central focus of this book is on business entities and business activities, although other economic units, such as hospitals and governmental units, will be mentioned at appropriate points in the text and assignment material.

Accounting provides a vital service by supplying the information that decision makers need in order to make "reasoned choices among alternative uses of scarce resources in the conduct of business and economic activities."[3] As shown in Figure 1, accounting is a link between business activities and decision makers. First, accounting measures business activities by recording data about them for future use. Second, the data are stored until needed and then processed to become useful information. Third, the information is communicated, through reports, to decision makers. We might say that data about business activities are the input to the accounting system and that useful information for decision makers is the output.

Business Goals, Activities, and Performance Measures

A **business** is an economic unit that aims to sell goods and services to customers at prices that will provide an adequate return to its owners. For example, listed

Key terms are highlighted in blue and followed by their definition.

Figure 1
Accounting as an Information System

Figures visually show relationships between concepts and/or processes.

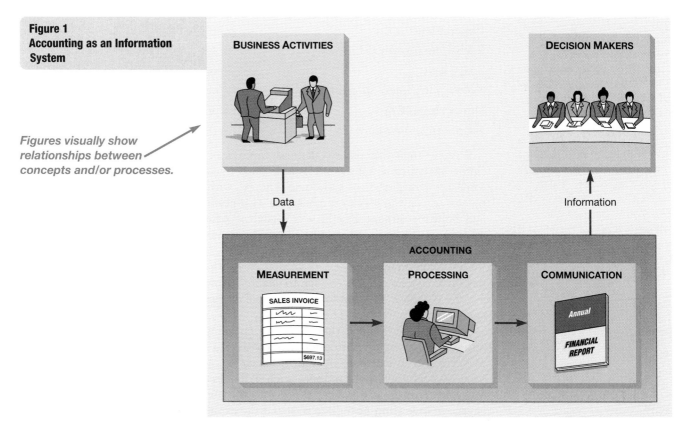

BUSINESS GOALS

BUSINESS ACTIVITIES

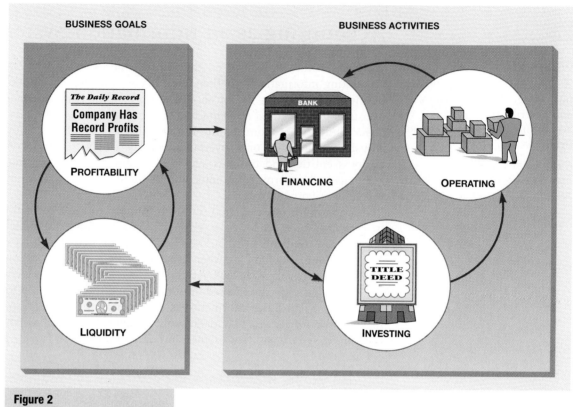

**Figure 2
Business Goals and Activities**

 below are some well-known companies and the principal goods or services that they sell:

Icons are visual guides to key features of text and supporting study aids. Look in the Preface for a complete list of icons and their meanings.

General Mills, Inc.	Food products
Reebok International Ltd.	Athletic footwear and clothing
Sony Corp.	Consumer electronics
Wendy's International Inc.	Food service
Hilton Hotels Corp.	Hotels and resorts service
Southwest Airlines Co.	Passenger airline service

Despite their differences, all these businesses have similar goals and engage in similar activities, as shown in Figure 2. Each must take in enough money from customers to pay all the costs of doing business, with enough left over as profit for the owners to want to stay in the business. This need to earn enough income to attract and hold investment capital is the goal of **profitability**. In addition, businesses must meet the goal of liquidity. **Liquidity** means having enough cash available to pay debts when they are due. For example, Toyota may meet the goal of profitability by selling many cars at a price that earns a profit. But if its customers do not pay for their cars quickly enough to enable Toyota to pay its suppliers and employees, the company may fail to meet the goal of liquidity. Both goals must be met if a company is to survive and be successful.

All businesses pursue their goals by engaging in similar activities. First, each business must engage in **financing activities** to obtain adequate funds, or capital, to begin and to continue operating. Financing activities include obtaining capital from owners and from creditors, such as banks and suppliers. They also include repaying creditors and paying a return to the owners. Second, each business must engage in **investing activities** to spend the capital it receives in ways that are productive and will help the business achieve its objectives. Investing activities include buying land, buildings, equipment, and other resources that are needed in the operation of the business, and selling these resources when they are no longer needed. Third, each business must engage in **operating activities**. In addition to the selling of goods and services to customers, operating activities include such actions as employing managers and workers, buying and producing goods and services, and paying taxes to the government.

An important function of accounting is to provide **performance measures**, which indicate whether managers are achieving their business goals and whether the business activities are well managed. It is important that these performance measures align with the goals of the business. For example, earned income is a measure of profitability and cash flow is a measure of liquidity. Ratios of accounting measures are also used as performance measures. For instance, one performance measure for operating activities might be the ratio of expenses to the revenue of the business. A performance measure for financing activities might be the ratio of money owed by the business to total resources controlled by the company. Because managers are usually evaluated on whether targeted levels of specific performance measures are achieved, they must have a knowledge of accounting to understand how they are evaluated and how they can improve their performance. Further, because managers will act to achieve the targeted performance measures, these measures must be crafted in such a way as to motivate managers to take actions that are in the best interests of the owners of the business.

The cash flow icon highlights discussion in the text of cash as a measure of liquidity.

The key ratio icon highlights discussion of a measure used to evaluate the performance of a company.

Financial and Management Accounting

Accounting's role of assisting decision makers by measuring, processing, and communicating information is usually divided into the categories of management accounting and financial accounting. Although there is considerable overlap in the functions of management accounting and financial accounting, the two can be distinguished by who the principal users of their information will be. **Management accounting** provides internal decision makers, who are charged with achieving the goals of profitability and liquidity, with information about financing, investing, and operating activities. Managers and employees, who conduct the activities of the business, need information that tells them how they have done in the past and what they can expect in the future. For example, The Gap, a retail clothing business, needs an operating report on each mall outlet that tells how much was sold at that outlet and what costs were incurred. It needs a budget for each outlet that projects the sales and costs for the next year. **Financial accounting** generates reports and communicates them to external decision makers so that they can evaluate how well the business has achieved its goals. These reports to external users are called **financial statements**. The Gap, for instance, will send its financial statements to its owners (called *stockholders*), its banks and other creditors, and government regulators. Financial statements report directly on the goals of profitability and liquidity and

The hot links to real companies icon highlights hot links to the Internet through the Needles Accounting Resource Center at http://college.hmco.com.

FOCUS ON BUSINESS PRACTICE

A study of chief executive officer bonus contracts shows that almost all companies use financial measures for determining annual bonuses. The most frequent measures are earnings per share, net income, operating income, return on equity, and cash flow. About one-third of the companies studied also use nonfinancial measures to determine bonuses. Examples of nonfinancial measures are customer satisfaction, product or service quality, nonfinancial strategic objectives, efficiency or productivity, and employee safety.[4]

Focus on Business boxes highlight the relevance of accounting in four different areas: practice, technology, ethics, and international.

FOCUS ON BUSINESS PRACTICE

Microsoft Corporation projects its performance in meeting the major business objectives in its annual report.[5]

Liquidity: "Management believes existing cash and short-term investments together with funds generated from operations will be sufficient to meet operating requirements ."

Profitability: "Because of the fixed nature of a significant portion of operating expenses, coupled with the possibility of slower revenue growth, operating margins [profitability] in 2001 may decrease from those in 2000."

Microsoft's main business activities are shown at the right.

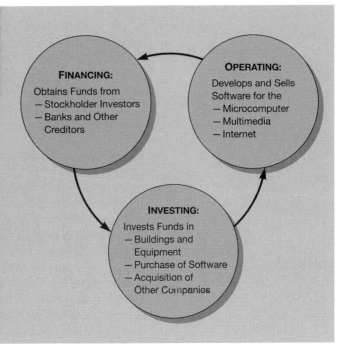

FINANCING:
Obtains Funds from
— Stockholder Investors
— Banks and Other Creditors

OPERATING:
Develops and Sells Software for the
— Microcomputer
— Multimedia
— Internet

INVESTING:
Invests Funds in
— Buildings and Equipment
— Purchase of Software
— Acquisition of Other Companies

are used extensively both inside and outside a business to evaluate the business's success. It is important for every person involved with a business to understand financial statements. They are a central feature of accounting and are the primary focus of this book.

Processing Accounting Information

To avoid misunderstandings, it is important to distinguish accounting itself from the ways in which accounting information is processed by bookkeeping, the computer, and management information systems.

People often fail to understand the difference between accounting and bookkeeping. **Bookkeeping** is the process of recording financial transactions and keeping financial records. Mechanical and repetitive, bookkeeping is only a small—but important—part of accounting. Accounting, on the other hand, includes the design of an information system that meets the user's needs. The major goals of accounting are the analysis, interpretation, and use of information.

The **computer** is an electronic tool that is used to collect, organize, and communicate vast amounts of information with great speed. Accountants were among the earliest and most enthusiastic users of computers, and today they use microcomputers in all aspects of their work. It may appear that the computer is doing the accountant's job; in fact, it is only a tool that is instructed to do routine bookkeeping and to perform complex calculations.

With the widespread use of the computer today, a business's many information needs are organized into what is called a **management information system (MIS)**. A management information system consists of the interconnected subsystems that provide the information needed to run a business. The accounting information system is the most important subsystem because it plays the key role of managing the flow of economic data to all departments within a business and to interested parties outside the business.

Decision Makers: The Users of Accounting Information

OBJECTIVE

2 Identify the many users of accounting information in society

The people who use accounting information to make decisions fall into three categories: (1) those who manage a business; (2) those outside a business enterprise who have a direct financial interest in the business; and (3) those people, organizations, and agencies that have an indirect financial interest in the business, as shown in Figure 3. These categories apply to government and not-for-profit organizations as well as to profit-oriented ventures.

Management

Management, collectively, is the people who have overall responsibility for operating a business and for meeting its profitability and liquidity goals. In a small business, management may include the owners. In a large business, management more often consists of people who have been hired. Managers must decide what to do, how to do it, and whether the results match their original plans. Successful managers consistently make the right decisions based on timely and relevant information. To make good decisions, managers need answers to such questions as: What was the company's net income during the past quarter? Is the rate of return to the owners adequate? Does the company have enough cash? Which products are most profitable? What is the cost of manufacturing each product? Because so many key decisions are based on accounting data, management is one of the most important users of accounting information.

In carrying out its decision-making process, management performs a set of functions that are essential to the operation of the business. Although larger businesses will have more elaborate operations, the same basic functions must be accomplished in businesses of all sizes. Each requires accounting information for decision making. The basic management functions are:

Financing the business Financial management obtains financial resources so that the company can begin and continue operating.

Investing the resources of the business Asset management invests the financial resources of the business in productive assets that support the company's goals.

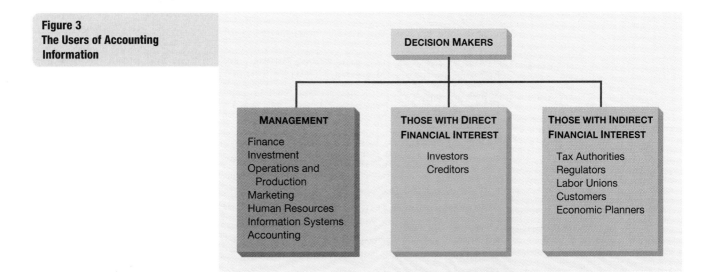

Figure 3
The Users of Accounting Information

Producing goods and services   Operations and production management develops and produces products and services.

Marketing goods and services   Marketing management sells, advertises, and distributes goods and services.

Managing employees   Human resource management encompasses the hiring, evaluation, and compensation of employees.

Providing information to decision makers   Information systems management captures data about all aspects of the company's operations, organizes the data into usable information, and provides reports to internal managers and appropriate outside parties. Accounting plays a key role in this function.

Users with a Direct Financial Interest

Another group of decision makers who need accounting information are those with a direct financial interest in a business. They depend on accounting to measure and report information about how a business has performed. Most businesses periodically publish a set of general-purpose financial statements that report their success in meeting the goals of profitability and liquidity. These statements show what has happened in the past, and they are important indicators of what will happen in the future. Many people outside the company carefully study these financial reports. The two most important outside groups are investors and creditors.

INVESTORS   Those who invest or may invest in a business are interested in its past performance and its potential earnings. A thorough study of a company's financial statements helps potential investors judge the prospects for a profitable investment. After investing in a company, investors must continually review their commitment. To accomplish this, they again examine the company's financial statements.

CREDITORS   Most companies borrow money for both long- and short-term operating needs. Creditors, those who lend money or deliver goods and services before being paid, are interested mainly in whether a company will have the cash to pay interest charges and repay debt at the appropriate time. They study a company's liquidity and cash flow as well as its profitability. Banks, finance companies, mortgage companies, securities firms, insurance firms, suppliers, and other lenders must analyze a company's financial position before they make a loan.

Users with an Indirect Financial Interest

In recent years, society as a whole, through government and public groups, has become one of the largest and most important users of accounting information. Users who need accounting information to make decisions on public issues include (1) tax authorities, (2) regulatory agencies, and (3) other groups.

TAX AUTHORITIES   Government at every level is financed through the collection of taxes. Under federal, state, and local laws, companies and individuals pay many kinds of taxes, including federal, state, and city income taxes; social security and other payroll taxes; excise taxes; and sales taxes. Each tax requires special tax returns, and often a complex set of records as well. Proper reporting is generally a matter of law and can be very complicated. The Internal Revenue Code, for instance, contains thousands of rules governing the preparation of the accounting information used in computing federal income taxes.

FOCUS ON BUSINESS PRACTICE

John Connors, corporate controller of Microsoft, emphasizes that providing information to decision makers is an important accounting function, as follows:

The way I look at it, the controller's principal job is providing information that the business needs to make good decisions. . . . The real purpose is getting the information that managers need to do their jobs better, whether it is in sales and marketing, research and development, in the support groups, or operations.[6]

REGULATORY AGENCIES   Most companies must report periodically to one or more regulatory agencies at the federal, state, and local levels. For example, all public corporations must report periodically to the **Securities and Exchange Commission (SEC)**. This body, which was set up by Congress to protect the public, regulates the issuing, buying, and selling of stocks in the United States. Companies that are listed on a stock exchange also must meet the special reporting requirements of their exchange.

OTHER GROUPS   Labor unions study the financial statements of corporations as part of preparing for contract negotiations. A company's income and costs often play an important role in these negotiations. Those who advise investors and creditors—financial analysts and advisers, brokers, underwriters, lawyers, economists, and the financial press—also have an indirect interest in the financial performance and prospects of a business. Consumer groups, customers, and the general public have become more concerned about the financing and earnings of corporations as well as the effects that corporations have on inflation, the environment, social problems, and the quality of life. Economic planners, among them members of the President's Council of Economic Advisers and the Federal Reserve Board, use aggregated accounting information to set economic policies and to evaluate economic programs.

Government and Not-for-Profit Organizations

More than 30 percent of the U.S. economy is generated by government and not-for-profit organizations (hospitals, universities, professional organizations, and charities). The managers of these diverse entities need to understand and to use accounting information to perform the same functions as managers in businesses. They need to raise funds from investors, creditors, taxpayers, and donors, and to deploy scarce resources. They need to plan to pay for operations and repay creditors on a timely basis. Moreover, they have an obligation to report their financial performance to legislators, boards, and donors, as well as to deal with tax authorities, regulators, and labor unions. Although most of the examples throughout this text focus on business enterprises, the same basic principles apply to government and not-for-profit organizations.

Accounting Measurement

OBJECTIVE

3 Explain the importance of business transactions, money measure, and separate entity to accounting measurement

Accounting is an information system that measures, processes, and communicates financial information. In this section, you begin the study of the measurement aspects of accounting. Here you learn what accounting actually measures and study the effects of certain transactions on a company's financial position.

To make an accounting measurement, the accountant must answer four basic questions:

1. What is measured?
2. When should the measurement be made?

3. What value should be placed on what is measured?

4. How should what is measured be classified?

All these questions deal with basic assumptions and generally accepted accounting principles, and their answers establish what accounting is and what it is not. Accountants in industry, professional associations, public accounting, government, and academic circles debate the answers to these questions constantly, and the answers change as new knowledge and practice require. But the basis of today's accounting practice rests on a number of widely accepted concepts and conventions, which are described in this book. We begin by focusing on the first question: What is measured?

What Is Measured?

The world contains an unlimited number of things to measure and ways to measure them. For example, consider a machine that makes bottle caps. How many measurements of this machine could you make? You might start with size and then go on to location, weight, cost, or many other units of measurement. Some of these measurements are relevant to accounting; some are not. Every system must define what it measures, and accounting is no exception. Basically, financial accounting uses money measures to gauge the impact of business transactions on separate business entities. The concepts of business transactions, money measure, and separate entity are discussed in the next sections.

Business Transactions as the Object of Measurement

Business transactions are economic events that affect the financial position of a business entity. Business entities can have hundreds or even thousands of transactions every day. These business transactions are the raw material of accounting reports.

A transaction can be an exchange of value (a purchase, sale, payment, collection, or loan) between two or more independent parties. A transaction also can be an economic event that has the same effect as an exchange transaction but does not involve an exchange. Some examples of "nonexchange" transactions are losses from fire, flood, explosion, and theft; physical wear and tear on machinery and equipment; and the day-by-day accumulation of interest.

 To be recorded, a transaction must relate directly to a business entity. For example, suppose a customer buys a shovel from Ace Hardware but has to buy a hoe from a competing store because Ace is out of hoes. The transaction in which the shovel was sold is entered in Ace's records. However, the purchase of the hoe from the competitor is not entered in Ace's records because even though it indirectly affects Ace economically, it does not involve a direct exchange of value between Ace and the customer.

Money Measure

All business transactions are recorded in terms of money. This concept is termed **money measure**. Of course, information of a nonfinancial nature may be recorded, but it is through the recording of monetary amounts that the diverse transactions and activities of a business are measured. Money is the only factor that is common to all business transactions, and thus it is the only practical unit of measure that can produce financial data that are alike and can be compared.

The monetary unit a business uses depends on the country in which the business resides. For example, in the United States, the basic unit of money is the dol-

Table 1. Partial Listing of Foreign Exchange Rates

Country	Price in $ U.S.	Country	Price in $ U.S.
Australia (dollar)	0.559	Hong Kong (dollar)	0.128
Brazil (real)	0.55	Japan (yen)	0.009
Britain (pound)	1.438	Mexico (peso)	0.10
Canada (dollar)	0.677	Russia (ruble)	0.359
Europe (euro)	0.871	Singapore (dollar)	0.577

Source: Data from *The Wall Street Journal*, September 7, 2000.

A table gives factual information referred to in the text.

lar. In Japan, it is the yen; in Europe, the euro; and in the United Kingdom, the pound. If there are transactions between countries, exchange rates must be used to translate from one currency to another. An **exchange rate** is the value of one currency in terms of another. For example, a British person purchasing goods from a U.S. company and paying in U.S. dollars must exchange British pounds for U.S. dollars before making payment. In effect, the currencies are goods that can be bought and sold. Table 1 illustrates the exchange rates for several currencies in dollars. It shows the exchange rate for British pounds as $1.438 per pound on a particular date. Like the prices of most goods or services, these prices change daily according to supply and demand for the currencies. For example, a few years earlier the exchange rate for British pounds was $1.64. Although our discussion in this book focuses on dollars, selected examples and certain assignments will be in foreign currencies.

The Concept of Separate Entity

For accounting purposes, a business is a **separate entity**, distinct not only from its creditors and customers but also from its owner or owners. It should have a completely separate set of records, and its financial records and reports should refer only to its own financial affairs.

For example, the Jones Florist Company should have a bank account that is separate from the account of Kay Jones, the owner. Kay Jones may own a home, a car, and other property, and she may have personal debts, but these are not the Jones Florist Company's resources or debts. Kay Jones also may own another business, say a stationery shop. If she does, she should have a completely separate set of records for each business.

Forms of Business Organization

OBJECTIVE

4 Identify the three basic forms of business organization

There are three basic forms of business organization: sole proprietorships, partnerships, and corporations. Accountants recognize each form as an economic unit separate from its owners, although legally only the corporation is considered separate from its owners. Other legal differences among the three forms are summarized in Table 2 and discussed briefly in the following sections. In this book, we begin with accounting for the sole proprietorship because it is the simplest form of accounting. At critical points, however, we call attention to its essential differences from accounting for partnerships and corporations.

Table 2. Comparative Features of the Forms of Business Organization

	Sole Proprietorship	Partnership	Corporation
1. Legal status	Not a separate legal entity	Not a separate legal entity	Separate legal entity
2. Risk of ownership	Owner's personal resources at stake	Partners' personal resources at stake	Limited to investment in corporation
3. Duration or life	Limited by choice or death of owner	Limited by choice or death of any partner	Indefinite, possibly unlimited
4. Transferability of ownership	Sale by owner establishes new company	Changes in any partner's percentage of interest requires new partnership	Transferable by sale of stock
5. Accounting treatment	Separate economic unit	Separate economic unit	Separate economic unit

Sole Proprietorships

A **sole proprietorship** is a business that is owned by one person and is not incorporated. This form of organization gives the individual a means of controlling the business apart from his or her personal interests. Legally, however, the proprietorship is the same economic unit as the individual. The individual receives all profits or losses and is liable for all obligations of the business. Proprietorships represent the largest number of businesses in the United States, but they transact far less business in dollar terms than do corporations. In addition, they are typically the smallest in size. The life of a sole proprietorship ends when the owner wants it to or when the owner dies or becomes incapacitated.

Partnerships

A **partnership** is like a proprietorship in most ways except that it has more than one owner. A partnership is not a legal entity separate from the owner; it is an unincorporated association that brings together the talents and resources of two or more people. The partners share the profits and losses of the partnership according to an agreed-upon formula. Generally, any partner can bind the partnership to another party, and, if necessary, the personal resources of each partner can be called on to pay the obligations of the partnership. In some cases, one or more partners limit their liability, but at least one partner must have unlimited liability. A partnership must be dissolved when ownership changes—for example, when a partner leaves or dies. For the business to continue as a partnership, a new partnership must be formed.

Corporations

A **corporation** is a business unit that is granted a state charter and is recognized as legally separate from its owners (the stockholders). The owners, whose ownership

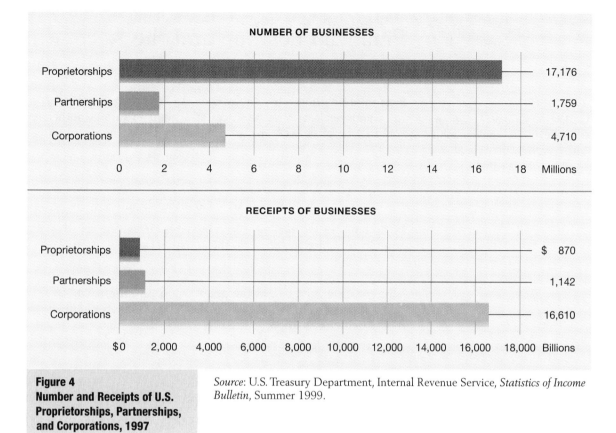

Figure 4
Number and Receipts of U.S.
Proprietorships, Partnerships,
and Corporations, 1997

Source: U.S. Treasury Department, Internal Revenue Service, *Statistics of Income Bulletin*, Summer 1999.

is represented by shares of stock in the corporation, do not control the operations of the corporation directly. Instead, they elect a board of directors, which appoints managers to run the corporation for the benefit of the stockholders. In exchange for limited involvement in the corporation's actual operations, stockholders enjoy limited liability. That is, their risk of loss is limited to the amount they paid for their shares. If they want, stockholders can sell their shares to other people, without affecting corporate operations. Because of this limited liability, stockholders often are willing to invest in riskier, but potentially more profitable, activities. Also, because ownership can be transferred without dissolving the corporation, the life of a corporation is unlimited; it is not subject to the whims or health of a proprietor or partner.

Corporations have several important advantages over proprietorships and partnerships that make them very efficient in amassing capital for the formation and growth of very large companies. Even though corporations are fewer in number than sole proprietorships and partnerships, they contribute much more to the U.S. economy in monetary terms (see Figure 4). For example, in 1999, General Motors generated more revenue than all but 30 of the world's countries.

FOCUS ON BUSINESS PRACTICE

Most people think of corporations as large national or global companies whose shares of stock are held by thousands of people and institutions. Indeed, corporations can be huge and have many stockholders. However, of the approximately 4.7 million corporations in the United States, only about 15,000 have stock that is publicly bought and sold. The vast majority of corporations are small businesses that are privately held by a few stockholders. In Illinois alone there are more than 250,000 corporations. For this reason, the study of corporations is just as relevant to small businesses as it is to large ones.

Financial Position and the Accounting Equation

OBJECTIVE

5 Define *financial position,* state the accounting equation, and show how they are affected by simple transactions

Financial position refers to the economic resources that belong to a company and the claims against those resources at a point in time. Another term for claims is *equities*. Therefore, a company can be viewed as economic resources and equities:

$$\text{Economic Resources} = \text{Equities}$$

Every company has two types of equities, creditors' equities and owner's equity:

$$\text{Economic Resources} = \text{Creditors' Equities} + \text{Owner's Equity}$$

In accounting terminology, economic resources are called *assets* and creditors' equities are called *liabilities*. So the equation can be written like this:

$$\text{Assets} = \text{Liabilities} + \text{Owner's Equity}$$

This equation is known as the **accounting equation**. The two sides of the equation always must be equal, or "in balance." To evaluate the financial effects of business activities, it is important to understand their effects on this equation.

Assets

Assets are economic resources owned by a business that are expected to benefit future operations. Certain kinds of assets—for example, cash and money owed to the company by customers (called *accounts receivable*)—are monetary items. Other assets—inventories (goods held for sale), land, buildings, and equipment—are nonmonetary physical things. Still other assets—the rights granted by patents, trademarks, or copyrights—are nonphysical.

Liabilities

Liabilities are present obligations of a business to pay cash, transfer assets, or provide services to other entities in the future. Among these obligations are debts of the business, amounts owed to suppliers for goods or services bought on credit (called *accounts payable*), borrowed money (for example, money owed on loans payable to banks), salaries and wages owed to employees, taxes owed to the government, and services to be performed.

As debts, liabilities are claims recognized by law. That is, the law gives creditors the right to force the sale of a company's assets if the company fails to pay its debts. Creditors have rights over owners and must be paid in full before the owners receive anything, even if payment of a debt uses up all the assets of a business.

Owner's Equity

Owner's equity represents the claims by the owner to the assets of the business. It equals the residual interest, or *residual equity*, in the assets of an entity that remains after deducting the entity's liabilities. Theoretically, it is what would be left if all the liabilities were paid, and it is sometimes referred to as **net assets**. By rearranging the accounting equation, we can define owner's equity this way:

$$\text{Owner's Equity} = \text{Assets} - \text{Liabilities}$$

The four types of transactions that affect owner's equity are shown in Figure 5. Two of these transactions, **owner's investments** and **owner's withdrawals**, are

Figure 5
Four Types of Transactions That Affect Owner's Equity

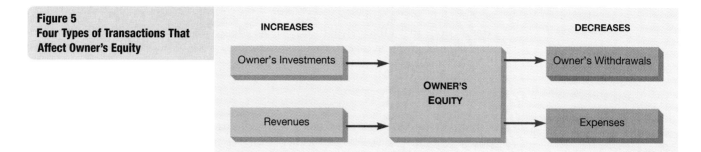

assets that the owner either puts into the business or takes out of the business. For instance, if the owner of Shannon Realty, John Shannon, takes cash out of his personal bank account and deposits it in the business bank account, he has made an owner's investment. The assets (cash) of the business increase, and John Shannon's equity in those assets also increases. Conversely, if John Shannon takes cash out of the business bank account and deposits it in his personal bank account, he has made a withdrawal from the business. The assets of the business decrease, and John Shannon's equity in the business also decreases.

The other two types of transactions that affect owner's equity are revenues and expenses. Simply stated, **revenues** and **expenses** are the increases and decreases in owner's equity that result from operating a business. For example, the amount a customer pays (or agrees to pay in the future) to Shannon Realty in return for a service provided by the company is a revenue. The assets (cash or accounts receivable) of Shannon Realty increase, and the owner's equity in those assets also increases. On the other hand, the amount Shannon Realty pays out (or agrees to pay in the future) in the process of providing a service is an expense. Now the assets (cash) decrease or the liabilities (accounts payable) increase, and the owner's equity in the assets decreases.

Generally speaking, a company is successful if its revenues exceed its expenses. When revenues exceed expenses, the difference is called **net income**; when expenses exceed revenues, the difference is called **net loss**.

Some Illustrative Transactions

Let us now examine the effects of some of the most common business transactions on the accounting equation. Suppose that John Shannon opens a real estate agency called Shannon Realty on December 1. During December, his business engages in the transactions described in the following paragraphs.

OWNER'S INVESTMENTS   John starts his business by depositing $50,000 in a bank account in the name of Shannon Realty. The transfer of cash from his personal account to the business account is an owner's investment. The first balance sheet of the new company would show the asset Cash and the owner's equity (John Shannon, Capital):

Assets	=	Owner's Equity (OE)	
Cash		John Shannon, Capital	Type of OE Transaction
1. $50,000		$50,000	Owner's Investments

At this point, the company has no liabilities, and assets equal the owner's equity. The labels Cash and John Shannon, Capital are called **accounts** and are used by accountants to accumulate amounts that result from similar transactions. Transactions that affect owner's equity are identified by type so that similar types may later be grouped together on accounting reports.

PURCHASE OF ASSETS WITH CASH John finds a good location and pays cash to purchase a lot for $10,000 and a small building on the lot for $25,000. This transaction does not change the total assets, liabilities, or owner's equity of Shannon Realty, but it does change the composition of the assets—it decreases Cash and increases Land and Building:

		Assets			=	Owner's Equity	
		Cash	Land	Building		John Shannon, Capital	Type of OE Transaction
bal.		$50,000				$50,000	
2.		−35,000	+$10,000	+$25,000			
bal.		$15,000	$10,000	$25,000		$50,000	

$50,000

PURCHASE OF ASSETS BY INCURRING A LIABILITY Assets do not always have to be purchased with cash. They may also be purchased on credit, that is, on the basis of an agreement to pay for them later. Suppose Shannon Realty buys some office supplies for $500 on credit. This transaction increases the assets (Supplies) and increases the liabilities of Shannon Realty. This liability is designated by an account called Accounts Payable:

		Assets			=	Liabilities	+	Owner's Equity	
	Cash	Supplies	Land	Building		Accounts Payable		John Shannon, Capital	Type of OE Transaction
bal.	$15,000		$10,000	$25,000				$50,000	
3.		+$500				+$500			
bal.	$15,000	$500	$10,000	$25,000		$500		$50,000	

$50,500 $50,500

Notice that this transaction increases both sides of the accounting equation to $50,500.

PAYMENT OF A LIABILITY If Shannon Realty later pays $200 of the $500 owed for the supplies, both assets (Cash) and liabilities (Accounts Payable) decrease, but Supplies is unaffected:

	Assets				= Liabilities	+ Owner's Equity	
	Cash	Supplies	Land	Building	Accounts Payable	John Shannon, Capital	Type of OE Transaction
bal.	$15,000	$500	$10,000	$25,000	$500	$50,000	
4.	−200				−200		
bal.	$14,800	$500	$10,000	$25,000	$300	$50,000	

$50,300 $50,300

Notice that both sides of the accounting equation are still equal, although now at a total of $50,300.

REVENUES   Shannon Realty earns revenues in the form of commissions by selling houses for clients. Sometimes these commissions are paid immediately in the form of cash, and sometimes the client agrees to pay the commission later. In either case, the commission is recorded when it is earned and Shannon Realty has a right to a current or future receipt of cash. A revenue is earned when a business provides a good or service to the buyer. First, assume that Shannon Realty sells a house and receives a commission of $1,500 in cash. This transaction increases both assets (Cash) and owner's equity (John Shannon, Capital):

	Assets				= Liabilities	+ Owner's Equity	
	Cash	Supplies	Land	Building	Accounts Payable	John Shannon, Capital	Type of OE Transaction
bal.	$14,800	$500	$10,000	$25,000	$300	$50,000	
5.	+1,500					+$1,500	Commissions Earned
bal.	$16,300	$500	$10,000	$25,000	$300	$51,500	

$51,800 $51,800

Now assume that Shannon Realty sells a house, in the process earning a commission of $2,000, and agrees to wait for payment of the commission. Because the commission has been earned now, a bill or invoice is sent to the client, and the transaction is recorded now. This revenue transaction increases both assets and owner's equity as before, but a new asset account, Accounts Receivable, shows that Shannon Realty is awaiting receipt of the commission:

	Assets					= Liabilities	+ Owner's Equity	
	Cash	Accounts Receivable	Supplies	Land	Building	Accounts Payable	John Shannon, Capital	Type of OE Transaction
bal.	$16,300		$500	$10,000	$25,000	$300	$51,500	
6.		+$2,000					+2,000	Commissions Earned
bal.	$16,300	$2,000	$500	$10,000	$25,000	$300	$53,500	

$53,800 $53,800

As you progress in your study of accounting, you will be shown the use of separate accounts for revenues, like Commissions Earned.

COLLECTION OF ACCOUNTS RECEIVABLE   Let us assume that a few days later Shannon Realty receives $1,000 from the client in transaction **6**. At that time, the asset Cash increases and the asset Accounts Receivable decreases:

		Assets				= Liabilities +	Owner's Equity	
	Cash	Accounts Receivable	Supplies	Land	Building	Accounts Payable	John Shannon, Capital	Type of OE Transaction
bal.	$16,300	$2,000	$500	$10,000	$25,000	$300	$53,500	
7.	+1,000	−1,000						
bal.	$17,300	$1,000	$500	$10,000	$25,000	$300	$53,500	
		$53,800					$53,800	

Notice that this transaction does not affect owner's equity because the commission revenue was already recorded in transaction **6**. Also notice that the balance of Accounts Receivable is $1,000, indicating that $1,000 is still to be collected.

EXPENSES   Just as revenues are recorded when they are earned, expenses are recorded when they are incurred. Expenses can be paid in cash when they occur, or they can be paid later. If payment is going to be made later, a liability—for example, Accounts Payable or Wages Payable—increases. In both cases, owner's equity decreases. Assume that Shannon Realty pays $1,000 to rent some equipment for the office and $400 in wages to a part-time helper. These transactions reduce assets (Cash) and owner's equity (John Shannon, Capital):

		Assets				= Liabilities +	Owner's Equity	
	Cash	Accounts Receivable	Supplies	Land	Building	Accounts Payable	John Shannon, Capital	Type of OE Transaction
bal.	$17,300	$1,000	$500	$10,000	$25,000	$300	$53,500	
8.	−1,000						−1,000	Equipment Rental Expense
9.	−400						−400	Wages Expense
bal.	$15,900	$1,000	$500	$10,000	$25,000	$300	$52,100	
		$52,400					$52,400	

Now assume that Shannon Realty has not paid the $300 bill for utilities expense incurred for December. In this case, the effect on owner's equity is the same as when the expense is paid in cash, but instead of a reduction in assets, there is an increase in liabilities (Accounts Payable):

		Assets			= Liabilities +	Owner's Equity	
	Cash	Accounts Receivable	Supplies	Land	Building	Accounts Payable	John Shannon, Capital	Type of OE Transaction
bal.	$15,900	$1,000	$500	$10,000	$25,000	$300	$52,100	
10.						+300	−300	Utilities Expense
bal.	$15,900	$1,000	$500	$10,000	$25,000	$600	$51,800	

$52,400 $52,400

As you progress in your study of accounting, you will be shown the use of separate accounts for expenses, like Equipment Rental Expense, Wages Expense, and Utilities Expense.

OWNER'S WITHDRAWALS   John now withdraws $600 in cash from Shannon Realty and deposits it in his personal account. This transaction reduces assets (Cash) and owner's equity (John Shannon, Capital). Although, as can be seen below, withdrawals have the same effect on the accounting equation as expenses (see transactions 8 and 9), it is important not to confuse them. Withdrawals are not expenses. Withdrawals are personal distributions of assets to the owner; expenses are incurred by the business in its operations.

		Assets			= Liabilities +	Owner's Equity	
	Cash	Accounts Receivable	Supplies	Land	Building	Accounts Payable	John Shannon, Capital	Type of OE Transaction
bal.	$15,900	$1,000	$500	$10,000	$25,000	$600	$51,800	
11.	−600						−600	Owner's Withdrawal
bal.	$15,300	$1,000	$500	$10,000	$25,000	$600	$51,200	

$51,800 $51,800

SUMMARY   Exhibit 1 (page 22) summarizes these 11 transactions.

Communication Through Financial Statements

OBJECTIVE

6 Identify the four financial statements

Financial statements are the primary means of communicating important accounting information to users. It is helpful to think of these statements as models of the business enterprise because they show the business in financial terms. As is true of all models, however, financial statements are not perfect pictures of the real thing, but rather the accountant's best effort to represent what is real. Four major financial statements are used to communicate accounting information about a business: the income statement, the statement of owner's equity, the balance sheet, and the statement of cash flows.

Exhibit 2 illustrates the relationship among the four financial statements by showing how they would appear for Shannon Realty after the 11 sample transactions

An exhibit illustrates financial information.

Exhibit 1
Summary of Effects of Illustrative Transactions on Financial Position

	Assets					= Liabilities +	Owner's Equity	
	Cash	Accounts Receivable	Supplies	Land	Building	Accounts Payable	John Shannon, Capital	Type of Owner's Equity Transaction
1.	$50,000						$50,000	Owner's Investments
2.	−35,000			+$10,000	+$25,000			
bal.	$15,000			$10,000	$25,000		$50,000	
3.			+$500			+$500		
bal.	$15,000		$500	$10,000	$25,000	$500	$50,000	
4.	−200					−200		
bal.	$14,800		$500	$10,000	$25,000	$300	$50,000	
5.	+1,500						+$1,500	Commissions Earned
bal.	$16,300		$500	$10,000	$25,000	$300	$51,500	
6.		+$2,000					+2,000	Commissions Earned
bal.	$16,300	$2,000	$500	$10,000	$25,000	$300	$53,500	
7.	+1,000	−1,000						
bal.	$17,300	$1,000	$500	$10,000	$25,000	$300	$53,500	
8.	−1,000						−1,000	Equipment Rental Expense
9.	−400						−400	Wages Expense
bal.	$15,900	$1,000	$500	$10,000	$25,000	$300	$52,100	
10.						+300	−300	Utilities Expense
bal.	$15,900	$1,000	$500	$10,000	$25,000	$600	$51,800	
11.	−600						−600	Owner's Withdrawal
bal.	$15,300	$1,000	$500	$10,000	$25,000	$600	$51,200	
			$51,800				$51,800	

Exhibit 2
Income Statement, Statement of Owner's Equity, Balance Sheet, and Statement of Cash Flows for Shannon Realty

Shannon Realty
Income Statement
For the Month Ended December 31, 20xx

Revenues		
Commissions Earned		$3,500
Expenses		
Equipment Rental Expense	$1,000	
Wages Expense	400	
Utilities Expense	300	
Total Expenses		1,700
Net Income		$1,800

Shannon Realty
Statement of Owner's Equity
For the Month Ended December 31, 20xx

John Shannon, Capital, December 1, 20xx		$ 0
Add: Investments by John Shannon	$50,000	
Net Income for the Month	1,800	51,800
Subtotal		$51,800
Less Withdrawals by John Shannon		600
John Shannon, Capital, December 31, 20xx		$51,200

Shannon Realty
Statement of Cash Flows
For the Month Ended December 31, 20xx

Cash Flows from Operating Activities		
Net Income		$ 1,800
Noncash Expenses and Revenues		
Included in Income		
Increase in Accounts		
Receivable	($ 1,000)*	
Increase in Supplies	(500)	
Increase in Accounts		
Payable	600	(900)
Net Cash Flows from		
Operating Activities		$ 900
Cash Flows from Investing Activities		
Purchase of Land	($10,000)	
Purchase of Building	(25,000)	
Net Cash Flows from		
Investing Activities		(35,000)
Cash Flows from Financing Activities		
Investments by		
John Shannon	$50,000	
Withdrawals by John		
Shannon	(600)	
Net Cash Flows from		
Financing Activities		49,400
Net Increase (Decrease) in Cash		$15,300
Cash at Beginning of Month		0
Cash at End of Month		$15,300

Shannon Realty
Balance Sheet
December 31, 20xx

Assets		**Liabilities**	
Cash	$15,300	Accounts Payable	$ 600
Accounts Receivable	1,000		
Supplies	500	**Owner's Equity**	
Land	10,000	John Shannon,	
Building	25,000	Capital	51,200
		Total Liabilities and Owner's	
Total Assets	$51,800	Equity	$51,800

*Parentheses indicate a negative impact or cash outflow.

shown in Exhibit 1. It is assumed that the time period covered is the month of December 20xx. Notice that each statement is headed in a similar way. Each heading identifies the company and the kind of statement. The income statement, the statement of owner's equity, and the statement of cash flows give the time period to which they apply; the balance sheet gives the specific date to which it applies. Much of this book deals with developing, using, and interpreting more complete versions of these basic statements.

The Income Statement

The **income statement** summarizes the revenues earned and expenses incurred by a business over a period of time. Many people consider it the most important financial report because it shows whether or not a business achieved its profitability goal of earning an acceptable income. In Exhibit 2, Shannon Realty had revenues in the form of commissions earned of $3,500 ($2,000 of revenue earned on credit and $1,500 of cash). From this amount, total expenses of $1,700 were deducted (equipment rental expense of $1,000, wages expense of $400, and utilities expense of $300), to arrive at a net income of $1,800. To show that it applies to a period of time, the statement is dated "For the Month Ended December 31, 20xx."

The Statement of Owner's Equity

The **statement of owner's equity** shows the change in the owner's capital over a period of time. In Exhibit 2, the beginning capital is zero because the company was started in this accounting period. During the month, John Shannon made an investment in the business of $50,000, and the company earned income (as shown on the income statement) of $1,800, for a total increase of $51,800. Deducted from this amount are the withdrawals for the month of $600, leaving an ending balance of $51,200 in the capital account.

The Balance Sheet

The purpose of a **balance sheet** is to show the financial position of a business on a certain date, usually the end of the month or year. For this reason, it often is called the *statement of financial position* and is dated as of a certain date. The balance sheet presents a view of the business as the holder of resources, or assets, that are equal to the claims against those assets. The claims consist of the company's liabilities and the owner's equity in the company. In Exhibit 2, Shannon Realty has several categories of assets, which total $51,800. These assets equal the total liabilities of $600 (Accounts Payable) plus the ending balance of owner's capital of $51,200. Notice that the owner's capital amount on the balance sheet comes from the ending balance on the statement of owner's equity.

The Statement of Cash Flows

Whereas the income statement focuses on a company's profitability goal, the **statement of cash flows** is directed toward the company's liquidity goal. **Cash flows** are the inflows and outflows of cash into and out of a business. Net cash flows are the difference between the inflows and outflows. The statement of cash flows shows the cash produced by operating a business as well as important investing and financing transactions that take place during an accounting period. Exhibit 2 shows the statement of cash flows for Shannon Realty. Notice that the statement explains how the Cash account changed during the period. Cash increased by $15,300. Operating activities produced net cash flows of $900, and financing activities produced net cash flows of $49,400. Investing activities used cash flows of $35,000.

This statement is related directly to the other three statements. Notice that net income comes from the income statement and that investments by owners and withdrawals come from the statement of owner's equity. The other items in the statement represent changes in the balance sheet accounts: Accounts Receivable, Supplies, Accounts Payable, Land, and Building.

Generally Accepted Accounting Principles

OBJECTIVE

7 State the relationship of generally accepted accounting principles (GAAP) to financial statements and the independent CPA's report, and identify the organizations that influence GAAP

To ensure that financial statements will be understandable to their users, a set of practices, called **generally accepted accounting principles (GAAP)**, has been developed to provide guidelines for financial accounting. Although the term has several meanings in the literature of accounting, perhaps this is the best definition: "Generally accepted accounting principles encompass the conventions, rules, and procedures necessary to define accepted accounting practice at a particular time."[7] In other words, GAAP arise from wide agreement on the theory and practice of accounting at a particular time. These "principles" are not like the unchangeable laws of nature found in chemistry or physics. They are developed by accountants and businesses to serve the needs of decision makers, and they can be altered as better methods evolve or as circumstances change.

In this book, we present accounting practice, or GAAP, as it is today. We also try to explain the reasons or theory on which the practice is based. Both theory and practice are important to the study of accounting. However, you should realize that accounting is a discipline that is always growing, changing, and improving. Just as years of research are necessary before a new surgical method or lifesaving drug can be introduced, it may take years for research and new discoveries in accounting to be commonly implemented. As a result, you may encounter practices that seem contradictory. In some cases, we point out new directions in accounting. Your instructor also may mention certain weaknesses in current theory or practice.

Financial Statements, GAAP, and the Independent CPA's Report

Financial statements are prepared by the management of a company and could be falsified for personal gain. All companies that sell ownership to the public and many companies that apply for sizable loans must have their financial statements audited by an independent certified public accountant. **Certified public accountants (CPAs)** are licensed by all states for the same reason that lawyers and doctors are—to protect the public by ensuring the quality of professional service. One important attribute of CPAs is independence: They have no financial or other compromising ties with the companies they audit. This gives the public confidence in their work. The firms listed in Table 3 employ about 25 percent of all CPAs.

Table 3. Large International Certified Public Accounting Firms		
Firm	**Home Office**	**Some Major Clients**
Arthur Andersen	Chicago	ITT, Texaco, United Airlines
Deloitte & Touche	New York	General Motors, Procter & Gamble, Sears
Ernst & Young	New York	Coca-Cola, McDonald's, Amgen
KPMG	New York	General Electric, Xerox, BMW
PricewaterhouseCoopers	New York	Du Pont, IBM, Ford

The CD-ROM icon indicates that data for the company in the text is available on the Fingraph® CD-ROM.

An independent CPA performs an **audit**, which is an examination of a company's financial statements and the accounting systems, controls, and records that produced them. The purpose of the audit is to ascertain that the financial statements have been prepared in accordance with generally accepted accounting principles. If the independent accountant is satisfied that this standard has been met, his or her report contains the following language:

> In our opinion, the financial statements . . . present fairly, in all material respects . . . in conformity with generally accepted accounting principles.

This wording emphasizes the fact that accounting and auditing are not exact sciences. The framework of GAAP provides room for interpretation, and the application of GAAP necessitates the making of estimates. As a result, the auditor can render an opinion or judgment only that the financial statements *present fairly* or conform *in all material respects* to GAAP. The accountant's report does not preclude minor or immaterial errors that might exist in the financial statements. However, it does imply that on the whole, investors and creditors can rely on those statements.

Historically, auditors have enjoyed a strong reputation for competence and independence. As a result, banks, investors, and creditors are willing to rely on an auditor's opinion when deciding to invest in a company or to make loans to a firm that has been audited. The independent audit is an important factor in the worldwide growth of financial markets.

Organizations That Influence Current Practice

Many organizations directly or indirectly influence GAAP and so influence much of what is in this book. The **Financial Accounting Standards Board (FASB)** is the most important body for developing and issuing rules on accounting practice. This independent body issues *Statements of Financial Accounting Standards*. The **American Institute of Certified Public Accountants (AICPA)** is the professional association of certified public accountants and influences accounting practice through the activities of its senior technical committees. The Securities and Exchange Commission (SEC) is an agency of the federal government that has the legal power to set and enforce accounting practices for companies whose securities are offered for sale to the general public. As such, it has enormous influence on accounting practice. The **Governmental Accounting Standards Board (GASB)**, which was established in 1984 under the same governing body as the Financial Accounting Standards Board, is responsible for issuing accounting standards for state and local governments.

With the growth of financial markets throughout the world, worldwide cooperation in the development of accounting principles has become a priority. The **International Accounting Standards Committee (IASC)** has approved more than 30 international standards, which have been translated into six languages.

U.S. tax laws that govern the assessment and collection of revenue for operating the federal government also influence accounting practice. Because a major source of the government's revenue is the income tax, these laws specify the rules for determining taxable income. These rules are interpreted and enforced by the **Internal Revenue Service (IRS)**. In some cases, these rules conflict with good accounting practice, but they still are an important influence on that practice. Businesses use certain accounting practices simply because they are required by the tax laws. Sometimes companies follow an accounting practice specified in the tax laws to take advantage of rules that can help them financially. Cases in which the tax laws affect accounting practice are noted throughout this book.

Professional Ethics and the Accounting Profession

Ethical issues are discussed in each chapter; they relate to real business situations that require ethical judgments.

Ethics is a code of conduct that applies to everyday life. It addresses the question of whether actions are right or wrong. Ethical actions are the product of individual decisions. You are faced with many situations involving ethical issues every day. Some may be potentially illegal—the temptation to take office supplies from your employer to use when you do homework, for example. Others are not illegal but are equally unethical—for example, deciding not to tell a fellow student who missed class that a test has been announced for the next class meeting.

When an organization is said to act ethically or unethically, it means that individuals within the organization have made a decision to act ethically or unethically. When a company uses false advertising, cheats customers, pollutes the environment, treats its employees poorly, or misleads investors by presenting false information in the financial statements, members of management and other employees have made a conscious decision to act unethically. In the same way, ethical behavior within a company is a direct result of the actions and decisions of the company's employees.

Professional ethics is a code of conduct that applies to the practice of a profession. Like the ethical conduct of a company, the ethical actions of a profession are a collection of individual actions. As members of a profession, accountants have a responsibility, not only to their employers and clients but to society as a whole, to uphold the highest ethical standards. Historically, accountants have been held in high regard. For example, a survey of over one thousand prominent people in business, education, and government ranked the accounting profession second only to the clergy as having the highest ethical standards.[8] It is the responsibility of every person who becomes an accountant to uphold the high standards of the profession, regardless of the field of accounting the individual enters.

To ensure that its members understand the responsibilities of being professional accountants, the AICPA and each state have adopted codes of professional conduct that must be followed by certified public accountants. Fundamental to these codes is responsibility to the public, including clients, creditors, investors, and anyone else who relies on the work of the certified public accountant. In resolving conflicts among these groups, the accountant must act with integrity, even to the sacrifice of personal benefit. **Integrity** means that the accountant is honest and candid, and subordinates personal gain to service and the public trust. The accountant must also be objective. **Objectivity** means that he or she is impartial and intellectually honest. Furthermore, the accountant must be independent. **Independence** means avoiding all relationships that impair or even appear to impair the accountant's objectivity.

One way in which the auditor of a company maintains independence is by having no direct financial interest in the company and by not being an employee of the company. The accountant must exercise **due care** in all activities, carrying out professional responsibilities with competence and diligence. For example, an accountant must not accept a job for which he or she is not qualified, even at the risk of losing a client to another firm, and careless work is not acceptable. These broad principles are supported by more specific rules that public accountants must follow. (For instance, with certain exceptions, client information must be kept strictly confidential.) Accountants who violate the rules can be disciplined or even suspended from practice.

A professional association, the **Institute of Management Accountants (IMA)**, has adopted the Code of Professional Conduct for Management Accountants. This ethical code emphasizes that management accountants have a responsibility to be competent in their jobs, to keep information confidential except when authorized or legally required to disclose it, to maintain integrity and avoid conflicts of interest, and to communicate information objectively and without bias.[9]

The Chapter Review restates each learning objective and its main ideas.

Chapter Review

REVIEW OF LEARNING OBJECTIVES

Check out ACE, a self-quizzing program on chapter content, at http://college.hmco.com.

1. **Define *accounting*, identify business goals and activities, and describe the role of accounting in making informed decisions.** Accounting is an information system that measures, processes, and communicates information, primarily financial in nature, about an identifiable entity for the purpose of making economic decisions. Management accounting focuses on the preparation of information primarily for internal decision making by management. Financial accounting is concerned with the development and use of accounting reports that are communicated to those external to the business organization as well as to management. Accounting is not an end in itself but a tool that provides the information that is necessary to make reasoned choices among alternative uses of scarce resources in the conduct of business and economic activities.

2. **Identify the many users of accounting information in society.** Accounting plays a significant role in society by providing information to managers of all institutions and to individuals with a direct financial interest in those institutions, including present or potential investors or creditors. Accounting information is also important to those with an indirect financial interest in the business—for example, tax authorities, regulatory agencies, and economic planners.

3. **Explain the importance of business transactions, money measure, and separate entity to accounting measurement.** To make an accounting measurement, the accountant must determine what is measured, when the measurement should be made, what value should be placed on what is measured, and how what is measured should be classified. Generally accepted accounting principles define the object of accounting measurement as business transactions that are measured in terms of money and are for separate entities. Relating these concepts, financial accounting uses money measure to gauge the impact of business transactions on a separate business entity.

4. **Identify the three basic forms of business organization.** The three basic forms of business organization are sole proprietorships, partnerships, and corporations. Legally, sole proprietorships, which are formed by one individual, and partnerships, which are formed by more than one individual, are not separate from their owners. In accounting, however, they are treated as separate. Corporations, whose ownership is represented by shares of stock, are separate entities for both legal and accounting purposes.

Want more review? The student study guide is a very thorough review of each learning objective, providing a detailed outline, true/false and multiple choice questions, and exercises. Answers are included. Ask for it at your bookstore.

5. **Define *financial position*, state the accounting equation, and show how they are affected by simple transactions.** Financial position is the economic resources that belong to a company and the claims against those

resources at a point in time. The accounting equation shows financial position in the equation form Assets = Liabilities + Owner's Equity. Business transactions affect financial position by decreasing or increasing assets, liabilities, or owner's equity in such a way that the accounting equation is always in balance.

6. **Identify the four financial statements.** Financial statements are the means by which accountants communicate the financial condition and activities of a business to those who have an interest in the business. The four basic financial statements are the income statement, the statement of owner's equity, the balance sheet, and the statement of cash flows.

7. **State the relationship of generally accepted accounting principles (GAAP) to financial statements and the independent CPA's report, and identify the organizations that influence GAAP.** Acceptable accounting practice consists of those conventions, rules, and procedures that make up generally accepted accounting principles at a particular time. GAAP are essential to the preparation and interpretation of financial statements and the independent CPA's report. Among the organizations that influence the formulation of GAAP are the Financial Accounting Standards Board, the American Institute of Certified Public Accountants, the Securities and Exchange Commission, and the Internal Revenue Service.

8. **Define *ethics* and describe the ethical responsibilities of accountants.** All accountants are required to follow a code of professional ethics, the foundation of which is responsibility to the public. Accountants must act with integrity, objectivity, and independence, and they must exercise due care in all their activities.

REVIEW OF CONCEPTS AND TERMINOLOGY

Notice that each chapter has a glossary that reviews the key concepts and terms defined in the chapter. For further discussion, see references to the LO next to each term.

The following concepts and terms were introduced in this chapter:

LO 1 **Accounting:** An information system that measures, processes, and communicates financial information about an identifiable economic entity.

LO 5 **Accounting equation:** Assets = Liabilities + Owner's Equity.

LO 5 **Accounts:** The labels used by accountants to accumulate the amounts produced from similar transactions.

LO 7 **American Institute of Certified Public Accountants (AICPA):** The professional association of certified public accountants.

LO 5 **Assets:** Economic resources owned by a business that are expected to benefit future operations.

LO 7 **Audit:** An examination of a company's financial statements in order to render an independent professional opinion that they have been presented fairly, in all material respects, in conformity with generally accepted accounting principles.

LO 6 **Balance sheet:** The financial statement that shows the assets, liabilities, and owner's equity of a business at a point in time. Also called a *statement of financial position*.

LO 1 **Bookkeeping:** The process of recording financial transactions and keeping financial records.

LO 1 **Business:** An economic unit that aims to sell goods and services to customers at prices that will provide an adequate return to its owners.

LO 3 **Business transactions:** Economic events that affect the financial position of a business entity.

LO 6 **Cash flows:** The inflows and outflows of cash into and out of a business.

LO 7 **Certified public accountants (CPAs):** Public accountants who have met the stringent licensing requirements set by the individual states.

LO 1 **Computer:** An electronic tool for the rapid collection, organization, and communication of large amounts of information.

LO 4 **Corporation:** A business unit granted a state charter recognizing it as a separate legal entity having its own rights, privileges, and liabilities distinct from those of its owners.

LO 8 **Due care:** The act of carrying out professional responsibilities competently and diligently.

LO 8 **Ethics:** A code of conduct that addresses whether everyday actions are right or wrong.

LO 3 **Exchange rate:** The value of one currency in terms of another.

LO 5 **Expenses:** Decreases in owner's equity that result from operating a business.

LO 1 **Financial accounting:** The process of generating and communicating accounting information in the form of financial statements to those outside the organization.

LO 7 **Financial Accounting Standards Board (FASB):** The most important body for developing and issuing rules on accounting practice, called *Statements of Financial Accounting Standards*.

LO 5 **Financial position:** The economic resources that belong to a company and the claims (equities) against those resources at a point in time.

LO 1 **Financial statements:** The primary means of communicating important accounting information to users. They include the income statement, statement of owner's equity, balance sheet, and statement of cash flows.

LO 1 **Financing activities:** Activities undertaken by management to obtain adequate funds to begin and to continue operating a business.

LO 7 **Generally accepted accounting principles (GAAP):** The conventions, rules, and procedures that define accepted accounting practice at a particular time.

LO 7 **Governmental Accounting Standards Board (GASB):** The board responsible for issuing accounting standards for state and local governments.

LO 6 **Income statement:** The financial statement that summarizes the revenues earned and expenses incurred by a business over a period of time.

LO 8 **Independence:** The avoidance of all relationships that impair or appear to impair an accountant's objectivity.

LO 8 **Institute of Management Accountants (IMA):** A professional organization made up primarily of management accountants.

LO 8 **Integrity:** Honesty, candidness, and the subordination of personal gain to service and the public trust.

LO 7 **Internal Revenue Service (IRS):** The federal agency that interprets and enforces the tax laws governing the assessment and collection of revenue for operating the national government.

LO 7 **International Accounting Standards Committee (IASC):** The organization that encourages worldwide cooperation in the development of accounting principles; it has approved more than 30 international standards of accounting.

LO 1 **Investing activities:** Activities undertaken by management to spend capital in ways that are productive and will help a business achieve its objectives.

LO 5 **Liabilities:** Present obligations of a business to pay cash, transfer assets, or provide services to other entities in the future.

LO 1 **Liquidity:** Having enough cash available to pay debts when they are due.

LO 2 **Management:** Collectively, the people who have overall responsibility for operating a business and meeting its goals.

LO 1 **Management accounting:** The process of producing accounting information for the internal use of a company's management.

LO 1   **Management information system (MIS):** The interconnected subsystems that provide the information needed to run a business.

LO 3   **Money measure:** The recording of all business transactions in terms of money.

LO 5   **Net assets:** Assets minus liabilities; owner's equity.

LO 5   **Net income:** The difference between revenues and expenses when revenues exceed expenses.

LO 5   **Net loss:** The difference between expenses and revenues when expenses exceed revenues.

LO 8   **Objectivity:** Impartiality and intellectual honesty.

LO 1   **Operating activities:** Activities undertaken by management in the course of running the business.

LO 5   **Owner's equity:** The residual interest in the assets of a business entity that remains after deducting the entity's liabilities. Also called *residual equity*.

LO 5   **Owner's investments:** The assets that the owner puts into the business.

LO 5   **Owner's withdrawals:** The assets that the owner takes out of the business.

LO 4   **Partnership:** A business owned by two or more people that is not incorporated.

LO 1   **Performance measures:** Indicators of whether managers are achieving business goals and whether the business activities are well managed.

LO 8   **Professional ethics:** A code of conduct that applies to the practice of a profession.

LO 1   **Profitability:** The ability to earn enough income to attract and hold investment capital.

LO 5   **Revenues:** Increases in owner's equity that result from operating a business.

LO 2   **Securities and Exchange Commission (SEC):** An agency of the federal government set up by the U.S. Congress to protect the public by regulating the issuing, buying, and selling of stocks. It has the legal power to set and enforce accounting practices for firms whose securities are sold to the general public.

LO 3   **Separate entity:** A business that is treated as distinct from its creditors, customers, and owners.

LO 4   **Sole proprietorship:** A business owned by one person that is not incorporated.

LO 6   **Statement of cash flows:** The financial statement that shows the inflows and outflows of cash from operating activities, investing activities, and financing activities over a period of time.

LO 6   **Statement of owner's equity:** The financial statement that shows the change in owner's capital over a period of time.

REVIEW PROBLEM

LO 5

Not sure you understood the techniques and calculations or want to check if you are ready for a chapter test? The review problem models main computations or analysis of the chapter and other problem assignments. The answer is provided for immediate feedback.

Effect of Transactions on the Accounting Equation

Charlene Rudek finished law school in June and immediately set up her own law practice. During the first month of operation, she completed these transactions.

a. Began the practice by placing $2,000 in a bank account established for the business.
b. Purchased a law library for $900 cash.
c. Purchased office supplies for $400 on credit.
d. Accepted $500 in cash for completing a contract.
e. Billed clients $1,950 for services rendered during the month.
f. Paid $200 of the amount owed for office supplies.
g. Received $1,250 in cash from one client who had been billed previously for services rendered.
h. Paid rent expense for the month in the amount of $1,200.
i. Withdrew $400 from the practice for personal use.

1. Show the effect of each of these transactions on the balance sheet equation by completing a table similar to Exhibit 1. Identify each owner's equity transaction.

2. Contrast the effects on cash flows of transactions **c** and **f** with transaction **b** and of transactions **e** and **g** with transaction **d**.

**ANSWER TO
REVIEW
PROBLEM**

1. Table of effects of transactions on the accounting equation

	Assets				= Liabilities +	Owner's Equity	
	Cash	Accounts Receivable	Office Supplies	Law Library	Accounts Payable	C. Rudek, Capital	Type of OE Transaction
a.	$2,000					$2,000	Owner's Investment
b.	−900			+$900			
bal.	$1,100			$900		$2,000	
c.			+$400		+$400		
bal.	$1,100		$400	$900	$400	$2,000	
d.	+500					+ 500	Legal Fees Earned
bal.	$1,600		$400	$900	$400	$2,500	
e.		+$1,950				+1,950	Legal Fees Earned
bal.	$1,600	$1,950	$400	$900	$400	$4,450	
f.	−200				−200		
bal.	$1,400	$1,950	$400	$900	$200	$4,450	
g.	+1,250	−1,250					
bal.	$2,650	$ 700	$400	$900	$200	$4,450	
h.	−1,200					−1,200	Rent Expense
bal.	$1,450	$ 700	$400	$900	$200	$3,250	
i.	−400					−400	Owner's Withdrawal
bal.	$1,050	$ 700	$400	$900	$200	$2,850	
			$3,050			$3,050	

2. Transaction **c**, a purchase on credit, enables the company to use the asset immediately and defer payment of cash until later. Cash is expended to partially pay for the asset in transaction **f**. The remainder is to be paid subsequently. This series of transactions contrasts with transaction **b**, in which cash is expended immediately for the asset. In each case, an asset is purchased, but the effects on cash flows are different.

Transaction **e**, a sale on credit, allows the customer to pay later for services provided. This payment is partially received in transaction **g**, and the remainder is to be received later. These transactions contrast with transaction **d**, in which payment is received immediately for the services performed. In each case, the revenue is earned at the time the service is provided to the customer, but the effect on cash flows is different.

Chapter Assignments

**BUILDING YOUR
KNOWLEDGE
FOUNDATION**

*Questions review key
concepts, terminology, and
topics of the chapter.*

QUESTIONS

1. Why is accounting considered an information system?
2. What is the role of accounting in the decision-making process, and what broad business goals and activities does it help management to achieve and manage?
3. Distinguish between management accounting and financial accounting.
4. Distinguish among these terms: *accounting, bookkeeping,* and *management information systems.*
5. Which decision makers use accounting information?
6. A business is an economic unit whose goal is to sell goods and services to customers at prices that will provide an adequate return to the business's owners. What functions must management perform to achieve that goal?
7. Why are investors and creditors interested in reviewing the financial statements of a company?
8. Among those who use accounting information are people and organizations that have an indirect interest in the business entity. Briefly describe these people and organizations.
9. Why has society, as a whole, become one of the largest users of accounting information?
10. Use the terms *business transactions, money measure,* and *separate entity* in a single sentence that demonstrates their relevance to financial accounting.
11. How do sole proprietorships, partnerships, and corporations differ?
12. Define *assets, liabilities,* and *owner's equity.*
13. Arnold Smith's company has assets of $22,000 and liabilities of $10,000. What is the amount of the owner's equity?
14. What four elements affect owner's capital? How?
15. Give examples of the types of transactions that (a) increase assets and (b) increase liabilities.
16. What is the function of the statement of owner's equity?
17. Why is the balance sheet sometimes called the statement of financial position?
18. Contrast the purpose of the balance sheet with that of the income statement.
19. A statement for an accounting period that ends in June can be headed "June 30, 20xx" or "For the Year Ended June 30, 20xx." Which heading is appropriate for (a) a balance sheet and (b) an income statement?
20. How does the income statement differ from the statement of cash flows?
21. What are GAAP? Why are they important to the readers of financial statements?
22. What do auditors mean by the phrase *in all material respects* when they state that financial statements "present fairly, in all material respects . . . in conformity with generally accepted accounting principles"?
23. What organization has the most influence on GAAP?
24. Discuss the importance of professional ethics in the accounting profession.

*Short exercises are a simple
application of chapter material
for a single learning objective.
Notice the reference to the
learning objective so you can
easily refer back to the text
for help.*

SHORT EXERCISES

SE 1.

LO 3   Accounting Concepts

Tell whether each of the following words or phrases relates most closely to (a) a business transaction, (b) a separate entity, or (c) a money measure.

1. Partnership
2. U.S. dollar
3. Payment of an expense
4. Corporation
5. Sale of an asset

SE 2.
LO 5 **The Accounting Equation**

Determine the amount missing from each accounting equation below.

	Assets	=	Liabilities	+	Owner's Equity
1.	?		$25,000		$35,000
2.	$ 78,000		$42,000		?
3.	$146,000		?		$96,000

SE 3.
LO 5 **The Accounting Equation**

Use the accounting equation to answer each question below.

1. The assets of Cruse Company are $480,000, and the liabilities are $360,000. What is the amount of the owner's equity?
2. The liabilities of Nabors Company equal one-fifth of the total assets. The owner's equity is $80,000. What is the amount of the liabilities?

SE 4.
LO 5 **The Accounting Equation**

Use the accounting equation to answer each question below.

1. At the beginning of the year, Gilbert Company's assets were $180,000, and its owner's equity was $100,000. During the year, assets increased by $60,000 and liabilities increased by $10,000. What was the owner's equity at the end of the year?
2. At the beginning of the year, Sailor Company had liabilities of $50,000 and owner's equity of $48,000. If assets increased by $20,000 and liabilities decreased by $15,000, what was the owner's equity at the end of the year?

SE 5.
LO 5 **The Accounting Equation and Net Income**

Use the following information and the accounting equation to determine the net income for the year for each alternative below.

	Assets	Liabilities
Beginning of the year	$ 70,000	$30,000
End of the year	100,000	50,000

1. No investments were made in the business and no withdrawals were made during the year.
2. Investments of $10,000 were made in the business, but no withdrawals were made during the year.
3. No investments were made in the business, but withdrawals of $2,000 were made during the year.

SE 6.
LO 5 **The Accounting Equation and Net Income**

Murillo Company had assets of $140,000 and liabilities of $60,000 at the beginning of the year, and assets of $200,000 and liabilities of $70,000 at the end of the year. During the year, there was an investment of $20,000 in the business, and withdrawals of $24,000 were made. What amount of net income was earned during the year?

SE 7.
LO 5 **Effect of Transactions on the Accounting Equation**

On a sheet of paper, list the numbers 1 through 6, with columns labeled Assets, Liabilities, and Owner's Equity. In the columns, indicate whether each transaction that follows caused an increase (+), a decrease (−), or no change (NC) in assets, liabilities, and owner's equity.

1. Purchased equipment on credit.
2. Purchased equipment for cash.
3. Billed customers for services performed.
4. Received and immediately paid a utility bill.
5. Received payment from a previously billed customer.
6. The owner made an additional investment.

SE 8.
LO 5 **Effect of Transactions on the Accounting Equation**

On a sheet of paper, list the numbers 1 through 6, with columns labeled Assets, Liabilities, and Owner's Equity. In the columns, indicate whether each transaction below caused an increase (+), a decrease (−), or no change (NC) in assets, liabilities, and owner's equity.

1. Purchased supplies on credit.
2. Paid for previously purchased supplies.
3. Paid employee's weekly wages.

4. Cash withdrawal by owner.
5. Purchased a truck with cash.
6. Received a telephone bill to be paid next month.

SE 9.

LO 6 Preparation and Completion of a Balance Sheet

Use the following accounts and balances to prepare a balance sheet for DeLay Company at June 30, 20x1, using Exhibit 2 as a model.

Accounts Receivable	$ 800
Wages Payable	250
Owner's Capital	13,750
Building	10,000
Cash	?

Exercises are richer applications of all chapter material referenced by LOs.

EXERCISES

E 1.

LO 1 The Nature of
LO 2 Accounting
LO 7

Match the terms on the left with the descriptions on the right.

_b_ 1. Bookkeeping
_c_ 2. Creditors
_a_ 3. Measurement
_d_ 4. Financial Accounting Standards Board (FASB)
_c_ 5. Tax authorities
_e_ 6. Computer
_a_ 7. Communication
_c_ _d_ 8. Securities and Exchange Commission (SEC)
_c_ 9. Investors
_a_ 10. Processing
_c_ 11. Management
_e_ 12. Management information system

a. Function of accounting
b. Often confused with accounting
c. User(s) of accounting information
d. Organization that influences current practice
e. Tool that facilitates the practice of accounting

E 2.

LO 3 Business Transactions

Lionel owns and operates a minimart. State which of the actions below are business transactions. Explain why any other actions are not regarded as transactions.

1. Lionel reduces the price of a gallon of milk in order to match the price offered by a competitor.
2. Lionel pays a high school student cash for cleaning up the driveway behind the market.
3. Lionel fills his son's car with gasoline in payment for restocking the vending machines and the snack food shelves.
4. Lionel pays interest to himself on a loan he made to the business three years ago.

E 3.

LO 3 Accounting Concepts
LO 4

Financial accounting uses money measures to gauge the impact of business transactions on a separate business entity. Tell whether each of the following words or phrases relates most closely to (a) a business transaction, (b) a separate entity, or (c) a money measure.

1. Corporation
2. French franc
3. Sales of products
4. Receipt of cash
5. Sole proprietorship
6. U.S. dollar
7. Partnership
8. Owner's investments
9. Japanese yen
10. Purchase of supplies

E 4.

LO 3 Money Measure

You have been asked to compare the sales and assets of four companies that make computer chips and determine which company is the largest in each category. You have gathered the following data, but they cannot be used for direct comparison because each company's sales and assets are in its own currency:

Company (Currency)	Sales	Assets
Inchip (U.S. dollar)	20,000,000	13,000,000
Wong (Singapore dollar)	50,000,000	24,000,000
Mitzu (Japanese yen)	3,500,000,000	2,500,000,000
Works (Euro)	35,000,000	49,000,000

Assuming that the exchange rates in Table 1 are current and appropriate, convert all the figures to U.S. dollars and determine which company is the largest in sales and which is the largest in assets.

E 5.

LO 5   The Accounting Equation

Use the accounting equation to answer each question that follows. Show any calculations you make.

1. The assets of Ortega Company are $650,000, and the owner's equity is $360,000. What is the amount of the liabilities?
2. The liabilities and owner's equity of Hires Company are $95,000 and $32,000, respectively. What is the amount of the assets?
3. The liabilities of Whitehead Company equal one-third of the total assets, and owner's equity is $120,000. What is the amount of the liabilities?
4. At the beginning of the year, Feinglass's assets were $220,000 and its owner's equity was $100,000. During the year, assets increased $60,000 and liabilities decreased $10,000. What is the owner's equity at the end of the year?

E 6.

LO 5   Owner's Equity Transactions

Identify the following transactions by marking each as an owner's investment (I), owner's withdrawal (W), revenue (R), expense (E), or not an owner's equity transaction (NOE).

a. Received cash for providing a service.
b. Took assets out of the business for personal expenses.
c. Received cash from a customer previously billed for a service.
d. Transferred assets to the business from a personal account.
e. Paid a service station for gasoline for a business vehicle.
f. Performed a service and received a promise of payment.
g. Paid cash to purchase equipment.
h. Paid cash to an employee for services performed.

E 7.

LO 5   Effect of Transactions on the Accounting Equation

During the month of April, Soo Corporation had the following transactions:

a. Paid salaries for April, $5,400.
b. Purchased equipment on credit, $9,000.
c. Purchased supplies with cash, $300.
d. Additional investment by owner, $12,000.
e. Received payment for services performed, $1,800.
f. Made partial payment on equipment purchased in transaction **b,** $3,000.
g. Billed customers for services performed, $4,800.
h. Cash withdrawal by owner, $4,500.
i. Received payment from customers billed in transaction **g,** $900.
j. Received utility bill, $210.

On a sheet of paper, list the letters **a** through **j,** with columns labeled Assets, Liabilities, and Owner's Equity. In the columns, indicate whether each transaction caused an increase (+), a decrease (−), or no change (NC) in assets, liabilities, and owner's equity.

E 8.

LO 5   Examples of Transactions

For each of the following categories, describe a transaction that would have the required effect on the elements of the accounting equation.

1. Increase one asset and decrease another asset.
2. Decrease an asset and decrease a liability.
3. Increase an asset and increase a liability.
4. Increase an asset and increase owner's equity.
5. Decrease an asset and decrease owner's equity.

E 9.

LO 5 **Effect of Transactions on the Accounting Equation**

The total assets and liabilities at the beginning and end of the year for Foskett Company are listed below.

	Assets	Liabilities
Beginning of the year	$110,000	$ 45,000
End of the year	200,000	120,000

Determine Foskett Company's net income for the year under each of the alternatives that follow. The owner made

1. No investments in or withdrawals from the business during the year.
2. No investments in the business but withdrew $22,000 during the year.
3. An investment of $13,000 in the business, but no withdrawals during the year.
4. An investment of $10,000 in the business and withdrew $22,000 during the year.

E 10.

LO 5 **Identification of Accounts**
LO 6

1. Indicate whether each of the following accounts is an asset (A), a liability (L), or a part of owner's equity (OE).
   a. Cash
   b. Salaries Payable
   c. Accounts Receivable
   d. F. Lane, Capital
   e. Land
   f. Accounts Payable
   g. Supplies

2. Indicate whether each account would be shown on the income statement (IS), the statement of owner's equity (OE), or the balance sheet (BS).
   a. Repair Revenue
   b. Automobile
   c. Fuel Expense
   d. Cash
   e. Rent Expense
   f. Accounts Payable
   g. F. Lane, Withdrawals

E 11.

LO 6 **Preparation of a Balance Sheet**

Listed in random order below are the balances for balance sheet items for the Bell Company as of June 30, 20xx.

Accounts Payable	$20,000	Accounts Receivable	$25,000
Building	45,000	Cash	10,000
N. Bell, Capital	85,000	Equipment	20,000
Supplies	5,000		

Sort the balances and prepare a balance sheet similar to the one in Exhibit 2.

E 12.

LO 6 **Completion of Financial Statements**

Determine the amounts that correspond to the letters by completing the following independent sets of financial statements. (Assume no new investments by the owners.)

Income Statement	Set A	Set B	Set C
Revenues	$1,100	$ g	$340
Expenses	a	5,200	m
Net Income	$ b	$ h	$180
Statement of Owner's Equity			
Beginning Balance	$2,900	$15,400	$200
Net Income	c	1,600	n
Less Withdrawals	200	i	o
Ending Balance	$3,000	$ j	$ p
Balance Sheet			
Total Assets	$ d	$21,000	$ q
Liabilities	$1,600	$ 5,000	$ r
Owner's Equity	e	k	380
Total Liabilities and Owner's Equity	$ f	$ l	$580

E 13.

LO 6 Preparation of Financial Statements

Wagoner Company engaged in the following activities during the year: Service Revenues, $52,800; Rent Expense, $4,800; Wages Expense, $33,080; Advertising Expense, $5,400; Utilities Expense, $3,600; and Sy Wagoner, Withdrawals, $2,800. In addition, the year-end balances of selected accounts were as follows: Cash, $6,200; Accounts Receivable, $3,000; Supplies, $400; Land, $4,000; Accounts Payable, $1,800; and Sy Wagoner, Capital, $8,680.

Using good form, prepare the income statement, statement of owner's equity, and balance sheet for Wagoner Company (assume the year ends on June 30, 20x2). (**Hint:** The amount given for Sy Wagoner, Capital is the beginning balance.)

E 14.

LO 6 Statement of Cash Flows

Buena Company began the year 20x2 with cash of $86,000. In addition to earning a net income of $50,000 and making an owner's withdrawal of $30,000 for his personal use, Buena borrowed $120,000 from the bank and purchased equipment for $180,000 with cash. Also, Accounts Receivable increased by $12,000 and Accounts Payable increased by $18,000.

Determine the amount of cash on hand at the end of the year (December 31) by preparing a statement of cash flows similar to the one in Exhibit 2.

E 15.

LO 7 Accounting Abbreviations

Identify the accounting meaning of each of the following abbreviations: AICPA, SEC, GAAP, FASB, IRS, GASB, IASC, IMA, and CPA.

PROBLEMS

P 1.

LO 5 Effect of Transactions on the Accounting Equation

Problems are comprehensive applications of chapter material often covering multiple learning objectives.

Frame-It Center was started by Brenda Kuzma in a small shopping center. In the first weeks of operation, she completed the following transactions.

a. Deposited $7,000 in an account in the name of the company to start the business.
b. Paid the current month's rent, $900.
c. Purchased store equipment on credit, $3,600.
d. Purchased framing supplies for cash, $1,700.
e. Received framing revenues, $800.
f. Billed customers for services, $700.
g. Paid utilities expense, $250.
h. Received payment from customers in transaction f, $200.
i. Made payment on store equipment purchased in transaction c, $1,800.
j. Withdrew cash for personal expenses, $400.

REQUIRED

1. Arrange the following asset, liability, and owner's equity accounts in an equation similar to Exhibit 1: Cash, Accounts Receivable, Framing Supplies, Store Equipment, Accounts Payable, and Brenda Kuzma, Capital.

2. Show by addition and subtraction, as in Exhibit 1, the effects of the transactions on the accounting equation. Show new balances after each transaction, and identify each owner's equity transaction by type.

3. Contrast the effects on cash flows of transactions c and i with transaction d and of transactions f and h with transaction e.

P 2.

LO 5 Effect of Transactions on the Accounting Equation

All problems can be worked on Excel Template Software.

The Jiffy Messenger Company was founded by Hector Moreno on December 1 and engaged in the following transactions.

a. Deposited $9,000 in a bank account established in the name of Jiffy Messenger Company to start the business.
b. Purchased a motorbike on credit, $3,100.
c. Purchased delivery supplies for cash, $200.
d. Billed a customer for a delivery, $100.
e. Received delivery fees in cash, $300.
f. Made a payment on the motorbike, $700.
g. Paid repair expense, $120.
h. Received payment from customer billed in transaction d, $50.
i. Withdrew cash for personal expenses, $150.

REQUIRED

1. Arrange the following asset, liability, and owner's equity accounts in an equation similar to Exhibit 1: Cash, Accounts Receivable, Delivery Supplies, Motorbike, Accounts Payable, and Hector Moreno, Capital.

2. Show by addition and subtraction, as in Exhibit 1, the effects of the transactions on the accounting equation. Show new balances after each transaction, and identify each owner's equity transaction by type.

P 3.

LO 5 Effect of Transactions on the Accounting Equation

After completing her Ph.D. in management, Delia Chan set up a consulting practice. At the end of her first month of operation, Dr. Chan had the following account balances: Cash, $2,930; Accounts Receivable, $1,400; Office Supplies, $270; Office Equipment, $4,200; Accounts Payable, $1,900; and Delia Chan, Capital, $6,900. Soon thereafter, the following transactions were completed.

a. Paid current month's rent, $800.
b. Made payment toward accounts payable, $450.
c. Billed clients for services performed, $800.
d. Received payment from clients billed last month, $1,000.
e. Purchased office supplies for cash, $80.
f. Paid part-time secretary's salary, $850.
g. Paid utilities expense, $90.
h. Paid telephone expense, $50.
i. Purchased additional office equipment for cash, $400.
j. Received cash from clients for services performed, $1,200.
k. Withdrew cash for personal expenses, $500.

REQUIRED

Curious if you got the right answer? Look at the Check Figures section before Chapter 1.

1. Arrange the following asset, liability, and owner's equity accounts in an equation similar to Exhibit 1: Cash, Accounts Receivable, Office Supplies, Office Equipment, Accounts Payable, and Delia Chan, Capital.

2. Enter the beginning balances of the assets, liabilities, and owner's equity.

3. Show by addition and subtraction, as in Exhibit 1, the effects of the transactions on the accounting equation. Show new balances after each transaction, and identify each owner's equity transaction by type.

P 4.

LO 6 Preparation of Financial Statements

At the end of its first month of operation, June, 20xx, Lerner Plumbing Company had the following account balances.

Cash	$29,300
Accounts Receivable	5,400
Delivery Truck	19,000
Tools	3,800
Accounts Payable	4,300

In addition, during the month of June, the following transactions affected owner's equity.

Initial investment by M. Lerner	$20,000
Withdrawals by M. Lerner	2,000
Further investment by M. Lerner	30,000
Contract revenue	11,600
Repair revenue	2,800
Salaries expense	8,300
Rent expense	700
Fuel expense	200

REQUIRED

Using Exhibit 2 as a model, prepare an income statement, a statement of owner's equity, and a balance sheet for Lerner Plumbing Company. (**Hint:** The final balance of M. Lerner, Capital is $53,200.)

P 5.

LO 5 Effect of Transactions on the
LO 6 Accounting Equation and Preparation of Financial Statements

Royal Copying Service began operations and engaged in the following transactions during July 20xx.

a. Linda Friedman deposited $5,000 in cash in an account in the name of the company to start the business.
b. Paid current month's rent, $950.
c. Purchased copier for cash, $2,500.
d. Paid cash for paper and other copier supplies, $190.
e. Received copying job payments in cash, $890.

f. Billed copying job to major customer, $680.
g. Paid wages to part-time employees, $280.
h. Purchased additional copier supplies on credit, $140.
i. Received partial payment from customer in transaction **f**, $300.
j. Paid current month's utility bill, $90.
k. Made partial payment on supplies purchased in transaction **h**, $70.
l. Withdrew cash for personal use, $700.

REQUIRED

1. Arrange the asset, liability, and owner's equity accounts in an equation similar to Exhibit 1, using these account titles: Cash, Accounts Receivable, Supplies, Copier, Accounts Payable, and L. Friedman, Capital.

2. Show by addition and subtraction, as in Exhibit 1, the effects of the transactions on the accounting equation. Show new balances after each transaction, and identify each owner's equity transaction by type.

3. Using Exhibit 2 as a guide, prepare an income statement, a statement of owner's equity, and a balance sheet for Royal Copying Service.

Looking for more practice? Alternate problems model an earlier problem in the chapter with the same format and learning objectives.

ALTERNATE PROBLEMS

P 6.
LO 5 **Effect of Transactions on the Accounting Equation**

Carmen Vega, after receiving her degree in computer science, started her own business, Custom Systems Company. She completed the following transactions soon after starting the business.

a. Deposited $9,000 in the bank and contributed a systems library valued at $920 to start the business.
b. Paid current month's rent on an office, $360.
c. Purchased a minicomputer for cash, $7,000.
d. Purchased computer supplies on credit, $600.
e. Received payment from a client for programming done, $800.
f. Billed a client on completion of a short programming project, $710.
g. Paid wages, $800.
h. Received a partial payment from the client billed in transaction **f**, $80.
i. Withdrew $250 in cash for personal expenses.
j. Made a partial payment on the computer supplies purchased in transaction **d**, $200.

REQUIRED

1. Arrange the asset, liability, and owner's equity accounts in an equation similar to Exhibit 1, using the following account titles: Cash, Accounts Receivable, Supplies, Equipment, Systems Library, Accounts Payable, and Carmen Vega, Capital.

2. Show by addition and subtraction, as in Exhibit 1, the effects of the transactions on the accounting equation. Show new balances after each transaction, and identify each owner's equity transaction by type.

3. Contrast the effects on cash flows of transactions **d** and **j** with transaction **c** and of transactions **f** and **h** with transaction **e**.

P 7.
LO 5 **Effect of Transactions on the Accounting Equation**

On June 1, Henry Redmond started a new business, the Redmond Transport Company. During the month of June, the firm completed the following transactions.

a. Deposited $66,000 in cash in a new bank account to establish the Redmond Transport Company.
b. Purchased a truck for cash, $43,000.
c. Purchased equipment on credit, $9,000.
d. Billed a customer for hauling goods, $1,200.
e. Received cash for hauling goods, $2,300.
f. Received cash payment from the customer billed in transaction **d**, $600.
g. Made a payment on the equipment purchased in transaction **c**, $5,000.
h. Paid wages expense in cash, $1,700.
i. Withdrew cash from the business for personal use, $1,200.

REQUIRED

1. Arrange the asset, liability, and owner's equity accounts in an equation similar to Exhibit 1, using the following account titles: Cash, Accounts Receivable, Trucks, Equipment, Accounts Payable, and Henry Redmond, Capital.

2. Show by addition and subtraction, as in Exhibit 1, the effects of the transactions on the accounting equation. Show new balances after each transaction, and identify each owner's equity transaction by type.

P 8.
LO 5 **Effect of Transactions on the**
LO 6 **Accounting Equation and**
Preparation of Financial
Statements

On April 1, 20xx, Dependable Taxi Service began operation. The company engaged in the following transactions during April.

a. Investment by owner, Suzy Maguire, $42,000.
b. Purchased taxi for cash, $19,000.
c. Purchased uniforms on credit, $400.
d. Received taxi fares in cash, $3,200.
e. Paid wages to part-time drivers, $500.
f. Purchased gasoline during month for cash, $800.
g. Purchased car washes during month on credit, $120.
h. Further investment by owner, $5,000.
i. Paid part of the amount owed for the uniforms purchased in transaction **c,** $200.
j. Billed major client for fares, $900.
k. Paid for automobile repairs, $250.
l. Withdrew cash from business for personal use, $1,000.

REQUIRED

1. Arrange the asset, liability, and owner's equity accounts in an equation similar to Exhibit 1, using the following account titles: Cash, Accounts Receivable, Uniforms, Taxi, Accounts Payable, and Suzy Maguire, Capital.

2. Show by addition and subtraction, as in Exhibit 1, the effects of the transactions on the accounting equation. Show new balances after each transaction, and identify each owner's equity transaction by type.

3. Using Exhibit 2 as a guide, prepare an income statement, a statement of owner's equity, and a balance sheet for Dependable Taxi Service.

EXPANDING YOUR CRITICAL THINKING, COMMUNICATION, AND INTERPERSONAL SKILLS

These cases focus on conceptual accounting issues based on real companies and situations.

SKILLS DEVELOPMENT

Conceptual Analysis

SD 1.
LO 1 **Business Activities and**
LO 2 **Management Functions**

J.C. Penney Company, Inc., is America's largest department store company. According to its letter to stockholders, financial results didn't meet company expectations.

> J.C. Penney is implementing a number of strategic initiatives to ensure our competitiveness, to meet our growth objectives, and to provide a strong return on our stockholders' investment. These initiatives include: accelerated growth in our top 10 markets; expand our women's apparel and accessories business; speed merchandise to market; reduce our cost structure and enhance customer service.[10]

To achieve its strategy, J.C. Penney must organize its management into functions that relate to the principal activities of a business. Discuss the three basic activities J.C. Penney will engage in to achieve its goals, and suggest some examples of each. What is the role of J.C. Penney's management, and what functions must its management perform to accomplish these activities?

| Cash Flow | CD-ROM | Communication | Critical Thinking | Ethics | General Ledger | Group Activity | Hot Links to Real Companies | International | Internet | Key Ratio | Memo | Spreadsheet |

SD 2.

LO 3 Concept of an Asset

Southwest Airlines Co. is one of the most successful airlines in the United States. Its annual report contains this statement: "We are a company of People, not Planes. That is what distinguishes us from other airlines and other companies. At Southwest Airlines, People are our most important asset."[11] Are employees considered assets in the financial statements? Discuss in what sense Southwest considers its employees to be assets.

Ethical Dilemma

SD 3.

LO 8 Professional Ethics

Ethical dilemmas provide practice in dealing with the tough choices businesses often face.

Discuss the ethical choices in the situations below. In each instance, determine the alternative courses of action, describe the ethical dilemma, and tell what you would do.

1. You are the payroll accountant for a small business. A friend asks you how much another employee is paid per hour.

2. As an accountant for the branch office of a wholesale supplier, you discover that several of the receipts the branch manager has submitted for reimbursement as selling expense actually stem from nights out with his spouse.

3. You are an accountant in the purchasing department of a construction company. When you arrive home from work on December 22, you find a large ham in a box marked "Happy Holidays—It's a pleasure to work with you." The gift is from a supplier who has bid on a contract your employer plans to award next week.

4. As an auditor with one year's experience at a local CPA firm, you are expected to complete a certain part of an audit in 20 hours. Because of your lack of experience, you know you cannot finish the job within that time. Rather than admit this, you are thinking about working late to finish the job and not telling anyone.

5. You are a tax accountant at a local CPA firm. You help your neighbor fill out her tax return, and she pays you $200 in cash. Because there is no record of this transaction, you are considering not reporting it on your tax return.

6. The accounting firm for which you work as a CPA has just won a new client, a firm in which you own 200 shares of stock that you received as an inheritance from your grandmother. Because it is only a small number of shares and you think the company will be very successful, you are considering not disclosing the investment.

Group Activity. Assign each case to a different group to resolve and report.

You are asked to gather information from the Internet or business publications and apply it to the accounting concepts in the chapter.

Research Activity

SD 4.

LO 1 Need for Knowledge of
LO 2 Accounting

Locate an article about a company from one of the following sources: the business section of your local paper or a nearby metropolitan daily, *The Wall Street Journal*, *Business Week*, *Forbes*, or the Needles Accounting Resource Center web site at http://college.hmco.com. List all the financial and accounting terms used in the article. Bring the article to class and be prepared to discuss how a knowledge of accounting would help a reader understand the content of the article.

Decision-Making Practice

SD 5.

LO 5 Effect of Transactions on the
LO 6 Balance Sheet

What are the relevant numbers and what do they mean? Practice making business decisions based on accounting information.

Instead of hunting for a summer job after finishing her junior year in college, Lucy Henderson organized a lawn service company in her neighborhood. To start her business on June 1, she deposited $1,350 in a new bank account in the name of her company. The $1,350 consisted of a $500 loan from her father and $850 of her own money. Using the money in this checking account, Henderson rented lawn equipment, purchased supplies, and hired neighborhood high school students to mow and trim the lawns of neighbors who had agreed to pay her for the service. At the end of each month, she mailed bills to her customers.

On August 31, Henderson was ready to dissolve her business and go back to school for the fall quarter. Because she had been so busy, she had not kept any records other than her checkbook and a list of amounts owed to her by customers.

Her checkbook had a balance of $1,760, and the amount owed to her by customers totaled $435. She expected these customers to pay her during October. She planned to return unused supplies to Suburban Landscaping Company for a full credit of $25. When she brought back the rented lawn equipment, Suburban Landscaping also would return a deposit of $100 she had made in June. She owed Suburban Landscaping $260 for equipment rentals and supplies. In addition, she owed the students who had worked for her $50, and she still owed her father $350. Although Henderson feels she did quite well, she is not sure just how successful she was.

1. Prepare a balance sheet dated June 1 and one dated August 31 for Henderson Lawn Care Company.
2. Comment on the performance of Henderson Lawn Care Company by comparing the two balance sheets. Did the company have a profit or a loss? (Assume that Henderson used none of the company's assets for personal purposes.)
3. If Henderson wants to continue her business next summer, what kind of information from her recordkeeping system would help make it easier to tell whether or not she is earning a profit?

FINANCIAL REPORTING AND ANALYSIS

Interpreting Financial Reports

FRA 1
LO 6 Nature of Cash, Assets, and Net Income

Using excerpts from business articles or annual reports of well-known companies, you are asked to extract relevant data, make computations, and interpret your results.

Charles Schwab Corporation is a rapidly growing financial services firm. Information for 1999 and 1998 adapted from the company's annual report is presented below.[12] (All numbers are in thousands.) Three students who were looking at Charles Schwab's annual report were overhead to make the following comments:

Student A: What a great year Charles Schwab had in 1999! The company earned net income of $7,034,671,000 because its total assets increased from $22,264,390,000 to $29,299,061,000.

Student B: But the change in total assets isn't the same as net income! The company had a net income of only $923,200,000 because cash increased from $1,155,928,000 to $2,079,128,000.

	Charles Schwab **Condensed Balance Sheets** **December 31, 1999 and 1998** **(in thousands)**	
	1999	**1998**
Assets		
Cash	$ 2,079,128	$ 1,155,928
Other Assets	27,219,933	21,108,462
Total Assets	$29,299,061	$22,264,390
Liabilities		
Total Liabilities	$27,025,126	$20,835,768
Owner's Equity		
Owner's Capital	2,273,935	1,428,622
Total Liabilities and Owner's Equity	$29,299,061	$22,264,390

Student C: I see from the annual report that Charles Schwab paid cash dividends (cash dividends are treated the same as owner's withdrawals) of $45,502,000 in 1999. Don't you have to take that into consideration when analyzing the company's performance?

REQUIRED

1. Comment on the interpretations of Students A and B, and then answer Student C's question.

2. Calculate Charles Schwab's net income for 1999. (**Hint:** Reconstruct the statement of owner's equity.)

Group Activity: After discussing **1**, let groups compete to see which one can come up with the answer to **2** first.

International Company

FRA 2.

LO 1 The Goal of Profitability

Explore accounting issues facing international companies.

The celebrated Danish toy company **Lego Group** reported its first loss since the 1930s in 1998. While its bright plastic bricks are famous around the globe, Lego is rapidly losing market share to computer and video games. The company's president said, "The Lego Group is not in critical condition, but action is needed. . . . We have to acknowledge that growth and innovation are not enough. We also have to be a profitable business."[13] Discuss the meaning of *profitability*. What other goal must a business achieve? Why is the goal of profitability important to Lego's president? What is the accounting measure of profitability, and on which statement is it determined?

Toys "R" Us Annual Report

FRA 3.

LO 6 The Four Financial Statements

Every financial chapter has a case on Toys "R" Us; the complete Toys "R" Us Annual Report for a recent year follows Chapter 6.

Refer to the Toys "R" Us annual report to answer the questions below. Keep in mind that every company, while following basic principles, adapts financial statements and terminology to its own special needs. Therefore, the complexity of the financial statements and the terminology in the Toys "R" Us statements will sometimes differ from those in the text. (Note that 2000 refers to the year ended January 29, 2000, and 1999 refers to the year ended January 30, 1999.)

1. What names does Toys "R" Us give its four basic financial statements? (Note that the use of the word "Consolidated" in the names of the financial statements means that these statements combine those of several companies owned by Toys "R" Us.)

2. Prove that the accounting equation works for Toys "R" Us on January 29, 2000, by finding the amounts for the following equation: Assets = Liabilities + Stockholders' Equity.

3. What were the total revenues of Toys "R" Us for the year ended January 29, 2000?

4. Was Toys "R" Us profitable in the year ended January 29, 2000? How much was net income (loss) in that year, and did it increase or decrease from the year ended January 30, 1999?

5. Did the company's cash and cash equivalents increase from January 30, 1999, to January 29, 2000? By how much? In what two places in the statements can this number be found or computed?

6. Did cash flows from operating activities, cash flows from investing activities, and cash flows from financing activities increase or decrease from 1999 to 2000?

Group Activity: Assign the above to in-class groups of three or four students. Set a time limit. The first group to answer all questions correctly wins.

Use the professional software Fingraph® to investigate annual reports and analyze financial data.

Fingraph® Financial Analyst™

FRA 4.

LO 1 Financial Statements,
LO 6 Business Activities, and
Goals

Choose any company in the Fingraph® Financial Analyst™ CD-ROM software.

1. In the company's annual report, find a description of the business. What is the nature of the company's business? How would you describe its operating activities?

2. Find and identify the company's four basic financial statements. Which statement shows the resources of the business and the various claims to those resources? From the balance sheet, prove the balance sheet equation by showing that the company's assets equal its liabilities plus stockholders' equity. What is the company's largest category of assets? Which statement shows changes in all or part of the company's stockholders' equity during the year? Did the company pay any dividends in the last year?

3. Which statement is most closely associated with the company's profitability goal? How much net income did the company earn in the last year? Which statement is most closely associated with the company's liquidity goal? Did cash (and cash equivalents) increase in the last year? Which provided the most positive cash flows in the last year: operating, investing, or financing activities?

4. Prepare a one-page executive summary that highlights what you have learned from parts **1**, **2**, and **3**. An executive summary is a short, easy-to-read report that emphasizes important information and conclusions by listing them by numbered paragraphs or bullet points.

Internet cases are accounting cases tailored to the Internet, based on concepts and applications from the chapter.

Internet Case

FRA 5.

LO 1 Financial Performance
LO 5 Comparison of Two High-Tech Companies

Microsoft Corporation and *Intel, Inc.,* are two of the most successful high-tech companies. Compare the two companies financial performance first by going to the Needles Accounting Resource Center web site at http://college.hmco.com and clicking on Intel under Chapter 1 companies. Utilizing the consolidated balance sheet and consolidated statement of income from the annual report, find the amount of total assets, revenues, and net income for the most recent year shown. Then compare these amounts to the same amounts for Microsoft shown in the first decision point of this chapter. Also compute net income to revenues and net income to total assets for both companies. Which company is larger? Which is more profitable?

ENDNOTES

1. Microsoft Corporation, *Annual Report*, 2000.
2. *Statement of Financial Accounting Concepts No. 1*, "Objectives of Financial Reporting by Business Enterprises" (Norwalk, Conn.: Financial Accounting Standards Board, 1978), par. 9.
3. Ibid.
4. Christopher D. Ittner, David F. Larcker, and Madhav V. Rajan, "The Choice of Performance Measures in Annual Bonus Contracts," *The Accounting Review*, April 1997.
5. Microsoft Corporation, *Annual Report*, 2000.
6. Kathy Williams and James Hart, "Microsoft: Tooling the Information Age," *Management Accounting*, May 1996, p. 42.
7. *Statement of the Accounting Principles Board No. 4*, "Basic Concepts and Accounting Principles Underlying Financial Statements of Business Enterprises" (New York: American Institute of Certified Public Accountants, 1970), par. 138.
8. Touche Ross & Co., "Ethics in American Business" (New York: Touche Ross & Co., 1988), p. 7.
9. *Statement Number IC*, "Standards of Ethical Conduct for Management Accountants" (Montvale, N.J.: Institute of Management Accountants, 1983, revised 1997).
10. J.C. Penney Company, Inc., *Annual Report*, 1995.
11. Southwest Airlines Co., *Annual Report*, 1996.
12. The Charles Schwab Corporation, *Annual Report*, 1999.
13. Robert Frank, "Facing a Loss, Lego Narrates a Sad Toy Story," *The Wall Street Journal*, January 22, 1999.

2 Measuring Business Transactions

Continental Airlines, Inc. & The Boeing Co.

In October 2000, Continental Airlines, Inc., announced that it had ordered 15 Boeing 757-300 jetliners.[1] The $1.2 billion order was part of an exclusive agreement Boeing negotiated with Continental. This exclusive 20-year agreement to purchase only Boeing aircraft was Boeing's fourth such agreement with a major airline and positioned the company favorably against Airbus, its European competitor. How should this important order have been recorded, if at all, in the records of Continental and Boeing? When should the purchase and sale that result from this order be recorded in the companies' records?

The order obviously was an important event, one with long-term consequences for both companies. But, as you will see in this chapter, it was not recorded in the accounting records of either company. At the time the order was placed, the aircraft were yet to be manufactured and would not begin to be delivered for several years. Even for "firm" orders, Boeing has cautioned that "an economic downturn could result in airline equipment requirements less than currently anticipated resulting in requests to negotiate the rescheduling or possible cancellation of firm orders."[2] The aircraft were not assets of Continental, and the company had not incurred a liability. No aircraft had been delivered or even built, so Continental was not obligated to pay at that point. And Boeing could not record any revenue until the aircraft were manufactured and delivered to Continental, and title to the aircraft shifted from Boeing to Continental. In fact, Boeing later experienced cancellation or extension of large previously firm orders from China because of the economic slowdown in Asia.[3]

To understand and use financial statements, it is important to know how to analyze events in order to determine the extent of their impact on those statements.

Measurement Issues

OBJECTIVE

1 Explain, in simple terms, the generally accepted ways of solving the measurement issues of recognition, valuation, and classification

Business transactions are economic events that affect the financial position of a business entity. To measure a business transaction, the accountant must decide when the transaction occurred (the recognition issue), what value to place on the transaction (the valuation issue), and how the components of the transaction should be categorized (the classification issue).

These three issues—recognition, valuation, and classification—underlie almost every major decision in financial accounting today. They lie at the heart of accounting for pension plans, for mergers of giant companies, and for international transactions. In discussing the three basic issues, we follow generally accepted accounting principles and use an approach that promotes an understanding of the basic ideas of accounting. Keep in mind, however, that controversy does exist, and that solutions to some problems are not as cut-and-dried as they appear.

The Recognition Issue

The **recognition** issue refers to the difficulty of deciding when a business transaction should be recorded. Often the facts of a situation are known, but there is disagreement about *when* the event should be recorded. Suppose, for instance, that a company orders, receives, and pays for an office desk. Which of the following actions constitutes a recordable event?

1. An employee sends a purchase requisition to the purchasing department.
2. The purchasing department sends a purchase order to the supplier.
3. The supplier ships the desk.
4. The company receives the desk.
5. The company receives the bill from the supplier.
6. The company pays the bill.

The answer to this question is important because amounts in the financial statements are affected by the date on which a purchase is recorded. According to accounting tradition, the transaction is recorded when title to the desk passes from the supplier to the purchaser, creating an obligation to pay. Thus, depending on the details of the shipping agreement, the transaction is recognized (recorded) at the time of either action **3** or action **4**. This is the guideline that we generally use in this book. However, in many small businesses that have simple accounting systems, the transaction is not recorded until the bill is received (action **5**) or paid (action **6**) because these are the implied points of title transfer. The predetermined time at which a transaction should be recorded is the **recognition point**.

The recognition issue is not always easy to solve. Consider the case of an advertising agency that is asked by a client to prepare a major advertising campaign. People may work on the campaign several hours a day for a number of weeks. Value is added to the plan as the employees develop it. Should this added value be recognized as the campaign is being produced or at the time it is completed? Normally, the increase in value is recorded at the time the plan is finished and the client is billed for it. However, if a plan is going to take a long period to develop, the agency and the client may agree that the client will be billed at key points during its development. A transaction is recorded at each billing.

The Valuation Issue

Valuation is perhaps the most controversial issue in accounting. The **valuation** issue focuses on assigning a monetary value to a business transaction. Generally accepted accounting principles state that the appropriate value to assign to all business transactions—and therefore to all assets, liabilities, and components of owner's equity, including revenues and expenses, recorded by a business—is the original cost (often called *historical cost*).

Cost is defined here as the exchange price associated with a business transaction at the point of recognition. According to this guideline, the purpose of accounting is not to account for value in terms of worth, which can change after a transaction occurs, but to account for value in terms of cost at the time of the transaction. For example, the cost of an asset is recorded when the asset is acquired, and the value is held at that level until the asset is sold, expires, or is consumed. In this context, *value* means the cost at the time of the transaction. The practice of recording transactions at cost is referred to as the **cost principle**.

Suppose that a person offers a building for sale at $120,000. It may be valued for real estate taxes at $75,000, and it may be insured for $90,000. One prospective buyer may offer $100,000 for the building, and another may offer $105,000. At this point, several different, unverifiable opinions of value have been expressed. Finally, suppose the seller and a buyer settle on a price and complete the sale for $110,000. All of these figures are values of one kind or another, but only the selling price of $110,000 is sufficiently reliable to be used in the records. The market value of the building may vary over the years, but the building will remain on the new buyer's records at $110,000 until it is sold again. At that point, the accountant will record the new transaction at the new exchange price, and a profit or loss will be recognized. The cost principle is used because the cost is verifiable. It results from the actions of independent buyers and sellers who come to an agreement on price. An exchange price is an objective price that can be verified by evidence created at the time of the transaction. It is this final price, verified by agreement of the two parties, at which the transaction is recorded.

FOCUS ON BUSINESS PRACTICE

With many aspects of accounting, there are sometimes exceptions to the general rules. For instance, the cost principle is not followed in all parts of the financial statements. Investments, for example, are often accounted for at fair or market value because these investments are available for sale. The fair or market value is the best measure of the potential benefit to the company. Intel Corp., the large microprocessor company, states in its annual report:

A substantial majority of the company's marketable investments are classified as available-for-sale as of the balance sheet date and are reported at fair value.[5]

The Classification Issue

The **classification** issue has to do with assigning all the transactions in which a business engages to appropriate categories, or accounts. For example, a company's ability to borrow money can be affected by the way in which its debts are categorized. Or a company's income can be affected by whether purchases of small items such as tools are considered repair expenses (a component of owner's equity) or equipment (assets).

FOCUS ON BUSINESS ETHICS

Not only are the accounting solutions related to recognition (when a transaction occurred), valuation (what value to place on the transaction), and classification (how the components of the transaction should be categorized) important for good financial reporting, but they are also designed to help a company's management fulfill its responsibilities to the owners and the public. Informix Corporation was one of the most suc-

cessful software companies and was a serious challenger in the market for large corporate databases. However, when the public discovered that Informix Corporation was using a questionable application of the recognition principle, its stock price plummeted, the NASDAQ stock market began actions to delist the company, and some questioned whether it would ultimately survive. Its problems occurred when management disclosed that a substantial portion of the company's revenue came from shipments to resellers that had not been sold to the final user, bringing into question whether sales had actually occurred.[6]

Proper classification depends not only on correctly analyzing the effect of each transaction on the business but also on maintaining a system of accounts that reflects that effect. The rest of this chapter explains the classification of accounts and the analysis and recording of transactions.

Accounts and the Chart of Accounts

OBJECTIVE

2 Describe the chart of accounts and recognize commonly used accounts

In the measurement of business transactions, large amounts of data are gathered. These data require a method of storage. Businesspeople should be able to retrieve transaction data quickly and in usable form. In other words, there should be a filing system to sort out or classify all the transactions that occur in a business. This filing system consists of accounts. Recall that accounts are the basic storage units for accounting data and are used to accumulate amounts from similar transactions. An accounting system has a separate account for each asset, each liability, and each component of owner's equity, including revenues and expenses. Whether a company keeps records by hand or by computer, management must be able to refer to accounts so that it can study the company's financial history and plan for the future. A very small company may need only a few dozen accounts; a multinational corporation may need thousands.

In a manual accounting system, each account is kept on a separate page or card. These pages or cards are placed together in a book or file called the **general ledger**. In the computerized systems that most companies have today, accounts are maintained on magnetic tapes or disks. However, as a matter of convenience, accountants still refer to the group of company accounts as the *general ledger*, or simply the *ledger*.

To help identify accounts in the ledger and to make them easy to find, the accountant often numbers them. A list of these numbers with the corresponding account names is called a **chart of accounts**. A very simple chart of accounts appears in Exhibit 1. Notice that the first digit refers to the major financial statement classifications. An account number that begins with the digit 1 represents an asset, an account number that begins with a 2 represents a liability, and so forth.

Exhibit 1
Chart of Accounts for a Small Business

Account Number	Account Name	Description
		Assets
111	Cash	Money and any medium of exchange, including coins, currency, checks, postal and express money orders, and money on deposit in a bank
112	Notes Receivable	Amounts due from others in the form of promissory notes (written promises to pay definite sums of money at fixed future dates)
113	Accounts Receivable	Amounts due from others for revenues or sales on credit (sales on account)
114	Fees Receivable	Amounts arising from services performed but not yet billed to customers
115	Art Supplies	Prepaid expense; art supplies purchased and not used
116	Office Supplies	Prepaid expense; office supplies purchased and not used
117	Prepaid Rent	Prepaid expense; rent paid in advance and not used
118	Prepaid Insurance	Prepaid expense; insurance purchased and not expired; unexpired insurance
141	Land	Property owned for use in the business
142	Buildings	Structures owned for use in the business
143	Accumulated Depreciation, Buildings	Sum of the periodic allocation of the cost of buildings to expense
144	Art Equipment	Art equipment owned for use in the business
145	Accumulated Depreciation, Art Equipment	Sum of the periodic allocation of the cost of art equipment to expense
146	Office Equipment	Office equipment owned for use in the business
147	Accumulated Depreciation, Office Equipment	Sum of the periodic allocation of the cost of office equipment to expense
		Liabilities
211	Notes Payable	Amounts due to others in the form of promissory notes
212	Accounts Payable	Amounts due to others for purchases on credit (purchases on account)
213	Unearned Art Fees	Unearned revenue; customer advances for artwork to be provided in future
214	Wages Payable	Amounts due to employees for wages earned and not paid
221	Mortgage Payable	Amounts due on loans that are backed by the company's property and buildings

(continued)

Exhibit 1
Chart of Accounts for a Small Business *(continued)*

Account Number	Account Name	Description
	Owner's Equity	
311	Capital	Owner's investment in the company
312	Withdrawals	Assets withdrawn from the business by the owner for personal use
313	Income Summary	Temporary account used at the end of the accounting period to summarize revenues and expenses for the period
	Revenues	
411	Advertising Fees Earned	Revenues derived from performing advertising services
412	Art Fees Earned	Revenues derived from performing art services
	Expenses	
511	Wages Expense	Amounts earned by employees
512	Utilities Expense	Amounts for utilities, such as water, electricity, and gas, used
513	Telephone Expense	Amounts for telephone services used
514	Rent Expense	Amounts for rent on property and buildings used
515	Insurance Expense	Amounts for insurance expired
516	Art Supplies Expense	Amounts for art supplies used
517	Office Supplies Expense	Amounts for office supplies used
518	Depreciation Expense, Buildings	Amount of buildings' cost allocated to expense
519	Depreciation Expense, Art Equipment	Amount of art equipment costs allocated to expense
520	Depreciation Expense, Office Equipment	Amount of office equipment costs allocated to expense
521	Interest Expense	Amount of interest on debts

The second and third digits refer to individual accounts. Notice the gaps in the sequence of numbers. These gaps allow the accountant to expand the number of accounts. The accounts shown in Exhibit 1 will be used in this chapter, as well as in the next two chapters, through the sample case of the Joan Miller Advertising Agency.

Owner's Equity Accounts

In the chart of accounts that appears in Exhibit 1, the revenue and expense accounts are separated from the other owner's equity accounts. The relationships of these accounts to each other and to the basic financial statements are illustrated

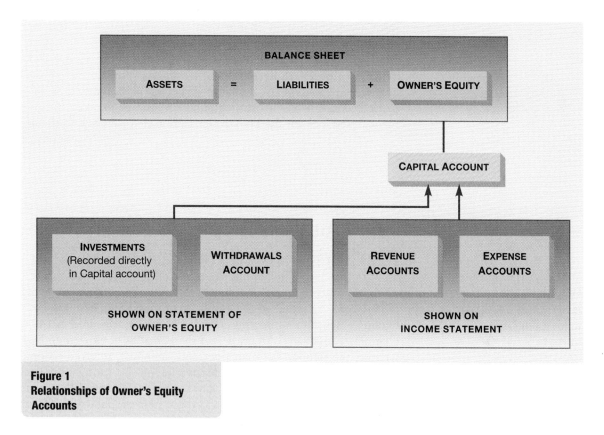

Figure 1
Relationships of Owner's Equity Accounts

in Figure 1. The distinctions among them are important for legal and financial reporting purposes.

First, for income tax reporting, financial reporting, and other purposes, the law requires that Capital and Withdrawals accounts be separated from revenues and expenses. The Capital account represents the owner's interest in the assets of the company. The Withdrawals account is used to record assets taken out of the business by the owner for personal use. These withdrawals are not described as salary or wages, although the owner may think of them as such, because there is no change in the ownership of the money withdrawn. In practice, the Withdrawals account often goes by other names, among them *Personal* and *Drawing.* Corporations do not use a Withdrawals account.

Second, management needs a detailed breakdown of revenues and expenses for budgeting and operating purposes. From these accounts, which are listed on the income statement, management can identify the sources of all revenues and the nature of all expenses. In this way, accounting gives management information about how it has achieved its primary goal of earning a net income.

Account Titles

The names of accounts often confuse beginning accounting students because some of the words are new or have technical meanings. Also, the same asset, liability, or owner's equity account can have different names in different companies. (Actually, this is not so strange. People, too, often are called different names by their friends, families, and associates.) For example, Fixed Assets, Plant and Equipment, Capital Assets, and Long-Lived Assets are all names for long-term asset accounts. Even the most acceptable names change over time, and, out of habit, some companies use names that are out of date.

In general, an account title should describe what is recorded in the account. When you come across an account title that you do not recognize, you should examine the context of the name—whether it is classified as an asset, liability, or owner's equity component, including revenue or expense, on the financial statements—and look for the kind of transaction that gave rise to the account.

The Double-Entry System: The Basic Method of Accounting

OBJECTIVE

3 Define *double-entry system* and state the rules for double entry

The double-entry system, the backbone of accounting, evolved during the Renaissance. As noted in the Focus on Business Practice box below, the first systematic description of double-entry bookkeeping appeared in 1494, two years after Columbus discovered America, in a mathematics book written by Fra Luca Pacioli. Goethe, the famous German poet and dramatist, referred to double-entry bookkeeping as "one of the finest discoveries of the human intellect." And Werner Sombart, an eminent economist and sociologist, believed that "double-entry bookkeeping is born of the same spirit as the system of Galileo and Newton."

What is the significance of the double-entry system? The system is based on the *principle of duality*, which means that every economic event has two aspects—effort and reward, sacrifice and benefit, source and use—that offset or balance each other. In the **double-entry system**, each transaction must be recorded with at least one debit and one credit, so that the total dollar amount of debits and the total dollar amount of credits equal each other. Because of the way it is designed, the whole system is always in balance. All accounting systems, no matter how sophisticated, are based on the principle of duality.

The T Account

The T account is a good place to begin the study of the double-entry system. In its simplest form, an account has three parts: (1) a title, which describes the asset, the liability, or the owner's equity account; (2) a left side, which is called the **debit** side; and (3) a right side, which is called the **credit** side. This form of an account, called a **T account** because it resembles the letter *T*, is used to analyze transactions. It looks like this:

Title of Account

Debit (left) side	Credit (right) side

Any entry made on the left side of the account is a debit, or debit entry; and any entry made on the right side of the account is a credit, or credit entry. The terms *debit* (abbreviated Dr., from the Latin *debere*) and *credit* (abbreviated Cr., from the Latin *credere*) are simply the accountant's words for "left" and "right" (not for "increase" or "decrease"). We present a more formal version of the T account later in this chapter, where we examine the ledger account form.

The T Account Illustrated

In the chapter on uses of accounting information and the basic financial statements, Shannon Realty had several transactions that involved the receipt or payment of cash. These transactions can be summarized in the Cash account by recording receipts on the left (debit) side of the account and payments on the right (credit) side:

Cash

(1)	50,000	(2)	35,000
(5)	1,500	(4)	200
(7)	1,000	(8)	1,000
		(9)	400
		(11)	600
	52,500		37,200
Bal.	15,300		

The cash receipts on the left total $52,500. (The total is written in small figures so that it cannot be confused with an actual debit entry). The cash payments on the right total $37,200. These totals are simply working totals, or **footings**. Footings, which are calculated at the end of each month, are an easy way to determine cash on hand. The difference in dollars between the total debit footing and the total credit footing is called the **balance**, or *account balance*. If the balance is a debit, it is written on the left side. If it is a credit, it is written on the right side. Notice that Shannon Realty's Cash account has a debit balance of $15,300 ($52,500 − $37,200). This is the amount of cash the business has on hand at the end of the month.

Analyzing and Processing Transactions

The two rules of double-entry bookkeeping are that every transaction affects at least two accounts and that the total of the debits must equal the total of the credits. In other words, for every transaction, one or more accounts must be debited and one or more accounts must be credited, and the total dollar amount of the debits must equal the total dollar amount of the credits.

Look again at the accounting equation:

$$\text{Assets} = \text{Liabilities} + \text{Owner's Equity}$$

You can see that if a debit increases assets, then a credit must be used to decrease assets on the same side of the equal sign or increase liabilities or owner's equity on opposite sides of the equal sign. Likewise, if a credit decreases assets, then a debit must be used to increase assets or decrease liabilities or owner's equity. These rules can be shown as follows:

Assets		=	Liabilities		+	Owner's Equity	
Debit for increases (+)	Credit for decreases (−)		Debit for decreases (−)	Credit for increases (+)		Debit for decreases (−)	Credit for increases (+)

1. Increases in assets are debited to asset accounts. Decreases in assets are credited to asset accounts.
2. Increases in liabilities and owner's equity are credited to liability and owner's equity accounts. Decreases in liabilities and owner's equity are debited to liability and owner's equity accounts.

One of the more difficult points to understand is the application of double-entry rules to the owner's equity components. The key is to remember that withdrawals and expenses are deductions from owner's equity. Thus, transactions that *increase* withdrawals or expenses *decrease* owner's equity. Consider this expanded version of the accounting equation:

Owner's Equity

$$\text{Assets} = \text{Liabilities} + \text{Capital} - \text{Withdrawals} + \text{Revenues} - \text{Expenses}$$

This equation may be rearranged by shifting withdrawals and expenses to the left side, as follows:

Assets		+	Withdrawals		+	Expenses		=	Liabilities		+	Capital		+	Revenues	
+ (debits)	− (credits)		+ (debits)	− (credits)		+ (debits)	− (credits)		− (debits)	+ (credits)		− (debits)	+ (credits)		− (debits)	+ (credits)

Note that the rules for double entry for all the accounts on the left of the equal sign are just the opposite of the rules for all the accounts on the right of the equal sign. Assets, withdrawals, and expenses are increased by debits and decreased by credits. Liabilities, capital, and revenues are increased by credits and decreased by debits.

With this basic information about double entry, it is possible to analyze and process transactions by following the five steps illustrated in Figure 2. To show how the steps are applied, assume that on June 1, Koenig Art Supplies borrows $100,000 from its bank on a promissory note. The transaction is analyzed and processed as follows:

1. *Analyze the transaction in order to determine its effect on assets, liabilities, and owner's equity.* In this case, both an asset (Cash) and a liability (Notes Payable) increase. A transaction is usually supported by some kind of **source**

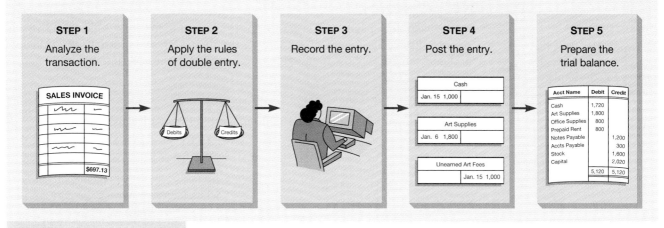

Figure 2
Analyzing and Processing Transactions

document—an invoice, a receipt, a check, or a contract. Here, a copy of the signed note would be the source document.

2. *Apply the rules of double entry*. Increases in assets are recorded by debits. Increases in liabilities are recorded by credits.

3. *Record the entry*. Transactions are recorded in chronological order in a journal. In one form of journal, which is explained in greater detail later on in this chapter, the date, the debit account, and the debit amount are recorded on one line, and the credit account and the credit amount are indented and recorded on the next line, as is shown below:

$$A = L + OE$$
$$+ \quad +$$

		Dr.	**Cr.**
June 1	Cash	100,000	
	Notes Payable		100,000

This form is referred to as **journal form** and carries an explanation immediately following the entry. If more than one account is debited or credited, additional lines are used.

4. *Post the entry*. The entry is posted to the general ledger by transferring the date and amounts to the proper accounts. The T account is one form of ledger account.

Cash			**Notes Payable**	
June 1	100,000		June 1	100,000

In formal records, step **3** is never omitted. However, for purposes of analysis, accountants often bypass step **3** and record entries directly in T accounts because doing so clearly and quickly shows the effects of transactions on the accounts. Some of the assignments in this chapter use the same approach to emphasize the analytical aspects of double entry.

5. *Prepare the trial balance to confirm the balance of the accounts*. Periodically, accountants prepare a trial balance to confirm that the accounts are still in balance after the recording and posting of transactions. Preparation of the trial balance is explained later in this chapter.

Transaction Analysis Illustrated

OBJECTIVE

4 Apply the steps for transaction analysis and processing to simple transactions

In the next few pages, we examine the transactions for Joan Miller Advertising Agency during the month of January. In the discussion, we illustrate the principle of duality and show how transactions are recorded in the accounts.

January 1: Joan Miller invests $10,000 to start her own advertising agency.

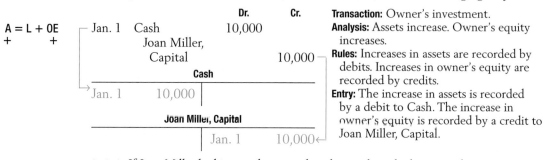

$A = L + OE$
$+ \qquad +$

Transaction: Owner's investment.
Analysis: Assets increase. Owner's equity increases.
Rules: Increases in assets are recorded by debits. Increases in owner's equity are recorded by credits.
Entry: The increase in assets is recorded by a debit to Cash. The increase in owner's equity is recorded by a credit to Joan Miller, Capital.

Analysis: If Joan Miller had invested assets other than cash in the business, the appropriate asset accounts would be debited.

January 2: Rents an office, paying two months' rent, $800, in advance.

$A = L + OE$
$+$
$-$

	Dr.	Cr.
Jan. 2 Prepaid Rent	800	
Cash		800

Cash

Jan. 1	10,000	Jan. 2	800

Prepaid Rent

Jan. 2	800	

Transaction: Rent paid in advance.
Analysis: Assets increase. Assets decrease.
Rules: Increases in assets are recorded by debits. Decreases in assets are recorded by credits.
Entry: The increase in assets is recorded by a debit to Prepaid Rent. The decrease in assets is recorded by a credit to Cash.

January 3: Orders art supplies, $1,800, and office supplies, $800.

Analysis: No entry is made because no transaction has occurred. According to the recognition issue, there is no liability until the supplies are shipped or received and there is an obligation to pay for them.

January 4: Purchases art equipment, $4,200, with cash.

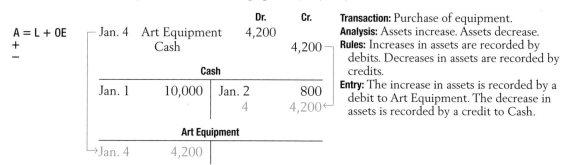

$A = L + OE$
$+$
$-$

Transaction: Purchase of equipment.
Analysis: Assets increase. Assets decrease.
Rules: Increases in assets are recorded by debits. Decreases in assets are recorded by credits.
Entry: The increase in assets is recorded by a debit to Art Equipment. The decrease in assets is recorded by a credit to Cash.

January 5: Purchases office equipment, $3,000, from Morgan Equipment; pays $1,500 in cash and agrees to pay the rest next month.

A = L + OE
+   +
−

		Dr.	Cr.
Jan. 5	Office Equipment	3,000	
	Cash		1,500
	Accounts Payable		1,500

Cash

Jan. 1	10,000	Jan. 2	800
		4	4,200
		5	1,500

Office Equipment

Jan. 5	3,000	

Accounts Payable

		Jan. 5	1,500

Transaction: Purchase of equipment and partial payment.
Analysis: Assets increase. Assets decrease. Liabilities increase.
Rules: Increases in assets are recorded by debits. Decreases in assets are recorded by credits. Increases in liabilities are recorded by credits.
Entry: The increase in assets is recorded by a debit to Office Equipment. The decrease in assets is recorded by a credit to Cash. The increase in liabilities is recorded by a credit to Accounts Payable.

January 6: Purchases art supplies, $1,800, and office supplies, $800, from Taylor Supply Company, on credit.

A = L + OE
+   +
+

		Dr.	Cr.
Jan. 6	Art Supplies	1,800	
	Office Supplies	800	
	Accounts Payable		2,600

Art Supplies

Jan. 6	1,800	

Office Supplies

Jan. 6	800	

Accounts Payable

		Jan. 5	1,500
		6	2,600

Transaction: Purchase of supplies on credit.
Analysis: Assets increase. Liabilities increase.
Rules: Increases in assets are recorded by debits. Increases in liabilities are recorded by credits.
Entry: The increase in assets is recorded by debits to Art Supplies and Office Supplies. The increase in liabilities is recorded by a credit to Accounts Payable.

January 8: Pays for a one-year life insurance policy, $480, with coverage effective January 1.

A = L + OE
+
−

		Dr.	Cr.
Jan. 8	Prepaid Insurance	480	
	Cash		480

Cash

Jan. 1	10,000	Jan. 2	800
		4	4,200
		5	1,500
		8	480

Prepaid Insurance

Jan. 8	480	

Transaction: Insurance purchased in advance.
Analysis: Assets increase. Assets decrease.
Rules: Increases in assets are recorded by debits. Decreases in assets are recorded by credits.
Entry: The increase in assets is recorded by a debit to Prepaid Insurance. The decrease in assets is recorded by a credit to Cash.

January 9: Pays Taylor Supply Company $1,000 of the amount owed.

A = L + OE
−   −

		Dr.	Cr.
Jan. 9	Accounts Payable	1,000	
	Cash		1,000

Cash

Jan. 1	10,000	Jan. 2	800
		4	4,200
		5	1,500
		8	480
		9	1,000

Accounts Payable

Jan. 9	1,000	Jan. 5	1,500
		6	2,600

Transaction: Partial payment on a liability.
Analysis: Assets decrease. Liabilities decrease.
Rules: Decreases in liabilities are recorded by debits. Decreases in assets are recorded by credits.
Entry: The decrease in liabilities is recorded by a debit to Accounts Payable. The decrease in assets is recorded by a credit to Cash.

January 10: Performs a service for an automobile dealer by placing advertisements in the newspaper and collects a fee, $1,400.

A = L + OE
+   +

		Dr.	Cr.
Jan. 10	Cash	1,400	
	Advertising Fees Earned		1,400

Cash

Jan. 1	10,000	Jan. 2	800
10	1,400	4	4,200
		5	1,500
		8	480
		9	1,000

Advertising Fees Earned

		Jan. 10	1,400

Transaction: Revenue earned and cash collected.
Analysis: Assets increase. Owner's equity increases.
Rules: Increases in assets are recorded by debits. Increases in owner's equity are recorded by credits.
Entry: The increase in assets is recorded by a debit to Cash. The increase in owner's equity is recorded by a credit to Advertising Fees Earned.

January 12: Pays the secretary two weeks' wages, $600.

A = L + OE
−   −

		Dr.	Cr.
Jan. 12	Wages Expense	600	
	Cash		600

Cash

Jan. 1	10,000	Jan. 2	800
10	1,400	4	4,200
		5	1,500
		8	480
		9	1,000
		12	600

Wages Expense

Jan. 12	600	

Transaction: Payment of wages expense.
Analysis: Assets decrease. Owner's equity decreases.
Rules: Decreases in owner's equity are recorded by debits. Decreases in assets are recorded by credits.
Entry: The decrease in owner's equity is recorded by a debit to Wages Expense. The decrease in assets is recorded by a credit to Cash.

January 15: Accepts an advance fee, $1,000, for artwork to be done for another agency.

A = L + OE
+   +

		Dr.	Cr.
Jan. 15	Cash	1,000	
	Unearned Art Fees		1,000

Cash

Jan. 1	10,000	Jan. 2	800
10	1,400	4	4,200
15	1,000	5	1,500
		8	480
		9	1,000
		12	600

Unearned Art Fees

		Jan. 15	1,000

Transaction: Payment received for future services.
Analysis: Assets increase. Liabilities increase.
Rules: Increases in assets are recorded by debits. Increases in liabilities are recorded by credits.
Entry: The increase in assets is recorded by a debit to Cash. The increase in liabilities is recorded by a credit to Unearned Art Fees.

January 19: Performs a service by placing several major advertisements for Ward Department Stores. The fee, $2,800, is billed now but will be collected next month.

A = L + OE
+   +

		Dr.	Cr.
Jan. 19	Accounts Receivable	2,800	
	Advertising Fees Earned		2,800

Accounts Receivable

Jan. 19	2,800		

Advertising Fees Earned

		Jan. 10	1,400
		19	2,800

Transaction: Revenue earned, to be received later.
Analysis: Assets increase. Owner's equity increases.
Rules: Increases in assets are recorded by debits. Increases in owner's equity are recorded by credits.
Entry: The increase in assets is recorded by a debit to Accounts Receivable. The increase in owner's equity is recorded by a credit to Advertising Fees Earned.

January 26: Pays the secretary two more weeks' wages, $600.

A = L + OE
−   −

		Dr.	Cr.
Jan. 26	Wages Expense	600	
	Cash		600

Cash

Jan. 1	10,000	Jan. 2	800
10	1,400	4	4,200
15	1,000	5	1,500
		8	480
		9	1,000
		12	600
		26	600

Wages Expense

Jan. 12	600		
26	600		

Transaction: Payment of wages expense.
Analysis: Assets decrease. Owner's equity decreases.
Rules: Decreases in owner's equity are recorded by debits. Decreases in assets are recorded by credits.
Entry: The decrease in owner's equity is recorded by a debit to Wages Expense. The decrease in assets is recorded by a credit to Cash.

January 29: Receives and pays the utility bill, $100.

A = L + OE
−   −

		Dr.	Cr.
Jan. 29	Utilities Expense	100	
	Cash		100

Cash

Jan.	1	10,000	Jan.	2	800
	10	1,400		4	4,200
	15	1,000		5	1,500
				8	480
				9	1,000
				12	600
				26	600
				29	100

Utilities Expense

Jan. 29	100	

Transaction: Payment of utilities expense.
Analysis: Assets decrease. Owner's equity decreases.
Rules: Decreases in owner's equity are recorded by debits. Decreases in assets are recorded by credits.
Entry: The decrease in owner's equity is recorded by a debit to Utilities Expense. The decrease in assets is recorded by a credit to Cash.

January 30: Receives (but does not pay) the telephone bill, $70.

A = L + OE
+   −

		Dr.	Cr.
Jan. 30	Telephone Expense	70	
	Accounts Payable		70

Accounts Payable

Jan.	9	1,000	Jan.	5	1,500
				6	2,600
				30	70

Telephone Expense

Jan. 30	70	

Transaction: Expense incurred, to be paid later.
Analysis: Liabilities increase. Owner's equity decreases.
Rules: Decreases in owner's equity are recorded by debits. Increases in liabilities are recorded by credits.
Entry: The decrease in owner's equity is recorded by a debit to Telephone Expense. The increase in liabilities is recorded by a credit to Accounts Payable.

January 31: Joan Miller withdraws $1,400 from the business for personal living expenses.

A = L + OE
−   −

		Dr.	Cr.
Jan. 31	Joan Miller, Withdrawals	1,400	
	Cash		1,400

Cash

Jan.	1	10,000	Jan.	2	800
	10	1,400		4	4,200
	15	1,000		5	1,500
				8	480
				9	1,000
				12	600
				26	600
				29	100
				31	1,400

Joan Miller, Withdrawals

Jan. 31	1,400	

Transaction: Owner's withdrawal for personal use.
Analysis: Assets decrease. Owner's equity decreases.
Rules: Decreases in assets are recorded by credits. Decreases in owner's equity are recorded by debits.
Entry: The decrease in owner's equity is recorded by a debit to Joan Miller, Withdrawals. The decrease in assets is recorded by a credit to Cash.

Summary of Transactions

In Exhibit 2 the transactions for January are shown in their accounts and in relation to the accounting equation. Note that all transactions have been recorded on the date they are recognized. Most of these transactions involve either the receipt or payment of cash as may be seen in the Cash account. There are important exceptions, however. For instance, on January 19 Advertising Fees were earned, but receipt of cash for these fees will come later. Also, on January 5, 6, and 30 there were transactions recognized that totaled $4,170 in Accounts Payable. This means the company can wait to pay. At the end of the month, only the $1,000 recorded on January 9 had been paid. These lags between recognition of transactions and the subsequent cash inflows or outflows impact achieving the goal of liquidity.

Exhibit 2
Summary of Sample Accounts and Transactions for Joan Miller Advertising Agency

Assets	=	Liabilities	+	Owner's Equity

Cash

Jan. 1	10,000	Jan. 2	800
10	1,400	4	4,200
15	1,000	5	1,500
		8	480
		9	1,000
		12	600
		26	600
		29	100
		31	1,400
	12,400		10,680
Bal.	1,720		

Accounts Payable

Jan. 9	1,000	Jan. 5	1,500
		6	2,600
		30	70
	1,000		4,170
		Bal.	3,170

Unearned Art Fees

		Jan. 15	1,000

Joan Miller, Capital

		Jan. 1	10,000

Joan Miller, Withdrawals

Jan. 31	1,400	

Advertising Fees Earned

		Jan. 10	1,400
		19	2,800
		Bal.	4,200

Wages Expense

Jan. 12	600	
26	600	
Bal.	1,200	

Utilities Expense

Jan. 29	100	

Telephone Expense

Jan. 30	70	

Accounts Receivable

Jan. 19	2,800	

Art Supplies

Jan. 6	1,800	

Office Supplies

Jan. 6	800	

Prepaid Rent

Jan. 2	800	

Prepaid Insurance

Jan. 8	480	

Art Equipment

Jan. 4	4,200	

Office Equipment

Jan. 5	3,000	

This account links to the statement of cash flows.

These accounts link to the income statement.

The Trial Balance

OBJECTIVE

5 Prepare a trial balance and describe its value and limitations

For every amount debited, an equal amount must be credited. This means that the total of debits and credits in the T accounts must be equal. To test this, the accountant periodically prepares a **trial balance**. Exhibit 3 shows a trial balance for Joan Miller Advertising Agency. It was prepared from the accounts in Exhibit 2.

The trial balance may be prepared at any time but is usually prepared on the last day of the month. Here are the steps in preparing a trial balance:

1. List each T account that has a balance, with debit balances in the left column and credit balances in the right column. Accounts are listed in the order in which they appear in the ledger.

2. Add each column.

3. Compare the totals of the columns.

In accounts in which increases are recorded by debits, the **normal balance** (the usual balance) is a debit balance; where increases are recorded by credits, the normal balance is a credit balance. Table 1 summarizes the normal account balances of the major account categories. According to the table, the T account Accounts Payable (a liability) typically has a credit balance and is copied into the trial balance as a credit balance.

Once in a while, a transaction leaves an account with a balance that is not "normal." For example, when a company overdraws its account at the bank, its Cash account (an asset) will show a credit balance instead of a debit balance. The "abnormal" balance should be copied into the trial balance columns as it stands, as a debit or a credit.

The trial balance proves whether or not the ledger is in balance. *In balance* means that the total of all debits recorded equals the total of all credits recorded.

Exhibit 3
Trial Balance

Joan Miller Advertising Agency Trial Balance January 31, 20xx		
Cash	$ 1,720	
Accounts Receivable	2,800	
Art Supplies	1,800	
Office Supplies	800	
Prepaid Rent	800	
Prepaid Insurance	480	
Art Equipment	4,200	
Office Equipment	3,000	
Accounts Payable		$ 3,170
Unearned Art Fees		1,000
Joan Miller, Capital		10,000
Joan Miller, Withdrawals	1,400	
Advertising Fees Earned		4,200
Wages Expense	1,200	
Utilities Expense	100	
Telephone Expense	70	
	$18,370	$18,370

Table 1. Normal Account Balances of Major Account Categories

Account Category	Increases Recorded by		Normal Balance	
	Debit	Credit	Debit	Credit
Assets	X		X	
Liabilities		X		X
Owner's Equity:				
Capital		X		X
Withdrawals	X		X	
Revenues		X		X
Expenses	X		X	

But the trial balance does not prove that the transactions were analyzed correctly or recorded in the proper accounts. For example, there is no way of determining from the trial balance that a debit should have been made in the Art Equipment account rather than the Office Equipment account. And the trial balance does not detect whether transactions have been omitted, because equal debits and credits will have been omitted. Also, if an error of the same amount is made in both a debit and a credit, it will not be discovered by the trial balance. The trial balance proves only that the debits and credits in the accounts are in balance.

If the debit and credit columns of the trial balance are not equal, look for one or more of the following errors: (1) a debit was entered in an account as a credit, or vice versa; (2) the balance of an account was computed incorrectly; (3) an error was made in carrying the account balance to the trial balance; or (4) the trial balance was summed incorrectly.

Other than simply incorrectly adding the columns, the two most common mistakes in preparing a trial balance are (1) recording an account with a debit balance as a credit, or vice versa, and (2) transposing two numbers when transferring an amount to the trial balance (for example, entering $23,459 as $23,549). The first of these mistakes causes the trial balance to be out of balance by an amount divisible by 2. The second causes the trial balance to be out of balance by a number divisible by 9. Thus, if a trial balance is out of balance and the addition has been verified, determine the amount by which the trial balance is out of balance and divide it first by 2 and then by 9. If the amount is divisible by 2, look in the trial balance for an amount equal to the quotient. If you find the amount, it is probably in the wrong column. If the amount is divisible by 9, trace each amount to the ledger account balance, checking carefully for a transposition error. If neither of these techniques identifies the error, first recompute the balance of each account in the ledger, then, if the error still has not been found, retrace each posting from the journal to the ledger.

Some Notes on Presentation

A ruled line appears in financial reports before each subtotal or total to indicate that the amounts above are added or subtracted. It is common practice to use a double line under a final total to show that it has been checked, or verified.

Dollar signs ($) are required in all financial statements, including the balance sheet and income statement, and in the trial balance and other schedules. On these

FOCUS ON INTERNATIONAL BUSINESS

Determining the dollar amount or valuation of a sale or purchase transaction is often not difficult because it equals the amount of cash that changes hands. However, in some areas of the world it is not so easy to determine. In a country where the currency is declining in value and there is high inflation, companies often are forced to resort to barter transactions, in which one good or service is traded for another. In Russia, for example, perhaps as many as two-thirds of all transactions are barter-type transactions. It is not uncommon for companies often to end up with piles of goods stacked around their offices and warehouses. In one case, an electric utility company provided a textile-machinery plant with electricity in exchange for wool blankets, which the plant had received in exchange for equipment sold to another company. Determining the value can be difficult in this case because it becomes a matter of determining the fair value of the goods being traded.[7]

statements, a dollar sign should be placed before the first amount in each column and before the first amount in a column following a ruled line. Dollar signs in the same column are aligned. Dollar signs are not used in journals and ledgers.

On unruled paper, commas and decimal points are used in dollar amounts. On paper with ruled columns—like the paper in journals and ledgers—commas and decimal points are not needed. In this book, because most problems and illustrations are in whole dollar amounts, the cents column usually is omitted. When accountants deal with whole dollars, they often use a dash in the cents column to indicate whole dollars rather than take the time to write zeros.

Recording and Posting Transactions

OBJECTIVE

6 Record transactions in the general journal

Let us now take a look at the formal process of recording transactions in the general journal and posting them to the ledger.

The General Journal

As you have seen, transactions can be entered directly into the accounts. But this method makes identifying individual transactions or finding errors very difficult because the debit is recorded in one account and the credit in another. The solution is to record all transactions chronologically in a **journal**. The journal is sometimes called the *book of original entry* because it is where transactions first enter the accounting records. Later, the debit and credit portions of each transaction can be transferred to the appropriate accounts in the ledger. A separate **journal entry** is used to record each transaction, and the process of recording transactions is called **journalizing**.

Most businesses have more than one kind of journal. The simplest and most flexible type is the **general journal**, the one we focus on in this chapter. Entries in the general journal include the following information about each transaction:

1. The date
2. The names of the accounts debited and the dollar amounts on the same lines in the debit column
3. The names of the accounts credited and the dollar amounts on the same lines in the credit column

4. An explanation of the transaction

5. The account identification numbers, if appropriate

Exhibit 4 displays two of the earlier transactions for Joan Miller Advertising Agency. The procedure for recording transactions in the general journal is as follows:

1. Record the date by writing the year in small figures on the first line at the top of the first column, and the month on the next line of the first column. Then record the day in the second column opposite the month. For subsequent entries on the same page for the same month and year, the month and year can be omitted.

2. Write the exact names of the accounts debited and credited in the Description column. Starting on the same line as the date, write the name(s) of the account(s) debited next to the left margin and indent the name(s) of the account(s) credited. The explanation is placed on the next line and further indented. The explanation should be brief but sufficient to explain and identify the transaction. A transaction can have more than one debit or credit entry; this is called a **compound entry**. In a compound entry, all debit accounts are listed before any credit accounts. (The January 6 transaction of Joan Miller Advertising Agency in Exhibit 4 is an example of a compound entry.)

3. Write the debit amounts in the Debit column opposite the accounts to be debited, and write the credit amounts in the Credit column opposite the accounts to be credited.

4. At the time the transactions are recorded, nothing is placed in the Post. Ref. (posting reference) column. (This column is sometimes called *LP* or *Folio*.) Later, if the company uses account numbers to identify accounts in the ledger, fill in the account numbers to provide a convenient cross-reference from the general journal to the ledger and to indicate that the entry has been posted to the ledger. If the accounts are not numbered, use a checkmark ($\sqrt{}$).

5. It is customary to skip a line after each journal entry.

Exhibit 4
The General Journal

Date		Description	Post. Ref.	Debit	Credit
General Journal					Page 1
20xx Jan.	6	Art Supplies		1,800	
		Office Supplies		800	
		Accounts Payable			2,600
		Purchased art and office supplies on credit			
	8	Prepaid Insurance		480	
		Cash			480
		Paid one-year life insurance premium			

A = L + OE
+   +
+

A = L + OE
+
−

The General Ledger

The general journal is used to record the details of each transaction. The general ledger is used to update each account.

THE LEDGER ACCOUNT FORM   The T account is a simple, direct means of recording transactions. In practice, a somewhat more complicated form of the account is needed in order to record more information. The **ledger account form**, which contains four columns for dollar amounts, is illustrated in Exhibit 5.

The account title and number appear at the top of the account form. The date of the transaction appears in the first two columns as it does in the journal. The Item column is used only rarely to identify transactions, because explanations already appear in the journal. The Post. Ref. column is used to note the journal page where the original entry for the transaction can be found. The dollar amount of the entry is entered in the appropriate Debit or Credit column, and a new account balance is computed in the final two columns after each entry. The advantage of this form of account over the T account is that the current balance of the account is readily available.

POSTING TO THE LEDGER   After transactions have been entered in the journal, they must be transferred to the ledger. The process of transferring journal entry information from the journal to the ledger is called **posting**. Posting is usually done after several entries have been made—for example, at the end of each day or less frequently, depending on the number of transactions. As shown in Exhibit 6, through posting, each amount in the Debit column of the journal is transferred into the Debit column of the appropriate account in the ledger, and each amount in the Credit column of the journal is transferred into the Credit column of the appropriate account in the ledger. The steps in the posting process are as follows:

1. In the ledger, locate the debit account named in the journal entry.
2. Enter the date of the transaction and, in the Post. Ref. column of the ledger, the journal page number from which the entry comes.
3. Enter in the Debit column of the ledger account the amount of the debit as it appears in the journal.
4. Calculate the account balance and enter it in the appropriate Balance column.

Exhibit 5
Accounts Payable in the General Ledger

General Ledger							
Accounts Payable							**Account No. 212**
						Balance	
Date		**Item**	**Post. Ref.**	**Debit**	**Credit**	**Debit**	**Credit**
20xx							
Jan.	5		J1		1,500		1,500
	6		J1		2,600		4,100
	9		J1	1,000			3,100
	30		J2		70		3,170

Exhibit 6
Posting from the General Journal to the Ledger

$A = L + OE$
$+ \quad -$

General Journal
② Page 2

Date		Description	Post. Ref.	Debit	Credit
20xx ②		①	⑤	③	
Jan.	30	Telephone Expense	513	70	
		Accounts Payable	212		70
		Received bill for			
		telephone expense			

General Ledger

Accounts Payable — Account No. 212

Date		Item	Post. Ref.	Debit	Credit	Balance Debit	Balance Credit
20xx							
Jan.	5		J1		1,500		1,500
	6		J1		2,600		4,100
	9		J1	1,000			3,100
	30		J2		70		3,170

General Ledger

Telephone Expense — Account No. 513

Date		Item	Post. Ref.	Debit	Credit	Balance Debit	Balance Credit
20xx						④	
Jan.	30		J2	70		70	

FOCUS ON BUSINESS TECHNOLOGY

In computerized accounting systems, posting is done automatically and the trial balance can be easily prepared as often as needed. Any accounts with abnormal balances are highlighted for investigation. Some general ledger software packages for small businesses list the trial balance amounts in a single column, with credit balances shown as minuses. In such cases, the trial balance is in balance if the total is zero.

5. Enter in the Post. Ref. column of the journal the account number to which the amount has been posted.

6. Repeat the same five steps for the credit side of the journal entry.

Notice that step **5** is the last step in the posting process for each debit and credit. In addition to serving as an easy reference between the journal entry and the ledger account, this entry in the Post. Ref. column of the journal indicates that all steps for the transaction have been completed. This allows accountants who have been called away from their work to easily find where they were before the interruption.

Chapter Review

1. **Explain, in simple terms, the generally accepted ways of solving the measurement issues of recognition, valuation, and classification.** To measure a business transaction, the accountant determines when the transaction occurred (the recognition issue), what value should be placed on the transaction (the valuation issue), and how the components of the transaction should be categorized (the classification issue). In general, recognition occurs when title passes, and a transaction is valued at the exchange price, the cost at the time the transaction is recognized. Classification refers to the categorizing of transactions according to a system of accounts.

2. **Describe the chart of accounts and recognize commonly used accounts.** An account is a device for storing data from transactions. There is one account for each asset, liability, and component of owner's equity, including revenues and expenses. The ledger is a book or file containing all of a company's accounts, arranged according to a chart of accounts. Commonly used asset accounts are Cash, Notes Receivable, Accounts Receivable, Prepaid Expenses, Land, Buildings, and Equipment. Common liability accounts are Notes Payable, Accounts Payable, Wages Payable, and Mortgage Payable. Common owner's equity accounts are Capital, Withdrawals, and revenue and expense accounts.

3. **Define *double-entry system* and state the rules for double entry.** In the double-entry system, each transaction must be recorded with at least one debit and one credit so that the total dollar amount of the debits equals the total dollar amount of the credits. The rules for double entry are (1) increases in assets are debited to asset accounts; decreases in assets are credited to asset accounts; and (2) increases in liabilities and owner's equity are credited to those accounts; decreases in liabilities and owner's equity are debited to those accounts.

4. **Apply the steps for transaction analysis and processing to simple transactions.** The procedure for analyzing transactions is (1) analyze the effect of the transaction on assets, liabilities, and owner's equity; (2) apply the appropriate double-entry rule; (3) record the entry; (4) post the entry; and (5) prepare a trial balance.

5. **Prepare a trial balance and describe its value and limitations.** A trial balance is used to check that the debit and credit balances are equal. It is prepared by listing each account with its balance in the Debit or Credit column. Then the two columns are added and the totals compared to test the balances. The major limitation of the trial balance is that even if debit and credit balances are equal, this does not guarantee that the transactions were analyzed correctly or recorded in the proper accounts.

6. **Record transactions in the general journal.** The general journal is a chronological record of all transactions. That record contains the date of each transaction, the names of the accounts and the dollar amounts debited and credited, an explanation of each entry, and the account numbers to which postings have been made.

7. **Post transactions from the general journal to the ledger.** After transactions have been entered in the general journal, they are posted to the ledger. Posting is done by transferring each amount in the Debit column of the general journal to the Debit column of the appropriate account in the ledger, and trans-

ferring each amount in the Credit column of the general journal to the Credit column of the appropriate account in the ledger. After each entry is posted, a new balance is entered in the appropriate Balance column.

REVIEW OF CONCEPTS AND TERMINOLOGY

The following concepts and terms were introduced in this chapter:

LO 3 **Balance:** The difference in dollars between the total debit footing and the total credit footing of an account. Also called *account balance*.

LO 2 **Chart of accounts:** A scheme that assigns a unique number to each account to facilitate finding the account in the ledger; also, the list of account numbers and titles.

LO 1 **Classification:** The process of assigning transactions to the appropriate accounts.

LO 6 **Compound entry:** An entry that has more than one debit or credit entry.

LO 1 **Cost:** The exchange price associated with a business transaction at the point of recognition.

LO 1 **Cost principle:** The practice of recording a transaction at cost.

LO 3 **Credit:** The right side of an account.

LO 3 **Debit:** The left side of an account.

LO 3 **Double-entry system:** The accounting system in which each transaction is recorded with at least one debit and one credit so that the total dollar amount of debits and the total dollar amount of credits equal each other.

LO 3 **Footings:** Working totals of columns of numbers. *To foot* means to total a column of numbers.

LO 6 **General journal:** The simplest and most flexible type of journal.

LO 2 **General ledger:** The book or file that contains all of the company's accounts, arranged in the order of the chart of accounts. Also called *ledger*.

LO 6 **Journal:** A chronological record of all transactions; the place where transactions first enter the accounting records. Also called *book of original entry*.

LO 6 **Journal entry:** The notations in the journal for recording a single transaction.

LO 3 **Journal form:** A form of journal in which the date, the debit account, and the debit amount of a transaction are recorded on one line and the credit account and credit amount on the next line.

LO 6 **Journalizing:** The process of recording transactions in a journal.

LO 7 **Ledger account form:** The form of account that has four dollar amount columns: one column for debit entries, one column for credit entries, and two columns (debit and credit) for showing the balance of the account.

LO 5 **Normal balance:** The usual balance of an account; also the side (debit or credit) that increases the account.

LO 7 **Posting:** The process of transferring journal entry information from the journal to the ledger.

LO 1 **Recognition:** The determination of when a business transaction should be recorded.

LO 1 **Recognition point:** The predetermined time at which a transaction should be recorded; usually, the point at which title passes to the buyer.

LO 3 **Source document:** An invoice, check, receipt, or other document that supports a transaction.

LO 3 **T account:** The simplest form of an account, used to analyze transactions.

LO 5 **Trial balance:** A comparison of the total of debit and credit balances in the accounts to check that they are equal.

LO 1 **Valuation:** The process of assigning a monetary value to a business transaction.

Transaction Analysis, General Journal, Ledger Accounts, and Trial Balance

LO 4
LO 5
LO 6
LO 7

After graduation from veterinary school, Laura Stors entered private practice. The transactions of the business through May 27 are as follows:

20xx

May 1   Laura Stors invested $2,000 in her business bank account.
     3   Paid $300 for two months' rent in advance for an office.
     9   Purchased medical supplies for $200 in cash.
    12   Purchased $400 of equipment on credit, making a 25 percent down payment.
    15   Delivered a calf for a fee of $35 (on credit).
    18   Made a partial payment of $50 on the equipment purchased May 12.
    27   Paid a utility bill of $40.

REQUIRED

1. Record these transactions in the general journal.
2. Post the transactions from the journal to the following accounts in the ledger: Cash (111); Accounts Receivable (112); Medical Supplies (115); Prepaid Rent (117); Equipment (144); Accounts Payable (212); Laura Stors, Capital (311); Veterinary Fees Earned (411); and Utilities Expense (512).
3. Prepare a trial balance as of May 31.
4. How does the transaction of May 15 relate to recognition and cash flows? Also compare the transactions of May 9 and May 27 with regard to classification.

ANSWER TO
REVIEW PROBLEM

1. Record the journal entries.

General Journal					Page 1
Date		Description	Post. Ref.	Debit	Credit
20xx May	1	Cash	111	2,000	
		Laura Stors, Capital	311		2,000
		Deposited $2,000 in the business bank account			
	3	Prepaid Rent	117	300	
		Cash	111		300
		Paid two months' rent in advance for an office			
	9	Medical Supplies	115	200	
		Cash	111		200
		Purchased medical supplies for cash			
	12	Equipment	144	400	
		Accounts Payable	212		300
		Cash	111		100
		Purchased equipment on credit, paying 25 percent down			
	15	Accounts Receivable	112	35	
		Veterinary Fees Earned	411		35
		Fee on credit for delivery of a calf			
	18	Accounts Payable	212	50	
		Cash	111		50
		Partial payment for equipment purchased May 12			
	27	Utilities Expense	512	40	
		Cash	111		40
		Paid utility bill			

REQUIRED

1. Prepare entries to record these transactions in journal form using the account titles in Part **2**.

2. Set up the following T accounts and post all the journal entries: Cash; Accounts Receivable; Supplies; Shed; Bicycles; Accounts Payable; Hassan Rahim, Capital; Hassan Rahim, Withdrawals; Rental Revenue; Wages Expense; Maintenance Expense; Repair Expense; and Concession Fee Expense.

3. Prepare a trial balance for Rahim Rentals as of June 30, 20xx.

4. Compare how recognition applies to the transactions of June 23 and 27 and their effects on cash flows and how classification applies to the transactions of June 8 and 13.

P 5.

LO 4 Transaction Analysis,
LO 5 General Journal,
LO 6 Ledger Accounts,
LO 7   and Trial Balance

Delta Security Service provides ushers and security personnel for athletic events and other functions. Delta's trial balance at the end of April was as shown below.

Delta Security Service Trial Balance April 30, 20xx		
Cash (111)	$ 13,300	
Accounts Receivable (113)	9,400	
Supplies (115)	560	
Prepaid Insurance (116)	600	
Equipment (141)	7,800	
Accounts Payable (211)		$ 5,300
Dennis Kinsella, Capital (311)		21,160
Dennis Kinsella, Withdrawals (312)	2,000	
Security Services Revenue (411)		28,000
Wages Expense (512)	16,000	
Rent Expense (513)	3,200	
Utilities Expense (514)	1,600	
	$54,460	$54,460

During May, Delta engaged in the following transactions.

May 1 Received cash from customers billed last month, $4,200.
2 Made a payment on accounts payable, $3,100.
3 Purchased a new one-year insurance policy in advance, $3,600.
5 Purchased supplies on credit, $430.
6 Billed a client for security services, $2,200.
7 Made a rent payment for May, $800.
9 Received cash from customers for security services, $1,600.
14 Paid wages for the security staff, $1,400.
16 Ordered equipment, $800.
17 Paid the current month's utility bill, $400.
18 Received and paid for the equipment ordered on May 16, $800.
19 Returned for full credit some of the supplies purchased on May 5 because they were defective, $120.
24 Withdrew cash for personal expenses, $1,000.
28 Paid for supplies purchased on May 5, less the return on May 19, $310.
30 Billed a customer for security services performed, $1,800.
31 Paid wages to the security staff, $1,050.

REQUIRED

1. Enter these transactions in the general journal (Pages 26 and 27).

2. Open ledger accounts for the accounts shown in the trial balance.

3. Enter the April 30, 20xx account balances from the trial balance in the appropriate ledger account.

4. Post the entries to the ledger accounts. Be sure to make the appropriate posting references in the journal and ledger as you post.

5. Prepare a trial balance as of May 31, 20xx.

ALTERNATE PROBLEMS

P 6. The following accounts are applicable to Jackson Communications:

LO 4   Transaction Analysis

1. Cash	7. Accounts Payable
2. Accounts Receivable	8. Capital
3. Supplies	9. Withdrawals
4. Prepaid Insurance	10. Service Revenue
5. Equipment	11. Rent Expense
6. Notes Payable	12. Repair Expense

Jackson Communications completed the following transactions:

	Debit	Credit
a. Paid for supplies purchased on credit last month.	7	1
b. Billed customers for services performed.	——	——
c. Paid the current month's rent.	——	——
d. Purchased supplies on credit.	——	——
e. Received cash from customers for services performed but not yet billed.	——	——
f. Purchased equipment on account.	——	——
g. Received a bill for repairs.	——	——
h. Returned a portion of the equipment that was purchased in **f** for a credit.	——	——
i. Received payments from customers previously billed.	——	——
j. Paid the bill received in **g**.	——	——
k. Received an order for services to be performed.	——	——
l. Paid for repairs with cash.	——	——
m. Made a payment to reduce the principal of the note payable.	——	——
n. Withdrew cash for personal expenses.	——	——

REQUIRED

Analyze each transaction and show the accounts affected by entering the corresponding numbers in the appropriate debit or credit column as shown in transaction **a**. Indicate no entry, if appropriate.

P 7. Tim Sauk is a house painter. During the month of June, he completed the following transactions:

LO 1   Transaction Analysis,
LO 4   Journal Form,
LO 5   T Accounts, and Trial Balance

June 3   Began his business with equipment valued at $2,460 and placed $14,200 in a business checking account.
     5   Purchased a used truck costing $3,800. Paid $1,000 in cash and signed a note for the balance.
     7   Purchased supplies on account for $640.
     8   Completed a painting job and billed the customer $960.
    10   Received $300 in cash for painting two rooms.
    11   Hired an assistant at $12 per hour.
    12   Purchased supplies for $320 in cash.
    13   Received a $960 check from the customer billed on June 8.
    14   Paid $800 for an insurance policy for eighteen months' coverage.
    16   Billed a customer $1,240 for a painting job.
    18   Paid the assistant $300 for twenty-five hours' work.
    19   Paid $80 for a tune-up for the truck.
    20   Paid for the supplies purchased on June 7.
    21   Purchased a new ladder (equipment) for $120 and supplies for $580, on account.
    23   Received a telephone bill for $120, due next month.
    24   Received $660 in cash from the customer billed on June 16.
    25   Transferred $600 to a personal checking account.

June 26   Received $720 in cash for painting a five-room apartment.
     28   Paid $400 on the note signed for the truck.
     29   Paid the assistant $360 for thirty hours' work.

REQUIRED

1. Prepare journal entries to record these transactions in journal form. Use the accounts listed below.

2. Set up the following T accounts and post all the journal entries: Cash; Accounts Receivable; Supplies; Prepaid Insurance; Equipment; Truck; Notes Payable; Accounts Payable; Tim Sauk, Capital; Tim Sauk, Withdrawals; Painting Fees Earned; Wages Expense; Telephone Expense; and Truck Expense.

3. Prepare a trial balance for Sank Painting Service as of June 30, 20xx.

4. Compare how recognition applies to the transactions of June 8 and 10 and their effects on cash flows and how classification applies to the transactions of June 14 and 18.

P 8.

LO 4 Transaction Analysis,
LO 5 General Journal,
LO 6 Ledger Accounts,
LO 7 and Trial Balance

The account balances for Lou's Landscaping Service at the end of July are shown in the trial balance below. During August, Mr. Jacobson completed these transactions:

Aug. 1   Paid for supplies purchased on credit last month, $140.
     2   Billed customers for services, $410.
     3   Paid the lease on a truck, $290.
     5   Purchased supplies on credit, $150.
     7   Received cash from customers not previously billed, $290.
     8   Purchased new equipment from Pendleton Manufacturing Company on account, $1,300.
     9   Received a bill for an oil change on the truck, $40.
    12   Returned a portion of the equipment that was purchased on August 8 for a credit, $320.
    13   Received payments from customers previously billed, $190.
    14   Paid the bill received on August 9.
    16   Took cash from the business for personal use, $110.
    19   Paid for the supplies purchased on August 5.
    20   Billed customers for services, $270.
    23   Purchased equipment from a friend who is retiring, $280. Payment was made from Lou's personal checking account, but the equipment will be used in the business. (**Hint:** Treat this as an owner's investment.)
    25   Received payments from customers previously billed, $390.
    27   Purchased gasoline for the truck with cash, $30.
    29   Made a payment to reduce the principal of the note payable, $600.

Lou's Landscaping Service
Trial Balance
July 31, 20xx

Cash (111)	$3,100	
Accounts Receivable (113)	220	
Supplies (115)	460	
Prepaid Insurance (116)	400	
Equipment (141)	4,400	
Notes Payable (211)		$3,000
Accounts Payable (212)		700
Lou Jacobson, Capital (311)		4,200
Lou Jacobson, Withdrawals (312)	420	
Service Revenue (411)		1,490
Lease Expense (511)	290	
Truck Expense (512)	100	
	$9,390	$9,390

1. Enter these transactions in the general journal (Pages 11 and 12).

2. Open accounts in the ledger for the accounts in the trial balance.

3. Enter the July 31, 20xx account balances from the trial balance.

4. Post the entries to the ledger accounts. Be sure to make the appropriate posting references in the journal and ledger as you post.

5. Prepare a trial balance as of August 31, 20xx.

EXPANDING YOUR CRITICAL THINKING, COMMUNICATION, AND INTERPERSONAL SKILLS

SKILLS DEVELOPMENT

Conceptual Analysis

SD 1.

LO 1 **Valuation Issue**

Nike, Inc., manufactures athletic shoes and related products. In one of its annual reports, Nike made this statement: "Property, plant, and equipment are recorded at cost."[8] Given that the property, plant, and equipment undoubtedly were purchased over several years and that the current value of those assets was likely to be very different from their original cost, tell what authoritative basis there is for carrying the assets at cost. Does accounting generally recognize changes in value subsequent to the purchase of property, plant, and equipment? Assume you are a Nike accountant. Write a memo to management explaining the rationale underlying Nike's approach.

SD 2.

LO 1 **Recognition, Valuation,**
LO 4 **and Classification Issues**

Chambers Development, a landfill development company, announced a change in its accounting practices. The company said the change would result in a restatement of its prior year's earnings. News of the accounting change caused the stock price to drop from $30½ to $11⅛ in one day, and it continued to decline to a low of $1⅞ two years later. According to one account,

> At the core of the problem was how Chambers accounted for millions of dollars it was spending to develop landfills. The company's choice: charge the costs in the year in which they were incurred or over the life of the landfill. The first method would increase operating costs, thereby depressing current earnings. On the other hand, writing off the costs gradually—"capitalizing" them in accounting parlance—would boost current earnings.[9]

Chambers initially chose to capitalize these costs (as an asset) and expense them gradually over future years. The change to immediate expensing led to a reduction of prior years' earnings of $362 million. The SEC required the restatement of Chambers' financial statements back to the year the company went public. The SEC determined that the amounts capitalized exceeded the reported pretax earnings. Instead of earning profits, the company had actually incurred losses.

The SEC discovered that management would set a target earnings level and back into the amount of costs to be capitalized to achieve the earnings target. The SEC investigation concluded "that the accounting practices that created millions of dollars in false profits were well outside the general bounds of generally accepted accounting practices. They were based on queered mathematics and an overzealous desire to please Wall Street, not an uncommon cause of corporate accounting scandals."[10]

1. Prepare the journal entry that Chambers made to record landfill costs as an asset (prepaid landfill costs). Prepare the journal entry to reduce its prepaid landfill costs by $362 million.

| Cash Flow | CD-ROM | Communication | Critical Thinking | Ethics | General Ledger | Group Activity | Hot Links to Real Companies | International | Internet | Key Ratio | Memo | Spreadsheet |

2. Three issues that must be addressed when recording a transaction are recognition, valuation, and classification. Which of these issues were of most concern to the SEC in the Chambers case? Explain how each applies to the transactions in part **1**.

Group Activity: Students work in groups to complete part **1**. Discuss part **2** as a class.

Ethical Dilemma

SD 3.

LO 1 **Recognition Point and Ethical Considerations**

One of **Penn Office Supplies Corporation**'s sales representatives, Jerry Hasbrow, is compensated on a commission basis and receives a substantial bonus for meeting his annual sales goal. The company's recognition point for sales is the day of shipment. On December 31, Hasbrow realizes that he needs sales of $2,000 to reach his sales goal and receive the bonus. He calls a purchasing agent for a local insurance company, whom he knows well, and asks him to buy $2,000 worth of copier paper today. The purchasing agent says, "But Jerry, that's more than a year's supply for us." Hasbrow says, "Buy it today. If you decide it's too much, you can return however much you want for full credit next month." The purchasing agent says, "Okay, ship it." The paper is shipped on December 31 and recorded as a sale. On January 15, the purchasing agent returns $1,750 worth of paper for full credit (okayed by Hasbrow) against the bill. Should the shipment on December 31 be recorded as a sale? Discuss the ethics of Hasbrow's action.

Group Activity: Divide the class into informal groups to discuss and report on the ethical issues of this case.

Research Activity

SD 4.

LO 4 **Transactions in a Business Article**

Locate an article on a company you recognize or on a company in a business that interests you in one of the following sources: a recent issue of a business journal (such as *Barron's, Fortune, The Wall Street Journal, Business Week,* or *Forbes*), or the Needles Accounting Resource Center web site at http://college.hmco.com. Read the article carefully, noting any references to transactions in which the company engages. These may be normal transactions (sales, purchases) or unusual transactions (a merger, the purchase of another company). Bring a copy of the article to class and be prepared to describe how you would analyze and record the transactions you have noted.

Decision-Making Practice

SD 5.

LO 4 **Transaction Analysis and**
LO 5 **Evaluation of a Trial Balance**

Ben Obi hired an attorney to help him start **Obi Repairs Company.** On June 1, Obi invested $23,000 in cash in the business. When he paid the attorney's bill of $1,400, the attorney advised him to hire an accountant to keep his records. However, Obi was so busy that it was June 30 before he asked you to straighten out his records. Your first task is to develop a trial balance based on the June transactions.

After making the investment and paying the attorney, Obi borrowed $10,000 from the bank. He later paid $520, which included interest of $120, on this loan. He also purchased a pickup truck in the company's name, paying $5,000 down and financing $14,800. The first payment on the truck is due July 15. Obi then rented an office and paid three months' rent, $1,800, in advance. Credit purchases of office equipment for $1,400 and repair tools for $1,000 must be paid for by July 13.

In June, Obi Repairs completed repairs of $2,600, of which $800 were cash transactions. Of the credit transactions, $600 were collected during June, and $1,200 remained to be collected at the end of June. Wages of $800 were paid to employees. On June 30, the company received a $150 bill for June utilities and a $100 check from a customer for work to be completed in July.

1. Record the June transactions in journal form.
2. Set up T accounts, post the general journal entries to the T accounts, and determine the balance of each account.
3. Prepare a June 30 trial balance for Obi Repairs Company.

4. Ben Obi is unsure how to evaluate the trial balance. His Cash account balance is $24,980, which exceeds his original investment of $23,000 by $1,980. Did he make a profit of $1,980? Explain why the Cash account is not an indicator of business earnings. Cite specific examples to show why it is difficult to determine net income by looking solely at figures in the trial balance.

FINANCIAL REPORTING AND ANALYSIS

Interpreting Financial Reports

FRA 1.

LO 2 Interpreting a Bank's
LO 4 Financial Statements

Mellon Bank is a large eastern bank holding company. Selected accounts from the company's 1999 annual report are as follows (in millions):[11]

Cash and Due from Banks	$ 3,410	Investment Securities	$ 1,193
Loans to Customers	30,248	Deposits by Customers	33,421

REQUIRED

1. Indicate whether each of the accounts just listed is an asset, a liability, or a component of owner's equity on Mellon's balance sheet.

2. Assume that you are in a position to do business with Mellon. Prepare the entry on the bank's books in journal form to record each of the following transactions:
   a. You sell securities in the amount of $2,000 to the bank.
   b. You deposit the $2,000 received in step **a** in the bank.
   c. You borrow $5,000 from the bank.

International Company

FRA 2.

LO 4 Transaction Analysis

Ajinomoto Company, a Japanese company with operations in 22 countries, is primarily engaged in the manufacture and sale of food products. The following selected aggregate cash transactions were reported in the statement of cash flows in Ajinomoto's annual report (amounts in millions of yen):[12]

Dividends paid	¥ 7,793
Purchase of property, plant, and equipment	46,381
Proceeds from long-term debt	10,357
Repayment of long-term debt	11,485

REQUIRED

Prepare entries in journal form to record the above transactions.

Toys "R" Us Annual Report

FRA 3.

LO 4 Transaction Analysis

Refer to the balance sheet in the Toys "R" Us annual report. Prepare T accounts for the accounts Cash and Cash Equivalents, Accounts and Other Receivables, Prepaid Expenses and Other Current Assets, Accounts Payable, and Income Taxes Payable. Properly place the balance of the account at January 29, 2000, in the T accounts. Below are some typical transactions in which Toys "R" Us would engage. Analyze each transaction, enter it in the T accounts, and determine the balance of each account. Assume all entries are in millions.

a. Paid cash in advance for certain expenses, $20.
b. Received cash from customers billed previously, $35.
c. Paid cash for income taxes previously owed, $70.
d. Paid cash to suppliers for amounts owed, $120.

Fingraph® Financial Analyst™

FRA 4.

LO 1 Transaction
LO 3 Identification
LO 4

Choose any company in the Fingraph® Financial Analyst™ CD-ROM software.

1. From the company's annual report, determine the industry(ies) in which the company operates.

2. Find the summary of significant accounting policies that appears following the financial statements. In these policies, find examples of the application of recognition, valuation, and classification.

3. Identify six types of transactions that your company would commonly engage in. Are any of these transactions more common in the industry in which your company operates than in other industries? For each transaction, tell what account would typically be debited and what account would be credited.

4. Prepare a one-page executive summary that highlights what you have learned from parts **1, 2,** and **3.**

Internet Case

FRA 5.

LO 2 **Comparison of Contrasting**
LO 4 **Companies**

Sun Microsystems and *Oracle Corporation* are leading computer and software companies. Compare and contrast the balance sheets of the two companies by first going to the Needles Accounting Resource Center web site at http://college.hmco.com. After choosing your textbook, click on "Chapter Resources" for Chapter 2. Then click on "Links to Companies in Text." Both companies are here. For each company, find its balance sheet. First, what differences and similarities do you find in the account titles used by Sun Microsystems and those used by Oracle? What differences and similarities do you find in the account titles used by the two companies and those used in your text? Second, although the companies are in the same general industry, their businesses differ. How are these differences reflected on the balance sheets? What types of transactions resulted in the differences?

ENDNOTES

1. "Boeing Scores a Deal to Sell 10 Planes to Air France for Long-Haul Routes," *The Wall Street Journal*, October 5, 2000.
2. The Boeing Co., *Annual Report*, 1994.
3. Craig S. Smith, "China Halts New Purchases of Jets," *The Wall Street Journal*, February 9, 1999.
4. Sun Microsystems Inc., *Annual Report*, 1999.
5. Intel Corp., *Annual Report*, 2000.
6. David Bank, "Informix Says Accounting Problems Were More Serious Than First Disclosed," *The Wall Street Journal*, September 23, 1997.
7. Patricia Kranz, "Rubles? Who Needs Rubles?" *Business Week*, April 13, 1998; Andrew Higgins, "Lacking Money to Pay, Russian Firms Survive on Deft Barter System," *The Wall Street Journal*, August 27, 1998.
8. Nike, Inc., *Annual Report*, 2000.
9. Len Boselovic, "A Look at How the SEC Disposed of Chambers' Claims," *Pittsburgh Post-Gazette*, May 14, 1995.
10. Ibid.
11. Mellon Bank, *Annual Report*, 1999.
12. Ajinomoto Company, *Annual Report*, 2000.

3

Measuring Business Income

DECISION POINT: A USER'S FOCUS

Southwest Airlines Co. Southwest Airlines Co. has become one of the most successful airlines by providing low-fare service between city pairs that are relatively close together. During any given year, Southwest incurs various operating expenses that are recorded as expenses when they are paid. However, at the end of the year, some expenses—including, for example, the wages of employees during the last days before the end of the year—will have been incurred but will not be paid until the next year. If these expenses are not accounted for correctly, they will appear in the wrong year—the year in which they are paid instead of the year in which Southwest benefited from them. The result is a misstatement of the company's income, a key profitability performance measure. How is this problem avoided?

According to the concepts of accrual accounting and the matching rule, which you will learn about in this chapter, the amount of expenses that have been incurred but not paid must be determined. Then they are recorded as expenses of the current year with corresponding liabilities to be paid the next year. The accompanying Financial Highlights shows the liabilities, called *accrued liabilities*, that resulted from this process at Southwest Airlines.[1] Accrued liabilities for aircraft rentals, employee profit sharing and savings plans, vacation pay, and other were $477,448,000 in 1998 and $535,024,000 in 1999. If these items had not been recorded in their respective years, income would have been misstated by a significant amount and the readers would have been misled.

Financial Highlights: Notes to the Financial Statements

3. ACCRUED LIABILITIES

(In thousands)	1999	1998
Aircraft rentals	$131,219	$121,868
Employee profitsharing and savings plans	138,566	123,195
Vacation pay	62,937	54,781
Other	202,302	177,604
Total accrued liabilities	$535,024	$477,448

Profitability Measurement: The Role of Business Income

Profitability is one of the two major goals of a business (the other being liquidity). For a business to succeed, or even to survive, it must earn a profit. The word **profit**, though, has many meanings. One is the increase in owner's equity that results from business operations. However, even this definition can be interpreted differently by economists, lawyers, businesspeople, and the public. Because the word *profit* has more than one meaning, accountants prefer to use the term *net income*, which can be precisely defined from an accounting point of view. Net income is reported on the income statement and is a performance measure used by management, owners, and others to monitor a business's progress in meeting the goal of profitability. Readers of income statements need to understand how the accountant defines net income and to be aware of its strengths and weaknesses as a measure of company performance.

Net Income

OBJECTIVE

1 Define *net income* and its two major components, *revenues* and *expenses*

Net income is the net increase in owner's equity that results from the operations of a company and is accumulated in the owner's Capital account. Net income, in its simplest form, is measured by the difference between revenues and expenses when revenues exceed expenses:

$$\text{Net Income} = \text{Revenues} - \text{Expenses}$$

When expenses exceed revenues, a **net loss** occurs.

REVENUES **Revenues** are increases in owner's equity resulting from selling goods, rendering services, or performing other business activities. Revenues are inflows, usually of cash or receivables, received in exchange for products or services. In the simplest case, revenues equal the price of goods sold and services rendered over a specific period of time. When a business delivers a product or provides a service to a customer, it usually receives either cash or a promise to pay cash in the near future. The promise to pay is recorded in either Accounts Receivable or Notes Receivable. The revenue for a given period equals the total of cash and receivables generated from goods and services provided to customers during that period.

Liabilities generally are not affected by revenues, and some transactions that increase cash and other assets do not produce revenues. For example a bank loan increases liabilities and cash but does not produce revenue. The collection of accounts receivable, which increases cash and decreases accounts receivable, does not produce revenue either. Remember that when a sale on credit takes place, the asset account Accounts Receivable increases; at the same time, an owner's equity revenue account increases. So counting the collection of the receivable as revenue later would be counting the same sale twice.

Not all increases in owner's equity arise from revenues. Owner investments increase owner's equity but are not revenue.

EXPENSES **Expenses** are decreases in owner's equity resulting from the costs of selling goods, rendering services, or performing other business activities. In other words, expenses are the costs of the goods and services used up in the course of earning revenues. Often called the *cost of doing business*, expenses include the cost of goods sold, the costs of activities necessary to carry on a business, and the costs of attracting and serving customers. Other examples are salaries, rent, advertising, telephone service, expired or used assets, and depreciation (allocation of cost) of a building or office equipment.

Just as not all cash receipts are revenues, not all cash payments are expenses. A cash payment to reduce a liability does not result in an expense because no good or service was used in the exchange. The liability, however, may have come from incurring a previous expense, such as advertising, that is to be paid later. There may also be two steps before an expenditure of cash becomes an expense. For example, prepaid expenses and plant assets (such as machinery and equipment) are recorded as assets when they are acquired. Later, as their usefulness expires in the operation of the business, their cost is allocated to expenses. In fact, expenses sometimes are called *expired costs*.

Not all decreases in owner's equity arise from expenses. Owner withdrawals decrease owner's equity, but they are not expenses.

The Accounting Period Issue

OBJECTIVE

2 Explain the difficulties of income measurement caused by the accounting period issue, the continuity issue, and the matching issue

The **accounting period issue** addresses the difficulty of assigning revenues and expenses to a short period of time, such as a month or a year. Not all transactions can be easily assigned to specific time periods. Purchases of buildings and equipment, for example, have effects that extend over many years. Accountants solve this problem by estimating the number of years the buildings or equipment will be in use and the cost that should be assigned to each year. In the process, they make an assumption about **periodicity**: that the net income for any period of time less than the life of the business, although tentative, is still a useful estimate of the entity's profitability for the period.

Generally, to make comparisons easier, the time periods are of equal length. Financial statements may be prepared for any time period. Accounting periods of less than one year—for example, a month or a quarter—are called *interim periods*. The 12-month accounting period used by a company is called its **fiscal year**. Many companies use the calendar year, January 1 to December 31, for their fiscal year. Others find it convenient to choose a fiscal year that ends during a slack season rather than a peak season. In this case, the fiscal year corresponds to the company's yearly cycle of business activity. The time period should always be noted in the financial statements.

The Continuity Issue

The process of measuring business income requires that certain expense and revenue transactions be allocated over several accounting periods. The number of accounting periods raises the **continuity issue**. How long will the business entity

FOCUS ON BUSINESS PRACTICE

The table on the right shows the diverse fiscal years used by some well-known companies. Many governmental and educational units use fiscal years that end June 30 or September 30.

Company	Last Month of Fiscal Year
American Greetings Corp.	February
Caesars World, Inc.	July
The Walt Disney Company	September
Eastman Kodak Company	December
Fleetwood Enterprises, Inc.	April
Lorimar Syndication	March
Mattel, Inc.	December
MGM-UA Communications Co.	August
Polaroid Corp.	December

last? Many businesses last less than five years; in any given year, thousands of businesses go bankrupt. To prepare financial statements for an accounting period, the accountant must make an assumption about the ability of the business to survive. Specifically, unless there is evidence to the contrary, the accountant assumes that the business will continue to operate indefinitely, that the business is a **going concern**. Justification for all the techniques of income measurement rests on the assumption of continuity. For example, this assumption allows the cost of certain assets to be held on the balance sheet until a future year, when it will become an expense on the income statement.

Another example has to do with the value of assets on the balance sheet. The accountant records assets at cost and does not record subsequent changes in their value. But the value of assets to a going concern is much higher than the value of assets to a firm facing bankruptcy. In the latter case, the accountant may be asked to set aside the assumption of continuity and to prepare financial statements based on the assumption that the firm will go out of business and sell all of its assets at liquidation value—that is, for what they will bring in cash.

The Matching Issue

Revenues and expenses can be accounted for on a cash received and cash paid basis. This practice is known as the **cash basis of accounting**. Individuals and some businesses may use the cash basis of accounting for income tax purposes. Under this method, revenues are reported in the period in which cash is received, and expenses are reported in the period in which cash is paid. Taxable income, therefore, is calculated as the difference between cash receipts from revenues and cash payments for expenses.

Although the cash basis of accounting works well for some small businesses and many individuals, it does not meet the needs of most businesses. As explained above, revenues can be earned in a period other than the one in which cash is received, and expenses can be incurred in a period other than the one in which cash is paid. To measure net income adequately, revenues and expenses must be assigned to the appropriate accounting period. The accountant solves this problem by applying the **matching rule**:

> Revenues must be assigned to the accounting period in which the goods are sold or the services performed, and expenses must be assigned to the accounting period in which they are used to produce revenue.

FOCUS ON BUSINESS ETHICS

Accounting practices are meant to inform the readers of financial statements, not to deceive them. Accounting assumptions and rules, such as the periodicity assumption and the matching rule, should not be applied in a way that will distort or obscure financial results. In recent years, Securities and Exchange Commission Chairman Arthur Levitt has waged a public campaign against corporate accounting practices that arise when companies manage or manipulate their earnings to meet Wall Street analysts' expectations. Management in these cases is fearful that a shortfall will trigger a big decline in its company's stock price. Companies, for instance, may increase expenses, inappropriately applying the matching rule and periodicity assumption by reducing earnings in a year of unusually high income and boosting income in subsequent years by reducing expenses. The SEC has challenged the accounting of many companies, including Sunbeam-Oster Company, Inc., and Cisco Systems.[2]

Direct cause-and-effect relationships seldom can be demonstrated for certain, but many costs appear to be related to particular revenues. The accountant recognizes these expenses and the related revenues in the same accounting period. Examples are the costs of goods sold and sales commissions. When there is no direct means of connecting expenses and revenues, the accountant tries to allocate costs in a systematic way among the accounting periods that benefit from the costs. For example, a building is converted from an asset to an expense by allocating its cost over the years during which the company benefits from its use.

Accrual Accounting

OBJECTIVE

3 Define *accrual accounting* and explain two broad ways of accomplishing it

To apply the matching rule, accountants have developed accrual accounting. **Accrual accounting** "attempts to record the financial effects on an enterprise of transactions and other events and circumstances . . . in the periods in which those transactions, events, and circumstances occur rather than only in the periods in which cash is received or paid by the enterprise."[3] That is, accrual accounting consists of all the techniques developed by accountants to apply the matching rule. It is done in two general ways: (1) by recording revenues when earned and expenses when incurred and (2) by adjusting the accounts.

Recognizing Revenues When Earned and Expenses When Incurred

The first application of accrual accounting is the recognition of revenues when earned and expenses when incurred. For example, when Joan Miller Advertising Agency makes a sale on credit by placing advertisements for a client, revenue is recorded at the time of the sale by debiting Accounts Receivable and crediting Advertising Fees Earned. This is how the accountant recognizes the revenue from a credit sale before the cash is collected. Accounts Receivable serves as a holding account until payment is received. The process of determining when revenue is earned, and consequently when it should be recorded, is referred to as **revenue recognition**.

When Joan Miller Advertising Agency receives its telephone bill, the expense is recognized both as having been incurred and as helping to produce revenue. The transaction is recorded by debiting Telephone Expense and crediting Accounts Payable. Until the bill is paid, Accounts Payable serves as a holding account. Notice that recognition of the expense does not depend on the payment of cash.

Adjusting the Accounts

The second application of accrual accounting is adjusting the accounts. Adjustments are necessary because the accounting period, by definition, ends on a particular day. The balance sheet must list all assets and liabilities as of the end of that day, and the income statement must contain all revenues and expenses applicable to the period ending on that day. Although operating a business is a continuous process, there must be a cutoff point for the periodic reports. Some transactions invariably span the cutoff point; thus, some accounts need adjustment.

For example, some of the accounts in the end-of-the-period trial balance for Joan Miller Advertising Agency (Exhibit 1) do not show the correct balances for preparing the financial statements. The January 31 trial balance lists prepaid rent

Exhibit 1
Trial Balance for Joan Miller Advertising Agency

Joan Miller Advertising Agency
Trial Balance
January 31, 20xx

Cash	$ 1,720	
Accounts Receivable	2,800	
Art Supplies	1,800	
Office Supplies	800	
Prepaid Rent	800	
Prepaid Insurance	480	
Art Equipment	4,200	
Office Equipment	3,000	
Accounts Payable		$ 3,170
Unearned Art Fees		1,000
Joan Miller, Capital		10,000
Joan Miller, Withdrawals	1,400	
Advertising Fees Earned		4,200
Wages Expense	1,200	
Utilities Expense	100	
Telephone Expense	70	
	$18,370	$18,370

of $800. At $400 per month, this represents rent for the months of January and February. So on January 31, one-half of the $800, or $400, represents rent expense for January; the remaining $400 represents an asset that will be used in February. An adjustment is needed to reflect the $400 balance in the Prepaid Rent account on the balance sheet and the $400 rent expense on the income statement. As you will see on the following pages, several other accounts in the Joan Miller Advertising Agency trial balance do not reflect their correct balances. Like the Prepaid Rent account, they need to be adjusted.

Accrual Accounting and Performance Measures

Accrual accounting can be difficult to understand. The related adjustments take time to calculate and enter in the records. Also, adjusting entries do not affect cash flows in the current period because they never involve the Cash account. You might ask, "Why go to all the trouble of making them? Why worry about them?" The Securities and Exchange Commission, in fact, has identified issues related to accrual accounting and adjustments to be an area of utmost importance because of the potential for abuse and misrepresentation.[4]

All adjustments are important because they are necessary to calculate key profitability performance measures. Adjusting entries affect net income on the income statement, and they affect profitability comparisons from one accounting period to the next. Adjusting entries also affect assets and liabilities on the balance sheet and thus provide information about a company's *future* cash inflows and outflows. This information is needed to assess management's short-term goal of achieving sufficient liquidity to meet its needs for cash to pay ongoing obligations. The potential for abuse arises from the fact that considerable judgment underlies the application of adjusting entries. Misuse of this judgment can result in misleading measures of performance.

The Adjustment Process

OBJECTIVE

4 State four principal situations that require adjusting entries

Accountants use **adjusting entries** to apply accrual accounting to transactions that span more than one accounting period. There are four situations in which adjusting entries are required, as illustrated in Figure 1. As shown, each situation affects one balance sheet account and one income statement account. Adjusting entries never involve the Cash account. The four types of adjusting entries may be stated as follows:

1. Costs have been recorded that must be allocated between two or more accounting periods. Examples are prepaid rent, prepaid insurance, supplies, and costs of a building. The adjusting entry in this case involves an asset account and an expense account.

2. Expenses have been incurred but are not yet recorded. Examples are the wages earned by employees in the current accounting period but after the last pay period. The adjusting entry involves an expense account and a liability account.

3. Unearned revenues have been recorded that must be allocated between two or more accounting periods. An example is payments collected for services yet to be rendered. The adjusting entry involves a liability account and a revenue account.

4. Revenues have been earned but not yet recorded. An example is fees earned but not yet collected or billed to customers. The adjusting entry involves an asset account and a revenue account.

Accountants often refer to adjusting entries as deferrals or accruals. A **deferral** is the postponement of the recognition of an expense already paid (Type 1 adjustment) or of a revenue received in advance (Type 3 adjustment). Recording of the receipt or payment of cash precedes the adjusting entry. An **accrual** is the recognition of a revenue (Type 4 adjustment) or expense (Type 2 adjustment) that has arisen but has not yet been recorded. No cash was received or paid prior to the adjusting entry; this will occur in a future accounting period. Once again, we use Joan Miller Advertising Agency to illustrate the kinds of adjusting entries that most businesses make.

Figure 1
The Four Types of Adjustments

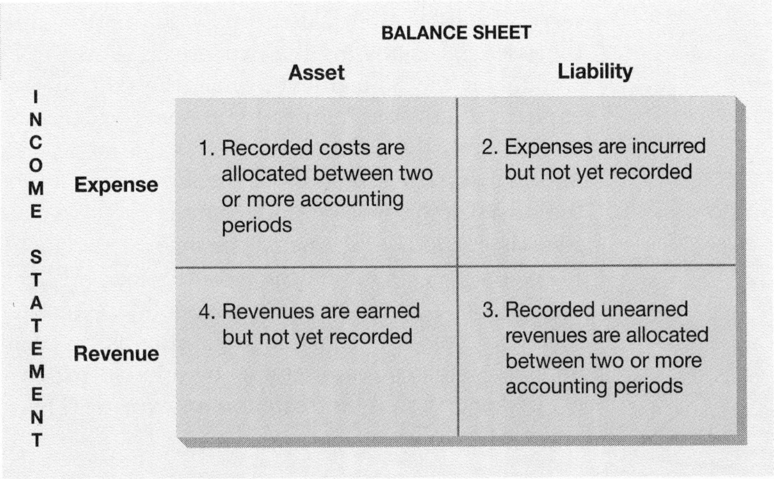

		BALANCE SHEET	
		Asset	**Liability**
INCOME STATEMENT	**Expense**	1. Recorded costs are allocated between two or more accounting periods	2. Expenses are incurred but not yet recorded
	Revenue	4. Revenues are earned but not yet recorded	3. Recorded unearned revenues are allocated between two or more accounting periods

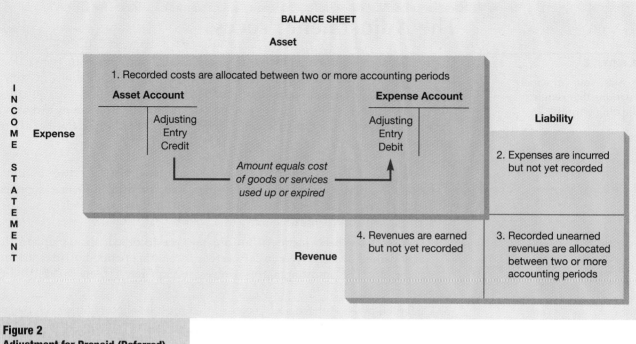

Figure 2
Adjustment for Prepaid (Deferred) Expenses

Type 1: Allocating Recorded Costs Between Two or More Accounting Periods (Deferred Expenses)

OBJECTIVE
5 Prepare typical adjusting entries

Organizations often make expenditures that benefit more than one period. These expenditures are usually debited to an asset account. At the end of the accounting period, the amount that has been used is transferred from the asset account to an expense account. Two of the more important kinds of adjustments are those for prepaid expenses and the depreciation of plant and equipment.

PREPAID EXPENSES   Some expenses customarily are paid in advance. These expenditures are called **prepaid expenses**. Among them are rent, insurance, and supplies. At the end of an accounting period, a portion (or all) of these goods or services will have been used up or will have expired. An adjusting entry reducing the asset and increasing the expense, as shown in Figure 2, is always required. The amount of the adjustment equals the cost of the goods or services used up or expired. If adjusting entries for prepaid expenses are not made at the end of the period, both the balance sheet and the income statement will present incorrect information: The assets of the organization will be overstated, and the expenses of the organization will be understated. This means that owner's equity on the balance sheet and net income on the income statement will be overstated.

At the beginning of the month, Joan Miller Advertising Agency paid two months' rent in advance. This expenditure resulted in an asset consisting of the right to occupy the office for two months. As each day in the month passed, part of the asset's cost expired and became an expense. By January 31, one-half had expired and should be treated as an expense. This economic event is analyzed and recorded as follows:

Prepaid Rent (Adjustment a)

	Dr.	Cr.
Jan. 31 Rent Expense	400	
Prepaid Rent		400

A = L + OE
−   −

Prepaid Rent

Jan. 2	800	Jan. 31	400

Rent Expense

Jan. 31	400	

Transaction: Expiration of one month's rent.
Analysis: Assets decrease. Owner's equity decreases.
Rules: Decreases in owner's equity are recorded by debits. Decreases in assets are recorded by credits.
Entries: The decrease in owner's equity is recorded by a debit to Rent Expense. The decrease in assets is recorded by a credit to Prepaid Rent.

The Prepaid Rent account now has a balance of $400, which represents one month's rent paid in advance. The Rent Expense account reflects the $400 expense for the month of January.

Besides rent, Joan Miller Advertising Agency prepaid expenses for insurance, art supplies, and office supplies, all of which call for adjusting entries.

On January 8, the agency purchased a one-year life insurance policy, paying for it in advance. Like prepaid rent, prepaid insurance offers benefits (in this case, protection) that expire day by day. By the end of the month, one-twelfth of the protection had expired.

The prepaid insurance adjustment is analyzed and recorded as follows:

Prepaid Insurance (Adjustment b)

	Dr.	Cr.
Jan. 31 Insurance Expense	40	
Prepaid Insurance		40

A = L + OE
−   −

Prepaid Insurance

Jan. 8	480	Jan. 31	40

Insurance Expense

Jan. 31	40	

Transaction: Expiration of one month's life insurance.
Analysis: Assets decrease. Owner's equity decreases.
Rules: Decreases in owner's equity are recorded by debits. Decreases in assets are recorded by credits.
Entries: The decrease in owner's equity is recorded by a debit to Insurance Expense. The decrease in assets is recorded by a credit to Prepaid Insurance.

The Prepaid Insurance account now shows the correct balance, $440, and Insurance Expense reflects the expired cost, $40 for the month of January.

Early in the month, Joan Miller Advertising Agency purchased art supplies and office supplies. As Joan Miller prepared advertising designs for various clients, art supplies were consumed, and her secretary used office supplies. There is no need to account for these supplies every day because the financial statements are not prepared until the end of the month and the recordkeeping would involve too much work. Instead, Joan Miller makes a careful inventory of the art and office supplies at the end of the month. This inventory records the quantity and cost of those supplies that are still assets of the company—that are yet to be consumed.

Suppose the inventory shows that art supplies costing $1,300 and office supplies costing $600 are still on hand. This means that of the $1,800 of art supplies originally purchased, $500 worth were used up (became an expense) in January. Of the original $800 of office supplies, $200 worth were consumed. These transactions are analyzed and recorded as follows:

Art Supplies and Office Supplies (Adjustments c and d)

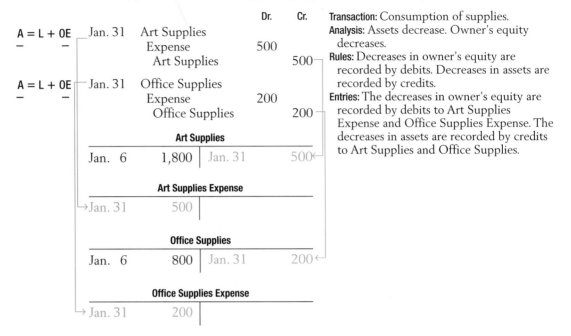

			Dr.	Cr.
A = L + OE	Jan. 31	Art Supplies Expense	500	
− −		Art Supplies		500
A = L + OE	Jan. 31	Office Supplies Expense	200	
− −		Office Supplies		200

Transaction: Consumption of supplies.
Analysis: Assets decrease. Owner's equity decreases.
Rules: Decreases in owner's equity are recorded by debits. Decreases in assets are recorded by credits.
Entries: The decreases in owner's equity are recorded by debits to Art Supplies Expense and Office Supplies Expense. The decreases in assets are recorded by credits to Art Supplies and Office Supplies.

Art Supplies

Jan. 6	1,800	Jan. 31	500

Art Supplies Expense

Jan. 31	500	

Office Supplies

Jan. 6	800	Jan. 31	200

Office Supplies Expense

Jan. 31	200	

The asset accounts Art Supplies and Office Supplies now reflect the correct balances, $1,300 and $600, respectively, of supplies that are yet to be consumed. In addition, the amount of art supplies used up during January is shown as $500 and the amount of office supplies used up is shown as $200.

DEPRECIATION OF PLANT AND EQUIPMENT When an organization buys a long-term asset—a building, trucks, computers, store fixtures, or furniture—it is, in effect, prepaying for the usefulness of that asset for as long as it benefits the organization. Because a long-term asset is a deferral of an expense, the accountant must allocate the cost of the asset over its estimated useful life. The amount allocated to any one accounting period is called **depreciation**, or *depreciation expense*. Depreciation, like other expenses, is incurred during an accounting period to produce revenue.

It is often impossible to tell how long an asset will last or how much of the asset is used in any one period. For this reason, depreciation has to be estimated. Accountants have developed a number of methods for estimating depreciation and for dealing with the related complex problems. Here we look at the simplest case.

FOCUS ON INTERNATIONAL BUSINESS

The privatization of businesses in Eastern Europe and the republics of the former Soviet Union has created a great need for Western accounting knowledge. Many managers from these countries want to study accounting. Under the old governmental systems, the concept of net income as Westerners know it did not exist because the state owned everything and there was no such thing as income. The new businesses, because they are private, require accounting systems that recognize the importance of net income. In these new systems, it is necessary to make adjusting entries to record such things as depreciation and accrued expenses. Many Eastern European businesses have been suffering losses for years without knowing it and, as a result, are now in poor financial and physical condition.

Suppose that Joan Miller Advertising Agency estimates that the art equipment for which it paid $4,200 and the office equipment for which it paid $3,000 will last five years (60 months) and will have zero value at the end of that time. The monthly depreciation of art equipment is $70 ($4,200 ÷ 60 months) and office equipment is $50 ($3,000 ÷ 60 months). These amounts represent the costs allocated to each month, and they are the amounts by which the asset accounts must be reduced and the expense accounts increased (reducing owner's equity).

Art Equipment and Office Equipment (Adjustments e and f)

		Dr.	Cr.
Jan. 31	Depreciation Expense, Art Equipment	70	
	Accumulated Depreciation, Art Equipment		70
Jan. 31	Depreciation Expense, Office Equipment	50	
	Accumulated Depreciation, Office Equipment		50

A = L + OE
−   −

A = L + OE
−   −

Transaction: Recording depreciation expense.
Analysis: Assets decrease. Owner's equity decreases.
Rules: Decreases in owner's equity are recorded by debits. Decreases in assets are recorded by credits.
Entries: The owner's equity is decreased by debits to Depreciation Expense, Art Equipment and Depreciation Expense, Office Equipment. The assets are decreased by credits to Accumulated Depreciation, Art Equipment and Accumulated Depreciation, Office Equipment.

Art Equipment

Jan. 4	4,200	

Accumulated Depreciation, Art Equipment

	Jan. 31	70

Office Equipment

Jan. 5	3,000	

Accumulated Depreciation, Office Equipment

	Jan. 31	50

Depreciation Expense, Art Equipment

Jan. 31	70	

Depreciation Expense, Office Equipment

Jan. 31	50	

ACCUMULATED DEPRECIATION—A CONTRA ACCOUNT   Notice that in the previous analysis, the asset accounts are not credited directly. Instead, as shown in Figure 3, new accounts—Accumulated Depreciation, Art Equipment and Accumulated Depreciation, Office Equipment—are credited. These **accumulated depreciation accounts** are contra-asset accounts used to total the past depreciation expense on specific long-term assets. A **contra account** is a separate account that is paired with a related account—in this case an asset account. The balance of the

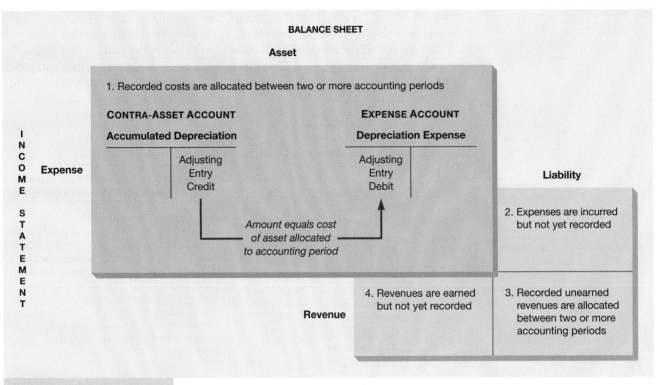

Figure 3
Adjustment for Depreciation

contra account is shown on the financial statement as a deduction from the related account.

There are several types of contra accounts. In this case, the balance of Accumulated Depreciation, Art Equipment is shown on the balance sheet as a deduction from the associated account Art Equipment. Likewise, Accumulated Depreciation, Office Equipment is a deduction from Office Equipment. Exhibit 2 shows the plant and equipment section of the balance sheet for Joan Miller Advertising Agency after these adjusting entries have been made.

A contra account is used for two very good reasons. First, it recognizes that depreciation is an estimate. Second, a contra account preserves the original cost of an asset: In combination with the asset account, it shows both how much of the asset has been allocated as an expense and the balance left to be depreciated. As

Exhibit 2
**Plant and Equipment Section
of the Balance Sheet**

Joan Miller Advertising Agency
Partial Balance Sheet
January 31, 20xx

Plant and Equipment		
Art Equipment	$4,200	
Less Accumulated Depreciation	70	$4,130
Office Equipment	$3,000	
Less Accumulated Depreciation	50	2,950
Total Plant and Equipment		$7,080

the months pass, the amount of accumulated depreciation grows, and the net amount shown as an asset declines. In six months, Accumulated Depreciation, Art Equipment will show a balance of $420; when this amount is subtracted from Art Equipment, a net amount of $3,780 will remain. The net amount is called the **carrying value**, or *book value*, of the asset.

Type 2: Recognizing Unrecorded Expenses (Accrued Expenses)

At the end of an accounting period, there usually are expenses that have been incurred but not recorded in the accounts. These expenses require adjusting entries. One such case is interest on borrowed money. Each day, interest accumulates on the debt. As shown in Figure 4, at the end of the accounting period, an adjusting entry is made to record this accumulated interest, which is an expense of the period, and the corresponding liability to pay the interest. Other common unrecorded expenses are wages and utilities. As the expense and the corresponding liability accumulate, they are said to *accrue*—hence the term **accrued expenses**.

ACCRUED WAGES   Suppose the calendar for January looks like this:

January

Su	M	T	W	Th	F	Sa
	1	2	3	4	5	6
7	8	9	10	11	12	13
14	15	16	17	18	19	20
21	22	23	24	25	26	27
28	29	30	31			

By the end of business on January 31, the secretary at Joan Miller Advertising Agency will have worked three days (Monday, Tuesday, and Wednesday) beyond

Figure 4
Adjustment for Unrecorded (Accrued) Expenses

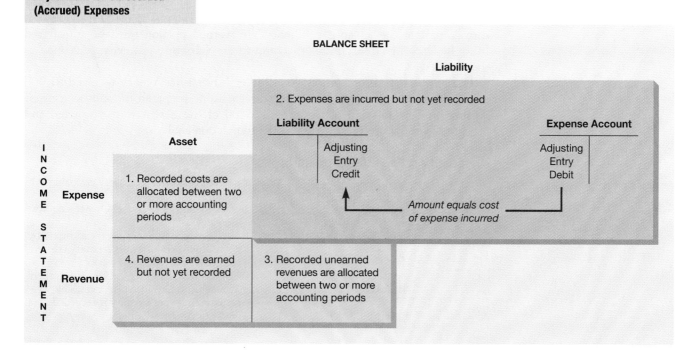

the last biweekly pay period, which ended on January 26. The employee has earned the wages for these days, but she will not be paid until the regular payday in February. The wages for these three days are rightfully an expense for January, and the liabilities should reflect the fact that the company owes the secretary for those days. Because the secretary's wage rate is $600 every two weeks, or $60 per day ($600 ÷ 10 working days), the expense is $180 ($60 × 3 days).

Accrued Wages (Adjustment g)

			Dr.	Cr.
A = L + OE	Jan. 31	Wages Expense	180	
+ −		Wages Payable		180

Wages Payable

			Jan. 31	180

Wages Expense

Jan. 12	600	
26	600	
31	180	

Transaction: Accrual of unrecorded expense.
Analysis: Liabilities increase. Owner's equity decreases.
Rules: Decreases in owner's equity are recorded by debits. Increases in liabilities are recorded by credits.
Entries: The decrease in owner's equity is recorded by a debit to Wages Expense. The increase in liabilities is recorded by a credit to Wages Payable.

The liability of $180 is now reflected correctly in the Wages Payable account. The actual expense incurred for wages during January, $1,380, is also correct.

Type 3: Allocating Recorded Unearned Revenues Between Two or More Accounting Periods (Deferred Revenues)

Just as expenses can be paid before they are used, revenues can be received before they are earned. When revenues are received in advance, the company has an obligation to deliver goods or perform services. Therefore, **unearned revenues** are shown in a liability account. For example, publishing companies usually receive payment in advance for magazine subscriptions. These receipts are recorded in a liability account. If the company fails to deliver the magazines, subscribers are entitled to their money back. As the company delivers each issue of the magazine, it earns a part of the advance payments. This earned portion must be transferred from the Unearned Subscriptions account to the Subscription Revenue account, as shown in Figure 5.

During the month of January, Joan Miller Advertising Agency received $1,000 as an advance payment for advertising designs to be prepared for another agency. Assume that by the end of the month, $400 of the design was completed and accepted by the other agency. Here is the transaction analysis:

Unearned Art Fees (Adjustment h)

			Dr.	Cr.
A = L + OE	Jan. 31	Unearned Art Fees	400	
− +		Art Fees Earned		400

Unearned Art Fees

Jan. 31	400	Jan. 15	1,000

Art Fees Earned

		Jan. 31	400

Transaction: Performance of services paid for in advance.
Analysis: Liabilities decrease. Owner's equity increases.
Rules: Decreases in liabilities are recorded by debits. Increases in owner's equity are recorded by credits.
Entries: The decrease in liabilities is recorded by a debit to Unearned Art Fees. The increase in owner's equity is recorded by a credit to Art Fees Earned.

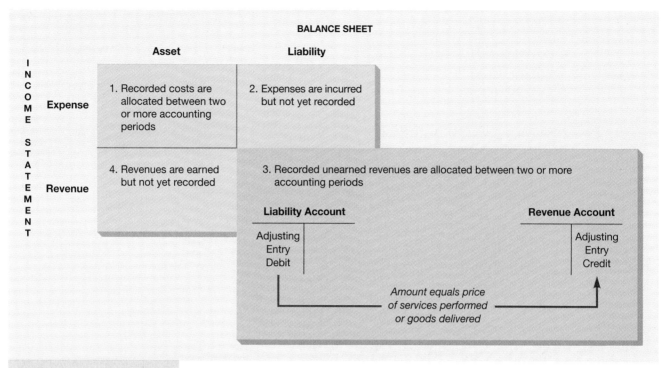

Figure 5
Adjustment for Unearned (Deferred) Revenues

The liability account Unearned Art Fees now reflects the amount of work still to be performed, $600. The revenue account Art Fees Earned reflects the services performed and the revenue earned for them during January, $400.

Type 4: Recognizing Unrecorded Revenues (Accrued Revenues)

Accrued revenues are revenues for which a service has been performed or goods delivered but for which no entry has been recorded. Any revenues earned but not recorded during the accounting period require an adjusting entry that debits an asset account and credits a revenue account, as shown in Figure 6. For example, the interest on a note receivable is earned day by day but may not be received until another accounting period. Interest Receivable should be debited and Interest Income should be credited for the interest accrued at the end of the current period.

FOCUS ON BUSINESS TECHNOLOGY

New businesses engaged in electronic commerce over the Internet have been receiving much attention in recent years. Electronic sales and purchases involving Web-based companies like Amazon.com, Webvan™, and BlueLight.com have been growing steadily.

The total value of goods and services traded on the Web will be $433 billion in 2002, of which $94 billion will be retail sales.[5]

It is important to realize that electronic transactions are analyzed and recorded in exactly the same way as transactions that take place in a physical store. In addition, companies operating on the Web require insurance, employee payrolls, buildings, and other assets and liabilities, and they must make the adjusting entries in the same way any other business does.

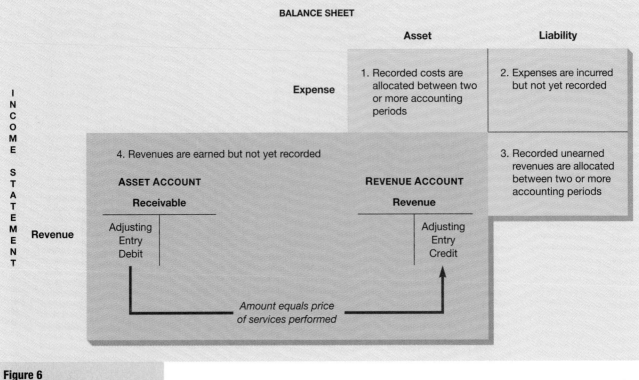

Figure 6
Adjustment for Unrecorded
(Accrued) Revenues

Suppose that Joan Miller Advertising Agency has agreed to place a series of advertisements for Marsh Tire Company and that the first advertisement appears on January 31, the last day of the month. The fee of $200 for this advertisement, which has been earned but not recorded, should be recorded this way:

Accrued Advertising Fees (Adjustment i)

	Dr.	Cr.
A = L + OE — Jan. 31 Fees Receivable	200	
Advertising Fees		
Earned		200

Transaction: Accrual of unrecorded revenue.
Analysis: Assets increase. Owner's equity increases.
Rules: Increases in assets are recorded by debits. Increases in owner's equity are recorded by credits.
Entries: The increase in assets is recorded by a debit to Fees Receivable. The increase in owner's equity is recorded by a credit to Advertising Fees Earned.

Fees Receivable

Jan. 31	200	

Advertising Fees Earned

	Jan. 10	1,400
	19	2,800
	31	200

Now both the asset and the revenue accounts show the correct balance: The $200 in Fees Receivable is owed to the company, and the $4,400 in Advertising Fees Earned has been earned by the company during January. Marsh Tire Company will be billed for the series of advertisements when they are completed.

A Note About Journal Entries

Thus far we have presented a full analysis of each journal entry. The analyses showed you the thought process behind each entry. By now, you should be fully

In a computerized accounting system, adjusting entries can be entered just like any other transactions. Some adjusting entries, such as those for insurance expense and depreciation expense, may be similar for each accounting period, and others, such as those for accrued wages, may always involve the same accounts. In such cases, the computer can be programmed to display the adjusting entries automatically so that all the accountant has to do is verify the amounts or enter the correct amounts. Then the adjusting entries are entered and posted, and the adjusted trial balance is prepared with the touch of a button.

aware of the effects of transactions on the accounting equation and the rules of debit and credit. For this reason, in the rest of the book, journal entries are presented without full analysis.

Using the Adjusted Trial Balance to Prepare Financial Statements

OBJECTIVE

6 Prepare financial statements from an adjusted trial balance

After adjusting entries have been recorded and posted, an **adjusted trial balance** is prepared by listing all accounts and their balances. If the adjusting entries have been posted to the accounts correctly, the adjusted trial balance should have equal debit and credit totals.

The adjusted trial balance for Joan Miller Advertising Agency is shown on the left side of Exhibit 3. Notice that some accounts, such as Cash and Accounts Receivable, have the same balances they have in the trial balance (see Exhibit 1) because no adjusting entries affected them. Some new accounts, such as Fees Receivable, depreciation accounts, and Wages Payable, appear in the adjusted trial balance, and other accounts, such as Art Supplies, Office Supplies, Prepaid Rent, and Prepaid Insurance, have balances different from those in the trial balance because adjusting entries did affect them.

From the adjusted trial balance, the financial statements can be easily prepared. The income statement is prepared from the revenue and expense accounts, as shown in Exhibit 3. Then, as shown in Exhibit 4, the statement of owner's equity and the balance sheet are prepared. Notice that the net income from the income statement is combined with withdrawals on the statement of owner's equity to give the net change in the Joan Miller, Capital account. The resulting balance of Joan Miller, Capital on January 31 is used on the balance sheet, as are the asset and liability accounts.

Cash Flows from Accrual-Based Information

SUPPLEMENTAL OBJECTIVE

7 Analyze cash flows from accrual-based information

Management has the short-range goal of achieving sufficient liquidity to meet its needs for cash to pay its ongoing obligations. It is important for managers to be able to use accrual-based financial information to analyze cash flows in order to plan payments to creditors and assess the need for short-term borrowing.

Exhibit 3
Relationship of Adjusted Trial Balance to Income Statement

Joan Miller Advertising Agency Adjusted Trial Balance January 31, 20xx		
Cash	$ 1,720	
Accounts Receivable	2,800	
Fees Receivable	200	
Art Supplies	1,300	
Office Supplies	600	
Prepaid Rent	400	
Prepaid Insurance	440	
Art Equipment	4,200	
Accumulated Depreciation, Art Equipment		$ 70
Office Equipment	3,000	
Accumulated Depreciation, Office Equipment		50
Accounts Payable		3,170
Wages Payable		180
Unearned Art Fees		600
Joan Miller, Capital		10,000
Joan Miller, Withdrawals	1,400	
Advertising Fees Earned		4,400
Art Fees Earned		400
Wages Expense	1,380	
Utilities Expense	100	
Telephone Expense	70	
Rent Expense	400	
Insurance Expense	40	
Art Supplies Expense	500	
Office Supplies Expense	200	
Depreciation Expense, Art Equipment	70	
Depreciation Expense, Office Equipment	50	
	$18,870	$18,870

Joan Miller Advertising Agency Income Statement For the Month Ended January 31, 20xx		
Revenues		
Advertising Fees Earned		$4,400
Art Fees Earned		400
Total Revenues		$4,800
Expenses		
Wages Expense	$1,380	
Utilities Expense	100	
Telephone Expense	70	
Rent Expense	400	
Insurance Expense	40	
Art Supplies Expense	500	
Office Supplies Expense	200	
Depreciation Expense, Art Equipment	70	
Depreciation Expense, Office Equipment	50	
Total Expenses		2,810
Net Income		$1,990

Every revenue or expense account on the income statement has one or more related accounts on the balance sheet. For instance, Supplies Expense is related to Supplies, Wages Expense to Wages Payable, and Art Fees Earned to Unearned Art Fees. As shown in this chapter, these accounts are related to one another through adjusting entries whose purpose is to apply the matching rule in the measurement of net income.

The cash flows generated or paid by company operations may also be determined by analyzing these relationships. For example, suppose that after receiving the financial statements in Exhibits 3 and 4, management wants to know how much cash was expended for art supplies. On the income statement, Art Supplies Expense is $500, and on the balance sheet, Art Supplies is $1,300. Because January

Exhibit 4
Relationship of Adjusted Trial Balance to Balance Sheet and Statement of Owner's Equity

Joan Miller Advertising Agency
Adjusted Trial Balance
January 31, 20xx

Cash	$ 1,720	
Accounts Receivable	2,800	
Fees Receivable	200	
Art Supplies	1,300	
Office Supplies	600	
Prepaid Rent	400	
Prepaid Insurance	440	
Art Equipment	4,200	
Accumulated Depreciation, Art Equipment		$ 70
Office Equipment	3,000	
Accumulated Depreciation, Office Equipment		50
Accounts Payable		3,170
Wages Payable		180
Unearned Art Fees		600
Joan Miller, Capital		10,000
Joan Miller, Withdrawals	1,400	
Advertising Fees Earned		4,400
Art Fees Earned		400
Wages Expense	1,380	
Utilities Expense	100	
Telephone Expense	70	
Rent Expense	400	
Insurance Expense	40	
Art Supplies Expense	500	
Office Supplies Expense	200	
Depreciation Expense, Art Equipment	70	
Depreciation Expense, Office Equipment	50	
	$18,870	$18,870

Joan Miller Advertising Agency
Balance Sheet
January 31, 20xx

Assets

Cash		$ 1,720
Accounts Receivable		2,800
Fees Receivable		200
Art Supplies		1,300
Office Supplies		600
Prepaid Rent		400
Prepaid Insurance		440
Art Equipment	$4,200	
Less Accumulated Depreciation	70	4,130
Office Equipment	$3,000	
Less Accumulated Depreciation	50	2,950
Total Assets		$14,540

Liabilities

Accounts Payable	$3,170	
Wages Payable	180	
Unearned Art Fees	600	
Total Liabilities		$ 3,950

Owner's Equity

Joan Miller, Capital	10,590
Total Liabilities and Owner's Equity	$14,540

Joan Miller Advertising Agency
Statement of Owner's Equity
For the Month Ended January 31, 20xx

Joan Miller, Capital, January 1, 20xx		—
Add: Investment by Joan Miller	$10,000	
Net Income	1,990	$11,990
Subtotal		$11,990
Less Withdrawals		1,400
Joan Miller, Capital, January 31, 20xx		$10,590

From Income Statement in Exhibit 3.

was the first month of operation for the company, there was no prior balance of art supplies, and so the amount of cash expended for art supplies during the month was $1,800. The cash flow used to purchase art supplies ($1,800) was much greater than the amount expensed in determining income ($500). In planning for February, management can anticipate that the cash needed may be less than the amount expensed because, given the large inventory of art supplies, it will probably not be necessary to buy art supplies for more than a month. Understanding these cash flow effects enables management to better predict the business's need for cash during February.

The general rule for determining the cash flow received from any revenue or paid for any expense (except depreciation, which is a special case not covered here) is to determine the potential cash payments or cash receipts and deduct the amount not paid or received. The application of the general rule varies with the type of asset or liability account, which is shown as follows:

Type of Account	Potential Payment or Receipt	Not Paid or Received	Result
Prepaid Expense	Ending Balance + Expense for the Period	− Beginning Balance	= Cash Payments for Expenses
Unearned Revenue	Ending Balance + Revenue for the Period	− Beginning Balance	= Cash Receipts from Revenues
Accrued Expense	Beginning Balance + Expense for the Period	− Ending Balance	= Cash Payments for Expenses
Accrued Revenue	Beginning Balance + Revenue for the Period	− Ending Balance	= Cash Receipts from Revenues

For instance, assume that on May 31 a company had a balance of $480 in Prepaid Insurance and that on June 30 the balance was $670. If the insurance expense during June was $120, the amount of cash expended on insurance during June can be computed as follows:

Prepaid Insurance at June 30	$670
Insurance Expense during June	120
Potential cash payments for insurance	$790
Less Prepaid Insurance at May 31	480
Cash payments for insurance during June	$310

The beginning balance is deducted because it was paid in a prior accounting period. Note that the cash payments equal the expense plus the increase in the balance of the Prepaid Insurance account [$120 + ($670 − $480) = $310]. In this case, the cash paid was almost three times the amount of insurance expense. In future months, cash payments are likely to be less than the expense.

Chapter Review

REVIEW OF LEARNING OBJECTIVES

1. **Define** *net income* **and its two major components,** *revenues* **and** *expenses.* Net income is the net increase in owner's equity that results from the operations of a company. Net income equals revenues minus expenses, unless expenses exceed revenues, in which case a net loss results. Revenues equal the price of goods sold and services rendered during a specific period. Expenses are the costs of goods and services used up in the process of producing revenues.

2. **Explain the difficulties of income measurement caused by the accounting period issue, the continuity issue, and the matching**

issue. The accounting period issue recognizes that net income measurements for short periods of time are necessarily tentative. The continuity issue recognizes that even though businesses face an uncertain future, without evidence to the contrary, accountants must assume that a business will continue indefinitely. The matching issue involves the difficulty of assigning revenues and expenses to a period of time. It is addressed by applying the matching rule: Revenues must be assigned to the accounting period in which the goods are delivered or the services performed, and expenses must be assigned to the accounting period in which they are used to produce revenue.

3. **Define *accrual accounting* and explain two broad ways of accomplishing it.** Accrual accounting consists of all the techniques developed by accountants to apply the matching rule. The two general ways of accomplishing accrual accounting are (1) by recognizing revenues when earned and expenses when incurred and (2) by adjusting the accounts.

4. **State four principal situations that require adjusting entries.** Adjusting entries are required (1) when recorded costs have to be allocated between two or more accounting periods, (2) when unrecorded expenses exist, (3) when recorded unearned revenues must be allocated between two or more accounting periods, and (4) when unrecorded revenues exist.

5. **Prepare typical adjusting entries.** The preparation of adjusting entries is summarized in the following table:

Type of Adjusting Entry	Type of Account		Balance Sheet Account Examples
	Debited	Credited	
1. Allocating recorded costs (previously paid, now expired)	Expense	Asset (or contra-asset)	Prepaid Rent Prepaid Insurance Supplies Accumulated Depreciation, Buildings Accumulated Depreciation, Equipment
2. Accrued expenses (previously incurred, now unpaid)	Expense	Liability	Wages Payable Interest Payable
3. Allocating recorded unearned revenues (previously received, now earned)	Liability	Revenue	Unearned Fees
4. Accrued revenues (previously earned, now not received)	Asset	Revenue	Fees Receivable Interest Receivable

6. **Prepare financial statements from an adjusted trial balance.** An adjusted trial balance is prepared after adjusting entries have been posted to the accounts. Its purpose is to test whether the adjusting entries are posted correctly before the financial statements are prepared. The income statement is prepared from the revenue and expense accounts in the adjusted trial balance.

The balance sheet is prepared from the asset and liability accounts in the adjusted trial balance and from the statement of owner's equity.

7. Analyze cash flows from accrual-based information. Cash flow information bears on management's liquidity goal. The general rule for determining the cash flow effect of any revenue or expense (except depreciation, which is a special case not covered here) is to determine the potential cash payments or cash receipts and deduct the amount not paid or received.

REVIEW OF CONCEPTS AND TERMINOLOGY

The following concepts and terms were introduced in this chapter:

LO 2 **Accounting period issue:** The difficulty of assigning revenues and expenses to a short period of time.

LO 4 **Accrual:** The recognition of an expense or revenue that has arisen but has not yet been recorded.

LO 3 **Accrual accounting:** The attempt to record the financial effects of transactions and other events in the periods in which those transactions or events occur, rather than only in the periods in which cash is received or paid by the business; all the techniques developed by accountants to apply the matching rule.

LO 5 **Accrued expenses:** Expenses that have been incurred but are not recognized in the accounts; unrecorded expenses.

LO 5 **Accrued revenues:** Revenues for which a service has been performed or goods delivered but for which no entry has been made; unrecorded revenues.

LO 5 **Accumulated depreciation accounts:** Contra-asset accounts used to accumulate the depreciation expense of specific long-lived assets.

LO 6 **Adjusted trial balance:** A trial balance prepared after all adjusting entries have been recorded and posted to the accounts.

LO 4 **Adjusting entries:** Entries made to apply accrual accounting to transactions that span more than one accounting period.

LO 5 **Carrying value:** The unexpired portion of the cost of an asset. Also called *book value*.

LO 2 **Cash basis of accounting:** Accounting for revenues and expenses on a cash received and cash paid basis.

LO 2 **Continuity issue:** The difficulty associated with not knowing how long a business entity will survive.

LO 5 **Contra account:** An account whose balance is subtracted from an associated account in the financial statements.

LO 4 **Deferral:** The postponement of the recognition of an expense that already has been paid or of a revenue that already has been received.

LO 5 **Depreciation:** The portion of the cost of a tangible long-term asset allocated to any one accounting period. Also called *depreciation expense*.

LO 1 **Expenses:** Decreases in owner's equity resulting from the costs of goods and services used up in the course of earning revenues. Also called *cost of doing business* or *expired costs*.

LO 2 **Fiscal year:** Any 12-month accounting period used by an economic entity.

LO 2 **Going concern:** The assumption, unless there is evidence to the contrary, that a business entity will continue to operate indefinitely.

LO 2 **Matching rule:** Revenues must be assigned to the accounting period in which the goods are sold or the services performed, and expenses must be assigned to the accounting period in which they are used to produce revenue.

LO 1 **Net income:** The net increase in owner's equity that results from business operations and is accumulated in the owner's Capital account; revenues less expenses when revenues exceed expenses.

LO 1 **Net loss:** The net decrease in owner's equity that results from business operations when expenses exceed revenues. It is accumulated in the owner's Capital account.

LO 2 **Periodicity:** The recognition that net income for any period less than the life of the business, although tentative, is still a useful measure.

LO 5 **Prepaid expenses:** Expenses paid in advance that have not yet expired; an asset account.

LO 1 **Profit:** The increase in owner's equity that results from business operations.

LO 3 **Revenue recognition:** In accrual accounting, the process of determining when revenue is earned.

LO 1 **Revenues:** Increases in owner's equity resulting from selling goods, rendering services, or performing other business activities.

LO 5 **Unearned revenues:** Revenues received in advance for which the goods have not yet been delivered or the services performed; a liability account.

REVIEW PROBLEM

Determining Adjusting Entries, Posting to T Accounts, Preparing Adjusted Trial Balance, and Preparing Financial Statements

LO 5
LO 6
The following is the unadjusted trial balance for Certified Answering Service on December 31, 20x2.

Certified Answering Service
Trial Balance
December 31, 20x2

Cash	$2,160	
Accounts Receivable	1,250	
Office Supplies	180	
Prepaid Insurance	240	
Office Equipment	3,400	
Accumulated Depreciation, Office Equipment		$ 600
Accounts Payable		700
Unearned Revenue		460
James Neal, Capital		4,870
James Neal, Withdrawals	400	
Answering Service Revenue		2,900
Wages Expense	1,500	
Rent Expense	400	
	$9,530	$9,530

The following information is also available:
a. Insurance that expired during December amounted to $40.
b. Office supplies on hand at the end of December totaled $75.
c. Depreciation for the month of December totaled $100.
d. Accrued wages at the end of December totaled $120.

e. Revenues earned for services performed in December but not yet billed on December 31 totaled $300.

f. Revenues earned in December for services performed that were paid in advance totaled $160.

REQUIRED

1. Prepare T accounts for the accounts in the trial balance and enter the balances.

2. Determine the required adjusting entries and record them directly to the T accounts. Open new T accounts as needed.

3. Prepare an adjusted trial balance.

4. Prepare an income statement, a statement of owner's equity, and a balance sheet for the month ended December 31, 20x2. The owner made no new investments during the month.

ANSWER TO REVIEW PROBLEM

1. T accounts set up and amounts from trial balance entered

2. Adjusting entries recorded

Cash	
Bal. 2,160	

Accounts Receivable	
Bal. 1,250	

Service Revenue Receivable	
(e) 300	

Office Supplies	
Bal. 180	(b) 105
Bal. 75	

Prepaid Insurance	
Bal. 240	(a) 40
Bal. 200	

Office Equipment	
Bal. 3,400	

Accumulated Depreciation, Office Equipment	
	Bal. 600
	(c) 100
	Bal. 700

Accounts Payable	
	Bal. 700

Unearned Revenue	
(f) 160	Bal. 460
	Bal. 300

Wages Payable	
	(d) 120

James Neal, Capital	
	Bal. 4,870

James Neal, Withdrawals	
Bal. 400	

Answering Service Revenue	
	Bal. 2,900
	(e) 300
	(f) 160
	Bal. 3,360

Wages Expense	
Bal. 1,500	
(d) 120	
Bal. 1,620	

Rent Expense	
Bal. 400	

Insurance Expense	
(a) 40	

Office Supplies Expense	
(b) 105	

Depreciation Expense, Office Equipment	
(c) 100	

3. Adjusted trial balance prepared

Certified Answering Service
Adjusted Trial Balance
December 31, 20x2

Cash	$ 2,160	
Accounts Receivable	1,250	
Service Revenue Receivable	300	
Office Supplies	75	
Prepaid Insurance	200	
Office Equipment	3,400	
Accumulated Depreciation, Office Equipment		$ 700
Accounts Payable		700
Unearned Revenue		300
Wages Payable		120
James Neal, Capital		4,870
James Neal, Withdrawals	400	
Answering Service Revenue		3,360
Wages Expense	1,620	
Rent Expense	400	
Insurance Expense	40	
Office Supplies Expense	105	
Depreciation Expense, Office Equipment	100	
	$10,050	$10,050

4. Financial statements prepared

Certified Answering Service
Income Statement
For the Month Ended December 31, 20x2

Revenues		
Answering Service Revenue		$3,360
Expenses		
Wages Expense	$1,620	
Rent Expense	400	
Insurance Expense	40	
Office Supplies Expense	105	
Depreciation Expense, Office Equipment	100	
Total Expenses		2,265
Net Income		$1,095

**Certified Answering Service
Statement of Owner's Equity
For the Month Ended December 31, 20x2**

James Neal, Capital, November 30, 20x2	$4,870
Net Income	1,095
Subtotal	$5,965
Less Withdrawals	400
James Neal, Capital, December 31, 20x2	$5,565

**Certified Answering Service
Balance Sheet
December 31, 20x2**

Assets

Cash		$2,160
Accounts Receivable		1,250
Service Revenue Receivable		300
Office Supplies		75
Prepaid Insurance		200
Office Equipment	$3,400	
Less Accumulated Depreciation	700	2,700
Total Assets		$6,685

Liabilities

Accounts Payable	$ 700
Unearned Revenue	300
Wages Payable	120
Total Liabilities	$1,120

Owner's Equity

James Neal, Capital	5,565
Total Liabilities and Owner's Equity	$6,685

Chapter Assignments

**BUILDING YOUR
KNOWLEDGE
FOUNDATION**

QUESTIONS

1. Why does the accountant use the term *net income* instead of *profit*?
2. Define the terms *revenues* and *expenses*.
3. Why does the need for an accounting period cause problems?
4. What is the significance of the continuity assumption?
5. "The matching rule is the most significant concept in accounting." Do you agree with this statement? Explain your answer.

6. What is the difference between the cash basis and the accrual basis of accounting?

7. In what two ways is accrual accounting accomplished?

8. Why are adjusting entries necessary?

9. What are the four situations that require adjusting entries? Give an example of each.

10. "Some assets are expenses that have not expired." Explain this statement.

11. What do plant and equipment, office supplies, and prepaid insurance have in common?

12. What is the difference between accumulated depreciation and depreciation expense?

13. What is a contra account? Give an example.

14. Why are contra accounts used to record depreciation?

15. How does unearned revenue arise? Give an example.

16. Where does unearned revenue appear in the financial statements?

17. What accounting problem exists for a magazine publisher who sells three-year subscriptions?

18. Under what circumstances does a company have accrued revenues? Provide an example. What asset arises when the adjustment is made?

19. What is an accrued expense? Give two examples.

20. "Why worry about adjustments? Doesn't it all come out in the wash?" Discuss these questions.

21. Why is the income statement usually the first statement prepared from the adjusted trial balance?

22. To what management goals do the measurements of net income and cash flow relate?

SHORT EXERCISES

SE 1.

LO 2 Accrual Accounting
LO 3 Concepts

Match the concepts of accrual accounting on the right with the assumptions or actions on the left.

1. Assumes expenses can be assigned to the accounting period in which they are used to produce revenues
2. Assumes a business will last indefinitely
3. Assumes revenues are earned at a point in time
4. Assumes net income measured for a short period of time, such as one quarter, is a useful measure

a. periodicity
b. going concern
c. matching rule
d. revenue recognition

SE 2.

LO 5 Adjustment for Prepaid
Insurance

The Prepaid Insurance account began the year with a balance of $230. During the year, insurance in the amount of $570 was purchased. At the end of the year (December 31), the amount of insurance still unexpired was $350. Make the year-end entry in journal form to record the adjustment for insurance expense for the year.

SE 3.

LO 5 Adjustment for Supplies

The Supplies account began the year with a balance of $190. During the year, supplies in the amount of $490 were purchased. At the end of the year (December 31), the inventory of supplies on hand was $220. Make the year-end entry in journal form to record the adjustment for supplies expense for the year.

SE 4.

LO 5 Adjustment for Depreciation

The depreciation expense on office equipment for the month of March is $50. This is the third month that the office equipment, which cost $950, has been owned. Prepare the adjusting entry in journal form to record depreciation for March and show the balance sheet presentation for office equipment and related accounts after the adjustment.

SE 5.

LO 5 Adjustment for Accrued
Wages

Wages are paid each Saturday for a six-day work week. Wages are currently running $690 per week. Make the adjusting entry required on June 30, assuming July 1 falls on a Tuesday.

SE 6.

LO 5 Adjustment for Unearned Revenue

During the month of August, deposits in the amount of $550 were received for services to be performed. By the end of the month, services in the amount of $380 had been performed. Prepare the necessary adjustment for Service Revenue at the end of the month.

SE 7.

LO 6 Preparation of an Income Statement from an Adjusted Trial Balance

The adjusted trial balance for Heller Company on December 31, 20x3, contains the following accounts and balances: Owner's Capital, $4,300; Withdrawals, $350; Service Revenue, $2,600; Rent Expense, $400; Wages Expense, $900; Utilities Expense, $200; Telephone Expense, $50; and Insurance Expense, $350. Prepare an income statement in proper form for the month of December.

SE 8.

LO 6 Preparation of a Statement of Owner's Equity

Using the data in **SE 7,** prepare a statement of owner's equity for Heller Company.

SE 9.

SO 7 Determination of Cash Flows

Wages Payable was $590 at the end of May and $920 at the end of June. Wages Expense for June was $2,300. How much cash was paid for wages during June?

SE 10.

SO 7 Determination of Cash Flows

Unearned Revenue was $1,300 at the end of November and $900 at the end of December. Service Revenue was $5,100 for the month of December. How much cash was received for services provided during December?

EXERCISES

E 1.

LO 2 Applications of
LO 3 Accounting Concepts
LO 4 Related to Accrual Accounting

The accountant for Pelias Company makes the assumptions or performs the activities listed below. Tell which of the following concepts of accrual accounting most directly relates to each assumption or action: (a) periodicity, (b) going concern, (c) matching rule, (d) revenue recognition, (e) deferral, and (f) accrual.

1. In estimating the life of a building, assumes that the business will last indefinitely.
2. Records a sale when the customer is billed.
3. Postpones the recognition of a one-year insurance policy as an expense by initially recording the expenditure as an asset.
4. Recognizes the usefulness of financial statements prepared on a monthly basis even though they are based on estimates.
5. Recognizes, by making an adjusting entry, wages expense that has been incurred but not yet recorded.
6. Prepares an income statement that shows the revenues earned and the expenses incurred during the accounting period.

E 2.

LO 5 Adjusting Entry for Unearned Revenue

Salt River Company of Louisville, Kentucky, publishes a monthly magazine featuring local restaurant reviews and upcoming social, cultural, and sporting events. Subscribers pay for subscriptions either one year or two years in advance. Cash received from subscribers is credited to an account called Magazine Subscriptions Received in Advance.

On December 31, 20x3, the end of the company's fiscal year, the balance of this account was $1,000,000. The earned revenue from expired subscriptions is as follows:

During 20x3 $200,000
During 20x4   500,000
During 20x5   300,000

Prepare the adjusting entry in journal form for December 31, 20x3.

E 3.

LO 5 Adjusting Entries for Prepaid Insurance

An examination of the Prepaid Insurance account reveals a balance of $4,112 at the end of an accounting period, before adjustment. Prepare entries in journal form to record the insurance expense for the period under each of the following independent assumptions.

1. An examination of the insurance policies shows unexpired insurance that cost $1,974 at the end of the period.

2. An examination of the insurance policies shows that insurance that cost $694 has expired during the period.

E 4.
LO 5 Supplies Account: Missing Data

Each column below represents a Supplies account:

	a	b	c	d
Supplies on hand, October 1	$396	$ 651	$294	$?
Supplies purchased during the month	78	?	261	2,892
Supplies consumed during the month	291	1,458	?	2,448
Supplies on hand, October 31	?	654	84	1,782

1. Determine the amounts indicated by the question marks in the columns.

2. Make the adjusting entry for Column **a,** assuming supplies purchased are debited to an asset account.

E 5.
LO 5 Adjusting Entry for Accrued Salaries

Azusa has a five-day work week and pays salaries of $70,000 each Friday.

1. Make the adjusting entry required on July 31, assuming that August 1 falls on a Wednesday.

2. Make the entry to pay the salaries on August 3.

E 6.
LO 5 Revenue and Expense Recognition

Uruk Company produces computer software that is sold by Ninevah Systems Company. Uruk receives a royalty of 15 percent of sales. Royalties are paid by Ninevah Systems and received by Uruk semiannually on May 1 for sales made July through December of the previous year and on November 1 for sales made January through June of the current year. Royalty expense for Ninevah Systems and royalty income for Uruk in the amount of $12,000 were accrued on December 31, 20x2. Cash in the amounts of $12,000 and $20,000 was paid and received on May 1 and November 1, 20x3, respectively. Software sales during the July to December 20x3 period totaled $300,000.

1. Calculate the amount of royalty expense for Ninevah Systems and royalty income for Uruk during 20x3.

2. Record the appropriate adjusting entry made by each company on December 31, 20x3.

E 7.
LO 5 Adjusting Entries

Prepare year-end adjusting entries for each of the following:

1. Office Supplies had a balance of $168 on January 1. Purchases debited to Office Supplies during the year amount to $830. A year-end inventory reveals supplies of $570 on hand.

2. Depreciation of office equipment is estimated to be $4,260 for the year.

3. Property taxes for six months, estimated at $1,750, have accrued but have not been recorded.

4. Unrecorded interest receivable on U.S. government bonds is $1,700.

5. Unearned Revenue has a balance of $1,800. Services for $600 received in advance have now been performed.

6. Services totaling $400 have been performed; the customer has not yet been billed.

E 8.
LO 5 Accounting for Revenue Received in Advance

Sonia Zumpen, a lawyer, was paid $72,000 on April 1 to represent a client in certain real estate negotiations over the next 12 months.

1. Record the entries required in Zumpen's records on April 1 and at the end of the year, December 31.

2. How would this transaction be reflected on the income statement and balance sheet on December 31?

E 9.

Prepare the monthly income statement, statement of owner's equity, and balance sheet for Musket Custodial Services from the data provided in this adjusted trial balance.

Musket Custodial Services Adjusted Trial Balance August 31, 20xx		
Cash	$ 4,590	
Accounts Receivable	2,592	
Prepaid Insurance	380	
Prepaid Rent	200	
Cleaning Supplies	152	
Cleaning Equipment	3,200	
Accumulated Depreciation, Cleaning Equipment		$ 320
Truck	7,200	
Accumulated Depreciation, Truck		720
Accounts Payable		420
Wages Payable		80
Unearned Janitorial Revenue		920
Joseph Musket, Capital		15,034
Joseph Musket, Withdrawals	2,000	
Janitorial Revenue		14,620
Wages Expense	5,680	
Rent Expense	1,200	
Gas, Oil, and Other Truck Expenses	580	
Insurance Expense	380	
Supplies Expense	2,920	
Depreciation Expense, Cleaning Equipment	320	
Depreciation Expense, Truck	720	
	$32,114	$32,114

E 10.

After adjusting entries had been made, the 20x3 and 20x4 balance sheets of Agheb Company showed the following asset and liability amounts at the end of each year:

	20x3	20x4
Prepaid Insurance	$1,450	$1,200
Wages Payable	1,100	600
Unearned Fees	950	2,100

From the accounting records, the following amounts of cash disbursements and cash receipts for 20x4 were determined:

Cash disbursed to pay insurance premiums	$1,900
Cash disbursed to pay wages	9,750
Cash received for fees	4,450

Calculate the amount of insurance expense, wages expense, and fees earned that should be reported on the 20x4 income statement.

E 11.

Medea Newspaper Agency delivers morning, evening, and Sunday city newspapers to subscribers who live in the suburbs. Customers can pay a yearly subscription fee in advance (at a savings) or pay monthly after delivery of their newspapers. The following data are available for the Subscriptions Receivable and Unearned Subscriptions accounts at the beginning and end of October 20xx:

	October 1	October 31
Subscriptions Receivable	$ 7,600	$ 9,200
Unearned Subscriptions	22,800	19,600

The income statement shows subscriptions revenue for October of $44,800. Determine the amount of cash received from customers for subscriptions during October. Why is this calculation important to management?

E 12.

SO 7 **Relationship of Expenses to Cash Paid**

The income statement for Griffon Company included the following expenses for 20xx:

Rent Expense	$ 5,200
Interest Expense	7,800
Salaries Expense	83,000

Listed below are the related balance sheet account balances at year end for last year and this year:

	Last Year	This Year
Prepaid Rent	—	$ 900
Interest Payable	$1,200	—
Salaries Payable	5,000	9,600

1. Compute the cash paid for rent during the year.
2. Compute the cash paid for interest during the year.
3. Compute the cash paid for salaries during the year.

PROBLEMS

P 1.

LO 5 **Determining Adjustments**

At the end of the first three months of operation, the trial balance of Thomas Answering Service appears as shown below. Lily Thomas, the owner, has hired an accountant to prepare financial statements to determine how well the company is doing after three months. Upon examining the accounting records, the accountant finds the following items of interest:

a. An inventory of office supplies reveals supplies on hand of $266.
b. The Prepaid Rent account includes the rent for the first three months plus a deposit for April's rent.
c. Depreciation on the equipment for the first three months is $416.
d. The balance of the Unearned Answering Service Revenue account represents a 12-month service contract paid in advance on February 1.
e. On March 31, accrued wages total $160.

The balance of the Capital account represents investments by Lily Thomas.

Thomas Answering Service Trial Balance March 31, 20x2		
Cash	$ 6,964	
Accounts Receivable	8,472	
Office Supplies	1,806	
Prepaid Rent	1,600	
Equipment	9,400	
Accounts Payable		$ 5,346
Unearned Answering Service Revenue		1,776
Lily Thomas, Capital		11,866
Lily Thomas, Withdrawals	4,260	
Answering Service Revenue		18,004
Wages Expense	3,800	
Office Cleaning Expense	690	
	$36,992	$36,992

All adjustments affect one balance sheet account and one income statement account. For each of the above situations, show the accounts affected, the amount of the adjustment (using a + or − to indicate an increase or decrease), and the balance of the account after the adjustment in the following format.

Balance Sheet Account	Amount of Adjustment (+ or −)	Balance After Adjustment	Income Statement Account	Amount of Adjustment (+ or −)	Balance After Adjustment

P 2.

LO 5 Preparing Adjusting Entries

On May 31, the end of the current fiscal year, the following information was available to help Viera Company's accountants make adjusting entries:

a. The Supplies account showed a beginning balance of $2,174. Purchases during the year were $4,526. The end-of-year inventory revealed supplies on hand that cost $1,397.

b. The Prepaid Insurance account showed the following on May 31:

Beginning Balance	$3,580
February 1	4,200
April 1	7,272

The beginning balance represents the portion of a one-year policy that remained unexpired at the beginning of the current fiscal year. The February 1 entry represents a new one-year policy, and the April 1 entry represents additional coverage in the form of a three-year policy.

c. The following table contains the cost and annual depreciation for buildings and equipment, all of which were purchased before the current year:

Account	Cost	Annual Depreciation
Buildings	$286,000	$14,500
Equipment	374,000	35,400

d. On March 1, the company completed negotiations with a client and accepted payment of $16,800, which represented one year's services paid in advance. The $16,800 was credited to Unearned Service Revenue.

e. The company calculated that as of May 31, it had earned $4,000 on an $11,000 contract that would be completed and billed in September.

f. Among the liabilities of the company is a note payable in the amount of $300,000. On May 31, the accrued interest on this note amounted to $15,000.

g. On Saturday, June 2, the company, which is on a six-day work week, will pay its regular salaried employees $12,300.

h. On May 29, the company completed negotiations and signed a contract to provide services to a new client at an annual rate of $17,500.

Prepare adjusting entries for each item listed above.

P 3.

LO 5 Determining Adjusting Entries, Posting to T Accounts, and Preparing an Adjusted Trial Balance

The trial balance for Fleet Relay Services on December 31, 20xx, is at the top of the next page.

The following information is also available:

a. Ending inventory of office supplies, $264.
b. Prepaid rent expired, $440.
c. Depreciation of office equipment for the period, $660.
d. Accrued interest expense at the end of the period, $550.
e. Accrued salaries at the end of the month, $330.
f. Fees still unearned at the end of the period, $1,166.
g. Fees earned but unrecorded, $2,200.

1. Open T accounts for the accounts in the trial balance plus the following: Fees Receivable; Interest Payable; Salaries Payable; Office Supplies Expense; Depreciation Expense, Office Equipment; and Interest Expense. Enter the balances.

2. Determine the adjusting entries and post them directly to the T accounts.

3. Prepare an adjusted trial balance.

	Fleet Relay Services Trial Balance December 31, 20xx	
Cash	$ 16,500	
Accounts Receivable	8,250	
Office Supplies	2,662	
Prepaid Rent	1,320	
Office Equipment	9,240	
Accumulated Depreciation, Office Equipment		$ 1,540
Accounts Payable		5,940
Notes Payable		11,000
Unearned Fees		2,970
Sandy Chee, Capital		24,002
Sandy Chee, Withdrawals	22,000	
Fees Revenue		72,600
Salaries Expense	49,400	
Rent Expense	4,400	
Utilities Expense	4,280	
	$118,052	$118,052

P 4.

LO 5 Determining Adjusting
LO 6 Entries and Tracing
Their Effects to Financial
Statements

The Crescent Custodial Service is owned by Mike Podgorney. After six months of operation, the June 30, 20xx, trial balance for the company, presented below, was prepared. The balance of the Capital account reflects investments made by Mike Podgorney.

	Crescent Custodial Service Trial Balance June 30, 20xx	
Cash	$ 762	
Accounts Receivable	914	
Prepaid Insurance	380	
Prepaid Rent	700	
Cleaning Supplies	1,396	
Cleaning Equipment	1,740	
Truck	3,600	
Accounts Payable		$ 170
Unearned Janitorial Fees		480
Mike Podgorney, Capital		7,095
Mike Podgorney, Withdrawals	3,000	
Janitorial Fees		7,487
Wages Expense	2,400	
Gas, Oil, and Other Truck Expenses	340	
	$15,232	$15,232

The following information is also available.

a. Cleaning supplies of $117 are on hand.
b. Prepaid insurance represents the cost of a one-year policy purchased on January 1.
c. Prepaid rent represents a $100 payment made on January 1 toward the last month's rent of a three-year lease plus $100 rent per month for each of the six past months.

d. The cleaning equipment and the truck are depreciated at the rate of 20 percent per year (10 percent for each six-month period).

e. The unearned revenue represents a six-month payment in advance made by a customer on May 1.

f. During the last week of June, Podgorney completed the first stage of work on a contract that will not be billed until the contract is completed. The amount that has been earned at this stage is $400.

g. On Saturday, July 3, Podgorney will owe his employees $540 for one week's work (six-day work week).

REQUIRED

1. Open T accounts for the accounts in the trial balance plus the following: Fees Receivable; Accumulated Depreciation, Cleaning Equipment; Accumulated Depreciation, Truck; Wages Payable; Rent Expense; Insurance Expense; Cleaning Supplies Expense; Depreciation Expense, Cleaning Equipment; and Depreciation Expense, Truck. Record the balances shown on the trial balance.

2. Determine the adjusting entries and post them directly to the T accounts.

3. Prepare an adjusted trial balance, an income statement, a statement of owner's equity, and a balance sheet.

P 5.

LO 5 Determining Adjusting
LO 6 Entries and Tracing
Their Effects to Financial
Statements

Here is the trial balance for New Wave Dance Studio at the end of its current fiscal year.

New Wave Dance Studio Trial Balance October 31, 20x2		
Cash (111)	$ 1,028	
Accounts Receivable (112)	517	
Supplies (115)	170	
Prepaid Rent (116)	400	
Prepaid Insurance (117)	360	
Equipment (141)	4,100	
Accumulated Depreciation, Equipment (142)		$ 400
Accounts Payable (211)		380
Unearned Dance Fees (213)		900
Midge Bronson, Capital (311)		2,500
Midge Bronson, Withdrawals (312)	12,000	
Dance Fees (411)		20,995
Wages Expense (511)	3,200	
Rent Expense (512)	2,200	
Utilities Expense (515)	1,200	
	$25,175	$25,175

Midge Bronson made no investments in the business during the year. The following information is available to assist in the preparation of adjusting entries.

a. An inventory of supplies reveals $92 still on hand.

b. The prepaid rent reflects the rent for October plus the rent for the last month of the lease.

c. Prepaid insurance consists of a two-year policy purchased on May 1, 20x2.

d. Depreciation on equipment is estimated at $800.

e. Accrued wages are $65 on October 31.

f. Two-thirds of the unearned dance fees have been earned by October 31.

REQUIRED

1. Record the adjusting entries in the general journal (Page 53).

2. Open ledger accounts for the accounts in the trial balance plus the following: Wages Payable (212); Supplies Expense (513); Insurance Expense (514); and Depreciation Expense, Equipment (516). Record the balances shown on the trial balance.

3. Post the adjusting entries from the general journal to the ledger accounts, showing the correct references.

4. Prepare an adjusted trial balance, an income statement, a statement of owner's equity, and a balance sheet.

ALTERNATE PROBLEMS

P 6.

LO 5 Determining Adjustments

At the end of its fiscal year, the trial balance for Scotch Cleaners appears as follows:

Scotch Cleaners Trial Balance November 30, 20x2		
Cash	$ 5,894	
Accounts Receivable	13,247	
Prepaid Insurance	1,700	
Cleaning Supplies	3,687	
Land	9,000	
Building	92,500	
Accumulated Depreciation, Building		$ 22,800
Accounts Payable		10,200
Unearned Dry Cleaning Revenue		800
Mortgage Payable		55,000
Regis Scot, Capital		28,280
Regis Scot, Withdrawals	5,000	
Dry Cleaning Revenue		60,167
Laundry Revenue		18,650
Wages Expense	50,665	
Cleaning Equipment Rent Expense	3,000	
Delivery Truck Expense	2,187	
Interest Expense	5,500	
Other Expenses	3,517	
	$195,897	$195,897

The following information is also available.

a. A study of insurance policies shows that $340 is unexpired at the end of the year.

b. An inventory of cleaning supplies shows $622 on hand.

c. Estimated depreciation on the building for the year is $6,400.

d. Accrued interest on the mortgage payable amounts to $500.

e. On November 1, the company signed a contract, effective immediately, with Boone County Hospital to dry clean, for a fixed monthly charge of $200, the uniforms used by doctors in surgery. Boone County Hospital paid for four months' service in advance.

f. Sales and delivery wages are paid on Saturday. The weekly payroll for Scotch Cleaners is $1,260. November 30 falls on a Thursday, and the company has a six-day pay week.

REQUIRED

All adjustments affect one balance sheet account and one income statement account. For each of the above situations, show the accounts affected, the amount of the adjustment (using a + or − to indicate an increase or decrease), and the balance of the account after the adjustment in the following format:

Balance Sheet Account	Amount of Adjustment (+ or −)	Balance After Adjustment	Income Statement Account	Amount of Adjustment (+ or −)	Balance After Adjustment

P 7.

LO 5 Preparing Adjusting Entries

On June 30, the end of the current fiscal year, the following information was available to aid the Hoosic Company's accountants in making adjusting entries:

a. Among the liabilities of the company is a mortgage payable in the amount of $480,000. On June 30, the accrued interest on this mortgage amounted to $24,000.

b. On Friday, July 2, the company, which is on a five-day work week and pays employees weekly, will pay its regular salaried employees $38,400.

c. On June 29, the company completed negotiations and signed a contract to provide services to a new client at an annual rate of $7,200.

d. The Supplies account showed a beginning balance of $3,230 and purchases during the year of $7,532. The end-of-year inventory revealed supplies on hand of $2,372.

e. The Prepaid Insurance account showed the following entries on June 30:

Beginning Balance	$3,060
January 1	5,800
May 1	6,732

The beginning balance represents the unexpired portion of a one-year policy purchased the previous fiscal year. The January 1 entry represents a new one-year policy, and the May 1 entry represents the additional coverage of a three-year policy.

f. The following table contains the cost and annual depreciation for buildings and equipment, all of which were purchased before the current year:

Account	Cost	Annual Depreciation
Buildings	$370,000	$14,600
Equipment	436,000	43,600

g. On June 1, the company completed negotiations with another client and accepted a payment of $42,000, representing one year's services paid in advance. The $42,000 was credited to Services Collected in Advance.

h. The company calculated that as of June 30 it had earned $7,000 on a $15,000 contract that would be completed and billed in August.

REQUIRED

Prepare adjusting entries for each item listed above.

P 8.

LO 5 Determining Adjusting Entries, Posting to T Accounts, and Preparing an Adjusted Trial Balance

The trial balance for the Alpha Advisory Company on March 31, 20x3, appears at the top of the next page.

The following information is also available:

a. Ending inventory of office supplies, $86.

b. Prepaid rent expired, $700.

c. Depreciation of office equipment for the period, $600.

d. Interest accrued on the note payable, $600.

e. Salaries accrued at the end of the period, $200.

f. Fees still unearned at the end of the period, $1,410.

g. Fees earned but not billed, $600.

REQUIRED

1. Open T accounts for the accounts in the trial balance plus the following: Fees Receivable; Interest Payable; Salaries Payable; Office Supplies Expense; Depreciation Expense, Office Equipment; and Interest Expense. Enter the balances.

2. Determine the adjusting entries and post them directly to the T accounts.

3. Prepare an adjusted trial balance.

Alpha Advisory Company		
Trial Balance		
March 31, 20x3		
Cash	$ 12,786	
Accounts Receivable	24,840	
Office Supplies	991	
Prepaid Rent	1,400	
Office Equipment	6,700	
Accumulated Depreciation, Office Equipment		$ 1,600
Accounts Payable		1,820
Notes Payable		10,000
Unearned Fees		2,860
Nils Haveczech, Capital		29,387
Nils Haveczech, Withdrawals	15,000	
Fees Revenue		58,500
Salaries Expense	33,000	
Utilities Expense	1,750	
Rent Expense	7,700	
	$104,167	$104,167

EXPANDING YOUR CRITICAL THINKING, COMMUNICATION, AND INTERPERSONAL SKILLS

SKILLS DEVELOPMENT

Conceptual Analysis

LO 2 **Importance of**
LO 3 **Adjustments**
LO 4

SD 1. *Never Flake Company,* which operated in the northeastern part of the United States, provided a rust-prevention coating for the underside of new automobiles. The company advertised widely and offered its services through new car dealers. When a dealer sold a new car, the salesperson attempted to sell the rust-prevention coating as an option. The protective coating was supposed to make cars last longer in the severe northeastern winters. A key selling point was Never Flake's warranty, which stated that it would repair any damage due to rust at no charge for as long as the buyer owned the car.

During the 1980s and most of the 1990s, Never Flake was very successful in generating enough cash to continue operations. But in 2002 the company suddenly declared bankruptcy. Company officials said that the firm had only $5.5 million in assets against liabilities of $32.9 million. Most of the liabilities represented potential claims under the company's lifetime warranty. It seemed that owners were keeping their cars longer in

Cash Flow

CD-ROM

Communication

Critical Thinking

Ethics

General Ledger

Group Activity

Hot Links to Real Companies

International

Internet

Key Ratio

Memo

Spreadsheet

recent years than they had in the 1980s. Therefore, more damage was being attributed to rust. Discuss what accounting decisions could have helped Never Flake to survive under these circumstances.

Group Activity: Divide the class into groups to discuss this case. Then debrief as a class by asking a person from each group to comment.

SD 2.

LO 3   **Application of Accrual**
LO 4   **Accounting**

The *Lyric Opera of Chicago* is one of the largest and best-managed opera companies in the United States. Managing opera productions requires advance planning, including the development of scenery, costumes, and stage properties and the sale of tickets. To measure how well the company is operating in any given year, accrual accounting must be applied to these and other transactions. At year end, April 30, 2000, Lyric Opera of Chicago's balance sheet showed Deferred Production Costs of $1,649,710 and Deferred Ticket Revenue of $18,665,544.[6] Be prepared to discuss what accounting policies and adjusting entries are applicable to these accounts. Why are they important to Lyric Opera's management?

Ethical Dilemma

SD 3.

LO 2   **Importance of**
LO 3   **Adjustments**
LO 4

Central Appliance Service Co. has achieved fast growth in the St. Louis area by selling service contracts on large appliances, such as washers, dryers, and refrigerators. For a fee, Central Appliance agrees to provide all parts and labor on an appliance after the regular warranty runs out. For example, by paying a fee of $200, a person who buys a dishwasher can add two years (years 2 and 3) to the regular one-year (year 1) warranty on the appliance. In 2002, the company sold service contracts in the amount of $1.8 million, all of which applied to future years. Management wanted all the sales recorded as revenues in 2002, contending that the amount of the contracts could be determined and the cash had been received. Discuss whether or not you agree with this logic. How would you record the cash receipts? What assumptions do you think should be made? Would you consider it unethical to follow management's recommendation? Who might be hurt or helped by this action?

Research Activity

SD 4.

LO 4   **Real World Observation of**
         Business Activities

Choose a company with which you are familiar. Visit the company and observe its operations. For example, it can be where you work, where you eat, or where you buy things. Identify at least two sources of revenue for the company and six types of expenses. For each type of revenue and each type of expense, determine whether it is probable that an adjusting entry is required at the end of the accounting period and specify the adjusting entry as a deferred revenue, deferred expense, accrued revenue, or accrued expense.

Decision-Making Practice

SD 5.

LO 1   **Adjusting Entries and**
LO 5   **Performance Evaluation**

Karen Jamison, the owner of a newsletter for managers of hotels and restaurants, has prepared the following condensed amounts from the financial statements for 20x3:

Revenues	$346,000
Expenses	282,000
Net Income	$ 64,000
Total Assets	$172,000
Liabilities	$ 48,000
Owner's Equity	124,000
Total Liabilities and Owner's Equity	$172,000

Given these figures, Jamison is planning to withdraw $50,000 for personal expenses. However, Jamison's accountant has found that the following items were overlooked:

a. Although the balance of the Printing Supplies account is $32,000, only $14,000 in supplies is on hand at the end of the year.

b. Depreciation of $20,000 on equipment has not been recorded.

c. Wages of $9,400 have been earned by employees but not recognized in the accounts.

d. A liability account called Unearned Subscriptions has a balance of $16,200, although it is determined that one-third of these subscriptions have been mailed to subscribers.

1. Prepare the necessary adjusting entries.

2. Recast the condensed financial statement figures after making the adjustments.

3. Discuss the performance of Jamison's business after the adjustments have been made. (**Hint:** Compare net income to revenues and total assets before and after the adjustments.) Do you think that making the withdrawal is advisable?

FINANCIAL REPORTING AND ANALYSIS

Interpreting Financial Reports

FRA 1.

LO 2 Analysis of an Asset
LO 5 Account

The Walt Disney Company is engaged in the financing, production, and distribution of motion pictures and television programming. In The Walt Disney Company's 1999 annual report, the balance sheet contains an asset called Film and Television Costs. Film and television costs, which consist of the cost associated with producing films and television programs less the amount expensed, were $4,071,000,000.

The statement of cash flows in the annual report reveals that the amount of film and television costs expensed (amortized) during 1999 was $2,472,000,000. The amount spent for new film productions was $3,020,000,000.[7]

REQUIRED

1. What are film and television costs and why would they be classified as an asset?

2. Prepare an entry to record the amount spent on new film and television production during 1999 (assume all expenditures are paid for in cash).

3. Prepare the adjusting entry that would be made to record the expense for film and television productions in 1999.

4. Can you suggest a method by which The Walt Disney Company might have determined the amount of the expense in **3** in accordance with the matching rule?

FRA 2.

LO 5 Identification of Accruals

H.J. Heinz Company, a major food company, had a net income of $474,341,000 in 1999 and had the following current liabilities at the end of 1999.[8]

Current Liabilities (In thousands)	1999
Short-term debt	$ 290,841
Portion of long-term debt due within one year	613,366
Accounts payable	945,488
Salaries and wages	74,098
Accrued marketing	182,024
Accrued restructuring costs	147,786
Other accrued liabilities	372,623
Income taxes	160,096
Total current liabilities	$2,786,322

1. Which of the current liabilities definitely arose as the result of an adjusting entry at the end of the year? Which ones may partially have arisen from an adjusting entry? Which ones probably did not arise from an adjusting entry?

2. What effect do adjustments that create new liabilities have on net income or loss? Based on your answer in **1,** what percentage of current liabilities was definitely the result of an adjusting entry? Assuming the adjusting entries for these items had not been performed, what would have been Heinz's net income or loss?

International Company

FRA 3.

LO 2 Account Identification
LO 3 and Accrual Accounting

Takashimaya Company, Limited, is Japan's largest department store chain. An account on Takashimaya's balance sheet called Gift Certificates contains ¥41,657 million ($404 million).[9] Is this account an asset or a liability? What transaction gives rise to the account? How is this account an example of the application of accrual accounting? Explain the conceptual issues that must be resolved for an adjusting entry to be valid.

Toys "R" Us Annual Report

FRA 4.

LO 4 Analysis of Balance Sheet
and Adjusting Entries

Refer to the balance sheet in the Toys "R" Us annual report. Examine the accounts listed in the current assets, property and equipment, and current liabilities sections. Which accounts are most likely to have had year-end adjusting entries? Tell the nature of the adjusting entries. For more information about the property and equipment section, refer to the notes to the consolidated financial statements.

Fingraph® Financial Analyst™

FRA 5.

LO 1 Income Measurement
LO 4 and Adjustments
SO 7

Choose any company in the Fingraph® Financial Analyst™ CD-ROM software.

1. Does the company have a calendar year end or use some other fiscal year? Do you think the year end corresponds to the company's natural business year?

2. Find the company's balance sheet. From the asset accounts and liability accounts, find four examples of accounts that might have been related to an adjusting entry at the end of the year. For each example, tell whether the adjustment is a deferral or an accrual and suggest an income statement account that might be associated with it.

3. Find the summary of significant accounting policies, which appears following the financial statements. In these policies, find examples of the application of going concern and accrual accounting. Explain your choices of examples.

4. Prepare a one-page executive summary that highlights what you have learned from parts **1, 2,** and **3.**

Internet Case

FRA 6.

LO 4 Comparison of Accrued
Expenses

How important are accrued expenses? Randomly choose the annual reports of four companies from the Needles Accounting Resource Center web site at http://college. hmco.com. For each company, find the section of the balance sheet labeled "Current Liabilities" and identify the current liabilities that are accrued expenses (sometimes called *accrued liabilities*). More than one account may be involved. On a pad, write the information you find in four columns: name of company, total current liabilities, total accrued liabilities, and total accrued liabilities as a percentage of total current liabilities. Write a memorandum to your instructor listing the companies you chose, telling how you obtained their reports, reporting the data you have gathered in the form of a table, and stating a conclusion, with reasons, as to the importance of accrued expenses to the companies you studied. (**Hint:** Compute the average percentage of total accrued expenses for the four companies you chose).

ENDNOTES

1. Southwest Airlines Co., Inc., *Annual Report*, 1999.
2. Elizabeth MacDonald, "SEC Says Earnings Scrutiny Goes Too Far," *The Wall Street Journal*, February 1, 1999.
3. *Statement of Financial Accounting Concepts No. 1*, "Objectives of Financial Reporting by Business Enterprises" (Norwalk, Conn.: Financial Accounting Standards Board, 1978), par. 44.
4. Michael Schroeder and Elizabeth MacDonald, "SEC Expects More Big Cases on Accounting," *The Wall Street Journal*, December 24, 1998.
5. PricewaterhouseCoopers presentation, 1999.
6. Lyric Opera of Chicago, *Annual Report*, 2000.
7. The Walt Disney Company, *Annual Report*, 1999.
8. H.J. Heinz Company, *Annual Report*, 1999.
9. Takashimaya Company, Limited, *Annual Report*, 2000.

4

Completing the Accounting Cycle

LEARNING OBJECTIVES

1 State all the steps in the accounting cycle.

2 Explain the purposes of closing entries.

3 Prepare the required closing entries.

4 Prepare the post-closing trial balance.

5 Prepare reversing entries as appropriate.

6 Prepare a work sheet.

7 Use a work sheet for three different purposes.

DECISION POINT: A USER'S FOCUS

Dell Computer Corporation Dell Computer Corporation is the world's largest computer company. As a company whose shares are traded on the New York Stock Exchange, Dell is required to prepare both annual and quarterly financial statements for its stockholders. Note the interim income statement from Dell's quarterly report, filed with the Securities and Exchange Commission, that appears here.[1] It shows that Dell's net revenue (sales) for the three months ended October 29, 1999, was greater than that for the same period of the preceding year by almost $2 billion, but that net income declined approximately 25 percent from $384,000,000 to $289,000,000 for the same period.

Whether required by law or not, the preparation of *interim financial statements* every quarter, or even every month, is a good idea for all businesses because such reports give stockholders an ongoing view of financial performance. What costs and time are involved in preparing interim financial statements?

The preparation of interim financial statements throughout the year requires more effort than the preparation of a single set of financial statements for the entire year. Each time the financial statements are prepared, adjusting entries must be determined, prepared, and recorded. Also, the ledger accounts must be prepared to begin the next accounting period. These procedures are time-

Financial Highlights: Interim Income Statement

(Unaudited—in millions)

	Three Months Ended	
	October 29, 1999	November 1, 1998
Net revenue	$6,784	$4,818
Cost of revenue	5,414	3,732
Gross margin	1,370	1,086
Operating expenses:		
Selling, general and administrative	622	471
Research, development and engineering	98	76
Purchased research & development	194	
Total operating expenses	914	547
Operating income	456	539
Financing and other	40	9
Income before income taxes	496	548
Provision for income taxes	207	164
Net income	$ 289	$ 384

133

consuming and costly. The advantages of preparing interim financial statements, even when they are not required, usually outweigh the costs, however, because such statements give management timely information for making decisions that will improve operations. This chapter explains the procedures used to prepare financial statements at the end of an accounting period, whether that period is a month, a quarter, or a year.

Overview of the Accounting Cycle

OBJECTIVE

1 State all the steps in the accounting cycle

The **accounting cycle** is a series of steps in the accounting system whose purpose is to measure business activities in the form of transactions and to transform these transactions into financial statements that will communicate useful information to decision makers. The steps in the accounting cycle, shown in Figure 1, are as follows:

1. *Analyze* business transactions from source documents.
2. *Record* the entries in the journal.
3. *Post* the entries to the ledger and prepare a trial balance.
4. *Adjust* the accounts and prepare an adjusted trial balance.
5. *Close* the accounts and prepare a post-closing trial balance.
6. *Prepare* financial statements.

You are already familiar with steps 1 through 4 and 6. Step 5 is covered in this chapter. The order of these steps can vary to some extent depending on the system in place. For instance, the financial statements (step 6) may be completed before the closing entries are prepared (step 5). In fact, in a computerized system, step 6 usually must be performed before step 5. The point is that all these steps must be accomplished to complete the accounting cycle. At key points in the accounting cycle, trial balances are prepared to ensure that the ledger remains in balance.

Closing Entries

OBJECTIVE

2 Explain the purposes of closing entries

Balance sheet accounts are considered to be **permanent accounts**, or *real accounts*, because they carry their end-of-period balances into the next accounting period. On the other hand, revenue and expense accounts are **temporary accounts**, or *nominal accounts*, because they begin each accounting period with a zero balance, accumulate a balance during the period, and are then cleared by means of closing entries.

Closing entries are journal entries made at the end of an accounting period. They have two purposes. First, closing entries set the stage for the next accounting period by clearing revenue, expense, and withdrawal accounts of their balances. Remember that the income statement reports net income (or loss) for a single accounting period and shows revenues and expenses for that period only. For the income statement to present the activity of a single accounting period, the revenue and expense accounts must begin each new period with zero balances. The zero balances are obtained by using closing entries to clear the balances in the revenue and expense accounts at the end of each accounting period. The Withdrawals account is closed in a similar manner.

Figure 1
Overview of the Accounting Cycle

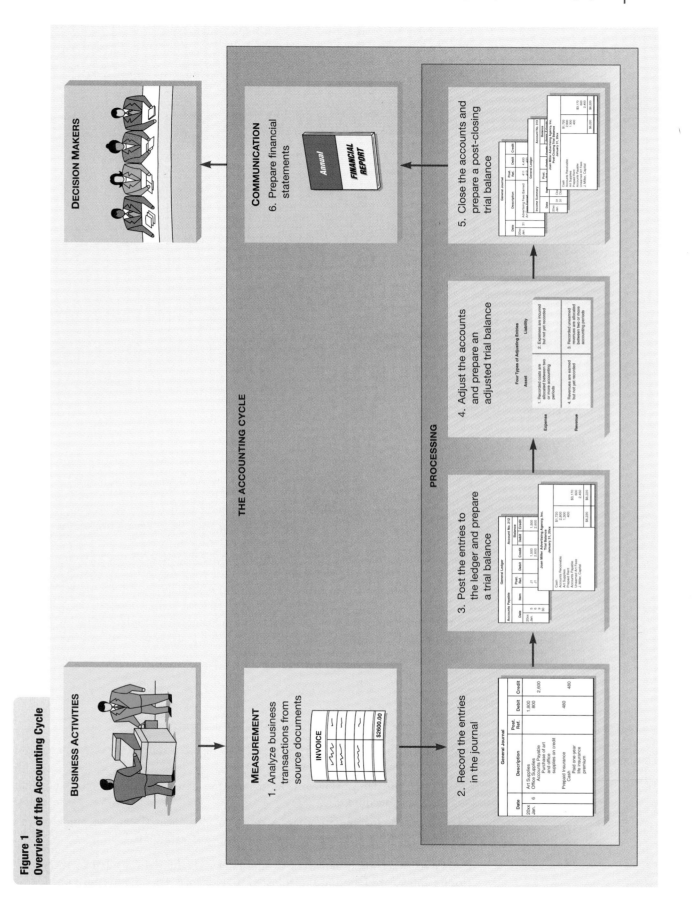

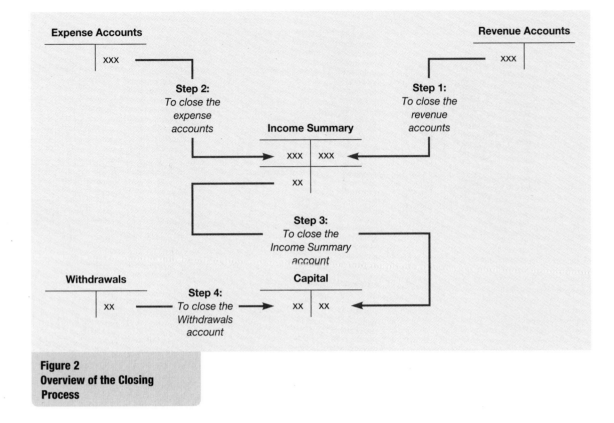

Figure 2
Overview of the Closing Process

Second, closing entries summarize a period's revenues and expenses. This is done by transferring the balances of revenue and expense accounts to the **Income Summary** account. This temporary account, which appears in the chart of accounts between the Withdrawals account and the first revenue account, provides a place to summarize all revenues and expenses. It is used only in the closing process and never appears in the financial statements.

The balance of the Income Summary account equals the net income or loss reported on the income statement. The net income or loss is then transferred to the Capital account. This is done because even though revenues and expenses are recorded in revenue and expense accounts, they actually represent increases and decreases in owner's equity. Closing entries transfer the net effect of increases (revenues) and decreases (expenses) to the owner's Capital account. An overview of the closing process is illustrated in Figure 2.

Required Closing Entries

OBJECTIVE

3 Prepare the required closing entries

There are four important steps in closing the accounts:

1. Closing the credit balances from the income statement accounts to the Income Summary account
2. Closing the debit balances from the income statement accounts to the Income Summary account
3. Closing the Income Summary account balance to the Capital account
4. Closing the Withdrawals account balance to the Capital account

Each step is accomplished by a closing entry. All the data needed to record the closing entries are found in the adjusted trial balance. The relationships of the four kinds of entries to the adjusted trial balance are shown in Exhibit 1.

Exhibit 1

**Preparing Closing Entries from
the Adjusted Trial Balance**

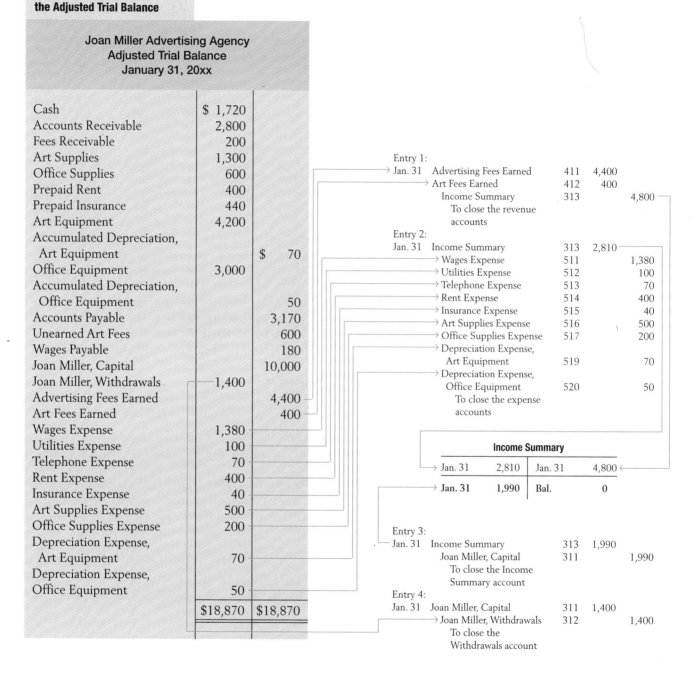

**Joan Miller Advertising Agency
Adjusted Trial Balance
January 31, 20xx**

Cash	$ 1,720	
Accounts Receivable	2,800	
Fees Receivable	200	
Art Supplies	1,300	
Office Supplies	600	
Prepaid Rent	400	
Prepaid Insurance	440	
Art Equipment	4,200	
Accumulated Depreciation, Art Equipment		$ 70
Office Equipment	3,000	
Accumulated Depreciation, Office Equipment		50
Accounts Payable		3,170
Unearned Art Fees		600
Wages Payable		180
Joan Miller, Capital		10,000
Joan Miller, Withdrawals	1,400	
Advertising Fees Earned		4,400
Art Fees Earned		400
Wages Expense	1,380	
Utilities Expense	100	
Telephone Expense	70	
Rent Expense	400	
Insurance Expense	40	
Art Supplies Expense	500	
Office Supplies Expense	200	
Depreciation Expense, Art Equipment	70	
Depreciation Expense, Office Equipment	50	
	$18,870	$18,870

Entry 1:

Jan. 31	Advertising Fees Earned	411	4,400	
	Art Fees Earned	412	400	
	Income Summary	313		4,800
	To close the revenue accounts			

Entry 2:

Jan. 31	Income Summary	313	2,810	
	Wages Expense	511		1,380
	Utilities Expense	512		100
	Telephone Expense	513		70
	Rent Expense	514		400
	Insurance Expense	515		40
	Art Supplies Expense	516		500
	Office Supplies Expense	517		200
	Depreciation Expense, Art Equipment	519		70
	Depreciation Expense, Office Equipment	520		50
	To close the expense accounts			

Income Summary

Jan. 31	2,810	Jan. 31	4,800
Jan. 31	1,990	Bal.	0

Entry 3:

Jan. 31	Income Summary	313	1,990	
	Joan Miller, Capital	311		1,990
	To close the Income Summary account			

Entry 4:

Jan. 31	Joan Miller, Capital	311	1,400	
	Joan Miller, Withdrawals	312		1,400
	To close the Withdrawals account			

**STEP 1: CLOSING THE CREDIT BALANCES FROM INCOME
STATEMENT ACCOUNTS TO THE INCOME SUMMARY ACCOUNT** On the credit side
of the adjusted trial balance in Exhibit 1, two revenue accounts show balances:
Advertising Fees Earned and Art Fees Earned. To close these two accounts, a journal entry must be made debiting each account in the amount of its balance and
crediting the total to the Income Summary account. The effect of posting the entry
is illustrated in Exhibit 2. Notice that the entry (1) sets the balances of the revenue
accounts to zero and (2) transfers the total revenues to the credit side of the
Income Summary account.

Exhibit 2
Posting the Closing Entry of the Credit Balances from the Income Statement Accounts to the Income Summary Account

Advertising Fees Earned — Account No. 411

Date	Item	Post. Ref.	Debit	Credit	Balance Debit	Balance Credit
Jan. 10		J2		1,400		1,400
19		J2		2,800		4,200
31	Adj. (i)	J3		200		4,400
31	Closing	J4	4,400			—

Income Summary — Account No. 313

Date	Item	Post. Ref.	Debit	Credit	Balance Debit	Balance Credit
Jan. 31	Closing	J4		4,800		4,800

4,400
400
4,800

Art Fees Earned — Account No. 412

Date	Item	Post. Ref.	Debit	Credit	Balance Debit	Balance Credit
Jan. 31	Adj. (h)	J3		400		400
31	Closing	J4	400			—

STEP 2: CLOSING THE DEBIT BALANCES FROM INCOME STATEMENT ACCOUNTS TO THE INCOME SUMMARY ACCOUNT Several expense accounts show balances on the debit side of the adjusted trial balance in Exhibit 1. A compound entry is needed to credit each of these expense accounts for its balance and to debit the Income Summary account for the total. The effect of posting the closing entry is shown in Exhibit 3. Notice how the entry (1) reduces the expense account balances to zero and (2) transfers the total of the account balances to the debit side of the Income Summary account.

STEP 3: CLOSING THE INCOME SUMMARY ACCOUNT TO THE CAPITAL ACCOUNT After the entries closing the revenue and expense accounts have been posted, the balance of the Income Summary account equals the net income or loss for the period. Since revenues are represented by the credit to Income Summary and expenses are represented by the debit to Income Summary, a net income is indicated by a credit balance (where revenues exceed expenses), and a net loss by a debit balance (where expenses exceed revenues). At this point, the Income Summary account balance, whatever its nature, must be closed to the Capital account, as shown in Exhibit 1. The effect

FOCUS ON BUSINESS PRACTICE

Performing routine accounting functions for other companies has become big business. The practice of managing a customer's information systems for a fixed fee is a form of *outsourcing*. If it leaves the information sys-

tems operations to an outside company, management can devote its attention to income-earning activities. Electronic Data Systems, Inc., founded by H. Ross Perot in 1962 and the source of his fortune, is the largest company in this business (it was owned for several years by General Motors until 1997 and now is a separate company again). EDS had revenues exceeding $18 billion in 1999 and is very profitable.

Exhibit 3

Posting the Closing Entry of the Debit Balances from the Income Statement Accounts to the Income Summary Account

Wages Expense — Account No. 511

Date	Item	Post. Ref.	Debit	Credit	Balance Debit	Balance Credit
Jan. 12		J2	600		600	
26		J2	600		1,200	
31	Adj. (g)	J3	180		1,380	
31	Closing	J4		1,380	—	

Income Summary — Account No. 313

Date	Item	Post. Ref.	Debit	Credit	Balance Debit	Balance Credit
Jan. 31	Closing	J4		4,800		4,800
31	Closing	J4	2,810			1,990

Utilities Expense — Account No. 512

Date	Item	Post. Ref.	Debit	Credit	Balance Debit	Balance Credit
Jan. 29		J2	100		100	
31	Closing	J4		100	—	

Telephone Expense — Account No. 513

Date	Item	Post. Ref.	Debit	Credit	Balance Debit	Balance Credit
Jan. 30		J2	70		70	
31	Closing	J4		70	—	

Rent Expense — Account No. 514

Date	Item	Post. Ref.	Debit	Credit	Balance Debit	Balance Credit
Jan. 31	Adj. (a)	J3	400		400	
31	Closing	J4		400	—	

Office Supplies Expense — Account No. 517

Date	Item	Post. Ref.	Debit	Credit	Balance Debit	Balance Credit
Jan. 31	Adj. (d)	J3	200		200	
31	Closing	J4		200	—	

Insurance Expense — Account No. 515

Date	Item	Post. Ref.	Debit	Credit	Balance Debit	Balance Credit
Jan. 31	Adj. (b)	J3	40		40	
31	Closing	J4		40	—	

Depreciation Expense, Art Equipment — Account No. 519

Date	Item	Post. Ref.	Debit	Credit	Balance Debit	Balance Credit
Jan. 31	Adj. (e)	J3	70		70	
31	Closing	J4		70	—	

Art Supplies Expense — Account No. 516

Date	Item	Post. Ref.	Debit	Credit	Balance Debit	Balance Credit
Jan. 31	Adj. (c)	J3	500		500	
31	Closing	J4		500	—	

Depreciation Expense, Office Equipment — Account No. 520

Date	Item	Post. Ref.	Debit	Credit	Balance Debit	Balance Credit
Jan. 31	Adj. (f)	J3	50		50	
31	Closing	J4		50	—	

Amounts posted to Income Summary: 1,380; 100; 70; 400; 40; 500; 50; 70; 200; 2,810

of posting the closing entry when the company has a net income is shown in Exhibit 4. Notice the dual effect of (1) closing the Income Summary account and (2) transferring the balance, net income in this case, to Joan Miller's Capital account.

STEP 4: CLOSING THE WITHDRAWALS ACCOUNT TO THE CAPITAL ACCOUNT The Withdrawals account shows the amount by which capital is reduced during the period by withdrawals of cash or other assets from the business for the owner's personal use. The debit balance of

Exhibit 4
Posting the Closing Entry of the Income Summary Account to the Capital Account

Income Summary						Account No. 313
					Balance	
Date	Item	Post. Ref.	Debit	Credit	Debit	Credit
Jan. 31	Closing	J4		4,800		4,800
31	Closing	J4	2,810			1,990
31	Closing	J4	1,990			—

Joan Miller, Capital						Account No. 311
					Balance	
Date	Item	Post. Ref.	Debit	Credit	Debit	Credit
Jan. 1		J1		10,000		10,000
31	Closing	J4		1,990		11,990

Exhibit 5
Posting the Closing Entry of the Withdrawals Account to the Capital Account

Joan Miller, Withdrawals						Account No. 312
					Balance	
Date	Item	Post. Ref.	Debit	Credit	Debit	Credit
Jan. 31		J2	1,400		1,400	
31	Closing	J4		1,400	—	

Joan Miller, Capital						Account No. 311
					Balance	
Date	Item	Post. Ref.	Debit	Credit	Debit	Credit
Jan. 1		J1		10,000		10,000
31	Closing	J4		1,990		11,990
31	Closing	J4	1,400			10,590

the Withdrawals account is closed to the Capital account, as shown in Exhibit 1. The effect of this closing entry, as shown in Exhibit 5, is to (1) close the Withdrawals account and (2) transfer the balance to the Capital account.

The Accounts After Closing

After all steps in the closing process have been completed and all closing entries have been posted to the accounts, everything is ready for the next accounting period. The ledger accounts of Joan Miller Advertising Agency, as they appear at this point, are shown in Exhibit 6. The revenue, expense, and Withdrawals accounts (temporary accounts) have zero balances. The Capital account has been increased to reflect the agency's net income and decreased for the owner's withdrawals. The balance sheet accounts (permanent accounts) show the correct balances, which are carried forward to the next period.

FOCUS ON BUSINESS TECHNOLOGY

When General Mills needed to speed up its year-end closing procedures, it selected a team from its Financial Reporting and Information Services Division to design an automated fiscal year-end accounting package. The team put together a system using software spreadsheets like Lotus and Microsoft Excel to record and consolidate annual results. Their effort accelerated the process, increased accuracy, reduced outside help and overtime, and provided flexibility. In addition, its cost was very low because it used PCs and software that the company already owned. The whole process was reduced from nine weeks to just six work days.[2]

Exhibit 6

The Accounts After Closing Entries Are Posted

Cash — Account No. 111

Date	Item	Post. Ref.	Debit	Credit	Balance Debit	Balance Credit
Jan. 1		J1	10,000		10,000	
2		J1		800	9,200	
4		J1		4,200	5,000	
5		J1		1,500	3,500	
8		J1		480	3,020	
9		J1		1,000	2,020	
10		J2	1,400		3,420	
12		J2		600	2,820	
15		J2	1,000		3,820	
26		J2		600	3,220	
29		J2		100	3,120	
31		J2		1,400	1,720	

Accounts Receivable — Account No. 113

Date	Item	Post. Ref.	Debit	Credit	Balance Debit	Balance Credit
Jan. 19		J2	2,800		2,800	

Fees Receivable — Account No. 114

Date	Item	Post. Ref.	Debit	Credit	Balance Debit	Balance Credit
Jan. 31	Adj. (i)	J3	200		200	

Art Supplies — Account No. 115

Date	Item	Post. Ref.	Debit	Credit	Balance Debit	Balance Credit
Jan. 6		J1	1,800		1,800	
31	Adj. (c)	J3		500	1,300	

Office Supplies — Account No. 116

Date	Item	Post. Ref.	Debit	Credit	Balance Debit	Balance Credit
Jan. 6		J1	800		800	
31	Adj. (d)	J3		200	600	

Prepaid Rent — Account No. 117

Date	Item	Post. Ref.	Debit	Credit	Balance Debit	Balance Credit
Jan. 2		J1	800		800	
31	Adj. (a)	J3		400	400	

Prepaid Insurance — Account No. 118

Date	Item	Post. Ref.	Debit	Credit	Balance Debit	Balance Credit
Jan. 8		J1	480		480	
31	Adj. (b)	J3		40	440	

Art Equipment — Account No. 144

Date	Item	Post. Ref.	Debit	Credit	Balance Debit	Balance Credit
Jan. 4		J1	4,200		4,200	

Accumulated Depreciation, Art Equipment — Account No. 145

Date	Item	Post. Ref.	Debit	Credit	Balance Debit	Balance Credit
Jan. 31	Adj. (e)	J3		70		70

Office Equipment — Account No. 146

Date	Item	Post. Ref.	Debit	Credit	Balance Debit	Balance Credit
Jan. 5		J1	3,000		3,000	

Accumulated Depreciation, Office Equipment — Account No. 147

Date	Item	Post. Ref.	Debit	Credit	Balance Debit	Balance Credit
Jan. 31	Adj. (f)	J3		50		50

Accounts Payable — Account No. 212

Date	Item	Post. Ref.	Debit	Credit	Balance Debit	Balance Credit
Jan. 5		J1		1,500		1,500
6		J1		2,600		4,100
9		J1	1,000			3,100
30		J2		70		3,170

Unearned Art Fees — Account No. 213

Date	Item	Post. Ref.	Debit	Credit	Balance Debit	Balance Credit
Jan. 15		J2		1,000		1,000
31	Adj. (h)	J3	400			600

Wages Payable — Account No. 214

Date	Item	Post. Ref.	Debit	Credit	Balance Debit	Balance Credit
Jan. 31	Adj. (g)	J3		180		180

(continued)

Exhibit 6
The Accounts After Closing Entries Are Posted *(continued)*

Joan Miller, Capital — Account No. 311

Date	Item	Post. Ref.	Debit	Credit	Balance Debit	Balance Credit
Jan. 1		J1		10,000		10,000
Jan. 31	Closing	J4		1,990		11,990
31	Closing	J4	1,400			10,590

Joan Miller, Withdrawals — Account No. 312

Date	Item	Post. Ref.	Debit	Credit	Balance Debit	Balance Credit
Jan. 31		J2	1,400		1,400	
31	Closing	J4		1,400	—	

Income Summary — Account No. 313

Date	Item	Post. Ref.	Debit	Credit	Balance Debit	Balance Credit
Jan. 31	Closing	J4		4,800		4,800
31	Closing	J4	2,810			1,990
31	Closing	J4	1,990			—

Advertising Fees Earned — Account No. 411

Date	Item	Post. Ref.	Debit	Credit	Balance Debit	Balance Credit
Jan. 10		J2		1,400		1,400
19		J2		2,800		4,200
31	Adj. (i)	J3		200		4,400
31	Closing	J4	4,400			—

Art Fees Earned — Account No. 412

Date	Item	Post. Ref.	Debit	Credit	Balance Debit	Balance Credit
Jan. 31	Adj. (h)	J3		400		400
31	Closing	J4	400			—

Wages Expense — Account No. 511

Date	Item	Post. Ref.	Debit	Credit	Balance Debit	Balance Credit
Jan. 12		J2	600		600	
26		J2	600		1,200	
31	Adj. (g)	J3	180		1,380	
31	Closing	J4		1,380	—	

Utilities Expense — Account No. 512

Date	Item	Post. Ref.	Debit	Credit	Balance Debit	Balance Credit
Jan. 29		J2	100		100	
31	Closing	J4		100	—	

Telephone Expense — Account No. 513

Date	Item	Post. Ref.	Debit	Credit	Balance Debit	Balance Credit
Jan. 30		J2	70		70	
31	Closing	J4		70	—	

Rent Expense — Account No. 514

Date	Item	Post. Ref.	Debit	Credit	Balance Debit	Balance Credit
Jan. 31	Adj. (a)	J3	400		400	
31	Closing	J4		400	—	

Insurance Expense — Account No. 515

Date	Item	Post. Ref.	Debit	Credit	Balance Debit	Balance Credit
Jan. 31	Adj. (b)	J3	40		40	
31	Closing	J4		40	—	

Art Supplies Expense — Account No. 516

Date	Item	Post. Ref.	Debit	Credit	Balance Debit	Balance Credit
Jan. 31	Adj. (c)	J3	500		500	
31	Closing	J4		500	—	

Office Supplies Expense — Account No. 517

Date	Item	Post. Ref.	Debit	Credit	Balance Debit	Balance Credit
Jan. 31	Adj. (d)	J3	200		200	
31	Closing	J4		200	—	

Depreciation Expense, Art Equipment — Account No. 519

Date	Item	Post. Ref.	Debit	Credit	Balance Debit	Balance Credit
Jan. 31	Adj. (e)	J3	70		70	
31	Closing	J4		70	—	

Depreciation Expense, Office Equipment — Account No. 520

Date	Item	Post. Ref.	Debit	Credit	Balance Debit	Balance Credit
Jan. 31	Adj. (f)	J3	50		50	
31	Closing	J4		50	—	

The Post-Closing Trial Balance

OBJECTIVE

4 Prepare the post-closing trial balance

Because errors may occur in posting the closing entries to the ledger accounts, a **post-closing trial balance** is prepared at the end of the accounting period after all adjusting and closing entries have been posted. This is necessary to determine that all temporary accounts have zero balances and to double-check that total debits equal total credits by preparing a new trial balance. The post-closing trial balance is shown in Exhibit 7 for Joan Miller Advertising Agency. Notice that only the balance sheet accounts show balances because the income statement accounts and the Withdrawals account have all been closed.

Exhibit 7
Post-Closing Trial Balance

Joan Miller Advertising Agency
Post-Closing Trial Balance
January 31, 20xx

Cash	$ 1,720	
Accounts Receivable	2,800	
Fees Receivable	200	
Art Supplies	1,300	
Office Supplies	600	
Prepaid Rent	400	
Prepaid Insurance	440	
Art Equipment	4,200	
Accumulated Depreciation, Art Equipment		$ 70
Office Equipment	3,000	
Accumulated Depreciation, Office Equipment		50
Accounts Payable		3,170
Unearned Art Fees		600
Wages Payable		180
Joan Miller, Capital		10,590
	$14,660	$14,660

Reversing Entries: The Optional First Step in the Next Accounting Period

OBJECTIVE

5 Prepare reversing entries as appropriate

At the end of each accounting period, adjusting entries are made to bring revenues and expenses into conformity with the matching rule. A **reversing entry** is a general journal entry made on the first day of a new accounting period that is the exact reverse of an adjusting entry made at the end of the previous period. Reversing entries are optional and, when made, simplify the bookkeeping process for transactions involving certain types of adjustments. Not all adjusting entries should be reversed. For the recording system used in this book, only adjustments for accruals (accrued revenues and accrued expenses) are reversed. Deferrals should not be reversed because such reversals would not simplify the bookkeeping process in future accounting periods.

To see how reversing entries can be helpful, consider the adjusting entry made in the records of Joan Miller Advertising Agency to accrue wages expense:

A = L + OE
    +   −

Jan. 31	Wages Expense	180	
	Wages Payable		180
	Accrued unrecorded wages		

When the secretary is paid on the next regular payday, the accountant would make this entry:

A = L + OE
   − −   −

Feb. 9	Wages Payable	180	
	Wages Expense	420	
	Cash		600
	Paid two weeks' wages to secretary, $180 of which accrued in the previous period		

Notice that when the payment is made, if there is no reversing entry, the accountant must look in the records to find out how much of the $600 applies to the current accounting period and how much is applicable to the previous period. This may seem easy in our example, but think how difficult and time-consuming it would be if a company had hundreds of employees, all working on different schedules.

A reversing entry helps solve the problem of applying revenues and expenses to the correct accounting period. It is exactly what its name implies: a reversal made by debiting the credits and crediting the debits of a previously made adjusting entry.

For example, notice the following sequence of entries and their effects on the ledger account Wages Expense:

1. Adjusting Entry

Jan. 31	Wages Expense	180
	Wages Payable	180

2. Closing Entry

Jan. 31	Income Summary	1,380
	Wages Expense	1,380

3. Reversing Entry

Feb. 1	Wages Payable	180
	Wages Expense	180

4. Payment Entry

Feb. 9	Wages Expense	600
	Cash	600

Wages Expense				Account No. 511	
				Balance	
Date	Post. Ref.	Debit	Credit	Debit	Credit
Jan. 12	J2	600		600	
26	J2	600		1,200	
31	J3	180		1,380	
31	J4		1,380	—	
Feb. 1	J5		180		180
9	J6	600		420	

Entry 1 adjusted Wages Expense to accrue $180 in the January accounting period.

Entry 2 closed the $1,380 in Wages Expense for January to Income Summary, leaving a zero balance.

Entry 3, the reversing entry, set up a credit balance of $180 on February 1 in Wages Expense, which is the expense recognized through the adjusting entry in January (and also reduced the liability account Wages Payable to a zero balance). The reversing entry always sets up an abnormal balance in the income statement account and produces a zero balance in the balance sheet account.

Entry 4 recorded the $600 payment of two weeks' wages as a debit to Wages Expense, automatically leaving a balance of $420, which represents the correct wages expense to date in February. The reversing entry simplified the process of making the payment entry on February 9.

Reversing entries apply to any accrued expenses or revenues. In the case of Joan Miller Advertising Agency, wages expense was the only accrued expense. However, the asset Fees Receivable was created as a result of the adjusting entry made to accrue fees earned but not yet billed. The adjusting entry for this accrued revenue would require the following reversing entry:

A = L + OE	Feb. 1	Advertising Fees Earned	200	
− −		Fees Receivable		200
		Reversed the adjusting entry for accrued fees receivable		

When the series of advertisements is finished, the company can credit all the proceeds to Advertising Fees Earned without regard to the amount accrued in the previous period. The credit will automatically be reduced to the amount earned during February by the $200 debit in the account.

As noted earlier, under the system of recording used in this book, reversing entries apply only to accruals. Reversing entries do not apply to deferrals, such as the entries that involve supplies, prepaid rent, prepaid insurance, depreciation, and unearned art fees.

The Work Sheet: An Accountant's Tool

OBJECTIVE

6 Prepare a work sheet

As seen earlier, the flow of information that affects a business does not stop arbitrarily at the end of an accounting period. In preparing financial reports, accountants must collect relevant data to determine what should be included. For example, they need to examine insurance policies to see how much prepaid insurance has expired, examine plant and equipment records to determine depreciation, take an inventory of supplies on hand, and calculate the amount of accrued wages. These calculations, together with other computations, analyses, and preliminary drafts of statements, make up the accountants' **working papers**. Working papers are important for two reasons. First, they help accountants organize their work and thus avoid omitting important data or steps that affect the financial statements. Second, they provide evidence of past work so that accountants or auditors can retrace their steps and support the information in the financial statements.

A special kind of working paper is the **work sheet**. The work sheet is often used as a preliminary step in recording adjusting and closing entries and the preparation of financial statements. Using a work sheet reduces the possibility of omitting an adjustment, helps the accountant check the arithmetical accuracy of the accounts, and facilitates the preparation of financial statements. The work sheet is never published and is rarely seen by management. It is a tool for the accountant. Because preparing a work sheet is a very mechanical process, many accountants use a microcomputer. In some cases, accountants use a spreadsheet program to prepare the work sheet. In other cases, they use general ledger software to prepare financial statements from the adjusted trial balance.

Preparing the Work Sheet

So far, adjusting entries have been entered directly in the journal and posted to the ledger, and the financial statements have been prepared from the adjusted trial balance. The process has been relatively simple because Joan Miller Advertising Agency is a small company. For larger companies, which may require many adjusting entries, a work sheet is essential. To illustrate the preparation of the work sheet, we continue with the Joan Miller Advertising Agency example.

A common form of work sheet has one column for account names and/or numbers and ten more columns with the headings shown in Exhibit 8. Notice that the work sheet is identified by a heading that consists of (1) the name of the company, (2) the title "Work Sheet," and (3) the period of time covered (as on the income statement).

There are five steps in the preparation of a work sheet:

1. Enter and total the account balances in the Trial Balance columns.
2. Enter and total the adjustments in the Adjustments columns.
3. Enter and total the adjusted account balances in the Adjusted Trial Balance columns.
4. Extend the account balances from the Adjusted Trial Balance columns to the Income Statement columns or the Balance Sheet columns.
5. Total the Income Statement columns and the Balance Sheet columns. Enter the net income or net loss in both pairs of columns as a balancing figure, and recompute the column totals.

1. **Enter and total the account balances in the Trial Balance columns.** The titles and balances of the accounts as of January 31 are copied directly from the ledger into the Trial Balance columns, as shown in Exhibit 8. When a work sheet is used, the accountant does not have to prepare a separate trial balance.

2. **Enter and total the adjustments in the Adjustments columns.** The required adjustments for Joan Miller Advertising Agency are entered in the Adjustments columns of the work sheet as shown in Exhibit 9. As each adjustment is entered, a letter is used to identify its debit and credit parts. The first adjustment, which is identified by the letter **a,** is to recognize rent expense, which results in a debit to Rent Expense and a credit to Prepaid Rent. In practice, this letter may be used to reference supporting computations or documentation underlying the adjusting entry, and it may simplify the recording of adjusting entries in the general journal.

If an adjustment calls for an account that has not been used in the trial balance, the new account is added below the accounts listed in the trial balance. The trial balance includes only those accounts that have balances. For example, Rent Expense has been added in Exhibit 9. The only exception to this rule is the Accumulated Depreciation accounts, which have a zero balance only in the initial period of operation. Accumulated Depreciation accounts are listed immediately after their associated asset accounts.

When all the adjustments have been made, the two Adjustments columns must be totaled. This step proves that the debits and credits of the adjustments are equal and generally reduces errors in the preparation of the work sheet.

3. **Enter and total the adjusted account balances in the Adjusted Trial Balance columns.** Exhibit 10 shows the adjusted trial balance. It is prepared by combining the amount of each account in the original Trial Balance columns with the corresponding amount in the Adjustments columns and entering each result in the Adjusted Trial Balance columns.

Some examples from Exhibit 10 illustrate **crossfooting**, or adding and subtracting a group of numbers horizontally. The first line shows Cash with a debit balance of $1,720. Because there are no adjustments to the Cash account, $1,720 is entered in the debit column of the Adjusted Trial Balance columns. The second line is Accounts Receivable, which shows a debit of $2,800 in the Trial Balance columns. Because there are no adjustments to Accounts Receivable, the $2,800 balance is carried over to the debit column of the Adjusted Trial Balance columns. The next line is Art Supplies, which shows a debit of $1,800 in the Trial Balance columns and a credit of $500 from adjustment c in the Adjustments columns. Subtracting $500 from $1,800 results in a $1,300 debit balance in the Adjusted Trial Balance columns. This process is followed for all the accounts, including those added below the trial balance totals. The Adjusted Trial Balance columns are then footed (totaled) to check the accuracy of the crossfooting.

4. **Extend the account balances from the Adjusted Trial Balance columns to the Income Statement columns or the Balance Sheet columns.** Every account in the adjusted trial balance is either a balance sheet account or an income statement account. Each account is extended to its proper place as a debit or credit in either the Income Statement columns or the Balance Sheet columns. The result of extending the accounts is shown in Exhibit 11. Revenue and expense accounts are copied to the Income Statement columns. Assets, liabilities, and the Capital and Withdrawals accounts are extended to the Balance Sheet columns. To avoid overlooking an account, extend the accounts line by line, beginning with the first line (which is Cash) and not omitting any subsequent lines. For instance, the Cash debit balance of $1,720 is extended to the debit column of the Balance Sheet columns, the Accounts Receivable debit balance of $2,800 is extended to the same debit column, and so forth. Each amount is carried across to only one column.

5. **Total the Income Statement columns and the Balance Sheet columns. Enter the net income or net loss in both pairs of columns as a balancing figure, and recompute the column totals.** This last step, as shown in Exhibit 12, is necessary to compute net income or net loss and to prove the arithmetical accuracy of the work sheet.

Net income (or net loss) is equal to the difference between the total debits and credits of the Income Statement columns. It also equals the difference between the total debits and credits of the Balance Sheet columns.

Revenue (Income Statement credit column total)	$4,800
Expenses (Income Statement debit column total)	(2,810)
Net Income	$1,990

In this case, revenues (credit column) exceed expenses (debit column). Consequently, the company has a net income of $1,990. The same difference is shown between the total debits and credits of the Balance Sheet columns.

The $1,990 is entered in the debit side of the Income Statement columns to balance the columns, and it is entered in the credit side of the Balance Sheet columns to balance the columns. Remember that the excess of revenues over expenses (net income) increases owner's equity and that increases in owner's equity are recorded by credits.

When a net loss occurs, the opposite rule applies. The excess of expenses over revenues—net loss—is placed in the credit side of the Income Statement columns as a balancing figure. It is then placed in the debit side of the Balance Sheet columns because a net loss decreases owner's equity, and decreases in owner's equity are recorded by debits.

As a final check, the four columns are totaled again. If the Income Statement columns and the Balance Sheet columns do not balance, an account may have been extended or sorted to the wrong column, or an error may have been made in adding the columns. Of course, equal totals in the two pairs of columns are not absolute proof of accuracy. If an asset has been carried to the Income Statement debit column and a similar error involving revenues or liabilities has been made, the work sheet will still balance, but the net income figure will be wrong.

Using the Work Sheet

OBJECTIVE

7 Use a work sheet for three different purposes

The completed work sheet assists the accountant in three principal tasks: (1) recording the adjusting entries, (2) recording the closing entries in the general journal to prepare the records for the beginning of the next period, and (3) preparing the financial statements.

RECORDING THE ADJUSTING ENTRIES   For Joan Miller Advertising Agency, the adjustments were determined while completing the work sheet because they are essential to the preparation of the financial statements. The adjusting entries may be recorded in the general journal at that point.

Recording the adjusting entries with appropriate explanations in the general journal, as shown in Exhibit 13, is an easy step. The information can be copied from the work sheet. Adjusting entries are then posted to the general ledger.

RECORDING THE CLOSING ENTRIES   The four closing entries for Joan Miller Advertising Agency are entered in the journal and posted to the ledger as shown in Exhibits 1 through 5. All accounts that need to be closed, except for Withdrawals, may be found in the Income Statement columns of the work sheet.

PREPARING THE FINANCIAL STATEMENTS   Once the work sheet has been completed, preparing the financial statements is simple because the account balances have been sorted into Income Statement and Balance Sheet columns. The income statement shown in Exhibit 14 was prepared from the account balances in the Income Statement columns of Exhibit 12. The statement of owner's equity and the

FOCUS ON BUSINESS TECHNOLOGY

The work sheet is a good application for electronic spreadsheet software programs like Lotus and Microsoft Excel. Constructing a work sheet using spreadsheet software takes time, but once it is done, the work sheet can be used over and over. The principal advantage of electronic preparation over manual preparation is that each time a number is entered or revised, the entire electronic work sheet is updated automatically, without the possibility of addition or extension mistakes. For example, if an error in an adjusting entry is corrected, the proper extensions to the other columns are made, all columns are re-added, and net income is recomputed. Of course, the software is purely mechanical. People are still responsible for inputting the correct numbers and equations initially.

Exhibit 13
Adjustments from Work Sheet Entered in the General Journal

		General Journal			Page 3
Date		Description	Post. Ref.	Debit	Credit
20xx Jan.	31	Rent Expense	514	400	
		Prepaid Rent	117		400
		To recognize expiration of one month's rent			
	31	Insurance Expense	515	40	
		Prepaid Insurance	118		40
		To recognize expiration of one month's insurance			
	31	Art Supplies Expense	516	500	
		Art Supplies	115		500
		To recognize art supplies used during the month			
	31	Office Supplies Expense	517	200	
		Office Supplies	116		200
		To recognize office supplies used during the month			
	31	Depreciation Expense, Art Equipment	519	70	
		Accumulated Depreciation, Art Equipment	145		70
		To record depreciation of art equipment for a month			
	31	Depreciation Expense, Office Equipment	520	50	
		Accumulated Depreciation, Office Equipment	147		50
		To record depreciation of office equipment for a month			
	31	Wages Expense	511	180	
		Wages Payable	214		180
		To accrue unrecorded wages			
	31	Unearned Art Fees	213	400	
		Art Fees Earned	412		400
		To recognize performance of services paid for in advance			
	31	Fees Receivable	114	200	
		Advertising Fees Earned	411		200
		To accrue advertising fees earned but unrecorded			

Joan Miller Advertising Agency
Income Statement
For the Month Ended January 31, 20xx

Revenues		
Advertising Fees Earned		$4,400
Art Fees Earned		400
Total Revenues		$4,800
Expenses		
Wages Expense	$1,380	
Utilities Expense	100	
Telephone Expense	70	
Rent Expense	400	
Insurance Expense	40	
Art Supplies Expense	500	
Office Supplies Expense	200	
Depreciation Expense, Art Equipment	70	
Depreciation Expense, Office Equipment	50	
Total Expenses		2,810
Net Income		$1,990

balance sheet for Joan Miller Advertising Agency are presented in Exhibits 15 and 16. The account balances for these statements are drawn from the Balance Sheet columns of the work sheet shown in Exhibit 12. Notice that the total assets and the total liabilities and owner's equity in the balance sheet are not the same as the totals of the Balance Sheet columns in the work sheet. The reason is that the Accumulated Depreciation and Withdrawals accounts have normal balances that appear in different columns from their associated accounts on the balance sheet. In addition, the owner's Capital account on the balance sheet is the amount determined on the statement of owner's equity. At this point, the financial statements have been prepared from the work sheet, not from the ledger accounts. For the ledger accounts to show the correct balances, the adjusting entries must be journalized and posted to the ledger.

Joan Miller Advertising Agency
Statement of Owner's Equity
For the Month Ended January 31, 20xx

Joan Miller, Capital, January 1, 20xx		—
Add: Investment by Joan Miller	$10,000	
Net Income	1,990	$11,990
Subtotal		$11,990
Less Withdrawals		1,400
Joan Miller, Capital, January 31, 20xx		$10,590

Exhibit 16
Balance Sheet for Joan Miller Advertising Agency

Joan Miller Advertising Agency
Balance Sheet
January 31, 20xx

Assets

Cash		$ 1,720
Accounts Receivable		2,800
Fees Receivable		200
Art Supplies		1,300
Office Supplies		600
Prepaid Rent		400
Prepaid Insurance		440
Art Equipment	$ 4,200	
Less Accumulated Depreciation	70	4,130
Office Equipment	$ 3,000	
Less Accumulated Depreciation	50	2,950
Total Assets		$14,540

Liabilities

Accounts Payable	$ 3,170	
Unearned Art Fees	600	
Wages Payable	180	
Total Liabilities		$ 3,950

Owner's Equity

Joan Miller, Capital, January 31, 20xx	10,590
Total Liabilities and Owner's Equity	$14,540

Chapter Review

1. **State all the steps in the accounting cycle.** The steps in the accounting cycle are (1) analyze business transactions from source documents, (2) record the entries in the journal, (3) post the entries to the ledger and prepare a trial balance, (4) adjust the accounts and prepare an adjusted trial balance, (5) close the accounts and prepare a post-closing trial balance, and (6) prepare the financial statements.

2. **Explain the purposes of closing entries.** Closing entries have two purposes. First, they clear the balances of all temporary accounts (revenue and expense accounts and owner's Withdrawals) so that they have zero balances at the beginning of the next accounting period. Second, they summarize a period's revenues and expenses in the Income Summary account so that the net income or loss for the period can be transferred as a total to owner's Capital.

3. **Prepare the required closing entries.** Closing entries are prepared by first transferring the revenue and expense account balances to the Income Summary account. Then the balance of the Income Summary account is transferred to the owner's Capital account. And, finally, the balance of the owner's Withdrawals account is transferred to the owner's Capital account.

4. **Prepare the post-closing trial balance.** As a final check on the balance of the ledger and to ensure that all temporary (nominal) accounts have been closed, a post-closing trial balance is prepared after the closing entries are posted to the ledger accounts.

5. **Prepare reversing entries as appropriate.** Reversing entries are optional entries dated the first day of the new accounting period to simplify routine bookkeeping procedures. They reverse certain adjusting entries made in the previous period. Under the system used in this text, they apply only to accruals.

6. **Prepare a work sheet.** There are five steps in the preparation of a work sheet: (1) Enter and total the account balances in the Trial Balance columns; (2) enter and total the adjustments in the Adjustments columns; (3) enter and total the adjusted account balances in the Adjusted Trial Balance columns; (4) extend the account balances from the Adjusted Trial Balance columns to the Income Statement or Balance Sheet columns; and (5) total the Income Statement and Balance Sheet columns, enter the net income or net loss in both pairs of columns as a balancing figure, and recompute the column totals.

7. **Use a work sheet for three different purposes.** A work sheet is useful in (1) recording the adjusting entries, (2) recording the closing entries, and (3) preparing the financial statements. The balance sheet and income statement can be prepared directly from the Balance Sheet and Income Statement columns of the completed work sheet. The statement of owner's equity is prepared using owner's Withdrawals, net income, additional investments, and the beginning balance of the owner's Capital account. Notice that the ending balance of owner's Capital does not appear on the work sheet. Adjusting entries can be recorded in the general journal directly from the Adjustments columns of the work sheet. Closing entries may be prepared from the Income Statement columns, except for owner's Withdrawals, which is found in the Balance Sheet columns.

REVIEW OF CONCEPTS AND TERMINOLOGY

The following concepts and terms were introduced in this chapter:

LO 1 **Accounting cycle:** The sequence of steps followed in the accounting system to measure business transactions and transform them into financial statements.

LO 2 **Closing entries:** Journal entries made at the end of an accounting period that set the stage for the next accounting period by clearing the temporary accounts of their balances and that summarize a period's revenues and expenses.

LO 6 **Crossfooting:** Adding and subtracting numbers across a row.

LO 2 **Income Summary:** A temporary account used during the closing process that holds a summary of all revenues and expenses before the net income or loss is transferred to the owner's Capital account.

LO 2 **Permanent accounts:** Balance sheet accounts; accounts whose balances can extend past the end of an accounting period. Also called *real accounts*.

LO 4 **Post-closing trial balance:** A trial balance prepared at the end of the accounting period after all adjusting and closing entries have been posted; a final check on the balance of the ledger to ensure that all temporary accounts have zero balances and that total debits equal total credits.

LO 5 **Reversing entry:** A journal entry dated the first day of a new accounting period that is the exact opposite of an adjusting entry made on the last day of the prior accounting period.

LO 2 **Temporary accounts:** Accounts that show the accumulation of revenues and expenses over one accounting period; at the end of the accounting period, these account balances are transferred to owner's equity. Also called *nominal accounts*.

LO 6 **Working papers:** Documents used by accountants to organize their work and to support the information in the financial statements.

LO 6 **Work sheet:** A type of working paper used as a preliminary step in recording adjusting and closing entries and in the preparation of financial statements.

REVIEW PROBLEM

Preparation of Closing Entries

LO 3 At the end of the current fiscal year, the adjusted trial balance for Westwood Movers Company appeared as shown below.

Westwood Movers Company Adjusted Trial Balance June 30, 20xx		
Cash	$ 14,200	
Accounts Receivable	18,600	
Packing Supplies	10,400	
Prepaid Insurance	7,900	
Land	4,000	
Building	80,000	
Accumulated Depreciation, Building		$ 7,500
Trucks	106,000	
Accumulated Depreciation, Trucks		27,500
Accounts Payable		7,650
Unearned Storage Fees		5,400
Mortgage Payable		70,000
Art Burton, Capital		104,740
Art Burton, Withdrawals	18,000	
Moving Services Earned		159,000
Storage Fees Earned		26,400
Driver Wages Expense	94,000	
Fuel Expense	19,000	
Office Wages Expense	14,400	
Office Equipment Rental Expense	3,000	
Utilities Expense	4,450	
Insurance Expense	4,200	
Depreciation Expense, Building	4,000	
Depreciation Expense, Trucks	6,040	
	$408,190	$408,190

REQUIRED

Prepare the necessary closing entries.

ANSWER TO REVIEW
PROBLEM

June 30	Moving Services Earned	159,000	
	Storage Fees Earned	26,400	
	Income Summary		185,400
	Closed the revenue accounts		
30	Income Summary	149,090	
	Driver Wages Expense		94,000
	Fuel Expense		19,000
	Office Wages Expense		14,400
	Office Equipment Rental Expense		3,000
	Utilities Expense		4,450
	Insurance Expense		4,200
	Depreciation Expense, Building		4,000
	Depreciation Expense, Trucks		6,040
	Closed the expense accounts		
30	Income Summary	36,310	
	Art Burton, Capital		36,310
	Closed the Income Summary account and		
	transferred the balance to the Capital account		
30	Art Burton, Capital	18,000	
	Art Burton, Withdrawals		18,000
	Closed the Withdrawals account		

Chapter Assignments

BUILDING YOUR
KNOWLEDGE
FOUNDATION

QUESTIONS

1. Resequence the following activities **a** through **f** to indicate the correct order of the accounting cycle.
   a. The transactions are entered in the journal.
   b. The financial statements are prepared.
   c. The transactions are analyzed from the source documents.
   d. The adjusting entries are prepared.
   e. The closing entries are prepared.
   f. The transactions are posted to the ledger.
2. What are the two purposes of closing entries?
3. What is the difference between adjusting entries and closing entries?
4. What is the purpose of the Income Summary account?
5. Which of the following accounts do not show a balance after the closing entries are prepared and posted?
   a. Insurance Expense   e. Owner's Withdrawals
   b. Accounts Receivable   f. Supplies
   c. Commission Revenue   g. Supplies Expense
   d. Prepaid Insurance   h. Owner's Capital
6. What is the significance of the post-closing trial balance?
7. Which of the following accounts would you expect to find on the post-closing trial balance?
   a. Insurance Expense   e. Owner's Withdrawals
   b. Accounts Receivable   f. Supplies
   c. Commission Revenue   g. Supplies Expense
   d. Prepaid Insurance   h. Owner's Capital
8. How do reversing entries simplify the bookkeeping process?

9. To what types of adjustments do reversing entries apply? To what types do they not apply?

10. Why are working papers important to accountants?

11. Why are work sheets never published and rarely seen by management?

12. Can the work sheet be used as a substitute for the financial statements? Explain your answer.

13. What is the normal balance (debit or credit) of the following accounts?
    a. Cash
    b. Accounts Payable
    c. Prepaid Rent
    d. Sam Jones, Capital
    e. Commission Revenue
    f. Sam Jones, Withdrawals
    g. Rent Expense
    h. Accumulated Depreciation, Office Equipment
    i. Office Equipment

14. Why should the Adjusted Trial Balance columns of the work sheet be totaled before the adjusted amounts are carried to the Income Statement and Balance Sheet columns?

15. What sequence should be followed in extending the amounts in the Adjusted Trial Balance columns to the Income Statement and Balance Sheet columns? Discuss your answer.

16. Do the Income Statement columns and the Balance Sheet columns of the work sheet balance after the amounts from the Adjusted Trial Balance columns are extended?

17. Do the totals of the Balance Sheet columns of the work sheet agree with the totals on the balance sheet? Explain your answer.

18. Should adjusting entries be posted to the ledger accounts before or after the closing entries? Explain your answer.

19. At the end of the accounting period, does the posting of adjusting entries to the ledger precede or follow the preparation of the work sheet?

SHORT EXERCISES

SE 1.

LO 1   Accounting Cycle

Resequence the following activities to indicate the usual order of the accounting cycle.
a. Close the accounts.
b. Analyze the transactions.
c. Post the entries to the ledger.
d. Prepare the financial statements.
e. Adjust the accounts.
f. Record the transactions in the journal.
g. Prepare the post-closing trial balance.
h. Prepare the initial trial balance.
i. Prepare the adjusted trial balance.

SE 2.

LO 3   Closing Revenue Accounts

Assuming credit balances at the end of the accounting period of $3,400 in Patient Services Revenues and $1,800 in Laboratory Fees Revenues, prepare the required closing entry. The accounting period ends December 31.

SE 3.

LO 3   Closing Expense Accounts

Assuming debit balances at the end of the accounting period of $1,400 in Rent Expense, $1,100 in Wages Expense, and $500 in Other Expenses, prepare the required closing entry. The accounting period ends December 31.

SE 4.

LO 3   Closing the Income Summary Account

Assuming that total revenues were $5,200 and total expenses were $3,000, prepare the journal entry to close the Income Summary account to the R. Richards, Capital account. The accounting period ends December 31.

LO 3 **Closing the Withdrawals Account**

SE 5. Assuming that withdrawals during the accounting period were $800, prepare the journal entry to close the R. Richards, Withdrawals account to the R. Richards, Capital account. The accounting period ends December 31.

LO 3 **Posting Closing Entries**

SE 6. Show the effects of the transactions in **SE 2, SE 3, SE 4,** and **SE 5** by entering beginning balances in appropriate T accounts and recording the transactions. Assume that the R. Richards, Capital account has a beginning balance of $1,300.

LO 5 **Preparation of Reversing Entries**

SE 7. Below, indicated by letters, are the adjusting entries at the end of March. Prepare the required reversing entry.

Account Name	Debit	Credit
Prepaid Insurance		(a) 180
Accumulated Depreciation, Office Equipment		(b) 1,050
Salaries Expense	(c) 360	
Insurance Expense	(a) 180	
Depreciation Expense, Office Equipment	(b) 1,050	
Salaries Payable		(c) 360
	1,590	1,590

LO 5 **Effects of Reversing Entries**

SE 8. Assume that prior to the adjustments in **SE 7**, Salaries Expense had a debit balance of $1,800 and Salaries Payable had a zero balance. Prepare a T account for each of these accounts. Enter the beginning balance; post the adjustment for accrued salaries, the appropriate closing entry, and the reversing entry; and enter the transaction in the T accounts for a payment of $480 for salaries on April 3.

LO 3 **Preparing Closing Entries**
LO 7 **from a Work Sheet**

SE 9. Prepare the required closing entries for the year ended December 31, using the following items from the Income Statement columns of a work sheet and assuming that withdrawals by the owner, R. Carrera, were $6,000:

	Income Statement	
Account Name	Debit	Credit
Repair Revenue		32,860
Wages Expense	12,260	
Rent Expense	1,800	
Supplies Expense	6,390	
Insurance Expense	1,370	
Depreciation Expense, Repair Equipment	2,020	
	23,840	32,860
Net Income	9,020	
	32,860	32,860

EXERCISES

LO 3 **Preparation of Closing Entries**

E 1. The adjusted trial balance for the Beede Realty Corporation at the end of its fiscal year is shown at the top of the next page. Prepare the required closing entries.

Beede Realty Corporation Adjusted Trial Balance December 31, 20xx		
Cash	$ 7,275	
Accounts Receivable	2,325	
Prepaid Insurance	585	
Office Supplies	440	
Office Equipment	6,300	
Accumulated Depreciation, Office Equipment		$ 765
Automobile	6,750	
Accumulated Depreciation, Automobile		750
Accounts Payable		1,700
Unearned Management Fees		1,500
P. Beede, Capital		14,535
P. Beede, Withdrawals	7,000	
Sales Commissions Earned		31,700
Office Salaries Expense	13,500	
Advertising Expense	2,525	
Rent Expense	2,650	
Telephone Expense	1,600	
	$50,950	$50,950

LO 5 Reversing Entries

E 2. Selected September T accounts for Quintera Company are as follows:

Supplies

9/1 Bal.	860	9/30 Adjust.	1,280
Sept. purchases	940		
Bal.	520		

Supplies Expense

9/30 Adjust.	1,280	9/30 Closing	1,280
Bal.	—		

Wages Payable

		9/30 Adjust.	640
		Bal.	640

Wages Expense

Sept. wages	3,940	9/30 Closing	4,580
9/30 Adjust.	640		
Bal.	—		

1. In which of these accounts would a reversing entry be helpful? Why?
2. Prepare the appropriate reversing entry.
3. Prepare the entry to record payments on October 3 for wages totaling $3,140. How much of this amount represents wages expense for October?

LO 6 Preparation of a Trial Balance

E 3. The following alphabetical list represents the accounts and balances for Ali Realty on June 30, 20x3. All the accounts have normal balances.

Accounts Payable	$15,420	Cash	$ 7,635
Accounts Receivable	7,650	Office Equipment	15,510
Accumulated Depreciation,		Prepaid Insurance	1,680
Office Equipment	1,350	Rent Expense	7,200
Advertising Expense	1,800	Revenue from Commissions	57,900
Ali, Capital	30,630	Supplies	825
Ali, Withdrawals	27,000	Wages Expense	36,000

Prepare a trial balance by listing the accounts in the correct order, with the balances in the appropriate debit or credit column.

E 4.
The following is an alphabetically arranged list of accounts and balances, in highly simplified form. This information is for the month ended March 31, 20xx.

Trial Balance Accounts and Balances

Accounts Payable	$ 4
Accounts Receivable	7
Accumulated Depreciation, Office Equipment	1
Cash	4
Office Equipment	8
Prepaid Insurance	2
Service Revenue	23
Supplies	4
Toni Smith, Capital	12
Toni Smith, Withdrawals	6
Unearned Revenues	3
Utilities Expense	2
Wages Expense	10

1. Prepare a work sheet, entering the trial balance accounts in the order in which they would normally appear, and arranging the balances in the correct debit or credit column.

2. Complete the work sheet using the following information:
   a. Expired insurance, $1.
   b. Of the unearned revenue balance, $2 has been earned by the end of the month.
   c. Estimated depreciation on office equipment, $1.
   d. Accrued wages, $1.
   e. Unused supplies on hand, $1.

E 5.
The Capital, Withdrawals, and Income Summary accounts for Axel's Barber Shop are shown in T account form below. The closing entries have been recorded for the year ended December 31, 20x1.

Axel Tyler, Capital

12/31/x1	4,500	12/31/x0	13,000
		12/31/x1	9,500
		Bal.	18,000

Income Summary

12/31/x1	21,500	12/31/x1	31,000
12/31/x1	9,500		
Bal.	—		

Axel Tyler, Withdrawals

4/1/x1	1,500	12/31/x1	4,500
7/1/x1	1,500		
10/1/x1	1,500		
Bal.	—		

Prepare a statement of owner's equity for Axel's Barber Shop.

E 6.
At the top of the next page is a partial work sheet in which the Trial Balance and Income Statement columns have been completed. All amounts shown are in dollars.

1. Show the adjustments that have been made in journal form without explanations.

2. Prepare a balance sheet.

Account Name	Trial Balance Debit	Trial Balance Credit	Income Statement Debit	Income Statement Credit
Cash	14			
Accounts Receivable	24			
Supplies	22			
Prepaid Insurance	16			
Building	50			
Accumulated Depreciation, Building		16		
Accounts Payable		8		
Unearned Revenues		4		
T.L., Capital		64		
Revenues		88		92
Wages Expense	54		60	
	180	180		
Insurance Expense			8	
Supplies Expense			16	
Depreciation Expense, Building			4	
Wages Payable				
			88	92
Net Income			4	
			92	92

E 7.

LO 5   Preparation of Adjusting
LO 7   and Reversing Entries from
Work Sheet Columns

The items below are from the Adjustments columns of a work sheet that is dated June 30.

Account Name	Adjustments Debit	Adjustments Credit
Prepaid Insurance		(a) 240
Office Supplies		(b) 630
Accumulated Depreciation, Office Equipment		(c) 1,400
Accumulated Depreciation, Store Equipment		(d) 2,200
Office Salaries Expense	(e) 240	
Store Salaries Expense	(e) 480	
Insurance Expense	(a) 240	
Office Supplies Expense	(b) 630	
Depreciation Expense, Office Equipment	(c) 1,400	
Depreciation Expense, Store Equipment	(d) 2,200	
Salaries Payable		(e) 720
	5,190	5,190

1. Prepare the adjusting entries.

2. Where required, prepare appropriate reversing entries.

E 8.

LO 3   Preparation of Closing
LO 7   Entries from the Work Sheet

The items at the top of the next page are from the Income Statement columns of the work sheet of the Saroyan Repair Shop for the year ended December 31, 20xx.

Prepare entries to close the revenue, expense, Income Summary, and Withdrawals accounts. Mr. Saroyan withdrew $5,000 during the year.

Account Name	Income Statement	
	Debit	Credit
Repair Revenue		25,620
Wages Expense	8,110	
Rent Expense	1,200	
Supplies Expense	4,260	
Insurance Expense	915	
Depreciation Expense, Repair Equipment	1,345	
	15,830	25,620
Net Income	9,790	
	25,620	25,620

PROBLEMS

P 1.

The adjusted trial balance for Glorry Bowling Lanes at the end of the company's fiscal year appears below.

Glorry Bowling Lanes
Adjusted Trial Balance
December 31, 20x3

	Debit	Credit
Cash	$ 8,107	
Accounts Receivable	3,694	
Supplies	78	
Prepaid Insurance	150	
Land	2,500	
Building	50,000	
Accumulated Depreciation, Building		$ 13,600
Equipment	62,500	
Accumulated Depreciation, Equipment		16,500
Accounts Payable		15,022
Notes Payable		35,000
Unearned Revenues		150
Wages Payable		1,981
Property Taxes Payable		5,000
Emma Glorry, Capital		30,406
Emma Glorry, Withdrawals	12,000	
Revenues		309,132
Wages Expense	190,538	
Advertising Expense	15,100	
Maintenance Expense	42,050	
Supplies Expense	574	
Insurance Expense	750	
Depreciation Expense, Building	2,400	
Depreciation Expense, Equipment	5,500	
Utilities Expense	21,100	
Miscellaneous Expense	4,750	
Property Taxes Expense	5,000	
	$426,791	$426,791

REQUIRED

1. Prepare T accounts and enter the balance for Emma Glorry, Capital; Emma Glorry, Withdrawals; Income Summary; and all revenue and expense accounts.

2. Enter in the T accounts the four required closing entries, labeling the components *a*, *b*, *c*, and *d* as appropriate.

3. Prepare an income statement, a statement of owner's equity, and a balance sheet.

P 2.

LO 3 Closing Entries Using Journal Form and Preparation of Financial Statements

Pines Recreational Park, owned by Emmett Howes, rents campsites in a wooded park. The adjusted trial balance for Pines Recreational Park on November 30, 20x3, the end of the current fiscal year, is shown below.

Pines Recreational Park
Adjusted Trial Balance
November 30, 20x3

Cash	$ 4,080	
Accounts Receivable	7,320	
Supplies	228	
Prepaid Insurance	1,188	
Land	30,000	
Building	91,800	
Accumulated Depreciation, Building		$ 21,000
Accounts Payable		3,450
Wages Payable		1,650
Emmett Howes, Capital		93,070
Emmett Howes, Withdrawals	36,000	
Campsite Rentals		88,200
Wages Expense	23,850	
Insurance Expense	3,784	
Utilities Expense	1,800	
Supplies Expense	1,320	
Depreciation Expense, Building	6,000	
	$207,370	$207,370

REQUIRED

1. From the information given, prepare an income statement, a statement of owner's equity, and a balance sheet. Assume no additional investments by the owner.

2. Record the closing entries in journal form.

3. Assuming that Wages Payable represents wages accrued at the end of the accounting period, record the optional reversing entry on December 1.

P 3.

LO 1 The Complete Accounting
LO 3 Cycle Without a Work Sheet:
LO 4 Two Months (*second month optional*)

Will Springer opened the Springer Repair Store on May 1, 20xx. During the month, he completed the following transactions for the company:

May 1 Began business by depositing $6,000 in a company bank account.
     1 Paid the premium on a one-year insurance policy, $600.
     1 Paid the current month's rent, $520.
     2 Purchased repair equipment from Fisk Company for $2,200. The terms were $300 down and $100 per month for nineteen months. The first payment is due June 1.
     5 Purchased repair supplies from Cordero Company on credit, $195.
   14 Paid the utilities bill for May, $77.
   15 Received cash bicycle repair revenue for the first half of May, $681.
   20 Paid Cordero Company on account, $100.
   29 Withdrew cash for personal expenses, $400.
   31 Received cash bicycle repair revenue for the last half of May, $655.

REQUIRED FOR MAY

1. Prepare journal entries to record the May transactions.
2. Open the following accounts: Cash (111); Prepaid Insurance (117); Repair Supplies (119); Repair Equipment (144); Accumulated Depreciation, Repair Equipment (145); Accounts Payable (212); Will Springer, Capital (311); Will Springer, Withdrawals (312); Income Summary (313); Bicycle Repair Revenue (411); Store Rent Expense (511); Utilities Expense (512); Insurance Expense (513); Repair Supplies Expense (514); and Depreciation Expense, Repair Equipment (515). Post the May journal entries to the ledger accounts.
3. Using the following information, record adjusting entries in the general journal and post to the ledger accounts.
    a. One month's insurance has expired.
    b. The remaining inventory of unused repair supplies is $97.
    c. The estimated depreciation on repair equipment is $35.
4. From the accounts in the ledger, prepare an adjusted trial balance. (Note: Normally a trial balance is prepared before adjustments, but this is omitted here to save time.)
5. From the adjusted trial balance, prepare an income statement, a statement of owner's equity, and a balance sheet for May.
6. Prepare and post closing entries for May.
7. Prepare a post-closing trial balance for May.

(*Optional*) During June, Will Springer completed the following transactions for the Springer Repair Store:

June 1 Paid the monthly rent, $520.
      1 Made the monthly payment to Fisk Company, $100.
      9 Purchased repair supplies on credit from Cordero Company, $447.
     15 Received cash bicycle repair revenue for the first half of June, $525.
     18 Paid the utilities bill for June, $83.
     19 Paid Cordero Company on account, $200.
     28 Withdrew cash for personal expenses, $400.
     30 Received cash bicycle repair revenue for the last half of June, $687.

REQUIRED FOR JUNE

8. Prepare and post journal entries to record the June transactions.
9. Using the following information, record adjusting entries in the general journal and post to the ledger accounts:
    a. One month's insurance has expired.
    b. The inventory of unused repair supplies is $209.
    c. The estimated depreciation on repair equipment is $35.
10. From the accounts in the ledger, prepare an adjusted trial balance.
11. From the adjusted trial balance, prepare an income statement, a statement of owner's equity, and a balance sheet for June.
12. Prepare and post closing entries for June.
13. Prepare a post-closing trial balance for June.

P 4.
LO 3 Preparation of a Work
LO 5 Sheet; Financial Statements;
LO 6 and Adjusting, Closing,
LO 7 and Reversing Entries

Roman Patel began his consulting practice immediately after earning his MBA. Several clients paid him retainers (payment in advance) for future services. Other clients paid when service was provided. After one year, the firm had the trial balance that appears at the top of the next page.

REQUIRED

1. Enter the trial balance amounts in the Trial Balance columns of a work sheet, and complete the work sheet using the following information.
    a. Inventory of unused supplies, $58.
    b. Estimated depreciation on office equipment, $600.
    c. Services rendered during the month but not yet billed, $725.
    d. Services rendered to clients who paid in advance that should be applied against unearned retainers, $3,150.
    e. Wages earned by employees, but not yet paid, $120.

Roman Patel, Consultant
Trial Balance
December 31, 20x3

Cash	$ 3,250	
Accounts Receivable	2,709	
Office Supplies	382	
Office Equipment	3,755	
Accounts Payable		$ 1,296
Unearned Retainers		5,000
Roman Patel, Capital		4,000
Roman Patel, Withdrawals	6,000	
Consulting Fees		18,175
Rent Expense	1,800	
Utilities Expense	717	
Wages Expense	9,858	
	$28,471	$28,471

2. Prepare an income statement, a statement of owner's equity, and a balance sheet. Assume no additional investments by Roman Patel.

3. Prepare adjusting, closing, and, when possible, reversing entries.

4. How would you evaluate Patel's first year in practice?

P 5.

LO 3 **Preparation of a Work**
LO 5 **Sheet; Financial Statements;**
LO 6 **and Adjusting, Closing,**
LO 7 **and Reversing Entries**

At the end of the current fiscal year, the trial balance of the Esquire Theater appeared as follows:

Esquire Theater
Trial Balance
December 31, 20x3

Cash	$ 15,900	
Accounts Receivable	9,272	
Prepaid Insurance	9,800	
Office Supplies	390	
Cleaning Supplies	1,795	
Land	10,000	
Building	200,000	
Accumulated Depreciation, Building		$ 19,700
Theater Furnishings	185,000	
Accumulated Depreciation, Theater Furnishings		32,500
Office Equipment	15,800	
Accumulated Depreciation, Office Equipment		7,780
Accounts Payable		22,753
Gift Books Liability		20,950
Mortgage Payable		150,000
Mildred Brown, Capital		156,324
Mildred Brown, Withdrawals	30,000	
Ticket Sales Revenue		205,700
Theater Rental		22,600
Usher Wages Expense	92,000	
Office Wages Expense	12,000	
Utilities Expense	56,350	
	$638,307	$638,307

REQUIRED

1. Enter the trial balance amounts in the Trial Balance columns of a work sheet, and complete the work sheet using the following information.
   a. Expired insurance, $8,700.
   b. Inventory of unused office supplies, $122.
   c. Inventory of unused cleaning supplies, $234.
   d. Estimated depreciation, building, $7,000.
   e. Estimated depreciation, theater furnishings, $18,000.
   f. Estimated depreciation, office equipment, $1,580.
   g. The company credits all gift books sold during the year to the Gift Books Liability account. A gift book is a booklet of ticket coupons purchased in advance as a gift. The recipient redeems the coupons at some point in the future. On December 31, it was estimated that $18,900 worth of the gift books had been redeemed.
   h. Accrued but unpaid usher wages at the end of the accounting period, $430.

2. Prepare an income statement, a statement of owner's equity, and a balance sheet. Assume no additional investments by Mildred Brown.

3. Prepare adjusting, closing, and, when possible, reversing entries from the work sheet.

ALTERNATE PROBLEMS

P 6.

LO 3   Closing Entries Using T Accounts and Preparation of Financial Statements

The adjusted trial balance for Palmetto Tennis Club at the end of the company's fiscal year appears below.

PalmettoTennis Club Adjusted Trial Balance June 30, 20x2		
Cash	$ 52,400	
Prepaid Advertising	19,200	
Supplies	2,400	
Land	200,000	
Building	1,290,400	
Accumulated Depreciation, Building		$ 520,000
Equipment	312,000	
Accumulated Depreciation, Equipment		100,800
Accounts Payable		146,000
Wages Payable		58,000
Property Taxes Payable		45,000
Unearned Revenues, Locker Fees		6,000
Bridget Lahey, Capital		942,300
Bridget Lahey, Withdrawals	108,000	
Revenues from Court Fees		1,356,200
Revenues from Locker Fees		19,200
Wages Expense	702,000	
Maintenance Expense	103,200	
Advertising Expense	79,500	
Utilities Expense	129,600	
Supplies Expense	52,000	
Depreciation Expense, Building	60,000	
Depreciation Expense, Equipment	24,000	
Property Taxes Expense	45,000	
Miscellaneous Expense	13,800	
	$3,193,500	$3,193,500

1. Prepare T accounts and enter the balance for Bridget Lahey, Capital; Bridget Lahey, Withdrawals; Income Summary; and all revenue and expense accounts.
2. Enter the four required closing entries in the T accounts, labeling the components *a*, *b*, *c*, and *d* as appropriate.
3. Prepare an income statement, a statement of owner's equity, and a balance sheet.

P 7.

LO 3 Closing Entries Using Journal Form and Preparation of Financial Statements

Quality Trailer Rental owns 30 small trailers that are rented by the day for local moving jobs. The adjusted trial balance for Quality Trailer Rental for the year ended June 30, 20x4, which is the end of the current fiscal year, is shown below.

Quality Trailer Rental Adjusted Trial Balance June 30, 20x4		
Cash	$ 692	
Accounts Receivable	972	
Supplies	119	
Prepaid Insurance	360	
Trailers	12,000	
Accumulated Depreciation, Trailers		$ 7,200
Accounts Payable		271
Wages Payable		200
Elena Mota, Capital		5,694
Elena Mota, Withdrawals	7,200	
Trailer Rentals		45,546
Wages Expense	23,400	
Insurance Expense	720	
Supplies Expense	266	
Depreciation Expense, Trailers	2,400	
Other Expenses	10,782	
	$58,911	$58,911

1. From the information given, record closing entries in journal form.
2. Prepare an income statement, a statement of owner's equity, and a balance sheet. Assume no additional investments by Elena Mota.

P 8.

LO 3 Preparation of a Work
LO 5 Sheet; Financial
LO 6 Statements; and Adjusting,
LO 7 Closing, and Reversing
Entries

The trial balance on the next page was taken from the ledger of Natchez Delivery Service on August 31, 20x2, the end of the company's fiscal year.

1. Enter the trial balance amounts in the Trial Balance columns of a work sheet and complete the work sheet using the following information:
   a. Expired insurance, $3,060.
   b. Inventory of unused delivery supplies, $1,430.
   c. Inventory of unused office supplies, $186.
   d. Estimated depreciation, building, $14,400.
   e. Estimated depreciation, trucks, $15,450.
   f. Estimated depreciation, office equipment, $2,700.
   g. The company credits the lockbox fees of customers who pay in advance to the Unearned Lockbox Fees account. Of the amount credited to this account during the year, $5,630 had been earned by December 31.

Natchez Delivery Service
Trial Balance
August 31, 20x2

Cash	$ 10,072	
Accounts Receivable	29,314	
Prepaid Insurance	5,340	
Delivery Supplies	14,700	
Office Supplies	2,460	
Land	15,000	
Building	196,000	
Accumulated Depreciation, Building		$ 53,400
Trucks	103,800	
Accumulated Depreciation, Trucks		30,900
Office Equipment	15,900	
Accumulated Depreciation, Office Equipment		10,800
Accounts Payable		9,396
Unearned Lockbox Fees		8,340
Mortgage Payable		72,000
Honore Natchez, Capital		128,730
Honore Natchez, Withdrawals	30,000	
Delivery Service Revenue		283,470
Lockbox Fees Earned		28,800
Truck Drivers' Wages Expense	120,600	
Office Salaries Expense	44,400	
Gas, Oil, and Truck Repairs Expense	31,050	
Interest Expense	7,200	
	$625,836	$625,836

h. Lockbox fees earned but unrecorded and uncollected at the end of the accounting period, $816.
i. Accrued but unpaid truck drivers' wages at the end of the year, $1,920.

2. Prepare an income statement, a statement of owner's equity, and a balance sheet. Assume no additional investments by Honore Natchez.

3. Prepare adjusting, closing, and, when possible, reversing entries from the work sheet.

EXPANDING YOUR CRITICAL THINKING, COMMUNICATION, AND INTERPERSONAL SKILLS

SKILLS DEVELOPMENT

Conceptual Analysis

LO 1 Interim Financial Statements

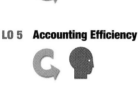

SD 1. *Ocean Oil Services Corporation* provides services for drilling operations off the coast of Louisiana. The company owes a significant amount of money to River National Bank in Baton Rouge. The bank requires the company to provide it with financial statements every quarter.

Explain what is involved in preparing financial statements every quarter.

LO 5 Accounting Efficiency

SD 2. *Way Heaters Company,* located just outside Milwaukee, Wisconsin, is a small, successful manufacturer of industrial heaters. The company's heaters are used, for instance, by candy manufacturers to heat chocolate. The company sells its heaters to some of its customers on credit with generous terms. The terms usually specify payment six months after purchase and an interest rate based on current bank rates. Because the interest on the loans accrues a little bit every day but is not paid until the due date of the note, it is necessary to make an adjusting entry at the end of each accounting period to debit Interest Receivable and credit Interest Income for the amount of the interest accrued but not received to date. The company prepares financial statements every month.

Keeping track of what has been accrued in the past is time-consuming because the notes carry different dates and interest rates. Discuss what the accountant can do to simplify the process of making the adjusting entry for accrued interest each month.

Ethical Dilemma

LO 1 Ethics and Time Pressure

SD 3. Jay Wheeler, the assistant accountant for *WB Company,* has made adjusting entries and is preparing the adjusted trial balance for the first six months of the year. Financial statements must be delivered to the bank by 5 o'clock to support a critical loan agreement. By noon, Wheeler cannot balance the adjusted trial balance. The figures are off by $1,320, so he increases the balance of the owner's Capital account by $1,320. He closes the accounts, prepares the statements, and sends them to the bank on time. Wheeler hopes that no one will notice the problem and believes that he can find the error and correct it by the end of next month.

Are Jay Wheeler's actions ethical? Explain why or why not. Did Wheeler have other alternatives?

Research Activity

LO 1 Interview of a Local
LO 2 Businessperson
LO 3
LO 4
LO 5
LO 7

SD 4. Arrange to spend about an hour interviewing the owner, manager, or accountant of a local service or retail business. Your goal is to learn as much as you can about the accounting cycle of the person's business. Ask the interviewee to show you his or her accounting records and to tell you how such transactions as sales, purchases, payments, and payroll are handled. Examine the documents used to support the transactions. Look at any journals, ledgers, or work sheets. Does the business use a computer? Does

| Cash Flow | CD-ROM |  Communication | Critical Thinking | Ethics | General Ledger | Group Activity | Hot Links to Real Companies | International | Internet | Key Ratio | Memo | Spreadsheet |

it use its own accounting system, or does it use an outside or centralized service? Does it use the cash or the accrual basis of accounting? When does it prepare adjusting entries? When does it prepare closing entries? How often does it prepare financial statements? Does it prepare reversing entries? How do its procedures differ from those described in the text?

When the interview is finished, organize and write up your findings and be prepared to present them to your class.

Group Activity: Divide the class into groups and assign each group to a different type of business, such as shoe store, fast food, grocery, hardware, records, and others. Have the groups give presentations in class.

Decision-Making Practice

SD 5.
LO 1 Conversion from Accrual
LO 3 to Cash Statement

Adele's Secretarial Service is a simple business. Adele provides typing services for students at the local university. Her accountant prepared the income statement that appears below for the year ended June 30, 20x4.

Adele's Secretarial Service **Income Statement** **For the Year Ended June 30, 20x4**		
Revenues		
Typing Services		$20,980
Expenses		
Rent Expense	$2,400	
Depreciation Expense, Office Equipment	2,200	
Supplies Expense	960	
Other Expenses	1,240	
Total Expenses		6,800
Net Income		$14,180

In reviewing this statement, Adele is puzzled. She knows she withdrew from the company $15,600 in cash for personal expenses, yet the cash balance in the company's bank account increased from $460 to $3,100 from last June 30 to this June 30. She wants to know how her net income could be less than the cash withdrawals she took out of the business if there is an increase in the cash balance.

Her accountant has completed the closing entries and shows her the balance sheets for June 30, 20x4, and June 30, 20x3. She explains that besides the change in the cash balance, accounts receivable from customers decreased by $1,480 and accounts payable increased by $380 (supplies are the only items Adele buys on credit). The only other asset or liability account that changed during the year was Accumulated Depreciation, Office Equipment, which increased by $2,200.

1. Verify the cash balance increase by preparing a statement that lists the receipts of cash and the expenditures of cash during the year.

2. Write a memorandum to Adele explaining why the accountant is answering her question by pointing out year-to-year changes in the balance sheet. Include in your memorandum an explanation of your treatment of depreciation expense, giving your reasons for the treatment.

FINANCIAL REPORTING AND ANALYSIS

Interpreting Financial Reports

FRA 1.

LO 2 **Closing Entries**
LO 3

H&R Block, Inc., is the world's largest tax preparation service firm. Information adapted from the statement of earnings (in thousands) from its annual report for the year ended April 30, 1999, is as follows:[3]

Revenues	
Service Revenues	$1,324,494
Product Sales	174,124
Royalties	123,201
Other Revenues	22,846
Total Revenues	$1,644,665
Expenses	
Employee Compensation and Benefits	$ 610,866
Occupancy and Equipment Expense	232,003
Marketing and Advertising Expense	90,056
Bad Debt Expense	71,662
Interest Expense	69,038
Supplies, Freight, and Postage Expense	57,457
Other Operating Expenses	158,509
Total Expenses	$1,289,591
Earnings Before Income Taxes	$ 355,074
Income Taxes	145,746
Net Earnings	$ 209,328

The company reported distributing cash in the amount of $95,004,000 to the owners in 1999.

REQUIRED

1. Prepare, in journal form, the closing entries that would have been made by H&R Block on April 30, 1999. Treat income taxes as an expense, and treat cash distributions as withdrawals.

2. Based on the way you handled expenses and cash distributions in 1 and their ultimate effect on the owner's capital, what theoretical reason can you give for not including expenses and cash distributions in the same closing entry?

International Company

FRA 2.

LO 1 **Accounting Cycle and**
LO 3 **Closing Entries**

Nestlé S.A., maker of such well-known products as Nescafé, Lean Cuisine, and Perrier, is one of the largest and most internationally diverse companies in the world. Only 2 percent of its $52.2 billion in revenues comes from its home country of Switzerland, with the rest coming from sales in almost every other country of the world. Nestlé has over 220,000 employees in 70 countries[4] and is highly decentralized; that is, many of its divisions operate as separate companies in their countries. Managing the accounting operations of such a vast empire is a tremendous challenge. In what ways do you think the accounting cycle, including the closing process, would be the same for Nestlé as it is for Joan Miller Advertising Agency, and in what ways would it be different?

Toys "R" Us Annual Report

FRA 3.

LO 1 **Fiscal Year, Closing Process, and Interim Reports**

Refer to the Notes to Consolidated Financial Statements in the Toys "R" Us annual report. When does Toys "R" Us end its fiscal year? What reasons can you give for the company's having chosen this date? From the standpoint of completing the accounting cycle, what advantages does this date have? Does Toys "R" Us prepare interim financial statements? What are the implications of interim financial statements for the accounting cycle?

Fingraph® Financial Analyst™

This activity is not applicable to the chapter.

Internet Case

FRA 4.

LO 1 **Interim Financial Statements**

Go to the Needles Accounting Resource Center web site at http://college.hmco.com and access the web site for *Dell Computer Corporation.* Find the latest quarterly financial report. Compare the results of the latest quarter available to you with the one in the Decision Point at the beginning of this chapter. Are Dell's net revenue (sales) and net income greater or less in the more recent quarter? What other information do you find in the quarterly report?

ENDNOTES

1. Dell Computer Corporation, *Annual Report*, 1999.
2. Earl E. Robertson, and Dean Lockwood, "Tapping the Power of the PC at General Mills," *Management Accounting*, August 1994.
3. Adapted from H&R Block, Inc., *Annual Report*, 1999.
4. Nestlé S.A., *Annual Report*, 1998.

Comprehensive Problem: Joan Miller Advertising Agency

This problem continues with the Joan Miller Advertising Agency, the company used to illustrate the accounting cycle in the chapters on measuring business transactions, measuring business income, and completing the accounting cycle. It is necessary in some instances to refer to those chapters in completing this problem.

The January 31, 20xx, post-closing trial balance for the Joan Miller Advertising Agency is as follows:

Joan Miller Advertising Agency
Post-Closing Trial Balance
January 31, 20xx

Cash	$ 1,720	
Accounts Receivable	2,800	
Fees Receivable	200	
Art Supplies	1,300	
Office Supplies	600	
Prepaid Rent	400	
Prepaid Insurance	440	
Art Equipment	4,200	
Accumulated Depreciation, Art Equipment		$ 70
Office Equipment	3,000	
Accumulated Depreciation, Office Equipment		50
Accounts Payable		3,170
Unearned Art Fees		600
Wages Payable		180
Joan Miller, Capital		10,590
	$14,660	$14,660

During February, the agency engaged in the following transactions.

Feb. 1 Received an additional investment of cash from Joan Miller, $6,300.
2 Purchased additional office equipment with cash, $1,200.

Feb. 5 Received art equipment transferred to the business from Joan Miller, $1,400.
6 Purchased additional office supplies with cash, $90.
7 Purchased additional art supplies on credit from Taylor Supply Company, $450.
8 Completed the series of advertisements for Marsh Tire Company that began on January 31 (see page 106) and billed Marsh Tire Company for the total services performed, including the accrued revenues (fees receivable) that had been recognized in an adjusting entry in January, $800.
9 Paid the secretary for two weeks' wages, $600.
12 Paid the amount due to Morgan Equipment for the office equipment purchased last month, $1,500.
13 Accepted an advance fee in cash for artwork to be done for another agency, $1,600.
14 Purchased a copier (office equipment) from Morgan Equipment for $2,100, paying $350 in cash and agreeing to pay the rest in equal payments over the next five months.
15 Performed advertising services and received a cash fee, $1,450.
16 Received payment on account from Ward Department Stores for services performed last month, $2,800.
19 Paid amount due for the telephone bill that was received and recorded at the end of January, $70.
20 Performed advertising services for Ward Department Stores and agreed to accept payment next month, $3,200.
21 Performed art services for a cash fee, $580.
22 Received and paid the utility bill for February, $110.
23 Paid the secretary for two weeks' wages, $600.
26 Paid the rent for March in advance, $400.
27 Received the telephone bill for February, which is to be paid next month, $80.
28 Paid out cash to Joan Miller as a withdrawal for personal living expenses, $1,400.

REQUIRED

1. Record in the general journal and post to the general ledger the optional reversing entries on February 1 for Wages Payable and Fees Receivable (see Adjustment **g** on page 104 and Adjustment **i** on page 106). (Begin the general journal on Page 5.)

2. Record the transactions for February in the general journal.

3. Post the February transactions to the general ledger accounts.

4. Prepare a trial balance in the Trial Balance columns of a work sheet.

5. Prepare adjusting entries and complete the work sheet using the information below.
   a. One month's prepaid rent has expired, $400.
   b. One month's prepaid insurance has expired, $40.
   c. An inventory of art supplies reveals $600 still on hand on February 28.
   d. An inventory of office supplies reveals $410 still on hand on February 28.
   e. Depreciation on art equipment for February is calculated to be $100.
   f. Depreciation on office equipment for February is calculated to be $100.
   g. Art services performed for which payment has been received in advance total $1,300.
   h. Advertising services performed that will not be billed until March total $290.
   i. Three days' wages had accrued by the end of February (assume a five-day week).

6. From the work sheet prepare an income statement, a statement of owner's equity, and a balance sheet.

7. Record the adjusting entries in the general journal, and post them to the general ledger.

8. Record the closing entries in the general journal, and post them to the general ledger.

9. Prepare a post-closing trial balance.

This Comprehensive Problem covers all of the Learning Objectives in the chapters on measuring business transactions, measuring business income, and completing the accounting cycle.

5

Merchandising Operations

Target Stores The management of merchandising businesses has two key decisions to make: the price at which merchandise is sold and the level of service the company provides. For example, a department store can set the price of its merchandise at a relatively high level and provide a great deal of service. A discount store, on the other hand, may price its merchandise at a relatively low level and provide limited service. The figures in the table below show that Target Stores, a division of Target Corp., is successful.[1] What decisions did Target Stores' management make about pricing and service to achieve this success?

Target distinguishes itself from other discounters by providing its guests with quality, trend-right merchandise, superior service, a convenient shopping experience, and competitive prices. In other words, Target emphasizes high-quality, name-brand merchandise that might be sold at full price in specialty stores, but sells it at discount prices that are competitive with the prices of other discount stores that sell less well-known merchandise. Target's chief executive officer says, "Our performance in 1999 was driven by superior results at our Target division. . . . At the core of Target's future growth and financial success is our differentiated merchandise strategy."[2]

Financial Highlights

(Millions of dollars, except stores and square feet)

	1999	1998	1997
Revenues	$26,080	$23,014	$20,368
Operating profit	$ 2,022	$ 1,578	$ 1,287
Stores	912	851	796
Retail square feet*	102,945	94,553	87,158

*In thousands, reflects total square feet, less office, warehouse, and vacant space.

Management Issues in Merchandising Businesses

OBJECTIVE

1 Identify the management issues related to merchandising businesses

Up to this point you have studied business and accounting issues related to the simplest type of business—the service business. **Service businesses**, such as advertising agencies and law firms, perform services for fees or commissions. **Merchandising businesses**, on the other hand, earn income by buying and selling products or merchandise. These companies, whether wholesale or retail, use the same basic accounting methods as do service companies, but the buying and selling of merchandise adds to the complexity of the process. As a foundation for discussing the accounting issues of merchandising businesses, we must first identify the management issues involved in running such a business.

VIDEO CASE

 ## Office Depot, Inc.

Objectives

■ To become familiar with the nature of merchandising operations.

■ To identify the management issues associated with a merchandising business.

■ To show how gross margin and operating expenses affect the business goal of profitability.

Background for the Case

All retailing companies are merchandising companies. Office Depot, Inc., is the world's largest office products

 retailer and one of the fastest-growing retailing companies in the world. Through its chain of office products superstores and delivery warehouses, the company serves the growing market of small and medium-size businesses, home offices, and individual consumers. A typical Office Depot store is 25,000 to 30,000 square feet in size and features over 6,000 name-brand products at prices that are generally 60 percent below manufacturers' suggested retail or catalogue prices. Office Depot's merchandise assortment includes office supplies, business electronics, state-of-the-art computer hardware and software, office furniture, and a complete business service center. The company operates a national network of Customer Service Centers where customers can pick up purchases or have them

delivered. The delivery business represents more than 30 percent of the company's total sales. Office Depot is expanding by opening megastores of approximately 50,000 square feet, free-standing furniture stores, and copying and publishing services outlets. The company is faced with intense competition from companies such as OfficeMax, Inc., and Staples, Inc.

For more information about Office Depot, Inc., visit the company's web site through the Needles Accounting Resource Center web site at:
    http://college.hmco.com

Required

▶ View the video on Office Depot, Inc., that accompanies this book. As you are watching the video, take notes related to the following questions:

1. All merchandising companies have inventories and need to control these inventories. In your own words, what is inventory, and why is it important to implement controls over it? Identify the types of products that Office Depot typically has in inventory and some ways in which the company might control its inventory.

2. All merchandising companies have an operating cycle. Describe the operating cycle and explain how it applies to Office Depot.

3. All merchandising companies try to achieve the goal of profitability by producing a satisfactory gross margin and maintaining acceptable levels of operating expenses. What is gross margin, and how does it relate to operating expenses? Describe how Office Depot's operations affect gross margin and operating expenses in a way that enables the company to achieve superior profitability.

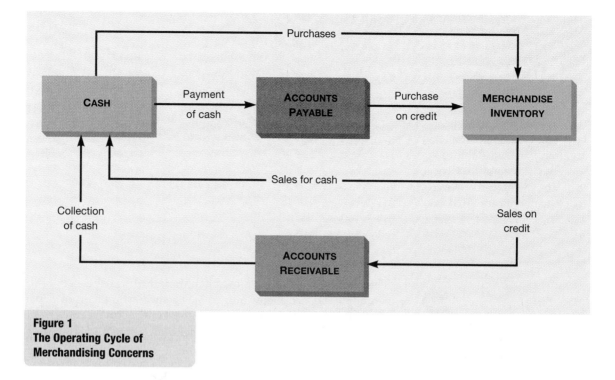

Figure 1
The Operating Cycle of Merchandising Concerns

Cash Flow Management

Merchandising businesses differ from service businesses in that they have goods on hand for sale to customers, called **merchandise inventory**, and they engage in a series of transactions called the **operating cycle**, as shown in Figure 1.

The transactions in the operating cycle of a merchandising business consist of (1) purchase of merchandise inventory for cash or on credit, (2) payment for purchases made on credit, (3) sales of merchandise inventory for cash or on credit, and (4) collection of cash from credit sales. Purchases of merchandise are usually made on credit, so the merchandiser has a period of time before payment is due, but this period is generally less than the time it takes to sell the merchandise. Therefore, management will have to plan for cash flows from within the company or from borrowing to finance the inventory until it is sold and the resulting revenue has been collected.

In the case of cash sales, the cash is collected immediately. Sales on bank credit cards, such as Visa or MasterCard, are considered cash sales because funds from these sales are available to the merchandiser immediately. In the case of credit sales, the merchandising concern must wait a period of time before receiving the cash. Some very small retail stores may have mostly cash or credit card sales and very few credit sales, whereas large wholesale concerns may have almost all credit sales. Most merchandising concerns, however, have a combination of cash sales and credit sales.

Regardless of the relationships of purchases, payments, cash and credit sales, and collections, the operators of a merchandising business must carefully manage cash flow, or liquidity. Such **cash flow management** involves planning the company's receipts and payments of cash. If a company is not able to pay its bills when they are due, it may be forced out of business. As mentioned above, merchandise that is purchased must often be paid for before it is sold and the cash from its sale collected. For example, if a retail business must pay for its purchases in 30 days, it must have cash available or arrange for borrowing if it cannot sell and collect payment for the merchandise in 30 days.

FOCUS ON BUSINESS TECHNOLOGY

An increasing percentage of merchandising transactions are conducted electronically. Credit cards have long been in use, but debit, purchase, and Smart cards are becoming integral parts of the so-called cashless society. The debit card allows consumers to access their bank accounts for ATM transactions or with any seller that accepts major credit cards. The price of the sale is withdrawn immediately from the customer's account when purchases are made at grocery stores, drugstores, gas stations, dry cleaners, or hardware stores. The purchase card, the business equivalent of a debit card, allows employees to purchase merchandise for their business. Smart cards have an embedded integrated circuit that stores information, such as prepaid amounts from which purchases are deducted at the point of purchase.

 The operating cycle for a merchandising firm can be 120 days, or even longer. For example, Dillard Dept. Stores, Inc., a successful chain of department stores in the South and Southwest regions of the United States, has an operating cycle of about 218 days. Its inventory is on hand an average of 78 days, and it takes, on average, 140 days to collect its receivables. Because the company pays for its merchandise in an average of 66 days, a much shorter time, management must carefully plan its cash flow.

Profitability Management

In addition to managing cash flow, management must achieve a satisfactory level of profitability in terms of performance measures. It must sell its merchandise at a price that exceeds its cost by a sufficient margin to pay operating expenses and have enough left to provide sufficient income, or profitability. **Profitability management** is a complex activity that includes, first, achieving a satisfactory gross margin and, second, maintaining acceptable levels of operating expenses. Achieving a satisfactory gross margin depends on setting appropriate prices for merchandise and purchasing merchandise at favorable prices and terms. Maintaining acceptable levels of operating expenses depends on controlling expenses and operating efficiently.

One of the more effective ways of controlling expenses is to use operating budgets. An **operating budget** reflects management's operating plans. It consists of detailed listings of projected selling expenses and general and administrative expenses for a company. At key times during the year and at the end of the year, management should compare the budget with actual expenses and make adjustments to operations as appropriate. An example of an operating budget for Fenwick Fashions Company is shown in Exhibit 1. Total selling expenses exceeded the budget by only $80, but four of the expense categories exceeded the budget by a total of $2,080. Management should investigate the possibility that underspending in advertising of $2,000 hid inefficiencies and waste in other areas. Also, sales may have been penalized by not spending the budgeted amount on advertising. Total general and administrative expenses exceeded the budget by $6,904. Management should determine why large differences occurred for office salaries expense, insurance expense, and office supplies expense. The amount of insurance expense is usually set by the insurance company; thus an error in the initial budgeting of insurance expense may have caused the unfavorable result. The operating budget helps management focus on the specific areas that need attention.

Exhibit 1
An Example of an Operating Budget

**Fenwick Fashions Company
Operating Budget
For the Year Ended December 31, 20x2**

Operating Expenses	Budget	Actual	Difference Under (Over) Budget
Selling Expenses			
Sales Salaries Expense	$22,000	$22,500	($ 500)
Freight Out Expense	5,500	5,740	(240)
Advertising Expense	12,000	10,000	2,000
Insurance Expense, Selling	800	1,600	(800)
Store Supplies Expense	1,000	1,540	(540)
Total Selling Expenses	$41,300	$41,380	($ 80)
General and Administrative Expenses			
Office Salaries Expense	$23,000	$26,900	($3,900)
Insurance Expense, General	2,100	4,200	(2,100)
Office Supplies Expense	500	1,204	(704)
Depreciation Expense, Building	2,600	2,600	—
Depreciation Expense, Office Equipment	2,000	2,200	(200)
Total General and Administrative Expenses	$30,200	$37,104	($6,904)
Total Operating Expenses	$71,500	$78,484	($6,984)

Choice of Inventory System

Another issue the management of a merchandising business must address is the choice of inventory system. Management must choose the system or combination of systems that is best for achieving the company's goals. There are two basic systems of accounting for the many items in the merchandise inventory: the perpetual inventory system and the periodic inventory system.

Under the **perpetual inventory system** continuous records are kept of the quantity and, usually, the cost of individual items as they are bought and sold. The detailed data available under the perpetual inventory system enable management to respond to customers' inquiries about product availability, to order inventory more effectively and thus avoid running out of stock, and to control the financial costs associated with investments in inventory. Under this system, the cost of each item is recorded in the Merchandise Inventory account when it is purchased. As merchandise is sold, its cost is transferred from the Merchandise Inventory account to the Cost of Goods Sold account. Thus, at all times the balance of the Merchandise Inventory account equals the cost of goods on hand, and the balance in Cost of Goods Sold equals the cost of merchandise sold to customers.

Under the **periodic inventory system**, the inventory not yet sold, or on hand, is counted periodically, usually at the end of the accounting period. No detailed records of the actual inventory on hand are maintained during the accounting period. The figure for inventory on hand is accurate only on the balance sheet date. As

FOCUS ON BUSINESS TECHNOLOGY

Many grocery stores, which traditionally used the periodic inventory system, now employ bar coding to update the physical inventory as items are sold. At the checkout counter, the cashier scans the electronic marking on each product, called a *bar code* or *universal product code* (UPC), into the cash register, which is linked to a computer. The price of the item appears on the cash register, and its sale is recorded by the computer. Bar coding has become common in all types of retail companies, and in manufacturing firms and hospitals as well. Some retail businesses now use the perpetual system for keeping track of the physical flow of inventory and the periodic system for preparing the financial statements.

soon as any purchases or sales are made, the figure becomes a historical amount, and it remains so until the new ending inventory amount is entered at the end of the next accounting period.

Some retail and wholesale businesses use periodic inventory systems to reduce the amount of clerical work. If a business is fairly small, management can maintain control over its inventory simply through observation or by the use of an off-line system of cards or computer records. On the other hand, for larger businesses, the lack of detailed records could lead to either lost sales or high operating costs.

Traditionally, the periodic inventory system has been used by companies that sell items of low value in high volume because of the difficulty and expense of accounting for the purchase and sale of each item. Examples of such companies are drugstores, automobile parts stores, department stores, discount stores, and grain companies. In contrast, companies that sell items of high unit value, such as appliances or automobiles, tend to use the perpetual inventory system. This distinction between high and low unit value for inventory systems has blurred considerably in recent years because of the widespread use of computers. Although use of the periodic inventory system is still widespread, use of the perpetual inventory system has increased greatly.

Control of Merchandising Operations

The principal transactions of merchandising businesses, such as buying and selling, involve assets—cash, accounts receivable, and merchandise inventory—that are vulnerable to theft and embezzlement. One reason for this vulnerability is that cash and inventory are fairly easy to steal. Another is that these assets are usually involved in a large number of transactions, such as cash receipts, receipts on account, payments for purchases, plus receipts and shipments of inventory, which can become difficult to monitor. If a merchandising company does not take steps to protect its assets, it can have high losses of cash and inventory. Management's responsibility is to establish an environment, accounting systems, and control procedures that will protect the company's assets. These systems and procedures are called **internal controls**.

Maintaining control over merchandise inventory is facilitated by taking a **physical inventory.** This process involves an actual count of all merchandise on hand. It can be a difficult task because it is easy to accidentally omit items or to count them twice. A physical inventory must be taken under both the periodic and the perpetual inventory systems.

Merchandise inventory includes all goods intended for sale that are owned by a concern, regardless of where they are located—on shelves, in storerooms, in warehouses, or in trucks between warehouses and stores. It also includes goods in transit from suppliers if title to the goods has passed to the merchant. Ending inventory does not include merchandise that has been sold but has not yet been delivered to customers or goods that cannot be sold because they are damaged or obsolete. If the damaged or obsolete goods can be sold at a reduced price, however, they should be included in ending inventory at their reduced value.

The actual count is usually taken after the close of business on the last day of the fiscal year. To facilitate taking the physical inventory, many companies end their fiscal year in a slow season, when inventories are at relatively low levels. Retail department stores often end their fiscal year in January or February, for example. After hours, at night, or on the weekend, employees count all items and record the results on numbered inventory tickets or sheets, following procedures to make sure that no items are missed. Sometimes a store closes for all or part of a day for inventory taking. The use of bar coding to take inventory electronically has greatly facilitated the taking of a physical inventory in many companies.

Income Statement for a Merchandising Concern

OBJECTIVE

2 Compare the income statements for service and merchandising concerns, and define the components of the merchandising income statement

Many service companies require only a simple income statement. For those companies, as shown in Figure 2, net income represents the difference between revenues and expenses. But merchandising companies, because they buy and sell merchandise inventory, require a more complex income statement. As shown in Figure 2, the income statement for a merchandiser consists of three major parts: (1) net

Figure 2
The Components of Income Statements for Service and Merchandising Companies

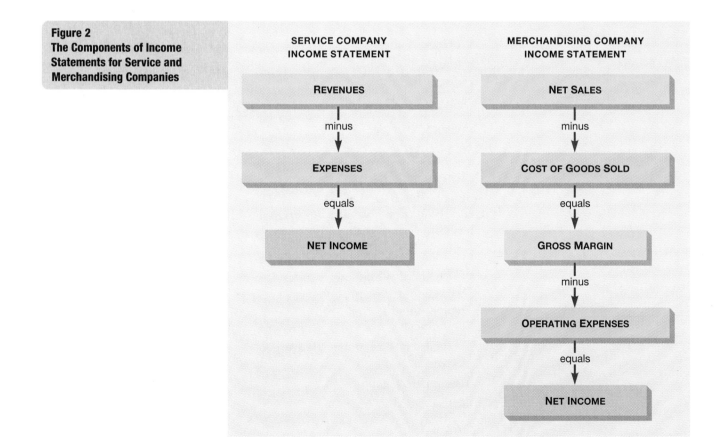

sales, (2) cost of goods sold, and (3) operating expenses. There is also a subtotal for gross margin.

The main difference between a merchandiser's income statement and that of a service business is that the merchandiser must compute gross margin before operating expenses are deducted. In the following discussion, the income statement for Fenwick Fashions Company, presented in Exhibit 2, will serve as an example of a merchandising income statement.

Net Sales

The first major part of the merchandising income statement is **net sales**, or often simply *sales*. Net sales consist of the gross proceeds from sales of merchandise, or gross sales, less sales returns and allowances. **Gross sales** consist of total cash sales and total credit sales occurring during an accounting period. Even though the cash may not be collected until the following accounting period, revenue is recognized, under the revenue recognition rule, as being earned when title for merchandise passes from seller to buyer at the time of sale. **Sales Returns and Allowances** is a contra-revenue account used to accumulate cash refunds, credits on account, and

---

Exhibit 2
Income Statement Under the Perpetual Inventory System

Fenwick Fashions Company
Income Statement
For the Year Ended December 31, 20x2

Net Sales			
Gross Sales			$246,350
Less Sales Returns and Allowances			7,025
Net Sales			$239,325
Cost of Goods Sold*			131,360
Gross Margin			$107,965
Operating Expenses			
Selling Expenses			
Sales Salaries Expense	$22,500		
Freight Out Expense	5,740		
Advertising Expense	10,000		
Insurance Expense, Selling	1,600		
Store Supplies Expense	1,540		
Total Selling Expenses		$41,380	
General and Administrative Expenses			
Office Salaries Expense	$26,900		
Insurance Expense, General	4,200		
Office Supplies Expense	1,204		
Depreciation Expense, Building	2,600		
Depreciation Expense, Office Equipment	2,200		
Total General and Administrative Expenses		37,104	
Total Operating Expenses			$ 78,484
Net Income			$ 29,481

*Freight In has been included in Cost of Goods Sold.

allowances off selling prices made to customers who have received defective or otherwise unsatisfactory products. If other discounts or allowances are given to customers (see supplemental objective 8, for instance), they also should be deducted from gross sales.

Management, investors, and others often use the amount of sales and trends suggested by sales as indicators of a firm's progress. Increasing sales suggest growth; decreasing sales indicate the possibility of decreased future earnings and other financial problems. To detect trends, comparisons are frequently made between the net sales of different accounting periods.

Cost of Goods Sold

Cost of goods sold, or simply *cost of sales*, is the amount a merchandiser paid for the merchandise sold during an accounting period or the cost to a manufacturer of manufacturing the products sold during an accounting period. It is the second part of the income statement for a merchandiser or manufacturer.

Gross Margin

The difference between net sales and cost of goods sold on the merchandising income statement is **gross margin**, or *gross profit*. To be successful, merchants must sell goods for an amount greater than cost—that is, gross margin must be great enough to pay operating expenses and provide an adequate income. Management is interested in both the amount and the percentage of gross margin. The percentage of gross margin is computed by dividing the dollar amount of gross margin by net sales. In the case of Fenwick Fashions, the dollar amount of gross margin is $107,965 and the percentage of gross margin is 45.1 percent ($107,965 ÷ $239,325). This information is helpful in planning business operations. For instance, management may try to increase total sales dollars by reducing the selling price. This strategy reduces the percentage of gross margin, but it will work if the total items sold increase enough to raise the absolute amount of gross margin. This is the strategy followed by a discount warehouse store like Sam's Clubs. On the other hand, management may keep a high gross margin and attempt to increase sales and the amount of gross margin by increasing operating expenses such as advertising. This is the strategy followed by upscale specialty stores like Neiman Marcus. Other strategies to increase gross margin, such as improving purchasing methods to reduce cost of goods sold, can also be explored.

Operating Expenses

The third major area of the merchandising income statement consists of **operating expenses**, which are the expenses other than cost of goods sold that are incurred in running a business. They are similar to the expenses of a service company. It is customary to group operating expenses into categories, such as selling expenses and general and administrative expenses. Selling expenses include the costs of storing goods and preparing them for sale, displaying, advertising, and otherwise promoting sales; making sales; and delivering goods to the buyer, if the seller bears the cost of delivery. The latter cost is often accumulated in an account called **Freight Out Expense** or *Delivery Expense*. Among the general and administrative expenses are general office expense, which includes expenses for accounting, personnel, credit and collections, and any other expenses that apply to overall operation. General occupancy expenses, such as rent expense, insurance expense, and utilities expense, are often classified as general and administrative expenses. However, they may also be allocated between the selling and the general and administrative categories. Careful planning and control of operating expenses can improve a company's profitability.

Net Income

Net income, the final figure or "bottom line" of the income statement, is what remains after operating expenses are deducted from gross margin. It is an important performance measure because it represents the amount of business earnings that accrue to the owners. It is the amount that is transferred to owner's equity from all the income-generating activities during the period. Both management and owners often use net income to measure whether a business has been operating successfully during the past accounting period.

Terms of Sale

OBJECTIVE

3 Define and distinguish the terms of sale for merchandising transactions

When goods are sold on credit, both parties should understand the amount and timing of payment as well as other terms of the purchase, such as who pays delivery or freight charges and what warranties or rights of return apply. Sellers quote prices in different ways. Many merchants quote the price at which they expect to sell their goods. Others, particularly manufacturers and wholesalers, provide a price list or catalogue and quote prices as a percentage (usually 30 percent or more) off the list or catalogue prices. Such a reduction of the list price is called a **trade discount.** For example, if an article was listed at $1,000 with a trade discount of 40 percent, or $400, the seller would record the sale at $600 and the buyer would record the purchase at $600. If the seller wishes to change the selling price, the trade discount can be raised or lowered. At times the trade discount may vary depending on the quantity purchased. The list price and trade discount are used only to reach agreement on price; they do not appear in the accounting records.

The terms of sale are usually printed on the sales invoice and thus constitute part of the sales agreement. Customary terms differ from industry to industry. In some industries, payment is expected in a short period of time, such as 10 or 30 days. In these cases, the invoice is marked "n/10" or "n/30" (read as "net 10" or "net 30"), meaning that the amount of the invoice is due either 10 days or 30 days after the invoice date. If the invoice is due 10 days after the end of the month, it is marked "n/10 eom."

In some industries it is customary to give a discount for early payment. This discount, called a **sales discount**, is intended to increase the seller's liquidity by reducing the amount of money tied up in accounts receivable. An invoice that offers a sales discount might be labeled "2/10, n/30," which means that the buyer either can pay the invoice within 10 days of the invoice date and take a 2 percent discount or can wait 30 days and then pay the full amount of the invoice. It is almost always advantageous for a buyer to take the discount because the saving of 2 percent over a period of 20 days (from the eleventh day to the thirtieth day) represents an effective annual rate of 36.5 percent (365 days ÷ 20 days × 2% = 36.5%). Most companies would be better off borrowing money to take the discount. The practice of giving sales discounts has been declining because it is costly to the seller and because, from the buyer's viewpoint, the amount of the discount is usually very small in relation to the price of the purchase. Accounting for sales discounts is covered in supplemental objective 8.

In some industries, it is customary for the seller to pay transportation costs and to charge a price that includes those costs. In other industries, it is customary for the purchaser to pay transportation charges on merchandise. Special terms designate whether the seller or the purchaser pays the freight charges. **FOB shipping point** means that the seller places the merchandise "free on board" at the point of origin, and the buyer bears the shipping costs. The title to the merchandise passes to the buyer at that point. For example, when the sales agreement for the purchase of a car says "FOB factory," the buyer must pay the freight from where the car was made to wherever he or she is located, and the buyer owns the car from the time it leaves the factory.

On the other hand, **FOB destination** means that the seller bears the transportation costs to the place where the merchandise is delivered. The seller retains title until the merchandise reaches its destination and usually prepays the shipping costs, in which case the buyer makes no accounting entry for freight. The effects of these special shipping terms are summarized as follows:

Shipping Term	Where Title Passes	Who Pays the Cost of Transportation
FOB shipping point	At origin	Buyer
FOB destination	At destination	Seller

Applying the Perpetual Inventory System

OBJECTIVE

4 Prepare an income statement and record merchandising transactions under the perpetual inventory system

The income statement for Fenwick Fashions Company under the perpetual inventory system is shown previously in Exhibit 2. The focal point of this income statement is cost of goods sold, which is deducted from net sales to arrive at gross margin. Under the perpetual inventory system, this account is continually updated during the accounting period as purchases, sales, and other inventory transactions take place. The Merchandise Inventory account on the balance sheet is updated at the same time. In Exhibit 2, freight in is included in cost of goods sold. Theoretically, freight in should be allocated between ending inventory and cost of goods sold, but most companies choose to include the cost of freight in with the cost of goods sold on the income statement because it is a relatively small amount.

Transactions Related to Purchases of Merchandise

The recording of typical transactions related to purchases of merchandise under the perpetual inventory system is illustrated in the following sections.

Purchases of Merchandise on Credit

Oct. 3 Received merchandise purchased on credit from Neebok Company, invoice dated October 1, terms n/10, FOB shipping point, $4,890.

$A = L + OE$
$+ \quad +$

Oct. 3	Merchandise Inventory	4,890	
	Accounts Payable		4,890
	Purchased merchandise from Neebok Company, terms n/10, FOB shipping point, invoice dated Oct. 1		

Under the perpetual inventory system, the cost of merchandise purchased is placed in the Merchandise Inventory account at the time of purchase.

Transportation Costs on Purchases

Oct. 4 Received bill from Transfer Freight Company for transportation costs on October 3 shipment, invoice dated October 1, terms n/10, $160.

$A = L + OE$
$\quad + \quad -$

Oct. 4	Freight In	160	
	Accounts Payable		160
	Received transportation charges on Oct. 3 purchase, Transfer Freight Company, terms n/10, invoice dated Oct. 1		

Freight in, also called *transportation in*, is the transportation cost of receiving merchandise. Transportation costs are accumulated in a Freight In account because most shipments contain multiple items. It is usually not practical to identify the specific cost of shipping each item of inventory.

In some cases, the seller pays the freight charges and bills them to the buyer as a separate item on the invoice. When this occurs, the entries are the same as in the October 3 example, except that a debit is made to Freight In for the amount of the freight charges and Accounts Payable is increased by a like amount.

Purchases Returns and Allowances

Oct. 6   Returned merchandise received from Neebok Company on October 3 for credit, $480.

A = L + OE   Oct. 6   Accounts Payable   480
–   –   Merchandise Inventory   480
                                   Returned merchandise from purchase
                                   of Oct. 3 to Neebok Company for
                                   full credit

If a seller sends the wrong product or one that is otherwise unsatisfactory, the buyer may be allowed to return the item for a cash refund or credit on account, or the buyer may be given an allowance off the sales price. Under the perpetual inventory system, the returned merchandise is removed from the Merchandise Inventory account.

Payments on Account

Oct. 10   Paid in full the amount due to Neebok Company for the purchase of October 3, part of which was returned on October 6.

A = L + OE   Oct. 10   Accounts Payable   4,410
–   –   Cash   4,410
                                      Made payment on account to
                                      Neebok Company
                                      $4,890 − $480 = $4,410

Transactions Related to Sales of Merchandise

Under the perpetual inventory system, at the time of a sale, the cost of the merchandise is transferred from the Merchandise Inventory account to the Cost of Goods Sold account. In the case of a return of sold merchandise, the cost of the merchandise is transferred from Cost of Goods Sold back to Merchandise Inventory. Transactions related to sales made by Fenwick Fashions Company follow.

Sales of Merchandise on Credit

Oct. 7   Sold merchandise on credit to Gonzales Distributors, terms n/30, FOB destination, $1,200; the cost of the merchandise was $720.

A = L + OE   Oct. 7   Accounts Receivable   1,200
+   +   Sales   1,200
                                   Sold merchandise to Gonzales
                                   Distributors, terms n/30, FOB destination

A = L + OE   Cost of Goods Sold   720
–   –   Merchandise Inventory   720
                                      Transferred cost of merchandise inventory
                                      sold to Cost of Goods Sold account

Under the perpetual inventory system, two entries are necessary. First, the sale is recorded. Second, Cost of Goods Sold is updated by a transfer from Merchandise Inventory. In the case of cash sales, Cash rather than Accounts Receivable is debited for the amount of the sale.

Payment of Delivery Costs

Oct. 8   Paid transportation costs for the sale on October 7, $78.

A = L + OE   Oct. 8   Freight Out Expense   78
−   −   Cash   78
                                Paid delivery costs on Oct. 7 sale

A seller will often absorb delivery or freight out costs in the belief that doing so will facilitate the sale of its products. These costs are accumulated in an account called Freight Out Expense, or *Delivery Expense*, which is shown as a selling expense on the income statement.

Returns of Merchandise Sold

Oct. 9   Merchandise sold on October 7 accepted back from Gonzales Distributors for full credit and returned to merchandise inventory, $300; the cost of the merchandise was $180.

A = L + OE   Oct. 9   Sales Returns and Allowances   300
−   −   Accounts Receivable   300
                                Accepted returned merchandise from
                                Gonzales Distributors

A = L + OE   Merchandise Inventory   180
+   +   Cost of Goods Sold   180
                                Transferred cost of merchandise returned
                                to the Merchandise Inventory account

Because returns and allowances to customers for wrong or unsatisfactory merchandise are often an indicator of customer dissatisfaction, such amounts are accumulated in a Sales Returns and Allowances account. This account is a contra-revenue account with a normal debit balance and is deducted from Sales on the income statement. Under the perpetual inventory system, the cost of the merchandise must also be transferred from the Cost of Goods Sold account back into the Merchandise Inventory account. If an allowance is made instead of accepting a return, or if the merchandise cannot be returned to inventory and resold, this transfer is not made.

FOCUS ON BUSINESS PRACTICE

In some industries a high percentage of sales returns is an accepted business practice. A book publisher like Simon & Schuster will produce and ship more copies of a best-seller than it expects to sell because, to gain the attention of potential buyers, copies must be distributed to a wide variety of outlets, such as bookstores, department stores, and discount stores. As a result, returns of unsold books may run as high as 30 to 50 percent of the books shipped. The same sales principles apply to magazines, such as *People*, that are sold on newsstands and to popular recordings produced by companies like Motown Records. In all these businesses, management scrutinizes the Sales Returns and Allowances account for ways to reduce returns and increase profitability.

Receipts on Account

Nov. 5 Received payment in full from Gonzales Distributors for sale of merchandise on October 7, less the return on October 9.

A = L + OE   Nov. 5   Cash   900
+
−
                       Accounts Receivable   900
                           Received on account from
                           Gonzales Distributors
                           $1,200 − $300 = $900

Credit Card Sales

Many retailers allow customers to charge their purchases to a third-party company that the customer will pay later. These transactions are normally handled with credit cards. Five of the most widely used credit cards are American Express, Discover Card, Diners Club, MasterCard, and Visa. The customer establishes credit with the lender (the credit card issuer) and receives a plastic card to use in making charge purchases. If the seller accepts the card, an invoice is prepared and signed by the customer at the time of the sale. The seller then deposits the invoice in the bank and receives cash.

Because the seller does not have to establish the customer's credit, collect from the customer, or tie money up in accounts receivable, the seller receives an economic benefit provided by the lender. As payment, the lender takes a discount of 2 to 6 percent on the credit card sales invoices rather than paying 100 percent of their total amount. The discount is a selling expense for the merchandiser. For example, assume that a restaurant made sales of $1,000 on Visa credit cards and that Visa takes a 4 percent discount on the sales. Assume also that the sales invoices are deposited in a special Visa bank account in the name of the company, in much the same way that checks from cash sales are deposited. The sales are recorded as follows:

A = L + OE   Cash   960
+   −   Credit Card Discount Expense   40
      +   Sales   1,000
                 Made sales on Visa cards

Inventory Losses

Most companies experience losses of merchandise inventory from spoilage, shoplifting, and theft by employees. When such losses occur, the periodic inventory system provides no means of identifying them because the costs are automatically included in the cost of goods sold. For example, assume that a company has lost $1,250 in stolen merchandise during an accounting period. When the physical inventory is taken, the missing items are not in stock, so they cannot be counted. Because the ending inventory does not contain these items, the amount subtracted from goods available for sale is less than it would be if the goods were in stock. The cost of goods sold, then, is overstated by $1,250. In a sense, the cost of goods sold is inflated by the amount of merchandise that has been lost.

The perpetual inventory system makes it easier to identify such losses. Because the Merchandise Inventory account is continuously updated for sales, purchases, and returns, the loss will show up as the difference between the inventory records and the physical inventory taken at the end of the accounting period. Once the amount of the loss has been identified, the ending inventory is updated by crediting the Merchandise Inventory account. The offsetting debit is usually an increase in Cost of Goods Sold because the loss is considered a cost that reduces the company's gross margin.

Applying the Periodic Inventory System

SUPPLEMENTAL OBJECTIVE

5 Prepare an income statement and record merchandising transactions under the periodic inventory system

The income statement for Fenwick Fashions Company under the periodic inventory system is shown in Exhibit 3 and illustrated in Figure 3. A major feature of this income statement is the computation of cost of goods sold. Cost of goods sold

Fenwick Fashions Company
Income Statement
For the Year Ended December 31, 20x2

Net Sales			
Gross Sales			$246,350
Less Sales Returns and Allowances			7,025
Net Sales			$239,325
Cost of Goods Sold			
Merchandise Inventory, December 31, 20x1		$ 52,800	
Purchases	$126,400		
Less Purchases Returns and Allowances	7,776		
Net Purchases	$118,624		
Freight In	8,236		
Net Cost of Purchases		126,860	
Goods Available for Sale		$179,660	
Less Merchandise Inventory, December 31, 20x2		48,300	
Cost of Goods Sold			131,360
Gross Margin			$107,965
Operating Expenses			
Selling Expenses			
Sales Salaries Expense	$ 22,500		
Freight Out Expense	5,740		
Advertising Expense	10,000		
Insurance Expense, Selling	1,600		
Store Supplies Expense	1,540		
Total Selling Expenses		$ 41,380	
General and Administrative Expenses			
Office Salaries Expense	$ 26,900		
Insurance Expense, General	4,200		
Office Supplies Expense	1,204		
Depreciation Expense, Building	2,600		
Depreciation Expense, Office Equipment	2,200		
Total General and Administrative Expenses		37,104	
Total Operating Expenses			78,484
Net Income			$ 29,481

Exhibit 3
Income Statement Under the Periodic Inventory System

Figure 3
The Components of Cost of
Goods Sold

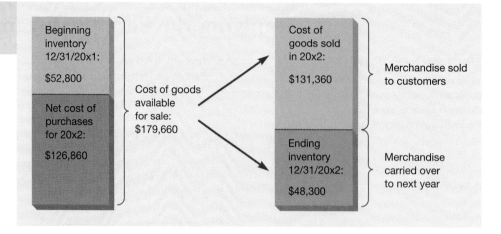

must be computed because it is not updated for purchases, sales, and other transactions during the accounting period as it is under the perpetual inventory system.

Cost of Goods Sold

The method of computing cost of goods sold when using the periodic inventory method is sometimes confusing because it must take into account both merchandise inventory on hand at the beginning of the accounting period, called the **beginning inventory**, and merchandise inventory on hand at the end of the accounting period, called the **ending inventory.** The ending inventory appears on the balance sheet at the end of the accounting period and becomes the beginning inventory for the next accounting period.

To calculate cost of goods sold, the **goods available for sale** must first be determined. The goods available for sale during the year is the sum of two factors, beginning inventory and the net cost of purchases during the year. In this case, the goods available for sale is $179,660 ($52,800 + $126,860).

If a company sold all the goods available for sale during an accounting period, the cost of goods sold would equal the goods available for sale. In most businesses, however, some merchandise will remain unsold and on hand at the end of the period. This merchandise, or ending inventory, must be deducted from the goods available for sale to determine the cost of goods sold. In the case of Fenwick Fashions Company, the ending inventory on December 31, 20x2, is $48,300. Thus, the cost of goods sold is $131,360 ($179,660 − $48,300).

An important component of the cost of goods sold section is **net cost of purchases**, which consists of net purchases plus any freight charges on the purchases. **Net purchases** equals total purchases less any deductions, such as purchases returns and allowances and any discounts allowed by suppliers for early payment (see supplemental objective 8). Because transportation charges, or freight in, are a necessary cost of receiving merchandise for sale, they are added to net purchases to arrive at the net cost of purchases, as shown in Exhibit 3.

Transactions Related to Purchases of Merchandise

The primary difference in accounting between the perpetual and the periodic inventory systems is that under the perpetual inventory system, the Merchandise Inventory account is continuously adjusted because purchases, sales, and other inventory transactions are entered in the account as they occur. Under the periodic inventory system, on the other hand, the Merchandise Inventory account stays at its beginning balance until the physical inventory is recorded at the end of the period. A Purchases account is used to accumulate the purchases of merchandise during the accounting period, and a Purchases Returns and Allowances account is used to accumulate returns of and allowances on purchases.

To illustrate the periodic inventory system, purchase transactions made by Fenwick Fashions Company follow.

Purchases of Merchandise on Credit

Oct. 3　Received merchandise purchased on credit from Neebok Company, invoice dated October 1, terms n/10, FOB shipping point, $4,890.

A = L + OE	Oct. 3	Purchases	4,890	
+ −		Accounts Payable		4,890
		Purchased merchandise from Neebok Company, terms n/10, FOB shipping point, invoice dated Oct. 1		

Under the periodic inventory system, **Purchases** is a temporary account. Its sole purpose is to accumulate the total cost of merchandise purchased for resale during an accounting period. (Purchases of other assets, such as equipment, are recorded in the appropriate asset account, not in the Purchases account.) The Purchases account does not indicate whether merchandise has been sold or is still on hand.

Transportation Costs on Purchases

Oct. 4　Received bill from Transfer Freight Company for transportation costs on October 3 shipment, invoice dated October 1, terms n/10, $160.

A = L + OE	Oct. 4	Freight In	160	
+ −		Accounts Payable		160
		Received transportation charges on Oct. 3 purchase, Transfer Freight Company, terms n/10, invoice dated Oct. 1		

Transportation costs on purchases are usually accumulated in a Freight In account. In some cases, the seller pays the freight charges and bills them to the buyer as a separate item on the invoice. When this occurs, the entries are the same as in the October 3 example, except that a debit is made to Freight In for the amount of the freight charges and Accounts Payable is increased by a like amount.

Purchases Returns and Allowances

Oct. 6　Returned merchandise received from Neebok Company on October 3 for credit, $480.

A = L + OE	Oct. 6	Accounts Payable	480	
− +		Purchases Returns and Allowances		480
		Returned merchandise from purchase of Oct. 3 to Neebok Company for full credit		

If a seller sends the wrong product or one that is otherwise unsatisfactory, the buyer may be allowed to return the item for a cash refund or credit on account, or the buyer may be given an allowance off the sales price. Under the periodic inventory system, the amount of the return or allowance is recorded in the **Purchases Returns and Allowances** account. This account is a contra-purchases account with a normal credit balance, and it is deducted from Purchases on the income statement.

Payments on Account

Oct. 10   Paid in full the amount due to Neebok Company for the purchase of October 3, part of which was returned on October 6.

A = L + OE
− −

Oct. 10	Accounts Payable	4,410	
	Cash		4,410
	Made payment on account to Neebok Company $4,890 − $480 = $4,410		

Transactions Related to Sales of Merchandise

The Cost of Goods Sold account, which is updated for sales and returns under the perpetual inventory system, is not used under the periodic inventory system because the Merchandise Inventory account is not updated until the end of the accounting period. Transactions related to sales made by Fenwick Fashions Company follow.

Sales of Merchandise on Credit

Oct. 7   Sold merchandise on credit to Gonzales Distributors, terms n/30, FOB destination, $1,200; the cost of the merchandise was $720.

A = L + OE
+ +

Oct. 7	Accounts Receivable	1,200	
	Sales		1,200
	Sold merchandise to Gonzales Distributors, terms n/30, FOB destination		

In the case of cash sales, Cash rather than Accounts Receivable is debited for the amount of the sale.

Payment of Delivery Costs

Oct. 8   Paid transportation costs for the sale on October 7, $78.

A = L + OE
− −

Oct. 8	Freight Out Expense	78	
	Cash		78
	Paid delivery costs on Oct. 7 sale		

Delivery or freight out costs are accumulated in the Freight Out Expense (also called Delivery Expense) account. This account is shown as a selling expense on the income statement.

Returns of Merchandise Sold

Oct. 9   Merchandise sold on October 7 accepted back from Gonzales Distributors for full credit and returned to merchandise inventory.

A = L + OE
− −

Oct. 9	Sales Returns and Allowances	300	
	Accounts Receivable		300
	Accepted returned merchandise from Gonzales Distributors		

Returns and allowances to customers for wrong or unsatisfactory merchandise are accumulated in the Sales Returns and Allowances account. This account is a contra-revenue account with a normal debit balance and is deducted from Sales on the income statement.

Receipts on Account

Nov. 5   Received payment in full from Gonzales Distributors for sale of merchandise on October 7, less the return on October 9.

A = L + OE					
+	Nov. 5	Cash		900	
−		Accounts Receivable			900
		Received on account from			
		Gonzales Distributors			
		$1,200 − $300 = $900			

The Merchandising Work Sheet and Closing Entries

The work sheet for a merchandising company is basically the same as for a service business, except that it includes the additional accounts needed to handle merchandising transactions. The treatment of these additional accounts differs depending on whether a company uses the perpetual or the periodic inventory system.

The Perpetual Inventory System

SUPPLEMENTAL OBJECTIVE

6 Prepare a work sheet and closing entries for a merchandising concern using the perpetual inventory system

The accounts for a merchandising company using the perpetual inventory system generally include Sales, Sales Returns and Allowances, Cost of Goods Sold, and Freight In. The Merchandise Inventory account is up to date at the end of the accounting period and therefore is not involved in the closing process. The reason for this is that, under the perpetual inventory system, purchases of merchandise are recorded directly in the Merchandise Inventory account and costs are transferred from the Merchandise Inventory account to the Cost of Goods Sold account as merchandise is sold. The work sheet for Fenwick Fashions Company, assuming the company uses the perpetual inventory system, is shown in Exhibit 4. Each pair of columns in the work sheet and the closing entries are discussed in the following paragraphs. Note that the ending merchandise inventory is $48,300 in both the Trial Balance and the Balance Sheet columns.

TRIAL BALANCE COLUMNS   The first step in the preparation of the work sheet is to enter the balances from the ledger accounts into the Trial Balance columns. You are already familiar with this procedure.

ADJUSTMENTS COLUMNS   The adjusting entries for Fenwick Fashions Company are entered in the Adjustments columns in the same way the adjusting entries were entered for service companies. Fenwick's adjusting entries involve insurance expired during the period (adjustment **a**), store and office supplies used during the period (adjustments **b** and **c**), and the depreciation of building and office equipment (adjustments **d** and **e**). No adjusting entry is made for merchandise inventory. After the adjusting entries are entered on the work sheet, the columns are totaled to prove that total debits equal total credits.

OMISSION OF ADJUSTED TRIAL BALANCE COLUMNS   These two columns, which appeared in the work sheet for a service company, can be omitted. They are optional and are used when there are many adjusting entries to record. When only a few adjusting entries are required, as in the case of Fenwick Fashions Company, these columns are not necessary and may be omitted to save time.

Exhibit 4
Work Sheet for Fenwick Fashions Company: Perpetual Inventory System

Fenwick Fashions Company
Work Sheet
For the Year Ended December 31, 20x2

Account Name	Trial Balance Debit	Trial Balance Credit	Adjustments Debit	Adjustments Credit	Income Statement Debit	Income Statement Credit	Balance Sheet Debit	Balance Sheet Credit
Cash	29,410						29,410	
Accounts Receivable	42,400						42,400	
Merchandise Inventory	48,300						48,300	
Prepaid Insurance	17,400			(a) 5,800			11,600	
Store Supplies	2,600			(b) 1,540			1,060	
Office Supplies	1,840			(c) 1,204			636	
Land	4,500						4,500	
Building	20,260						20,260	
Accumulated Depreciation, Building		5,650		(d) 2,600				8,250
Office Equipment	8,600						8,600	
Accumulated Depreciation, Office Equipment		2,800		(e) 2,200				5,000
Accounts Payable		25,683						25,683
Gloria Fenwick, Capital		118,352						118,352
Gloria Fenwick, Withdrawals	20,000						20,000	
Sales		246,350				246,350		
Sales Returns and Allowances	7,025				7,025			
Cost of Goods Sold	123,124				123,124			
Freight In	8,236				8,236			
Sales Salaries Expense	22,500				22,500			
Freight Out Expense	5,740				5,740			
Advertising Expense	10,000				10,000			
Office Salaries Expense	26,900				26,900			
	398,835	398,835						
Insurance Expense, Selling			(a) 1,600		1,600			
Insurance Expense, General			(a) 4,200		4,200			
Store Supplies Expense			(b) 1,540		1,540			
Office Supplies Expense			(c) 1,204		1,204			
Depreciation Expense, Building			(d) 2,600		2,600			
Depreciation Expense, Office Equipment			(e) 2,200		2,200			
			13,344	13,344	216,869	246,350	186,766	157,285
Net Income					29,481			29,481
					246,350	246,350	186,766	186,766

INCOME STATEMENT AND BALANCE SHEET COLUMNS   After the Trial Balance columns have been totaled, the adjustments entered, and the equality of the columns proved, the balances are extended to the Income Statement and Balance Sheet columns. Again, begin with the Cash account at the top of the work sheet and move sequentially down the work sheet, one account at a time, entering each account balance in the correct Income Statement or Balance Sheet column.

ADJUSTING ENTRIES   The adjusting entries from the work sheet are now entered into the general journal and posted to the ledger, as they would be in a service company. There is no difference in this procedure between a service company and a merchandising company.

CLOSING ENTRIES   The closing entries for Fenwick Fashions Company are shown in Exhibit 5. The Cost of Goods Sold account is closed to Income Summary along with the expense accounts because the Cost of Goods Sold account has a debit balance. No closing entries affect the Merchandise Inventory account.

Exhibit 5
Closing Entries for Fenwick Fashions Company: Perpetual Inventory System

		General Journal			Page 10
Date		Description	Post. Ref.	Debit	Credit
20x2 Dec.	31	*Closing entries:* Income Summary		216,869	
		Sales Returns and Allowances			7,025
		Cost of Goods Sold			123,124
		Freight In			8,236
		Sales Salaries Expense			22,500
		Freight Out Expense			5,740
		Advertising Expense			10,000
		Office Salaries Expense			26,900
		Insurance Expense, Selling			1,600
		Insurance Expense, General			4,200
		Store Supplies Expense			1,540
		Office Supplies Expense			1,204
		Depreciation Expense, Building			2,600
		Depreciation Expense, Office Equipment			2,200
		To close the temporary expense and revenue accounts having debit balances			
	31	Sales		246,350	
		Income Summary			246,350
		To close the temporary revenue account having a credit balance			
	31	Income Summary		29,481	
		Gloria Fenwick, Capital			29,481
		To close the Income Summary account			
	31	Gloria Fenwick, Capital		20,000	
		Gloria Fenwick, Withdrawals			20,000
		To close the Withdrawals account			

The Periodic Inventory System

SUPPLEMENTAL OBJECTIVE

7 Prepare a work sheet and closing entries for a merchandising concern using the periodic inventory system

The accounts for a merchandising company using the periodic inventory system generally include Sales, Sales Returns and Allowances, Sales Discounts, Purchases, Purchases Returns and Allowances, Purchases Discounts, Freight In, and Merchandise Inventory. Except for Merchandise Inventory, these accounts are treated in much the same way as revenue and expense accounts for a service company. On the work sheet, they are extended to the Income Statement columns. In the closing process, they are transferred to the Income Summary account.

The Merchandise Inventory account requires special treatment because, under the periodic inventory system, purchases of merchandise are accumulated in the Purchases account, and no entries are made to Merchandise Inventory during the accounting period. As a result, at the end of the period, the balance in Merchandise Inventory is the same as it was at the beginning of the period: the beginning inventory amount. To calculate net income, the closing entries must (1) remove the beginning inventory from the Merchandise Inventory account, (2) enter the ending inventory in the Merchandise Inventory account, and (3) transfer both inventory amounts to the Income Summary account. The following T accounts illustrate the flow of the inventory amounts at Fenwick Fashions.

Merchandise Inventory

Dec. 31, 20x1	Beg. Bal.	52,800	Dec. 31, 20x2	52,800
Dec. 31, 20x2	End. Bal.	48,300		

Income Summary

Dec. 31, 20x2	52,800	Dec. 31, 20x2	48,300

The beginning merchandise inventory was $52,800. This amount is removed from the Merchandise Inventory account by a credit, which leaves a zero balance, and transferred to the Income Summary account by a debit. The ending inventory was $48,300. This amount is entered in the Merchandise Inventory account by a debit and recorded in the Income Summary account by a credit. The results of the two closing entries mirror the calculation of cost of goods sold, in which beginning inventory is added to net cost of purchases and ending inventory is then subtracted. When beginning inventory is debited to the Income Summary account, it is, in effect, added to net purchases because the balance in the Purchases account is also debited to Income Summary through a closing entry. And when ending inventory is credited to Income Summary, it is, in effect, deducted from the sum of beginning inventory and net cost of purchases. Keep these effects in mind while studying the work sheet for Fenwick Fashions Company shown in Exhibit 6.

INCOME STATEMENT AND BALANCE SHEET COLUMNS   As explained earlier, the Merchandise Inventory row requires special treatment. The beginning inventory balance of $52,800 (which is already in the trial balance) is extended to the debit column of the Income Statement columns, as shown in Exhibit 6. This procedure has the effect of adding beginning inventory to net purchases because the Purchases account is also in the debit column of the Income Statement columns. The ending inventory balance of $48,300 (determined by the physical inventory and not in the trial balance) is then inserted in the credit column of the Income Statement columns. This procedure has the effect of subtracting the ending inventory from goods available for sale in order to calculate the cost of goods sold. Finally, the ending merchandise inventory ($48,300) is inserted in the debit side of the Balance Sheet columns because it will appear on the balance sheet.

After all the items have been extended into the correct columns, the four columns are totaled. The net income or net loss is the difference between the debit

**Work Sheet for Fenwick Fashions
Company: Periodic Inventory System**

Fenwick Fashions Company
Work Sheet
For the Year Ended December 31, 20x2

Account Name	Trial Balance Debit	Trial Balance Credit	Adjustments Debit	Adjustments Credit	Income Statement Debit	Income Statement Credit	Balance Sheet Debit	Balance Sheet Credit
Cash	29,410						29,410	
Accounts Receivable	42,400						42,400	
Merchandise Inventory	52,800				52,800	48,300	48,300	
Prepaid Insurance	17,400			(a) 5,800			11,600	
Store Supplies	2,600			(b) 1,540			1,060	
Office Supplies	1,840			(c) 1,204			636	
Land	4,500						4,500	
Building	20,260						20,260	
Accumulated Depreciation, Building		5,650		(d) 2,600				8,250
Office Equipment	8,600						8,600	
Accumulated Depreciation, Office Equipment		2,800		(e) 2,200				5,000
Accounts Payable		25,683						25,683
Gloria Fenwick, Capital		118,352						118,352
Gloria Fenwick, Withdrawals	20,000						20,000	
Sales		246,350				246,350		
Sales Returns and Allowances	7,025				7,025			
Purchases	126,400				126,400			
Purchases Returns and Allowances		7,776				7,776		
Freight In	8,236				8,236			
Sales Salaries Expense	22,500				22,500			
Freight Out Expense	5,740				5,740			
Advertising Expense	10,000				10,000			
Office Salaries Expense	26,900				26,900			
	406,611	406,611						
Insurance Expense, Selling			(a) 1,600		1,600			
Insurance Expense, General			(a) 4,200		4,200			
Store Supplies Expense			(b) 1,540		1,540			
Office Supplies Expense			(c) 1,204		1,204			
Depreciation Expense, Building			(d) 2,600		2,600			
Depreciation Expense, Office Equipment			(e) 2,200		2,200			
			13,344	13,344	272,945	302,426	186,766	157,285
Net Income					29,481			29,481
					302,426	302,426	186,766	186,766

and credit Income Statement columns. In this case, Fenwick Fashions Company has earned a net income of $29,481, which is extended to the credit side of the Balance Sheet columns. The four columns are then added to prove that total debits equal total credits.

CLOSING ENTRIES The closing entries for Fenwick Fashions Company appear in Exhibit 7. Notice that Merchandise Inventory is credited for the amount of the beginning inventory ($52,800) in the first entry and debited for the amount of the ending inventory ($48,300) in the second entry. Otherwise, these closing entries

Exhibit 7		General Journal			Page 10
Closing Entries for Fenwick Fashions Company: Periodic Inventory System			Post.		
Date	Description	Ref.	Debit	Credit

Date		Description	Post. Ref.	Debit	Credit
20x2		*Closing entries:*			
Dec.	31	Income Summary		272,945	
		Merchandise Inventory			52,800
		Sales Returns and Allowances			7,025
		Purchases			126,400
		Freight In			8,236
		Sales Salaries Expense			22,500
		Freight Out Expense			5,740
		Advertising Expense			10,000
		Office Salaries Expense			26,900
		Insurance Expense, Selling			1,600
		Insurance Expense, General			4,200
		Store Supplies Expense			1,540
		Office Supplies Expense			1,204
		Depreciation Expense, Building			2,600
		Depreciation Expense, Office Equipment			2,200
		To close the temporary expense and revenue accounts having debit balances and to remove the beginning inventory			
	31	Merchandise Inventory		48,300	
		Sales		246,350	
		Purchases Returns and Allowances		7,776	
		Income Summary			302,426
		To close the temporary expense and revenue accounts having credit balances and to establish the ending inventory			
	31	Income Summary		29,481	
		Gloria Fenwick, Capital			29,481
		To close the Income Summary account			
	31	Gloria Fenwick, Capital		20,000	
		Gloria Fenwick, Withdrawals			20,000
		To close the Withdrawals account			

are very similar to those for a service company except that the merchandising accounts also must be closed to Income Summary. All income statement accounts with debit balances, including the merchandising accounts of Sales Returns and Allowances, Purchases, and Freight In, are credited in the first entry. The total of these accounts ($272,945) equals the total of the debit column in the Income Statement columns of the work sheet. All income statement accounts with credit balances—Sales and Purchases Returns and Allowances—are debited in the second entry. The total of these accounts ($302,426) equals the total of the Income Statement credit column in the work sheet. The third and fourth entries are used to close the Income Summary account and transfer net income to the Capital account, and to close the Withdrawals account to the Capital account.

Accounting for Discounts

Sales Discounts

SUPPLEMENTAL OBJECTIVE

8 Apply sales and purchases discounts to merchandising transactions

As mentioned earlier, some industries give sales discounts for early payment. Because it usually is not possible to know at the time of the sale whether the customer will pay in time to take advantage of them, sales discounts are recorded only at the time the customer pays. For example, assume that Fenwick Fashions Company sells merchandise to a customer on September 20 for $300, on terms of 2/10, n/60. This is the entry at the time of the sale:

A = L + OE				
+ +	Sept. 20	Accounts Receivable	300	
		Sales		300
		Sold merchandise on credit, terms 2/10, n/60		

The customer can take advantage of the sales discount any time on or before September 30, ten days after the date of the invoice. If the customer pays on September 29, the entry in Fenwick's records would look like this:

A = L + OE				
+ −	Sept. 29	Cash	294	
−		Sales Discounts	6	
		Accounts Receivable		300
		Received payment for Sept. 20 sale; discount taken		

If the customer does not take advantage of the sales discount but waits until November 19 to pay for the merchandise, the entry would be as follows:

A = L + OE				
+	Nov. 19	Cash	300	
−		Accounts Receivable		300
		Received payment for Sept. 20 sale; no discount taken		

At the end of the accounting period, the Sales Discounts account has accumulated all the sales discounts taken during the period. Because sales discounts reduce revenues from sales, Sales Discounts is a contra-revenue account with a normal debit balance that is deducted from gross sales in the income statement. Sales Discounts is treated the same as Sales Returns and Allowances on the work sheet and in the closing entries.

Purchases Discounts

Merchandise purchases are usually made on credit and sometimes involve **purchases discounts** for early payment. Purchases discounts are discounts taken for early payment for merchandise purchased for resale. They are to the buyer what sales discounts are to the seller. The amount of discounts taken is recorded in a separate account. Assume that Fenwick made a credit purchase of merchandise on November 12 for $1,500 with terms of 2/10, n/30 and returned $200 in merchandise on November 14. When payment is made, the journal entry looks like this:

A = L + OE
−   −   +

Nov. 22	Accounts Payable		1,300	
	Purchases Discounts			26
	Cash			1,274
	Paid the invoice of Nov. 12			
	Purchase Nov. 12	$1,500		
	Less return Nov. 14	200		
	Net purchase	$1,300		
	Discount: 2%	26		
	Cash paid	$1,274		

If the purchase is not paid for within the discount period, this is the entry:

A = L + OE
−   −

Dec. 12	Accounts Payable	1,300	
	Cash		1,300
	Paid the invoice of Nov. 12, less the return,		
	on due date; no discount taken		

Like Purchases Returns and Allowances, Purchases Discounts is a contra-purchases account with a normal credit balance that is deducted from Purchases on the income statement. If a company makes only a partial payment on an invoice, most creditors allow the company to take the discount applicable to the partial payment. The discount usually does not apply to freight, postage, taxes, or other charges that might appear on the invoice. Purchases Discounts is treated the same as Purchases Returns and Allowances on the work sheet and in the closing entries.

Chapter Review

REVIEW OF LEARNING OBJECTIVES

Check out ACE, a self-quizzing program on chapter content, at http://college.hmco.com.

1. **Identify the management issues related to merchandising businesses.** Merchandising companies differ from service companies in that they earn income by buying and selling products or merchandise. The buying and selling of merchandise adds to the complexity of the business and raises four issues that management must address. First, the series of transactions that merchandising companies engage in (the operating cycle) requires careful cash flow management. Second, profitability management requires the company to price goods and control costs and expenses in ways that ensure the earning of an adequate income after operating expenses have been paid. Third, the company must choose whether to use the perpetual or the periodic inventory system. Fourth, management must establish an internal control structure that protects the assets of cash, merchandise inventory, and accounts receivable.

2. **Compare the income statements for service and merchandising concerns, and define the components of the merchandising income statement.** In the simplest case, the income statement for a service company consists only of revenues and expenses. The income statement for a merchandising company has three major parts: (1) net sales, (2) cost of goods sold, and (3) operating expenses. Gross margin is the difference between revenues from net sales and the cost of goods sold. Net income is the "bottom line" after operating expenses are deducted from the gross margin.

3. **Define and distinguish the terms of sale for merchandising transactions.** Trade discounts are a reduction from the catalogue or list price of a product. A sales discount is a discount given for early payment of a sale on credit. FOB shipping point means the buyer bears the cost of transportation, and title to the goods passes to the buyer at the shipping origin. FOB destination means that the seller bears the cost of transportation, and title does not pass to the buyer until the goods reach their destination.

4. **Prepare an income statement and record merchandising transactions under the perpetual inventory system.** Under the perpetual inventory system, records of the quantity and, usually, the cost of individual items of inventory are kept throughout the year. The cost of goods sold is recorded as goods are transferred to customers, and the inventory balance is kept current throughout the year as items are bought and sold. The main advantage of the perpetual inventory system is that it provides management with timely information about the status of the inventory. The main disadvantages are that it is more difficult to maintain and more costly than a periodic inventory system. A physical inventory, or physical count, is taken at the end of the accounting period to establish a basis for accuracy and detect possible inventory losses under the perpetual inventory system. The Merchandise Inventory account is continuously adjusted by entering purchases, sales, and other inventory transactions as they occur. Purchases increase the Merchandise Inventory account, and purchases returns decrease it. As goods are sold, their cost is transferred from the Merchandise Inventory account to the Cost of Goods Sold account.

SUPPLEMENTAL OBJECTIVES

5. **Prepare an income statement and record merchandising transactions under the periodic inventory system.** Under the periodic inventory system, no detailed records of the actual inventory on hand are maintained during the accounting period. A physical count of inventory is made at the end of the accounting period to update the Inventory account and to determine cost of goods sold. The main advantages of the periodic inventory system are that it is simpler and less costly than the perpetual inventory system. The main disadvantage of the periodic inventory system is that the lack of detailed records may lead to inefficiencies, lost sales, and higher operating costs. When the periodic inventory system is used, the income statement must include a cost of goods sold section that includes the following elements:

$$\text{Gross Purchases} - \text{Purchases Returns and Allowances} + \text{Freight In} = \text{Net Cost of Purchases}$$

$$\text{Beginning Merchandise Inventory} + \text{Net Cost of Purchases} = \text{Goods Available for Sale}$$

$$\text{Goods Available for Sale} - \text{Ending Merchandise Inventory} = \text{Cost of Goods Sold}$$

Under the periodic inventory system, the Merchandise Inventory account stays at the beginning level until the physical inventory is recorded at the end of the period. A Purchases account is used to accumulate purchases of merchandise during the accounting period, and a Purchases Returns and Allowances account is used to accumulate returns of and allowances on purchases.

6. **Prepare a work sheet and closing entries for a merchandising concern using the perpetual inventory system.** Preparing a work sheet for a merchandising concern is much like preparing one for a service concern, except that there are additional accounts relating to merchandising transactions, such as Sales, Sales Returns and Allowances, Cost of Goods Sold, and Freight In. These accounts must be extended to the appropriate Income Statement columns. Also, since the Merchandise Inventory account is kept up to date, its

ending balance is extended directly to the debit column of the Balance Sheet columns. There is no need to place it in the Income Statement columns. Further, the Cost of Goods Sold account replaces the Purchases and Purchases Returns and Allowances accounts and is extended to the debit column of the Income Statement columns. The closing entries for a merchandising concern under the perpetual inventory system are the same as those for a service business. There is no need to include the Merchandise Inventory account.

7. **Prepare a work sheet and closing entries for a merchandising concern using the periodic inventory system.** The work sheet under the periodic inventory system is the same as under the perpetual inventory system with the exception that the beginning merchandise inventory from the trial balance is extended to the debit column of the Income Statement columns, and the ending balance of Merchandise Inventory is inserted in both the credit column of the Income Statement columns and the debit column of the Balance Sheet columns. The closing entries for a merchandising concern under the periodic inventory system are similar to those for a service business, with one exception. The exception is that the closing entries include a credit to Merchandise Inventory for the amount of the beginning inventory and a debit to Merchandise Inventory for the amount of the ending inventory.

8. **Apply sales and purchases discounts to merchandising transactions.** Sales discounts are discounts for early payment. Terms of 2/10, n/30 mean that the buyer can take a 2 percent discount if the invoice is paid within ten days of the invoice date. Otherwise, the buyer is obligated to pay the full amount in thirty days. Discounts on sales are recorded in the Sales Discounts account, and discounts on purchases are recorded in the Purchases Discounts account.

REVIEW OF CONCEPTS AND TERMINOLOGY

The following concepts and terms were introduced in this chapter:

SO 5 **Beginning inventory:** Merchandise on hand at the start of an accounting period.

LO 1 **Cash flow management:** The planning of a company's receipts and payments of cash.

LO 2 **Cost of goods sold:** The amount a merchant paid for the merchandise sold during an accounting period. Also called *cost of sales*.

SO 5 **Ending inventory:** Merchandise on hand at the end of an accounting period.

LO 3 **FOB destination:** A shipping term that means that the seller bears transportation costs to the place of delivery.

LO 3 **FOB shipping point:** A shipping term that means that the buyer bears transportation costs from the point of origin.

LO 4 **Freight in:** Transportation charges on merchandise purchased for resale. Also called *transportation in*.

LO 2 **Freight Out Expense:** The account that accumulates transportation charges on merchandise sold, which are shown as an operating expense. Also called *Delivery Expense*.

SO 5 **Goods available for sale:** The sum of beginning inventory and the net cost of purchases during the period; the total goods available for sale to customers during an accounting period.

LO 2 **Gross margin:** The difference between net sales and cost of goods sold. Also called *gross profit*.

LO 2 **Gross sales:** Total sales for cash and on credit occurring during an accounting period.

LO 1 **Internal controls:** The environment, accounting systems, and control procedures established by management and designed to safeguard the assets of a business and provide reliable accounting records.

LO 1   **Merchandise inventory:** The goods on hand at any one time that are available for sale to customers.

LO 1   **Merchandising business:** A business that earns income by buying and selling products or merchandise.

SO 5   **Net cost of purchases:** Net purchases plus any freight charges on the purchases.

LO 2   **Net income:** For merchandising companies, what is left after deducting operating expenses from gross margin.

SO 5   **Net purchases:** Total purchases less any deductions, such as purchases returns and allowances and purchases discounts.

LO 2   **Net sales:** The gross proceeds from sales of merchandise less sales returns and allowances and any discounts. Also called *sales* on income statements.

LO 1   **Operating budget:** Management's operating plans as reflected by detailed listings of projected selling and general and administrative expenses.

LO 1   **Operating cycle:** A series of transactions that includes purchases of merchandise inventory for cash or on credit, payment for purchases made on credit, sales of merchandise inventory for cash or on credit, and collection of the cash from the sales.

LO 2   **Operating expenses:** The expenses other than cost of goods sold that are incurred in running a business.

LO 1   **Periodic inventory system:** A system for determining inventory on hand and cost of goods sold by a physical count at the end of an accounting period.

LO 1   **Perpetual inventory system:** A system for determining inventory and cost of goods sold by keeping continuous records of the quantity and, usually, the cost of individual items as they are bought and sold.

LO 1   **Physical inventory:** An actual count of all merchandise on hand at the end of an accounting period.

LO 1   **Profitability management:** The process of setting appropriate prices on merchandise, purchasing merchandise at favorable prices and terms, and maintaining acceptable levels of expenses.

SO 5   **Purchases:** A temporary account used under the periodic inventory system to accumulate the total cost of all merchandise purchased for resale during an accounting period.

SO 8   **Purchases discounts:** Discounts taken for prompt payment for merchandise purchased for resale; the Purchases Discounts account is a contra-purchases account.

SO 5   **Purchases Returns and Allowances:** A contra-purchases account used under the periodic inventory system to accumulate cash refunds, credits on account, and other allowances made by suppliers on merchandise originally purchased for resale.

LO 3   **Sales discount:** A discount given to a buyer for early payment for a sale made on credit; the Sales Discounts account is a contra-revenue account.

LO 2   **Sales Returns and Allowances:** A contra-revenue account used to accumulate cash refunds, credits on account, and other allowances made to customers who have received defective or otherwise unsatisfactory products.

LO 1   **Service business:** A business that earns income by performing a service for fees or commissions.

LO 3   **Trade discount:** A deduction (usually 30 percent or more) off a list or catalogue price.

REVIEW PROBLEM

Merchandising Transactions: Perpetual and Periodic Inventory Systems

LO 4
SO 5

Dawkins Company engaged in the following transactions.

Oct. 1   Sold merchandise to Ernie Devlin on credit, terms n/30, FOB shipping point, $1,050 (cost, $630).

Oct. 2 Purchased merchandise on credit from Ruland Company, terms n/30, FOB shipping point, $1,900.

2 Paid Custom Freight $145 for freight charges on merchandise received.

6 Purchased store supplies on credit from Arizin Supply House, terms n/30, $318.

9 Purchased merchandise on credit from LNP Company, terms n/30, FOB shipping point, $1,800, including $100 freight costs paid by LNP Company.

11 Accepted from Ernie Devlin a return of merchandise, which was returned to inventory, $150 (cost, $90).

14 Returned for credit $300 of merchandise received on October 2.

15 Returned for credit $100 of store supplies purchased on October 6.

16 Sold merchandise for cash, $500 (cost, $300).

22 Paid Ruland Company for purchase of October 2 less return of October 14.

23 Received full payment from Ernie Devlin for his October 1 purchase, less return on October 11.

REQUIRED

1. Prepare entries in journal form to record the transactions, assuming the perpetual inventory system is used.

2. Prepare entries in journal form to record the transactions, assuming the periodic inventory system is used.

ANSWER TO REVIEW PROBLEM

Accounts that differ under the two systems are highlighted in color.

1. Perpetual Inventory System

2. Periodic Inventory System

20xx

Date	Perpetual	Dr	Cr	Periodic	Dr	Cr
Oct. 1	Accounts Receivable	1,050		Accounts Receivable	1,050	
	Sales		1,050	Sales		1,050
	Sold merchandise on account to Ernie Devlin, terms n/30, FOB shipping point			Sold merchandise on account to Ernie Devlin, terms n/30, FOB shipping point		
	Cost of Goods Sold	630				
	Merchandise Inventory		630			
	Transferred cost of merchandise sold to Cost of Goods Sold account					
2	Merchandise Inventory	1,900		Purchases	1,900	
	Accounts Payable		1,900	Accounts Payable		1,900
	Purchased merchandise on account from Ruland Company, terms n/30, FOB shipping point			Purchased merchandise on account from Ruland Company, terms n/30, FOB shipping point		
2	Freight In	145		Freight In	145	
	Cash		145	Cash		145
	Paid freight on previous purchase			Paid freight on previous purchase		
6	Store Supplies	318		Store Supplies	318	
	Accounts Payable		318	Accounts Payable		318
	Purchased store supplies on account from Arizin Supply House, terms n/30			Purchased store supplies on account from Arizin Supply House, terms n/30		
9	Merchandise Inventory	1,700		Purchases	1,700	
	Freight In	100		Freight In	100	
	Accounts Payable		1,800	Accounts Payable		1,800
	Purchased merchandise on account from LNP Company, terms n/30, FOB shipping point, freight paid by supplier			Purchased merchandise on account from LNPCompany, terms n/30, FOB shipping point, freight paid by supplier		

1. Perpetual Inventory System (*continued*)			2. Periodic Inventory System (*continued*)		
20xx					
Oct. 11 Sales Returns and Allowances	150		Sales Returns and Allowances	150	
Accounts Receivable		150	Accounts Receivable		150
Accepted return of merchandise from Ernie Devlin			Accepted return of merchandise from Ernie Devlin		
Merchandise Inventory	90				
Cost of Goods Sold		90			
Transferred cost of merchandise returned to Merchandise Inventory account					
14 Accounts Payable	300		Accounts Payable	300	
Merchandise Inventory		300	Purchases Returns and Allowances		300
Returned portion of merchandise purchased from Ruland Company			Returned portion of merchandise purchased from Ruland Company		
15 Accounts Payable	100		Accounts Payable	100	
Store Supplies		100	Store Supplies		100
Returned store supplies (not merchandise) purchased on October 6 for credit			Returned store supplies (not merchandise) purchased on October 6 for credit		
16 Cash	500		Cash	500	
Sales		500	Sales		500
Sold merchandise for cash			Sold merchandise for cash		
Cost of Goods Sold	300				
Merchandise Inventory		300			
Transferred cost of merchandise sold to Cost of Goods Sold account					
22 Accounts Payable	1,600		Accounts Payable	1,600	
Cash		1,600	Cash		1,600
Made payment on account to Ruland Company $1,900 − $300 = $1,600			Made payment on account to Ruland Company $1,900 − $300 = $1,600		
23 Cash	900		Cash	900	
Accounts Receivable		900	Accounts Receivable		900
Received payment on account of Ernie Devlin $1,050 − $150 = $900			Received payment on account of Ernie Devlin $1,050 − $150 = $900		

Chapter Assignments

BUILDING YOUR KNOWLEDGE FOUNDATION

QUESTIONS

1. What four issues must be faced by managers of merchandising businesses?
2. What is the operating cycle of a merchandising business and why is it important?
3. What is the primary difference between the operations of a merchandising business and those of a service business? How is this difference reflected on the income statement?
4. What is the difference between the perpetual inventory system and the periodic inventory system?
5. Under the periodic inventory system, how must the amount of inventory at the end of the year be determined?

6. What are the principal differences in the handling of merchandise inventory in the accounting records under the perpetual inventory system and the periodic inventory system?

7. Discuss this statement: "The perpetual inventory system is the best system because management always needs to know how much inventory it has."

8. Define *gross margin*. Why is it important?

9. During its first year in operation, D'Andrea Nursery had a cost of goods sold of $64,000 and a gross margin equal to 40 percent of sales. What was the dollar amount of the company's sales?

10. Could D'Andrea Nursery (in Question **9**) have a net loss for the year? Explain your answer.

11. What is the difference between a trade discount and a sales discount?

12. The following prices and terms on 50 units of product were quoted by two companies. Which supplier is quoting the better deal? Explain your answer.

	Price	Terms
Supplier A	$20 per unit	FOB shipping point
Supplier B	$21 per unit	FOB destination

13. What is the principal difference in accounting for the purchase and sale of merchandise under the perpetual inventory system and the periodic inventory system?

14. Is *freight in* an operating expense? Explain your answer.

15. Lorres Hardware purchased the following items: (a) a delivery truck, (b) two dozen hammers, (c) supplies for its office workers, and (d) a broom for the janitor. Which items should be debited to the Purchases account under the periodic inventory system?

16. Under which inventory system is a Cost of Goods Sold account maintained? Why?

17. Why is it advisable to maintain a Sales Returns and Allowances account when the same result could be obtained by debiting each return or allowance to the Sales account?

18. Why is special treatment of the Merchandise Inventory account at the end of the accounting period of particular importance in the determination of net income under the periodic inventory system? What must be achieved in the account?

19. What are the principal differences between the work sheet for a merchandising company and that for a service company? Discuss in terms of the periodic and the perpetual inventory systems.

20. What are the principal differences between the closing entries for a merchandising company using the perpetual inventory system and those for a company using the periodic inventory system?

21. What is the normal balance of the Sales Discounts account? Is it an asset, a liability, an expense, or a contra-revenue account?

SHORT EXERCISES

LO 1 Identification of Management Issues

SE 1. Identify each of the following decisions as most directly related to (a) cash flow management, (b) profitability management, (c) choice of inventory system, or (d) control of merchandising operations.

1. Determination of how to protect cash from theft or embezzlement
2. Determination of the selling price of goods for sale
3. Determination of policies governing sales of merchandise on credit
4. Determination of whether to use the periodic or the perpetual inventory system

LO 2 Merchandising Income Statement

SE 2. Using the following data, prepare an income statement for Melchior Hardware for the month ended February 28.

Cost of Goods Sold	$30,000
General and Administrative Expenses	8,000
Net Sales	50,000
Selling Expenses	7,000

SE 3.

LO 3   Terms of Sale

A machine tool dealer buys machines from a manufacturer and resells the machines to its customers.

a. The manufacturer sets a list or catalogue price of $6,000 for a machine. The manufacturer offers its dealers a 40 percent trade discount.
b. The manufacturer sells the machine under terms of FOB shipping point. The cost of shipping is $350.
c. The manufacturer offers a sales discount of 2/10, n/30. The sales discount does not apply to shipping costs.

What is the net cost of the machine tool to the dealer, assuming it is paid for within ten days of purchase? **3,878**

SE 4.

LO 4   Purchases of Merchandise: Perpetual Inventory System

Record in journal form each of the following transactions, assuming the perpetual inventory system is used.

Aug. 2   Purchased merchandise on credit from Gear Company, invoice dated August 1, terms n/10, FOB shipping point, $2,300.
       3   Received bill from State Shipping Company for transportation costs on August 2 shipment, invoice dated August 1, terms n/30, $210.
       7   Returned damaged merchandise received from Gear Company on August 2 for credit, $360.
      10   Paid in full the amount due to Gear Company for the purchase of August 2, part of which was returned on August 7.

SE 5.

LO 4   Sales of Merchandise: Perpetual Inventory System

Record in journal form the following transactions, assuming the perpetual inventory system is used.

Freight-out/Del. Exp. ←
Cash

Aug. 4   Sold merchandise on credit to Kwai Corporation, terms n/30, FOB destination, $1,200. (Cost = $720)
       5   Paid transportation costs for sale of August 4, $110.
       9   Part of the merchandise sold on August 4 was accepted back from Kwai Corporation for full credit and returned to the merchandise inventory, $350. (Cost = $210)
Sept. 3   Received payment in full from Kwai Corporation for merchandise sold on August 4, less the return on August 9.

SE 6.

LO 4   Credit Card Sales Transaction

Record in journal form the following transaction for Jenny's Novelties Store.

Apr. 19   A tabulation of invoices at the end of the day showed $400 in Visa invoices, which are deposited in a special bank account at full value less 5 percent discount.   *Cash*
✱e.e · Exp. or Fees/Financing Exp. **380 20**
✱credit card = e.e   *Cash*   **400**

SE 7.

SO 5   Purchases of Merchandise: Periodic Inventory System

Record in journal form the transactions in SE 4, assuming the periodic inventory system is used.

SE 8.

SO 5   Cost of Goods Sold: Periodic Inventory System

Using the following data and assuming cost of goods sold is $230,000, prepare the cost of goods sold section of a merchandising income statement (periodic inventory system), including computation of the amount of purchases for the month of October.

Freight In	$12,000
Merchandise Inventory, Sept. 30, 20xx	33,000
Merchandise Inventory, Oct. 31, 20xx	44,000
Purchases	?
Purchases Returns and Allowances	9,000

SE 9.

SO 5   Sales of Merchandise: Periodic Inventory System

Record in journal form the transactions in SE 5 using the periodic inventory system.

SE 10.

SO 6   Merchandise Inventory
SO 7   on the Work Sheet and in Closing Entries

Friedland Company had beginning merchandise inventory of $14,800 and ending merchandise inventory of $19,200. Where would these numbers appear on the work sheet and in the closing entries under (1) the perpetual inventory system and (2) the periodic inventory system?   *$19,200 trial bal.*
debit

SE 11.
SO 8 **Sales and Purchases Discounts**

On April 15, the Hassi Company sold merchandise to Swallow Company for $1,500 on terms of 2/10, n/30. Record the entries in both Hassi's and Swallow's records for (1) the sale, (2) a return of merchandise on April 20 of $300, and (3) payment in full on April 25. Assume both companies use the periodic inventory system.

EXERCISES

E 1.
LO 1 **Management Issues and Decisions**

The decisions and actions below were undertaken by the management of Malouf Shoe Company. Indicate whether each action pertains primarily to (a) cash flow management, (b) profitability management, (c) choice of inventory system, or (d) control of merchandise operations.

1. Decided to mark each item of inventory with a magnetic tag that sets off an alarm if the tag is removed from the store before being deactivated.
2. Decided to reduce the credit terms offered to customers from 30 days to 20 days to speed up collection of accounts.
3. Decided that the benefits of keeping track of each item of inventory as it is bought and sold would exceed the costs of such a system and acted on the decision.
4. Decided to raise the price of each item of inventory to achieve a higher gross margin to offset an increase in rent expense.
5. Decided to purchase a new type of cash register that can be operated only by a person who knows a predetermined code.
6. Decided to switch to a new cleaning service that will provide the same service at a lower cost.

E 2.
LO 1 **Operating Budget**

The operating budget and actual performance for the six months ended June 30, 20x1, for Bearclaw Hardware Company appear as follows:

	Budget	Actual
Selling Expenses		
Sales Salaries Expense	$ 90,000	$102,030
Sales Supplies Expense	2,000	1,642
Rent Expense, Selling Space	18,000	18,000
Utilities Expense, Selling Space	12,000	11,256
Advertising Expense	15,000	21,986
Depreciation Expense, Selling Fixtures	6,500	6,778
Total Selling Expenses	$143,500	$161,692
General and Administrative Expenses		
Office Salaries Expense	$ 50,000	$ 47,912
Office Supplies Expense	1,000	782
Rent Expense, Office Space	4,000	4,000
Depreciation Expense, Office Equipment	3,000	3,251
Utilities Expense, Office Space	3,000	3,114
Postage Expense	500	626
Insurance Expense	2,000	2,700
Miscellaneous Expense	500	481
Total General and Administrative Expenses	$ 64,000	$ 62,866
Total Operating Expenses	$207,500	$224,558

1. Prepare an operating report that shows budget, actual, and difference.
2. Discuss the results, including identifying which differences most likely should be investigated by management.

E 3.
LO 2 **Parts of the Income Statement: Missing Data**

Compute the dollar amount of each item indicated by a letter in the following table. Treat each horizontal row of numbers as a separate problem.

Sales	Cost of Goods Sold	Gross Margin	Operating Expenses	Net Income (Loss)
$250,000	$ a	$ 80,000	$ b	$24,000
c	216,000	120,000	80,000	40,000
460,000	d	100,000	e	(2,000)
780,000	f	g	240,000	80,000

E 4.

LO 3 Terms of Sale

A household appliance dealer buys refrigerators from a manufacturer and resells them to its customers.

a. The manufacturer sets a list or catalogue price of $1,000 for a refrigerator. The manufacturer offers its dealers a 30 percent trade discount.
b. The manufacturer sells the machine under terms of FOB destination. The cost of shipping is $100.
c. The manufacturer offers a sales discount of 2/10, n/30. Sales discounts do not apply to shipping costs.

What is the net cost of the refrigerator to the dealer, assuming it is paid for within ten days of purchase?

E 5.

LO 4 Preparation of the Income Statement: Perpetual Inventory System

Using the selected account balances at December 31, 20xx, for Tents, Etc. Store that follow, prepare an income statement for the year ended December 31, 20xx. Show detail of net sales. The company uses the perpetual inventory system, and Freight In has not been included in Cost of Goods Sold.

Account Name	Debit	Credit
Sales		$237,500
Sales Returns and Allowances	$ 11,750	
Cost of Goods Sold	140,000	
Freight In	6,750	
Selling Expenses	21,500	
General and Administrative Expenses	43,500	
Income Taxes	5,000	

E 6.

LO 4 Recording Purchases: Perpetual Inventory System

Give the entries to record each of the following transactions under the perpetual inventory system:

a. Purchased merchandise on credit, terms n/30, FOB shipping point, $2,500.
b. Paid freight on the shipment in transaction **a**, $135.
c. Purchased merchandise on credit, terms n/30, FOB destination, $1,400.
d. Purchased merchandise on credit, terms n/30, FOB shipping point, $2,600, which includes freight paid by the supplier of $200.
e. Returned part of the merchandise purchased in transaction **c**, $500.
f. Paid the amount owed on the purchase in transaction **a**.
g. Paid the amount owed on the purchase in transaction **d**.
h. Paid the amount owed on the purchase in transaction **c** less the return in **e**.

E 7.

LO 4 Recording Sales: Perpetual Inventory System

On June 15, Vega Company sold merchandise for $1,300 on terms of n/30 to Whist Company. On June 20, Whist Company returned some of the merchandise for a credit of $300, and on June 25, Whist paid the balance owed. Give Vega's entries to record the sale, return, and receipt of payment under the perpetual inventory system. The cost of the merchandise sold on June 15 was $750, and the cost of the merchandise returned to inventory on June 20 was $175.

E 8.

SO 5 Preparation of the Income Statement: Periodic Inventory System

Using the selected year-end account balances at December 31, 20x2, for the Boston General Store shown at the top of the next page, prepare a 20x2 income statement. Show detail of net sales. The company uses the periodic inventory system. Beginning merchandise inventory was $52,000; ending merchandise inventory is $44,000.

Account Name	Debit	Credit
Sales		$594,000
Sales Returns and Allowances	$ 30,400	
Purchases	229,600	
Purchases Returns and Allowances		8,000
Freight In	11,200	
Selling Expenses	97,000	
General and Administrative Expenses	74,400	
Income Taxes	30,000	

E 9.

SO 5 Merchandising Income Statement: Missing Data, Multiple Years

Determine the missing data for each letter in the following three income statements for Leseur Wholesale Paper Company (in thousands):

	20x3	20x2	20x1
Gross Sales	$ p	$ h	$286
Sales Returns and Allowances	24	19	a
Net Sales	q	317	b
Merchandise Inventory, Beginning	r	i	38
Purchases	192	169	c
Purchases Returns and Allowances	31	j	17
Freight In	s	29	22
Net Cost of Purchases	189	k	d
Goods Available for Sale	222	212	182
Merchandise Inventory, Ending	39	l	42
Cost of Goods Sold	t	179	e
Gross Margin	142	m	126
Selling Expenses	u	78	f
General and Administrative Expenses	39	n	33
Total Operating Expenses	130	128	g
Income Before Income Taxes	v	o	27
Income Taxes	3	2	5
Net Income	w	8	22

E 10.

SO 5 Recording Purchases: Periodic Inventory System

Using the data in **E 6,** give the entries to record each of the transactions under the periodic inventory system.

E 11.

SO 5 Recording Sales: Periodic Inventory System

Using the relevant data in **E 7,** give the entries to record each of the transactions under the periodic inventory system.

E 12.

SO 6 Preparation of Closing Entries: Perpetual Inventory System

Below are selected account balances of Li Company for the year ended December 31, 20xx.

Account Name	Debit	Credit
Sales		$297,000
Sales Returns and Allowances	$ 15,200	
Cost of Goods Sold	113,000	
Freight In	5,600	
Selling Expenses	48,500	
General and Administrative Expenses	37,200	

Prepare closing entries, assuming that the owner of Li Company, Su Li, withdrew $40,000 for personal expenses during the year.

E 13.

SO 7 Preparation of Closing Entries: Periodic Inventory System

Selected account balances of the Coastal Grocery Store for the year ended December 31, 20xx, follow.

Account Name	Debit	Credit
Sales		$297,000
Sales Returns and Allowances	$ 11,000	
Sales Discounts	4,200	
Purchases	114,800	
Purchases Returns and Allowances		1,800
Purchases Discounts		2,200
Freight In	5,600	
Selling Expenses	48,500	
General and Administrative Expenses	37,200	

Beginning merchandise inventory was $26,000, and ending merchandise inventory is $22,000. Prepare closing entries, assuming that the owner of Coastal Grocery, John Verplanck, withdrew $34,000 for personal expenses during the year.

E 14.

SO 8 Sales Involving Discounts

Give the entries to record the following transactions engaged in by Cortes Company, which uses the periodic inventory system.

Mar. 1 Sold merchandise on credit to Smith Company, terms 2/10, n/30, FOB shipping point, $500.
      3 Accepted a return from Smith Company for full credit, $200.
      10 Received payment from Smith Company for the sale, less the return and discount.
      11 Sold merchandise on credit to Smith Company, terms 2/10, n/30, FOB destination, $800.
      31 Received payment for amount due from Smith Company for the sale of March 11.

E 15.

SO 8 Purchases Involving Discounts

Give the entries to record the following transactions engaged in by Aquad Company, which uses the periodic inventory system.

July 2 Purchased merchandise on credit from Ordner Company, terms 2/10, n/30, FOB destination, invoice dated July 1, $800.
      6 Returned merchandise to Ordner Company for full credit, $100.
      11 Paid Ordner Company for purchase less return and discount.
      14 Purchased merchandise on credit from Ordner Company, terms 2/10, n/30, FOB destination, invoice dated July 12, $900.
      31 Paid amount owed to Ordner Company for purchase of July 14.

E 16.

SO 8 Purchases and Sales Involving Discounts

The Whalen Company purchased $9,200 of merchandise, terms 2/10, n/30, from the Midori Company and paid for the merchandise within the discount period. Give the entries (1) by the Whalen Company to record the purchase and payment and (2) by the Midori Company to record the sale and receipt of payment. Both companies use the periodic inventory system.

PROBLEMS

P 1.

LO 1 Merchandising Income
LO 4 Statement: Perpetual Inventory System

At the end of the fiscal year, August 31, 20x2, selected accounts from the adjusted trial balance for Alan's Accessories appeared as shown on the next page.

REQUIRED

1. Using the information given, prepare an income statement for Alan's Accessories. Combine Freight In with Cost of Goods Sold. Store Salaries Expense; Advertising Expense; Store Supplies Expense; and Depreciation Expense, Store Equipment are

Alan's Accessories Partial Adjusted Trial Balance August 31, 20x2		
Sales		$162,000
Sales Returns and Allowances	$ 2,000	
Cost of Goods Sold	61,400	
Freight In	2,300	
Store Salaries Expense	32,625	
Office Salaries Expense	12,875	
Advertising Expense	24,300	
Rent Expense	2,400	
Insurance Expense	1,200	
Utilities Expense	1,560	
Store Supplies Expense	2,880	
Office Supplies Expense	1,175	
Depreciation Expense, Store Equipment	1,050	
Depreciation Expense, Office Equipment	800	

selling expenses. The other expenses are general and administrative expenses. The company uses the perpetual inventory system. Show details of net sales and operating expenses.

2. Based on your knowledge to this point in the course, how would you use the income statement for Alan's Accessories to evaluate the company's profitability? What other financial statement should be considered and why?

P 2.

LO 4 Merchandising Transactions: Perpetual Inventory System

Tattle Company engaged in the following transactions in October 20xx.

Oct. 7 Sold merchandise on credit to Lina Ortiz, terms n/30, FOB shipping point, $6,000 (cost, $3,600).

8 Purchased merchandise on credit from Ruff Company, terms n/30, FOB shipping point, $12,000.

9 Paid Curry Company for shipping charges on merchandise purchased on October 8, $508.

10 Purchased merchandise on credit from Sewall Company, terms n/30, FOB shipping point, $19,200, including $1,200 freight costs paid by Sewall.

13 Purchased office supplies on credit from Door Company, terms n/30, $4,800.

14 Sold merchandise on credit to Peter Watts, terms n/30, FOB shipping point, $4,800 (cost, $2,880).

14 Returned damaged merchandise received from Ruff Company on October 8 for credit, $1,200.

17 Received check from Lina Ortiz for her purchase of October 7.

18 Returned a portion of the office supplies received on October 13 for credit because the wrong items were sent, $800.

19 Sold merchandise for cash, $3,600 (cost, $2,160).

20 Paid Sewall Company for purchase of October 10.

21 Paid Ruff Company the balance from the transactions of October 8 and October 14.

24 Accepted from Peter Watts a return of merchandise, which was put back in inventory, $400 (cost, $240).

REQUIRED

Prepare entries in journal form to record the transactions, assuming the perpetual inventory system is used.

P 3.

LO 1 Merchandising Income
SO 5 Statement: Periodic Inventory System

Selected accounts from the adjusted trial balance for Carol's Kitchen Shop, as of March 31, 20x4, the end of the fiscal year, are shown on the next page. The merchandise inventory for Carol's Kitchen Shop was $38,200 at the beginning of the year and $29,400 at the end of the year.

Carol's Kitchen Shop Partial Adjusted Trial Balance March 31, 20x4		
Sales		$165,000
Sales Returns and Allowances	$ 2,000	
Purchases	70,200	
Purchases Returns and Allowances		2,600
Freight In	2,300	
Store Salaries Expense	32,625	
Office Salaries Expense	12,875	
Advertising Expense	24,300	
Rent Expense	2,400	
Insurance Expense	1,200	
Utilities Expense	1,560	
Store Supplies Expense	2,880	
Office Supplies Expense	1,175	
Depreciation Expense, Store Equipment	1,050	
Depreciation Expense, Office Equipment	800	

REQUIRED

1. Using the information given, prepare an income statement for Carol's Kitchen Shop. Store Salaries Expense; Advertising Expense; Store Supplies Expense; and Depreciation Expense, Store Equipment are selling expenses. The other expenses are general and administrative expenses. The company uses the periodic inventory system. Show detail of net sales and operating expenses.

2. Based on your knowledge at this point in the course, how would you use the income statement for Carol's Kitchen Shop to evaluate the company's profitability? What other financial statements should be considered and why?

P 4.

SO 5 Merchandising Transactions: Periodic Inventory System

Use the data in **P 2** for this problem.

REQUIRED

Prepare entries in journal form to record the transactions, assuming the periodic inventory system is used.

P 5.

SO 6 Work Sheet, Financial Statements, and Closing Entries for a Merchandising Company: Perpetual Inventory System

The trial balance at the top of the next page was taken from the ledger of Metzler Music Store at the end of its annual accounting period.

REQUIRED

1. Assuming the company uses the perpetual inventory system, enter the trial balance on a work sheet, and complete the work sheet using the following information: ending store supplies inventory, $912; unexpired prepaid insurance, $600; estimated depreciation on store equipment, $12,900; sales salaries payable, $240; and accrued utilities expense, $450.

2. Prepare an income statement, a statement of owner's equity, and a balance sheet. Sales Salaries Expense; Other Selling Expenses; Store Supplies Expense; and Depreciation Expense, Store Equipment are all selling expenses.

3. From the work sheet, prepare the closing entries.

Metzler Music Store
Trial Balance
November 30, 20x4

Cash	$ 18,075	
Accounts Receivable	27,840	
Merchandise Inventory	99,681	
Store Supplies	5,733	
Prepaid Insurance	4,800	
Store Equipment	111,600	
Accumulated Depreciation, Store Equipment		$ 46,800
Accounts Payable		36,900
Susan Metzler, Capital		167,313
Susan Metzler, Withdrawals	36,000	
Sales		306,750
Sales Returns and Allowances	2,961	
Cost of Goods Sold	156,567	
Freight In	6,783	
Sales Salaries Expense	64,050	
Rent Expense	10,800	
Other Selling Expenses	7,842	
Utilities Expense	5,031	
	$557,763	$557,763

P 6.

SO 7 Work Sheet, Financial Statements, and Closing Entries for a Merchandising Company: Periodic Inventory System

The year-end trial balance below was taken from the ledger of Le Bere Office Supplies Company at the end of its annual accounting period, on September 30, 20x4.

Le Bere Office Supplies Company
Trial Balance
September 30, 20x4

Cash	$ 21,150	
Accounts Receivable	74,490	
Merchandise Inventory	214,200	
Store Supplies	11,400	
Prepaid Insurance	14,400	
Store Equipment	253,900	
Accumulated Depreciation, Store Equipment		$ 76,500
Accounts Payable		116,850
Grace Le Bere, Capital		484,050
Grace Le Bere, Withdrawals	72,000	
Sales		1,225,750
Sales Returns and Allowances	25,440	
Purchases	754,800	
Purchases Returns and Allowances		18,150
Freight In	31,200	
Sales Salaries Expense	193,800	
Rent Expense	144,000	
Other Selling Expenses	98,730	
Utilities Expense	11,790	
	$1,921,300	$1,921,300

REQUIRED

1. Assuming the company uses the periodic inventory system, enter the trial balance on a work sheet, and complete the work sheet using the following information: end-

ing merchandise inventory, $266,700; ending store supplies inventory, $1,650; expired insurance, $7,200; estimated depreciation on store equipment, $15,000; sales salaries payable, $1,950; and accrued utilities expense, $300.

2. Prepare an income statement, a statement of owner's equity, and a balance sheet. Sales Salaries Expense; Other Selling Expenses; Store Supplies Expense; and Depreciation Expense, Store Equipment are selling expenses.

3. From the work sheet, prepare the closing entries.

P 7.
SO 5 **Merchandising Transactions,**
SO 8 **Including Discounts:**
Periodic Inventory System

The following is a list of transactions for Attention Promotions Company for the month of March 20xx:

Mar. 1 Sold merchandise on credit to M. Gaberman, terms 2/10, n/60, FOB shipping point, $2,200.

3 Purchased merchandise on credit from King Company, terms 2/10, n/30, FOB shipping point, $12,800.

4 Received freight bill for shipment received on March 3, $900.

6 Sold merchandise for cash, $1,100.

7 Sold merchandise on credit to B. Gomez, terms 2/10, n/60, $2,400.

9 Purchased merchandise from Armstrong Company, terms 1/10, n/30, FOB shipping point, $6,180, which includes freight charges of $400.

10 Sold merchandise on credit to G. Horn, terms 2/10, n/20, $4,400.

10 Received check from M. Gaberman for payment in full for sale of March 1.

11 Purchased merchandise from King Company, terms 2/10, n/30, FOB shipping point, $16,400.

12 Received freight bill for shipment of March 11, $1,460.

13 Paid King Company for purchase of March 3.

14 Returned merchandise from the March 9 shipment that was the wrong size and color, for credit, $580.

16 G. Horn returned some of the merchandise sold to him on March 10 for credit, $400.

17 Received payment from B. Gomez for half of his purchase on March 7. A discount is allowed on partial payment.

18 Paid Armstrong Company balance due on account from transactions on March 9 and 14.

20 In checking the purchase of March 11 from King Company, the accounting department found an overcharge of $800. King agreed to issue a credit.

21 Paid freight company for freight charges of March 4 and 12.

23 Purchased cleaning supplies on credit from Moon Company, terms n/5, $500.

24 Discovered that some of the cleaning supplies purchased on March 23 had not been ordered. Returned them to Moon Company for credit, $100.

25 Sold merchandise for cash, $1,600.

27 Paid Moon Company for the March 23 purchase less the March 24 return.

28 Received payment in full from G. Horn for transactions on March 10 and 16.

29 Paid King Company for purchase of March 11 less allowance of March 20.

31 Received payment for balance of amount owed from B. Gomez from transactions of March 7 and 17.

REQUIRED

Prepare entries in journal form to record the transactions, assuming that the periodic inventory system is used.

ALTERNATE PROBLEMS

P 8.
LO 1 **Merchandising Income**
LO 4 **Statement: Perpetual**
Inventory System

At the end of the fiscal year, June 30, 20x3, selected accounts from the adjusted trial balance for Hans' Video Store appeared as shown on the next page.

REQUIRED

1. Prepare a multistep income statement for Hans' Video Store. Freight In should be combined with Cost of Goods Sold. Store Salaries Expense; Advertising Expense; Store Supplies Expense; and Depreciation Expense, Store Equipment are selling expenses. The other expenses are general and administrative expenses. Hans' Video

Hans' Video Store
Partial Adjusted Trial Balance
June 30, 20x3

Sales		$867,824
Sales Returns and Allowances	$ 22,500	
Cost of Goods Sold	442,370	
Freight In	20,156	
Store Salaries Expense	215,100	
Office Salaries Expense	53,000	
Advertising Expense	36,400	
Rent Expense	28,800	
Insurance Expense	5,600	
Utilities Expense	17,520	
Store Supplies Expense	4,928	
Office Supplies Expense	3,628	
Depreciation Expense, Store Equipment	3,600	
Depreciation Expense, Office Equipment	3,700	

Store uses the perpetual inventory system. Show detail of net sales and operating expenses.

2. Based on your knowledge to this point in the course, how would you use the income statement for Hans' Video Store to evaluate the company's profitability? What other financial statement should be considered and why?

P 9.

LO 4 Merchandising Transactions: Perpetual Inventory System

Tonia Company engaged in the following transactions in July 20xx:

July 1 Sold merchandise to Su Long on credit, terms n/30, FOB shipping point, $4,200 (cost, $2,520).
3 Purchased merchandise on credit from Angier Company, terms n/30, FOB shipping point, $7,600.
5 Paid Mix Freight for freight charges on merchandise received, $580.
6 Purchased store supplies on credit from Exto Supply Company, terms n/20, $1,272.
8 Purchased merchandise on credit from Ginn Company, terms n/30, FOB shipping point, $7,200, which includes $400 freight costs paid by Ginn Company.
12 Returned some of the merchandise received on July 3 for credit, $1,200.
15 Sold merchandise on credit to Pete Smith, terms n/30, FOB shipping point, $2,400 (cost, $1,440).
16 Returned some of the store supplies purchased on July 6 for credit, $400.
17 Sold merchandise for cash, $2,000 (cost, $1,200).
18 Accepted for full credit a return from Su Long and returned merchandise to inventory, $400 (cost, $240).
24 Paid Angier Company for purchase of July 3 less return of July 12.
25 Received full payment from Su Long for her July 1 purchase less the return on July 18.

REQUIRED

Prepare entries in journal form to record the transactions, assuming use of the perpetual inventory system.

P 10.

LO 1 Merchandising Income
SO 5 Statement: Periodic Inventory System

The data on the next page come from Dan's Sports Equipment's adjusted trial balance as of September 30, 20x5, the fiscal year end. The company's beginning merchandise inventory was $81,222, and ending merchandise inventory is $76,664 for the period.

REQUIRED

1. Prepare a multistep income statement for Dan's Sports Equipment. Store Salaries Expense; Advertising Expense; Store Supplies Expense; and Depreciation Expense, Store Equipment are selling expenses. The other expenses are general and adminis-

Dan's Sports Equipment Partial Adjusted Trial Balance September 30, 20x5		
Sales		$433,912
Sales Returns and Allowances	$ 11,250	
Purchases	221,185	
Purchases Returns and Allowances		30,238
Freight In	10,078	
Store Salaries Expense	107,550	
Office Salaries Expense	26,500	
Advertising Expense	18,200	
Rent Expense	14,400	
Insurance Expense	2,800	
Utilities Expense	18,760	
Store Supplies Expense	464	
Office Supplies Expense	814	
Depreciation Expense, Store Equipment	1,800	
Depreciation Expense, Office Equipment	1,850	

trative expenses. The company uses the periodic inventory system. Show detail of net sales and operating expenses.

2. Based on your knowledge at this point in the course, how would you use the income statement for Dan's Sports Equipment to evaluate the company's profitability? What other financial statements should be considered and why?

P 11.

SO 5   Merchandising Transactions: Periodic Inventory System

Use the data in **P 9** for this problem.

REQUIRED

Prepare entries in journal form to record the transactions, assuming the periodic inventory system is used.

EXPANDING YOUR CRITICAL THINKING, COMMUNICATION, AND INTERPERSONAL SKILLS

SKILLS DEVELOPMENT

Conceptual Analysis

SD 1.

LO 1   Merchandising Income
LO 2   Statement

Village TV and *TV Warehouse* sell television sets and other video equipment in the Phoenix area. Village TV gives each customer individual attention, with employees explaining the features, advantages, and disadvantages of each video component. When a customer buys a television set or video system, Village provides free delivery, installs and adjusts the equipment, and teaches the family how to use it. TV Warehouse sells the same video components through showroom display. If a customer wants to buy a

Cash Flow

CD-ROM

Communication

Critical Thinking

Ethics

General Ledger

Group Activity

Hot Links to Real Companies

International

Internet

Key Ratio

Memo

Spreadsheet

video component or a system, he or she fills out a form and takes it to the cashier for payment. After paying, the customer drives to the back of the warehouse to pick up the component, which he or she then takes home and installs. Village TV charges higher prices than TV Warehouse for the same components. Discuss how you would expect the income statements of Village TV and TV Warehouse to differ. Is it possible to tell which approach is more profitable?

Group Activity: Divide the class into informal groups. In addition to answering the above questions, ask each group to decide which store they would prefer to shop in and why. Allow 15 minutes and debrief immediately.

SD 2.

LO 1 **Periodic Versus Perpetual**
LO 4 **Inventory Systems**
SO 5

The Book Nook is a well-established chain of 20 bookstores in eastern Michigan. In recent years the company has grown rapidly, adding five new stores in regional malls. Management has relied on the manager of each store to place orders keyed to the market in his or her neighborhood, selected from a master list of available titles provided by the central office. Every six months, a physical inventory is taken, and financial statements are prepared using the periodic inventory system. At that time, books that have not sold well are placed on sale or, whenever possible, returned to the publisher. As a result of the company's fast growth, there are many new store managers, who management has found do not have the same ability to judge the market as do managers of the older, established stores. Thus, management is considering a recommendation to implement a perpetual inventory system and carefully monitor sales from the central office. Do you think The Book Nook should switch to the perpetual inventory system or stay with the periodic inventory system? Discuss the advantages and disadvantages of each system.

Ethical Dilemma

SD 3.

SO 8 **Ethics and Purchases**
Discounts

The purchasing power of some customers is such that they can exert pressure on suppliers to go beyond the suppliers' customary allowances. For example, *Wal-Mart* represents more than 10 percent of annual sales for many suppliers, such as Fruit of the Loom, Rubbermaid, Sunbeam, and Coleman. *Forbes* magazine reports that while many of these suppliers allow a 2 percent discount if bills are paid within 15 days, "Wal-Mart routinely pays its bills closer to 30 days and takes the 2 percent discount anyway on the gross amount of the invoice, not the net amount, which deducts for [trade] discounts and things like freight costs."[3] Identify three ways in which Wal-Mart's practice benefits Wal-Mart. Do you think this practice is unethical, or is it just good cash management on the part of Wal-Mart? Are the suppliers harmed by it?

Research Activity

SD 4.

LO 1 **Merchandising Companies**
LO 2

Conduct an individual field trip by visiting any retail or wholesale business. It may be a business where you buy a product, a company where you work, or a family business. It is not necessary for you to talk to anyone at the business, but it may be helpful to do so. Determine why the business is a merchandising business. List the products or groups of products that the company sells. Does the company offer any services? How do services differ from merchandise? Make a list of the types of transactions the business engages in. Also identify and list all the operating expenses you can think of that would be relevant to this business. Organize your findings in the form of a memo to your instructor.

Decision-Making Practice

SD 5.

LO 2 **Analysis of Merchandising**
Income Statement

In 20x5 Les Solty opened a small retail store in a suburban mall. Called *Solty Denim Company,* the shop sold designer jeans. Solty worked 14 hours a day and controlled all aspects of the operation. All sales were for cash or bank credit card. The business was such a success that in 20x6 Solty decided to open a second store in another mall. Because the new shop needed his attention, he hired a manager to work in the original store with two sales clerks. During 20x6 the new store was successful, but the operations of the original store did not match the first year's performance.

Concerned about this turn of events, Solty compared the two years' results for the original store. The figures are as follows:

	20x6	20x5
Net Sales	$325,000	$350,000
Cost of Goods Sold	225,000	225,000
Gross Margin	$100,000	$125,000
Operating Expenses	75,000	50,000
Net Income	$ 25,000	$ 75,000

In addition, Solty's analysis revealed that the cost and selling price of jeans were about the same in both years and that the level of operating expenses was roughly the same in both years, except for the new manager's $25,000 salary. Sales returns and allowances were insignificant amounts in both years.

Studying the situation further, Solty discovered the following facts about the cost of goods sold:

	20x6	20x5
Gross purchases	$200,000	$271,000
Total purchases allowances	15,000	20,000
Freight in	19,000	27,000
Physical inventory, end of year	32,000	53,000

Still not satisfied, Solty went through all the individual sales and purchases records for the year. Both sales and purchases were verified. However, the 20x6 ending inventory should have been $57,000, given the unit purchases and sales during the year. After puzzling over all this information, Solty comes to you for accounting help.

1. Using Solty's new information, recompute the cost of goods sold for 20x5 and 20x6, and account for the difference in net income between 20x5 and 20x6.

2. Suggest at least two reasons for the discrepancy in the 20x6 ending inventory. How might Solty improve the management of the original store?

FINANCIAL REPORTING AND ANALYSIS

Interpreting Financial Reports

FRA 1.

LO 2 Comparison of Operating Performance

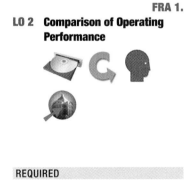

Wal-Mart Stores, Inc., and *Kmart Corp.,* two of the largest retailers in the United States, have different approaches to retailing. Their success has been different also. At one time, Kmart was larger than Wal-Mart. Today, Wal-Mart is almost three times as large. You can see the difference by analyzing their respective income statements and merchandise inventories. Selected information from their annual reports for the year ended January 31, 2000, is presented below. (All amounts are in millions.)[4]

Wal-Mart: Net Sales, $165,013; Cost of Goods Sold, $129,664; Operating Expenses, $27,040; Ending Inventory, $19,793

Kmart: Net Sales, $35,925; Cost of Goods Sold, $28,102; Operating Expenses, $6,523; Ending Inventory, $7,101

REQUIRED

1. Prepare a schedule computing the gross margin and income from operations for both companies as dollar amounts and as percentages of net sales. Also, compute inventory as a percentage of the cost of goods sold.

2. From what you know about the different retailing approaches of these two companies, do the gross margins and incomes from operations you computed in 1 seem compatible with these approaches? What is it about the nature of Wal-Mart's operations that produces lower gross margin and lower operating expenses in percentages in comparison to Kmart? Which company's approach was more successful in the fiscal year ending January 31, 2000? Explain your answer.

3. Both companies have chosen a fiscal year that ends on January 31. Why do you suppose they made this choice? How realistic do you think the inventory figures are as indicators of inventory levels during the rest of the year? Which company appears to make most efficient use of its inventory?

FRA 2.

LO 1 Business Objectives and
LO 2 Income Statements

Superior Products, Inc., is one of the nation's largest discount retailers, operating 216 stores in 30 states. In a letter to stockholders in the 1999 annual report (fiscal year ended January 31, 2000), the chairman and chief executive officer of the company stated, "Our operating plan for fiscal 2000 (year ended January 31, 2001) calls for moderate sales increases, continued improvement in gross margins, and a continuation of aggressive expense reduction programs." The following data are taken from the income statements presented in the 2000 annual report (dated January 30, 2001) (in millions):

| | Year Ended | | |
	January 30, 2001	January 31, 2000	February 1, 1999
Net Sales	$2,067	$2,142	$2,235
Cost of Goods Sold	1,500	1,593	1,685
Operating Expenses	466	486	502

REQUIRED

Did Superior Products, Inc., achieve the objective stated by its chairman? (**Hint:** Prepare an income statement for each year and compute gross margin and operating expenses as percentages of net sales.)

International Company

FRA 3.

LO 3 Terminology for
LO 4 Merchandising
SO 5 Transactions in England

Harrods is a large English retailer with department stores throughout England and in other European countries. Merchandising terms in England differ from those in the United States. For instance, in England, the income statement is called the profit and loss account, sales is called turnover, merchandise inventory is called stocks, accounts receivable is called debtors, and accounts payable is called creditors. Of course, the amounts are stated in terms of the pound (£). In today's business world, it is important to understand and use terminology employed by professionals from other countries. Explain in your own words why the English may use the terms *profit and loss account, turnover, stocks, debtors,* and *creditors* in place of the American terms.

Toys "R" Us Annual Report

FRA 4.

LO 1 Operating Cycle

Refer to the Toys "R" Us annual report at the end of Chapter 6 and to Figure 1 in this chapter. Write a memorandum to your instructor on the subject of the Toys "R" Us operating cycle. This memorandum should identify the most common transactions in the operating cycle as it applies to Toys "R" Us and should support the answer by referring to the importance of accounts receivable, accounts payable, and merchandise inventory in the Toys "R" Us financial statements. Complete the memorandum by explaining why this operating cycle is favorable to Toys "R" Us.

Fingraph® Financial Analyst™

FRA 5.

LO 1 Income Statement Analysis
LO 2

Choose any retail company from the Fingraph® Financial Analyst™ CD-ROM software and display the Income Statements Analysis: Income from Operations in tabular and graphical form for the company. Write an executive summary that analyzes the change in the company's income from operations from the first to the second year. In preparing your response, focus on the reasons the change occurred by answering the following questions: Did the company's income from operations improve or decline from the first to the second year? What was the relationship of the change to the change in net sales? Was the change in income from operations primarily due to a change in gross margin or a change in operating expenses? Suggest some possible reasons for the change in gross margin or operating expenses. Use percentages to support your answer.

Internet Case

FRA 6.

LO 1 **Comparison of Traditional**
LO 3 **Merchandising to**
LO 4 **E-commerce**

E-commerce is a word coined to describe merchandising companies that attempt to establish retail business over the Internet. This type of business is similar in some ways to traditional retailing, but it also presents new challenges. Choose a company with traditional retail outlets that is also selling over the Internet and go to its web site. Some examples to choose from are **Wal-Mart Stores, Inc., Kmart Corp., Toys "R" Us, Barnes & Noble**, and **Lands End.** Investigate and list the steps a customer makes to purchase a good on the site. How do these steps differ from those in a traditional retail store? What are some of the accounting challenges in recording the transaction? Be prepared to discuss your results in class.

ENDNOTES

1. Target Corp., *Annual Report*, 1999.
2. Ibid.
3. Matthew Schifrin, "The Big Squeeze," *Forbes*, March 11, 1996.
4. Wal-Mart Stores, Inc., *Annual Report*, 1999; and Kmart Corp., *Annual Report*, 1999.

6 Financial Reporting and Analysis

General Mills, Inc. The management of a corporation is judged by the company's financial performance. This financial performance is reported to stockholders and others outside the business in the company's published annual report, which includes the company's financial statements and other relevant information. Performance measures are usually based on the relationships of key data in the financial statements and are communicated by management to the reader. For large companies, this often means condensing a tremendous amount of information to a few numbers considered important by management. For example, what key measures does the management of General Mills, Inc., a successful food products company with brands such as Cheerios, Wheaties, Hamburger Helper, and Fruit Roll-ups, choose to focus on as its goals?

After restoring double-digit earnings per share growth over the last two years (see chart), General Mills' management, in a recent press release, presented the company's growth model for 2000–2010, which included the following goals:

- *To generate 7 to 8 percent compound annual sales growth over the next decade.*
- *To generate continued double-digit earnings per share growth over the next decade.*

The General Mills' chief executive stated, "We believe that if we meet these growth goals, our performance will result in superior returns to our shareholders."[1]

Of course, investors and creditors will want to conduct their own analysis of General Mills as well. This will require reading and interpretation of the financial statements and the calculation of other ratios. However, this analysis will be meaningless unless the reader understands financial statements and generally accepted accounting principles, on

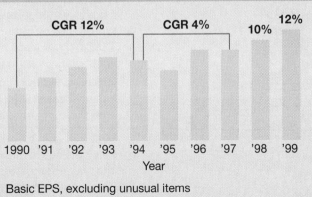

General Mills Earnings Per Share (EPS) Growth

CGR 12%   CGR 4%   10%   12%

1990 '91 '92 '93 '94 '95 '96 '97 '98 '99
Year

Basic EPS, excluding unusual items
CGR = Compound growth rate

which the statements are based. Also important to learning how to read and interpret financial statements is a comprehension of the categories and classifications used in balance sheets and income statements. Key financial ratios used in financial statement analysis are based on those categories. The chapter begins by describing the objectives, characteristics, and conventions that underlie the preparation of financial statements.

Objectives of Financial Information

The United States has a highly developed exchange economy. In this kind of economy, most goods and services are exchanged for money or claims to money instead of being used or bartered by their producers. Most business is carried on through corporations, including many extremely large firms that buy, sell, and obtain financing in U.S. and world markets.

By issuing stocks and bonds that are traded in financial markets, businesses can raise capital for production and marketing activities. Investors are interested mainly in returns from dividends and increases in the market price of their investments. Creditors want to know if the business can repay a loan plus interest in accordance with required terms. Thus, investors and creditors both need to know if a company can generate adequate cash flows. Financial statements are important to both groups in making that judgment. They offer valuable information that helps investors and creditors judge a company's ability to pay dividends and repay debts with interest. In this way, the market puts scarce resources to work in the companies that can use them most efficiently.

The information needs of users and the general business environment are the basis for the Financial Accounting Standards Board's (FASB) three objectives of financial reporting:[2]

1. *To furnish information that is useful in making investment and credit decisions.* Financial reporting should offer information that can help present and potential investors and creditors make rational investment and credit decisions. The reports should be in a form that makes sense to those who have some understanding of business and are willing to study the information carefully.

2. *To provide information useful in assessing cash flow prospects.* Financial reporting should supply information to help present and potential investors and creditors judge the amounts, timing, and risk of expected cash receipts from dividends or interest and the proceeds from the sale, redemption, or maturity of stocks or loans.

3. *To provide information about business resources, claims to those resources, and changes in them.* Financial reporting should give information about the company's assets, liabilities, and stockholders' equity, and the effects of transactions on the company's assets, liabilities, and stockholders' equity.

Financial statements are the most important way of periodically presenting to parties outside the business the information that has been gathered and processed in the accounting system. For this reason, the financial statements—the balance sheet, the income statement, the statement of owner's equity, and the statement of cash flows—are the most important output of the accounting system. These financial statements are "general purpose" because of their wide audience. They are "external" because their users are outside the business. Because of a potential conflict of interest between managers, who must prepare the statements, and investors or creditors, who invest in or lend money to the business, these statements often are audited by outside accountants to increase confidence in their reliability.

Qualitative Characteristics of Accounting Information

OBJECTIVE

2 State the qualitative characteristics of accounting information and describe their interrelationships

It is easy for students in their first accounting course to get the idea that accounting is 100 percent accurate. This idea is reinforced by the fact that all the problems in this and other introductory books can be solved. The numbers all add up; what is supposed to equal something else does. Accounting seems very much like mathematics in its precision. In this course, the basics of accounting are presented in a simple form to help you understand them. In practice, however, accounting information is neither simple nor precise, and it rarely satisfies all criteria. The FASB emphasizes this fact in the following statement:

> The information provided by financial reporting often results from approximate, rather than exact, measures. The measures commonly involve numerous estimates, classifications, summarizations, judgments and allocations. The outcome of economic activity in a dynamic economy is uncertain and results from combinations of many factors. Thus, despite the aura of precision that may seem to surround financial reporting in general and financial statements in particular, with few exceptions the measures are approximations, which may be based on rules and conventions, rather than exact amounts.[3]

The goal of accounting information—to provide the basic data that different users need to make informed decisions—is an ideal. The gap between the ideal and the actual provides much of the interest and controversy in accounting. To facilitate interpretation, the FASB has described the **qualitative characteristics** of accounting information, which are standards for judging that information. In addition, there are generally accepted conventions for recording and reporting that simplify interpretation. The relationships among these concepts are shown in Figure 1.

The most important qualitative characteristics are understandability and usefulness. **Understandability** depends on both the accountant and the decision maker. The accountant prepares the financial statements in accordance with accepted practices, generating important information that is believed to be understandable. But the decision maker must interpret the information and decide how to use it in making decisions.

For accounting information to meet the standard of **usefulness**, it must have two major qualitative characteristics: relevance and reliability. **Relevance** means that the information can affect the outcome of a decision. In other words, a different decision would be made if the relevant information were not available. To be relevant, information must provide feedback, help predict future conditions, and be timely. For example, the income statement provides information about how a company performed over the past year (feedback), and it helps in planning for the next year (prediction). In order to be useful, however, it also must be communicated soon enough after the end of the accounting period to enable the reader to make decisions (timeliness).

In addition to being relevant, accounting information must have **reliability**. In other words, the user must be able to depend on the information. It must represent what it is meant to represent. It must be verifiable by independent parties using the same methods of measuring. It also must be neutral. Accounting should

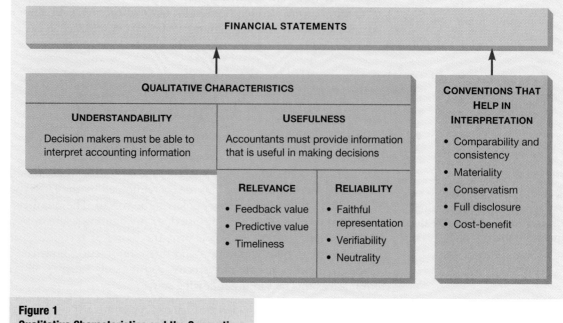

Figure 1
Qualitative Characteristics and the Conventions of Accounting Information

convey information about business activity as faithfully as possible without influencing anyone in a specific direction. For example, the balance sheet should represent the economic resources, obligations, and owner's equity of a business as faithfully as possible in accordance with generally accepted accounting principles, and this balance sheet should be verifiable by an auditor.

Conventions That Help in the Interpretation of Financial Information

OBJECTIVE

3 Define and describe the use of the conventions of *comparability* and *consistency, materiality, conservatism, full disclosure,* and *cost-benefit*

To a large extent, financial statements are based on estimates and application of accounting rules for recognition and allocation. In this book, we point out a number of difficulties with financial statements. One is failing to recognize the changing value of the dollar caused by inflation. Another is treating intangibles, such as research and development costs, as assets if they are purchased outside the company and as expenses if they are developed within the company. Such problems do not mean that financial statements are useless; they are essential. However, users must know how to interpret them. To help in this interpretation, accountants depend on five **conventions**, or rules of thumb, in recording transactions and preparing financial statements: (1) comparability and consistency, (2) materiality, (3) conservatism, (4) full disclosure, and (5) cost-benefit.

Comparability and Consistency

A characteristic that increases the usefulness of accounting information is comparability. Information about a company is more useful if it can be compared with similar facts about the same company over several time periods or about another company for the same time period. **Comparability** means that the information is presented in such a way that a decision maker can recognize similarities, differences, and trends over different time periods or between different companies.

Consistent use of accounting measures and procedures is important in achieving comparability. The **consistency** convention requires that an accounting procedure, once adopted by a company, remain in use from one period to the next unless users are informed of the change. Thus, without a note to the contrary, users of financial statements can assume that there has been no arbitrary change in the treatment of a particular transaction, account, or item that would affect the interpretation of the statements.

If management decides that a certain procedure is no longer appropriate and should be changed or if reporting requirements change, generally accepted accounting principles require that the change and its dollar effect be described in the notes to the financial statements:

> The nature of and justification for a change in accounting principle and its effect on income should be disclosed in the financial statements of the period in which the change is made. The justification for the change should explain clearly why the newly adopted accounting principle is preferable.[4]

 For example, in a recent year, Reynolds Metals Company changed its method of accounting for business start-up costs because the AICPA changed the requirements for accounting for this type of cost.[5]

Materiality

The term **materiality** refers to the relative importance of an item or event. If an item or event is material, it is probably relevant to the user of financial statements. In other words, an item is material if users would have done something differently if they had not known about the item. The accountant is often faced with decisions about small items or events that make little difference to users no matter how they are handled. For example, a large company may decide that expenditures for durable items of less than $500 should be charged as expenses rather than recorded as long-term assets and depreciated.

In general, an item is material if there is a reasonable expectation that knowing about it would influence the decisions of users of financial statements. The materiality of an item normally is determined by relating its dollar value to an element of the financial statements, such as net income or total assets. Some accountants feel that when an item is 5 percent or more of net income, it is material. However, materiality also depends on the nature of the item, not just its value. For example, in a multimillion-dollar company, a mistake of $5,000 in recording an item may not be important, but the discovery of a $5,000 bribe or theft can be very important. Also, many small errors can combine into a material amount. Accountants judge the materiality of many things, and the users of financial statements depend on their judgments being fair and accurate. The SEC has recently questioned companies' judgment in using the materiality convention to avoid showing certain items in the financial statements.

Conservatism

Accountants try to base their decisions on logic and evidence that lead to the fairest report of what happened. In judging and estimating, however, accountants often are faced with uncertainties. In these cases, they look to the convention of **conservatism**. This convention means that when accountants face major uncertainties about which accounting procedure to use, they generally choose the one that is least likely to overstate assets and income.

One of the most common applications of the conservatism convention is the use of the lower-of-cost-or-market method in accounting for inventories. Under this method, if an item's market value is greater than its cost, the more conservative cost figure is used. If the market value falls below the cost, the more conservative market value is used. The latter situation often occurs in the computer industry.

Conservatism can be a useful tool in doubtful cases, but its abuse leads to incorrect and misleading financial statements. Suppose that someone incorrectly applies the conservatism convention by expensing a long-term asset of material cost in the period of purchase. In this case, there is no uncertainty. Income and assets for the current period would be understated, and income in future periods would be overstated. For this reason, accountants depend on the conservatism convention only when there is uncertainty about which accounting procedure to use.

Full Disclosure

The convention of **full disclosure** requires that financial statements and their notes present all information that is relevant to the users' understanding of the statements. That is, the statements should offer any explanation that is needed to keep them from being misleading. Explanatory notes are considered an integral part of the financial statements. For instance, a change from one accounting procedure to another should be reported. In general, the form of the financial statements can affect their usefulness in making certain decisions. In addition, certain items, such as the amount of depreciation expense on the income statement and the accumulated depreciation on the balance sheet, are essential to the readers of financial statements.

Other examples of disclosures required by the Financial Accounting Standards Board and other official bodies are the accounting procedures used in preparing the statements, important terms of the company's debt, commitments and contingencies, and important events taking place after the date of the statements. However, there is a point at which the statements become so cluttered that notes impede rather than help understanding. Beyond required disclosures, the application of the full-disclosure convention is based on the judgment of management and of the accountants who prepare the financial statements. In recent years, the principle of full disclosure also has been influenced by users of accounting information.

FOCUS ON BUSINESS PRACTICE

When is "full disclosure" too much? When does the cost exceed the benefits? The big-five accounting firm of Ernst & Young reports that over a 20-year period the total number of pages in the annual reports of 25 large, well-known companies increased an average of 84 percent and the number of pages of notes increased 325 percent—from 4 pages to 17 pages. Management's discussion and analysis increased 300 percent, from 3 pages to 12.[6] Because some people feel that "these documents are so daunting that people don't read them at all," the Securities and Exchange Commission (SEC) allows companies to issue "summary reports" to the public that would eliminate many of the current notes. These reports would be more accessible and less costly. This is a controversial action because many analysts feel that it is in the notes that one gets the detailed information necessary to understand complex business operations. One analyst remarked, "To banish the notes for fear they will turn off readers would be like eliminating fractions from math books on the theory that the average student prefers to work with whole numbers."[7] Where this controversy will end, nobody knows. Detailed reports still must be filed with the SEC, but more and more companies are providing summary reports to the public.

To protect investors and creditors, independent auditors, the stock exchanges, and the SEC have made more demands for disclosure by publicly owned companies. The SEC has been pushing especially hard for the enforcement of full disclosure. As a result, more and better information about corporations is available to the public today than ever before.

Cost-Benefit

The **cost-benefit** convention underlies all the qualitative characteristics and conventions. It holds that the benefits to be gained from providing accounting information should be greater than the costs of providing it. Of course, minimum levels of relevance and reliability must be reached if accounting information is to be useful. Beyond the minimum levels, however, it is up to the FASB and the SEC, which require the information, and the accountant, who provides the information, to judge the costs and benefits in each case. Most of the costs of providing information fall at first on the preparers; the benefits are reaped by both preparers and users. Finally, both the costs and the benefits are passed on to society in the form of prices and social benefits from more efficient allocation of resources.

The costs and benefits of a particular requirement for accounting disclosure are both direct and indirect, immediate and deferred. For example, it is hard to judge the final costs and benefits of a far-reaching and costly regulation. The FASB, for instance, allows certain large companies to make a supplemental disclosure in their financial statements of the effects of changes in current costs. Most companies choose not to present this information because they believe the costs of producing and providing it exceed its benefits to the readers of their financial statements. Cost-benefit is a question faced by all regulators, including the FASB and the SEC. Even though there are no definitive ways of measuring costs and benefits, much of an accountant's work deals with these concepts.

Management's Responsibility for Ethical Reporting

OBJECTIVE

4 Explain management's responsibility for ethical financial reporting and define *fraudulent financial reporting*

The users of financial statements depend on the good faith of those who prepare these statements. This dependence places a duty on a company's management and its accountants to act ethically in the reporting process. That duty is often expressed in the report of management that accompanies financial statements. For example, the report of the management of Quaker Oats Co., a company known for strong financial reporting and controls, states:

> Management is responsible for the preparation and integrity of the Company's financial statements. The financial statements have been prepared in accordance with generally accepted accounting principles and necessarily include some amounts that are based on management's estimates and judgment.[8]

Quaker Oats' management also tells how it meets this responsibility:

> To fulfill its responsibility, management's goal is to maintain strong systems of internal controls, supported by formal policies and procedures that are communicated throughout the Company. Management regularly evaluates its systems of internal control with an eye toward improvement. Management also

maintains a staff of internal auditors who evaluate the adequacy of and investigate the adherence to these controls, policies, and procedures.[10]

The intentional preparation of misleading financial statements is called **fraudulent financial reporting**.[11] It can result from the distortion of records (the manipulation of inventory records), falsified transactions (fictitious sales or orders), or the misapplication of accounting principles (treating as an asset an item that should be expensed). There are a number of possible motives for fraudulent reporting—for instance, to obtain a higher price when a company is sold, to meet the expectations of stockholders, or to obtain a loan. Other times, the incentive is personal gain, such as additional compensation, promotion, or avoidance of penalties for poor performance. The personal costs of such actions can be high—individuals who authorize or prepare fraudulent financial statements may face criminal penalties and financial loss. Others, including investors and lenders to the company, employees, and customers, suffer from fraudulent financial reporting as well.

Incentives for fraudulent financial reporting exist to some extent in every company. It is management's responsibility to insist on honest financial reporting, but it is also the company accountants' responsibility to maintain high ethical standards. Ethical reporting demands that accountants apply financial accounting concepts to present a fair view of the company's operations and financial position and to avoid misleading readers of the financial statements.

Classified Balance Sheet

OBJECTIVE

5 Identify and describe the basic components of a classified balance sheet

The balance sheets you have seen in the chapters thus far categorize accounts as assets, liabilities, and owner's equity. Because even a fairly small company can have hundreds of accounts, simply listing accounts in such broad categories is not particularly helpful to a statement user. Setting up subcategories within the major categories often makes financial statements much more useful. Investors and creditors study and evaluate the relationships among the subcategories. General-purpose external financial statements that are divided into useful subcategories are called **classified financial statements**.

The balance sheet presents the financial position of a company at a particular time. The subdivisions of the classified balance sheet shown in Exhibit 1 are typical of most companies in the United States. The subdivisions under owner's equity, of course, depend on the form of business.

Exhibit 1
Classified Balance Sheet for
Shafer Auto Parts Company

Shafer Auto Parts Company
Balance Sheet
December 31, 20xx

Assets

Current Assets

Cash	$10,360	
Short-Term Investments	2,000	
Notes Receivable	8,000	
Accounts Receivable	35,300	
Merchandise Inventory	60,400	
Prepaid Insurance	6,600	
Store Supplies	1,060	
Office Supplies	636	
Total Current Assets		$124,356

Investments

Land Held for Future Use	5,000

Property, Plant, and Equipment

Land		$ 4,500	
Building	$20,650		
Less Accumulated Depreciation	8,640	12,010	*book value/carrying value*
Delivery Equipment	$18,400		
Less Accumulated Depreciation	9,450	8,950	
Office Equipment	$ 8,600		
Less Accumulated Depreciation	5,000	3,600	
Total Property, Plant, and Equipment			29,060

Intangible Assets

other intangible assets:
★ patent →
★ franchise
★ special license
★ copyright

Trademark	500
Total Assets	$158,916

Liabilities

Current Liabilities

Notes Payable	$15,000	
Accounts Payable	23,883	
Salaries Payable	2,000	
Current Portion of Mortgage Payable	1,800	
Total Current Liabilities		$ 42,683

Long-Term Liabilities

Mortgage Payable	17,800
Total Liabilities	$ 60,483

Owner's Equity

Fred Shafer, Capital	98,433
Total Liabilities and Owner's Equity	$158,916

Assets

A company's assets are often divided into four categories: (1) current assets; (2) investments; (3) property, plant, and equipment; and (4) intangible assets. For simplicity, some companies group investments, intangible assets, and other miscellaneous assets into a category called "other assets." The categories are listed in the order of their presumed ease of conversion into cash. For example, current assets are usually more easily converted to cash than are property, plant, and equipment.

CURRENT ASSETS   **Current assets** are cash or other assets that are reasonably expected to be converted to cash, sold, or consumed within the next year or within the normal operating cycle of the business, whichever is longer. The normal operating cycle of a company is the average time needed to go from cash to cash. For example, cash is used to buy merchandise inventory, which is sold for cash or for a promise of cash if the sale is made on account. If a sale is made on account, the resulting receivable must be collected before the cycle is completed.

The normal operating cycle for most companies is less than one year, but there are exceptions. Boeing Company, for example, can take more than one year to make commercial aircraft. The cost of those aircraft are considered current assets while they are being made because they will be sold in the current operating cycle. Another example is a company that sells on the installment basis. The payments for a television set or stove can be extended over 24 or 36 months, but such receivables are still considered current assets.

Cash is obviously a current asset. Temporary investments, notes and accounts receivable, and inventory are also current assets because they are expected to be converted to cash within the next year or during the normal operating cycle. On the balance sheet, they are listed in the order of their ease of conversion into cash.

Prepaid expenses, such as rent and insurance paid for in advance, and inventories of supplies bought for use rather than for sale should also be classified as current assets. Such assets are current in the sense that if they had not been bought earlier, a current outlay of cash would be needed to obtain them.[12]

In deciding whether an asset is current or noncurrent, the idea of "reasonable expectation" is important. For example, Short-Term Investments is an account used for temporary investments of idle cash or cash that is not immediately required for operating purposes. Management can reasonably expect to sell those securities as cash needs arise over the next year or operating cycle. Investments in securities that management does not expect to sell within the next year and that do not involve the temporary use of idle cash should be shown in the investments category of a classified balance sheet.

INVESTMENTS   The **investments** category includes assets, usually long term, that are not used in the normal operation of the business and that management does not plan to convert to cash within the next year. Items in that category are securities held for long-term investment, long-term notes receivable, land held for future use, plant or equipment not used in the business, and special funds established to pay off a debt or buy a building. Also included are large permanent investments in another company for the purpose of controlling that company.

PROPERTY, PLANT, AND EQUIPMENT   The **property, plant, and equipment** category includes long-term assets used in the continuing operation of the business. They represent a place to operate (land and buildings) and equipment to produce, sell, deliver, and service the company's goods. Consequently, they may also be called *operating assets* or, sometimes, *fixed assets, tangible assets, long-lived assets,* or *plant assets.* Through depreciation, the costs of such assets (except land) are spread over the periods they benefit. Past depreciation is recorded in the Accumulated

Depreciation accounts. The exact order in which property, plant, and equipment are listed on the balance sheet is not the same everywhere. In practice, accounts are often combined to make the financial statements less cluttered. For example:

Property, Plant, and Equipment

Land		$ 4,500
Buildings and Equipment	$47,650	
Less Accumulated Depreciation	23,090	24,560
Total Property, Plant, and Equipment		$29,060

Many companies simply show a single line with a total for property, plant, and equipment and provide the details in a note to the financial statements.

Property, plant, and equipment also includes natural resources owned by the company, such as forest lands, oil and gas properties, and coal mines. Assets that are not used in the regular course of business are listed in the investments category, as noted above.

INTANGIBLE ASSETS **Intangible assets** are long-term assets that have no physical substance but that have a value based on the rights or privileges that belong to their owner. Examples are patents, copyrights, goodwill, franchises, and trademarks. An intangible asset is recorded at cost, which is spread over the expected life of the right or privilege.

OTHER ASSETS Some companies use the category **other assets** to group all owned assets other than current assets and property, plant, and equipment. Other assets can include investments and intangible assets.

Liabilities

Liabilities are divided into two categories, based on when the liabilities fall due: current liabilities and long-term liabilities.

CURRENT LIABILITIES The category **current liabilities** consists of obligations due to be paid or performed within one year or within the normal operating cycle of the business, whichever is longer. Current liabilities are typically paid from current assets or by incurring new short-term liabilities. They include notes payable, accounts payable, the current portion of long-term debt, salaries and wages payable, taxes payable, and customer advances (unearned revenues).

LONG-TERM LIABILITIES The debts of a business that fall due more than one year in the future or beyond the normal operating cycle, or that are to be paid out of non-current assets, are **long-term liabilities**. Mortgages payable, long-term notes, bonds payable, employee pension obligations, and long-term lease liabilities generally fall in the category of long-term liabilities.

Owner's Equity

The terms *owner's equity, proprietorship, capital,* and *net worth* are used interchangeably to denote the owner's interest in a company. The first three terms are preferred to *net worth* because most assets are recorded at original cost rather than at current value. Consequently, the ownership section does not represent "worth." It really represents a claim against the assets of the company.

The accounting treatment of assets and liabilities is not usually affected by the form of business organization. However, the equity section of the balance sheet differs depending on whether the business is a sole proprietorship, a partnership, or a corporation.

SOLE PROPRIETORSHIP   You already are familiar with the owner's equity section of a sole proprietorship, like the one shown in the balance sheet for Shafer Auto Parts Company in Exhibit 1:

Owner's Equity

Fred Shafer, Capital	$98,433

PARTNERSHIP   The equity section of the balance sheet for a partnership is called *partners' equity* and is much like that of the sole proprietorship. It might appear as follows:

Partners' Equity

A. J. Martin, Capital	$21,666	
R. C. Moore, Capital	35,724	
Total Partners' Equity		$57,390

CORPORATION   Corporations are by law separate, legal entities that are owned by their stockholders. The equity section of a balance sheet for a corporation is called stockholders' equity and has two parts: contributed, or paid-in, capital and retained earnings. It might appear like this:

Stockholders' Equity

Contributed Capital		
Common Stock, $10 par value, 5,000 shares		
authorized, issued, and outstanding	$50,000	
Paid-in Capital in Excess of Par Value	10,000	
Total Contributed Capital		$60,000
Retained Earnings		37,500
Total Stockholders' Equity		$97,500

Remember that owner's equity accounts show the sources of and claims on assets. Of course, the claims are not on any particular asset but on the assets as a whole. It follows, then, that a corporation's contributed and earned capital accounts measure its stockholders' claims on assets and also indicate the sources of the assets. The **contributed capital**, also called *paid-in capital*, accounts reflect the amounts of assets invested by stockholders. Generally, contributed capital is shown on corporate balance sheets by two amounts: (1) the face, or par, value of issued stock and (2) the amounts paid in, or contributed, in excess of the par value per share. In the illustration above, stockholders invested amounts equal to par value of the outstanding stock (5,000 × $10) plus $10,000 more.

The **Retained Earnings** account is sometimes called *Earned Capital* because it represents the stockholders' claim to the assets that are earned from operations and reinvested in corporate operations. Distributions of assets to shareholders, which are called *dividends*, reduce the Retained Earnings account balance just as withdrawals of assets by the owner of a business lower the Capital account balance. Thus the Retained Earnings account balance, in its simplest form, represents the earnings of the corporation less dividends paid to stockholders over the life of the business.

Reading and Graphing Real Company Balance Sheets

Although financial statements usually follow the same general form as illustrated for Shafer Auto Parts Company, no two companies will have statements that are exactly alike. The balance sheet of Dell Computer Corp., the world's leading direct seller of computer systems, is a good example (see Exhibit 2). Note that two years

Exhibit 2
Balance Sheet for Dell Computer Corp.

Dell Computer Corp.
Consolidated Statement of Financial Position

(In millions)

	Jan. 28, 2000	Jan. 29, 1999
ASSETS		
CURRENT ASSETS:		
Cash and cash equivalents	$ 3,809	$1,726
Short term investments	323	923
Accounts receivable, net	2,608	2,094
Inventories	391	273
Other	550	791
Total current assets	7,681	5,807
PROPERTY, PLANT, AND EQUIPMENT:		
Land and buildings	229	172
Computer equipment	277	205
Equipment and other	634	398
Total	1,140	775
Less accumulated depreciation	375	252
Property, plant, and equipment, net	765	523
Long term investments	1,048	532
Equity securities and other investments	1,673	—
Goodwill and other	304	15
Total Assets	$11,471	$6,877
LIABILITIES AND STOCKHOLDERS' EQUITY		
CURRENT LIABILITIES:		
Accounts payable	$ 3,538	$2,397
Accrued and other	1,654	1,298
Total current liabilities	5,192	3,695
Long-term debt	508	512
Other liabilities	463	349
TOTAL LIABILITIES	6,163	4,556
STOCKHOLDERS' EQUITY:		
Common stock	3,583	1,781
Retained earnings	1,260	606
Other comprehensive income	533	(36)
Other	(68)	(30)
Total stockholders' equity	5,308	2,321
Total liabilities and stockholders' equity	$11,471	$6,877

Source: Dell Computer Corp., *Annual Report*, 2000.

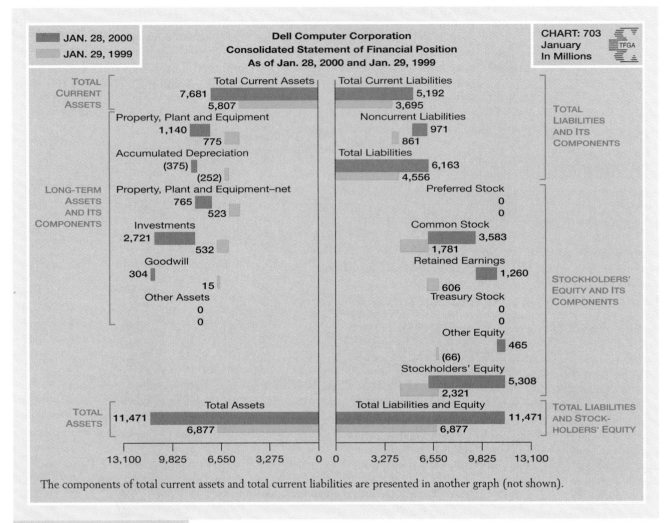

Figure 2
Graphical Presentation of Dell Computer Corp.'s Balance Sheets

of data are provided so that the change from one year to the next can be evaluated. Also note that the major classifications are similar but not identical to those for Shafer Auto Parts. For instance, the assets of Shafer Auto Parts include investments and intangible assets categories, whereas Dell Computer Corp. lists equity securities and other investments, as well as goodwill, separately from long-term investments. Also notice that there is a category called "Other Liabilities." Because this category appears after long-term debt, it represents longer-term liabilities, due more than one year from the balance sheet dates.

We may also observe that Dell's stockholders' equity section differs from the stockholders' equity section of Shafer Auto Parts Company because it is a corporation. However, it is possible to look at the total stockholders' equity and know that this amount relates to the claims by the stockholders on the company and is similar in nature to the capital account for Shafer.

When we look at columns of numbers, it is sometimes difficult to see the patterns. Graphical presentation of the statements is helpful in visualizing the changes that are taking place in a company's financial position. For example, Dell's balance sheet from Exhibit 2 is presented graphically in Figure 2 using the Fingraph® Financial Analyst™ CD-ROM software that accompanies this text. In the graph, total assets and its components are graphed on the left side, and total liabilities and its components, together with total stockholders' equity, are on the right side. The composition of the assets and liabilities, their relation to stockholders' equity, and the changes in them from 1999 to 2000 are clearly seen. These graphs show that overall there was significant growth in both totals and most components for Dell from 1999 to 2000. Also note that showing the balance sheet visually reduces the detailed clutter of the statement. For instance, all current assets are combined and represented by a single component line.

Forms of the Income Statement

OBJECTIVE

6 Prepare multistep and single-step classified income statements

For internal management, a detailed income statement is helpful in analyzing the company's performance. But for external reporting purposes, the income statement is usually presented in condensed form. **Condensed financial statements** present only the major categories of the detailed financial statements. There are two common forms of the condensed income statement, the multistep form and the single-step form. The **multistep form**, illustrated in Exhibit 3, derives net income in the same step-by-step fashion as a detailed income statement would, except that only the totals of significant categories are given. Usually, some breakdown is shown for operating expenses, such as the totals for selling expenses and for general and administrative expenses. In the Shafer statement, gross margin less operating expenses is called **income from operations** and a new section, **other revenues and expenses**, has been added to include nonoperating revenues and expenses. The latter section includes revenues from investments (such as dividends and interest from stocks, bonds, and savings accounts) and interest earned on credit or notes extended to customers. It also includes interest expense and other expenses

Exhibit 3
Condensed Multistep Income Statement for Shafer Auto Parts Company

Shafer Auto Parts Company
Income Statement
For the Year Ended December 31, 20xx

Net Sales		$289,656
Cost of Goods Sold		181,260
Gross Margin		$108,396
Operating Expenses		
Selling Expenses	$54,780	
General and Administrative Expenses	34,504	
Total Operating Expenses		89,284
Income from Operations		$ 19,112
Other Revenues and Expenses		
Interest Income	$ 1,400	
Less Interest Expense	2,631	
Excess of Other Expenses over Other Revenues		1,231
Net Income		$ 17,881

Exhibit 4

Condensed Single-Step Income Statement for Shafer Auto Parts Company

Shafer Auto Parts Company
Income Statement
For the Year Ended December 31, 20xx

Revenues		
Net Sales		$289,656
Interest Income		1,400
Total Revenues		$291,056
Costs and Expenses		
Cost of Goods Sold	$181,260	
Selling Expenses	54,780	
General and Administrative Expenses	34,504	
Interest Expense	2,631	
Total Costs and Expenses		273,175
Net Income		$ 17,881

that result from borrowing money or from credit extended to the company. If the company has other revenues and expenses that are not related to normal business operations, they too are included in this part of the income statement. Thus an analyst who wants to compare two companies independent of their financing methods—that is, before considering other revenues and expenses—would focus on income from operations.

The **single-step form** of income statement, illustrated in Exhibit 4, derives net income in a single step by putting the major categories of revenues in the first part of the statement and the major categories of costs and expenses in the second part. The multistep form and the single-step form each have advantages. The multistep form shows the components that are used in deriving net income; the single-step form has the advantage of simplicity. Approximately an equal number of large U.S. companies use each form in their public reports.

Net income from the income statement becomes an element of the statement of owner's equity.

Reading and Graphing Real Company Income Statements

As with the presentation of balance sheets, you will rarely find income statements that are exactly like the one for Shafer Auto Parts Company. You will encounter terms and structure that differ, such as those on the multistep income statement for Dell Computer Corp. in Exhibit 5, where management provides three years of data for comparison purposes. Sometimes there may be components in the income statement that are not covered in this chapter. If this occurs, refer to the index at the end of the book to find the topic and read about it.

Using the Fingraph® Financial Analyst™ CD-ROM software that accompanies this text to graphically present Dell's income from operations, as shown in Figure 3, helps to show the company's progress in meeting its profitability objectives. On the left side of the graph are the components of income from operations, beginning with net revenues at the top and ending with income from operations at the bottom. On the right side, the changes in the components are graphed. Increases are shown on the right of the vertical column, and decreases are shown on the left. Income from operations increased by only $217 million (10.6 percent), even

Exhibit 5
**Income Statement for
Dell Computer Corp.**

**Dell Computer Corp.
Consolidated Statements of Income**

(In millions)

	Fiscal Year Ended		
	Jan. 28, 2000	Jan. 29, 1999	Feb. 1, 1998
Net revenues	**$25,265**	$18,243	$12,327
Cost of revenue	**20,047**	14,137	9,605
Gross margin	**5,218**	4,106	2,722
Operating expenses:			
Selling, general and administrative	**2,387**	1,788	1,202
Research and development	**374**	272	204
Purchased in-process research and development	**194**	—	—
Total operating expenses	**2,955**	2,060	1,406
Operating income	**2,263**	2,046	1,316
Financing and other income	**188**	38	52
Income before income taxes	**2,451**	2,084	1,368
Provision for income taxes	**785**	624	424
Net income	**$ 1,666**	$ 1,460	$ 944

Source: Dell Computer Corp.,
Annual Report, 2000.

Figure 3
Graphical Presentation of Dell Computer Corp.'s Income Statement

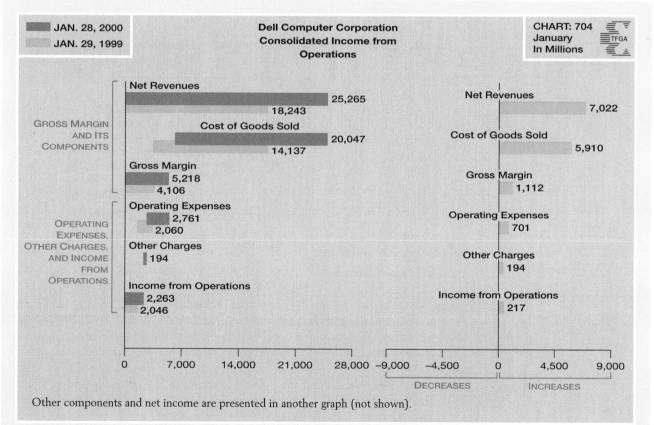

Other components and net income are presented in another graph (not shown).

Nike, Inc.
Consolidated Statements of Income

(In millions, except per share data)

	Year Ended May 31		
	1999	1998	1997
Revenues	**$8,776.9**	$9,553.1	$9,186.5
Costs and expenses:			
Costs of sales	**$5,493.5**	$6,065.5	$5,503.0
Selling and administrative	**2,426.6**	2,623.8	2,303.7
Interest expense	**44.1**	60.0	52.3
Other income/expense, net	**21.5**	20.9	32.2
Restructuring charge	**45.1**	129.9	—
	$8,030.8	$8,900.1	$7,891.3
Income before income taxes	**$ 746.1**	$ 653.0	$1,295.2
Income taxes	**294.7**	253.4	499.4
Net income	**$ 451.4**	$ 399.6	$ 795.8
Basic income per common share	**$ 1.59**	$ 1.38	$ 2.76

The accompanying notes to consolidated financial statements are an integral part
of this statement.

Source: Nike, Inc., *Annual Report*, 1999.

though gross margin increased by $1,112 million (27.1 percent) because operating expenses increased by $701 million (34.0 percent) and other charges increased $194 million from zero the prior year.

A separate graphical presentation (not shown) is used to show the remainder of the income statement, starting with income from operations and ending with net income. The income statement shows annual increases in net income similar to increases in operating income.

When a company uses the single-step form, as Nike, Inc., the footwear company, does in Exhibit 6, most analysts will still calculate gross margin and income from operations and each component's percentages of revenues, as shown below for Nike, Inc.:

	1999	Percent	1998	Percent
Revenues	$8,776.9	100.0	$9,553.1	100.0
Cost of Sales	5,493.5	62.6	6,065.5	63.5
Gross Margin	3,283.4	37.4	$3,487.6	36.5
Selling and Administrative	2,426.6	27.6	2,623.8	27.5
Income from Operations	$ 856.8	9.8	$ 863.8	9.0

From this analysis, it may be seen that Nike's profitability results are mixed. Despite declines in the amounts of revenues, gross margin, and income from operations, the gross margin percentage and operating margin percentage improved. Cost of sales declined faster than revenue, creating a higher gross margin percentage in 1999. However, selling and administrative expenses declined only slightly slower than revenues, giving up a small amount of the gross margin percentage gain. This type of analysis is often performed because a majority of public companies use some form of the single-step income statement.

Using Classified Financial Statements

Earlier in this chapter, you learned that financial reporting, according to the Financial Accounting Standards Board, seeks to provide information that is useful in making investment and credit decisions, in judging cash flow prospects, and in understanding business resources, claims to those resources, and changes in them. These objectives are related to two of the more important goals of management—maintaining adequate liquidity and achieving satisfactory profitability—because investors and creditors base their decisions largely on their assessment of a company's potential liquidity and profitability. The following analysis focuses on those two important goals.

In this section a series of charts shows average ratios for six industries based on data obtained from *Industry Norms and Key Business Ratios*, a publication of Dun and Bradstreet. There are two examples from service industries, advertising agencies and interstate trucking; two examples from merchandising industries, auto and home supply and grocery stores; and two examples from manufacturing industries, pharmaceuticals and computers. Shafer Auto Parts Company, the example used in this chapter, falls into the auto and home supply industry.

Evaluation of Liquidity

Liquidity means having enough money on hand to pay bills when they are due and to take care of unexpected needs for cash. Two measures of liquidity are working capital and the current ratio.

WORKING CAPITAL The first measure, **working capital**, is the amount by which total current assets exceed total current liabilities. This is an important measure of liquidity because current liabilities are debts that must be paid or obligations that must be performed within one year, and current assets are assets that will be realized in cash or that will be used up within one year or one operating cycle, whichever is longer. By definition, current liabilities are paid out of current assets. So the excess of current assets over current liabilities is the net current assets on hand to continue business operations. It is the working capital that can be used to buy inventory, obtain credit, and finance expanded sales. Lack of working capital can lead to a company's failure.

For Shafer Auto Parts Company, working capital is computed as shown on the next page.

FOCUS ON BUSINESS PRACTICE

Caldor, a discounter that was based in Connecticut, had plans for a major expansion and remodeling. To finance this growth, the company could have issued stock, borrowed using long-term debt, or used working capital. Caldor's management chose to use working capital to fund the expansion. In less than a year the company was forced to declare bankruptcy because it could not pay its short-term debt, even though it was still earning a profit. Caldor had violated a fundamental rule of financial management. Working capital should be used to maintain liquidity, and long-term sources, such as debt and stock, should be used to finance long-term expansion. Because its working capital dropped from $80 million to zero and its stock price dropped from $32 to $5, Caldor's creditors no longer saw the company as credit-worthy and would not extend any further credit. As one creditor summed it up, "They were expanding using working capital—which, of course, is supposed to be used for short-term liquidity."[13]

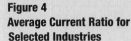

Figure 4
Average Current Ratio for Selected Industries

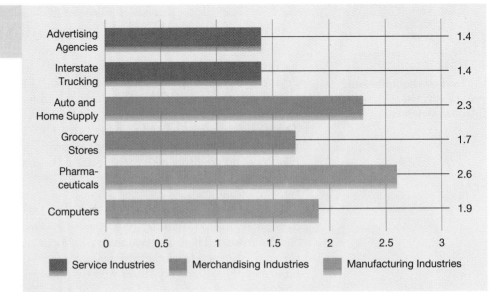

Source: Data from Dun and Bradstreet, *Industry Norms and Key Business Ratios*, 1999–2000.

Current assets	$124,356
Less current liabilities	42,683
Working capital	$ 81,673

CURRENT RATIO   The second measure of liquidity, the current ratio, is closely related to working capital and is believed by many bankers and other creditors to be a good indicator of a company's ability to pay its bills and to repay outstanding loans. The **current ratio** is the ratio of current assets to current liabilities. For Shafer Auto Parts Company, it would be computed like this:

$$\text{Current Ratio} = \frac{\text{Current Assets}}{\text{Current Liabilities}} = \frac{\$124,356}{\$42,683} = 2.9$$

Thus Shafer has $2.90 of current assets for each $1.00 of current liabilities. Is that good or bad? The answer requires the comparison of this year's ratio with ratios of earlier years and with similar measures for successful companies in the same industry. The average current ratio varies widely from industry to industry, as shown in Figure 4. For advertising agencies, which have no merchandise inventory, the current ratio is 1.4. In contrast, auto and home supply companies, which carry large merchandise inventories, have an average current ratio of 2.3. Shafer Auto Parts Company, with a ratio of 2.9, exceeds the average for its industry. A very low current ratio, of course, can be unfavorable, but so can a very high one. The latter may indicate that the company is not using its assets effectively.

Evaluation of Profitability

Just as important as paying bills on time is **profitability**—the ability to earn a satisfactory income. As a goal, profitability competes with liquidity for managerial attention because liquid assets, although important, are not the best profit-producing resources. Cash, for example, means purchasing power, but a satisfactory profit can be made only if purchasing power is used to buy profit-producing (and less liquid) assets, such as inventory and long-term assets.

Among the common measures of a company's ability to earn income are (1) profit margin, (2) asset turnover, (3) return on assets, (4) debt to equity, and (5) return on equity. To evaluate a company meaningfully, one must relate its profit performance to its past performance and prospects for the future as well as to the averages for other companies in the same industry.

PROFIT MARGIN The **profit margin** shows the percentage of each sales dollar that results in net income. It is figured by dividing net income by net sales. It should not be confused with gross margin, which is not a ratio but rather the amount by which revenues exceed the cost of goods sold.

Shafer Auto Parts Company has a profit margin of 6.2 percent:

$$\text{Profit Margin} = \frac{\text{Net Income}}{\text{Net Sales}} = \frac{\$17,881}{\$289,656} = .062 \ (6.2\%)$$

On each dollar of net sales, Shafer Auto Parts Company made 6.2 cents. A difference of 1 or 2 percent in a company's profit margin can mean the difference between a fair year and a very profitable one.

ASSET TURNOVER **Asset turnover** measures how efficiently assets are used to produce sales. Computed by dividing net sales by average total assets, it shows how many dollars of sales were generated by each dollar of assets. A company with a higher asset turnover uses its assets more productively than one with a lower asset turnover. Average total assets is computed by adding total assets at the beginning of the year to total assets at the end of the year and dividing by 2.

Assuming that total assets for Shafer Auto Parts Company were $148,620 at the beginning of the year, its asset turnover is computed as follows:

$$\begin{aligned} \text{Asset Turnover} &= \frac{\text{Net Sales}}{\text{Average Total Assets}} \\[2mm] &= \frac{\$289,656}{(\$158,916 + \$148,620) \div 2} \\[2mm] &= \frac{\$289,656}{\$153,768} = 1.9 \text{ times} \end{aligned}$$

Shafer Auto Parts Company produces $1.90 in sales for each $1.00 invested in average total assets. This ratio shows a meaningful relationship between an income statement figure and a balance sheet figure.

RETURN ON ASSETS Both the profit margin and the asset turnover ratios have some limitations. The profit margin ratio does not take into consideration the assets necessary to produce income, and the asset turnover ratio does not take into account the amount of income produced. The **return on assets** ratio overcomes these deficiencies by relating net income to average total assets. It is computed like this:

$$\begin{aligned} \text{Return on Assets} &= \frac{\text{Net Income}}{\text{Average Total Assets}} \\[2mm] &= \frac{\$17,881}{(\$158,916 + \$148,620) \div 2} \\[2mm] &= \frac{\$17,881}{\$153,768} = .116 \ (11.6\%) \end{aligned}$$

For each dollar invested, Shafer Auto Parts Company's assets generated 11.6 cents of net income. This ratio indicates the income-generating strength (profit margin) of the company's resources and how efficiently the company is using all its assets (asset turnover).

Return on assets, then, combines profit margin and asset turnover, as follows:

Figure 5
Average Profit Margin for Selected Industries

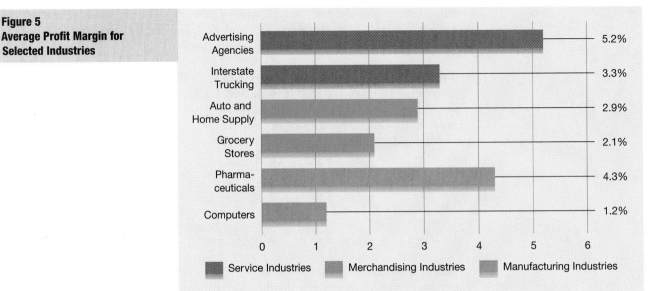

Source: Data from Dun and Bradstreet, *Industry Norms and Key Business Ratios*, 1999–2000.

$$\frac{\text{Net Income}}{\text{Net Sales}} \times \frac{\text{Net Sales}}{\text{Average Total Assets}} = \frac{\text{Net Income}}{\text{Average Total Assets}}$$

$$\text{Profit Margin} \times \quad \text{Asset Turnover} \quad = \quad \text{Return on Assets}$$
$$6.2\% \quad \times \quad 1.9 \text{ times} \quad = \quad 11.8\%*$$

* The slight difference between 11.6 and 11.8 is due to rounding.

Thus a company's management can improve overall profitability by increasing the profit margin, the asset turnover, or both. Similarly, in evaluating a company's overall profitability, the financial statement user must consider the interaction of both ratios to produce return on assets.

Careful study of Figures 5, 6, and 7 shows the different ways in which the selected industries combine profit margin and asset turnover to produce return on

Figure 6
Asset Turnover for Selected Industries

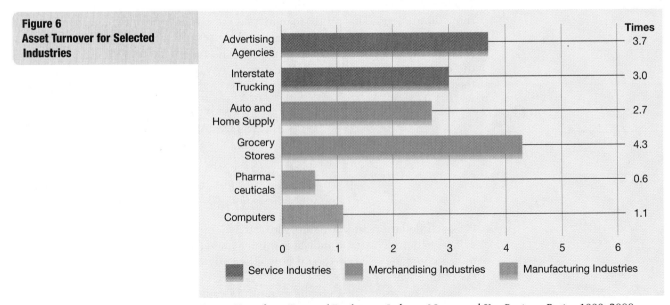

Source: Data from Dun and Bradstreet, *Industry Norms and Key Business Ratios*, 1999–2000.

Figure 7
Return on Assets for Selected Industries

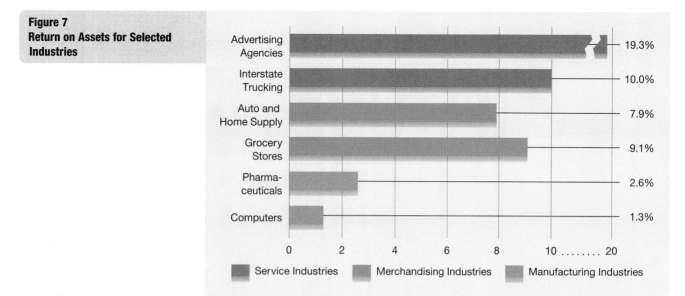

Source: Data from Dun and Bradstreet, *Industry Norms and Key Business Ratios*, 1999–2000.

assets. For instance, compare the return on assets for grocery stores and auto and home supply, and see how they achieve it in very different ways. Grocery stores have a smaller profit margin, 2.1 percent, which when multiplied by a higher asset turnover, 4.3 times, gives a return on assets of 9.1 percent. Auto and home supply stores, on the other hand, have a higher profit margin, 2.9 percent, and a lower asset turnover, 2.7 times, which produces a return on assets of 7.9 percent.

Shafer Auto Parts Company's profit margin of 6.2 percent is well above the auto and home supply industry average of 2.9 percent, but its turnover of 1.9 times lags behind the industry average of 2.7 times. Shafer is sacrificing asset turnover to achieve a high profit margin. It is clear that the strategy is working, because Shafer's return on assets of 11.6 percent exceeds the industry average of 7.9 percent.

DEBT TO EQUITY   Another useful measure is the **debt to equity** ratio, which shows the proportion of the company financed by creditors in comparison to that financed by the owners. This ratio is computed by dividing total liabilities by owner's equity. Since the balance sheets of many companies do not show total liabilities, a short way of determining total liabilities is to deduct owner's equity from total assets. A debt to equity ratio of 1.0 means that total liabilities equal owner's equity—that half of the company's assets are financed by creditors. A ratio of .5 would mean that one-third of the assets are financed by creditors. A company with a high debt to equity ratio is more vulnerable in poor economic times because it must continue to repay creditors. Owner's investments, on the other hand, do not have to be repaid, and withdrawals can be deferred if the company is suffering because of a poor economy.

Shafer Auto Parts Company's debt to equity ratio is computed as follows:

$$\text{Debt to Equity} = \frac{\text{Total Liabilities}}{\text{Owner's Equity}} = \frac{\$60,483}{\$98,433} = .614 \ (61.4\%)$$

A debt to equity ratio of 61.4 percent, which is less than 100 percent, means that Shafer Auto Parts Company receives less than half its financing from creditors and more than half from its owner, Fred Shafer.

The debt to equity ratio does not fit neatly into either the liquidity or the profitability category. It is clearly very important to liquidity analysis because it relates to debt and its repayment. However, the debt to equity ratio is also relevant to

Figure 8
Average Debt to Equity for Selected Industries

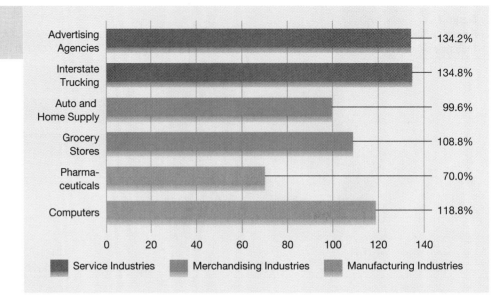

Advertising Agencies	134.2%
Interstate Trucking	134.8%
Auto and Home Supply	99.6%
Grocery Stores	108.8%
Pharmaceuticals	70.0%
Computers	118.8%

■ Service Industries ■ Merchandising Industries ■ Manufacturing Industries

Source: Data from Dun and Bradstreet, *Industry Norms and Key Business Ratios*, 1999–2000.

profitability for two reasons. First, creditors are interested in the proportion of the business that is debt financed because the more debt a company has, the more profit it must earn to protect the payment of interest to its creditors. Second, an owner is interested in the proportion of the business that is debt financed, because the amount of interest that must be paid on the debt affects the amount of profit that is left to provide a return on the owner's investment. The debt to equity ratio also shows how much expansion is possible by borrowing additional long-term funds. Figure 8 shows that the debt to equity ratio in our selected industries varies from a low of 70.0 percent in the pharmaceutical industry to a high of 134.8 percent in interstate trucking and 134.2 percent in the advertising agency industry.

RETURN ON EQUITY   Of course, Fred Shafer is interested in how much he has earned on his investment in the business. His **return on equity** is measured by the ratio of net income to average owner's equity. Taking the ending owner's equity

FOCUS ON BUSINESS PRACTICE

To what level of profitability should a company aspire? At one time, a company earning a 20 percent return on equity was considered among the elite. Walt Disney, Wal-Mart, Coca-Cola, and a few other companies were able to achieve this level of profitability. However, *The Wall Street Journal* reported that in the first quarter of 1995, for the first time, the average company of the Standard & Poor's 500 companies made a return on equity of 20.12 percent. It said that this performance was "akin to the average ball player hitting .350."[14] This means that stockholders' equity will double every four years.

Why did this happen? First, a good business environment and cost cutting led to more profitable operations. Second, special charges and other accounting transactions reduced the amount of stockholders' equity for many companies.

The number of companies with a return on equity of 20 percent or more has also continued to increase as profits have grown.

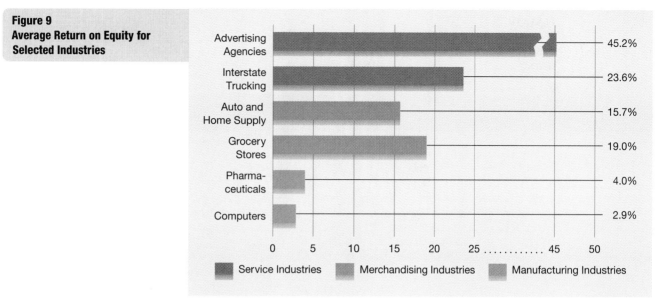

Figure 9
Average Return on Equity for Selected Industries

Advertising Agencies	45.2%
Interstate Trucking	23.6%
Auto and Home Supply	15.7%
Grocery Stores	19.0%
Pharma-ceuticals	4.0%
Computers	2.9%

0   5   10   15   20   25 45   50

■ Service Industries   ■ Merchandising Industries   ■ Manufacturing Industries

Source: Data from Dun and Bradstreet, *Industry Norms and Key Business Ratios*, 1999–2000.

from the balance sheet and assuming that beginning owner's equity is $100,553, Shafer's return on equity is computed as follows:

$$\text{Return on Equity} = \frac{\text{Net Income}}{\text{Average Owner's Equity}}$$

$$= \frac{\$17,881}{(\$98,433 + \$100,553) \div 2}$$

$$= \frac{\$17,881}{\$99,493} = .180 \ (18.0\%)$$

In 20xx, Shafer Auto Parts Company earned 18.0 cents for every dollar invested by the owner, Fred Shafer.

Whether or not this is an acceptable return depends on several factors, such as how much the company earned in prior years and how much other companies in the same industry earned. As measured by return on equity (Figure 9), advertising agencies are the most profitable of our sample industries, with a return on equity of 45.2 percent. Shafer Auto Parts Company's average return on equity of 18.0 percent exceeds the average of 15.7 percent for the auto and home supply industry.

GRAPHING RATIO ANALYSIS   Using the Fingraph® Financial Analyst™ CD-ROM software that accompanies this text to graphically present Dell Computer Corp.'s profitability ratios involving net income, shown in Figure 10, helps us visualize the progress of the company in meeting its profitability objectives. On the left of the figure are the components of the ratios. On the right of the figure are the ratios for the past two years. It may be seen that the changes in Dell Computer Corp.'s return on equity and return on assets are linked to changes in profit margin or asset turnover.

The Fingraph® Financial Analyst™ CD-ROM software graphs all the ratios used in this book and provides narrative analysis. The asset turnover ratio is shown graphically with the balance sheet analysis.

**Figure 10
Graphical Presentation of Dell Computer Corp.'s Profitability Ratios**

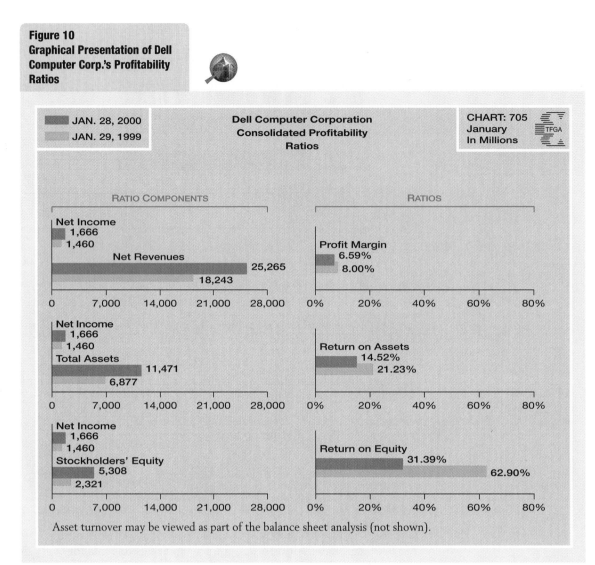

■ JAN. 28, 2000	**Dell Computer Corporation**
■ JAN. 29, 1999	**Consolidated Profitability Ratios**

CHART: 705
January
In Millions
TFGA

RATIO COMPONENTS

Net Income
1,666
1,460
Net Revenues
25,265
18,243

0   7,000   14,000   21,000   28,000

Net Income
1,666
1,460
Total Assets
11,471
6,877

0   7,000   14,000   21,000   28,000

Net Income
1,666
1,460
Stockholders' Equity
5,308
2,321

0   7,000   14,000   21,000   28,000

RATIOS

Profit Margin
6.59%
8.00%

0%   20%   40%   60%   80%

Return on Assets
14.52%
21.23%

0%   20%   40%   60%   80%

Return on Equity
31.39%
62.90%

0%   20%   40%   60%   80%

Asset turnover may be viewed as part of the balance sheet analysis (not shown).

Chapter Review

1. **State the objectives of financial reporting.** The objectives of financial reporting are (1) to furnish information that is useful in making investment and credit decisions; (2) to provide information that can be used to assess cash flow prospects; and (3) to provide information about business resources, claims to those resources, and changes in them.

2. **State the qualitative characteristics of accounting information and describe their interrelationships.** Understandability depends on the knowledge of the user and the ability of the accountant to provide useful information. Usefulness is a function of two primary characteristics, relevance and reliability. Information is relevant when it affects the outcome of a decision. Information that is relevant has feedback value and predictive value, and is

timely. To be reliable, information must represent what it is supposed to represent, must be verifiable, and must be neutral.

3. **Define and describe the use of the conventions of *comparability* and *consistency*, *materiality*, *conservatism*, *full disclosure*, and *cost-benefit*.** Because accountants' measurements are not exact, certain conventions have come to be applied in current practice to help users interpret financial statements. One of these conventions is consistency, which requires the use of the same accounting procedures from period to period and enhances the comparability of financial statements. The second is materiality, which has to do with the relative importance of an item. The third is conservatism, which entails using the procedure that is least likely to overstate assets and income. The fourth is full disclosure, which means including all relevant information in the financial statements. The fifth is cost-benefit, which suggests that above a minimum level of information, additional information should be provided only if the benefits derived from the information exceed the costs of providing it.

4. **Explain management's responsibility for ethical financial reporting and define *fraudulent financial reporting*.** Management is responsible for the preparation of financial statements in accordance with generally accepted accounting principles and for the internal controls that provide assurance that this objective is achieved. Fraudulent financial reporting is the intentional preparation of misleading financial statements.

5. **Identify and describe the basic components of a classified balance sheet.** The classified balance sheet is subdivided as follows:

Assets	Liabilities
Current Assets	Current Liabilities
Investments	Long-Term Liabilities
Property, Plant, and Equipment	
Intangible Assets	**Owner's Equity**
(Other Assets)	(Content depends on the form of business)

A current asset is an asset that can reasonably be expected to be realized in cash or consumed during the next year or the normal operating cycle, whichever is longer. Investments are long-term assets that are not usually used in the normal operation of a business. Property, plant, and equipment are long-term assets that are used in day-to-day operations. Intangible assets are long-term assets whose value stems from the rights or privileges they extend to the owner. A current liability is a liability that can reasonably be expected to be paid or performed during the next year or the normal operating cycle, whichever is longer. Long-term liabilities are debts that fall due more than one year in the future or beyond the normal operating cycle. The equity section of the balance sheet for a corporation differs from that for a proprietorship in that it has subdivisions of contributed capital (the value of assets invested by stockholders) and retained earnings (stockholders' claim to assets earned from operations and reinvested in operations).

6. **Prepare multistep and single-step classified income statements.** Condensed income statements for external reporting can be in multistep or single-step form. The multistep form arrives at net income through a series of steps; the single-step form arrives at net income in a single step. There is usually a separate section in the multi-step form for other revenues and expenses.

7. **Evaluate liquidity and profitability using classified financial statements.** One important use of classified financial statements is to evaluate a company's liquidity and profitability. Two simple measures of liquidity are

working capital and the current ratio. Five simple measures of profitability are profit margin, asset turnover, return on assets, debt to equity, and return on equity.

The following concepts and terms were introduced in this chapter:

LO 7 **Asset turnover:** A measure of profitability that shows how efficiently assets are used to produce sales; net sales divided by average total assets.

LO 5 **Classified financial statements:** General-purpose external financial statements divided into useful subcategories.

LO 3 **Comparability:** The convention of presenting information in a way that enables decision makers to recognize similarities, differences, and trends over different time periods or between different companies.

LO 6 **Condensed financial statements:** Financial statements for external reporting that present only the major categories of information.

LO 3 **Conservatism:** The convention that requires that, when faced with equally acceptable alternatives, accountants must choose the one least likely to overstate assets and income.

LO 3 **Consistency:** The convention that requires that an accounting procedure, once adopted, not be changed from one period to another unless users are informed of the change.

LO 5 **Contributed capital:** The accounts that reflect the stockholders' investment in a corporation. Also called *paid-in capital*.

LO 3 **Conventions:** Rules of thumb or customary ways of recording transactions or preparing financial statements.

LO 3 **Cost-benefit:** The convention that holds that benefits gained from providing accounting information should be greater than the costs of providing that information.

LO 5 **Current assets:** Cash or other assets that are reasonably expected to be converted to cash, sold, or consumed within one year or within the normal operating cycle, whichever is longer.

LO 5 **Current liabilities:** Obligations due to be paid or performed within one year or within the normal operating cycle, whichever is longer.

LO 7 **Current ratio:** A measure of liquidity; current assets divided by current liabilities.

LO 7 **Debt to equity:** A ratio that measures the relationship of assets financed by creditors to those financed by owners; total liabilities divided by owner's equity.

LO 4 **Fraudulent financial reporting:** The intentional preparation of misleading financial statements.

LO 3 **Full disclosure:** The convention that requires that financial statements and their notes present all information relevant to the users' understanding of the company's financial condition.

LO 6 **Income from operations:** Gross margin less operating expenses.

LO 5 **Intangible assets:** Long-term assets that have no physical substance but that have a value based on rights or privileges that belong to their owner.

LO 5 **Investments:** Assets, usually long term, that are not used in the normal operation of a business and that management does not intend to convert to cash within the next year.

LO 7 **Liquidity:** Having enough money on hand to pay bills when they are due and to take care of unexpected needs for cash.

LO 5 **Long-term liabilities:** Debts that fall due more than one year in the future or beyond the normal operating cycle, or that are to be paid out of noncurrent assets.

LO 3   **Materiality:** The convention that refers to the relative importance of an item or event in a financial statement and its influence on the decisions of the users of financial statements.

LO 6   **Multistep form:** A form of condensed income statement that arrives at net income in the same steps as a detailed income statement but that presents only the totals of significant categories.

LO 5   **Other assets:** The balance sheet category that may include various types of assets other than current assets and property, plant, and equipment.

LO 6   **Other revenues and expenses:** The section of a multistep income statement that includes nonoperating revenues and expenses.

LO 7   **Profitability:** The ability of a business to earn a satisfactory income.

LO 7   **Profit margin:** A measure of profitability that shows the percentage of each sales dollar that results in net income; net income divided by net sales.

LO 5   **Property, plant, and equipment:** Tangible long-term assets used in the continuing operation of a business. Also called *operating assets, fixed assets, tangible assets, long-lived assets,* or *plant assets.*

LO 2   **Qualitative characteristics:** Standards for judging the information that accountants give to decision makers.

LO 2   **Relevance:** The qualitative characteristic of information bearing directly on the outcome of a decision.

LO 2   **Reliability:** The qualitative characteristic of information being representationally faithful, verifiable, and neutral.

LO 5   **Retained Earnings:** The account that reflects the stockholders' claim to the assets earned from operations and reinvested in corporate operations. Also called *Earned Capital.*

LO 7   **Return on assets:** A measure of profitability that shows how efficiently a company uses its assets to produce income; net income divided by average total assets.

LO 7   **Return on equity:** A measure of profitability that relates the amount earned by a business to the owner's investment in the business; net income divided by average owner's equity.

LO 6   **Single-step form:** A form of condensed income statement that arrives at net income in a single step.

LO 2   **Understandability:** The qualitative characteristic of communicating an intended meaning.

LO 2   **Usefulness:** The qualitative characteristic of accounting information being relevant and reliable.

LO 7   **Working capital:** A measure of liquidity equal to the net current assets on hand to continue business operations; total current assets minus total current liabilities.

REVIEW PROBLEM

Analyzing Liquidity and Profitability Using Ratios

LO 7   Flavin Shirt Company has faced increased competition from overseas shirtmakers in recent years. Key information for the last two years is as follows:

	20x2	20x1
Current Assets	$ 200,000	$ 170,000
Total Assets	880,000	710,000
Current Liabilities	90,000	50,000
Long-Term Liabilities	150,000	50,000
Owner's Equity	640,000	610,000
Sales	1,200,000	1,050,000
Net Income	60,000	80,000

Total assets and owner's equity at the beginning of 20x1 were $690,000 and $590,000, respectively.

REQUIRED

Use (1) liquidity analysis and (2) profitability analysis to document the declining financial position of Flavin Shirt Company.

ANSWER TO REVIEW PROBLEM

1. Liquidity analysis

	Current Assets	Current Liabilities	Working Capital	Current Ratio
20x1	$170,000	$50,000	$120,000	3.4
20x2	200,000	90,000	110,000	2.2
Decrease in working capital			($ 10,000)	
Decrease in current ratio				1.2

Both working capital and the current ratio declined because, although current assets increased by $30,000 ($200,000 − $170,000), current liabilities increased by a greater amount, $40,000 ($90,000 − $50,000), from 20x1 to 20x2.

2. Profitability analysis

	Net Income	Sales	Profit Margin	Average Total Assets	Asset Turnover	Return on Assets	Average Owners' Equity	Return on Equity
20x1	$80,000	$1,050,000	7.6%	$700,000[1]	1.50	11.4%	$600,000[3]	13.3%
20x2	60,000	1,200,000	5.0	795,000[2]	1.51	7.5	625,000[4]	9.6
Increase (decrease)	($20,000)	$ 150,000	(2.6)%	$ 95,000	0.01	(3.9)%	$ 25,000	(3.7)%

[1]($710,000 + $690,000) ÷ 2   [3]($610,000 + $590,000) ÷ 2
[2]($880,000 + $710,000) ÷ 2   [4]($640,000 + $610,000) ÷ 2

Net income decreased by $20,000 despite an increase in sales of $150,000 and an increase in average total assets of $95,000. The results were decreases in profit margin from 7.6 percent to 5.0 percent and in return on assets from 11.4 percent to 7.5 percent. Asset turnover showed almost no change and so did not contribute to the decline in profitability. The decrease in return on equity from 13.3 percent to 9.6 percent was not as great as the decrease in return on assets because the growth in total assets was financed by debt instead of owner's equity, as shown by the following capital structure analysis.

	Total Liabilities	Owner's Equity	Debt to Equity Ratio
20x1	$100,000	$610,000	16.4%
20x2	240,000	640,000	37.5
Increase	$140,000	$ 30,000	21.1%

Total liabilities increased by $140,000 while owner's equity increased by $30,000. As a result, the amount of the business financed by debt in relation to the amount of the business financed by owner's equity increased from 20x1 to 20x2.

Chapter Assignments

BUILDING YOUR
KNOWLEDGE
FOUNDATION

QUESTIONS

1. What are the three objectives of financial reporting?
2. What are the qualitative characteristics of accounting information, and what is their significance?
3. What are the accounting conventions? How does each help in the interpretation of financial information?
4. Who is responsible for preparing reliable financial statements, and what is a principal way of fulfilling the responsibility?
5. What is the purpose of classified financial statements?
6. What are four common categories of assets?
7. What criteria must an asset meet to be classified as current? Under what condition is an asset considered current even though it will not be realized as cash within a year? What are two examples of assets that fall into this category?
8. In what order should current assets be listed?
9. What is the difference between a short-term investment in the current assets section and a security in the investments section of the balance sheet?
10. What is an intangible asset? Give at least three examples.
11. Name the two major categories of liabilities.
12. What are the primary differences between the equity section of the balance sheet for a sole proprietorship or partnership and the corresponding section for a corporation?
13. Explain the difference between contributed capital and retained earnings.
14. Explain how the multistep form of income statement differs from the single-step form. What are the relative merits of each?
15. Why are other revenues and expenses separated from operating revenues and expenses in the multistep income statement?
16. Define *liquidity* and name two measures of liquidity.
17. How is the current ratio computed and why is it important?
18. Which is the more important goal—liquidity or profitability? Explain your answer.
19. Name five measures of profitability.
20. Evaluate the following statement: "Return on assets is a better measure of profitability than profit margin."

SHORT EXERCISES

SE 1.
LO 3 Accounting Conventions

State which of the accounting conventions—comparability and consistency, materiality, conservatism, full disclosure, or cost-benefit—is being followed in each of these cases:

1. Management provides detailed information about the company's long-term debt in the notes to the financial statements.
2. A company does not account separately for discounts received for prompt payment of accounts payable because few such transactions occur and the total amount of the discounts is small.
3. Management eliminates a weekly report on property, plant, and equipment acquisitions and disposals because no one finds it useful.

4. A company follows the policy of recognizing a loss on inventory when the market value of an item falls below its cost but does nothing if the market value rises.

5. When several accounting methods are acceptable, management chooses a single method and follows that method from year to year.

SE 2.
LO 5   Classification of Accounts: Balance Sheet

Tell whether each of the following accounts is a current asset; an investment; property, plant, and equipment; an intangible asset; a current liability; a long-term liability; owner's equity; or not on the balance sheet.

1. Delivery Trucks
2. Accounts Payable
3. Note Payable (due in 90 days)
4. Delivery Expense
5. Y. San, Capital

6. Prepaid Insurance
7. Trademark
8. Investment to Be Held Six Months
9. Interest Payable
10. Factory Not Used in Business

SE 3.
LO 5   Classified Balance Sheet

Using the following accounts, prepare a classified balance sheet at year end, May 31, 20xx: Accounts Payable, $400; Accounts Receivable, $550; Accumulated Depreciation, Equipment, $350; Cash, $100; Equipment, $2,000; Franchise, $100; Investments (long-term), $250; Merchandise Inventory, $300; Notes Payable (long-term), $200; B. Pamp, Capital, ?; and Wages Payable, $50.

SE 4.
LO 6   Classification of Accounts: Income Statement

Tell whether each of the following accounts is part of net sales, cost of goods sold, operating expenses, other revenues and expenses, or not on the income statement.

1. Delivery Expense
2. Interest Expense
3. Unearned Revenue
4. Sales Returns and Allowances

5. Purchases
6. Depreciation Expense
7. Investment Income
8. Withdrawals

SE 5.
LO 6   Single-Step Income Statement

Using the following accounts, prepare a single-step income statement at year end, May 31, 20xx: Cost of Goods Sold, $280; General Expenses, $150; Interest Expense, $70; Interest Income, $30; Net Sales, $800; and Selling Expenses, $185.

SE 6.
LO 6   Multistep Income Statement

Using the accounts presented in **SE 5,** prepare a multistep income statement.

SE 7.
LO 7   Liquidity Ratios

Using the following information from a year-end balance sheet, compute working capital and the current ratio.

Accounts Payable	$ 7,000
Accounts Receivable	10,000
Cash	4,000
V. Smyth, Capital	20,000
Marketable Securities	2,000
Merchandise Inventory	12,000
Notes Payable in Three Years	13,000
Property, Plant, and Equipment	40,000

SE 8.
LO 7   Profitability Ratios

Using the following information from a balance sheet and an income statement, compute the (1) profit margin, (2) asset turnover, (3) return on assets, (4) debt to equity, and (5) return on equity. (The previous year's total assets were $100,000 and owner's equity was $70,000.)

Total Assets	$120,000	Net Sales	$130,000
Total Liabilities	30,000	Cost of Goods Sold	70,000
Total Owner's Equity	90,000	Operating Expenses	45,000

EXERCISES

E 1.
LO 3   Accounting Concepts and Conventions

Each of the following statements violates a convention in accounting. State which of the following accounting conventions is violated: comparability and consistency, materiality, conservatism, full disclosure, or cost-benefit.

1. A series of reports that are time-consuming and expensive to prepare is presented to the board of directors each month even though the reports are never used.

2. A company changes its method of accounting for depreciation.

3. The company in **2** does not indicate in the financial statements that the method of depreciation was changed, nor does it specify the effect of the change on net income.

4. A new office building next to the factory is debited to the Factory account because it represents a fairly small dollar amount in relation to the factory.

5. The asset account for a pickup truck still used in the business is written down to what the truck could be sold for even though the carrying value under conventional depreciation methods is higher.

E 2.

LO 1 Financial Accounting
LO 2 Concepts
LO 3

The lettered items below represent a classification scheme for the concepts of financial accounting. Match each numbered term with the letter of the category in which it belongs.

a. Decision makers (users of accounting information)
b. Business activities or entities relevant to accounting measurement
c. Objectives of accounting information
d. Accounting measurement considerations
e. Accounting processing considerations
f. Qualitative characteristics
g. Accounting conventions
h. Financial statements

1. Conservatism
2. Verifiability
3. Statement of cash flows
4. Materiality
5. Reliability
6. Recognition
7. Cost-benefit
8. Understandability
9. Business transactions
10. Consistency
11. Full disclosure
12. Furnishing information useful to investors and creditors

13. Specific business entities
14. Classification
15. Management
16. Neutrality
17. Internal accounting control
18. Valuation
19. Investors
20. Timeliness
21. Relevance
22. Furnishing information useful in assessing cash flow prospects

E 3.

LO 5 Classification of Accounts:
Balance Sheet

The lettered items below represent a classification scheme for a balance sheet, and the numbered items are account titles. Match each account with the letter of the category in which it belongs.

a. Current assets
b. Investments
c. Property, plant, and equipment
d. Intangible assets
e. Current liabilities
f. Long-term liabilities
g. Owner's equity
h. Not on balance sheet

1. Patent
2. Building Held for Sale
3. Prepaid Rent
4. Wages Payable
5. Note Payable in Five Years
6. Building Used in Operations
7. Fund Held to Pay Off Long-Term Debt
8. Inventory

9. Prepaid Insurance
10. Depreciation Expense
11. Accounts Receivable
12. Interest Expense
13. Unearned Revenue
14. Short-Term Investments
15. Accumulated Depreciation
16. B. Dobecki, Capital

E 4.

LO 5 Classified Balance Sheet
Preparation

The following data pertain to a corporation: Cash, $31,200; Investment in Six-Month Government Securities, $16,400; Accounts Receivable, $38,000; Inventory, $40,000; Prepaid Rent, $1,200; Investment in Corporate Securities (long-term), $20,000; Land, $8,000; Building, $70,000; Accumulated Depreciation, Building, $14,000; Equipment, $152,000; Accumulated Depreciation, Equipment, $17,000; Copyright, $6,200;

Accounts Payable, $51,000; Revenue Received in Advance, $2,800; Bonds Payable, $60,000; Common Stock, $10 par, 10,000 shares authorized, issued, and outstanding, $100,000; Paid-in Capital in Excess of Par Value, $50,000; and Retained Earnings, $88,200.

Prepare a classified balance sheet; omit the heading.

E 5.

LO 6 Classification of Accounts: Income Statement

Using the classification scheme below for a multistep income statement, match each account with the letter of the category in which it belongs.

a. Net sales
b. Cost of goods sold
c. Selling expenses
d. General and administrative expenses
e. Other revenues and expenses
f. Not on income statement

1. Purchases
2. Sales Discounts
3. Merchandise Inventory (beginning)
4. Interest Income
5. Advertising Expense
6. Office Salaries Expense
7. Freight Out Expense
8. Prepaid Insurance
9. Utilities Expense

10. Sales Salaries Expense
11. Rent Expense
12. Purchases Returns and Allowances
13. Freight In
14. Depreciation Expense, Delivery Equipment
15. Taxes Payable
16. Interest Expense

E 6.

LO 6 Preparation of Income Statements

The following data pertain to a sole proprietorship: Sales, $405,000; Cost of Goods Sold, $220,000; Selling Expenses, $90,000; General and Administrative Expenses, $60,000; Interest Expense, $4,000; and Interest Income, $3,000.

1. Prepare a condensed single-step income statement.

2. Prepare a condensed multistep income statement.

E 7.

LO 6 Condensed Multistep Income Statement

A condensed single-step income statement appears below. Present this information in a condensed multistep income statement, and tell what insights can be obtained from the multistep form as opposed to the single-step form.

Rosala Housewares Company
Income Statement
For the Year Ended June 30, 20xx

Revenues		
Net Sales	$1,197,132	
Interest Income	5,720	
Total Revenues		$1,202,852
Costs and Expenses		
Cost of Goods Sold	$ 777,080	
Selling Expenses	203,740	
General and Administrative Expenses	100,688	
Interest Expense	13,560	
Total Costs and Expenses		1,095,068
Net Income		$ 107,784

E 8.
LO 7   Liquidity Ratios

The following accounts and balances are taken from the general ledger of Quan Company.

Accounts Payable	$ 49,800
Accounts Receivable	30,600
Cash	4,500
Current Portion of Long-Term Debt	30,000
Long-Term Investments	31,200
Marketable Securities	37,800
Merchandise Inventory	76,200
Notes Payable, 90 days	45,000
Notes Payable, 2 years	60,000
Notes Receivable, 90 days	78,000
Notes Receivable, 2 years	30,000
Prepaid Insurance	1,200
Property, Plant, and Equipment	180,000
F. Abruzzi, Capital	84,900
Salaries Payable	2,550
Supplies	1,050
Property Taxes Payable	3,750
Unearned Revenue	2,250

Compute the (1) working capital and (2) current ratio.

E 9.
LO 7   Profitability Ratios

The following end-of-year amounts are taken from the financial statements of Van Guyse Company: Total Assets, $852,000; Total Liabilities, $344,000; Owner's Equity, $508,000; Net Sales, $1,564,000; Cost of Goods Sold, $972,000; Operating Expenses, $404,000; and Withdrawals, $80,000.

During the past year, total assets increased by $150,000. Total owner's equity was affected only by net income and withdrawals.

Compute (1) profit margin, (2) asset turnover, (3) return on assets, (4) debt to equity, and (5) return on equity.

E 10.
LO 7   Computation of Ratios

The simplified balance sheet and income statement for a sole proprietorship appear below and on the following page.

Total assets and owner's equity at the beginning of 20xx were $360,000 and $280,000, respectively.

Balance Sheet December 31, 20xx			
Assets		**Liabilities**	
Current Assets	$100,000	Current Liabilities	$ 40,000
Investments	20,000	Long-Term Liabilities	60,000
Property, Plant, and Equipment	293,000	Total Liabilities	$100,000
Intangible Assets	27,000	**Owner's Equity**	
		P. Cavafy, Capital	340,000
Total Assets	$440,000	Total Liabilities and Owner's Equity	$440,000

Income Statement
For the Year Ended December 31, 20xx

Net Sales	$820,000
Cost of Goods Sold	500,000
Gross Margin	$320,000
Operating Expenses	270,000
Net Income	$ 50,000

1. Compute the following liquidity measures: (a) working capital and (b) current ratio.
2. Compute the following profitability measures: (a) profit margin, (b) asset turnover, (c) return on assets, (d) debt to equity, and (e) return on equity.

PROBLEMS

P 1.

LO 3 Accounting Conventions

In each case below, accounting conventions may have been violated.

1. Figuero Manufacturing Company uses the cost method for computing the balance sheet amount of inventory unless the market value of the inventory is less than the cost, in which case the market value is used. At the end of the current year, the market value is $77,000 and the cost is $80,000. Figuero uses the $77,000 figure to compute net income because management feels it is the more cautious approach.
2. Margolis Company has annual sales of $5,000,000. It follows the practice of charging any items costing less than $100 to expenses in the year purchased. During the current year, it purchased several chairs for the executive conference rooms at $97 each, including freight. Although the chairs were expected to last for at least ten years, they were charged as an expense in accordance with company policy.
3. Choi Company closed its books on December 31, 20x3, before preparing its annual report. On December 30, 20x3, a fire destroyed one of the company's two factories. Although the company had fire insurance and would not suffer a loss on the building, a significant decrease in sales in 20x4 was expected because of the fire. The fire damage was not reported in the 20x3 financial statements because the operations for that year were not affected by the fire.
4. Shumate Drug Company spends a substantial portion of its profits on research and development. The company has been reporting its $2,500,000 expenditure for research and development as a lump sum, but management recently decided to begin classifying the expenditures by project even though the recordkeeping costs will increase.
5. During the current year, McMillan Company changed from one generally accepted method of accounting for inventories to another method.

REQUIRED

In each case, state the convention that applies, tell whether or not the treatment is in accord with the convention and generally accepted accounting principles, and briefly explain why.

P 2.

LO 6 Forms of the Income Statement

The income statement accounts from the September 30, 20x2, year-end adjusted trial balance of Muramoto Hardware Company appear at the top of the next page. Beginning merchandise inventory was $350,400 and ending merchandise inventory is $315,300. The company is a sole proprietorship.

REQUIRED

From the information provided, prepare the following:

1. A detailed income statement.

Account Name	Debit	Credit
Sales		$1,082,460
Sales Returns and Allowances	$ 30,596	
Purchases	424,672	
Purchases Returns and Allowances		12,318
Freight In	22,442	
Sales Salaries Expense	204,060	
Sales Supplies Expense	3,284	
Rent Expense, Selling Space	36,000	
Utilities Expense, Selling Space	22,512	
Advertising Expense	43,972	
Depreciation Expense, Selling Fixtures	13,556	
Office Salaries Expense	95,824	
Office Supplies Expense	1,564	
Rent Expense, Office Space	8,000	
Depreciation Expense, Office Equipment	6,502	
Utilities Expense, Office Space	6,228	
Postage Expense	1,252	
Insurance Expense	5,400	
Miscellaneous Expense	962	
Interest Expense	7,200	
Interest Income		1,600

2. A condensed income statement in multistep form.

3. A condensed income statement in single-step form.

P 3.

LO 5 Classified Balance Sheet

The following information was taken from the September 30, 20x2, post-closing trial balance of Tasheki Hardware Company.

Account Name	Debit	Credit
Cash	$ 48,000	
Short-Term Investments	26,300	
Notes Receivable	90,000	
Accounts Receivable	153,140	
Merchandise Inventory	313,500	
Prepaid Rent	4,000	
Prepaid Insurance	2,400	
Sales Supplies	852	
Office Supplies	194	
Land Held for Future Expansion	23,000	
Selling Fixtures	144,800	
Accumulated Depreciation, Selling Fixtures		$ 44,000
Office Equipment	48,200	
Accumulated Depreciation, Office Equipment		24,100
Trademark	8,000	
Accounts Payable		219,490
Salaries Payable		1,574
Interest Payable		1,200
Notes Payable (due in three years)		72,000
Thomas Tasheki, Capital		500,022

REQUIRED

From the information provided, prepare a classified balance sheet.

P 4.

LO 7 Ratio Analysis: Liquidity and Profitability

Below is a summary of data taken from the income statements and balance sheets of Heard Construction Supply for the past two years.

	20x4	20x3
Current Assets	$ 183,000	$ 155,000
Total Assets	1,160,000	870,000
Current Liabilities	90,000	60,000
Long-Term Liabilities	300,000	290,000
Owner's Equity	670,000	520,000
Net Sales	2,300,000	1,740,000
Net Income	150,000	102,000

Total assets and owner's equity at the beginning of 20x3 were $680,000 and $420,000, respectively.

REQUIRED

1. Compute the following liquidity measures for 20x3 and 20x4: (a) working capital and (b) current ratio. Comment on the differences between the years.

2. Compute the following measures of profitability for 20x3 and 20x4: (a) profit margin, (b) asset turnover, (c) return on assets, (d) debt to equity, and (e) return on equity. Comment on the change in performance from 20x3 to 20x4.

P 5.

**LO 5 Classified Financial
LO 6 Statement Preparation
LO 7 and Evaluation**

The following accounts (in alphabetical order) and amounts were taken or calculated from the December 31, 20x4 year-end adjusted trial balance of Blossom Lawn Equipment Center: Accounts Payable, $36,300; Accounts Receivable, $84,700; Accumulated Depreciation, Building, $26,200; Accumulated Depreciation, Equipment $17,400; Building, $110,000; Cash, $10,640; Cost of Goods Sold, $246,000; Dividend Income, $1,280; Equipment, $75,600; General and Administrative Expenses, $60,600; Nancy Gregorio, Capital, $211,210; Nancy Gregorio, Withdrawals, $23,900; Interest Expense, $12,200; Inventory, $56,150; Land (used in operations), $29,000; Land Held for Future Use, $20,000; Mortgage Payable, $90,000; Notes Payable (short term), $25,000; Notes Receivable, $12,000; Sales (net), $448,000; Selling Expenses, $101,350; Short-Term Investment (100 shares of General Motors), $6,500; and Trademark, $6,750. Total assets on December 31, 20x3 were $343,950.

REQUIRED

1. From the information above, prepare (a) an income statement in condensed multi-step form, (b) a statement of owner's equity, and (c) a classified balance sheet.

2. Calculate the following measures of liquidity: (a) working capital and (b) current ratio.

3. Calculate the following measures of profitability: (a) profit margin, (b) asset turnover, (c) return on assets, (d) debt to equity, and (e) return on equity.

ALTERNATE PROBLEMS

P 6.

LO 3 Accounting Conventions

In each case that follows, accounting conventions *may* have been violated.

1. After careful study, Hawthorne Company, which has offices in 40 states, has determined that in the future its method of depreciating office furniture should be changed. The new method is adopted for the current year, and the change is noted in the financial statements.

2. In the past, Regalado Corporation has recorded operating expenses in general accounts for each classification (for example, Salaries Expense, Depreciation Expense, and Utilities Expense). Management has determined that despite the additional recordkeeping costs, the company's income statement should break down each operating expense into its components of selling expense and administrative expense.

3. Callie Watts, the auditor of Burleson Corporation, discovered that an official of the company may have authorized the payment of a $1,000 bribe to a local official. Management argued that because the item was so small in relation to the size of the company ($1,000,000 in sales), the illegal payment should not be disclosed.

4. Kuberski's Bookstore built a small addition to its main building to house a new computer games section. Because no one could be sure that the computer games section would succeed, the accountant took a conservative approach and recorded the addition as an expense.

5. Since its origin ten years ago, Hsu Company has used the same generally accepted inventory method. Because there has been no change in the inventory method, the company does not declare in its financial statements what inventory method it uses.

REQUIRED

In each case, state the convention that applies, tell whether or not the treatment is in accord with the convention and generally accepted accounting principles, and briefly explain why.

P 7.

LO 6 Forms of the Income Statement

The March 31, 20x3, year-end income statement accounts that follow are for O'Dell Hardware Company. Beginning merchandise inventory was $86,400 and ending merchandise inventory is $72,500. O'Dell Hardware Company is a sole proprietorship.

Account Name	Debit	Credit
Sales		$461,100
Sales Returns and Allowances	$ 26,900	
Purchases	224,500	
Purchases Returns and Allowances		11,920
Freight In	17,400	
Sales Salaries Expense	62,160	
Sales Supplies Expense	1,640	
Rent Expense, Selling Space	7,200	
Utilities Expense, Selling Space	2,960	
Advertising Expense	16,800	
Depreciation Expense, Delivery Equipment	4,400	
Office Salaries Expense	29,240	
Office Supplies Expense	9,760	
Rent Expense, Office Space	2,400	
Utilities Expense, Office Space	1,000	
Postage Expense	2,320	
Insurance Expense	2,680	
Miscellaneous Expense	1,440	
General Management Salaries Expense	42,000	
Interest Expense	5,600	
Interest Income		420

REQUIRED

From the information provided, prepare the following:

1. A detailed income statement.
2. A condensed income statement in multistep form.
3. A condensed income statement in single-step form.

P 8.

LO 7 Ratio Analysis: Liquidity and Profitability

Sambito Products Company has been disappointed with its operating results for the past two years. As the accountant for the company, you have the following information available to you:

	20x4	20x3
Current Assets	$ 90,000	$ 70,000
Total Assets	290,000	220,000
Current Liabilities	40,000	20,000
Long-Term Liabilities	40,000	—
Owner's Equity	210,000	200,000
Net Sales	524,000	400,000
Net Income	32,000	22,000

Total assets and owner's equity at the beginning of 20x3 were $180,000 and $160,000, respectively.

REQUIRED

1. Compute the following measures of liquidity for 20x3 and 20x4: (a) working capital and (b) current ratio. Comment on the differences between the years.

2. Compute the following measures of profitability for 20x3 and 20x4: (a) profit margin, (b) asset turnover, (c) return on assets, (d) debt to equity, and (e) return on equity. Comment on the change in performance from 20x3 to 20x4.

EXPANDING YOUR CRITICAL THINKING, COMMUNICATION, AND INTERPERSONAL SKILLS

SKILLS DEVELOPMENT

Conceptual Analysis

SD 1.
LO 3 **Accounting Conventions**

Sulu Parking, which operates a seven-story parking building in downtown Chicago, has a calendar year end. It serves daily and hourly parkers, as well as monthly parkers who pay a fixed monthly rate in advance. The company traditionally has recorded all cash receipts as revenues when received. Most monthly parkers pay in full during the month prior to that in which they have the right to park. The company's auditors have said that beginning in 2001, the company should consider recording the cash receipts from monthly parking on an accrual basis, crediting Unearned Revenues. Total cash receipts for 2001 were $2,500,000, and the cash receipts received in 2001 and applicable to January 2002 were $125,000. Discuss the relevance of the accounting conventions of consistency, materiality, and full disclosure to the decision to record the monthly parking revenues on an accrual basis.

SD 2.
LO 3 **Materiality**

Brown Electronics, Inc., operates a chain of consumer electronics stores in the Atlanta area. This year the company achieved annual sales of $50 million, on which it earned a net income of $2 million. At the beginning of the year, management implemented a new inventory system that enabled it to track all purchases and sales. At the end of the year, a physical inventory revealed that the actual inventory was $80,000 below what the new system indicated it should be. The inventory loss, which probably resulted from shoplifting, is reflected in a higher cost of goods sold. The problem concerns management but seems to be less important to the company's auditors. What is materiality? Why might the inventory loss concern management more than it does the auditors? Do you think the amount is material?

Ethical Dilemma

SD 3.
LO 4 **Ethics and Financial Reporting**

Dawes Software, located outside Boston, develops computer software and licenses it to financial institutions. The firm uses an aggressive accounting method that records revenues from the software it has developed on a percentage of completion basis. Consequently, revenue for partially completed projects is recognized based on the proportion of the project that is completed. If a project is 50 percent completed, then 50 percent of the contracted revenue is recognized. In 20x2, preliminary estimates for a $5 million project are that the project is 75 percent complete. Because the estimate of completion is a matter of judgment, management asks for a new report showing the

 Cash Flow   CD-ROM   Communication   Critical Thinking   Ethics   General Ledger   Group Activity   Hot Links to Real Companies   International   Internet   Key Ratio   Memo   Spreadsheet

project to be 90 percent complete. The change will enable senior managers to meet their financial goals for the year and thus receive substantial year-end bonuses. Do you think management's action is ethical? If you were the company controller and were asked to prepare the new report, would you do it? What action would you take?

Group Activity: Use in-class groups to debate the ethics of the action.

SD 4.

LO 4 Ethics and Financial Reporting

Orion Microsystems, Inc., a Silicon Valley manufacturer of microchips for personal computers, has just completed its year-end physical inventory in advance of preparing financial statements. To celebrate, the entire accounting department goes out for a New Year's Eve party at a local establishment. As senior accountant, you join the fun. At the party, you fall into conversation with an employee of one of your main competitors. After a while, the employee reveals that the competitor plans to introduce a new product in 60 days that will make Orion's principal product obsolete.

On Monday morning, you go to the financial vice president with this information, stating that the inventory may have to be written down and net income reduced. To your surprise, the financial vice president says that you were right to come to her, but urges you to say nothing about the problem. She says, "It is probably a rumor, and even if it is true, there will be plenty of time to write down the inventory in sixty days." You wonder if this is the appropriate thing to do. You feel confident that your source knew what he was talking about. You know that the salaries of all top managers, including the financial vice president, are tied to net income. What is fraudulent financial reporting? Is this an example of fraudulent financial reporting? What action would you take?

Research Activity

SD 5.

LO 4 Accounting and Fraud

Most university and public libraries have access to indexes of leading newspapers such as *The Wall Street Journal* and *The New York Times* on CD-ROM. Go to a library and do a search for a recent year using the key words "accounting and fraud," "accounting and restatement," or "accounting and irregularities." Choose one of the articles you find and read it. What company is involved and how is accounting connected with the fraud, restatement, or irregularity? Describe the situation. Does it involve an apparently legal or illegal activity? Does it involve fraudulent financial reporting? Explain your answer and be prepared to discuss it in class.

Decision-Making Practice

SD 6.

LO 7 Financial Analysis for Loan Decision

Rosa Corona was recently promoted to loan officer at the *First National Bank*. She has authority to issue loans up to $50,000 without approval from a higher bank official. This week two small companies, Handy Harvey, Inc., and Sheila's Fashions, Inc., have each submitted a proposal for a six-month $50,000 loan. To prepare financial analyses of the two companies, Rosa has obtained the information summarized below.

Handy Harvey, Inc., is a local lumber and home improvement company. Because sales have increased so much during the past two years, Handy Harvey has had to raise additional working capital, especially as represented by receivables and inventory. The $50,000 loan is needed to assure the company of enough working capital for the next year. Handy Harvey began the year with total assets of $740,000 and stockholders' equity of $260,000. During the past year the company had a net income of $40,000 on net sales of $760,000. The company's current unclassified balance sheet appears as follows:

Assets		Liabilities and Stockholders' Equity	
Cash	$ 30,000	Accounts Payable	$200,000
Accounts Receivable (net)	150,000	Notes Payable (short term)	100,000
Inventory	250,000	Notes Payable (long term)	200,000
Land	50,000	Common Stock	250,000
Buildings (net)	250,000	Retained Earnings	50,000
Equipment (net)	70,000	Total Liabilities and	
Total Assets	$800,000	Stockholders' Equity	$800,000

Sheila's Fashions, Inc., has for three years been a successful clothing store for young professional women. The leased store is located in the downtown financial district. Sheila's loan proposal asks for $50,000 to pay for stocking a new line of women's suits during the coming season. At the beginning of the year, the company had total assets of $200,000 and total stockholders' equity of $114,000. Over the past year, the company earned a net income of $36,000 on net sales of $480,000. The firm's unclassified balance sheet at the current date appears as follows:

Assets		Liabilities and Stockholders' Equity	
Cash	$ 10,000	Accounts Payable	$ 80,000
Accounts Receivable (net)	50,000	Accrued Liabilities	10,000
Inventory	135,000	Common Stock	50,000
Prepaid Expenses	5,000	Retained Earnings	100,000
Equipment (net)	40,000	Total Liabilities and	
Total Assets	$240,000	Stockholders' Equity	$240,000

1. Prepare a financial analysis of each company's liquidity before and after receiving the proposed loan. Also compute profitability ratios before and after, as appropriate. Write a brief summary of the effect of the proposed loan on each company's financial position.

2. Assume you are Rosa Corona and you can make a loan to only one of these companies. Write a memorandum to the bank's vice president naming the company to which you would recommend loaning $50,000. Be sure to state what positive and negative factors could affect each company's ability to pay back the loan in the next year. Also indicate what other information of a financial or nonfinancial nature would be helpful in making a final decision.

FINANCIAL REPORTING AND ANALYSIS

Interpreting Financial Reports

FRA 1.
LO 7 Comparison of Profitability

Two of the largest chains of grocery/drugstores in the United States are *Albertson's Inc.* and *Safeway, Inc.* In its fiscal year ended February 3, 2000, Albertson's had a net income of $955 million, and in its fiscal year ended December 28, 1999, Safeway had a net income of $971 million. It is difficult to judge which company is more profitable from those figures alone because they do not take into account the relative sales, sizes, and investments of the companies. Data (in millions) to complete a financial analysis of the two companies follow:[15]

	Albertson's	Safeway
Net Sales	$37,478	$28,860
Beginning Total Assets	15,131	11,390
Ending Total Assets	15,701	14,900
Beginning Total Liabilities	9,609	8,308
Ending Total Liabilities	10,000	10,814
Beginning Stockholders' Equity	5,522	3,082
Ending Stockholders' Equity	5,701	4,086

REQUIRED

1. Determine which company was more profitable by computing profit margin, asset turnover, return on assets, debt to equity, and return on equity for the two companies. Comment on the relative profitability of the two companies.

2. What do the ratios tell you about the factors that go into achieving an adequate return on assets in the grocery industry? For industry data, refer to Figures 5 through 9.

3. How would you characterize the use of debt financing in the grocery industry and the use of debt by the two companies?

Group Activity: Assign each ratio or company to a group and hold a class discussion.

FRA 2.
LO 7 Evaluation of Profitability

Walt Half-Moon is the principal stockholder and president of *Half-Moon Tapestries, Inc.,* which wholesales fine tapestries to retail stores. Because Half-Moon was not satisfied with the company earnings in 20x3, he raised prices in 20x4, increasing gross margin from sales from 30 percent in 20x3 to 35 percent in 20x4. Half-Moon is pleased that net income did go up from 20x3 to 20x4, as shown in the following comparative income statements.

	20x4	20x3
Revenues		
Net Sales	$611,300	$693,200
Costs and Expenses		
Cost of Goods Sold	$397,345	$485,240
Selling and Administrative Expenses	154,199	152,504
Total Costs and Expenses	$551,544	$637,744
Income Before Income Taxes	$ 59,756	$ 55,456
Income Taxes	15,000	14,000
Net Income	$ 44,756	$ 41,456

Total assets for Half-Moon Tapestries, Inc., at year end for 20x2, 20x3, and 20x4 were $623,390, $693,405, and $768,455, respectively. Has Half-Moon Tapestries' profitability really improved? (**Hint:** Compute profit margin and return on assets, and comment.) What factors has Half-Moon overlooked in evaluating the profitability of the company? (**Hint:** Compute asset turnover and comment on the role it plays in profitability.)

FRA 3.
LO 7 Financial Analysis with Industry Comparison

REQUIRED

Exhibits 2 and 5 in this chapter contain the comparative balance sheet and income statement for *Dell Computer Corp.* Assume you are the chief financial officer.

1. Compute liquidity ratios (working capital and current ratio) and profitability ratios (profit margin, asset turnover, return on assets, debt to equity, and return on equity) for 1999 and 2000 and show the industry ratios (except working capital) from Figures 4 to 9 in the chapter. In 1998, total assets were $4,268 million and stockholders' equity was $1, 293 million.

2. Write a short memorandum to the board of directors in executive summary form summarizing changes in Dell's liquidity and profitability performance from 1999 to 2000 compared with the industry averages.

International Company

FRA 4.
LO 5 Interpretation and
LO 7 Analysis of British Financial Statements

REQUIRED

At the top of the next page are the classified balance sheets for the British company *Glaxo Wellcome plc,* a pharmaceutical firm with marketing and manufacturing operations in 57 countries.[16]

In the United Kingdom, the format used for classified financial statements is usually different from that used in the United States. To compare the financial statements of companies in different countries, it is important to develop the ability to interpret a variety of formats.

1. For each line on Glaxo Wellcome plc's balance sheet, indicate the corresponding term that would be found on a U.S. balance sheet. (For this exercise, consider Provisions for Liabilities and Charges to be long-term liabilities.) What is the focus or rationale behind the format of the U.K. balance sheet?

Glaxo Wellcome plc and Subsidiaries Consolidated Balance Sheets		
	1999 £m	1998 £m
Fixed assets		
Goodwill	144	106
Tangible assets	3,720	3,633
Investments	483	98
	4,347	3,837
Current assets		
Stocks	1,537	1,154
Debtors	2,577	2,470
Equity investments	52	28
Liquid investments	1,697	1,617
Cash at bank	217	240
	6,080	5,509
Creditors: amounts due within one year		
Loans and overdrafts	2,250	1,317
Other creditors	3,013	2,828
	5,263	4,145
Net current (liabilities)/assets	817	1,364
Total assets less current liabilities	5,164	5,201
Creditors: amounts due after one year		
Loans	1,260	1,804
Other creditors	116	161
	1,376	1,965
Provisions for liabilities and charges	595	468
Net assets	3,193	2,768
Capital and reserves		
Called up share capital	910	906
Share premium account	1,249	1,149
Other reserves	983	647
Equity shareholders' funds	3,142	2,702
Equity minority interests	51	66
Capital employed	3,193	2,768

2. Assuming that Glaxo Wellcome plc earned a net income of £1,951 million and £1,836 million in 1999 and 1998, respectively, compute the current ratio, debt to equity, return on assets, and return on equity for 1999 and 1998. (Use year-end amounts to compute ratios.)

Toys "R" Us Annual Report

FRA 5.

LO 5 Reading and Analyzing
LO 6 an Annual Report
LO 7

Refer to the Toys "R" Us annual report to answer the following questions. (Note that 2000 refers to the year ended January 29, 2000, and 1999 refers to the year ended January 30, 1999.)

1. Consolidated balance sheets: (a) Did the amount of working capital increase or decrease from 1999 to 2000? By how much? (b) Did the current ratio improve from 1999 to 2000? (c) Does the company have long-term investments or intangible

assets? (d) Did the debt to equity ratio of Toys "R" Us change from 1999 to 2000? (e) What is the contributed capital for 2000? How does it compare with retained earnings?

2. Consolidated statements of earnings: (a) Does Toys "R" Us use a multistep or a single-step form of income statement? (b) Is it a comparative statement? (c) What is the trend of net earnings? (d) How significant are income taxes for Toys "R" Us? (e) Did the profit margin increase from 1999 to 2000? (f) Did asset turnover improve from 1999 to 2000? (g) Did the return on assets increase from 1999 to 2000? (h) Did the return on equity increase from 1999 to 2000? Total assets and total stockholders' equity for 1998 may be obtained from the financial highlights.

3. Multistep income statement: In Toys "R" Us's 1987 annual report, management stated that the company's "[operating] expense levels were among the best controlled in retailing [at] 18.8 percent. . . . We were able to operate with lower merchandise margins and still increase our earnings and return on sales."[17] Prepare a multistep income statement for Toys "R" Us down to income from operations for 1999 and 2000, excluding the restructuring, and compute the ratios of gross margin, operating expenses, and income from operations to net sales. Comment on whether the company continued, as of 2000, to maintain the level of performance indicated by management in 1987. In 1987, gross margin was 31.2 percent and income from operations was 12.4 percent of net sales.

Fingraph® Financial Analyst™

FRA 6.

LO 7 Analysis of Dell Computer Corp. or Toys "R" Us

Choose one or both of the following analyses:

1. *Alternative to FRA 3:* Analyze Dell Computer Corp.'s balance sheet and income statement using Fingraph® Financial Analyst™ CD-ROM software. To do this assignment, you will need to enter the data from Dell's financial statements shown in this chapter. Complete part 1 of **FRA 3.** Prepare the memorandum required in part 2 of **FRA 3** separately.

2. *Alternative to FRA 5:* Analyze the Toys "R" Us balance sheet and income statement using Fingraph® Financial Analyst™ CD-ROM software. The CD-ROM contains the 2000 Toys "R" Us data entry spreadsheet for the annual report that appears in this textbook. Complete requirements 1, 2, and 3 of **FRA 5.**

Internet Case

FRA 7.

LO 7 Annual Reports and Financial Analysis

Obtain the annual report for a large, well-known company from either your college's library or the Needles Accounting Resource Center web site at http://college.hmco.com. Companies in this chapter include General Mills, Dell Computer, Nike, and Quaker Oats. In the annual report, identify the four basic financial statements and the notes to the financial statements. Perform a liquidity analysis, including the calculation of working capital and the current ratio. Perform a profitability analysis, calculating profit margin, asset turnover, return on assets, debt to equity, and return on equity. Be prepared to present your findings in class.

ENDNOTES

1. General Mills, Inc., "General Mills Outlines Year 2010 Growth Goals," press release, February 22, 2000.

2. *Statement of Financial Accounting Concepts No. 1*, "Objectives of Financial Reporting by Business Enterprises" (Norwalk, Conn.: Financial Accounting Standards Board, 1978), pars. 32–54.

3. *Statement of Financial Accounting Concepts No. 1*, "Qualitative Characteristics of Accounting Information" (Norwalk, Conn.: Financial Accounting Standards Board, 1980), par. 20.

4. Accounting Principles Board, "Accounting Changes," *Opinion No. 20* (New York: American Institute of Certified Public Accountants, 1971), par. 17.
5. Reynolds Metals Company, *Annual Report*, 1998.
6. Ray J. Groves, "Here's the Annual Report. Got a Few Hours?" *The Wall Street Journal Europe*, August 26–27, 1994.
7. Roger Lowenstein, "Investors Will Fish for Footnotes in 'Abbreviated' Annual Reports," *The Wall Street Journal*, September 14, 1995.
8. Quaker Oats Co., *Annual Report*, 1998.
9. Emily Nelson and Joann J. Lublin, "How Whistle-Blowers Set Off a Fraud Probe that Crushed Cendant," *The Wall Street Journal*, August 13, 1998.
10. Quaker Oats Co., *Annual Report*, 1998.
11. National Commission on Fraudulent Financial Reporting, *Report of the National Commission on Fraudulent Financial Reporting* (Washington, D.C., 1987), p. 2.
12. *Accounting Research and Terminology Bulletin*, final ed. (New York: American Institute of Certified Public Accountants, 1961), p. 20.
13. Roger Lowenstein, "Lenders' Stampede Tramples Caldor," *The Wall Street Journal*, October 26, 1995.
14. Roger Lowenstein, "The '20% Club' No Longer Is Exclusive," *The Wall Street Journal*, May 4, 1995.
15. Albertson's Inc. and Safeway, Inc., *Annual Reports*, February 3, 2000, and December 28, 1999, respectively.
16. Glaxo Wellcome plc, *Annual Report*, 1999.
17. Toys "R" Us, *Annual Report*, 1987.

SUPPLEMENT TO CHAPTER 6

How to Read an Annual Report

More than 4 million corporations are chartered in the United States. Most of these corporations are small, usually family-owned, businesses. They are called *private* or *closely held corporations* because their common stock is held by only a few people and is not available for sale to the public. Larger companies usually find it desirable to raise investment funds from many investors by issuing common stock to the public. These companies are called *public companies*. Although they are fewer in number than private companies, the total economic impact of public companies is much greater.

Public companies must register their common stock with the Securities and Exchange Commission (SEC), which regulates the issuance and subsequent trading of the stock of public companies. One important responsibility of the management of public companies under SEC rules is to report each year to the company's stockholders on the financial performance of the company. This report, called an *annual report*, contains the annual financial statements and other information about the company. Annual reports, which are a primary source of financial information about public companies, are distributed to all the company's stockholders and filed with the SEC. When filed with the SEC, the annual report is called the 10-K because a Form 10-K is used to file the report. The general public may obtain a company's annual report by calling or writing the company. Many libraries have files of annual reports or have them available on electronic media such as *Compact Disclosure*. The annual reports of many companies can be accessed on the Internet by going to a company's home page on the World Wide Web. Also, many large companies file their 10-Ks electronically with the SEC. These annual reports and other filings may be accessed on the Internet at http://www.freeedgar.com.

This supplement describes the major sections of the typical annual report and contains the complete annual report for one of the most successful retailers of this generation, *Toys "R" Us, Inc.* In addition to stores that sell toys and other items for children, the company has opened a chain of stores that sell children's clothes, called Kids "R" Us. The Toys "R" Us annual report should be referred to in completing the case assignments related to the company in each chapter.

The Components of an Annual Report

In addition to the financial statements, the annual report contains the notes to the financial statements, a letter to the stockholders (or shareholders), a multiyear summary of financial highlights, a description of the business, management's discussion of operating results and financial condition, a report of management's responsibility, the auditors' report, and a list of directors and officers of the company.

Letter to the Stockholders

Traditionally, at the beginning of the annual report, there is a letter in which the top officers of a corporation tell stockholders about the performance of and prospects for the company. The president and chief executive officer of Toys "R" Us wrote to the stockholders about the highlights of the past year, the key priorities for the new year, store format and redeployment plans, corporate citizenship, and other aspects of the business. For example, they reported on future prospects as follows:

> It comes as no surprise to anyone that Toys "R" Us needs to improve its performance. No doubt many of you have been frustrated by the performance of the company over the last few years, including the holiday season of 1999 which yielded disappointing results. Those financials are thoroughly examined in this report. While we can't change the past, we can learn from it. I believe we have, and I want to tell you why I'm optimistic about the future of Toys "R" Us, and what our priorities are for the next 24 months.
>
> We've got a strong organization of talented and dedicated people, a brand that is second to none in the toy industry, and a solid financial foundation.

Financial Highlights

The financial highlights section of the annual report presents key financial statistics for a ten-year period and is often accompanied by graphs. The Toys "R" Us annual report, for example, gives key figures for operations, financial position, and number of stores at year end. Other key figures are also shown graphically at appropriate points in the report. Note that the financial highlights section often includes nonfinancial data, such as number of stores.

In addition to financial highlights, an annual report will contain a detailed description of the products and divisions of the company. Some analysts tend to scoff at this section of the annual report because it often contains glossy photographs and other image-building material, but it should not be overlooked because it may provide useful information about past results and future plans.

Financial Statements

All companies present four basic financial statements. Toys "R" Us presents statements of earnings, balance sheets, statements of cash flows, and statements of stockholders' equity. Refer to the Toys "R" Us statements following this supplement during the discussion.

All of the Toys "R" Us financial statements are preceded by the word *consolidated*. A corporation issues *consolidated financial statements* when it consists of several companies and has combined their data for reporting purposes. For example, Toys "R" Us also operates Kids "R" Us and has combined that company's financial data with those of the Toys "R" Us stores.

Toys "R" Us also provides several years of data for each financial statement: two years for the balance sheet and three years for the others. Financial statements presented in this fashion are called *comparative financial statements*. Such statements are in accordance with generally accepted accounting principles and help readers to assess the company's performance over several years.

You may notice that the fiscal year for Toys "R" Us, instead of ending on the same date each year, ends on the Saturday nearest to the end of January. The reason is that Toys "R" Us is a retail company. It is common for retailers to end their fiscal years at a slow period after the busiest time of year.

In a note at the bottom of each page of the financial statements, the company reminds the reader that the accompanying notes are an integral part of the statements and must be consulted in interpreting the data.

CONSOLIDATED STATEMENTS OF EARNINGS   Toys "R" Us uses a multistep form of the income statement that shows gross margin as the difference between net sales and cost of goods sold. Total operating expenses are deducted from gross margin to arrive at operating income. Interest expense is shown separately, and income taxes are deducted in another step.

Net earnings is an alternative name for net income. The company also discloses the earnings per share, which is the net earnings divided by the weighted average number of shares of common stock held by stockholders during the year.

CONSOLIDATED BALANCE SHEETS   Toys "R" Us has a typical balance sheet for a merchandising company. In the assets and liabilities sections, the company separates out the current assets and the current liabilities. These are assets that will become available as cash or be used up in the next year and liabilities that will have to be paid or satisfied in the next year. These groupings help in understanding the company's liquidity.

Several items in the stockholders' equity section need additional explanation. Common stock represents the number of shares outstanding at par value. Additional paid-in capital represents amounts invested by stockholders in excess of the par value of the common stock. Foreign currency translation adjustments occur because Toys "R" Us has foreign operations (see the appendixes on international accounting and long-term investments). Treasury shares is a deduction from stockholders' equity that represents the cost of previously issued shares that have been bought back and held by the company.

CONSOLIDATED STATEMENTS OF CASH FLOWS   The preparation of the consolidated statement of cash flows is presented in the chapter on the statement of cash flows. Whereas the income statement reflects a company's profitability, the statement of cash flows reflects its liquidity. The statement provides information about a company's cash receipts, cash payments, and investing and financing activities during an accounting period.

Refer to the consolidated statements of cash flows in the Toys "R" Us annual report. The first major section shows cash flows from operating activities. It begins with the net earnings (income) from the consolidated statements of earnings and adjusts that figure to a figure that represents the net cash flows provided by operating activities. Among the adjustments are increases for depreciation and amortization, which are expenses that do not require the use of cash, and increases and decreases for the changes in the working capital accounts. In the year ended January 29, 2000, Toys "R" Us had net earnings of $279,000,000, and its net cash inflow from operating activities was $865,000,000. Added to net income are expenses that do not require a current outlay of cash, such as depreciation, amortization, and asset write-offs of $278,000,000. A decrease of $35,000,000 in accounts and other receivables, and a large increase in accounts payable, accrued expenses and other liabilities of $497,000,000 had positive effects on cash flows. Cash was used to increase inventories ($192,000,000) and prepaid expenses and other operating assets ($69,000,000) and to decrease income taxes payable ($119,000,000).

The second major section of the consolidated statements of cash flows is cash flows from investing activities. The main item in this category is capital expenditures, net, of $533,000,000. This shows that Toys "R" Us is a growing company.

The third major section of the consolidated statements of cash flows is cash flows from financing activities. You can see here that the sources of cash from financing are short-term and long-term borrowings of $95,000,000 and $593,000,000, respectively, and exercise of stock options of $14,000,000, which were helpful in making long-term debt repayments of $604,000,000 and share repurchases of $200,000,000. In total, the company used $102,000,000 for financing activities during the year.

At the bottom of the consolidated statements of cash flows, the net effect of the operating, investing, and financing activities on the cash balance may be seen. Toys "R" Us had an increase in cash and cash equivalents during the year of $174,000,000 and ended the year with $584,000,000 of cash and cash equivalents on hand.

The supplemental disclosures of cash flow information show income tax and interest payments for the last three years.

CONSOLIDATED STATEMENTS OF STOCKHOLDERS' EQUITY   Instead of a simple statement of retained earnings, Toys "R" Us presents a *statement of stockholders' equity*. This statement explains the changes in five components of stockholders' equity.

Notes to Consolidated Financial Statements

To meet the requirements of full disclosure, the company must add *notes to the financial statements* to help users interpret some of the more complex items. The notes are considered an integral part of the financial statements. In recent years, the need for explanation and further details has become so great that the notes often take more space than the statements themselves. The notes to the financial statements can be put into three broad groups: summary of significant accounting policies, explanatory notes, and supplementary information notes.

SUMMARY OF SIGNIFICANT ACCOUNTING POLICIES   Generally accepted accounting principles require that the financial statements include a *summary of significant accounting policies*. In most cases, this summary is presented in the first note to the financial statements or as a separate section just before the notes. In this summary, the company tells which generally accepted accounting principles it has followed in preparing the statements. For example, in the Toys "R" Us report the company states the principles followed for property and equipment:

> Property and equipment are recorded at cost. Depreciation and amortization are provided using the straight-line method over the estimated useful lives of the assets or, where applicable, the terms of the respective leases, whichever is shorter.

Other important accounting policies listed by Toys "R" Us deal with fiscal year, reclassification, principles of consolidation, cash and cash equivalents, merchandise inventories, financial instruments, forward foreign exchange contracts, and the use of estimates.

EXPLANATORY NOTES   Other notes explain some of the items in the financial statements. For example, Toys "R" Us showed the details of its Property and Equipment account, which is reproduced at the top of the next page. Other notes had to do with seasonal financing and long-term debt, leases, stockholders' equity, earnings per share, taxes on income, stock options, the profit-sharing plan, acquisition, segments, restructuring and other charges, and other matters.

Property and Equipment			
	Useful Life (in years)	**January 29, 2000**	January 30, 1999
Land		**$ 827**	$ 829
Buildings	45–50	**1,859**	1,842
Furniture and equipment	5–20	**2,046**	1,861
Leaseholds and leasehold improvements	12½–35	**1,432**	1,213
Construction in progress		**42**	42
Leased property under capital leases		**26**	27
		6,232	5,814
Less accumulated depreciation and amortization		**1,777**	1,588
		$4,455	$4,226

SUPPLEMENTARY INFORMATION NOTES   In recent years, the FASB and the SEC have ruled that certain supplemental information must be presented with financial statements. Examples are the quarterly reports that most companies present to their stockholders and to the Securities and Exchange Commission. These quarterly reports, which are called *interim financial statements*, are in most cases reviewed but not audited by the company's independent CPA firm. In its annual report, Toys "R" Us presented unaudited quarterly financial data from its 1999 quarterly statements, which are shown in the following table (for the year ended January 29, 2000; dollars in millions, except per share amounts):

	First Quarter	Second Quarter	Third Quarter	Fourth Quarter
1999				
Net Sales	$2,166	$2,204	$2,465	$5,027
Cost of Sales	1,505	1,522	1,704	3,590
Net Earnings	17	12[a]	15[a]	235[a]
Basic Earnings per Share	$ .07	$ .05	$ .06	$ .98
Diluted Earnings per Share	$ .07	$ .05	$ .06	$ .98

[a] Includes cost to establish and operate toysrus.com, the company's Internet subsidiary.

Interim data were presented for the prior year as well. Toys "R" Us also provides supplemental information on the market price of its common stock during the years and data on its store locations.

Report of Management's Responsibilities

A statement of management's responsibility for the financial statements and the internal control structure may accompany the financial statements. The management report of Toys "R" Us acknowledges management's responsibility for the integrity and objectivity of the financial information and for the system of internal controls. It mentions the company's internal audit program and its distribution of company policies to employees. It also states that the company's financial statements have been audited.

Management's Discussion and Analysis

Management also presents a discussion and analysis of financial condition and results of operations. In this section, management explains the difference from one year to the next. For example, the management of Toys "R" Us describes the company's sales performance in the following way:

> The company's total sales increased 6% to $11.9 billion from $11.2 billion. The total sales growth was primarily driven by a 3% increase in comparable store sales, as well as continued new store expansion, partially offset by the closing of 46 under-performing stores in 1999 and 1998 (see "Restructuring and Other Charges" below). Comparable store sales for the USA toy store division increased 3%. The USA comparable toy store sales increases were driven primarily by improved merchandising trends and strong sales of Pokémon and electronic and video products. These gains were partially offset by the deflationary impact of video hardware sales, and were limited by industry-wide shortages of electronic and other products during the holiday season.

Its management of cash flows is described as follows:

> The seasonal nature of the business (approximately 42% of sales take place in the fourth quarter) typically causes cash to decline from the beginning of the year through October as inventory increases for the holiday selling season and funds are used for land purchases and construction of new stores, which usually open in the first ten months of the year. The company has a $1 billion multi-currency unsecured committed revolving credit facility expiring in December 2002, from a syndicate of financial institutions. There were no outstanding balances under this revolver at January 2000, 1999 and 1998. Cash requirements for operations, capital expenditures, lease commitments and the share repurchase program will be met primarily through operating activities, borrowings under the $1 billion revolving credit facility, issuance of commercial paper and/or other bank borrowings of foreign subsidiaries.

Report of Certified Public Accountants

The *independent auditors' report* deals with the credibility of the financial statements. This report by independent certified public accountants gives the accountants' opinion about how fairly these statements have been presented. Using financial statements prepared by managers without an independent audit would be like having a judge hear a case in which he or she was personally involved. Management, through its internal accounting system, is logically responsible for recordkeeping because it needs similar information for its own use in operating the business. The certified public accountants, acting independently, add the necessary credibility to management's figures for interested third parties. They report to the board of directors and the stockholders rather than to management.

In form and language, most auditors' reports are like the one shown in Figure 11. Usually such a report is short, but its language is very important. The report is divided into three parts.

**Figure 11
Auditors' Report for Toys "R"
Us, Inc.**

REPORT OF INDEPENDENT AUDITORS

To the Board of Directors and Stockholders
Toys"R"Us, Inc.

(1) We have audited the accompanying consolidated balance sheets of Toys"R"Us, Inc. and subsidiaries as of January 29, 2000 and January 30, 1999, and the related consolidated statements of earnings, stockholders' equity and cash flows for each of the three years in the period ended January 29, 2000. These financial statements are the responsibility of the Company's management. Our responsibility is to express an opinion on these financial statements based on our audits.

(2) We conducted our audits in accordance with auditing standards generally accepted in the United States. Those standards require that we plan and perform the audit to obtain reasonable assurance about whether the financial statements are free of material misstatement. An audit includes examining, on a test basis, evidence supporting the amounts and disclosures in the financial statements. An audit also includes assessing the accounting principles used and significant estimates made by management,

as well as evaluating the overall financial statement presentation. We believe that our audits provide a reasonable basis for our opinion.

(3) In our opinion, the financial statements referred to above present fairly, in all material respects, the consolidated financial position of Toys"R"Us, Inc. and subsidiaries at January 29, 2000 and January 30, 1999, and the consolidated results of their operations and their cash flows for each of the three years in the period ended January 29, 2000, in conformity with accounting principles generally accepted in the United States.

Ernst & Young LLP

New York, New York
March 8, 2000

Source: Reprinted courtesy of Toys "R" Us, Inc. The notes to the financial statement, which are an integral part of the report, are not included.

1. The first paragraph identifies the financial statements subject to the auditors' report. This paragraph also identifies responsibilities. Company management is responsible for the financial statements, and the auditor is responsible for expressing an opinion on the financial statements based on the audit.

2. The second paragraph, or *scope section*, states that the examination was made in accordance with generally accepted auditing standards. These standards call for an acceptable level of quality in ten areas established by the American Institute of Certified Public Accountants. This paragraph also contains a brief description of the objectives and nature of the audit.

3. The third paragraph, or *opinion section*, states the results of the auditors' examination. The use of the word *opinion* is very important because the auditor does not certify or guarantee that the statements are absolutely correct. To do so would go beyond the truth, since many items, such as depreciation, are based on estimates. Instead, the auditors simply give an opinion about whether, overall, the financial statements "present fairly," in all material respects, the financial position, results of operations, and cash flows. This means that the statements are prepared in accordance with generally accepted accounting principles. If, in the auditors' opinion, the statements do not meet accepted standards, the auditors must explain why and to what extent.

The Annual Report Project

Many instructors assign a term project that requires reading and analyzing a real annual report. The Annual Report Project described here is one that has proved successful in the authors' classes. It may be used with the annual report of any company, including the Toys "R" Us Annual Report that is provided with this supplement.

The extent to which the financial analysis is required depends on the point in the course at which the Annual Report Project is assigned. Several options are provided in Instruction 3E, below.

Instructions:

1. Select an annual report of a company from those available on the Fingraph® Financial Analyst™ CD-ROM database that accompanies this text, or obtain one from the company, your library, or another source.

2. Library and Internet Research
   Go to the library or use the Web Resources at the Needles Accounting Resource Center web site (http://college.hmco.com) to learn about the company you have chosen and the industry in which it operates. Find at least two articles or other references to the industry and the company and summarize your findings.

   Also, access the company's Internet home page directly or through the Needles Accounting Resource Center web site. Review the company's products and services and find its financial information. Summarize what you have learned.

3. Your term project should consist of five or six double-spaced pages organized according to the following outline:

   A. **Introduction**
      Identify your company by writing a summary that includes the following elements:
      - Name of the chief executive officer
      - Location of the home office
      - Ending date of latest fiscal year
      - Description of the principal products or services that the company provides
      - Main geographic area of activity

- Name of the company's independent accountants (auditors). In your own words, what did the accountants say about the company's financial statements?
- The most recent price of the company's stock and its dividend per share. Be sure to provide the date for this information.

B. Industry Situation and Company Plans

Describe the industry and its outlook; then summarize the company's future plans based on your library research and on reading the annual report. Be sure to read the letter to the stockholders. Include relevant information about the company's plans from that discussion.

C. Financial Statements

Income Statement: Is the format most like a single-step or multistep format? Determine gross profit, income from operations, and net income for the last two years; comment on the increases or decreases in these amounts.

Balance Sheet: Show that Assets = Liabilities + Stockholders' Equity for the past two years.

Statement of Cash Flows: Are cash flows from operations more or less than net income for the past two years? Is the company expanding through investing activities? What is the company's most important source of financing? Overall, has cash increased or decreased over the past two years?

D. Accounting Policies

What are the significant accounting policies, if any, relating to revenue recognition, cash, short-term investments, merchandise inventories, property and equipment, and preopening costs?

What are the topics of the notes to the financial statements?

E. Financial Analysis

For the past two years, calculate and discuss the significance of the following ratios:

Option (a): Basic (After Completing Chapters 1–6)

Liquidity Ratios
    Working capital
    Current ratio

Profitability Ratios
    Profit margin
    Asset turnover
    Return on assets
    Debt to equity
    Return on equity

Option (b): Basic with Enhanced Liquidity Analysis (After Completing Chapters 1–10)

Liquidity Ratios
    Working capital
    Current ratio
    Receivable turnover
    Average days' sales uncollected
    Inventory turnover
    Average days' inventory on hand

Profitability Ratios
  Profit margin
  Asset turnover
  Return on assets
  Debt to equity
  Return on equity

Option (c): Comprehensive (After Completing Chapters 1–18)

Liquidity Ratios
  Working capital
  Current ratio
  Receivable turnover
  Average days' sales uncollected
  Inventory turnover
  Average days' inventory on hand

Profitability Ratios
  Profit margin
  Asset turnover
  Return on assets
  Return on equity

Long-Term Solvency Ratios
  Debt to equity
  Interest coverage

Cash Flow Adequacy
  Cash flow yield
  Cash flows to sales
  Cash flows to assets
  Free cash flow

Market Strength Ratios
  Price/earnings per share
  Dividends yield

Option (d): Comprehensive Using Fingraph® Financial Analyst™ Software on the CD-ROM That Accompanies This Text

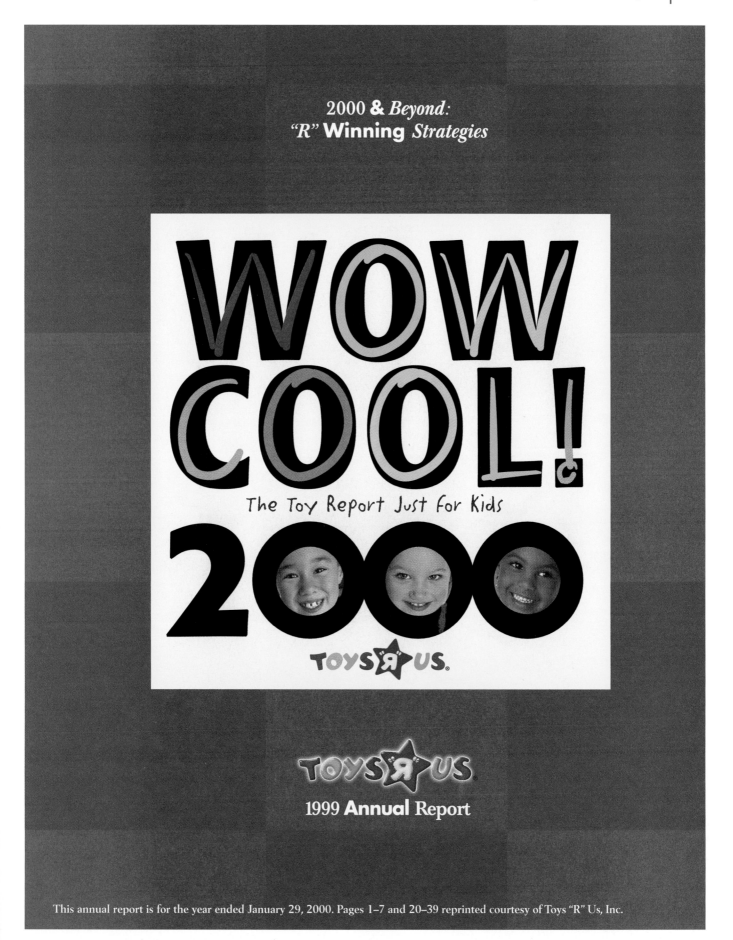

Table Of Contents

Financial Highlights
TOYS"R"US, INC. AND SUBSIDIARIES

(Dollars in millions except per share data)   Fiscal Year Ended

	Jan. 29, 2000*	Jan. 30, 1999**	Jan. 31, 1998	Feb.1, 1997**	Feb. 3, 1996**	Jan. 28, 1995	Jan. 29, 1994	Jan. 30, 1993	Feb. 1, 1992	Feb. 2, 1991
OPERATIONS:										
Net Sales	$11,862	$11,170	$11,038	$9,932	$9,427	$8,746	$7,946	$7,169	$6,124	$5,510
Net Earnings/(Loss)	279	(132)	490	427	148	532	483	438	340	326
Basic Earnings/(Loss) Per Share	1.14	(0.50)	1.72	1.56	0.54	1.88	1.66	1.51	1.18	1.12
Diluted Earnings/(Loss) Per Share	1.14	(0.50)	1.70	1.54	0.53	1.85	1.63	1.47	1.15	1.11
FINANCIAL POSITION AT YEAR END:										
Working Capital	$ 35	$ 106	$ 579	$ 619	$ 326	$ 484	$ 633	$ 797	$ 328	$ 177
Real Estate - Net	2,342	2,354	2,435	2,411	2,336	2,271	2,036	1,877	1,751	1,433
Total Assets	8,353	7,899	7,963	8,023	6,738	6,571	6,150	5,323	4,583	3,582
Long-Term Debt	1,230	1,222	851	909	827	785	724	671	391	195
Stockholders' Equity	3,680	3,624	4,428	4,191	3,432	3,429	3,148	2,889	2,426	2,046
NUMBER OF STORES AT YEAR END:										
Toys"R"Us - United States	710	704	700	682	653	618	581	540	497	451
Toys"R"Us - International	462	452	441	396	337	293	234	167	126	97
Kids"R"Us - United States	205	212	215	212	213	204	217	211	189	164
Babies"R"Us - United States	131	113	98	82	–	–	–	–	–	–
Imaginarium	40	–	–	–	–	–	–	–	–	–
Total Stores	1,548	1,481	1,454	1,372	1,203	1,115	1,032	918	812	712

*Includes the company's Internet subsidiary, toysrus.com.

**After restructuring and other charges.

To Our Shareholders

This is my first formal opportunity to communicate with many of you, and I'm pleased to share with you my enthusiasm for the future of Toys"R"Us.

As a relative newcomer, I have a different perspective of the company, and I'd like you to take a moment to see it through my eyes. When I look at Toys"R"Us, I see a great family of brands and a financially healthy company with a solid cash flow. I also see lots of opportunity.

It comes as no surprise to anyone that Toys"R"Us needs to improve its performance. No doubt many of you have been frustrated by the performance of the company over the last few years, including the holiday season of 1999 which yielded disappointing results. Those financials are thoroughly examined in this report. While we can't change the past, we can learn from it. I believe we have, and I want to tell you why I'm optimistic about the future of Toys"R"Us, and what our priorities are for the next 24 months.

We've got a strong organization of talented and dedicated people, a brand that is second to none in the toy industry, and a solid financial foundation. Let me share with you the strategies that we are focused on executing in 2000 and 2001.

Differentiation.

We're going to focus on four key priorities, beginning with our merchandise offering. It is essential that we differentiate our content from that of our competitors. We will still be the headquarters for the toy brands known and loved by our customers, but we'll be more. We are committed to offering new and exciting products first, and to that end we will be focusing a significant amount of time and attention on developing exclusive new concepts and technologies to offer more unique, fun and interesting products.

We made important strides in that effort here in the U.S. recently. In February, we announced a new line of exclusive branded products with Animal Planet. Animal Planet is the fastest growing cable station in the U.S., and this unique, interactive product line will be unlike anything else on the market. The Animal Planet line will be introduced in our stores this fall, and it is only the beginning of new, exclusive products to come.

The company has also entered into an exclusive partnership with Home Depot. Together with Home Depot, we'll be the store where kids and their parents can buy "real" tools for kids — actual working tools that are scaled appropriately to a kid's size and capability. These will come complete with accessories like tool belts, safety goggles and work aprons. We'll also offer construction kits for kids that will enable them to build things such as a birdhouse or a bookshelf on their own or under the guidance of an adult. And the Home Depot line of toys will also include role-play items like workbenches or drills that actually simulate the motion of a real drill. We will begin introducing these products in our stores in May with a full assortment rolled out by the end of the summer. We are very excited about this partnership and this line of creative and interactive toys available only at Toys"R"Us.

We've signed a unique licensing agreement with OshKosh B'Gosh, Inc., for a line of baby products under the well-known OshKosh brand. These products, which will be available in our stores in August, bring additional equity to our juvenile line and will include items such as basic juvenile toys, dolls, plush, soft toys and other items.

Toys"R"Us will also develop exclusive products with our most important resources that support their principal brands. This will further strengthen our relationships with key manufacturers while providing interesting and unique products available only at Toys"R"Us.

The Animal Planet Line is only the beginning of new, exclusive products to come.

Our focus is on better category segmentation

Refining our Store Format.

There is no question that we have made significant financial investment in remodeling stores over the last few years, both in the C-3 and the Concept 2000 formats. The good news is that the new store formats are out performing the old ones — and the gap continues to widen with this more customer-friendly format. The new format is a major step forward, and provides a solid foundation on which to build. We also think it provides us with further opportunity to unlock additional performance gains.

The best news, though, is that even with the progress we've made, we're not yet close to maximizing the potential of our new format. That's why we've developed 16 test stores across the country to provide us with laboratories for experimenting with new concepts and refinements.

This test store effort focuses on the reconfiguration of fixturing, better category segmentation and clear projection of merchandising concepts — all designed to make the shopping experience more pleasant and productive for our guests, the customers who shop at Toys"R"Us. It also includes the addition of many new business categories, the addition of Imaginarium as a child development center, demonstration areas where we can delight our guests with the newest products, and a redefinition of our service level. These test stores include selling specialists and a truly service-focused management commitment. We believe the opportunities for sales growth and guest satisfaction are material. As these concepts are validated, we expect to execute significant rollout by holiday season 2000.

Redeployment of Inventory Investment.

We are redeploying inventory investment to ensure major intensification supporting the most important volume-producing toys in our assortment. We missed many selling opportunities during the holiday season in 1999 by not having enough investment behind the top 1,000 items. We will dramatically improve this process in 2000, and have already begun substantial order placements to ensure key item availability.

Our objective this year is to fund a doubling of the investment in our top 1,000 items by reducing our current levels of non-key inventory and by working with our resources to more tightly focus our investment behind their most important properties. We will still offer the broadest selection of any bricks and mortar store in the world, but this redeployment of inventory depth behind the most important items will help to energize our sales this coming holiday season by ensuring that we have the most wanted items.

Redeployment of Expense Dollars.

We have challenged each operating and support division worldwide to analyze every expense dollar and to eliminate spending that does not productively serve our guests, generate sales or improve productivity.

Those expense dollars are being redeployed to fund guest service, pricing and marketing initiatives designed to drive sales growth in our stores.

Unlocking the Value of our Assets.

There are many assets within this company that offer tremendous value to our shareholders. This was evident in our recent announcement regarding an initial public offering (IPO) plan for Toys"R"Us - Japan. Under the IPO plan, Toys"R"Us - Japan and the company will offer primary and secondary shares, respectively, to the public in Japan. Such shares should begin trading on the

Demonstration areas delight our customers

Babies"R"Us is a clear winner

Japanese OTC market on April 25, 2000. Following that offering, the company will retain a 48% ownership stake of Toys"R"Us - Japan.

This action is beneficial to our shareholders in several ways: we will continue to derive benefits from our 48% share of Toys"R"Us - Japan's future earnings, as well as through royalty income. In addition, the IPO will enable Toys"R"Us - Japan to fund its future growth without support from the company, therefore greatly enhancing our financial flexibility. Furthermore, we expect that the sale of shares, which reduces our ownership position from 80% to 48%, will result in a significant gain for the company.

We will continue to explore other opportunities and alternatives as appropriate to further unlock the value of our assets.

Other Aspects of the Business.

We have begun many initiatives in our U.S. toy stores already, and more are planned in the months ahead. But we're making strides in other areas of our business as well.

Babies"R"Us is a clear winner in the juvenile products market. This division marked the new millenium by reaching the billion-dollar sales mark in January. Babies"R"Us has excelled in all areas of the business, including outstanding guest service, terrific juvenile assortment and strong merchandising and operational capabilities. In addition, the success we have had with our Baby Registry is second to none — Babies"R"Us registers more expectant parents than any other retailer in the U.S. We're pleased with the strong growth of Babies"R"Us and expect to open 20 new stores this year.

Performance of Kids"R"Us has reached a plateau, but we are making substantial progress in rethinking how to rekindle growth in sales and profits for this division. We have seen significant success with leveraging our Kids"R"Us buying expertise and infrastructure up to our combo stores — essentially placing Kids"R"Us stores within Toys"R"Us stores — and we expect to roll out many more of these in 2000.

I mentioned the addition of Imaginarium child development centers within our Toys"R"Us stores earlier in this letter. Based on the tremendous success of the 19 initial tests of this concept, we plan to have upwards of 100 Imaginarium worlds within our Toys"R"Us stores by year-end. In addition, we expect to open five or more free-standing Imaginarium "neighborhood stores" this year as well.

Our International business had a terrific year with a much-improved performance, as the financials indicate. Our International stores have been the vanguard of the redeployment of expense and inventory dollars to maximize their opportunities for this past holiday. We think the future has never been brighter for that segment of our business. A

major milestone for the year 2000 will include the opening of our 100th store in Japan, our largest International market.

Finally, our toysrus.com business has proven the power of our brand on the Internet, and we are confident that our "clicks and mortar" strategy will be a long-term winner.

During the last few months of 1999, toysrus.com became one of the fastest growing Web sites on the Internet. With its new management, the advantage of an unbeatable brand name, and brick and mortar assets, we are confident that toysrus.com will become the undisputed one-stop shop for kids, parents and grandparents anywhere in the world.

We took a giant step forward in achieving that goal in February when we announced an exciting strategic partnership between Toys"R"Us, toysrus.com and SOFTBANK, the world's leading Internet venture capital firm. SOFTBANK's $57 million investment is a strong endorsement of our Internet business. SOFTBANK's investment capital will be used to accelerate the development of toysrus.com's infrastructure to support further growth. Their track record, international savvy and unbeatable industry experience will help us in building a world-class e-commerce platform.

Conclusion.

As we look at the months ahead and as we begin to write a new chapter in Toys"R"Us history, it's important to remember that we're building on a strong foundation. Ours is a profitable business that can and will do much better.

We're moving ahead aggressively with our store refinements, adding new products and pockets of excitement as we go. Our stores are going to be more fun and interactive, and more guest-friendly. Our merchandise assortments will be more interesting and captivating with greater guest appeal than competitors can offer. These are realistic, achievable goals, and my commitment to you is that our company will put every resource we have against these goals. We're going to get better, we're going to perform better, and we're going to maintain that momentum.

Many people have asked me over the past few months about my decision to join Toys"R"Us. I can say in all honesty that after working with this organization and looking at what needs to be done, I am even more optimistic and enthusiastic than I was when I first joined. We know what we need to do. Some of you may be skeptical and say that you've heard this before. My request to you, as a shareholder, is to have the patience and the faith in Toys"R"Us to let this strategy unfold. We are moving forward with the greatest possible energy, emotion and commitment. When I look ahead to the future of Toys"R"Us, I see a bright future, and I know that the best days of this company are still in front of us.

John H. Eyler Jr.
President and
Chief Executive Officer
March 27, 2000

Financial Section

20

Management's Discussion and Analysis

OF RESULTS OF OPERATIONS AND FINANCIAL CONDITION

RESULTS OF OPERATIONS*
Comparison of Fiscal Year 1999 to 1998

The company's total sales increased 6% to $11.9 billion from $11.2 billion. The total sales growth was primarily driven by a 3% increase in comparable store sales, as well as continued new store expansion, partially offset by the closing of 46 under-performing stores in 1999 and 1998 (see "Restructuring and Other Charges" below). Comparable store sales for the USA toy store division increased 3%. The USA comparable toy store sales increases were driven primarily by improved merchandising trends and strong sales of Pokémon and electronic and video products. These gains were partially offset by the deflationary impact of video hardware sales, and were limited by industry-wide shortages of electronic and other products during the holiday season. The International toy store division results of operations discussed below include the results of Toys"R"Us - Japan. Total sales for the International toy store division increased 7% and comparable international toy store sales, on a local currency basis, increased 2%. The comparable international toy store sales increases reflect improved performances in several merchandise categories, in particular, the juvenile, toy and electronics categories. Total sales for the Babies"R"Us division exceeded the $1 billion milestone in 1999 and increased 28%. Comparable store sales for Babies"R"Us increased 9%. The Kids"R"Us division reported a 3% comparable store sales decrease. The company's toysrus.com Internet subsidiary reported total sales of $49 million from its inception in May 1999.

International sales were favorably impacted by the translation of local currency into U.S. dollars by approximately $59 million in 1999 and unfavorably impacted by approximately $30 million in 1998. Neither the translation of currency into U.S. dollars nor inflation had a material effect on the company's operating results for 1999.

In 1998, the company recorded restructuring and other non-recurring charges of $698 million to reposition its world-wide business, as set forth below. For comparability purposes, the following discussion regarding results of operations excludes the impact of these charges.

On a consolidated basis, 1999's cost of sales as a percentage of sales was 70.1% versus 70.2%. The USA toy store division reported cost of sales as a percentage of sales of 71.6% as compared to 71.0%. This increase was a result of increased markdowns to keep inventory fresh. The International toy store division reported cost of sales as a percentage of sales of 69.2% versus 69.1%. The Babies"R"Us division reported cost of sales as a percentage of sales of 67.2% versus 69.0%, reflecting a favorable change in the sales mix.

On a consolidated basis, selling, general and administrative expenses (SG&A) as a percentage of sales increased to 23.1% from 21.3%. This increase was due in part to establishing and

operating toysrus.com, the company's Internet subsidiary, the implementation of strategic initiatives targeted to improve the company's long-term performance, and costs related to the reformatting of the company's toy stores to the C-3 format. The USA toy store division reported SG&A as a percentage of sales of 19.8% versus 18.6%, while the International toy store division reported SG&A as a percentage of sales of 23.4% versus 23.6%. The Babies"R"Us division reported SG&A as a percentage of sales of 24.0% versus 25.0%.

Depreciation and amortization increased to $278 million from $255 million. This increase was due in part to additional new stores and renovations to the C-3 format, as well as strategic investments to improve management information systems.

Interest expense decreased by $11 million. This decrease was due primarily to lower average interest rates in 1999. Also included in 1998 interest expense is $6 million relating to the early extinguishment of long-term debt.

Included in the company's 1999 results are net costs to establish and operate the company's Internet subsidiary, toysrus.com. Excluding the impact of these net costs, 1999 earnings before income taxes, net earnings and diluted earnings per share would have been $526 million, $334 million and $1.36, respectively.

The company's effective tax rate was unchanged at 36.5%, excluding the restructuring and other charges.

Comparison of Fiscal Year 1998 to 1997

The company's total sales increased to $11.2 billion from $11.0 billion. In 1998, sales were negatively impacted by the overall weakness in the worldwide toy industry which was cycling against strong sales of virtual pets, action figures and plush from the prior year. In addition, sales were negatively impacted by sales of video hardware and software at lower price points as well as the deflationary effect from sales of clearance merchandise related to the company's inventory reduction program. Comparable store sales for the USA toy store division declined 4%, while the International toy store division had a 2% comparable store sales decline, in local currency. The Babies"R"Us division reported a 19% comparable store sales increase and the Kids"R"Us division reported a 2% comparable store sales decrease.

International sales were unfavorably impacted by the translation of local currency into U.S. dollars by approximately $30 million in 1998 and $250 million in 1997. Neither the translation of currency into U.S. dollars nor inflation had a material effect on the company's operating results for 1998 and 1997.

---

* References to 1999, 1998 and 1997, are for the 52 weeks ended January 29, 2000, January 30, 1999 and January 31, 1998, respectively.

Management's Discussion and Analysis

OF RESULTS OF OPERATIONS AND FINANCIAL CONDITION

On a consolidated basis, cost of sales as a percentage of sales was 70.2% versus 69.8%. The USA toy store division reported cost of sales as a percentage of sales of 71.0% versus 70.5%. The International toy store division reported cost of sales as a percentage of sales of 69.1% versus 68.8%. These increases were due to a shift in the sales mix to lower margin video software merchandise from higher margin action figures and virtual pet products. The Babies"R"Us division reported cost of sales as a percentage of sales of 69.0% versus 70.7%.

On a consolidated basis, SG&A as a percentage of sales was 21.3% versus 20.2%. The USA toy store division reported SG&A as a percentage of sales of 18.6% versus 17.5%, the International toy store division reported SG&A as a percentage of sales of 23.6% versus 23.1%. These increases were primarily a result of the implementation of strategic initiatives, as well as store expansion. The Babies"R"Us division reported SG&A as a percentage of sales of 25.0% versus 27.1%.

Depreciation, amortization and write-offs were $255 million as compared to $253 million.

Interest expense increased by $17 million primarily due to higher average borrowings outstanding throughout the year as a result of the company's share repurchase programs. Also included in 1998 interest expense is $6 million relating to the early extinguishment of long-term debt.

The company's effective tax rate for 1998 was unfavorably affected by the restructuring and other charges recorded in 1998. Excluding the impact of these charges, the company's effective tax rate was unchanged at 36.5%.

Restructuring and Other Charges

During 1998, the company announced strategic initiatives to reposition its worldwide business and other charges including the customer-focused reformatting of its toy stores into the new C-3 format, as well as the restructuring of its international operations, all of which resulted in a charge of $353 million ($279 million net of tax benefits, or $1.05 per share). The strategic initiatives resulted in a restructuring charge of $294 million. The other charges of $59 million primarily consisted of changes in accounting estimates and provisions for legal settlements. The company has closed 46 under-performing stores and 7 administrative offices, as well as 4 distribution centers. The company is continuing to aggressively negotiate the closing/downsizing of the remaining stores and distribution centers included in its repositioning program and intends to execute the remainder of the initiatives included in the program. Details on the components of the charges are described in the notes to the consolidated financial statements and are as follows:

Description	Charge	Utilized in 1998	Reserve Balance 1/30/99	Utilized in 1999	Reserve Balance 1/29/00
Closings/downsizings:					
Lease commitments	$ 81	$ -	$ 81	$ 19	$ 62
Severance and other closing costs	29	4	25	11	14
Write-down of property, plant and equipment	155	155	-	-	-
Other	29	5	24	13	11
Total restructuring	$ 294	$ 164	$ 130	$ 43	$ 87
Changes in accounting estimates and provisions for legal settlements	$ 59	$ 20	$ 39	$ 9	$ 30

In 1998, the company also announced markdowns and other charges of $345 million ($229 million net of tax benefits, or $0.86 per share). Of this charge, $253 million related to markdowns required to clear excess inventory from stores, primarily to enable the company to proceed with the C-3 conversions on an accelerated basis. The company's objective with its new C-3 concept is to provide customers with a better shopping experience leading to increased sales and higher inventory turns. In addition, the company recorded $29 million in markdowns related to the store closings discussed previously. The company also recorded charges to cost of sales of $63 million related to inventory system refinements and changes in accounting estimates. Unused reserves at January 29, 2000 are expected to be utilized in the company's upcoming business cycle. Details of the markdowns and other charges are as follows:

Description	Charge	Utilized in 1998	Reserve Balance 1/30/99	Utilized in 1999	Reserve Balance 1/29/00
Markdowns					
Clear excess inventory	$ 253	$ 179	$ 74	$ 72	$ 2
Store closings	29	2	27	15	12
Change in accounting estimates and other	63	57	6	6	–
Total cost of sales	$ 345	$ 238	$ 107	$ 93	$ 14

The company has substantially completed its restructuring program that was announced in 1995, with the exception of long-term lease commitment reserves that will be utilized throughout 2000 and thereafter.

The company believes all reserves are adequate to complete its restructuring programs.

Liquidity and Capital Resources

The company's cash flow from operations were $865 million in 1999 and $964 million in 1998. The difference relates primarily to the non-cash portion of the 1998 restructuring charge as well as a significant decrease in inventories in 1998, partially offset by higher net earnings in 1999. Cash flows from operations increased to $964 million in 1998 from $509 million in 1997 primarily due to a significant reduction in inventories during 1998 as well as higher accounts payable, accrued expenses and other liabilities.

Management's Discussion and Analysis

OF RESULTS OF OPERATIONS AND FINANCIAL CONDITION

Cash flows used for investing activities increased by $182 million in 1999, due to new store expansion in the Babies"R"Us division and International toy store division, USA toy store conversions to the C-3 format, as well as capital requirements to establish and operate the company's toysrus.com Internet subsidiary. The company now operates 170 toy stores in the U.S. in the C-3 format and 163 additional toy stores in the U.S. with retrofitted "front-ends". In addition, the company invested $43 million for the purchase of Imaginarium (see "Other Matters" below). Cash flows used for investing activities decreased by $94 million in 1998 from 1997, primarily due to fewer new store openings in 1998, as well as fewer store conversions in 1998.

Cash flows used for financing activities decreased to $102 million in 1999 from $344 million in 1998. As discussed above, the company increased the number of toy stores converted to its C-3 format in 1999 and thus decreased the amount of cash used for its share repurchase program to $200 million in 1999, from $723 million in 1998. In addition, net borrowings decreased by $279 million for 1999 verses 1998. Cash flows used for financing activities decreased to $344 million in 1998 from $498 million in 1997 primarily due to repayment of a $115 million Baby Superstore obligation in 1997.

For 2000, capital requirements for new stores, conversions of existing stores and other capital investments are estimated at approximately $550 million. These plans include the addition of approximately 20 new Babies"R"Us stores in the United States, approximately 30 new International toy stores, including 17 new stores in Japan and 10 franchise stores. The company is also planning the conversion of approximately 70 toy stores in the U.S. into C-3 combo stores. In addition, the company's capital investment plans also include major revisions to its distribution center structure and enhancements to its management information systems.

In 1999, the company repurchased 12 million shares of its common stock through its share repurchase programs for a total of $200 million. At January 29, 2000, the company has $130 million remaining in its $1 billion share repurchase program announced in January 1998. On March 20,2000, the company announced that its Board of Directors approved a new $1 billion share repurchase program. The company will continue to repurchase additional shares when appropriate.

The company announced several major strategic initiatives regarding online retailing, as part of the company's strategy to become a global leader in the online retail market for toys and children's products. Although online sales currently represent only a very small percentage of the overall toy business, it is a rapidly growing retail segment. Over the next five years, the number of online users around the world is forecasted to increase more than three fold to over 400 million. The key initiatives include the establishment of toysrus.com as a separate subsidiary of the company and the acquisition of a 500,000 square foot distribution center dedicated solely to the fulfillment of orders placed with toysrus.com. In addition, on February 24, 2000, the company entered into a partnership with SOFTBANK Venture Capital and affiliates that included an investment of $57 million in toysrus.com. During the last few months of 1999, toysrus.com became one of the fastest growing web sites on the Internet. The company plans to continue making strategic investments in toysrus.com to capitalize on the company's brand names, brick and mortar assets, and SOFTBANK's Internet expertise to reach the goal of making toysrus.com a global leader in the online retail market for toys and children's products.

The seasonal nature of the business (approximately 42% of sales take place in the fourth quarter) typically causes cash to decline from the beginning of the year through October as inventory increases for the holiday selling season and funds are used for land purchases and construction of new stores, which usually open in the first ten months of the year. The company has a $1 billion multi-currency unsecured committed revolving credit facility expiring in December 2002, from a syndicate of financial institutions. There were no outstanding balances under this revolver at January 2000, 1999 and 1998. Cash requirements for operations, capital expenditures, lease commitments and the share repurchase program will be met primarily through operating activities, borrowings under the $1 billion revolving credit facility, issuance of commercial paper and/or other bank borrowings of foreign subsidiaries.

Other Matters

On August 20, 1999, the company acquired all of the capital stock of Imaginarium Toy Centers, Inc. for approximately $43 million in cash and the assumption of certain liabilities. The company believes this acquisition will accelerate its strategy to establish a leadership position in the learning and educational category and will provide further opportunities for new growth. The company is currently operating existing Imaginarium stores under the Imaginarium name. The operating results of Imaginarium from the date of acquisition were not material to the overall results or financial condition of the company.

On August 26, 1999, Robert C. Nakasone resigned as the company's Chief Executive Officer and as a director. Also on that date Michael Goldstein, Chairman of the Board of Directors, was named Chief Executive Officer on an interim basis. Mr. Goldstein was Chief Executive Officer of the company from 1994 to 1998. On January 17, 2000, John H. Eyler, Jr. was named President and Chief Executive Officer and a director of the company. Mr. Goldstein remains Chairman of the Board of Directors. In connection with the resignation of Mr. Nakasone as Chief Executive Officer and a director, the company entered into a Separation and Release Agreement with Mr. Nakasone providing for cash payments, the immediate vesting of all unvested options and unvested profit shares held by Mr. Nakasone, as well as the prorated vesting of other unvested equity based awards on the second anniversary of the termination date. The company accrued all costs related to this matter as of January 29, 2000. These amounts were not material to the overall results or financial condition of the company.

Management's Discussion and Analysis

OF RESULTS OF OPERATIONS AND FINANCIAL CONDITION

On March 20, 2000, the company announced the planned initial public offering ("IPO") in Japan of shares of Toys"R"Us - Japan. Under the initial public offering plan, Toys"R"Us - Japan and the company will offer primary and secondary shares respectively, to the public in Japan during the first half of fiscal 2000. This offering is subject to Japanese government approval and risks associated with market conditions. After the offering, the company will retain a significant ownership stake of Toys"R"Us - Japan, although less than 50% of the then outstanding shares. Accordingly, subsequent to the completion of the planned IPO, the company will no longer consolidate the financial statements of Toys"R"Us - Japan. Toys"R"Us - Japan will operate as a licensee of Toys"R"Us, Inc.

Quantitative and Qualitative Disclosures About Market Risks

The company is exposed to market risk from potential changes in interest rates and foreign exchange rates. The company regularly evaluates these risks and has taken the following measures to mitigate these risks: the countries in which the company owns assets and operates stores are politically stable; the company's foreign exchange risk management objectives are to stabilize cash flow from the effects of foreign currency fluctuations; the company will, whenever practical, offset local investments in foreign currencies with borrowings denominated in the same currencies; the company also enters into foreign exchange contracts or purchases options to eliminate specific transaction risk. The market risk related to these derivative contracts is offset by the changes in value of the underlying items being hedged. Approximately half of the company's long-term debt is at fixed interest rates and therefore, the fair value is affected by changes in market interest rates. The company believes the amount of risk and the use of derivative financial instruments described above are not material to the company's financial condition or results of operations.

Impact of Year 2000

In prior years, the company discussed the nature and progress of its plans to become Year 2000 ready. In late 1999, the company completed its remediation and testing of systems. As a result of those planning and implementation efforts, the company experienced no significant disruptions in mission critical information technology and non-information technology systems and believes those systems successfully responded to the Year 2000 date change. The company is not aware of any material problems resulting from Year 2000 issues, either with its products, its internal systems, or the products and services of third parties. The company will continue to monitor its mission-critical computer applications and those of its suppliers and vendors throughout the Year 2000 to ensure that any latent Year 2000 matters that may arise are addressed promptly.

Recent Accounting Pronouncements

In June 1999, the Financial Accounting Standards Board issued Statement of Financial Accounting Standards (SFAS) No. 137, *Accounting for Derivative Instruments and Hedging Activities – Deferral of the Effective Date of FASB Statement No. 133*. This pronouncement requires the company to adopt SFAS No 133, *Accounting for Derivative Instruments and Hedging Activities*, on February 4, 2001. SFAS No. 133 requires the company to recognize all derivative instruments as assets or liabilities in its balance sheet and measure them at fair value. The company does not expect the adoption of SFAS No. 133 to have a material impact on its financial position, results of operations or cash flows.

Euro Conversion

The company has developed a plan to ensure business and systems continuity during the introduction of the Euro currency in certain of the company's European operations. The initial phase of this plan was implemented prior to the January 1, 1999 (Phase 1) introduction of the Euro. Further implementation of this plan is scheduled to coincide with the transition phases (Phases 2 and 3) of completely converting from local denominated currencies to the Euro (the "Euro conversion"). Total costs for the entire Euro conversion program are not expected to be material. Based on the actions taken to date, the company does not expect the Euro conversion to have a material effect on the consolidated financial position, results of operations or cash flows of the company.

Forward Looking Statements

This annual report contains "forward looking" statements within the meaning of Section 27A of the Securities Act of 1933, as amended, and Section 21E of the Securities Exchange Act of 1934, which are intended to be covered by the safe harbors created thereby. All statements that are not historical facts, including statements about the company's beliefs or expectations, are forward-looking statements. Such statements involve risks and uncertainties that exist in the company's operations and business environment that could render actual outcomes and results materially different than predicted. The company's forward-looking statements are based on assumptions about many factors, including, but not limited to, ongoing competitive pressures in the retail industry, changes in consumer spending, general economic conditions in the United States and other jurisdictions in which the company conducts business (such as interest rates and consumer confidence) and normal business uncertainty. While the company believes that its assumptions are reasonable at the time forward-looking statements were made, it cautions that it is impossible to predict the actual outcome of numerous factors and, therefore, readers should not place undue reliance on such statements. Forward-looking statements speak only as of the date they are made, and the company undertakes no obligation to update such statements in light of new information or future events that involve inherent risks and uncertainties. Actual results may differ materially from those contained in any forward looking statement.

Consolidated Statements of Earnings

TOYS"R"US, INC. AND SUBSIDIARIES

		Year Ended	
	January 29,	January 30,	January 31,
(In millions except per share data)	**2000**	1999	1998
Net sales	**$11,862**	$11,170	$11,038
Cost of sales	**8,321**	8,191	7,710
Gross Profit	**3,541**	2,979	3,328
Selling, general and administrative expenses	**2,743**	2,443	2,231
Depreciation, amortization and asset write-offs	**278**	255	253
Restructuring charge	**-**	294	–
Total Operating Expenses	**3,021**	2,992	2,484
Operating Income/(Loss)	**520**	(13)	844
Interest expense	**91**	102	85
Interest and other income	**(11)**	(9)	(13)
Interest Expense, Net	**80**	93	72
Earnings/(loss) before income taxes	**440**	(106)	772
Income taxes	**161**	26	282
Net earnings/(loss)	**$ 279**	$ (132)	$ 490
Basic earnings/(loss) per share	**$ 1.14**	$ (0.50)	$ 1.72
Diluted earnings/(loss) per share	**$ 1.14**	$ (0.50)	$ 1.70

See notes to consolidated financial statements.

Consolidated Balance Sheets

TOYS"R"US, INC. AND SUBSIDIARIES

(In millions)	January 29, 2000	January 30, 1999
ASSETS		
Current Assets:		
Cash and cash equivalents	$ 584	$ 410
Accounts and other receivables	182	204
Merchandise inventories	2,027	1,902
Prepaid expenses and other current assets	80	81
Total current assets	2,873	2,597
Property and Equipment:		
Real estate, net	2,342	2,354
Other, net	2,113	1,872
Total property and equipment	4,455	4,226
Goodwill, net	374	347
Other assets	651	729
	$ 8,353	$ 7,899
LIABILITIES AND STOCKHOLDERS' EQUITY		
Current Liabilities:		
Short-term borrowings	$ 278	$ 156
Accounts payable	1,617	1,415
Accrued expenses and other current liabilities	836	696
Income taxes payable	107	224
Total current liabilities	2,838	2,491
Long-Term Debt	1,230	1,222
Deferred Income Taxes	362	333
Other Liabilities	243	229
Stockholders' Equity:		
Common stock	30	30
Additional paid-in capital	453	459
Retained earnings	4,757	4,478
Foreign currency translation adjustments	(137)	(100)
Treasury shares, at cost	(1,423)	(1,243)
Total stockholders' equity	3,680	3,624
	$ 8,353	$ 7,899

See notes to consolidated financial statements.

Consolidated Statements of Cash Flows

TOYS"R"US, INC. AND SUBSIDIARIES

			Year Ended
(In millions)	**January 29, 2000**	January 30, 1999	January 31, 1998
CASH FLOWS FROM OPERATING ACTIVITIES			
Net Earnings/(Loss)	**$ 279**	$ (132)	$ 490
Adjustments to reconcile net earnings/(loss) to net cash provided by operating activities:			
Depreciation, amortization and asset write-offs	**278**	255	253
Deferred income taxes	**156**	(90)	18
Restructuring and other charges	**-**	546	–
Changes in operating assets and liabilities:			
Accounts and other receivables	**35**	(43)	(40)
Merchandise inventories	**(192)**	233	(265)
Prepaid expenses and other operating assets	**(69)**	(27)	(9)
Accounts payable, accrued expenses and other liabilities	**497**	229	22
Income taxes payable	**(119)**	(7)	40
Net Cash Provided by Operating Activities	**865**	964	509
CASH FLOWS FROM INVESTING ACTIVITIES			
Capital expenditures, net	**(533)**	(373)	(494)
Other assets	**(28)**	(49)	(22)
Purchase of Imaginarium, net of cash acquired	**(43)**	–	–
Net Cash Used in Investing Activities	**(604)**	(422)	(516)
CASH FLOWS FROM FINANCING ACTIVITIES			
Short-term borrowings, net	**95**	4	(142)
Long-term borrowings	**593**	771	11
Long-term debt repayments	**(604)**	(412)	(176)
Exercise of stock options	**14**	16	62
Share repurchase program	**(200)**	(723)	(253)
Net Cash Used in Financing Activities	**(102)**	(344)	(498)
Effect of exchange rate changes on cash and cash equivalents	**15**	(2)	(42)
CASH AND CASH EQUIVALENTS			
Increase/(decrease) during year	**174**	196	(547)
Beginning of year	**410**	214	761
End of Year	**$ 584**	$ 410	$ 214
SUPPLEMENTAL DISCLOSURES OF CASH FLOW INFORMATION			
Income tax payments	**$ 126**	$ 122	$ 192
Interest payments	**$ 92**	$ 109	$ 83

See notes to consolidated financial statements.

Consolidated Statements of Stockholders' Equity

TOYS"R"US, INC. AND SUBSIDIARIES

(In millions)	Common Stock Issued Shares	Common Stock Issued Amount	In Treasury Shares	In Treasury Amount	Additional paid-in capital	Foreign currency translation adjustments	Retained earnings	Total stockholders' equity
Balance, February 1, 1997	300.4	$ 30	(12.6)	$ (388)	$ 489	$ (60)	$ 4,120	$ 4,191
Net earnings for the year	–	–	–	–	–	–	490	490
Foreign currency translation adjustments	–	–	–	–	–	(62)	–	(62)
Comprehensive income								428
Share repurchase program	–	–	(8.2) •	(253)	–	–	–	(253)
Exercise of stock options, net	–	–	2.8	84	(22)	–	–	62
Balance, January 31, 1998	300.4	30	(18.0)	(557)	467	(122)	4,610	4,428
Net loss for the year	–	–	–	–	–	–	(132)	(132)
Foreign currency translation adjustments	–	–	–	–	–	22	–	22
Comprehensive loss								(110)
Share repurchase program	–	–	(32.2)	(723)	–	–	–	(723)
Issuance of restricted stock	–	–	–	15	(2)	–	–	13
Exercise of stock options, net	–	–	.4	22	(6)	–	–	16
Balance, January 30, 1999	300.4	30	(49.8)	(1,243)	459	(100)	4,478	3,624
Net earnings for the year	–	–	–	–	–	–	279	279
Foreign currency translation adjustments	–	–	–	–	–	(37)	–	(37)
Comprehensive income								242
Share repurchase program	–	–	(12.0)	(200)	–	–	–	(200)
Issuance of restricted stock, net	–	–	–	3	(4)	–	–	(1)
Exercise of stock options, net	–	–	.7	17	(2)	–	–	15
Balance, January 29, 2000	**300.4**	**$ 30**	**(61.1)**	**$(1,423)**	**$ 453**	**$ (137)**	**$ 4,757**	**$ 3,680**

See notes to consolidated financial statements.

Notes to Consolidated Financial Statements

TOYS"R"US, INC. AND SUBSIDIARIES

(Amounts in millions except per share data)
SUMMARY OF SIGNIFICANT ACCOUNTING POLICIES

Fiscal Year
The company's fiscal year ends on the Saturday nearest to January 31. References to 1999, 1998 and 1997 are for the 52 weeks ended January 29, 2000, January 30, 1999 and January 31, 1998, respectively.

Reclassification
Certain amounts in the 1998 Consolidated Balance Sheet have been reclassified to conform with the 1999 presentation.

Principles of Consolidation
The consolidated financial statements include the accounts of the company and its subsidiaries. All material intercompany balances and transactions have been eliminated. Assets and liabilities of foreign operations are translated at current rates of exchange at the balance sheet date while results of operations are translated at average rates in effect for the period. Translation gains or losses are shown as a separate component of stockholders' equity.

Cash and Cash Equivalents
The company considers its highly liquid investments with original maturities of less than three months to be cash equivalents.

Merchandise Inventories
Merchandise inventories for the U.S.A. toy store operations, which represent approximately 60% of total inventories, are stated at the lower of LIFO (last-in, first-out) cost or market, as determined by the retail inventory method. If inventories had been valued at the lower of FIFO (first-in, first-out) cost or market, inventories would show no change at January 29, 2000 or January 30, 1999. All other merchandise inventories are stated at the lower of FIFO cost or market as determined by the retail inventory method.

Property and Equipment
Property and equipment are recorded at cost. Depreciation and amortization are provided using the straight-line method over the estimated useful lives of the assets or, where applicable, the terms of the respective leases, whichever is shorter. The company evaluates the need to recognize impairment losses relating to long-lived assets based on several factors including, but not limited to, management's plans for future operations, recent operating results and projected cash flows.

Financial Instruments
The carrying amounts reported in the balance sheets for cash and cash equivalents and short and long-term borrowings approximate their fair market values.

Forward Foreign Exchange Contracts
The company enters into forward foreign exchange contracts to eliminate the risk associated with currency movement relating to its short-term intercompany loan program with foreign subsidiaries and inventory purchases denominated in foreign currency. Gains and losses, which offset the movement in the underlying transactions, are recognized as part of such transactions. Gross deferred unrealized gains and losses on the forward contracts were not material at either January 29, 2000 or January 30, 1999. The related receivable, payable and deferred gain or loss are included on a net basis in the balance sheet. The company had $59 and $209 of short term outstanding forward contracts at January 29, 2000 and January 30, 1999, maturing in 2000 and 1999, respectively. These contracts are entered into with counterparties that have high credit ratings and with which the company has the contractual right to net forward currency settlements. In addition, the company had a $342 currency swap obligation outstanding at January 29, 2000 and January 30, 1999, respectively, related to its 475 Swiss franc note payable due 2004.

Use of Estimates
The preparation of financial statements in conformity with generally accepted accounting principles requires management to make estimates and assumptions that affect the amounts reported in the consolidated financial statements and accompanying notes. Actual results could differ from those estimates.

PROPERTY AND EQUIPMENT

	Useful Life (in years)	January 29, 2000	January 30, 1999
Land		$ 827	$ 829
Buildings	45-50	1,859	1,842
Furniture and equipment	5-20	2,046	1,861
Leaseholds and leasehold improvements	12½-35	1,432	1,213
Construction in progress		42	42
Leased property under capital leases		26	27
		6,232	5,814
Less accumulated depreciation and amortization		1,777	1,588
		$ 4,455	$ 4,226

SEASONAL FINANCING AND LONG-TERM DEBT

	January 29, 2000	January 30, 1999
Commercial Paper interest rates from 5.64% to 5.98%	$ 368	$ 368
475 Swiss franc note payable, due 2004 (a)	342	342
8¾% debentures, due 2021, net of expenses	198	198
Japanese yen loans with interest payable at annual rates from 1.49% to 6.47%, due in varying amounts through 2012	242	198
Industrial revenue bonds, net of expenses (b)	52	60
7% British pound sterling loan payable, due quarterly through 2001 (c)	19	33
8¼% sinking fund debentures, due 2017, net of discounts	12	24
Mortgage notes payable at annual interest rates from 10.16% to 11.00% (d)	10	11
Obligations under capital leases	8	11
	1,251	1,245
Less current portion (e)	21	23
	$ 1,230	$ 1,222

(a) Supported by a 406 Swiss franc bank letter of credit. This note has been converted by an interest rate and currency swap to a floating rate, US dollar obligation at 3 month LIBOR less approximately 95 basis points.

(b) Bank letters of credit of $35, expiring in 2001, support certain of these industrial revenue bonds. The company expects that the bank letters of credit will be renewed. The bonds have fixed or variable interest rates with an average rate of 4.1% and 3.6% at January 29, 2000 and January 30, 1999, respectively.

(c) Collateralized by property with a carrying value of $156 and $160 at January 29, 2000 and January 30, 1999, respectively.

(d) Collateralized by property and equipment with an aggregate carrying value of $12 and $15 at January 29, 2000 and January 30, 1999, respectively.

(e) Included in accrued expenses and other current liabilities on the consolidated balance sheets.

The fair market value of the company's long-term debt at January 29, 2000 and January 30, 1999, exclusive of commercial paper, was approximately $932 and $980, respectively. The fair market value was estimated using quoted market rates for publicly traded debt and estimated interest rates for non-public debt.

The company has a $1 billion unsecured committed revolving credit facility expiring in December 2002. This multi-currency facility permits the company to borrow at the lower of LIBOR plus a fixed spread or a rate set by competitive auction. The facility is available to support domestic commercial paper borrowings and to meet worldwide cash requirements.

Commercial paper of $368 is classified as long-term debt at January 29, 2000 and January 30, 1999, as the company maintains long-term committed credit agreements, as described above, to support these borrowings and intends to refinance them on a long-term basis through continued commercial paper borrowings. Commercial paper of $152 at January 29, 2000 was included in short-term debt.

Additionally, the company has lines of credit with various banks to meet the short-term financing needs of its foreign subsidiaries.

The weighted-average interest rates on short-term borrowings outstanding at January 29, 2000 and January 30, 1999 were 4.8% and 3.8%, respectively.

The annual maturities of long-term debt at January 29, 2000, excluding commercial paper of $368, are as follows:

2000	$ 21
2001	55
2002	10
2003	352
2004	10
2005 and subsequent	435
	$ 883

LEASES

The company leases a portion of the real estate used in its operations. Most leases require the company to pay real estate taxes and other expenses; some require additional amounts based on percentages of sales.

Minimum rental commitments under noncancelable operating leases having a term of more than one year as of January 29, 2000 are as follows:

	Gross minimum rentals	Sublease income	Net minimum rentals
2000	$ 353	$ 23	$ 330
2001	349	20	329
2002	344	18	326
2003	341	15	326
2004	333	12	321
2005 and subsequent	2,968	59	2,909
	$ 4,688	$ 147	$ 4,541

Total rent expense, net of sublease income was $350, $334 and $309 in 1999, 1998 and 1997, respectively.

STOCKHOLDERS' EQUITY

The common shares of the company, par value $0.10 per share, were as follows:

	January 29, 2000	January 30, 1999
Authorized shares	650.0	650.0
Issued shares	300.4	300.4
Treasury shares	61.1	49.8
Issued and outstanding shares	239.3	250.6

EARNINGS PER SHARE

The following table sets forth the computation of basic and diluted earnings per share:

	1999	1998	1997
Numerator:			
Net income/(loss) available to common stockholders	$ 279	$ (132)	$ 490
Denominator for basic earnings per share - weighted average shares	244.8	265.4	285.3
Effect of diluted securities: Stock options, etc.	.6	–	3.1
Denominator for diluted earnings per share - adjusted weighted average shares	245.4	265.4	288.4
Basic earnings/(loss) per share	$ 1.14	$ (0.50)	$ 1.72
Diluted earnings/(loss) per share	$ 1.14	$ (0.50)	$ 1.70

Options to purchase approximately 38.7, 25.0 and 6.0 shares of common stock were outstanding during 1999, 1998 and 1997, respectively, but were not included in the computation of diluted earnings/(loss) per share because either the option exercise prices were greater than the average market price of the common shares, or the effect would be antidilutive.

TAXES ON INCOME

The provisions for income taxes consist of the following:

	1999	1998	1997
Current:			
Federal	$ (12)	$ 78	$ 199
Foreign	17	18	35
State	-	20	30
	5	116	264
Deferred:			
Federal	31	(64)	32
Foreign	124	(9)	(17)
State	1	(17)	3
	156	(90)	18
Total tax provision	$ 161	$ 26	$ 282

The tax effects of temporary differences and carry forwards that give rise to significant portions of deferred tax assets and liabilities consist of the following:

	January 29, 2000	January 30, 1999
Deferred tax assets:		
Foreign loss carryforwards	$ 330	$ 311
Restructuring	67	92
Other	48	51
Gross deferred tax assets	445	454
Valuation allowances related to foreign loss carryforwards	(273)	(141)
	$ 172	$ 313
Deferred tax liabilities:		
Property, plant and equipment	316	281
LIFO inventory	30	50
Gross deferred tax liabilities	$ 346	$ 331
Net deferred tax liability	$ 174	$ 18

On January 29, 2000, the company had $845 of foreign loss carryforwards of which $340 must be utilized within the next five years and $505 over an indefinite period.

The valuation allowances related to foreign loss carryforwards increased to $273 from $141 in recognition of the uncertainty of obtaining tax benefit from foreign loss carryforwards.

A reconciliation of the federal statutory tax rate with the effective tax rate follows:

	1999	1998	1997
Statutory tax rate	35.0%	(35.0)%	35.0%
State income taxes, net of federal income tax benefit	0.6	4.2	3.2
Foreign taxes	(2.6)	(22.4)	(2.3)
Valuation allowances for foreign loss carryforwards	30.0	74.7	–
Tax benefit of branch election	(22.5)	–	–
Subpart F income	1.0	8.5	–
Foreign tax credits	(1.6)	(6.8)	–
Amortization of goodwill	0.7	3.0	0.4
Other, net	(4.1)	(1.7)	0.2
Effective tax rate	36.5%	24.5%	36.5%

In 1999, the company elected to treat two of its foreign subsidiaries as U.S. branches, claimed deductions for its investments in these subsidiaries, and reduced its current tax expense. In future years, income earned by these foreign subsidiaries can be offset by foreign loss carryforwards but will be subject to current U.S. income tax.

In 1998, certain foreign tax benefits have been offset by valuation allowances related to foreign loss carryforwards due in part to the restructuring and other charges recorded in 1998.

Deferred income taxes are not provided on unremitted earnings of foreign subsidiaries that are intended to be indefinitely invested. Exclusive of amounts, that if remitted would result in little or no tax under current U.S. tax laws, unremitted earnings were approximately $568 at January 29, 2000. Net income taxes of approximately $167 would be due if these earnings were to be remitted.

STOCK OPTIONS

The company has Stock Option Plans (the "Plans") which provide for the granting of options to purchase the company's common stock. The plans cover substantially all employees and directors of the company and provide for the issuance of non-qualified options, incentive stock options, performance share options, performance units, stock appreciation rights, restricted shares, restricted units and unrestricted shares. Of the total number of shares reserved for the Plans, 3.0 shares of company stock have been reserved for the issuance of restricted shares, restricted units, performance units, and unrestricted shares. The Plans provide for a variety of vesting dates with the majority of the options vesting approximately five years from the date of grant. Prior to June 10, 1999, options granted to directors are exercisable 20% each year on a cumulative basis commencing one year from the date of grant. Effective June 10, 1999, the options granted to directors are exercisable one-third on a cumulative basis commencing on the third, fourth and fifth anniversaries from the date of grant.

In addition to the aforementioned plans, 1.0 stock options were granted to certain senior executives during the period from 1993 to 1996 pursuant to stockholder approved individual plans. Of this total, 0.25 options vest 20% each on a cumulative basis commencing one year from the date of grant with the balance of the options vesting five years from the date of grant. Of this total, 0.25 options became vested on September 5, 1999, 1998 and 1997.

The exercise price per share of all options granted has been the average of the high and low market price of the company's common stock on the date of grant. All options must be exercised within ten years from the date of grant.

At January 29, 2000, an aggregate of 45.3 shares of authorized common stock were reserved for all of the Plans noted above, of which 5.5 were available for future grants. All outstanding options expire at dates ranging from January 31, 2000 to January 17, 2010.

Stock option transactions are summarized as follows:

	Shares	Exercise Price Per Share	Weighted-Average Exercise Price
Outstanding at February 1, 1997	23.2	$12.33 - $40.94	$ 25.82
Granted	6.8	25.38 - 36.47	34.74
Exercised	(3.3)	12.33 - 33.13	22.11
Canceled	(2.6)	13.00 - 40.94	28.82
Outstanding at January 31, 1998	**24.1**	**14.78 - 40.94**	**29.12**
Granted	17.7	16.94 - 28.38	22.18
Exercised	(0.7)	14.78 - 27.81	17.99
Canceled	(4.3)	14.99 - 39.88	28.89
Outstanding at January 30, 1999	**36.8**	**14.78 - 40.94**	**26.02**
Granted	9.7	11.69 - 24.22	18.63
Exercised	(1.3)	18.16 - 25.44	17.71
Canceled	(5.4)	18.16 - 39.88	25.34
Outstanding at January 29, 2000	**39.8**	**$11.69 - $40.94**	**$ 24.59**

Options exercisable and the weighted-average exercise prices were 8.4 and $26.38 at January 31, 1998, 10.8 and $28.25 at January 30, 1999, and 20.7 and $23.94 at January 29, 2000, respectively.

The company utilizes a restoration feature to encourage the early exercise of certain options and retention of shares, thereby promoting increased employee ownership. This feature provides for the grant of new options when previously owned shares of company stock are used to exercise existing options. Restoration option grants are non-dilutive as they do not increase the combined number of shares of company stock and options held by an employee prior to exercise. The new options are granted at a price equal to the fair market value on the date of the new grant, and generally expire on the same date as the original options that were exercised.

The company has adopted the disclosure only provisions of SFAS No. 123, Accounting for Stock-Based Compensation, issued in October 1995. In accordance with the provisions of SFAS No. 123, the company applies APB Opinion 25 and related interpretations in accounting for its stock option plans and, accordingly, does not recognize compensation cost. If the company had elected to recognize compensation cost based on the fair value of the options granted at grant date as prescribed by SFAS No. 123, net income and earnings per share would have been reduced to the pro forma amounts indicated in the table below:

	1999	1998	1997
Net income/(loss) – as reported	$ 279	$ (132)	$ 490
Net income/(loss) – pro forma	232	(162)	470
Basic earnings/(loss) per share – as reported	1.14	(0.50)	1.72
Basic earnings/(loss) per share – pro forma	0.95	(0.61)	1.65
Diluted earnings/(loss) per share – as reported	1.14	(0.50)	1.70
Diluted earnings/(loss) per share – pro forma	0.95	(0.61)	1.63

The weighted-average fair value at date of grant for options granted in 1999, 1998 and 1997 was $6.26, $5.31 and $7.66, respectively. The fair value of each option grant is estimated on the date of grant using the Black-Scholes option pricing model. As there were a number of options granted during the years of 1997 through 1999, a range of assumptions are provided below:

	1999	1998	1997
Expected stock price volatility	**.351-.568**	.283-.347	.294-.334
Risk-free interest rate	**4.7%-6.7%**	4.7%-5.8%	5.0%-6.9%
Weighted average expected life of options	**6 years**	6 years	6 years

The effects of applying SFAS No.123 and the results obtained through the use of the Black-Scholes option pricing model are not necessarily indicative of future values.

PROFIT SHARING PLAN

The company has a profit sharing plan with a 401(k) salary deferral feature for eligible domestic employees. The terms of the plan call for annual contributions by the company as determined by the Board of Directors, subject to certain limitations. The profit sharing plan may be terminated at the company's discretion. Provisions of $48, $41 and $39 have been charged to earnings in 1999, 1998 and 1997, respectively.

ACQUISITION

On August 20, 1999, the company acquired all of the capital stock of Imaginarium Toy Centers, Inc. ("Imaginarium"), a leading educational specialty retailer with 41 stores in 13 states, for approximately $43 in cash and the assumption of certain liabilities. The acquisition is accounted for using the purchase method of accounting and the results of Imaginarium operations have been combined with those of the company from the date of acquisition. The excess of purchase price over net assets acquired of approximately $38 has been recorded as goodwill and is being amortized on a straight-line basis over the estimated useful life of 10 years. The operating results of Imaginarium from the date of acquisition were not material to the overall results or financial condition of the company, as such, proforma information has not been provided.

SEGMENTS

The company's reportable segments are Toys"R"Us - USA, Toys"R"Us - International, Toys"R"Us - Japan, Babies"R"Us and toysrus.com. The division that does not meet quantitative reportable thresholds is Kids"R"Us. Toys"R"Us - USA operates toy stores in 49 states and Puerto Rico and Toys"R"Us - International operates or franchises toy stores in 26 countries outside the United States. Information on segments and a reconciliation to income/(loss) before income taxes, are as follows:

		Year ended	
	January 29, 2000	January 30, 1999	January 31, 1998
Sales			
Toys"R"Us - USA	**$ 6,819**	$ 6,581	$ 6,814
Toys"R"Us - International [b]	**1,990**	2,090	2,072
Toys"R"Us - Japan [c]	**1,208**	906	795
Babies"R"Us	**1,036**	810	563
toysrus.com	**49**	-	-
Kids"R"Us	**760**	783	794
Total	**$11,862**	$11,170	$11,038
Operating earnings/(loss)			
Toys"R"Us - USA	**$ 386**	$ 501	$ 654
Toys"R"Us - International [b]	**73**	85	106
Toys"R"Us - Japan, net of minority interest [c]	**88**	61	59
Babies"R"Us	**69**	30	(6)
toysrus.com	**(86)**	-	-
Kids"R"Us	**18**	29	47
General corporate expenses	**(28)**	(21)	(16)
Interest expense, net	**(80)**	(93)	(72)
Restructuring and other charges	**-**	(698)	-
Earnings/(loss) before taxes on income	**$ 440**	$ (106)	$ 772
Identifiable assets			
Toys"R"Us - USA	**$ 4,801**	$ 4,300	$ 4,732
Toys"R"Us - International [b]	**1,274**	1,742	1,734
Toys"R"Us - Japan [c]	**813**	680	548
Babies"R"Us	**389**	295	232
toysrus.com	**65**	-	-
Kids"R"Us	**427**	472	504
Corporate [a]	**584**	410	213
Total	**$ 8,353**	$ 7,899	$ 7,963
Depreciation, amortization and asset write-offs			
Toys"R"Us - USA	**$ 172**	$ 154	$ 158
Toys"R"Us - International [b]	**47**	52	52
Toys"R"Us - Japan [c]	**16**	11	9
Babies"R"Us	**22**	19	15
toysrus.com	**2**	-	-
Kids"R"Us	**19**	19	19
Total	**$ 278**	$ 255	$ 253

(a) Consists primarily of cash and cash equivalents.
(b) Excludes Toys"R"Us - Japan.
(c) 80% owned.

RESTRUCTURING AND OTHER CHARGES

On September 16, 1998, the company announced strategic initiatives to reposition its worldwide business. The cost to implement these initiatives, as well as other charges resulted in a total charge of $333 ($266 net of tax benefits, or $1.00 per share). The company determined that the strategic initiatives required a restructuring charge of $294 to close and/or downsize stores, distribution centers and administrative functions. This worldwide plan included the closing of 50 toy stores in the International division, predominately in continental Europe, and 9 in the United States that did not meet the company's return on investment objectives. The plan also included the closing of

31 Kids"R"Us stores and conversion of 28 nearby USA toy stores into combination stores in the company's C-3 format. Combination stores include toys and an apparel selling space of approximately 5,000 square feet. Other charges consisted primarily of changes in accounting estimates and provisions for legal settlements of $39 recorded in selling, general and administrative expenses. Of the total restructuring and other charges, $149 related to domestic operations and $184 related to international operations.

Also on September 16, 1998, the company announced markdowns and other charges to cost of sales of $345 ($229 net of tax benefits, or $0.86 per share). Of this charge, $253 related to markdowns required to clear excess inventory from its stores so the company could proceed with its new C-3 store format on an accelerated basis. Another component of the charge was inventory markdowns of $29 related to the closing and/or downsizing of stores discussed above. The company also recorded charges to cost of sales of $63 related to inventory system refinements and changes in accounting estimates. Of these charges, $288 related to domestic operations and $57 related to International operations. Remaining reserves of $14 are expected to be used in the company's upcoming business cycle.

Additionally, in the fourth quarter of 1998 the company recorded a charge of $20 ($13 net of tax benefits, or $0.05 per share), related to the resolution of third party claims asserted from allegations made by the Federal Trade Commission. This charge was in addition to a $15 charge relating to the same matter, included in the charges mentioned above. (See Other Matters).

The company intends to execute the remainder of the initiatives included in its repositioning program and will utilize the remaining reserves of $117 as these initiatives are completed.

The company has substantially completed its restructuring program that was announced in 1995, with the exception of long-term lease commitment reserves that will be utilized throughout 2000 and thereafter.

The company believes all reserves are adequate to complete its restructuring programs.

Other Matters

On May 22, 1996, the Staff of the Federal Trade Commission (the "FTC") filed an administrative complaint against the company alleging that the company is in violation of Section 5 of the Federal Trade Commission Act for its practices relating to warehouse clubs. The complaint alleges that the company reached understandings with various suppliers that such suppliers not sell to the clubs the same items that they sell to the company. The complaint also alleges that the company "facilitated

understandings" among the manufacturers that such manufacturers not sell to clubs. The complaint seeks an order that the company cease and desist from this practice. The matter was tried before an administrative law judge in the period from March through May of 1997. On September 30, 1997, the administrative law judge filed an Initial Decision upholding the FTC's complaint against the company. On October 13, 1998, the FTC issued a final order and opinion upholding the FTC's complaint against the company.

The company has appealed the FTC's decision to the United States Court of Appeals for the Seventh Circuit. The appeal was argued on May 18, 1999 and is awaiting decision from the Court.

After the filing of the FTC complaint, several class action suits were filed against the company in State courts in Alabama and California, alleging that the company had violated certain state competition laws as a consequence of the behavior alleged in the FTC complaint. After the Initial Decision was handed down, more than thirty purported class actions were filed in federal and state courts in various jurisdictions alleging that the company had violated the federal antitrust laws as a consequence of the behavior alleged in the FTC complaint. In addition, the attorneys general of forty-four states, the District of Columbia and Puerto Rico filed a suit against the company in their capacity as representatives of the consumers of their states, alleging that the company had violated federal and state antitrust laws as a consequence of the behavior alleged in the FTC complaint. These suits sought damages in unspecified amounts and other relief under state and/or federal law and were consolidated in the United States District Court for the Eastern District of New York.

The company believes that it has always acted fairly and in the best interests of its customers and that both its policy and its conduct in connection with the foregoing have been and are within the law. However, to avoid the cost and uncertainty of protracted litigation the company has reached an agreement to settle all of the class action and attorney general lawsuits in a manner which will not have a material adverse effect on its financial condition, results of operations or cash flow. The Court granted final approval of the agreement on February 17, 2000. The company had accrued all anticipated costs relating to this matter as of January 30, 1999.

The company is party to certain other litigation which, in management's judgement, based in part on the opinion of legal counsel, will not have a material adverse effect on the company's financial position.

REPORT OF MANAGEMENT

Responsibility for the integrity and objectivity of the financial information presented in this Annual Report rests with the management of Toys"R"Us. The accompanying financial statements have been prepared from accounting records which management believes fairly and accurately reflect the operations and financial position of the company. Management has established a system of internal controls to provide reasonable assurance that assets are maintained and accounted for in accordance with its policies and that transactions are recorded accurately on the company's books and records.

The company's comprehensive internal audit program provides for constant evaluation of the adequacy of the adherence to management's established policies and procedures. The company has distributed to key employees its policies for conducting business affairs in a lawful and ethical manner.

The Audit Committee of the Board of Directors, which is comprised solely of outside directors, provides oversight to the financial reporting process through periodic meetings with our independent auditors, internal auditors and management.

The financial statements of the company have been audited by Ernst & Young LLP, independent auditors, in accordance with auditing standards generally accepted in the United States, including a review of financial reporting matters and internal controls to the extent necessary to express an opinion on the consolidated financial statements.

Louis Lipschitz
Executive Vice President
and Chief Financial Officer

REPORT OF INDEPENDENT AUDITORS

The Board of Directors and Stockholders
Toys"R"Us, Inc.

We have audited the accompanying consolidated balance sheets of Toys"R"Us, Inc. and subsidiaries as of January 29, 2000 and January 30, 1999, and the related consolidated statements of earnings, stockholders' equity and cash flows for each of the three years in the period ended January 29, 2000. These financial statements are the responsibility of the company's management. Our responsibility is to express an opinion on these financial statements based on our audits.

We conducted our audits in accordance with auditing standards generally accepted in the United States. Those standards require that we plan and perform the audit to obtain reasonable assurance about whether the financial statements are free of material misstatement. An audit includes examining, on a test basis, evidence supporting the amounts and disclosures in the financial statements. An audit also includes assessing the accounting principles used and significant estimates made by management, as well as evaluating the overall financial statement presentation. We believe that our audits provide a reasonable basis for our opinion.

In our opinion, the financial statements referred to above present fairly, in all material respects, the consolidated financial position of Toys"R"Us, Inc. and subsidiaries at January 29, 2000 and January 30, 1999, and the consolidated results of their operations and their cash flows for each of the three years in the period ended January 29, 2000, in conformity with accounting principles generally accepted in the United States.

Ernst & Young LLP

New York, New York
March 8, 2000

Directors and Officers

Note of Thanks

On behalf of the "R"Us family, we would like to express our deep appreciation to Robert A. Bernhard and Howard W. Moore who are retiring from our Board of Directors this year. Bob became a member of the Board of Directors in 1980 and Howard in 1984. They both served our Board and our company with distinction, and their insight and counsel will be greatly missed. Their commitment and dedication to our company was exemplary, and we sincerely thank them for their tireless efforts on behalf of us all. Bob and Howard may be leaving our Board of Directors, but we know that in their hearts they will always be true Toys"R"Us kids.

> With deepest appreciation,
> The "R"Us Family

Directors

CHARLES LAZARUS
Chairman Emeritus of the company

MICHAEL GOLDSTEIN
Chairman of the Board of the company

ROBERT A. BERNHARD
Real Estate Developer

ROANN COSTIN
President,
Reservoir Capital Management, Inc.

JOHN H. EYLER, JR.
President and Chief Executive Officer
of the company

CALVIN HILL
Consultant

SHIRLEY STRUM KENNY
President, State University of
New York at Stony Brook

NORMAN S. MATTHEWS
Consultant and former Vice Chairman
of the Board and President of
Federated Department Stores

HOWARD W. MOORE
Consultant

ARTHUR B. NEWMAN
Senior Managing Director,
Blackstone Group

Corporate and Administrative

JOHN H. EYLER, JR.
President and Chief Executive Officer

MICHAEL G. SHANNON
President - Administration and Logistics

WARREN F. KORNBLUM
Executive Vice President - Worldwide
Marketing and Brand Management

LOUIS LIPSCHITZ
Executive Vice President -
Chief Financial Officer

FRANCESCA L. BROCKETT
Senior Vice President -
Strategic Planning/Business Development

ROGER C. GASTON
Senior Vice President -
Human Resources

JOHN HOLOHAN
Senior Vice President -
Chief Information Officer

REBECCA A. CARUSO
Vice President -
Corporate Communications

MICHAEL J. CORRIGAN
Vice President -
Compensation and Benefits

RICHARD N. CUDRIN
Vice President -
Associate Relations

MARIANITA HOWARD
Vice President -
Creative Services

JON W. KIMMINS
Vice President - Treasurer

DAVID P. PICOT
Vice President - Real Estate,
Design and Construction

DION C. ROONEY
Vice President - Systems Development

MICHAEL L. TUMOLO
Vice President - Counsel

PETER W. WEISS
Vice President - Taxes

DENNIS J. BLOCK
Secretary
Partner - Cadwalader, Wickersham & Taft

Toys"R"Us United States

GREGORY R. STALEY
President

JAMES E. FELDT
Executive Vice President
President - Merchandising and Marketing

DENNIS J. WILLIAMS
Senior Vice President - Operations

KRISTOPHER M. BROWN
Vice President - Logistics

STEVEN M. COOK
Vice President - Distribution Operations

THOMAS F. DELUCA
Vice President - Imports, Product
Development and Safety Assurance

ANDREW R. GATTO
Vice President -
Product Development

ALBERT FORTIER
Vice President - World Leader

EMANUEL J. FRANCIONE
Vice President - World Leader

JONATHAN M. FRIEDMAN
Vice President - Chief Financial Officer

DANIEL D. HLAVATY
Vice President - Loss Prevention

JEREL G. HOLLENS
Vice President -
Merchandise Planning

FREDERICK L. HURLEY
Vice President - World Leader

ELIZABETH S. JORDAN
Vice President - Human Resources

MITCHELL B. LOUKOTA
Vice President - World Leader

JULIE E. LYNN
Vice President - World Leader

THOMAS J. LYNN
Vice President and President of
Imaginarium Stores

CHARLENE MADY
Vice President -
Area Merchandise Planning

GERALD S. PARKER
Vice President -
Sales and Service

TIMOTHY J. SLADE
Vice President - Store Planning

WILLIAM A. STEPHENSON
Vice President -
Merchandise Planning and Allocation

DAVID S. WALKER
Vice President - Advertising

THOMAS A. DRUGAN
Regional Vice President - Midwest

HARVEY J. FINKEL
Regional Vice President - Northeast

MICHAEL K. HEFFNER
Regional Vice President - West

SAMUEL M. MARTIN
Regional Vice President - Pacific

JOHN J. PRAWLOCKI
Regional Vice President - Southeast

EDWARD F. SIEGLER
Regional Vice President - Mid-Atlantic

KEVIN VANDERGRIEND
Regional Vice President - Great Lakes

Toys"R"Us International

ERNEST V. SPERANZA
Senior Vice President - Marketing

ROBERT J. BAKER
Vice President - Finance

JOAN W. DONOVAN
Vice President -
General Merchandise Manager

LARRY D. GARDNER
Vice President - Operations

MICHAEL C. TAYLOR
Vice President - Franchising/Logistics

DAVID RURKA
Managing Director -
Toys"R"Us United Kingdom and Chairman
of the European Management Board

JOHANNES DERCKS
President -
Toys"R"Us Central Europe

JACQUES LEFOLL
President -
Toys"R"Us France

MONIKA MERZ
President - Toys"R"Us Canada

JOHN SCHRYVER
Managing Director -
Toys"R"Us Australia

MANABU TAZAKI
President -
Toys"R"Us Japan

ANTONIO URCELAY
Managing Director -
Toys"R"Us Iberia

Babies"R"Us and Kids"R"Us*

RICHARD L. MARKEE
President - Babies"R"Us and
Chairman - Kids"R"Us

JAMES G. PARROS
Senior Vice President -
Stores and Distribution Center Operations

*Kids"R"Us Officer,
unless otherwise indicated.

THERESE R. DENA
Vice President -
Planning and Allocation

JAMES L. EASTON
Vice President -
General Merchandise Manager

MARTIN E. FOGELMAN
Vice President -
General Merchandise Manager
Babies"R"Us and Toys"R"Us

VINCENT A. SCARFONE
Vice President - Human Resources

CHRISTOPHER M. SCHERM
Vice President - Advertising

DAVID E. SCHOENBECK
Vice President -
Operations - Babies"R"Us

SANDEE A. SPRINGER
Vice President -
Divisional Merchandise Manager

PAMELA B. WALLACK
Vice President -
Divisional Merchandise Manager

ROBERT S. ZARRA
Vice President - Chief Financial Officer
Kids"R"Us and Babies"R"Us

toysrus.com

JOHN BARBOUR
Chief Executive Officer

JONATHAN F. FOSTER
Executive Vice President -
Chief Operating Officer and
Chief Financial Officer

JOEL D. ANDERSON
Vice President - General Manager

RAYMOND L. ARTHUR
Vice President - Finance and Controller

LAWRENCE MC GUIRE
Vice President - Human Resources

JOHN P. SULLIVAN
Vice President - General Manager

GREGG TREADWAY
Vice President - Logistics

Quarterly Financial Data and Market Information

TOYS"R"US, INC. AND SUBSIDIARIES

Quarterly Financial Data

(In millions except per share data)

The following table sets forth certain unaudited quarterly financial information.

	First Quarter	Second Quarter	Third Quarter	Fourth Quarter
1999				
Net Sales	$ 2,166	$ 2,204	$ 2,465	$ 5,027
Cost of Sales	1,505	1,522	1,704	3,590
Net Earnings	17	12[a]	15[a]	235[a]
Basic Earnings per Share	$ .07	$ .05	$ .06	$ .98
Diluted Earnings per Share	$ .07	$ .05	$ .06	$ .98
1998				
Net Sales	$ 2,043	$ 2,020	$ 2,171	$ 4,936
Cost of Sales	1,417	1,390	1,831	3,553
Net Earnings/(Loss)	19	14	(475)[b]	310[c]
Basic Earnings/(Loss) per Share	$ .07	$ .05	$ (1.85)	$ 1.23
Diluted Earnings/(Loss) per Share	$ .07	$ .05	$ (1.85)	$ 1.23

(a) Includes costs to establish and operate toysrus.com, the company's Internet subsidiary as follows:
  Second quarter - $5 million ($3 million net of tax, or $0.01 per share).
  Third quarter - $17 million ($11 million net of tax, or $0.04 per share).
  Fourth quarter - $64 million ($41 million net of tax, or $0.17 per share).
(b) Includes restructuring and other charges of $678 ($495 net of tax benefits, or $1.93 per share)
(c) Includes provisions for legal settlements of $20 ($13 net of tax benefits, or $.05 per share).

Market Information

The company's common stock is listed on the New York Stock Exchange. The following table reflects the high and low prices (rounded to the nearest one-sixteenth) based on New York Stock Exchange trading since January 31, 1998.

The company has not paid any cash dividends, however, the Board of Directors of the company reviews this policy annually.

The company had approximately 31,100 Stockholders of Record on March 7, 2000.

		High	Low
1998	1st Quarter	30 7/8	25 7/8
	2nd Quarter	29 1/2	22 5/16
	3rd Quarter	23 13/16	15 5/8
	4th Quarter	21 1/2	14 7/16
1999	1st Quarter	23 1/4	13 5/8
	2nd Quarter	24 3/4	15 15/16
	3rd Quarter	17 3/16	13 1/8
	4th Quarter	19	9 3/4

Store Locations

Stores Across the United States

	Toys	Kids	Babies	Imaginarium
Alabama	8	1	2	–
Alaska	1	–	–	–
Arizona	12	–	3	1
Arkansas	4	–	–	–
California	88	22	13	7
Colorado	11	–	2	–
Connecticut	11	5	–	2
Delaware	2	1	1	–
Florida	47	10	10	–
Georgia	20	4	6	–
Hawaii	1	–	–	–
Idaho	2	–	–	–
Illinois	35	19	6	2
Indiana	13	7	2	–
Iowa	8	1	–	–
Kansas	5	1	1	–
Kentucky	8	–	2	1
Louisiana	11	–	1	–
Maine	2	1	–	–
Maryland	19	8	3	4
Massachusetts	19	6	4	–
Michigan	25	13	6	–
Minnesota	11	2	1	2
Mississippi	5	–	–	–
Missouri	13	4	3	–
Montana	1	–	–	–

	Toys	Kids	Babies	Imaginarium
Nebraska	3	–	–	–
Nevada	4	–	2	–
New Hampshire	5	2	–	–
New Jersey	26	18	8	7
New Mexico	4	–	–	–
New York	47	24	6	3
North Carolina	16	1	5	–
North Dakota	1	–	–	–
Ohio	33	18	8	5
Oklahoma	5	–	1	–
Oregon	8	–	2	1
Pennsylvania	33	15	3	–
Rhode Island	1	1	1	–
South Carolina	9	–	3	–
South Dakota	2	–	–	–
Tennessee	15	2	4	–
Texas	54	8	13	–
Utah	6	3	1	–
Vermont	1	–	–	–
Virginia	22	5	6	2
Washington	15	–	2	3
West Virginia	4	–	–	–
Wisconsin	10	3	–	–
Puerto Rico	4	–	–	–
	710	205	131	40

Toys"R"Us International–462

Australia - 23	Portugal - 6
Austria - 7	Qatar - 1[a]
Bahrain - 1[a]	Saudi Arabia - 3[a]
Canada - 63	Singapore - 4[a]
Denmark - 10[a]	South Africa - 7[a]
France - 31	Spain - 30
Germany - 53	Sweden - 7[a]
Hong Kong - 5[a]	Switzerland - 4
Indonesia - 3[a]	Taiwan - 6[a]
Israel - 19[b]	Turkey - 7[a]
Japan - 91[b]	United Arab
Malaysia - 5[a]	Emirates - 2[a]
Netherlands - 10[a]	United Kingdom - 63
Norway - 1[a]	

(a) Franchise or joint venture.
(b) 80 % owned.

Corporate Data and Citizenship
TOYS"R"US, INC. AND SUBSIDIARIES

Annual Meeting

The Annual Meeting of the Stockholders of Toys"R"Us will be held at The 200 Fifth Club, 200 Fifth Avenue, New York, New York, on June 7, 2000 at 10:00 A.M.

The Offices of The Company are Located at

461 From Road
Paramus, New Jersey 07652
Telephone: 201-262-7800

225 Summit Avenue
Montvale, New Jersey 07645
Telephone: 201-802-5000

General Counsel

Cadwalader, Wickersham & Taft
100 Maiden Lane
New York, New York 10036

Independent Auditors

Ernst & Young LLP
787 Seventh Avenue
New York, New York 10019

Registrar and Transfer Agent

American Stock Transfer and Trust Company
40 Wall Street
New York, New York 10005
Telephone: 718-921-8200

Common Stock Listed

New York Stock Exchange, Symbol: TOY

Stockholder Information

The company will supply to any owner of its common stock, upon written request to Mr. Louis Lipschitz of the company at the above address and without charge, a copy of the annual report on Form 10-K for the year ended January 29, 2000, which has been filed with the Securities and Exchange Commission.

Stockholder information, including quarterly earnings and other corporate news releases, can be obtained by calling 800-785-TOYS, or at our web site on the Internet at www.toysrus.com

Significant news releases are anticipated to be available as follows:

Call after...	For the following...
May 15, 2000	1st Quarter Results
Aug. 14, 2000	2nd Quarter Results
Nov. 13, 2000	3rd Quarter Results
Jan. 4, 2001	Holiday Sales Results
Mar. 14, 2001	2000 Results

Corporate Citizenship

Toys"R"Us maintains a company-wide giving program focused on improving the health care needs of children by supporting many national and regional children's health care organizations. The Counsel on Economic Priority awarded Toys"R"Us the Pioneer Award in Global Ethics. This award was the direct result of the implementation of our Code of Conduct for suppliers which outlines the company's position against child labor and unsafe working conditions. In order for a vendor's product to be sold in any of our stores, they must comply with our Code of Conduct. If you would like to receive more information on Toys"R"Us' corporate citizenship please write to Mr. Roger Gaston of the company at the above address.

Visit us on the Internet at www.toysrus.com and www.imaginarium.com.

7

Accounting Information Systems

LEARNING OBJECTIVES

1 Identify the principles of accounting systems design.

2 Describe how general ledger software and spreadsheet software are used in accounting.

3 Describe the use of microcomputer systems in small businesses.

4 Explain how accountants use the Internet.

5 Explain the objectives and uses of special-purpose journals.

6 Explain the purposes and relationships of controlling accounts and subsidiary ledgers.

7 Construct and use a sales journal, purchases journal, cash receipts journal, cash payments journal, and other special-purpose journals.

Fine Arts Gallery and Framing

Fine Arts Gallery and Framing, located in the South Fork Mall, was established two years ago to provide framing services. At that time, Gary Hoben, the owner, set up a computerized accounting system using Peachtree Complete Accounting™ for Windows®. His business is a sole proprietorship service business that uses Peachtree Complete's general journal and general ledger features. Because all sales were for cash or by credit card and because Hoben made a practice of paying all bills by the end of the month, the gallery had few receivables or payables. Over the past year, however, Hoben has added an inventory of color prints and posters, which carry a high profit margin. In addition, the new suppliers offer generous terms for payment. As a result, Hoben has allowed customers who buy framed prints or posters to pay over a period of three months. With the increased number of transactions involving inventory, accounts receivable, and accounts payable, Hoben's general journal/general ledger accounting system is now outdated. What kind of accounting system could Hoben use to handle the increased number and complexity of the store's transactions?

After analyzing the transactions in which his business engages, Hoben divided these transactions into five categories: credit sales, credit purchases, cash receipts, cash payments, and miscellaneous. Because more than 95 percent of the store's transactions fall into the first four categories, he decided to use Peachtree Complete's accounts payable and accounts receivable system. The accounts payable and accounts receivable system includes a separate or special-purpose journal for each of the categories that he defined. Hoben will use the general journal for his adjusting entries and some miscellaneous transactions. Because Hoben has been using Peachtree Complete's general journal/general ledger features for two years, he is eager to learn how to use the software's special journals and subsidiary ledgers. This chapter identifies the principles to consider when designing or buying a computerized accounting system and describes the basic features of computer hardware and software.

Principles of Accounting Systems Design

Accounting systems summarize financial data about a business and organize the data into useful forms. Accountants communicate the results to management. The means by which an accounting system accomplishes these objectives is called **data processing**. Management uses the resulting information to make a variety of business decisions. As businesses have grown larger and more complex, the role of accounting systems has also grown. Today, the need for a total information system with accounting as its base is more pressing. For this reason, accountants must understand all phases of their company's operations as well as the latest developments in systems design and technology.

Most businesses use computerized accounting systems that can be set up, monitored, and operated by accountants. However, their primary role is to provide timely accounting information to decision makers. Computer use does not eliminate the need to understand the accounting process. In fact, it is impossible to use accounting software without a basic knowledge of accounting. The opposite is also true: An accountant must have a basic knowledge of computer systems.

Analysis of computer system choices begins with the four general principles of accounting systems design: (1) cost-benefit principle, (2) control principle, (3) compatibility principle, and (4) flexibility principle.

Cost-Benefit Principle

The most important systems principle, the **cost-benefit principle**, holds that the benefits derived from an accounting system and the information it generates must be equal to or greater than the system's cost. In addition to certain routine tasks—preparing payroll and tax reports and financial statements, and maintaining internal control—management may want or need other information. The benefits from that information must be weighed against both the tangible and the intangible costs of gathering it. Among the tangible costs are those for personnel, forms, and equipment. One of the intangible costs is the cost of wrong decisions stemming from the lack of good information. For instance, wrong decisions can lead to loss of sales, production stoppages, or inventory losses. Some companies have spent thousands of dollars on computer systems that do not offer enough benefits. On the other hand, some managers have failed to realize the important benefits that could be gained from investing in more advanced systems. It is the job of the accountant and the systems designer or analyst to weigh the costs and benefits.

Control Principle

The **control principle** requires that an accounting system provide all the features of internal control needed to protect the firm's assets and ensure that data are reliable. For example, before expenditures are made, they should be approved by a responsible member of management.

Compatibility Principle

The **compatibility principle** holds that the design of an accounting system must be in harmony with the organizational and human factors of the business. The organizational factors have to do with the nature of a company's business and the formal roles its units play in meeting business objectives. For example, a company can organize its marketing efforts by region or by product. If a company is organized by region, its accounting system should report revenues and expenses by region. If a company is organized by product, its system should report revenues and expenses first by product and then by region.

The human factors of business have to do with the people within the organization and their abilities, behaviors, and personalities. The interest, support, and competence of a company's employees are very important to the success or failure of the system. In changing systems or installing new ones, the accountant must deal with the people who are presently carrying out or supervising existing procedures. Such people must understand, accept, and, in many cases, be trained in the new procedures.

Flexibility Principle

The **flexibility principle** holds that an accounting system must be flexible enough to allow the volume of transactions to grow and organizational changes to be made. Businesses do not stay the same. They grow, offer new products, add new branch offices, sell existing divisions, or make other changes that require adjustments in the accounting system. A carefully designed system allows a business to grow and change without making major alterations in the accounting system. For example, the chart of accounts should be designed to allow the addition of new asset, liability, owner's equity, revenue, and expense accounts.

Computer Software for Accounting

OBJECTIVE

2 Describe how general ledger software and spreadsheet software are used in accounting

Accountants use a variety of software programs to assist them in performing their jobs. Two of the most important types of these are general ledger software and spreadsheet software.

General Ledger Software

General ledger software is the term commonly used to identify the group of integrated software programs that an accountant uses to perform major functions such as accounting for sales and accounts receivable, purchases and accounts payable, and payroll. Today, most general ledger software is written using the Windows® operating system. Windows® has a **graphical user interface (GUI)**. A graphical user interface employs symbols called **icons** to represent common operations. Examples of icons include a file folder, eraser, hourglass, and magnifying glass. When programs use Windows® as their graphical user interface, the program is termed *Windows®-compatible*. The keyboard can be used in the traditional way, or a *mouse* or *trackball* may be used. The visual format and the ability to use a mouse or trackball make Windows®-compatible software easy to use.

Figure 1 shows how Peachtree Complete Accounting™ for Windows® uses a combination of text and icons. It is an example of what a graphical user interface looks like on your computer.

One of the benefits of Windows®-compatible software is the use of standardized terms and operations within software programs. Once you know how to use Peachtree Complete, you can use other Windows®-compatible applications, as they are similar.

Two software programs available for this book are General Ledger Software and Peachtree Complete Accounting™ for Windows®. General Ledger Software is used to supplement end-of-chapter problems. It is designed for educational use and cannot be purchased commercially. Peachtree Complete can be purchased through retail stores. It can also be used with selected end-of-chapter problems.

Figure 1
Graphical User Interface

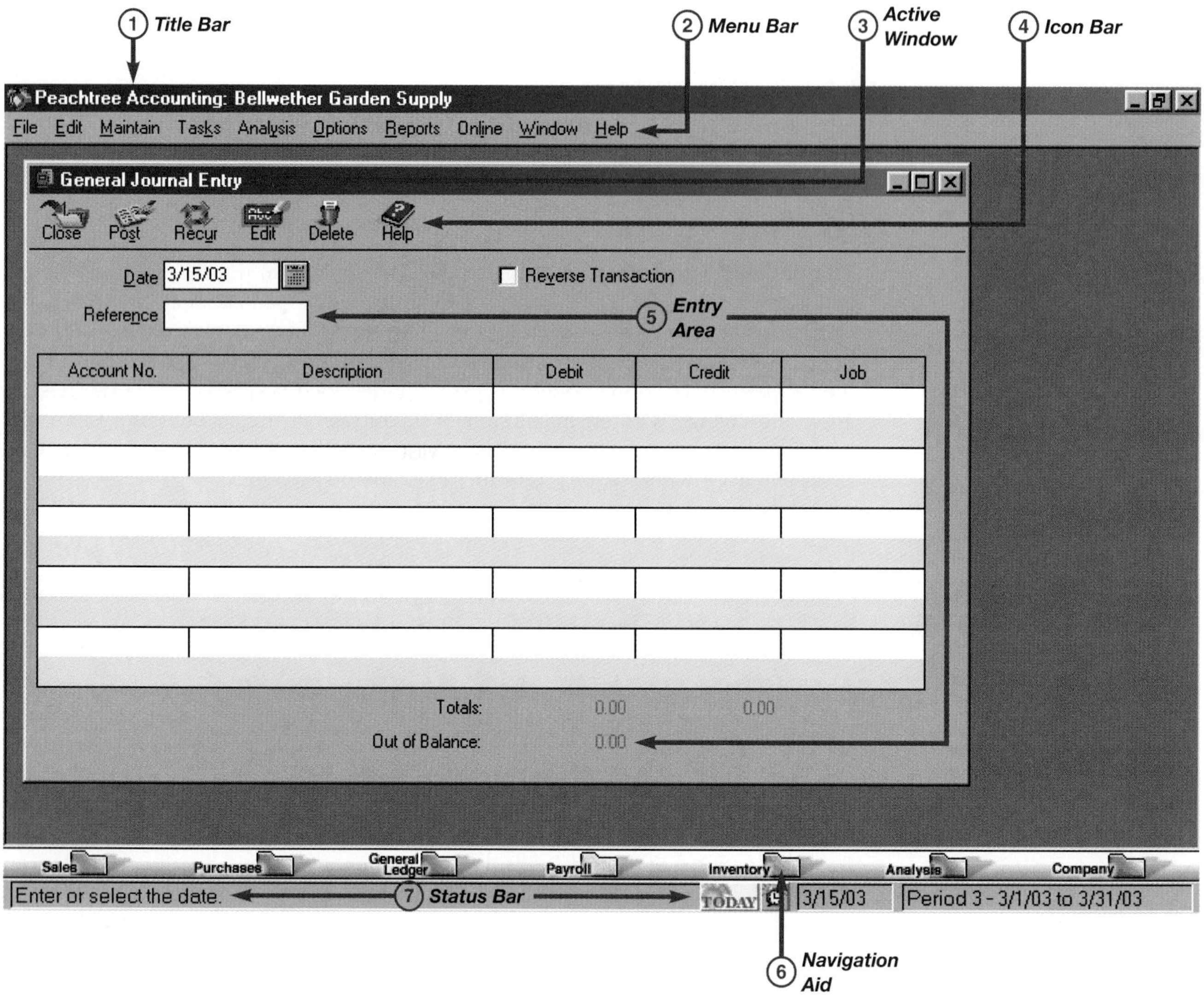

1. **Title Bar:** The title bar is the bar at the top of your screen. When you enter the program, the name of the company is displayed on the title bar with Peachtree Accounting.

2. **Menu Bar:** When you click on one of the menu bar headings, a submenu of options is pulled down or opened. These options are selected with a mouse or by holding down the <Alt> key and pressing the letter that is underlined in the desired menu bar option.

3. **Active Window:** The "General Journal Entry" window has been chosen here in order to record an entry. This bar shows what window is open or "active."

4. **Icon Bar:** The icon bar shows visual images that pertain to the window. Some icons are common to all windows, whereas other

icons are specific to a particular window. You click on an icon to perform that function.

5. **Entry Area:** This part of the screen is where information is entered for the journal entry.

6. **Navigation Aid:** The navigation aid offers a graphical supplement to the menu bar. The major functions of the program are represented as icons or pictures that show you how tasks flow through the system.

7. **Status Bar:** The gray bar (screen colors may vary) at the bottom of the window shows "help" information about the window, the current date, and the current accounting period.

Source: From Peachtree Complete Accounting™ for Windows®. Reprinted by permission.

Spreadsheet Software

Accountants use spreadsheet software in addition to general ledger software. General ledger software is effective for transactions that require double-entry accounting. Spreadsheets are used to analyze data. A **spreadsheet** is a grid made up of columns and rows into which are placed data or formulas used for financial planning, cost estimating, and other accounting tasks. Windows® Excel and Lotus are popular commercial spreadsheet programs used for financial analysis and other spreadsheet applications.

Computerized Accounting Systems

OBJECTIVE

3 Describe the use of microcomputer systems in small businesses

Most businesses use computerized accounting systems. The parts of such systems may be put together in many ways, and companies use their computers for many different purposes. A company's overall goal is to meet all its computing needs at the lowest possible cost. The computer system is the nerve center of the company. Large, multinational companies have vast computer resources and increasingly make use of **enterprise resource management (ERM)** systems. An ERM system is a very complex software system developed by companies like SAP AG from Germany and PeopleSoft from the United States. These systems use very powerful computers that are linked together to provide communication and data transfer around the world. Their objective is to integrate not just the financial operations but all functions of the business in a vast information network. However, even in these large companies and in most small companies, the microcomputer system has become a critical element in the processing of information. This will be more critical as the Internet develops and companies expand the use of the Internet to communicate and transact business.

Most small businesses purchase commercial accounting software that is already programmed to perform accounting functions. Most of these programs are organized so that each module performs a major task of the accounting system. A typical configuration of general ledger software is shown in Figure 2. Note that there is a software module, or function, for each major accounting function—sales/accounts receivable, purchases/accounts payable, cash receipts, cash disbursements, payroll, and general journal. When these features interact with one another, the software is called an *integrated program.*

Each transaction entered into the accounting system should be supported by **source documents**, or written evidence. Source documents verify that a transaction occurred and provide the details of the transaction. For example, a customer's invoice should support each sale on account, and a vendor's invoice should support each purchase. Even though the transactions are recorded by the computer in a file (on floppy disks or hard disks), the documents should be kept so that they can be examined at a later date if a question arises about the accuracy of the accounting records. After transactions are processed, a procedure is followed to post them to and update the ledgers and to prepare the trial balance. Finally, the financial statements and other accounting reports are printed.

Peachtree Complete Accounting™ for Windows'® general ledger program allows either batch posting or real-time posting. In a batch posting system, source documents are recorded in the appropriate journal and saved. Posting is done at the end of the day, week, or month. In a real-time posting system, documents are posted as they are recorded in the journal. The basic goal of general ledger software is to computerize existing accounting tasks to make them less time-consuming and more accurate and dependable. However, it is important to understand, in principle, just what the computer is accomplishing. Knowledge of the underlying

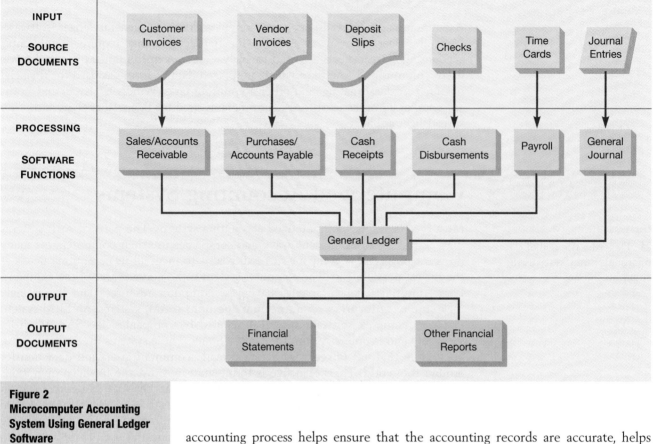

INPUT SOURCE DOCUMENTS	Customer Invoices	Vendor Invoices	Deposit Slips	Checks	Time Cards	Journal Entries
PROCESSING SOFTWARE FUNCTIONS	Sales/Accounts Receivable	Purchases/ Accounts Payable	Cash Receipts	Cash Disbursements	Payroll	General Journal

General Ledger

| OUTPUT

OUTPUT
DOCUMENTS | Financial
Statements | Other Financial
Reports |

Figure 2
Microcomputer Accounting
System Using General Ledger
Software

accounting process helps ensure that the accounting records are accurate, helps protect the assets of the business, and aids in the analysis of financial statements.

Accountants and the Internet

OBJECTIVE

4 Explain how accountants use the Internet

The **Internet** is the world's largest computer network. The Internet allows any computer on the network to communicate with any other computer on the network. Internet usage is the fastest-growing part of the computer revolution. To access the Internet, a computer needs a modem that connects it to a phone line. A subscription to an Internet service provider (ISP) is usually necessary. Some ISPs are America Online (AOL), MCI World Com, and AT&T. Local Internet service providers are also available.

The Internet has many capabilities:

- **Electronic mail** **Electronic mail (E-mail)** is the sending and receiving of communications over a computer network. *Electronic mailing lists* are subscriptions to organizations that share a common interest.

- **World Wide Web** The **World Wide Web** is a repository that provides access to enormous amounts of information over the Internet. It can be compared to the biggest library in the world. When people type in a World Wide Web address, they may not only get access to the material at that location, but be in a position to do what is commonly called "surfing the Web." The software used to navigate the Web is known as a *browser*. The most popular browsers today are Netscape Navigator and Microsoft Internet Explorer.

- **Information retrieval** **Information retrieval** is the downloading of files from the Internet to an individual's computer. Companies sometimes offer upgrades

FOCUS ON BUSINESS TECHNOLOGY

Every year the American Institute of CPAs identifies the ten most important technological challenges facing businesses. In 2000, the list emphasized the growing role of the Internet in business activities and related issues of security, controls, training, reliability, and privacy. The latest list of the top ten technology priorities is as follows:[1]

1. E-business
2. Information security and controls
3. Training and technology competency
4. Disaster recovery
5. High availability and resiliency of systems
6. Technology management and budgeting
7. Electronic financial reporting
8. Other Internet issues
9. The virtual office
10. Privacy

of their software this way. Sometimes the information is free and sometimes there is a charge.

- **Bulletin boards**   **Bulletin boards** allow people who have common interests to share information with one another over the Internet. Many hardware and software companies offer bulletin boards for technical support and troubleshooting.

- **E-business**   **E-business** is a term used to describe the broadest use of the Internet by business. It involves the use of the Internet to perform a wide array of business functions including, but not limited to, electronic commerce. Examples of other uses include human resource planning, business planning, and collaborating with strategic partners.

- **Electronic commerce**   Businesses and consumers increasingly are using the Internet for transacting business with vendors, suppliers, and customers. Such activities as selling books, buying stocks, and paying bills are examples. These practices and others using computers to conduct business transactions are called **electronic commerce** and provide new challenges for accountants in terms of keeping records of transactions and maintaining good internal controls.

- **Search engines**   **Search engines** such as Yahoo!, Lycos, and Excite are Internet sites that enable the user to research or search for information on any topic of interest.

Manual Data Processing: Journals and Procedures

OBJECTIVE

5 Explain the objectives and uses of special-purpose journals

The method of accounting described in prior chapters, and presented in Figure 3, is a form of **manual data processing**. It has been a useful way to present basic accounting theory and practice in small businesses. Data are fed into the system manually by entering each transaction from a source document into the general journal. Then each debit and credit is posted to the correct ledger account. A work sheet is used as a tool to prepare the financial statements that are distributed to users. This system, although useful for explaining the basic concepts of accounting, is actually used in only the smallest of companies.

Companies involved in more transactions, perhaps hundreds or thousands every week or every day, must have a more efficient and economical way of recording transactions in the journal and posting entries to the ledger. The easiest approach is to group typical transactions into common categories and use an input device

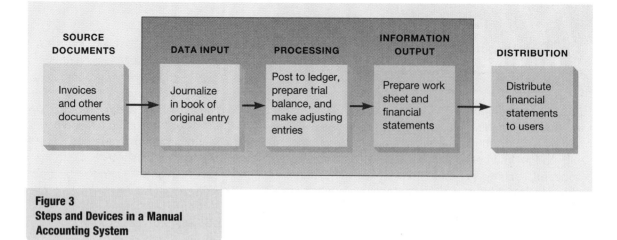

Figure 3
Steps and Devices in a Manual Accounting System

called a **special-purpose journal** for each category. The objectives of special-purpose journals are efficiency, economy, and control. Although manual special-purpose journals are used by companies that have not yet computerized their systems, the concepts underlying special-purpose journals also underlie the software programs that drive computerized accounting systems.

Most business transactions—90 to 95 percent—fall into one of the following four categories. Each kind of transaction can be recorded in a special-purpose journal.

Transaction	Special-Purpose Journal	Posting Abbreviation
Sale of merchandise on credit	Sales journal	S
Purchase on credit	Purchases journal	P
Receipt of cash	Cash receipts journal	CR
Disbursement of cash	Cash payments journal	CP

Notice that these special-purpose journals correspond to the accounting functions shown in the microcomputer system in Figure 2, except for payroll.

The general journal is used to record transactions that do not fall into any of the special categories. For example, purchase returns, sales returns, and adjusting and closing entries are recorded in the general journal. (When transactions are posted from the general journal to the ledger accounts, the posting abbreviation is J.)

Using special-purpose journals greatly reduces the work involved in entering and posting transactions. For example, instead of posting every debit and credit for each transaction, in most cases only column totals—the sum of many transactions—are posted. In addition, labor can be divided, with each journal assigned to a different employee. This division of labor is important in establishing good internal control.

Controlling Accounts and Subsidiary Ledgers

OBJECTIVE

6 Explain the purposes and relationships of controlling accounts and subsidiary ledgers

Controlling accounts and subsidiary ledgers contain important details about the figures in special-purpose journals and other books of original entry. A **controlling account**, also called a *control account*, is an account in the general ledger that maintains the total balance of all related accounts in a subsidiary ledger. A **subsidiary ledger** is a ledger separate from the general ledger that contains a group of related accounts; the total of the balances in the subsidiary ledger accounts equals or ties in with the balance in the corresponding controlling account. For example, up to this point a single Accounts Receivable account has been used. But the balance in the single Accounts Receivable account does not tell how much each cus-

FOCUS ON BUSINESS PRACTICE

Accounting information systems are obviously important for financial reporting, but they are increasingly becoming a means of providing good customer service as well. For instance, Walgreens, the world's largest prescription pharmacy company, has established direct communications with the insurance companies, employers, and government agencies that pay the bills of Walgreens' customers. From an accounting perspective, such links enhance Walgreens' profitability by eliminating rejected prescriptions, facilitating billing, and speeding collections. From the customers' point of view, instant communication with payers means faster service and immediate confirmation of payments—no forms, no paperwork, and no-hassle service.[2]

tomer bought and paid for and how much each customer owes. Consequently, in practice, all companies that sell on credit keep an individual accounts receivable record for each customer. If a company has 6,000 credit customers, it has 6,000 accounts receivable. Including all those accounts with the other assets, liabilities, and owner's equity accounts would make the ledger very bulky. Therefore, companies take the individual customers' accounts out of the general ledger and place them in a separate, subsidiary ledger. In the accounts receivable subsidiary ledger, customers' accounts are filed either alphabetically or numerically (if account numbers are used).

When individual customers' accounts are put in an accounts receivable subsidiary ledger, the total balance is maintained in one Accounts Receivable account in the general ledger. The Accounts Receivable account in the general ledger is the controlling account in that its balance should equal the total of the individual account balances in the subsidiary ledger, as shown in Figure 4. Entries that involve accounts receivable, such as credit sales, must be posted to the individual customers' accounts every day. Postings to the controlling account in the general ledger are made at least once a month. When the amounts in the subsidiary ledger and the controlling account do not match, the accountant knows there is an error that must be found and corrected.

Figure 4
Relationship of Subsidiary Accounts to the Controlling Account

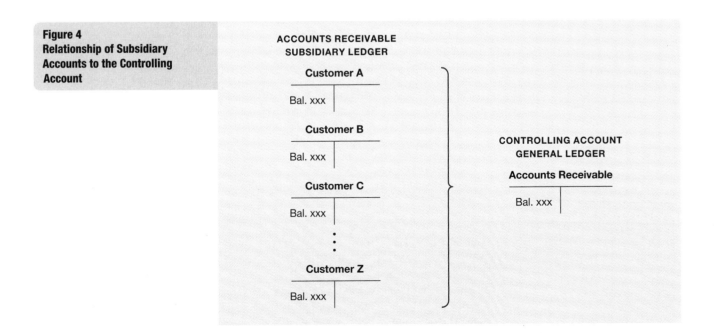

Most companies use an accounts payable subsidiary ledger as well. It is possible to use a subsidiary ledger for almost any account in the general ledger, such as Notes Receivable, Short-Term Investments, and Equipment, when management wants specific information on individual items.

Sales Journal

OBJECTIVE

7 Construct and use a sales journal, purchases journal, cash receipts journal, cash payments journal, and other special-purpose journals

The **sales journal** is designed to contain all credit sales, and only credit sales. Cash sales are recorded in the cash receipts journal. Exhibit 1 illustrates a page from a typical sales journal. It shows the recording of six sales transactions involving five customers.

Notice how the sales journal saves time:

1. Only one line is needed to record each transaction. Each entry consists of a debit to a customer in Accounts Receivable and a corresponding credit to Sales.

2. The account names do not have to be written out because each entry automatically is debited to Accounts Receivable and credited to Sales.

3. No explanations are necessary because the function of the special-purpose journal is to record just one type of transaction. Only credit sales are recorded in the sales journal. Sales for cash are recorded in the cash receipts journal.

4. Only one amount—the total credit sales for the month—has to be posted to the general ledger accounts. It is posted twice: once as a debit to Accounts Receivable and once as a credit to Sales. You can see the time this saves in Exhibit 1, with just six transactions. Imagine the time saved when there are hundreds of sales transactions.

Exhibit 1
Sales Journal and Related Ledger Accounts

Sales Journal   Page 1

Date		Account Debited	Invoice Number	Terms	Post. Ref.	Amount (Debit/ Credit Accounts Receivable/Sales)
July	1	Peter Clark	721	2/10, n/30	√	750
	5	Georgetta Jones	722	2/10, n/30	√	500
	8	Eugene Cumberland	723	2/10, n/30	√	335
	12	Maxwell Gertz	724	2/10, n/30	√	1,165
	18	Peter Clark	725	1/10, n/30	√	1,225
	25	Michael Powers	726	2/10, n/30	√	975
						4,950
						(114/411)

Post total at end of month.

Accounts Receivable   114

Date	Post. Ref.	Debit	Credit	Balance Debit	Balance Credit
July 31	S1	4,950		4,950	

Sales   411

Date	Post. Ref.	Debit	Credit	Balance Debit	Balance Credit
July 31	S1		4,950		4,950

Exhibit 2
Relationship of Sales Journal, General Ledger, and Accounts Receivable Subsidiary Ledger and the Posting Procedure

Sales Journal — Page 1

Date		Account Debited	Invoice Number	Terms	Post. Ref.	Amount (Debit/Credit Accounts Receivable/Sales)
July	1	Peter Clark	721	2/10, n/30	√	750
	5	Georgetta Jones	722	2/10, n/30	√	500
	8	Eugene Cumberland	723	2/10, n/30	√	335
	12	Maxwell Gertz	724	2/10, n/30	√	1,165
	18	Peter Clark	725	1/10, n/30	√	1,225
	25	Michael Powers	726	2/10, n/30	√	975
						4,950
						(114/411)

Post individual amounts **daily** to subsidiary ledger accounts.

Post total at **end of month** to general ledger accounts.

Accounts Receivable Subs. Ledger

Peter Clark

Date		Post. Ref.	Debit	Credit	Balance
July	1	S1	750		750
	18	S1	1,225		1,975

Eugene Cumberland

Date		Post. Ref.	Debit	Credit	Balance
July	8	S1	335		335

Continue posting to Maxwell Gertz, Georgetta Jones, and Michael Powers.

General Ledger

Accounts Receivable — 114

Date		Post. Ref.	Debit	Credit	Balance Debit	Balance Credit
July	31	S1	4,950		4,950	

Sales — 411

Date		Post. Ref.	Debit	Credit	Balance Debit	Balance Credit
July	31	S1		4,950		4,950

SUMMARY OF THE SALES JOURNAL PROCEDURE Exhibit 2 shows the relationships among the sales journal, the accounts receivable subsidiary ledger, and the general ledger accounts. It also illustrates the procedure for using a sales journal, the steps of which are outlined in the list that follows.

1. Enter each sales invoice in the sales journal on a single line. Record the date, the customer's name, the invoice number, and the amount. No column is needed for the terms if the terms on all sales are the same.

Mitchell's Used Car Sales
Schedule of Accounts Receivable
July 31, 20xx

Peter Clark	$1,975
Eugene Cumberland	335
Maxwell Gertz	1,165
Georgetta Jones	500
Michael Powers	975
Total Accounts Receivable	$4,950

Exhibit 3
Schedule of Accounts Receivable

2. At the end of each day, post each individual sale to the customer's account in the accounts receivable ledger. As each sale is posted, place a checkmark (or customer account number, if one is used) in the Post. Ref. (posting reference) column of the sales journal to indicate that the sale has been posted. In the Post. Ref. column of each customer's account, place an **S** and the sales journal page number (**S1** means Sales Journal—Page 1) to indicate the source of the entry.

3. At the end of the month, sum the entries in the Amount column in the sales journal to determine the total credit sales and post the total to the general ledger accounts (debit Accounts Receivable and credit Sales). Place the numbers of the accounts debited and credited beneath the total in the sales journal to indicate that this step in the procedure has been completed. In the general ledger, indicate the source of the entry in the Post. Ref. column of each account.

4. Verify the accuracy of the posting by adding the account balances of the accounts receivable ledger and matching the total with the Accounts Receivable controlling account balance in the general ledger. You can do this by listing the accounts in a schedule of accounts receivable. As shown in Exhibit 3, the accounts are listed in the order in which they are maintained. This step is performed after collections on account in the cash receipts journal have been posted.

The single controlling Accounts Receivable account in the general ledger summarizes all the individual accounts in the subsidiary ledger. Because the individual accounts are posted daily and the controlling account is posted monthly, the total of the individual accounts in the accounts receivable ledger equals the controlling account only after the monthly posting. The monthly trial balance is prepared using only the general ledger accounts.

SALES TAXES Many retailers are required to collect a sales tax from their customers and periodically remit the total collected to the city or state. In such cases, an additional column is needed in the sales journal to record the credit to Sales Tax Payable on credit sales. The form of the entry is shown in Exhibit 4. The procedure for posting to the ledger is exactly the same as described above, except that the total of the Sales Tax Payable column must be posted as a credit to the Sales Tax Payable account at the end of the month.

						Debit	Credits	
Date		Account Debited	Invoice Number	Terms	Post. Ref.	Accounts Receivable	Sales Tax Payable	Sales
Sept.	1	Ralph P. Hake	727	2/10, n/30	√	206	6	200

Sales Journal   Page 7

Exhibit 4

Section of a Sales Journal with a Column for Sales Tax

Purchases Journal

The **purchases journal** is used to record purchases on credit. It can take the form of either a single-column journal or a multicolumn journal. In a single-column journal, shown in Exhibit 5, only credit purchases of merchandise for resale to customers are recorded. This kind of transaction is recorded with a debit to Purchases and a credit to Accounts Payable. When a single-column purchases journal is used, credit purchases of things other than merchandise are recorded in the general journal. Cash purchases are never recorded in the purchases journal; they are recorded in the cash payments journal, which we explain later.

Like Accounts Receivable, the Accounts Payable account in the general ledger is commonly used as a controlling account. The company keeps a separate account for each supplier in an accounts payable subsidiary ledger in order to know how much it owes each supplier. The process described above for using the accounts receivable subsidiary ledger and the general ledger controlling account also applies to the accounts payable subsidiary ledger and the general ledger controlling account. Thus, the total of the separate accounts in the accounts payable subsidiary ledger should equal the balance of the Accounts Payable controlling account in the general ledger. Here, too, the monthly total of the credit purchases posted to the individual accounts each day must equal the total credit purchases posted to the controlling account each month.

The procedure for using the purchases journal is much like that for using the sales journal.

1. Enter each purchase invoice in the purchases journal on a single line. Record the date, the supplier's name, the invoice date, the terms (if given), and the amount. It is not necessary to record the shipping terms in the Terms column because they do not affect the payment date.

2. At the end of each day, post each individual purchase to the supplier's account in the accounts payable subsidiary ledger. As each purchase is posted, place a checkmark in the Post. Ref. column of the purchases journal to show that it has been posted. Also place a **P** and the page number in the purchases journal (**P1** stands for Purchases Journal—Page 1) in the Post. Ref. column of each supplier's account to show the source of the entry.

3. At the end of the month, sum the Amount column and post the total to the general ledger accounts (a debit to Purchases and a credit to Accounts Payable). Place the numbers of the accounts debited and accounts credited beneath the total in the purchases journal to show that this step has been carried out.

4. Check the accuracy of the posting by adding the balances of the accounts payable ledger accounts and matching the total with the balance of the

Exhibit 5

Relationship of Single-Column Purchases Journal to the General Ledger and the Accounts Payable Subsidiary Ledger

		Purchases Journal				Page 1
Date	Account Credited	Date of Invoice	Terms	Post. Ref.	Amount (Debit/Credit Purchases/ Accounts Payable)	
July 1	Jones Chevrolet	7/1	2/10, n/30	√	2,500	
2	Marshall Ford	7/2	2/15, n/30	√	300	
3	Dealer Sales	7/3	n/30	√	700	
12	Thomas Auto	7/11	n/30	√	1,400	
17	Dealer Sales	7/17	2/10, n/30	√	3,200	
19	Thomas Auto	7/17	n/30	√	1,100	
					9,200	
					(511/212)	

Post individual amounts **daily**.

Post total at **end of month**.

Accounts Payable Subs. Ledger

Dealer Sales

Date	Post. Ref.	Debit	Credit	Balance
July 3	P1		700	700
17	P1		3,200	3,900

Jones Chevrolet

Date	Post. Ref.	Debit	Credit	Balance
July 1	P1		2,500	2,500

Continue posting to Marshall Ford and Thomas Auto.

General Ledger

Accounts Payable   212

Date	Post. Ref.	Debit	Credit	Balance Debit	Balance Credit
July 31	P1		9,200		9,200

Purchases   511

Date	Post. Ref.	Debit	Credit	Balance Debit	Balance Credit
July 31	P1	9,200		9,200	

Accounts Payable controlling account in the general ledger. This step can be carried out by preparing a schedule of accounts payable.

The single-column purchases journal can be expanded to record credit purchases of things other than merchandise by adding separate debit columns for other accounts that are used often. For example, the multicolumn purchases journal in Exhibit 6 has columns for Freight In, Store Supplies, Office Supplies, and Other Accounts. Here, the total credits to Accounts Payable ($9,637) equal the

Exhibit 6
A Multicolumn Purchases Journal

Purchases Journal   Page 1

Date		Account Credited	Date of Invoice	Terms	Post. Ref.	Credit — Accounts Payable	Purchases	Freight In	Store Supplies	Office Supplies	Other Accounts — Account	Post. Ref.	Amount
July	1	Jones Chevrolet	7/1	2/10, n/30	√	2,500	2,500						
	2	Marshall Ford	7/2	2/15, n/30	√	300	300						
	2	Shelby Car Delivery	7/2	n/30	√	50		50					
	3	Dealer Sales	7/3	n/30	√	700	700						
	12	Thomas Auto	7/11	n/30	√	1,400	1,400						
	17	Dealer Sales	7/17	2/10, n/30	√	3,200	3,200						
	19	Thomas Auto	7/17	n/30	√	1,100	1,100						
	25	Osborne Supply	7/21	n/10	√	187			145	42			
	28	Auto Supply	7/28	n/10	√	200					Parts	120	200
						9,637	9,200	50	145	42			200
						(212)	(511)	(514)	(132)	(133)			(√)

total debits to Purchases, Freight In, Store Supplies, Office Supplies, and Other Accounts ($9,200 + $50 + $145 + $42 + $200). Again, the individual transactions in the Accounts Payable column are posted regularly to the accounts payable subsidiary ledger, and the totals of each named account column in the journal are posted monthly to the correct general ledger accounts. Entries in the Other Accounts column are posted individually to the named accounts, and the column total is not posted.

Cash Receipts Journal

All transactions involving receipts of cash are recorded in the **cash receipts journal**. Examples of such transactions are cash from cash sales, cash from credit customers in payment of their accounts, and cash from other sources. The cash receipts journal must have several columns because, although all cash receipts require a debit to Cash, they require a variety of credit entries. Note the use of an

FOCUS ON BUSINESS TECHNOLOGY

In manual accounting systems, subsidiary ledgers are often maintained in alphabetical order because that is a convenient way for people to organize information. With computers, however, numbers are much faster and easier to process than letters. For this reason, numbers are essential for all types of computer data processing. There are customer numbers, order numbers, social security numbers, product numbers, credit card numbers, and many more. When numbers are used, every account can be given a unique identification number. Then the potential confusion of having more than one Janet Smith or Juan Sanchez as customers can be avoided because each customer is assigned a different number.

Other Accounts column, the use of account numbers in the Post. Ref. column, and the daily posting of the credits to other accounts.

The cash receipts journal shown in Exhibit 7 has three debit columns and three credit columns. The three debit columns are as follows:

1. *Cash* Each entry must have an amount in this column because each transaction must be a receipt of cash.

2. *Sales Discounts* This company allows a 2 percent discount for prompt payment. Therefore, it is useful to have a column for sales discounts. Notice that in the transactions of July 8 and 28, the total of debits to Cash and Sales Discounts equals the credit to Accounts Receivable.

3. *Other Accounts* The Other Accounts column (sometimes called *Sundry Accounts*) is used for transactions that involve both a debit to Cash and a debit to some other account besides Sales Discounts.

These are the credit columns:

1. *Accounts Receivable* This column is used to record collections on account from customers. The customer's name is written in the Account Debited/Credited column so that the payment can be entered in the corresponding account in the accounts receivable subsidiary ledger. Postings to the individual accounts receivable accounts are usually done daily so that each customer's account balance is up-to-date.

2. *Sales* This column is used to record all cash sales during the month. Retail firms that use cash registers would make an entry at the end of each day for the total sales from each cash register for that day. The debit, of course, is in the Cash debit column.

3. *Other Accounts* This column is used for the credit portion of any entry that is neither a cash collection from accounts receivable nor a cash sale. The name of the account to be credited is indicated in the Account Debited/Credited column. For example, the transactions of July 1, 20, and 24 involve credits to accounts other than Accounts Receivable or Sales. These individual postings should be done daily (or weekly if there are just a few of them). If a company finds that it is consistently crediting a certain account in the Other Accounts column, it can add another credit column to the cash receipts journal for that particular account.

The procedure for posting the cash receipts journal, which is shown in Exhibit 7, is as follows:

1. Post the Accounts Receivable column daily to each individual account in the accounts receivable subsidiary ledger. The amount credited to the customer's account is the same as that credited to Accounts Receivable. A checkmark in the Post. Ref. column of the cash receipts journal indicates that the amount has been posted, and a **CR** plus the cash receipts journal page number (**CR1** means Cash Receipts Journal—Page 1) in the Post. Ref. column of each ledger account indicates the source of the entry.

2. Post the debits/credits in the Other Accounts columns daily, or at convenient short intervals during the month, to the general ledger accounts. As the individual items are posted, write the account number in the Post. Ref. column of the cash receipts journal to indicate that the posting has been done. Write **CR** and the page number of the cash receipts journal in the Post. Ref. column of each ledger account to indicate the source of the entry.

3. At the end of the month, total the columns in the cash receipts journal. The sum of the Debits column totals must equal the sum of the Credits column totals (see page 322). This step is called *crossfooting*.

Exhibit 7
Relationship of the Cash Receipts Journal to the General Ledger and the Accounts Receivable Subsidiary Ledger

Cash Receipts Journal — Page 1

Date		Account Debited/Credited	Post. Ref.	Debits Cash	Debits Sales Discounts	Debits Other Accounts	Credits Accounts Receivable	Credits Sales	Credits Other Accounts
July	1	Henry Mitchell, Capital	311	20,000					20,000
	5	Sales		1,200				1,200	
	8	Georgetta Jones	√	490	10		500		
	13	Sales		1,400				1,400	
	16	Peter Clark	√	750			750		
	19	Sales		1,000				1,000	
	20	Store Supplies	132	500					500
	24	Notes Payable	213	5,000					5,000
	26	Sales		1,600				1,600	
	28	Peter Clark	√	588	12		600		
				32,528	22		1,850	5,200	25,500
				(111)	(412)		(114)	(411)	(√)

Post individual amounts in Accounts Receivable ledger columns daily.

Post totals at end of month.

Total not posted.

Post individual amounts in Other Accounts column daily.

General Ledger

Cash — 111

Date	Post Ref.	Debit	Credit	Balance Debit	Balance Credit
July 31	CR1	32,528		32,528	

Accounts Receivable — 114

Date	Post. Ref.	Debit	Credit	Balance Debit	Balance Credit
July 31	S1	4,950		4,950	
31	CR1		1,850	3,100	

Store Supplies — 132

Date	Post. Ref.	Debit	Credit	Balance Debit	Balance Credit
Bal.				500	
July 20	CR1		500	—	

Accounts Receivable Subsidiary Ledger

Peter Clark

Date	Post. Ref.	Debit	Credit	Balance
July 1	S1	750		750
16	CR1		750	—
18	S1	1,225		1,225
28	CR1		600	625

Georgetta Jones

Date	Post. Ref.	Debit	Credit	Balance
July 5	S1	500		500
8	CR1		500	—

Continue posting to Notes Payable and Henry Mitchell, Capital.

Continue posting to Sales and Sales Discounts.

Debits Column Totals		Credits Column Totals	
Cash	$32,528	Accounts Receivable	$ 1,850
Sales Discounts	22	Sales	5,200
Other Accounts	—	Other Accounts	25,500
Total Debits	$32,550	Total Credits	$32,550

4. Post the Debits column totals as follows:
   a. Post the total of the Cash column as a debit to the Cash account.
   b. Post the total of the Sales Discounts column as a debit to the Sales Discounts account.

5. Post the Credits column totals as follows:
   a. Post the total of the Accounts Receivable column as a credit to the Accounts Receivable controlling account.
   b. Post the total of the Sales column as a credit to the Sales account.

6. Write the account numbers below each column in the cash receipts journal as the totals are posted to indicate that this step has been completed. A **CR** and the page number of the cash receipts journal are written in the Post. Ref. column of each account to indicate the source of the entry.

7. Notice that the total of the Other Accounts column is not posted to a general ledger account, because each entry is posted separately when the transaction occurs. The individual accounts are posted in step **2.** Place a checkmark (√) at the bottom of each Other Accounts column to show that postings in that column have been made and that the total is not posted.

Cash Payments Journal

All transactions involving payments of cash are recorded in the **cash payments journal** (also called the *cash disbursements journal*). The cash payments journal shown in Exhibit 8 has three credit columns and two debit columns. The credit columns for the cash payments journal are as follows:

1. *Cash* Each entry must have an amount in this column because each transaction must involve a payment of cash.

2. *Purchases Discounts* When purchases discounts are taken, they are recorded in this column.

3. *Other Accounts* This column is used to record credits to accounts other than Cash or Purchases Discounts. Notice that the July 31 transaction shows a purchase of land for $15,000, with a check for $5,000 and a note payable for $10,000.

The debit columns are as follows:

1. *Accounts Payable* This column is used to record payments to suppliers that have extended credit to the company. Each supplier's name is written in the Payee column so that the payment can be entered in his or her account in the accounts payable subsidiary ledger.

2. *Other Accounts* Cash can be expended for many reasons. Thus, an Other Accounts or Sundry Accounts column is needed in the cash payments journal. The title of the account to be debited is written in the Account Credited/Debited column, and the amount is entered in the Other Accounts debit column. If a company finds that a particular account appears often in the Other Accounts column, it can add another debit column to the cash payments journal.

Exhibit 8
Relationship of the Cash Payments Journal to the General Ledger and the Accounts Payable Subsidiary Ledger

Cash Payments Journal Page 1

						Credits			Debits	
Date	Ck. No.	Payee	Account Credited/Debited	Post. Ref.	Cash	Purchases Discounts	Other Accounts	Accounts Payable	Other Accounts
July 2	101	Sondra Tidmore	Purchases	511	400				400
6	102	Daily Journal	Advertising Expense	612	200				200
8	103	Siviglia Agency	Rent Expense	631	250				250
11	104	Jones Chevrolet		√	2,450	50		2,500	
16	105	Charles Kuntz	Salary Expense	611	600				600
17	106	Marshall Ford		√	294	6		300	
24	107	Grabow & Company	Prepaid Insurance	119	480				480
27	108	Dealer Sales		√	3,136	64		3,200	
30	109	A&B Equipment Company	Office Equipment Service Equipment	144 146	900				400 500
31	110	Burns Real Estate	Notes Payable Land	213 141	5,000		10,000		15,000
					13,710	120	10,000	6,000	17,830
					(111)	(512)	(√)	(212)	(√)

Post individual amounts in Other Accounts column **daily.**

Post individual amounts in Accounts Payable column **daily.**

Post totals at end of month.

Totals not posted.

General Ledger

Cash   111

Date	Post. Ref.	Debit	Credit	Balance Debit	Balance Credit
July 31	CR1	32,528		32,528	
31	CP1		13,710	18,818	

Prepaid Insurance   119

Date	Post. Ref.	Debit	Credit	Balance Debit	Balance Credit
July 24	CP1	480		480	

Continue posting to Land, Office Equipment, Service Equipment, Notes Payable, Purchases, Salary Expense, Advertising Expense, and Rent Expense.

Continue posting to Purchases Discounts and Accounts Payable.

Accounts Payable Subsidiary Ledger

Dealer Sales

Date	Post. Ref.	Debit	Credit	Balance
July 3	P1		700	700
17	P1		3,200	3,900
27	CP1	3,200		700

Jones Chevrolet

Date	Post. Ref.	Debit	Credit	Balance
July 1	P1		2,500	2,500
11	CP1	2,500		—

Marshall Ford

Date	Post. Ref.	Debit	Credit	Balance
July 2	P1		300	300
17	CP1	300		—

The procedure for posting the cash payments journal, shown in Exhibit 8, is as follows:

1. Post the Accounts Payable column daily to the individual accounts in the accounts payable subsidiary ledger. Place a checkmark in the Post. Ref. column of the cash payments journal to indicate that the posting has been made.

2. Post the debits/credits in the Other Accounts debit/credit columns to the general ledger daily or at convenient short intervals during the month. As the individual items are posted, write the account number in the Post. Ref. column of the cash payments journal to indicate that the posting has been completed and **CP** plus the cash payments journal page number (**CP1** means Cash Payments Journal—Page 1) in the Post. Ref. column of each ledger account.

3. At the end of the month, the columns are footed and crossfooted. That is, the sum of the Credits column totals must equal the sum of the Debits column totals, as follows:

Credits Column Totals		Debits Column Totals	
Cash	$ 13,710	Accounts Payable	$ 6,000
Purchases Discounts	120	Other Accounts	17,830
Other Accounts	10,000	Total Debits	$23,830
Total Credits	$23,830		

4. Post the column totals for Cash, Purchases Discounts, and Accounts Payable at the end of the month to their respective accounts in the general ledger. Write the account number below each column in the cash payments journal as the total is posted to indicate that this step has been completed and **CP** plus the cash payments journal page number in the Post. Ref. column of each ledger account. Place a checkmark under the total of each Other Accounts column in the cash payments journal to indicate that the postings in the column have been made and that the total is not posted.

General Journal

Transactions that do not involve sales, purchases, cash receipts, or cash payments should be recorded in the general journal. Usually, there are only a few such transactions. The two examples in Exhibit 9 require entries that do not fit in a special-purpose journal. They are a return of merchandise and an allowance from a supplier for credit. Adjusting and closing entries are also recorded in the general journal.

Exhibit 9
Transactions Recorded in the General Journal

General Journal					Page 1
Date		Description	Post. Ref.	Debit	Credit
July	25	Accounts Payable, Thomas Auto	212/√	700	
		Purchases Returns and			
		Allowances	513		700
		Returned used car for			
		credit; invoice date 7/11			
	26	Sales Returns and Allowances	413	35	
		Accounts Receivable, Maxwell			
		Gertz	114/√		35
		Allowance for faulty tire			

Confidentiality is an important issue in the design and use of accounting information systems. For example, computer operators and other employees who have access to accounting records may know customers' credit histories as well as what they have purchased, how much they owe the company, and how punctually they pay their bills. In many cases, customers may include friends, neighbors, and acquaintances. The payroll records also contain such sensitive information as salary levels. To avoid problems, it is good practice for businesses to restrict access to sensitive records to only those employees whose work depends on them and to make it clear that strict confidentiality must be maintained. The Institute of Management Accountants states that information should not be communicated to anyone inside or outside the company who is not authorized to receive it, except when disclosure is required by law.

Notice that the entries in Exhibit 9 include a debit or a credit to a controlling account (Accounts Payable or Accounts Receivable). The name of the customer or supplier is also given. When this kind of debit or credit is made to a controlling account in the general journal, the entry must be posted twice: once to the controlling account and once to the individual account in the subsidiary ledger. This procedure keeps the subsidiary ledger equal to the controlling account as far as entries from the general journal are concerned. Notice that the July 26 transaction is posted by a debit to Sales Returns and Allowances in the general ledger (shown by the account number 413), by a credit to the Accounts Receivable controlling account in the general ledger (account number 114), and by a credit to the Maxwell Gertz account in the accounts receivable subsidiary ledger (checkmark).

The Flexibility of Special-Purpose Journals

Special-purpose journals reduce and simplify the work of accounting and allow for the division of labor. Such journals should be designed to fit the business in which they are used. As noted earlier, if certain accounts show up often in the Other Accounts column of a journal, it is a good idea to add a column for them when a new page of a special-purpose journal is prepared. Also, if certain transactions appear repeatedly in the general journal, it is a good idea to set up a new special-purpose journal.

Chapter Review

REVIEW OF LEARNING OBJECTIVES

1. **Identify the principles of accounting systems design.** The developers of an accounting system must keep in mind the four principles of systems design: the cost-benefit principle, the control principle, the compatibility principle, and the flexibility principle.

2. **Describe how general ledger software and spreadsheet software are used in accounting.** General ledger software is a group of integrated software programs that perform major accounting functions such as general ledger,

↑
Check out ACE, a self-quizzing program on chapter content, at http://college.hmco.com.

purchases and accounts payable, sales and accounts receivable, payroll, and others in an integrated fashion. Some software uses icons in a graphical user interface to easily guide the accountant through the tasks. Spreadsheet software is also used widely by accountants for analysis.

3. **Describe the use of microcomputer systems in small businesses.** In contrast to large companies, most small companies use microcomputer accounting systems that use general ledger software to perform the major accounting functions. These systems require forms to document each transaction recorded by the software.

4. **Explain how accountants use the Internet.** Accountants are increasingly using the Internet for electronic mail, for obtaining information or help on many issues via the World Wide Web and information retrieval, and for exchanging information on bulletin boards. Businesses are using the Internet for electronic commerce, which provides new challenges to the accountant.

5. **Explain the objectives and uses of special-purpose journals.** The typical manual data processing system uses several special-purpose journals, each designed to record one kind of transaction. Recording only one kind of transaction in each journal reduces and simplifies the accounting task and allows for the division of labor. The division of labor is important for internal control.

6. **Explain the purposes and relationships of controlling accounts and subsidiary ledgers.** Subsidiary ledgers contain individual accounts of a specific kind, such as customers' accounts (accounts receivable) or suppliers' accounts (accounts payable). The individual account records are kept separately in a subsidiary ledger to avoid making the general ledger too bulky. The total of the balances of the subsidiary ledger accounts should equal the balance of the controlling account in the general ledger because the individual items are posted daily to the subsidiary ledger accounts and the column totals are posted to the general ledger account monthly from the special-purpose journal.

7. **Construct and use a sales journal, purchases journal, cash receipts journal, cash payments journal, and other special-purpose journals.** A special-purpose journal is constructed by devoting a single column to a particular account (for example, debits to Cash in the cash receipts journal and credits to Cash in the cash payments journal). Other columns in the journal depend on the kinds of transactions in which the company normally engages. Special-purpose journals also have columns for transaction dates, explanations or subsidiary account names, and posting references.

REVIEW OF CONCEPTS AND TERMINOLOGY

The following concepts and terms were introduced in this chapter.

LO 1 **Accounting systems:** The process that gathers data and puts them into useful form for communication of the results to management.

LO 4 **Bulletin boards:** A method for individuals with common interests to share information on the Internet.

LO 7 **Cash payments journal:** A multicolumn special-purpose journal used to record payments of cash. Also called *cash disbursements journal.*

LO 7 **Cash receipts journal:** A multicolumn special-purpose journal used to record transactions involving the receipt of cash.

LO 1 **Compatibility principle:** The principle that holds that the design of an accounting system must be in harmony with the organizational and human factors of the business.

LO 6 **Controlling account:** An account in the general ledger that summarizes the total balance of a group of related accounts in a subsidiary ledger. Also called *control account*.

LO 1 **Control principle:** The principle that holds that an accounting system must provide all the features of internal control needed to protect the firm's assets and ensure that data are reliable.

LO 1 **Cost-benefit principle:** The principle that holds that the benefits derived from an accounting system and the information it generates must be equal to or greater than its cost.

LO 1 **Data processing:** The means by which an accounting system gathers data, organizes them into useful forms, and issues the resulting information to users.

LO 4 **E-business:** The use of the Internet to perform a wide array of business functions, including, but not limited to, electronic commerce.

LO 4 **Electronic commerce:** The use of the Internet to transact business directly with vendors, suppliers, and customers.

LO 4 **Electronic mail (E-mail):** The sending and receiving of communications on the Internet.

LO 3 **Enterprise resource management (ERM):** Complex software systems that integrate financial operations with all functions of a business creating a vast information network.

LO 1 **Flexibility principle:** The principle that holds that an accounting system must be flexible enough to allow the volume of transactions to grow and organizational changes to be made.

LO 2 **General ledger software:** A group of integrated software programs that an accountant uses to direct the computer to carry out the major accounting functions.

LO 2 **Graphical user interface (GUI):** The employment of symbols, called *icons*, to represent common operations, making software easier to use.

LO 2 **Icon:** A symbol representing a common operation that appears on the screen as part of a graphical user interface.

LO 4 **Information retrieval:** The downloading of files from the Internet to an individual's computer.

LO 4 **Internet:** The world's largest computer network; it allows communication among computers of individuals and organizations around the world.

LO 5 **Manual data processing:** A system of accounting in which each transaction is entered manually from a source document into the general journal (input device) and each debit and credit is posted manually to the correct ledger account (processor and memory device) for the eventual preparation of financial statements (output devices).

LO 7 **Purchases journal:** A single-column or multicolumn special-purpose journal used to record all purchases on credit.

LO 7 **Sales journal:** A type of special-purpose journal used to record credit sales.

LO 4 **Search engines:** Internet sites that enable the user to research or search for information on any topic.

LO 3 **Source documents:** The written evidence that supports each accounting transaction for each major accounting function.

LO 5 **Special-purpose journal:** An input device in an accounting system that is used to record a single type of transaction.

LO 2 **Spreadsheet:** A computerized grid of columns and rows into which are placed data or formulas used for financial planning, cost estimating, and other accounting tasks.

LO 6 **Subsidiary ledger:** A ledger separate from the general ledger that contains a group of related accounts; the total of the balances in the subsidiary ledger accounts must equal the balance of the related controlling account in the general ledger.

LO 4 **World Wide Web:** The repository of vast amounts of information on the Internet.

REVIEW PROBLEM

Purchases Journal

LO 1
LO 5
LO 7

Caraban Company is a retail seller of hiking and camping gear. The company is installing a manual accounting system, and the accountant is trying to decide whether to use a single-column or a multicolumn purchases journal. Here is a list of several transactions related to purchases in the month of January.

Jan. 5 Received a shipment of merchandise from Simons Corporation, terms 2/10, n/30, FOB shipping point, invoice dated January 4, $2,875.

10 Received a bill from Allied Freight for the freight charges on the January 5 shipment, terms n/30, invoice dated January 4, $416.

15 Returned some of the merchandise received from Simons Corporation because it was not what was ordered, $315.

20 Purchased store supplies of $56 and office supplies of $117 from Mason Company, terms n/30, invoice dated January 20.

25 Received a shipment from Thomas Manufacturing, $1,882, which included supplier-paid freight charges of $175, terms n/30, FOB shipping point, invoice dated January 23.

REQUIRED

1. Record the transactions using a single-column purchases journal and a general journal, and show the posting reference for each journal entry. Use the following accounts: Store Supplies (116), Office Supplies (117), Accounts Payable (211), Purchases (611), Purchases Returns and Allowances (612), and Freight In (613).

2. Record the transactions using a multicolumn purchases journal and a general journal, total the purchases journal, and show the posting reference for each entry.

3. Using the principles of systems design, compare the single-column and multicolumn systems in terms of the number of journal entries and postings.

ANSWER TO REVIEW PROBLEM

1. Record the transactions in a single-column purchases journal and the general journal. Show the posting references.

		Purchases Journal				Page 1
Date		Account Credited	Date of Invoice	Terms	Post. Ref.	Amount
Jan.	5	Simons Corporation	1/4	2/10, n/30	√	2,875

		General Journal			Page 1
Date		**Description**	**Post. Ref.**	**Debit**	**Credit**
Jan.	10	Freight In	613	416	
		Accounts Payable, Allied Freight	211/√		416
		Freight charges on Simons Corporation shipment, terms n/30, invoice dated January 4			
	15	Accounts Payable, Simons Corporation	211/√	315	
		Purchases Returns and Allowances	612		315
		Returned merchandise not ordered			
	20	Store Supplies	116	56	
		Office Supplies	117	117	
		Accounts Payable, Mason Company	211/√		173
		Purchased supplies, terms n/30, invoice dated January 20			
	25	Purchases	611	1,707	
		Freight In	613	175	
		Accounts Payable, Thomas Manufacturing	211/√		1,882
		Purchased merchandise, terms n/30; supplier paid shipping, invoice dated January 23			

2. Record the transactions in a multicolumn purchases journal and the general journal. Total the purchases journal and show posting references.

		Purchases Journal								Page 1
						Credit	**Debits**			
Date		**Account Credited**	**Date of Invoice**	**Terms**	**Post. Ref.**	**Accounts Payable**	**Purchases**	**Freight In**	**Store Supplies**	**Office Supplies**
Jan.	5	Simons Corporation	1/4	2/10, n/30	√	2,875	2,875			
	10	Allied Freight	1/4	n/30	√	416		416		
	20	Mason Company	1/20	n/30	√	173			56	117
	25	Thomas Manufacturing	1/23	n/30	√	1,882	1,707	175		
						5,346	4,582	591	56	117
						(211)	(611)	(613)	(116)	(117)

Each of these amounts is posted **daily** to the appropriate account in the subsidiary ledger.

Each of these totals is posted **monthly** to the applicable general ledger account.

		General Journal			Page 1
Date		Description	Post. Ref.	Debit	Credit
Jan.	15	Accounts Payable, Simons Corporation Purchases Returns and Allowances Returned merchandise not ordered	211/√ → 612	315	315 ←

This amount is posted both to the controlling account and to the subsidiary account.

This amount is posted to the general ledger account.

3. The single-column purchases journal requires four general journal entries plus one purchases journal entry, or 20 separate lines, including explanations. In addition, 15 postings to the general ledger and the accounts payable subsidiary ledger are necessary. (Also, the total of the purchases journal must be posted twice at the end of the month: once as a debit to Purchases and once as a credit to Accounts Payable.) The multicolumn purchases journal calls for just one general journal entry and four purchases journal entries. Only eight lines need to be written, and only seven postings must be made. (In addition, the column totals in the purchases journal must be posted at the end of the month.)

In applying the cost-benefit principle, the benefits of the multicolumn purchases journal in terms of journalizing and posting time saved are clear from this analysis. In addition, there are fewer chances for error when using the multicolumn purchases journal. So the control principle is better achieved under the second system. It is not possible to decide which system better meets the compatibility principle because we do not know the relative proportion of transaction types. For instance, if the number of transactions like the one for January 5 exceeds all the others by ten to one, the first system may be more compatible with the needs of the company. On the other hand, if there are many transactions like those for January 10, 20, and 25, the second system may be more compatible. Finally, in terms of the flexibility principle, the multicolumn purchases journal is obviously more flexible because it can handle more kinds of transactions and can be expanded to include columns for other accounts if necessary.

Chapter Assignments

BUILDING YOUR KNOWLEDGE FOUNDATION

QUESTIONS

1. What is the relationship of accounting systems to data processing?
2. Describe the four principles of accounting systems design.
3. What are two common types of software used by accountants, and how do they differ in terms of their use?
4. Why is a graphical user interface important to the successful use of general ledger software?
5. Define and contrast *enterprise resource management* (ERM), *electronic commerce*, and *E-business*.
6. Data are the raw material of a computer system. Trace the flow of data through the different parts of a microcomputer accounting system.

7. How does a microcomputer accounting system using general ledger software relate to the major accounting functions?

8. In what ways can the Internet assist an individual in performing a job?

9. How do special-purpose journals save time in entering and posting transactions?

10. What is the purpose of the Accounts Receivable controlling account? What is its relationship to the accounts receivable subsidiary ledger?

11. Long Transit had 1,700 sales on credit during the current month.
    a. If the firm uses a two-column general journal to record sales, how many times will the word *Sales* be written?
    b. How many postings to the Sales account will have to be made?
    c. If the firm uses a sales journal, how many times will the word *Sales* be written?
    d. How many postings to the Sales account will have to be made?

12. Why are the cash receipts journal and cash payments journal crossfooted? When is this step performed?

13. A company has the following accounts with balances: 18 asset accounts, including the Accounts Receivable account but not the individual customers' accounts; 200 customer accounts; 8 liability accounts, including the Accounts Payable account but not the individual creditors' accounts; 100 creditor accounts; and 35 owner's equity accounts, including income statement accounts—a total of 361 accounts. How many accounts in total would appear in the general ledger?

SHORT EXERCISES

SE 1.
LO 1 Principles of Accounting Information System Design

Indicate whether each of the following statements concerning a newly installed accounting information system is most closely related to the (a) cost-benefit principle, (b) control principle, (c) compatibility principle, or (d) flexibility principle.

1. Procedures are put in place to make sure that the data entered into the system are reliable.
2. The system allows for growth in the number and types of transactions entered into by the company.
3. The system was installed after careful consideration of the additional costs in relation to the improved decision making that will result.
4. The system takes into account the various operations of the business and the capabilities of the people who will interact with the system.

SE 2.
LO 3 Microcomputer Accounting System

Assuming that a company uses a general ledger package for a microcomputer accounting system, indicate whether each source document listed below would provide input to (a) sales/accounts receivable, (b) purchases/accounts payable, (c) cash receipts, (d) cash disbursements, (e) payroll, or (f) the general journal.

1. Deposit slips
2. Time cards
3. Vendor invoices
4. Checks issued
5. Customer invoices
6. Documents for other journal entries

SE 3.
LO 5 Transactions and Special-Purpose Journals

Indicate whether each transaction listed below should be recorded in the (a) sales journal, (b) multicolumn purchases journal, (c) cash receipts journal, (d) cash payments journal, or (e) general journal.

1. Receipt on account
2. Purchase return on account
3. Sale on account
4. Purchase on account
5. Sale for cash
6. Payment on account

SE 4.
LO 7 Sales Journal Transactions

Using Exhibit 2 as a model, show how each of the following transactions should be entered in a sales journal. All terms are 2/10, n/30. If a transaction should not appear in the sales journal, tell where it should be recorded.

Oct. 1 Sold merchandise to S. Ruiz on credit, invoice no. 301, $350.
    8 Sold merchandise to J. Sizemore for cash, $150.
   15 Sold merchandise to F. Thomas on credit, invoice no. 302, $200.

Total and rule the journal.

SE 5.

LO 6 **Sales Journal Postings**
LO 7 **and Subsidiary Ledger**

Assuming the transactions in **SE 4** are the only sales transactions for the month of October, describe all the postings that would be made from the sales journal to the general ledger and the accounts receivable subsidiary ledger.

SE 6.

LO 7 **Multicolumn Purchases**
Journal

Using Exhibit 6 as a model, show how each of the following transactions should be entered in a multicolumn purchases journal. If a transaction should not appear in this journal, tell where it should be recorded.

Oct. 2   Purchased merchandise on credit from Carlson Electronics, invoice dated October 1, terms 2/10, n/30, $500.

    4   Purchased merchandise on credit from Boyer Electrics, invoice dated October 2, terms 2/10, n/30, $650, including freight charges of $50.

    6   Purchased supplies on credit from Ace Supplies, invoice dated October 5, terms n/30, $180, to be allocated one-third to store and two-thirds to office.

    8   Purchased postage stamps at the post office for cash (check no. 101), $58.

    9   Purchased equipment on credit from Jones Furniture Co., invoice dated October 9, terms n/EOM, $1,000.

Total and rule the journal.

SE 7.

LO 6 **Purchases Journal**
LO 7 **Postings and Subsidiary**
Ledger

Assuming the transactions in **SE 6** are the only purchases transactions for the month of October, describe all the postings that would be made from the purchases journal to the general ledger and the accounts payable subsidiary ledger.

SE 8.

LO 6 **Cash Receipts Journal**
LO 7

Using Exhibit 7 as a model, show how each of the following transactions should be entered in the cash receipts journal. If a transaction should not appear in this journal, tell where it should be recorded.

Oct. 8   Sold merchandise for cash to J. Sizemore, $150.

    9   Received payment on account from S. Ruiz, $350 less 2 percent discount.

    17   F. Thomas returned purchase of October 15 for full credit, $200.

Describe the postings that are required for each transaction.

SE 9.

LO 6 **Cash Payments Journal**
LO 7

Using Exhibit 8 as a model, show how each of the following transactions should be entered in the cash payments journal. If a transaction should not appear in this journal, tell where it should be recorded.

Oct. 8   Issued check no. 101 to the U.S. Postal Service for postage, $58.

    12   Issued check no. 102 to Carlson Electronics, $500 less 2 percent discount.

Describe the postings that are required for each transaction.

EXERCISES

E 1.

LO 5 **Matching Transactions to**
Special-Purpose Journals

A company uses a single-column sales journal, a single-column purchases journal, a cash receipts journal, a cash payments journal, and a general journal. In which journal would each of the following transactions be recorded?

1. Sold merchandise on credit
2. Sold merchandise for cash
3. Gave a customer credit for merchandise purchased on credit and returned
4. Paid a creditor
5. Paid office salaries
6. Received a customer's payment for merchandise previously purchased on credit
7. Recorded adjusting and closing entries
8. Purchased merchandise on credit
9. Purchased sales department supplies on credit
10. Purchased office equipment for cash
11. Returned merchandise purchased on credit
12. Paid income taxes

LO 5 **Characteristics of**
LO 6 **Special-Purpose**
LO 7 **Journals**

E 2. Fano Corporation uses a single-column sales journal, a single-column purchases journal, a cash receipts journal, a cash payments journal, and a general journal.

1. In which of the journals listed above would you expect to find the fewest transactions recorded?

2. At the end of the accounting period, to which account or accounts should the total of the sales journal be posted as a debit and/or credit?

3. At the end of the accounting period, to which account or accounts should the total of the purchases journal be posted as a debit and/or credit?

4. What two subsidiary ledgers would probably be associated with the journals listed above? From which journals would postings normally be made to each of the two subsidiary ledgers?

5. In which of the journals are adjusting and closing entries made?

LO 7 **Identifying the Content of a**
Special-Purpose Journal

E 3. Shown below is a page from a special-purpose journal.

Date		Account Credited	Post. Ref.	Debits		Credits		
				Cash	Sales Discount	Accounts Receivable	Sales	Other Accounts
May	25	Balance Forward		79,598	1,574	20,408	8,564	52,200
	26	Edna Jefferson	√	980	20	1,000		
		Notes Receivable	115	2,240				2,000
		Interest Income	715					240
	27	Cash Sale		1,920			1,920	
	31	Herb Jones	√	400		400		
				85,138	1,594	21,808	10,484	54,440
				(111)	(412)	(114)	(411)	(√)

1. What kind of journal is this?

2. Explain each transaction.

3. Explain the following: (a) the numbers under the double rule, (b) the checkmarks entered in the Post. Ref. column, (c) the numbers 115 and 715 in the Post. Ref. column, and (d) the checkmark below the Other Accounts credit column.

LO 7 **Multicolumn Purchases**
Journal

E 4. Hizick Company uses a multicolumn purchases journal similar to the one shown in Exhibit 6.

During the month of July, Hizick made the following purchases:

July 1 Purchased merchandise from Breslin Company on account for $5,400, invoice dated July 1, terms 2/10, n/30.

3 Received freight bill dated July 1 from Wong Freight for merchandise purchased July 1, $350, terms n/30.

18 Purchased supplies from Leeds Company for $240; allocated half to the store and half to the office; invoice dated July 16, terms n/30.

23 Purchased merchandise from Viola Company on account for $1,974; total included freight in of $174; invoice dated July 20, terms n/30, FOB shipping point.

27 Purchased office supplies from Leeds Company for $96, invoice dated July 27, terms n/30.

31 Purchased a one-year insurance policy from Smithers Associates, $480, invoice dated July 31, terms n/30.

1. Set up a multicolumn purchases journal similar to the one in Exhibit 6.

2. Enter the transactions listed above in the purchases journal. Then foot and crossfoot the columns.

E 5.

LO 6 Finding Errors in
LO 7 Special-Purpose Journals

A company records purchases in a single-column purchases journal and records purchases returns in its general journal. During the past month, an accounting clerk made each of the errors described below. Explain how each error might be discovered.

1. Correctly recorded a $191 purchase in the purchases journal but posted it to the creditor's account as a $119 purchase.

2. Made an error in totaling the Amount column of the purchases journal.

3. Posted a purchases return from the general journal to the Purchases Returns and Allowances account and the Accounts Payable account but did not post it to the creditor's account.

4. Made an error in determining the balance of a creditor's account.

5. Posted a purchases return to the Accounts Payable account but did not post it to the Purchases Returns and Allowances account.

E 6.

LO 6 Posting from a Sales
LO 7 Journal

Fern Corporation began business on June 1. The company maintains a sales journal. The sales journal at the end of the month is shown below.

	Sales Journal				Page 1
Date		Account Debited	Invoice Number	Post. Ref.	Amount
June	3	Sue Lang	1001		516
	8	Ed Kohl	1002		951
	12	Ye Sang	1003		642
	18	Sue Lang	1004		291
	27	Gina Colantos	1005		1,299
					3,699

1. Open general ledger accounts for Accounts Receivable (112) and Sales (411) and an accounts receivable subsidiary ledger with an account for each customer. Make the appropriate postings from the sales journal, inserting the posting references in the sales journal and in the ledger accounts as you work.

2. Prove the accounts receivable subsidiary ledger by preparing a schedule of accounts receivable.

E 7.

LO 6 Identification of
LO 7 Transactions

Obrero Company uses a manual accounting system with a sales journal, purchases journal, cash receipts journal, cash payments journal, and general journal similar to those illustrated in the text. On October 31, the Sales account in the general ledger looked like this:

Sales						Account No. 411	
			Post Ref.	Debit	Credit	Balance	
Date		Item				Debit	Credit
Oct.	31		S11		74,842		74,842
	31		CR7		42,414		117,256
	31		J17	117,256			—

On October 31, the T. Bearn account in the accounts receivable subsidiary ledger looked like this:

T. Bearn					Account No. 10012
Date	Item	Post. Ref.	Debit	Credit	Balance
Oct. 8		S10	4,216		4,216
12		J14		564	3,652
18		CR6		1,000	2,652

1. Write an explanation of each entry in the Sales account; include the journal from which the entry was posted.
2. Write an explanation of each entry in the T. Bearn account in the accounts receivable subsidiary ledger; include the journal from which the entry was posted.

LO 6 Identification of
LO 7 Transactions

E 8. Rudy Company uses a sales journal, single-column purchases journal, cash receipts journal, cash payments journal, and general journal similar to those shown in the text. On April 30, the D. Yousif account in the accounts receivable subsidiary ledger appeared as shown below.

D. Yousif					
Date	Item	Post. Ref.	Debit	Credit	Balance
Mar. 31		S4	2,448		2,448
Apr. 7		J7		192	2,256
12		CR5		600	1,656
17		S6	684		2,340

On April 30, the Dao Company account in the accounts payable subsidiary ledger appeared as follows:

Dao Company					
Date	Item	Post. Ref.	Debit	Credit	Balance
Apr. 18		P7		6,078	6,078
20		J9	636		5,442
25		CP8	5,442		—

1. Write an explanation of each entry that affected the D. Yousif account receivable, including the journal from which the entry was posted.
2. Write an explanation of each entry that affected the Dao Company account payable, including the journal from which the entry was posted.

PROBLEMS

P 1.

LO 6 Special-Purpose Journals
LO 7 and Subsidiary Ledgers

Lamb Company, a small retail business, uses a manual accounting system similar to the one illustrated in this chapter. At the end of August 20xx, the accounts in the accounts receivable and accounts payable subsidiary ledgers showed the following balances:

Accounts Receivable		Accounts Payable	
S. Adams	$ 870	Halcom, Inc.	$2,900
M. Alwin	650	Wolcord Company	460
Total Accounts Receivable	$1,520	Total Accounts Payable	$3,360

During September, the company engaged in the following transactions:

Sept. 2 Sold merchandise on credit to M. Alwin, $920, terms 2/10, n/30, invoice no. 4001.
   4 Received payment in full from M. Alwin for the amount due at the beginning of September less a 2 percent discount.
   5 Paid Halcom, Inc., the full amount owed less a 2 percent discount, check no. 501.
   8 Accepted a return of merchandise from M. Alwin, $220.
   9 Paid Wolcord Company the full amount owed, no discount allowed, check no. 502.
   12 Received payment from M. Alwin for the amount due less the discount.
   15 Received partial payment from S. Adams, no discount allowed, $300.
   22 Purchased merchandise from Wolcord Company, $1,700, terms 2/10, n/30, FOB destination, invoice dated September 21.
   23 Sold merchandise on credit to I. Yancy, $2,450, terms 2/10, n/30, invoice no. 4002.
   26 Purchased merchandise from Halcom, Inc., $1,500, terms 2/10, n/30, FOB destination, invoice dated September 24.
   30 Returned merchandise to Wolcord Company for full credit, $600.

REQUIRED

1. Prepare a sales journal, a single-column purchases journal, a cash receipts journal, a cash payments journal, and a general journal similar to the ones illustrated in the chapter. Use Page 1 for all references.

2. Open the following general ledger accounts: Accounts Receivable (112) and Accounts Payable (211).

3. Open the following accounts receivable subsidiary ledger accounts: S. Adams, M. Alwin, and I. Yancy.

4. Open the following accounts payable subsidiary ledger accounts: Halcom, Inc., and Wolcord Company.

5. Enter the transactions in the journals and post to the appropriate subsidiary ledger and general ledger accounts.

6. Foot and crossfoot the journals, and make the end-of-month postings applicable to Accounts Receivable and Accounts Payable.

7. Prove the control balances of Accounts Receivable and Accounts Payable by preparing schedules of accounts receivable and accounts payable.

P 2.

LO 7 Cash Receipts and Cash
Payments Journals

The following items detail all cash transactions by Vanissi Company for the month of March. The company uses multicolumn cash receipts and cash payments journals similar to those illustrated in the chapter.

Mar. 1 The owner, Gene Vanissi, invested $50,000 cash and $24,000 in equipment in the business.
   2 Paid rent to Camus Agency, $600, with check no. 75.
   3 Cash sales, $2,200.
   6 Purchased store equipment for $5,000 from Jilson Company, with check no. 76.
   7 Purchased merchandise for cash, $6,500, from Felipe Company, with check no. 77.

Mar. 8 Paid Borski Company invoice, $1,800, less 2 percent discount, with check no. 78 (assume that a payable has already been recorded).

9 Paid advertising bill, $350, to WOSU, with check no. 79.

10 Cash sales, $3,910.

12 Received $800 on account from L. Trout.

13 Purchased used truck for cash, $3,520, from Debes Company, with check no. 80.

19 Received $4,180 from Madison Company, in settlement of a $4,000 note plus interest.

20 Received $1,078 ($1,100 less $22 cash discount) from Sue Stibb.

21 Paid Vanissi $2,000 from business for personal use by issuing check no. 81.

23 Paid Dornor Company invoice, $2,500, less 2 percent discount, with check no. 82.

26 Paid Hebert Company for freight on merchandise received, $60, with check no. 83.

27 Cash sales, $4,800.

28 Paid Chan Yu for monthly salary, $1,400, with check no. 84.

31 Purchased land from L. Armbruster for $20,000, paying $5,000 with check no. 85 and signing a note payable for $15,000.

REQUIRED

1. Enter the preceding transactions in the cash receipts and cash payments journals.

2. Foot and crossfoot the journals.

P 3.

LO 6 Purchases and General
LO 7 Journals

Below are the credit transactions for McGarry Company during the month of August. The company uses a multicolumn purchases journal and a general journal similar to those illustrated in the text.

Aug. 2 Purchased merchandise from Alvarez Company, $1,400.

5 Purchased a truck to be used in the business from Meriweather Company, $8,000.

8 Purchased office supplies from Dandridge Company, $400.

12 Purchased filing cabinets from Dandridge Company, $550.

14 Purchased merchandise, $1,400, and store supplies, $200, from Petrie Company.

17 Purchased store supplies from Alvarez Company, $100, and office supplies from Hollins Company, $50.

20 Purchased merchandise from Petrie Company, $1,472.

24 Purchased merchandise from Alvarez Company, $2,452; the $2,452 invoice total included shipping charges, $232.

26 Purchased office supplies from Dandridge Company, $150.

30 Purchased merchandise from Petrie Company, $290.

31 Returned defective merchandise purchased from Petrie Company on August 20 for full credit, $432.

REQUIRED

1. Enter the preceding transactions in the purchases journal and the general journal. Assume that all terms are n/30 and that invoice dates are the same as the transaction dates. Use Page 1 for all references.

2. Foot and crossfoot the purchases journal.

3. Open the following general ledger accounts: Store Supplies (116), Office Supplies (117), Trucks (142), Office Equipment (144), Accounts Payable (211), Purchases (611), Purchases Returns and Allowances (612), and Freight In (613). Open accounts payable subsidiary ledger accounts as needed. Post from the journals to the ledger accounts.

P 4.

LO 6 Comprehensive Use of
LO 7 Special-Purpose Journals

The following transactions were completed by Lezcano's Men's Wear during the month of July, its first month of operation:

July 2 Carlos Lezcano deposited $20,000 in the new company's bank account.

3 Issued check no. 101 to Rollins Realty for one month's rent, $1,200.

4 Received merchandise from Garnett Company, invoice dated July 3, terms 2/10, n/60, FOB shipping point, $7,000.

July 5 Received from Wiggins Company freight bill on merchandise purchased, terms n/20, $964.

6 Issued check no. 102 to Bagley Company for store equipment, $7,400.

7 Signed a 90-day, 9 percent note for a bank loan and received $8,000 in cash.

8 Cash sales for the first week, $1,982. (To shorten this problem, cash sales are recorded weekly instead of daily, as they would be in actual practice.)

10 Sold merchandise to Midlands School, terms 2/10, n/30, invoice no. 1001, $900.

11 Sold merchandise to Charlotte Soo, terms n/20, invoice no. 1002, $300.

12 Purchased advertising in the *Journal-Citizen*, terms n/15, $150.

13 Issued check no. 103 for purchase of July 4 less discount.

14 Issued a credit memorandum for merchandise returned by Charlotte Soo, $30.

15 Cash sales for the second week, $3,492

17 Received merchandise from Garnett Company, invoice dated July 16, terms 2/10, n/60, FOB shipping point, $1,900.

18 Received from Wiggins Company freight bill on merchandise purchased, terms n/20, $262.

19 Received merchandise from Law Company, invoice dated July 17, terms 1/10, n/60, FOB destination, $1,400.

20 Received payment in full less discount from Midlands School.

21 Received a credit memorandum from Garnett Company for merchandise returned, $100.

22 Cash sales for third week, $2,912.

24 Issued check no. 104 for total amount owed Wiggins Company.

25 Sold merchandise to Midlands School, terms 2/10, n/30, invoice no. 1003, $684.

26 Issued check no. 105 in payment of amount owed Garnett Company less discount.

27 Sold merchandise to Al Kaiser, terms n/20, invoice no. 1004, $372.

28 Issued check no. 106 for amount owed the *Journal-Citizen*.

29 Cash sales for the fourth week, $1,974.

31 Issued check no. 107 to Payroll for sales salaries for the month of July, $3,600.

REQUIRED

1. Prepare a sales journal, a multicolumn purchases journal, a cash receipts journal, a cash payments journal, and a general journal. Use Page 1 for all journal references.

2. Open the following general ledger accounts: Cash (111); Accounts Receivable (112); Store Equipment (141); Accounts Payable (211); Notes Payable (212); Carlos Lezcano, Capital (311); Sales (411); Sales Discounts (412); Sales Returns and Allowances (413); Purchases (511); Purchases Discounts (512); Purchases Returns and Allowances (513); Freight In (514); Sales Salaries Expense (611); Advertising Expense (612); and Rent Expense (613).

3. Open accounts receivable subsidiary ledger accounts for Al Kaiser, Midlands School, and Charlotte Soo.

4. Open accounts payable subsidiary ledger accounts for Garnett Company, the *Journal-Citizen*, Law Company, and Wiggins Company.

5. Enter the transactions in the journals and post as appropriate.

6. Foot and crossfoot the journals, and make the end-of-month postings.

7. Prepare a trial balance of the general ledger and prove the control balances of Accounts Receivable and Accounts Payable by preparing schedules of accounts receivable and accounts payable.

P 5.

LO 6 Comprehensive Use of
LO 7 Special-Purpose Journals

During May, Chung Refrigerating Company completed the following transactions:

May 1 Received merchandise from Costello Company, invoice dated April 29, terms 2/10, n/30, FOB shipping point, $2,500.

2 Issued check no. 230 to Roundfield Realtors for May rent, $2,000.

3 Received merchandise from Vranes Manufacturing, invoice dated May 1, terms 2/10, n/30, FOB shipping point, $5,400.

May 5 Issued check no. 231 to Dukes Company for repairs, $560.

6 Received credit memorandum pertaining to May 3 shipment from Vranes Manufacturing for return of unsatisfactory merchandise, $400.

7 Issued check no. 232 to Orta Company for freight charges on May 1 and May 3 shipments, $184.

8 Sold merchandise to C. Share, terms 1/10, n/30, invoice no. 725, $1,000.

9 Issued check no. 233 to Costello Company in full payment less discount.

10 Sold merchandise to R. Bell, terms 1/10, n/30, invoice no. 726, $1,250.

11 Issued check no. 234 to Vranes Manufacturing for balance of account less discount.

12 Purchased advertising on credit from WXYR, terms n/20, $450.

14 Issued credit memorandum to R. Bell for merchandise returned, $50.

15 Cash sales for the first half of the month, $9,670. (To shorten this problem, cash sales are recorded only twice a month instead of daily, as they would be in actual practice.)

16 Sold merchandise to L. Stokes, terms 1/10, n/30, invoice no. 727, $700.

17 Received check from C. Share for May 8 sale less discount.

19 Received check from R. Bell for balance of account less discount.

20 Received merchandise from Costello Company, invoice dated May 19, terms 2/10, n/30, FOB shipping point, $2,800.

21 Received from Noh Company freight bill on merchandise purchased, terms n/5, $570.

22 Issued check no. 235 for advertising purchase of May 12.

23 Received merchandise from Vranes Manufacturing, invoice dated May 22, terms 2/10, n/30, FOB shipping point, $3,600.

24 Issued check no. 236 for freight charge of May 21.

26 Sold merchandise to C. Share, terms 1/10, n/30, invoice no. 728, $800.

27 Received credit memorandum from Vranes Manufacturing for defective merchandise received May 23, $300.

28 Issued check no. 237 to Espinoza Company for purchase of office equipment, $350.

29 Issued check no. 238 to Costello Company for half of May 20 purchase less discount.

30 Received check in full from L. Stokes, discount not allowed.

31 Cash sales for the last half of month, $11,560.

31 Issued check no. 239, payable to Payroll for monthly sales salaries, $4,300.

REQUIRED

1. Prepare a sales journal, a multicolumn purchases journal, a cash receipts journal, a cash payments journal, and a general journal for Chung Refrigerating Company similar to the ones illustrated in this chapter. Use Page 1 for all journal references.

2. Open the following general ledger accounts: Cash (111), Accounts Receivable (112), Office Equipment (141), Accounts Payable (211), Sales (411), Sales Discounts (412), Sales Returns and Allowances (413), Purchases (511), Purchases Discounts (512), Purchases Returns and Allowances (513), Freight In (514), Sales Salaries Expense (521), Advertising Expense (522), Rent Expense (531), and Repairs Expense (532).

3. Open accounts receivable subsidiary ledger accounts for R. Bell, C. Share, and L. Stokes.

4. Open accounts payable subsidiary ledger accounts for Costello Company, Noh Company, Vranes Manufacturing, and WXYR.

5. Enter the transactions in the journals and post as appropriate.

6. Foot and crossfoot the journals, and make the end-of-month postings.

7. Prepare a trial balance of the accounts used in this problem and prove the control balances of Accounts Receivable and Accounts Payable by preparing schedules of accounts receivable and accounts payable.

ALTERNATE PROBLEMS

P 6.

LO 6 Special-Purpose Journals
LO 7 and Subsidiary Ledgers

Dune Company is a small retail business that uses a manual accounting system similar to the one described in this chapter. At the end of June 20xx, the firm's accounts receivable and accounts payable subsidiary ledgers showed the following balances:

Accounts Receivable		Accounts Payable	
R. Costa	$430	Donlevy Company	$1,300
Y. Paik	330	Mintol Company	890
Total Accounts Receivable	$760	Total Accounts Payable	$2,190

During July, the company engaged in the following transactions:

July 2 Sold merchandise on credit to L. Stone, a new customer, $570, terms 2/10, n/30, invoice no. 1001.
   4 Received payment in full from Y. Paik, no discount allowed.
   5 Paid Donlevy Company the full amount owed less a 2 percent discount, check no. 201.
   8 Accepted a return of merchandise for credit from L. Stone, $170.
   9 Paid Mintol Company the full amount owed, no discount allowed, check no. 202.
   12 Received payment from L. Stone for amount due less discount.
   15 Received partial payment from R. Costa, no discount allowed, $230.
   22 Purchased merchandise from Donlevy Company, $1,200, terms 2/10, n/30, FOB destination, invoice dated July 22.
   23 Sold merchandise on credit to Y. Paik, $670, terms 2/10, n/30, invoice no. 1002.
   26 Purchased merchandise from Mintol Company, $1,500, terms 2/10, n/30, FOB destination, invoice dated July 23.
   31 Returned merchandise to Mintol Company for full credit, $600.

REQUIRED

1. Prepare a single-column sales journal, a single-column purchases journal, a cash receipts journal, a cash payments journal, and a general journal similar to the ones illustrated in the chapter. Use Page 1 for all references.

2. Open the following general ledger accounts: Accounts Receivable (112) and Accounts Payable (211).

3. Open the following accounts receivable subsidiary ledger accounts: R. Costa, Y. Paik, and L. Stone.

4. Open the following accounts payable subsidiary ledger accounts: Donlevy Company and Mintol Company.

5. Enter the transactions in the journals and post to the appropriate subsidiary ledger and general ledger accounts.

6. Foot and crossfoot the journals, and make the end-of-month postings applicable to Accounts Receivable and Accounts Payable.

7. Prove the control balances of Accounts Receivable and Accounts Payable by preparing schedules of accounts receivable and accounts payable.

P 7.

LO 7 Cash Receipts and Cash
Payments Journals

Caron Company is a small retail business that uses a manual data processing system similar to the one described in the chapter. Among its special-purpose journals are multicolumn cash receipts and cash payments journals. These were the cash transactions for Caron Company during the month of April:

Apr. 1 Paid April rent to V. Kregsy, $1,000, with check no. 782.
   3 Paid Panos Wholesale on account, $2,300 less a 2 percent discount, check no. 783.
   4 Received payment on account of $1,000, within the 2 percent discount period, from P. Waller.
   5 Cash sales, $2,632.
   8 Paid Fast Freight on account, $598, with check no. 784.
   9 The owner, Harry Caron, invested an additional $10,000 in cash and a truck valued at $14,000 in the business.

Apr. 11 Paid Slowik Supply on account, $284, with check no. 785.

14 Cash sales, $2,834.

15 Paid Fast Freight $310 for the freight on a shipment of merchandise received today, with check no. 786.

16 Paid Hales Company on account, $1,568 net a 2 percent discount, with check no. 787.

17 Received payment on account from R. Tomayo, $120.

18 Cash sales, $1,974.

19 Received payment on a note receivable, $1,800 plus $36 interest.

20 Purchased office supplies from Slowik Supply, $108, with check no. 788.

21 Paid a note payable in full to Wadsworth Bank, $4,100 including $100 interest, with check no. 789.

24 Cash sales, $2,964.

25 Paid $500 less a 2 percent discount to Panos Wholesale, with check no. 790.

26 Paid Patrice Quiero, a sales clerk, $1,100 for her monthly salary, with check no. 791.

27 Purchased equipment from Helena Corporation for $16,000, paying $4,000 with check no. 792 and signing a note payable for the difference.

30 Harry Caron withdrew $1,200 from the business, using check no. 793.

REQUIRED

1. Enter these transactions in the cash receipts and cash payments journals.

2. Foot and crossfoot the journals.

P 8.

LO 6 Comprehensive Use of
LO 7 Special-Purpose Journals

Scott Bookstore opened its doors for business on September 1. During September, the following transactions took place:

Sept. 1 Cynthia Scott began the business by depositing $21,000 in the new company's bank account.

2 Issued check no. C001 to Page Rentals for one month's rent, $500.

3 Received a shipment of books from Gray Books, Inc., invoice dated September 2, terms 5/10, n/60, FOB shipping point, $7,840.

4 Received a bill for freight from All Points Shippers for the previous day's shipment, terms n/30, $395.

5 Received a shipment from Choice Books, invoice dated September 5, terms 2/10, n/30, FOB shipping point, $5,650.

6 Issued check no. C002 to Selby Freight, Inc., for transportation charges on the previous day's shipment, $287.

8 Issued check no. C003 to Urban Equipment Company for store equipment, $5,200.

9 Sold books to Spectrum Center, terms 5/10, n/30, invoice no. 1001, $782.

10 Returned books to Gray Books, Inc., for credit, $380.

11 Issued check no. C004 to WBNS for radio commercials, $235.

12 Issued check no. C005 to Gray Books, Inc., for balance of amount owed less discount.

13 Cash sales for the first two weeks, $2,009. (To shorten this problem, cash sales are recorded every two weeks instead of daily, as they would be in actual practice.)

15 Issued check no. C006 to Choice Books, $3,000 less discount.

16 Signed a 90-day, 10 percent note for a bank loan and received $10,000 in cash.

17 Sold books to Joe Prokop, terms n/30, invoice no. 1002, $130.

18 Issued a credit memorandum to Spectrum Center for returned books, $62.

19 Received payment in full from Spectrum Center for balance owed less discount.

20 Sold books to Joyce Monsoya, terms n/30, invoice no. 1003, $97.

22 Received a shipment from Temple Publishing Company, invoice dated September 21, terms 5/10, n/60, $2,302.

23 Returned additional books purchased on September 3 to Gray Books, Inc., for credit at gross price, $718.

24 Sold books to Spectrum Center, terms 5/10, n/30, invoice no. 1004, $817.

Sept. 25 Received a shipment from Gray Books, Inc., invoice dated September 22, terms 5/10, n/60, FOB shipping point, $1,187.

26 Issued check no. C007 to All Points Shippers for balance owed on account plus shipping charges of $97 on previous day's shipment.

27 Cash sales for the second two weeks, $3,744.

29 Issued check no. C008 to Payroll for sales salaries for first four weeks of the month, $700.

30 Cash sales for the last two days of the month, $277.

REQUIRED

1. Prepare a sales journal, a multicolumn purchases journal, a cash receipts journal, a cash payments journal, and a general journal. Use Page 1 for all journal references.

2. Open the following general ledger accounts: Cash (111); Accounts Receivable (112); Store Equipment (141); Accounts Payable (211); Notes Payable (212); Cynthia Scott, Capital (311); Sales (411); Sales Discounts (412); Sales Returns and Allowances (413); Purchases (511); Purchases Discounts (512); Purchases Returns and Allowances (513); Freight In (514); Sales Salaries Expense (611); Advertising Expense (612); and Rent Expense (613).

3. Open accounts receivable subsidiary ledger accounts for Joyce Monsoya, Joe Prokop, and Spectrum Center.

4. Open accounts payable subsidiary ledger accounts for All Points Shippers; Choice Books; Gray Books, Inc.; and Temple Publishing Company.

5. Enter the transactions in the journals and post as appropriate.

6. Foot and crossfoot the journals, and make the end-of-month postings.

7. Prepare a trial balance of the general ledger and prove the control balances of Accounts Receivable and Accounts Payable by preparing schedules of accounts receivable and accounts payable.

EXPANDING YOUR CRITICAL THINKING, COMMUNICATION, AND INTERPERSONAL SKILLS

SKILLS DEVELOPMENT

Conceptual Analysis

SD 1.

LO 1 **Accounting System**
LO 3 **Evaluation**
LO 5

Lessing Interiors is an interior design company that was started three years ago by Loretta Lessing. For the first two years of the company's life, Lessing helped clients plan the decorating of their luxury apartments in Manhattan. Lessing did not sell any furnishings herself but was paid an hourly fee plus a percentage of the total purchases made by her clients. Although the business was successful, it was very simple. And it required just a simple manual accounting system consisting of a general journal and a general ledger. During the past year, Lessing expanded. She opened a second-floor studio and began displaying and selling selected furnishings. She hired her first employees and began buying and selling on credit. As the number of her company's daily transactions multiplied, Lessing began to find the manual accounting system very burdensome. It was taking far too much time to record and post all the transactions. The company does not have a computer at present, but Lessing is thinking about buying one.

Cash Flow   CD-ROM   Communication   Critical Thinking   Ethics   General Ledger   Group Activity   Hot Links to Real Companies   International   Internet   Key Ratio   Memo   Spreadsheet

She has come to you for help. Evaluate Lessing's current accounting system in terms of the principles of systems design (excluding the control principle) and make a recommendation about the types of accounting systems Lessing should consider installing. Write a memorandum to Lessing providing your analysis and recommendation.

LO 2 **Switching to a General**
LO 3 **Ledger Accounting System**

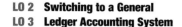

SD 2. *Krock's & Marici's* operates a growing full-service bookstore in the Louisville area. The firm is known for excellent service and large inventories of books in a wide number of fields, such as art, history, business, technology, travel, fiction, and juvenile. To increase traffic and project a casual image, the company has a coffee shop in the bookstore. The owner's accountant has recommended that it install a general ledger software system. Tell what a general ledger software system is and identify the source documents, software function, and output documents that would constitute the system. What do you think the advantages of this system will be?

Ethical Dilemma

LO 6 **Confidentiality of**
Accounting Records

SD 3. Frank Santino is the accounting manager at the Ford and Toyota dealership in Petersburg, Texas, a town with a population of 50,000. At a barbecue, José Martinez, a close friend, mentions that he is planning to sell some land to Louis Johnson for $20,000 and will allow Johnson to pay him over a five-year period. Santino, who happened to have been reviewing the delinquent accounts at the dealership earlier in the day, knows that Johnson has a poor payment history and that his car may have to be repossessed. Martinez asks Santino what he thinks about the sale. What ethical issue is involved here? If you were Santino, would you warn Martinez about Johnson's credit record?

Research Activity

LO 4 **Using the Internet**

SD 4. Assume you have been asked by your boss, the owner of a small dress shop, to investigate general ledger software for her business. Both *Peachtree Software* and *Intuit Software*, the publisher of Quickbooks®, have web pages. Access these web sites through the Needles Accounting Resource Center web site at http://college.hmco.com. Study the information you find, and write a summary of the information and its usefulness. Can you assess the differences in the software approaches of the two companies and their applicability to a small dress shop?

Decision-Making Practice

LO 5 **Design of Special-**
LO 6 **Purpose Journals**
LO 7

SD 5. *RW Finer Foods Company,* owned by Robert Washington, is a neighborhood grocery store that accepts cash or checks in payment for food. Known for its informality, the store has been very successful and has grown with the community. Along with that growth, however, has come an increase in the number of bad checks customers have written for purchases. Washington is concerned about the difficulty of accounting for these returned checks, so he has asked you to look into the problem.

In addition to a purchases journal and a cash payments journal, the company has a combination single-column sales and cash receipts journal. The combination journal has worked in the past because all sales are for cash (including checks), and almost all cash receipts represent sales transactions. Thus, the single column represents a debit to Cash and a credit to Sales.

The bad checks are recorded individually in the general journal by debiting Accounts Receivable and crediting Cash for the amount of the check. When a customer pays off a bad check, another entry is made in the general journal debiting Cash and crediting Accounts Receivable. Returned Check Revenue for the amount of $10, which represents reimbursement of the service charge by the bank, will be recorded in the Sales/Cash Receipts journal when the bad check is collected. Washington keeps the returned checks in an envelope. When a customer comes in to pay one off, Washington gives the check back. No other records of the returned checks are maintained.

In studying the problem, you discover that the company is averaging ten returned checks per day, totaling $1,000. As part of the solution, you recommend that

Washington issue check-cashing cards to customers whose credit is approved in advance. The card must be presented when a customer offers a check in payment for groceries. You recommend further that a special-purpose journal be established for the returned checks and returned check revenue, that a subsidiary ledger be maintained, and that the combination sales/cash receipts journal be expanded.

1. Draw and label the columns for the new returned checks journal and the expanded sales/cash receipts journal.

2. Assume that there are 300 returned checks and 280 collections per month and that the records are closed each month. How many written lines can be saved each month by recording returned checks and subsequent collections in the special journals? How many postings can be saved each month? (Ignore the effect of the subsidiary ledger.)

3. Describe the nature and use of the subsidiary ledger. What advantages do you see in having a subsidiary ledger?

4. Assuming that it takes approximately two and a half minutes to make each entry and related postings under the old system of recording bad checks and one minute to make each entry and related postings under the new system, what are the monthly savings if the cost is $20 an hour? What further, and possibly more significant, savings may be realized by using the new system?

Group Activity: After presenting parts **1** and **3** in class, divide the class into teams to work on parts **2** and **4**. Compare and discuss results.

FINANCIAL REPORTING AND ANALYSIS

Interpreting Financial Reports

FRA 1.
LO 1 Electronic Commerce on
LO 4 the Internet

Amazon.com, which describes itself as the "Earth's Biggest Bookstore," is the leading Internet book seller. It might be described as a "virtual" bookstore because it carries only a relatively few books in its Seattle warehouse, far fewer than the average superstore, like Borders or Barnes & Noble. Buyers choose from a selection of 2.5 million books on the Internet and give credit card information to place an order. Amazon.com verifies the information and electronically sends the order to a wholesaler that packages and sends the order, usually within one day. Ninety-five percent of the books Amazon.com sells are delivered by these wholesalers, which charge a wholesale markup for handling and shipping. The cost of having to rely on wholesalers for distribution is one reason that Amazon.com has not yet reached profitability in spite of its success. As a result, the company is planning to expand its own distribution capability, which it believes it can do at a lower cost.[3]

1. Define e-business and electronic commerce and describe generally how conducting business on the Internet differs from conducting business in a retail store.

2. Describe how you believe the four principles of systems design apply to Amazon.com's sale and distribution of books as compared to a more traditional bookstore.

3. What changes in the application of these principles will occur if Amazon.com begins to do more of its own distribution?

International Company

This category is not applicable to this chapter.

Toys "R" Us Annual Report

FRA 2.
LO 1 Principles of Accounting
Systems Design

In its Letter to Stockholders, the management of Toys "R" Us states that the company "missed many selling opportunities during the holiday season in 1999 by not having enough investment behind the top 1,000 items." The objective in 2000 is "a doubling of the investment in the top 1,000 items by reducing our current levels of non-key inventory and by working with our resources to more tightly focus our investment behind the most important properties." To do this, the company uses satellite technology in

North America that instantaneously links stores with headquarters' computer data bases to make ordering, inventory control, and customer transaction authorization more cost-efficient. Explain how this computer technology and centralized data bases comply with the principles of cost-benefit, control, compatibility, and flexibility.

Fingraph® Financial Analyst™

This category is not applicable to this chapter.

Internet Case

FRA 3.

LO 1 Accounting and Systems Careers

Many accountants are involved in systems careers. Go to the Needles Accounting Resource Center at http://college.hmco.com. Under Companies Web Links, go to the annual reports on the web sites for *PeopleSoft*, *Accenture* (formerly *Andersen Consulting*), and *PricewaterhouseCoopers*. Find information describing these firms' businesses and look for the sections on career opportunities that relate to accounting and systems. For each firm, summarize its business and the career opportunities and be prepared to discuss what you find in class.

ENDNOTES

1. "E-Business Tops Tech Priorities for CPAs," *Journal of Accountancy*, March 2000.
2. Walgreen, *Annual Report*, 1993.
3. Anthony Bianco, "Virtual Bookstores to Get Real," *Business Week*, October 27, 1997.

8

Internal Control

LEARNING OBJECTIVES

1 Define *internal control*, identify the five components of internal control, and explain seven examples of control activities.

2 Describe the inherent limitations of internal control.

3 Apply internal control activities to common merchandising transactions.

4 Demonstrate the control of cash by preparing a bank reconciliation.

SUPPLEMENTAL OBJECTIVES

5 Demonstrate the use of a simple imprest system.

6 Define *voucher system* and describe the components of a voucher system.

7 Describe and carry out the five steps in operating a voucher system.

Dell Computer Corporation Dell Computer Corporation is one of the fastest-growing businesses in the history of merchandising. The company sells computers by mail order and is known for providing good, fast service. But the fast growth causes problems for the company. In its early years, management acknowledged that "[the company's] internal controls are having difficulty keeping up with its zooming growth. . . . The problems have made it difficult for the company to track its inventory and to accurately project supply and demand for the components that go into its personal computers. . . . The systems and the processes in the company didn't grow as fast as the business."[1] Why were these problems serious for Dell Computer, and what action should management have taken?

Problems with controls and systems are serious for all companies, including Dell, because they lead to lost inventory, lost sales, and disgruntled customers. The mail-order computer business is very competitive, and Dell Computer could easily have lost its business and gone bankrupt if it had not addressed its growth-related problems. Management needed to institute new internal controls over purchases and inventory so that it could track all components and ship to customers soon after they placed their orders. As you will see in the next section, this goal can be achieved through a good internal control structure: a good control environment with an accounting and computer system that has specific procedures designed to manage and safeguard the inventory. Dell Computer Corporation was successful in remedying its problems and continues to be the leading mail-order computer company in the world.

Internal Control: Basic Components and Control Activities

OBJECTIVE

1 Define *internal control,* identify the five components of internal control, and explain seven examples of control activities

A merchandising company can have inaccurate accounting records as well as high losses of cash and inventory if it does not take steps to protect its assets. The best way to do this is to set up and maintain a good system of internal control.

Management's Responsibility for Internal Control

Management is responsible for establishing a satisfactory system of internal control. **Internal control** is defined as all the policies and procedures management uses to ensure the reliability of financial reporting, compliance with laws and regulations, and the effectiveness and efficiency of operations. In other words, management must safeguard the firm's assets and have reliable accounting records. It must ensure that employees comply with legal requirements and operate the company in the best way possible.

Management comments on its responsibility and effectiveness in achieving the goals of internal control in the "Report of Management" in the company's annual report to stockholders. For example, a portion of this statement from the annual report of Circuit City Stores, Inc., follows:

> Management is responsible for maintaining an internal control structure designed to provide reasonable assurance that the books and records reflect the transactions of the Company and that the Company's established policies and procedures are carefully followed. Because of inherent limitations in any system, there can be no absolute assurance that errors or irregularities will not occur. Nevertheless, management believes that the internal control structure provides reasonable assurance that assets are safeguarded and that financial information is objective and reliable.[2]

Components of Internal Control

To accomplish the objectives of internal control, management must establish five interrelated components of internal control:[3]

1. *Control environment*   The **control environment** is created by the overall attitude, awareness, and actions of management. It includes management's integrity and ethics, philosophy and operating style, organizational structure, method of assigning authority and responsibility, and personnel policies and practices. Personnel should be qualified to handle responsibilities, which means that employees must be trained and informed. For example, the manager of a retail store should train employees to follow prescribed procedures for handling cash sales, credit card sales, and returns and refunds.

2. *Risk assessment*   **Risk assessment** is the identification of areas where risks of loss of assets or inaccuracies in the accounting records are high so that adequate controls can be implemented. For example, among the greater risks in a retail store are the risks that employees will take cash or that customers will shoplift merchandise.

3. *Information and communication*   **Information and communication** relates to the accounting systems established by management to identify, assemble, ana-

lyze, classify, record, and report a company's transactions. Management should establish clear communication of individual responsibilities in achieving these functions.

4. *Control activities* **Control activities** are the policies and procedures management puts in place to see that the directives related to internal control are carried out. Control activities are discussed in more detail below.

5. *Monitoring* **Monitoring** involves management's regular assessment of the quality of internal control including periodic review of compliance with all policies and procedures. For example, large companies often have a staff of internal auditors who review the company's system of internal control to determine if it is working properly and if procedures are being followed. In smaller businesses, owners and managers should conduct these reviews.

Control Activities

Control activities are a principal way in which internal control is implemented in the accounting system. They safeguard a company's assets and ensure the reliability of accounting records. These control activities include the following:

1. *Authorization* All transactions and activities should be properly authorized by management. In a retail store, for example, some transactions, such as normal cash sales, are authorized routinely; others, such as issuing a refund, may require a manager's approval.

2. *Recording transactions* To facilitate preparation of financial statements and to establish accountability for assets, all transactions should be recorded. In a retail store, for example, the cash register records sales, refunds, and other transactions internally on a paper tape or computer disk so that the cashier can be held responsible for the cash received and the merchandise removed during his or her shift.

3. *Documents and records* The design and use of adequate documents help ensure the proper recording of transactions. For example, to ensure that all transactions are recorded, invoices and other documents should be prenumbered and all numbers should be accounted for.

4. *Physical controls* Physical controls permit access to assets only with management's authorization. For example, retail stores should use cash registers, and only the cashier responsible for the cash in a register should have access to it. Other employees should not be able to open the cash drawer if the cashier is not present. Likewise, warehouses and storerooms should be accessible only to authorized personnel. Access to accounting records, including company computers, should also be controlled.

5. *Periodic independent verification* The records should be checked against the assets by someone other than the persons responsible for those records and assets. For example, at the end of each shift or day, the owner or store manager should count the cash in the cash drawer and compare the amount to the amounts recorded on the tape or computer disk in the cash register. Other examples of independent verification are the monthly bank reconciliation and periodic counts of physical inventory.

6. *Separation of duties* The organizational plan should separate functional responsibilities. Within a department, no one person should be in charge of authorizing transactions, operating the department, handling assets, and keeping records of assets. For example, in a stereo store, each employee should oversee only a single part of a transaction. A sales employee takes the order and creates an invoice. Another employee receives the customer's cash or credit card payment and issues a receipt. Once the customer has a paid receipt, and only then, a third employee obtains the item from the warehouse and gives it to the customer. A person in the accounting department subsequently records the sales from the tape in the cash register, comparing them with the sales invoices and updating the inventory in the records. The separation of duties ensures that a deviation from a prescribed system, whether done in error or intentionally, cannot be made without being seen by at least one other person.

7. *Sound personnel procedures* Sound practices should be followed in managing the people who carry out the functions of each department. Among those practices are supervision, rotation of key people among different jobs, insistence that employees take vacations, and bonding of personnel who handle cash or inventories. **Bonding** is the process of carefully checking an employee's background and insuring the company against loss due to theft by that person. Bonding does not guarantee against theft, but it does prevent or reduce economic loss if theft occurs. Prudent personnel procedures help to ensure that employees know their jobs, are honest, and will find it difficult to carry out and conceal embezzlement over time.

Limitations of Internal Control

OBJECTIVE

2 Describe the inherent limitations of internal control

No system of internal control is without weaknesses. As long as control procedures are performed by people, the internal control system is vulnerable to human error. Errors may arise from misunderstandings, mistakes in judgment, carelessness, distraction, or fatigue. Separation of duties can be defeated through collusion by employees who secretly agree to deceive the company. Also, established procedures may be ineffective against employees' errors or dishonesty, or controls that were initially effective may become ineffective because conditions have changed.[4] In some cases, the costs of establishing and maintaining elaborate systems may exceed the benefits. In a small business, for example, active involvement by the owner can be a practical substitute for the separation of some duties.

FOCUS ON BUSINESS ETHICS

A survey of 5,000 large U.S. businesses disclosed that 21 percent suffered frauds in excess of $1 million. Common frauds were credit card frauds, check frauds, inventory theft, false invoices and phantom vendors, and expense account abuse. The most common ways in which the frauds were allowed to take place were through poor internal controls, management override of internal controls, and collusion. The frauds were most commonly detected by notification by an employee, internal controls, internal auditor review, notification by a customer, and by accident. Companies successful in preventing fraud have a good system of internal control and a formal code of ethics with a program to monitor compliance. The company routinely communicates the existence of the program to employees, which includes a system to report incidents of fraud.[5]

Internal Control over Merchandising Transactions

OBJECTIVE

3 Apply internal control activities to common merchandising transactions

Sound internal control activities are needed in all aspects of a business, but particularly when assets are involved. Assets are especially vulnerable when they enter or leave a business. When sales are made, for example, cash or other assets enter the business, and goods or services leave the business. Activities must be set up to prevent theft during those transactions.

Likewise, purchases of assets and payments of liabilities must be controlled. The majority of those transactions can be safeguarded by adequate purchasing and payment systems. In addition, assets on hand, such as cash, investments, inventory, plant, and equipment, must be protected.

In this section, you will see how internal control activities are applied to such merchandising transactions as cash sales, receipts, purchases, and cash payments. Similar activities are applicable to service and manufacturing businesses.

Internal Control and Management Goals

When a system of internal control is applied effectively to merchandising transactions, it can achieve important management goals. For example, two key goals for the success of a merchandising business are:

1. To prevent losses of cash or inventory owing to theft or fraud
2. To provide accurate records of merchandising transactions and account balances

Three broader goals for management are:

1. To keep enough inventory on hand to sell to customers without overstocking
2. To keep enough cash on hand to pay for purchases in time to receive discounts
3. To keep credit losses as low as possible by making credit sales only to customers who are likely to pay on time

One control used in meeting broad management goals is the cash budget, which projects future cash receipts and disbursements. By maintaining adequate cash balances, a company is able to take advantage of discounts on purchases, prepare to borrow money when necessary, and avoid the damaging effects of being unable to pay bills when they are due. By investing excess cash, the company can earn interest until the cash is needed.

A more specific accounting control is the separation of duties that involve the handling of cash. Such separation makes theft without detection extremely unlikely, unless two or more employees conspire. The separation of duties is easier in large businesses than in small ones, where one person may have to carry out several duties. The effectiveness of internal control over cash varies, based on the size and nature of the company. Most firms, however, should use the following procedures:

1. Separate the functions of authorization, recordkeeping, and custodianship of cash.
2. Limit the number of people who have access to cash.
3. Designate specific people who are responsible for handling cash.
4. Use banking facilities as much as possible, and keep the amount of cash on hand to a minimum.
5. Bond all employees who have access to cash.

6. Physically protect cash on hand by using cash registers, cashiers' cages, and safes.

7. Have a person who does not handle or record cash make unannounced audits of the cash on hand.

8. Record all cash receipts promptly.

9. Deposit all cash receipts promptly.

10. Make payments by check rather than by currency.

11. Have a person who does not authorize, handle, or record cash transactions reconcile the Cash account.

Notice that each of the foregoing procedures helps to safeguard cash by making it more difficult for any one individual who has access to cash to steal or misuse it without being detected.

Control of Cash Sales Receipts

 Cash payments for sales of goods and services can be received by mail or over the counter in the form of checks or currency. Whatever the source of the payments, cash should be recorded immediately upon receipt. This is usually done by making an entry in a cash receipts journal. Such a journal establishes a written record of cash receipts that should prevent errors and make theft more difficult.

CONTROL OF CASH RECEIVED THROUGH THE MAIL Cash receipts that arrive by mail are vulnerable to theft by the employees who handle them. Payment by mail is increasing because of the expansion of mail-order sales. Therefore, to control mailed receipts, customers should be urged to pay by check or credit card instead of with currency.

Cash that comes in through the mail should be handled by two or more employees. The employee who opens the mail should make a list in triplicate of the money received. The list should contain each payer's name, the purpose for which the money was sent, and the amount. One copy goes with the cash to the cashier, who deposits the money. The second copy goes to the accounting department for recording. The third copy is kept by the person who opens the mail. Errors can be easily caught because the amount deposited by the cashier must agree with the amount received and the amount recorded in the cash receipts journal.

CONTROL OF CASH RECEIVED OVER THE COUNTER Two common tools for controlling cash sales receipts are cash registers and prenumbered sales tickets. The amount of a cash sale should be rung up on a cash register at the time of the sale. The cash register should be placed so that the customer can see the amount recorded. Each cash register should have a locked-in tape on which it prints the day's transactions. At the end of the day, the cashier counts the cash in the cash register and turns it in to the cashier's office. Another employee takes the tape out of the cash register and records the cash receipts for the day in the cash receipts journal. The amount of cash turned in and the amount recorded on the tape should agree; if not, any differences must be explained.

Large retail chains commonly monitor cash receipts by having each cash register tied directly into a computer that records each transaction as it occurs. Whether the elements are performed manually or by computer, separating responsibility for cash receipts, cash deposits, and recordkeeping is necessary to ensure good internal control.

In some stores, internal control is further strengthened by the use of prenumbered sales tickets and a central cash register or cashier's office, where all sales are rung up and collected by a person who does not participate in the sale. The salesperson completes a prenumbered sales ticket at the time of the sale, giving one copy to the customer and keeping a copy. At the end of the day, all sales tickets must be accounted for, and the sales total computed from the sales tickets should equal the total sales recorded on the cash register.

Control of Purchases and Cash Disbursements

 Cash disbursements are particularly vulnerable to fraud and embezzlement. In one recent case, the treasurer of one of the nation's largest jewelry retailers was charged with having stolen over $500,000 by systematically overpaying federal income taxes and keeping the refund checks as they came back to the company.

To avoid such theft, cash should be paid only after the receipt of specific authorization supported by documents that establish the validity and amount of the claim. In addition, maximum possible use should be made of the principle of separation of duties in the purchase of goods and services and the payment for them. The degree of separation of duties varies, depending on the size of the business. Figure 1 shows how separation of duties can be maximized in large companies. In the figure, five internal units (the requesting department, the purchasing department, the accounting department, the receiving department, and the treasurer) and two external contacts (the supplier and the banking system) all play a role in the internal control plan. Notice that business documents are also crucial components of the plan.

As shown in Figure 2, every action is documented and verified by at least one other person. For instance, the requesting department cannot work out a kickback

Figure 1
Internal Control for Purchasing and Paying for Goods and Services

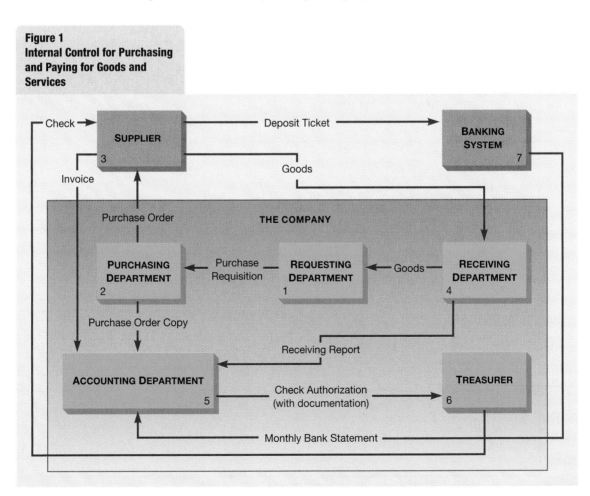

Figure 2
Internal Control Plan for Purchases and Cash Disbursements

① PURCHASE REQUISITION   No. 7077

Martin Maintenance Company

From: Credit Office   Date: September 6, 20xx

To: Purchasing Department   Suggested Vendor: Henderson Supply Company

Please purchase the following items:

Quantity	Number	Description
20 boxes	X 144	FAX paper rolls

Reason for Request   To be filled in by Purchasing Department

Six months' supply for office

Date ordered 9/8/20xx   P.O. No. J 102

Approved _J.P._

---

② PURCHASE ORDER   No. J 102

Martin Maintenance Company
8428 Rocky Island Avenue
Chicago, Illinois 60643

To: Henderson Supply Company   Date: September 8, 20xx
2525 25th Street
Mesa, Illinois 61611   FOB: Destination

        Ship by: September 12, 20xx

Ship to: Martin Maintenance Company   Terms: 2/10, n/30
Above Address

Please ship the following:

Quantity	✓	Number	Description	Price	Per	Amount
20 boxes		X 144	FAX paper rolls	12.00	box	$240.00

Purchase order number must appear on all shipments and invoices.

Ordered by _Marsha Owen_

---

③ INVOICE   No. 0468

Henderson Supply Company   Date: September 12, 20xx
2525 25th Street
Mesa, Illinois 61611   Your Order No.: J 102

Sold to: Ship to:

Martin Maintenance Company   Same
8428 Rocky Island Avenue
Chicago, Illinois 60643

Sales Representative: Joe Jacobs

Quantity		Description	Price	Per	Amount
Ordered	Shipped				
20	20	X 144 FAX paper rolls	12.00	box	$240.00

FOB Destination | Terms: 2/10, n/30 | Date Shipped: 9/12/20xx | Via: Self

---

④ RECEIVING REPORT   No. JR065

Martin Maintenance Company
8428 Rocky Island Avenue
Chicago, Illinois 60643

Date: September 12, 20xx

Quantity	Number	Description	Condition
20 boxes	X 144	FAX paper rolls	O.K.

Received by _B.M._

---

⑤ CHECK AUTHORIZATION

	NO.	CHECK
Purchase Order	J 102	✓
Receiving Report	JR065	✓
INVOICE	0468	✓
Price		✓
Calculations		✓
Terms		✓

Approved for Payment _J Joseph_

---

⑥

Martin Maintenance Company   NO. 2570
8428 Rocky Island Avenue   61-153/313
Chicago, Illinois 60643

       9/21   20 xx

PAY TO
THE ORDER OF Henderson Supply Company $ 235.20

Two hundred thirty-five and 20/100 — — — — — — — Dollars

THE LAKE PARK NATIONAL BANK   Martin Maintenance Company
Chicago, Illinois

⑈03130153⑈ ⑈8030 647 4⑈   by _Arthur Martin_

Remittance Advice

Date	P.O. No.	DESCRIPTION	AMOUNT
9/21/20xx	J 102	20 X 144 FAX paper rolls	$240.00
		Supplier Inv. No. 0468	
		Less 2% discount	4.80
		Net	$235.20
		Martin Maintenance Company	

Business Document	Prepared by	Sent to	Verification and Related Procedures
(1) Purchase requisition	Requesting department	Purchasing department	Purchasing verifies authorization.
(2) Purchase order	Purchasing department	Supplier	Supplier sends goods or services in accordance with purchase order.
(3) Invoice	Supplier	Accounting department	Accounting receives invoice from supplier.
(4) Receiving report	Receiving department	Accounting department	Accounting compares invoice, purchase order, and receiving report. Accounting verifies prices.
(5) Check authorization	Accounting department	Treasurer	Accounting attaches check authorization to invoice, purchase order, and receiving report.
(6) Check	Treasurer	Supplier	Treasurer verifies all documents before preparing check.
(7) Bank statement	Buyer's bank	Accounting department	Accounting compares amount and payee's name on returned check with check authorization.

(7)

Statement of Account with
THE LAKE PARK NATIONAL BANK
Chicago, Illinois

Martin Maintenance Company
8428 Rocky Island Avenue
Chicago, Illinois 60643

Checking Acct No
8030-647-4
Period covered
Sept.30-Oct.31,20xx

Previous Balance	Checks/Debits—No.	Deposits/Credits—No.	S.C.	Current Balance
$2,645.78	$4,319.33 --16	$5,157.12 --7	$12.50	$3,471.07

CHECKS/DEBITS			DEPOSITS/CREDITS		DAILY BALANCES	
Posting Date	Check No.	Amount	Posting Date	Amount	Date	Amount
					09/30	2,645.78
10/01	2564	100.00	10/01	586.00	10/01	2,881.78
10/01	2565	250.00	10/05	1,500.00	10/04	2,825.60
10/04	2567	56.18	10/06	300.00	10/05	3,900.46
10/05	2566	425.14	10/16	1,845.50	10/06	4,183.34
10/06	2568	17.12	10/21	600.00	10/12	2,242.34
10/12	2569	1,705.80	10/24	300.00CM	10/16	3,687.84
10/12	2570	235.20	10/31	25.62IN	10/17	3,589.09
10/16	2571	400.00			10/21	4,189.09
10/17	2572	29.75			10/24	3,745.59
10/17	2573	69.00			10/25	3,586.09
10/24	2574	738.50			10/28	3,457.95
10/24		5.00DM			10/31	3,471.07
10/25	2575	7.50				
10/25	2577	152.00				
10/28		118.14NSF				
10/28		10.00DM				
10/31		12.50SC				

Explanation of Symbols:

CM – Credit Memo	SC – Service Charge	The last amount
DM – Debit Memo	EC – Error Correction	in this column
NSF – Non-Sufficient Funds	OD – Overdraft	is your balance.
	IN – Interest on Average Balance	

Please examine; if no errors are reported within ten (10) days, the account will be considered to be correct.

FOCUS ON BUSINESS TECHNOLOGY

One of the more difficult challenges facing computer programmers is to build good internal controls into computerized accounting programs. Such computer programs must include controls that prevent unintentional errors as well as unauthorized access and tampering. The programs prevent errors through reasonableness checks that, for example, may allow no transactions over a specified amount, mathematical checks that verify the arithmetic of transactions, and sequence checks that require documents and transactions to be in their proper order. They typically use passwords and questions about randomly selected personal data to prevent unauthorized access to computer records. With unauthorized Internet access easily available in many systems, data encryption and firewalls are important. Data encryption is a way of coding data so that if they are stolen, they are useless to the thief. A firewall is a strong electronic barrier to access from outside a computer system.

scheme to make illegal payments to the supplier because the receiving department independently records receipts and the accounting department verifies prices. The receiving department cannot steal goods because the receiving report must equal the invoice. For the same reason, the supplier cannot bill for more goods than it ships. The accounting department's work is verified by the treasurer, and the treasurer ultimately is checked by the accounting department.

Using the forms shown with Figure 2, follow the typical sequence of documents used in this internal control plan for the purchase of 20 boxes of fax paper rolls. To begin, the credit office (requesting department) of Martin Maintenance Company fills out a formal request for a purchase, or **purchase requisition**, for 20 boxes of fax paper rolls (item 1). The department head approves it and forwards it to the purchasing department. The people in the purchasing department prepare a **purchase order**, as shown in item 2. The purchase order is addressed to the vendor (seller) and contains a description of the items ordered; the expected price, terms, and shipping date; and other shipping instructions. Martin Maintenance Company does not pay any bill that is not accompanied by a purchase order number.

After receiving the purchase order, the vendor, Henderson Supply Company, ships the goods and sends an **invoice** or bill (item 3) to Martin Maintenance Company. The invoice gives the quantity and description of the goods delivered and the terms of payment. If goods cannot all be shipped immediately, the estimated date for shipment of the remainder is indicated.

When the goods reach the receiving department of Martin Maintenance Company, an employee writes the description, quantity, and condition of the goods on a form called a **receiving report** (item 4). The receiving department does not receive a copy of the purchase order or the invoice, so its employees do not know what should be received or its value. Thus, they are not tempted to steal any excess that may be delivered.

The receiving report is sent to the accounting department, where it is compared with the purchase order and the invoice. If everything is correct, the accounting department completes a **check authorization** and attaches it to the three supporting documents. The check authorization form shown in item 5 has a space for each item to be checked off as it is examined. Notice that the accounting department has all the documentary evidence for the transaction but does not have access to the assets purchased. Nor does it write the check for payment. This means that the people performing the accounting function cannot gain by falsifying documents in an effort to conceal fraud.

Finally, the treasurer examines all the documents and issues an order to the bank for payment, called a **check** (item 6), for the amount of the invoice less any

appropriate discount. In some systems, the accounting department fills out the check so that all the treasurer has to do is inspect and sign it. The check is then sent to the supplier, with a remittance advice that shows the reason the check was issued. A supplier who is not paid the proper amount will complain, of course, thus providing a form of outside control over the payment. Using a deposit ticket, the supplier deposits the check in the bank, which returns the canceled check with Martin Maintenance Company's next bank statement (item 7). If the treasurer has made the check out for the wrong amount (or altered a pre-filled-in check), the problem will show up in the bank reconciliation.

There are many variations of the system just described. This example is offered as a simple system that provides adequate internal control.

Preparing a Bank Reconciliation

OBJECTIVE

4 Demonstrate the control of cash by preparing a bank reconciliation

Rarely will the balance of a company's Cash account exactly equal the cash balance shown on the bank statement. Certain transactions shown in the company's records may not have been recorded by the bank, and certain bank transactions may not appear in the company's records. Therefore, a necessary step in internal control is to prove both the balance shown on the bank statement and the balance of Cash in the accounting records. A **bank reconciliation** is the process of accounting for the differences between the balance appearing on the bank statement and the balance of Cash according to the company's records. This process involves making additions to and subtractions from both balances to arrive at the adjusted cash balance.

The most common examples of transactions shown in the company's records but not entered in the bank's records are the following:

1. *Outstanding checks* These are checks that have been issued and recorded by the company but that do not yet appear on the bank statement.

2. *Deposits in transit* These are deposits that were mailed or taken to the bank but that were not received in time to be recorded on the bank statement.

Transactions that may appear on the bank statement but that have not been recorded by the company include the following:

1. *Service charges (SC)* Banks often charge a fee, or service charge, for the use of a checking account. Many banks base the service charge on a number of factors, such as the average balance of the account during the month or the number of checks drawn.

2. *NSF (nonsufficient funds) checks* An NSF check is a check deposited by the company that is not paid when the company's bank presents it to the maker's bank. The bank charges the company's account and returns the check so that the company can try to collect the amount due. If the bank has deducted the NSF check from the bank statement but the company has not deducted it from its book balance, an adjustment must be made in the bank reconciliation. The depositor usually reclassifies the NSF check from Cash to Accounts Receivable because the company must now collect from the person or company that wrote the check.

3. *Interest income* It is very common for banks to pay interest on a company's average balance. These accounts are sometimes called NOW or money market accounts, but they can take other forms. Such interest is reported on the bank statement.

4. *Miscellaneous charges and credits* Banks also charge for other services, such as collection and payment of promissory notes, stopping payment on checks, and printing checks. The bank notifies the depositor of each deduction by including a debit memorandum with the monthly statement. A bank will sometimes serve as an agent in collecting on promissory notes for the depositor. In such a case, a credit memorandum will be included.

An error by either the bank or the depositor will, of course, require immediate correction.

Illustration of a Bank Reconciliation

Assume that the October bank statement for Martin Maintenance Company indicates a balance on October 31 of $3,471.07 and that, in its records, Martin Maintenance Company has a cash balance on October 31 of $2,415.91. The purpose of a bank reconciliation is to identify the items that make up the difference between these amounts and to determine the correct cash balance. The bank reconciliation for Martin Maintenance Company is given in Exhibit 1. The numbered items in the exhibit refer to the following:

1. A deposit in the amount of $276.00 was mailed to the bank on October 31 and has not been recorded by the bank.

2. Five checks issued in October or prior months have not yet been paid by the bank, as follows:

Check No.	Date	Amount
551	Sept. 14	$150.00
576	Oct. 30	40.68
578	Oct. 31	500.00
579	Oct. 31	370.00
580	Oct. 31	130.50

3. The deposit for cash sales of October 6 was incorrectly recorded in Martin Maintenance Company's records as $330.00. The bank correctly recorded the deposit as $300.00.

Exhibit 1
Bank Reconciliation

Martin Maintenance Company
Bank Reconciliation
October 31, 20xx

Balance per bank, October 31		$3,471.07
① Add deposit of October 31 in transit		276.00
		$3,747.07
② Less outstanding checks:		
No. 551	$150.00	
No. 576	40.68	
No. 578	500.00	
No. 579	370.00	
No. 580	130.50	1,191.18
Adjusted bank balance, October 31		**$2,555.89**
Balance per books, October 31		$2,415.91
Add:		
④ Note receivable collected by bank	$280.00	
④ Interest income on note	20.00	
⑦ Interest income	15.62	315.62
		$2,731.53
Less:		
③ Overstatement of deposit of October 6	$ 30.00	
④ Collection fee	5.00	
⑤ NSF check of Arthur Clubb	128.14	
⑥ Service charge	12.50	175.64
Adjusted book balance, October 31		**$2,555.89**

Note: The circled numbers refer to the items listed in the text on the previous page and below.

4. Among the returned checks was a credit memorandum showing that the bank had collected a promissory note from A. Jacobs in the amount of $280.00, plus $20.00 in interest on the note. A debit memorandum was also enclosed for the $5.00 collection fee. No entry had been made on Martin Maintenance Company's records.

5. Also returned with the bank statement was an NSF check for $128.14. This check had been received from a customer named Arthur Clubb. The NSF check from Clubb was not reflected in the company's accounting records.

6. A debit memorandum was enclosed for the regular monthly service charge of $12.50. This charge had not yet been recorded by Martin Maintenance Company.

7. Interest earned by Martin Maintenance Company on the average balance was reported as $15.62.

Note in Exhibit 1 that, starting from their separate balances, both the bank and book amounts are adjusted to the amount of $2,555.89. This adjusted balance is the amount of cash owned by the company on October 31 and thus is the amount that should appear on its October 31 balance sheet.

Recording Transactions After Reconciliation

The adjusted balance of cash differs from both the bank statement and Martin Maintenance Company's records. The bank balance will automatically become correct when outstanding checks are presented for payment and the deposit in transit is received and recorded by the bank. Entries must be made by the depositor (company) only for the transactions necessary to update the book balance. Only the items reported by the bank but not yet recorded by the company are recorded in the general journal by means of the following entries:

A = L + OE
+
–
	+	Oct. 31 Cash
		  Notes Receivable
		  Interest Income
		    Note receivable of $280.00
		    and interest of $20.00 collected
		    by bank from A. Jacobs
			300.00	280.00
				20.00

A = L + OE
+
	+	31 Cash
		  Interest Income
		    Interest on average bank
		    account balance
			15.62	15.62

A = L + OE
–
	–	31 Sales
		  Cash
		    Correction of error in recording
		    a $300.00 deposit as $330.00
			30.00	30.00

A = L + OE
+
–
		31 Accounts Receivable
		  Cash
		    NSF check of Arthur Clubb
		    returned by bank
			128.14	128.14

A = L + OE
–
	–	31 Bank Service Charges Expense
		  Cash
		    Bank service charge ($12.50)
		    and collection fee ($5.00) for October
			17.50	17.50

It is acceptable to record these entries in one or two compound entries to save time and space.

Petty Cash Procedures

SUPPLEMENTAL OBJECTIVE

5 Demonstrate the use of a simple imprest system

It is not always practical to make every disbursement by check. For example, it is sometimes necessary to make small payments of cash for such things as postage stamps, incoming postage, shipping charges due, or minor purchases of pens, paper, and the like.

For situations in which it is inconvenient to pay by check, most companies set up a **petty cash fund**. One of the best methods of maintaining control over the fund is to use an **imprest system**. Under this system, a petty cash fund is established for a fixed amount. Each cash payment from the fund is documented by a voucher. Then the fund is periodically reimbursed, based on the vouchers, for the exact amount necessary to restore the original cash balance.

Establishing the Petty Cash Fund

Some companies have a regular cashier or other employee who administers the petty cash fund. To establish the fund, the company issues a check for an amount that is intended to cover two to four weeks of small expenditures. The check is cashed, and the money is placed in the petty cash box, drawer, or envelope.

The only entry required when the fund is established is to record the check.

A = L + OE Oct. 14   Petty Cash   100.00
+   Cash   100.00
−   To establish the petty cash fund

Making Disbursements from the Petty Cash Fund

The custodian of the petty cash fund should prepare a **petty cash voucher**, or written authorization, for each expenditure, as shown in Figure 3. On each petty cash voucher, the custodian enters the date, amount, and purpose of the expenditure. The voucher is signed by the person who receives the payment.

The custodian should be informed that unannounced audits of the fund will be made occasionally. The cash in the fund plus the sum of the petty cash vouchers should at all times equal the amount shown in the Petty Cash account.

Reimbursing the Petty Cash Fund

At specified intervals, when the fund becomes low, and at the end of an accounting period, the petty cash fund is replenished by a check issued to the custodian for the exact amount of the expenditures. From time to time, there may be minor discrepancies in the amount of cash left in the fund at the time of reimbursement. In those cases, the amount of the discrepancy is recorded in a Cash Short or Over account, as a debit if short or as a credit if over.

Assume that after two weeks the petty cash fund established earlier has a cash balance of $14.27 and petty cash vouchers as follows: postage, $25.00; supplies, $30.55; and freight in, $30.00. The entry to replenish, or replace, the fund would be:

A = L + OE Oct. 28   Postage Expense   25.00
+   =   Supplies   30.55
−   −   Freight In   30.00
          −   Cash Short or Over   .18
                                Cash   85.73
                                    To replenish the petty cash fund

Notice that the Petty Cash account was not affected by the entry to replenish the fund. The Petty Cash account is debited when the fund is established or the fund level is changed. Expense or asset accounts are debited each time the fund is replenished, including in this case $.18 to Cash Short or Over for a small cash shortage. In most cases, no further entries to the Petty Cash account are needed unless the firm wants to change the fixed amount of the fund.

Figure 3
Petty Cash Voucher

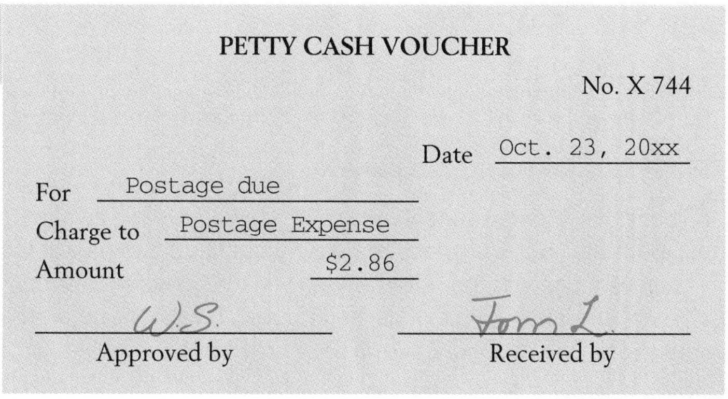

PETTY CASH VOUCHER

No. X 744

Date Oct. 23, 20xx

For _____Postage due_____

Charge to _____Postage Expense_____

Amount _____$2.86_____

_____W.S._____   _____Tom L_____
Approved by   Received by

The petty cash fund should be replenished at the end of an accounting period to bring it up to its fixed amount and ensure that changes in the other accounts involved are reflected in the current period's financial statements. If, through an oversight, the petty cash fund is not replenished at the end of the period, expenditures for the period still must appear on the income statement. They are shown through an adjusting entry debiting the expense accounts and crediting Petty Cash. The result is a reduction in the petty cash fund and the Petty Cash account by the amount of the adjusting entry. On the financial statements, the balance of the Petty Cash account is usually combined with other cash accounts.

Voucher Systems

SUPPLEMENTAL OBJECTIVE

6 Define *voucher system* and describe the components of a voucher system

A **voucher system** is any system that gives documentary proof of and written authorization for business transactions. In this section, we present a voucher system designed to keep the tightest possible control over a company's expenditures. It consists of records and procedures for systematically gathering, recording, and paying expenditures. The system provides strong internal control by separating duties and responsibilities in the following functions:

1. Authorization of expenditures
2. Receipt of goods and services
3. Validation of liability by examination of invoices from suppliers for correctness of prices, extensions (quantity times price), shipping costs, and credit terms
4. Payment of expenditure by check, taking discounts when possible

Under a voucher system, every liability must be recorded as soon as it is incurred. A written authorization, called a **voucher**, is prepared for each expenditure when it becomes an obligation to pay, and checks are written only for approved vouchers. No one person has the authority both to incur expenses and to issue checks. In large companies, the duties of authorizing expenditures, verifying receipt of goods and services, checking invoices, recording liabilities, and issuing checks are divided among different people. So, for both accounting and management control, every expenditure must be carefully and routinely reviewed and verified before payment. For each transaction, the written approval leaves a trail of documentary evidence, or what is called an **audit trail**.

Although there is more than one way to set up a voucher system, most systems use (1) vouchers, (2) voucher checks, (3) a voucher register, and (4) a check register.

FOCUS ON BUSINESS PRACTICE

E-tailing, the selling of business (goods) to consumers (B-to-C), gets the most publicity, but the most rapidly growing segment of business use of the Internet is business to business (B-to-B) transactions. It is projected that B-to-B transactions will exceed $14 trillion, compared with $7 trillion for B-to-C transactions. Industries leading in B-to-B transactions are automotive, chemicals, paper and office products, computers and electronics, and utilities. Manual voucher systems are obviously not sufficient for this volume of activity. B-to-B voucher systems will require strong internal controls that ensure proper delivery, precise product specifications, high levels of customer service, and timely, accurate bill payment.[7]

Figure 4
Front and Back of a Typical Voucher Form

Thomas Appliance Company

Payee	Belmont Products		Voucher No.	704
Address	Gary, Indiana		Date Due	7/13
			Date Paid	7/13
Terms	2/10, n/30		Check No.	205

Date	Invoice No.	Description	Amount
7/3	XL1066	10 cases Model 70X14	1,200--

Approved _____ M. N. _____   Approved _____ A. Thomas _____
        Controller   Treasurer

BACK OF VOUCHER

Account Debited	Acct. No.	Amount
Purchases	511	1,200.00
Freight In	512	
Rent Expense	631	
Salary Expense	611	
Utilities Expense	635	
Total		$1,200.00

Voucher No.	704
Payee	Belmont Products
Address	Gary, Indiana
Invoice Amount	1,200.00
Less Discount	24.00
Net	1,176.00
Date Due	7/13
Date Paid	7/13
Check No.	205

Vouchers

Any business can use vouchers to control expenditures. A voucher serves as the basis of an accounting entry. To facilitate tracking, all vouchers are sequentially numbered, and a separate voucher is attached to each bill as it comes in. In the cash disbursement system introduced earlier in this chapter, a voucher would replace the check authorization form. On the face of a typical voucher (Figure 4) is important information about the expenditure and the authorizing signatures required for payment. On the reverse side of the voucher is information about the accounts and amounts to be debited and credited. The voucher identifies the transaction by both voucher number and check number and is recorded in both the voucher register and the check register, as described in the following sections.

Voucher Checks

Although regular checks can be used effectively with a voucher system, many businesses use a form of **voucher check**, which tells the payee the reason the check was issued. The information is written either on the check itself or on a detachable stub.

Exhibit 2
Voucher Register

Voucher Register

Date	Voucher No.	Payee	Payment Date	Check No.	Credit Vouchers Payable	Debits Purchases	Freight In	Store Supplies
20xx July 1	701	Common Utility	7/6	203	75			
2	702	Ade Realty	7/2	201	400			
2	703	Buy Rite Supplies	7/6	202	25			
3	704	Belmont Products	7/13	205	1,200	1,200		
6	705	M&M Freight			60		60	
7	706	J. Jay, Petty Cash	7/7	204	50			
8	707	Belmont Products	7/18	208	600	600		
11	708	M&M Freight			30		30	
11	709	Mack Truck			5,600			
12	710	Livingstone Wholesale	7/22	209	785	750	35	
14	711	Payroll	7/14	206	2,200			
17	712	First National Bank	7/17	207	4,250			
20	713	Livingstone Wholesale			525	500	25	
21	714	Belmont Products			400	400		
24	715	M&M Freight			18		18	
30	716	Payroll	7/30	210	2,200			
31	717	J. Jay, Petty Cash	7/31	211	47		17	
31	718	Maintenance Company			175			
31	719	Store Supply Company			350			350
					18,990	3,450	185	350
					(211)	(511)	(512)	(116)

Voucher Register

The **voucher register** is the book of original entry in which vouchers are recorded after they have been approved. The voucher register takes the place of the purchases journal in companies that use special-purpose journals. There is one important difference between the two journals: All expenditures—expenses, payroll, plant, and equipment, as well as purchases of merchandise—are recorded in a voucher register; only purchases of merchandise on credit are recorded in a single-column purchases journal.

A voucher register appears in Exhibit 2. Notice that a column called Vouchers Payable replaces the Accounts Payable column. As you can see, the first entry in

						Page 1
				Debits				
Office Supplies	Sales Salaries Expense	Office Salaries Expense	Main- tenance Expense, Selling	Main- tenance Expense, Office	Utilities Expense	**Other Accounts**		
						Name	No.	Amount
25					75	Rent Expense	631	400
						Petty Cash	121	50
						Trucks	148	5,600
	1,400	800				Notes Payable	212	4,000
						Interest Expense	645	250
20	1,400	800				Misc. Expense	649	10
			100	75				
45	2,800	1,600	100	75	75			10,310
(117)	(611)	(612)	(621)	(622)	(635)			(√)

the voucher register records the receipt of a utility bill. It is recorded as a debit to Utilities Expense and a credit to Vouchers Payable (not Accounts Payable). On July 6, this utility bill was paid with check number 203.

Check Register

In a voucher system, the **check register**, as shown in Exhibit 3, is the journal in which checks are listed as they are written. Consequently, it replaces the cash payments journal. Carefully study the connection between the voucher register and the check register. The incurrence of a liability is recorded in the voucher register; its payment is recorded in the check register.

Operation of a Voucher System

There are five steps in the operation of a voucher system:

1. Preparing the voucher
2. Recording the voucher
3. Paying the voucher
4. Posting the voucher and check registers
5. Summarizing unpaid vouchers

1. *Preparing the voucher*   A voucher is prepared for each expenditure. All documents—purchase orders, invoices, and receiving reports—should be attached to the voucher when it is submitted for approval.

   Many companies pay their employees out of a separate payroll account. In such cases, a voucher is prepared to cover the total payroll. The check for the voucher is then deposited in the payroll account, and individual payroll checks are drawn on that account.

2. *Recording the voucher*   All approved vouchers should be recorded in the voucher register, as shown in Exhibit 2. For example, the entry for Voucher 704 corresponds to the information that is presented in Figure 4. Vouchers that do not have appropriate approvals or supporting documents should be investigated immediately.

3. *Paying the voucher*   After a voucher has been recorded, it is placed in an unpaid voucher file. Many companies file their vouchers by due date and by vendor within due date, so that checks can be written at the appropriate times. Such a practice ensures that all discounts for prompt payment can be taken. After payment, vouchers are filed by voucher number.

   A few days before a voucher is due, a check for the correct amount, accompanied by the voucher and supporting documents, is presented to the individual who is authorized to sign checks. The payment is entered in the check register, as shown in Exhibit 3. For example, Belmont Products is paid with check no. 205. Both the date of payment and the check number are then entered in the voucher register on the same line as the corresponding voucher. This information is helpful in the preparation of a schedule of unpaid vouchers (see step **5**).

   Extra steps are required when there has been a purchase return or allowance that applies to a voucher. For example, suppose that part of a shipment of merchandise is defective and is returned to the supplier for credit. At the time the merchandise is returned or the allowance is given, an entry should be made in the general journal debiting Vouchers Payable and crediting Purchases Returns and Allowances, and a notation should be made on the voucher in the voucher file. At the time of payment, only the *net amount* of the voucher—the original amount less the return or allowance and any applicable discount—should be paid and recorded in the check register. Rather than noting the change on the voucher, some companies cancel the original voucher and prepare a new one for the amount to be paid.

4. *Posting the voucher and check registers*   Posting the voucher and check registers is very similar to posting the purchases journal and cash payments journal. The only difference is that the Vouchers Payable account is substituted for the Accounts Payable account.

5. *Summarizing unpaid vouchers*   Because the sum of the vouchers in the unpaid vouchers file should always equal the credit balance of the Vouchers Payable

Exhibit 3
Check Register

Check Register

Date		Check No.	Payee	Voucher No.	Debit Vouchers Payable	Credits Purchases Discounts	Cash
20xx							
July	2	201	Ade Realty	702	400		400
	6	202	Buy Rite Supplies	703	25		25
	6	203	Common Utility	701	75		75
	7	204	J. Jay, Petty Cash	706	50		50
	13	205	Belmont Products	704	1,200	24	1,176
	14	206	Payroll	711	2,200		2,200
	17	207	First National Bank	712	4,250		4,250
	18	208	Belmont Products	707	600	12	588
	22	209	Livingstone Wholesale	710	785	15	770
	30	210	Payroll	716	2,200		2,200
	31	211	J. Jay, Petty Cash	717	47		47
					11,832	51	11,781
					(211)	(513)	(111)

account, a subsidiary ledger is unnecssary. At the end of each accounting period, the unpaid voucher file should be totaled to prove the balance of the Vouchers Payable account. Exhibit 4 shows a schedule of unpaid vouchers, which is a list of all the unpaid vouchers according to the voucher register in Exhibit 2. The voucher register and the check register (Exhibit 3) are reconciled by simple subtraction:

Exhibit 4
Schedule of Unpaid Vouchers

Thomas Appliance Company
Schedule of Unpaid Vouchers
July 31, 20xx

Payee	Voucher Number	Amount
M&M Freight	705	$ 60
M&M Freight	708	30
Mack Truck	709	5,600
Livingstone Wholesale	713	525
Belmont Products	714	400
M&M Freight	715	18
Maintenance Company	718	175
Store Supply Company	719	350
Total Unpaid Vouchers		$7,158

Vouchers Payable credit from the voucher register	$18,990
Less Vouchers Payable debit from the check register	11,832
Vouchers Payable credit balance from the schedule of unpaid vouchers	$ 7,158

Sometimes the account title *Vouchers Payable* appears on a company's balance sheet. The preferred practice, however, is to use the more widely known and accepted term *Accounts Payable*, even when a voucher system is in place.

Chapter Review

REVIEW OF LEARNING OBJECTIVES

Check out ACE, a self-quizzing program on chapter content, at http://college.hmco.com.

1. **Define *internal control*, identify the five components of internal control, and explain seven examples of control activities.** Internal control is the policies and procedures management uses to protect the organization's assets and to ensure the accuracy and reliability of accounting records. It also works to maintain efficient operations and compliance with management's polices. Internal control consists of five components: the control environment, risk assessment, information and communication, control activities, and monitoring. Examples of control activities are proper authorization of transactions; recording transactions to facilitate preparation of financial statements and to establish accountability for assets; use of well-designed documents and records; physical controls; periodic independent verification of records and assets; separation of duties into the functions of authorization, operations, custody of assets, and recordkeeping; and use of sound personnel policies.

2. **Describe the inherent limitations of internal control.** A system of internal control relies on the people who implement it. Thus, the effectiveness of internal control is limited by the people involved. Human error, collusion, and failure to recognize changed conditions all can contribute to a system's failure.

3. **Apply internal control activities to common merchandising transactions.** Certain procedures strengthen internal control over sales, cash receipts, purchases, and cash disbursements. First, the functions of authorization, recordkeeping, and custody should be kept separate. Second, the accounting system should provide for physical protection of assets (especially cash and merchandise inventory), use of banking services, prompt recording and deposit of cash receipts, and payment by check. Third, the people who have access to cash and merchandise inventory should be specifically designated and their number limited. Fourth, employees who have access to cash or merchandise inventory should be bonded. Fifth, the Cash account should be reconciled each month. Unannounced audits of cash on hand should be made by an individual who does not authorize, handle, or record cash transactions.

4. **Demonstrate the control of cash by preparing a bank reconciliation.** The term *bank reconciliation* means accounting for the difference between the balance that appears on the bank statement and the balance in the company's Cash account. It involves adjusting both balances to arrive at the adjusted cash balance. The bank balance is adjusted for outstanding checks and deposits in transit. The depositor's book balance is adjusted for service charges, NSF checks, interest earned, and miscellaneous debits and credits.

SUPPLEMENTAL OBJECTIVES

5. Demonstrate the use of a simple imprest system. An imprest system is a method of controlling small cash expenditures by setting up a fund at a fixed amount and periodically reimbursing the fund by the amount necessary to restore the original balance. A petty cash fund, one example of an imprest system, is established by a debit to Petty Cash and a credit to Cash. It is replenished by debits to various expense or asset accounts and a credit to Cash. Each expenditure should be supported by a petty cash voucher.

6. Define *voucher system* and describe the components of a voucher system. A voucher system is any system that gives documentary proof of and written authorization for business transactions. It consists of authorizations (vouchers), voucher checks, a special journal to record the vouchers (voucher register), and a special journal to record the voucher checks (check register).

7. Describe and carry out the five steps in operating a voucher system. The five steps in operating a voucher system are (1) preparing the voucher, (2) recording the voucher, (3) paying the voucher, (4) posting the voucher and check registers, and (5) summarizing unpaid vouchers.

REVIEW OF CONCEPTS AND TERMINOLOGY

The following concepts and terms were introduced in this chapter:

SO 6 **Audit trail:** The documentary evidence of written approval created by key people as they routinely review and verify an expenditure before payment is made.

LO 4 **Bank reconciliation:** A procedure to account for the difference between the cash balance that appears on the bank statement and the balance of the Cash account in the depositor's records.

LO 1 **Bonding:** The process of carefully checking an employee's background and insuring the company against loss due to theft by that person.

LO 3 **Check:** A written order to a bank to pay the amount specified from funds on deposit.

LO 3 **Check authorization:** A form prepared by the accounting department after it has compared the receiving report for goods received with the purchase order and the invoice.

SO 6 **Check register:** In a voucher system, the journal in which voucher checks are listed as they are written.

LO 1 **Control activities:** Procedures and policies established by management to ensure that the directives related to internal control are met.

LO 1 **Control environment:** The overall attitude, awareness, and actions of management of a business, as reflected in philosophy and operating style, organizational structure, methods of assigning authority and responsibility, and personnel policies and practices.

SO 5 **Imprest system:** A system for controlling small cash disbursements by establishing a fund at a fixed amount and periodically reimbursing the fund by the amount necessary to restore the original cash balance.

LO 1 **Information and communication:** The accounting system established by management and the communication of responsibilities with regard to the accounting system.

LO 1 **Internal control:** All the policies and procedures a company uses to ensure the reliability of financial reporting, compliance with laws and regulations, and the effectiveness and efficiency of operations.

LO 3 **Invoice:** A form sent to the purchaser by the vendor that describes the quantity and price of the goods or services delivered and the terms of payment.

LO 1 **Monitoring:** Management's regular assessment of the quality of internal control.

SO 5 **Petty cash fund:** A fund for making small payments of cash when it is inconvenient to pay by check.

SO 5 **Petty cash voucher:** A form signed by a person who receives a cash payment from a petty cash fund; lists the date, amount, and purpose of the expenditure.

LO 3 **Purchase order:** A form prepared by a company's purchasing department and sent to a vendor. It describes the items ordered; their expected price, terms, and shipping date; and other shipping instructions.

LO 3 **Purchase requisition:** A formal written request for a purchase, prepared by the requesting department in an organization and sent to the purchasing department.

LO 3 **Receiving report:** A form prepared by the receiving department of a company; describes the quantity and condition of goods received.

LO 1 **Risk assessment:** The identification of areas where risks of loss of assets or inaccuracies in the accounting records are high.

SO 6 **Voucher:** A written authorization prepared for each business expenditure when it becomes a liability or obligation to pay.

SO 6 **Voucher check:** A form of check, used in a voucher system, that describes the reason for issuing the check.

SO 6 **Voucher register:** The book of original entry in which vouchers are recorded after they have been approved.

SO 6 **Voucher system:** Any system that gives documentary proof of and written authorization for business transactions.

REVIEW PROBLEM

Bank Reconciliation

LO 4 The information that follows comes from the records of the Maynard Company. The credit memorandum on April 15 is for the collection of a note and includes $100 in

From the Cash Receipts Journal	Page 14
Date	Debit Cash
Apr. 1	560
10	1,440
17	780
30	2,900
	5,680

From the Cash Payments Journal		Page 18
Date	Check Number	Credit Cash
Apr. 4	1716	580
6	1717	800
17	1718	1,050
25	1719	110
		2,540

From the General Ledger

Cash							Account No. 111
						Balance	
Date		Item	Post. Ref.	Debit	Credit	Debit	Credit
Mar.	31	Balance				4,200	
Apr.	30		CR14	5,680		9,880	
	30		CP18		2,540	7,340	

From the Company's Bank Statement

Checks and Other Debits						
Date	Check Number	Amount	Deposits		Balance	
					4/1	4,480
4/5	1714	210	4/2	560	4/2	5,040
4/5	1716	580	4/11	1,440	4/5	4,250
4/12	1717	800	4/15	1,500CM	4/11	5,690
4/28		20SC	4/17	780	4/12	4,890
			4/28	10IN	4/15	6,390
					4/17	7,170
					4/28	7,160

CM—Credit Memo SC—Service Charge IN—Interest

interest. Checks numbered 1714 for $210 and 1715 for $70 were outstanding on March 31.

REQUIRED

1. Prepare a bank reconciliation as of April 30, 20xx.
2. Prepare the necessary journal entries.

Answer to Review Problem

1. Prepare a bank reconciliation.

Maynard Company
Bank Reconciliation
April 30, 20xx

Balance per bank, April 30, 20xx		$ 7,160
Add deposit of April 30, in transit		2,900
		$10,060
Less outstanding checks:		
No. 1715	$ 70	
No. 1718	1,050	
No. 1719	110	1,230
Adjusted bank balance, April 30, 20xx		$ 8,830
Balance per books, April 30, 20xx		$ 7,340
Add: Note collected by bank	$1,400	
Interest income on note	100	
Interest income	10	1,510
		$ 8,850
Less service charge		20
Adjusted book balance, April 30, 20xx		$ 8,830

2. Prepare the journal entries.

Apr. 30	Cash		1,500	
	Notes Receivable			1,400
	Interest Income			100
	Collection of note by bank			
30	Cash		10	
	Interest Income			10
	Interest on bank account			
30	Bank Service Charges Expense		20	
	Cash			20
	Bank service charge for April			

Chapter Assignments

BUILDING YOUR
KNOWLEDGE
FOUNDATION

QUESTIONS

1. Most people think of internal control as a means of making fraud harder to commit and easier to detect. What are some other important purposes of internal control?

2. What are the five components of internal control?

3. What are some examples of control activities?

4. Why is the separation of duties necessary to ensure sound internal control? What does this principle assume about the relationships of employees in a company and the possibility of two or more of them stealing from the company?

5. In a small business, it is sometimes impossible to separate duties completely. What are three other practices that a small business can follow to achieve the objectives of internal control over cash?

6. At Thrifty Variety Store, each sales clerk counts the cash in his or her cash drawer at the end of the day and then removes the cash register tape and prepares a daily cash form, noting any discrepancies. The information is checked by an employee in the cashier's office, who counts the cash, compares the total with the form, and then gives the cash to the cashier. What is the weakness in this system of internal control?

7. How does a movie theater control cash receipts?

8. For each of the following business documents, tell what department or person prepares it and what department or person receives it: purchase requisition, purchase order, invoice, receiving report, check authorization, check, deposit ticket, and bank statement.

9. Why is a bank reconciliation prepared?

10. Assume that each of the following items appeared on a bank reconciliation. Which item would be (1) an addition to the balance on the bank statement, (2) a deduction from the balance on the bank statement, (3) an addition to the balance on the books, or (4) a deduction from the balance on the books? Write the correct number next to each item.

   a. Outstanding checks
   b. Deposits in transit
   c. Bank service charge
   d. NSF check returned with statement
   e. Note collected by bank

   Which of the above items requires a journal entry?

11. What is the purpose of a petty cash fund? From the standpoint of internal control, what is the significance of the level at which the fund is established?

12. What account or accounts are debited when a petty cash fund is established? What account or accounts are debited when a petty cash fund is replenished?

13. What does a credit balance in the Cash Short or Over account indicate?

14. At the end of the day, the combined count of cash for all cash registers in a store reveals a cash shortage of $17.20. In what account would this cash shortage be recorded? Would the account be debited or credited?

15. Should a petty cash fund be replenished as of the last day of the accounting period? Explain your answer.

16. Explain how each of the following can contribute to internal control over cash: (a) a bank reconciliation; (b) a petty cash fund; (c) a cash register with printed receipts; (d) printed, prenumbered cash sales receipts; (e) regular vacations for the cashier; (f) two signatures on checks; and (g) prenumbered checks.

17. What is the greatest advantage of a voucher system?

18. Before a voucher for the purchase of merchandise is approved for payment, three documents should be compared to verify the amount of the liability. What are the three documents?

19. A company that presently uses a general journal, a sales journal, a purchases journal, a cash receipts journal, and a cash payments journal decides to adopt the voucher system. Which of the five journals would be changed or replaced? What would replace them?

20. What is the correct order for filing (a) unpaid vouchers and (b) paid vouchers?

21. When the voucher system is used, is there an Accounts Payable controlling account and an accounts payable subsidiary ledger? Be prepared to explain your answer.

SHORT EXERCISES

SE 1.
LO 1 Purposes of Internal Control

Sara Morgan owns a gourmet coffee shop. Identify four ways in which good internal controls can help her operate her business.

SE 2.
LO 1 Components of Internal Control

Fell Company is a men's clothing store. Indicate whether each of the following components of internal control is part of the (a) control environment, (b) risk assessment, (c) information and communication, (d) control activities, or (e) monitoring.

1. An organization plan calls for separation of duties in the handling of cash sales.
2. Charles Fell emphasizes to employees the importance of following specific procedures in the handling of cash.
3. All cash transactions are recorded automatically in the company's computer when the sales are rung up on the cash register.
4. Management identifies the ways clothes could be stolen.
5. Management observes that employees are following proper procedures.

SE 3.
LO 1 Internal Control
LO 3 Activities

Match each of the following control activities to the appropriate check-writing policy for a small business listed below.

a. Authorization
b. Recording transactions
c. Documents and records
d. Physical controls
e. Periodic independent verification
f. Separation of duties
g. Sound personnel policies

1. The person who writes the checks to pay bills is different from the persons who authorize the payments and who keep the records of the payments.
2. The checks are kept in a locked drawer. The only person who has the key is the person who writes the checks.
3. The person who writes the checks is bonded.

4. Once each month the owner compares and reconciles the amount of money shown in the accounting records with the amount in the bank account.
5. Each check is approved by the owner of the business before it is mailed.
6. A check stub recording pertinent information is completed for each check.
7. Every day, all checks are recorded in the accounting records, using the information on the check stubs.

SE 4.
LO 2 Limitations of Internal Control

Internal control is subject to several inherent limitations. Indicate whether each of the following situations is an example of (a) human error, (b) collusion, (c) changed conditions, or (d) cost-benefit considerations.

1. Effective separation of duties in a restaurant is impractical because the business is too small.
2. The cashier and the manager of a retail shoe store work together to circumvent the internal controls for the purpose of embezzling funds.
3. The cashier in a pizza shop does not understand the procedures for operating the cash register and thus fails to ring up all sales and to count the cash at the end of the day.
4. At a law firm, computer supplies were mistakenly delivered to the reception area instead of the receiving area because the supplier began using a different means of shipment. As a result, the receipt of the supplies was not recorded.

SE 5.
LO 3 Internal Control Documents for Purchases and Payments

Indicate the letter of where each of the following documents would be prepared and the letter of where each document would be sent.

a. Requesting department
b. Purchasing department
c. Receiving department
d. Accounting department
e. Treasurer
f. Supplier

1. Purchase requisition
2. Receiving report
3. Invoice
4. Check authorization
5. Check

SE 6.
LO 4 Elements of a Bank Reconciliation

When a bank reconciliation is performed, is each of the following items (a) an addition to the balance per bank, (b) a deduction from the balance per bank, (c) an addition to the balance per books, or (d) a deduction from the balance per books?

1. Service charges (by the bank)
2. Deposits in transit
3. Interest income (shown on bank statement)
4. Outstanding checks

SE 7.
LO 4 Bank Reconciliation

Prepare a bank reconciliation from the following information.

a. Balance per bank statement as of June 30, $2,586.58
b. Balance per books as of June 30, $1,308.87
c. Deposits in transit, $348.00
d. Outstanding checks, $1,611.11
e. Interest on average balance, $14.60

SE 8.
SO 5 Petty Cash Fund

A petty cash fund was established at $100. At the end of May, the fund has a cash balance of $36 and petty cash vouchers for postage, $29, and office supplies, $34. Prepare the entry on May 31 to replenish the fund.

SE 9.

SO 6 Components of a Voucher System

Identify which of the following statements describes the purpose of a (a) voucher, (b) voucher check, (c) voucher register, and (d) check register.

1. Provides a record of the payment of vouchers
2. Serves as a means of payment and notes the reason for the issuance of the payment
3. Provides a written authorization for each expenditure
4. Provides a record of all authorized expenditures

SE 10.

SO 7 Operation of a Voucher System

Arrange the following actions in the order in which they would take place in the operation of a voucher system.

1. A voucher check is written for each recorded voucher on the due date and is recorded in the check register.
2. A voucher is prepared authorizing each expenditure.
3. A list of unpaid vouchers is prepared to prove the balance of the Vouchers Payable account.
4. Each authorized voucher is recorded in the voucher register.
5. Column totals in the voucher register and the check register and individual items in the Other Accounts column of the voucher register are posted to the appropriate accounts.

EXERCISES

E 1.

LO 1 Use of Accounting Records in Internal Control

Careful scrutiny of accounting records and financial statements can lead to the discovery of fraud or embezzlement. Each of the following situations may indicate a possible breakdown in internal control. Indicate the nature of the possible fraud or embezzlement in each situation.

1. Wages expense for a branch office was 30 percent higher in 20x2 than in 20x1, even though the office was authorized to employ only the same four employees and raises were only 5 percent in 20x2.
2. Sales returns and allowances increased from 5 percent to 20 percent of sales in the first two months of 20x2, after record sales in 20x1 resulted in large bonuses being paid to the sales staff.
3. Gross margin decreased from 40 percent of net sales in 20x1 to 30 percent in 20x2, even though there was no change in pricing. Ending inventory was 50 percent less at the end of 20x2 than it was at the beginning of the year. There is no immediate explanation for the decrease in inventory.
4. A review of daily records of cash register receipts shows that one cashier consistently accepts more discount coupons for purchases than do the other cashiers.

E 2.

LO 1 Internal Control Activities

Colby Strong, who operates a small grocery store, has established the following policies with regard to the check-out cashiers.

1. Each cashier has his or her own cash drawer, to which no one else has access.
2. Each cashier may accept checks for purchases under $50 with proper identification. Checks over $50 must be approved by Strong before they are accepted.
3. Every sale must be rung up on the cash register and a receipt given to the customer. Each sale is recorded on a tape inside the cash register.
4. At the end of each day Strong counts the cash in the drawer and compares it to the amount on the tape inside the cash register.

Identify by letter which of the following conditions for internal control applies to each of the above policies.

a. Transactions are executed in accordance with management's general or specific authorization.
b. Transactions are recorded as necessary to permit preparation of financial statements and maintain accountability for assets.
c. Access to assets is permitted only as allowed by management.
d. At reasonable intervals, the records of assets are compared with the existing assets.

E 3.
LO 1 Internal Control Activities

Lily's Video Store maintains the following policies with regard to purchases of new videotapes at each of its branch stores:

1. Employees are required to take vacations, and the duties of employees are rotated periodically.
2. Once each month a person from the home office visits each branch to examine the receiving records and to compare the inventory of tapes with the accounting records.
3. Purchases of new tapes must be authorized by purchase order in the home office and paid for by the treasurer in the home office. Receiving reports are prepared in each branch and sent to the home office.
4. All new personnel receive one hour of training in how to receive and catalogue new tapes.
5. The company maintains a perpetual inventory system that keeps track of all tapes purchased, sold, and on hand.

Indicate by letter which of the following control activities apply to each of the above policies (some may have several answers).

a. Authorization
b. Recording transactions
c. Documents and records
d. Physical controls
e. Periodic independent verification
f. Separation of duties
g. Sound personnel policies

E 4.
LO 1 Internal Control Evaluation

Developing a convenient means of providing sales representatives with cash for their incidental expenses, such as entertaining a client at lunch, is a problem many companies face. Under one company's plan, the sales representatives receive advances in cash from the petty cash fund. Each advance is supported by an authorization from the sales manager. The representative returns the receipt for the expenditure and any unused cash, which is replaced in the petty cash fund. The cashier of the petty cash fund is responsible for seeing that the receipt and the cash returned equal the advance. When the petty cash fund is reimbursed, the amount of the representative's expenditure is debited to Direct Sales Expense.

What is the weak point in this system? What fundamental principle of internal control is being ignored? What improvement in the procedure can you suggest?

E 5.
LO 1 Internal Control Evaluation

An accountant is responsible for the following procedures: (1) receiving all cash; (2) maintaining the general ledger; (3) maintaining the accounts receivable subsidiary ledger that includes the individual records of each customer; (4) maintaining the journals for recording sales, purchases, and cash receipts; and (5) preparing monthly statements to be sent to customers. As a service to customers and employees, the company allows the accountant to cash checks of up to $50 with money from the cash receipts. When deposits are made, the checks are included in place of the cash receipts.

What weakness in internal control exists in this system?

E 6.
LO 4 Bank Reconciliation

Prepare a bank reconciliation from the following information.

a. Balance per bank statement as of August 31, $8,454.54
b. Balance per books as of August 31, $6,138.04
c. Deposits in transit, $1,134.42
d. Outstanding checks, $3,455.92
e. Bank service charge, $5.00

E 7.
LO 4 Bank Reconciliation:
Missing Data

Compute the correct amounts to replace each letter in the following table.

Balance per bank statement	$ a	$26,700	$945	$5,970
Deposits in transit	1,800	b	150	375
Outstanding checks	4,500	3,000	c	225
Balance per books	10,350	28,200	675	d

E 8.
LO 4   Collection of a Note by a Bank

Hickes Corporation received a notice with its bank statement that the bank had collected a note for $4,000 plus $20 interest from J. Piero and credited Hickes Corporation's account for the total less a collection charge of $30.

Explain the effect that these items have on the bank reconciliation. Prepare a journal entry to record the information on the books of Hickes Corporation.

E 9.
SO 5   Petty Cash Entries

The petty cash fund of Soto Company appeared as follows on July 31, 20xx (the end of the accounting period):

Cash on hand		$122.46
Petty cash vouchers		
Freight in	$45.72	
Postage	42.38	
Flowers for a sick employee	37.00	
Office supplies	52.44	177.54
Total		$300.00

Because there is cash on hand, is there a need to replenish the petty cash fund on July 31? Explain your answer. Prepare, in journal form, an entry to replenish the fund.

E 10.
SO 5   Petty Cash Transactions

A small company maintains a petty cash fund for minor expenditures. In June and July, the following transactions took place:

a. The fund was established in the amount of $100.00 on June 1 from the proceeds of check no. 2707.

b. On June 30, the petty cash fund had cash of $15.46 and the following receipts on hand: postage, $40.00; supplies, $24.94; delivery service, $12.40; and rubber stamp, $7.20. Check no. 2778 was drawn to replenish the fund.

c. On July 31, the petty cash fund had cash of $22.06 and these receipts on hand: postage, $34.20; supplies, $32.84; and delivery service, $6.40. The petty cash custodian could not account for the shortage. Check no. 2847 was drawn to replenish the fund.

Prepare journal entries necessary to record each transaction.

Problems

P 1.

LO 4 **Bank Reconciliation**

The following information is available for Miguel Beirios Company as of March 31, 20xx:

a. Cash on the books as of March 31 amounted to $21,327.08. Cash on the bank statement for the same date was $26,175.73.

b. A deposit of $2,610.47, representing cash receipts of March 31, did not appear on the bank statement.

c. Outstanding checks totaled $1,968.40.

Book Error

d. A check for $960.00 returned with the statement was recorded incorrectly in the check register as $690.00. The check was made for a cash purchase of merchandise.

e. Bank service charges for October amounted to $12.50.

f. The bank collected for Miguel Beirios Company $6,120.00 on a note. The face value of the note was $6,000.00.

g. An NSF check for $91.78 from a client, Lyn Eckstein, came back with the bank statement.

h. The bank mistakenly charged to the company account a check for $425.00 drawn by another company.

i. The bank reported that it had credited the account for $170.00 in interest on the average balance for March.

REQUIRED

1. Prepare a bank reconciliation for Miguel Beirios Company as of March 31, 20xx.

2. Prepare the journal entries necessary to adjust the accounts.

3. State the amount of cash that should appear on the balance sheet as of March 31.

P 2.

LO 4 **Bank Reconciliation**

The following information comes from the records of the Janesville Company:

From the Cash Receipts Journal	Page 22		From the Cash Payments Journal		Page 12
Date	Debit Cash		Date	Check Number	Credit Cash
Feb. 1	1,416		Feb. 1	2076	1,218
8	14,486		3	2077	22
15	13,214		6	2078	6
22	10,487		7	2079	19,400
28	7,802		8	2080	2,620
	47,405		12	2081	9,135
			16	2082	14
			17	2083	186
			18	2084	5,662
					38,263

not in transit

From the General Ledger							
Cash						Account No. 111	
Date		Item	Post. Ref.	Debit	Credit	Balance Debit	Balance Credit
Jan. 31		Balance				10,570	
Feb. 28			CR22	47,405		57,975	
28			CP12		38,263	19,712	

FIRST NATIONAL BANK					Statement of Janesville Company Janesville, OH	
Checks/Debits			Deposits/Credits		Daily Balances	
Posting Date	Check No.	Amount	Posting Date	Amount	Date	Amount
02/02	2056	510	02/02	1,614	02/01	12,416
02/02	2075	32	02/09	14,486	02/02	13,488
02/03	2076	1,218	02/12	1,654CM	02/03	12,266
02/03	2072	4	02/16	13,214	02/05	12,244
02/05	2077	22	02/23	10,487	02/09	26,730
02/10	2079	19,400	02/28	101IN	02/10	6,065
02/10	2074	1,265			02/11	3,445
02/11	2080	2,620			02/12	5,099
02/17	2081	9,135			02/16	18,313
02/17	2082	14			02/17	9,164
02/18		30NSF			02/18	9,134
02/18		10DM			02/18	9,124
02/24	2084	5,662			02/23	19,611
02/28		17SC			02/24	13,949
					02/28	14,033

Code:	CM—Credit Memo	IN—Interest	NSF—Nonsufficient
	DM—Debit Memo	SC—Service Charge	Funds

On the bank statement, the NSF check was received from customer T. Lambeth for merchandise. The debit memo is for the NSF check. The credit memorandum represents a $1,600 note, plus interest, collected by the bank. The February 2 deposit, recorded by Janesville as $1,416 in cash sales, was recorded correctly by the bank as $1,614. On February 1, there were the following outstanding checks: no. 2056 at $510, no. 2072 at $4, no. 2073 at $35, no. 2074 at $1,265, and no. 2075 at $32.

REQUIRED

1. Prepare a bank reconciliation as of February 28, 20xx.
2. Prepare journal entries to update the accounts.
3. What amount should appear on the balance sheet for Cash as of February 28?

P 3.

SO 5 Petty Cash Transactions

The UpTown Theater Company established a petty cash fund in its snack bar so that payment could be made for small deliveries upon receipt. The following transactions occurred in October and November.

Oct. 1   The fund was established in the amount of $200.00 from the proceeds of a check drawn for that purpose.

31   The petty cash fund has cash of $15.71 and receipts on hand for merchandise received, $102.15; freight in, $32.87; laundry service, $42.00; and miscellaneous expense, $7.27. A check was drawn to replenish the fund.

Nov. 30   The petty cash fund has cash of $27.50 and receipts on hand for merchandise, $98.42; freight in, $38.15; laundry service, $42.00; and miscellaneous expense, $3.93. The petty cash custodian cannot account for the excess cash in the fund. A check is drawn to replenish the fund.

REQUIRED

In journal form, prepare the entries necessary to record each of the UpTown Theater Company's transactions.

LO 1 **Internal Control**
LO 3 **Activities**

P 4. Daxell Printers makes printers for personal computers and maintains a factory outlet showroom through which it sells its products to the public. The company's management has set up a system of internal controls over the inventory of printers to prevent theft and to ensure the accuracy of the accounting records.

All printers in inventory at the factory outlet are kept in a secured warehouse behind the showroom, except for the sample printers on display. Only authorized personnel may enter the warehouse. When a customer buys a printer, a sales invoice is written in triplicate by the cashier and is marked "paid." The sales invoices are sequentially numbered, and all must be accounted for. The cashier sends the pink copy of the completed invoice to the warehouse, gives the blue copy to the customer, and keeps the green copy. The customer drives around to the warehouse entrance. The warehouse attendant takes the blue copy of the invoice from the customer and gives the customer the printer and the pink copy of the invoice.

The company maintains a perpetual inventory system for the printers at the outlet. The warehouse attendant at the outlet signs an inventory transfer sheet for each printer received. An accountant at the factory is assigned responsibility for maintaining the inventory records based on copies of the inventory transfer sheets and the sales invoices. The records are updated daily and may be accessed by computer but not modified by the sales personnel and the warehouse attendant. The accountant also sees that all prenumbered inventory transfer sheets are accounted for and compares copies of them with the ones signed by the warehouse attendant. Once every three months the company's internal auditor takes a physical count of the printer inventory and compares the results with the perpetual inventory records.

All new employees are required to read a sales and inventory manual and receive a two-hour training session about the internal controls. They must demonstrate that they can perform the functions required of them.

REQUIRED

Give an example of how each of the following internal control activities is applied to the printer inventory at Daxell Printers' outlet showroom: authorization, recording transactions, documents and records, physical controls, periodic independent verification, separation of duties, and sound personnel procedures. Do not address controls over cash.

SO 7 **Voucher System**
Transactions

P 5. In January, M and S Company had the following transactions affecting vouchers payable:

Jan. 2 Prepared voucher no. 7901, payable to Banyan Realty, for January rent, $700.
2 Issued check no. 5501 for voucher no. 7901.
3 Prepared voucher no. 7902, payable to Fishman Company for merchandise, $4,200, invoice dated January 2, terms 2/10, n/30, FOB destination.
5 Prepared voucher no. 7903, payable to Holiday Supply House, for supplies, $650, to be allocated $450 to Store Supplies and $200 to Office Supplies, terms n/10.
6 Prepared voucher no. 7904, payable to City Power and Light, for monthly service, $314.
6 Issued check no. 5502 for voucher no. 7904.
9 Prepared voucher no. 7905, payable to Crandall Company, for merchandise, $1,700, invoice dated January 7, terms 2/10, n/60, FOB shipping point. Crandall Company prepaid freight charges of $146 and added them to the invoice, for a total of $1,846.
12 Issued check no. 5503 for voucher no. 7902.
15 Issued check no. 5504 for voucher no. 7903.
16 Prepared voucher no. 7906, payable to Lopez Company, for merchandise, $970, invoice dated January 14, terms 2/10, n/30, FOB shipping point.
16 Prepared voucher no. 7907, payable to Kidd Freight Company, for the shipment from Lopez Company, $118, terms n/10 EOM.
17 Issued check no. 5505 for voucher no. 7905.
18 Returned $220 in defective merchandise to Lopez Company for credit.
22 Prepared voucher no. 7908, payable to Holiday Supply House, for supplies, $375, to be allocated $200 to Store Supplies and $175 to Office Supplies, terms n/10.

Jan. 23 Prepared voucher no. 7909, payable to Expo National Bank, for a 90-day note that is due, $5,000 plus $150 interest.

23 Issued check no. 5506 for voucher no. 7909.

24 Issued check no. 5507 for voucher no. 7906, less the return on January 18.

26 Prepared voucher no. 7910, payable to Crandall Company, for merchandise, $2,100, invoice dated January 25, terms 2/10, n/30, FOB shipping point. Crandall Company prepaid freight charges of $206 and added them to the invoice, for a total of $2,306.

27 Prepared voucher no. 7911, payable to Midlands Telephone Company, $37. Payments for telephone are considered a utilities expense.

27 Issued check no. 5508 for voucher no. 7911.

30 Prepared voucher no. 7912, payable to Payroll account, for monthly payroll, $17,200, to be allocated $13,300 to Sales Salaries Expense and $3,900 to Office Salaries Expense.

30 Issued check no. 5509 for voucher no. 7912.

31 Prepared voucher no. 7913, payable to Chang Maintenance Company, $360, to be allocated two-thirds to Maintenance Expense, Selling, and one-third to Maintenance Expense, Office.

REQUIRED

1. Record the transactions in a voucher register (Page 18), a check register (Page 28), and a general journal (Page 25). Record purchases at gross amounts. Total the voucher and check registers.

2. Prepare a Vouchers Payable account (211), and post those portions of the journal and register entries that affect this account. Assume that the December 31 balance of Vouchers Payable was zero.

3. Prove the balance of the Vouchers Payable account by preparing a schedule of unpaid vouchers.

ALTERNATE PROBLEMS

P 6.

LO 1 Internal Control
LO 3 Activities

Mayamura Sports is a small neighborhood sporting goods store. The store's owner, Sara Mayamura, has set up a system of internal control over sales to prevent theft and to ensure the accuracy of the accounting records.

When a customer buys a product, the cashier writes up a sales invoice that describes the purchase, including the total price. All sales invoices are prenumbered sequentially.

If the sale is by credit card, the cashier runs the credit card through a scanner that verifies the customer's credit. The scanner prints out a receipt and a slip for the customer to sign. The signed slip is put in the cash register, and the customer is given the receipt and a copy of the sales invoice.

If the sale is by cash or check, the cashier rings it up on the cash register and gives change, if appropriate. Checks must be written for the exact amount of the purchase and must be accompanied by identification. The sale is recorded on a tape inside the cash register that cannot be accessed by the cashier. The cash register may be locked with a key. The cashier is the only person other than Mayamura who has a key. The cash register must be locked when the cashier is not present. Refunds are made only with Mayamura's approval, are recorded on prenumbered credit memorandum forms, and are rung up on the cash register.

At the end of each day, Mayamura counts the cash and checks in the cash register and compares the total with the amount recorded on the tape inside the register. Mayamura totals all the signed credit card slips and ensures that the total equals the amount recorded by the scanner. Mayamura also makes sure that she accounts for all sales invoices and credit memoranda. Mayamura prepares a bank deposit ticket for the cash, checks, and signed credit card slips, less $40 in change to be put in the cash register the next day, and removes the record of the day's credit card sales from the scanner. All the records are placed in an envelope that is sealed and sent to the company's accountant for verification and recording in the company records. On the way home, Mayamura places the bank deposit in the night deposit box.

The company hires experienced cashiers who are bonded. The owner spends the first half-day with new cashiers, showing them the procedures and observing their work.

REQUIRED

Give an example of how each of the following control activities is applied to internal control over sales and cash at Mayamura Sports: authorization, recording transactions, documents and records, physical controls, periodic independent verification, separation of duties, and sound personnel procedures. Do not address controls over inventory.

P 7.

LO 4 Bank Reconciliation

The following information is available for Sagan Company as of June 30, 20xx:

a. Cash on the books as of June 30 amounted to $56,837.64. Cash on the bank statement for the same date was $70,858.54.

b. A deposit of $7,124.92, representing cash receipts of June 30, did not appear on the bank statement.

c. Outstanding checks totaled $3,646.82.

d. A check for $1,210.00 returned with the statement was recorded in the cash payments journal in error as $1,012.00. The check was for advertising.

e. Bank service charges for June amounted to $13.00.

f. The bank collected for Sagan Company $18,200.00 on a note. The face value of the note was $18,000.00.

g. An NSF check for $560.00 from a customer, Louise Bryant, was returned with the statement. The bank charged a $10.00 fee.

h. The bank mistakenly deducted a check for $400.00 drawn by Sherod Corporation.

i. The bank reported a credit of $480.00 for interest on the average balance.

REQUIRED

1. Prepare a bank reconciliation for Sagan Company as of June 30, 20xx.

2. Prepare the journal entries necessary from the reconciliation.

3. State the amount of cash that should appear on the balance sheet as of June 30.

P 8.

SO 5 Petty Cash Transactions

A small company maintains a petty cash fund for minor expenditures. The following transactions occurred in November and December.

a. The fund was established in the amount of $600.00 on November 1 from the proceeds of check no. 1515.

b. On November 30, the petty cash fund had cash of $92.76 and the following receipts on hand: postage, $240.00; supplies, $149.64; delivery service, $74.40; and rubber stamp, $43.20. Check no. 1527 was drawn to replenish the fund.

c. On December 31, the petty cash fund had cash of $132.36 and the following receipts on hand: postage, $205.20; supplies, $197.04; and delivery service, $38.40. The petty cash custodian could not account for the shortage. Check no. 1621 was written to replenish the fund.

REQUIRED

Prepare the journal entries necessary to record each transaction.

EXPANDING YOUR CRITICAL THINKING, COMMUNICATION, AND INTERPERSONAL SKILLS

SKILLS DEVELOPMENT

Conceptual Analysis

SD 1.

LO 1 **System for Control of**
LO 2 **Supplies**
LO 3

Industrial Services Company provides maintenance services to factories in the West Bend, Wisconsin, area. The company, which buys large amounts of cleaning supplies, has consistently been over budget in its expenditures for those items. In the past, supplies were left open in the warehouse so that the on-site supervisors could take them as needed. Periodically, a clerk in the accounting department ordered additional supplies from a long-time supplier. The only records maintained were records of purchases. Once a year, an inventory of supplies was made for the preparation of the financial statements.

To solve the budgetary problem, management recently implemented a new system for controlling and purchasing supplies. Under the new system, the cleaning supplies were placed in a secured storeroom overseen by a supplies clerk. Supplies are requisitioned by the supervisors of specific jobs. Each job receives a predetermined amount of supplies based on a study of the needs of that job. In the storeroom, the supplies clerk notes the levels of supplies and completes a purchase requisition when supplies are needed. The purchase requisition goes to the purchasing clerk, a new position, who is solely responsible for authorizing purchases and who prepares the purchase orders for suppliers. The prices of several suppliers are constantly monitored to ensure that the lowest price is obtained. When supplies are received from a vendor, the supplies clerk checks them in and prepares a receiving report, which is sent to accounting, where each payment to a supplier is documented by the purchase requisition, the purchase order, and the receiving report. The accounting department also maintains a record of supplies inventory, supplies requisitioned by supervisors, and supplies received. Once each month, a physical inventory of cleaning supplies in the storeroom is made by the warehouse manager and compared against the supplies inventory records maintained by the accounting department.

Demonstrate how the new system applies or does not apply to each of the seven control activities described in this chapter. Is each new control activity an improvement over the old system?

Ethical Dilemma

SD 2.

LO 4 **Inflating the Cash Account and the Bank Reconciliation**

Jean McGuire is the accountant for *Slate Company*. Among her responsibilities are the payment of bills and the preparation of the monthly bank reconciliation. On December 31, year end, McGuire's boss, Lydia Grunwald, instructed her to write checks for all the outstanding bills so that their amounts could be deducted for income tax purposes. Since payment of all the outstanding bills would have overdrawn the company's checking account by $78,000, McGuire had to hold the checks until sufficient funds were received. On January 2, a check for $100,000 was received from a customer in payment of an account receivable. Grunwald did not want to report the negative balance of cash on the previous year's balance sheet. She thus instructed McGuire to record the receipt as of December 31 and to show the check as a deposit in transit on the bank reconciliation. The checks written by McGuire on December 31 were mailed on January 3 and listed as outstanding checks on the bank reconciliation. Which, if any, of

 Cash Flow   CD-ROM   Communication   Critical Thinking   Ethics   General Ledger   Group Activity   Hot Links to Real Companies   International   Internet   Key Ratio   Memo   Spreadsheet

McGuire's and Grunwald's actions are unethical? Who may be harmed by their actions? What alternative actions could McGuire have taken?

Research Activity

SD 3.

LO 1 **Internal Controls**
LO 3

Identify a retail business in your local shopping area or a local shopping mall, such as a bookstore, a clothing shop, a gift shop, a grocery, a hardware store, or a car dealership. Speak to someone who is knowledgeable about the store's internal controls. Find out the answers to the following questions and be prepared to discuss your findings in class.

1. How does the company protect against inventory theft and loss?
2. What control activities, including authorization, recording transactions, documents and records, physical controls, periodic independent verification, separation of duties, and sound personnel policies, does the company use?
3. Can you see these control procedures in use?

Group Activity: Assign teams to carry out the above assignment.

Decision-Making Practice

SD 4.

LO 1 **Identifying Internal**
LO 2 **Control Weaknesses**
LO 3

Fleet's is a retail store with several departments. Its internal control procedures for cash sales and purchases are described in the following paragraphs.

Cash sales. Every cash sale is rung up on the department cash register by the sales clerk assigned to that department. The cash register produces a sales slip that is given to the customer with the merchandise. A carbon copy of the sales ticket is made on a continuous tape locked inside the machine. At the end of each day, a "total" key is pressed, and the machine prints the total sales for the day on the continuous tape. Then, the sales clerk unlocks the machine, reads the total sales figure, and makes the entry in the accounting records for the day's cash sales. Next, she counts the cash in the drawer, places the basic $100 change fund back in the drawer, and gives the cash received to the cashier. Finally, the sales clerk files the cash register tape and is ready for the next day's business.

Purchases. All goods are ordered by the purchasing agent upon the requests of the various department heads. When the goods are received, the receiving clerk prepares a receiving report in triplicate. One copy is sent to the purchasing agent, one copy is forwarded to the department head, and one copy is kept by the receiving clerk. Invoices are forwarded immediately to the accounting department to ensure payment before the discount period elapses. After payment, the invoice is forwarded to the purchasing agent for comparison with the purchase order and the receiving report and is then returned to the accounting office for filing.

Fleet's president has asked you to evaluate these control procedures for cash sales and purchases. Write a memorandum to the president identifying the significant internal control weakness for each of the above situations and in each case recommend changes that would improve the current system.

FINANCIAL REPORTING AND ANALYSIS

Interpreting Financial Reports

FRA 1.

LO 1 **Effect of E-commerce**
LO 3 **on Internal**
Control

Many retailers, such as *Crate & Barrel, Eddie Bauer Inc.*, and *Sears, Roebuck and Co.*, are selling to customers on the Internet. In what ways do Internet transactions differ from retail store transactions? How will each difference affect internal controls?

Group Activity: Divide the class into teams and ask each team to identify as many differences as they can. Debrief by asking each team to give one difference and describe its effect on internal controls. Write the results on the board. Continue until no team can add another difference.

International Company

FRA 2.

LO 1 Internal Control and Accounting Education in a Developing Country

Zambia, a country in southern Africa, has 8.5 million inhabitants. It has an elected government and is moving toward capital markets through privatization of government-owned business. For example, the government-owned beer company was recently sold to private interests for $13 million. One national priority calls for the training of competent professional accountants, and the ***Zambian Centre for Accountancy Studies*** has been established with the assistance of the World Bank. There are only about 250 native-born certified accountants in all of Zambia. A state with a comparable population in the United States would have more than 20,000 certified public accountants. One reason for placing a priority on the training of accountants is the importance of good internal controls to the development of a country like Zambia. What are the purposes of internal control, and what are some ways in which such controls would aid the development of a country like Zambia? What are some other reasons for making accounting education a high national priority?

Toys "R" Us Annual Report

FRA 3.

LO 1 Internal Control
LO 3 Considerations

Refer to the annual report for Toys "R" Us in the supplement to Chapter 6. How many stores did Toys "R" Us operate in the United States and abroad in the most recent year? The typical store contains a showroom where customers wheel grocery carts down aisles to select toys and other products for purchase, a warehouse where larger items may be picked up after purchase, a bank of cash registers, and a service desk where returns and other unusual transactions can be authorized. Identify the main activities or transactions for which Toys "R" Us management would need to establish internal controls in each new store. Discuss the objectives of internal controls in each case.

Fingraph® Financial Analyst™

This activity is not appropriate for this chapter.

Internet Case

FRA 4.

LO 1 Comparison of Reports of Management on Internal Control

Through the Needles Accounting Resource Center at http://college.hmco.com, go to the annual reports in the web sites for ***Tandy Corporation*** and ***Circuit City Stores, Inc.*** Find the "Report of Management on Internal Accounting Controls" in the case of Tandy and "Management's Report" in the case of Circuit City in the companies' respective annual reports. A portion of the Circuit City's report is quoted in the text. Compare management statements. What similarities do you find in the content? What is a difference in the reports? Which, in your opinion, does a better job of explaining what management has done to fulfill its responsibility of internal control?

ENDNOTES

1. Kyle Pope, "Dell Refocuses on Groundwork to Cope with Rocketing Sales," *The Wall Street Journal*, June 18, 1993.
2. Circuit City Stores, *Annual Report*, 1998.
3. *Professional Standards*, Vol. 1 (New York: American Institute of Certified Public Accountants, June 1, 1999), Sec. AU 322.07.
4. Ibid., Sec. AU 325.16.
5. "1998 Fraud Survey," KPMG Peat Marwick, 1998.
6. Lynnette Khalfani, "Information-Destruction Finds Lucrative Business in Going to Waste," *The Wall Street Journal*, December 6, 1996.
7. "B-to-B Communities," *Business 2.0*, December 1999.

9

Short-Term Liquid Assets

LEARNING OBJECTIVES

1 Identify and explain the management issues related to short-term liquid assets.

2 Explain *cash*, *cash equivalents*, and the importance of electronic funds transfer.

3 Account for short-term investments.

4 Define *accounts receivable* and apply the allowance method of accounting for uncollectible accounts, using both the percentage of net sales method and the accounts receivable aging method.

5 Define and describe a *promissory note*, and make calculations and journal entries involving promissory notes.

Pioneer Electronic Corporation A company must use its assets to maximize income earned while maintaining liquidity. Pioneer Electronic Corporation, a leading provider of electronics for home, commerce, and industry, manages about $2.4 billion in short-term liquid assets. Short-term liquid assets are financial assets that arise from cash transactions, the investment of cash, and the extension of credit. What is the composition of these assets? Why are they important to Pioneer's management?

Pioneer's short-term liquid assets (in millions), as reported on the balance sheet in this Japanese company's annual report, are shown here.[1] These assets make up almost 43 percent of Pioneer's total assets, and they are very important to the company's strategy for meeting its goals. Effective asset management techniques ensure that these assets remain liquid and usable for the company's operations.

A commonly used ratio for measuring the adequacy of short-term liquid assets is the quick ratio. The quick ratio is the ratio of short-term liquid assets to current liabilities. Because Pioneer's current liabilities are (in millions) ¥202,735 ($1,912.6), its quick ratio is 1.26, which is computed as follows:

$$\text{Quick Ratio} = \frac{\text{Short-Term Liquid Assets}}{\text{Current Liabilities}} = \frac{\$2,409,400,000}{\$1,912,600,000} = 1.26$$

A quick ratio of about 1.0 is a common benchmark. However, it is more important to look at industry characteristics and at the trends for a particular company to see if the ratio is improving or not. A lower ratio may mean that a company is a very good manager of its short-term liquid assets. Pioneer has maintained a quick ratio of over 1.0 for several years. Through

Financial Highlights

(In millions)

	Yen	Dollars
Cash and Cash Equivalents	¥151,805	$1,432.1
Short-Term Investments	1,606	15.1
Accounts Receivable, Net of Allowances of ¥5,077 ($47.9)	94,813	894.5
Notes Receivable	7,174	67.7
Total Short-Term Liquid Assets	¥255,398	$2,409.4

good cash management, the company has not tied up excess funds in quick assets relative to current liabilities. This chapter emphasizes management of, and accounting for, short-term liquid assets to achieve liquidity.

Management Issues Related to Short-Term Liquid Assets

OBJECTIVE

1 Identify and explain the management issues related to short-term liquid assets

The management of short-term liquid assets is critical to the goal of providing adequate liquidity. In dealing with short-term liquid assets, management must address three key issues: managing cash needs during seasonal cycles, setting credit policies, and financing receivables.

Managing Cash Needs During Seasonal Cycles

Most companies experience seasonal cycles of business activity during the year. These cycles involve some periods when sales are weak and other periods when sales are strong. There are also periods when expenditures are greater and periods when expenditures are smaller. In some companies, such as toy companies, college publishers, amusement parks, construction companies, and sports equipment companies, the cycles are dramatic, but all companies experience them to some degree.

Seasonal cycles require careful planning of cash inflows, cash outflows, borrowing, and investing. For example, Figure 1 might represent the seasonal cycles for a home improvement company like The Home Depot, Inc. As you can see, cash receipts from sales are highest in the late spring, summer, and fall because that is when most people make home improvements. Sales are relatively low in the winter months. On the other hand, cash expenditures are highest in late winter and spring as the company builds up inventory for spring and summer selling. During the late summer, fall, and winter, the company has excess cash on hand that it needs to invest in a way that will earn a return, but still permit access as needed. During the late spring and early summer, the company needs to plan for short-term borrowing to tide it over until cash receipts pick up later in the year. The discussion in this

FOCUS ON BUSINESS PRACTICE

Big buyers often have significant power over small suppliers, and their cash management decisions can cause severe cash flow problems for the little companies that depend on them. For instance, in an effort to control costs and optimize cash flow, Ameritech Corp. told 70,000 suppliers that it would begin paying its bills in 45 days instead of 30 days. Other large com-

panies routinely take 90 days or more to pay. Small suppliers are so anxious to get the big companies' business that they fail to realize the implications of the deals they make until it is too late. When Earthly Elements, Inc., accepted a $10,000 order for dried floral gifts from a national home shopping network, management was ecstatic because the deal increased sales by 25 percent. But in four months, the resulting cash crunch forced the company to close down. When the shopping network finally paid for the big order six months later, it was too late to revive Earthly Elements.[2]

Figure 1
Seasonal Cycles and Cash
Requirements for a Home
Improvement Company

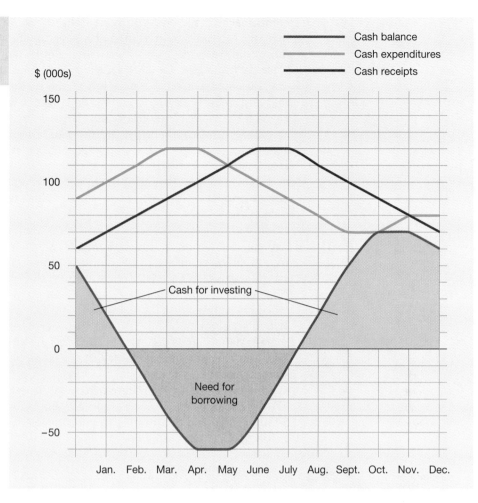

chapter of accounting for cash, cash equivalents, and short-term investments is directly related to managing for the seasonal cycles of a business.

Setting Credit Policies

Companies that sell on credit do so in order to be competitive and to increase sales. In setting credit terms, management must keep in mind both the terms the company's competitors are offering and the needs of its customers. Obviously,

FOCUS ON BUSINESS PRACTICE

To be profitable, not only must a company sell goods and services, it also must generate cash flows by collecting on those sales. When Bally Total Fitness, the nation's largest health-club chain, announced a successful new membership program that generated $100 million in new revenue, the stock market responded by pushing up the price of the company's stock. Under the new membership program, a $1,300 three-year membership could be paid in monthly installments. It quickly became apparent, however, that as much as 40 percent of the memberships were not paid or were canceled. The memberships were not profitable and the company's stock dropped by half. The Securities and Exchange Commission (SEC) has now told health clubs to stop recognizing memberships as revenue until payments are received.[3]

companies that sell on credit want to have customers who will pay the debts they incur. To increase the likelihood of selling only to customers who will pay on time, most companies develop control procedures and maintain a credit department. The credit department's responsibilities include the examination of each person or company that applies for credit and the approval or rejection of a credit sale to that customer. Typically, the credit department will ask for information about the customer's financial resources and debts. It may also check personal references and credit bureaus for further information. Then, based on the information it has gathered, the credit department will decide whether or not to extend credit to the customer.

Two common measures of the effect of a company's credit policies are **receivable turnover** and **average days' sales uncollected**. The receivable turnover reflects the relative size of a company's accounts receivable and the success of its credit and collection policies. It may also be affected by external factors, such as seasonal conditions and interest rates. It shows how many times, on average, the receivables were turned into cash during the accounting period. The average days' sales uncollected is a related measure that shows, on average, how long it takes to collect accounts receivable.

Turnover ratios usually consist of one balance sheet account and one income statement account. The receivable turnover is computed by dividing net sales by average net accounts receivable. Theoretically, the numerator should be net credit sales, but the amount of net credit sales is rarely made available in public reports, so total net sales is used. American Greetings Corp. is the second largest producer of greeting cards in the United States. The company's net sales in 2000 were $2,175,236,000, and its net trade accounts receivable in 2000 and 1999 were $430,825,000 and $390,740,000, respectively.[4] Its receivable turnover is computed as follows:

$$\text{Receivable Turnover} = \frac{\text{Net Sales}}{\text{Average Net Accounts Receivable}}$$

$$= \frac{\$2,175,236,000}{(\$430,825,000 + \$390,740,000) \div 2}$$

$$= \frac{\$2,175,236,000}{\$410,782,500} = 5.3 \text{ times}$$

To find the average days' sales uncollected, the number of days in a year is divided by the receivable turnover, as follows:

$$\text{Average Days' Sales Uncollected} = \frac{365 \text{ days}}{\text{Receivable Turnover}} = \frac{365 \text{ days}}{5.3} = 68.9 \text{ days}$$

American Greetings turns its receivables 5.3 times a year, for an average of every 68.9 days. While this turnover period is longer than those of many companies, it is not unusual for greeting card companies because their credit terms allow retail outlets to receive and sell cards for various holidays, such as Easter, Thanksgiving, and Christmas, before paying for them. This example demonstrates the need to interpret ratios in light of the specific industry's practice.

As may be seen from Figure 2, the receivable turnover ratio varies substantially from industry to industry. Grocery stores, for example, have a high turnover because that type of business has few receivables; the turnover in interstate trucking is 10.8 times because the typical credit terms in that industry are 30 days. The turnover in the pharmaceutical industry and computer industry is lower because those industries tend to have longer credit terms.

Figure 2
Receivable Turnover for Selected Industries

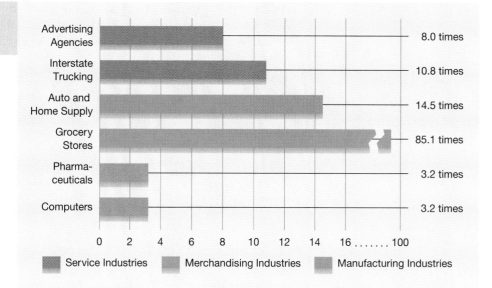

Advertising Agencies	8.0 times
Interstate Trucking	10.8 times
Auto and Home Supply	14.5 times
Grocery Stores	85.1 times
Pharmaceuticals	3.2 times
Computers	3.2 times

Service Industries Merchandising Industries Manufacturing Industries

Source: Data from Dun and Bradstreet, *Industry Norms and Key Business Ratios,* 1999–2000.

Financing Receivables

Financial flexibility is important to most companies. Companies that have significant amounts of assets tied up in accounts receivable may be unwilling or unable to wait until the receivables are collected to receive the cash they represent. Many companies have set up finance companies to help their customers finance the purchase of their products. For example, Ford Motor Co. has Ford Motor Credit Co. (FMCC), General Motors Corp. has General Motors Acceptance Corp. (GMAC), and Sears, Roebuck and Co. has Sears Roebuck Acceptance Corp. (SRAC). Some companies borrow funds by pledging their accounts receivable as collateral. If a company does not pay back its loan, the creditor can take the collateral, in this case the accounts receivable, and convert it to cash to satisfy the loan.

Companies can also raise funds by selling or transferring accounts receivable to another entity, called a **factor**. The sale or transfer of accounts receivable, called **factoring**, can be done with or without recourse. *Without recourse* means that the factor that buys the accounts receivable bears any losses from uncollectible accounts. A company's acceptance of credit cards like Visa, MasterCard, or American Express is an example of factoring without recourse because the credit card issuers accept the risk of nonpayment.

With recourse means that the seller of the receivables is liable to the purchaser if the receivable is not collected. The factor, of course, charges a fee for its service. The fee for sales with recourse is usually about 1 percent of the accounts receivable. The fee is higher for sales without recourse because the factor's risk is greater. In accounting terminology, the seller of the receivables with recourse is said to be contingently liable. A **contingent liability** is a potential liability that can develop into a real liability if a possible subsequent event occurs. A contingent liability generally requires note disclosure in the notes to the financial statements. In this case, the subsequent event would be nonpayment of the receivable by the customer.

Circuit City Stores, Inc., is one of the nation's largest electronics, appliance, and car retailers. To sell its products, the company offers its customers generous terms through its installment programs, under which customers pay over a number of months. The company is growing rapidly and needs the cash from these installment receivables sooner than the customers have agreed to pay. To generate cash immediately from these receivables, the company sells them. After generating $160.8 million from selling receivables in 2000, the cumulative total amount of receivables sold but not yet collected was $2.844 billion, as follows:[5]

Financial Highlights	
(Amounts in thousands)	2000
Securitized receivables	$2,844,377
Interest retained by company	(163,094)
Net receivables sold	$2,681,283
Net receivables sold with recourse	229,000
Net receivables sold without recourse	$2,452,283

Securitized receivables are those receivables sold both with and without recourse. The interest retained by the company is in effect a provision or allowance for customers who do not pay. The finance charges paid by customers on the accounts go to the buyers of the receivables to cover interest costs, uncollectible accounts, and servicing fees. The net receivables sold with recourse represents a contingent liability for the company. If the receivables are paid as expected, Circuit City will have no further liability.

Another method of financing receivables is through the **discounting**, or selling, of promissory notes held as notes receivable. Selling notes receivable is called discounting because the bank deducts the interest from the maturity value of the note to determine the proceeds. The holder of the note (usually the payee) endorses the note and delivers it to the bank. The bank expects to collect the maturity value of the note (principal plus interest) on the maturity date but also has recourse against the endorser or seller of the note. If the maker fails to pay, the endorser is liable to the bank for payment. The endorser has a contingent liability in the amount of the discounted notes plus interest that must be disclosed in the notes to the financial statements.

Cash and Cash Equivalents

OBJECTIVE

2 Explain *cash, cash equivalents,* and the importance of electronic funds transfer

The annual report of Pioneer Electronic Corporation refers to *cash and cash equivalents.* Of the two terms, *cash* is the easier to understand. It is the most liquid of all assets and the most readily available to pay debts. On the balance sheet, **cash** normally consists of currency and coins on hand, checks and money orders from customers, and deposits in bank checking accounts. Cash may also include a **compensating balance,** an amount that is not entirely free to be spent. A compensating balance is a minimum amount that a bank requires a company to keep in its bank account as part of a credit-granting arrangement. Such an arrangement restricts cash, increases the effective interest of the loan, and may reduce a company's liquidity. Therefore, the SEC requires companies to disclose the amount of any compensating balances in a note to the financial statements.

The term *cash equivalents* is a little harder to understand. At times a company may find that it has more cash on hand than it needs to pay current obligations. Excess cash should not remain idle, especially during periods of high interest rates. Thus, management may periodically invest idle funds in time deposits or certificates of deposit at banks and other financial institutions, in government securities such as U.S. Treasury notes, or in other securities. Such actions are rightfully called investments. However, if the investments have a term of 90 days or less when they are purchased, they are called **cash equivalents** because the funds revert to cash so quickly that they are regarded as cash on the balance sheet. For example, Verizon (formerly Bell Atlantic Corp.) follows this practice. Its policy is stated as follows: "The Company considers all highly liquid investments with a maturity of 90 days or less when purchased to be cash equivalents. Cash equivalents are stated at cost, which approximates market value."[6] A survey of 600 large U.S. corporations found that 57 of them, or 9 percent, used the term *cash* as the balance sheet caption and 502, or 84 percent, used the phrase *cash and cash equivalents* or *cash and equivalents*. Thirty-one companies, or 5 percent, combined cash with marketable securities.[7] The average amount of cash held can also vary by industry.

Most companies need to keep some currency and coins on hand. Currency and coins are needed for cash registers and for paying expenses that are impractical to pay by check. A company may need to advance cash to sales representatives for travel expenses, to divisions to cover their payrolls, and to individual employees to cash their paychecks.

One way to control a cash fund or cash advances is through the use of an **imprest system**. A common form of imprest system is a petty cash fund, which is established at a fixed amount. Each cash payment from the fund is documented by a receipt. Then the fund is periodically reimbursed, based on the documented expenditures, by the exact amount necessary to restore its original cash balance. The person responsible for the petty cash fund must always be able to account for its contents by having cash and receipts whose total equals the originally fixed amount.

Banking and Electronic Funds Transfer

Banks greatly help businesses to control both cash receipts and cash disbursements. Banks serve as safe depositories for cash, negotiable instruments, and other valuable business documents, such as stocks and bonds. The checking accounts that banks provide improve control by minimizing the amount of currency a company needs to keep on hand and by supplying permanent records of all cash payments. Banks can also serve as agents in a variety of transactions, such as the collection and payment of certain kinds of debts and the exchange of foreign currencies.

Many companies commonly conduct transactions through a means of electronic communication called **electronic funds transfer (EFT)**. Instead of writing checks to pay for purchases or to repay loans, the company arranges to have cash transferred electronically from its bank to another company's bank. Wal-Mart Stores,

FOCUS ON BUSINESS ETHICS

To combat the laundering of money by drug dealers, U.S. law requires banks to report cash transactions in excess of $10,000. Not to be deterred, money launderers began to sidestep the regulation by electronically transferring funds from overseas to banks, money exchanges, and brokerage firms. In response, the Treasury Department set up rules that require those institutions to keep records about the sources and recipients of all electronic transfers. Given the widespread use of electronic transfers in today's business world, it is questionable how much effect this action will have in the ongoing battle against drugs. Looking for drug money by combing the millions of transfers that occur every day is "like looking for a needle in a haystack."[8]

Inc., for example, operates the largest electronic funds network in the retail industry and makes 75 percent of its payments to suppliers by this method. The actual cash, of course, is not transferred. For the banks, an electronic transfer is simply a bookkeeping entry.

In serving customers, banks may also offer automated teller machines (ATMs) for making deposits, withdrawing cash, transferring funds among accounts, and paying bills. Large consumer banks like Citibank, BankOne, and Bank of America will process hundreds of thousands of ATM transactions each week. Many banks also give customers the option of paying bills over the telephone and with *debit cards*. When a customer makes a retail purchase using a debit card, the amount of the purchase is deducted directly from the buyer's bank account. The bank usually documents debit card transactions for the retailer, but the retailer must develop new internal controls to ensure that the transactions are recorded properly and that unauthorized transfers are not permitted. It is expected that within a few years 25 percent of all retail activity will be handled electronically.

Short-Term Investments

OBJECTIVE

3 Account for short-term investments

When investments have a maturity of more than 90 days but are intended to be held only until cash is needed for current operations, they are called **short-term investments** or **marketable securities**.

Investments that are intended to be held for more than one year are called *long-term investments*. Long-term investments are reported in an investments section of the balance sheet, not in the current assets section. Although long-term investments may be just as marketable as short-term assets, management intends to hold them for an indefinite period of time.

Securities that may be held as short-term or long-term investments fall into three categories, as specified by the Financial Accounting Standards Board: held-to-maturity securities, trading securities, and available-for-sale securities.[9] Trading securities are classified as short-term investments. Held-to-maturity securities and available-for-sale securities, depending on their length to maturity or management's intent to hold them, may be classified as either short-term or long-term investments. The three categories of securities when held as short-term investments are discussed here.

Held-to-Maturity Securities

Held-to-maturity securities are debt securities that management intends to hold to their maturity date and whose cash value is not needed until that date. Such securities are recorded at cost and valued on the balance sheet at cost adjusted for the effects of interest. For example, suppose that on December 1, 20x1, Lowes Company pays $97,000 for U.S. Treasury bills, which are short-term debt of the federal government. The bills will mature in 120 days at $100,000. The following entry would be made by Lowes:

20x1			
Dec. 1	Short-Term Investments	97,000	
	Cash		97,000
	Purchase of U.S. Treasury bills that mature in 120 days		

A = L + OE
+
−

At Lowes' year end on December 31, the entry to accrue the interest income earned to date would be as follows:

A = L + OE
\+ \+

20x1
Dec. 31   Short-Term Investments   750
                Interest Income   750
                Accrual of interest on U.S. Treasury bills
                $3,000 × 30/120 = $750

On December 31, the U.S. Treasury bills would be shown on the balance sheet as a short-term investment at their amortized cost of $97,750 ($97,000 + $750). When Lowes receives the maturity value on March 31, 20x2, the entry is as follows:

A = L + OE
\+ \+
\-

20x2
Mar. 31   Cash   100,000
                   Short-Term Investments   97,750
                   Interest Income   2,250
                   Receipt of cash at maturity of
                   U.S. Treasury bills and recognition
                   of related income

Trading Securities

Trading securities are debt and equity securities bought and held principally for the purpose of being sold in the near term. Such securities are frequently bought and sold to generate profits on short-term changes in their prices. Trading securities are classified as current assets on the balance sheet and valued at fair value, which is usually the same as market value—for example, when securities are traded on a stock exchange or in the over-the-counter market.

An increase or decrease in the fair value of the total trading portfolio (the group of securities held for trading purposes) is included in net income in the accounting period in which the increase or decrease occurs. For example, assume that Franklin Company purchases 10,000 shares of Exxon Mobil Corporation for $900,000 ($90 per share) and 5,000 shares of Texaco Inc. for $300,000 ($60 per share) on October 25, 20x1. The purchase is made for trading purposes; that is, management intends to realize a gain by holding the shares for only a short period. The entry to record the investment at cost follows:

A = L + OE
\+
\-

20x1
Oct. 25   Short-Term Investments   1,200,000
                   Cash   1,200,000
                   Investment in stocks for trading
                   ($900,000 + $300,000 = $1,200,000)

Assume that at year end Exxon Mobil's stock price has decreased to $80 per share and Texaco's has risen to $64 per share. The trading portfolio is now valued at $1,120,000:

Security	Market Value	Cost	Gain (Loss)
Exxon Mobil (10,000 shares)	$ 800,000	$ 900,000	
Texaco (5,000 shares)	320,000	300,000	
Totals	$1,120,000	$1,200,000	($80,000)

Because the current fair value of the portfolio is $80,000 less than the original cost of $1,200,000, an adjusting entry is needed, as follows:

A = L + OE
\- \-

20x1
Dec. 31   Unrealized Loss on Investments   80,000
                   Allowance to Adjust Short-Term
                   Investments to Market   80,000
                   Recognition of unrealized loss
                   on trading portfolio

The unrealized loss will appear on the income statement as a reduction in income. (The loss is unrealized because the securities have not been sold.) The Allowance to Adjust Short-Term Investments to Market account appears on the balance sheet as a contra-asset, as follows:

Short-Term Investments (at cost)	$1,200,000
Less Allowance to Adjust Short-Term Investments to Market	80,000
Short-Term Investments (at market)	$1,120,000

or more simply,

Short-Term Investments (at market value, cost is $1,200,000)	$1,120,000

If Franklin sells its 5,000 shares of Texaco for $70 per share on March 2, 20x2, a realized gain on trading securities is recorded as follows:

<table>
<tr><td colspan="4">20x2</td></tr>
<tr><td>Mar. 2</td><td>Cash</td><td>350,000</td><td></td></tr>
<tr><td></td><td>   Short-Term Investments</td><td></td><td>300,000</td></tr>
<tr><td></td><td>   Realized Gain on Investments</td><td></td><td>50,000</td></tr>
<tr><td></td><td>   Sale of 5,000 shares of Texaco</td><td></td><td></td></tr>
<tr><td></td><td>   for $70 per share; cost was $60 per share</td><td></td><td></td></tr>
</table>

A = L + OE
+   +
−

The realized gain will appear on the income statement. Note that the realized gain is unaffected by the adjustment for the unrealized loss at the end of 20x1. The two transactions are treated independently. If the stock had been sold for less than cost, a realized loss on investments would have been recorded. Realized losses also appear on the income statement.

Let's assume that during 20x2 Franklin buys 2,000 shares of BP Amoco Corporation at $64 per share and has no transactions involving Exxon Mobil. Also assume that by December 31, 20x2, the price of Exxon Mobil's stock has risen to $95 per share, or $5 per share more than the original cost, and that BP Amoco's stock price has fallen to $58, or $6 less than the original cost. The trading portfolio now can be analyzed as follows:

Security	Market Value	Cost	Gain (Loss)
Exxon Mobil (10,000 shares)	$ 950,000	$ 900,000	
BP Amoco (2,000 shares)	116,000	128,000	
Totals	$1,066,000	$1,028,000	$38,000

The market value of the portfolio now exceeds the cost by $38,000 ($1,066,000 − $1,028,000). This amount represents the targeted ending balance for the Allowance to Adjust Short-Term Investments to Market account. Recall that at the end of 20x1, that account had a credit balance of $80,000, meaning that the market value of the trading portfolio was less than the cost. The account has no entries during 20x2 and thus retains its balance until adjusting entries are made at the end of the year. The adjustment for 20x2 must be $118,000—enough to result in a debit balance of $38,000 in the allowance account.

<table>
<tr><td colspan="4">20x2</td></tr>
<tr><td>Dec. 31</td><td>Allowance to Adjust Short-Term</td><td></td><td></td></tr>
<tr><td></td><td>   Investments to Market</td><td>118,000</td><td></td></tr>
<tr><td></td><td>   Unrealized Gain on Investments</td><td></td><td>118,000</td></tr>
<tr><td></td><td>   Recognition of unrealized gain</td><td></td><td></td></tr>
<tr><td></td><td>   on trading portfolio</td><td></td><td></td></tr>
<tr><td></td><td>   ($80,000 + $38,000 = $118,000)</td><td></td><td></td></tr>
</table>

A = L + OE
+   +

The 20x2 ending balance of the allowance account may be determined as follows:

Allowance to Adjust Short-Term Investments to Market

Dec. 31, 20x2 adj.	118,000	Dec. 31, 20x1 bal.	80,000
Dec. 31, 20x2 bal.	**38,000**		

The balance sheet presentation of short-term investment is as follows:

Short-Term Investments (at cost)	$1,028,000
Allowance to Adjust Short-Term Investments to Market	38,000
Short-Term Investments (at market)	$1,066,000

or, more simply,

Short-Term Investments (at market value, cost is $1,028,000)	$1,066,000

If the company also holds held-to-maturity securities, they are included in short-term investments at cost adjusted for the effects of interest if they will mature within one year.

Available-for-Sale Securities

Available-for-sale securities are debt and equity securities that do not meet the criteria for either held-to-maturity or trading securities. They are accounted for in exactly the same way as trading securities, except that the unrealized gain or loss is not reported on the income statement, but is reported as a special item in the stockholders' equity section of the balance sheet. For example, Pioneer Electronic states in its annual report that "all debt securities and marketable equity securities held by the Company are classified as available-for-sale securities, and are carried at their fair values with unrealized gains and losses reported as a component of shareholders' equity."[10] This latter component is called Accumulated Other Comprehensive Income.

Dividend and Interest Income

Dividend and interest income for all three categories of investments is shown in the Other Income and Expenses section of the income statement.

Accounts Receivable

OBJECTIVE

4 Define *accounts receivable* and apply the allowance method of accounting for uncollectible accounts, using both the percentage of net sales method and the accounts receivable aging method

The other major types of short-term liquid assets are accounts receivable and notes receivable. Both result from credit sales to customers. Retail companies such as Sears, Roebuck and Co. have made credit available to nearly every responsible person in the United States. Every field of retail trade has expanded by allowing customers to make payments a month or more after the date of sale. What is not so apparent is that credit has expanded even more in the wholesale and manufacturing industries than at the retail level. The levels of accounts receivable in selected industries are shown in Figure 3.

Accounts receivable are short-term liquid assets that arise from sales on credit to customers by wholesalers or retailers. This type of credit is often called **trade credit**. Terms on trade credit usually range from five to 60 days, depending on industry practice. For some companies that sell to consumers, **installment accounts receivable** constitute a significant portion of accounts receivable. Installment accounts receivable arise from the sale of goods on terms that allow the buyer to make a series of time payments. Department stores, appliance stores,

Figure 3
Accounts Receivable as a Percentage of Total Assets for Selected Industries

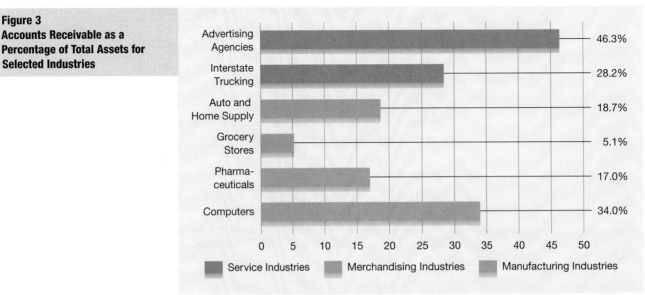

Source: Data from Dun and Bradstreet, *Industry Norms and Key Business Ratios,* 1999–2000.

furniture stores, used car companies, and other retail businesses often offer installment credit. Retailers such as J.C. Penney Company, Inc., and Sears, Roebuck and Co. have millions of dollars in installment accounts receivable. Although the payment period may be 24 months or more, installment accounts receivable are classified as current assets if such credit policies are customary in the industry.

On the balance sheet, the title Accounts Receivable is used for amounts arising from sales made to customers in the ordinary course of business. If loans or sales that do not fall into this category are made to employees, officers of the corporation, or owners, they should be shown separately with an asset title such as Receivables from Employees because of the increased risk of uncollectibility and conflict of interest.

Normally, individual customer accounts receivable have debit balances, but sometimes customers overpay their accounts either by mistake or in anticipation of future purchases. When individual customer accounts show credit balances, the total of the credits should be shown on the balance sheet as a current liability because the amounts must be refunded if future sales are not made to those customers.

Uncollectible Accounts and the Direct Charge-Off Method

A company will always have some customers who cannot or will not pay their debts. The accounts owed by such customers are called **uncollectible accounts**, or *bad debts*, and are a loss or an expense of selling on credit. Why does a company sell on credit if it expects that some of its accounts will not be paid? The answer is that the company expects to sell much more than it would if it did not sell on credit, thereby increasing its earnings.

Some companies recognize the loss from an uncollectible account receivable at the time it is determined to be uncollectible by reducing Accounts Receivable directly and increasing Uncollectible Accounts Expense. Many small companies use this method because it is required in computing taxable income under federal tax regulations. However, companies that follow generally accepted accounting principles do not use the **direct charge-off method** in their financial statements because it makes no attempt to match revenues and expenses. The direct charge-off is often recorded in a different accounting period from the one in which the sale takes place. They prefer the allowance method, which is explained in the next section.

Uncollectible Accounts and the Allowance Method

Under the **allowance method** of accounting for uncollectible accounts, bad debt losses are matched against the sales they help to produce. As mentioned earlier, when management extends credit to increase sales, it knows that it will incur some losses from uncollectible accounts. Those losses are expenses that occur at the time sales on credit are made and should be matched to the revenues they help to generate. Of course, at the time the sales are made, management cannot identify which customers will not pay their debts, nor can it predict the exact amount of money that will be lost. Therefore, to observe the matching rule, losses from uncollectible accounts must be estimated, and the estimate becomes an expense in the fiscal year in which the sales are made.

For example, let us assume that Cottage Sales Company made most of its sales on credit during its first year of operation, 20x2. At the end of the year, accounts receivable amounted to $100,000. On December 31, 20x2, management reviewed the collectible status of the accounts receivable. Approximately $6,000 of the $100,000 of accounts receivable were estimated to be uncollectible. Therefore, the uncollectible accounts expense for the first year of operation was estimated to be $6,000. The following adjusting entry would be made on December 31 of that year:

	20x2			
A = L + OE	Dec. 31	Uncollectible Accounts Expense	6,000	
− −		Allowance for Uncollectible Accounts		6,000
		To record the estimated uncollectible accounts expense for the year		

Uncollectible Accounts Expense appears on the income statement as an operating expense. **Allowance for Uncollectible Accounts** appears on the balance sheet as a contra account that is deducted from Accounts Receivable.* It reduces the accounts receivable to the amount expected to be realized, or collected in cash, as follows:

Current Assets		
Cash		$ 10,000
Short-Term Investments		15,000
Accounts Receivable	$100,000	
Less Allowance for Uncollectible Accounts	6,000	94,000
Inventory		56,000
Total Current Assets		$175,000

Accounts receivable may also be shown on the balance sheet as follows:

Accounts Receivable (net of allowance for uncollectible accounts of $6,000)	$94,000

Or they may be shown at "net," with the amount of the allowance for uncollectible accounts identified in a note to the financial statements. The estimated uncollectible amount cannot be identified with any particular customer; therefore, it is credited to a separate contra-asset account—Allowance for Uncollectible Accounts.

---

*The purpose of Allowance for Uncollectible Accounts is to reduce the gross accounts receivable to the amount estimated to be collectible (net realizable value). The purpose of another contra account, Accumulated Depreciation, is *not* to reduce the gross plant and equipment accounts to realizable value. Rather, its purpose is to show how much of the cost of the plant and equipment has been allocated as an expense to previous accounting periods.

The allowance account will often have other titles, such as *Allowance for Doubtful Accounts* or *Allowance for Bad Debts*. Once in a while, the older phrase *Reserve for Bad Debts* will be seen, but in modern practice it should not be used. *Bad Debts Expense* is another title often used for Uncollectible Accounts Expense.

Estimating Uncollectible Accounts Expense

As noted, it is necessary to estimate the expense to cover the expected losses for the year. Of course, estimates can vary widely. If management takes an optimistic view and projects a small loss from uncollectible accounts, the resulting net accounts receivable will be larger than if management takes a pessimistic view. The net income will also be larger under the optimistic view because the estimated expense will be smaller. The company's accountant makes an estimate based on past experience and current economic conditions. For example, losses from uncollectible accounts are normally expected to be greater in a recession than during a period of economic growth. The final decision, made by management, on the amount of the expense will depend on objective information, such as the accountant's analyses, and on certain qualitative factors, such as how investors, bankers, creditors, and others may view the performance of the debtor company. Regardless of the qualitative considerations, the estimated losses from uncollectible accounts should be realistic.

The accountant may choose from two common methods for estimating uncollectible accounts expense for an accounting period: the percentage of net sales method and the accounts receivable aging method.

PERCENTAGE OF NET SALES METHOD The **percentage of net sales method** asks, How much of this year's net sales will not be collected? The answer determines the amount of uncollectible accounts expense for the year. For example, the following balances represent the ending figures for Hassel Company for the year 20x9:

Sales		Sales Returns and Allowances	
	Dec. 31 645,000	Dec. 31 40,000	

Sales Discounts		Allowance for Uncollectible Accounts	
Dec. 31 5,000			Dec. 31 3,600

Below are the actual losses from uncollectible accounts for the past three years:

Year	Net Sales	Losses from Uncollectible Accounts	Percentage
20x6	$ 520,000	$10,200	1.96
20x7	595,000	13,900	2.34
20x8	585,000	9,900	1.69
Total	$1,700,000	$34,000	2.00

In many businesses, net sales is understood to approximate net credit sales. If there are substantial cash sales, then net credit sales should be used. Management believes that uncollectible accounts will continue to average about 2 percent of net sales. The uncollectible accounts expense for the year 20x9 is therefore estimated to be

$$.02 \times (\$645,000 - \$40,000 - \$5,000) = .02 \times \$600,000 = \$12,000$$

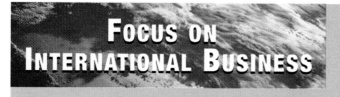

FOCUS ON INTERNATIONAL BUSINESS

Companies in emerging economies do not always follow the accounting practices accepted in the United States. The Shanghai Stock Exchange is one of the fastest-growing stock markets in the world. Few Chinese companies acknowledge that uncollected receivables are not worth full value even though many receivables have been outstanding for a year or more. It is common practice in the United States to write off receivables more than six months old. Now that Chinese companies like Shanghai Steel Tube and Shanghai Industrial Sewing Machine are making their shares of stock available to outsiders, they must estimate uncollectible accounts in accordance with international accounting standards. Recognition of this expense could easily wipe out annual earnings.[11]

The entry to record this estimate is as follows:

A = L + OE	20x9		
− −	Dec. 31 Uncollectible Accounts Expense	12,000	
	Allowance for Uncollectible Accounts		12,000
	To record uncollectible accounts expense		
	at 2 percent of $600,000 net sales		

After the above entry is posted, Allowance for Uncollectible Accounts will have a balance of $15,600.

Allowance for Uncollectible Accounts

	Dec. 31	3,600
	Dec. 31 adj.	12,000
	Dec. 31 bal.	15,600

The balance consists of the $12,000 estimated uncollectible accounts receivable from 20x9 sales and the $3,600 estimated uncollectible accounts receivable from previous years.

ACCOUNTS RECEIVABLE AGING METHOD The **accounts receivable aging method** asks the question, How much of the year-end balance of accounts receivable will not be collected? Under this method, the year-end balance of Allowance for Uncollectible Accounts is determined directly by an analysis of accounts receivable. The difference between the amount determined to be uncollectible and the actual balance of Allowance for Uncollectible Accounts is the expense for the year. In theory, this method should produce the same result as the percentage of net sales method, but in practice it rarely does.

The **aging of accounts receivable** is the process of listing each customer's receivable account according to the due date of the account. If the customer's account is past due, there is a possibility that the account will not be paid. And the further past due an account is, the greater that possibility. The aging of accounts receivable helps management evaluate its credit and collection policies and alerts it to possible problems.

The aging of accounts receivable for Myer Company is illustrated in Exhibit 1. Each account receivable is classified as being not yet due or as 1–30 days, 31–60 days, 61–90 days, or over 90 days past due. The estimated percentage uncollectible in each category is multiplied by the amount in each category in order to determine the estimated, or target, balance of Allowance for Uncollectible Accounts. In total, it is estimated that $2,459 of the $44,400 accounts receivable will not be collected.

Customer	Total	Not Yet Due	1–30 Days Past Due	31–60 Days Past Due	61–90 Days Past Due	Over 90 Days Past Due
A. Arnold	$ 150		$ 150			
M. Benoit	400			$ 400		
J. Connolly	1,000	$ 900	100			
R. Deering	250				$ 250	
Others	42,600	21,000	14,000	3,800	2,200	$1,600
Totals	$44,400	$21,900	$14,250	$4,200	$2,450	$1,600
Estimated percentage uncollectible		1.0	2.0	10.0	30.0	50.0
Allowance for Uncollectible Accounts	$ 2,459	$ 219	$ 285	$ 420	$ 735	$ 800

Myer Company
Analysis of Accounts Receivable by Age
December 31, 20xx

Exhibit 1
Analysis of Accounts Receivable by Age

Once the target balance for Allowance for Uncollectible Accounts has been found, it is necessary to determine how much the adjustment is. The amount of the adjustment depends on the current balance of the allowance account. Let us assume two cases for the December 31 balance of Myer Company's Allowance for Uncollectible Accounts: (1) a credit balance of $800 and (2) a debit balance of $800.

In the first case, an adjustment of $1,659 is needed to bring the balance of the allowance account to $2,459, calculated as follows:

Targeted Balance for Allowance for Uncollectible Accounts	$2,459
Less Current Credit Balance of Allowance for Uncollectible Accounts	800
Uncollectible Accounts Expense	$1,659

The uncollectible accounts expense is recorded as follows:

$A = L + OE$

20x2
Dec. 31 Uncollectible Accounts Expense ... 1,659
                Allowance for Uncollectible Accounts ... 1,659
                To bring the allowance for
                uncollectible accounts to the
                level of estimated losses

The resulting balance of Allowance for Uncollectible Accounts is $2,459, as follows:

Allowance for Uncollectible Accounts

	Dec. 31	800
	Dec. 31 adj.	1,659
	Dec. 31 bal.	2,459

In the second case, because Allowance for Uncollectible Accounts has a debit balance of $800, the estimated uncollectible accounts expense for the year will have to be $3,259 to reach the targeted balance of $2,459. This calculation is as follows:

Targeted Balance for Allowance for Uncollectible Accounts	$2,459
Plus Current Debit Balance of Allowance for Uncollectible Accounts	800
Uncollectible Accounts Expense	$3,259

The uncollectible accounts expense is recorded as follows:

$$A = L + OE$$
$$- \quad -$$

20x2			
Dec. 31	Uncollectible Accounts Expense	3,259	
	Allowance for Uncollectible Accounts		3,259
	To bring the allowance for		
	uncollectible accounts to the		
	level of estimated losses		

After this entry, Allowance for Uncollectible Accounts has a credit balance of $2,459, as shown below:

Allowance for Uncollectible Accounts

Dec. 31	800	Dec. 31 adj.	3,259
		Dec. 31 bal.	2,459

COMPARISON OF THE TWO METHODS   Both the percentage of net sales method and the accounts receivable aging method estimate the uncollectible accounts expense in accordance with the matching rule, but as shown in Figure 4, they do so in different ways. The percentage of net sales method is an income statement approach. It assumes that a certain proportion of sales will not be collected, and this proportion is the *amount of Uncollectible Accounts Expense* for the accounting period. The accounts receivable aging method is a balance sheet approach. It assumes that a certain proportion of accounts receivable outstanding will not be collected. This proportion is the *targeted balance of the Allowance for Uncollectible*

Figure 4
Two Methods of Estimating Uncollectible Accounts

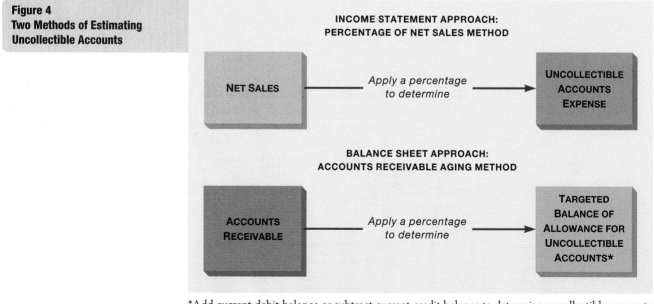

*Add current debit balance or subtract current credit balance to determine uncollectible accounts expense.

Accounts account. The expense for the accounting period is the difference between the targeted balance and the current balance of the allowance account.

WHY ACCOUNTS WRITTEN OFF WILL DIFFER FROM ESTIMATES   Regardless of the method used to estimate uncollectible accounts, the total of accounts receivable written off in any given year will rarely equal the estimated uncollectible amount. The allowance account will show a credit balance when the total of accounts written off is less than the estimated uncollectible amount. The allowance account will show a debit balance when the total of accounts written off is greater than the estimated uncollectible amount.

Writing Off an Uncollectible Account

When it becomes clear that a specific account receivable will not be collected, the amount should be written off to Allowance for Uncollectible Accounts. Remember that the uncollectible amount was already accounted for as an expense when the allowance was established. For example, assume that on January 15, 20x3, R. Deering, who owes Myer Company $250, is declared bankrupt by a federal court. The entry to *write off* this account is as follows:

	20x3			
A = L + OE	Jan. 15	Allowance for Uncollectible Accounts	250	
+		Accounts Receivable		250
−		To write off receivable from		
		R. Deering as uncollectible;		
		Deering declared bankrupt		
		on January 15		

Although the write-off removes the uncollectible amount from Accounts Receivable, it does not affect the estimated net realizable value of accounts receivable. The write-off simply reduces R. Deering's account to zero and reduces Allowance for Uncollectible Accounts by a similar amount, as shown below:

	Balances Before Write-off	Balances After Write-off
Accounts Receivable	$44,400	$44,150
Less Allowance for Uncollectible Accounts	2,459	2,209
Estimated Net Realizable Value of Accounts Receivable	$41,941	$41,941

RECOVERY OF ACCOUNTS RECEIVABLE WRITTEN OFF   Occasionally, a customer whose account has been written off as uncollectible will later be able to pay some or all of the amount owed. When this happens, two journal entries must be made: one to reverse the earlier write-off (which is now incorrect) and another to show the collection of the account. For example, assume that on September 1, 20x3, R. Deering, after his bankruptcy on January 15, notified the company that he could pay $100 of his account and sent a check for $50. The entries to record this transaction follow:

	20x3			
A = L + OE	Sept. 1	Accounts Receivable	100	
+		Allowance for Uncollectible Accounts		100
−		To reinstate the portion of		
		the account of R. Deering		
		now considered collectible;		
		originally written off January 15		

A = L + OE	Sept. 1	Cash	50	
+		Accounts Receivable		50
–		Collection from R. Deering		

The collectible portion of R. Deering's account must be restored to his account and credited to Allowance for Uncollectible Accounts for two reasons. First, it turned out to be wrong to write off the full $250 on January 15 because only $150 was actually uncollectible. Second, the accounts receivable subsidiary account for R. Deering should reflect his ability to pay a portion of the money he owed despite his declaration of bankruptcy. Documentation of this action will give a clear picture of R. Deering's credit record for future credit action.

Notes Receivable

OBJECTIVE

5 Define and describe a *promissory note,* and make calculations and journal entries involving promissory notes

A **promissory note** is an unconditional promise to pay a definite sum of money on demand or at a future date. The entity who signs the note and thereby promises to pay is called the *maker* of the note. The entity to whom payment is to be made is called the *payee*.

The promissory note illustrated in Figure 5 is dated May 20, 20x1, and is an unconditional promise by the maker, Samuel Mason, to pay a definite sum, or principal ($1,000), to the payee, Cook County Bank & Trust Company, at the future date of August 18, 20x1. The promissory note bears an interest rate of 8 percent. The payee regards all promissory notes it holds that are due in less than one year as **notes receivable** in the current assets section of the balance sheet. The maker regards them as **notes payable** in the current liabilities section of the balance sheet.

This portion of the chapter is concerned primarily with notes received from customers. The nature of a business generally determines how frequently promissory notes are received from customers. Firms selling durable goods of high value,

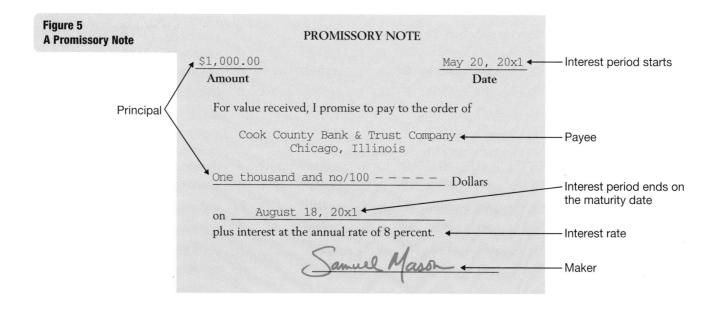

Figure 5
A Promissory Note

PROMISSORY NOTE

$1,000.00   May 20, 20x1 ◄——— Interest period starts
Amount   **Date**

Principal

For value received, I promise to pay to the order of

Cook County Bank & Trust Company ◄——— Payee
Chicago, Illinois

One thousand and no/100 – – – – – Dollars ——— Interest period ends on the maturity date

on   August 18, 20x1 ◄———

plus interest at the annual rate of 8 percent. ◄——— Interest rate

Samuel Mason ◄——— Maker

such as farm machinery and automobiles, will often accept promissory notes. Among the advantages of promissory notes are that they produce interest income and represent a stronger legal claim against a debtor than do accounts receivable. In addition, selling or discounting promissory notes to banks is a common financing method. Almost all companies will occasionally receive a note, and many companies obtain notes receivable in settlement of past-due accounts.

Computations for Promissory Notes

In accounting for promissory notes, the following terms are important to remember: (1) maturity date, (2) duration of note, (3) interest and interest rate, and (4) maturity value.

MATURITY DATE   The **maturity date** is the date on which the note must be paid. This date must either be stated on the promissory note or be determinable from the facts stated on the note. Among the most common statements of maturity date are the following:

1. A specific date, such as "November 14, 20xx"
2. A specific number of months after the date of the note, for example, "three months after date"
3. A specific number of days after the date of the note, for example, "60 days after date"

The maturity date is obvious when a specific date is stated. And when the maturity date is a number of months from the date of the note, one simply uses the same day in the appropriate future month. For example, a note that is dated January 20 and that is due in two months would be due on March 20.

When the maturity date is a specific number of days from the date of the note, however, the exact maturity date must be determined. In computing the maturity date, it is important to exclude the date of the note. For example, a note dated May 20 and due in 90 days would be due on August 18, computed as follows:

Days remaining in May (31 − 20)	11
Days in June	30
Days in July	31
Days in August	18
Total days	90

DURATION OF NOTE   The **duration of note** is the length of time in days between a promissory note's issue date and its maturity date. Knowing the duration of the note is important because interest is calculated for the exact number of days. Identifying the duration is easy when the maturity date is stated as a specific number of days from the date of the note because the two numbers are the same. However, if the maturity date is stated as a specific date, the exact number of days must be determined. Assume that a note issued on May 10 matures on August 10. The duration of the note is 92 days, determined as follows:

Days remaining in May (31 − 10)	21
Days in June	30
Days in July	31
Days in August	10
Total days	92

of May Financial Corporation of Dallas, Texas, states in its customer loan agreement, "Interest is calculated on a 360-day basis." In Europe, use of a 360-day year is common. Financial institutions that use the 360-day basis earn slightly more interest than those that use the 365-day basis. In this book, we use a 360-day year to keep the computations simple.

Practice as to the computation of interest varies. Most banks use a 365-day year for all loans, but some use a 360-day year for commercial loans. The brokerage firm

INTEREST AND INTEREST RATE   The **interest** is the cost of borrowing money or the return for lending money, depending on whether one is the borrower or the lender. The amount of interest is based on three factors: the principal (the amount of money borrowed or lent), the rate of interest, and the loan's length of time. The formula used in computing interest is as follows:

$$\text{Principal} \times \text{Rate of Interest} \times \text{Time} = \text{Interest}$$

Interest rates are usually stated on an annual basis. For example, the interest on a one-year, 8 percent, $1,000 note would be $80 ($1,000 × 8/100 × 1 = $80). If the term, or time period, of the note were three months instead of a year, the interest charge would be $20 ($1,000 × 8/100 × 3/12 = $20).

When the term of a note is expressed in days, the exact number of days must be used in computing the interest. To keep the computation simple, let us compute interest on the basis of 360 days per year. Therefore, if the term of the above note were 45 days, the interest would be $10, computed as follows: $1,000 × 8/100 × 45/360 = $10.

MATURITY VALUE   The **maturity value** is the total proceeds of a note at the maturity date. The maturity value is the face value of the note plus interest. The maturity value of a 90-day, 8 percent, $1,000 note is computed as follows:

$$
\begin{aligned}
\text{Maturity Value} &= \text{Principal} + \text{Interest} \\
&= \$1,000 + (\$1,000 \times 8/100 \times 90/360) \\
&= \$1,000 + \$20 \\
&= \$1,020
\end{aligned}
$$

There are also so-called non-interest-bearing notes. The maturity value is the face value, or principal amount. In this case, the principal includes an implied interest cost.

Illustrative Accounting Entries

The accounting entries for promissory notes receivable fall into these four groups: (1) recording receipt of a note, (2) recording collection on a note, (3) recording a dishonored note, and (4) recording adjusting entries.

RECORDING RECEIPT OF A NOTE   Assume that on June 1 a 30-day, 12 percent note is received from a customer, J. Halsted, in settlement of an existing account receivable of $4,000. The entry for this transaction is as follows:

A = L + OE
\+
−

June 1   Notes Receivable   4,000
              Accounts Receivable   4,000
                   Received 30-day, 12 percent note in
                   payment of account of J. Halsted

RECORDING COLLECTION ON A NOTE   When the note plus interest is collected 30 days later, the entry is as follows:

A = L + OE
\+   +
−

July 1   Cash   4,040
              Notes Receivable   4,000
              Interest Income   40
                   Collected 30-day, 12 percent
                   note from J. Halsted

RECORDING A DISHONORED NOTE   When the maker of a note does not pay the note at maturity, the note is said to be dishonored. The holder, or payee, of a **dishonored note** should make an entry to transfer the total amount due from Notes Receivable to an account receivable from the debtor. If J. Halsted dishonors her note on July 1, the following entry would be made:

A = L + OE
\+   +
−

July 1   Accounts Receivable   4,040
              Notes Receivable   4,000
              Interest Income   40
                   30-day, 12 percent note
                   dishonored by J. Halsted

The interest earned is recorded because, although J. Halsted did not pay the note, she is still obligated to pay both the principal and the interest.

Two things are accomplished by transferring a dishonored note receivable into an Accounts Receivable account. First, this leaves the Notes Receivable account with only notes that have not matured and are presumably negotiable and collectible. Second, it establishes a record in the borrower's accounts receivable account that he or she has dishonored a note receivable. Such information may be helpful in deciding whether to extend future credit to the customer.

RECORDING ADJUSTING ENTRIES   A promissory note received in one period may not be due until a following accounting period. Because the interest on a note accrues by a small amount each day of the note's duration, it is necessary, according to the matching rule, to apportion the interest earned to the periods in which it belongs. For example, assume that on August 31 a 60-day, 8 percent, $2,000 note was received and that the company prepares financial statements monthly. The following adjusting entry is necessary on September 30 to show how the interest earned for September has accrued.

A = L + OE
\+   +

Sept. 30   Interest Receivable   13.33
                 Interest Income   13.33
                      To accrue 30 days' interest
                      earned on a note receivable
                      $2,000 × 8/100 × 30/360 = $13.33

The account Interest Receivable is a current asset on the balance sheet. When payment of the note plus interest is received on October 30, the following entry is made:*

*Some firms may follow the practice of reversing the September 30 adjusting entry. Here we assume that a reversing entry is not made.

A = L + OE	Oct. 30	Cash	2,026.67	
+ +		Notes Receivable		2,000.00
–		Interest Receivable		13.33
–		Interest Income		13.34
		Receipt of note receivable		
		plus interest		

As seen from these transactions, both September and October receive the benefit of one-half the interest earned.

Chapter Review

1. Identify and explain the management issues related to short-term liquid assets. In managing short-term liquid assets, management must (1) consider the effects of seasonal cycles on the need for short-term investing and borrowing as the business's balance of cash fluctuates, (2) establish credit policies that balance the need for sales with the ability to collect, and (3) assess the need for additional cash flows through the financing of receivables.

2. Explain *cash, cash equivalents*, and the importance of electronic funds transfer. Cash consists of coins and currency on hand, checks and money orders received from customers, and deposits in bank accounts. Cash equivalents are investments that have a term of 90 days or less. Conducting transactions through electronic communication or electronic funds transfer is important because of its efficiency: Much of the paperwork associated with traditional recordkeeping is eliminated.

3. Account for short-term investments. Short-term investments may be classified as held-to-maturity securities, trading securities, or available-for-sale securities. Held-to-maturity securities are debt securities that management intends to hold to the maturity date; they are valued on the balance sheet at cost adjusted for the effects of interest. Trading securities are debt and equity securities bought and held principally for the purpose of being sold in the near term; they are valued at fair value or at market value. Unrealized gains or losses on trading securities appear on the income statement. Available-for-sale securities are debt and equity securities that do not meet the criteria for either held-to-maturity or trading securities. They are accounted for in the same way as trading securities, except that an unrealized gain or loss is reported as a special item in the stockholders' equity section of the balance sheet.

4. Define *accounts receivable* and apply the allowance method of accounting for uncollectible accounts, using both the percentage of net sales method and the accounts receivable aging method. Accounts receivable are amounts still to be collected from credit sales to customers. Because credit is offered to increase sales, uncollectible accounts associated with credit sales should be charged as expenses in the period in which the sales are made. However, because of the time lag between the sales and the time the accounts are judged uncollectible, the accountant must estimate the amount of bad debts in any given period.

Uncollectible accounts expense is estimated by either the percentage of net sales method or the accounts receivable aging method. When the first method is used, bad debts are judged to be a certain percentage of sales during the period. When the second method is used, percentages are applied to groups of accounts receivable that have been arranged by due dates.

Allowance for Uncollectible Accounts is a contra-asset account to Accounts Receivable. The estimate of uncollectible accounts is debited to Uncollectible Accounts Expense and credited to the allowance account. When an individual account is determined to be uncollectible, it is removed from Accounts Receivable by debiting the allowance account and crediting Accounts Receivable. If the written-off account should later be collected, the earlier entry should be reversed and the collection recorded in the normal way.

5. **Define and describe a *promissory note*, and make calculations and journal entries involving promissory notes.** A promissory note is an unconditional promise to pay a definite sum of money on demand or at a future date. Companies selling durable goods of high value, such as farm machinery and automobiles, often accept promissory notes, which can be sold to banks as a financing method.

In accounting for promissory notes, it is important to know how to calculate the maturity date, duration of note, interest and interest rate, and maturity value. The accounting entries for promissory notes receivable fall into four groups: recording receipt of a note, recording collection on a note, recording a dishonored note, and recording adjusting entries.

REVIEW OF CONCEPTS AND TERMINOLOGY

The following concepts and terms were introduced in this chapter:

LO 4 **Accounts receivable:** Short-term liquid assets that arise from sales on credit at the wholesale or retail level.

LO 4 **Accounts receivable aging method:** A method of estimating uncollectible accounts based on the assumption that a predictable proportion of each dollar of accounts receivable outstanding will not be collected.

LO 4 **Aging of accounts receivable:** The process of listing each customer's receivable account according to the due date of the account.

LO 4 **Allowance for Uncollectible Accounts:** A contra-asset account that reduces accounts receivable to the amount that is expected to be collected in cash; also called *Allowance for Bad Debts*.

LO 4 **Allowance method:** A method of accounting for uncollectible accounts by expensing estimated uncollectible accounts in the period in which the related sales take place.

LO 3 **Available-for-sale securities:** Debt and equity securities that do not meet the criteria for either held-to-maturity or trading securities.

LO 1 **Average days' sales uncollected:** A ratio that shows on average how long it takes to collect accounts receivable; 365 days divided by receivable turnover.

LO 2 **Cash:** Coins and currency on hand, checks and money orders from customers, and deposits in bank checking accounts.

LO 2 **Cash equivalents:** Short-term investments that will revert to cash in 90 days or less from when they are purchased.

LO 2 **Compensating balance:** A minimum amount that a bank requires a company to keep in its account as part of a credit-granting arrangement.

LO 1 **Contingent liability:** A potential liability that can develop into a real liability if a possible subsequent event occurs.

LO 4 **Direct charge-off method:** A method of accounting for uncollectible accounts by directly debiting an expense account when bad debts are discovered instead of using the allowance method; this method violates the matching rule but is required for federal income tax computations.

LO 1 **Discounting:** A method of selling notes receivable in which the bank deducts the interest from the maturity value of the note to determine the proceeds.

LO 5 **Dishonored note:** A promissory note that the maker cannot or will not pay at the maturity date.

LO 5 **Duration of note:** The length of time in days between a promissory note's issue date and its maturity date.

LO 2 **Electronic funds transfer (EFT):** The transfer of funds from one bank to another through electronic communication.

LO 1 **Factor:** An entity that buys accounts receivable.

LO 1 **Factoring:** The selling or transferring of accounts receivable.

LO 3 **Held-to-maturity securities:** Debt securities that management intends to hold to their maturity or their payment date and whose cash value is not needed until that date.

LO 2 **Imprest system:** A system for controlling small cash disbursements by establishing a fund at a fixed amount and periodically reimbursing the fund by the amount necessary to restore its original cash balance.

LO 4 **Installment accounts receivable:** Accounts receivable that are payable in a series of time payments.

LO 5 **Interest:** The cost of borrowing money or the return for lending money, depending on whether one is the borrower or the lender.

LO 3 **Marketable securities:** Short-term investments intended to be held until needed to pay current obligations; also called *short-term investments*.

LO 5 **Maturity date:** The date on which a promissory note must be paid.

LO 5 **Maturity value:** The total proceeds of a promissory note, including principal and interest, at the maturity date.

LO 5 **Notes payable:** Collective term for promissory notes owed by the entity (maker) who promises payment to other entities.

LO 5 **Notes receivable:** Collective term for promissory notes held by the entity to whom payment is promised (payee).

LO 4 **Percentage of net sales method:** A method of estimating uncollectible accounts based on the assumption that a predictable proportion of each dollar of sales will not be collected.

LO 5 **Promissory note:** An unconditional promise to pay a definite sum of money on demand or at a future date.

LO 1 **Quick ratio:** A ratio for measuring the adequacy of short-term liquid assets; short-term liquid assets divided by current liabilities.

LO 1 **Receivable turnover:** A ratio for measuring the average number of times receivables were turned into cash during an accounting period; net sales divided by average net accounts receivable.

LO 3 **Short-term investments:** Temporary investments of excess cash, intended to be held until needed to pay current obligations; also called *marketable securities*.

LO 1 **Short-term liquid assets:** Financial assets that arise from cash transactions, the investment of cash, and the extension of credit.

LO 4 **Trade credit:** Credit granted to customers by wholesalers or retailers.

LO 3 **Trading securities:** Debt and equity securities bought and held principally for the purpose of being sold in the near term.

LO 4 **Uncollectible accounts:** Accounts receivable owed by customers who cannot or will not pay; also called *bad debts*.

REVIEW PROBLEM

Estimating Uncollectible Accounts, Receivables Analysis, and Notes Receivable Transactions

LO 1
LO 4
LO 5

The Farm Implement Company sells merchandise on credit and also accepts notes for payment. During the year ended June 30, the company had net sales of $1,200,000, and at the end of the year it had Accounts Receivable of $400,000 and a debit balance in Allowance for Uncollectible Accounts of $2,100. In the past, approximately 1.5 percent of net sales have proved uncollectible. Also, an aging analysis of accounts receivable reveals that $17,000 in accounts receivable appears to be uncollectible.

The Farm Implement Company sold a tractor to R. C. Sims. Payment was received in the form of a 90-day, 9 percent, $15,000 note dated March 16. On June 14, Sims dishonored the note. On June 29, the company received payment in full from Sims plus additional interest from the date of the dishonored note.

REQUIRED

1. Compute Uncollectible Accounts Expense and determine the ending balance of Allowance for Uncollectible Accounts and Accounts Receivable, Net under (a) the percentage of net sales method and (b) the accounts receivable aging method.

2. Compute the receivable turnover and average days' sales uncollected using the data from the accounts receivable aging method in **1** and assuming that the prior year's net accounts receivable were $353,000.

3. Prepare entries in journal form relating to the note received from R. C. Sims.

ANSWER TO REVIEW PROBLEM

1. Uncollectible Accounts Expense computed and balances determined

   a. Percentage of net sales method:

      Uncollectible Accounts Expense = 1.5 percent × $1,200,000 = $18,000

      Allowance for Uncollectible Accounts = $18,000 − $2,100 = $15,900

      Accounts Receivable, Net = $400,000 − $15,900 = $384,100

   b. Accounts receivable aging method:

      Uncollectible Accounts Expense = $2,100 + $17,000 = $19,100

      Allowance for Uncollectible Accounts = $17,000

      Accounts Receivable, Net = $400,000 − $17,000 = $383,000

2. Receivable turnover and average days' sales uncollected computed

$$\text{Receivable Turnover} = \frac{\$1,200,000}{(\$383,000 + \$353,000) \div 2} = 3.3 \text{ times}$$

$$\text{Average Days' Sales Uncollected} = \frac{365 \text{ days}}{3.3} = 110.6 \text{ days}$$

3. Journal entries related to the note prepared

A = L + OE
+   +

Mar. 16	Notes Receivable	15,000.00	
	Sales		15,000.00
	Tractor sold to R. C. Sims;		
	terms of note: 90 days, 9 percent		

A = L + OE
+   +
−

June 14	Accounts Receivable	15,337.50	
	Notes Receivable		15,000.00
	Interest Income		337.50
	The note was dishonored by R. C. Sims		
	Maturity value:		
	$15,000 + ($15,000 × 9/100		
	× 90/360) = $15,337.50		

A = L + OE
+   +
−

June 29	Cash	15,395.02	
	Accounts Receivable		15,337.50
	Interest Income		57.52

         Received payment in full from R. C. Sims
         $15,337.50 + ($15,337.50 \times 9/100 \times$
         15/360)
         $15,337.50 + $57.52 = $15,395.02

Chapter Assignments

**BUILDING YOUR
KNOWLEDGE
FOUNDATION**

QUESTIONS

1. Why does a business need short-term liquid assets? What three issues does management face in managing short-term liquid assets?

2. What is a factor, and what do the terms *factoring with recourse* and *factoring without recourse* mean?

3. What items are included in the Cash account? What is a compensating balance?

4. How do cash equivalents differ from cash? From short-term investments?

5. What are the three kinds of securities held as short-term investments, and how are they valued at the balance sheet date?

6. What are unrealized gains and losses on trading securities? On what statement are they reported?

7. Which of the following lettered items should be in Accounts Receivable? If an item does not belong in Accounts Receivable, tell where on the balance sheet it does belong: (a) installment accounts receivable from regular customers, due monthly for three years; (b) debit balances in customers' accounts; (c) receivables from employees; (d) credit balances in customers' accounts; (e) receivables from officers of the company.

8. Why does a company sell on credit if it expects that some of the accounts will not be paid? What role does a credit department play in selling on credit?

9. What accounting rule is violated by the direct charge-off method of recognizing uncollectible accounts? Why?

10. According to generally accepted accounting principles, at what point in the cycle of selling and collecting does a loss on an uncollectible account occur?

11. Are the following terms different in any way: allowance for bad debts, allowance for doubtful accounts, allowance for uncollectible accounts?

12. What is the effect on net income of management's taking an optimistic versus a pessimistic view of estimated uncollectible accounts?

13. In what ways is Allowance for Uncollectible Accounts similar to Accumulated Depreciation? In what ways is it different?

14. What is the reasoning behind the percentage of net sales method and the accounts receivable aging method of estimating uncollectible accounts?

15. What procedure for estimating uncollectible accounts also gives management a view of the status of collections and the overall quality of accounts receivable?

16. After adjusting and closing the accounts at the end of the year, suppose that Accounts Receivable is $176,000 and Allowance for Uncollectible Accounts is $14,500. (a) What is the collectible value of Accounts Receivable? (b) If the $450 account of a bankrupt customer is written off in the first month of the new year, what will be the resulting collectible value of Accounts Receivable?

17. Why should an account that has been written off as uncollectible be reinstated if the amount owed is subsequently collected?

18. What is a promissory note? Who is the maker? Who is the payee?

19. What are the maturity dates of these notes: (a) a three-month note dated August 16, (b) a 90-day note dated August 16, and (c) a 60-day note dated March 25?

SHORT EXERCISES

SE 1.
LO 1 Management Issues

Indicate whether each of the actions below is related to (a) managing cash needs during seasonal cycles, (b) setting credit policies, or (c) financing receivables.

1. Selling accounts receivable to a factor
2. Borrowing funds for short-term needs during slow periods
3. Conducting thorough checks of new customers' ability to pay
4. Investing cash that is not currently needed for operations

SE 2.
LO 1 Short-Term Liquidity Ratios

Slater Company has cash of $20,000, short-term investments of $25,000, net accounts receivable of $45,000, inventory of $44,000, accounts payable of $60,000, and net sales of $360,000. Last year's net accounts receivable were $35,000. Compute the following ratios: quick ratio, receivable turnover, and average days' sales uncollected. Assume there are no current liabilities other than accounts payable.

SE 3.
LO 2 Cash and Cash Equivalents

Compute the amount of cash and cash equivalents on Quay Company's balance sheet if, on the balance sheet date, it has currency and coins on hand of $500, deposits in checking accounts of $3,000, U.S. Treasury bills due in 80 days of $30,000, and U.S. Treasury bonds due in 200 days of $50,000.

SE 4.
LO 3 Held-to-Maturity Securities

On May 31, Renata Company invested $49,000 in U.S. Treasury bills. The bills mature in 120 days at $50,000. Prepare entries to record the purchase on May 31; the adjustment to accrue interest on June 30, which is the end of the fiscal year; and the receipt of cash at the maturity date of September 28.

SE 5.
LO 3 Trading Securities

Monika Corporation began investing in trading securities this year. At the end of 20x1, the following trading portfolio existed:

Security	Cost	Market Value
Sara Lee (10,000 shares)	$220,000	$330,000
Skyline (5,000 shares)	100,000	75,000
Totals	$320,000	$405,000

Prepare the necessary year-end adjusting entry on December 31 and the entry for the sale of all the Skyline shares on the following March 23 for $95,000.

SE 6.
LO 4 Percentage of Net Sales Method

At the end of October, Mafa Company management estimates the uncollectible accounts expense to be 1 percent of net sales of $2,770,000. Give the entry to record the uncollectible accounts expense, assuming that the Allowance for Uncollectible Accounts has a debit balance of $14,000.

SE 7.
LO 4 Accounts Receivable Aging Method

An aging analysis on June 30 of the accounts receivable of Texbar Corporation indicates uncollectible accounts of $43,000. Give the entry to record uncollectible accounts expense under each of the following independent assumptions: (a) Allowance for Uncollectible Accounts has a credit balance of $9,000 before adjustment, and (b) Allowance for Uncollectible Accounts has a debit balance of $7,000 before adjustment.

SE 8.
LO 4 Write-off of Accounts Receivable

Key Company, which uses the allowance method, has an account receivable from Sandy Burgess of $4,400 that it deems to be uncollectible. Prepare the entries on May 31 to write off the account and on August 13 to record an unexpected receipt of $1,000 from Burgess. The company does not expect to collect more from Burgess.

SE 9.
LO 5 Notes Receivable Entries

On August 25, Rostin Company received a 90-day, 9 percent note in settlement of an account receivable in the amount of $10,000. Record the receipt of the note, the accrual of interest at fiscal year end on September 30, and collection of the note on the due date.

EXERCISES

E 1.
LO 1 Management Issues

Indicate whether each of the following actions is primarily related to (a) managing cash needs during seasonal cycles, (b) setting credit policies, or (c) financing receivables.

1. Buying a U.S. Treasury bill with cash that is not needed for a few months
2. Comparing receivable turnovers for two years
3. Setting policy on which customers may buy on credit
4. Selling notes receivable to a financing company
5. Borrowing funds for short-term needs during the period of the year when sales are low
6. Changing the terms for credit sales in an effort to reduce the average days' sales uncollected
7. Using a factor to provide operating funds
8. Establishing a department whose responsibility is to approve customers' credit

E 2.
LO 1 Short-Term Liquidity Ratios

Using the following data from the financial statements of Phillipi Company, compute the quick ratio, the receivable turnover, and the average days' sales uncollected:

Current Assets	
Cash	$ 70,000
Short-Term Investments	170,000
Notes Receivable	240,000
Accounts Receivable, Net	200,000
Inventory	500,000
Prepaid Assets	50,000
Total Current Assets	$1,230,000
Current Liabilities	
Notes Payable	$ 300,000
Accounts Payable	150,000
Accrued Liabilities	20,000
Total Current Liabilities	$ 470,000
Net Sales	$1,600,000
Last Period's Accounts Receivable, Net	$ 180,000

E 3.
LO 2 Cash and Cash Equivalents

At year end, Burkes Company had currency and coins in cash registers of $2,800, money orders from customers of $5,000, deposits in checking accounts of $32,000, U.S. Treasury bills due in 80 days of $90,000, certificates of deposits at the bank that mature in six months of $100,000, and U.S. Treasury bonds due in one year of $50,000. Calculate the amount of cash and cash equivalents that will be shown on the company's year-end balance sheet.

E 4.
LO 3 Held-to-Maturity Securities

Isak Company experiences heavy sales in the summer and early fall, after which time it has excess cash to invest until the next spring. On November 1, 20x1, the company invested $194,000 in U.S. Treasury bills. The bills mature in 180 days at $200,000. Prepare entries to record the purchase on November 1; the adjustment to accrue interest on December 31, which is the end of the fiscal year; and the receipt of cash at the maturity date of April 30.

E 5.
LO 3 Trading Securities

Vida Corporation began investing in trading securities and engaged in the following transactions:

Jan. 6 Purchased 7,000 shares of Quaker Oats stock, $30 per share.
Feb. 15 Purchased 9,000 shares of EG&G, $22 per share.

At June 30 year end, Quaker Oats was trading at $40 per share and EG&G was trading at $18 per share. Record the entries for the purchases. Then record the necessary year-end adjusting entry. (Include a schedule of the trading portfolio cost and market in the explanation.) Also record the entry for the sale of all the EG&G shares on August 20 for $16 per share. Is the last entry affected by the June 30 adjustment?

E 6.

LO 4 **Percentage of Net Sales Method**

At the end of the year, Nassis Enterprises estimates the uncollectible accounts expense to be .7 percent of net sales of $30,300,000. The current credit balance of Allowance for Uncollectible Accounts is $51,600. Prepare the entry in journal form to record the uncollectible accounts expense. What is the balance of Allowance for Uncollectible Accounts after this adjustment?

E 7.

LO 4 **Accounts Receivable Aging Method**

Accounts Receivable of Cho Company shows a debit balance of $52,000 at the end of the year. An aging analysis of the individual accounts indicates estimated uncollectible accounts to be $3,350.

Prepare the entry in journal form to record the uncollectible accounts expense under each of the following independent assumptions: (a) Allowance for Uncollectible Accounts has a credit balance of $400 before adjustment, and (b) Allowance for Uncollectible Accounts has a debit balance of $400 before adjustment. What is the balance of Allowance for Uncollectible Accounts after this adjustment?

E 8.

LO 4 **Aging Method and Net Sales Method Contrasted**

At the beginning of 20xx, the balances for Accounts Receivable and Allowance for Uncollectible Accounts were $430,000 and $31,400, respectively. During the current year, credit sales were $3,200,000 and collections on account were $2,950,000. In addition, $35,000 in uncollectible accounts were written off.

Using T accounts, determine the year-end balances of Accounts Receivable and Allowance for Uncollectible Accounts. Then make the year-end adjusting entry to record the uncollectible accounts expense, and show the year-end balance sheet presentation of Accounts Receivable and Allowance for Uncollectible Accounts under each of the following conditions:

a. Management estimates the percentage of uncollectible credit sales to be 1.2 percent of total credit sales.
b. Based on an aging of accounts receivable, management estimates the end-of-year uncollectible accounts receivable to be $38,700.

Post the results of each of the entries to the T account for Allowance for Uncollectible Accounts.

E 9.

LO 4 **Aging Method and Net Sales Method Contrasted**

During 20x1, Days Supply Company had net sales of $2,850,000. Most of the sales were on credit. At the end of 20x1, the balance of Accounts Receivable was $350,000 and Allowance for Uncollectible Accounts had a debit balance of $12,000. Management has two methods of estimating uncollectible accounts expense: (a) The percentage of uncollectible sales is 1.5 percent of net sales, and (b) based on an aging of accounts receivable, the end-of-year uncollectible accounts total $35,000. Make the end-of-year adjusting entry to record the uncollectible accounts expense under each method, and tell what the balance of Allowance for Uncollectible Accounts will be after each adjustment. Why are the results different? Which method is likely to be more reliable?

E 10.

LO 4 **Aging Method and Net Sales Method Contrasted**

The Washington Parts Company sells merchandise on credit. During the fiscal year ended July 31, the company had net sales of $4,600,000. At the end of the year, it had Accounts Receivable of $1,200,000 and a debit balance in Allowance for Uncollectible Accounts of $6,800. In the past, approximately 1.4 percent of net sales have proved uncollectible. Also, an aging analysis of accounts receivable reveals that $60,000 of the receivables appear to be uncollectible. Prepare entries in journal form to record uncollectible accounts expense using: (a) the percentage of net sales method and (b) the accounts receivable aging method.

What is the resulting balance of Allowance for Uncollectible Accounts under each method? How would your answers under each method change if Allowance for Uncollectible Accounts had a credit balance of $6,800 instead of a debit balance? Why do the methods result in different balances?

E 11.

LO 4 **Accounts Receivable Transactions**

Assuming that the allowance method is being used, prepare entries in journal form to record the following transactions:

July 12, 20x4   Sold merchandise to Bea Johnson for $1,800, terms n/10.
Oct. 18, 20x4   Received $600 from Bea Johnson on account.

May 8, 20x5 Wrote off as uncollectible the balance of the Bea Johnson account when she declared bankruptcy.

June 22, 20x5 Unexpectedly received a check for $200 from Bea Johnson.

E 12.

LO 5 Interest Computations

Determine the interest on the following notes:

a. $22,800 at 10 percent for 90 days
b. $16,000 at 12 percent for 60 days
c. $18,000 at 9 percent for 30 days
d. $30,000 at 15 percent for 120 days
e. $10,800 at 6 percent for 60 days

E 13.

LO 5 Notes Receivable Transactions

Prepare entries in journal form to record the following transactions:

Jan. 16 Sold merchandise to Katz Corporation on account for $36,000, terms n/30.
Feb. 15 Accepted a 90-day, 10 percent, $36,000 note from Katz Corporation in lieu of payment of account.
May 16 Katz Corporation dishonored the note.
June 15 Received payment in full from Katz Corporation, including interest at 10 percent from the date the note was dishonored.

E 14.

LO 5 Adjusting Entries: Interest Income

Prepare entries in journal form (assuming reversing entries were not made) to record the following:

Dec. 1 Received a 90-day, 12 percent note for $10,000 from a customer for a sale of merchandise.
     31 Made end-of-year adjustment for interest income.
Mar. 1 Received payment in full for note and interest.

E 15.

LO 5 Notes Receivable Transactions

Prepare entries in journal form to record these transactions:

Jan. 5 Accepted a 60-day, 10 percent, $4,800 note dated this day in granting a time extension on the past-due account of S. Lavelle.
Mar. 6 S. Lavelle paid the maturity value of his $4,800 note.
     9 Accepted a 60-day, 12 percent, $3,000 note dated this day in granting a time extension on the past-due account of R. Tamayo.
May 8 When asked for payment, R. Tamayo dishonored his note.
June 7 R. Tamayo paid in full the maturity value of the note plus interest at 12 percent for the period since May 8.

PROBLEMS

P 1.

LO 3 Held-to-Maturity and Trading Securities

During certain periods, Weller Company invests its excess cash until it is needed. During 20x1 and 20x2, the company engaged in the following transactions:

20x1

Jan. 16 Invested $146,000 in 120-day U.S. Treasury bills that had a maturity value of $150,000.
Apr. 15 Purchased 10,000 shares of Rani Tools common stock at $40 per share and 5,000 shares of Soder Gas common stock at $30 per share as trading securities.
May 16 Received maturity value of U.S. Treasury bills in cash.
June 2 Received dividends of $2.00 per share from Rani Tools and $1.50 per share from Soder Gas.
     30 Made year-end adjusting entry for trading securities. Market price of Rani Tools shares is $32 per share and of Soder Gas shares is $35 per share.
Nov. 14 Sold all the shares of Rani Tools for $42 per share.

20x2

Feb. 15 Purchased 9,000 shares of MKD Communications for $50 per share.
Apr. 1 Invested $195,500 in 120-day U.S. Treasury bills that had a maturity value of $200,000.

June 1 Received dividends of $2.20 per share from Soder Gas.
  30 Made year-end adjusting entry for held-to-maturity securities.
  30 Made year-end adjusting entry for trading securities. Market price of Soder Gas shares is $33 per share and of MKD Communications shares is $60 per share.

1. Prepare entries in journal form to record the preceding transactions, assuming that Weller Company's fiscal year ends on June 30.

2. Show the balance sheet presentation of short-term investments on June 30, 20x2.

P 2.
LO 1 Methods of Estimating
LO 4 Uncollectible Accounts and Receivables Analysis

On December 31 of last year, the balance sheet of Vaslor Company had Accounts Receivable of $298,000 and a credit balance in Allowance for Uncollectible Accounts of $20,300. During the current year, the company's records included the following selected activities: (a) sales on account, $1,195,000; (b) sales returns and allowances, $73,000; (c) collections from customers, $1,150,000; (d) accounts written off as worthless, $16,000. In the past, the company had found that 1.6 percent of net sales would not be collected.

1. Prepare T accounts for Accounts Receivable and Allowance for Uncollectible Accounts. Enter the beginning balances, and show the effects on these accounts of the items listed above, summarizing the year's activity. Determine the ending balance of each account.

2. Compute Uncollectible Accounts Expense and determine the ending balance of Allowance for Uncollectible Accounts under (a) the percentage of net sales method and (b) the accounts receivable aging method, assuming an aging of the accounts receivable shows that $20,000 may be uncollectible.

3. Compute the receivable turnover and average days' sales uncollected, using the data from the accounts receivable aging method in **2**.

4. How do you explain the fact that the two methods in **2** result in different amounts for Uncollectible Accounts Expense? What rationale underlies each method?

P 3.
LO 4 Accounts Receivable Aging Method

Thant Company uses the accounts receivable aging method to estimate uncollectible accounts. The Accounts Receivable account had a debit balance of $88,430 and Allowance for Uncollectible Accounts had a credit balance of $7,200 at the beginning of the year. During the year, the company had sales on account of $473,000, sales returns and allowances of $4,200, worthless accounts written off of $7,900, and collections from customers of $450,730. At the end of the year (December 31), a junior accountant for the company was preparing an aging analysis of accounts receivable. At the top of page 6 of the report, the following totals appeared:

Customer Account	Total	Not Yet Due	1–30 Days Past Due	31–60 Days Past Due	61–90 Days Past Due	Over 90 Days Past Due
Balance Forward	$89,640	$49,030	$24,110	$9,210	$3,990	$3,300

The following accounts remained to be classified to finish the analysis:

Account	Amount	Due Date
B. Singh	$ 930	Jan. 14 (next year)
L. Wells	620	Dec. 24
A. Roc	1,955	Sept. 28
T. Cila	2,100	Aug. 16
M. Mix	375	Dec. 14
S. Price	2,685	Jan. 23 (next year)
J. Wendt	295	Nov. 5
	$8,960	

From past experience, the company has found that the following rates are realistic to estimate uncollectible accounts:

Time	Percentage Considered Uncollectible
Not yet due	2
1–30 days past due	4
31–60 days past due	20
61–90 days past due	30
Over 90 days past due	50

1. Complete the aging analysis of accounts receivable.

2. Determine the end-of-year balances (before adjustments) of Accounts Receivable and Allowance for Uncollectible Accounts.

3. Prepare an analysis computing the estimated uncollectible accounts.

4. Prepare the entry in journal form to record the estimated uncollectible accounts expense for the year (round the adjustment to the nearest whole dollar).

P 4.

LO 5   Notes Receivable Transactions

Abraham Manufacturing Company sells engines. The company engaged in the following transactions involving promissory notes:

Jan. 10   Sold engines to Anton Company for $60,000, terms n/10.

20   Accepted a 90-day, 12 percent promissory note in settlement of the account from Anton.

Apr. 20   Received payment from Anton Company for the note and interest.

May   5   Sold engines to Yu Company for $40,000, terms n/10.

15   Received $8,000 cash and a 60-day, 13 percent note for $32,000 in settlement of the Yu account.

July 14   When asked to pay, Yu dishonored the note.

Aug. 2   Wrote off the Yu account as uncollectible after receiving news that the company declared bankruptcy.

5   Received a 90-day, 11 percent note for $30,000 from Vila Company in settlement of an account receivable.

Nov. 3   When asked to pay, Vila dishonored the note.

9   Received payment in full from Vila, including 15 percent interest for the six days since the note was dishonored.

REQUIRED   Prepare entries in journal form to record the preceding transactions.

ALTERNATE PROBLEMS

P 5.

LO 3   Held-to-Maturity and Trading Securities

Smitty Distributions follows a policy of investing excess cash until it is needed. During 20x1 and 20x2, the company engaged in the following transactions:

20x1

Feb.   1   Invested $97,000 in 120-day U.S. Treasury bills that had a maturity value of $100,000.

Mar. 30   Purchased 20,000 shares of Files Company common stock at $16 per share and 12,000 shares of Sun's Fruit, Inc., common stock at $10 per share as trading securities.

June 1   Received maturity value of U.S. Treasury bills in cash.

June 10   Received dividends of $.50 per share from Files Company and $.25 per share from Sun's Fruit, Inc.

30   Made year-end adjusting entry for trading securities. Market price of Files Company shares is $13 per share and of Sun's Fruit, Inc., shares is $12 per share.

Dec.   3   Sold all the shares of Files Company for $12 per share.

20x2

Mar. 17   Purchased 15,000 shares of Bytes, Inc., for $9 per share.

May 31   Invested $116,000 in 120-day U.S. Treasury bills that had a maturity value of $120,000.

June 10   Received dividends of $.30 per share from Sun's Fruit, Inc.
      30   Made year-end adjusting entry for held-to-maturity securities.
      30   Made year-end adjusting entry for trading securities. Market price of Sun's Fruit, Inc., shares is $6 per share and of Bytes, Inc., shares is $11 per share.

REQUIRED

1. Prepare entries in journal form to record these transactions, assuming that Smitty Distributions' fiscal year ends on June 30.
2. Show the balance sheet presentation of short-term investments on June 30, 20x2.

P 6.
LO 1   Methods of Estimating
LO 4   Uncollectible Accounts and Receivables Analysis

Hernandez Company had an Accounts Receivable balance of $320,000 and a credit balance in Allowance for Uncollectible Accounts of $16,700 at January 1, 20xx. During the year, the company recorded the following transactions:

a. Sales on account, $1,052,000
b. Sales returns and allowances by credit customers, $53,400
c. Collections from customers, $993,000
d. Worthless accounts written off, $19,800

The company's past history indicates that 2.5 percent of its net credit sales will not be collected.

REQUIRED

1. Prepare T accounts for Accounts Receivable and Allowance for Uncollectible Accounts. Enter the beginning balances, and show the effects on these accounts of the items listed above, summarizing the year's activity. Determine the ending balance of each account.
2. Compute Uncollectible Accounts Expense and determine the ending balance of Allowance for Uncollectible Accounts under (a) the percentage of net sales method and (b) the accounts receivable aging method, assuming an aging of the accounts receivable shows that $24,000 may be uncollectible.
3. Compute the receivable turnover and average days' sales uncollected, using the data from the accounts receivable aging method in **2.**
4. How do you explain the fact that the two methods in **2** result in different amounts for Uncollectible Accounts Expense? What rationale underlies each method?

P 7.
LO 4   Accounts Receivable Aging Method

The Forsell Fashions Store uses the accounts receivable aging method to estimate uncollectible accounts. The balance of the Accounts Receivable account was a debit of $446,341 and the balance of Allowance for Uncollectible Accounts was a credit of $43,000 at February 1, 20x1. During the year, the store had sales on account of $3,724,000, sales returns and allowances of $63,000, worthless accounts written off of $44,300, and collections from customers of $3,214,000. As part of the end-of-year (January 31, 20x2) procedures, an aging analysis of accounts receivable is prepared. The totals of the analysis, which is partially complete, follow:

Customer Account	Total	Not Yet Due	1–30 Days Past Due	31–60 Days Past Due	61–90 Days Past Due	Over 90 Days Past Due
Balance Forward	$793,791	$438,933	$149,614	$106,400	$57,442	$41,402

The following accounts remain to be classified to finish the analysis:

Account	Amount	Due Date
J. Curtis	$10,977	Jan. 15
T. Dawson	9,314	Feb. 15 (next fiscal year)
L. Zapata	8,664	Dec. 20
R. Copa	780	Oct. 1
E. Land	14,810	Jan. 4
S. Qadri	6,316	Nov. 15
A. Rosenthal	4,389	Mar. 1 (next fiscal year)
	$55,250	

From past experience, the company has found that the following rates are realistic to estimate uncollectible accounts:

Time	Percentage Considered Uncollectible
Not yet due	2
1–30 days past due	5
31–60 days past due	15
61–90 days past due	25
Over 90 days past due	50

REQUIRED

1. Complete the aging analysis of accounts receivable.

2. Determine the end-of-year balances (before adjustments) of Accounts Receivable and Allowance for Uncollectible Accounts.

3. Prepare an analysis computing the estimated uncollectible accounts.

4. Prepare the entry in journal form to record the estimated uncollectible accounts expense for the year (round the adjustment to the nearest whole dollar).

P 8.

LO 5   Notes Receivable Transactions

Ault Importing Company engaged in the following transactions involving promissory notes:

Jan. 14 Sold merchandise to Riordan Company for $37,000, terms n/30.

Feb. 13 Received $8,400 in cash from Riordan Company and received a 90-day, 8 percent promissory note for the balance of the account.

May 14 Received payment in full from Riordan Company.

15 Received a 60-day, 12 percent note from Calvin Eng Company in payment of a past-due account, $12,000.

July 14 When asked to pay, Calvin Eng Company dishonored the note.

20 Received a check from Calvin Eng Company for payment of the maturity value of the note and interest at 12 percent for the six days beyond maturity.

25 Sold merchandise to Leona Fancy Company for $36,000, with payment of $6,000 cash down and the remainder on account.

31 Received a 45-day, 10 percent, $30,000 promissory note from Leona Fancy Company for the outstanding account receivable.

Sept. 14 When asked to pay, Leona Fancy Company dishonored the note.

25 Wrote off the Leona Fancy Company account as uncollectible following news that the company had declared bankruptcy.

REQUIRED

Prepare entries in journal form to record the preceding transactions.

EXPANDING YOUR CRITICAL THINKING, COMMUNICATION, AND INTERPERSONAL SKILLS

SKILLS DEVELOPMENT

Conceptual Analysis

SD 1.

LO 1   Management of Cash
LO 2
LO 3

Academia Publishing Company publishes college textbooks in the sciences and humanities. More than 50 percent of the company's sales occur in July, August, and December. Its cash balances are largest in August, September, and January. During the rest of the year, its cash receipts are low. The corporate treasurer keeps the cash in a bank checking account earning little or no interest and pays bills from this account as they come due. To survive, the company has borrowed money during some slow sales

 Cash Flow   CD-ROM   Communication   Critical Thinking   Ethics   General Ledger   Group Activity   Hot Links to Real Companies International Internet   Key Ratio Memo Spreadsheet

months. The loans were repaid in the months when cash receipts were largest. A management consultant has suggested that the company institute a new cash management plan under which cash would be invested in marketable securities as it is received and securities would be sold when the funds are needed. In this way, the company will earn income on the cash and may realize a gain through an increase in the value of the securities, thus reducing the need for borrowing. The president of the company has asked you to assess the plan. Write a memorandum to the president that lays out the accounting implications of this cash management plan for cash and cash equivalents and for the three types of marketable securities. Include an assessment of the plan and any disadvantages to it.

SD 2.

LO 1 **Role of Credit Sales**
LO 4

Mitsubishi Corp.,[12] a broadly diversified Japanese corporation, instituted a credit plan called Three Diamonds for customers who buy its major electronic products, such as large-screen televisions and videotape recorders, from specified retail dealers. Under the plan, approved customers who make purchases in July of one year do not have to make any payments until September of the next year and pay no interest for the intervening months. Mitsubishi pays the dealer the full amount less a small fee, sends the customer a Mitsubishi credit card, and collects from the customer at the specified time. What was Mitsubishi's motivation for establishing such generous credit terms? What costs are involved? What are the accounting implications?

SD 3.

LO 1 **Receivables Financing**

Siegel Appliances, Inc., is a small manufacturer of washing machines and dryers located in central Michigan. Siegel sells most of its appliances to large, established discount retail companies that market the appliances under their own names. Siegel sells the appliances on trade credit terms of n/60. If a customer wants a longer term, however, Siegel will accept a note with a term of up to nine months. At present, the company is having cash flow troubles and needs $5 million immediately. Its cash balance is $200,000, its accounts receivable balance is $2.3 million, and its notes receivable balance is $3.7 million. How might Siegel's management use its accounts receivable and notes receivable to raise the cash it needs? What are the company's prospects for raising the needed cash?

Group Activity: Assign to in-class groups and debrief.

Ethical Dilemma

SD 4.

LO 1 **Ethics, Uncollectible**
LO 4 **Accounts, and Short-Term**
Objectives

Fitzsimmons Designs, a successful retail furniture company, is located in an affluent suburb where a major insurance company has just announced a restructuring that will lay off 4,000 employees. Fitzsimmons sells quality furniture, usually on credit. Accounts Receivable represents one of the major assets of the company and, although the company's annual uncollectible accounts losses are not out of line, they represent a sizable amount. The company depends on bank loans for its financing. Sales and net income have declined in the past year, and some customers are falling behind in paying their accounts. George Fitzsimmons, owner of the business, knows that the bank's loan officer likes to see a steady performance. Therefore, he has instructed the controller to underestimate the uncollectible accounts this year to show a small growth in earnings. Fitzsimmons believes the short-term action is justified because future successful years will average out the losses, and since the company has a history of success, the adjustments are meaningless accounting measures anyway. Are Fitzsimmons's actions ethical? Would any parties be harmed by his actions? How important is it to try to be accurate in estimating losses from uncollectible accounts?

Group Activity: Assign to in-class groups and debate the ethical issues.

Research Activity

SD 5.

LO 1 **Stock and Treasury**
LO 3 **Investments**

Find a recent issue of *The Wall Street Journal* in your school library. Turn to the third, or C, section, entitled "Money & Investing." From the index at the top of the page, locate the listing of New York Stock Exchange (NYSE) stocks and turn to that page. From the

listing of stocks, find five companies you have heard of, such as IBM, Deere, McDonald's, or Ford. Copy down the range of each company's stock price for the last year and the current closing price. Also copy down the dividend, if any, per share. How much did the market values of the common stocks you picked vary in the last year? Do these data demonstrate the need to value short-term investments of this type at market? How does accounting for short-term investments in these common stocks differ from accounting for short-term investments in U.S. Treasury bills? How are dividends received on investments in these common stocks accounted for?

Be prepared to hand in your notes and to discuss the results of your investigation during class.

Decision-Making Practice

SD 6.

LO 3 Accounting for Short-Term Investments

Norman Christmas Tree Company's business—the growing and selling of Christmas trees—is seasonal. By January 1, after its heavy selling season, the company has cash on hand that will not be needed for several months. The company has minimal expenses from January to October and heavy expenses during the harvest and shipping months of November and December. The company's management follows the practice of investing the idle cash in marketable securities, which can be sold as the funds are needed for operations. The company's fiscal year ends on June 30. On January 10 of the current year, the company has cash of $597,300 on hand. It keeps $20,000 on hand for operating expenses and invests the rest as follows:

$100,000 three-month Treasury bills	$ 97,800
1,000 shares of Ford Motor Co. ($50 per share)	50,000
2,500 shares of McDonald's ($50 per share)	125,000
2,100 shares of IBM ($145 per share)	304,500
Total short-term investments	$577,300

During the next few months, Norman Christmas Tree Company receives two quarterly cash dividends from each company (assume February 10 and May 10): $.50 per share from Ford, $.05 per share from McDonald's, and $.25 per share from IBM. The Treasury bills are redeemed at face value on April 10. On June 1 management sells 500 shares of McDonald's at $55 per share. On June 30 the market values of the investments are:

Ford Motor Co.	$61 per share
McDonald's	$46 per share
IBM	$140 per share

Another quarterly dividend is received from each company (assume August 10). All the remaining shares are sold on November 1 at the following prices:

Ford Motor Co.	$55 per share
McDonald's	$44 per share
IBM	$160 per share

1. Record the investment transactions that occurred on January 10, February 10, April 10, May 10, and June 1. The Treasury bills are accounted for as held-to-maturity securities, and the stocks are trading securities. Prepare the required adjusting entry on June 30, and record the investment transactions on August 10 and November 1.

2. Explain how the short-term investments would be shown on the balance sheet on June 30.

3. After November 1, what is the balance of Allowance to Adjust Short-Term Investments to Market, and what will happen to this account next June?

4. What is your assessment of Norman Christmas Tree Company's strategy with regard to idle cash?

FINANCIAL REPORTING AND ANALYSIS

Interpreting Financial Reports

FRA 1.

LO 4 **Accounting for Accounts Receivable**

Bex Co. is a major consumer goods company that sells over 3,000 products in 135 countries. The company's annual report to the Securities and Exchange Commission presented the following data (in thousands) pertaining to net sales and accounts related to accounts receivable for 1999, 2000, and 2001.

	2001	2000	1999
Net Sales	$4,910,000	$4,865,000	$4,888,000
Accounts Receivable	523,000	524,000	504,000
Allowance for Uncollectible Accounts	18,600	21,200	24,500
Uncollectible Accounts Expense	15,000	16,700	15,800
Uncollectible Accounts Written Off	19,300	20,100	17,700
Recoveries of Accounts Previously Written Off	1,700	100	1,000

REQUIRED

1. Compute the ratios of Uncollectible Accounts Expense to Net Sales and to Gross Accounts Receivable and of Allowance for Uncollectible Accounts to Gross Accounts Receivable for 1999, 2000, and 2001.

2. Compute the receivable turnover and average days' sales uncollected for each year, assuming 1998 net accounts receivable are $465,000,000.

3. What is your interpretation of the ratios? What appears to be management's attitude with respect to the collectibility of accounts receivable over the three-year period?

International Company

FRA 2.

LO 1 **Comparison and Interpretation of Ratios**

Philips Electronics, N.V., and **Heineken N.V.** are two of the most famous Dutch companies. Philips is a large, diversified electronics, music, and media company, and Heineken makes a popular beer. Philips is about four times bigger than Heineken, with 1999 revenues of 31.5 billion euros versus 7.1 billion euros for Heineken. Ratios can help in comparing and understanding the companies. For example, the receivable turnovers for the companies for two past years are as follows:[13]

	1999	1998
Philips	6.6 times	7.2 times
Heineken	7.8 times	8.1 times

What do the ratios tell you about the credit policies of the two companies? How long does it take each on average to collect a receivable? What do the ratios tell about the companies' relative needs for capital to finance receivables? Can you tell which company has a better credit policy? Explain your answers.

Toys "R" Us Annual Report

FRA 3.

LO 1 **Analysis of Short-Term**
LO 2 **Liquid Assets**
LO 4

Refer to the Toys "R" Us annual report to answer the following questions.

1. How much cash and cash equivalents did Toys "R" Us have in 2000? Do you suppose most of that amount is cash in the bank or cash equivalents?

2. Toys "R" Us does not disclose an allowance for uncollectible accounts. How do you explain the lack of disclosure?

3. Compute the quick ratios for 1999 and 2000 and comment on them.

4. Compute receivable turnover and average days' sales uncollected for 1999 and 2000 and comment on Toys "R" Us credit policies. Accounts Receivable in 1998 were $175,000,000.

Fingraph® Financial Analyst™

FRA 4.

LO 1 Comparison and Analysis of Short-Term Liquid Assets

Choose any two companies from the same industry in the Fingraph® Financial Analyst™ CD-ROM software. The industry chosen should be one in which accounts receivable is likely to be an important current asset. Suggested industries from which to choose are manufacturing, consumer products, consumer food and beverage, and computers.

1. Find and read in the annual reports for the companies you have selected any reference to cash and cash equivalents, short-term or marketable securities, and accounts receivable in the summary of significant accounting policies or notes to the financial statements.

2. Display and print for the companies you have selected (a) the Current Assets and Current Liabilities Analysis page and (b) the Liquidity and Asset Utilization Analysis page in tabular and graphical form. Prepare a table that compares the quick ratio, receivable turnover, and average days' sales uncollected for both companies for two years.

3. Find and read the liquidity analysis section of management's discussion and analysis in each annual report.

4. Write a one-page executive summary that highlights the accounting policies for short-term liquid assets and compares the short-term liquidity position of the two companies. Include your assessment of the companies' relative liquidity and make reference to management's assessment. Include the Fingraph® pages and your table as an attachment to your report.

Internet Case

FRA 5.

LO 4 Comparison of J.C. Penney and Sears

Go to the Needles Accounting Resource Center at http://college.hmco.com. Under web links, go to the annual reports on the web sites for *J.C. Penney Company, Inc.,* and *Sears, Roebuck and Co.* Find the accounts receivable and marketable securities (if any) on each company's balance sheet and the notes related to these accounts in the notes to the financial statements. If either company has marketable securities, what is the cost and what is the market value of the securities? Does the company currently have a gain or loss on the securities? Which company has the most accounts receivable as a percentage of total assets? What is the percentage of the allowance account to gross accounts receivable for each company? Which company experienced the highest loss rate on its receivables? Why do you think there is a difference? Do the companies finance their receivables? Be prepared to discuss your findings in class.

ENDNOTES

1. Pioneer Electronic Corporation, *Annual Report*, 2000.
2. Michael Selz, "Big Customers' Late Bills Choke Small Suppliers," *The Wall Street Journal*, June 22, 1994.
3. Linda Sandler, "Bally Total Fitness's Accounting Procedures Are Getting Some Skeptical Investors Exercised," *The Wall Street Journal*, August 28, 1998.
4. American Greetings Corp., *Annual Report*, 2000.
5. Adapted from Circuit City Stores, Inc., *Annual Report*, 2000.
6. Bell Atlantic Corp., *Annual Report*, 2000.
7. *Accounting Trends & Techniques* (New York: American Institute of CPAs, 1999), p. 140.
8. Jeffrey Taylor, "Rules on Electronic Transfers of Money Are Being Tightened by U.S. Treasury," *The Wall Street Journal*, September 26, 1994.
9. *Statement of Financial Accounting Standards No. 115,* "Accounting for Certain Investments in Debt and Equity Securities" (Norwalk, Conn.: Financial Accounting Standards Board, 1993).
10. Pioneer Electronic Corporation, *Annual Report*, 1999.
11. Craig S. Smith, "Chinese Companies Writing off Old Debt," *The Wall Street Journal*, December 28, 1995.
12. Information based on promotional brochures received from Mitsubishi Electric Corp.
13. Philips Electronics, N.V., *Annual Report*, 1999; and Heineken N.V., *Annual Report*, 1999.

10

Inventories

DECISION POINT: A USER'S FOCUS

J.C. Penney Company, Inc. The management of inventory for profit is one of management's most complex and challenging tasks. In terms of dollars, the inventory of goods held for sale is one of the largest assets of a merchandising business. As a major retailer, with department stores in all 50 states and Puerto Rico, J.C. Penney Company, Inc., devotes 25 percent, or $6.0 billion, of its $23.6 billion in assets to inventories. What challenges does J.C. Penney's management face in managing its inventory?

Not only must J.C. Penney's management purchase fashions and other merchandise that customers will want to buy, but it must also have the merchandise available in the right locations at the times when customers want to buy it. Management also must try to minimize the cost of inventory while maintaining quality. To these ends, J.C. Penney maintains purchasing offices throughout the world, including Hong Kong, Taipei, Osaka, Seoul, Bangkok, Singapore, Bombay, and Florence. Quality assurance experts operate out of 22 domestic and 14 international offices. Further, the amount of money tied up in inventory must be controlled because of the high cost of borrowing funds and storing inventory. Important accounting decisions include what assumptions to make about the flow of inventory costs, what prices to put on inventory, what inventory systems to use, and how to protect inventory against loss. Proper management of inventory helped J.C. Penney earn net income of $594 million in 1998, but small variations in any inventory decision can mean the difference between a net profit and a net loss.

After three years of steady or increasing profits, J.C. Penney's 1999 net income was down 43 percent to $336 million. Gross margin percentage was lower on higher net sales. J.C. Penney's chairman said, "Improving the profitability of our core department store and drug store business is our top priority." The company announced its plans to close underperforming stores and liquidate certain inventories in the coming year.[1]

Management Issues Associated with Accounting for Inventories

Inventory is considered a current asset because it will normally be sold within a year's time or within a company's operating cycle. For a merchandising business like J.C. Penney or Toys "R" Us, **merchandise inventory** consists of all goods owned and held for sale in the regular course of business.

Inventories are also important for manufacturing companies. Because manufacturers are engaged in the actual making of products, they have three kinds of inventory: raw materials to be used in the production of goods, partially completed products (often called *work in process*), and finished goods ready for sale. For example, in its 1999 annual report, Illinois Tool Works, Inc., disclosed the following inventories (in thousands):

Financial Highlights		
	1999	1998
Inventories		
Raw materials	$ 409,532	$ 376,892
Work in process	94,815	89,073
Finished goods	579,865	570,852
Total inventories	$1,084,212	$1,036,817

In manufacturing operations, the costs of the work in process and the finished goods inventories include not only the cost of the raw materials that go into the product, but also the cost of the labor used to convert the raw materials to finished goods and the overhead costs that support the production process. Included in this latter category are such costs as indirect materials (for example, paint, glue, and nails), indirect labor (such as the salaries of supervisors), factory rent, depreciation of plant assets, utilities costs, and insurance costs. The methods for maintaining and pricing inventory explained in this chapter are applicable to manufactured goods, but because the details of accounting for manufacturing companies are usually covered as a management accounting topic, this chapter focuses on accounting for merchandising firms.

Applying the Matching Rule to Inventories

The American Institute of Certified Public Accountants states, "A major objective of accounting for inventories is the proper determination of income through the process of matching appropriate costs against revenues."[2] Note that the objective is the proper determination of income through the matching of costs and revenues, not the determination of the most realistic inventory value. These two objectives are sometimes incompatible, in which case the objective of income determination takes precedence.

The reason inventory accounting is so important to income measurement is linked to the way income is measured on the merchandising income statement. Recall that gross margin is computed as the difference between net sales and cost of goods sold and that cost of goods sold is dependent on the cost assigned to inventory or goods not sold. Because of those relationships, the higher the cost of ending inventory, the lower the cost of goods sold and the higher the resulting gross margin. Conversely, the lower the value assigned to ending inventory, the higher the cost of goods sold and the lower the gross margin. Because the amount of gross margin has a direct effect on the amount of net income, the amount assigned to ending inventory directly affects the amount of net income. *In effect, the value assigned to the ending inventory determines what portion of the cost of goods available for sale is assigned to cost of goods sold and what portion is assigned to the balance sheet as inventory to be carried over into the next accounting period.*

Assessing the Impact of Inventory Decisions

Figure 1 summarizes the management choices with regard to inventory systems and methods. The decisions usually result in different amounts of reported net income. As a result, the choices affect both the external evaluation of the company by investors and creditors and such internal evaluations as performance reviews, bonuses, and executive compensation. Because income is affected, the valuation of inventory may also have a considerable effect on the amount of income taxes paid. Federal income tax authorities have specific regulations about the acceptability of different methods. As a result, management is sometimes faced with balancing the goal of proper income determination with that of minimizing income taxes. Another consideration is that since the choice of inventory valuation method affects the amount of income taxes paid, it also affects a company's cash flows.

Evaluating the Level of Inventory

The level of inventory has important economic consequences for a company. Ideally, management wants to have a great variety and quantity on hand so that

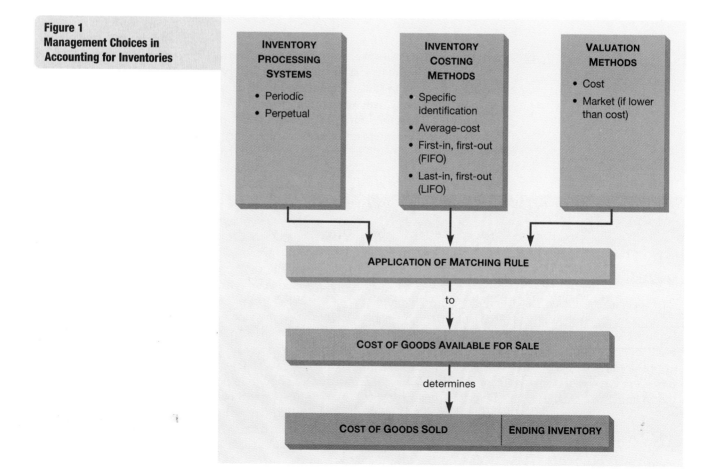

Figure 1
Management Choices in Accounting for Inventories

customers have a large choice and do not have to wait. Such an inventory policy is not costless, however. The cost of handling and storage and the interest cost of the funds necessary to maintain high inventory levels are usually substantial. On the other hand, the maintenance of low inventory levels may result in lost sales and disgruntled customers. Common measures used in the evaluation of inventory levels are inventory turnover and its related measure, average days' inventory on hand. **Inventory turnover** is a measure similar to receivable turnover. It indicates the number of times a company's average inventory is sold during an accounting period. Inventory turnover is computed by dividing cost of goods sold by average inventory. For example, J.C. Penney's cost of goods sold was $23,374 million in 1999, and its merchandise inventory was $5,947 million at the end of 1999 and $6,031 million at the end of 1998. Its inventory turnover is computed as follows:

$$\text{Inventory Turnover} = \frac{\text{Cost of Goods Sold}}{\text{Average Inventory}}$$

$$= \frac{\$23,374,000,000}{(\$5,947,000,000 + \$6,031,000,000) \div 2}$$

$$= \frac{\$23,374,000,000}{\$5,989,000,000} = 3.9 \text{ times}$$

The **average days' inventory on hand** indicates the average number of days required to sell the inventory on hand. It is found by dividing the number of days in a year by the inventory turnover, as follows:

$$\text{Average Days' Inventory on Hand} = \frac{\text{Number of Days in a Year}}{\text{Inventory Turnover}}$$

$$= \frac{365 \text{ days}}{3.9 \text{ times}} = 93.6 \text{ days}$$

J.C. Penney turned its inventory over 3.9 times in 1999, or on average every 93.6 days. These figures are reasonable because J.C. Penney is in a business where fashions change every season, or about every 100 days. Management would want to sell all of each season's inventory within 90 days, even while making purchases for the next season. There are natural levels of inventory in every industry, as shown for selected merchandising and manufacturing industries in Figures 2 and 3. However,

FOCUS ON BUSINESS TECHNOLOGY

Computer maker Dell Computer Corporation has long been a model of excellent inventory management with high inventory turnover ratios and keen cost controls. The use of computer technology has been critical to its success in these areas. Dell's speed from order to delivery sets the industry standard. Consider that a computer ordered by 9 A.M. can be delivered the next day by 9 P.M. How can Dell do this when it doesn't start ordering components and assembling computers until an order is booked? First, Dell's suppliers keep components warehoused just minutes from Dell's factories, making possible efficient, just-in-time operations. Another time and money saver is the handling of monitors. Dell sends an e-mail message to a shipper such as United Parcel Service. The shipper pulls a computer monitor from supplier stocks and schedules it to arrive with the PC. Monitors are no longer shipped first to Dell and then on to buyers. In addition to contributing to a high inventory turnover, this practice saves Dell about $30 per monitor in freight costs. Dell is showing the world how to run a business in the cyber age by selling more than $1 million worth of computers a day on its web site.[3]

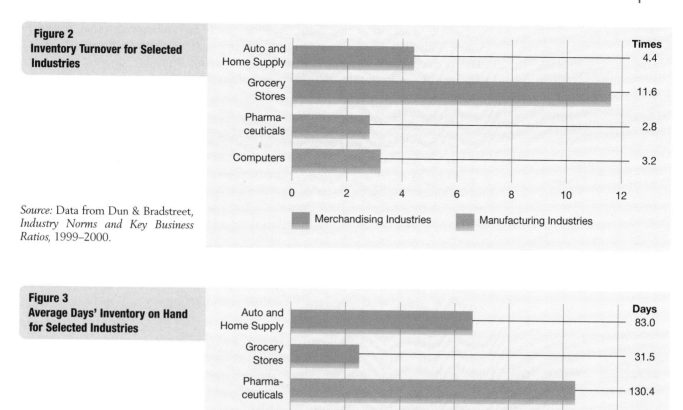

Figure 2
Inventory Turnover for Selected Industries

Source: Data from Dun & Bradstreet, *Industry Norms and Key Business Ratios*, 1999–2000.

Figure 3
Average Days' Inventory on Hand for Selected Industries

Source: Data from Dun & Bradstreet, *Industry Norms and Key Business Ratios*, 1999–2000.

companies that are able to maintain their inventories at lower levels and still satisfy customer needs are the most successful.

Merchandising and manufacturing companies are attempting to reduce their levels of inventory by changing to a **just-in-time operating environment**. In such an environment, rather than stockpiling inventories for later use, companies work closely with suppliers to coordinate and schedule shipments so that goods arrive just at the time they are needed. Less money is tied up in inventories, and the costs associated with carrying inventories are reduced. For example, Pacific Bell was able to close six warehouses by implementing just-in-time inventory management.

Pricing Inventory Under the Periodic Inventory System

OBJECTIVE

2 Define *inventory cost* and relate it to goods flow and cost flow

According to the AICPA, "The primary basis of accounting for inventories is cost, which has been defined generally as the price paid or consideration given to acquire an asset."[4] This definition of **inventory cost** has generally been interpreted to include the following costs: (1) invoice price less purchases discounts; (2) freight or transportation in, including insurance in transit; and (3) applicable taxes and tariffs. There are other costs—for ordering, receiving, and storing—that should in principle also be included in inventory cost. In practice, however, it is so difficult to allocate such costs to specific inventory items that they are usually considered expenses of the accounting period instead of inventory costs.

Merchandise in Transit

Because merchandise inventory includes all items owned by a company and held for sale, the status of any merchandise in transit, whether it is being sold or being purchased by the inventorying company, must be examined to determine if the merchandise should be included in the inventory count. As Figure 4 illustrates, neither the customer nor the buyer has physical possession of the merchandise. Ownership of these goods in transit is determined by the terms of the shipping agreement, which indicate whether title has passed. Outgoing goods shipped FOB (free on board) destination would be included in the seller's merchandise inventory, whereas those shipped FOB shipping point would not. Conversely, incoming goods shipped FOB shipping point would be included in the buyer's merchandise inventory, but those shipped FOB destination would not.

Merchandise on Hand Not Included in Inventory

At the time a physical inventory is taken, there may be merchandise on hand to which the company does not hold title. One category of such goods is merchandise that has been sold and is awaiting delivery to the buyer. Since the sale has been completed, title to the goods has passed to the buyer, and the merchandise should be included in the inventory of the buyer and not of the seller. A second category is goods held on consignment. A **consignment** is merchandise placed by its owner (known as the *consignor*) on the premises of another company (the *consignee*) with the understanding that payment is expected only when the merchandise is sold and that unsold items may be returned to the consignor. Title to consigned goods remains with the consignor until the consignee sells the goods. Consigned goods should not be included in the physical inventory of the consignee because they still belong to the consignor.

Methods of Pricing Inventory at Cost

The prices of most kinds of merchandise vary during the year. Identical lots of merchandise may have been purchased at different prices. Also, when identical items

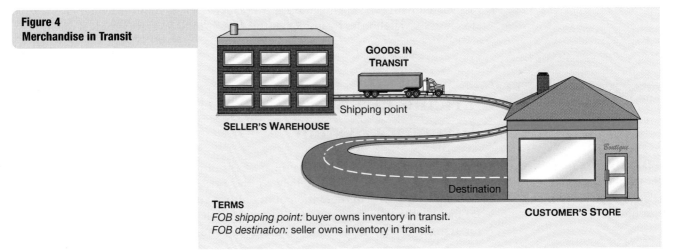

Figure 4
Merchandise in Transit

GOODS IN TRANSIT

Shipping point

SELLER'S WAREHOUSE

Destination

CUSTOMER'S STORE

TERMS
FOB shipping point: buyer owns inventory in transit.
FOB destination: seller owns inventory in transit.

are bought and sold, it is often impossible to tell which have been sold and which are still in inventory. For this reason, it is necessary to make an assumption about the order in which items have been sold. Because the assumed order of sale may or may not be the same as the actual order of sale, the assumption is really about the *flow of costs* rather than the *flow of physical inventory*.

The term **goods flow** refers to the actual physical movement of goods in the operations of a company, and the term **cost flow** refers to the association of costs with their *assumed* flow in the operations of a company. The assumed cost flow may or may not be the same as the actual goods flow. The possibility of a difference between cost flow and goods flow may seem strange at first, but it arises because several choices of assumed cost flow are available under generally accepted accounting principles. In fact, it is sometimes preferable to use an assumed cost flow that bears no relationship to goods flow because it gives a better estimate of income, which is the main goal of inventory valuation.

Accountants usually price inventory by using one of the following generally accepted methods, each based on a different assumption of cost flow: (1) specific identification method; (2) average-cost method; (3) first-in, first-out (FIFO) method; and (4) last-in, first-out (LIFO) method. The choice of method depends on the nature of the business, the financial effects of the methods, and the costs of implementing the methods.

To illustrate the four methods under the periodic inventory system, the following data for the month of June will be used:

Inventory Data—June 30

June	1	Inventory	50 units @ $1.00	$ 50
	6	Purchase	50 units @ $1.10	55
	13	Purchase	150 units @ $1.20	180
	20	Purchase	100 units @ $1.30	130
	25	Purchase	150 units @ $1.40	210
Goods available for sale			500 units	$625
Sales			280 units	
On hand June 30			220 units	

Notice that there is a total of 500 units available for sale at a total cost of $625. Stated simply, the problem of inventory pricing is to divide the $625 between the 280 units sold and the 220 units on hand. Recall that under the periodic inventory system, the inventory is not updated after each purchase and sale. Thus it is not necessary to know when the individual sales take place.

SPECIFIC IDENTIFICATION METHOD   If the units in the ending inventory can be identified as coming from specific purchases, the **specific identification method** may be used to price the inventory by identifying the cost of each item in ending inventory. For instance, assume that the June 30 inventory consisted of 50 units from the June 1 inventory, 100 units from the purchase of June 13, and 70 units from the purchase of June 25. The cost assigned to the inventory under the specific identification method would be $268, determined as follows:

OBJECTIVE

3 Calculate the pricing of inventory, using the cost basis under the periodic inventory system, according to the specific identification method; average-cost method; first-in, first-out (FIFO) method; and last-in, first-out (LIFO) method

Periodic Inventory System—Specific Identification Method

50 units @ $1.00	$ 50	Cost of goods available	
100 units @ $1.20	120	for sale	$625
70 units @ $1.40	98	Less June 30 inventory	268
220 units at a cost of	$268	Cost of goods sold	$357

The specific identification method might be used in the purchase and sale of high-priced articles, such as automobiles, heavy equipment, and works of art. Although this method may appear logical, it is not used by many companies because it has two definite disadvantages. First, in many cases, it is difficult and impractical to keep track of the purchase and sale of individual items. Second, when a company deals in items that are identical but were purchased at different costs, deciding which items are sold becomes arbitrary; thus the company can raise or lower income by choosing to sell the lower- or higher-cost items.

AVERAGE-COST METHOD Under the **average-cost method**, inventory is priced at the average cost of the goods available for sale during the period. Average cost is computed by dividing the total cost of goods available for sale by the total units available for sale. This gives an average unit cost that is applied to the units in ending inventory. In our illustration, the ending inventory would be $275, or $1.25 per unit, determined as follows:

Periodic Inventory System—Average-Cost Method

Cost of Goods Available for Sale ÷ Units Available for Sale = Average Unit Cost
$625 ÷ 500 units = $1.25

Ending inventory: 220 units @ $1.25 =	$275
Cost of goods available for sale	$625
Less June 30 inventory	275
Cost of goods sold	$350

The average-cost method tends to level out the effects of cost increases and decreases because the cost for the ending inventory calculated under this method is influenced by all the prices paid during the year and by the beginning inventory price. Some, however, criticize the average-cost method because they believe that recent costs are more relevant for income measurement and decision making.

FIRST-IN, FIRST-OUT (FIFO) METHOD The **first-in, first-out (FIFO) method** is based on the assumption that the costs of the first items acquired should be assigned to the first items sold. The costs of the goods on hand at the end of a period are assumed to be from the most recent purchases, and the costs assigned to goods that have been sold are assumed to be from beginning inventory and the earliest purchases. The FIFO method of determining inventory cost may be adopted by any business, regardless of the actual physical flow of goods, because the assumption is made regarding the flow of costs and not the flow of goods.

In our illustration, the June 30 inventory would be $301 when the FIFO method is used. It is computed as follows:

Periodic Inventory System—First-In, First-Out Method

150 units @ $1.40 from purchase of June 25	$210
70 units @ $1.30 from purchase of June 20	91
220 units at a cost of	$301
Cost of goods available for sale	$625
Less June 30 inventory	301
Cost of goods sold	$324

The effect of the FIFO method is to value the ending inventory at the most recent costs and include earlier costs in cost of goods sold. During periods of consistently rising prices, the FIFO method yields the highest possible amount of net income because cost of goods sold will show the earliest costs incurred, which are lower during periods of inflation. Another reason for this result is that businesses tend to increase selling prices as costs rise, even when inventories were purchased before the price rise. The reverse effect occurs in periods of price decreases. Consequently, a major criticism of FIFO is that it magnifies the effects of the business cycle on income.

LAST-IN, FIRST-OUT (LIFO) METHOD   The **last-in, first-out (LIFO) method** of costing inventories is based on the assumption that the costs of the last items purchased should be assigned to the first items sold and that the cost of ending inventory reflects the cost of the merchandise purchased earliest.

Under this method, the June 30 inventory would be $249, computed as follows:

Periodic Inventory System—Last-In, First-Out Method

50 units @ $1.00 from June 1 inventory	$ 50
50 units @ $1.10 from purchase of June 6	55
120 units @ $1.20 from purchase of June 13	144
220 units at a cost of	$249
Cost of goods available for sale	$625
Less June 30 inventory	249
Cost of goods sold	$376

The effect of LIFO is to value inventory at the earliest prices and to include in cost of goods sold the cost of the most recently purchased goods. This assumption, of course, does not agree with the actual physical movement of goods in most businesses.

There is, however, a strong logical argument to support LIFO, based on the fact that a certain size inventory is necessary in a going concern. When inventory is sold, it must be replaced with more goods. The supporters of LIFO reason that the fairest determination of income occurs if the current costs of merchandise are matched against current sales prices, regardless of which physical units of merchandise are sold. When prices are moving either upward or downward, the cost of goods sold will, under LIFO, show costs closer to the price level at the time the goods were sold. As a result, the LIFO method tends to show a smaller net income during inflationary times and a larger net income during deflationary times than other methods of inventory valuation. The peaks and valleys of the business cycle tend to be smoothed out. In inventory valuation, the flow of costs, and hence income determination, is more important than the physical movement of goods and balance sheet valuation.

An argument may also be made against the LIFO method. Because the inventory valuation on the balance sheet reflects earlier prices, it often gives an unrealistic picture of the current value of the inventory. Such balance sheet measures as working capital and current ratio may be distorted and must be interpreted carefully.

FOCUS ON BUSINESS PRACTICE

A new type of retail business called the "category killer" seems to ignore the tenets of good inventory management. These retailers, such as The Home Depot, Inc., in home improvements; Barnes & Noble Inc. in bookstores; Wal-Mart Stores, Inc., in groceries and dry goods; Toys "R" Us, Inc., in toys; and Blockbuster Entertainment Corporation in videos, maintain huge inventories at such low prices that smaller competitors find it hard to compete. Although these companies have a large amount of money tied up in inventories, they maintain very sophisticated just-in-time operating environments that require suppliers to meet demanding standards for delivery of products and reduction of inventory costs. Some suppliers are required to stock the shelves and keep track of inventory levels. By minimizing handling and overhead costs and buying at favorably low prices, the category killers achieve great success.

Figure 5
Summary of Cost Flow Assumptions' Impact on Income Statement and Balance Sheet Using Periodic Inventory System

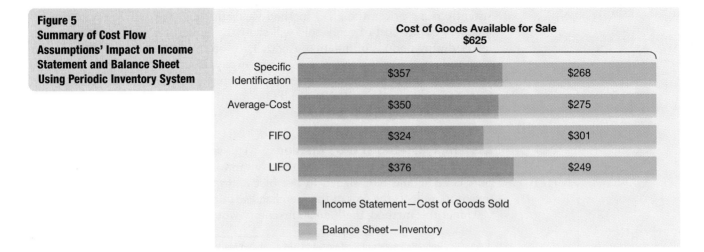

Figure 5 summarizes the impact of the four inventory cost allocation methods on the cost of goods sold as reported on the income statement and on inventory as reported on the balance sheet when a company uses the periodic inventory system. In periods of rising prices, the FIFO method yields the highest inventory valuation, the lowest cost of goods sold, and hence a higher net income. The LIFO method yields the lowest inventory valuation, the highest cost of goods sold, and thus a lower net income.

Pricing Inventory Under the Perpetual Inventory System

OBJECTIVE

4 Apply the perpetual inventory system to the pricing of inventories at cost

The pricing of inventories under the perpetual inventory system differs from pricing under the periodic inventory system. The difference occurs because under the perpetual inventory system, a continuous record of quantities and costs of merchandise is maintained as purchases and sales are made. Under the periodic inventory system, only the ending inventory is counted and priced. Cost of goods sold is determined by deducting the cost of the ending inventory from the cost of goods available for sale. Under the perpetual inventory system, cost of goods sold is accumulated as sales are made and costs are transferred from the Inventory account to Cost of Goods Sold. The cost of the ending inventory is the balance of the Inventory account. To illustrate pricing methods under the perpetual inventory system, the same data will be used as before, but specific sales dates and amounts will be added, as follows:

Inventory Data—June 30

June 1	Inventory	50 units @ $1.00
6	Purchase	50 units @ $1.10
10	Sale	70 units
13	Purchase	150 units @ $1.20
20	Purchase	100 units @ $1.30
25	Purchase	150 units @ $1.40
30	Sale	210 units
30	Inventory	220 units

Pricing the inventory and cost of goods sold using the specific identification method is the same under the perpetual system as it was under the periodic system because cost of goods sold and ending inventory are based on the cost of the identified items sold and on hand. The perpetual system facilitates the use of the specific identification method because detailed records of purchases and sales are maintained.

Pricing the inventory and cost of goods sold using the average-cost method differs when the perpetual system is used. Under the periodic system, the average cost is computed for all goods available for sale during the month. Under the perpetual system, a moving average is computed after each purchase or series of purchases preceding the next sale, as follows:

Perpetual Inventory System—Average-Cost Method

June 1	Inventory	50 units @ $1.00	$ 50.00
6	Purchase	50 units @ $1.10	55.00
6	Balance	100 units @ $1.05	$105.00
10	Sale	70 units @ $1.05	(73.50)
10	Balance	30 units @ $1.05	$ 31.50
13	Purchase	150 units @ $1.20	180.00
20	Purchase	100 units @ $1.30	130.00
25	Purchase	150 units @ $1.40	210.00
25	Balance	430 units @ $1.28*	$551.50
30	Sale	210 units @ $1.28	(268.80)
30	Inventory	220 units @ $1.29*	$282.70
Cost of goods sold		($73.50 + $268.80)	$342.30

*Rounded.

The sum of the costs applied to sales becomes the cost of goods sold, $342.30. The ending inventory is the balance, or $282.70.

When pricing the inventory using the FIFO and LIFO methods, it is necessary to keep track of the components of inventory at each step of the way because as sales are made, the costs must be assigned in the proper order. To apply the FIFO method, the approach is as follows:

Perpetual Inventory System—FIFO Method

June 1	Inventory	50 units @ $1.00		$ 50.00
6	Purchase	50 units @ $1.10		55.00
10	Sale	50 units @ $1.00	($ 50.00)	
		20 units @ $1.10	(22.00)	(72.00)
10	Balance	30 units @ $1.10		$ 33.00
13	Purchase	150 units @ $1.20		180.00
20	Purchase	100 units @ $1.30		130.00
25	Purchase	150 units @ $1.40		210.00
30	Sale	30 units @ $1.10	($ 33.00)	
		150 units @ $1.20	(180.00)	
		30 units @ $1.30	(39.00)	(252.00)
30	Inventory	70 units @ $1.30	$ 91.00	
		150 units @ $1.40	210.00	$301.00
Cost of goods sold		($72.00 + $252.00)		$324.00

FOCUS ON BUSINESS TECHNOLOGY

Using the LIFO method under the perpetual inventory system is a very tedious process, especially if done manually. However, the development of faster and less expensive computer systems has made it easier for many companies to switch to LIFO and still use the perpetual inventory system. The availability of better technology may partially account for the increasing use of LIFO in the United States and may enable more companies to enjoy LIFO's economic benefits.

Note that the ending inventory of $301 and the cost of goods sold of $324 are the same as the figures computed earlier under the periodic inventory system. This will always occur because the ending inventory under both systems will always consist of the last items purchased—in this case, the entire purchase of June 25 and 70 units from the purchase of June 20.

To apply the LIFO method, the approach is as follows:

Perpetual Inventory System—LIFO Method

June	1	Inventory	50 units @ $1.00		$ 50.00
	6	Purchase	50 units @ $1.10		55.00
	10	Sale	50 units @ $1.10	($ 55.00)	
			20 units @ $1.00	(20.00)	(75.00)
	10	Balance	30 units @ $1.00		$ 30.00
	13	Purchase	150 units @ $1.20		180.00
	20	Purchase	100 units @ $1.30		130.00
	25	Purchase	150 units @ $1.40		210.00
	30	Sale	150 units @ $1.40	($210.00)	
			60 units @ $1.30	(78.00)	(288.00)
	30	Inventory	30 units @ $1.00	$ 30.00	
			150 units @ $1.20	180.00	
			40 units @ $1.30	52.00	$262.00
Cost of goods sold			($75.00 + $288.00)		$363.00

Notice that the ending inventory of $262 includes 30 units from the beginning inventory, all the units from the purchase of June 13, and 40 units from the purchase of June 20.

Figure 6
Summary of Cost Flow Assumptions' Impact on Income Statement and Balance Sheet Using Perpetual Inventory System

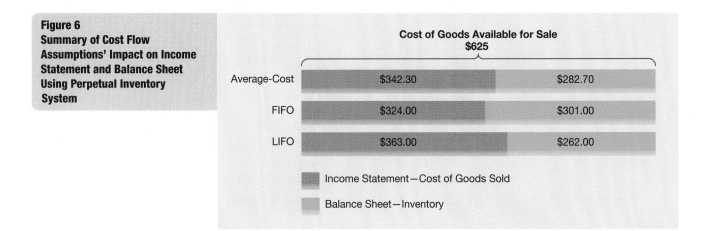

A comparison of the three cost flow assumptions or methods using a perpetual inventory system is shown in Figure 6. The relative relationship of the methods is the same as their relationship under the periodic inventory system, but some amounts have changed. For example, LIFO has the lowest inventory valuation regardless of the inventory system used, but the amount is $262 using the perpetual system versus $249 using the periodic system.

Comparison and Impact of Inventory Decisions and Misstatements

OBJECTIVE

5 State the effects of inventory methods and misstatements of inventory on income determination, income taxes, and cash flows

The specific identification, average-cost, FIFO, and LIFO methods of pricing inventory under both the periodic and the perpetual inventory systems have now been illustrated. The effects of the four methods on gross margin are shown in Exhibit 1, using the same data as before and assuming June sales of $500. Because the specific identification method is based on actual cost, it is the same under both systems.

Keeping in mind that June was a period of rising prices, we can see that LIFO, which charges the most recent, and, in this case, the highest, prices to cost of goods sold, resulted in the lowest gross margin under both systems. Conversely, FIFO, which charges the earliest, and, in this case, the lowest, prices to cost of goods sold, produced the highest gross margin. The gross margin under the average-cost method is somewhere between those under LIFO and FIFO. Thus, it is clear that the average-cost method has a less pronounced effect. Note that ending inventory and gross margin under FIFO are always the same under both the periodic and the perpetual inventory systems.

During a period of declining prices, the reverse would occur. The LIFO method would produce a higher gross margin than the FIFO method. It is apparent that

Exhibit 1

Effects of Inventory Systems and Methods Computed

	Specific Identification Method	Periodic Inventory System			Perpetual Inventory System*		
		Average-Cost Method	First-In, First-Out Method	Last-In, First-Out Method	Average-Cost Method	First-In, First-Out Method	Last-In, First-Out Method
Sales	$500	$500	$500	$500	$500	$500	$500
Cost of Goods Sold							
Beginning Inventory	$ 50	$ 50	$ 50	$ 50			
Purchases	575	575	575	575			
Cost of Goods Available for Sale	$625	$625	$625	$625			
Less Ending Inventory	268	275	301	249	$283[†]	$301	$262
Cost of Goods Sold	$357	$350	$324	$376	$342[†]	$324	$363
Gross Margin	$143	$150	$176	$124	$158	$176	$137

*Ending inventory under the perpetual inventory system is provided for comparison only. It is not used in the computation of cost of goods sold.
[†]Rounded.

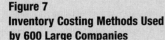

Figure 7
Inventory Costing Methods Used by 600 Large Companies

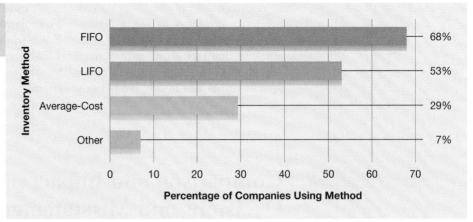

Total percentage exceeds 100 because some companies used different methods for different types of inventory.

Source: Reprinted with permission from *Accounting Trends & Techniques.* Copyright © 1999 by the American Institute of Certified Public Accountants, Inc.

the method of inventory valuation has the greatest importance during prolonged periods of price changes in one direction, either up or down.

Because the specific identification method depends on the particular items sold, no generalization can be made about the effect of changing prices.

Effects on the Financial Statements

Each of the four methods of inventory pricing is acceptable for use in published financial statements. The FIFO, LIFO, and average-cost methods are widely used, as can be seen in Figure 7, which shows the inventory costing methods used by 600 large companies. Each has its advantages and disadvantages, and none can be considered best or perfect. The factors that should be considered in choosing an inventory method are the trend of prices and the effects of each method on financial statements, income taxes, and cash flows.

A basic problem in determining the best inventory measure for a particular company stems from the fact that inventory affects both the balance sheet and the income statement. As we have seen, the LIFO method is best suited for the income statement because it matches revenues and cost of goods sold. But it is not the best measure of the current balance sheet value of inventory, particularly during a prolonged period of price increases or decreases. The FIFO method, on the other hand, is best suited to the balance sheet because the ending inventory is closest to current values and thus gives a more realistic view of the current financial assets of a business. Readers of financial statements must be alert to inventory methods and be able to assess their effects.

Effects on Income Taxes

The Internal Revenue Service has developed several rules for valuing inventories for federal income tax purposes. A company has a wide choice of methods, including specific identification, average-cost, FIFO, and LIFO, as well as lower-of-cost-or-market. But once a method has been chosen, it must be used consistently from one year to the next. The IRS must approve any change in the inventory valuation method for income tax purposes.* This requirement agrees with the rule of consis-

*A single exception to this rule is that taxpayers must notify the IRS of a change to LIFO from another method, but they do not need to have advance IRS approval.

Does the accounting method a company uses affect management's operating decisions? It certainly does when taxes are involved! Recent research shows that among firms that use the LIFO inventory method, those with high tax rates are more likely to buy extra inventory at year end than are those with low tax rates.[5] This behavior is predictable because LIFO deducts the most recent purchases, which are likely to have higher costs than earlier purchases, in determining taxable income. This action will result in lower income taxes.

tency in accounting, since changes in inventory method may cause income to fluctuate too much and would make income statements hard to interpret from year to year. A company may change its inventory method if there is a good reason for doing so. The nature and effect of the change must be shown on the company's financial statements.

Many accountants believe that the use of the FIFO and average-cost methods in periods of rising prices causes businesses to report more than their true profit, resulting in the payment of excess income taxes. The profit is overstated because cost of goods sold is understated, relative to current prices. The company must buy replacement inventory at higher prices, but additional funds are also needed to pay income taxes. During the rapid inflation of 1979 to 1982, billions of dollars reported as profits and paid in income taxes were believed to be the result of poor matching of current costs and revenues under the FIFO and average-cost methods. Consequently, many companies, encouraged by the belief that prices will continue to rise, have since switched to the LIFO inventory method.

If a company uses the LIFO method in reporting income for tax purposes, the IRS requires that the same method be used in the accounting records. Also, the IRS will not allow the use of the lower-of-cost-or-market rule if LIFO is used to determine inventory cost. In such a case, only the LIFO cost can be used. This rule, however, does not preclude a company from using lower-of-LIFO-cost-or-market for financial reporting purposes (discussed later in this chapter).

Over a period of rising prices, a business that uses the LIFO method may find that for balance sheet purposes, its inventory is valued at a cost figure far below what it currently pays for the same items. Management must monitor this situation carefully, because if it should let the inventory quantity at year end fall below the beginning-of-the-year level, the company will find itself paying higher income taxes. Higher income before taxes results because the company would expense historical costs of inventory, which are below current costs. When this occurs, it is called a **LIFO liquidation** because sales have reduced inventories below the levels set in prior years; that is, units sold exceed units purchased for the period.

A LIFO liquidation may be prevented by making enough purchases prior to year end to restore the desired inventory level. Sometimes a LIFO liquidation cannot be avoided because products are discontinued or supplies are interrupted, as in the case of a strike. In a recent year, 28 of 600 large companies reported a LIFO liquidation in which net income was increased because of the matching of older historical cost with present sales dollars.[6]

Effects of Misstatements in Inventory Measurement

The basic problem of separating goods available for sale into two components—goods sold and goods not sold—is that of assigning a cost to the goods not sold, the ending inventory. The portion of the goods available for sale not assigned to the ending inventory is used to determine the cost of goods sold.

Because the figures for ending inventory and cost of goods sold are related, a misstatement in the inventory figure at the end of the period will cause an equal misstatement in gross margin and income before income taxes in the income statement. The amount of assets and owners' equity on the balance sheet will also be misstated by the same amount. The consequences of overstatement and understatement of inventory are illustrated in the three simplified examples that follow. In each case, beginning inventory, net purchases, and cost of goods available for sale have been stated correctly. In the first example, ending inventory has been stated correctly. In the second example, ending inventory is overstated by $6,000; in the third example, ending inventory is understated by $6,000.

Example 1. Ending Inventory Correctly Stated at $10,000

Cost of Goods Sold for the Year		Income Statement for the Year	
Beginning Inventory	$12,000	Net Sales	$100,000
Net Cost of Purchases	58,000	→ Cost of Goods Sold	60,000
Cost of Goods Available for Sale	$70,000	Gross Margin	$ 40,000
Ending Inventory	10,000	Operating Expenses	32,000
		Income Before Income	
Cost of Goods Sold	$60,000 ←	Taxes	$ 8,000

Example 2. Ending Inventory Overstated by $6,000

Cost of Goods Sold for the Year		Income Statement for the Year	
Beginning Inventory	$12,000	Net Sales	$100,000
Net Cost of Purchases	58,000	→ Cost of Goods Sold	54,000
Cost of Goods Available for Sale	$70,000	Gross Margin	$ 46,000
Ending Inventory	16,000	Operating Expenses	32,000
		Income Before Income	
Cost of Goods Sold	$54,000 ←	Taxes	$ 14,000

Example 3. Ending Inventory Understated by $6,000

Cost of Goods Sold for the Year		Income Statement for the Year	
Beginning Inventory	$12,000	Net Sales	$100,000
Net Cost of Purchases	58,000	→ Cost of Goods Sold	66,000
Cost of Goods Available for Sale	$70,000	Gross Margin	$ 34,000
Ending Inventory	4,000	Operating Expenses	32,000
		Income Before Income	
Cost of Goods Sold	$66,000 ←	Taxes	$ 2,000

In all three examples, the total cost of goods available for sale was $70,000. The difference in income before income taxes resulted from how this $70,000 was divided between ending inventory and cost of goods sold.

Because the ending inventory in one period becomes the beginning inventory in the following period, it is important to recognize that a misstatement in inventory valuation affects not only the current period but also the following period. Over a two-year period, the errors in income before income taxes will offset, or counterbalance, each other. In Example **2** above, for instance, the overstatement of ending inventory in 20x1 caused a $6,000 overstatement of beginning inventory in the

Table 1. Ending Inventory Overstated by $6,000

	With Inventory Correctly Stated	With Inventory at December 31, 20x1, Overstated	
		Reported Income Before Income Taxes Will Be	Reported Income Before Income Taxes Will Be Overstated (Understated)
Income Before Income Taxes for 20x1	$ 8,000	$14,000	$6,000
Income Before Income Taxes for 20x2	15,000	9,000	(6,000)
Total Income Before Income Taxes for Two Years	$23,000	$23,000	—

following year, resulting in an understatement of income by $6,000 in the second year. This offsetting effect is illustrated in Table 1.

Because the total income before income taxes for the two years is the same, it may appear that one need not worry about inventory misstatements. However, the misstatements violate the matching rule. In addition, management, creditors, and investors make many decisions on an annual basis and depend on the accountant's determination of net income. The accountant has an obligation to make the net income figure for each year as useful as possible.

The effects of misstatements in inventory on income before income taxes are as follows:

Year 1	Year 2
Ending inventory overstated	**Beginning inventory overstated**
Cost of goods sold understated	Cost of goods sold overstated
Income before income taxes overstated	Income before income taxes understated
Ending inventory understated	**Beginning inventory understated**
Cost of goods sold overstated	Cost of goods sold understated
Income before income taxes understated	Income before income taxes overstated

A misstatement in inventory results in a misstatement in income before income taxes of the same amount. Thus the measurement of inventory is important.

FOCUS ON BUSINESS ETHICS

Income may be easily manipulated through accounting for inventory. For example, it is easy to overstate or understate inventory by including end-of-the-year purchase and sale transactions in the wrong fiscal year. In one case, *The Wall Street Journal* reported that Leslie Fay Company restated its earnings for three past years to reverse $81 million of pretax earnings. The situation was a "carefully concealed case of fraud" involving many members of the financial accounting staff. "Inventory was overstated, while the cost of making garments was understated in order to enhance profit figures." Such actions are obviously unethical and, in this case, led the company to bankruptcy and ruined the careers of most of its senior officers.[7]

Inventory Measurement and Cash Flows

A company's inventory methods affect not only its reported profitability but also its reported liquidity and cash flows. In the case of a large company like International Paper Co., these effects can be complex and material. In a note on inventories, International Paper provides more detail on these effects:

> The company uses the last-in, first-out inventory method to value substantially all of its domestic inventories. Approximately 73% of the company's total raw materials and finished products inventories were valued using this method. If the first-in, first-out method had been used, it would have increased total inventory balances by approximately $250 million, $321 million and $348 million at December 31, 1999, 1998, and 1997, respectively.[8]

By using LIFO, the company usually reports a lower income before taxes. This will have a favorable effect on cash flows because of the lower amount of income taxes to be paid. The reader of the financial statements may determine what International Paper's inventory value would have been if it were valued at current prices under FIFO rather than older prices under LIFO. More realistic comparison of the company's liquidity ratios may be made. For example, the more realistic FIFO figure would show a better short-term liquidity position as measured by the current ratio than the reported LIFO figures on the face of the balance sheet would seem to indicate. However, the company's inventory turnover and average days' inventory on hand will be adversely affected if the more realistic FIFO figures are used.

Valuing Inventory at the Lower of Cost or Market (LCM)

OBJECTIVE

6 Apply the lower-of-cost-or-market (LCM) rule to inventory valuation

Although cost is usually the most appropriate basis for valuation of inventory, there are times when inventory may properly be shown in the financial statements at less than its cost. If by reason of physical deterioration, obsolescence, or decline in price level the market value of inventory falls below its cost, a loss has occurred. This loss may be recognized by writing the inventory down to **market** or current replacement cost of inventory. For a merchandising company, market is the amount that the company would pay at the present time for the same goods, purchased from the usual suppliers and in the usual quantities. The **lower-of-cost-or-market (LCM) rule** requires that when the replacement cost of inventory falls below historical cost, the inventory is written down to the lower value and a loss is recorded. This rule is an example of the application of the convention of conservatism because the loss is recognized before an actual transaction takes place. Under historical cost accounting, the inventory remains at cost until it is sold. It may help in applying the LCM rule to think of it as the "lower-of-cost-or-replacement-cost" rule.* Approximately 90 percent of 600 large companies report applying the LCM rule to their inventories.[9]

There are two basic methods of valuing inventories at the lower of cost or market accepted both by GAAP and for federal income tax purposes: (1) the item-by-item method and (2) the major category method. For example, a stereo shop

---

*In some cases, *market value* is determined by the *realizable value* of the inventory—the amount for which the goods can be sold—rather than by the amount for which the goods can be replaced. The circumstances in which realizable value determines market value are encountered in practice only occasionally, and the valuation procedures are technical enough to be addressed in a more advanced accounting course.

Table 2. Lower of Cost or Market with Item-by-Item Method

	Quantity	Per Unit Cost	Per Unit Market	Lower of Cost or Market
Category I				
Item a	200	$1.50	$1.70	$ 300
Item b	100	2.00	1.80	180
Item c	100	2.50	2.60	250
Category II				
Item d	300	5.00	4.50	1,350
Item e	200	4.00	4.10	800
Inventory at the lower of cost or market				$2,000
				2,880

could determine lower of cost or market for each kind of speaker, receiver, and turntable (item by item) or for all speakers, all receivers, and all turntables (major categories).

Item-by-Item Method

When the **item-by-item method** is used, cost and market values are compared for each item in inventory. Each individual item is then valued at its lower price (see Table 2).

Major Category Method

Under the **major category method**, the total cost and total market values for each category of items are compared. Each category is then valued at its lower amount (see Table 3).

Table 3. Lower of Cost or Market with Major Category Method

	Quantity	Per Unit Cost	Per Unit Market	Total Cost	Total Market	Lower of Cost or Market
Category I						
Item a	200	$1.50	$1.70	$ 300	$ 340	
Item b	100	2.00	1.80	200	180	
Item c	100	2.50	2.60	250	260	
Totals				$ 750	$ 780	$ 750
Category II						
Item d	300	5.00	4.50	$1,500	$1,350	
Item e	200	4.00	4.10	800	820	
Totals				$2,300	$2,170	2,170
Inventory at the lower of cost or market						$2,920

Valuing Inventory by Estimation

SUPPLEMENTAL OBJECTIVE

7 Estimate the cost of ending inventory using the retail inventory method and gross profit method

It is sometimes necessary or desirable to estimate the value of ending inventory. The methods most commonly used for this purpose are the retail method and the gross profit method.

Retail Method of Inventory Estimation

The **retail method**, as its name implies, is used in retail merchandising businesses to estimate the cost of ending inventory by using the ratio of cost to retail price. There are two principal reasons for its use. First, management usually requires that financial statements be prepared at least once a month. As taking a physical inventory is time-consuming and expensive, the retail method is used instead to estimate the cost of inventory on hand. Second, because items in a retail store normally have a price tag or a universal product code, it is a common practice to take the physical inventory at retail from these price tags and codes and reduce the total value to cost through use of the retail method. The term *at retail* means the amount of the inventory at the marked selling prices of the inventory items.

When the retail method is used to estimate ending inventory, the records must show the beginning inventory at cost and at retail. The records must also show the amount of goods purchased during the period both at cost and at retail. The net sales at retail is, of course, the balance of the Sales account less returns and allowances. A simple example of the retail method is shown in Table 4.

Goods available for sale is determined both at cost and at retail by listing beginning inventory and net purchases for the period at cost and at their expected selling price, adding freight to the cost column, and totaling. The ratio of these two amounts (cost to retail price) provides an estimate of the cost of each dollar of retail sales value. The estimated ending inventory at retail is then determined by deducting sales for the period from the retail price of the goods that were available for sale during the period. The inventory at retail is then converted to cost on the basis of the ratio of cost to retail.

Table 4. Retail Method of Inventory Valuation

	Cost	Retail
Beginning Inventory	$ 40,000	$ 55,000
Net Purchases for the Period (excluding Freight In)	107,000	145,000
Freight In	3,000	
Merchandise Available for Sale	$150,000	$200,000
Ratio of Cost to Retail Price: $\frac{\$150,000}{\$200,000} = 75\%$		
Net Sales During the Period		160,000
Estimated Ending Inventory at Retail		$ 40,000
Ratio of Cost to Retail	75%	
Estimated Cost of Ending Inventory	$ 30,000	

Table 5. Gross Profit Method of Inventory Valuation

1. Beginning Inventory at Cost		$ 50,000
Purchases at Cost (including Freight In)		290,000
Cost of Goods Available for Sale		$340,000
2. Less Estimated Cost of Goods Sold		
Sales at Selling Price	$400,000	
Less Estimated Gross Margin		
(30% × 400,000)	120,000	
Estimated Cost of Goods Sold		280,000
3. Estimated Cost of Ending Inventory		$ 60,000

The cost of ending inventory may also be estimated by applying the ratio of cost to retail price to the total retail value of the physical count of the ending inventory. Applying the retail method in practice is often more difficult than this simple example because of such complications as changes in retail price during the year, different markups on different types of merchandise, and varying volumes of sales for different types of merchandise.

Gross Profit Method of Inventory Estimation

The **gross profit method** assumes that the ratio of gross margin for a business remains relatively stable from year to year. The gross profit method is used in place of the retail method when records of the retail prices of beginning inventory and purchases are not kept. It is considered acceptable for estimating the cost of inventory for interim reports, but it is not acceptable for valuing inventory in the annual financial statements. It is also useful in estimating the amount of inventory lost or destroyed by theft, fire, or other hazards. Insurance companies often use this method to verify loss claims.

The gross profit method is simple to use. First, figure the cost of goods available for sale in the usual way (add purchases to beginning inventory). Second, estimate the cost of goods sold by deducting the estimated gross margin of 30 percent from sales. Finally, deduct the estimated cost of goods sold from the goods available for sale to arrive at the estimated cost of ending inventory. This method is shown in Table 5.

Chapter Review

REVIEW OF LEARNING OBJECTIVES

1. Identify and explain the management issues associated with accounting for inventories. Included in inventory are goods owned, whether produced or purchased, that are held for sale in the normal course of business. Manufacturing companies also include raw materials and work in process. Among the issues management must face in accounting for inventories are allocating the cost of inventories in accordance with the matching rule, assessing the impact of inventory decisions, and evaluating the levels of inventory. The objective of accounting for inventories is the proper determination of income

Check out ACE, a self-quizzing program on chapter content, at http://college.hmco.com.

through the matching of costs and revenues, not the determination of the most realistic inventory value. Because the valuation of inventory has a direct effect on a company's net income, the choice of inventory systems and methods affects not only the amount of income taxes and cash flows but also the external and internal evaluation of the company. The level of inventory as measured by the inventory turnover and its related measure, average days' inventory on hand, is important to managing the amount of investment needed by a company.

2. **Define *inventory cost* and relate it to goods flow and cost flow.** The cost of inventory includes (1) invoice price less purchases discounts; (2) freight or transportation in, including insurance in transit; and (3) applicable taxes and tariffs. Goods flow relates to the actual physical flow of merchandise, whereas cost flow refers to the assumed flow of costs in the operations of the business.

3. **Calculate the pricing of inventory, using the cost basis under the periodic inventory system, according to the specific identification method; average-cost method; first-in, first-out (FIFO) method; and last-in, first-out (LIFO) method.** The value assigned to ending inventory is the result of two measurements: quantity and price. Quantity is determined by taking a physical inventory. The pricing of inventory is usually based on the assumed cost flow of the goods as they are bought and sold. One of four assumptions is usually made regarding cost flow. These assumptions are represented by four inventory methods. Inventory pricing can be determined by the specific identification method, which associates the actual cost with each item of inventory, but this method is rarely used. The average-cost method assumes that the cost of inventory is the average cost of goods available for sale during the period. The first-in, first-out (FIFO) method assumes that the costs of the first items acquired should be assigned to the first items sold. The last-in, first-out (LIFO) method assumes that the costs of the last items acquired should be assigned to the first items sold. The inventory method chosen may or may not be equivalent to the actual physical flow of goods.

4. **Apply the perpetual inventory system to the pricing of inventories at cost.** The pricing of inventories under the perpetual inventory system differs from pricing under the periodic system because under the perpetual system a continuous record of quantities and costs of merchandise is maintained as purchases and sales are made. Cost of goods sold is accumulated as sales are made and costs are transferred from the Inventory account to Cost of Goods Sold. The cost of the ending inventory is the balance of the Inventory account. Under the perpetual inventory system, the specific identification method and the FIFO method will produce the same results as under the periodic method. The results will differ for the average-cost method because a moving average is calculated prior to each sale rather than at the end of the accounting period, and for the LIFO method because the cost components of inventory change constantly as goods are bought and sold.

5. **State the effects of inventory methods and misstatements of inventory on income determination, income taxes, and cash flows.** During periods of rising prices, the LIFO method will show the lowest net income; FIFO, the highest; and average cost, in between. The opposite effects occur in periods of falling prices. No generalization can be made regarding the specific identification method. The Internal Revenue Service requires that if LIFO is used for tax purposes, it must also be used for financial statement purposes, and that the lower-of-cost-or-market rule cannot be applied to the LIFO method. If the value of ending inventory is understated or overstated, a corresponding error—dollar for dollar—will be made in income before income taxes. Furthermore, because the ending inventory of one period is the beginning inventory of the

next, the misstatement affects two accounting periods, although the effects are opposite.

6. **Apply the lower-of-cost-or-market (LCM) rule to inventory valuation.** The lower-of-cost-or-market rule can be applied to the above methods of determining inventory at cost. This rule states that if the replacement cost (market) of the inventory is lower than the inventory cost, the lower figure should be used. Valuation can be determined on an item-by-item or major category basis.

SUPPLEMENTAL OBJECTIVE

7. **Estimate the cost of ending inventory using the retail inventory method and gross profit method.** Two methods of estimating the value of inventory are the retail inventory method and the gross profit method. Under the retail inventory method, inventory is determined at retail prices and is then reduced to estimated cost by applying a ratio of cost to retail price. Under the gross profit method, cost of goods sold is estimated by reducing sales by estimated gross margin. The estimated cost of goods sold is then deducted from the cost of goods available for sale to estimate the inventory.

REVIEW OF CONCEPTS AND TERMINOLOGY

The following concepts and terms were introduced in this chapter:

LO 3   **Average-cost method:** An inventory costing method in which inventory is priced at the average cost of the goods available for sale during the period.

LO 1   **Average days' inventory on hand:** The average number of days required to sell the inventory on hand; number of days in a year divided by inventory turnover.

LO 2   **Consignment:** Merchandise placed by its owner (the *consignor*) on the premises of another company (the *consignee*) with the understanding that payment is expected only when the merchandise is sold and that unsold items may be returned to the consignor.

LO 2   **Cost flow:** The association of costs with their assumed flow in the operations of a company.

LO 3   **First-in, first-out (FIFO) method:** An inventory costing method based on the assumption that the costs of the first items acquired should be assigned to the first items sold.

LO 2   **Goods flow:** The actual physical movement of goods in the operations of a company.

SO 7   **Gross profit method:** A method of inventory estimation based on the assumption that the ratio of gross margin for a business remains relatively stable from year to year.

LO 2   **Inventory cost:** The price paid or consideration given to acquire an asset; includes invoice price less purchases discounts, plus freight or transportation in, and plus applicable taxes and tariffs.

LO 1   **Inventory turnover:** A ratio indicating the number of times a company's average inventory is sold during an accounting period; cost of goods sold divided by average inventory.

LO 6   **Item-by-item method:** A lower-of-cost-or-market method of valuing inventory in which cost and market values are compared for each item in inventory, with each item then valued at its lower price.

LO 1   **Just-in-time operating environment:** An inventory management system in which companies seek to reduce their levels of inventory by working closely with suppliers to coordinate and schedule deliveries so that goods arrive just at the time they are needed.

LO 3   **Last-in, first-out (LIFO) method:** An inventory costing method based on the assumption that the costs of the last items purchased should be assigned to the first items sold.

LO 5 **LIFO liquidation:** The reduction of inventory below previous levels so that income is increased by the amount by which current prices exceed the historical cost of the inventory under LIFO.

LO 6 **Lower-of-cost-or-market (LCM) rule:** A method of valuing inventory at an amount below cost if the replacement (market) value is less than cost.

LO 6 **Major category method:** A lower-of-cost-or-market method of valuing inventory in which the total cost and total market values for each category of items are compared, with each category then valued at its lower amount.

LO 6 **Market:** Current replacement cost of inventory.

LO 1 **Merchandise inventory:** All goods owned and held for sale in the regular course of business.

SO 7 **Retail method:** A method of inventory estimation, used in retail merchandising businesses, under which inventory at retail value is reduced by the ratio of cost to retail price.

LO 3 **Specific identification method:** An inventory costing method in which the price of inventory is computed by identifying the cost of each item in ending inventory as coming from a specific purchase.

REVIEW PROBLEM

LO 1
LO 3
LO 4

Periodic and Perpetual Inventory Systems

The table below summarizes the beginning inventory, purchases, and sales of Psi Company's single product during January.

Date		Beginning Inventory and Purchases			Sales Units
		Units	Cost	Total	
Jan. 1	Inventory	1,400	$19	$26,600	
4	Sale				300
8	Purchase	600	20	12,000	
10	Sale				1,300
12	Purchase	900	21	18,900	
15	Sale				150
18	Purchase	500	22	11,000	
24	Purchase	800	23	18,400	
31	Sale				1,350
Totals		4,200		$86,900	3,100

REQUIRED

1. Assuming that the company uses the periodic inventory system, compute the cost that should be assigned to ending inventory and to cost of goods sold using (a) the average-cost method, (b) the FIFO method, and (c) the LIFO method.

2. Assuming that the company uses the perpetual inventory system, compute the cost that should be assigned to ending inventory and to cost of goods sold using (a) the average-cost method, (b) the FIFO method, and (c) the LIFO method.

3. Compute inventory turnover and average days' inventory on hand under each of the inventory cost flow assumptions in 1. What conclusion can be made from this comparison?

**ANSWER TO REVIEW
PROBLEM**

	Units	Amount
Beginning inventory	1,400	$26,600
Purchases	2,800	60,300
Available for sale	4,200	$86,900
Sales	3,100	
Ending inventory	1,100	

1. Periodic inventory system:
   a. Average-cost method

Cost of goods available for sale	$86,900
Less ending inventory consists of 1,100 units at $20.69*	22,759
Cost of goods sold	$64,141

   *$86,900 ÷ 4,200 = $20.69 (rounded).

   b. FIFO method

Cost of goods available for sale		$86,900
Less ending inventory consists of		
Jan. 24 purchase (800 × $23)	$18,400	
Jan. 18 purchase (300 × $22)	6,600	25,000
Cost of goods sold		$61,900

   c. LIFO method

Cost of goods available for sale	$86,900
Less ending inventory consists of beginning inventory (1,100 × $19)	20,900
Cost of goods sold	$66,000

2. Perpetual inventory system:
   a. Average-cost method

Date		Units	Cost*	Amount*
Jan. 1	Inventory	1,400	$19.00	$26,600
4	Sale	(300)	19.00	(5,700)
4	Balance	1,100	19.00	$20,900
8	Purchase	600	20.00	12,000
8	Balance	1,700	19.35	$32,900
10	Sale	(1,300)	19.35	(25,155)
10	Balance	400	19.36	$ 7,745
12	Purchase	900	21.00	18,900
12	Balance	1,300	20.50	$26,645
15	Sale	(150)	20.50	(3,075)
15	Balance	1,150	20.50	$23,570
18	Purchase	500	22.00	11,000
24	Purchase	800	23.00	18,400
24	Balance	2,450	21.62	$52,970
31	Sale	(1,350)	21.62	(29,187)
31	Inventory	1,100	21.62	$23,783

   Cost of goods sold ($5,700 + $25,155 + $3,075 + $29,187) $63,117

   *Rounded.

b. FIFO method

Date			Units	Cost*	Amount*
Jan.	1	Inventory	1,400	$19	$26,600
	4	Sale	(300)	19	(5,700)
	4	Balance	1,100	19	$20,900
	8	Purchase	600	20	12,000
	8	Balance	1,100	19	
			600	20	$32,900
	10	Sale	(1,100)	19	
			(200)	20	(24,900)
	10	Balance	400	20	$ 8,000
	12	Purchase	900	21	18,900
	12	Balance	400	20	
			900	21	$26,900
	15	Sale	(150)	20	(3,000)
	15	Balance	250	20	
			900	21	$23,900
	18	Purchase	500	22	11,000
	24	Purchase	800	23	18,400
	24	Balance	250	20	
			900	21	
			500	22	
			800	23	$53,300
	31	Sale	(250)	20	
			(900)	21	
			(200)	22	(28,300)
	31	Inventory	300	22	
			800	23	$25,000

Cost of goods sold ($5,700 + $24,900 + $3,000 + $28,300) $61,900

*Rounded.

c. LIFO method

Date			Units	Cost*	Amount*
Jan.	1	Inventory	1,400	$19	$26,600
	4	Sale	(300)	19	(5,700)
	4	Balance	1,100	19	$20,900
	8	Purchase	600	20	12,000
	8	Balance	1,100	19	
			600	20	$32,900
	10	Sale	(600)	20	
			(700)	19	(25,300)
	10	Balance	400	19	$ 7,600
	12	Purchase	900	21	18,900
	12	Balance	400	19	
			900	21	$26,500
	15	Sale	(150)	21	(3,150)
	15	Balance	400	19	
			750	21	$23,350
	18	Purchase	500	22	11,000
	24	Purchase	800	23	18,400

*Rounded.

(continued)

Date		Units	Cost*	Amount*
Jan. 24	Balance	400	19	
		750	21	
		500	22	
		800	23	$52,750
31	Sale	(800)	23	
		(500)	22	
		(50)	21	(30,450)
31	Inventory	400	19	
		700	21	$22,300

Cost of goods sold ($5,700 + $25,300 + $3,150 + $30,450)　　$64,600

*Rounded.

3. Ratios computed:

	Average-Cost	FIFO	LIFO
Cost of goods sold	$64,141	$61,900	$66,000
Average inventory	$24,680*	$25,800	$23,750
	($22,759 + $26,600) ÷ 2	($25,000 + $26,600) ÷ 2	($20,900 + $26,600) ÷ 2
Inventory turnover	2.6 times	2.4 times	2.8 times
	($64,141 ÷ $24,680)	($61,900 ÷ $25,800)	($66,000 ÷ $23,750)
Average days' inventory on hand	140.4 days	152.1 days	130.4 days
	(365 days ÷ 2.6 times)	(365 days ÷ 2.4 times)	(365 days ÷ 2.8 times)

*Rounded.

In periods of rising prices, the LIFO method will always result in a higher inventory turnover and lower average days' inventory on hand. When comparing inventory ratios for two or more companies, the inventory methods used by the companies should be considered.

Chapter Assignments

BUILDING YOUR KNOWLEDGE FOUNDATION

QUESTIONS

1. What is merchandise inventory, and what is the primary objective of inventory measurement?
2. How does inventory for a manufacturing company differ from that for a merchandising company?
3. Why is the level of inventory important, and what are two common measures of inventory level?
4. What items should be included in the cost of inventory?
5. Fargo Sales Company is very busy at the end of its fiscal year on June 30. There is an order for 130 units of product in the warehouse. Although the shipping department tries, it cannot ship the product by June 30, and title has not yet passed. Should the 130 units be included in the year-end count of inventory? Why or why not?
6. What is the difference between goods flow and cost flow?
7. Do the FIFO and LIFO inventory methods result in different quantities of ending inventory?
8. Under which method of cost flow are (a) the earliest costs assigned to inventory, (b) the latest costs assigned to inventory, and (c) the average costs assigned to inventory?

9. What are the relative advantages and disadvantages of FIFO and LIFO from management's point of view?

10. Why do you think it is more expensive to maintain a perpetual inventory system?

11. In periods of steadily rising prices, which inventory method—average-cost, FIFO, or LIFO—will give the (a) highest ending inventory cost, (b) lowest ending inventory cost, (c) highest net income, and (d) lowest net income?

12. May a company change its inventory cost method from year to year? Explain.

13. What is the relationship between income tax rules and inventory valuation methods?

14. If the merchandise inventory is mistakenly overstated at the end of 20x0, what is the effect on the (a) 20x0 net income, (b) 20x0 year-end balance sheet value, (c) 20x1 net income, and (d) 20x1 year-end balance sheet value?

15. In the phrase *lower of cost or market*, what is meant by the word *market*?

16. What methods can be used to determine the lower of cost or market?

17. Does using the retail inventory method mean that inventories are measured at retail value on the balance sheet? Explain.

18. For what reasons might management use the gross profit method of estimating inventory?

19. Which of the following inventory systems or methods do not require the taking of a physical inventory: (a) perpetual, (b) periodic, (c) retail, and (d) gross profit?

SHORT EXERCISES

SE 1.

LO 1   Management Issues

Indicate whether each item listed below is associated with (a) allocating the cost of inventories in accordance with the matching rule, (b) assessing the impact of inventory decisions, or (c) evaluating the level of inventory.

1. Calculating the average days' inventory on hand

2. Ordering a supply of inventory to satisfy customer needs

3. Calculating the income tax effect of an inventory method

4. Deciding the cost to place on ending inventory

SE 2.

LO 1   Inventory Turnover and Average Days' Inventory on Hand

During 20x1, Certeen Clothiers had beginning inventory of $240,000, ending inventory of $280,000, and cost of goods sold of $1,100,000. Compute the inventory turnover and average days' inventory on hand.

SE 3.

LO 3   Specific Identification Method

Assume the following data with regard to inventory for Alexis Company:

Aug.	1	Inventory	80 units @ $10 per unit	$ 800
	8	Purchase	100 units @ $11 per unit	1,100
	22	Purchase	70 units @ $12 per unit	840
		Goods available for sale	250 units	$2,740
Aug.	15	Sale	90 units	
	28	Sale	50 units	
		Inventory, Aug. 31	110 units	

Assuming that the inventory consists of 60 units from the August 8 purchase and 50 units from the purchase of August 22, calculate the cost of ending inventory and cost of goods sold.

SE 4.

LO 3   Average-Cost Method— Periodic Inventory System

Using the data in **SE 3,** calculate the cost of ending inventory and cost of goods sold according to the average-cost method under the periodic inventory system.

SE 5. **LO 3 FIFO Method—Periodic** **Inventory System**	Using the data in **SE 3,** calculate the cost of ending inventory and cost of goods sold according to the FIFO method under the periodic inventory system.
SE 6. **LO 3 LIFO Method—Periodic** **Inventory System**	Using the data in **SE 3,** calculate the cost of ending inventory and cost of goods sold according to the LIFO method under the periodic inventory system.
SE 7. **LO 4 Average-Cost Method—** **Perpetual Inventory System**	Using the data in **SE 3,** calculate the cost of ending inventory and cost of goods sold according to the average-cost method under the perpetual inventory system.
SE 8. **LO 4 FIFO Method—Perpetual** **Inventory System**	Using the data in **SE 3,** calculate the cost of ending inventory and cost of goods sold according to the FIFO method under the perpetual inventory system.
SE 9. **LO 4 LIFO Method—Perpetual** **Inventory System**	Using the data in **SE 3,** calculate the cost of ending inventory and cost of goods sold according to the LIFO method under the perpetual inventory system.
SE 10. **LO 5 Effects of Methods and** **Changing Prices**	Following the pattern of Exhibit 1, prepare a table with seven columns that shows the ending inventory and cost of goods sold for each of the results from your calculations in SE 3 through SE 9. Comment on the results, including the effects of the different prices at which the merchandise was purchased. Which method(s) would result in the lowest income taxes?

SE 11.
LO 6 Lower of Cost or Market

The following schedule is based on a physical inventory and replacement costs for one product line of men's shirts:

Item	Quantity	Cost per Unit	Market per Unit
Short sleeve	280	$24	$20
Long sleeve	190	28	29
Extra-long sleeve	80	34	35

Determine the value of this category of inventory at the lower of cost or market using (1) the item-by-item method and (2) the major category method.

EXERCISES

E 1.
LO 1 Management Issues Related
to Inventory

Indicate whether each item listed below is associated with (a) allocating the cost of inventories in accordance with the matching rule, (b) assessing the impact of inventory decisions, or (c) evaluating the level of inventory.

1. Computing inventory turnover
2. Application of the just-in-time operating environment
3. Determining the effects of inventory decisions on cash flows
4. Apportioning the cost of goods available for sale to ending inventory and cost of goods sold
5. Determining the effects of inventory methods on income taxes
6. Determining the assumption about the flow of costs into and out of the company

E 2.
LO 1 Inventory Ratios

Dollar Discount Stores is assessing its levels of inventory for 20x2 and 20x3 and has gathered the following data:

	20x3	20x2	20x1
Ending inventory	$128,000	$108,000	$92,000
Cost of goods sold	640,000	600,000	

Compute the inventory turnover and average days' inventory on hand for 20x2 and 20x3 and comment on the results.

E 3.

LO 3 **Periodic Inventory System and Inventory Costing Methods**

Ray's Farm Store recorded the following purchases and sales of fertilizer during the year:

Jan.	1	Beginning inventory	250 cases @ $23	$ 5,750
Feb.	25	Purchased	100 cases @ $26	2,600
June	15	Purchased	400 cases @ $28	11,200
Aug.	15	Purchased	100 cases @ $26	2,600
Oct.	15	Purchased	300 cases @ $28	8,400
Dec.	15	Purchased	200 cases @ $30	6,000
		Total goods available for sale	1,350	$36,550
		Total sales	1,000 cases	
		Dec. 31 Ending inventory	350 cases	

[Handwritten annotations: "200" above Jan 1; "4600", "11200", "5600" (over 200 300 cases @ $28), "6,000"; "27400 COST ☺ 9,150 E.I. ☺"]

[Handwritten left margin notes: "Sales 1000", "E.I. 350"]

[Handwritten box: "② ave. cost method 36,550 / 1,350 = 27.07   1,000 × 27.07 = 27,070 COGS   9,480 EI"]

Assume that all of the June 15 purchase and 200 cases each from the January 1 beginning inventory, the October 15 purchase, and the December 15 purchase were sold.

Determine the costs that should be assigned to ending inventory and cost of goods sold under each of the following assumptions: (1) costs are assigned by the specific identification method; (2) costs are assigned by the average-cost method; (3) costs are assigned by the FIFO method; (4) costs are assigned by the LIFO method. What conclusions can be drawn about the effect of each method on the income statement and the balance sheet of Ray's Farm Store? Round your answers to the nearest whole number and assume the periodic inventory system.

[Handwritten: "● Specific identification method"]

[Handwritten: "③ FIFO COGS = 26,350 E.I. = 10,200"   "④ LIFO"]

E 4.

LO 3 **Periodic Inventory System and Inventory Costing Methods**

During its first year of operation, Bellows Company purchased 5,600 units of a product at $21 per unit. During the second year, it purchased 6,000 units of the same product at $24 per unit. During the third year, it purchased 5,000 units at $30 per unit. Bellows Company managed to have an ending inventory each year of 1,000 units. The company uses the periodic inventory system.

Prepare cost of goods sold statements that compare the value of ending inventory and the cost of goods sold for each of the three years using (1) the FIFO method and (2) the LIFO method. From the resulting data, what conclusions can you draw about the relationships between changes in unit price and changes in the value of ending inventory?

E 5.

LO 3 **Periodic Inventory System and Inventory Costing Methods**

In chronological order, the inventory, purchases, and sales of a single product for a recent month are as follows:

			Units	Amount per Unit
June	1	Beginning inventory	300	$30
	4	Purchase	800	33
	8	Sale	400	60
	12	Purchase	1,000	36
	16	Sale	700	60
	20	Sale	500	66
	24	Purchase	1,200	39
	28	Sale	600	66
	29	Sale	400	66

Using the periodic inventory system, compute the cost of ending inventory, cost of goods sold, and gross margin. Use the average-cost, FIFO, and LIFO inventory costing methods. Explain the differences in gross margin produced by the three methods. Round unit costs to cents and totals to dollars.

E 6.

LO 4 Perpetual Inventory System and Inventory Costing Methods

Using the data provided in **E 5** and assuming the perpetual inventory system, compute the cost of ending inventory, cost of goods sold, and gross margin. Use the average-cost, FIFO, and LIFO inventory costing methods. Explain the reasons for the differences in gross margin produced by the three methods. Round unit costs to cents and totals to dollars.

E 7.

LO 3 Inventory Costing Methods:
LO 4 Periodic and Perpetual Systems

During July 20x1, Toan, Inc., sold 250 units of its product Velt for $4,000. The following units were available:

	Units	Cost
Beginning inventory	100	$ 2
Purchase 1	40	4
Purchase 2	60	6
Purchase 3	70	8
Purchase 4	80	10
Purchase 5	90	12

A sale of 100 units was made after purchase 1, and a sale of 150 units was made after purchase 4. Of the units sold, 100 came from beginning inventory and 150 from purchases 3 and 4.

Determine cost of goods available for sale and ending inventory in units. Then determine the costs that should be assigned to cost of goods sold and ending inventory under each of the following assumptions: (1) Costs are assigned under the periodic inventory system using (a) the specific identification method, (b) the average-cost method, (c) the FIFO method, and (d) the LIFO method. (2) Costs are assigned under the perpetual inventory system using (a) the average-cost method, (b) the FIFO method, and (c) the LIFO method. For each alternative, show the gross margin. Round unit costs to cents and totals to dollars.

E 8.

LO 5 Effects of Inventory Methods on Cash Flows

Won Products, Inc., sold 120,000 cases of glue at $40 per case during 20x1. Its beginning inventory consisted of 20,000 cases at a cost of $24 per case. During 20x1, it purchased 60,000 cases at $28 per case and later 50,000 cases at $30 per case. Operating expenses were $1,100,000, and the applicable income tax rate was 30 percent.

Using the periodic inventory system, compute net income using the FIFO method and the LIFO method for costing inventory. Which alternative produces the larger cash flow? The company is considering a purchase of 10,000 cases at $30 per case just before the year end. What effect on net income and on cash flow will this proposed purchase have under each method? (**Hint:** What are the income tax consequences?)

E 9.

LO 3 Inventory Costing Method
LO 5 Characteristics

The lettered items in the list below represent inventory costing methods. Write the letter of the method that each of the following statements *best* describes.

a. Specific identification
b. Average-cost
c. First-in, first-out (FIFO)
d. Last-in, first-out (LIFO)

1. Matches recent costs with recent revenues
2. Assumes that each item of inventory is identifiable
3. Results in the most realistic balance sheet valuation
4. Results in the lowest net income in periods of deflation
5. Results in the lowest net income in periods of inflation
6. Matches the oldest costs with recent revenues
7. Results in the highest net income in periods of inflation
8. Results in the highest net income in periods of deflation
9. Tends to level out the effects of inflation
10. Is unpredictable as to the effects of inflation

E 10.
LO 5 Effects of Inventory Errors

Condensed income statements for Elan Company for two years are shown below.

	20x4	20x3
Sales	$126,000	$105,000
Cost of Goods Sold	75,000	54,000
Gross Margin	$ 51,000	$ 51,000
Operating Expenses	30,000	30,000
Income Before Income Taxes	$ 21,000	$ 21,000

(handwritten annotations: income = 12,000; income = 30,700; higher; no effects; will balance out after correction in 2004)

After the end of 20x4, the company discovered that an error had resulted in a $9,000 understatement of the 20x3 ending inventory.

Compute the corrected income before income taxes for 20x3 and 20x4. What effect will the error have on income before income taxes and owners' equity for 20x5?

E 11.
LO 6 Lower-of-Cost-or-Market Rule

Rumore Company values its inventory, shown below, at the lower of cost or market. Compute Rumore's inventory value using (1) the item-by-item method and (2) the major category method.

	Quantity	Per Unit Cost	Per Unit Market
Category I			
Item aa	200	$ 2.00	$ 1.80
Item bb	240	4.00	4.40
Item cc	400	8.00	7.50
Category II			
Item dd	300	12.00	13.00
Item ee	400	18.00	18.20

E 12.
SO 7 Retail Inventory Method

Irene's Dress Shop had net retail sales of $500,000 during the current year. The following additional information was obtained from the accounting records:

	At Cost	At Retail
Beginning inventory	$ 80,000	$120,000
Net purchases (excluding freight in)	280,000	440,000
Freight in	20,800	

1. Using the retail method, estimate the company's ending inventory at cost.
2. Assume that a physical inventory taken at year end revealed an inventory on hand of $36,000 at retail value. What is the estimated amount of inventory shrinkage (loss due to theft, damage, and so forth) at cost using the retail method?

E 13.
SO 7 Gross Profit Method

Lind Bales was at home watching television when he received a call from the fire department. His business was a total loss from fire. The insurance company asked him to prove his inventory loss. For the year, until the date of the fire, Bales's company had sales of $450,000 and purchases of $280,000. Freight in amounted to $13,700, and the beginning inventory was $45,000. It was Bales's custom to price goods to achieve a gross margin of 40 percent.

Compute Bales's estimated inventory loss.

PROBLEMS

P 1.
LO 1 Periodic Inventory
LO 3 System and Inventory Costing Methods

Lobo Company merchandises a single product called Piel. The following data represent beginning inventory and purchases of Piel during the past year: January 1 inventory, 68,000 units at $11.00; February purchases, 80,000 units at $12.00; March purchases, 160,000 units at $12.40; May purchases, 120,000 units at $12.60; July purchases,

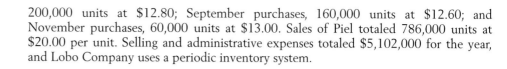

200,000 units at $12.80; September purchases, 160,000 units at $12.60; and November purchases, 60,000 units at $13.00. Sales of Piel totaled 786,000 units at $20.00 per unit. Selling and administrative expenses totaled $5,102,000 for the year, and Lobo Company uses a periodic inventory system.

REQUIRED

1. Prepare a schedule to compute the cost of goods available for sale.

2. Compute income before income taxes under each of the following inventory cost flow assumptions: (a) the average-cost method; (b) the FIFO method; and (c) the LIFO method.

3. Compute inventory turnover and average days' inventory on hand under each of the inventory cost flow assumptions listed in **2.** What conclusion can be made from this comparison?

P 2.

LO 3 Periodic Inventory System and Inventory Methods

The inventory of Product EL and data on purchases and sales for a two-month period follow. The company closes its books at the end of each month. It uses a periodic inventory system.

June 1	Inventory	50 units @ $204
5	Sale	30 units
10	Purchase	100 units @ $220
17	Sale	60 units
30	Inventory	60 units
July 2	Purchase	100 units @ $216
8	Sale	110 units
14	Purchase	50 units @ $224
18	Sale	40 units
22	Purchase	60 units @ $234
26	Sale	30 units
30	Sale	20 units
31	Inventory	70 units

REQUIRED

1. Compute the cost of ending inventory of Product EL on June 30 and July 31 using the average-cost method. In addition, determine cost of goods sold for June and July. Round unit costs to cents and totals to dollars.

2. Compute the cost of the ending inventory on June 30 and July 31 using the FIFO method. In addition, determine cost of goods sold for June and July.

3. Compute the cost of the ending inventory on June 30 and July 31 using the LIFO method. In addition, determine cost of goods sold for June and July.

P 3.

LO 4 Perpetual Inventory System and Inventory Methods

Use the data provided in **P 2,** but assume that the company uses the perpetual inventory system. (**Hint:** In preparing the solutions required below, it is helpful to determine the balance of inventory after each transaction, as shown in the Review Problem for this chapter.)

REQUIRED

1. Determine the cost of ending inventory and cost of goods sold for June and July using the average-cost method. Round unit costs to cents and totals to dollars.

2. Determine the cost of ending inventory and cost of goods sold for June and July using the FIFO method.

3. Determine the cost of ending inventory and cost of goods sold for June and July using the LIFO method.

P 4.

SO 7 Retail Inventory Method

Overland Company switched recently to the retail inventory method to estimate the cost of ending inventory. To test this method, the company took a physical inventory one month after its implementation. Cost, retail, and the physical inventory data are presented at the top of the next page.

	At Cost	At Retail
July 1 Beginning inventory	$472,132	$ 622,800
Purchases	750,000	1,008,400
Purchases returns and allowances	(25,200)	(34,800)
Freight in	8,350	
Sales		1,060,000
Sales returns and allowances		(28,000)
July 31 Physical inventory		508,200

REQUIRED

1. Prepare a schedule to estimate the dollar amount of Overland's July 31 inventory using the retail method.

2. Use Overland's cost ratio to reduce the retail value of the physical inventory to cost.

3. Calculate the estimated amount of inventory shortage at cost and at retail.

P 5.

SO 7 Gross Profit Method

Brandon Oil Products stores its oil field products in a West Texas warehouse. The warehouse and most of its inventory were completely destroyed by a tornado on April 27. The company found some of its records, but it does not keep perpetual inventory records. The warehouse manager must estimate the amount of the loss. He found the following information in the records:

Beginning inventory, Jan. 1	$1,320,000
Purchases, Jan. 2 to Apr. 27	780,000
Purchases returns, Jan. 2 to Apr. 27	(30,000)
Freight in since Jan. 2	16,000
Sales, Jan. 2 to Apr. 27	1,840,000
Sales returns, Jan. 2 to Apr. 27	(40,000)

Inventory costing $420,000 was recovered and could be sold. The manager remembers that the average gross margin on oil field products is 48 percent.

REQUIRED

Prepare a schedule to estimate the inventory destroyed by the tornado.

ALTERNATE PROBLEMS

P 6.

LO 1 Periodic Inventory System
LO 3 and Inventory Costing Methods

The Knapp Door Company sold 2,200 doors during 20x2 at $320 per door. Its beginning inventory on January 1 was 130 doors at $112. Purchases made during the year were as follows:

Feb.	225 doors @ $124
Apr.	350 doors @ $130
June	700 doors @ $140
Aug.	300 doors @ $132
Oct.	400 doors @ $136
Nov.	250 doors @ $144

The company's selling and administrative expenses for the year were $202,000, and the company uses the periodic inventory system.

REQUIRED

1. Prepare a schedule to compute the cost of goods available for sale.

2. Compute income before income taxes under each of the following inventory cost flow assumptions: (a) the average-cost method; (b) the FIFO method; and (c) the LIFO method.

3. Compute inventory turnover and average days' inventory on hand under each of the inventory cost flow assumptions in **2.** What conclusion can be drawn from this comparison?

P 7.

LO 3 Periodic Inventory System and Inventory Methods

The inventory, purchases, and sales of Product ISO for March and April follow. The company closes its books at the end of each month and uses a periodic inventory system.

Mar.	1	Inventory	60 units @ $49
	7	Sale	20 units
	10	Purchase	100 units @ $52
	19	Sale	70 units
	31	Inventory	70 units
Apr.	4	Purchase	120 units @ $53
	11	Sale	110 units
	15	Purchase	50 units @ $54
	23	Sale	80 units
	25	Purchase	100 units @ $55
	27	Sale	100 units
	30	Inventory	50 units

REQUIRED

1. Compute the cost of the ending inventory on March 31 and April 30 using the average-cost method. In addition, determine cost of goods sold for March and April. Round unit costs to cents and totals to dollars.

2. Compute the cost of the ending inventory on March 31 and April 30 using the FIFO method. In addition, determine cost of goods sold for March and April.

3. Compute the cost of the ending inventory on March 31 and April 30 using the LIFO method. In addition, determine cost of goods sold for March and April.

P 8.
LO 4 Perpetual Inventory System and Inventory Methods

Use the data provided in **P 7,** but assume that the company uses the perpetual inventory system. (**Hint:** In preparing the solutions required, it is helpful to determine the balance of inventory after each transaction, as shown in the Review Problem for this chapter.)

REQUIRED

1. Determine the cost of ending inventory and cost of goods sold for March and April using the average-cost method. Round unit costs to cents and totals to dollars.

2. Determine the cost of ending inventory and cost of goods sold for March and April using the FIFO method.

3. Determine the cost of ending inventory and cost of goods sold for March and April using the LIFO method.

EXPANDING YOUR CRITICAL THINKING, COMMUNICATION, AND INTERPERSONAL SKILLS

SKILLS DEVELOPMENT

Conceptual Analysis

SD 1.
LO 1 Evaluation of Inventory Levels

The Gap Inc. is one of the most important retailers of casual clothing for all members of the family. *Business Week* reports, "The Gap Inc. is hell-bent on becoming to apparel what McDonald's is to food." With more than 1,100 stores already open, the company plans to open about 150 new stores per year for the next half decade. How does the company stay ahead of the competition? "One way is through frequent replenishment

Cash Flow	CD-ROM	Communication	Critical Thinking	Ethics	General Ledger	Group Activity	Hot Links to Real Companies	International	Internet	Key Ratio	Memo	Spreadsheet

of mix-and-match inventory. That enables the company to clear out unpopular items fast—which prompts shoppers to check in on the new selections more often." The Gap replaces inventory 6.1 times a year.[10] That compares with 3.5 times at other specialty apparel stores. One way in which The Gap controls inventory is by applying a just-in-time operating environment. How many days of inventory does The Gap have on hand on average compared to the competition? Discuss why those comparisons are important to The Gap. (Think of as many business and financial reasons as you can.) What is a just-in-time operating environment? Why is it important to achieving a favorable inventory turnover?

SD 2.

LO 5   **LIFO Inventory Method**

Ninety-three percent of paper companies use the LIFO inventory method for the costing of inventories, whereas only 11 percent of computer equipment companies use LIFO.[11] Describe the LIFO inventory method. What effects does it have on reported income, cash flows, and income taxes during periods of price changes? Discuss why the paper industry would use LIFO but most of the computer industry would not.

Ethical Dilemma

SD 3.

LO 1   **Inventories, Income**
LO 5   **Determination, and Ethics**

Flare, Inc., which has a December 31 year end, designs and sells fashions for young professional women. Sandra Mason, president of the company, feared that the forecasted 20x1 profitability goals would not be reached. She was pleased when Flare received a large order on December 30 from The Executive Woman, a retail chain of upscale stores for businesswomen. Mason immediately directed the controller to record the sale, which represented 13 percent of Flare's annual sales, but directed the inventory control department not to separate the goods for shipment until after January 1. Separated goods are not included in inventory because they have been sold. On December 31, the company's auditors arrived to observe the year-end taking of the physical inventory under the periodic inventory system. What will be the effect of Mason's action on Flare's 20x1 profitability? What will be the effect on 20x2 profitability? Was Mason's action ethical?

Research Activity

SD 4.

LO 2   **Retail Business**
LO 4   **Inventories**

Make an appointment to visit a local retail business—a grocery, clothing, book, music, or appliance store, for example—and interview the manager for 30 minutes about the company's inventory accounting system. The store may be a branch of a larger company. Find out answers to the following questions, summarize your findings in a paper to be handed in, and be prepared to discuss your results in class.

What is the physical flow of merchandise into the store, and what documents are used in connection with this flow?

What documents are prepared when merchandise is sold?

Does the store keep perpetual inventory records? If so, does it keep the records in units only, or does it keep track of cost as well? If not, what system does the store use?

How often does the company take a physical inventory?

How are financial statements generated for the store?

What method does the company use to cost its inventory for financial statements?

Group Activity: Assign teams to various types of businesses in your community.

Decision-Making Practice

SD 5.

LO 5   **Inventory Methods, Income
         Taxes, and Cash Flows**

The *Osaka Trading Company* began business in 20x1 for the purpose of importing and marketing an electronic component used widely in digital appliances. It is now December 20, 20x1, and management is considering its options. Among its considerations is which inventory method to choose. It has decided to choose either the FIFO or the LIFO method. Under the periodic inventory system, the effects on net income of using the two methods are as follows:

	FIFO Method	LIFO Method
Sales (500,000 units × $12)	$6,000,000	$6,000,000
Cost of Goods Sold		
Purchases		
200,000 × $4	$ 800,000	$ 800,000
400,000 × $6	2,400,000	2,400,000
Total Purchases	$3,200,000	$3,200,000
Less Ending Inventory		
FIFO (100,000 × $6)	(600,000)	
LIFO (100,000 × $4)		(400,000)
Cost of Goods Sold	$2,600,000	$2,800,000
Gross Margin	$3,400,000	$3,200,000
Operating Expenses	2,400,000	2,400,000
Income Before Income Taxes	$1,000,000	$ 800,000
Income Taxes	300,000	240,000
Net Income	$ 700,000	$ 560,000

Also, management has an option to purchase an additional 100,000 units of inventory before year end at a price of $8 per unit, the price that is expected to prevail during 20x2. The income tax rate applicable to the company in 20x1 is 30 percent.

Business conditions are expected to be favorable in 20x2, as they were in 20x1. Management has asked you for advice. Analyze the effects of making the additional purchase. Then prepare a memorandum to Osaka management in which you compare cash outcomes under the four alternatives and advise management which inventory method to choose and whether to order the additional inventory. Be prepared to discuss your recommendations.

FINANCIAL REPORTING AND ANALYSIS

Interpreting Financial Reports

FRA 1.
LO 5 Misstatement of Inventory

The Wall Street Journal reported that **Crazy Eddie Inc.,** a discount consumer electronics chain, seemed to be missing $45 million in merchandise inventory. "It was a shock," Elias Zinn, the new president and chief executive officer, was quoted as saying.[12]

The article went on to say that Zinn headed a management team that had taken control of Crazy Eddie after a new board of directors was elected at a shareholders' meeting. A count turned up only $75 million in inventory, compared with $126.7 million reported by the old management. Net sales could account for only $6.7 million of the difference. Zinn said he didn't know whether bookkeeping errors in prior years or an actual physical loss created the shortfall, although at least one store manager felt it was a bookkeeping error, because security is strong. "It would be hard for someone to steal anything," he said.

REQUIRED

1. What is the effect of the misstatement of inventory on Crazy Eddie's reported earnings in prior accounting periods?

2. Is this a situation you would expect in a company that is experiencing financial difficulty? Explain.

FRA 2.
LO 5 LIFO Liquidation

At December 31, 1997 and 1996, **RJR Nabisco, Inc.,** reported approximately $592 million and $194 million, respectively, of domestic tobacco inventories valued under the LIFO method. As explained in the annual report,

The current cost of LIFO inventories at December 31, 1997, and 1996, was greater than the amount at which these inventories were carried on the Consolidated Balance Sheets by $151 million and $166 million respectively. For the years ended December 31, 1997, 1996, and 1995, net income was increased by approximately $14 million, $35 million, and $29 million respectively, as a result of LIFO inventory liquidations. The LIFO liquidations resulted from programs to reduce domestic leaf durations consistent with forecasts of future operating requirements.[13]

RJR Nabisco's average income tax rates for 1997 and 1996 were 52 percent and 49 percent, respectively.

REQUIRED

1. Explain why a reduction in the quantity of inventory resulted in an increase in net income. Would the same result have occurred if RJR Nabisco had used the FIFO method to value inventory? Explain your answer.

2. What is the income tax effect of the LIFO liquidation? Is this a favorable outcome?

International Company

FRA 3.
LO 1   Comparison of Inventory
LO 5   Levels and Methods

Two large Japanese diversified electronics companies are *Pioneer Electronic Corporation* and *Yamaha Motor Co., Ltd.* Both companies use the average-cost method and the lower-of-cost-or-market rule to account for inventories. The following data are for their 1999 fiscal years (in millions of yen):[14]

	Pioneer	Yamaha
Beginning inventory	¥116,081	¥137,628
Ending inventory	107,374	142,436
Cost of goods sold	398,947	561,801

Compare the inventory efficiency of Pioneer and Yamaha by computing the inventory turnover and average days' inventory on hand for both companies in 1999. Comment on the results. Most companies in the United States use the LIFO inventory method. How would inventory method affect your evaluation if you were to compare Pioneer and Yamaha to a U.S. company? What could you do to make the results comparable?

Toys "R" Us Annual Report

FRA 4.
LO 1   Retail Inventory Method
LO 5   and Inventory Ratios
LO 6
SO 7

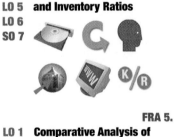

Refer to the note related to inventories in the Toys "R" Us annual report to answer the following questions: What inventory method(s) does Toys "R" Us use? Why do you think that if LIFO inventories had been valued at FIFO, there would be no difference? Do you think many of the company's inventories are valued at market? Even though few companies use the retail inventory method, why do you think Toys "R" Us uses this method? Compute and compare the inventory turnover and average days' inventory on hand for Toys "R" Us for 1999 and 2000. Beginning 1998 inventory was $2,464 million.

Fingraph® Financial Analyst™

FRA 5.
LO 1   Comparative Analysis of
Inventories and Operating
Cycle

Select any two companies from the same industry on the Fingraph® Financial Analyst™ CD-ROM software. Choose an industry, such as manufacturing, consumer products, consumer food and beverage, or computers, in which inventory is likely to be an important current asset.

1. In the annual reports for the companies you have selected, read any reference to inventories in the summary of significant accounting policies or notes to the financial statements. What inventory method does the company use? What are the changes in and relative importance of raw materials, work in process, and finished goods inventories?

2. Display and print in tabular and graphical form the Liquidity and Asset Utilization Analysis page. Prepare a table that compares the inventory turnover and average days' inventory on hand for both companies for two years. Also include in your table the operating cycle by combining average days' inventory on hand with average days' sales uncollected.

3. Find and read references to inventories in the liquidity analysis section of management's discussion and analysis in each annual report.

4. Write a one-page executive summary that highlights the accounting policies for inventories, the relative importance and changes in raw materials, work in process,

and finished goods, and compares the inventory utilization of the two companies, including reference to management's assessment. Comment specifically on the financing implications of the companies' relative operating cycles. Include the Fingraph® page and your table as an attachment to your report.

Internet Case

Maytag Corporation, an appliance manufacturer, uses the LIFO inventory method. Go to www.maytagcorp.com and select "About Maytag." Then select "Financial Center." After finding the income statement and inventory note, calculate what net income would have been had the company used FIFO. Calculate how much cash the company saved for the year and cumulatively by using LIFO. What is the difference between the LIFO and FIFO gross margin and profit margin results? Which reporting alternative is better for the company?

ENDNOTES

1. J.C. Penney Company, Inc., *Annual Report*, 1999.
2. American Institute of Certified Public Accountants, *Accounting Research Bulletin No. 43* (New York: AICPA, 1953), ch. 4.
3. Gary McWilliams, "Whirlwind on the Web," *Business Week*, April 7, 1997.
4. American Institute of Certified Public Accountants, *Accounting Research Bulletin No. 43* (New York: AICPA, 1953), ch. 4.
5. Micah Frankel and Robert Trezevant, "The Year-End LIFO Inventory Purchasing Decision: An Empirical Test," *The Accounting Review*, April 1994.
6. American Institute of Certified Public Accountants, *Accounting Trends & Techniques* (New York: AICPA, 1999).
7. Teri Agins, "Report Is Said to Show Pervasive Fraud at Leslie" and "Leslie Fay Co.'s Profits Restated for Past 3 Years," *The Wall Street Journal*, September 27 and 30, 1993.
8. International Paper Company, *Annual Report*, 1999.
9. American Institute of Certified Public Accountants, *Accounting Trends & Techniques* (New York: AICPA, 1999).
10. "Everybody's Falling into The Gap," *Business Week*, September 23, 1991, p. 36; and The Gap Inc., *Annual Report*, 1999.
11. American Institute of Certified Public Accountants, *Accounting Trends & Techniques* (New York: AICPA, 1999).
12. Based on Ann Hagedorn, "Crazy Eddie Says About $45 Million of Goods Missing," *The Wall Street Journal*, November 20, 1987, p. 47.
13. RJR Nabisco, Inc., *Annual Report*, 1997.
14. Pioneer Electronic Corporation, *Annual Report*, 1999; and Yamaha Motor Co. Ltd., *Annual Report*, 1999.

11

Long-Term Assets

LEARNING
OBJECTIVES

1 Identify the types of long-term assets and explain the management issues related to accounting for them.

2 Distinguish between capital and revenue expenditures, and account for the cost of property, plant, and equipment.

3 Define *depreciation*, state the factors that affect its computation, and show how to record it.

4 Compute periodic depreciation under the straight-line method, production method, and declining-balance method.

5 Account for the disposal of depreciable assets not involving exchanges.

6 Account for the disposal of depreciable assets involving exchanges.

7 Identify the issues related to accounting for natural resources and compute depletion.

8 Apply the matching rule to intangible assets, including research and development costs and goodwill.

SUPPLEMENTAL
OBJECTIVE

9 Apply depreciation methods to problems of partial years, revised rates, groups of similar items, special types of capital expenditures, and cost recovery.

DECISION POINT: A USER'S FOCUS

H. J. Heinz Company The effects of management's decisions regarding long-term assets are most apparent in the areas of reported total assets and net income. How does one learn about the significance of those items to a company? An idea of the extent of a company's long-term assets and their importance can be gained from the financial statements. For example, this list of assets (in thousands of dollars) is taken from the annual report of H. J. Heinz Company, one of the world's largest food companies.

Of the company's approximately $8.9 billion in total assets, about 27 percent consists of property, plant, and equipment, and another 37.5 percent is goodwill and other noncurrent assets. On the income statement, depreciation and amortization expenses associated with those assets are more than $306 million, or about 34 percent of net income. On the statement of cash flows, more than $452 million was spent on new long-term assets.[1] This chapter deals with long-term assets: property, plant, and equipment and intangible assets.

Financial Highlights

(In thousands)

	2000	1999
Property, Plant, and Equipment:		
Land	$ 45,959	$ 48,649
Buildings and leasehold improvements	860,873	798,307
Equipment, furniture, and other	3,440,915	3,227,019
	$4,347,747	$4,073,975
Less accumulated depreciation	1,988,994	1,902,951
Total property, plant, and equipment, net	$2,358,753	$2,171,024
Other Noncurrent Assets:		
Goodwill (net of amortization: 2000—$312,433 and 1999—$352,209)	$1,609,672	$1,781,466
Trademarks (net of amortization: 2000—$104,125 and 1999—$84,672)	674,279	511,608
Other intangibles (net of amortization: 2000—$147,343 and 1999—$117,038)	127,779	177,290
Other noncurrent assets	910,225	525,468
Total other noncurrent assets	$3,321,955	$2,995,832

Management Issues Related to Accounting for Long-Term Assets

OBJECTIVE

1 Identify the types of long-term assets and explain the management issues related to accounting for them

Long-term assets are assets that (1) have a useful life of more than one year, (2) are acquired for use in the operation of a business, and (3) are not intended for resale to customers. For many years, it was common to refer to long-term assets as *fixed assets*, but use of this term is declining because the word *fixed* implies that they last forever. The relative importance of long-term assets to various industries is shown in Figure 1. Long-term assets range from 17.1 percent of total assets in computers to 53.5 percent in interstate trucking.

VIDEO CASE

 Fermi National Accelerator Laboratory

Objectives

- To describe the characteristics of long-term assets.
- To identify the four issues that must be addressed in applying the matching rule to long-term assets.
- To define depreciation and state the principal causes of depreciation.
- To identify the issues related to intangible assets, including research and development.

Background for the Case

The Fermi National Accelerator Laboratory (Fermilab), located 30 miles west of Chicago, is a U.S. Department of Energy national laboratory. Its primary mission is to advance the understanding of the fundamental nature of matter and energy.

Fermilab operates the world's highest-energy particle accelerator, the Trevatron, or "atom-smasher." Circling through rings of magnets four miles in circumference, particle beams generate experimental conditions equivalent to those that existed in the first quadrillionth of a second after the birth of the universe. This capability to re-create such high energy levels places Fermilab at the frontier of global physics research. It provides leadership and resources for qualified experimenters to conduct basic research at the leading edge of high-energy physics and related disciplines. In the year 2000, with Collider Run II, Fermilab began probing the smallest dimensions that humans have ever examined. These scientists have the best opportunity to make important discoveries that could answer some of today's questions in particle physics.

Although a unit of the U.S. government, Fermilab is a financially independent nonprofit corporation with a governing body consisting of the presidents of 87 member research universities. With annual revenues of about $300 million, consisting mostly of government contracts, and annual expenses of about $260 million, Fermilab faces the same management challenges that a for-profit corporation faces. It must make huge investments in long-term assets. Other than salaries, depreciation is the lab's largest expense. In addition, Fermilab creates intellectual capital through basic research that it shares cooperatively with U.S. industry to encourage economic development.

For more information about Fermi National Accelerator Laboratory, visit the laboratory's web site through the Needles Accounting Resource Center at:
http://college.hmco.com

Required

View the video on Fermi National Accelerator Laboratory that accompanies this book. As you are watching the video, take notes related to the following questions:

1. What are the characteristics that distinguish long-term assets? What are some examples of long-term assets at Fermilab?

2. What four issues must be addressed in applying the matching rule to long-term assets?

3. What is depreciation and what are the two major causes of depreciation?

4. What are research and development costs and how does Fermilab account for them? How might this method understate the assets of Fermilab?

**Figure 1
Long-Term Assets as a
Percentage of Total Assets for
Selected Industries**

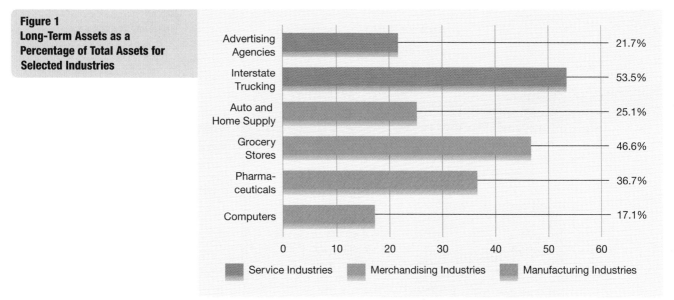

Source: Data from Dun & Bradstreet, *Industry Norms and Key Business Ratios,* 1999–2000.

Although there is no strict minimum useful life an asset must have to be classified as long term, the most common criterion is that the asset must be capable of repeated use for a period of at least a year. Included in this category is equipment used only in peak or emergency periods, such as generators.

Assets that are not used in the normal course of business should not be included in this category. Thus, land held for speculative reasons or buildings no longer used in ordinary business operations should not be included in the property, plant, and equipment category. Instead, they should be classified as long-term investments.

Finally, if an item is held for resale to customers, it should be classified as inventory—not plant and equipment—no matter how durable it is. For example, a printing press that is held for sale by a printing press manufacturer would be considered inventory, whereas the same printing press would be considered plant and equipment for a printing company that buys it for use in operations.

Long-term assets differ from current assets in that they support the operating cycle instead of being a part of it. They are also expected to benefit the business for a longer period than do current assets. Current assets are expected to be used up or converted to cash within one year or during the operating cycle, whichever is longer. Long-term assets are expected to last beyond that period. Long-term assets and their related expenses are summarized in Figure 2.

Generally, long-lived assets are reported at carrying value, as presented in Figure 3. **Carrying value** is the unexpired part of the cost of an asset, not its market value; it is also called *book value.* If a long-lived asset loses some or all of its revenue-generating potential prior to the end of its useful life, the asset may be deemed impaired and its carrying value reduced. **Asset impairment** occurs when the sum of the expected cash flows from the asset is less than the carrying value of the asset.[2] Reducing carrying value to fair value, as measured by the present value of future cash flows, is an application of conservatism. All long-term assets are subject to an asset impairment evaluation. A reduction in carrying value as a result of impairment is recorded as a loss.

Facing deregulation and competition for the first time, six of the seven Baby Bell regional telephone companies, including Pacific Telesis, Bell South, and NYNEX, took writedowns in the billions of dollars. In the past, the cost of old equipment

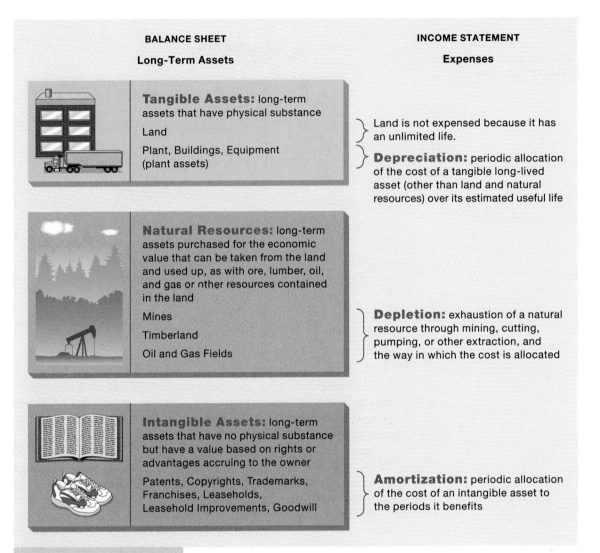

BALANCE SHEET

Long-Term Assets

INCOME STATEMENT

Expenses

Tangible Assets: long-term assets that have physical substance

Land

Plant, Buildings, Equipment (plant assets)

Land is not expensed because it has an unlimited life.

Depreciation: periodic allocation of the cost of a tangible long-lived asset (other than land and natural resources) over its estimated useful life

Natural Resources: long-term assets purchased for the economic value that can be taken from the land and used up, as with ore, lumber, oil, and gas or other resources contained in the land

Mines

Timberland

Oil and Gas Fields

Depletion: exhaustion of a natural resource through mining, cutting, pumping, or other extraction, and the way in which the cost is allocated

Intangible Assets: long-term assets that have no physical substance but have a value based on rights or advantages accruing to the owner

Patents, Copyrights, Trademarks, Franchises, Leaseholds, Leasehold Improvements, Goodwill

Amortization: periodic allocation of the cost of an intangible asset to the periods it benefits

**Figure 2
Classification of Long-Term Assets and Corresponding Expenses**

could be passed on to consumers through regulated rate increases, but with competition, rates are decreasing, not increasing. As a result, the future cash flows cannot justify the recorded asset carrying values of aging copper telephone lines, switching gear, and other equipment. Estimated useful lives for these assets have been reduced by 50 percent or more. The writedowns have caused the companies to report operating losses.[3]

Deciding to Acquire Long-Term Assets

The decision to acquire a long-term asset involves a complex process. Methods of evaluating data to make rational decisions in this area are grouped under a topic called *capital budgeting*, which is usually covered as a management accounting topic. However, an awareness of the general nature of the problem is helpful in understanding the accounting issues related to long-term assets. To illustrate the

Plant Assets	Natural Resources	Intangible Assets
Less Accumulated Depreciation	Less Accumulated Depletion	Less Accumulated Amortization
Carrying Value	Carrying Value	Carrying Value

Figure 3
Carrying Value of Long-Term
Assets on Balance Sheet

acquisition decision, let us assume that Irena Markova, M.D., is considering the purchase of a $5,000 computer for her office. Dr. Markova estimates that if she purchases the computer, she can reduce the hours of a part-time employee sufficiently to save net cash flows of $2,000 per year for four years and that the computer will be worth about $1,000 at the end of that period. These data are summarized as follows:

	20x1	20x2	20x3	20x4
Acquisition cost	($5,000)			
Net annual savings in cash flows	$2,000	$2,000	$2,000	$2,000
Disposal price				1,000
Net cash flows	($3,000)	$2,000	$2,000	$3,000

To place the cash flows on a comparable basis, it is helpful to use present value tables such as Tables 3 and 4 in the appendix on future value and present value tables. Assuming that the appropriate interest rate is 10 percent compounded annually, the purchase may be evaluated as follows:

		Present Value
Acquisition cost	Present value factor = 1.000	
	1.000 × $5,000	($5,000)
Net annual savings in cash flows	Present value factor = 3.170	
	(Table 4: 4 periods, 10%)	
	3.170 × $2,000	6,340
Disposal price	Present value factor = .683	
	(Table 3: 4 periods, 10%)	
	.683 × $1,000	683
Net present value		$2,023

As long as the net present value is positive, Dr. Markova will earn at least 10 percent on the investment. In this case, the return is greater than 10 percent because the net present value is a positive $2,023. Based on this analysis, Dr. Markova makes the decision to purchase. However, there are other important considerations that have to be taken into account, such as the costs of training and maintenance, and the possibility that, because of unforeseen circumstances, the savings may not be as great as expected. In Dr. Markova's case, the decision to purchase is likely to be a good one because the net present value is both positive and large relative to the investment.

Information about a company's acquisitions of long-term assets may be found under investing activities in the statement of cash flows. For example, in referring to this section of its annual report, the management of Ford Motor Company, a manufacturer of automobiles, makes the following statement: "We spent $7.9 billion for capital goods, such as machinery, equipment, tooling, and facilities."[4]

Financing Long-Term Assets

In addition to deciding whether or not to acquire a long-term asset, management must decide how to finance the asset if it is acquired. Some companies are profitable enough to pay for long-term assets out of cash flows from operations, but when financing is needed, some form of long-term arrangement related to the life of the asset is usually most appropriate. For example, an automobile loan generally spans four or five years, whereas a mortgage loan on a house may span as many as 30 years.

For a major long-term acquisition, a company may issue capital stock, long-term notes, or bonds. A good place to study a company's long-term financing is in the financing activities section of the statement of cash flows. For instance, in discussing this section, Ford Motor Company's management states, "Our automotive debt totaled $7.9 billion, which was 31 percent of total capitalization (stockholders' equity and Automotive debt), compared with 30 percent of total capitalization a year ago."[5]

Applying the Matching Rule to Long-Term Assets

Accounting for long-term assets requires the proper application of the matching rule through the resolution of two important issues. The first is how much of the total cost to allocate to expense in the current accounting period. The second is how much to retain on the balance sheet as an asset to benefit future periods. To resolve these issues, four important questions about the acquisition, use, and disposal of each long-term asset, as illustrated in Figure 4, must be answered:

1. How is the cost of the long-term asset determined?
2. How should the expired portion of the cost of the long-term asset be allocated against revenues over time?
3. How should subsequent expenditures, such as repairs and additions, be treated?
4. How should disposal of the long-term asset be recorded?

Because of the long life of long-term assets and the complexity of the transactions involving them, management has many choices and estimates to make. For example, acquisition cost may be complicated by group purchases, trade-ins, or construction costs. In addition, to allocate the cost of the asset to future periods effectively, management must estimate how long the asset will last and what it will be worth at the end of its use.

When making such estimates, it is helpful to think of a long-term asset as a bundle of services to be used in the operation of the business over a period of years. A delivery truck may provide 100,000 miles of service over its life. A piece of equipment may have the potential to produce 500,000 parts. A building may provide shelter for 50 years. As each of those assets is purchased, the company is paying in advance for 100,000 miles, the capacity to produce 500,000 parts, or 50 years of service. In essence, each asset is a type of long-term prepaid expense. The accounting problem is to spread the cost of the services over the useful life of the asset. As the services benefit the company over the years, the cost becomes an expense rather than an asset.

**Figure 4
Issues of Accounting for
Long-Term Assets**

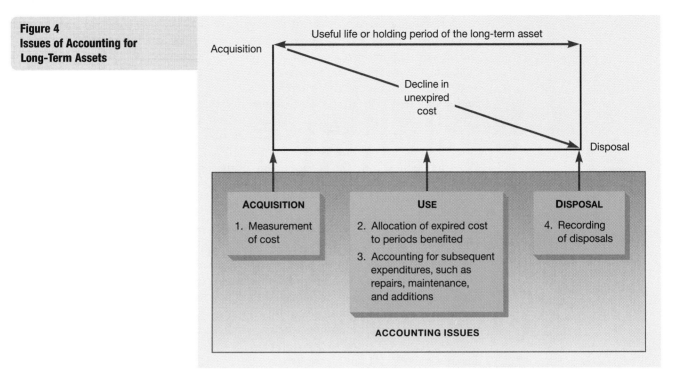

Acquisition Cost of Property, Plant, and Equipment

OBJECTIVE

2 Distinguish between capital and revenue expenditures, and account for the cost of property, plant, and equipment

The term **expenditure** refers to a payment or an obligation to make future payment for an asset, such as a truck, or a service, such as a repair. Expenditures may be classified as capital expenditures or revenue expenditures. A **capital expenditure** is an expenditure for the purchase or expansion of a long-term asset. Capital expenditures are recorded in the asset accounts because they benefit several future accounting periods. A **revenue expenditure** is an expenditure related to the repair, maintenance, and operation of a long-term asset. These expenditures do not extend the asset's original useful life but are necessary to enable the asset to fulfill its original useful life. Revenue expenditures are recorded in the expense accounts because their benefits are realized in the current period.

Careful distinction between capital and revenue expenditures is important to the proper application of the matching rule. For example, if the purchase of an automobile is mistakenly recorded as a revenue expenditure, the total cost of the automobile is recorded as an expense on the income statement. As a result, current net income is reported at a lower amount (understated) and assets are understated. In future periods net income will be overstated because depreciation expense is understated. Assets are also understated because the asset was completely expensed in the period that it was purchased. If, on the other hand, a revenue expenditure, such as the painting of a building, were charged to an asset account, the expense of the current period would be understated. Current net income and assets would be overstated by the same amount, and the net income of future periods would be understated because of the erroneous future depreciation expense that was recorded.

Determining when a payment is an expense and when it is an asset is a matter of judgment, in the exercise of which management takes a leading role. For example, inconsistencies have existed in accounting for the costs of computer programs that run the systems for businesses. Some companies immediately write off the expenditure as an expense, whereas others treat it as a long-term intangible asset and amortize it year after year. Companies spend billions of dollars a year on this type of software, and it is an important variable in the profitability of many companies. Although the AICPA has issued new rules to try to bring more standardization to these accounting issues, considerable latitude does still exist, such as in determining how long the economic life of the software will be.[6]

General Approach to Acquisition Costs

The acquisition cost of property, plant, and equipment includes all expenditures reasonable and necessary to get the asset in place and ready for use. For example, the cost of installing and testing a machine is a legitimate cost of the machine. However, if the machine is damaged during installation, the cost of repairs is an operating expense and not an acquisition cost.

Cost is easiest to determine when a purchase is made for cash. In that case, the cost of the asset is equal to the cash paid for the asset plus expenditures for freight, insurance while in transit, installation, and other necessary related costs. If a debt is incurred in the purchase of the asset, the interest charges are not a cost of the asset but a cost of borrowing the money to buy the asset. They are therefore an operating expense. An exception to this principle is that interest costs incurred during the construction of an asset are properly included as a cost of the asset.[7]

Expenditures such as freight, insurance while in transit, and installation are included in the cost of the asset because they are necessary if the asset is to function. Following the matching rule, they are allocated to the useful life of the asset rather than charged as expenses in the current period.

For practical purposes, many companies establish policies defining when an expenditure should be recorded as an expense or as an asset. For example, small expenditures for items that would normally be treated as assets may be treated as expenses because the amounts involved are not material in relation to net income. Thus, a wastebasket, which might last for years, would be recorded as a supplies expense rather than as a depreciable asset.

Some of the problems of determining the cost of a long-lived asset are demonstrated in the illustrations for land, land improvements, buildings, equipment, and group purchases presented in the next few sections.

LAND There are often expenditures in addition to the purchase price of land that should be debited to the Land account. Some examples are commissions to real estate agents; lawyers' fees; accrued taxes paid by the purchaser; costs of preparing the land to build on, such as draining, tearing down old buildings, clearing, and grading; and assessments for local improvements, such as streets and sewage systems. The cost of landscaping is usually debited to the Land account because such improvements are relatively permanent. Land is not subject to depreciation because it does not have a limited useful life.

Let us assume that a company buys land for a new retail operation. It pays a net purchase price of $170,000, pays brokerage fees of $6,000 and legal fees of $2,000, pays $10,000 to have an old building on the site torn down, receives $4,000 salvage from the old building, and pays $1,000 to have the site graded. The cost of the land will be $185,000.

Net purchase price		$170,000
Brokerage fees		6,000
Legal fees		2,000
Tearing down old building	$10,000	
Less salvage	4,000	6,000
Grading		1,000
Total cost		$185,000

LAND IMPROVEMENTS Improvements to real estate, such as driveways, parking lots, and fences, have a limited life and are thus subject to depreciation. They should be recorded in an account called Land Improvements rather than in the Land account.

BUILDINGS When an existing building is purchased, its cost includes the purchase price plus all repairs and other expenditures required to put it in usable condition. Buildings are subject to depreciation because they have a limited useful life. When a business constructs its own building, the cost includes all reasonable and necessary expenditures, such as those for materials, labor, part of the overhead and other indirect costs, architects' fees, insurance during construction, interest on construction loans during the period of construction, lawyers' fees, and building permits. If outside contractors are used in the construction, the net contract price plus other expenditures necessary to put the building in usable condition are included.

EQUIPMENT The cost of equipment includes all expenditures connected with purchasing the equipment and preparing it for use. Those expenditures include the invoice price less cash discounts; freight or transportation, including insurance; excise taxes and tariffs; buying expenses; installation costs; and test runs to ready the equipment for operation. Equipment is subject to depreciation.

GROUP PURCHASES Sometimes land and other assets are purchased for a lump sum. Because land is a nondepreciable asset that has an unlimited life, it must have

FOCUS ON BUSINESS ETHICS

Determining the acquisition price of a long-term asset is not always as clear-cut as some might imagine, especially in the case of constructed assets. Management has considerable leeway, but if choices are questioned, the results can sometimes be costly. *The Wall Street Journal* reported that Chambers Development Co., a waste-disposal company, wrote off nearly $50 million when it decided to stop deferring costs related to the development of landfills. Previously, Chambers had been including certain indirect costs, such as executives' salaries and travel, legal, and public relations fees, as capital expenditures to be written off over the life of the landfill. *The Wall Street Journal* reported that Chambers portrayed the accounting change as the outcome of a theoretical debate about good accounting practice, but SEC investigators concluded that the accounting practices created fictitious profit beyond generally accepted accounting practices. Further write-offs may follow because of the large amount of interest the company was capitalizing as a cost of the landfill. On news of the accounting change, the company's stock price dropped 63 percent in one day.[8] After straightening out its accounting, Chambers was acquired by USA Waste for $424 million.

a separate ledger account, and the lump-sum purchase price must be apportioned between the land and the other assets. For example, assume that a building and the land on which it is situated are purchased for a lump-sum payment of $85,000. The apportionment can be made by determining the price of each if purchased separately and applying the appropriate percentages to the lump-sum price. Assume that appraisals yield estimates of $10,000 for the land and $90,000 for the building, if purchased separately. In that case, 10 percent of the lump-sum price, or $8,500, would be allocated to the land and 90 percent, or $76,500, would be allocated to the building, as follows:

	Appraisal	Percentage	Apportionment
Land	$ 10,000	10% ($10,000 ÷ $100,000)	$ 8,500 ($85,000 × 10%)
Building	90,000	90 ($90,000 ÷ $100,000)	76,500 ($85,000 × 90%)
Totals	$100,000	100%	$85,000

Accounting for Depreciation

OBJECTIVE

3 Define *depreciation,* state the factors that affect its computation, and show how to record it

Depreciation accounting is described by the AICPA as follows:

> The cost of a productive facility is one of the costs of the services it renders during its useful economic life. Generally accepted accounting principles require that this cost be spread over the expected useful life of the facility in such a way as to allocate it as equitably as possible to the periods during which services are obtained from the use of the facility. This procedure is known as depreciation accounting, a system of accounting which aims to distribute the cost or other basic value of tangible capital assets, less salvage (if any), over the estimated useful life of the unit . . . in a systematic and rational manner. It is a process of allocation, not of valuation.[9]

This description contains several important points. First, all tangible assets except land have a limited useful life. Because of this limited useful life, the costs of these assets must be distributed as expenses over the years they benefit. Physical deterioration and obsolescence are the major causes of the limited useful life of a depreciable asset. The **physical deterioration** of tangible assets results from use and from exposure to the elements, such as wind and sun. Periodic repairs and a sound maintenance policy may keep buildings and equipment in good operating order and extract the maximum useful life from them, but every machine or building at some point must be discarded. The need for depreciation is not eliminated by repairs. **Obsolescence** is the process of becoming out of date. Because of fast-changing technology and fast-changing demands, machinery and even buildings often become obsolete before they wear out. Accountants do not distinguish between physical deterioration and obsolescence because they are interested in the length of an asset's useful life regardless of what limits that useful life.

Second, the term *depreciation,* as used in accounting, does not refer to an asset's physical deterioration or decrease in market value over time. Depreciation means the allocation of the cost of a plant asset to the periods that benefit from the services of that asset. The term is used to describe the gradual conversion of the cost of the asset into an expense.

Third, depreciation is not a process of valuation. Accounting records are kept in accordance with the cost principle; they are not indicators of changing price levels.

It is possible that, because of an advantageous purchase and specific market conditions, the market value of a building may rise. Nevertheless, depreciation must continue to be recorded because it is the result of an allocation, not a valuation, process. Eventually the building will wear out or become obsolete regardless of interim fluctuations in market value.

Factors That Affect the Computation of Depreciation

Four factors affect the computation of depreciation: (1) cost, (2) residual value, (3) depreciable cost, and (4) estimated useful life.

COST   As explained earlier in the chapter, cost is the net purchase price plus all reasonable and necessary expenditures to get the asset in place and ready for use.

RESIDUAL VALUE   The **residual value** of an asset is its estimated net scrap, salvage, or trade-in value as of the estimated date of disposal. Other terms often used to describe residual value are *salvage value* and *disposal value*.

DEPRECIABLE COST   The **depreciable cost** of an asset is its cost less its residual value. For example, a truck that costs $12,000 and has a residual value of $3,000 would have a depreciable cost of $9,000. Depreciable cost must be allocated over the useful life of the asset.

ESTIMATED USEFUL LIFE   **Estimated useful life** is the total number of service units expected from a long-term asset. Service units may be measured in terms of years the asset is expected to be used, units expected to be produced, miles expected to be driven, or similar measures. In computing the estimated useful life of an asset, an accountant should consider all relevant information, including (1) past experience with similar assets, (2) the asset's present condition, (3) the company's repair and maintenance policy, (4) current technological and industry trends, and (5) local conditions such as weather.

Depreciation is recorded at the end of the accounting period by an adjusting entry that takes the following form:

A = L + OE   Depreciation Expense, Asset Name   xxx
–   –   Accumulated Depreciation, Asset Name   xxx
                    To record depreciation for the period

FOCUS ON BUSINESS PRACTICE

Most airlines depreciate airplanes over an estimated useful life of 10 to 20 years. But how long will a properly maintained airplane really last? In July 1968 Western Airlines paid $3.3 million for a new Boeing 737. More than 78,000 flights and 30 years later this aircraft was still flying for a no-frills airline named Vanguard Airlines. During the course of its life, the owners of this aircraft have included Piedmont, Delta, US Airways, and other airlines. Virtually every part of the plane has been replaced over the years. Boeing believes the plane could theoretically make double the number of flights before it is retired.

The useful lives of many types of assets can be extended indefinitely if the assets are correctly maintained, but proper accounting in accordance with the matching rule requires depreciation over a "reasonable" useful life. Each airline that owned the plane would have accounted for the plane in this way.

Methods of Computing Depreciation

OBJECTIVE

4 Compute periodic depreciation under the straight-line method, the production method, and the declining-balance method

Many methods are used to allocate the cost of plant assets to accounting periods through depreciation. Each is proper for certain circumstances. The most common methods are (1) the straight-line method, (2) the production method, and (3) an accelerated method known as the declining-balance method.

STRAIGHT-LINE METHOD   When the **straight-line method** is used to calculate depreciation, the depreciable cost of the asset is spread evenly over the estimated useful life of the asset. The straight-line method is based on the assumption that depreciation depends only on the passage of time. The depreciation expense for each period is computed by dividing the depreciable cost (cost of the depreciating asset less its estimated residual value) by the number of accounting periods in the asset's estimated useful life. Under this method, the rate of depreciation is the same in each year.

Suppose, for example, that a delivery truck costs $10,000 and has an estimated residual value of $1,000 at the end of its estimated useful life of five years. The annual depreciation would be $1,800 under the straight-line method, calculated as follows:

$$\frac{\text{Cost} - \text{Residual Value}}{\text{Estimated Useful Life}} = \frac{\$10,000 - \$1,000}{5 \text{ years}} = \$1,800 \text{ per year}$$

The depreciation for the five years would be as follows:

Depreciation Schedule, Straight-Line Method

	Cost	Yearly Depreciation	Accumulated Depreciation	Carrying Value
Date of purchase	$10,000	—	—	$10,000
End of first year	10,000	$1,800	$1,800	8,200
End of second year	10,000	1,800	3,600	6,400
End of third year	10,000	1,800	5,400	4,600
End of fourth year	10,000	1,800	7,200	2,800
End of fifth year	10,000	1,800	9,000	1,000

There are three important points to note from the depreciation schedule for the straight-line depreciation method. First, the depreciation is the same each year. Second, the accumulated depreciation increases uniformly. Third, the carrying value decreases uniformly until it reaches the estimated residual value.

PRODUCTION METHOD   The **production method** of depreciation is based on the assumption that depreciation is solely the result of use and that the passage of time plays no role in the depreciation process. If we assume that the delivery truck from the previous example has an estimated useful life of 90,000 miles, the depreciation cost per mile would be determined as follows:

$$\frac{\text{Cost} - \text{Residual Value}}{\text{Estimated Units of Useful Life}} = \frac{\$10,000 - \$1,000}{90,000 \text{ miles}} = \$.10 \text{ per mile}$$

If we assume that the use of the truck was 20,000 miles for the first year, 30,000 miles for the second, 10,000 miles for the third, 20,000 miles for the fourth, and 10,000 miles for the fifth, the depreciation schedule for the delivery truck would appear as follows:

Depreciation Schedule, Production Method

	Cost	Miles	Yearly Depreciation	Accumulated Depreciation	Carrying Value
Date of purchase	$10,000	—	—	—	$10,000
End of first year	10,000	20,000	$2,000	$2,000	8,000
End of second year	10,000	30,000	3,000	5,000	5,000
End of third year	10,000	10,000	1,000	6,000	4,000
End of fourth year	10,000	20,000	2,000	8,000	2,000
End of fifth year	10,000	10,000	1,000	9,000	1,000

There is a direct relation between the amount of depreciation each year and the units of output or use. Also, the accumulated depreciation increases each year in direct relation to units of output or use. Finally, the carrying value decreases each year in direct relation to units of output or use until it reaches the estimated residual value.

Under the production method, the unit of output or use employed to measure the estimated useful life of each asset should be appropriate for that asset. For example, the number of items produced may be an appropriate measure for one machine, but the number of hours of use may be a better measure for another. The production method should be used only when the output of an asset over its useful life can be estimated with reasonable accuracy.

DECLINING-BALANCE METHOD   An **accelerated method** of depreciation results in relatively large amounts of depreciation in the early years of an asset's life and smaller amounts in later years. Such a method, which is based on the passage of time, assumes that many kinds of plant assets are most efficient when new, and so provide more and better service in the early years of their useful life. It is consistent with the matching rule to allocate more depreciation to earlier years than to later years if the benefits or services received in the earlier years are greater.

An accelerated method also recognizes that changing technologies make some equipment lose service value rapidly. Thus, it is realistic to allocate more to depreciation in earlier years than in later years. New inventions and products result in obsolescence of equipment bought earlier, making it necessary to replace equipment sooner than if technology changed more slowly.

Another argument in favor of an accelerated method is that repair expense is likely to be greater in later years than in earlier years. Thus, the total of repair and depreciation expense remains fairly constant over a period of years. This result naturally assumes that the services received from the asset are roughly equal from year to year.

The **declining-balance method** is the most common accelerated method of depreciation. Under this method, depreciation is computed by applying a fixed rate to the carrying value (the declining balance) of a tangible long-lived asset, resulting in higher depreciation charges during the early years of the asset's life. Though any fixed rate can be used, the most common rate is a percentage equal to twice the straight-line percentage. When twice the straight-line rate is used, the method is usually called the **double-declining-balance method**.

In our earlier example, the delivery truck had an estimated useful life of five years. Consequently, under the straight-line method, the depreciation rate for each year was 20 percent (100 percent ÷ 5 years).

Under the double-declining-balance method, the fixed rate is 40 percent (2 × 20 percent). This fixed rate is applied to the *remaining carrying value* at the end of each year. Estimated residual value is not taken into account in figuring depreciation except in a year when calculated depreciation exceeds the amount necessary to bring the carrying value down to the estimated residual value. The depreciation schedule for this method is as follows:

Depreciation Schedule, Double-Declining-Balance Method

	Cost	Yearly Depreciation		Accumulated Depreciation	Carrying Value
Date of purchase	$10,000	—		—	$10,000
End of first year	10,000	(40% × $10,000)	$4,000	$4,000	6,000
End of second year	10,000	(40% × $6,000)	2,400	6,400	3,600
End of third year	10,000	(40% × $3,600)	1,440	7,840	2,160
End of fourth year	10,000	(40% × $2,160)	864	8,704	1,296
End of fifth year	10,000		296*	9,000	1,000

*Depreciation limited to amount necessary to reduce carrying value to residual value: $296 = $1,296 (previous carrying value) − $1,000 (residual value).

Note that the fixed rate is always applied to the carrying value at the end of the previous year. The depreciation is greatest in the first year and declines each year after that. Finally, the depreciation in the fifth year is limited to the amount necessary to reduce carrying value to residual value.

COMPARING THE THREE METHODS   A visual comparison may provide a better understanding of the three depreciation methods described above. Figure 5 compares yearly depreciation and carrying value under the three methods. In the left-hand graph, which shows yearly depreciation, straight-line depreciation is uniform at $1,800 per year over the five-year period. However, the double-declining-balance method begins at an amount greater than straight-line ($4,000) and decreases each year to amounts that are less than straight-line (ultimately, $296). The production method does not generate a regular pattern because of the random fluctuation of the depreciation from year to year. The three yearly depreciation patterns are reflected in the graph of carrying value. In that graph, each method starts in the same place (cost of $10,000) and ends at the same place (residual value of $1,000). It is the patterns during the useful life of the asset that differ for each method. For instance, the carrying value under the straight-line method is always greater than that under the double-declining-balance method, except at the beginning and end of useful life.

Figure 5
Graphical Comparison of Three Methods of Determining Depreciation

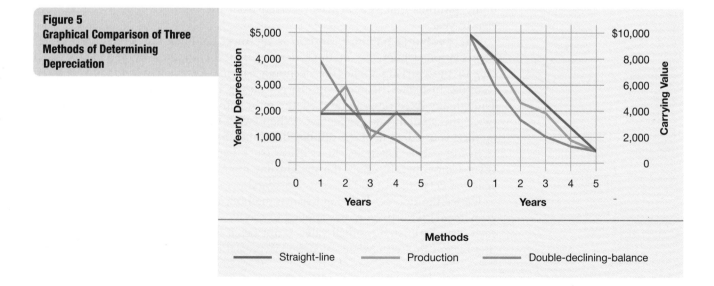

FOCUS ON BUSINESS PRACTICE

Most companies choose the straight-line method of depreciation for financial reporting purposes, as shown in Figure 6. Only about 13 percent use some type of accelerated method and 6 percent use the production method. These figures tend to be misleading about the importance of accelerated depreciation methods, how-

ever, especially when it comes to income taxes. Federal income tax laws allow either the straight-line method or an accelerated method. For tax purposes, according to *Accounting Trends & Techniques*, about 75 percent of the 600 large companies studied preferred an accelerated method. Companies use different methods of depreciation for good reason. The straight-line method can be advantageous for financial reporting because it can produce the highest net income, and an accelerated method can be beneficial for tax purposes because it can result in lower income taxes.

Figure 6
Depreciation Methods Used by 600 Large Companies

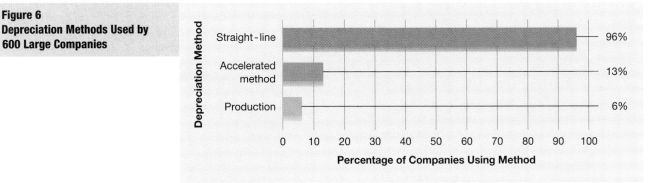

Total percentage exceeds 100 because some companies used different methods for different types of depreciable assets.
Source: Reprinted with permission from *Accounting Trends & Techniques,* Copyright © 1999 by the American Institute of Certified Public Accountants, Inc.

Disposal of Depreciable Assets

OBJECTIVE

5 Account for the disposal of depreciable assets not involving exchanges

When plant assets are no longer useful because they are worn out or obsolete, they may be discarded, sold, or traded in on the purchase of new plant and equipment. For accounting purposes, a plant asset may be disposed of in three different ways: It may be (1) discarded, (2) sold for cash, or (3) exchanged for another asset. To illustrate how each of these cases is recorded, assume that MGC Company purchased a machine on January 1, 20x0, for $6,500 and planned to depreciate it on a straight-line basis over an estimated useful life of ten years. The residual value at the end of ten years was estimated to be $500. On January 1, 20x7, the balances of the relevant accounts in the plant asset ledger appear as follows:

On September 30, 20x7, management disposes of the asset. The next few sections illustrate the accounting treatment to record depreciation for the partial year and the disposal under several assumptions.

Depreciation for Partial Year

When a plant asset is discarded or disposed of in some other way, it is first necessary to record depreciation expense for the partial year up to the date of disposal. This step is required because the asset was used until that date and, under the matching rule, the accounting period should receive the proper allocation of depreciation expense.

In this illustration, MGC Company disposes of the machinery on September 30. The entry to record the depreciation for the first nine months of 20x7 (nine-twelfths of a year) is as follows:

A = L + OE
−   −

Sept. 30	Depreciation Expense, Machinery	450	
	Accumulated Depreciation, Machinery		450

To record depreciation up to date of disposal

$$\frac{\$6{,}500 - \$500}{10} \times \frac{9}{12} = \$450$$

The relevant accounts in the plant asset ledger appear as follows after the entry is posted:

Machinery		Accumulated Depreciation, Machinery	
6,500			4,650

Discarded Plant Assets

A plant asset rarely lasts exactly as long as its estimated life. If it lasts longer than its estimated life, it is not depreciated past the point at which its carrying value equals its residual value. The purpose of depreciation is to spread the depreciable cost of an asset over the estimated life of the asset. Thus, the total accumulated depreciation should never exceed the total depreciable cost. If an asset remains in use beyond the end of its estimated life, its cost and accumulated depreciation remain in the ledger accounts. Proper records will thus be available for maintaining control over plant assets. If the residual value is zero, the carrying value of a fully depreciated asset is zero until the asset is disposed of. If such an asset is discarded, no gain or loss results.

In the illustration, however, the discarded equipment has a carrying value of $1,850 at the time of its disposal. The carrying value is computed from the ledger accounts above as machinery of $6,500 less accumulated depreciation of $4,650. A loss equal to the carrying value should be recorded when the machine is discarded.

A = L + OE
+
−

Sept. 30	Accumulated Depreciation, Machinery	4,650	
	Loss on Disposal of Machinery	1,850	
	Machinery		6,500

Discarded machine no longer used in the business

Gains and losses on disposals of plant assets are classified as other revenues and expenses on the income statement.

Plant Assets Sold for Cash

The entry to record a plant asset sold for cash is similar to the one just illustrated except that the receipt of cash should also be recorded. The following entries show how to record the sale of a machine under three assumptions about the selling price. In the first case, the $1,850 cash received is exactly equal to the $1,850 carrying value of the machine; therefore, no gain or loss results.

A = L + OE   Sept. 30   Cash   1,850
+
+   Accumulated Depreciation, Machinery   4,650
–   Machinery   6,500
                  Sale of machine for carrying value;
                  no gain or loss

In the second case, the $1,000 cash received is less than the carrying value of $1,850, so a loss of $850 is recorded.

A = L + OE   Sept. 30   Cash   1,000
+   –
+   Accumulated Depreciation, Machinery   4,650
–   Loss on Sale of Machinery   850
              Machinery   6,500
                  Sale of machine at less than carrying
                  value; loss of $850 ($1,850 – $1,000)
                  recorded

In the third case, the $2,000 cash received exceeds the carrying value of $1,850, so a gain of $150 is recorded.

A = L + OE   Sept. 30   Cash   2,000
+   +
+   Accumulated Depreciation, Machinery   4,650
–   Gain on Sale of Machinery   150
              Machinery   6,500
                  Sale of machine at more than the
                  carrying value; gain of $150
                  ($2,000 – $1,850) recorded

Exchanges of Plant Assets

OBJECTIVE

6 Account for the disposal of depreciable assets involving exchanges

Businesses also dispose of plant assets by trading them in on the purchase of other plant assets. Exchanges may involve similar assets, such as an old machine traded in on a newer model, or dissimilar assets, such as a machine traded in on a truck. In either case, the purchase price is reduced by the amount of the trade-in allowance.

The basic accounting for exchanges of plant assets is similar to accounting for sales of plant assets for cash. If the trade-in allowance received is greater than the carrying value of the asset surrendered, there has been a gain. If the allowance is less, there has been a loss. There are special rules for recognizing these gains and losses, depending on the nature of the assets exchanged.

Exchange	Losses Recognized	Gains Recognized
For financial accounting purposes		
Of dissimilar assets	Yes	Yes
Of similar assets	Yes	No
For income tax purposes		
Of dissimilar assets	Yes	Yes
Of similar assets	No	No

Both gains and losses are recognized when a company exchanges dissimilar assets. Assets are dissimilar when they perform different functions or do not meet specific monetary and type of business criteria for being considered similar assets. For financial accounting purposes, most exchanges are considered to be exchanges of dissimilar assets. In rare cases, when exchanges meet the specific criteria for them to be considered exchanges of similar assets, the gains are not recognized. In these cases, you could think of the trade-in as an extension of the life and usefulness of the original machine. Instead of recognizing a gain at the time of the exchange, the company records the new machine at the sum of the carrying value of the older machine plus any cash paid.[10]

For income tax purposes, similar assets are defined as those performing the same function. Neither gains nor losses on exchanges of these assets are recognized in computing a company's income tax liability. Thus, in practice, accountants face cases where both gains and losses are recognized (exchanges of dissimilar assets), cases where losses are recognized and gains are not recognized (exchanges of similar assets), and cases where neither gains nor losses are recognized (exchanges of similar assets for income tax purposes). Since all these options are used in practice, they are all illustrated in the following paragraphs.

LOSS RECOGNIZED ON THE EXCHANGE   A loss is recognized for financial accounting purposes on all exchanges in which a material loss occurs. A loss occurs when the trade-in allowance is less than the carrying value of the old asset. To illustrate the recognition of a loss, let us assume that the firm in our example exchanges the machine for a newer, more modern machine on the following terms:

List price of new machine	$12,000
Trade-in allowance for old machine	(1,000)
Cash payment required	$11,000

In this case the trade-in allowance ($1,000) is less than the carrying value ($1,850) of the old machine. The loss on the exchange is $850 ($1,850 − $1,000). The following journal entry records this transaction under the assumption that the loss is to be recognized.

A = L + OE				
+	Sept. 30	Machinery (new)	12,000	
+		Accumulated Depreciation, Machinery	4,650	
−		Loss on Exchange of Machinery	850	
−		Machinery (old)		6,500
		Cash		11,000
		Exchange of machines		

LOSS NOT RECOGNIZED ON THE EXCHANGE   In the previous example, in which a loss was recognized, the new asset was recorded at the purchase price of $12,000 and a loss of $850 was recorded. If the transaction involves similar assets and is to be recorded for income tax purposes, the loss should not be recognized. In this case, the cost basis of the new asset will reflect the effect of the unrecorded loss. The cost basis is computed by adding the cash payment to the carrying value of the old asset:

Carrying value of old machine	$ 1,850
Cash paid	11,000
Cost basis of new machine	$12,850

Note that no loss is recognized in the entry to record this transaction.

A = L + OE				
+	Sept. 30	Machinery (new)	12,850	
+		Accumulated Depreciation, Machinery	4,650	
−		Machinery (old)		6,500
−		Cash		11,000
		Exchange of machines		

Note that the new machinery is reported at the purchase price of $12,000 plus the unrecognized loss of $850. The nonrecognition of the loss on the exchange is, in effect, a postponement of the loss. Since depreciation of the new machine will be computed based on a cost of $12,850 instead of $12,000, the "unrecognized" loss results in more depreciation each year on the new machine than if the loss had been recognized.

GAIN RECOGNIZED ON THE EXCHANGE   Gains on exchanges are recognized for accounting purposes when dissimilar assets are involved. To illustrate the recognition of a gain, we continue with our example, assuming the following terms and assuming the machines being exchanged serve different functions:

List price of new machine	$12,000
Trade-in allowance for old machine	(3,000)
Cash payment required	$ 9,000

Here the trade-in allowance ($3,000) exceeds the carrying value ($1,850) of the old machine by $1,150. Thus, there is a gain on the exchange, assuming that the price of the new machine has not been inflated to allow for an excessive trade-in value. In other words, a gain exists if the trade-in allowance represents the fair market value of the old machine. Assuming that this condition is true, the entry to record the transaction is as follows:

A = L + OE
\+   \+
\+
–
–

Sept. 30	Machinery (new)	12,000	
	Accumulated Depreciation, Machinery	4,650	
	Gain on Exchange of Machinery		1,150
	Machinery (old)		6,500
	Cash		9,000
	Exchange of machines		

GAIN NOT RECOGNIZED ON THE EXCHANGE   When assets meeting the criteria for similar assets are exchanged, gains are not recognized for accounting or income tax purposes. The cost basis of the new machine must reflect the effect of the unrecorded gain. This cost basis is computed by adding the cash payment to the carrying value of the old asset.

Carrying value of old machine	$ 1,850
Cash paid	9,000
Cost basis of new machine	$10,850

The entry to record the transaction is as follows:

A = L + OE
\+
\+
–
–

Sept. 30	Machinery (new)	10,850	
	Accumulated Depreciation, Machinery	4,650	
	Machinery (old)		6,500
	Cash		9,000
	Exchange of machines		

As with the nonrecognition of losses, the nonrecognition of the gain on an exchange is, in effect, a postponement of the gain. In this illustration, when the new machine is eventually discarded or sold, its cost basis will be $10,850 instead of its original price of $12,000. Since depreciation will be computed on the cost basis of $10,850, the "unrecognized" gain is reflected in lower depreciation each year on the new machine than if the gain had been recognized.

Accounting for Natural Resources

OBJECTIVE

7 Identify the issues related to accounting for natural resources and compute depletion

Natural resources are shown on the balance sheet as long-term assets with such descriptive titles as Timberlands, Oil and Gas Reserves, and Mineral Deposits. The distinguishing characteristic of these assets is that they are converted into inventory by cutting, pumping, or mining. In terms of two of our examples, an oil field is a reservoir of unpumped oil, and a coal mine is a deposit of unmined coal. When the timber is cut, the oil is pumped, or the coal is mined, it becomes an inventory of the product to be sold. Natural resources are recorded at acquisition cost, which may also include some costs of development. As the resource is converted through the process of cutting, pumping, or mining, the asset account must be proportionally reduced. The carrying value of oil reserves on the balance sheet, for example, is reduced by a small amount for each barrel of oil pumped. As a result, the original cost of the oil reserves is gradually reduced, and depletion is recognized in the amount of the decrease.

Depletion

The term *depletion* is used to describe not only the exhaustion of a natural resource but also the proportional allocation of the cost of a natural resource to the units extracted. The costs are allocated in a way that is much like the production method used to calculate depreciation. When a natural resource is purchased or developed, there must be an estimate of the total units that will be available, such as barrels of oil, tons of coal, or board-feet of lumber. The depletion cost per unit is determined by dividing the cost of the natural resource (less residual value, if any) by the estimated number of units available. The amount of the depletion cost for each accounting period is then computed by multiplying the depletion cost per unit by the number of units pumped, mined, or cut and sold. For example, for a mine having an estimated 1,500,000 tons of coal, a cost of $1,800,000, and an estimated residual value of $300,000, the depletion charge per ton of coal is $1. Thus, if 115,000 tons of coal are mined and sold during the first year, the depletion charge for the year is $115,000. This charge is recorded as follows:

A = L + OE   Dec. 31   Depletion Expense, Coal Deposits   115,000
 –   –   Accumulated Depletion, Coal Deposits   115,000
                   To record depletion of coal mine:
                   $1 per ton for 115,000 tons mined
                   and sold

On the balance sheet, the mine would be presented as follows:

Coal Deposits	$1,800,000	
Less Accumulated Depletion	115,000	$1,685,000

Sometimes a natural resource that is extracted in one year is not sold until a later year. It is important to note that it would then be recorded as a depletion *expense* in the year it is *sold*. The part not sold is considered inventory.

Depreciation of Closely Related Plant Assets

Natural resources often require special on-site buildings and equipment, such as conveyors, roads, tracks, and drilling and pumping devices that are necessary to extract the resource. If the useful life of those assets is longer than the estimated time it will take to deplete the resource, a special problem arises. Because such long-term assets are often abandoned and have no useful purpose once all the resources have been extracted, they should be depreciated on the same basis as the depletion is computed. For example, if machinery with a useful life of ten years is installed on an oil field that is expected to be depleted in eight years, the machinery should be depreciated over the eight-year period, using the production method. That way, each year's depreciation will be proportional to the year's depletion. If one-sixth of the oil field's total reserves is pumped in one year, then the depreciation should be one-sixth of the machinery's cost minus the residual value. If the useful life of a long-term asset is less than the expected life of the depleting asset, the shorter life should be used to compute depreciation. In such cases, or when an asset will not be abandoned once the reserves have been fully depleted, other depreciation methods, such as straight-line or declining-balance, are appropriate.

Development and Exploration Costs in the Oil and Gas Industry

The costs of exploration and development of oil and gas resources can be accounted for under either of two methods. Under the **successful efforts method**, successful exploration—for example, the cost of a producing oil well—is a cost of the resource. This cost should be recorded as an asset and depleted over the estimated life of the resource. An unsuccessful exploration—such as the cost of a dry well—is written off immediately as a loss. Because of these immediate write-offs, successful efforts accounting is considered the more conservative method and is used by most large oil companies.

Exploration-minded independent oil companies, on the other hand, argue that the cost of dry wells is part of the overall cost of the systematic development of an oil field and thus a part of the cost of producing wells. Under this **full-costing method**, all costs, including the cost of dry wells, are recorded as assets and depleted over the estimated life of the producing resources. This method tends to improve earnings performance in the early years for companies using it. Either method is permitted by the Financial Accounting Standards Board.[11]

Accounting for Intangible Assets

OBJECTIVE

8 Apply the matching rule to intangible assets, including research and development costs and goodwill

The purchase of an intangible asset is a special kind of capital expenditure. An intangible asset is long term, but it has no physical substance. Its value comes from the long-term rights or advantages it offers to its owner. The most common examples—patents, copyrights, leaseholds, leasehold improvements, trademarks and brand names, franchises, licenses, and goodwill—are described in Table 1. Some current assets, such as accounts receivable and certain prepaid expenses, have no physical substance, but they are not classified as intangible assets because they are short term. Intangible assets are both long term and nonphysical.

Intangible assets are accounted for at acquisition cost—that is, the amount that was paid for them. Some intangible assets, such as goodwill and trademarks, may be acquired at little or no cost. Even though they may have great value and be needed for profitable operations, they should not appear on the balance sheet unless they have been purchased from another party at a price established in the marketplace.

The accounting issues connected with intangible assets are the same as those connected with other long-lived assets. The Accounting Principles Board, in its *Opinion No. 17*, lists them as follows:

1. Determining an initial carrying amount
2. Accounting for that amount after acquisition under normal business conditions —that is, through periodic write-off or amortization—in a manner similar to depreciation
3. Accounting for that amount if the value declines substantially and permanently[12]

Besides these three problems, an intangible asset has no physical substance and, in some cases, may be impossible to identify. For these reasons, its value and its useful life may be quite hard to estimate.

Table 1. Accounting for Intangible Assets

Type	Description	Accounting Treatment
Patent	An exclusive right granted by the federal government for a period of 20 years to make a particular product or use a specific process. A design may be granted a patent for 14 years.	The cost of successfully defending a patent in a patent infringement suit is added to the acquisition cost of the patent. Amortize over the useful life, which may be less than the legal life.
Copyright	An exclusive right granted by the federal government to the possessor to publish and sell literary, musical, or other artistic materials for a period of the author's life plus 70 years; includes computer programs.	Record at acquisition cost and amortize over the useful life, which is often much shorter than the legal life, but not to exceed 40 years. For example, the cost of paperback rights to a popular novel would typically be amortized over a useful life of two to four years.
Leasehold	A right to occupy land or buildings under a long-term rental contract. For example, Company A, which owns but does not want to use a prime retail location, sells or subleases Company B the right to use it for ten years in return for one or more rental payments. Company B has purchased a leasehold.	Debit Leasehold for the amount of the rental payment, and amortize it over the remaining life of the lease. Payments to the lessor during the life of the lease should be debited to Lease Expense.
Leasehold improvements	Improvements to leased property that become the property of the lessor (the person who owns the property) at the end of the lease.	Debit Leasehold Improvements for the cost of improvements, and amortize the cost of the improvements over the remaining life of the lease.
Trademark, brand name	A registered symbol or name that can be used only by its owner to identify a product or service.	Debit Trademark or Brand Name for the acquisition cost, and amortize it over a reasonable life, not to exceed 40 years.
Franchise, license	A right to an exclusive territory or market, or the right to use a formula, technique, process, or design.	Debit Franchise or License for the acquisition cost, and amortize it over a reasonable life, not to exceed 40 years.
Goodwill	The excess of the cost of a group of assets (usually a business) over the fair market value of the net assets if purchased individually.	Debit Goodwill for the acquisition cost, and amortize it over a reasonable life, not to exceed 40 years.*

*The FASB is considering several alternative changes in accounting for goodwill and other acquired intangible assets, including the elimination of amortization altogether.

The Accounting Principles Board has decided that a company should record as assets the costs of intangible assets acquired from others. However, the company should record as expenses the costs of developing intangible assets. Also, intangible assets that have a determinable useful life, such as patents, copyrights, and lease-holds, should be written off through periodic amortization over that useful life in much the same way that plant assets are depreciated. Even though some intangible assets, such as goodwill and trademarks, have no measurable limit on their lives, they should still be amortized over a reasonable length of time (not to exceed 40 years).

One of the most valuable intangible assets some companies have is a list of subscribers. For example, the Newark Morning Ledger Co., a newspaper chain, purchased a chain of Michigan newspapers whose list of 460,000 subscribers was valued at $68 million. In a 1993 decision, the U.S. Supreme Court upheld the company's right to amortize the value of the subscribers list because the company showed that the list had a limited useful life. The Internal Revenue Service had argued that the list had an indefinite life and therefore could not provide tax deductions through amortization. This ruling will benefit other types of businesses that purchase everything from bank deposits to pharmacy prescription files.[13]

However, this may change for goodwill because the FASB is considering a proposal to eliminate goodwill amortization. Under this proposal, no amortization would be required, but if goodwill were impaired, it would be written down to fair market value.

To illustrate these procedures, assume that Soda Bottling Company purchases a patent on a unique bottle cap for $18,000. The entry to record the patent would include $18,000 in the asset account Patents. Note that if Soda Bottling Company had developed the bottle cap internally instead of purchasing it from others, the costs of developing the cap, such as salaries of researchers, supplies used in testing, and costs of equipment, would have been expensed as incurred.

Assume now that Soda's management determines that, although the patent for the bottle cap will last for 17 years, the product using the cap will be sold for only the next six years. The entry to record the annual amortization expense would be for $3,000 ($18,000 ÷ 6 years). Note that the Patents account is reduced directly by the amount of the amortization expense. This is in contrast to the treatment of other long-term asset accounts, for which depreciation or depletion is accumulated in separate contra accounts. If the patent becomes worthless before it is fully amortized, the remaining carrying value is written off as a loss by removing it from the Patents account.

Research and Development Costs

Most successful companies carry out activities, possibly within a separate department, involving research and development. Among these activities are development of new products, testing of existing and proposed products, and pure research. In the past, some companies would record as assets those costs of research and development that could be directly traced to the development of specific patents, formulas, or other rights. Other costs, such as those for testing and pure research, were treated as expenses of the accounting period and deducted from income.

The Financial Accounting Standards Board has stated that all research and development costs should be treated as revenue expenditures and charged to expense in the period when incurred.[14] The board argues that it is too hard to trace specific costs to specific profitable developments. Also, the costs of research and development are continuous and necessary for the success of a business and so should be treated as current expenses. To support this conclusion, the board cites studies showing that 30 to 90 percent of all new products fail and that three-fourths of new-product expenses go to unsuccessful products. Thus, their costs do not represent future benefits.

Computer Software Costs

Many companies develop computer programs or software to be sold or leased to individuals and companies. The costs incurred in creating a computer software product are considered research and development costs until the product has proven to be technologically feasible. As a result, costs incurred before that point in the process should be charged to expense as incurred. A product is deemed to be technologically feasible when a detailed working program has been designed.

After the working program has been developed, all software production costs are recorded as assets and amortized over the estimated economic life of the product using the straight-line method. If at any time the company cannot expect to realize from a software product the amount of its unamortized costs on the balance sheet, the asset should be written down to the amount expected to be realized.[17] Under new rules developed by the AICPA, software programs developed for internal use by a company may be capitalized and amortized over their estimated economic life.

Goodwill

The term *goodwill* is widely used by businesspeople, lawyers, and the public to mean different things. In most cases goodwill is taken to mean the good reputation of a company. From an accounting standpoint, goodwill exists when a purchaser pays more for a business than the fair market value of the net assets if purchased separately. Because the purchaser has paid more than the fair market value of the physical assets, there must be intangible assets. If the company being purchased does not have patents, copyrights, trademarks, or other identifiable intangible assets of value, the excess payment is assumed to be for goodwill. Goodwill exists because most businesses are worth more as going concerns than as collections of assets. Goodwill reflects all the factors that allow a company to earn a higher-than-market rate of return on its assets, including customer satisfaction, good management, manufacturing efficiency, the advantages of holding a monopoly, good locations, and good employee relations. The payment above and beyond the fair market value of the tangible assets and other specific intangible assets is properly recorded in the Goodwill account. As mentioned earlier, the FASB is considering a proposal that would not require periodic amortization of goodwill and other acquired intangible assets with indefinite useful lives. The proposal would continue to require the writedown of these intangibles if the assets have been deemed impaired. Current practice does require amortization of goodwill as follows.

In *Opinion No. 17*, the Accounting Principles Board states that the benefits arising from purchased goodwill will in time disappear. It is hard for a company to keep having above-average earnings unless new factors of goodwill replace the old ones. For this reason, goodwill should be amortized or written off by systematic charges to income over a reasonable number of future time periods. The total time period should in no case be more than 40 years.[18]

Goodwill, as stated, should not be recorded unless it is paid for in connection with the purchase of a whole business. The amount to be recorded as goodwill can be determined by writing the identifiable net assets up to their fair market values at the time of purchase and subtracting the total from the purchase price. For example, assume that the owners of Company A agree to sell the company for

$11,400,000. If the net assets (total assets − total liabilities) are fairly valued at $10,000,000, then the amount of the goodwill is $1,400,000 ($11,400,000 − $10,000,000). If the fair market value of the company's net assets is later determined to be more or less than $10,000,000, an entry is made in the accounting records to adjust the assets to the fair market value. The goodwill would then represent the difference between the adjusted net assets and the purchase price of $11,400,000.

Special Problems of Depreciating Plant Assets

SUPPLEMENTAL OBJECTIVE

9 Apply depreciation methods to problems of partial years, revised rates, groups of similar items, special types of capital expenditures, and cost recovery

The illustrations used so far in this chapter have been simplified to explain the concepts and methods of depreciation. In actual business practice, there is often a need to (1) calculate depreciation for partial years, (2) revise depreciation rates based on new estimates of useful life or residual value, (3) group like items when calculating depreciation, (4) account for special types of capital expenditures, and (5) use the accelerated cost recovery method for tax purposes. The next sections discuss these five cases.

Depreciation for Partial Years

So far, the illustrations of depreciation methods have assumed that plant assets were purchased at the beginning or end of an accounting period. In most cases, however, businesses buy assets when they are needed and sell or discard them when they are no longer useful or needed. The time of year is normally not a factor in the decision. Consequently, it is often necessary to calculate depreciation for partial years.

For example, assume that a piece of equipment is purchased for $3,600 and that it has an estimated useful life of six years and an estimated residual value of $600. Assume also that it is purchased on September 5 and that the yearly accounting period ends on December 31. Depreciation must be recorded for four months, September through December, or four-twelfths of the year. This factor is applied to the calculated depreciation for the entire year. The four months' depreciation under the straight-line method is calculated as follows:

$$\frac{\$3,600 - \$600}{6 \text{ years}} \times 4/12 = \$167$$

For the other depreciation methods, most companies will compute the first year's depreciation and then multiply by the partial year factor. For example, if the company used the double-declining-balance method on the preceding equipment, the depreciation on the asset would be computed as follows:

$$\$3,600 \times 1/3 \times 4/12 = \$400$$

Typically, the depreciation calculation is rounded off to the nearest whole month because a partial month's depreciation is rarely material and the calculation is easier. In this case, depreciation was recorded from the beginning of September even though the purchase was made on September 5.

For all methods, the remainder (eight-twelfths) of the first year's depreciation is recorded in the next annual accounting period together with four-twelfths of the second year's depreciation.

Revision of Depreciation Rates

Because a depreciation rate is based on an estimate of an asset's useful life, the periodic depreciation charge is seldom precise. Sometimes it is very inadequate or excessive. This situation may result from an underestimate or overestimate of the asset's useful life or from a wrong estimate of the residual value. What action should be taken when it is found, after several years of use, that a piece of equipment will last less time—or longer—than originally thought? Sometimes it is necessary to revise the estimate of useful life so that the periodic depreciation expense increases or decreases. Then, to reflect the revised situation, the remaining depreciable cost of the asset is spread over the remaining years of useful life.

With this technique, the annual depreciation expense is increased or decreased to reduce the asset's carrying value to its residual value at the end of its remaining useful life. To illustrate, assume that a delivery truck was purchased for $7,000 and has a residual value of $1,000. At the time of the purchase, the truck was expected to last six years, and it was depreciated on the straight-line basis. However, after two years of intensive use, it is determined that the truck will last only two more years, but that its estimated residual value at the end of the two years will still be $1,000. In other words, at the end of the second year, the truck's estimated useful life is reduced from six years to four years. At that time, the asset account and its related accumulated depreciation account would appear as follows:

Delivery Truck		Accumulated Depreciation, Delivery Truck	
Cost 7,000		Depreciation, year 1	1,000
		Depreciation, year 2	1,000

The remaining depreciable cost is computed as follows:

Cost	minus	Depreciation Already Taken	minus	Residual Value	
$7,000	−	$2,000	−	$1,000	= $4,000

The new annual periodic depreciation charge is computed by dividing the remaining depreciable cost of $4,000 by the remaining useful life of two years. Therefore, the new periodic depreciation charge is $2,000. The annual adjusting entry for depreciation for the next two years would be as follows:

$$A = L + OE$$
$$- \qquad -$$

Dec. 31 Depreciation Expense, Delivery Truck   2,000
         Accumulated Depreciation, Delivery Truck   2,000
             To record depreciation expense for the year

This method of revising depreciation is used widely in industry. It is also supported by the Accounting Principles Board of the AICPA in Accounting Principles Board *Opinion No. 9* and *Opinion No. 20*.

Group Depreciation

To say that the estimated useful life of an asset, such as a piece of equipment, is six years means that the average piece of equipment of that type is expected to last six years. In reality, some pieces may last only two or three years, and others may last eight or nine years, or longer. For this reason, and for reasons of convenience, large companies will group similar items, such as trucks, power lines, office equipment, or transformers, to calculate depreciation. This method is called **group depreciation**. Group depreciation is widely used in all fields of industry and business. A survey of large businesses indicated that 65 percent used group depreciation for all or part of their plant assets.[19]

Special Types of Capital Expenditures

In addition to the acquisition of plant assets, natural resources, and intangible assets, capital expenditures also include additions and betterments. An **addition** is an enlargement to the physical layout of a plant asset. As an example, if a new wing is added to a building, the benefits from the expenditure will be received over several years, and the amount paid for it should be debited to the asset account. A **betterment** is an improvement that does not add to the physical layout of a plant asset but rather increases the quality of the asset or its output. Installation of an air-conditioning system is an example of a betterment that will offer benefits over a period of years; thus its cost should be charged to an asset account.

Among the more usual kinds of revenue expenditures for plant equipment are the repairs, maintenance, lubrication, cleaning, and inspection necessary to keep an asset in good working condition. Repairs fall into two categories: ordinary repairs and extraordinary repairs. **Ordinary repairs** are expenditures that are necessary to maintain an asset in good operating condition in order to achieve its original intended useful life. Trucks must have periodic tune-ups, their tires and batteries must be regularly replaced, and other routine repairs must be made. Offices and halls must be painted regularly, and broken tiles or woodwork must be replaced. Such repairs are a current expense.

Extraordinary repairs are repairs of a more significant nature—they affect the estimated residual value or estimated useful life of an asset. For example, a boiler for heating a building may be given a complete overhaul, at a cost of several thousand dollars, that will extend its useful life by five years. Typically, extraordinary repairs are recorded by debiting the Accumulated Depreciation account, under the assumption that some of the depreciation previously recorded has now been eliminated. The effect of this reduction in the Accumulated Depreciation account is to increase the carrying value of the asset by the cost of the extraordinary repair. Consequently, the new carrying value of the asset should be depreciated over the new estimated useful life.

Let us assume that a machine that cost $10,000 had no estimated residual value and an original estimated useful life of ten years. After eight years, the accumulated depreciation under the straight-line method was $8,000, and the carrying value was $2,000 ($10,000 − $8,000). At that point, the machine was given a major overhaul costing $1,500. This expenditure extended the machine's useful life three years beyond the original ten years. The entry for the extraordinary repair would be as follows:

A = L + OE				
+	Jan. 4	Accumulated Depreciation, Machinery	1,500	
−		Cash		1,500
		Extraordinary repair		
		to machinery		

The annual periodic depreciation for each of the five years remaining in the machine's useful life would be calculated as follows:

Carrying value before extraordinary repairs	$2,000
Extraordinary repairs	1,500
Total	$3,500

$$\text{Annual periodic depreciation} = \frac{\$3,500}{5 \text{ years}} = \$700$$

If the machine remains in use for the five years expected after the major overhaul, the total of the five annual depreciation charges of $700 will exactly equal the new carrying value, including the cost of the extraordinary repair.

Cost Recovery for Federal Income Tax Purposes

In 1986, Congress passed the Tax Reform Act of 1986, arguably the most sweeping revision of federal tax laws since the original enactment of the Internal Revenue Code in 1913. First, a company may elect to expense the first $17,500 (which increases to $25,000 by tax year 2003) of equipment expenditures rather than recording them as an asset. Second, a new method for writing off expenditures recorded as assets, the **Modified Accelerated Cost Recovery System (MACRS)**, may be elected. MACRS discards the concepts of estimated useful life and residual value. Instead, it requires that a cost recovery allowance be computed (1) on the unadjusted cost of property being recovered and (2) over a period of years prescribed by the law for all property of similar types. The accelerated method prescribed under MACRS for most property other than real estate is 200 percent declining balance with a half-year convention (only one half-year's depreciation is allowed in the year of purchase, and one half-year's depreciation is taken in the last year). In addition, the period over which the cost may be recovered is specified. Recovery of the cost of property placed in service after December 31, 1986, is calculated as prescribed in the 1986 law.

Congress hoped that MACRS would encourage businesses to invest in new plant and equipment by allowing them to write off such assets rapidly. MACRS accelerates the write-off of these investments in two ways. First, the prescribed recovery periods are often shorter than the estimated useful lives used for calculating depreciation for the financial statements. Second, the accelerated method allowed under the new law enables businesses to recover most of the cost of their investments early in the depreciation process.

Tax methods of depreciation are not usually acceptable for financial reporting under generally accepted accounting principles because the recovery periods are shorter than the depreciable assets' estimated useful lives.

Chapter Review

REVIEW OF LEARNING OBJECTIVES

Check out ACE, a self-quizzing program on chapter content, at http://college.hmco.com.

1. **Identify the types of long-term assets and explain the management issues related to accounting for them.** Long-term assets are assets that are used in the operation of a business, are not intended for resale, and have a useful life of more than one year. Long-term assets are either tangible or intangible. In the former category are land, plant assets, and natural resources. In the latter are trademarks, patents, franchises, goodwill, and other rights. The accounting issues associated with long-term assets relate to the decision to acquire the assets, the means of financing the assets, and the methods of accounting for the assets.

2. **Distinguish between capital and revenue expenditures, and account for the cost of property, plant, and equipment.** It is important to distinguish between capital expenditures, which are recorded as assets, and revenue expenditures, which are recorded as expenses of the current period. The error of classifying one as the other will have an important effect on net income. The acquisition cost of property, plant, and equipment includes all expenditures

that are reasonable and necessary to get such an asset in place and ready for use. Among these expenditures are purchase price, installation cost, freight charges, and insurance during transit.

3. **Define *depreciation*, state the factors that affect its computation, and show how to record it.** Depreciation is the periodic allocation of the cost of a plant asset over its estimated useful life. It is recorded by debiting Depreciation Expense and crediting a related contra-asset account called Accumulated Depreciation. Factors that affect the computation of depreciation are cost, residual value, depreciable cost, and estimated useful life.

4. **Compute periodic depreciation under the straight-line method, production method, and declining-balance method.** Depreciation is commonly computed by the straight-line method, the production method, or an accelerated method. The straight-line method is related directly to the passage of time, whereas the production method is related directly to use. An accelerated method results in relatively large amounts of depreciation in earlier years and reduced amounts in later years. It is based on the assumption that plant assets provide greater economic benefit in their earlier years than in later years. The most common accelerated method is the declining-balance method.

5. **Account for the disposal of depreciable assets not involving exchanges.** Long-term depreciable assets may be disposed of by being discarded, sold, or exchanged. When long-term assets are disposed of, it is necessary to record the depreciation up to the date of disposal and to remove the carrying value from the accounts by removing the cost from the asset account and the depreciation to date from the accumulated depreciation account. If a long-term asset is sold at a price that differs from its carrying value, there is a gain or loss that should be recorded and reported on the income statement.

6. **Account for the disposal of depreciable assets involving exchanges.** In recording exchanges of similar plant assets, a gain or loss may arise. According to the Accounting Principles Board, losses, but not gains, should be recognized at the time of the exchange. When a gain is not recognized, the new asset is recorded at the carrying value of the old asset plus any cash paid. For income tax purposes, neither gains nor losses are recognized in the exchange of similar assets. When dissimilar assets are exchanged, gains and losses are recognized under both accounting and income tax rules.

7. **Identify the issues related to accounting for natural resources and compute depletion.** Natural resources are wasting assets that are converted to inventory by cutting, pumping, mining, or other forms of extraction. Natural resources are recorded at cost as long-term assets. They are allocated as expenses through depletion charges as the resources are sold. The depletion charge is based on the ratio of the resource extracted to the total estimated resource. A major issue related to this subject is accounting for oil and gas reserves.

8. **Apply the matching rule to intangible assets, including research and development costs and goodwill.** The purchase of an intangible asset should be treated as a capital expenditure and recorded at acquisition cost, which in turn should be amortized over the useful life of the asset. The FASB requires that research and development costs be treated as revenue expenditures and charged as expenses in the periods of expenditure. Software costs are treated as research and development costs and expensed until a feasible working program is developed, after which time the costs may be capitalized and amortized over a reasonable estimated life. Goodwill is the excess of the amount paid for the purchase of a business over the fair market value of the net

assets and is usually related to the superior earning potential of the business. It should be recorded only if paid for in connection with the purchase of a business, and it should be amortized over a period not to exceed 40 years.

9. Apply depreciation methods to problems of partial years, revised rates, groups of similar items, special types of capital expenditures, and cost recovery. In actual business practice, many factors affect depreciation calculations. It may be necessary to calculate depreciation for partial years because assets are bought and sold throughout the year, or to revise depreciation rates because of changed conditions. Because it is often difficult to estimate the useful life of a single item, and because it is more convenient, many large businesses group similar items for purposes of depreciation. Companies must also consider certain special capital expenditures when calculating depreciation. For example, expenditures for additions and betterments are capital expenditures. Extraordinary repairs, which increase the residual value or extend the life of an asset, are also treated as capital expenditures, but ordinary repairs are revenue expenditures. For income tax purposes, rapid write-offs of depreciable assets are allowed through the Modified Accelerated Cost Recovery System. Such rapid write-offs are not usually acceptable for financial accounting because the shortened recovery periods violate the matching rule.

REVIEW OF CONCEPTS AND TERMINOLOGY

The following concepts and terms were introduced in this chapter:

LO 4   **Accelerated method:** A method of depreciation that allocates relatively large amounts of the depreciable cost of an asset to earlier years and reduced amounts to later years.

SO 9   **Addition:** An enlargement to the physical layout or capacity of a plant asset.

LO 1   **Amortization:** The periodic allocation of the cost of an intangible asset to the periods it benefits.

LO 1   **Asset impairment:** Loss of revenue-generating potential of a long-lived asset prior to the end of its useful life. The loss is computed as the difference between the asset's carrying value and its fair value, as measured by the present value of the sum of the expected net cash inflows.

SO 9   **Betterment:** An improvement that does not add to the physical layout of a plant asset but rather increases the quality of the asset or its output.

LO 8   **Brand name:** A registered name that can be used only by its owner to identify a product or service.

LO 2   **Capital expenditure:** An expenditure for the purchase or expansion of a long-term asset, recorded in an asset account.

LO 1   **Carrying value:** The unexpired part of the cost of an asset, not its market value; also called *book value*.

LO 8   **Copyright:** An exclusive right granted by the federal government to the possessor to publish and sell literary, musical, or other artistic materials for a period of the author's life plus 50 years; includes computer programs.

LO 4   **Declining-balance method:** An accelerated method of depreciation in which depreciation is computed by applying a fixed rate to the carrying value (the declining balance) of a tangible long-lived asset.

LO 1   **Depletion:** The exhaustion of a natural resource through mining, cutting, pumping, or other extraction, and the way in which the cost is allocated.

LO 3   **Depreciable cost:** The cost of an asset less its residual value.

LO 1   **Depreciation:** The periodic allocation of the cost of a tangible long-lived asset (other than land and natural resources) over its estimated useful life.

LO 4   **Double-declining-balance method:** An accelerated method of depreciation in which a fixed rate equal to twice the straight-line percentage is applied to the carrying value (the declining balance) of a tangible long-lived asset.

LO 3   **Estimated useful life:** The total number of service units expected from a long-term asset.

LO 2   **Expenditure:** A payment or an obligation to make future payment for an asset or a service.

SO 9   **Extraordinary repairs:** Repairs that affect the estimated residual value or estimated useful life of an asset, whereby the carrying value of the asset is increased.

LO 8   **Franchise:** The right or license to an exclusive territory or market.

LO 7   **Full-costing method:** A method of accounting for the costs of exploration and development of oil and gas resources in which all costs are recorded as assets and depleted over the estimated life of the producing resources.

LO 8   **Goodwill:** The excess of the cost of a group of assets (usually a business) over the fair market value of the identifiable net assets if purchased individually.

SO 9   **Group depreciation:** The grouping of similar items to calculate depreciation.

LO 1   **Intangible assets:** Long-term assets that have no physical substance but have a value based on rights or advantages accruing to the owner.

LO 8   **Leasehold:** A right to occupy land or buildings under a long-term rental contract.

LO 8   **Leasehold improvements:** Improvements to leased property that become the property of the lessor at the end of the lease.

LO 8   **License:** The right to use a formula, technique, process, or design.

LO 1   **Long-term assets:** Assets that (1) have a useful life of more than one year, (2) are acquired for use in the operation of a business, and (3) are not intended for resale to customers; less commonly called *fixed assets*.

SO 9   **Modified Accelerated Cost Recovery System (MACRS):** A mandatory system of depreciation for income tax purposes, enacted by Congress in 1986, that requires a cost recovery allowance to be computed (1) on the unadjusted cost of property being recovered and (2) over a period of years prescribed by the law for all property of similar types.

LO 1   **Natural resources:** Long-term assets purchased for the economic value that can be taken from the land and used up rather than for the value associated with the land's location.

LO 3   **Obsolescence:** The process of becoming out of date; a contributor, with physical deterioration, to the limited useful life of tangible assets.

SO 9   **Ordinary repairs:** Expenditures, usually of a recurring nature, that are recorded as current period expenses. They are necessary to maintain an asset in good operating condition in order to attain its originally intended useful life.

LO 8   **Patent:** An exclusive right granted by the federal government to make a particular product or use a specific process for a specified period of time.

LO 3   **Physical deterioration:** Limitations on the useful life of a depreciable asset resulting from use and from exposure to the elements.

LO 4   **Production method:** A method of depreciation that assumes that depreciation is solely the result of use and that the passage of time plays no role in the depreciation process; it allocates depreciation based on the units of output or use during each period of an asset's useful life.

LO 3   **Residual value:** The estimated net scrap, salvage, or trade-in value of a tangible asset at the estimated date of disposal; also called *salvage value* or *disposal value*.

LO 2   **Revenue expenditure:** An expenditure for repairs, maintenance, or other services needed to maintain or operate a plant asset for its original useful life; recorded by a debit to an expense account.

LO 4 **Straight-line method:** A method of depreciation that assumes that depreciation depends only on the passage of time and that allocates an equal amount of depreciation to each accounting period in an asset's useful life.

LO 7 **Successful efforts method:** A method of accounting for oil and gas resources in which successful exploration is recorded as an asset and depleted over the estimated life of the resource; all unsuccessful efforts are immediately written off as losses.

LO 1 **Tangible assets:** Long-term assets that have physical substance.

LO 8 **Trademark:** A registered symbol or brand name that can be used only by its owner to identify a product or service.

REVIEW PROBLEM

LO 3
LO 4

Comparison of Depreciation Methods

Norton Construction Company purchased a cement mixer on January 1, 20x1, for $14,500. The mixer was expected to have a useful life of five years and a residual value of $1,000. The company engineers estimated that the mixer would have a useful life of 7,500 hours. It was used 1,500 hours in 20x1, 2,625 hours in 20x2, 2,250 hours in 20x3, 750 hours in 20x4, and 375 hours in 20x5. The company's year end is December 31.

REQUIRED

1. Compute the depreciation expense and carrying value for 20x1 to 20x5, using the following three methods: (a) straight-line, (b) production, and (c) double-declining-balance.

2. Prepare the adjusting entry to record the depreciation for 20x1 calculated in **1(a)**.

3. Show the balance sheet presentation for the cement mixer after the entry in **2** on December 31, 20x1.

4. What conclusions can you draw from the patterns of yearly depreciation?

ANSWER TO REVIEW PROBLEM

1. Depreciation computed:

Depreciation Method	Year	Computation	Depreciation	Carrying Value
a. Straight-line	20x1	$13,500 × 1/5	$2,700	$11,800
	20x2	13,500 × 1/5	2,700	9,100
	20x3	13,500 × 1/5	2,700	6,400
	20x4	13,500 × 1/5	2,700	3,700
	20x5	13,500 × 1/5	2,700	1,000
b. Production	20x1	$13,500 × $\frac{1,500}{7,500}$	$2,700	$11,800
	20x2	13,500 × $\frac{2,625}{7,500}$	4,725	7,075
	20x3	13,500 × $\frac{2,250}{7,500}$	4,050	3,025
	20x4	13,500 × $\frac{750}{7,500}$	1,350	1,675
	20x5	13,500 × $\frac{375}{7,500}$	675	1,000
c. Double-declining-balance	20x1	$14,500 × .4	$5,800	$ 8,700
	20x2	8,700 × .4	3,480	5,220
	20x3	5,220 × .4	2,088	3,132
	20x4	3,132 × .4	1,253*	1,879
	20x5		879*†	1,000

*Rounded.
†Remaining depreciation to reduce carrying value to residual value ($1,879 − $1,000 = $879).

2. Adjusting entry prepared—straight-line method:

20x1
Dec. 31   Depreciation Expense, Cement Mixer   2,700
                Accumulated Depreciation, Cement Mixer   2,700
                To record depreciation expense,
                straight-line method

3. Balance sheet presentation for 20x1 shown:

Property, Plant, and Equipment
    Cement Mixer $14,500
    Less Accumulated Depreciation   2,700
                                                          $11,800

4. Conclusions drawn from depreciation patterns: The pattern of depreciation for the straight-line method differs significantly from that for the double-declining-balance method. In the earlier years, the amount of depreciation under the double-declining-balance method is significantly greater than the amount under the straight-line method. In the later years, the opposite is true. The carrying value under the straight-line method is greater than that under the double-declining-balance method at the end of all years except the fifth year. Depreciation under the production method differs from that under the other methods in that it follows no regular pattern. It varies with the amount of use. Consequently, depreciation is greatest in 20x2 and 20x3, which are the years of greatest use. Use declined significantly in the last two years.

Chapter Assignments

BUILDING YOUR KNOWLEDGE FOUNDATION

QUESTIONS

1. What are the characteristics of long-term assets?
2. Which of the following items would be classified as plant assets on the balance sheet? (a) A truck held for sale by a truck dealer, (b) an office building that was once the company headquarters but is now to be sold, (c) a typewriter used by a secretary of the company, (d) a machine that is used in manufacturing operations but is now fully depreciated, (e) pollution-control equipment that does not reduce the cost or improve the efficiency of a factory, and (f) a parking lot for company employees.
3. Why is land different from other long-term assets?
4. What do accountants mean by the term *depreciation*, and what is its relationship to depletion and amortization?
5. What is asset impairment, and how does it affect the valuation of long-term assets?
6. How do cash flows relate to the decision to acquire a long-term asset, and how does the useful life of an asset relate to the means of financing it?
7. Why is it useful to think of a plant asset as a bundle of services?
8. What is the distinction between revenue expenditures and capital expenditures, why is it important, and what in general is included in the cost of a long-term asset?
9. Which of the following expenditures stemming from the purchase of a computer system would be charged to the asset account? (a) The purchase price of the equipment, (b) interest on the debt incurred to purchase the equipment, (c) freight charges, (d) installation charges, (e) the cost of special communications outlets at

the computer site, (f) the cost of repairing a door that was damaged during installation, and (g) the cost of adjustments to the system during the first month of operation.

10. Hale's Grocery obtained bids on the construction of a receiving dock at the back of its store. The lowest bid was $22,000. The company decided to build the dock itself, however, and was able to do so for $20,000, which it borrowed. The activity was recorded as a debit to Buildings for $22,000 and credits to Notes Payable for $20,000 and Gain on Construction for $2,000. Do you agree with the entry?

11. A firm buys technical equipment that is expected to last 12 years. Why might the equipment have to be depreciated over a shorter period of time?

12. A company purchased a building five years ago. The market value of the building is now greater than it was when the building was purchased. Explain why the company should continue depreciating the building.

13. Evaluate the following statement: "A parking lot should not be depreciated because adequate repairs will make it last forever."

14. Is the purpose of depreciation to determine the value of equipment? Explain your answer.

15. Contrast the assumptions underlying the straight-line depreciation method with the assumptions underlying the production depreciation method.

16. What is the principal argument supporting an accelerated depreciation method?

17. If a plant asset is sold during the year, why should depreciation be computed for the partial year prior to the date of the sale?

18. If a plant asset is discarded before the end of its useful life, how is the amount of loss measured?

19. When similar assets are exchanged, at what amount is the new asset recorded for federal income tax purposes?

20. When an exchange of similar assets occurs in which there is an unrecorded loss, is the taxpayer ever able to deduct or receive federal income tax credit for the loss?

21. Old Stake Mining Company computes the depletion rate of ore to be $2 per ton. During 20xx the company mined 400,000 tons of ore and sold 370,000 tons. What is the total depletion expense for the year?

22. Under what circumstances can a mining company depreciate its plant assets over a period of time that is less than their useful lives?

23. Because accounts receivable have no physical substance, can they be classified as intangible assets?

24. Under what circumstances can a company have intangible assets that do not appear on the balance sheet?

25. When the Accounting Principles Board indicates that accounting for intangible assets involves the same issues as accounting for tangible assets, what issues is it referring to?

26. How does the Financial Accounting Standards Board recommend that research and development costs be treated?

27. After spending three years developing a new software program for designing office buildings, Archi Draw Company recently completed the detailed working program. How does accounting for the costs of software development differ before and after the completion of a successful working program?

28. How is accounting for software development costs similar to and different from accounting for research and development costs?

29. Under what conditions should goodwill be recorded? Should it remain in the records permanently once it is recorded?

30. What basic procedure should be followed in revising a depreciation rate?

31. On what basis can depreciation be taken on a group of assets rather than on individual items?

32. What will be the effect on future years' income of charging an addition to a building to repair expense?

33. In what ways do an addition, a betterment, and an extraordinary repair differ?
34. How does an extraordinary repair differ from an ordinary repair? What is the accounting treatment for each?
35. What is the difference between depreciation for accounting purposes and the Modified Accelerated Cost Recovery System for income tax purposes?

SHORT EXERCISES

SE 1.
LO 1 Management Issues

Indicate whether each of the following actions is primarily related to (a) acquisition of long-term assets, (b) financing of long-term assets, or (c) choosing methods and estimates related to long-term assets.

1. Deciding between common stock and long-term notes for the raising of funds
2. Relating the acquisition cost of a long-term asset to cash flows generated by the asset
3. Determining how long an asset will benefit the company
4. Deciding to use cash flows from operations to purchase long-term assets
5. Determining how much an asset will sell for when it is no longer useful to the company

SE 2.
LO 2 Determining Cost of Long-Term Assets

Denecker Auto purchased a neighboring lot for a new building and parking lot. Indicate whether each of the following expenditures is properly charged to (a) Land, (b) Land Improvements, or (c) Buildings.

1. Paving costs
2. Architects' fee for building design
3. Cost of clearing the property
4. Cost of the property
5. Building construction costs
6. Lights around the property
7. Building permit
8. Interest on the construction loan

SE 3.
LO 2 Group Purchase

Altshuler Company purchased property with a warehouse and parking lot for $750,000. An appraiser valued the components of the property if purchased separately as follows:

Land	$200,000
Land improvements	100,000
Building	500,000
Total	$800,000

Determine the cost to be assigned to each component.

SE 4.
LO 4 Straight-Line Method

Vermont Sun Fitness Center purchased a new step machine for $5,500. The apparatus is expected to last four years and have a residual value of $500. What will be the depreciation expense for each year under the straight-line method?

SE 5.
LO 4 Production Method

Assuming that the step machine in **SE 4** has an estimated useful life of 8,000 hours and was used for 2,400 hours in year 1, for 2,000 hours in year 2, for 2,200 hours in year 3, and for 1,400 hours in year 4, how much would depreciation expense be in each year?

SE 6.
LO 4 Double-Declining-Balance Method

Assuming that the step machine in **SE 4** is depreciated using the declining-balance method at double the straight-line rate, how much would depreciation expense be in each year?

SE 7.
LO 5 Disposal of Plant Assets: No Trade-In

New England Printing had a piece of equipment that cost $8,100 and on which $4,500 of accumulated depreciation had been recorded. The equipment was disposed of on January 4, the first day of business of the current year. Prepare the entries in journal form to record the disposal under each of the following assumptions:

1. It was discarded as having no value.
2. It was sold for $1,500 cash.
3. It was sold for $4,000 cash.

SE 8.
LO 6 Disposal of Plant Assets: Trade-In

Prepare the entries in journal form to record the disposal referred to in **SE 7** under each of the following assumptions:

1. The equipment was traded in on dissimilar equipment that had a list price of $12,000. A $3,800 trade-in was allowed, and the balance was paid in cash. Gains and losses are to be recognized.

2. The equipment was traded in on dissimilar equipment that had a list price of $12,000. A $1,750 trade-in was allowed, and the balance was paid in cash. Gains and losses are to be recognized.

3. Same as **2,** with the exception that the items are similar and gains and losses are not to be recognized.

SE 9.
LO 7 Natural Resources

Lincoln Hills Company purchased land containing an estimated 4,000,000 tons of ore for $8,000,000. The land will be worth $1,200,000 without the ore after eight years of active mining. Although the equipment needed for the mining will have a useful life of 20 years, it is not expected to be usable and will have no value after the mining on this site is complete. Compute the depletion charge per ton and the amount of depletion expense for the first year of operation, assuming that 600,000 tons of ore were mined and sold. Also, compute the first-year depreciation on the mining equipment using the production method, assuming a cost of $9,600,000 with no residual value.

SE 10.
LO 8 Intangible Assets: Computer Software

Alpha-Links created a new software application for PCs. Its costs during research and development were $500,000, and its costs after the working program was developed were $350,000. Although its copyright may be amortized over 40 years, management believes that the product will be viable for only five years. How should the costs be accounted for? At what value will the software appear on the balance sheet after one year?

EXERCISES

E 1.
LO 1 Management Issues

Indicate whether each of the following actions is primarily related to (a) acquisition of long-term assets, (b) financing of long-term assets, or (c) choosing methods and estimates related to long-term assets.

1. Deciding to use the production method of depreciation
2. Allocating costs on a group purchase
3. Determining the total units a machine will produce
4. Deciding to borrow funds to purchase equipment
5. Estimating the savings a new machine will produce and comparing the amount to cost
6. Deciding whether to rent or buy a piece of equipment

E 2.
LO 1 Purchase Decision—Present Value Analysis

Management is considering the purchase of a new machine for a cost of $12,000. It is estimated that the machine will generate positive net cash flows of $3,000 per year for five years and will have a disposal price at the end of that time of $1,000. Assuming an interest rate of 9 percent, determine if management should purchase the machine. Use Tables 3 and 4 in the appendix on future value and present value tables to determine the net present value of the new machine.

E 3.
LO 2 Determining Cost of Long-Term Assets

Winkle Manufacturing purchased land next to its factory to be used as a parking lot. Expenditures incurred by the company were as follows: purchase price, $150,000; broker's fees, $12,000; title search and other fees, $1,100; demolition of a shack on the property, $4,000; general grading of property, $2,100; paving parking lots, $20,000; lighting for parking lots, $16,000; and signs for parking lots, $3,200. Determine the amounts that should be debited to the Land account and the Land Improvements account.

E 4.
LO 2 Group Purchase

Nikki Hopper purchased a car wash for $480,000. If purchased separately, the land would have cost $120,000, the building $270,000, and the equipment $210,000.

Determine the amount that should be recorded in the new business's records for land, building, and equipment.

E 5.

LO 2 Cost of Long-Term Asset
LO 4 and Depreciation

Ed Ruzicka purchased a used tractor for $35,000. Before the tractor could be used, it required new tires, which cost $2,200, and an overhaul, which cost $2,800. Its first tank of fuel cost $150. The tractor is expected to last six years and have a residual value of $4,000. Determine the cost and depreciable cost of the tractor and calculate the first year's depreciation under the straight-line method.

E 6.

LO 3 Depreciation Methods
LO 4

Trujillo Oil Company purchased a drilling truck for $90,000. The company expected the truck to last five years or 200,000 miles, with an estimated residual value of $15,000 at the end of that time. During 20x5, the truck was driven 48,000 miles. The company's year end is December 31. Compute the depreciation for 20x5 under each of the following methods, assuming that the truck was purchased on January 13, 20x4: (1) straight-line, (2) production, and (3) double-declining-balance. Using the amount computed in **3,** prepare the entry in journal form to record depreciation expense for the second year and show how the Drilling Truck account would appear on the balance sheet.

E 7.

LO 4 Declining-Balance Method

Irgan Burglar Alarm Systems Company purchased a word processor for $2,240. It has an estimated useful life of four years and an estimated residual value of $240. Compute the depreciation charge for each of the four years using the double-declining-balance method.

E 8.

LO 5 Disposal of Plant Assets
LO 6

A piece of equipment that cost $32,400 and on which $18,000 of accumulated depreciation had been recorded was disposed of on January 2, the first day of business of the current year. Prepare entries in journal form to record the disposal under each of the following assumptions:

1. It was discarded as having no value.
2. It was sold for $6,000 cash.
3. It was sold for $18,000 cash.
4. It was traded in on dissimilar equipment having a list price of $48,000. A $16,200 trade-in was allowed, and the balance was paid in cash. Gains and losses are to be recognized.
5. It was traded in on dissimilar equipment having a list price of $48,000. A $7,500 trade-in was allowed, and the balance was paid in cash. Gains and losses are to be recognized.
6. Same as **5,** with the exception that the items are similar and gains and losses are not to be recognized.

E 9.

LO 5 Disposal of Plant Assets
LO 6

A microcomputer was purchased by Aristotle Company on January 1, 20x1, at a cost of $5,000. It is expected to have a useful life of five years and a residual value of $500. Assuming that the computer is disposed of on July 1, 20x4, record the partial year's depreciation for 20x4 using the straight-line method, and record the disposal under each of the following assumptions:

1. The microcomputer is discarded.
2. The microcomputer is sold for $800.
3. The microcomputer is sold for $2,200.
4. The microcomputer is exchanged for a new microcomputer with a list price of $9,000. A $1,200 trade-in is allowed on the cash purchase. The accounting approach to gains and losses is followed.
5. Same as **4,** except a $2,400 trade-in is allowed.
6. Same as **4,** except the income tax approach is followed.
7. Same as **5,** except the income tax approach is followed.
8. Same as **4,** except the microcomputer is exchanged for dissimilar office equipment.
9. Same as **5,** except the microcomputer is exchanged for dissimilar office equipment.

E 10.

LO 7 **Natural Resource Depletion and Depreciation of Related Plant Assets**

Loess Mining Company purchased land containing an estimated 10 million tons of ore for a cost of $8,800,000. The land without the ore is estimated to be worth $1,600,000. The company expects that all the usable ore can be mined in ten years. Buildings costing $800,000 with an estimated useful life of 30 years were erected on the site. Equipment costing $960,000 with an estimated useful life of ten years was installed. Because of the remote location, neither the buildings nor the equipment has an estimated residual value. During its first year of operation, the company mined and sold 800,000 tons of ore.

1. Compute the depletion charge per ton.
2. Compute the depletion expense that Loess Mining should record for the year.
3. Determine the depreciation expense for the year for the buildings, making it proportional to the depletion.
4. Determine the depreciation expense for the year for the equipment under two alternatives: (a) making the expense proportional to the depletion and (b) using the straight-line method.

E 11.

LO 8 **Amortization of Copyrights and Trademarks**

1. Okumura Publishing Company purchased the copyright to a basic computer textbook for $20,000. The usual life of a textbook is about four years. However, the copyright will remain in effect for another 70 years. Calculate the annual amortization of the copyright.

2. Austin Company purchased a trademark from a well-known supermarket for $160,000. The management of the company argued that because the trademark's value would last forever and might even increase, no amortization should be charged. Calculate the minimum amount of annual amortization that should be charged, according to guidelines of the appropriate Accounting Principles Board opinion.

E 12.

SO 9 **Depreciation Methods: Partial Years**

Using the data given for Trujillo Oil Company in **E 6,** compute the depreciation for calendar year 20x4 under each of the following methods, assuming that the truck was purchased on July 1, 20x4, and was driven 20,000 miles during 20x4: (1) straight-line, (2) production, and (3) double-declining-balance.

E 13.

SO 9 **Revision of Depreciation Rates**

Exmoor Hospital purchased a special x-ray machine for its operating room. The machine, which cost $311,560, was expected to last ten years, with an estimated residual value of $31,560. After two years of operation (and depreciation charges using the straight-line method), it became evident that the x-ray machine would last a total of only seven years. The estimated residual value, however, would remain the same. Given this information, determine the new depreciation charge for the third year on the basis of the revised estimated useful life.

E 14.

LO 2 **Special Types of Capital**
SO 9 **Expenditures**

Tell whether each of the following transactions related to an office building is a revenue expenditure (RE) or a capital expenditure (CE). In addition, indicate whether each transaction is an ordinary repair (OR), an extraordinary repair (ER), an addition (A), a betterment (B), or none of these (N).

1. The hallways and ceilings in the building are repainted at a cost of $8,300.
2. The hallways, which have tile floors, are carpeted at a cost of $28,000.
3. A new wing is added to the building at a cost of $175,000.
4. Furniture is purchased for the entrance to the building at a cost of $16,500.
5. The air-conditioning system is overhauled at a cost of $28,500. The overhaul extends the useful life of the air-conditioning system by ten years.
6. A cleaning firm is paid $200 per week to clean the newly installed carpets.

E 15.

SO 9 **Extraordinary Repairs**

Collinson Manufacturing has an incinerator that originally cost $187,200 and now has accumulated depreciation of $132,800. The incinerator has completed its fifteenth year of service in an estimated useful life of 20 years. At the beginning of the sixteenth year, the company spent $42,800 repairing and modernizing the incinerator to comply with pollution-control standards. Therefore, the incinerator is now expected to last ten more years instead of five more years. It will not, however, have more capacity than it did in the past or a residual value at the end of its useful life.

1. Prepare the entry to record the cost of the repair.
2. Compute the carrying value of the incinerator after the entry.
3. Prepare the entry to record straight-line depreciation for the current year.

PROBLEMS

P 1.

LO 2 Determining Cost of Assets

Oslo Company began operation on January 1 of the current year. At the end of the year, the company's auditor discovered that all expenditures involving long-term assets had been debited to an account called Fixed Assets. An analysis of the account, which had a year-end balance of $2,644,972, disclosed that it contained the following items:

Cost of land	$ 316,600
Surveying costs	4,100
Transfer of title and other fees required by the county	920
Broker's fees for land	21,144
Attorney's fees associated with land acquisition	7,048
Cost of removing unusable timber from land	50,400
Cost of grading land	4,200
Cost of digging building foundation	34,600
Architect's fee for building and land improvements (80 percent building)	64,800
Cost of building construction	710,000
Cost of sidewalks	11,400
Cost of parking lots	54,400
Cost of lighting for grounds	80,300
Cost of landscaping	11,800
Cost of machinery	989,000
Shipping cost on machinery	55,300
Cost of installing machinery	176,200
Cost of testing machinery	22,100
Cost of changes in building to comply with safety regulations pertaining to machinery	12,540
Cost of repairing building that was damaged in the installation of machinery	8,900
Cost of medical bill for injury received by employee while installing machinery	2,400
Cost of water damage to building during heavy rains prior to opening the plant for operation	6,820
Account balance	$2,644,972

The timber that was cleared from the land was sold to a firewood dealer for $5,000. This amount was credited to Miscellaneous Income. During the construction period, two supervisors devoted their full time to the construction project. They earn annual salaries of $48,000 and $42,000, respectively. They spent two months on the purchase and preparation of the land, six months on the construction of the building (approximately one-sixth of which was devoted to improvements on the grounds), and one month on machinery installation. The plant began operation on October 1, and the supervisors returned to their regular duties. Their salaries were debited to Factory Salaries Expense.

REQUIRED

Prepare a schedule with the following column headings: Land, Land Improvements, Buildings, Machinery, and Expense. List the items and place each in the proper account. Negative amounts should be shown in parentheses. Total the columns.

**LO 3 Comparison of
LO 4 Depreciation Methods**

REQUIRED

P 2. Myles Construction Company purchased a new crane for $360,500 at the beginning of year 1. The crane has an estimated residual value of $35,000 and an estimated useful life of six years. The crane is expected to last 10,000 hours. It was used 1,800 hours in year 1; 2,000 in year 2; 2,500 in year 3; 1,500 in year 4; 1,200 in year 5; and 1,000 in year 6.

1. Compute the annual depreciation and carrying value for the new crane for each of the six years (round to nearest dollar where necessary) under each of the following methods: (a) straight-line, (b) production, and (c) double-declining-balance.

2. Prepare the adjusting entry that would be made each year to record the depreciation calculated under the straight-line method.

3. Show the balance sheet presentation for the crane after the adjusting entry in year 2 using the straight-line method.

4. What conclusions can you draw from the patterns of yearly depreciation and carrying value in **1**?

**LO 4 Depreciation Methods
SO 9 and Partial Years**

P 3. Chen Company operates three types of equipment. Because of the equipment's varied functions, company accounting policy requires the application of three different depreciation methods. Data on this equipment are summarized in the table below. Equipment 3 was used 2,000 hours in 20x1; 4,200 hours in 20x2; and 3,200 hours in 20x3.

Equipment	Date Purchased	Cost	Installation Cost	Estimated Residual Value	Estimated Life	Depreciation Method
1	1/12/x1	$171,000	$ 9,000	$18,000	10 years	Double-declining-balance
2	7/9/x1	191,100	15,900	21,000	10 years	Straight-line
3	10/2/x1	290,700	8,100	33,600	20,000 hours	Production

REQUIRED

Assuming that the fiscal year ends December 31, compute the depreciation expense on each type of equipment and the total depreciation expense for 20x1, 20x2, and 20x3 by filling in a table with the headings shown below.

		Depreciation		
Equipment No.	Computations	20x1	20x2	20x3

**LO 5 Recording Disposals
LO 6**

P 4. Laughlin Designs, Inc., purchased a computer that will assist it in designing factory layouts. The cost of the computer was $23,500. Its expected useful life is six years. The company can probably sell the computer for $2,500 at the end of six years.

REQUIRED

Prepare journal entries to record the disposal of the computer at the end of the third year, after the depreciation is recorded, assuming that it was depreciated using the straight-line method and making the following assumptions:

a. The computer is sold for $19,000.
b. It is sold for $10,000.
c. It is traded in on a dissimilar item (equipment) costing $36,000, a trade-in allowance of $17,500 is given, the balance is paid in cash, and gains and losses are recognized.
d. Same as **c** except the trade-in allowance is $11,000.
e. Same as **c** except it is traded for a similar computer and APB accounting rules are followed with regard to the recognition of gains or losses.
f. Same as **d** except it is traded for a similar computer and APB accounting rules are followed with regard to the recognition of gains or losses.
g. Same as **c** except it is traded for a similar computer and gains and losses are not recognized (income tax method).
h. Same as **d** except it is traded for a similar computer and gains and losses are not recognized (income tax method).

**LO 8 Leasehold, Leasehold
Improvements, and
Amortization of Patent**

P 5. **Part A:** At the beginning of the fiscal year, Chang Company purchased an eight-year leasehold or sublease on a warehouse in Peoria for $48,000. Chang will also pay rent of $1,000 a month. The warehouse needs the following improvements to meet Chang's needs:

Lighting fixtures	$18,000	Heating system	$30,000
Replacement of a wall	25,000	Break room	12,200
Office carpet	14,400	Loading dock	8,400

The expected life of the loading dock and carpet is eight years. The other items are expected to last ten years. None of the improvements will have a residual value.

REQUIRED

Prepare entries in journal form to record the following: (a) payment for the leasehold, (b) first-year lease expense payment, (c) payments for the improvements, (d) amortization of the leasehold for the year, and (e) leasehold improvement amortization for the year.

Part B: At the beginning of the fiscal year, Ricks Company purchased for $1,030,000 a patent that applies to the manufacture of a unique tamper-proof lid for medicine bottles. Ricks incurred legal costs of $450,000 in successfully defending the patent against use of the lid by a competitor. Ricks estimated that the patent would be valuable for at least ten years. During the first two years of operation, Ricks successfully marketed the lid. At the beginning of the third year, a study appeared in a consumers' magazine showing that the lid could, in fact, be removed by children. As a result, all orders for the lids were canceled, and the patent was rendered worthless.

REQUIRED

Prepare entries in journal form to record the following: (a) purchase of the patent, (b) successful defense of the patent, (c) amortization expense for the first year, and (d) write-off of the patent as worthless.

ALTERNATE PROBLEMS

P 6.
LO 2 Determining Cost of Assets

Georgakis Computers constructed a new training center in 20x2. You have been hired to manage the training center. A review of the accounting records lists the following expenditures debited to an asset account titled "Training Center":

Attorney's fee, land acquisition	$ 34,900
Cost of land	598,000
Architect's fee, building design	102,000
Building	1,020,000
Parking lot and sidewalk	135,600
Electrical wiring, building	164,000
Landscaping	55,000
Cost of surveying land	9,200
Training equipment, tables, and chairs	136,400
Installation of training equipment	68,000
Cost of grading the land	14,000
Cost of changes in building to soundproof rooms	59,200
Total account balance	$2,396,300

During the center's construction, someone from Georgakis Computers worked full time on the project. He spent two months on the purchase and preparation of the site, six months on the construction, one month on land improvements, and one month on equipment installation and training room furniture purchase and setup. His salary of $64,000 during this ten-month period was charged to Administrative Expense. The training center was placed in operation on November 1.

REQUIRED

Prepare a schedule with the following four column (Account) headings: Land, Land Improvements, Building, and Equipment. Place each of the expenditures above in the appropriate column. Total the columns.

P 7.
LO 3 Comparison of
LO 4 Depreciation Methods

Gent Manufacturing Company purchased a robot for $1,440,000 at the beginning of year 1. The robot has an estimated useful life of four years and an estimated residual value of $120,000. The robot, which should last 20,000 hours, was operated 6,000 hours in year 1; 8,000 hours in year 2; 4,000 hours in year 3; and 2,000 hours in year 4.

REQUIRED

1. Compute the annual depreciation and carrying value for the robot for each year assuming the following depreciation methods: (a) straight-line, (b) production, and (c) double-declining-balance.

2. Prepare the adjusting entry that would be made each year to record the depreciation calculated under the straight-line method.

3. Show the balance sheet presentation for the robot after the adjusting entry in year 2 using the straight-line method.

4. What conclusions can you draw from the patterns of yearly depreciation and carrying value in 1?

P 8.

LO 4 **Depreciation Methods**
SO 9 **and Partial Years**

Rita Montes purchased a laundry company. In addition to the washing machines, Montes installed a tanning machine and a refreshment center. Because each type of asset performs a different function, she has decided to use different depreciation methods. Data on each type of asset are summarized in the table below. The tanning machine was operated 2,100 hours in 20x2, 3,000 hours in 20x3, and 2,400 hours in 20x4.

Asset	Date Purchased	Cost	Installation Cost	Residual Value	Estimated Life	Depreciation Method
Washing machines	3/5/x2	$30,000	$4,000	$5,200	4 years	Straight-line
Tanning machine	4/1/x2	68,000	6,000	2,000	7,500 hours	Production
Refreshment center	10/1/x2	6,800	1,200	1,200	10 years	Double-declining-balance

REQUIRED

Assume the fiscal year ends December 31. Compute the depreciation expense for each item and the total depreciation expense for 20x2, 20x3, and 20x4. Round your answers to the nearest dollar and present them in a table with the headings shown below.

		Depreciation		
Asset	Computations	20x2	20x3	20x4

EXPANDING YOUR CRITICAL THINKING, COMMUNICATION, AND INTERPERSONAL SKILLS

SKILLS DEVELOPMENT

Conceptual Analysis

SD 1.

LO 3 **Change of Depreciation**
LO 4 **Method**

Polaroid Corporation, a manufacturer of instant cameras and films, changed from an accelerated depreciation method for financial reporting purposes to the straight-line method for assets acquired after January 1, 1997. As noted in Polaroid's 1997 annual report:

> The company changed its method of depreciation for financial reporting for the cost of buildings, machinery, and equipment acquired on or after January 1, 1997, from primarily accelerated method to the straight-line method.[20]

What reasons can you give for Polaroid's choosing to switch to a straight-line method of depreciation? Discuss which of the two depreciation methods is more conservative. How does the change of depreciation method for financial reporting affect the company's cash flows?

| Cash Flow | CD-ROM | Communication | Critical Thinking | Ethics | General Ledger | Group Activity | Hot Links to Real Companies | International | Internet | Key Ratio | Memo | Spreadsheet |

LO 8 Trademarks

SD 2. *America Online* (AOL), America's largest online Internet service, filed a trademark-infringement lawsuit against *AT&T*'s WorldNet Service seeking to block its use of such terms and phrases as "You Have Mail" and "You've Got Mail." A district court judge denied AOL's request for a temporary restraining order against AT&T's using these phrases, saying it was not clear that AOL owned them. AOL claims these terms are historically associated with its service, but AT&T says they are common Internet phrases available to all.

The Internet community is watching this case and others like it closely because the Internet is a relatively new medium in which it is not clear what rules apply. Whatever the outcome, it can have significant financial effects.[21]

What is a trademark, and why is it considered an intangible asset? Why does a trademark have value? For whom does a trademark have value? Be prepared to discuss how your answers apply to the case of AOL's use of "You Have Mail" or "You've Got Mail."

Ethical Dilemma

LO 2 Ethics and Allocation of Acquisition Costs

SD 3. *Signal Company* has purchased land and a warehouse for $18,000,000. The warehouse is expected to last 20 years and to have a salvage value equal to 10 percent of its cost. The chief financial officer (CFO) and the controller are discussing the allocation of the purchase price. The CFO believes that the largest amount possible should be assigned to the land because this action will improve reported net income in the future. Depreciation expense will be lower because land is not depreciated. He suggests allocating one-third, or $6,000,000, of the cost to the land. This results in depreciation expense each year of $540,000 [($12,000,000 − $1,200,000) ÷ 20 years].

The company's controller disagrees with the CFO. The controller argues that the smallest amount possible, say one-fifth of the purchase price, should be allocated to the land, thereby saving income taxes, since the depreciation, which is tax deductible, will be greater. Under this plan, annual depreciation would be $648,000 [($14,400,000 − $1,440,000) ÷ 20 years]. The annual tax savings at a 30 percent tax rate is $32,400 [($648,000 − $540,000) × .30]. How will this decision affect the company's cash flows? Ethically speaking, how should the purchase cost be allocated? Who will be affected by the decision?

Group Activity: Have each group develop the position of one of the two roles for presentation and debate.

LO 2 Ethics of Aggressive
LO 8 Accounting Policies

SD 4. Is it ethical to choose aggressive accounting practices to advance a company's business? *America Online* (AOL), the largest online service and Internet service provider in the United States, is one of the hottest stocks on Wall Street. From its initial stock offering in 1992, its stock price was up several thousand percent. Accounting is very important to AOL because earnings enable it to sell shares of stock and raise more cash to fund its phenomenal growth.

In its early years, AOL was one of the most aggressive companies in its choice of accounting principles. AOL's strategy called for building the largest customer base in the industry. Consequently, it spent many millions of dollars each year marketing its services to new customers. Such costs are usually recognized as operating expenses in the year in which they are incurred. However, AOL treated these costs as long-term assets, called "deferred subscriber acquisition costs," and expensed them over several years, because the company said the average customer was going to stay with the company for three years or more. The company also recorded research and development costs as "product development costs" and amortized them over five years. Both of these practices are justifiable theoretically, but they are not common practice. If the standard or more conservative practice had been followed, the company would have had a net loss in every year it has been in business.[22] This result would have greatly limited AOL's ability to raise money and grow as it has.

Explain in your own words management's rationale for adopting the accounting policies that it did. What could go wrong with management's plan? How would you evaluate the ethics of AOL's actions? Who benefits from the actions? Who is harmed by the actions? Have you seen any developments about AOL in the news?

Research Activity

Visit a fast-food restaurant. Make a list of all the intangible and property, plant, and equipment assets you can identify. For each one, identify one management issue that relates to that asset. In addition, identify at least one capital expenditure and one revenue expenditure that is applicable to property, plant, and equipment assets (not to each one on your list). Bring your list to class for discussion.

Decision-Making Practice

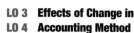

Morningside Machine Works has successfully obtained a subcontract to manufacture parts for a new military aircraft. The parts are to be delivered over the next five years, and Morningside will be paid as the parts are delivered. To make the parts, new equipment will have to be purchased. Two types of equipment are available. Type A is conventional equipment that can be put into service immediately, and Type B requires one year to be put into service but is more efficient. Type A requires an immediate cash investment of $1,000,000 and will produce enough parts to provide net cash receipts of $340,000 each year for the five years. Type B may be purchased by signing a two-year non-interest-bearing note for $1,346,000. It is projected that Type B will produce net cash receipts of zero in year 1, $500,000 in year 2, $600,000 in year 3, $600,000 in year 4, and $200,000 in year 5. Neither type of equipment can be used on other contracts or will have any useful life remaining at the end of the contract. Morningside currently pays an interest rate of 16 percent to borrow money.

1. What is the present value of the investment required for each type of equipment? (Use Table 3 in the appendix on future value and present value tables.)

2. Compute the net present value of each type of equipment based on your answer in **1** and the present value of the net cash receipts projected to be received. (Use Tables 3 and 4 in the appendix on future value and present value tables.)

3. Write a memorandum to the board of directors that recommends the option that appears to be best for Morningside based on your analysis (include **1** and **2** as attachments) and that explains why.

FINANCIAL REPORTING AND ANALYSIS

Interpreting Financial Reports

Depreciation expense is a significant expense for companies in which plant assets are a high proportion of assets. The amount of depreciation expense in a given year is affected by estimates of useful life and choice of depreciation method. In 2000, **Century Steelworks Company,** a major integrated steel producer, changed the estimated useful lives for its major production assets. In addition, Century Steelworks changed the method of depreciation for other steel-making assets from straight-line to the production method.

The company's 2000 annual report states, "A recent study conducted by management shows that actual years-in-service figures for our major production equipment and machinery are, in most cases, higher than the estimated useful lives assigned to these assets. We have recast the depreciable lives of such assets so that equipment previously assigned a useful life of 8 to 26 years now has an extended depreciable life of 10 to 32 years."

The report goes on to explain that the new production method of depreciation "recognizes that depreciation of production equipment and machinery correlates directly to both physical wear and tear and the passage of time. The production method of depreciation, which we have now initiated, more closely allocates the cost of these assets to the periods in which products are manufactured."

The report summarized the effects of both actions on the year 2000 in the following manner:

Incremental Increase in Net Income	In Millions	Per Share
Lengthened lives	$11.0	$ .80
Production method		
Current year	7.3	.53
Prior years	2.8	.20
Total increase	$21.1	$1.53

During 2000, Century Steelworks reported a net loss of $83,156,500 ($6.03 per share). Depreciation expense for 2000 was $87,707,200.

In explaining the changes, the controller of Century Steelworks was quoted in an article in *Business Journal* as follows: "There is no reason for Century Steelworks to continue to depreciate our assets more conservatively than our competitors do." But the article quotes an industry analyst who argues that by slowing its method of depreciation, Century Steelworks could be viewed as reporting lower-quality earnings.

REQUIRED

1. Explain the accounting treatment when there is a change in the estimated lives of depreciable assets. What circumstances must exist for the production method to produce the effect it did in relation to the straight-line method? What would Century Steelworks' net income or loss have been if the changes had not been made? What may have motivated management to make the changes?

2. What does the controller of Century Steelworks mean when he says that Century had been depreciating "more conservatively than our competitors do"? Why might the changes at Century Steelworks indicate, as the analyst asserts, "lower-quality earnings"? What risks might Century face as a result of its decision to use the production method of depreciation?

International Company

FRA 2.
LO 8 Accounting for Trademarks: U.S. and British Rules

When the British company **Grand Metropolitan** (Grand Met) purchased **Pillsbury**, it adopted British accounting policies with regard to intangibles. Many analysts felt this gave British companies advantages over U.S. companies, especially in buyout situations.[23] For example, under the U.S. rules, as discussed in this chapter, intangible assets such as trademarks are recorded at their acquisition cost, which is often nominal, and the cost is amortized over a reasonable life. Under British accounting standards, on the other hand, firms are able to record the value of trademarks for the purpose of increasing the total assets on their balance sheets. Further, they do not have to amortize the value if management can show that the value can be preserved through extensive brand support. Grand Met, therefore, elected to record such famous Pillsbury trademarks as the Pillsbury Doughboy, Green Giant vegetables, Häagen Dazs ice cream, and Van de Kamp fish at an estimated value and not to amortize them. Analysts say that British rules made Pillsbury more valuable to Grand Met than to Pillsbury stockholders and thus led to Pillsbury's being bought by the British firm.

Write a one-page paper that addresses the following questions: What is the rationale behind the argument that the British company has an advantage due to the differences between U.S. and British accounting principles? Do you agree with U.S. or British accounting rules regarding trademarks? Defend your answers.

Toys "R" Us Annual Report

FRA 3.
LO 1 Long-Term Assets
LO 2
LO 3
LO 4
LO 8

1. Refer to the consolidated balance sheets and to the note on property and equipment in the notes to consolidated financial statements in the Toys "R" Us annual report to answer the following questions: What percentage of total assets in 2000 was property and equipment? What is the most significant type of property and equipment? Does Toys "R" Us have a significant investment in land? What other kinds of things are included in the property and equipment category? (Ignore leased property under capital leases for now.)

2. Refer to the summary of significant accounting policies and to the note on property and equipment in the Toys "R" Us annual report. What method of depreciation does Toys "R" Us use? How long does management estimate its buildings to last as compared to furniture and equipment? What does this say about Toys "R" Us's need to remodel its stores?

3. Refer to the statement of cash flows in the Toys "R" Us annual report. How much did Toys "R" Us spend on property and equipment (capital expenditures, net) during 2000? Is this an increase or a decrease from prior years?

4. Refer again to the income statement and note on property and equipment. What are leaseholds and leasehold improvements? How significant are these items? How does the amount of rent expense (see note on leases) and appreciation and amortization compare with the net earnings in 2000?

Fingraph® Financial Analyst™

FRA 4.
LO 1 Comparison of Long-Term
LO 4 Assets
LO 7
LO 8

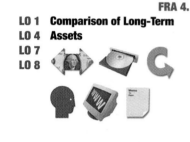

Choose any two companies from the same industry in the Fingraph® Financial Analyst™ CD-ROM software. The industry chosen should be one in which long-term assets are likely to be important. Choose an industry such as airlines, manufacturing, consumer products, consumer food and beverage, or computers.

1. In the annual reports for the companies you have selected, read the long-term asset section of the balance sheet and any reference to any long-term assets in the summary of significant accounting policies or notes to the financial statements. What are the most important long-term assets for each company? What depreciation methods do the companies use? Are there any long-term assets that appear to be characteristic of the industry? What intangible assets do the companies have, and how important are they?

2. Display and print in tabular and graphical form the Balance Sheet Analysis page. Prepare a table that compares the gross and net property, plant, and equipment.

3. Locate the statements of cash flows in the two companies' annual reports. Prepare another table that compares depreciation (and amortization) expense from the operating activities section with the net purchases of property, plant, and equipment (net capital expenditures) from the investing activities section for two years. Does depreciation (and amortization) expense exceed replacement of long-term assets? Are the companies expanding or reducing their property, plant, and equipment?

4. Find and read references to long-term assets and capital expenditures in management's discussion and analysis in each annual report.

5. Write a one-page executive summary that highlights the most important long-term assets and the accounting policies for long-term assets, and compares the investing activities of the two companies, including reference to management's assessment. Include the Fingraph® page and your tables as attachments to your report.

Internet Case

FRA 5.
LO 4 SEC and Forms 10-K
LO 5
LO 8

Public corporations are required not only to communicate with their stockholders by means of an annual report, but also to submit an annual report to the Securities and Exchange Commission (SEC). The annual report to the SEC is called a Form 10-K and is a source of the latest information about a company. Through the Needles Accounting Resource Center web site at http://college.hmco.com, access the SEC's EDGAR files to locate either H. J. Heinz Company's or Ford Motor Company's Form 10-K. Find the financial statements and the notes to the financial statements. Scan through the notes to the financial statements and prepare a list of information you find related to long-term assets, including intangibles. For instance, what depreciation methods does the company use? What are the useful lives of its property, plant, and equipment? What intangible assets does the company have? Does the company have goodwill? How much does the company spend on research and development? In the statement of cash flows, how much did the company spend on new property, plant, and equipment (capital expenditures)? Summarize your results and be prepared to discuss them as well as your experience in using the SEC's EDGAR database.

Group Activity: Divide students into groups according to the company researched and have each group compile a comprehensive list of information about its company.

ENDNOTES

1. H. J. Heinz Company, *Annu al Report*, 2000.
2. *Statement of Financial Accounting Standards No. 121*, "Accounting for the Impairment of Long-Lived Assets and for Long-Lived Assets to Be Disposed Of" (Norwalk, Conn.: Financial Accounting Standards Board, 1995).
3. Leslie Canley, "Pacific Telesis Plans a Charge of $3.3 Billion," *The Wall Street Journal*, September 8, 1995.
4. Ford Motor Company, *Annual Report*, 1999.
5. Ibid.
6. *Statement of Position No. 98-1*, "Accounting for the Costs of Computer Software Developed or Planned for Internal Use" (New York: American Institute of Certified Public Accountants, 1996).
7. *Statement of Financial Accounting Standards No. 34*, "Capitalization of Interest Cost" (Norwalk, Conn.: Financial Accounting Standards Board, 1979), par. 9–11.
8. Len Boselovic, "A Look at How the SEC Disposed of Chambers' Claims," *Pittsburgh Post-Gazette*, May 14, 1995.
9. *Financial Accounting Standards: Original Pronouncements as of July 1, 1977* (Norwalk, Conn.: Financial Accounting Standards Board, 1977), ARB No. 43, Ch. 9, Sec. C, par. 5.
10. Accounting Principles Board, *Opinion No. 29*, "Accounting for Nonmonetary Transactions" (New York: American Institute of Certified Public Accountants, 1973) and Emerging Issues Task Force, *EITF Issue Summary 86-29*, "Nonmonetary Transactions: Magnitude of Boot and the Exceptions to the Use of Fair Value" (Norwalk, Conn.: Financial Accounting Standards Board, 1986). The specific criteria for similar assets are the subject of more advanced courses.
11. *Statement of Financial Accounting Standards No. 25*, "Suspension of Certain Accounting Requirements for Oil and Gas Producing Companies" (Norwalk, Conn.: Financial Accounting Standards Board, 1979).
12. Adapted from Accounting Principles Board, *Opinion No. 17*, "Intangible Assets" (New York: American Institute of Certified Public Accountants, 1970), par. 2.
13. "What's in a Name?" *Time*, May 3, 1993.
14. *Statement of Financial Accounting Standards No. 2*, "Accounting for Research and Development Costs" (Norwalk, Conn.: Financial Accounting Standards Board, 1974), par. 12.
15. General Motors, *Annual Report*, 1998.
16. Abbott Laboratories, *Annual Report*, 1998; and Roche Group, *Annual Report*, 1998.
17. *Statement of Financial Accounting Standards No. 86*, "Accounting for the Costs of Computer Software to be Sold, Leased, or Otherwise Marketed" (Norwalk, Conn.: Financial Accounting Standards Board, 1985).
18. Accounting Principles Board, *Opinion No. 17*, par. 29. See note 13 above.
19. Edward P. McTague, "Accounting for Trade-Ins of Operational Assets," *National Public Accountant* (January 1986), p. 39.
20. Polaroid Corporation, *Annual Report*, 1997.
21. "AOL Loses Round in AT&T Suit," Times Mirror Company web site <www.TimesMirror.com>, January 5, 1999.
22. "Stock Gives Case the Funds He Needs to Buy New Technology," *Business Week*, April 15, 1996.
23. Joanne Lipman, "British Value Brand Names—Literally," *The Wall Street Journal*, February 9, 1989, p. B4; and "Brand Name Policy Boosts Assets," *Accountancy*, October 1988, pp. 38–39.

Current Liabilities

LEARNING OBJECTIVES

1 Identify the management issues related to recognition, valuation, classification, and disclosure of current liabilities.

2 Identify, compute, and record definitely determinable and estimated current liabilities.

3 Define *contingent liability*.

SUPPLEMENTAL OBJECTIVE

4 Compute and record the liabilities associated with payroll accounting.

DECISION POINT: A USER'S FOCUS

US Airways, Inc. Liabilities are one of the three major parts of the balance sheet. They are legal obligations for the future payment of assets or the future performance of services that result from past transactions. For example, the current and long-term liabilities of US Airways, Inc., which has total assets of almost $7.7 billion, are shown here.[1] Current Maturities of Long-Term Debt; Accounts Payable; Accrued Aircraft Rent; Accrued Salaries, Wages, and Vacation; and Other Accrued Expenses for the most part will require an outlay of cash in the next year. Traffic Balances Payable will require payments to other airlines, but those may be partially offset by amounts owed from other airlines. Unused Tickets are tickets already paid for by passengers and represent services that must be performed. Long-Term Debt will require cash outlays in future years. Altogether these liabilities represent 60 percent of total assets. How does the decision of US Airways' management to incur so much debt relate to the goals of the business?

Liabilities are important because they are closely related to the goals of profitability and liquidity. Liabilities are sources of cash for operating and financing activities when they are incurred, but they are also obligations that use cash when they are paid as required. Achieving the appropriate level of liabilities is critical to business success. A company that has too few liabilities may not be earning up to its potential. A company that has too many liabilities, however, may be incurring excessive risks. This chapter focuses on the management and accounting issues involving current liabilities, including payroll liabilities and contingent liabilities.

Financial Highlights

(In millions)

Current Liabilities	1999	1998	1997
Current Maturities of Long-Term Debt	$ 116	$ 71	$ 186
Accounts Payable	474	430	323
Traffic Balances Payable and Unused Tickets	635	752	707
Accrued Aircraft Rent	236	166	187
Accrued Salaries, Wages and Vacation	341	329	311
Other Accrued Expenses	699	521	492
Total Current Liabilities	$2,501	$2,269	$2,206
Long-Term Debt, Net of Current Maturities	$2,113	$1,955	$2,426

Management Issues Related to Accounting for Current Liabilities

The primary reason for incurring current liabilities is to meet needs for cash during the operating cycle. The proper identification and management of current liabilities also requires an understanding of how they are recognized, valued, classified, and disclosed.

Managing Liquidity and Cash Flows

The operating cycle is the process of converting cash to purchases, to sales, to accounts receivable, and back to cash. Most current liabilities arise in support of this cycle, as when accounts payable arise from purchases of inventory, accrued expenses arise from operating costs, and unearned revenues arise from customers' advance payments. Short-term debt is used to raise cash during periods of inventory buildup or while waiting for collection of receivables. Cash is used to pay current maturities of long-term debt and to pay off liabilities arising from operations.

Failure to manage the cash flows related to current liabilities can have serious consequences for a business. For instance, if suppliers are not paid on time, they may withhold shipments that are vital to a company's operations. Continued failure to pay current liabilities can lead to bankruptcy. To evaluate a company's ability to pay its current liabilities, three measures of liquidity—working capital, the current ratio, and the quick ratio—are often used. Current liabilities are a key component of each of these measures. They typically equal from 25 to 50 percent of total assets.

US Airways' short-term liquidity as measured by working capital deteriorated from 1997 to 1999 (in millions):

	Current Assets	−	Current Liabilities	=	Working Capital
1999	$2,096	−	$2,501	=	($405)
1998	$2,364	−	$2,269	=	$ 95
1997	$2,777	−	$2,206	=	$571

This measure highlights the need for US Airways' management to focus on the management of short-term liquidity because it has deteriorated significantly over the three-year period. It is common for airlines to have low or negative working capital because unearned ticket revenue is a current liability, but the cash from these ticket sales is quickly consumed in operations. On the assumption that only a small portion of unearned ticket revenues will be repaid to customers, unearned ticket revenue might be excluded from current liabilities for purposes of analysis. The healthiest airlines have positive working capital when unearned ticket revenue is excluded.

Another consideration with managing a company's liquidity position and cash flows is the amount of time its creditors are willing to give it to pay its accounts payable. Common measures of this time are the **payables turnover** and the **average days' payable**. The payables turnover is the number of times on average that accounts payable are paid in an accounting period and shows the relative size of a company's accounts payable. The average days' payable measures how long, on average, a company takes to pay its accounts payables.

For example, Radio Shack Corporation, which operates more than 7,000 electronics retail locations, must carefully plan its purchases and payables. It had accounts payable of $234.8 million in 1999 and $206.4 million in 1998. Its purchases are determined by cost of goods sold adjusted for the change in inventory. An increase in inventory means purchases were more than cost of goods sold, and a

Figure 1
Payables Turnover for Selected Industries

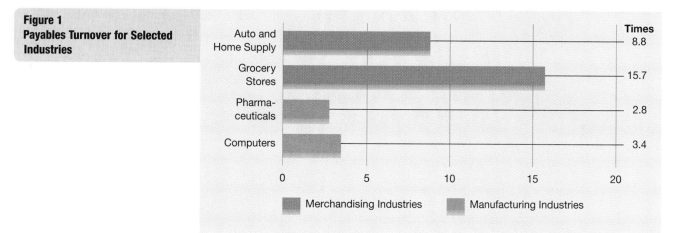

Source: Data from Dun & Bradstreet, *Industry Norms and Key Business Ratios,* 1999–2000.

decrease in inventory means that purchases were less than cost of goods sold. Radio Shack's cost of goods sold was $2,042.7 million and its inventory decreased by $50.7 million.[2] Its payables turnover is computed as follows:

$$\text{Payables Turnover} = \frac{\text{Cost of Goods Sold} \pm \text{Change in Merchandise Inventory}}{\text{Average Accounts Payable}}$$

$$= \frac{\$2,042.7 - \$50.7}{(\$234.8 + \$206.4) \div 2}$$

$$= \frac{\$1,992.0}{\$220.6} = 9.0 \text{ times}$$

To find the average days' payable, the number of days in a year is divided by the payables turnover:

$$\text{Average Days' Payable} = \frac{365 \text{ days}}{\text{Payables Turnover}} = \frac{365 \text{ days}}{9.0} = 40.6 \text{ days}$$

The payables turnover of 9.0 times and the resulting average days' payable of 40.6 days are consistent with customary 30-day credit terms, with some purchases having longer terms.

The chart in Figure 1 shows the payables turnover for various other industries. The payables turnover should be considered in relation to the inventory turnover and the receivables turnover to get a full picture of a company's operating cycle and liquidity position.

Recognition of Liabilities

Timing is important in the recognition of liabilities. Failure to record a liability in an accounting period very often goes along with failure to record an expense. The two errors lead to an understatement of expense and an overstatement of income.

A liability is recorded when an obligation occurs. This rule is harder to apply than it might appear. When a transaction obligates a company to make future payments, a liability arises and is recognized, as when goods are bought on credit. However, current liabilities often are not represented by direct transactions. One of the key reasons for making adjusting entries at the end of an accounting period is to recognize unrecorded liabilities. Among these accrued liabilities are salaries payable and interest payable. Other liabilities that can only be estimated, such as taxes payable, must also be recognized through adjusting entries.

On the other hand, companies often enter into agreements for future transactions. For instance, a company may agree to pay an executive $50,000 a year for a period of three years, or a public utility may agree to buy an unspecified quantity of coal at a certain price over the next five years. Such contracts, though they are definite commitments, are not considered liabilities because they are for future—not past—transactions. As there is no current obligation, no liability is recognized.

Valuation of Liabilities

On the balance sheet, a liability is generally valued at the amount of money needed to pay the debt or the fair market value of goods or services to be delivered. For most liabilities the amount is definitely known, but for some it must be estimated. For example, an automobile dealer who sells a car with a one-year warranty must provide parts and service during the year. The obligation is definite because the sale of the car has occurred, but the amount of the obligation can only be estimated. Such estimates are usually based on past experience and anticipated changes in the business environment. Additional disclosures of the fair value of liabilities may be required in the notes to the financial statements, as explained below.

Classification of Liabilities

The classification of liabilities directly matches the classification of assets. **Current liabilities** are debts and obligations expected to be satisfied within one year or within the normal operating cycle, whichever is longer. Such liabilities are normally paid out of current assets or with cash generated from operations. **Long-term liabilities**, which are liabilities due beyond one year or beyond the normal operating cycle, have a different purpose. They are used to finance long-term assets, such as aircraft in the case of US Airways. The distinction between current and long-term liabilities is important because it affects the evaluation of a company's liquidity.

Disclosure of Liabilities

To explain some accounts, supplemental disclosure in the notes to the financial statements may be required. For example, if a company has a large amount of notes payable, an explanatory note may disclose the balances, maturities, interest rates, and other features of the debts. Any special credit arrangements, such as issues of commercial paper and lines of credit, should also be disclosed. For example, The Goodyear Tire & Rubber Company, which manufactures and sells tires, vehicle components, industrial rubber products, and rubber-related chemicals, disclosed its credit arrangements in the notes to the financial statements. Excerpts from that note follow:

> **Note 10. Short-Term Debt and Financing Arrangements**
> At December 31, 1999, the Company had short-term uncommitted credit arrangements totaling $2.0 billion, of which $.83 billion were unused. These arrangements are available to the Company or certain of its international subsidiaries through various international banks at quoted market interest rates. There are no commitment fees or compensating balances associated with these arrangements.
> The company had outstanding debt obligations which are due within one year amounting to $2.32 billion at December 31, 1999. Commercial paper

The company had outstanding debt obligations which are due within one year amounting to $2.32 billion at December 31, 1999. Commercial paper

and domestic short-term bank debt represented $1.46 billion of this total with a weighted average interest rate of 6.29% at December 31, 1999. . . . The remaining $.86 billion was international subsidiary short-term debt with a weighted average interest rate of 4.79% at December 31, 1999.[3]

This type of disclosure is helpful in assessing whether a company has additional borrowing power, because unused lines of credit allow a company to borrow on short notice, up to the agreed credit limit, with little or no negotiations.

Common Categories of Current Liabilities

Current liabilities fall into two major groups: (1) definitely determinable liabilities and (2) estimated liabilities.

Definitely Determinable Liabilities

OBJECTIVE

2 Identify, compute, and record definitely determinable and estimated current liabilities

Current liabilities that are set by contract or by statute and can be measured exactly are called **definitely determinable liabilities**. The related accounting problems are to determine the existence and amount of each such liability and to see that it is recorded properly. Definitely determinable liabilities include accounts payable, bank loans and commercial paper, notes payable, accrued liabilities, dividends payable, sales and excise taxes payable, current portions of long-term debt, payroll liabilities, and unearned or deferred revenues.

ACCOUNTS PAYABLE Accounts payable, sometimes called trade accounts payable, are short-term obligations to suppliers for goods and services. The amount in the Accounts Payable account is generally supported by an accounts payable subsidiary ledger, which contains an individual account for each person or company to which money is owed.

BANK LOANS AND COMMERCIAL PAPER Management will often establish a **line of credit** from a bank; this arrangement allows the company to borrow funds when they are needed to finance current operations. For example, Lowe's Companies, Inc., a large home improvement center and consumer durables company, reported in its 1999 annual report that "the company had a $300 million revolving credit facility with a syndicate of 11 banks, expiring lines of credit of $218 million . . . and $50 million available, on an unsecured basis, for the purposes of short-term borrowing."[4]

A promissory note for the full amount of the line of credit is signed when the credit is granted, but the company has great flexibility in using the available funds. The company can increase its borrowing up to the limit when it needs cash and reduce the amount borrowed when it generates enough cash of its own. Both the amount borrowed and the interest rate charged by the bank may change daily. The bank may require the company to meet certain financial goals (such as maintaining specific profit margins, current ratios, or debt to equity ratios) in order to retain the line of credit.

Figure 2
Two Promissory Notes:
One with Interest Stated
Separately; One with Interest
in Face Amount

CASE 1: INTEREST STATED SEPARATELY

Chicago, Illinois   August 31, 20xx

Sixty days after date I promise to pay First Federal Bank
the sum of $5,000 with interest at the rate of 12% per
annum.

                    Sandra Caron
                    Caron Corporation

CASE 2: INTEREST IN FACE AMOUNT

Chicago, Illinois   August 31, 20xx

Sixty days after date I promise to pay First Federal Bank
the sum of $5,000.

                    Sandra Caron
                    Caron Corporation

Companies with excellent credit ratings may borrow short-term funds by issuing **commercial paper**, unsecured loans that are sold to the public, usually through professionally managed investment firms. The portion of a line of credit currently borrowed and the amount of commercial paper issued are usually combined with notes payable in the current liabilities section of the balance sheet. Details are disclosed in a note to the financial statements.

NOTES PAYABLE Short-term notes payable, which also arise out of the ordinary course of business, are obligations represented by promissory notes. These notes may be used to secure bank loans, to pay suppliers for goods and services, and to secure credit from other sources.

The interest may be stated separately on the face of the note (Case 1 in Figure 2), or it may be deducted in advance by discounting it from the face value of the note (Case 2 in Figure 2). The entries to record the note in each case follow.

Case 1—Interest Stated Separately

Case 2—Interest in Face Amount

Case 1
A = L + OE
+   +

Aug. 31 Cash   5,000
              Notes Payable   5,000
              Issued 60-day,
              12 percent promissory
              note with interest
              stated separately

Case 2
A = L + OE
+   −
     +

Aug. 31 Cash   4,900
              Discount on Notes Payable   100
              Notes Payable   5,000
              Issued 60-day
              promissory note with
              $100 interest included
              in face amount

Note that in Case 1 the money received equaled the face value of the note, whereas in Case 2 the money received ($4,900) was less than the face value ($5,000) of the note. The discount of $100 ($5,000 × .12 × 60/360) equals the amount of the interest for 60 days. Although the dollar amount of interest on each of these notes is the same, the effective interest rate is slightly higher in Case 2 because the amount received is slightly less ($4,900 in Case 2 versus $5,000 in

Case 1). Discount on Notes Payable is a contra account to Notes Payable and is deducted from Notes Payable on the balance sheet.

On October 30, when the note is paid, each alternative is recorded as follows:

Case 1—Interest Stated Separately

Case 1
A = L + OE
−   −   −

Case 2
A = L + OE
−   −
A = L + OE
  +   −

Oct. 30	Notes Payable	5,000	
	Interest Expense	100	
	Cash		5,100
	Payment of note with interest stated separately		

$$\$5,000 \times \frac{60}{360} \times .12 = \$100$$

Case 2—Interest in Face Amount

Oct. 30	Notes Payable	5,000	
	Cash		5,000
	Payment of note with interest included in face amount		
30	Interest Expense	100	
	Discount on Notes Payable		100
	Interest expense on note payable		

ACCRUED LIABILITIES   A key reason for making adjusting entries at the end of an accounting period is to recognize and record liabilities that are not already in the accounting records. This practice applies to any type of liability. As you will see, accrued liabilities can include estimated liabilities.

Here the focus is on interest payable, a definitely determinable liability. Interest accrues daily on interest-bearing notes. At the end of the accounting period, an adjusting entry should be made in accordance with the matching rule to record the interest obligation up to that point in time. Let us again use the example of the two notes presented above. If we assume that the accounting period ends on September 30, or 30 days after the issuance of the 60-day notes, the adjusting entries for each case would be as follows:

Case 1—Interest Stated Separately

Case 1
A = L + OE
  +   −

Case 2
A = L + OE
  +   −

Sept. 30	Interest Expense	50	
	Interest Payable		50
	To record interest expense for 30 days on note with interest stated separately		

$$\$5,000 \times \frac{30}{360} \times .12 = \$50$$

Case 2—Interest in Face Amount

Sept. 30	Interest Expense	50	
	Discount on Notes Payable		50
	To record interest expense for 30 days on note with interest included in face amount		

$$\$100 \times \frac{30}{60} = \$50$$

In Case 2, Discount on Notes Payable will now have a debit balance of $50, which will become interest expense during the next 30 days.

DIVIDENDS PAYABLE   Cash dividends are a distribution of earnings by a corporation. The payment of dividends is solely the decision of the corporation's board of directors. A liability does not exist until the board declares the dividends. There is usually a short time between the date of declaration and the date of payment of dividends. During that short time, the dividends declared are considered current liabilities of the corporation.

SALES AND EXCISE TAXES PAYABLE   Most states and many cities levy a sales tax on retail transactions. There is a federal excise tax on some products, such as automobile tires. A merchant who sells goods subject to these taxes must collect the taxes and forward them periodically to the appropriate government agency. The amount of tax collected represents a current liability until it is remitted to the government. For example, assume that a merchant makes a $100 sale that is subject to a 5 percent sales tax and a 10 percent excise tax. Assuming that the sale takes place on June 1, the entry to record the sale is as follows:

A = L + OE
+   +   +
    +

June 1	Cash	115	
	Sales		100
	Sales Tax Payable		5
	Excise Tax Payable		10
	Sale of merchandise and collection of sales and excise taxes		

The sale is properly recorded at $100, and the taxes collected are recorded as liabilities to be remitted at the proper times to the appropriate government agencies.

CURRENT PORTIONS OF LONG-TERM DEBT   If a portion of long-term debt is due within the next year and is to be paid from current assets, then that current portion is properly classified as a current liability. For example, suppose that a $500,000 debt is to be paid in installments of $100,000 per year for the next five years. The $100,000 installment due in the current year should be classified as a current liability. The remaining $400,000 should be classified as a long-term liability. Note that no journal entry is necessary. The total debt of $500,000 is simply reclassified when the financial statements are prepared, as follows:

Current Liabilities	
Current Portion of Long-Term Debt	$100,000
Long-Term Liabilities	
Long-Term Debt	400,000

PAYROLL LIABILITIES   For most organizations, the cost of labor and related payroll taxes is a major expense. In some industries, such as banking and airlines, payroll costs represent more than half of all operating costs. Payroll accounting is important because complex laws and significant liabilities are involved. The employer is liable to employees for wages and salaries and to various agencies for amounts withheld from wages and salaries and for related taxes. The term **wages** refers to payment for the services of employees at an hourly rate. The term **salaries** refers to the compensation of employees who are paid at a monthly or yearly rate.

Because payroll accounting applies only to the employees of an organization, it is therefore important to distinguish between employees and independent contractors. Employees are paid a wage or salary by the organization and are under its direct supervision and control. Independent contractors are not employees of the organization, so they are not accounted for under the payroll system. They offer services to the organization for a fee, but they are not under its direct control or supervision. Some examples of independent contractors are certified public accountants, advertising agencies, and lawyers.

Figure 3 provides an illustration of payroll liabilities and their relationship to employee earnings and employer taxes and other costs. Two important observations may be made. First, the amount payable to employees is less than the amount of earnings. This occurs because employers are required by law or are requested by employees to withhold certain amounts from wages and send them directly to government agencies or other organizations. Second, the total employer liabilities exceed employee earnings because the employer must pay additional taxes and make other contributions, such as for pensions and medical care, that increase the cost and liabilities. The most common withholdings, taxes, and other payroll costs are described on page 524.

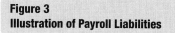

Figure 3
Illustration of Payroll Liabilities

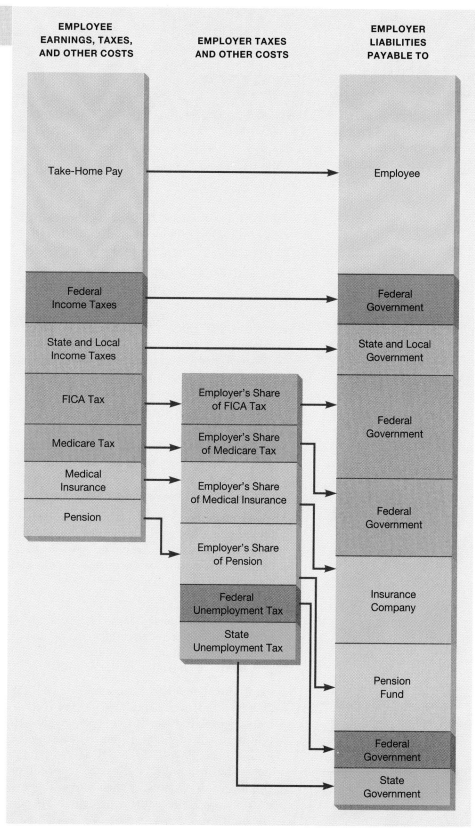

The processing of payroll is an ideal application for computers because it is a very routine and complex procedure that must be done with absolute accuracy: Employees want to be paid exactly what they are owed, and failure to pay the taxes and other costs as required can result in severe penalties and high interest charges. Consequently, many companies purchase carefully designed and tested computer software for use in preparing the payroll. Other companies do not process their own payroll but rely on outside businesses that specialize in providing such services. Many of these service suppliers, such as Automatic Data Processing, Inc., are successful and fast growing.

Federal Income Taxes Federal income taxes are collected on a "pay as you go" basis. Employers are required to withhold appropriate taxes from employees' paychecks and pay them to the United States Treasury.

State and Local Income Taxes Most states and some local governments have income taxes. In most cases, the procedures for withholding are similar to those for federal income taxes.

Social Security (FICA) Tax The social security program (the Federal Insurance Contribution Act) offers retirement and disability benefits and survivor's benefits. About 90 percent of the people working in the United States fall under the provisions of this program. The 2001 social security tax rate of 6.2 percent was paid by *both* employee and employer on the first $80,400 earned by an employee during the calendar year. Both the rate and the base to which it applies are subject to change in future years.

Medicare Tax A major extension of the social security program is Medicare, which provides hospitalization and medical insurance for persons over age 65. In 1999, the Medicare tax rate was 1.45 percent of gross income, with no limit, paid by *both* employee and employer.

Medical Insurance Many organizations provide medical benefits to employees. Often, the employee contributes a portion of the cost through withholdings from income and the employer pays the rest, usually a greater amount, to the insurance company. Some proposals for national health-care reform, if they become law, could change substantially the way medical insurance is funded and provided in this country.

Pension Contributions Many organizations also provide pension benefits to employees. In a manner similar to that for medical insurance, a portion of the pension contribution is withheld from the employee's income and the rest is paid by the organization to the pension fund.

Federal Unemployment Insurance (FUTA) Tax This tax, referred to as FUTA after the Federal Unemployment Tax Act, is intended to pay for programs to help unemployed workers. It is paid *only* by employers and recently was 6.2 percent of the first $7,000* earned by each employee. Against this federal tax, however, the employer is allowed a credit for unemployment taxes paid to the state. The maximum credit is 5.4 percent of the first $7,000 earned by each employee. Most states set their rate at this maximum. Thus, the FUTA tax most often paid is .8 percent (6.2 percent − 5.4 percent) of the taxable wages.

State Unemployment Insurance Tax All state unemployment programs provide for unemployment compensation to be paid to eligible unemployed workers.

* This amount may vary from state to state.

This compensation is paid out of the fund provided by the 5.4 percent of the first $7,000 (varies in some states) earned by each employee. In some states, employers with favorable employment records may be entitled to pay less than 5.4 percent.

To illustrate the recording of the payroll, assume that on February 15 total employee wages are $32,500, with withholdings of $5,400 for federal income taxes, $1,200 for state income taxes, $2,015 for social security tax, $471 for Medicare tax, $900 for medical insurance, and $1,300 for pension contributions. The entry to record this payroll follows:

A = L + OE				
+ −	Feb. 15	Wages Expense	32,500	
+		Employees' Federal Income Taxes Payable		5,400
+		Employees' State Income Taxes Payable		1,200
+		Social Security Tax Payable		2,015
+		Medicare Tax Payable		471
+		Medical Insurance Payable		900
+		Pension Contributions Payable		1,300
		Wages Payable		21,214
		To record payroll		

Note that the employees' take-home pay is only $21,214, although $32,500 was earned.

Using the same data, the additional employer taxes and other benefits costs would be recorded as follows, assuming that the payroll taxes correspond to the discussion above and that the employer pays 80 percent of the medical insurance premiums and half of the pension contributions:

A = L + OE				
+ −	Feb. 15	Payroll Taxes and Benefits Expense	9,401	
+		Social Security Tax Payable		2,015
+		Medicare Tax Payable		471
+		Medical Insurance Payable		3,600
+		Pension Contributions Payable		1,300
+		Federal Unemployment Tax Payable		260
		State Unemployment Tax Payable		1,755
		To record payroll taxes and other costs		

Note that the payroll taxes and benefits increase the total cost of the payroll to $41,901 ($9,401 + $32,500), which exceeds by almost 29 percent the amount earned by employees. This is a typical situation.

UNEARNED REVENUES   **Unearned revenues** represent obligations for goods or services that the company must provide or deliver in a future accounting period in return for an advance payment from a customer. For example, a publisher of a monthly magazine who receives annual subscriptions totaling $240 would make the following entry:

A = L + OE			
+ +	Cash	240	
	Unearned Subscriptions		240
	Receipt of annual subscriptions in advance		

The publisher now has a liability of $240 that will be reduced gradually as monthly issues of the magazine are mailed.

A = L + OE			
− +	Unearned Subscriptions	20	
	Subscription Revenues		20
	Delivery of monthly magazine issues		

Many businesses, such as repair companies, construction companies, and special-order firms, ask for a deposit or advance from a customer before they will begin work. Such advances are also current liabilities until the goods or services are actually delivered.

Estimated Liabilities

Estimated liabilities are definite debts or obligations of which the exact dollar amount cannot be known until a later date. Since there is no doubt about the existence of the legal obligation, the primary accounting problem is to estimate and record the amount of the liability. Examples of estimated liabilities are income taxes, property taxes, product warranties, and vacation pay.

INCOME TAXES   The income of a corporation is taxed by the federal government, most state governments, and some cities and towns. The amount of income taxes liability depends on the results of operations. Often the results are not known until after the end of the year. However, because income taxes are an expense in the year in which income is earned, an adjusting entry is necessary to record the estimated tax liability. The entry is as follows:

$A = L + OE$	Dec. 31	Income Taxes Expense	53,000	
+ −		Estimated Income Taxes Payable		53,000
		To record estimated federal income taxes		

Sole proprietorships and partnerships do *not* pay income taxes. Their owners must report their share of the firm's income on their individual tax returns.

PROPERTY TAX PAYABLE   Property taxes are levied on real property, such as land and buildings, and on personal property, such as inventory and equipment. Property taxes are a main source of revenue for local governments. They are usually assessed annually against the property involved. Because the fiscal years of local governments and their assessment dates rarely correspond to a firm's fiscal year, it is necessary to estimate the amount of property tax that applies to each month of the year. Assume, for instance, that a local government has a fiscal year of July 1 to June 30, that its assessment date is November 1 for the current fiscal year, and that its payment date is December 15. Assume also that on July 1, Janis Corporation estimates that its property tax assessment for the coming year will be $24,000. The adjusting entry to be made on July 31, which would be repeated on August 31, September 30, and October 31, would be as follows:

A = L + OE   July 31   Property Tax Expense   2,000
   +   −   Estimated Property Tax Payable   2,000
                  To record estimated property tax
                  expense for the month
                  $24,000 ÷ 12 months = $2,000

On November 1, the firm receives a property tax bill for $24,720. The estimate that was made in July was too low. The charge should have been $2,060 per month. Because the difference between the actual assessment and the estimate is small, the company decides to absorb in November the amount undercharged in the previous four months. Therefore, the property tax expense for November is $2,300 [$2,060 + 4($60)] and is recorded as follows:

A = L + OE   Nov. 30   Property Tax Expense   2,300
   +   −   Estimated Property Tax Payable   2,300
                  To record estimated property tax

The Estimated Property Tax Payable account now has a balance of $10,300. The entry to record payment on December 15 would be as follows:

A = L + OE   Dec. 15   Estimated Property Tax Payable   10,300
 + −   Prepaid Property Tax   14,420
 −   Cash   24,720
                  Payment of property tax

Beginning December 31 and each month afterward until June 30, property tax expense is recorded by a debit to Property Tax Expense and a credit to Prepaid Property Tax in the amount of $2,060. The total of these seven entries will reduce the Prepaid Property Tax account to zero on June 30.

PRODUCT WARRANTY LIABILITY   When a firm places a warranty or guarantee on its product at the time of sale, a liability exists for the length of the warranty. The cost of the warranty is properly debited to an expense account in the period of sale because it is a feature of the product or service sold and thus is included in the price paid by the customer for the product. On the basis of experience, it should be possible to estimate the amount the warranty will cost in the future. Some products or services will require little warranty service; others may require much. Thus, there will be an average cost per product or service.

For example, assume that a muffler company guarantees that it will replace free of charge any muffler it sells that fails during the time the buyer owns the car. The company charges a small service fee for replacing the muffler. This guarantee is an important selling feature for the firm's mufflers. In the past, 6 percent of the mufflers sold have been returned for replacement under the guarantee. The average cost of a muffler is $25. Assume that during July, 350 mufflers were sold. The accrued liability would be recorded as an adjustment at the end of July as shown below:

A = L + OE   July 31   Product Warranty Expense   525
   +   −   Estimated Product Warranty Liability   525
                  To record estimated product
                  warranty expense:
                  Number of units sold   350
                  Rate of replacement under warranty   × .06
                  Estimated units to be replaced   21
                  Estimated cost per unit   ×$ 25
                  Estimated liability for product warranty $525

When a muffler is returned for replacement under the warranty, the cost of the muffler is charged against the Estimated Product Warranty Liability account. For example, assume that on December 5 a customer returns with a defective muffler and pays a $10 service fee to have the muffler replaced. Assume that this particular muffler cost $20. The entry is as follows:

A = L + OE	Dec. 5	Cash	10	
+ − +		Estimated Product Warranty Liability	20	
−		Service Revenue		10
		Merchandise Inventory		20
		Replacement of muffler under warranty		

VACATION PAY LIABILITY   In most companies, employees earn the right to paid vacation days or weeks as they work during the year. For example, an employee may earn two weeks of paid vacation for each 50 weeks of work. Therefore, the person is paid 52 weeks' salary for 50 weeks' work. Theoretically, the cost of the two weeks' vacation should be allocated as an expense over the whole year so that month-to-month costs will not be distorted. The vacation pay represents 4 percent (two weeks' vacation divided by 50 weeks) of a worker's pay. Every week worked earns the employee a small fraction (4 percent) for vacation pay.

Vacation pay liability can amount to a substantial amount of money. For example, in its annual report Delta Air Lines, Inc., reported at its 1999 year end a vacation pay liability of $470 million.[6]

Suppose that a company with a vacation policy of two weeks of paid vacation for each 50 weeks of work has a payroll of $21,000, of which $1,000 was paid to employees on vacation for the week ended April 20. Because of turnover and rules regarding term of employment, not every employee in the company will collect vacation pay, and so it is assumed that 75 percent of employees will ultimately collect vacation pay. The computation of vacation pay expense based on the payroll of employees not on vacation ($21,000 − $1,000) is as follows: $20,000 × 4 percent × 75 percent = $600. The entry to record vacation pay expense for the week ended April 20 is as follows:

A = L + OE	Apr. 20	Vacation Pay Expense	600	
+ −		Estimated Liability for Vacation Pay		600
		Estimated vacation pay expense		

At the time employees receive their vacation pay, an entry is made debiting Estimated Liability for Vacation Pay and crediting Cash or Wages Payable. For

FOCUS ON BUSINESS PRACTICE

In the early 1980s, American Airlines, Inc., developed a frequent-flier program that gave free trips and other awards to customers based on the number of miles they flew on the airline. Since then, the number of similar programs by other airlines has mushroomed, and it is estimated that 38 million people now belong to airlines' frequent-flier programs. Today, U.S. airlines have more than 3 trillion miles outstanding. Seven to eight percent of all passengers are traveling on free tickets. Estimated liabilities for these tickets have become an important consideration in evaluating an airline's financial position. Complicating the estimate is that almost half the "miles" have been earned on purchases from hotel, car rental, and telephone companies and from the use of credit cards. In the latter cases, the companies giving the miles must pay the airlines at the rate of $.02 per mile. Thus, a free ticket obtained with 25,000 miles provides revenue to the airline of $500.[7]

example, the entry to record the $1,000 paid to employees on vacation during August is as follows:

A* = L + OE
— —
*Assumes cash paid.

Aug. 31	Estimated Liability for Vacation Pay	1,000	
	Cash (or Wages Payable)		1,000
	Wages of employees on vacation		

The treatment of vacation pay presented in this example may also be applied to other payroll costs, such as bonus plans and contributions to pension plans.

Contingent Liabilities

OBJECTIVE
3 Define *contingent liability*

A **contingent liability** is not an existing liability. Rather, it is a potential liability because it depends on a future event arising out of a past transaction. For instance, a construction company that built a bridge may have been sued by the state for using poor materials. The past transaction is the building of the bridge under contract. The future event is the outcome of the lawsuit, which is not yet known.

Two conditions have been established by the FASB for determining when a contingency should be entered in the accounting records: (1) the liability must be probable and (2) it must be reasonably estimated.[8] Estimated liabilities such as the estimated income taxes liability, warranty liability, and vacation pay liability that were described earlier meet those conditions. Therefore, they are accrued in the accounting records. Potential liabilities that do not meet both conditions (probable and reasonably estimated) are reported in the notes to the financial statements. Losses from such potential liabilities are recorded when the conditions set by the FASB are met.

According to a survey of 600 large companies, the most common types of contingencies reported were litigation, which can involve many different issues, and environmental concerns.[9] The following example of contingent liabilities comes from the notes in the annual report of General Motors Corp., the world's largest automobile manufacturer:

> GM is subject to potential liability under government regulations and various claims and legal actions which are pending or may be asserted against them. Some of the pending actions purport to be class actions. The aggregate ultimate liability of GM under these government regulations and under these claims and actions, was not determinable at December 31, 1999. After discussion with counsel, it is the opinion of management that such liability is not expected to have a material adverse effect on the Corporation's consolidated financial statements.[10]

Payroll Accounting Illustrated

SUPPLEMENTAL OBJECTIVE
4 Compute and record the liabilities associated with payroll accounting

Earlier in this chapter, the liabilities associated with payroll accounting were identified and discussed. This section will focus on the calculations, records, and control requirements of payroll accounting. To demonstrate the concepts, the illustrations are shown in manual format, but, in actual practice, most businesses (including small businesses) use a computer to process payroll.

Computation of an Employee's Take-Home Pay

Besides setting minimum wage levels, the federal Fair Labor Standards Act (also called the Wages and Hours Law) regulates overtime pay. Employers who take part in interstate commerce must pay overtime to employees who work beyond 40 hours a week or more than eight hours a day. This pay must be at least one and one-half times the regular rate. Work on Saturdays, Sundays, or holidays may also call for overtime pay or some sort of premium pay under separate wage agreements. Overtime pay under union or other employment contracts may exceed these minimums.

For example, suppose that the employment contract of Robert Jones calls for a regular wage of $8 an hour, one and one-half times the regular rate for work over eight hours in any weekday, and twice the regular rate for work on Saturdays, Sundays, or holidays. He works the following days and hours during the week of January 18, 20xx:

Day	Total Hours Worked	Regular Time	Overtime
Monday	10	8	2
Tuesday	8	8	0
Wednesday	8	8	0
Thursday	9	8	1
Friday	10	8	2
Saturday	2	0	2
	47	40	7

Jones's wages would be calculated as follows:

Regular time	40 hours × $8	$320
Overtime, weekdays	5 hours × $8 × 1.5	60
Overtime, weekend	2 hours × $8 × 2	32
Total wages		$412

Once Jones's wages are known, his take-home pay can be calculated. Since his total earnings for the week of January 18 are $412.00, his social security tax is 6.2 percent, or $25.54 (he has not earned over $80,400), and his Medicare tax is 1.45 percent, or $5.97. The amount to be withheld for federal income taxes depends in part on Jones's earnings and in part on the number of his exemptions. All employees are required by law to indicate exemptions by filing a Form W-4 (Employee's Withholding Exemption Certificate). Every employee is entitled to one exemption for himself or herself and one for each dependent.

Based on the information in the Form W-4, the amount of withholding is determined by referring to a withholding table provided by the Internal Revenue Service. For example, the withholding table in Figure 4 shows that for Jones, a married employee who has a total of four exemptions and is paid weekly, the withholding on total wages of $412 is $31. Actual withholding tables change periodically to reflect changes in tax rates and tax laws. Assume also that Jones's union dues are $2.00, his medical insurance premiums are $7.60, his life insurance premium is $6.00, he places $15.00 per week in savings bonds, and he contributes $1.00 per week to United Charities.

Jones's net (take-home) pay can now be computed as follows:

	WEEKLY PAYROLL PERIOD—EMPLOYEE MARRIED										
	And the number of withholding allowances claimed is —										
And the wages are —	0	1	2	3	4	5	6	7	8	9	10 or more
At least — But less than	The amount of income tax to be withheld will be —										
$300 — $310	$37	$31	$26	$20	$14	$9	$3	$0	$0	$0	$0
310 — 320	38	33	27	22	16	10	5	0	0	0	0
320 — 330	40	34	29	23	17	12	6	1	0	0	0
330 — 340	41	36	30	25	19	13	8	2	0	0	0
340 — 350	43	37	32	26	20	15	9	4	0	0	0
350 — 360	44	39	33	28	22	16	11	5	0	0	0
360 — 370	46	40	35	29	23	18	12	7	1	0	0
370 — 380	47	42	36	31	25	19	14	8	2	0	0
380 — 390	49	43	38	32	26	21	15	10	4	0	0
390 — 400	50	45	39	34	28	22	17	11	5	0	0
400 — 410	52	46	41	35	29	24	18	13	7	1	0
410 — 420	53	48	42	37	31	25	20	14	8	3	0
420 — 430	55	49	44	38	32	27	21	16	10	4	0

Figure 4
Sample Withholding Table

Total earnings		$412.00
Deductions		
Federal income taxes withheld	$31.00	
Social security tax	25.54	
Medicare tax	5.97	
Union dues	2.00	
Medical insurance	7.60	
Life insurance	6.00	
Savings bonds	15.00	
United Charities contribution	1.00	
Total deductions		94.11
Net (take-home) pay		$317.89

Payroll Register

The **payroll register**, which is prepared each pay period, is a detailed listing of the firm's total payroll. A payroll register is presented in Exhibit 1. Note that the name, hours, earnings, deductions, and net pay of each employee are listed. Compare the entry for Robert Jones in the payroll register with the January 18 entry in the employee earnings record of Robert Jones presented in Exhibit 2. Except for the first column, which lists the employee names, and the last two columns, which show the wage or salary as either sales or office expense, the columns are the same. The columns help employers record the payroll in the accounting records and meet legal reporting requirements. The last two columns in Exhibit 1 are needed to divide the expenses in the accounting records into selling and administrative categories.

Exhibit 1
Payroll Register

		Earnings			Deductions								Payment		Distribution	
Employee	Total Hours	Regular	Overtime	Gross	Federal Income Taxes	Social Security Tax	Medicare Tax	Union Dues	Medical Insurance	Life Insurance	Savings Bonds	Other: A—United Charities	Net Earnings	Check No.	Sales Wages Expense	Office Wages Expense
Linda Duval	40	160.00		160.00	11.00	9.92	2.32		5.80				130.96	923		160.00
John Franks	44	160.00	24.00	184.00	14.00	11.41	2.67	2.00	7.60			A 10.00	136.32	924	184.00	
Samuel Goetz	40	400.00		400.00	53.00	24.80	5.80		10.40	14.00		A 3.00	289.00	925	400.00	
Robert Jones	47	320.00	92.00	412.00	31.00	25.54	5.97	2.00	7.60	6.00	15.00	A 1.00	317.89	926	412.00	
Billie Matthews	40	160.00		160.00	14.00	9.92	2.32		5.80				127.96	927		160.00
Rosaire O'Brien	42	200.00	20.00	220.00	22.00	13.64	3.19	2.00	5.80				173.37	928	220.00	
James Van Dyke	40	200.00		200.00	20.00	12.40	2.90		5.80				158.90	929		200.00
		1,600.00	136.00	1,736.00	165.00	107.63	25.17	6.00	48.80	20.00	15.00	14.00	1,334.40		1,216.00	520.00

Exhibit 2
Employee Earnings Record

Employee Earnings Record

Employee's Name Robert Jones   **Social Security Number** 444-66-9999

Address 777 20th Street   **Sex** Male   **Employee No.** 705

Marshall, Michigan 52603   **Single** ____ **Married** X   **Weekly Pay Rate** ____

Date of Birth September 20, 1962   **Exemptions (W-4)** 4   **Hourly Rate** $8

Position Sales Assistant   **Date of Employment** July 15, 1988   **Date Employment Ended** ____

20xx		Earnings			Deductions								Payment		
Period Ended	Total Hours	Regular	Overtime	Gross	Federal Income Taxes	Social Security Tax	Medicare Tax	Union Dues	Medical Insurance	Life Insurance	Savings Bonds	Other: A—United Charities	Net Earnings	Check No.	Cumulative Gross Earnings
Jan 4	40	320.00	0	320.00	17.00	19.84	4.64	2.00	7.60	6.00	15.00	A 1.00	246.92	717	320.00
11	44	320.00	48.00	368.00	23.00	22.82	5.34	2.00	7.60	6.00	15.00	A 1.00	285.24	822	688.00
18	47	320.00	92.00	412.00	31.00	25.54	5.97	2.00	7.60	6.00	15.00	A 1.00	317.89	926	1,100.00

Recording the Payroll

The journal entry for recording the payroll is based on the column totals from the payroll register. The journal entry to record the January 18 payroll follows. Note that each account debited or credited is a total from the payroll register. If the payroll register is considered a special-purpose journal, the column totals can be posted directly to the ledger accounts, with the correct account numbers shown at the bottom of each column.

	Jan. 18	Sales Wages Expense	1,216.00	
A = L + OE		Office Wages Expense	520.00	
+ −		Employees' Federal Income Taxes Payable		165.00
+		Social Security Tax Payable		107.63
+		Medicare Tax Payable		25.17
+		Union Dues Payable		6.00
+		Medical Insurance Premiums Payable		48.80
+		Life Insurance Premiums Payable		20.00
+		Savings Bonds Payable		15.00
		United Charities Payable		14.00
		Wages Payable		1,334.40
		To record payroll		

Employee Earnings Record

Each employer must keep a record of earnings and withholdings for each employee. Most companies today use computers to maintain such records, but some small companies may still use manual records. The manual form of **employee earnings record** for Robert Jones is shown in Exhibit 2. This form is designed to help the employer meet legal reporting requirements. Each deduction must be shown to have been paid to the proper agency, and the employee must receive a report of the deductions made each year.

Most of the columns in Exhibit 2 are self-explanatory. Note, however, the column on the far right for cumulative gross earnings (total earnings to date). This record helps the employer comply with the rule of applying social security and unemployment taxes only up to the maximum wage levels. At the end of the year, the employer reports to the employee on Form W-2, the Wage and Tax Statement, the total earnings and tax deductions for the year, which the employee uses to complete his or her individual tax return. The employer sends a copy of the W-2 to the Internal Revenue Service. Thus, the IRS can check whether the employee has reported all income earned from that employer.

Recording Payroll Taxes

According to Exhibit 1, the gross payroll for the week ended January 18 was $1,736.00. Because it was the first month of the year, all employees had accumulated less than the $80,400 and $7,000 maximum taxable salaries. Therefore, the total social security tax was $107.63 and the total Medicare tax was $25.17 (equal to the tax on employees), the total FUTA tax was $13.89 (.008 × $1,736.00), and the total state unemployment tax was $93.74 (.054 × $1,736.00). The entry to record this expense and related liability is as follows:

A = L + OE	Jan. 18	Payroll Taxes Expense	240.43	
+		Social Security Tax Payable		107.63
+ −		Medicare Tax Payable		25.17
+		Federal Unemployment Tax Payable		13.89
		State Unemployment Tax Payable		93.74
		To record payroll taxes		

Payment of Payroll and Payroll Taxes

After the weekly payroll is recorded, as illustrated earlier, a liability of $1,334.40 exists for wages payable. How this liability will be paid depends on the system used by the company. Many companies use a special payroll account against which payroll checks are drawn. Under this system, a check for total net earnings for this payroll ($1,334.40) must be drawn on the regular checking account and deposited in the special payroll account before the payroll checks are issued to the employees. If a voucher system is combined with a special payroll account, a voucher for the total wages payable is prepared and recorded in the voucher register as a debit to Payroll Bank Account and a credit to Vouchers Payable.

The combined social security and Medicare taxes (both employees' and employer's shares) and the federal income taxes must be paid at least quarterly. More frequent payments are required when the total liability exceeds $500. The federal unemployment insurance tax is paid yearly if the amount is less than $100. If the liability for the federal unemployment insurance tax exceeds $100 at the end of any quarter, a payment is necessary. Payment dates vary among the states. Other payroll deductions must be paid in accordance with the particular contracts or agreements involved.

Chapter Review

REVIEW OF LEARNING OBJECTIVES

↑
Check out ACE, a self-quizzing program on chapter content, at http://college.hmco.com.

1. **Identify the management issues related to recognition, valuation, classification, and disclosure of current liabilities.** Liabilities represent present legal obligations for future payment of assets or future performance of services. They result from past transactions and should be recognized when there is a transaction that obligates the company to make future payments. Liabilities are valued at the amount of money necessary to satisfy the obligation or the fair value of goods or services that must be delivered. Liabilities are classified as current or long term. Supplemental disclosure is required when the nature or details of the obligations would help in understanding the liability. Liabilities are an important consideration in assessing a company's liquidity. Key measures are working capital, payables turnover, and average days' payable.

2. **Identify, compute, and record definitely determinable and estimated current liabilities.** Two principal categories of current liabilities are definitely determinable liabilities and estimated liabilities. Although definitely determinable liabilities, such as accounts payable, notes payable, dividends payable, accrued liabilities, and the current portion of long-term debt, can be measured exactly, the accountant must still be careful not to overlook existing liabilities in these categories. Estimated liabilities, such as liabilities for income taxes, prop-

erty taxes, and product warranties, definitely exist, but the amounts must be estimated and recorded properly.

3. **Define** *contingent liability.* A contingent liability is a potential liability arising from a past transaction and dependent on a future event. Examples are lawsuits, income tax disputes, discounted notes receivable, guarantees of debt, and failure to follow government regulations.

**SUPPLEMENTAL
OBJECTIVE**

4. **Compute and record the liabilities associated with payroll accounting.** Computations for payroll liabilities must be made for the compensation to each employee, for withholdings from each employee's total pay, and for the employer's portion of payroll taxes. The salary and deductions for each employee are recorded each pay period in the payroll register. From the payroll register, the details of each employee's earnings are transferred to the employee's earnings record. The column totals of the payroll register are used to prepare an entry that records the payroll and accompanying liabilities. The employer's share of social security and Medicare taxes and the federal and state unemployment taxes as well as any liabilities for other fringe benefits must then be recorded.

**REVIEW OF
CONCEPTS AND
TERMINOLOGY**

The following concepts and terms were introduced in this chapter:

LO 1 **Average days' payable:** How long, on average, a company takes to pay its accounts payable; 365 days divided by payables turnover.

LO 2 **Commercial paper:** A means of borrowing short-term funds by using unsecured loans that are sold directly to the public, usually through professionally managed investment firms.

LO 3 **Contingent liability:** A potential liability that depends on a future event arising out of a past transaction.

LO 1 **Current liabilities:** Debts and obligations expected to be satisfied within one year or within the normal operating cycle, whichever is longer.

LO 2 **Definitely determinable liabilities:** Current liabilities that are set by contract or by statute and can be measured exactly.

SO 4 **Employee earnings record:** A record of earnings and withholdings for an individual employee.

LO 2 **Estimated liabilities:** Definite debts or obligations of which the exact amounts cannot be known until a later date.

LO 1 **Liabilities:** Legal obligations for the future payment of assets or the future performance of services that result from past transactions.

LO 2 **Line of credit:** A preapproved arrangement with a commercial bank that allows a company to borrow funds as needed.

LO 1 **Long-term liabilities:** Debts or obligations due beyond one year or beyond the normal operating cycle.

LO 1 **Payables turnover:** Number of times on average that accounts payable are paid in an accounting period; cost of goods sold plus (or minus) change in merchandise inventory divided by average accounts payable.

SO 4 **Payroll register:** A detailed listing of a firm's total payroll that is prepared each pay period.

LO 2 **Salaries:** Compensation to employees who are paid at a monthly or yearly rate.

LO 2 **Unearned revenues:** Revenues received in advance for which the goods will not be delivered or the services performed during the current accounting period.

LO 2 **Wages:** Payment for services of employees at an hourly rate.

REVIEW PROBLEM

LO 2

Notes Payable Transactions and End-of-Period Entries

McLaughlin, Inc., whose fiscal year ends June 30, 20xx, completed the following transactions involving notes payable.

May 11 Purchased a small crane by issuing a 60-day, 12 percent note for $54,000. The face of the note does not include interest.

16 Obtained a $40,000 bank loan to finance a temporary increase in receivables by signing a 90-day, 10 percent note. The face value includes interest.

June 30 Made the end-of-year adjusting entry to accrue interest expense.

30 Made the end-of-year adjusting entry to recognize discount expired on the note.

30 Made the end-of-year closing entry pertaining to interest expense.

July 10 Paid the note plus interest on the crane purchase.

Aug. 14 Paid off the note to the bank.

REQUIRED

Prepare entries in journal form for the above transactions.

ANSWER TO REVIEW PROBLEM

20xx

May 11	Equipment		54,000	
	Notes Payable			54,000
	Purchase of crane with 60-day, 12 percent note			
16	Cash		39,000	
	Discount on Notes Payable		1,000	
	Notes Payable			40,000
	Loan from bank obtained by signing 90-day, 10 percent note; discount equals $40,000 \times .10 \times 90 \div 360 = \$1,000$			
June 30	Interest Expense		900	
	Interest Payable			900
	To accrue interest expense $\$54,000 \times .12 \times 50 \div 360 = \$900$			
30	Interest Expense		500	
	Discount on Notes Payable			500
	To recognize interest on note $\$1,000 \times 45 \div 90 = \$500$			
30	Income Summary		1,400	
	Interest Expense			1,400
	To close interest expense			
July 10	Notes Payable		54,000	
	Interest Payable		900	
	Interest Expense		180	
	Cash			55,080
	Payment of note on equipment $\$54,000 \times .12 \times 60 \div 360 = \$1,080$			
Aug. 14	Notes Payable		40,000	
	Cash			40,000
	Payment of bank loan			
14	Interest Expense		500	
	Discount on Notes Payable			500
	Interest expense on matured note $\$1,000 - \$500 = \$500$			

Chapter Assignments

QUESTIONS

1. What are liabilities?
2. Why is the timing of liability recognition important in accounting?
3. At the end of the accounting period, Janson Company had a legal obligation to accept delivery of and pay for a truckload of hospital supplies the following week. Is this legal obligation a liability?
4. Ned Johnson, a star college basketball player, received a contract from the Midwest Blazers to play professional basketball. The contract calls for a salary of $300,000 a year for four years, dependent on his making the team in each of those years. Should this contract be considered a liability and recorded on the books of the basketball team?
5. What is the rule for classifying a liability as current?
6. What are a line of credit and commercial paper? Where do they appear on the balance sheet?
7. A bank is offering Diane Wedge two alternatives for borrowing $2,000. The first alternative is a 30-day, 12 percent, $2,000 note. The second alternative is a 30-day, $2,000 note discounted at 12 percent. (a) What entries are required by Diane Wedge to record the two loans? (b) What entries are needed by Wedge to record the payment of the two loans? (c) Which alternative favors Wedge, and why?
8. Where should the Discount on Notes Payable account appear on the balance sheet?
9. When can a portion of long-term debt be classified as a current liability?
10. What are three types of employer-related payroll liabilities?
11. How does an employee differ from an independent contractor?
12. Who pays social security and Medicare taxes?
13. Why are unearned revenues classified as liabilities?
14. What is definite about an estimated liability?
15. Why are income taxes payable considered to be estimated liabilities?
16. When does a company incur a liability for a product warranty?
17. What is a contingent liability, and how does it differ from an estimated liability?
18. What are some examples of contingent liabilities? For what reason is each a contingent liability?
19. What role does the W-4 form play in determining the withholding for estimated federal income taxes?
20. How can the payroll register be used as a special-purpose journal?
21. Why is an employee earnings record necessary, and how does it relate to the W-2 form?

SHORT EXERCISES

SE 1.

LO 1 Issues in Accounting for Liabilities

Indicate whether each of the following actions relates to (a) managing liquidity and cash flow, (b) recognition of liabilities, (c) valuation of liabilities, (d) classification of liabilities, or (e) disclosure of liabilities.

1. Determining that a liability will be paid in less than one year
2. Estimating the amount of a liability
3. Providing information about when liabilities are due and the interest rate that they carry
4. Determining when a liability arises
5. Assessing working capital and payables turnover

SE 2.

LO 1 **Measuring Short-Term Liquidity**

Turnbow Company has current assets of $130,000 and current liabilities of $80,000, of which accounts payable are $70,000. Turnbow's cost of goods sold is $460,000, its merchandise inventory increased by $20,000, and accounts payable were $50,000 the prior year. Calculate Turnbow's working capital, payables turnover, and average days' payable.

SE 3.

LO 2 **Types of Liabilities**
LO 3

Indicate whether each of the following is (a) a definitely determinable liability, (b) an estimated liability, or (c) a contingent liability.

1. Dividends Payable
2. Pending litigation
3. Income Taxes Payable
4. Current portion of long-term debt
5. Vacation Pay Liability
6. Guaranteed loans of another company

SE 4.

LO 2 **Interest Expense: Interest Not Included in Face Value of Note**

On the last day of August, Gross Company borrowed $60,000 on a bank note for 60 days at 10 percent interest. Assume that interest is stated separately. Prepare the following entries in journal form: (1) August 31, recording of note; and (2) October 30, payment of note plus interest.

SE 5.

LO 2 **Interest Expense: Interest Included in Face Value of Note**

Assume the same facts as in **SE 4,** except that interest of $1,000 is included in the face amount of the note and the note is discounted at the bank on August 31. Prepare the following entries in journal form: (1) August 31, recording of note; and (2) October 30, payment of note and recording of interest expense.

SE 6.

LO 2 **Payroll Entries**

The following payroll totals for the month of April were taken from the payroll register of Coover Corporation: salaries, $223,000.00; federal income taxes withheld, $31,440.00; social security tax withheld, $13,826.00; Medicare tax withheld, $3,233.50; medical insurance deductions, $6,580.00; and salaries subject to unemployment taxes, $156,600.00. Prepare journal entries to record (1) the monthly payroll and (2) employer's payroll expense, assuming social security and Medicare taxes equal to the amounts for employees, a federal unemployment insurance tax of .8 percent, a state unemployment tax of 5.4 percent, and medical insurance premiums for which the employer pays 80 percent of the cost.

SE 7.

LO 2 **Product Warranty Liability**

Rainbow Corp. manufactures and sells travel clocks. Each clock costs $25 to produce and sells for $50. In addition, each clock carries a warranty that provides for free replacement if it fails during the two years following the sale. In the past, 5 percent of the clocks sold have had to be replaced under the warranty. During October, Rainbow sold 52,000 clocks, and 2,800 clocks were replaced under the warranty. Prepare journal entries to record the estimated liability for product warranties during the month and the clocks replaced under warranty during the month.

SE 8.

LO 2 **Vacation Pay Liability**

The employees of Chan Services receive two weeks of paid vacation each year. Seventy percent of the employees qualify for vacation. Assuming the September payroll is $150,000, including $12,000 paid to employees on vacation, how much is the vacation pay expense for September? What is the ending balance of the Estimated Liability for Vacation Pay account, assuming a beginning balance of $16,000?

SE 9.

SO 4 **Payroll Taxes**

Kristof Company and its employees are subject to a 6.2 percent social security tax on wages up to $80,400 and a 1.45 percent Medicare tax with no limit. The company is subject to a 5.4 percent state unemployment tax and a .8 percent federal unemployment tax up to $7,000 per employee. The company has two employees: A. Burns, who has cumulative earnings of $81,000 and earned $7,000 in the month of December, and C. Dunn, who has cumulative earnings of $5,000 and earned $1,000 during December. Compute the total payroll taxes for the employees and the employer for December.

SE 10.

SO 4 **Payroll Earnings, Withholdings, and Taxes**

Last week, Manuel Kardo worked 44 hours. He is paid $10 per hour and receives one and one-half times his regular rate for hours worked over 40. Kardo has withholdings of $45 for federal income taxes, $10 for state income taxes, $23 for health insurance, 6.2 percent for social security tax, and 1.45 percent for Medicare tax. Compute Kardo's take-home pay. Also compute the total cost of Kardo to his employer, assuming that Kardo's cumulative wages are over the limit for unemployment taxes and that the company makes a health-care contribution of $75.

EXERCISES

E 1.
LO 1 Issues in Accounting for Liabilities

Indicate whether each of the following actions relates to (a) managing liquidity and cash flows, (b) recognition of liabilities, (c) valuation of liabilities, (d) classification of liabilities, or (e) disclosure of liabilities.

1. Setting a liability at the fair market value of goods to be delivered
2. Relating the payment date of a liability to the length of the operating cycle
3. Recording a liability in accordance with the matching rule
4. Providing information about financial instruments on the balance sheet
5. Estimating the amount of "cents-off" coupons that will be redeemed
6. Categorizing a liability as long-term debt
7. Measuring working capital
8. Comparing average days' payable with last year

E 2.
LO 1 Measuring Short-Term Liquidity

In 20x1, Rady Company had current assets of $310,000 and current liabilities of $200,000, of which accounts payable were $130,000. Cost of goods sold was $850,000, merchandise inventory increased by $40,000, and accounts payable were $110,000 in the prior year. In 20x2, Rady Company had current assets of $420,000 and current liabilities of $320,000, of which accounts payable were $150,000. Cost of goods sold was $950,000 and merchandise inventory decreased by $30,000. Calculate Rady's working capital, payables turnover, and average days' payable for 20x1 and 20x2. Assess Rady's liquidity and cash flows in relation to the change in payables turnover from 20x1 to 20x2.

E 3.
LO 2 Interest Expense: Interest Not Included in Face Value of Note

On the last day of October, Thespian Company borrows $30,000 on a bank note for 60 days at 12 percent interest. Assume that interest is not included in the face amount. Prepare the following entries in journal form: (1) October 31, recording of note; (2) November 30, accrual of interest expense; and (3) December 30, payment of note plus interest.

E 4.
LO 2 Interest Expense: Interest Included in Face Value of Note

Assume the same facts as in **E 3,** except that interest is included in the face amount of the note and the note is discounted at the bank on October 31. Prepare the following entries in journal form: (1) October 31, recording of note; (2) November 30, recognition of interest accrued on note; and (3) December 30, payment of note and recording of interest expense.

E 5.
LO 2 Sales and Excise Taxes

Quick Dial Service billed its customers a total of $980,400 for the month of August, including 9 percent federal excise tax and 5 percent sales tax.

1. Determine the proper amount of service revenue to report for the month.
2. Prepare an entry in journal form to record the revenue and related liabilities for the month.

E 6.
LO 2 Payroll Entries

At the end of October, the payroll register for Echo Tool and Die Corporation contained the following totals: wages, $185,500; federal income taxes withheld, $47,442; state income taxes withheld, $7,818; social security tax withheld, $11,501; Medicare tax withheld, $2,689.75; medical insurance deductions, $6,435; and wages subject to unemployment taxes, $28,620.

Prepare entries in journal form to record the (1) monthly payroll and (2) employer payroll expenses, assuming social security and Medicare taxes equal to the amount for employees, a federal unemployment insurance tax of .8 percent, a state unemployment tax of 5.4 percent, and medical insurance premiums for which the employer pays 80 percent of the cost.

E 7.
LO 2 Product Warranty Liability

Ziggy Company manufactures and sells electronic games. Each game costs $25 to produce and sells for $45. In addition, each game carries a warranty that provides for free replacement if it fails during the two years following the sale. In the past, 7 percent of the games sold had to be replaced under the warranty. During July, Ziggy sold 26,000 games and 2,800 games were replaced under the warranty.

1. Prepare an entry in journal form to record the estimated liability for product warranties during the month.

2. Prepare an entry in journal form to record the games replaced under warranty during the month.

E 8.

LO 2   Vacation Pay Liability

Rochester Corporation currently allows each employee who has worked at the company for one year three weeks' paid vacation. Based on studies of employee turnover and previous experience, management estimates that 65 percent of the employees will qualify for vacation pay this year.

1. Assume that Rochester's July payroll is $600,000, of which $40,000 is paid to employees on vacation. Figure the estimated employee vacation benefit for the month.

2. Prepare an entry in journal form to record Rochester Corporation's employee benefit for July.

3. Prepare an entry in journal form to record Rochester Corporation's pay to employees on vacation.

E 9.

LO 2   Property Tax Liability

Sarro Corporation prepares monthly financial statements and ends its fiscal year on June 30, the same as the local government. In July 20x1, your first month as accountant for the company, you find that the company has not previously accrued estimated liabilities. In the past, the company, which has a large property tax bill, has charged the property tax to the month in which the bill is paid. The tax bill for the year ended June 30, 20x1, was $72,000, and it is estimated that the tax will increase by 8 percent for the year ending June 30, 20x2. The tax bill is usually received on September 1, to be paid November 1.

Figure the proper monthly charge to property tax expense and prepare entries in journal form for the following:

July   31   Accrual of property tax expense
Aug. 31   Accrual of property tax expense
Sept. 30   Accrual of property tax expense (assume the actual bill is $81,720)
Oct.   31   Accrual of property tax expense
Nov.   1   Payment of property tax
        30   Recording of monthly property tax expense

E 10.

**SO 4   Social Security, Medicare,
and Unemployment Taxes**

Muzzy Company is subject to a 5.4 percent state unemployment insurance tax and a .8 percent federal unemployment insurance tax after credits. Assume both federal and state unemployment taxes apply to the first $7,000 earned by each employee. Social security and Medicare taxes in effect at this time are 6.2 and 1.45 percent, respectively. The social security tax is levied for both employee and employer on the first $80,400 earned by each employee during the year.

During the current year, the cumulative earnings for each employee of the company are as follows:

Employee	Cumulative Earnings	Employee	Cumulative Earnings
Botala, J.	$28,620	Gosliga, M.	$16,760
Cohn, A.	5,260	Harrington, P.	6,420
Dwyer, G.	32,820	Lebeau, C.	51,650
Esposito, R.	30,130	Miklos, D.	32,100
Furchgott, B.	82,000	Offray, V.	36,645
Gonzalez, N.	5,120	Tung, S.	5,176

1. Prepare and complete a schedule with the following columns: Employee Name, Cumulative Earnings, Earnings Subject to Social Security Tax, Earnings Subject to Medicare Tax, and Earnings Subject to Unemployment Taxes. Total the columns.

2. Compute the social security and Medicare taxes and the federal and state unemployment taxes for Muzzy Company for the year.

E 11.

SO 4 **Net Pay Calculation and Payroll Entries**

Linda Lightfoot is an employee whose overtime pay is regulated by the Fair Labor Standards Act. Her hourly rate is $8, and during the week ended July 11, she worked 42 hours. She claims two exemptions on her W-4 form. So far this year she has earned $8,650. Each week $12 is deducted from her paycheck for medical insurance.

1. Compute the following items related to the pay for Linda Lightfoot for the week of July 11: (a) total pay, (b) federal income taxes withholding (use Figure 4), (c) social security and Medicare taxes (assume rates of 6.2 percent and 1.45 percent, respectively), and (d) net pay.

2. Prepare an entry in journal form to record the wages expense and related liabilities for Linda Lightfoot for the week ended July 11.

E 12.

SO 4 **Payroll Transactions**

Jian-Jin Ye earns a salary of $82,000 per year. Social security and Medicare taxes are, respectively, 6.2 percent on salary up to $80,400 and 1.45 percent on total salary. Federal unemployment insurance taxes are 6.2 percent of the first $7,000; however, a credit is allowed equal to the state unemployment insurance taxes of 5.4 percent on the $7,000. During the year, $15,000 was withheld for federal income taxes, $3,000 for state income taxes, and $1,500 for medical insurance.

1. Prepare an entry in journal form summarizing the payment of $82,000 to Ye during the year.

2. Prepare an entry in journal form summarizing the employer payroll taxes and other costs on Ye's salary for the year. Assume the company pays 80 percent of the total premiums for medical insurance.

3. Determine the total cost paid by Jian-Jin Ye's employer to employ Ye for the year.

PROBLEMS

P 1.

LO 1 **Identification and Analysis**
LO 2 **of Current Liabilities**

Jerry Highland opened a small television repair shop, Highland Television Repair, on January 2, 20x0. He also sold a small line of television sets. In January 20x1, Highland realized that he had failed to file any tax reports for his business since its inception and therefore probably owed a considerable amount of taxes. Since Highland has limited experience in running a business, he has brought all his business records to you and is asking for your help. The records include a checkbook, canceled checks, deposit slips, invoices from his suppliers, a notice of annual property taxes of $4,620 due to the city, and a promissory note to his father-in-law for $5,000. He wants you to determine what his business owes the government and other parties.

You analyze all his records and determine the following as of December 31, 20x0:

Unpaid invoices for televisions	$ 18,000
Television sales (excluding sales tax)	88,540
Cost of televisions sold	62,250
Workers' salaries	20,400
Repair revenues	120,600
Current assets	32,600
Television inventory	23,500

You learn that the company has deducted $952 from the two employees' salaries for federal income taxes owed to the government. The current social security tax is 6.2 percent on maximum earnings of $80,400 for each employee, and the current Medicare tax is 1.45 percent (no maximum earnings). The FUTA tax is 5.4 percent to the state and .8 percent to the federal government on the first $7,000 earned by each employee, and each employee earned more than $7,000. Highland has not filed a sales tax report to the state (5 percent of sales).

REQUIRED

1. Given these limited facts, determine Highland Television Repair's current liabilities as of December 31, 20x0.

2. What additional information would you want from Highland to satisfy yourself that all current liabilities have been identified?

3. Evaluate Highland's liquidity by calculating working capital, payables turnover, and average days' payable. Comment on the results. (Assume average accounts payable were the same as year-end accounts payable.)

P 2.

LO 2 **Notes Payable Transactions and End-of-Period Entries**

Botjen Corporation, whose fiscal year ends June 30, completed the following transactions involving notes payable:

May 11 Signed a 90-day, 12 percent, $66,000 note payable to Shire Bank for a working capital loan. The face value included interest. Proceeds received were $64,020.

21 Obtained a 60-day extension on an $18,000 trade account payable owed to a supplier by signing a 60-day, $18,000 note. Interest is in addition to the face value, at the rate of 14 percent.

June 30 Made end-of-year adjusting entry to accrue interest expense on supplier note.

30 Made end-of-year adjusting entry to recognize interest accrued on bank note.

July 20 Paid off the note plus interest due the supplier.

Aug. 9 Paid amount due to the bank on the 90-day note.

REQUIRED

Prepare entries in journal form for the notes payable transactions.

P 3.

LO 2 **Product Warranty Liability**

Maide Company is engaged in the retail sale of washing machines. Each machine has a 24-month warranty on parts. If a repair under warranty is required, a charge for the labor is made. Management has found that 20 percent of the machines sold require some work before the warranty expires. Furthermore, the average cost of replacement parts has been $120 per repair. At the beginning of June, the account for the estimated liability for product warranties had a credit balance of $28,600. During June, 112 machines were returned under the warranty. The cost of the parts used in repairing the machines was $17,530, and $18,884 was collected as service revenue for the labor involved. During the month, Maide Company sold 450 new machines.

REQUIRED

1. Prepare entries in journal form to record each of the following: (a) the warranty work completed during the month, including related revenue; (b) the estimated liability for product warranties for machines sold during the month.

2. Compute the balance of the Estimated Product Warranty Liability account at the end of the month.

P 4.

LO 2 **Payroll Entries**

The following payroll totals for the month of April were taken from the payroll register of Meingold Corporation: sales salaries, $116,400; office salaries, $57,000; general salaries, $49,600; social security tax withheld, $13,826; Medicare tax withheld, $3,233.50; income taxes withheld, $31,440; medical insurance premiums, $3,290; life insurance premiums, $1,880; salaries subject to unemployment taxes, $156,600. Fifty percent of medical and life insurance premiums are paid by the employee. The rest are paid by the employer.

REQUIRED

Prepare entries in journal form to record the following: (1) accrual of the monthly payroll, (2) payment of the net payroll, (3) accrual of employer's payroll taxes and expenses (assuming social security and Medicare taxes equal to the amounts for employees, a federal unemployment insurance tax of .8 percent, and a state unemployment tax of 5.4 percent), and (4) payment of all liabilities related to the payroll (assuming that all are paid at the same time).

P 5.

SO 4 **Payroll Register and Related Entries**

Huizenga Dairy Company has seven employees. Employees paid hourly receive a set rate for regular hours plus one and one-half times their hourly rate for overtime hours. They are paid every two weeks. The salaried employees are paid monthly on the last biweekly payday of each month. The employees and company are subject to social security tax of 6.2 percent up to a maximum of $80,400 for each employee and to Medicare tax of 1.45 percent. The unemployment insurance tax rates are 5.4 percent for the state and .8 percent for the federal government. The unemployment insurance tax applies to the first $7,000 earned by each employee and is levied only on the employer.

The company maintains a supplemental benefits plan that includes medical insurance, life insurance, and additional retirement funds for employees. Under the plan, each employee contributes 4 percent of her or his gross income as a payroll withholding, and the company matches the amount. Data for the November 30 payroll, the last payday of November, follow.

Employee	Hours		Pay Rate	Cumulative Gross Pay Excluding Current Pay Period	Federal Income Taxes to Be Withheld
	Regular	Overtime			
Epstein, D.	80	5	$ 8.00	$ 4,867.00	$ 71.00
Hladik, W.	80	4	6.50	3,954.00	76.00
Melchior, P.*	Salary	—	5,000.00	55,000.00	985.00
Nuovo, V.	80	—	5.00	8,250.00	32.00
Rasmussen, L.*	Salary	—	2,000.00	20,000.00	294.00
Tang, M.	80	20	10.00	12,000.00	103.00
Von Bruns, B.*	Salary	—	1,500.00	15,000.00	210.00

*Denotes administrative personnel; the rest are sales. P. Melchior's cumulative gross pay includes a $5,000 bonus paid early in the year.

REQUIRED

1. Prepare a payroll register for the pay period ended November 30. The payroll register should have the following columns:

Employee	Deductions	Net Pay
Total Hours	Federal Income Taxes	Distribution
Earnings	Social Security Tax	Sales Wages Expense
Regular	Medicare Tax	Administrative Salaries
Overtime	Supplemental Benefits Plan	
Gross		
Cumulative		

2. Prepare an entry in journal form to record the payroll and related liabilities for deductions for the period ended November 30.

3. Prepare entries in journal form to record the employer's payroll taxes and contribution to the supplemental benefits plan.

4. Prepare the November 30 entries (a) to transfer sufficient cash from the company's regular checking account to a special payroll disbursement account and (b) to pay the employees.

ALTERNATE PROBLEMS

P 6.
LO 2 Notes Payable Transactions and End-of-Period Entries

Csizczak Plywood Company, whose fiscal year ends December 31, completed the following transactions involving notes payable:

20x1
Nov. 25 Purchased a new loading cart by issuing a 60-day, 10 percent note for $21,600.
Dec. 16 Borrowed $25,000 from the bank to finance inventory by signing a 90-day note. The face value of the note includes interest of $750. Proceeds received were $24,250.
31 Made the end-of-year adjusting entry to accrue interest expense on cart note.
31 Made the end-of-year adjusting entry to recognize the interest accrued on the note to the bank.

20x2
Jan. 24 Paid off the loading cart note.
Mar. 16 Paid off the inventory note to the bank.

REQUIRED

Prepare entries in journal form for these transactions.

P 7.
LO 2 Product Warranty Liability

The Whirling Company manufactures and sells food processors. The company guarantees the processors for five years. If a processor fails, it is replaced free, but the customer is charged a service fee for handling. In the past, management has found that only 3 percent of the processors sold required replacement under the warranty. The average food processor costs the company $120. At the beginning of September, the account for estimated liability for product warranties had a credit balance of $104,000. During September, 250 processors were returned under the warranty. Service fees of $4,930 were collected for handling. During the month, the company sold 2,800 food processors.

1. Prepare entries in journal form to record (a) the cost of food processors replaced under warranty and (b) the estimated liability for product warranties for processors sold during the month.

2. Compute the balance of the Estimated Product Warranty Liability account at the end of the month.

P 8.

LO 2 Payroll Entries

At the end of October, the payroll register for Lindos Corporation contained the following totals: sales salaries, $176,220; office salaries, $80,880; administrative salaries, $113,900; federal income taxes withheld, $94,884; state income taxes withheld, $15,636; social security tax withheld, $23,002; Medicare tax withheld, $5,379.50; medical insurance premiums, $12,870; life insurance premiums, $11,712; union dues deductions, $1,368; and salaries subject to unemployment taxes, $57,240. Fifty percent of medical and life insurance premiums are paid by the employer.

Prepare entries in journal form to record the (1) accrual of the monthly payroll, (2) payment of the net payroll, (3) accrual of employer's payroll taxes and expenses (assuming social security and Medicare taxes equal to the amount for employees, a federal unemployment insurance tax of .8 percent, and a state unemployment tax of 5.4 percent), and (4) payment of all liabilities related to the payroll (assuming that all are paid at the same time).

EXPANDING YOUR CRITICAL THINKING, COMMUNICATION, AND INTERPERSONAL SKILLS

SKILLS DEVELOPMENT

Conceptual Analysis

SD 1.

LO 2 Frequent-Flier Plan

America South Airways instituted a frequent-flier program under which passengers accumulate points based on the number of miles they fly on the airline. One point is awarded for each mile flown, with a minimum of 750 miles given for any flight. Because of competition in 2001, the company began a triple mileage bonus plan under which passengers received triple the normal mileage points. In the past, about 1.5 percent of passenger miles were flown by passengers who had converted points to free flights. With the triple mileage program, it is expected that a 2.5 percent rate will be more appropriate for future years. During 2001 the company had passenger revenues of $966.3 million and passenger transportation operating expenses of $802.8 million before depreciation and amortization. Operating income was $86.1 million. What is the appropriate rate to use to estimate free miles? What would be the effect of the estimated liability for free travel by frequent fliers on 2001 net income? Describe several ways to estimate the amount of this liability. Be prepared to discuss the arguments for and against recognizing this liability.

| Cash Flow | CD-ROM | Communication | Critical Thinking | Ethics | General Ledger | Group Activity | Hot Links to Real Companies | International | Internet | Key Ratio | Memo | Spreadsheet |

LO 2 **Nature and Recognition of**
LO 3 **an Estimated Liability**

SD 2. Sometimes the decision to recognize and record a liability is a matter of judgment. People who use **General Motors** credit cards earn rebates toward the purchase of new cars in relation to the amount of purchases made using their cards. General Motors chooses to discuss these outstanding rebates as "Commitments" in the notes to the financial statements in the following way:

> GM sponsors a credit card program, entitled the GM Card program, that offers rebates that can be applied against the purchase or lease of GM vehicles. The amount of rebates available to qualified cardholders at December 31, 1999, 1998, and 1997 was $3.7 billion, $3.7 billion, and $3.5 billion, respectively. Provisions for GM Card rebates are recorded as reductions in revenues at the time of vehicle sale.[11]

Using the two criteria established by the FASB for recognizing and recording a contingency, what reasoning do you think General Motors management uses to show this commitment in the notes, where it will likely receive less attention by analysts, rather than on the income statement as an expense and on the balance sheet as an estimated liability? Do you agree with this position? (**Hint:** Apply the matching rule.)

Ethical Dilemma

LO 2 **Known Legal Violations**

SD 3. *Tower Restaurant* is a large seafood restaurant in the suburbs of Chicago. Joe Murray, an accounting student at a nearby college, recently secured a full-time accounting job at the restaurant. He felt fortunate to have a good job that accommodated his class schedule because the local economy was very bad. After a few weeks on the job, Murray realized that his boss, the owner of the business, was paying the kitchen workers in cash and was not withholding federal and state income taxes or social security and Medicare taxes. Murray understands that federal and state laws require these taxes to be withheld and paid to the appropriate agency in a timely manner. He also realizes that if he raises this issue, he may lose his job. What alternatives are available to Murray? What action would you take if you were in his position? Why did you make this choice?

Group Activity: Use in class groups. Debrief by asking each group for an alternative. Then debate the ethics of each alternative.

Research Activity

LO 2 **Basic Research Skills**
LO 3

SD 4. Indexes for business periodicals, in which you can look up topics of interest, are available in your school library. Three of the most important of these indexes are the *Business Periodicals Index*, *The Wall Street Journal Index*, and the *Accountants' Index*. Using one or more of these indexes, locate and photocopy two articles related to bank financing, commercial paper, product warranties, airline frequent-flier plans, or contingent liabilities. Keep in mind that you may have to look under related topics to find an article. For example, to find articles about contingent liabilities, you might look under litigation, debt guarantees, environmental losses, or other topics. For each of the two articles, write a short summary of the situation and tell how it relates to accounting for the topic as described in the text. Be prepared to discuss your results in class.

Decision-Making Practice

LO 1 **Identification of Current**
LO 2 **Liabilities**
SO 4

SD 5. Sandra Miller opened a bicycle repair shop, Miller Bicycles, in 20x1. She also sold bicycles. The new business was such a success that she hired three assistants on June 1, 20x1. In December, Miller realized that she had failed to file any tax reports for her business since its inception and therefore probably owed a considerable amount of taxes. Since Miller has limited experience in running a business, she has brought all her business records to you and is asking for help. The records include a checkbook, canceled checks, deposit slips, invoices from her suppliers, a notice of annual property taxes of $9,240 due to the city on January 1, 20x2, and a one-year promissory note to the bank for $10,000. She wants you to determine what her business owes the government and other parties.

You analyze all her records and determine the following:

Unpaid supplies invoices	$ 6,320
Sales (excluding sales tax)	177,080
Workers' salaries	40,800
Repair revenues	241,200

You learn that the company has deducted $1,904 from the two employees' salaries for federal income taxes owed to the government. The current social security tax is 6.2 percent on maximum earnings of $80,400 for each employee, and the current Medicare tax is 1.45 percent (no maximum earnings). The FUTA tax is 5.4 percent to the state and .8 percent to the federal government on the first $7,000 earned by each employee, and each employee earned more than $7,000. Miller has not filed a sales tax report to the state (5 percent of sales).

1. Given these limited facts, determine Miller Bicycle's current liabilities as of December 31, 20x2.
2. What additional information would you want from Miller to satisfy yourself that all current liabilities have been identified?

FINANCIAL REPORTING AND ANALYSIS

Interpreting Financial Reports

FRA 1.

LO 1 Comparison of Two Companies with Industry Ratios

Two computer companies are **Sun Microsystems Inc.** and **Cisco Systems.** The following data are for their 1999 fiscal year ends (amounts are in thousands):[12]

	Sun	Cisco
Average Accounts Payable	$ 624,720	$ 305,500
Cost of Goods Sold	4,674,390	4,240,000
Increase (Decrease) Inventory	(38,573)	290,000

Compare the payables turnover ratio and average days' payable for both companies in 1999. Comment on the results. How are cash flows affected by average days' payable? How do Sun Microsystems and Cisco Systems compare to the 1999 industry result shown in Figure 1 of this chapter?

International Company

FRA 2.

LO 1 Classification and LO 2 Disclosure of Current LO 3 Liabilities and Contingent Liabilities

The German company **Man Nutzfahrzeuge Aktiengesellschaft** is one of the largest truck companies in the world. Accounting in Germany differs in some respects from that in the United States. A good example of the difference is the placement and classification of liabilities. On the balance sheet, Man places liabilities below a detailed stockholders' equity section. Man does not distinguish between current and long-term liabilities; however, a note to the financial statements does disclose the amount of the liabilities due within one year. Those liabilities are primarily what we call *definitely determinable liabilities*, such as loans and accounts and notes payable. Estimated liabilities do not seem to appear in this category. In contrast, there is an asset category called *current assets*, which is similar to that found in the United States. In another note to the financial statements, the company lists what it calls *contingent liabilities*, which have not been recorded and do not appear on the balance sheet. These include liabilities for hire and leasing contracts, guarantees of loans of other companies, and warranties on trucks.[13] What do you think of the idea of combining all liabilities, whether short-term or long-term, as a single item on the balance sheet? Do you think any of the contingent liabilities should be recorded and shown on the balance sheet?

Toys "R" Us Annual Report

FRA 3.

LO 1 Short-Term Liabilities and Seasonality

Refer to the balance sheet and the liquidity and capital resources section of Management's Discussion—Results of Operations and Financial Condition in the Toys "R" Us annual report. Compute the payables turnover and average days' payable for 2000 for

Toys "R" Us. How does this ratio compare to that in other industries, as represented by Figure 1? Toys "R" Us is a seasonal business. Would you expect short-term borrowings and accounts payable to be unusually high or unusually low at the balance sheet date of January 29, 2000? How does management use short-term financing to meet its needs for cash during the year?

Fingraph® Financial Analyst™

FRA 4.

LO 1 Comparison of
LO 2 Current Liabilities and
LO 3 Working Capital

Choose any two companies from the same industry in the Fingraph® Financial Analyst™ CD-ROM software. The industry chosen should be one in which current liabilities are likely to be important. Choose an industry such as airlines, manufacturing, consumer products, consumer food and beverage, or computers.

1. In the annual reports for the companies you have selected, read the current liability section of the balance sheet and any reference to any current liabilities in the summary of significant accounting policies or notes to the financial statements. What are the most important current liabilities for each company? Are there any current liabilities that appear to be characteristic of the industry? Which current liabilities are definitely determinable and which appear to be accrued liabilities?

2. Display and print in tabular and graphical form the Current Assets and Current Liabilities Analysis page. Prepare a table that compares the current ratio and working capital for both companies for two years.

3. Find and read references to current liabilities in the liquidity analysis section of management's discussion and analysis in each annual report.

4. Write a one-page executive summary that highlights the most important types of current liabilities for this industry and compares the current ratio and working capital trends of the two companies, including reference to management's assessment. Include the Fingraph® page and your table as an attachment to your report.

Internet Case

FRA 5.

LO 3 Investigation of Status of
Famous Contingencies

Some of the most famous contingent liabilities in history include the suits against tobacco companies such as **RJR Nabisco, Inc.,** and **Philip Morris Incorporated** and the **Valdez** oil spill case against **Exxon Corporation.** Investigate the current status of any one of these cases, including Texaco, by first going to the Needles Accounting Resource Center web site at http://college.hmco.com and clicking on one of these companies' web links. Then find the company's latest annual report and look in the notes to the financial statements under Contingencies. Report what you find about the case, including the possibility that the case has been settled or is no longer reported.

ENDNOTES

1. US Airways, Inc., *Annual Report*, 1999.
2. Radio Shack Corporation, *Annual Report*, 1999.
3. The Goodyear Tire & Rubber Company, *Annual Report*, 1999.
4. Lowe's Companies, Inc., *Annual Report*, 1999.
5. Raju Narisetti, "P&G Ad Chief Plots Demise of the Coupon," *The Wall Street Journal*, April 17, 1996.
6. Delta Air Lines, Inc., *Annual Report*, 1999.
7. Scott McCartney, "Free Airline Miles Become a Potent Tool for Selling Everything," *The Wall Street Journal*, April 16, 1996.
8. *Statement of Financial Accounting Standards No. 5*, "Accounting for Contingencies" (Norwalk, Conn.: Financial Accounting Standards Board, 1975).
9. American Institute of Certified Public Accountants, *Accounting Trends & Techniques*, 1999.
10. General Motors Corp., *Annual Report*, 1999.
11. Ibid.
12. Sun Microsystems Inc., *Annual Report*, 1999; Cisco Systems, *Annual Report*, 1999.
13. Man Nutzfahrzeuge Aktiengesellschaft, *Annual Report*, 1997.

13

Partnerships

LEARNING OBJECTIVES

1 Identify the principal characteristics, advantages, and disadvantages of the partnership form of business.

2 Record partners' investments of cash and other assets when a partnership is formed.

3 Compute and record the income or losses that partners share, based on stated ratios, capital balance ratios, and partners' salaries and interest.

4 Record a person's admission to a partnership.

5 Record a person's withdrawal from a partnership.

6 Compute the distribution of assets to partners when they liquidate their partnership.

KPMG International Many people think of partnerships as relatively small business organizations, and usually they are right. However, some partnerships, among them law firms, investment companies, real estate companies, and accounting firms, are very large. An example is KPMG International, an integrated professional services firm with 800 offices in 150 countries. The firm provides accounting and auditing services, tax services, and management consulting services. With over 100,000 employees, it is one of the largest partnerships in the world. In 1999, the firm was growing rapidly with revenues of over $12 billion, $5.7 billion of which came from the United States. How does a partnership this large organize to accomplish its objectives?[1]

KPMG International is organized as a limited liability partnership. In a normal partnership, the personal financial resources of all partners are subject to risk of loss if the partnership suffers a loss it cannot bear. Accounting firms are at risk of suffering large losses as a result of lawsuits from investors who lose money investing in a company audited by the accounting firm. Because KPMG is organized as a limited liability partnership, partners are liable to the extent of their partnership interest in the firm but do not subject their other personal assets to risk.

Financial Highlights

(In millions of dollars)

	1999	1998	1997
Annual revenue	$12,200	$10,400	$9,000

Partnership Characteristics

The Uniform Partnership Act, which has been adopted by most states, defines a **partnership** as "an association of two or more persons to carry on as co-owners of a business for profit." Partnerships are treated as separate entities in accounting. They differ in many ways from the other forms of business. The next few paragraphs describe some of the important characteristics of a partnership.

Voluntary Association

A partnership is a voluntary association of individuals rather than a legal entity in itself. Therefore, a partner is responsible under the law for his or her partners' business actions within the scope of the partnership. A partner also has unlimited liability for the debts of the partnership. Because of these potential liabilities, an individual must be allowed to choose the people who join the partnership. A person should select as partners individuals who share his or her business objectives.

PARTNERSHIP AGREEMENT   A partnership is easy to form. Two or more competent people simply agree to be partners in a common business purpose. Their agreement is known as a **partnership agreement**. The partnership agreement does not have to be in writing; however, good business practice calls for a written document that clearly states the details of the arrangement. The contract should specify the name, location, and purpose of the business; the partners and their respective duties; the investments of each partner; the methods for distributing income and losses; and the procedures for the admission and withdrawal of partners, the withdrawal of assets allowed each partner, and the liquidation (termination) of the business.

LIMITED LIFE   Because a partnership is formed by a contract between partners, it has a **limited life**: Anything that ends the contract dissolves the partnership. A partnership is dissolved when (1) a new partner is admitted, (2) a partner withdraws, (3) a partner goes bankrupt, (4) a partner is incapacitated (to the point where he or she cannot perform as obligated), (5) a partner retires, (6) a partner dies, or (7) the partnership ends according to the partnership agreement (for example, when a large project is completed). However, if the partners want the partnership to continue legally, the partnership agreement can be written to cover each of these situations. For example, the partnership agreement can state that if a partner dies, the remaining partner or partners must purchase the deceased partner's capital at book value from the heirs.

FOCUS ON INTERNATIONAL BUSINESS

American businesses are expanding into emerging markets throughout the world. Many of these markets, such as those of Hungary, Poland, the Czech Republic, India, and China, are in the process of privatizing public entities. This means that operations such as steel mills, cement factories, and utilities that were previously run by the government are being converted into private enterprises. Many countries require that local investors own a substantial proportion of the newly formed businesses. One way of accomplishing this is to form joint ventures, which match a country's need for outside capital and operational know-how with investors' interest in business expansion and profitability. Joint ventures often take the form of partnerships among two or more corporations and other investors. Any income or losses from operations will be divided among the participants according to a predetermined agreement.

Mutual Agency   Each partner is an agent of the partnership within the scope of the business. Because of this **mutual agency**, any partner can bind the partnership to a business agreement as long as he or she acts within the scope of the company's normal operations. For example, a partner in a used-car business can bind the partnership through the purchase or sale of used cars. But this partner cannot bind the partnership to a contract to buy men's clothing or any other goods that are not related to the used-car business. Because of mutual agency, it is very important for an individual to choose business partners who have integrity and who share his or her business objectives.

Unlimited Liability   All partners have **unlimited liability** for their company's debt, which means that each partner is personally liable for all the debts of the partnership. If a partnership is in poor financial condition and cannot pay its debts, the creditors must first satisfy their claims from the assets of the partnership. If the assets are not enough to pay all debts, the creditors can seek payment from the personal assets of each partner. If one partner's personal assets are used up before the debts are paid, the creditors can claim additional assets from the remaining partners who are able to pay. Each partner, then, could be required by law to pay all the debts of the partnership.

Co-ownership of Partnership Property   When individuals invest property in a partnership, they give up the right to their separate use of the property. The property has become an asset of the partnership and is now owned jointly by all the partners.

Participation in Partnership Income   Each partner has the right to share in the company's income and the responsibility to share in its losses. The partnership agreement should state the method of distributing income and losses to each partner. If the agreement describes how income should be shared but does not mention losses, losses are distributed in the same way as income. If the partners fail to describe the method of income and loss distribution in the partnership agreement, the law states that income and losses must be shared equally.

Advantages and Disadvantages of Partnerships   Partnerships have both advantages and disadvantages. One advantage is that a partnership is easy to form, change, and dissolve. Also, a partnership facilitates the pooling of capital resources and individual talents; it has no corporate tax burden (because a partnership is not a legal entity for tax purposes, it does not have to pay a federal income tax, as do corporations, but must file an informational return); and it gives the partners a certain amount of freedom and flexibility.

On the other hand, there are the following disadvantages: the life of a partnership is limited; one partner can bind the partnership to a contract (mutual agency); the partners have unlimited personal liability; and it is more difficult for a partnership to raise large amounts of capital and to transfer ownership interests than it is for a corporation.

Other Forms of Association

Two other common forms of association that are a type of partnership or similar to a partnership are limited partnerships and joint ventures.

Limited Partnerships   A **limited partnership** is a special type of partnership that, like corporations, confines the limited partner's potential loss to the amount of his or her investment. Under this type of partnership the unlimited liability disadvantage of a partnership can be overcome. Usually, the limited partner-

FOCUS ON BUSINESS PRACTICE

Limited partnerships are sometimes used in place of the corporate form to raise funds from the public. Because possible investor losses are normally restricted to the amount of the investment, the limited partnership has some characteristics of the corporate form. Limited partnerships are used to obtain financing for many projects, such as locating and drilling oil and gas wells, manufacturing airplanes, and developing real estate (including shopping centers, office buildings, and apartment complexes). For example, Alliance Capital Management Limited Partnership is one of the largest investment advisors, managing more than $90 billion in assets for corporate and individual investors. The company's partnership units, or shares of ownership, sell on the New York Stock Exchange and can be purchased by the individual investor. In 2000, the units were selling at about $48 each and paid an annual dividend of $3.16 per share.[2]

ship has a general partner who has unlimited liability but allows other partners to limit their potential loss. The potential loss of all partners in an ordinary partnership is limited only by personal bankruptcy laws.

JOIN VENTURES   In today's global environment, more companies are looking to form alliances similar to partnerships, called *joint ventures*, with other companies rather than to venture out on their own. A **joint venture** is an association of two or more entities for the purpose of achieving a specific goal, such as the manufacture of a product in a new market. Many joint ventures have an agreed-upon limited life. The entities forming joint ventures usually involve companies but can sometimes involve governments, especially in emerging economies. A joint venture brings together the resources, technical skills, political ties, and other assets of each of the parties for a common goal. Profits and losses are shared on an agreed-upon basis.

Accounting for Partners' Equity

OBJECTIVE

2 Record partners' investments of cash and other assets when a partnership is formed

Although accounting for a partnership is very similar to accounting for a sole proprietorship, there are differences. One is that the owner's equity in a partnership is called **partners' equity**. In accounting for partners' equity, it is necessary to maintain separate Capital and Withdrawals accounts for each partner and to divide the income and losses of the company among the partners. The differences in the Capital accounts of a sole proprietorship and a partnership are shown below:

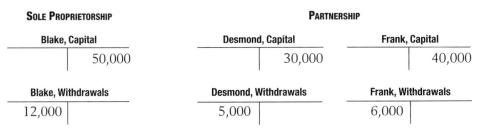

SOLE PROPRIETORSHIP	**PARTNERSHIP**	
Blake, Capital	**Desmond, Capital**	**Frank, Capital**
50,000	30,000	40,000
Blake, Withdrawals	**Desmond, Withdrawals**	**Frank, Withdrawals**
12,000	5,000	6,000

In the partners' equity section of the balance sheet, the balance of each partner's Capital account is listed separately:

Liabilities and Partners' Equity

Total Liabilities		$28,000
Partners' Equity		
Desmond, Capital	$25,000	
Frank, Capital	34,000	
Total Partners' Equity		59,000
Total Liabilities and Partners' Equity		$87,000

Each partner invests cash or other assets or a combination of the two in the partnership according to the partnership agreement. Noncash assets should be valued at their fair market value on the date they are transferred to the partnership. The assets invested by a partner are debited to the proper account, and the total amount is credited to the partner's Capital account.

To show how partners' investments are recorded, let's assume that Jerry Adcock and Rose Villa have agreed to combine their capital and equipment in a partnership to operate a jewelry store. According to their partnership agreement, Adcock will invest $28,000 in cash and $37,000 worth of furniture and displays, and Villa will invest $40,000 in cash and $30,000 worth of equipment. Related to the equipment is a note payable for $10,000, which the partnership assumes. The journal entries to record the partners' initial investments are as follows:

	20x1			
A = L + OE	July 1	Cash	28,000	
+ +		Furniture and Displays	37,000	
+		Jerry Adcock, Capital		65,000
		Initial investment of Jerry Adcock in Adcock and Villa		
A = L + OE	1	Cash	40,000	
+ + +		Equipment	30,000	
+		Note Payable		10,000
		Rose Villa, Capital		60,000
		Initial investment of Rose Villa in Adcock and Villa		

FOCUS ON BUSINESS TECHNOLOGY

The Internet is fostering the formation of many joint ventures by companies that are normally competitors. Among recent developments of this type are the following:

- Eight metals companies, including Allegheny Technologies Inc. and Alcoa Inc., have formed a joint venture to establish online service to provide products to businesses in the metals industries.

- Accor, Europe's largest hotel chain; Hilton International; and Forte Hotels have launched an Internet joint venture enabling customers to make online bookings at their hotels. This counters a similar effort involving seven other hotel chains including Marriott, Hyatt, and Holiday Inn.

- General Motors Corporation and other companies have formed an Internet joint venture to consolidate and coordinate the purchase of parts and supplies in the manufacture of automobiles.

The values assigned to the assets would be included in the partnership agreement. These values can differ from those carried on the partners' personal books. For example, the equipment that Rose Villa contributed had a value of only $22,000 on her books, but its market value had increased considerably after she purchased it. The book value of Villa's equipment is not important. The fair market value of the equipment at the time of transfer *is* important, however, because that value represents the amount of money Villa has invested in the partnership. Later investments are recorded the same way.

Distribution of Partnership Income and Losses

OBJECTIVE

3 Compute and record the income or losses that partners share, based on stated ratios, capital balance ratios, and partners' salaries and interest

Income and losses can be distributed according to whatever method the partners specify in the partnership agreement. To avoid later disputes, the agreement should be specific and clear. If a partnership agreement does not mention the distribution of income and losses, the law requires that they be shared equally by all partners. Also, if a partnership agreement mentions only the distribution of income, the law requires that losses be distributed in the same ratio as income.

The income of a partnership normally has three components: (1) return to the partners for the use of their capital (called *interest on partners' capital*), (2) compensation for direct services the partners have rendered (partners' salaries), and (3) other income for any special characteristics or risks individual partners may bring to the partnership. The breakdown of total income into its three components helps clarify how much each partner has contributed to the firm.

If all partners contribute equal capital, have similar talents, and spend the same amount of time in the business, then an equal distribution of income and losses would be fair. However, if one partner works full time in the firm and another devotes only a fourth of his or her time, then the distribution of income or losses should reflect the difference. (This concept would apply to any situation in which the partners contribute unequally to the business.)

Several ways for partners to share income are (1) by stated ratios, (2) by capital balance ratios, and (3) by salaries to the partners and interest on partners' capital, with the remaining income shared according to stated ratios. *Salaries* and *interest* here are not the same as *salaries expense* and *interest expense* in the ordinary sense of the terms. They do not affect the amount of reported net income. Instead, they refer to ways of determining each partner's share of net income or loss on the basis of time spent and money invested in the partnership.

Stated Ratios

One method of distributing income and losses is to give each partner a stated ratio of the total income or loss. If each partner is making an equal contribution to the firm, each can assume the same share of income and losses. It is important to understand that an equal contribution to the firm does not necessarily mean an equal capital investment in the firm. One partner may devote more time and talent to the firm, whereas the second partner may make a larger capital investment. And, if the partners contribute unequally to the firm, unequal stated ratios—60 percent and 40 percent, perhaps—can be appropriate.

Let's assume that Adcock and Villa had a net income last year of $30,000. Their partnership agreement states that the percentages of income and losses distributed to Jerry Adcock and Rose Villa should be 60 percent and 40 percent, respectively.

The computation of each partner's share of the income and the journal entry to show the distribution are as follows:

Adcock ($30,000 × .60)	$18,000
Villa ($30,000 × .40)	12,000
Net Income	$30,000

A = L + OE
−
+
+

20x2
June 30

Income Summary	30,000	
Jerry Adcock, Capital		18,000
Rose Villa, Capital		12,000
Distribution of income for the year to the partners' Capital accounts		

Capital Balance Ratios

If invested capital produces the most income for the partnership, then income and losses may be distributed according to capital balances. The ratio used to distribute income and losses here may be based on each partner's capital balance at the beginning of the year or on the average capital balance of each partner during the year. The partnership agreement must describe the method to be used.

RATIOS BASED ON BEGINNING CAPITAL BALANCES To show how the first method works, let's look at the beginning capital balances of the partners in Adcock and Villa. At the start of the fiscal year, July 1, 20x1, Jerry Adcock, Capital showed a $65,000 balance, and Rose Villa, Capital showed a $60,000 balance. (Actually, these balances reflect the partners' initial investment; the partnership was formed on July 1, 20x1.) The total partners' equity in the firm, then, was $125,000 ($65,000 + $60,000). Each partner's capital balance at the beginning of the year divided by the total partners' equity at the beginning of the year is that partner's beginning capital balance ratio:

	Beginning Capital Balance	Beginning Capital Balance Ratio
Jerry Adcock	$ 65,000	65,000 ÷ 125,000 = .52 = 52%
Rose Villa	60,000	60,000 ÷ 125,000 = .48 = 48%
	$125,000	

The income that each partner should receive when distribution is based on beginning capital balance ratios is determined by multiplying the total income by each partner's capital ratio. If we assume that income for the year was $140,000, Jerry Adcock's share of that income was $72,800, and Rose Villa's share was $67,200.

Jerry Adcock	$140,000 × .52 = $ 72,800
Rose Villa	140,000 × .48 = 67,200
	$140,000

RATIOS BASED ON AVERAGE CAPITAL BALANCES If Adcock and Villa use beginning capital balance ratios to determine the distribution of income, they do not consider any investments or withdrawals made during the year. But investments and withdrawals usually change the partners' capital ratios. If the partners believe that their capital balances are going to change dramatically during the year, they can choose average capital balance ratios as a fairer means of distributing income and losses.

The following T accounts show the activity over the year in Adcock and Villa's partners' Capital and Withdrawals accounts:

Jerry Adcock, Capital			Jerry Adcock, Withdrawals		
	7/1/x1	65,000	1/1/x2	10,000	

Rose Villa, Capital			Rose Villa, Withdrawals		
	7/1/x1	60,000	11/1/x1	10,000	
	2/1/x2	8,000			

Jerry Adcock withdrew $10,000 on January 1, 20x2, and Rose Villa withdrew $10,000 on November 1, 20x1, and invested an additional $8,000 of equipment on February 1, 20x2. Again, the income for the year's operation (July 1, 20x1, to June 30, 20x2) was $140,000. The calculations for the average capital balances and the distribution of income are as follows:

Average Capital Balances

Partner	Date	Capital Balance ×	Months Unchanged	=	Total	Average Capital Balance
Adcock	July–Dec.	$65,000 ×	6	=	$390,000	
	Jan.–June	55,000 ×	6	=	330,000	
			12		$720,000 ÷ 12 =	$ 60,000
Villa	July–Oct.	$60,000 ×	4	=	$240,000	
	Nov.–Jan.	50,000 ×	3	=	150,000	
	Feb.–June	58,000 ×	5	=	290,000	
			12		$680,000 ÷ 12 =	56,667
					Total average capital	$116,667

Average Capital Balance Ratios

$$\text{Adcock} = \frac{\text{Adcock's Average Capital Balance}}{\text{Total Average Capital}} = \frac{\$60,000}{\$116,667} = .514 = 51.4\%$$

$$\text{Villa} = \frac{\text{Villa's Average Capital Balance}}{\text{Total Average Capital}} = \frac{\$56,667}{\$116,667} = .486 = 48.6\%$$

Distribution of Income

Partner	Income	×	Ratio	=	Share of Income
Adcock	$140,000	×	.514	=	$ 71,960
Villa	140,000	×	.486	=	68,040
				Total income	$140,000

Notice that to determine the distribution of income (or loss), you have to determine (1) the average capital balances, (2) the average capital balance ratios, and (3) each partner's share of income or loss. To compute each partner's average capital balance, you have to examine the changes that have taken place during the year in each partner's capital balance, changes that are the product of further investments and withdrawals. The partner's beginning capital is multiplied by the number of months the balance remains unchanged. After the balance changes, the new balance is multiplied by the number of months it remains unchanged. The process continues until the end of the year. The totals of these computations are added, and then they are divided by 12 to determine the average capital balances. Once the average capital balances are determined, the method of figuring capital balance ratios for sharing income and losses is the same as the method used for beginning capital balances.

Salaries, Interest, and Stated Ratios

Partners generally do not contribute equally to a firm. To make up for unequal contributions, a partnership agreement can allow for partners' salaries, interest on partners' capital balances, or a combination of both in the distribution of income. Again, salaries and interest of this kind are not deducted as expenses before the partnership income is determined. They represent a method of arriving at an equitable distribution of income or loss.

To illustrate an allowance for partners' salaries, we assume that Adcock and Villa have agreed that they will receive salaries—$8,000 for Adcock and $7,000 for Villa—and that any remaining income will be divided equally between them. Each salary is charged to the appropriate partner's Withdrawals account when paid. Assuming the same $140,000 income for the first year, the calculations for Adcock and Villa are as follows:

	Income of Partner		Income Distributed
	Adcock	Villa	
Total Income for Distribution			$140,000
Distribution of Salaries			
Adcock	$ 8,000		
Villa		$ 7,000	(15,000)
Remaining Income After Salaries			$125,000
Equal Distribution of Remaining Income			
Adcock ($125,000 × .50)	62,500		
Villa ($125,000 × .50)		62,500	(125,000)
Remaining Income			—
Income of Partners	$70,500	$69,500	$140,000

Salaries allow for differences in the services that partners provide the business. However, they do not take into account differences in invested capital. To allow for capital differences, each partner can receive a stated interest on his or her invested capital in addition to salary. Suppose that Jerry Adcock and Rose Villa agree to pay annual salaries of $8,000 for Adcock and $7,000 for Villa, to receive 10 percent interest on their beginning capital balances, and to share any remaining income equally. If we assume income of $140,000, the calculations for Adcock and Villa are as follows:

	Income of Partner		Income Distributed
	Adcock	Villa	
Total Income for Distribution			$140,000
Distribution of Salaries			
Adcock	$ 8,000		
Villa		$ 7,000	(15,000)
Remaining Income After Salaries			$125,000
Distribution of Interest			
Adcock ($65,000 × .10)	6,500		
Villa ($60,000 × .10)		6,000	(12,500)
Remaining Income After Salaries and Interest			$112,500
Equal Distribution of Remaining Income			
Adcock ($112,500 × .50)	56,250		
Villa ($112,500 × .50)		56,250	(112,500)
Remaining Income			—
Income of Partners	$70,750	$69,250	$140,000

If the partnership agreement allows for the distribution of salaries or interest or both, the amounts must be allocated to the partners even if profits are not enough to cover the salaries and interest. In fact, even if the company has a loss, these allocations must still be made. The negative balance or loss after the allocation of salaries and interest must be distributed according to the stated ratio in the partnership agreement, or equally if the agreement does not mention a ratio.

For example, let's assume that Adcock and Villa agreed to the following conditions for the distribution of income and losses:

	Salaries	Interest	Beginning Capital Balance
Adcock	$70,000	10 percent of beginning	$65,000
Villa	60,000	capital balances	60,000

FOCUS ON BUSINESS PRACTICE

Partners in professional accounting firms are often held in high esteem and envied for the high incomes that some of them make. Partners in large accounting firms can make over $250,000 per year, with top partners drawing over $800,000. However, consideration of those incomes should take into account the risks that partners take and the fact that the incomes of partners in small accounting firms are often much lower.

Partners are not compensated in the same way as managers in corporations. Partners' income is not guaranteed, but rather is based on the performance of the partnership. Also, each partner is required to make a substantial investment of capital in the partnership. This capital remains at risk for as long as the partner chooses to stay in the partnership. For instance, in one notable instance, when many savings and loan institutions were failing, the partners in a major accounting firm lost their total investments as well as their income when their firm was subjected to lawsuits and other losses. The firm was eventually liquidated.

The income for the first year of operation was $140,000. The computation for the distribution of the income and loss is as follows:

	Income of Partner		Income Distributed
	Adcock	Villa	
Total Income for Distribution			$140,000
Distribution of Salaries			
Adcock	$70,000		
Villa		$60,000	(130,000)
Remaining Income After Salaries			$ 10,000
Distribution of Interest			
Adcock ($65,000 × .10)	6,500		
Villa ($60,000 × .10)		6,000	(12,500)
Negative Balance After Salaries and Interest			($ 2,500)
Equal Distribution of Negative Balance*			
Adcock ($2,500 × .50)	(1,250)		
Villa ($2,500 × .50)		(1,250)	2,500
Remaining Income			—
Income of Partners	$75,250	$64,750	$140,000

*Notice that the negative balance is distributed equally because the agreement does not indicate how income and losses should be distributed after salaries and interest are paid.

On the income statement for the partnership, the distribution of income or losses is shown below the net income figure. Exhibit 1 shows how this is done.

Exhibit 1
Partial Income Statement for Adcock and Villa

Adcock and Villa
Partial Income Statement
For the Year Ended June 30, 20x2

Net Income		$140,000
Distribution to the Partners		
Adcock		
Salary Distribution	$70,000	
Interest on Beginning Capital Balance	6,500	
Total	$76,500	
One-Half of Remaining Negative Amount	(1,250)	
Share of Net Income		$ 75,250
Villa		
Salary Distribution	$60,000	
Interest on Beginning Capital Balance	6,000	
Total	$66,000	
One-Half of Remaining Negative Amount	(1,250)	
Share of Net Income		64,750
Net Income Distributed		$140,000

Dissolution of a Partnership

Dissolution of a partnership occurs whenever there is a change in the original association of partners. When a partnership is dissolved, the partners lose their authority to continue the business as a going concern. That the partners lose this authority does not necessarily mean that the business operation is ended or interrupted. However, it does mean—from a legal standpoint as well as an accounting one—that the separate entity ceases to exist. The remaining partners can act for the partnership in finishing the affairs of the business or form a new partnership that will be a new accounting entity. The dissolution of a partnership takes place through the admission of a new partner, the withdrawal of a partner, or the death of a partner.

Admission of a New Partner

The admission of a new partner dissolves the old partnership because a new association has been formed. Dissolving the old partnership and creating a new one require the consent of all the old partners and the ratification of a new partnership agreement. When a new partner is admitted, a new partnership agreement should be in place.

An individual can be admitted into a partnership in one of two ways: (1) by purchasing an interest in the partnership from one or more of the original partners or (2) by investing assets in the partnership.

PURCHASING AN INTEREST FROM A PARTNER When an individual is admitted to a firm by purchasing an interest from an old partner, each partner must agree to the change. The transaction is a personal one between the old and new partners, but the interest purchased must be transferred from the Capital account of the selling partner to the Capital account of the new partner.

Suppose that Jerry Adcock decides to sell his interest, assumed to be $70,000, in Adcock and Villa to Richard Davis for $100,000 on August 31, 20x3, and that Rose Villa agrees to the sale. The entry to record the sale on the partnership books looks like this:

	20x3			
A = L + OE	Aug. 31	Jerry Adcock, Capital	70,000	
−		Richard Davis, Capital		70,000
+		Transfer of Jerry Adcock's equity to Richard Davis		

Notice that the entry records the book value of the equity, not the amount Davis pays. The amount Davis pays is a personal matter between him and Adcock. Because the amount paid does not affect the assets or liabilities of the firm, it is not entered in the records.

Here's another example of a purchase: Assume that Richard Davis purchases half of Jerry Adcock's $70,000 interest in the partnership and half of Rose Villa's interest, assumed to be $80,000, by paying a total of $100,000 to the two partners on August 31, 20x3. The entry to record this transaction on the partnership books would be as follows:

20x3

A = L + OE
−
−
+

Aug. 31   Jerry Adcock, Capital 35,000

Rose Villa, Capital 40,000

Richard Davis, Capital 75,000

Transfer of half of Jerry Adcock's
and Rose Villa's equity to
Richard Davis

INVESTING ASSETS IN A PARTNERSHIP   When a new partner is admitted through an investment in the partnership, both the assets and the partners' equity in the firm increase. The increase occurs because the assets the new partner invests become partnership assets, and as partnership assets increase, partners' equity increases as well. For example, assume that Jerry Adcock and Rose Villa have agreed to allow Richard Davis to invest $75,000 in return for a one-third interest in their partnership. The Capital accounts of Jerry Adcock and Rose Villa are assumed to be $70,000 and $80,000, respectively. Davis's $75,000 investment equals a one-third interest in the firm after the investment is added to the previously existing capital of the partnership:

Jerry Adcock, Capital	$ 70,000
Rose Villa, Capital	80,000
Davis's investment	75,000
Total capital after Davis's investment	$225,000
One-third interest ($225,000 ÷ 3)	$ 75,000

The journal entry to record Davis's investment is as follows:

20x3

A = L + OE
+   +

Aug. 31   Cash 75,000

Richard Davis, Capital 75,000

Admission of Richard Davis to a
one-third interest in the company

BONUS TO THE OLD PARTNERS   Sometimes a partnership may be so profitable or otherwise advantageous that a new investor is willing to pay more than the actual dollar interest he or she receives in the partnership. For instance, suppose an individual pays $100,000 for an $80,000 interest in a partnership. The $20,000 excess of the payment over the interest purchased is a **bonus** to the original partners. The bonus must be distributed to the original partners according to the partnership agreement. When the agreement does not cover the distribution of bonuses, a bonus should be distributed to the original partners in accordance with the method for distributing income and losses.

Assume that Adcock and Villa has operated for several years and that the partners' capital balances and the stated ratios for distribution of income and loss are as follows:

Partners	Capital Balances	Stated Ratios
Adcock	$160,000	55%
Villa	140,000	45
	$300,000	100%

Richard Davis wants to join the firm. He offers to invest $100,000 on December 1 in return for a one-fifth interest in the business and income. The original partners agree to the offer. The computation of the bonus to the original partners follows:

Partners' equity in the original partnership		$300,000
Cash investment by Richard Davis		100,000
Partners' equity in the new partnership		$400,000
Partners' equity assigned to Richard Davis ($400,000 × ⅕)		$ 80,000
Bonus to the original partners		
Investment by Richard Davis	$100,000	
Less equity assigned to Richard Davis	80,000	$ 20,000
Distribution of bonus to original partners		
Jerry Adcock ($20,000 × .55)	$ 11,000	
Rose Villa ($20,000 × .45)	9,000	$ 20,000

The journal entry that records Davis's admission to the partnership is as follows:

	20x3			
A = L + OE	Dec. 1	Cash	100,000	
+ +		Jerry Adcock, Capital		11,000
+		Rose Villa, Capital		9,000
+		Richard Davis, Capital		80,000
		Investment by Richard Davis for a one-fifth interest in the firm, and the bonus paid to the original partners		

BONUS TO THE NEW PARTNER There are several reasons for a partnership to want a new partner. A firm in financial trouble might need additional cash. Or the original partners, wanting to expand the firm's markets, might need more capital than they themselves can provide. Also, the partners might know a person who would bring a unique talent to the firm. Under such conditions, a new partner could be admitted to the partnership with the understanding that part of the original partners' capital will be transferred (credited) to the new partner's Capital account as a bonus.

For example, suppose that Jerry Adcock and Rose Villa have invited Richard Davis to join the firm. Davis is going to invest $60,000 on December 1 for a one-fourth interest in the company. The stated ratios for distribution of income or loss for Adcock and Villa are 55 percent and 45 percent, respectively. If Davis is to receive a one-fourth interest in the firm, the interest of the original partners represents a three-fourths interest in the business. The computation of Davis's bonus is as follows:

Total equity in partnership		
Jerry Adcock, Capital		$160,000
Rose Villa, Capital		140,000
Investment by Richard Davis		60,000
Partners' equity in the new partnership		$360,000
Partners' equity assigned to Richard Davis ($360,000 × ¼)		$ 90,000
Bonus to new partner		
Equity assigned to Richard Davis	$90,000	
Less cash investment by Richard Davis	60,000	$ 30,000
Distribution of bonus from original partners		
Jerry Adcock ($30,000 × .55)	$16,500	
Rose Villa ($30,000 × .45)	13,500	$ 30,000

The journal entry to record the admission of Davis to the partnership is shown below:

	20x3			
A = L + OE	Dec. 1	Cash	60,000	
+		Jerry Adcock, Capital	16,500	
−		Rose Villa, Capital	13,500	
+		Richard Davis, Capital		90,000
		To record the investment by		
		Richard Davis of cash and a		
		bonus from Adcock and Villa		

Withdrawal of a Partner

OBJECTIVE

5 Record a person's withdrawal from a partnership

Since a partnership is a voluntary association, a partner usually has the right to withdraw at any time. However, to avoid disputes when a partner does decide to withdraw or retire, a partnership agreement should describe the procedures to be followed. The agreement should specify (1) whether or not an audit will be performed, (2) how the assets will be reappraised, (3) how a bonus will be determined, and (4) by what method the withdrawing partner will be paid.

An individual can withdraw from a partnership in several ways. A partner can (1) sell his or her interest to another partner with the consent of the remaining partners, (2) sell his or her interest to an outsider with the consent of the remaining partners, (3) withdraw assets equal to his or her capital balance, (4) withdraw assets that are less than his or her capital balance (in which case the remaining partners receive a bonus), or (5) withdraw assets that are greater than his or her capital balance (in which case the withdrawing partner receives a bonus). These alternatives are illustrated in Figure 1.

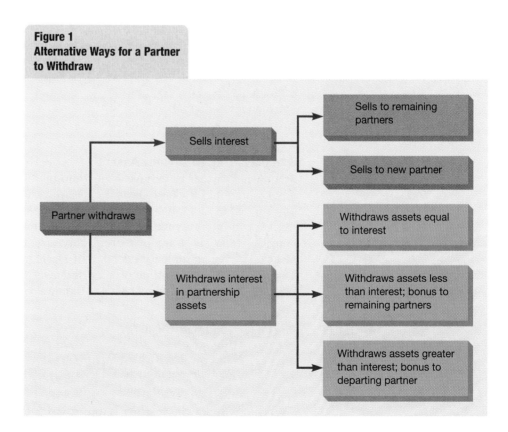

Figure 1
Alternative Ways for a Partner to Withdraw

FOCUS ON BUSINESS PRACTICE

The withdrawal of partners can cause a financial strain on a partnership. For instance, several years ago Goldman, Sachs & Co., the last major Wall Street investment company still organized as a partnership, was scrambling to raise more than $250 million to compensate for the withdrawal of twenty-three partners.

The retirements caused a decrease in equity capital of about $400 million, which represented almost 10 percent of the firm's capital. Goldman was looking for private investors to make up for the losses.[3] The majority of Wall Street investment companies, such as Merrill Lynch & Co., Inc., and Salomon Brothers Inc., are organized as corporations. An advantage of this form of organization is that managers who want to leave their jobs can sell their stock to other investors without affecting the firm's capital.

WITHDRAWAL BY SELLING INTEREST   When a partner sells his or her interest to another partner or to an outsider with the consent of the other partners, the transaction is personal; it does not change the partnership assets or the partners' equity. For example, let's assume that the capital balances of Adcock, Villa, and Davis are $140,000, $100,000, and $60,000, respectively, for a total of $300,000.

Villa wants to withdraw from the partnership and is reviewing two offers for her interest. The offers are (1) to sell her interest to Davis for $110,000 or (2) to sell her interest to Judy Jones for $120,000. The remaining partners have agreed to either potential transaction. Because Davis and Jones would pay for Villa's interest from their personal assets, the partnership accounting records would show only the transfer of Villa's interest to Davis or Jones. The entries to record these possible transfers are as follows:

1. If Villa's interest is purchased by Davis:

$A = L + OE$
$-$
$+$

Rose Villa, Capital	100,000	
Richard Davis, Capital		100,000
Sale of Villa's partnership interest to Davis		

2. If Villa's interest is purchased by Jones:

$A = L + OE$
$-$
$+$

Rose Villa, Capital	100,000	
Judy Jones, Capital		100,000
Sale of Villa's partnership interest to Jones		

WITHDRAWAL BY REMOVING ASSETS   A partnership agreement can allow a withdrawing partner to remove assets from the firm equal to his or her capital balance. Assume that Richard Davis decides to withdraw from Adcock, Villa, Davis & Company. Davis's capital balance is $60,000. The partnership agreement states that he can withdraw cash from the firm equal to his capital balance. If there is not enough cash, he must accept a promissory note from the new partnership for the balance. The remaining partners ask that Davis take only $50,000 in cash because of a cash shortage at the time of his withdrawal; he agrees to this request. The following journal entry records Davis's withdrawal:

$A = L + OE$
$-$ $+$ $-$

20x3

Jan. 21	Richard Davis, Capital	60,000	
	Cash		50,000
	Notes Payable, Richard Davis		10,000
	Withdrawal of Richard Davis from the partnership		

When a withdrawing partner removes assets that represent less than his or her capital balance, the equity he or she leaves in the business is divided among the remaining partners according to their stated ratios. This distribution is considered a bonus to the remaining partners. When a withdrawing partner takes out assets greater than his or her capital balance, the excess is treated as a bonus to the withdrawing partner. The remaining partners absorb the bonus according to their stated ratios. Alternative arrangements can be spelled out in the partnership agreement.

Death of a Partner

When a partner dies, the partnership is dissolved because the original association has changed. The partnership agreement should state the actions to be taken. Normally, the books are closed and financial statements are prepared. Those actions are necessary to determine the capital balance of each partner on the date of the death. The agreement may also indicate whether an audit should be conducted, assets appraised, and a bonus recorded, as well as the procedures for settling with the heirs. The remaining partners may purchase the deceased's equity, sell it to outsiders, or deliver specified business assets to the estate. If the firm intends to continue, a new partnership must be formed.

Liquidation of a Partnership

OBJECTIVE

6 Compute the distribution of assets to partners when they liquidate their partnership

The **liquidation** of a partnership is the process of ending the business, of selling enough assets to pay the partnership's liabilities, and distributing any remaining assets among the partners. Liquidation is a special form of dissolution. When a partnership is liquidated, the business will not continue.

The partnership agreement should indicate the procedures to be followed in the case of liquidation. Usually, the books are adjusted and closed, with the income or loss distributed to the partners. As the assets of the business are sold, any gain or loss should be distributed to the partners according to the stated ratios. As cash becomes available, it must be applied first to outside creditors, then to partners' loans, and finally to the partners' capital balances.

The process of liquidation can have a variety of financial outcomes. We look at two: (1) assets sold for a gain and (2) assets sold for a loss. For both alternatives, we make the assumptions that the books have been closed for Adcock, Villa, Davis & Company and that the following balance sheet exists before liquidation:

Adcock, Villa, Davis & Company			
Balance Sheet			
February 2, 20x4			
Assets		**Liabilities**	
Cash	$ 60,000	Accounts Payable	$120,000
Accounts Receivable	40,000	**Partners' Equity**	
Merchandise Inventory	100,000		
Plant Assets (net)	200,000	Adcock, Capital	85,000
Total Assets	$400,000	Villa, Capital	95,000
		Davis, Capital	100,000
		Total Liabilities and Partners' Equity	$400,000

The stated ratios of Adcock, Villa, and Davis are 3:3:4, or 30, 30, and 40 percent, respectively.

Gain on Sale of Assets

Suppose that the following transactions took place in the liquidation of Adcock, Villa, Davis & Company:

1. The accounts receivable were collected for $35,000.
2. The inventory was sold for $110,000.
3. The plant assets were sold for $200,000.
4. The accounts payable of $120,000 were paid.
5. The gain of $5,000 from the realization of the assets was distributed according to the partners' stated ratios.
6. The partners received cash equivalent to the balances of their Capital accounts.

These transactions are summarized in the statement of liquidation in Exhibit 2. The journal entries with their assumed transaction dates are as follows:

Explanation on Statement of
Liquidation

	20x4			
A = L + OE	Feb. 13	Cash	35,000		1
+		Gain or Loss from Realization	5,000	
−		Accounts Receivable		40,000
		Collection of accounts		
		receivable		
A = L + OE	14	Cash	110,000		2
+ +		Merchandise Inventory		100,000
−		Gain or Loss from Realization		10,000
		Sale of inventory		
A = L + OE	16	Cash	200,000		3
+		Plant Assets		200,000
−		Sale of plant assets		
A = L + OE	16	Accounts Payable	120,000		4
− −		Cash		120,000
		Payment of accounts payable		
A = L + OE	20	Gain or Loss from Realization	5,000		5
−		Jerry Adcock, Capital		1,500
+		Rose Villa, Capital		1,500
+		Richard Davis, Capital		2,000
+		Distribution of the gain		
		on assets ($10,000 gain		
		minus $5,000 loss) to the partners		
A = L + OE	20	Jerry Adcock, Capital	86,500		6
− −		Rose Villa, Capital	96,500	
−		Richard Davis, Capital	102,000	
−		Cash		285,000
		Distribution of cash to the partners		

Exhibit 2
Statement of Liquidation Showing Gain on Sale of Assets

Adcock, Villa, Davis & Company
Statement of Liquidation
February 2–20, 20x4

Explanation	Cash	Other Assets	Accounts Payable	Adcock, Capital (30%)	Villa, Capital (30%)	Davis, Capital (40%)	Gain (or Loss) from Realization
Balance 2/2/x4	$ 60,000	$340,000	$120,000	$85,000	$95,000	$100,000	
1. Collection of Accounts Receivable	35,000	(40,000)					($ 5,000)
	$ 95,000	$300,000	$120,000	$85,000	$95,000	$100,000	($ 5,000)
2. Sale of Inventory	110,000	(100,000)					10,000
	$205,000	$200,000	$120,000	$85,000	$95,000	$100,000	$ 5,000
3. Sale of Plant Assets	200,000	(200,000)					
	$405,000	—	$120,000	$85,000	$95,000	$100,000	$ 5,000
4. Payment of Liabilities	(120,000)		(120,000)				
	$285,000		—	$85,000	$95,000	$100,000	$ 5,000
5. Distribution of Gain (or Loss) from Realization				1,500	1,500	2,000	(5,000)
	$285,000			$86,500	$96,500	$102,000	—
6. Distribution to Partners	(285,000)			(86,500)	(96,500)	(102,000)	
	—			—	—	—	

Notice that the cash distributed to the partners is the balance in their respective Capital accounts. Cash is not distributed according to the partners' stated ratios.

Loss on Sale of Assets

We discuss two cases involving losses on the sale of a company's assets. In the first, the losses are small enough to be absorbed by the partners' capital balances. In the second, one partner's share of the losses is too large for his capital balance to absorb.

When a firm's assets are sold at a loss, the partners share the loss on liquidation according to their stated ratios. For example, assume that during the liquidation of Adcock, Villa, Davis & Company, the total cash received from the collection of accounts receivable and the sale of inventory and plant assets was $140,000. The statement of liquidation appears in Exhibit 3, and the journal entries for the liquidation are as follows:

<table>
<tr><td></td><td></td><td></td><td></td><td></td><td colspan="2">Explanation on Statement of Liquidation</td></tr>
<tr><td></td><td>20x4</td><td></td><td></td><td></td><td></td><td></td></tr>
<tr><td>A = L + OE</td><td>Feb. 15</td><td>Cash</td><td></td><td>140,000</td><td></td><td>1</td></tr>
<tr><td>+   −</td><td></td><td>Gain or Loss from Realization</td><td></td><td>200,000</td><td></td><td></td></tr>
<tr><td>−</td><td></td><td> Accounts Receivable</td><td></td><td></td><td>40,000</td><td></td></tr>
<tr><td>−</td><td></td><td> Merchandise Inventory</td><td></td><td></td><td>100,000</td><td></td></tr>
<tr><td>−</td><td></td><td> Plant Assets</td><td></td><td></td><td>200,000</td><td></td></tr>
<tr><td></td><td></td><td>   Collection of accounts receivable and the sale of inventory and plant assets</td><td></td><td></td><td></td><td></td></tr>
<tr><td>A = L + OE</td><td>16</td><td>Accounts Payable</td><td></td><td>120,000</td><td></td><td>2</td></tr>
<tr><td>−   −</td><td></td><td> Cash</td><td></td><td></td><td>120,000</td><td></td></tr>
<tr><td></td><td></td><td>   Payment of accounts payable</td><td></td><td></td><td></td><td></td></tr>
<tr><td>A = L + OE</td><td>20</td><td>Jerry Adcock, Capital</td><td></td><td>60,000</td><td></td><td>3</td></tr>
<tr><td>−</td><td></td><td>Rose Villa, Capital</td><td></td><td>60,000</td><td></td><td></td></tr>
<tr><td>−</td><td></td><td>Richard Davis, Capital</td><td></td><td>80,000</td><td></td><td></td></tr>
<tr><td>+</td><td></td><td> Gain or Loss from Realization</td><td></td><td></td><td>200,000</td><td></td></tr>
<tr><td></td><td></td><td>   Distribution of the loss on assets to the partners</td><td></td><td></td><td></td><td></td></tr>
<tr><td>A = L + OE</td><td>20</td><td>Jerry Adcock, Capital</td><td></td><td>25,000</td><td></td><td>4</td></tr>
<tr><td>−   −</td><td></td><td>Rose Villa, Capital</td><td></td><td>35,000</td><td></td><td></td></tr>
<tr><td>−</td><td></td><td>Richard Davis, Capital</td><td></td><td>20,000</td><td></td><td></td></tr>
<tr><td>−</td><td></td><td> Cash</td><td></td><td></td><td>80,000</td><td></td></tr>
<tr><td></td><td></td><td>   Distribution of cash to the partners</td><td></td><td></td><td></td><td></td></tr>
</table>

In some liquidations, a partner's share of the loss is greater than his or her capital balance. In such a situation, because partners are subject to unlimited liability, the partner must make up the deficit in his or her Capital account from personal assets. For example, suppose that after the sale of assets and the payment of liabilities, the remaining assets and partners' equity of Adcock, Villa, Davis & Company look like this:

Assets
Cash $ 30,000

Partners' Equity
  Adcock, Capital $25,000
  Villa, Capital   20,000
  Davis, Capital   (15,000) $ 30,000

Richard Davis must pay $15,000 into the partnership from personal funds to cover his deficit. If he pays cash to the partnership, the following entry would record the cash contribution:

<table>
<tr><td></td><td>20x4</td><td></td><td></td><td></td></tr>
<tr><td>A = L + OE</td><td>Feb. 20</td><td>Cash</td><td>15,000</td><td></td></tr>
<tr><td>+   +</td><td></td><td> Richard Davis, Capital</td><td></td><td>15,000</td></tr>
<tr><td></td><td></td><td>   Additional investment of Richard Davis to cover the negative balance in his Capital account</td><td></td><td></td></tr>
</table>

Exhibit 3
**Statement of Liquidation
Showing Loss on Sale of Assets**

Adcock, Villa, Davis & Company
Statement of Liquidation
February 2–20, 20x4

Explanation	Cash	Other Assets	Accounts Payable	Adcock, Capital (30%)	Villa, Capital (30%)	Davis, Capital (40%)	Gain (or Loss) from Realization
Balance 2/2/x4	$ 60,000	$340,000	$120,000	$85,000	$95,000	$100,000	
1. Collection of Accounts Receivable and Sale of Inventory and Plant Assets	140,000	(340,000)					($200,000)
	$200,000	—	$120,000	$85,000	$95,000	$100,000	($200,000)
2. Payment of Liabilities	(120,000)		(120,000)				
	$ 80,000		—	$85,000	$95,000	$100,000	($200,000)
3. Distribution of Gain (or Loss) from Realization				(60,000)	(60,000)	(80,000)	200,000
	$ 80,000			$25,000	$35,000	$ 20,000	—
4. Distribution to Partners	(80,000)			(25,000)	(35,000)	(20,000)	
	—			—	—	—	

After Davis pays $15,000, there is enough cash to pay Adcock and Villa their capital balances and, thus, to complete the liquidation. The transaction is recorded like this:

		20x4			
A = L + OE	Feb. 20	Jerry Adcock, Capital	25,000	
—	—	Rose Villa, Capital	20,000	
	—	Cash		45,000
		Distribution of cash to the partners		

If a partner does not have the cash to cover his or her obligations to the partnership, the remaining partners share the loss according to their established stated ratios. Remember that all partners have unlimited liability. As a result, if Richard Davis cannot pay the $15,000 deficit in his Capital account, Adcock and Villa must share the deficit according to their stated ratios. Each has a 30 percent stated ratio, so each must pay 50 percent of the losses that Davis cannot pay. The new stated ratios are computed as follows:

	Old Ratios	New Ratios	
Adcock	30%	30 ÷ 60 = .50 =	50%
Villa	30	30 ÷ 60 = .50 =	50
	60%		100%

And the journal entries to record the transactions are as follows:

			20x4			
A = L + OE		Feb. 20	Jerry Adcock, Capital		7,500	
−			Rose Villa, Capital		7,500	
−			Richard Davis, Capital			15,000
+			Transfer of Davis's deficit			
			to Adcock and Villa			
A = L + OE		20	Jerry Adcock, Capital		17,500	
−	−		Rose Villa, Capital		12,500	
−			Cash			30,000
			Distribution of cash to the partners			

Davis's inability to meet his obligations at the time of liquidation does not relieve him of his liabilities to Adcock and Villa. If he is able to pay his liabilities at some time in the future, Adcock and Villa can collect the amount of Davis's deficit that they absorbed.

Chapter Review

REVIEW OF LEARNING OBJECTIVES

Check out ACE, a self-quizzing program on chapter content, at http://college.hmco.com.

1. Identify the principal characteristics, advantages, and disadvantages of the partnership form of business. A partnership has several major characteristics that distinguish it from the other forms of business. It is a voluntary association of two or more people who combine their talents and resources to carry on a business. Their joint effort should be supported by a partnership agreement that spells out the venture's operating procedures. A partnership is dissolved by a partner's admission, withdrawal, or death, and therefore has a limited life. Each partner acts as an agent of the partnership within the scope of normal operations and is personally liable for the partnership's debts. Property invested in the partnership becomes an asset of the partnership, owned jointly by all the partners. And, finally, each partner has the right to share in the company's income and the responsibility to share in its losses.

The advantages of a partnership are the ease of its formation and dissolution, the opportunity to pool several individuals' talents and resources, the lack of corporate tax burden, and the freedom of action each partner enjoys. The disadvantages are the limited life of a partnership, mutual agency, the unlimited personal liability of the partners, and the difficulty of raising large amounts of capital and transferring partners' interest. Two other common forms of association that are a type of partnership or similar to a partnership are limited partnerships and joint ventures.

2. **Record partners' investments of cash and other assets when a partnership is formed.** A partnership is formed when the partners contribute cash, other assets, or a combination of both to the business. The details are stated in the partnership agreement. Initial investments are recorded with a debit to Cash or another asset account and a credit to the investing partner's Capital account. The recorded amount of the other assets should be their fair market value on the date of transfer to the partnership. In addition, a partnership can assume an investing partner's liabilities. When this occurs, the partner's Capital account is credited with the difference between the assets invested and the liabilities assumed.

3. **Compute and record the income or losses that partners share, based on stated ratios, capital balance ratios, and partners' salaries and interest.** The partners must share income and losses in accordance with the partnership agreement. If the agreement says nothing about the distribution of income and losses, the partners share them equally. Common methods used for distributing income and losses include stated ratios, capital balance ratios, and salaries and interest on capital investments. Each method tries to measure the individual partner's contribution to the operations of the business. Stated ratios usually are based on the partners' relative contributions to the partnership. When capital balance ratios are used, income or losses are divided strictly on the basis of each partner's capital balance. The use of salaries and interest on capital investment takes into account both efforts (salary) and capital investment (interest) in dividing income or losses among the partners.

4. **Record a person's admission to a partnership.** An individual is admitted to a partnership by purchasing a partner's interest or by contributing additional assets. When an interest is purchased, the withdrawing partner's capital is transferred to the new partner. When the new partner contributes assets to the partnership, it may be necessary to recognize a bonus shared or borne by the original partners or by the new partner.

5. **Record a person's withdrawal from a partnership.** A person can withdraw from a partnership by selling his or her interest in the business to the remaining partners or a new partner, or by withdrawing company assets. When assets are withdrawn, the amount can be equal to, less than, or greater than the partner's capital interest. When assets that have a value less than or greater than the partner's interest are withdrawn, a bonus is recognized and distributed among the remaining partners or to the departing partner.

6. **Compute the distribution of assets to partners when they liquidate their partnership.** The liquidation of a partnership entails selling the assets necessary to pay the company's liabilities and then distributing any remaining assets to the partners. Any gain or loss on the sale of the assets is shared by the partners according to their stated ratios. When a partner has a deficit balance in a Capital account, that partner must contribute personal assets equal to the deficit. When a partner does not have personal assets to cover a capital deficit, the deficit must be absorbed by the solvent partners according to their stated ratios.

REVIEW OF CONCEPTS AND TERMINOLOGY

The following concepts and terms were introduced in this chapter:

LO 4 **Bonus:** An amount that accrues to the original partners when a new partner pays more to the partnership than the interest received or that accrues to the new partner when the amount paid to the partnership is less than the interest received.

LO 4 **Dissolution:** The loss of authority to continue a partnership as a separate entity due to a change in the original association of partners.

LO 1 **Joint venture:** An association of two or more entities for the purpose of achieving a specific goal, such as the manufacture of a product in a new market.

LO 1 **Limited life:** A characteristic of a partnership; the fact that any event that breaches the partnership agreement—including the admission, withdrawal, or death of a partner—terminates the partnership.

LO 1 **Limited partnership:** A form of partnership in which limited partners' liabilities are limited to their investment.

LO 6 **Liquidation:** A special form of dissolution in which a business ends by selling assets, paying liabilities, and distributing any remaining assets to the partners.

LO 1 **Mutual agency:** A characteristic of a partnership; the authority of each partner to act as an agent of the partnership within the scope of the business's normal operations.

LO 2 **Partners' equity:** The owner's equity in a partnership.

LO 1 **Partnership:** An association of two or more people to carry on as co-owners of a business for profit.

LO 1 **Partnership agreement:** The contractual relationship between partners that identifies the details of their partnership.

LO 1 **Unlimited liability:** A characteristic of a partnership; the fact that each partner has personal liability for all the debts of the partnership.

REVIEW PROBLEM

Distribution of Income and Admission of a Partner

LO 3
LO 4
Jack Holder and Dan Williams reached an agreement in 20x7 to pool their resources and form a partnership to manufacture and sell university T-shirts. In forming the partnership, Holder and Williams contributed $100,000 and $150,000, respectively. They drafted a partnership agreement stating that Holder was to receive an annual salary of $6,000 and Williams was to receive 3 percent interest annually on his original investment of $150,000 in the business. Income and losses after salary and interest were to be shared by Holder and Williams in a 2:3 ratio.

REQUIRED

1. Compute the income or loss that Holder and Williams share, and prepare the required entries in journal form, assuming the partnership made $27,000 income in 20x7 and suffered a $2,000 loss in 20x8 (before salary and interest).

2. Assume that Jean Ratcliffe offers Holder and Williams $60,000 for a 15 percent interest in the partnership on January 1, 20x9. Holder and Williams agree to Ratcliffe's offer because they need her resources to expand the business. The capital balances of Holder and Williams are $113,600 and $161,400, respectively, on January 1, 20x9. Record the admission of Ratcliffe to the partnership, assuming that her investment represents a 15 percent interest in the total partners' capital and that a bonus will be distributed to Holder and Williams in the ratio of 2:3.

1. Compute the income or loss distribution to the partners.

	Income of Partner		Income Distributed
	Holder	Williams	
20x7			
Total Income for Distribution			$27,000
Distribution of Salary			
Holder	$ 6,000		(6,000)
Remaining Income After Salary			$21,000
Distribution of Interest			
Williams ($150,000 × .03)		$ 4,500	(4,500)
Remaining Income After Salary and Interest			$16,500
Distribution of Remaining Income			
Holder ($16,500 × ⅖)	6,600		
Williams ($16,500 × ⅗)		9,900	(16,500)
Remaining Income			—
Income of Partners	$12,600	$14,400	$27,000
20x8			
Total Loss for Distribution			($ 2,000)
Distribution of Salary			
Holder	$ 6,000		(6,000)
Negative Balance After Salary			($ 8,000)
Distribution of Interest			
Williams ($150,000 × .03)		$ 4,500	(4,500)
Negative Balance After Salary and Interest			($12,500)
Distribution of Negative Balance			
Holder ($12,500 × ⅖)	(5,000)		
Williams ($12,500 × ⅗)		(7,500)	12,500
Remaining Loss			—
Income and Loss of Partners	$ 1,000	($ 3,000)	($ 2,000)

Entry in Journal Form—20x7

Income Summary	27,000	
Jack Holder, Capital		12,600
Dan Williams, Capital		14,400
Distribution of income for the year to the partners' Capital accounts		

Entry in Journal Form—20x8

Dan Williams, Capital	3,000	
Income Summary		2,000
Jack Holder, Capital		1,000
Distribution of the loss for the year to the partners' Capital accounts		

2. Record the admission of a new partner.

Capital Balance and Bonus Computation

$$\text{Ratcliffe, Capital} = (\text{Original Partners' Capital} + \text{New Partner's Investment}) \times 15\%$$
$$= (\$113,600 + \$161,400 + \$60,000) \times .15 = \$50,250$$
$$\text{Bonus} = \text{New Partner's Investment} - \text{Ratcliffe, Capital}$$
$$= \$60,000 - \$50,250$$
$$= \$9,750$$

Distribution of Bonus

$$\text{Holder} = \$9,750 \times \tfrac{2}{5} = \$3,900$$

$$\text{Williams} = \$9,750 \times \tfrac{3}{5} = \underline{5,850}$$

$$\text{Total bonus} \quad \underline{\underline{\$9,750}}$$

Entry in Journal Form

20x9			
Jan. 1	Cash	60,000	
	Jack Holder, Capital		3,900
	Dan Williams, Capital		5,850
	Jean Ratcliffe, Capital		50,250
	Sale of a 15 percent interest in the partnership to Jean Ratcliffe and the bonus paid to the original partners		

Chapter Assignments

BUILDING YOUR KNOWLEDGE FOUNDATION

QUESTIONS

1. Briefly define *partnership* and list several important characteristics of the partnership form of business.
2. Leon and Jon are partners in a drilling operation. Leon purchased a drilling rig to be used in the partnership's operations. Is Leon's purchase binding on Jon even though Jon was not involved in it? Explain your answer.
3. What is the meaning of unlimited liability when applied to a partnership? Describe a form of partnership that limits investors' liability.
4. The partnership agreement for Anne and Jin-Li does not disclose how they will share income and losses. How would the income and losses be shared in this partnership?
5. What are several key advantages of a partnership? What are some disadvantages?
6. How does a limited partnership overcome a key disadvantage of ordinary partnerships?
7. What form of association is becoming more prevalent in conducting global business? Define it.

8. Charles contributes $10,000 in cash and a building with a book value of $40,000 and fair market value of $50,000 to the Charles and Dean partnership. What is the balance of Charles's Capital account in the partnership?

9. Oscar Perez and Leah Torn are forming a partnership. What are some factors they should consider in deciding how income is to be divided?

10. Sue and Ari share income and losses in their partnership in a 3:2 ratio. The firm's net income for the current year is $80,000. How would the distribution of income be recorded in the journal?

11. Kathy and Roger share income in their partnership in a 2:4 ratio. Kathy and Roger receive salaries of $6,000 and $10,000, respectively. How would they share a net income of $22,000 before salaries?

12. Carol purchases Mary's interest in the Mary and Leo partnership for $62,000. Mary has a $57,000 capital interest in the partnership. How would this transaction be recorded in the partnership books?

13. Dan and Augie each own a $50,000 interest in a partnership. They agree to admit Bea as a partner by selling her a one-third interest for $80,000. How large a bonus will be distributed to Dan and Augie?

14. Describe how the dissolution of a partnership differs from the liquidation of a partnership.

15. In the liquidation of a partnership, José's Capital account showed a $5,000 debit balance after all the creditors had been paid. What obligation does José have to the partnership?

SHORT EXERCISES

SE 1.
LO 1 Partnership Characteristics

Indicate whether each statement below is a reflection of (a) voluntary association, (b) a partnership agreement, (c) limited life, (d) mutual agency, or (e) unlimited liability.

1. A partner may be required to pay the debts of the partnership out of personal assets.
2. A partnership must be dissolved when a partner is admitted, withdraws, retires, or dies.
3. Any partner can bind the partnership to a business agreement.
4. A partner does not have to remain a partner if he or she does not want to.
5. Details of the arrangements among partners are specified in a written contract.

SE 2.
LO 2 Partnership Formation

Bob contributes cash of $12,000 and Kim contributes office equipment that cost $10,000 but is valued at $8,000 to the formation of a new partnership. Prepare the entry in journal form to form the partnership.

SE 3.
LO 3 Distribution of Partnership Income

During the first year, the Bob and Kim partnership (see **SE 2**) earned an income of $5,000. Assume the partners agreed to share income and losses in the ratio of the beginning balances of their capital accounts. How much income should be transferred to each Capital account?

SE 4.
LO 3 Distribution of Partnership Income

During the first year, the Bob and Kim partnership (see **SE 2**) earned an income of $5,000. Assume the partners agreed to share income and losses by figuring interest on the beginning capital balances at 10 percent and dividing the remainder equally. How much income should be transferred to each Capital account?

SE 5.
LO 3 Distribution of Partnership Income

During the first year, the Bob and Kim partnership (see **SE 2**) earned an income of $5,000. Assume the partners agreed to share income and losses by figuring interest on the beginning capital balances at 10 percent, allowing a salary of $6,000 to Bob, and dividing the remainder equally. How much income (or loss) should be transferred to each Capital account?

SE 6.

LO 4 **Withdrawal of a Partner**
LO 5 **and Admission of a Partner**

After a year of operating as partners, the Capital accounts of Bob and Kim are $15,000 and $10,000, respectively. Kim withdraws from the partnership by selling her interest in the business to Sonia for $8,000. What will be the Capital account balances of the partners in the new Bob and Sonia partnership? Prepare the journal entry to record the transfer of ownership on the partnership books.

SE 7.

LO 4 **Admission of a New Partner**

After a year of operating as partners, the Capital accounts of Bob and Kim are $15,000 and $10,000, respectively. Sonia buys a one-sixth interest in the partnership by investing cash of $11,000. What will be the Capital account balances of the partners in the new Bob, Kim, and Sonia partnership, assuming a bonus to the old partners, who share income and losses equally? Prepare the entry in journal form to record the transfer of ownership on the partnership books.

SE 8.

LO 4 **Admission of a New Partner**

After a year of operating as partners, the Capital accounts of Bob and Kim are $15,000 and $10,000, respectively. Sonia buys a one-fourth interest in the partnership by investing cash of $5,000. What will be the Capital account balances of the partners in the new Bob, Kim, and Sonia partnership, assuming that the new partner receives a bonus and that Bob and Kim share income and losses equally? Prepare the entry in journal form to record the transfer of ownership on the partnership books.

SE 9.

LO 5 **Withdrawal of a Partner**

After several years of operating as partners, the Capital accounts of Bob, Kim, and Sonia are $25,000, $16,000, and $9,000, respectively. Sonia decides to leave the partnership and is allowed to withdraw $9,000 in cash. Prepare the entry in journal form to record the withdrawal on the partnership books.

SE 10.

LO 6 **Liquidation of a Partnership**

After a year of operating as partners, the Capital accounts of Bob and Kim are $15,000 and $10,000, respectively. The firm has cash of $12,000 and office equipment of $13,000. The partners decide to liquidate the partnership. The office equipment is sold for only $4,000. Assuming the partners share income and losses in the ratio of one-third to Bob and two-thirds to Kim, how much cash will be distributed to each partner in liquidation?

EXERCISES

E 1.

LO 2 **Partnership Formation**

Jorge Miguel and August Jones are watch repairmen who want to form a partnership and open a jewelry store. They have an attorney prepare their partnership agreement, which indicates that assets invested in the partnership will be recorded at their fair market value and that liabilities will be assumed at book value.

The assets contributed by each partner and the liabilities assumed by the partnership are as follows:

Assets	Jorge Miguel	August Jones	Total
Cash	$40,000	$30,000	$70,000
Accounts Receivable	52,000	20,000	72,000
Allowance for Uncollectible			
Accounts	4,000	3,000	7,000
Supplies	1,000	500	1,500
Equipment	20,000	10,000	30,000
Liabilities			
Accounts Payable	32,000	9,000	41,000

Prepare the entry in journal form necessary to record the original investments of Miguel and Jones in the partnership.

E 2.
LO 3   Distribution of Income

Eldridge Samms and Tom Winston agreed to form a partnership. Samms contributed $200,000 in cash, and Winston contributed assets with a fair market value of $400,000. The partnership, in its initial year, reported net income of $120,000. Calculate the distribution of the first year's income to the partners under each of the following conditions:

1. Samms and Winston failed to include stated ratios in the partnership agreement.
2. Samms and Winston agreed to share income and losses in a 3:2 ratio.
3. Samms and Winston agreed to share income and losses in the ratio of their original investments.
4. Samms and Winston agreed to share income and losses by allowing 10 percent interest on original investments and sharing any remainder equally.

E 3.
LO 3   Distribution of Income or
Losses: Salary and Interest

Assume that the partnership agreement of Samms and Winston in **E 2** states that Samms and Winston are to receive salaries of $20,000 and $24,000, respectively; that Samms is to receive 6 percent interest on his capital balance at the beginning of the year; and that the remainder of income and losses are to be shared equally. Calculate the distribution of the income or losses under the following conditions:

1. Income totaled $120,000 before deductions for salaries and interest.
2. Income totaled $48,000 before deductions for salaries and interest.
3. There was a loss of $2,000.
4. There was a loss of $40,000.

E 4.
LO 3   Distribution of Income:
Average Capital Balance

Bess and Crystal operate a furniture rental business. Their capital balances on January 1, 20x7, were $160,000 and $240,000, respectively. Bess withdrew cash of $32,000 from the business on April 1, 20x7. Crystal withdrew $60,000 cash on October 1, 20x7. Bess and Crystal distribute partnership income based on their average capital balances each year. Income for 20x7 was $160,000. Compute the income to be distributed to Bess and Crystal using their average capital balances in 20x7.

E 5.
LO 4   Admission of a New Partner:
Recording a Bonus

Elias, Ray, and Gerry have equity in a partnership of $40,000, $40,000, and $60,000, respectively, and they share income and losses in a ratio of 1:1:3. The partners have agreed to admit Hollis to the partnership. Prepare entries in journal form to record the admission of Hollis to the partnership under the following conditions:

1. Hollis invests $60,000 for a 20 percent interest in the partnership, and a bonus is recorded for the original partners.
2. Hollis invests $60,000 for a 40 percent interest in the partnership, and a bonus is recorded for Hollis.

E 6.
LO 5   Withdrawal of a Partner

Donald, Sam, and Hitoshi are partners. They share income and losses in the ratio of 3:2:1. Hitoshi's Capital account has a $120,000 balance. Donald and Sam have agreed to let Hitoshi take $160,000 of the company's cash when he retires from the business. What entry in journal form must be made on the partnership's books when Hitoshi retires, assuming that a bonus to Hitoshi is recognized and absorbed by the remaining partners?

E 7.
LO 6   Partnership Liquidation

Assume the following assets, liabilities, and partners' equity in the Phung and Dordek partnership on December 31, 20xx:

$$\text{Assets} = \text{Liabilities} + \text{Phung, Capital} + \text{Dordek, Capital}$$
$$\$160,000 = \$10,000 + \$90,000 + \$60,000$$

The partnership has no cash. When the partners agree to liquidate the business, the assets are sold for $120,000 and the liabilities are paid. Phung and Dordek share income and losses in a ratio of 3:1.

1. Prepare a statement of liquidation.

2. Prepare entries in journal form for the sale of assets, payment of liabilities, distribution of loss from realization, and final distribution of cash to Phung and Dordek.

E 8.

LO 6   Partnership Liquidation

Alice, Meg, and Terry are partners in a tanning salon. The assets, liabilities, and capital balances as of July 1, 20x7, are as follows:

Assets	$480,000
Liabilities	160,000
Alice, Capital	140,000
Meg, Capital	40,000
Terry, Capital	140,000

Because competition is strong, business is declining, and the partnership has no cash, the partners have decided to sell the business. Alice, Meg, and Terry share income and losses in a ratio of 3:1:1, respectively. The assets were sold for $260,000, and the liabilities were paid. Meg has no other assets and will not be able to cover any deficits in her Capital account. How will the ending cash balance be distributed to the partners?

PROBLEMS

P 1.

LO 2   Partnership Formation
LO 3   and Distribution of Income

On January 1, 20x1, Joyce Chan and Kim Nichols agreed to form a partnership to operate an educational consulting business. Chan and Nichols invested cash of $90,000 and $60,000, respectively, in the partnership. The business had normal first-year problems, but during the second year the operation was very successful. For 20x1, they reported a $30,000 loss; for 20x2, an $80,000 income.

REQUIRED

1. Prepare the entry in journal form to record the investment of both partners in the partnership.

2. Determine Chan's and Nichols's share of the income or loss for each year, assuming each of the following methods of sharing income and losses: (a) The partners agreed to share income and losses equally. (b) They agreed to share income and losses in the ratio of 7:3 for Chan and Nichols, respectively. (c) They agreed to share income according to their original capital investment ratio, but the agreement did not mention losses. (d) They agreed to share income and losses in the ratio of their capital balances at the beginning of each year. (e) They agreed to share income and losses by allowing interest of 10 percent on original investments and dividing the remainder equally. (f) They agreed to share income and losses by paying salaries of $20,000 to Chan and $15,000 to Nichols, allowing interest of 10 percent on original investments, and dividing the remainder equally.

P 2.

LO 3   Distribution of Income:
Salary and Interest

Gregory, Jerome, and Owen are partners in the Custom Tech Company. The partnership agreement states that Gregory is to receive 8 percent interest on his capital balance at the beginning of the year, Jerome is to receive a salary of $50,000 a year, and Owen will be paid interest of 6 percent on his average capital balance during the year. Gregory, Jerome, and Owen will share any income or loss after salary and interest in a 5:3:2 ratio. Gregory's capital balance at the beginning of the year was $300,000, and Owen's average capital balance for the year was $360,000.

REQUIRED

Determine each partner's share of income and losses under each of the following conditions. In each case, the income or loss is stated before the distribution of salary and interest.

1. Income was $272,600.
2. Income was $77,800.
3. The loss was $28,400.

P 3.
LO 4 Admission and Withdrawal
LO 5 of a Partner

REQUIRED

Alicia, Roberta, and Joanne are partners in the Image Gallery. The balances in the Capital accounts of Alicia, Roberta, and Joanne as of November 30, 20xx, are $50,000, $60,000, and $90,000, respectively. The partners share income and losses in a ratio of 2:3:5.

Prepare journal entries for each of the following independent conditions: (a) Luke pays Joanne $100,000 for four-fifths of Joanne's interest. (b) Luke is to be admitted to the partnership with a one-third interest for a $100,000 cash investment. (c) Luke is to be admitted to the partnership with a one-third interest for a $160,000 cash investment. A bonus, based on the partners' ratio for income and losses, is to be distributed to the original partners when Luke is admitted. (d) Luke is to be admitted to the partnership with a one-third interest for an $82,000 cash investment. A bonus is to be given to Luke on admission. (e) Alicia withdraws from the partnership, taking $66,000 in cash. (f) Alicia withdraws from the partnership by selling her interest directly to Luke for $70,000.

P 4.
LO 6 Partnership Liquidation

The balance sheet of the GDL Partnership as of August 31, 20xx, is as follows:

GDL Partnership
Balance Sheet
August 31, 20xx

Assets		Liabilities	
Cash	$ 12,000	Accounts Payable	$ 960,000
Accounts Receivable	240,000	**Partners' Equity**	
Inventory	528,000		
Equipment (net)	924,000	Gary, Capital	144,000
Total Assets	$1,704,000	Dawn, Capital	360,000
		Leslie, Capital	240,000
		Total Liabilities and Partners' Equity	$1,704,000

The partners—Gary, Dawn, and Leslie—share income and losses in the ratio of 5:3:2. Because of a mutual disagreement, the partners have decided to liquidate the business.

Assume that Gary cannot contribute any additional personal assets to the company during liquidation and that the following transactions occurred during liquidation: (a) Accounts receivable were sold for 60 percent of their book value. (b) Inventory was sold for $552,000. (c) Equipment was sold for $600,000. (d) Accounts payable were paid in full. (e) Gain or loss from realization was distributed to the partners' Capital accounts. (f) Gary's deficit was transferred to the remaining partners in their new income and loss ratio. (g) The remaining cash was distributed to Dawn and Leslie.

REQUIRED

1. Prepare a statement of liquidation.
2. Prepare journal entries to liquidate the partnership and distribute any remaining cash.

P 5.

LO 2 **Comprehensive Partnership**
LO 3 **Transactions**
LO 4
LO 6

Sam Flippo and Henry McCovey formed a partnership on January 1, 20x1, to operate a computer software store. To begin the partnership, Flippo transferred cash totaling $116,000 and office equipment valued at $84,000 to the partnership. McCovey transferred cash of $56,000, land valued at $36,000, and a building valued at $300,000. In addition, the partnership assumed the mortgage of $232,000 on the building.

On December 31, the partnership reported a loss of $16,000 for its first year. In the partnership agreement, the owners had specified the distribution of income and losses by allowing salaries of $20,000 to Flippo and $48,000 to McCovey, interest of 10 percent on beginning capital, and the remaining amount to be divided in the ratio of 3:2.

On January 1, 20x2, the partners brought Mel Stanford, who was experienced in the software business, into the partnership. Stanford invested $56,000 in the partnership for a 20 percent interest. The bonus to Stanford was transferred from the original partners' accounts in the ratio of 3:2.

During 20x2, the partnership earned an income of $108,000. The new partnership agreement required that income and losses be divided by allowing salaries of $20,000, $48,000, and $60,000 for Flippo, McCovey, and Stanford, and by paying interest of 10 percent on capital balances at the beginning of the year. Remaining amounts were to be divided equally.

Unhappy with the level of income, the partners decided to liquidate the partnership on January 1, 20x3. On that date, the assets and liabilities of the partnership were as follows: Cash, $244,000; Accounts Receivable, $152,000; Land, $36,000; Building (net), $280,000; Office Equipment (net), $108,000; Accounts Payable, $108,000; and Mortgage Payable, $204,000.

The office equipment was sold for $72,000, and the accounts receivable were valued at $128,000. The accounts payable were paid. The losses were distributed equally to the partners' Capital accounts. Flippo agreed to accept the accounts receivable plus cash in payment for his partnership interest. McCovey accepted the land, building, and mortgage payable at book value plus cash for his share in the liquidation. Stanford was paid in cash.

REQUIRED

Prepare entries in journal form to record all the facts above. Support your computations with schedules, and prepare a statement of liquidation in connection with the January 1, 20x3, entries.

ALTERNATE PROBLEMS

P 6.

LO 3 **Distribution of Income:**
Salary and Interest

Gloria and Dennis are partners in a tennis shop. They have agreed that Gloria will operate the store and receive a salary of $52,000 per year. Dennis will receive 10 percent interest on his average capital balance during the year of $250,000. The remaining income or losses are to be shared by Gloria and Dennis in a 2:3 ratio.

REQUIRED

Determine each partner's share of income and losses under each of the following conditions. In each case, the income or loss is stated before the distribution of salary and interest.

1. Income was $84,000.
2. Income was $44,000.
3. The loss was $12,800.

P 7.

LO 4 **Admission and Withdrawal**
LO 5 **of a Partner**

Renee, Esther, and Jane are partners in Seabury Woodwork Company. Their capital balances as of July 31, 20x4, are as follows:

Renee, Capital		Esther, Capital		Jane, Capital	
	90,000		30,000		60,000

Each partner has agreed to admit Maureen to the partnership.

REQUIRED

Prepare the journal entries to record Maureen's admission to or Renee's withdrawal from the partnership under each of the following independent conditions: (a) Maureen pays Renee $25,000 for 20 percent of Renee's interest in the partnership. (b) Maureen invests $40,000 cash in the partnership and receives an interest equal to her investment. (c) Maureen invests $60,000 cash in the partnership for a 20 percent interest in the business. A bonus is to be recorded for the original partners on the basis of their capital balances. (d) Maureen invests $60,000 cash in the partnership for a 40 percent interest in the business. The original partners give Maureen a bonus according to the ratio of their capital balances on July 31, 20x4. (e) Renee withdraws from the partnership, taking $105,000. The excess of assets over the partnership interest is distributed according to the balances of the Capital accounts. (f) Renee withdraws by selling her interest directly to Maureen for $120,000.

P 8.

LO 6   Partnership Liquidation

Nguyen, Waters, and Leach are partners in a retail lighting store. They share income and losses in the ratio of 2:2:1, respectively. The partners have agreed to liquidate the partnership. Here is the partnership balance sheet before the liquidation.

Nguyen, Waters, and Leach Partnership
Balance Sheet
May 31, 20x3

Assets		Liabilities	
Cash	$140,000	Accounts Payable	$180,000
Other Assets	440,000	**Partners' Equity**	
Total Assets	$580,000		
		Nguyen, Capital	200,000
		Waters, Capital	120,000
		Leach, Capital	80,000
		Total Liabilities and	
		Partners' Equity	$580,000

The other assets were sold on June 1, 20x3, for $360,000. Accounts payable were paid on June 4, 20x3. The remaining cash was distributed to the partners on June 11, 20x3.

REQUIRED

1. Prepare a statement of liquidation.
2. Prepare the following journal entries: (a) the sale of the other assets, (b) payment of the accounts payable, (c) the distribution of the partners' gain or loss on liquidation, and (d) the distribution to the partners of the remaining cash.

EXPANDING YOUR CRITICAL THINKING, COMMUNICATION, AND INTERPERSONAL SKILLS

SKILLS DEVELOPMENT

Conceptual Analysis

SD 1.
LO 1 Partnership Agreement

Form a partnership with one or two of your classmates. Assume that the two or three of you are forming a small service business. For example, you might form a company that hires college students to paint houses during the summer. Working together, draft a partnership agreement for your business. The agreement can be a simple one, with just a sentence or two for each provision, but it should include the name, location, and purpose of the business; the partners and their respective duties; the investments of each partner; methods for distributing profits and losses; and procedures for dealing with the admission or withdrawal of partners, the withdrawal of assets, the death of a partner, and liquidation of the business. Include a title, date, and signature lines.

Group Activity: Assign groups to prepare partnership agreements.

SD 2.
LO 3 Distribution of Partnership Income and Losses

List, Donohue, and Han, who are forming a partnership to operate an antiques gallery, are discussing how income and losses should be distributed. Among the facts they are considering are the following:

a. List will contribute cash for operations of $100,000, Donohue will contribute a collection of antiques valued at $300,000, and Han will not contribute any assets.
b. List and Han will handle day-to-day business operations. Han will work full time, and List will devote about half-time to the partnership. Donohue will not devote time to day-to-day operations. A full-time clerk in a retail store would make about $20,000 in a year, and a full-time manager would receive about $30,000.
c. The current interest rate on long-term bonds is 8 percent.

You have just been hired as the partnership's accountant. Write a memorandum describing an equitable plan for distributing income and losses. State your reasons why this plan is equitable. According to your plan, which partner will gain the most if the partnership is very profitable, and which will lose the most if the partnership has large losses?

Ethical Dilemma

SD 3.
LO 1 Death of Partner
LO 2
LO 5

South Shore Realty was started 20 years ago when J. B. Taylor, C. L. Sklar, and L. A. Hodges established a partnership to sell real estate near Galveston, Texas. The partnership has been extremely successful. In 20xx, Taylor, the senior partner, who in recent years had not been very active in the partnership, died. Unfortunately, the partnership agreement is vague about how the partnership interest of a partner who dies should be valued. It simply states that "the estate of a deceased partner shall receive compensation for his or her interest in the partnership in a reasonable time after death." The attorney for Taylor's family believes that the estate should receive one-third of the assets of the partnership based on the fair market value of the net assets (total assets less total liabilities). The total assets of the partnership are $10 million in the accounting records, but the assets are worth at least $20 million. Because the firm's total liabilities are $4 million, the attorney is asking for $5.3 million (one-third of $16 million).

Cash Flow   CD-ROM   Communication   Critical Thinking   Ethics   General Ledger   Group Activity   Hot Links to Real Companies   International   Internet   Key Ratio   Memo   Spreadsheet

Sklar and Hodges do not agree, but all parties want to avoid a protracted, expensive lawsuit. They have decided to put the question to an arbitrator, who will make a determination of the settlement.

Here are some other facts that may or may not be relevant. The current balances in the partners' Capital accounts are $1.5 million for Taylor, $2.5 million for Sklar, and $2.0 million for Hodges. Net income in 20xx is to be distributed to the Capital accounts in the ratio of 1:4:3. Before Taylor's semiretirement, the distribution ratio was 3:3:2. Assume you or your group is the arbitrator and develop what you would consider a fair distribution of assets to Taylor's estate. Defend your solution.

Research Activity

SD 4.

LO 1 Basic Research Skills

The limited partnership is a form of business that was particularly important to the U.S. economy in the 1980s. To find the latest developments or to study the practical applications of a particular subject, such as limited partnerships, it is helpful to use periodical indexes in the library to find articles relating to that subject. Three periodical indexes relevant to accounting and business are *The Accountant's Index*, the *Business Periodicals Index*, and *The Wall Street Journal Index*. Use one or more of those periodical indexes in your school library to find three articles about limited partnerships. Sometimes the articles are not listed under the heading "Limited Partnerships"; instead, they appear under the uses of limited partnerships. Some examples are real estate, investments, research and development, and cattle or livestock. Write a short summary of each article, relating the content of the article to the content of this chapter or explaining why the limited partnership form of business was important in the situation described in the article.

Decision-Making Practice

SD 5.

LO 4 Potential Partnership Purchase

The *A-One Fitness Center*, owned by John Kiel and Sunjat Patel, has been very successful since its inception five years ago. Kiel and Patel work 10 to 11 hours a day at the business. They have decided to expand by opening up another fitness center in the north part of town. Kiel has approached you about becoming a partner in the business. He and Patel are interested in you because of your experience in operating a small gym. Also, they need additional funds to expand their business. Projected income after the expansion but before partners' salaries for the next five years is as follows:

20x1	20x2	20x3	20x4	20x5
$100,000	$120,000	$130,000	$140,000	$150,000

Currently, Kiel and Patel each draw a $25,000 salary and share remaining profits equally. They are willing to give you an equal share of the business for $142,000. You will receive a $25,000 salary and one-third of the remaining profits. You would work the same hours as Kiel and Patel. Your salary for the next five years where you currently work is expected to be as follows:

20x1	20x2	20x3	20x4	20x5
$34,000	$38,000	$42,000	$45,000	$50,000

Here is financial information for the A-One Fitness Center:

Current Assets	$ 45,000	Long-Term Liabilities	$100,000
Plant and Equipment, net	365,000	John Kiel, Capital	140,000
Current Liabilities	50,000	Sunjat Patel, Capital	120,000

1. Compute your capital balance if you decide to join Kiel and Patel in the fitness center partnership.

2. Analyze your expected income for the next five years.

3. Should you invest in the A-One Fitness Center?

4. Assume that you do not consider Kiel and Patel's offer of partnership to be a good one. Develop a counteroffer that you would be willing to accept (be realistic).

FINANCIAL REPORTING AND ANALYSIS

Interpreting Financial Reports

FRA 1.

LO 1 **Effects of Lawsuit on**
LO 3 **Partnership**

The *Springfield Clinic* is owned and operated by ten local doctors as a partnership. Recently, a paralyzed patient sued the clinic for malpractice, for a total of $20 million. The clinic carries malpractice liability insurance in the amount of $10 million. There is no provision for the possible loss from this type of lawsuit in the partnership's financial statements. The condensed balance sheet for 20xx is as follows:

Springfield Clinic Condensed Balance Sheet December 31, 20xx		
Assets		
Current Assets	$246,000	
Property, Plant, and Equipment (net)	750,000	
Total Assets		$996,000
Liabilities and Partners' Equity		
Current Liabilities	$180,000	
Long-Term Debt	675,000	
Total Liabilities		$855,000
Partners' Equity		141,000
Total Liabilities and Partners' Equity		$996,000

1. How should information about the lawsuit be disclosed in the December 31, 20xx, financial statements of the partnership?

2. Assume that the clinic and its insurance company settle out of court by agreeing to pay a total of $10.1 million, of which $100,000 must be paid by the partnership. What effect will the payment have on the clinic's December 31, 20xx, financial statements? Discuss the effect of the settlement on the Springfield Clinic doctors' personal financial situations.

International Company

FRA 2.

LO 1 **International Joint Ventures**

Nokia, the Finnish telecommunications company, has formed an equally owned joint venture with **Capital Corporation,** a state-owned Chinese company, to develop a center for the manufacture and development of telecommunications equipment in China, the world's fastest-growing market for this kind of equipment. The main aim of the development is to persuade Nokia's suppliers to move close to the company's main plant. The Chinese government looks favorably on companies that involve local suppliers.[4] What advantages does a joint venture have over a single company in entering a new market in another country? What are the potential disadvantages?

Toys "R" Us Annual Report

The partnership chapter is not applicable to Toys "R" Us.

Fingraph® Financial Analysis™

The partnership chapter is not applicable to this case.

Internet Case

FRA 3.

LO 1 Comparison of Career Opportunities in Partnerships and Corporations

Accounting firms are among the world's largest partnerships and provide a wide range of attractive careers for business and accounting majors. Through the Needles Accounting Resource Center at http://college.hmco.com, you can explore careers in public accounting by linking to the web site of one of the big five accounting firms. The firms are Arthur Andersen, Deloitte & Touche, Ernst & Young, KPMG International, and PricewaterhouseCoopers. Each firm's home page has a career opportunity section. For the firm you choose, compile a list of facts about the firm—size, locations, services, and career opportunities. Do you have the interest and background for a career in public accounting? Why or why not? How do you think working for a large partnership would differ from or be the same as working for a large corporation? Be prepared to discuss your findings in class.

ENDNOTES

1. KPMG International, Internet site, May 16, 2000. KPMG has announced plans to separate its consulting practice as a corporation.
2. Information excerpted from the 1990 and 2000 annual reports of Alliance Capital Management Limited Partnership; wsj.com, November 17, 2000.
3. Anita Raghavan, "Goldman Scrambles to Find $250 Million in Equity Capital from Private Investors," *The Wall Street Journal*, September 15, 1994.
4. "Nokia Unveils Plans for Chinese Centre," *Financial Times London*, May 9, 2000.

14

Contributed Capital

DECISION POINT: A USER'S FOCUS

General Motors Corporation One way corporations raise new capital is by issuing stock. General Motors Corporation, a major automotive manufacturer, has issued common stock, including over $2.9 billion in a recent three-year period, as shown in the Financial Highlights from the statement of cash flows.[1] Why does General Motors' management choose to issue common stock to satisfy some of its needs for new capital? What are some disadvantages of this approach?

There are advantages to financing with common stock. First, financing with common stock is less risky than financing with bonds, because dividends on common stock are not paid unless the board of directors decides to pay them. In contrast, if the interest on bonds is not paid, a company can be forced into bankruptcy. Second, when a company does not pay a cash dividend, the cash generated by profitable operations can be invested in the company's operations. Third, and most important for General Motors, a company may need the proceeds of a common stock issue to improve the balance between liabilities and stockholders' equity. The company lost more than $23.5 billion in 1992, drastically reducing its stockholders' equity. However, by issuing common stock over the next several years, General Motors improved its debt to equity ratio and its credit rating.

Financial Highlights

(In millions of dollars)

	1999	1998	1997
Proceeds from issuing common stock	$2,005	$343	$614

On the other hand, issuing common stock has certain disadvantages. Unlike the interest on bonds, dividends paid on stock are not tax deductible. Furthermore, when it issues more stock, the corporation dilutes its ownership. This means that the current stockholders must yield some control to the new stockholders. It is important for accountants to understand the nature and characteristics of corporations as well as the process of accounting for a stock issue and other types of stock transactions.

Management Issues Related to Contributed Capital

A **corporation** is defined as "a body of persons granted a charter recognizing them as a separate legal entity having its own rights, privileges, and liabilities distinct from those of its members."[2] In other words, a corporation is a legal entity separate and distinct from its owners.

VIDEO CASE

 ## Lotus Development Corporation

Objectives

- To become familiar with the advantages of a corporation, especially in equity financing.
- To identify the ways investors obtain return on investment in a corporation.
- To show how stock buybacks affect return on equity as a measure of profitability.

Background for the Case

The story of software giant Lotus Development Corporation is a prototype of the recent history of high-technology com-

panies. When Lotus was founded in the early 1980s, its landmark spreadsheet program Lotus 1-2-3 was an overnight sensation at corporations because of its ability to make rapid calculations based on mathematical relationships in large databases. Lotus 1-2-3 went far beyond the rudimentary spreadsheets that preceded it by incorporating a database module and graphics capability. In October 1983, investors stampeded for the company's initial public offering of 2.6 million shares at $18 per share for a total of $46.8 million. For several years the company had no real competition. By 1992, more than 11 million units of Lotus 1-2-3 had been sold, but the company was unable to solidify its position by developing any new blockbuster products. Microsoft gained on Lotus and eventually passed it with its spreadsheet program Excel. Finally, Lotus developed a hit "groupware" product called Lotus Notes, which boosts productivity by enabling co-workers to share information and work together electronically on complex tasks. The large audit firm Coopers & Lybrand (now PricewaterhouseCoopers), for example, networks more than 2,000 auditors all over the world and the knowledge of experts in various parts of the firm via Lotus Notes. Many other big companies such as Ford, Unilever, and Citicorp (now Citigroup) are also using Lotus Notes successfully. The success of Lotus Notes attracted the notice of IBM, which had failed to develop its own groupware product. In 1995, IBM made a hostile takeover bid for Lotus and bought out the company. In fewer than 15 years, Lotus had gone from an intriguing startup to a mature company with sales of more than $1 billion and, finally, to a takeover candidate for a giant competitor.

For more information about Lotus, which is now a division of IBM, visit the company's or IBM's web site through the Needles Accounting Resource Center at:
http://college.hmco.com

Required

View the video on Lotus Development Corporation that accompanies this book. As you are watching the video, take notes related to the following questions:

1. All corporations must raise equity capital in the form of common stock. In your own words, what is common stock? What is the relationship of par value to market value of the common stock? What is an initial public offering (IPO)? Why was this IPO important in Lotus's early history?

2. Investors in corporations desire to receive an adequate return on their investment. What are the ways investors can receive a return? In what way did Lotus's shareholders receive a return?

3. From 1991 to 1993, the Lotus board of directors authorized the repurchase of 7,700,000 shares of the company's approximately 44,000,000 shares. What impact will the repurchase of these shares have on the investors' return? What role did the takeover by IBM play in achieving an adequate return to Lotus shareholders?

4. Return on equity is a common measure of management's ability to meet the company's profitability goal. What role do common stock buybacks (purchases of treasury stock) play in the company's increasing return on equity?

The management of contributed capital is a critical component in the financing of a corporation. Important issues faced by management in the area of contributed capital are managing under the corporate form of business, using equity financing, determining dividend policies, and evaluating performance using return on equity.

Forming a Corporation

To form a corporation, most states require individuals, called incorporators, to sign an application and file it with the proper state official. This application contains the **articles of incorporation**. If approved by the state, these articles become, in effect, a contract, called the company charter, between the state and the incorporators. The company is then authorized to do business.

The authority to manage the corporation is delegated by the stockholders to the board of directors and by the board of directors to the corporate officers (see Figure 1). That is, the stockholders elect the board of directors, which sets company policies and chooses the corporate officers, who in turn carry out the corporate policies by managing the business.

STOCKHOLDERS   A unit of ownership in a corporation is called a **share of stock**. The articles of incorporation state the maximum number of shares of stock that the corporation will be allowed, or authorized, to issue. The number of shares held by stockholders is the outstanding capital stock; this is generally less than the number authorized in the articles of incorporation. To invest in a corporation, a stockholder transfers cash or other resources to the corporation. In return, the stockholder receives shares of stock representing a proportionate share of ownership in the corporation. The stockholder may then transfer the shares at will. Corporations may have more than one kind of capital stock, but we will refer only to common stock.

BOARD OF DIRECTORS   As noted, the stockholders elect the board of directors, which in turn decides on the major business policies of the corporation. Among the specific duties of the board are authorizing contracts, setting executive salaries, and arranging major loans with banks. The declaration of dividends is also an important function. Only the board has the authority to declare dividends. **Dividends** are distributions of resources, generally in the form of cash, to the stockholders. Paying dividends is one way of rewarding stockholders for their investment when the corporation has been successful in earning a profit. (The other way is through a rise in the market value of the stock.) There is usually a delay of two or three weeks between the time the board declares a dividend and the date of the actual payment.

The board of directors varies in composition from company to company, but it usually contains several corporate officers and several outsiders. Today, the formation of an **audit committee** with several outside directors is encouraged to make sure that the board will be objective in evaluating management's performance. One function of the audit committee is to engage the company's independent auditors and review their work. Another is to ensure that proper systems safeguard the company's resources and that reliable accounting records are kept.

Figure 1
The Corporate Form of Business

STOCKHOLDERS		BOARD OF DIRECTORS		MANAGEMENT
invest in shares of capital stock and elect board of directors	→	determines corporate policy, declares dividends, and appoints management	→	executes policy and carries out day-to-day operations

MANAGEMENT The board of directors appoints managers to carry out the corporation's policies and run day-to-day operations. The management consists of the operating officers, who are generally the president, vice presidents, controller, treasurer, and secretary. Besides being responsible for running the business, management has the duty of reporting the financial results of its administration to the board of directors and the stockholders. Though management must, at a minimum, make a comprehensive annual report, it may and generally does report more often. The annual reports of large public corporations are available to the public. Excerpts from many of them are used throughout this book.

Managing Under the Corporate Form of Business

Although sole proprietorships and partnerships outnumber corporations in the United States, corporations dominate the economy in total dollars of assets and output of goods and services. Corporations are well suited to today's trends toward large organizations, international trade, and professional management. Figure 2 shows the amount and sources of new funds raised by corporations in recent years. The amount raised increased dramatically after 1990. In 1998, the amount of new corporate capital was $1,802 billion, of which $1,650 billion, or 92 percent, came

**Figure 2
Sources of Capital Raised
by Corporations in the
United States**

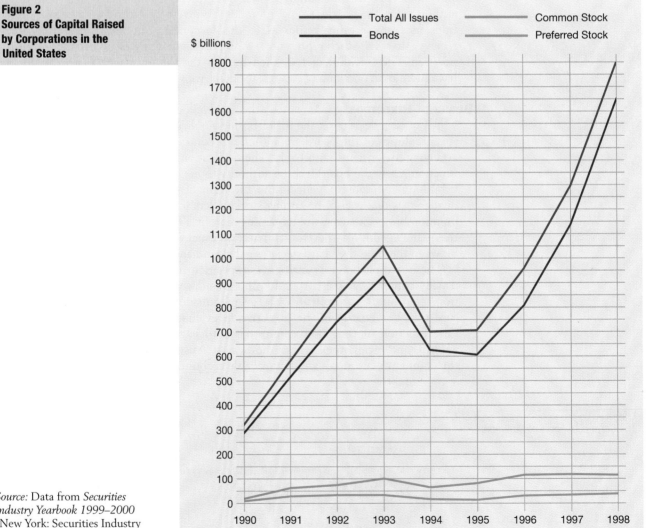

Source: Data from *Securities Industry Yearbook 1999–2000* (New York: Securities Industry Association, 1999), p. 1001.

from new bond issues; $114 billion, or 6 percent, came from new common stock issues; and $38 billion, or 2 percent, came from preferred stock issues.

In managing the corporation, the advantages and disadvantages of this form of business must be considered. Some of the advantages are as follows.

SEPARATE LEGAL ENTITY A corporation is a separate legal entity that has most of the rights of a person except those such as voting and marrying. As such, a corporation can buy, sell, or own property; sue and be sued; enter into contracts; hire and fire employees; and be taxed.

LIMITED LIABILITY Because a corporation is a separate legal entity, it is responsible for its own actions and liabilities. This means that a corporation's creditors can satisfy their claims only against the assets of the corporation, not against the personal property of the corporation's owners. Because the owners are not responsible for the corporation's debts, their liability is limited to the amount of their investment. The personal property of sole proprietors and partners, however, generally is available to creditors.

EASE OF CAPITAL GENERATION It is fairly easy for a corporation to raise capital because shares of ownership in the business are available to a great number of potential investors for a small amount of money. As a result, a single corporation can be owned by many people.

EASE OF TRANSFER OF OWNERSHIP A share of stock, a unit of ownership in a corporation, is transferable. A stockholder can normally buy and sell shares without affecting the corporation's activities or needing the approval of other owners.

LACK OF MUTUAL AGENCY There is no mutual agency in the corporate form of business. If a stockholder, acting as an owner, tries to enter into a contract for the corporation, the corporation is not bound by the contract. But in a partnership, because of mutual agency, all the partners can be bound by one partner's actions.

CONTINUOUS EXISTENCE Because a corporation is a separate legal entity, an owner's death, incapacity, or withdrawal does not affect the life of the corporation. The life of a corporation is set by its charter and regulated by state laws.

CENTRALIZED AUTHORITY AND RESPONSIBILITY The board of directors represents the stockholders and delegates the responsibility and authority for the day-to-day operation of the corporation to a single person, usually the president. Operating power is not divided among the many owners of the business. The president may delegate authority over certain segments of the business to others, but he or she is held accountable to the board of directors. If the board is dissatisfied with the performance of the president, it can replace him or her.

PROFESSIONAL MANAGEMENT Large corporations are owned by many people, the vast majority of whom are unequipped to make timely decisions about business operations. So, in most cases, management and ownership are separate. This allows a corporation to hire the best talent available to manage the business.

The disadvantages of the corporation are as follows.

GOVERNMENT REGULATION Corporations must meet the requirements of state laws. As "creatures of the state," corporations are subject to greater control and regulation by the state than are other forms of business. Corporations must file many reports with the state in which they are chartered. Also, corporations that are publicly held must file reports with the Securities and Exchange Commission and with the stock exchanges. Meeting those requirements is very costly.

TAXATION A major disadvantage of the corporate form of business is **double taxation**. Because a corporation is a separate legal entity, its earnings are subject to federal and state income taxes, which may be as much as 35 percent of corporate earnings. If any of the corporation's after-tax earnings are then paid out as dividends, the earnings are taxed again as income to the stockholders. In contrast, the earnings of sole proprietorships and partnerships are taxed only once, as personal income to the owners.

LIMITED LIABILITY Above, we cited limited liability as an advantage of incorporation, but it also can be a disadvantage. Limited liability restricts the ability of a small corporation to borrow money. Because creditors can lay claim only to the assets of the corporation, they limit their loans to the level secured by those assets or ask stockholders to guarantee the loans personally.

SEPARATION OF OWNERSHIP AND CONTROL Just as limited liability can be a drawback, so can the separation of ownership and control. Sometimes management makes decisions that are not good for the corporation as a whole. Poor communication can also make it hard for stockholders to exercise control over the corporation or even to recognize that management's decisions are harmful.

Using Equity Financing

A share of stock is a unit of ownership in a corporation. A **stock certificate** is issued to the owner. It shows the number of shares of the corporation's stock owned by the stockholder. Stockholders can transfer their ownership at will. When they do, they must sign their stock certificate and send it to the corporation's secretary. In large corporations that are listed on the organized stock exchanges, stockholders' records are hard to maintain. Such companies can have millions of shares of stock, thousands of which change ownership every day. Therefore, they often appoint independent registrars and transfer agents (usually banks and trust companies) to help perform the secretary's duties. The outside agents are responsible for transferring the corporation's stock, maintaining stockholders' records, preparing a list of stockholders for stockholders' meetings, and paying dividends.

When a corporation applies for a charter, the articles of incorporation specify the maximum number of shares of stock the corporation is allowed to issue. This number represents **authorized stock**. Most corporations are authorized to issue more shares of stock than are necessary at the time of organization, which allows for future stock issues to raise additional capital. For example, if a corporation plans to expand in the future, it will be able to sell the unissued shares of stock that were authorized in its charter. If a corporation immediately issues all of its authorized stock, it cannot issue more stock unless it applies to the state for a change in its charter.

The charter also shows the par value of the stock that has been authorized. **Par value** is an arbitrary amount assigned to each share of stock. It must be recorded in the capital stock accounts and constitutes the legal capital of a corporation. **Legal capital** equals the number of shares issued times the par value; it is the minimum amount that can be reported as contributed capital. Par value usually bears little if any relationship to the market value or book value of the shares. When a corporation is formed, a memorandum entry can be made in the general journal giving the number and description of authorized shares.

To help with the initial issue of capital stock, called an **initial public offering (IPO)**, a corporation often uses an **underwriter**—an intermediary between the corporation and the investing public. For a fee—usually less than 1 percent of the selling price—the underwriter guarantees the sale of the stock. The corporation records the amount of the net proceeds of the offering—what the public paid less the underwriter's fee, legal and printing expenses, and any other direct costs of the offering—in its capital stock and additional paid-in capital accounts. In one of the most unique IPOs, Goldman, Sachs, & Co., the renowned 130-year-old investment bank, went public in one of the largest IPOs ever of about $3.6 billion.

Determining Dividend Policies

The board of directors has sole authority to declare dividends, but the dividend policies are influenced by senior managers, who usually serve as members of the board. Receiving dividends from a corporation is one of the two ways stockholders can earn a return on their investment in the company. The other way is to sell their shares of stock for more than they paid for them. Investors evaluate the amount of dividends received with the ratio **dividends yield**. Dividends yield measures the current return to an investor in the form of dividends and is computed by dividing the dividends per share by the market price per share. For instance, the dividends yield (shown in Figure 3) for Abbott Laboratories, a large, successful pharmaceutical company, is computed as follows:

$$\text{Dividends Yield} = \frac{\text{Dividends per Share}}{\text{Market Price per Share}} = \frac{\$.76}{\$42.75} = 1.8\%$$

Since the yield on corporate bonds exceeds 8 percent, the shareholders of Abbott Labs must expect some of their return to come from increases in the price of the shares. A measure of investors' confidence in a company's future is the **price/earnings (P/E) ratio**, which is calculated by dividing the market price per share by the earnings per share. The price/earnings ratio will vary as market price per share fluctuates daily and the amount of earnings per share changes. From Figure 3, the price/earnings ratio for Abbott Labs is 27 times, which was computed by using its most recent annual earnings per share, as follows:

$$\text{Price/Earnings (P/E) Ratio} = \frac{\text{Market Price per Share}}{\text{Earnings per Share}} = \frac{\$42.75}{\$1.58} = 27 \text{ times}$$

Figure 3
Stock Quotations on the New York Stock Exchange

NYSE COMPOSITE TRANSACTIONS

52 Weeks Hi	Lo	Stock	Sym	Div	Yld %	PE	Vol 100's	Hi	Lo	Close	Net Chg
61	34^{1}/$_{16}$	AT&T	T	.88	2.6	18	186798	34^{15}/$_{16}$	33^{5}/$_{8}$	34	− ^{13}/$_{16}$
100	19^{13}/$_{16}$ ♦	AVX Cp	AVX	.28	.5	32	6532	61^{3}/$_{8}$	56^{13}/$_{16}$	57^{3}/$_{4}$	− ^{3}/$_{4}$
79^{15}/$_{16}$	53^{3}/$_{4}$	AXA ADS	AXA	2.16e	3.2	...	1147	68^{1}/$_{8}$	67^{1}/$_{4}$	67^{9}/$_{16}$	+ 2^{7}/$_{16}$
39^{7}/$_{16}$	25^{1}/$_{2}$ ♦	AXA Fnl	AXF	.10	.3	15	16294	40^{3}/$_{16}$	37^{15}/$_{16}$	39^{3}/$_{8}$	+ ^{1}/$_{2}$
9^{3}/$_{8}$	1	AamesFnl	AAM		...	dd	1181	1^{1}/$_{16}$	^{13}/$_{16}$	^{15}/$_{16}$	− ^{1}/$_{8}$
22^{1}/$_{4}$	12^{1}/$_{2}$	AaronRent	RNT	.04	.3	10	293	13	12^{9}/$_{16}$	12^{7}/$_{8}$	...
20	14^{5}/$_{8}$	AaronRent A	RNTA	.04	.3	14	8	15^{5}/$_{8}$	15^{5}/$_{16}$	15^{5}/$_{16}$	− ^{5}/$_{8}$
24^{11}/$_{16}$	19	AbbeyNtl	SUA	1.75	8.9	...	83	19^{7}/$_{8}$	19^{5}/$_{8}$	19^{11}/$_{16}$	− ^{1}/$_{8}$
23^{15}/$_{16}$	19^{1}/$_{2}$	AbbeyNtl 7 ^{1}/$_{4}$%	SUD	1.81	8.7	...	77	20^{11}/$_{16}$	20^{7}/$_{8}$	20^{11}/$_{16}$	+ ^{1}/$_{4}$
26^{5}/$_{8}$	22^{1}/$_{8}$	AbbeyNtl pfA		2.19	9.3	...	642	23^{7}/$_{16}$	23^{1}/$_{4}$	23^{7}/$_{16}$	+ ^{1}/$_{16}$
45^{15}/$_{16}$	29^{3}/$_{8}$	AbbottLab	ABT	.76f	1.8	27	29393	43^{1}/$_{4}$	42^{1}/$_{2}$	42^{3}/$_{4}$	− ^{183}/$_{256}$
49^{11}/$_{16}$	8	Abercrombie A	ANF		...	6	22687	9^{1}/$_{8}$	8^{15}/$_{16}$	8^{7}/$_{8}$	+ ^{11}/$_{16}$
13^{13}/$_{16}$	7^{3}/$_{4}$	Abitibi g	ABY	.40g	...	...	2099	10^{5}/$_{8}$	10	10^{1}/$_{16}$	− ^{11}/$_{16}$
6^{1}/$_{8}$	4^{3}/$_{4}$ ♦	AcadiaRlty	AKR	.48	8.2	18	27	5^{7}/$_{8}$	5^{7}/$_{8}$	5^{7}/$_{8}$	− ^{1}/$_{8}$
15^{15}/$_{16}$	2^{3}/$_{4}$ ♦	AcceptIns	AIF		...	dd	184	4^{5}/$_{8}$	4^{3}/$_{8}$	4^{1}/$_{2}$	+ ^{1}/$_{16}$
20	11^{1}/$_{8}$	AckrlyGp	AK	.02	.2	...	136	12^{9}/$_{16}$	12^{1}/$_{8}$	12^{1}/$_{8}$	− ^{1}/$_{4}$
32^{3}/$_{4}$	16^{5}/$_{16}$	ACNielsen	ART		...	19	980	23^{3}/$_{16}$	22^{3}/$_{16}$	22^{3}/$_{16}$	− ^{1}/$_{16}$

Source: Republished with permission of Dow Jones, from *The Wall Street Journal*, May 26, 2000; permission conveyed through Copyright Clearance Center, Inc.

Since the market price is 27 times earnings, investors are paying what for most companies would be a high price in relation to earnings, expecting this drug company to continue its success. Caution must be taken in interpreting high P/E ratios because unusually low earnings can produce a high result.

Companies usually pay dividends to stockholders only when they have experienced profitable operations. For example, Apple Computer, Inc., paid a dividend beginning in 1987 but suspended its dividend payments in 1996 to conserve cash after large operating losses in 1995. Factors other than earnings affect the decision to pay dividends. First, the expected volatility of earnings is a factor. If a company has years of good earnings followed by years of poor earnings, the board may want to keep dividends low to avoid giving a false impression of sustained high earnings. For years General Motors Corporation followed the practice of having a fairly stable dividend yield and paying a bonus dividend in especially good years. Second, the level of dividends affects cash flows. Some companies may not have the cash to pay higher dividends because operations are not generating cash at the level of earnings or because the companies are investing the cash in future operations. For instance, Abbott Labs pays a dividend of only $.76 per share in spite of earning $1.58 per share. Management believes the cash generated by the earnings is better spent for other purposes, such as researching and developing new drugs that will generate revenue in the future. It is partly due to Abbott's investment in new products that stockholders are willing to pay a high price for Abbott Labs stock. In recent years, many investors have shown a preference for companies like Abbott that have strong earnings growth but that pay low or no dividends because the tax rates favor capital gains made by selling shares for a profit over dividend income.

Evaluating Performance Using Return on Equity

The ratio **return on equity** is the most important ratio associated with the stockholders' equity section because it is a common measure of management's performance. For instance, when *Business Week* and *Forbes* rate companies on their success, return on equity is the major basis of this evaluation. Also, the compensation of top executives is often tied to return on equity benchmarks. This ratio is computed for Abbott Labs from information in the company's 1999 annual report, as follows:

$$\text{Return on Equity} = \frac{\text{Net Income}}{\text{Average Stockholders' Equity}}$$

$$= \frac{\$2,445,759,000}{(\$7,427,595,000 + \$5,753,591,000) \div 2}$$

$$= 37.1\%$$

Abbott Labs' healthy return on equity of 37.1 percent depends, of course, on the amount of net income the company earns, but it also depends on the level of stockholders' equity. This level can be affected by management decisions. First, it depends on the amount of stock a company sells to the public. Management can keep the stockholders' equity at a minimum by financing the business with cash flows from operations and with debt instead of with stock. However, the use of debt to finance the business increases a company's risk because the interest and principal of the debt must be paid in a timely manner. In the case of common stock, dividends may be suspended if there is a cash shortage. Abbott Labs has a debt to equity ratio of over 1.3 and thus is taking advantage of the leverage provided by debt. Second, management can reduce the number of shares in the hands of the public by buying back its shares on the open market. The cost of these shares, which are called *treasury stock*, has the effect of reducing the amount of stockholders' equity and thereby increasing the return on equity. Many companies follow this practice instead of paying or increasing dividends because it puts money into the hands of stockholders in the form of market price appreciation without creating a commitment to higher dividends in the future. For example, during the three years ended 1999, Abbott Labs purchased its common stock at a cost of $1.9 billion.[3] Abbott Labs' stock repurchases improved the company's return on equity, increased its earnings per share, and lowered its price/earnings ratio.

Start-up and Organization Costs

OBJECTIVE

2 Define *start-up and organization costs* and state their effects on financial reporting

The costs of forming a corporation are called **start-up and organization costs**. Such costs, which are incurred before the corporation begins operations, include state incorporation fees and attorneys' fees for drawing up the articles of incorporation. They also include the cost of printing stock certificates, accountants' fees for services rendered in registering the firm's initial stock, and other expenditures necessary for forming the corporation.

Theoretically, start-up and organization costs benefit the entire life of the corporation. For that reason, a case can be made for recording them as intangible assets and amortizing them over the years of the life of the corporation. However, the life of a corporation normally is not known, so accountants expense start-up and organization costs as they are incurred.[4]

Components of Stockholders' Equity

OBJECTIVE

3 Identify the components of stockholders' equity

In a corporation's balance sheet, the owners' claims to the business are called *stockholders' equity*. Look at the sample stockholders' equity section of a balance sheet that follows.

Stockholders' Equity		
Contributed Capital		
Preferred Stock, $50 par value, 1,000 shares authorized, issued, and outstanding		$ 50,000
Common Stock, $5 par value, 30,000 shares authorized, 20,000 shares issued and outstanding	$100,000	
Paid-in Capital in Excess of Par Value, Common	50,000	150,000
Total Contributed Capital		$200,000
Retained Earnings		60,000
Total Stockholders' Equity		$260,000

Notice that the equity section of the corporate balance sheet is divided into two parts: (1) contributed capital and (2) retained earnings. Contributed capital represents the investments made by the stockholders in the corporation. Retained earnings are the earnings of the corporation since its inception, less any losses, dividends, or transfers to contributed capital. Retained earnings are not a pool of funds to be distributed to the stockholders; they represent, instead, earnings reinvested in the corporation.

In keeping with the convention of full disclosure, the contributed-capital part of the stockholders' equity section of the balance sheet gives a great deal of information about the corporation's stock: the kinds of stock; their par value; and the number of shares authorized, issued, and outstanding.

Common Stock

A corporation can issue two basic types of stock: common stock and preferred stock. If only one kind of stock is issued by the corporation, it is called **common stock**. Common stock is the company's **residual equity**. This means that all other creditors' and preferred stockholders' claims to the company's assets rank ahead of those of the common stockholders in case of liquidation. Because common stock is generally the only stock that carries voting rights, it represents the means of controlling the corporation.

The **issued stock** of a corporation is the shares sold or otherwise transferred to stockholders. For example, a corporation can be authorized to issue 500,000 shares of stock but may choose to issue only 300,000 shares when the company is organized. The holders of those 300,000 shares own 100 percent of the corporation. The remaining 200,000 shares of stock are unissued shares. No rights or privileges are associated with them until they are issued.

Outstanding stock is stock that has been issued and is still in circulation. A share of stock is not outstanding if the issuing corporation has repurchased it or if a stockholder has given it back to the company that issued it, so a company can have more shares issued than are currently outstanding. Issued shares that are bought back and held by the corporation are called *treasury stock*, which we discuss in detail later in this chapter. The relationship of authorized, issued, unissued, outstanding, and treasury shares is illustrated in Figure 4.

Dividends

OBJECTIVE
4 Account for cash dividends

Dividends can be paid quarterly, semiannually, annually, or at other times decided on by the board. Most states do not allow the board to declare a dividend that exceeds retained earnings. When a dividend that exceeds retained earnings is declared, the corporation is, in essence, returning to the stockholders part of their contributed capital. It is called a **liquidating dividend** and is usually paid when a company is going out of business or reducing its operations. Having sufficient retained earnings in itself does not justify the distribution of a dividend. If cash or other readily distributable assets are not available for distribution, the company might have to borrow money to pay a dividend—an action most boards of directors want to avoid.

Figure 4
Relationship of Authorized, Unissued, Issued, Outstanding, and Treasury Shares

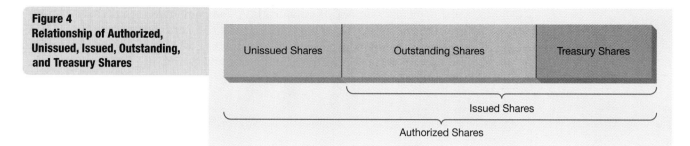

There are three important dates associated with dividends. In order of occurrence, they are (1) the date of declaration, (2) the date of record, and (3) the date of payment. The **date of declaration** is the date on which the board of directors formally declares that a dividend is going to be paid. The **date of record** is the date on which ownership of the stock of a company, and therefore of the right to receive a dividend, is determined. Individuals who own the stock on the date of record will receive the dividend. Between that date and the date of payment, the stock is said to be **ex-dividend**. If the owner on the date of record later sells the shares of stock, the right to the cash dividend remains with that person; it does not transfer with the shares to the second owner. The **date of payment** is the date on which the dividend is paid to the stockholders of record.

To illustrate the accounting for cash dividends, we assume that the board of directors has decided that sufficient cash is available to pay a $56,000 cash dividend to the common stockholders. The process has two steps. First, the board declares the dividend as of a certain date. Second, the dividend is paid. Assume that the dividend is declared on February 21, 20xx, for stockholders of record on March 1, 20xx, to be paid on March 11, 20xx. Here are the entries to record the declaration and payment of the cash dividend.

Date of Declaration

$A = L + OE$	Feb. 21	Cash Dividends Declared	56,000	
$+$ $-$		Cash Dividends Payable		56,000
		Declared cash dividend		
		to common stockholders		

Date of Record

Mar. 1   No entry is required. This date is used simply to determine the owners of the stock who will receive the dividends. After this date (starting March 2), the shares are ex-dividend.

Date of Payment

$A = L + OE$	Mar. 11	Cash Dividends Payable	56,000	
$-$ $-$		Cash		56,000
		Paid cash dividends		
		declared on February 21		

Notice that the liability for the dividend is recorded on the date of declaration because the legal obligation to pay the dividend is established on that date. No entry is required on the date of record. The liability is liquidated, or settled, on the date of payment. The Cash Dividends Declared account is a temporary stockholders' equity account that is closed at the end of the accounting period by debiting Retained Earnings and crediting Cash Dividends Declared. Retained Earnings are thereby reduced by the total dividends declared during the period.

Some companies do not pay dividends. A company may not have any earnings, or the cash generated by operations may need to be kept in the company for business purposes, perhaps expansion of the plant. Investors in growth companies expect a return on their investment in the form of an increase in the market value of their stock.

Preferred Stock

OBJECTIVE

5 Identify the characteristics of preferred stock, including the effect on distribution of dividends

The second kind of stock a company can issue is called **preferred stock**. Preferred stock has preference over common stock in one or more areas. Most preferred stock has one or more of the following characteristics: preference as to dividends, preference as to assets of the business in liquidation, convertibility, and a callable option. Both common stock and preferred stock are sold to raise money. But investors in preferred stock and investors in common stock have different investment goals. In fact, a corporation may offer several different classes of preferred stock, each with distinctive characteristics to attract different investors.

PREFERENCE AS TO DIVIDENDS   Preferred stocks ordinarily have a preference over common stock in the receipt of dividends; that is, the holders of preferred shares must receive a certain amount of dividends before the holders of common shares can receive dividends. The amount that preferred stockholders must be paid before common stockholders can be paid is usually stated in dollars per share or as a percentage of the par value of the preferred shares. For example, a corporation can issue a preferred stock and pay an annual dividend of $4 per share, or it might issue a preferred stock at $50 par value and pay a yearly dividend of 8 percent of par value, also $4 per share.

Preferred stockholders have no guarantee of ever receiving dividends. The company must have earnings and the board of directors must declare dividends on preferred shares before any liability arises. The consequences of not declaring a dividend to preferred stockholders in the current year vary according to the exact terms under which the shares were issued. In the case of **noncumulative preferred stock**, if the board of directors fails to declare a dividend to preferred stockholders in a given year, the company is under no obligation to make up the missed dividend in future years. In the case of **cumulative preferred stock**, however, the fixed dividend amount per share accumulates from year to year, and the whole amount must be paid before any common dividends can be paid. Dividends not paid in the year they are due are called **dividends in arrears**.

Assume that a corporation has been authorized to issue 10,000 shares of $100 par value, 5 percent cumulative preferred stock, and that the shares have been issued and are outstanding. If no dividends were paid in 20x1, at the end of the year there would be preferred dividends of $50,000 (10,000 shares × $100 × .05 = $50,000) in arrears. If dividends are paid in 20x2, the preferred stockholders' dividends in arrears plus the 20x2 preferred dividends must be paid before any dividends on common stock can be paid.

Dividends in arrears are not recognized as liabilities because no liability exists until the board declares a dividend. A corporation cannot be sure it is going to make a profit, so, of course, it cannot promise dividends to stockholders. However, if a company has dividends in arrears, the amount should be reported either in the body of the financial statements or in a note. The following note appeared in a steel company's annual report.

On January 1, 20xx, the company was in arrears by $37,851,000 ($1.25 per share) on dividends to its preferred stockholders. The company must pay all dividends in arrears to preferred stockholders before paying any dividends to common stockholders.

Suppose that on January 1, 20x1, a corporation issued 10,000 shares of $10 par, 6 percent cumulative preferred stock and 50,000 shares of common stock. The first year's operations resulted in income of only $4,000. The corporation's board of directors declared a $3,000 cash dividend to the preferred stockholders. The dividend picture at the end of 20x1 was as follows:

20x1 dividends due preferred stockholders ($100,000 × .06)	$6,000
Less 20x1 dividends declared to preferred stockholders	3,000
20x1 preferred stock dividends in arrears	$3,000

Now, suppose that in 20x2 the company earned income of $30,000 and wanted to pay dividends to both the preferred and the common stockholders. Because the preferred stock is cumulative, the corporation must pay the $3,000 in arrears on the preferred stock, plus the current year's dividends on its preferred stock, before it can distribute a dividend to the common stockholders. For example, assume that the corporation's board of directors declared a $12,000 dividend to be distributed to preferred and common stockholders. It would be distributed as follows:

20x2 declaration of dividends	$12,000
Less 20x1 preferred stock dividends in arrears	3,000
Available for 20x2 dividends	$ 9,000
Less 20x2 dividends due preferred stockholders ($100,000 × .06)	6,000
Remainder available to common stockholders	$ 3,000

And this is the journal entry when the dividend is declared:

A = L + OE	Dec. 31	Cash Dividends Declared	12,000	
+ −		Cash Dividends Payable		12,000
		Declared a $9,000 cash dividend to preferred stockholders and a $3,000 cash dividend to common stockholders		

PREFERENCE AS TO ASSETS Many preferred stocks have preference in terms of the assets of the corporation in the case of liquidation. If the corporation's existence is terminated, the preferred stockholders have a right to receive the par value of their stock or a larger stated liquidation value per share before the common stockholders receive any share of the company's assets. This preference can also include any dividends in arrears owed to the preferred stockholders.

CONVERTIBLE PREFERRED STOCK A corporation can make its preferred stock more attractive to investors by adding convertibility. People who hold **convertible preferred stock** can exchange their shares of preferred stock for shares of the company's common stock at a ratio stated in the preferred stock contract. Convertibility appeals to investors for two reasons. First, like all preferred stockholders, owners of convertible stock are more likely to receive regular dividends than are common stockholders. Second, if the market value of a company's common stock rises, the conversion feature allows the preferred stockholders to share in the increase. The rise in value would come either through increases in the value of the preferred stock or through conversion to common stock.

Preferred stock represents a flexible means of achieving goals that cannot be achieved with common stock. For example, Microsoft Corporation issued almost $1 billion in preferred stock even though the company probably did not need the cash.[6] Since Microsoft does not pay and has no plans to pay a dividend on its common stock, this preferred stock satisfies the desire of investors who want to own Microsoft stock but who want to buy stocks that pay a dividend. The preferred stock pays a fixed dividend and is convertible into common stock or convertible notes, or the company guarantees it can be redeemed at face value for cash in three years. In return for this flexibility and low risk, the possible gain of converting the preferred stock into common stock is limited to 25 to 30 percent. A Microsoft vice president said, "If you own the preferred, you get a dividend yield and downside protection, but the upside is capped."[7]

For example, suppose that a company issues 1,000 shares of 8 percent, $100 par value convertible preferred stock for $100 per share. Each share of stock can be converted into five shares of the company's common stock at any time. The market value of the common stock is now $15 per share. In the past, an owner of the common stock could expect dividends of about $1 per share per year. The owner of one share of preferred stock, on the other hand, now holds an investment that is approaching a value of $100 on the market and is more likely to receive dividends than is the owner of common stock.

Assume that in the next several years, the corporation's earnings increase, and the dividends paid to common stockholders also increase, to $3 per share. In addition, assume that the market value of a share of common stock rises from $15 to $30. Preferred stockholders can convert each of their preferred shares into five common shares and increase their dividends from $8 on each preferred share to the equivalent of $15 ($3 on each of five common shares). Furthermore, the market value of each share of preferred stock will be close to the $150 value of the five shares of common stock because each share can be converted into five shares of common stock.

CALLABLE PREFERRED STOCK Most preferred stock is **callable preferred stock**. That is, it can be redeemed or retired at the option of the issuing corporation at a price stated in the preferred stock contract. A stockholder must surrender nonconvertible preferred stock to the corporation when asked to do so. If the preferred stock is convertible, the stockholder can either surrender the stock to the corporation or convert it into common stock when the corporation calls the stock. The *call price*, or redemption price, is usually higher than the par value of the stock. For example, a $100 par value preferred stock might be callable at $103 per share. When preferred stock is called and surrendered, the stockholder is entitled to (1) the par value of the stock, (2) the call premium, (3) any dividends in arrears, and (4) a portion of the current period's dividend, prorated by the proportion of the year to the call date.

A corporation may call its preferred stock for several reasons. First, the company may want to force conversion of the preferred stock to common stock because the cash dividend paid on the equivalent common stock is lower than the dividend paid on the preferred shares. Second, it may be possible to replace the outstanding preferred stock on the current market with a preferred stock at a lower dividend rate or with long-term debt, which can have a lower after-tax cost. Third, the company may simply be profitable enough to retire the preferred stock.

Accounting for Stock Issuance

A share of capital stock may be either par or no-par. The value of par stock is stated in the corporate charter and must be printed on each share of stock. Par value can be $.10, $1, $5, $100, or any other amount established by the organizers of the corporation. The par values of common stocks tend to be lower than those of preferred stocks.

Par value is the amount per share that is entered into the corporation's capital stock accounts and that makes up the legal capital of the corporation. A corporation cannot declare a dividend that would cause stockholders' equity to fall below the legal capital of the firm. Therefore, the par value is a minimum cushion of capital that protects creditors. Any amount in excess of par value received from the issuance of stock is recorded in the Paid-in Capital in Excess of Par Value account and represents a portion of the company's contributed capital.

No-par stock is capital stock that does not have a par value. There are several reasons for issuing stock without a par value. One is that some investors confuse par value with the market value of stock instead of recognizing it as an arbitrary figure. Another reason is that most states do not allow an original stock issue below par value and thereby limit a corporation's flexibility in obtaining capital.

No-par stock can be issued with or without a stated value. The board of directors of a corporation issuing no-par stock may be required by state law to place a **stated value** on each share of stock or may choose to do so as a matter of convenience. The stated value can be any value set by the board, although some states specify a minimum amount. The stated value can be set before or after the shares are issued if the state law is not specific.

If a company issues no-par stock without a stated value, all proceeds are recorded in the Capital Stock account. That amount becomes the corporation's legal capital unless a different amount is specified by state law. Because additional shares of the stock can be issued at different prices, the per-share credit to the Capital Stock account will not be uniform. This is a key way in which no-par stock without a stated value differs from par value stock or no-par stock with a stated value.

When no-par stock with a stated value is issued, the shares are recorded in the Capital Stock account at the stated value. Any amount that is received in excess of the stated value is recorded in the Paid-in Capital in Excess of Stated Value account. The amount in excess of the stated value is part of the corporation's contributed capital. However, the stated value is normally considered to be the legal capital of the corporation.

Par Value Stock

When par value stock is issued, the appropriate capital stock account (usually Common Stock or Preferred Stock) is credited for the par value regardless of whether the proceeds are more or less than the par value. For example, assume that Bradley Corporation is authorized to issue 20,000 shares of $10 par value common stock and actually issues 10,000 shares at $10 per share on January 1, 20xx. The entry to record the stock issue at par value would be as follows:

A = L + OE	Jan. 1	Cash	100,000	
+ +		Common Stock		100,000
		Issued 10,000 shares of $10 par value common stock for $10 per share		

Cash is debited for $100,000 (10,000 shares × $10), and Common Stock is credited for an equal amount because the stock was sold for par value.

When stock is issued for a price greater than par, the proceeds in excess of par are credited to a capital account called Paid-in Capital in Excess of Par Value, Common. For example, assume that the 10,000 shares of Bradley common stock sold for $12 per share on January 1, 20xx. The entry to record the issuance of the stock at the price in excess of par value would be as follows:

A = L + OE
+   +
         +

Jan. 1	Cash	120,000	
	Common Stock		100,000
	Paid-in Capital in Excess of Par Value, Common		20,000
	Issued 10,000 shares of $10 par value common stock for $12 per share		

Cash is debited for the proceeds of $120,000 (10,000 shares × $12), and Common Stock is credited for the total par value of $100,000 (10,000 shares × $10). Paid-in Capital in Excess of Par Value, Common is credited for the difference of $20,000 (10,000 shares × $2). The amount in excess of par value is part of the corporation's contributed capital and will be included in the stockholders' equity section of the balance sheet. The stockholders' equity section for Bradley Corporation immediately following the stock issue would appear as follows:

Contributed Capital		
Common Stock, $10 par value, 20,000 shares authorized, 10,000 shares issued and outstanding		$100,000
Paid-in Capital in Excess of Par Value, Common		20,000
Total Contributed Capital		$120,000
Retained Earnings		—
Total Stockholders' Equity		$120,000

If a corporation issues stock for less than par, an account called Discount on Capital Stock is debited for the difference. The issuance of stock at a discount rarely occurs because it is illegal in many states.

No-Par Stock

As mentioned earlier, stock can be issued without a par value. However, most states require that all or part of the proceeds from the issuance of no-par stock be designated as legal capital, which cannot be withdrawn except in liquidation. The purpose of this requirement is to protect the corporation's assets for creditors. Assume that Bradley Corporation's capital stock is no-par common and that 10,000 shares are issued on January 1, 20xx, at $15 per share. The $150,000 (10,000 shares × $15) in proceeds would be recorded as shown in the following entry:

A = L + OE
+   +

Jan. 1	Cash	150,000	
	Common Stock		150,000
	Issued 10,000 shares of no-par common stock for $15 per share		

Because the stock does not have a stated or par value, all proceeds of the issue are credited to Common Stock and are part of the company's legal capital.

Most states allow the board of directors to put a stated value on no-par stock, and that value represents the corporation's legal capital. Assume that Bradley's board puts a $10 stated value on its no-par stock. The entry to record the issue of

10,000 shares of no-par common stock with a $10 stated value for $15 per share would appear as follows:

A = L + OE
+   +
       +

Jan. 1	Cash	150,000	
	Common Stock		100,000
	Paid-in Capital in Excess of		
	Stated Value, Common		50,000
	Issued 10,000 shares of no-par		
	common stock with $10 stated value		
	for $15 per share		

Notice that the legal capital credited to Common Stock is the stated value decided by the board of directors. Notice also that the account Paid-in Capital in Excess of Stated Value, Common is credited for $50,000. The $50,000 is the difference between the proceeds ($150,000) and the total stated value ($100,000). Paid-in Capital in Excess of Stated Value is presented on the balance sheet in the same way as Paid-in Capital in Excess of Par Value.

Issuance of Stock for Noncash Assets

Stock can be issued for assets or services other than cash. The problem is to determine the dollar amount that should be recorded for the exchange. The generally preferred rule is to record the transaction at the fair market value of what the corporation is giving up—in this case, the stock. If the fair market value of the stock cannot be determined, the fair market value of the assets or services received can be used. Transactions of this kind usually involve the use of stock to pay for land or buildings or for the services of attorneys and others who helped organize the company.

When there is an exchange of stock for noncash assets, the board of directors has the right to determine the fair market value of the property. Suppose that when Bradley Corporation was formed on January 1, 20xx, its attorney agreed to accept 100 shares of its $10 par value common stock for services rendered. At the time the stock was issued, its market value could not be determined. However, for similar services the attorney would have billed the company $1,500. The entry to record the noncash transaction is as follows:

A = L + OE
+   +
       +

Jan. 1	Start-up and Organization Expense	1,500	
	Common Stock		1,000
	Paid-in Capital in Excess of		
	Par Value, Common		500
	Issued 100 shares of $10 par		
	value common stock for attorney's		
	services		

Now suppose that two years later Bradley Corporation exchanged 1,000 shares of its $10 par value common stock for a piece of land. At the time of the exchange, the stock was selling on the market for $16 per share. The following entry records the exchange:

A = L + OE
+   +
       +

Jan. 1	Land	16,000	
	Common Stock		10,000
	Paid-in Capital in Excess of		
	Par Value, Common		6,000
	Issued 1,000 shares of $10 par value		
	common stock with a market value		
	of $16 per share for a piece of land		

Treasury Stock

Treasury stock is capital stock, either common or preferred, that has been issued and later reacquired by the issuing company but that has not subsequently been resold or retired. The company normally gets the stock back by purchasing the shares on the market. It is common for companies to buy and hold their own stock. In a recent year, 392, or 65 percent, of 600 large companies held treasury stock.[8] Although the purchase of treasury stock can be a severe drain on cash, a company may purchase its own stock for several reasons:

1. It may want stock to distribute to employees through stock option plans.

2. It may be trying to maintain a favorable market for its stock.

3. It may want to increase its earnings per share or stock price per share.

4. It may want to have additional shares of stock available for such activities as purchasing other companies.

5. It may want to prevent a hostile takeover.

A treasury stock purchase reduces the assets and stockholders' equity of the company. It is not considered a purchase of assets, as the purchase of shares in another company would be. Treasury stock is capital stock that has been issued but is no longer outstanding. Treasury shares can be held for an indefinite period of time, reissued, or retired. Like unissued stock, treasury stock has no rights until it is reissued. Treasury stock does not have voting rights, rights to cash dividends and stock dividends, or rights to share in assets during liquidation of the company, and it is not considered to be outstanding in the calculation of book value. However, there is one major difference between unissued shares and treasury shares: A share of stock that originally was issued at par value or greater and fully paid for, and that then was reacquired as treasury stock, can be reissued at less than par value without negative consequences.

PURCHASE OF TREASURY STOCK   When treasury stock is purchased, it is normally recorded at cost. The transaction reduces both the assets and the stockholders' equity of the firm. For example, assume that on September 15 the Caprock Corporation purchases 1,000 shares of its common stock on the market at a price of $50 per share. The purchase would be recorded as follows:

A = L + OE
−   −

Sept. 15	Treasury Stock, Common	50,000	
	Cash		50,000
	Acquired 1,000 shares of the company's common stock for $50 per share		

The treasury shares are recorded at cost. The par value, stated value, or original issue price of the stock is ignored.

The stockholders' equity section of Caprock's balance sheet shows the cost of the treasury stock as a deduction from the total of contributed capital and retained earnings:

Contributed Capital	
Common Stock, $5 par value, 100,000 shares authorized, 30,000 shares issued, 29,000 shares outstanding	$ 150,000
Paid-in Capital in Excess of Par Value, Common	30,000
Total Contributed Capital	$ 180,000
Retained Earnings	900,000
Total Contributed Capital and Retained Earnings	$1,080,000
Less Treasury Stock, Common (1,000 shares at cost)	50,000
Total Stockholders' Equity	$1,030,000

A = L + OE   Mar. 30   Cash   50,000
  +   +   Common Stock   20,000
         +   Paid-in Capital in Excess of
                               Par Value, Common   30,000
                                 Issued 2,000 shares of $10 par
                                 value common stock under
                                 employee stock option plan

In other cases, the stock option plan gives employees the right to purchase stock in the future at a fixed price. This type of plan, which is usually offered only to management personnel, both compensates and motivates management because the market value of a company's stock is tied to the company's performance. As the market value of the stock goes up, the difference between the option price and the market price grows, which increases management's compensation. On the date stock options are granted, the fair value of the options must be estimated and the amount in excess of the exercise price must be either recorded as compensation expense over the grant period or reported in the notes to the financial statements.[12] If a company chooses to record compensation expense, additional paid-in capital will increase as a result. Almost all companies report the excess of fair value over exercise price in the notes to the financial statements. The notes must include the impact on net income and earnings per share of not recording compensation expense.

If note disclosure is the preferred method of reporting compensation costs, then when an option eventually is exercised and the stock is issued, the entry is similar to the one above. For example, assume that on July 1, 20x1, a company grants its key management personnel the option to purchase 50,000 shares of $10 par value common stock at its then-current market value of $15 per share. Suppose that one of the firm's vice presidents exercises the option to purchase 2,000 shares on March 30, 20x2, when the market price is $25 per share. The following entry would record the issue:

20x2
A = L + OE   Mar. 30   Cash   30,000
  +   +   Common Stock   20,000
         +   Paid-in Capital in Excess of
                               Par Value, Common   10,000
                                 Issued 2,000 shares of $10 par
                                 value common stock under the
                                 employee stock option plan

FOCUS ON BUSINESS PRACTICE

Stock options have an earnings advantage for corporations that use them, and their impact varies depending on the size of a company's options program and its industry. Specifically, the cost of options and its effect on earnings may be reported in the notes and not in the income statement as compensation expense. However, salaries and other cash bonuses are included as compensation expense and reported on the income statement. A recent study by Bears Sterns indicates that options grants would completely wipe out corporate profits and operating income at some fast growing high-tech companies, which tend to rely heavily on generous options grants to attract top talent. The effect for the high-tech industry ranged from 10 to 100 percent. However, the impact of options costs for industrial companies was much less, an average of 3 percent, because they do not have large options programs and the earnings of these firms was quite large.[13]

Although the vice president has a gain of $20,000 (the $50,000 market value less the $30,000 option price), no compensation expense is recorded. Estimation of the fair value of options at the grant date is the subject of more advanced courses. Information pertaining to employee stock option plans should be discussed in the notes to the financial statements.*

Chapter Review

REVIEW OF LEARNING OBJECTIVES

Check out ACE, a self-quizzing program on chapter content, at http://college.hmco.com.

1. Identify and explain the management issues related to contributed capital. The management of contributed capital is a critical component in the financing of a corporation, which is a legal entity separate and distinct from its owners. The issues faced by management in the area of contributed capital are forming a corporation, managing under the corporate form of business, using equity financing, determining dividend policies, and evaluating performance using return on equity.

2. Define *start-up and organization costs* and state their effects on financial reporting. The costs of organizing a corporation are recorded as expenses when they are incurred. They increase the initial loss or reduce the initial income of a corporation.

3. Identify the components of stockholders' equity. Stockholders' equity consists of contributed capital and retained earnings. Contributed capital includes two basic types of stock: common stock and preferred stock. When only one type of security is issued, it is common stock. Common stockholders have voting rights; they also share in the earnings of the corporation.

Retained earnings, the other component of stockholders' equity, represents the claim of stockholders to the assets of the company resulting from profitable operations. These are earnings that have been invested in the corporation.

4. Account for cash dividends. The liability for payment of cash dividends arises on the date of declaration by the board of directors. The declaration is recorded with a debit to Cash Dividends Declared and a credit to Cash Dividends Payable. The date of record, on which no entry is required, establishes the stockholders who will receive the cash dividend on the date of payment. Payment is recorded with a debit to Cash Dividends Payable and a credit to Cash.

5. Identify the characteristics of preferred stock, including the effect on distribution of dividends. Preferred stock, like common stock, is sold to raise capital. But the investors in preferred stock have different objectives. To attract such investors, corporations usually give them a preference—in terms of

*Stock options are discussed here in the context of employee compensation. They can also be important features of complex corporate capitalization arrangements.

receiving dividends and assets—over common stockholders. The dividend on preferred stock is generally figured first; then the remainder goes to common stock. If the preferred stock is cumulative and in arrears, the amount in arrears must be allocated to preferred stockholders before any allocation is made to common stockholders. In addition, certain preferred stock is convertible. Preferred stock is often callable at the option of the corporation.

6. **Account for the issuance of stock for cash and other assets.** A corporation's stock is normally issued for cash and other assets. The majority of states require that stock be issued at a minimum value called *legal capital*. Legal capital is represented by the par or stated value of the stock.

When stock is issued for cash at par or stated value, Cash is debited and Common Stock or Preferred Stock is credited. When stock is sold at an amount greater than par or stated value, the excess is recorded in Paid-in Capital in Excess of Par or Stated Value.

Sometimes stock is issued for noncash assets. Then the accountant must decide how to value the stock. The general rule is to record the stock at its market value. If this value cannot be determined, the fair market value of the asset received is used to record the transaction.

7. **Account for treasury stock.** Treasury stock is stock that a company has issued and later reacquired but not resold or retired. A company may acquire its own stock to create stock option plans, maintain a favorable market for the stock, increase earnings per share, or purchase other companies. Treasury stock is similar to unissued stock in that it does not have rights until it is reissued. However, treasury stock can be resold at less than par value without penalty. The accounting treatment for treasury stock is as shown below.

Treasury Stock Transaction	Accounting Treatment
Purchase of treasury stock	Debit Treasury Stock and credit Cash for the cost of the shares.
Sale of treasury stock at the same price as the cost of the shares	Debit Cash and credit Treasury Stock for the cost of the shares.
Sale of treasury stock at an amount greater than the cost of the shares	Debit Cash for the reissue price of the shares, and credit Treasury Stock for the cost of the shares and Paid-in Capital, Treasury Stock for the excess.
Sale of treasury stock at an amount less than the cost of the shares	Debit Cash for the reissue price; debit Paid-in Capital, Treasury Stock for the difference between the reissue price and the cost of the shares; and credit Treasury Stock for the cost of the shares. If Paid-in Capital, Treasury Stock does not exist or its balance is not large enough to cover the difference, Retained Earnings should absorb the difference.

8. **Account for the exercise of stock options.** Companywide stock option plans are used to encourage employees to own a part of the company. Other plans are offered only to management personnel, both to compensate and to motivate them. Usually, the issue of stock to employees under stock option plans is recorded like the issue of stock to any outsider.

The following concepts and terms were introduced in this chapter:

LO 1   **Articles of incorporation:** An official document filed with and approved by a state that authorizes the incorporators to do business as a corporation.

LO 1   **Audit committee:** A subgroup of the board of directors of a corporation charged with ensuring that the board will be objective in reviewing management's performance; it engages the company's independent auditors and reviews their work.

LO 1   **Authorized stock:** The maximum number of shares a corporation can issue without changing its charter with the state.

LO 5   **Callable preferred stock:** Preferred stock that can be redeemed or retired at a stated price at the option of the corporation.

LO 3   **Common stock:** Shares of stock that carry voting rights but that rank below preferred stock in terms of dividends and the distribution of assets.

LO 5   **Convertible preferred stock:** Preferred stock that can be exchanged for common stock at the option of the holder.

LO 1   **Corporation:** A separate legal entity having its own rights, privileges, and liabilities distinct from those of its owners.

LO 5   **Cumulative preferred stock:** Preferred stock on which unpaid dividends accumulate over time and must be satisfied in any given year before a dividend can be paid to common stockholders.

LO 4   **Date of declaration:** The date on which the board of directors declares a dividend.

LO 4   **Date of payment:** The date on which payment of a dividend is made.

LO 4   **Date of record:** The date on which ownership of stock for the purpose of receiving a dividend is determined.

LO 1   **Dividend:** The distribution of a corporation's assets (usually cash generated by past earnings) to its stockholders.

LO 5   **Dividends in arrears:** Past dividends on cumulative preferred stock that remain unpaid.

LO 1   **Dividends yield:** Current return to stockholders in the form of dividends; dividends per share divided by market price per share.

LO 1   **Double taxation:** The act of taxing corporate earnings twice—once as the income of the corporation and once as the dividends distributed to stockholders.

LO 4   **Ex-dividend:** A description of capital stock between the date of record and the date of payment, when the right to a dividend already declared on the stock remains with the person who sells the stock and does not transfer to the person who buys it.

LO 1   **Initial public offering (IPO):** Common stock issue of a company that is selling its stock to the public for the first time.

LO 3   **Issued stock:** The shares of stock sold or otherwise transferred to stockholders.

LO 1   **Legal capital:** The number of shares of stock issued times the par value; the minimum amount that can be reported as contributed capital.

LO 4   **Liquidating dividend:** A dividend that exceeds retained earnings; usually paid when a corporation goes out of business or reduces its operations.

LO 5   **Noncumulative preferred stock:** Preferred stock that does not oblige the issuer to make up a missed dividend in a subsequent year before paying dividends to common stockholders.

LO 6   **No-par stock:** Capital stock that does not have a par value.

LO 3   **Outstanding stock:** Stock that has been issued and is still in circulation.

LO 1   **Par value:** An arbitrary amount assigned to each share of stock; used to determine the legal capital of a corporation.

LO 5   **Preferred stock:** Stock that has preference over common stock, usually in terms of dividends and the distribution of assets.

LO 1   **Price/earnings (P/E) ratio:** A measure of confidence in a company's future; market price per share divided by earnings per share.

LO 3   **Residual equity:** The common stock of a corporation.

LO 1   **Return on equity:** A measure of management performance; net income divided by average stockholders' equity.

LO 1   **Share of stock:** A unit of ownership in a corporation.

LO 2   **Start-up and organization costs:** The costs of forming a corporation.

LO 6   **Stated value:** A value assigned by the board of directors of a corporation to no-par stock.

LO 1   **Stock certificate:** A document issued to a stockholder indicating the number of shares of stock the stockholder owns.

LO 8   **Stock option plan:** An agreement to issue stock to employees according to specified terms.

LO 7   **Treasury stock:** Capital stock, either common or preferred, that has been issued and reacquired by the issuing company but that has not subsequently been resold or retired.

LO 1   **Underwriter:** An intermediary between the corporation and the investing public who facilitates an issue of stock or other securities for a fee.

REVIEW PROBLEM

Stock Journal Entries and Stockholders' Equity

LO 1
LO 2
LO 3
LO 4
LO 5
LO 6
LO 7

The Beta Corporation was organized in 20x1 in the state of Arizona. Its charter authorized the corporation to issue 1,000,000 shares of $1 par value common stock and an additional 25,000 shares of 4 percent, $20 par value cumulative convertible preferred stock. Here are the transactions that related to the company's stock during 20x1:

Feb. 1   Issued 100,000 shares of common stock for $125,000.

15   Issued 3,000 shares of common stock for accounting and legal services. The services were billed to the company at $3,600.

Mar. 15   Issued 120,000 shares of common stock to Edward Jackson in exchange for a building and land that had appraised values of $100,000 and $25,000, respectively.

Apr. 2   Purchased 20,000 shares of common stock for the treasury at $1.25 per share from a person who changed his mind about investing in the company.

July 1   Issued 25,000 shares of preferred stock for $500,000.

Sept. 30   Sold 10,000 of the shares in the treasury for $1.50 per share.

Dec. 31   The board declared dividends of $24,910 payable on January 15 to stockholders of record on January 8. Dividends included preferred stock cash dividends for one-half year.

For the period ended December 31, 20x1, the company reported net income of $40,000 and earnings per common share of $.14. At December 31, the market price per common share was $1.60.

REQUIRED

1. Record these transactions in journal form. Following the December 31 entry to record dividends, show dividends payable for each class of stock.

2. Prepare the stockholders' equity section of the Beta Corporation balance sheet as of December 31, 20x1. (**Hint:** Use net income and dividends to calculate retained earnings.)

3. Calculate dividends yield on common stock, price/earnings ratio of common stock, and return on equity.

1. Prepare the entries in journal form.

20x1

Feb.	1	Cash		125,000	
			Common Stock		100,000
			Paid-in Capital in Excess of Par Value, Common		25,000
			Issued 100,000 shares of $1 par value common stock for $1.25 per share		
	15	Start-up and Organization Expense		3,600	
			Common Stock		3,000
			Paid-in Capital in Excess of Par Value, Common		600
			Issued 3,000 shares of $1 par value common stock for billed accounting and legal services of $3,600		
Mar.	15	Building		100,000	
		Land		25,000	
			Common Stock		120,000
			Paid-in Capital in Excess of Par Value, Common		5,000
			Issued 120,000 shares of $1 par value common stock for a building and land appraised at $100,000 and $25,000, respectively		
Apr.	2	Treasury Stock, Common		25,000	
			Cash		25,000
			Purchased 20,000 shares of common stock for the treasury at $1.25 per share		
July	1	Cash		500,000	
			Preferred Stock		500,000
			Issued 25,000 shares of $20 par value preferred stock for $20 per share		
Sept.	30	Cash		15,000	
			Treasury Stock, Common		12,500
			Paid-in Capital, Treasury Stock		2,500
			Sold 10,000 shares of treasury stock at $1.50 per share; original cost was $1.25 per share		
Dec.	31	Cash Dividends Declared		24,910	
			Cash Dividends Payable		24,910
			Declared a $24,910 cash dividend to preferred and common stockholders		

Total dividend	$24,910	
Less preferred stock cash dividend $500,000 × .04 × 6/12		10,000
Common stock cash dividend		$14,910

2. Prepare the stockholders' equity section of the balance sheet.

Beta Corporation
Balance Sheet
December 31, 20x1

Stockholders' Equity

Contributed Capital		
Preferred Stock, 4 percent cumulative convertible, $20 par value, 25,000 shares authorized, issued, and outstanding		$500,000
Common Stock, $1 par value, 1,000,000 shares authorized, 223,000 shares issued, and 213,000 shares outstanding	$223,000	
Paid-in Capital in Excess of Par Value, Common	30,600	
Paid-in Capital, Treasury Stock	2,500	256,100
Total Contributed Capital		$756,100
Retained Earnings		15,090*
Total Contributed Capital and Retained Earnings		$771,190
Less Treasury Stock, Common (10,000 shares, at cost)		12,500
Total Stockholders' Equity		$758,690

*Retained Earnings = $40,000 − $24,910 = $15,090.

3. Calculate dividends yield on common stock, price/earnings ratio of common stock, and return on equity.

$$\text{Dividends per Share} = \$14,910 \text{ Common Stock Dividend} \div 213,000 \text{ Common Shares Outstanding} = \$.07$$

$$\text{Dividends Yield} = \frac{\text{Dividends per Share}}{\text{Market Price per Share}} = \frac{\$.07}{\$1.60} = 4.4\%$$

$$\text{Price/Earnings (P/E) Ratio} = \frac{\text{Market Price per Share}}{\text{Earnings per Share}} = \frac{\$1.60}{\$.15} = 10.7 \text{ times}$$

The opening balance of stockholders' equity on February 1, 20x1, was $125,000.

$$\text{Return on Equity} = \frac{\text{Net Income}}{\text{Average Stockholders' Equity}}$$

$$= \frac{\$40,000}{(\$758,690 + \$125,000) \div 2}$$

$$= 9.1\%$$

Chapter Assignments

BUILDING YOUR KNOWLEDGE FOUNDATION

QUESTIONS

1. What issues faced by management are related to contributed capital?
2. Identify and explain several advantages of the corporate form of business.

3. Identify and explain several disadvantages of the corporate form of business.

4. What is dividends yield, and what do investors learn from it?

5. What is the price/earnings (P/E) ratio, and what does it measure?

6. What are the start-up and organization costs of a corporation?

7. What is the proper accounting treatment of start-up and organization costs?

8. What is the legal capital of a corporation, and what is its significance?

9. Describe the significance of the following dates as they relate to dividends: (a) date of declaration, (b) date of record, and (c) date of payment.

10. Explain the accounting treatment of cash dividends.

11. What are dividends in arrears, and how should they be disclosed in the financial statements?

12. Define the terms *cumulative, convertible,* and *callable* as they apply to preferred stock.

13. How is the value of stock determined when stock is issued for noncash assets?

14. Define *treasury stock* and explain why a company would purchase its own stock.

15. What is the proper classification of the following accounts on the balance sheet? Indicate whether stockholders' equity accounts are contributed capital, retained earnings, or contra stockholders' equity. (a) Common Stock; (b) Treasury Stock; (c) Paid-in Capital, Treasury Stock; (d) Paid-in Capital in Excess of Par Value, Common; (e) Paid-in Capital in Excess of Stated Value, Common; and (f) Retained Earnings.

16. What is a stock option plan and why would a company have one?

SHORT EXERCISES

SE 1.

LO 1 Management Issues

Indicate whether each of the actions below is related to (a) forming a corporation, (b) managing under the corporate form of business, (c) using equity financing, (d) determining dividend policies, or (e) evaluating performance using return on equity.

1. Considering whether to make a distribution to stockholders
2. Controlling day-to-day operations not necessarily by the owners
3. Determining whether to issue preferred or common stock
4. Compensating management based on the company's meeting or exceeding the targeted return on equity
5. Issuing shares (not to exceed the maximum of authorized shares)
6. Transferring shares from one owner to another without the approval of other owners
7. Deciding who will be the officers and board of directors

SE 2.

LO 1 Advantages and Disadvantages of a Corporation

Identify whether each of the following characteristics is an advantage or a disadvantage of the corporate form of business:

1. Ease of transfer of ownership
2. Taxation
3. Separate legal entity
4. Lack of mutual agency
5. Government regulation
6. Continuous existence

SE 3.

LO 2 Effect of Start-up and Organization Costs

At the beginning of 20x1, Matson Company incurred two start-up and organization costs: (1) attorneys' fees with a market value of $5,000, paid with 3,000 shares of $1 par value common stock, and (2) incorporation fees paid to the state of $3,000. Calculate total start-up and organization costs. What will be the effect of these costs on the balance sheet and income statement?

SE 4.

LO 3 Stockholders' Equity

Prepare the stockholders' equity section of Lincoln Corporation's balance sheet from the following accounts and balances on December 31, 20xx.

Account	Balance Debit	Balance Credit
Common Stock, $10 par value, 60,000 shares authorized, 40,000 shares issued, and 39,000 shares outstanding		$400,000
Paid-in Capital in Excess of Par Value, Common		200,000
Retained Earnings		30,000
Treasury Stock, Common (1,000 shares, at cost)	$15,000	

SE 5.

LO 4 Cash Dividends

Blancone Corporation has authorized 100,000 shares of $1 par value common stock, of which 80,000 are issued and 70,000 are outstanding. On May 15, the board of directors declared a cash dividend of $.10 per share payable on June 15 to stockholders of record on June 1. Prepare the entries, as necessary, for each of the three dates.

SE 6.

LO 5 Preferred Stock Dividends with Dividends in Arrears

The Vergennes Corporation has 1,000 shares of its $100, 8 percent cumulative preferred stock outstanding and 20,000 shares of its $1 par value common stock outstanding. In its first three years of operation, the board of directors of Vergennes Corporation paid cash dividends as follows: 20x1, none; 20x2, $20,000; and 20x3, $40,000.

Determine the total cash dividends and dividends per share paid to the preferred and common stockholders during each of the three years.

SE 7.

LO 6 Issuance of Stock

Ferrisburg Company is authorized to issue 100,000 shares of common stock. The company sold 5,000 shares at $12 per share. Prepare journal entries to record the sale of stock for cash under each of the following independent alternatives: (1) The stock has a par value of $5, and (2) the stock has no par value but a stated value of $1 per share.

SE 8.

LO 6 Issuance of Stock for Noncash Assets

Borneo Corporation issued 8,000 shares of its $1 par value common stock in exchange for land that had a fair market value of $50,000. Prepare the journal entries necessary to record the issuance of the stock for the land under each of these conditions: (1) The stock was selling for $7 per share on the day of the transaction; (2) management attempted to place a value on the common stock but could not do so.

SE 9.

LO 7 Treasury Stock Transactions

Prepare the journal entries necessary to record the following stock transactions of the Lemner Company during 20xx:

Oct. 1   Purchased 1,000 shares of its own $2 par value common stock for $20 per share, the current market price.
      17   Sold 250 shares of treasury stock purchased on October 1 for $25 per share.
      21   Sold 400 shares of treasury stock purchased on October 1 for $18 per share.

SE 10.

LO 7 Retirement of Treasury Stock

On October 28, 20xx, the Lemner Company (**SE 9**) retired the remaining 350 shares of treasury stock. The shares were originally issued at $5 per share. Prepare the necessary journal entry.

SE 11.

LO 8 Exercise of Stock Options

On June 6, Winston Leno exercised his option to purchase 10,000 shares of Plunkett Company $1 par value common stock at an option price of $4. The market price per share was $4 on the grant date and $18 on the exercise date. Record the transaction on Plunkett's books.

EXERCISES

E 1. In 20x1, Caps Corporation earned $2.20 per share and paid a dividend of $1.00 per share. At year end, the price of its stock was $33 per share. Calculate the dividends yield and the price/earnings ratio.

E 2. The accounts and balances below were taken from the records of Hagor Corporation on December 31, 20xx.

Account	Balance Debit	Balance Credit
Preferred Stock, $100 par value, 9 percent cumulative, 20,000 shares authorized, 12,000 shares issued and outstanding		$1,200,000
Common Stock, $12 par value, 90,000 shares authorized, 60,000 shares issued, and 57,000 shares outstanding		720,000
Paid-in Capital in Excess of Par Value, Common		388,000
Retained Earnings		46,000
Treasury Stock, Common (3,000 shares, at cost)	$60,000	

Prepare a stockholders' equity section for Hagor Corporation's balance sheet.

E 3. Indicate whether each characteristic listed below is more closely associated with common stock (C) or preferred stock (P).

1. Often receives dividends at a set rate
2. Is considered the residual equity of a company
3. Can be callable
4. Can be convertible
5. More likely to have dividends that vary in amount from year to year
6. Can be entitled to receive dividends not paid in past years
7. Likely to have full voting rights
8. Receives assets first in liquidation
9. Generally receives dividends before other classes of stock

E 4. The Prada Hospital Supply Corporation was organized in 20xx. The company was authorized to issue 100,000 shares of no-par common stock with a stated value of $5 per share, and 20,000 shares of $100 par value, 6 percent noncumulative preferred stock.

On March 1 the company issued 60,000 shares of its common stock for $15 per share and 8,000 shares of its preferred stock for $100 per share.

1. Prepare the journal entries to record the issuance of the stock.
2. Prepare the company's stockholders' equity section of the balance sheet immediately after the common and preferred stock was issued.

E 5. Cardosa Corporation has secured authorization from the state for 200,000 shares of $10 par value common stock. There are 160,000 shares issued and 140,000 shares outstanding. On June 5, the board of directors declared a $.50 per share cash dividend to be paid on June 25 to stockholders of record on June 15. Prepare the journal entries necessary to record these events.

E 6. Bodi Corporation has 500,000 authorized shares of $1 par value common stock, of which 400,000 are issued, including 40,000 shares of treasury stock. On October 15, the board of directors declared a cash dividend of $.25 per share payable on November 15 to stockholders of record on November 1. Prepare the entries, as necessary, for each of the three dates.

LO 5 Cash Dividends with Dividends in Arrears

E 7. The Hachiya Corporation has 10,000 shares of its $100 par value, 7 percent cumulative preferred stock outstanding, and 50,000 shares of its $1 par value common stock outstanding. In its first four years of operation, the board of directors of Hachiya Corporation paid cash dividends as follows: 20x1, none; 20x2, $120,000; 20x3, $140,000; 20x4, $140,000.

Determine the dividends per share and total cash dividends paid to the preferred and common stockholders during each of the four years.

LO 5 Preferred and Common Cash Dividends

E 8. The McCay Corporation pays dividends at the end of each year. The dividends paid for 20x1, 20x2, and 20x3 were $80,000, $60,000, and $180,000, respectively.

Calculate the total amount of dividends paid each year to the common and preferred stockholders if each of the following capital structures is assumed: (1) 20,000 shares of $100 par, 6 percent noncumulative preferred stock and 60,000 shares of $10 par common stock. (2) 10,000 shares of $100 par, 7 percent cumulative preferred stock and 60,000 shares of $10 par common stock. There were no dividends in arrears at the beginning of 20x1.

LO 6 Issuance of Stock

E 9. Seong Company is authorized to issue 200,000 shares of common stock. On August 1, the company issued 10,000 shares at $25 per share. Prepare journal entries to record the issuance of stock for cash under each of the following independent alternatives:

1. The stock has a par value of $25.
2. The stock has a par value of $10.
3. The stock has no par value.
4. The stock has a stated value of $1 per share.

LO 6 Issuance of Stock for Noncash Assets

E 10. On July 1, 20xx, Whitesides, a new corporation, issued 20,000 shares of its common stock for a corporate headquarters building. The building has a fair market value of $600,000 and a book value of $400,000. Because the corporation is new, it is not possible to establish a market value for the common stock.

Record the issuance of stock for the building, assuming the following conditions: (1) the par value of the stock is $10 per share; (2) the stock is no-par stock; and (3) the stock has a stated value of $4 per share.

LO 7 Treasury Stock Transactions

E 11. Prepare the necessary journal entries for the Skoglund Company to record the following stock transactions, representing all of the company's treasury stock transactions, during 20xx:

May 5 Purchased 400 shares of its own $2 par value common stock for $20 per share, the current market price.
17 Sold 150 shares of treasury stock purchased on May 5 for $22 per share.
21 Sold 100 shares of treasury stock purchased on May 5 for $20 per share.
28 Sold the remaining 150 shares of treasury stock purchased on May 5 for $19 per share.

LO 7 Treasury Stock Transactions Including Retirement

E 12. Prepare the journal entries necessary to record the following stock transactions of Vazquez Corporation, which represent all of its treasury stock transactions.

June 1 Purchased 2,000 shares of its own $30 par value common stock for $70 per share, the current market price.
10 Sold 500 shares of treasury stock purchased on June 1 for $80 per share.
20 Sold 700 shares of treasury stock purchased on June 1 for $58 per share.
30 Retired the remaining shares purchased on June 1. The original issue price was $42 per share.

LO 8 Grant and Exercise of Stock Options

E 13. On January 1, 20x3, Ho-Young Wang received an option to purchase 10,000 shares of $1 par value common stock at the January 1, 20x3, market price of $13 per share. The fair market value of the options on the date of grant was $16 per share, and the options expire on December 31, 20x3. Record the entry to recognize compensation expense for 20x3 and describe the alternative method of reporting in the notes to the financial statements. Ho-Young Wang exercised her options on November 30, 20x3. Record the issuance of stock.

PROBLEMS

P 1. Sussex Corporation began operations on September 1, 20xx. The corporation's charter authorized 300,000 shares of $8 par value common stock. Sussex Corporation engaged in the following transactions during its first quarter:

Sept. 1 Issued 50,000 shares of common stock, $500,000.
1 Paid an attorney $32,000 to help start up and organize the corporation and obtain the corporate charter from the state.
Oct. 2 Issued 80,000 shares of common stock, $960,000.
Nov. 30 The board of directors declared a cash dividend of $.40 per share to be paid on December 15 to stockholders of record on December 10.

1. Prepare journal entries to record the first-quarter transactions shown above.

2. Prepare the stockholders' equity section of Sussex Corporation's November 30, 20xx, balance sheet. Net income for the quarter was $80,000.

P 2. The DeMeo Corporation had both common stock and preferred stock outstanding from 20x2 through 20x4. Information about each stock for the three years is as follows:

Type	Par Value	Shares Outstanding	Other
Preferred	$100	40,000	7% cumulative
Common	20	600,000	

The company paid $140,000, $800,000, and $1,100,000 in dividends for 20x2 through 20x4, respectively. The market price per common share was $15 and $17 per share at year end 20x3 and 20x4, respectively.

1. Determine the dividends per share and total dividends paid to the common and preferred stockholders each year.

2. Repeat the computations performed in **1**, with the assumption that the preferred stock was noncumulative.

3. Calculate the 20x3 and 20x4 dividends yield for common stock using dividends per share computed in **2**.

P 3. The Spivy Corporation was involved in the following treasury stock transactions during 20x1:

a. Purchased 80,000 shares of its $1 par value common stock at $2.50 per share.
b. Purchased 16,000 shares of its common stock at $2.80 per share.
c. Sold 44,000 shares purchased in **a** for $131,000.
d. Sold the other 36,000 shares purchased in **a** for $72,000.
e. Sold 6,000 of the remaining shares of treasury stock for $1.60 per share.
f. Retired all the remaining shares of treasury stock. All shares originally were issued at $1.50 per share.

Record the treasury stock transactions in journal form.

P 4. Kokaly Plastics Corporation was chartered in the state of Massachusetts. The company was authorized to issue 20,000 shares of $100 par value, 6 percent preferred stock and 100,000 shares of no-par common stock. The common stock has a $2 stated value. The stock-related transactions for the quarter ended October 31, 20xx, were as follows:

Aug. 3 Issued 10,000 shares of common stock for $120,000 worth of services rendered in organizing and chartering the corporation.
15 Issued 16,000 shares of common stock for land, which had an asking price of $200,000. The common stock had a market value of $12 per share.
22 Issued 10,000 shares of preferred stock for $1,000,000.
Oct. 4 Issued 10,000 shares of common stock for $120,000.
10 Purchased 5,000 shares of common stock for the treasury for $13,000.
15 Declared a quarterly cash dividend on the outstanding preferred stock and $.10 per share on common stock outstanding, payable on October 31 to stockholders of record on October 25.
25 Date of record for cash dividends.
31 Paid cash dividends.

REQUIRED

1. Record transactions for the quarter ended October 31, 20xx, in journal form.

2. Prepare the stockholders' equity section of the company's balance sheet as of October 31, 20xx. Net income for the quarter was $46,000.

P 5.

LO 2 **Comprehensive**
LO 3 **Stockholders' Equity**
LO 4 **Transactions and**
LO 5 **T Accounts**
LO 6
LO 7
LO 8

In January 20xx, the Jones Corporation was organized and authorized to issue 2,000,000 shares of no-par common stock and 50,000 shares of 5 percent, $50 par value, noncumulative preferred stock. The stock-related transactions for the first year's operations were as follows:

Jan. 19   Sold 15,000 shares of the common stock for $31,500. State law requires a minimum of $1 stated value per share.

21   Issued 5,000 shares of common stock to attorneys and accountants for services valued at $11,000 and provided during the organization of the corporation.

Feb. 7   Issued 30,000 shares of common stock for a building that had an appraised value of $78,000.

Mar. 22   Purchased 10,000 shares of common stock for the treasury at $3 per share.

July 15   Issued 5,000 shares of common stock to employees under a stock option plan that allows any employee to buy shares at the current market price, which today is $3 per share.

Aug. 1   Sold 2,500 shares of treasury stock for $4 per share.

Sept. 1   Declared a cash dividend of $.15 per common share to be paid on September 25 to stockholders of record on September 15.

15   Cash dividends date of record.

25   Paid cash dividends to stockholders of record on September 15.

Oct. 30   Issued 4,000 shares of common stock for a piece of land. The stock was selling for $3 per share, and the land had a fair market value of $12,000.

Dec. 15   Issued 2,200 shares of preferred stock for $50 per share.

REQUIRED

1. Record the above transactions in T accounts. Prepare T accounts for Cash; Land; Building; Cash Dividends Payable; Preferred Stock; Common Stock; Paid-in Capital in Excess of Stated Value, Common; Paid-in Capital, Treasury Stock; Retained Earnings; Treasury Stock, Common; Cash Dividends Declared; and Start-up and Organization Expense.

2. Prepare the stockholders' equity section of Jones Corporation's balance sheet as of December 31, 20xx. Net income earned during the year was $100,000.

ALTERNATE PROBLEMS

P 6.

LO 2 **Start-up and**
LO 3 **Organization Costs,**
LO 4 **Stock and Dividend**
LO 6 **Journal Entries, and**
 Stockholders' Equity

On March 1, 20xx, Carmel Corporation began operations with a charter from the state that authorized 100,000 shares of $4 par value common stock. Over the next quarter, the firm engaged in the following transactions:

Mar. 1   Issued 30,000 shares of common stock, $200,000.

2   Paid fees associated with obtaining the charter and starting up and organizing the corporation, $24,000.

Apr. 10   Issued 13,000 shares of common stock, $130,000.

May 31   The board of directors declared a $.20 per share cash dividend to be paid on June 15 to shareholders of record on June 10.

REQUIRED

1. Record the transactions indicated above in journal form.

2. Prepare the stockholders' equity section of Carmel Corporation's balance sheet on May 31, 20xx. Net income earned during the first quarter was $30,000.

P 7.

LO 1 **Preferred and Common**
LO 5 **Stock Dividends and**
 Dividends Yield

The Clockwork Corporation had the following stock outstanding from 20x1 through 20x4:

Preferred stock: $100 par value, 8 percent cumulative, 10,000 shares authorized, issued, and outstanding

Common stock: $10 par value, 200,000 shares authorized, issued, and outstanding

The company paid $60,000, $60,000, $188,000, and $260,000 in dividends during 20x1, 20x2, 20x3, and 20x4, respectively. The market price per common share was $7.25 and $8.00 per share at year end 20x3 and 20x4, respectively.

REQUIRED

1. Determine the dividends per share and the total dividends paid to common stockholders and preferred stockholders in 20x1, 20x2, 20x3, and 20x4.

2. Perform the same computations, with the assumption that the preferred stock was noncumulative.

3. Calculate the 20x3 and 20x4 dividends yield for common stock, using the dividends per share computed in **2**.

P 8.

LO 2 **Comprehensive**
LO 3 **Stockholders' Equity**
LO 4 **Transactions**
LO 5
LO 6
LO 7

Vanowski, Inc., was organized and authorized to issue 10,000 shares of $100 par value, 9 percent preferred stock and 100,000 shares of no-par, $5 stated value common stock on July 1, 20xx. Stock-related transactions for Vanowski were as follows:

July   1   Issued 20,000 shares of common stock at $11 per share.

      1   Issued 1,000 shares of common stock at $11 per share for services rendered in connection with the organization of the company.

      2   Issued 2,000 shares of preferred stock at par value for cash.

    10   Issued 5,000 shares of common stock for land on which the asking price was $70,000. Market value of the stock was $12. Management wishes to record the land at full market value of the stock.

Aug.   2   Purchased 3,000 shares of common stock for the treasury at $13 per share.

   10   Declared a cash dividend for one month on the outstanding preferred stock and $.02 per share on common stock outstanding, payable on August 22 to stockholders of record on August 12.

   12   Date of record for cash dividends.

   22   Paid cash dividends.

REQUIRED

1. Record the transactions in journal form.

2. Prepare the stockholders' equity section of the balance sheet as it would appear on August 31, 20xx. Net income for July and August was $25,000.

EXPANDING YOUR CRITICAL THINKING, COMMUNICATION, AND INTERPERSONAL SKILLS

SKILLS DEVELOPMENT

Conceptual Analysis

SD 1.

LO 1 **Reasons for Issuing**
LO 3 **Common Stock**

In a recent year, **Safeway, Inc.,** one of the largest grocery chains in the United States, issued 19,750,000 shares of common stock for $52^{11}/_{16}$ for a total of $1,040,578,125.[14] As a large, profitable company, Safeway could have raised this significant amount of money by issuing long-term bonds. What are some advantages of issuing common stock as opposed to bonds? What are some disadvantages?

SD 2.

LO 5 **Reasons for Issuing**
      Preferred Stock

Preferred stock is a hybrid security that has some of the characteristics of stock and some of the characteristics of bonds. Historically, preferred stock has not been a popular means of financing. In the past few years, however, it has become more attractive to companies and individual investors alike, and investors are buying large amounts because of high yields. Large preferred stock issues have been made by banks such as **Chase Manhattan, Citibank, Republic New York,** and **Wells Fargo,** as well as other companies. The dividends yields on these stocks are over 9 percent, higher than the interest rates on comparable bonds.[15] Especially popular are preferred equity redemption

Cash Flow   CD-ROM   Communication   Critical Thinking   Ethics   General Ledger   Group Activity   Hot Links to Real Companies   International   Internet   Key Ratio   Memo   Spreadsheet

convertible stocks, or PERCs, which are automatically convertible into common stock after three years if the company does not redeem or call them first and retire them. What reasons can you give for the popularity of preferred stock, and of PERCs in particular, when the tax-deductible interest on bonds is less costly? Discuss both the company's and the investor's standpoints.

SD 3.
LO 7 Purposes of Treasury Stock

Many companies in recent years have bought back their common stock. For example, *IBM,* with large cash holdings, has spent almost $27 billion over five years buying back its stock. What are the reasons that companies buy back their own shares? What is the effect of common stock share buybacks on earnings per share, return on equity, return on assets, debt to equity, and the current ratio?

Ethical Dilemma

SD 4.
LO 1 Ethics of Incorporating an Accounting Firm

Traditionally, accounting firms have organized as partnerships or as professional corporations, a form of corporation that in many ways resembles a partnership. In recent years, some accounting firms have had large judgments imposed upon them as a result of lawsuits by investors who lost money when they invested in companies the firms have audited that went bankrupt. Because of the increased risk of large losses from malpractice suits, accounting firms are allowed to incorporate as long as they maintain a minimum level of partners' capital and carry malpractice insurance. Some accounting practitioners feel that incorporating would be a violation of their responsibility to the public. What features of the corporate form of business would be most advantageous to the partners of an accounting firm? Do you think it is a violation of the public trust for an accounting firm to incorporate?

Research Activity

SD 5.
LO 1 Comparison of
LO 3 Stockholders' Equity
LO 4 Characteristics
LO 5
LO 6
LO 8

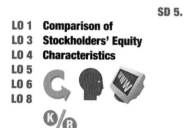

Select the annual reports of three corporations using either your library or the Fingraph® Financial Analyst™ CD-ROM software that accompanies this text. You can choose them from the same industry or at random, at the direction of your instructor. (Note: You may be asked to use these companies again in the Research Activities in later chapters.) Prepare a table with a column for each corporation. Then answer the following questions for each corporation: Does the corporation have preferred stock? If so, what are the par value and the indicated dividend, and is the preferred stock cumulative or convertible? Is the common stock par value or no-par? What is the par value or stated value? What cash dividends, if any, were paid in the past year? What is the dividends yield? From the notes to the financial statements, determine whether the company has an employee stock option plan. What are some of its provisions? What is the return on equity? Be prepared to discuss the characteristics of the stocks and dividends for your selected companies in class.

Decision-Making Practice

SD 6.
LO 1 Analysis of Alternative
LO 3 Financing Methods

Companies offering services to the computer technology industry are growing quickly. Participating in this growth, **Northeast Servotech Corporation** has expanded rapidly in recent years. Because of its profitability, the company has been able to grow without obtaining external financing. This fact is reflected in its current balance sheet, which contains no long-term debt. The liability and stockholders' equity sections of the balance sheet on March 31, 20xx, are shown at the top of the next page.

The company now has the opportunity to double its size by purchasing the operations of a rival company for $4,000,000. If the purchase goes through, Northeast Servotech will become the top company in its specialized industry in the northeastern part of the country. The problem for management is how to finance the purchase. After much study and discussion with bankers and underwriters, management has prepared three financing alternatives to present to the board of directors, which must authorize the purchase and the financing.

Alternative A: The company could issue $4,000,000 of long-term debt. Given the company's financial rating and the current market rates, management believes the company will have to pay an interest rate of 12 percent on the debt.

Northeast Servotech Corporation
Balance Sheet
March 31, 20xx

Liabilities

Current Liabilities	$ 500,000

Stockholders' Equity

Common Stock, $10 par value, 500,000 shares authorized, 100,000 shares issued and outstanding	$1,000,000	
Paid-in Capital in Excess of Par Value, Common	1,800,000	
Retained Earnings	1,700,000	
Total Stockholders' Equity		4,500,000
Total Liabilities and Stockholders' Equity		$5,000,000

Alternative B: The company could issue 40,000 shares of 8 percent, $100 par value preferred stock.

Alternative C: The company could issue 100,000 additional shares of $10 par value common stock at $40 per share.

Management explains to the board that the interest on the long-term debt is tax-deductible and that the applicable income tax rate is 40 percent. The board members know that a dividend of $.80 per share of common stock was paid last year, up from $.60 and $.40 per share in the two years before that. The board has had a policy of regular increases in dividends of $.20 per share. The board feels that each of the three financing alternatives is feasible and now wants to study the financial effects of each alternative.

1. Prepare a schedule to show how the liabilities and stockholders' equity sections of Northeast Servotech's balance sheet would look under each alternative, and compute the debt to equity ratio (total liabilities ÷ total stockholders' equity) for each.

2. Compute and compare the cash needed to pay the interest or dividends for each kind of new financing net of income taxes in the first year.

3. How might the cash needed to pay for the financing change in future years under each alternative?

4. Prepare a memorandum to the board of directors that evaluates the alternatives in order of preference based on cash flow effects, giving arguments for and against each one.

Group Activity: Assign the alternatives to different groups to analyze and present to the class as the "board of directors."

FINANCIAL REPORTING AND ANALYSIS

Interpreting Financial Reports

FRA 1.

LO 1 **Effect of Stock Issue**
LO 3
LO 6

Netscape Communications Corporation, now a part of AOL–Time Warner, is a leading provider of software, applications, and tools that link people and information over networks, the Internet, and the World Wide Web. It is one of the great success stories of the Internet age. Netscape went public with an IPO in June 1995 and issued shares at a price of $14 per share. On November 14, 1996, Netscape announced a common stock issue in an ad in *The Wall Street Journal:*

6,440,000 Shares
NETSCAPE
Common Stock
Price $53¾ a share

If Netscape sold all these shares at the offering price of $53.75, the net proceeds before issue costs would be $346.15 million.

A portion of the stockholders' equity section of the balance sheet adapted from Netscape's 1995 annual report is shown below.

	1995	1994
	(In thousands)	
Common Stock, $.0001 par value, 200,000,000 shares authorized, 12,003,594 shares in 1994 and 81,063,158 shares in 1995 issued and outstanding	$ 8	$ 1
Additional Paid-in Capital	196,749	18,215
Accumulated Deficit	(16,314)	(12,873)

REQUIRED

1. Assume the net proceeds from the sale of 6,440,000 shares at $53.75 were $342.6 million after issue costs. Record the stock issuance on Netscape's accounting records in journal form.

2. Prepare the portion of the stockholders' equity section of the balance sheet shown above after the issue of the common stock, based on the information given. Round all answers to the nearest thousand.

3. Based on your answer in **2,** did Netscape have to increase its authorized shares to undertake this stock issue?

4. What amount per share did Netscape receive and how much did Netscape's underwriters receive to help in issuing the stock if investors paid $53.75 per share? What do the underwriters do to earn their fee?

International Company

FRA 2.

LO 3   Stockholders' Equity
LO 4   and Dividends

Roche Group is a giant Swiss pharmaceutical company. Its stockholders' equity shows how little importance common stock, called *share capital*, typically plays in the financing of Swiss companies:[16]

	1999	1998
Shareholders' Equity (in millions of Swiss francs)		
Share Capital	160	160
Retained Earnings	26,669	21,655
Total Shareholders' Equity	26,829	21,815

When Swiss companies need financing, they often rely on debt financing from large Swiss banks and from other debt markets. With only 160 million Swiss francs (1.6 million shares) in share capital, Roche has had few stock issues in its history. This amount compares to over 43 billion Swiss francs in liabilities. Also, Roche has been enormously profitable, having built up retained earnings of more than 26 billion Swiss francs over the years. The company also pays a substantial dividend that totaled 750 million Swiss francs in 1999. Calculate the dividends per share and dividends yield assuming a share price of 18,100 Swiss francs. Also, assuming that dividends and net income were the only factors that affected retained earnings during 1999, how much did Roche earn in 1999 in U.S. dollars (use an exchange rate of 1.7 Swiss francs to the dollar)? What was Roche's return on equity?

Toys "R" Us Annual Report

FRA 3.

LO 1   Stockholders' Equity
LO 3
LO 7
LO 8

Refer to the Toys "R" Us annual report to answer the following questions:

1. What type of capital stock does Toys "R" Us have? What is the par value? How many shares are authorized, issued, and outstanding at the end of 2000?

2. What is the dividends yield for Toys "R" Us and its relationship to the investors' total return? Does the company rely mostly on stock or on earnings for its stockholders' equity?

3. From the statement of stockholders' equity, how has management's policy with regard to treasury stock changed over the past three years? What favorable effects did the stock buybacks have?

4. Does the company have a stock option plan? To whom do the stock options apply? Do employees have significant stock options? Given the market price of the stock shown in the report, do these options represent significant value to the employees?

5. Calculate and discuss the price/earnings ratio and return on equity for 1999 and 2000. The average share price for the fourth quarter was $18 and $15 for 1999 and 2000, respectively.

Fingraph® Financial Analyst™

FRA 4.

LO 1 Comparative
LO 3 Analysis of
LO 7 Stockholders' Equity
LO 8

Select any two companies from the same industry in the Fingraph® Financial Analyst™ CD-ROM software.

1. In the annual reports for the companies you have selected, identify the stockholders' equity section of the balance sheet and reference to any stockholders' equity accounts in the summary of significant accounting policies or notes to the financial statements. Do the companies have more than one kind of capital stock? What are the characteristics of each type of capital stock? Do the companies have treasury stock? Do the companies have an employee stock option plan?

2. Find the earnings per share and dividends per share in the annual reports for both companies. Also, find in the financial section of your local paper the current market prices of the companies' common stock. Prepare a table that summarizes this information and that shows the price/earnings ratio and the dividends yield.

3. Locate the statements of cash flows in the two companies' annual reports. Has the company issued capital stock or repurchased its stock in the last three years?

4. Find and read references to capital stock in management's discussion and analysis in each annual report.

5. Write a one-page executive summary that highlights the types of capital stock for these companies, the significance of treasury stock, and any employee stock option plan; also compare the price/earnings ratio and the dividends yield trends of the two companies, including reference to management's assessment. Include your table as an attachment to your report.

Internet Case

FRA 5.

LO 1 Comparison of Financing of
LO 4 Internet Companies
LO 5
LO 6
LO 7
LO 8

Many Internet start-up companies have gone public in recent years. These companies are generally unprofitable and require a great deal of cash to finance expansion. They also reward their employees with stock options. Choose any two of the following Internet companies: *Amazon.com, Yahoo, eBay Inc.,* and *AOL–Time Warner*. Through the Needles Accounting Resource Center at http://college.hmco.com, find companies under web links and go to the web sites for the two companies you have selected. In the latest annual report for each of the companies, look at the financing activities section of the statement of cash flows for the last three years. How have your two companies financed their businesses? Have they issued stock or long-term debt? Have they purchased treasury stock, paid dividends, or issued stock under stock option plans? Are the companies profitable (see net income or earnings at the top of the statement)? Are your findings in line with your expectations about these young Internet companies? Find each company's stock price, either on the Web (many companies have it on their homepage) or in the newspaper, and compare it to the average issue price of that company's past stock issues. Summarize your findings and conclusions.

ENDNOTES

1. General Motors Corporation, *Annual Report*, 1999.
2. Copyright © 2000 by Houghton Mifflin Company. Adapted and reproduced by permission from *The American Heritage Dictionary of the English Language*, Fourth Edition.
3. Abbott Laboratories, *Annual Report*, 1999.
4. *Statement of Position No. 98-5*, "Report on the Costs of Start up Activities" (New York: American Institute of Certified Public Accountants, 1998).
5. Suzanne McGee, "Europe's New Markets for IPOs of Growth Start-Ups Fly High," *The Wall Street Journal*, February 22, 1999.
6. Microsoft Corporation, Inc., *Annual Report*, 1997.
7. G. Christian Hill, "Microsoft Plans Preferred Issue of $750 Million," *The Wall Street Journal*, December 3, 1996.
8. American Institute of Certified Public Accountants, *Accounting Trends & Techniques* (New York: AICPA, 1999).
9. The Coca-Cola Company, *Annual Report*, 1999, and IBM Corporation, *Annual Report*, 1999.
10. Fred P. Bleakley, "Management Problem: Reinvest High Profits or Please Institutions?" *The Wall Street Journal*, October 16, 1995.
11. American Institute of Certified Public Accountants, *Accounting Trends & Techniques* (New York: AICPA, 1999).
12. *Statement of Accounting Standards No. 123*, "Accounting for Stock-Based Compensation" (Norwalk, Conn.: Financial Accounting Standards Board, 1995).
13. Elizabeth MacDonald, "Options' Effect on Earnings Sparks Debate," *The Wall Street Journal*, May 13, 1999.
14. Announcement, *The Wall Street Journal*, February 19, 1999, p. C19.
15. Tom Herman, "Preferreds' Rich Yields Blind Some Investors to Risks," *The Wall Street Journal*, March 24, 1992.
16. Roche Group, *Annual Report*, 1999.

15

The Corporate Income Statement and the Statement of Stockholders' Equity

LEARNING OBJECTIVES

1 Identify the issues related to evaluating the quality of a company's earnings.

2 Prepare a corporate income statement.

3 Show the relationships among income taxes expense, deferred income taxes, and net of taxes.

4 Describe the disclosure on the income statement of discontinued operations, extraordinary items, and accounting changes.

5 Compute earnings per share.

6 Prepare a statement of stockholders' equity.

7 Account for stock dividends and stock splits.

8 Calculate book value per share.

DaimlerChrysler AG DaimlerChrysler AG is one of the largest automobile companies in the world. Interpreting the operating results of such a company is not always easy. For instance, consider DaimlerChrysler's performance for the three-year period from 1997 to 1999, as measured by earnings per share.[1] The company's statements are presented in Euros, the new European currency. Net income per share declined from e6.90 to e5.03 in 1998 but rebounded to e5.73 in 1999. However, income before extraordinary items declined from e6.90 in 1997 to e5.09 in 1999. Someone not familiar with the structure and use of corporate income statements might be confused by this apparent contradiction. Which is the best measure of DaimlerChrysler's performance?

Financial Highlights

	1999	1998	1997
Earnings per share (in Euros):			
Basic earnings per share			
Income before extraordinary items	5.09	5.16	6.90
Extraordinary items	.64	(.13)	—
Net income	5.73	5.03	6.90

Earnings or net income per share is the "bottom line" that many investors look at to judge the success or failure of a company. Just looking at the bottom line, however, can be misleading. The corporate income statement contains a number of infrequent increases and decreases made more or less at the discretion of management that will result in variations in results. In 1998, DaimlerChrysler had a loss on early extinguishment of debt that reduced its earnings per share by e.13. In 1999, the company had a gain on the disposal of a business that increased earnings per share by e.64. These latter items are called *extraordinary items,* or rare items that occur because management has made the decision to engage in these transactions. Because of these items, net income per share is not the best gauge of DaimlerChrysler's ongoing performance in its normal operations. Net income before extraordinary items is a better measure. Knowledge of issues involving quality of earnings and the components of corporate income statements is essential to understanding and analyzing the operations of companies like DaimlerChrysler.

Performance Measurement: Quality of Earnings Issues

OBJECTIVE

1 Identify the issues related to evaluating the quality of a company's earnings

Current and expected earnings are important factors to consider in evaluating a company's performance and analyzing its prospects. In fact, a survey of 2,000 members of the Association for Investment Management and Research indicated that the two most important economic indicators in evaluating common stocks were expected changes in earnings per share and expected return on equity.[2] Net income is a key component of both measures.

Because of the importance of net income, or the "bottom line," in measuring a company's prospects, there is significant interest in evaluating the quality of the net income figure, or the **quality of earnings**. The quality of a company's earnings refers to the substance of earnings and their sustainability into future accounting periods. The quality of earnings may be affected by (1) the accounting methods and estimates the company's management chooses and (2) the nature of nonoperating items on the income statement.

Choice of Accounting Methods and Estimates

Choices of accounting methods and estimates affect a firm's operating income. To assure proper matching of revenues and expenses, accounting requires cost allocations and estimates of data that will not be known with certainty until some future date. For example, accountants estimate the useful life of assets when they are acquired. However, technological obsolescence could shorten the expected useful life, or excellent maintenance and repairs could lengthen it. The actual useful life will not be known with certainty until some future date. The choice of estimate affects both current and future operating income.

Because there is considerable latitude in the choice of estimates, management and other financial statement users must be aware of the impact of accounting estimates on reported operating income. Estimates include percentage of uncollectible accounts receivable, sales returns, useful life, residual or salvage value, total units of production, total recoverable units of natural resource, amortization period, expected warranty claims, and expected environmental cleanup costs.

These estimates are not all equally important to every firm. The relative importance of each estimate depends on the industry in which the firm operates. For example, the estimate of uncollectible receivables for a credit card firm, such as American Express, or a financial services firm, such as Bank of America, can have a

FOCUS ON BUSINESS PRACTICE

Quality of earnings is an important issue for investors. For example, analysts for Twentieth Century Mutual Funds, a major investment company, make adjustments to a company's reported financial performance to create a more accurate picture of the company's ongoing operations. Assume a paper company reports earnings of $1.30 per share, which makes year-to-year comparisons unusually strong. Upon further investigation, however, it is found that the per share number includes a one-time gain on the sale of assets of $.25 per share. Twentieth Century would list the company in its data base as earning only $1.05 per share. "These kinds of adjustments help assure long-term decisions aren't based on one-time events."[3]

material impact on earnings, but the choice of useful life may be less important because depreciable assets represent only a small percentage of total assets. Toys "R" Us has very few receivables, but it has substantial investment in depreciable assets; thus choice of useful life and residual value are much more important than uncollectible accounts receivable.

The choice of methods also affects a firm's operating income. Generally accepted accounting methods include uncollectible receivable methods (net sales or aging of accounts receivable), inventory methods (last-in, first-out [LIFO], first-in, first-out [FIFO], or average cost), depreciation methods (accelerated, production, or straight-line), and revenue recognition methods. These methods are designed to match revenues and expenses. Costs are allocated based on a determination of the benefits to the current period (expenses) versus the benefits to future periods (assets). The expenses are estimates, and the period or periods benefited cannot be demonstrated conclusively. The estimates are also subjective, because in practice it is hard to justify one method of estimation over another.

For these reasons, management, the accountant, and the financial statement user need to understand the possible effects of different accounting procedures on net income and financial position. Some methods and estimates are more conservative than others because they tend to produce a lower net income in the current period. For example, suppose that two companies have similar operations, but one uses FIFO for inventory costing and straight-line (SL) for computing depreciation, whereas the other uses LIFO for inventory costing and double-declining-balance (DDB) for computing depreciation. The income statements of the two companies might appear as follows:

	FIFO and SL	LIFO and DDB
Net Sales	$500,000	$500,000
Goods Available for Sale	$300,000	$300,000
Less Ending Inventory	60,000	50,000
Cost of Goods Sold	$240,000	$250,000
Gross Margin	$260,000	$250,000
Less: Depreciation Expense	$ 40,000	$ 80,000
Other Expenses	170,000	170,000
Total Operating Expenses	$210,000	$250,000
Operating Income	$ 50,000	$ —

The operating income for the firm using LIFO and DDB is lower because, in periods of rising prices, the LIFO inventory costing method produces a higher cost of goods sold, and, in the early years of an asset's useful life, accelerated depreciation yields a higher depreciation expense. The result is lower operating income. However, future operating income is expected to be higher.

The $50,000 difference in operating income stems only from the differences in accounting methods. Differences in the estimated lives and residual values of the plant assets could lead to an even greater variation. In practice, of course, differences in net income occur for many reasons, but the user must be aware of the discrepancies that can occur as a result of the accounting methods chosen by management. In general, an accounting method or estimate that results in lower current earnings is considered to produce a better quality of operating income.

The existence of such alternatives could cause problems in the interpretation of financial statements were it not for the conventions of full disclosure and consistency. Full disclosure requires that management explain the significant accounting policies used in preparing the financial statements in a note to the statements.

Consistency requires that the same accounting procedures be followed from year to year. If a change in procedure is made, the nature of the change and its monetary effect must be explained in a note.

Nature of Nonoperating Items

The corporate income statement consists of several components, as shown in Exhibit 1. The top of the statement presents income from current ongoing operations, called *income from continuing operations.* The lower part of the statement can contain such nonoperating items as discontinued operations, extraordinary gains and losses, and effects of accounting changes. Those items may drastically affect the bottom line, or net income, of the company. In fact, in Exhibit 1, earnings per common share associated with continuing operations were $2.81, but net income per share was $3.35, or 19.2 percent higher.

For practical reasons, the calculations of trends and ratios are based on the assumption that net income and other components are comparable from year to year and from company to company. However, in making interpretations, the astute analyst will always look beyond the ratios to the quality of the components. For example, restructuring charges, if they are large enough, can make a company's

Exhibit 1
A Corporate Income Statement

Junction Corporation
Income Statement
For the Year Ended December 31, 20x1

Revenues		$925,000
Less Costs and Expenses		500,000
Income from Continuing Operations Before Income Taxes		$425,000
Income Taxes Expense		144,500
Income from Continuing Operations		$280,500
Discontinued Operations		
Income from Operations of Discontinued Segment		
(net of taxes, $35,000)	$90,000	
Loss on Disposal of Segment (net of taxes, $42,000)	(73,000)	17,000
Income Before Extraordinary Items and		
Cumulative Effect of Accounting Change		$297,500
Extraordinary Gain (net of taxes, $17,000)		43,000
Subtotal		$340,500
Cumulative Effect of a Change in Accounting		
Principle (net of taxes, $5,000)		(6,000)
Net Income		$334,500
Earnings per Common Share:		
Income from Continuing Operations		$ 2.81
Discontinued Operations (net of taxes)		.17
Income Before Extraordinary Items and		
Cumulative Effect of Accounting Change		$ 2.98
Extraordinary Gain (net of taxes)		.43
Cumulative Effect of Accounting Change (net of taxes)		(.06)
Net Income		$ 3.35

disclose wrongdoing on the part of their company. For example, after the internal audit chief of W. R. Grace, a chemical company, was fired, he made known to the SEC his concerns of deliberate deferral of reporting of income by W. R. Grace. The goal was to show growth in earnings within the targeted range of 20–24 percent, which analysts were expecting. Later the company reversed the deferral of income to offset poor operating results. The SEC is currently investigating W. R. Grace for fraudulently manipulated earnings.[4]

External users of financial statements depend on management's honesty and openness in disclosing factual information about a company. In the vast majority of cases, management's reports are reliable, but on occasion, employees (called *whistle-blowers*) may publicly

---

return on equity look better. In a recent year, Boeing Company, an aircraft manufacturer, took charges of $4 billion resulting in a loss of $178 million. The effect of this charge reduced equity by almost 20 percent. Return on equity should increase in next period.[5] Although such write-offs reduce a company's net worth, they usually do not affect current cash flows or operations and in most cases are ignored by analysts assessing current performance.

In some cases, a company may boost income by including one-time gains. For example, Sears, Roebuck and Co., a multiline retailer providing a wide array of merchandise and services, used a gain from the change of an accounting principle to bolster its net income by $136 million, or $.35 per share, in 1997. Without the gain, earnings per share (EPS) actually decreased from $3.12 to $2.92, not increased as Sears originally reported.[6] The quality of Sears's earnings is in fact lower than it might appear on the surface. Unless analysts are prepared to go beyond the "bottom line" in analyzing and interpreting financial reports, they can come to the wrong conclusions.

The Corporate Income Statement

OBJECTIVE

2 Prepare a corporate income statement

Accounting organizations have not specified the format of the income statement because they have considered flexibility more important than a standard format. Either the single-step or the multistep form can be used. However, the accounting profession has taken the position that income for a period should be all-inclusive, **comprehensive income**, which is different from net income.[7] Comprehensive income is the change in a company's equity during a period from sources other than owners and includes net income, change in unrealized investment gains and losses, and other items affecting equity. Companies are reporting comprehensive income and its components as a separate financial statement, or as part of another financial statement.

In the first year of this requirement, 347 of 600 large companies reported comprehensive income. Of these, 78 percent reported comprehensive income on the statement of stockholders' equity, 10 percent reported it on a separate statement, and only 2 percent reported it on the income statement.[8]

Net income or loss for a period includes all revenues, expenses, gains, and losses over the period, except for prior period adjustments. As a result, several items must be added to the income statement, among them discontinued operations, extraordinary items, and accounting changes. The Financial Accounting Standards Board has proposed adding goodwill amortization to this list, moving it down from income from operations. In addition, earnings per share figures must be disclosed. Exhibit 1 illustrated a corporate income statement and the required disclosures. The following sections discuss the components of the corporate income statement, beginning with income taxes expense.

Income Taxes Expense

OBJECTIVE

3 Show the relationships among income taxes expense, deferred income taxes, and net of taxes

Corporations determine their taxable income (the amount on which taxes are paid) by subtracting allowable business deductions from includable gross income. The federal tax laws determine which business expenses may be deducted and which cannot be deducted from taxable gross income.*

The tax rates that apply to a corporation's taxable income are shown in Table 1. A corporation with taxable income of $70,000 would have a federal income tax liability of $12,500: $7,500 (the tax on the first $50,000 of taxable income) plus $5,000 (25 percent of the $20,000 earned in excess of $50,000).

Income taxes expense is the expense recognized in the accounting records on an accrual basis that applies to income from continuing operations. This expense may or may not equal the amount of taxes actually paid by the corporation and recorded as income taxes payable in the current period. The amount payable is determined from taxable income, which is measured according to the rules and regulations of the income tax code.

For the sake of convenience, most small businesses keep their accounting records on the same basis as their tax records, so that the income taxes expense on the income statement equals the income taxes liability to be paid to the Internal Revenue Service (IRS). This practice is acceptable when there is no material difference between the income on an accounting basis and the income on an income tax basis. However, the purpose of accounting is to determine net income in accordance with generally accepted accounting principles, not to determine taxable income and tax liability.

Management has an incentive to use methods that minimize the firm's tax liability, but accountants, who are bound by accrual accounting and the materiality concept, cannot let tax procedures dictate their method of preparing financial statements if the result would be misleading. As a consequence, there can be a material difference between accounting and taxable incomes, especially in larger businesses. This discrepancy can result from differences in the timing of the recognition of revenues and expenses under the two accounting methods. Some possible variations are shown below.

	Accounting Method	Tax Method
Expense recognition	Accrual or deferral	At time of expenditure
Accounts receivable	Allowance	Direct charge-off
Inventories	Average cost	FIFO
Depreciation	Straight-line	Modified Accelerated Cost Recovery System

Deferred Income Taxes

The accounting method used to accrue income taxes expense on the basis of accounting income whenever there are differences between accounting and taxable income is called **income tax allocation**. The account used to record the difference between the income taxes expense and income taxes payable is called **Deferred Income Taxes**. For example, Junction Corporation shows income taxes expense of $144,500 on its income statement but has actual income taxes payable

---

*Rules for calculating and reporting taxable income in specialized industries such as banking, insurance, mutual funds, and cooperatives are highly technical and may vary significantly from those discussed in this chapter.

Table 1. Tax Rate Schedule for Corporations, 2000

Taxable Income		Tax Liability	
Over	But Not Over		Of the Amount Over
—	$ 50,000	0 + 15%	—
$ 50,000	75,000	$ 7,500 + 25%	$ 50,000
75,000	100,000	13,750 + 34%	75,000
100,000	335,000	22,250 + 39%	100,000
335,000	10,000,000	113,900 + 34%	335,000
10,000,000	15,000,000	3,400,000 + 35%	10,000,000
15,000,000	18,333,333	5,150,000 + 38%	15,000,000
18,333,333	—	6,416,667 + 35%	18,333,333

Note: Tax rates are subject to change by Congress.

to the IRS of $92,000. The entry that follows is to record the estimated income taxes expense applicable to income from continuing operations using the income tax allocation procedure.

A = L + OE
\ + −
\ +

Dec. 31	Income Taxes Expense	144,500	
	Income Taxes Payable		92,000
	Deferred Income Taxes		52,500
	To record estimated current and deferred income taxes		

In other years, it is possible for Income Taxes Payable to exceed Income Taxes Expense, in which case the same entry is made except that Deferred Income Taxes is debited.

The Financial Accounting Standards Board has issued specific rules for recording, measuring, and classifying deferred income taxes.[9] Deferred income taxes are recognized for the estimated future tax effects resulting from temporary differences in the valuation of assets, liabilities, equity, revenues, expenses, gains, and losses for tax and financial reporting purposes. Temporary differences include revenues and expenses or gains and losses that are included in taxable income before or after they are included in financial income. In other words, the recognition point for revenues, expenses, gains, and losses is not the same for tax and financial reporting. For example, advance payments for goods and services, such as magazine subscriptions, are not recognized in financial income until the product is shipped, but for tax purposes they are usually recognized as revenue when cash is received. The result is that taxes paid exceed tax expense, which creates a deferred income tax asset (or prepaid taxes).

Classification of deferred income taxes as current or noncurrent depends on the classification of the related asset or liability that created the temporary difference. For example, the deferred income tax asset mentioned above would be classified as current if unearned subscription revenue is classified as a current liability. On the other hand, the temporary difference arising from depreciation is related to a long-term depreciable asset. Therefore, the resulting deferred income tax would be classified as long-term. However, if a temporary difference is not related to an asset or liability, then it is classified as current or noncurrent based on its expected date of reversal. Temporary differences and the classification of deferred income taxes that results are covered in depth in more advanced courses.

Each year, the balance of the Deferred Income Taxes account is evaluated to determine whether it still accurately represents the expected asset or liability in light of legislated changes in income tax laws and regulations. If changes have occurred, an adjusting entry to bring the account balance into line with current laws is required. For example, a decrease in corporate income tax rates, like the one that occurred in 1987, means that a company with deferred income tax liabilities will pay less in taxes in future years than the amount indicated by the credit balance of its Deferred Income Taxes account. As a result, the company would debit Deferred Income Taxes to reduce the liability and credit Gain from Reduction in Income Tax Rates. This credit increases the reported income on the income statement. If the tax rate increases in future years, a loss would be recorded and the deferred income tax liability would be increased.

In any given year, the amount a company pays in income taxes is determined by subtracting (or adding, as the case may be) the deferred income taxes for that year, as reported in the notes to the financial statements, from (or to) income taxes expense, which is reported in the financial statements. In subsequent years, the amount of deferred income taxes can vary based on changes in tax laws and rates.

Some understanding of the importance of deferred income taxes to financial reporting can be gained from studying a survey of the financial statements of 600 large companies. About 67 percent reported deferred income taxes with a credit balance in the long-term liability section of the balance sheet.[10]

Net of Taxes

The phrase **net of taxes**, as used in Exhibit 1, means that the effect of applicable taxes (usually income taxes) has been considered in determining the overall effect of an item on the financial statements. The phrase is used on the corporate income statement when a company has items that must be disclosed in a separate section. Each such item should be reported net of the applicable income taxes to avoid distorting the income taxes expense associated with ongoing operations and the resulting net operating income. For example, assume that a corporation with operating income before taxes of $120,000 has a total tax expense of $66,000 and that the total income includes a gain of $100,000 on which a tax of $30,000 is due. Also assume that the gain is not part of normal operations and must be disclosed separately on the income statement as an extraordinary item (explained later). This is how the tax expense would be reported on the income statement:

Operating Income Before Taxes	$120,000
Income Taxes Expense	36,000
Income Before Extraordinary Item	$ 84,000
Extraordinary Gain (net of taxes, $30,000)	70,000
Net Income	$154,000

If all the tax expense were deducted from operating income before taxes, both the income before extraordinary item and the extraordinary gain would be distorted.

A company follows the same procedure in the case of an extraordinary loss. For example, assume the same facts as before except that the total tax expense is only $6,000 because of a $100,000 extraordinary loss. The result is a $30,000 tax savings, shown as follows:

Operating Income Before Taxes	$120,000
Income Taxes Expense	36,000
Income Before Extraordinary Item	$ 84,000
Extraordinary Loss (net of taxes, $30,000)	(70,000)
Net Income	$ 14,000

In Exhibit 1, the total of the income tax items is $149,500. That amount is allocated among five statement components, as follows:

Income taxes expense on income from continuing operations	$144,500
Income tax on income from a discontinued segment	35,000
Income tax savings on the loss on the disposal of the segment	(42,000)
Income tax on the extraordinary gain	17,000
Income tax savings on the cumulative effect of a change in accounting principle	(5,000)
Total income taxes expense	$149,500

Discontinued Operations

OBJECTIVE

4 Describe the disclosure on the income statement of discontinued operations, extraordinary items, and accounting changes

Large companies in the United States usually have many **segments**. A segment may be a separate major line of business or serve a separate class of customer. For example, a company that makes heavy drilling equipment may also have another line of business, such as the manufacture of mobile homes. A large company may discontinue or otherwise dispose of certain segments of its business that do not fit its future plans or are not profitable. **Discontinued operations** are segments of a business that are no longer part of its ongoing operations. Generally accepted accounting principles require that gains and losses from discontinued operations be reported separately on the income statement. Such separation makes it easier to evaluate the ongoing activities of the business.

In Exhibit 1, the disclosure of discontinued operations has two parts. One part shows that after the date of the decision to discontinue, the income from operations of the segment that has been disposed of was $90,000 (net of $35,000 taxes). The other part shows that the loss from the disposal of the segment was $73,000 (net of $42,000 tax savings). Computation of the gains or losses is covered in more advanced accounting courses. The disclosure has been described, however, to give a complete view of the corporate income statement.

Extraordinary Items

The Accounting Principles Board, in its *Opinion No. 30*, defines **extraordinary items** as "events or transactions that are distinguished by their unusual nature *and* by the infrequency of their occurrence."[11] Unusual and infrequent occurrences are explained in the opinion as follows:

> Unusual Nature—the underlying event or transaction should possess a high degree of abnormality and be of a type clearly unrelated to, or only incidentally related to, the ordinary and typical activities of the entity, taking into account the environment in which the entity operates.

> Infrequency of Occurrence—the underlying event or transaction should be of a type that would not reasonably be expected to recur in the foreseeable future, taking into account the environment in which the entity operates.[12]

If an item is both unusual and infrequent (and material in amount), it should be reported separately from continuing operations on the income statement. The disclosure allows readers to identify gains or losses in income that would not be expected to happen again soon. Items usually treated as extraordinary include (1) an uninsured loss from flood, earthquake, fire, or theft; (2) a gain or loss resulting from the passage of a new law; (3) the expropriation (taking) of property by a foreign government; and (4) a gain or loss from the early retirement of debt. Gains or losses from extraordinary items should be reported on the income statement after discontinued operations. And they should be shown net of applicable taxes. In a recent year, 74 (12 percent) of 600 large companies reported extraordinary items on their income statements.[13] In Exhibit 1, the extraordinary gain was $43,000 after applicable taxes of $17,000.

Accounting Changes

Consistency, which is one of the basic conventions of accounting, means that companies must apply the same accounting principles from year to year. However, a company is allowed to make accounting changes if current procedures are incorrect or inappropriate. For example, a change from the FIFO to the LIFO inventory method can be made if there is adequate justification for the change. Adequate justification usually means that if the change occurs, the financial statements will better show the financial activities of the company. A company's desire to lower the amount of income taxes it pays is not considered adequate justification for an accounting change. If justification does exist and an accounting change is made, generally accepted accounting principles require the disclosure of the change in the financial statements.

The **cumulative effect of an accounting change** is the effect that the new accounting principle would have had on net income in prior periods if it had been applied instead of the old principle. This effect is shown on the income statement immediately after extraordinary items.[14] For example, assume that in the five years prior to 20xx, Junction Corporation had used the straight-line method to depreciate its machinery. This year, the company retroactively changed to the double-declining-balance method of depreciation. The controller computed the cumulative effect of the change in depreciation charges (net of taxes) as $6,000, as follows:

Cumulative, five-year double-declining-balance depreciation	$29,000
Less cumulative, five-year straight-line depreciation	18,000
Before tax effect	$11,000
Income tax savings	5,000
Cumulative effect of accounting change	$ 6,000

Relevant information about the accounting change is shown in the notes to the financial statements. The change results in $11,000 of depreciation expense for prior years being deducted in the current year, in addition to the current year's depreciation costs included in the $500,000 costs and expenses section of the income statement. This expense must be shown in the current year's income statement as a reduction in income (see Exhibit 1). In 1997, 62, or 10 percent, of 600 large companies reported changes in accounting procedures.[15] Further study of accounting changes is left to more advanced accounting courses.

Earnings per Share

OBJECTIVE

5 Compute earnings per share

Readers of financial statements use earnings per share information to judge a company's performance and to compare it with the performance of other companies. Because such information is so important, the Accounting Principles Board concluded that earnings per share of common stock should be presented on the face of the income statement.[16] As shown in Exhibit 1, the information is usually disclosed just below the net income.

An earnings per share amount is always shown for (1) income from continuing operations, (2) income before extraordinary items and the cumulative effect of accounting changes, (3) the cumulative effect of accounting changes, and (4) net income. If the statement shows a gain or loss from discontinued operations or a gain or loss on extraordinary items, earnings per share amounts can also be presented for them. The following per share data from the income statement of Minnesota Mining and Manufacturing Company (3M) show why it is a good idea to study the components of earnings per share.[17]

Financial Highlights

	Years Ended December 31		
	1999	1998	1997
Earnings per share—Basic:			
Continuing operations	$4.39	$3.01	$5.14
Extraordinary loss	–	(.10)	–
Net income	$4.39	$2.91	$5.14

Note that net income was influenced by a special item in 1998: An extraordinary loss decreased income from continuing operations by $.10 per share to a basic net income of $2.91 per share. In 1999, the company had no special items; thus, 100 percent of 3M's basic earnings per share were attributable to continuing operations.

Basic earnings per share is net income applicable to common stock divided by the weighted-average number of common shares outstanding. To compute this figure, one must determine if during the year the number of common shares outstanding changed, and if the company paid preferred stock dividends.

When a company has only common stock and has the same number of shares outstanding throughout the year, the earnings per share computation is simple. From Exhibit 1, we know that Junction Corporation reported net income of $334,500. Assume that the company had 100,000 shares of common stock outstanding for the entire year. The earnings per share of common stock is computed as follows:

$$\text{Earnings per Share} = \frac{\$334,500}{100,000 \text{ shares}} = \$3.35 \text{ per share}$$

If the number of shares outstanding changes during the year, it is necessary to figure the weighted-average number of shares outstanding for the year. Suppose that Junction Corporation had the following amounts of common shares outstanding during various periods of the year: January–March, 100,000 shares; April–September, 120,000 shares; and October–December, 130,000 shares. The weighted-average number of common shares outstanding and basic earnings per share would be found this way:

100,000 shares $\times$ $^3/_{12}$ year	25,000
120,000 shares $\times$ $^6/_{12}$ year	60,000
130,000 shares $\times$ $^3/_{12}$ year	32,500
Weighted-average common shares outstanding	117,500

$$\text{Basic Earnings per Share} = \frac{\text{Net Income}}{\text{Weighted-Average Common Shares Outstanding}}$$

$$= \frac{\$334,500}{117,500 \text{ shares}} = \$2.85 \text{ per share}$$

If a company has nonconvertible preferred stock outstanding, the dividend for that stock must be subtracted from net income before earnings per share for common stock are computed. Suppose that Junction Corporation has preferred stock on which the annual dividend is $23,500. Earnings per share on common stock would be $2.65 [($334,500 − $23,500) ÷ 117,500 shares].

Companies with a capital structure in which there are no bonds, stocks, or stock options that could be converted into common stock are said to have a **simple**

capital structure. The earnings per share for these companies is computed as shown on the previous page. Some companies, however, have a **complex capital structure**, which includes exercisable stock options or convertible stocks and bonds. Those convertible securities have the potential of diluting the earnings per share of common stock. *Potential dilution* means that a stockholder's proportionate share of ownership in a company could be reduced through the conversion of stocks or bonds or the exercise of stock options, which would increase the total shares outstanding.

For example, suppose that a person owns 10,000 shares of a company, which equals 2 percent of the outstanding shares of 500,000. Now suppose that holders of convertible bonds convert the bonds into 100,000 shares of stock. The person's 10,000 shares would then equal only 1.67 percent (10,000 ÷ 600,000) of the outstanding shares. In addition, the added shares outstanding would lower earnings per share and would most likely lower market price per share.

Because stock options and convertible preferred stocks or bonds have the potential to dilute earnings per share, they are referred to as **potentially dilutive securities**. When a company has a complex capital structure, it must report two earnings per share figures: basic earnings per share and diluted earnings per share.[18] **Diluted earnings per share** are calculated by adding all potentially dilutive securities to the denominator of the basic earnings per share calculation. This figure shows stockholders the maximum potential effect of dilution of their ownership position in the company.

The difference between basic and diluted earnings per share can be significant. For example, consider the results reported by Dollar General Corporation, a successful retail discount chain:

Financial Highlights

	Years Ended December 31		
	1999	1998	1997
Basic earnings per share	$.89	$.81	$.64
Diluted earnings per share	.81	.68	.54

Note that while both measures of earnings per share are increasing, the pattern of increase is different and basic earnings per share are greater by at least 10 percent in every year.[19]

The computation of diluted earnings per share is a complex process and is reserved for more advanced courses.

The Statement of Stockholders' Equity

OBJECTIVE

6 Prepare a statement of stockholders' equity

The **statement of stockholders' equity**, also called the *statement of changes in stockholders' equity*, summarizes the changes in the components of the stockholders' equity section of the balance sheet. More and more companies are using this statement in place of the statement of retained earnings because it reveals much more about the year's stockholders' equity transactions. In the statement of stockholders' equity in Exhibit 2, for example, the first line shows the beginning balance of each account in the stockholders' equity section. Each subsequent line discloses the effects of transactions on those accounts. It is possible to determine from the statement that during 20x1 Tri-State Corporation issued 5,000 shares of common stock for $250,000, had a conversion of $100,000 of preferred stock into

Exhibit 2
A Statement of Stockholders' Equity

Tri-State Corporation
Statement of Stockholders' Equity
For the Year Ended December 31, 20x1

	Preferred Stock $100 Par Value 8% Convertible	Common Stock $10 Par Value	Paid-in Capital in Excess of Par Value, Common	Retained Earnings	Treasury Stock	Accumulated Other Comprehensive Income	Total
Balance, December 31, 20x0	$400,000	$300,000	$300,000	$600,000	—		$1,600,000
Issuance of 5,000 Shares of Common Stock		50,000	200,000				250,000
Conversion of 1,000 Shares of Preferred Stock into 3,000 Shares of Common Stock	(100,000)	30,000	70,000				—
10 Percent Stock Dividend on Common Stock, 3,800 Shares		38,000	152,000	(190,000)			—
Purchase of 500 Shares of Treasury Stock					($24,000)		(24,000)
Foreign Currency Translation Adjustment						($10,000)	(10,000)
Net Income				270,000			270,000
Cash Dividends							
Preferred Stock				(24,000)			(24,000)
Common Stock				(47,600)			(47,600)
Balance, December 31, 20x1	$300,000	$418,000	$722,000	$608,400	($24,000)	($10,000)	$2,014,400

common stock, declared and issued a 10 percent stock dividend on common stock, had a net purchase of treasury shares of $24,000, had a foreign currency translation loss of $10,000 reported as accumulated other comprehensive income, earned net income of $270,000, and paid cash dividends on both preferred and common stock. The ending balances of the accounts are presented at the bottom of the statement. Those accounts and balances make up the stockholders' equity section of Tri-State's balance sheet on December 31, 20x1, as shown in Exhibit 3.

Retained Earnings

Notice that in Exhibit 2 the Retained Earnings column has the same components as the statement of retained earnings. The **retained earnings** of a company are the part of stockholders' equity that represents stockholders' claims to assets arising from the earnings of the business. Retained earnings equal a company's profits since the date of its inception, less any losses, dividends to stockholders, or transfers to contributed capital.

It is important to remember that retained earnings are not the assets themselves. The existence of retained earnings means that assets generated by profitable operations have been kept in the company to help it grow or meet other business needs. A credit balance in Retained Earnings is *not* directly associated with a

Exhibit 3
Stockholders' Equity Section of a Balance Sheet

Tri-State Corporation
Stockholders' Equity
December 31, 20x1

Contributed Capital		
Preferred Stock, $100 par value, 8 percent convertible, 10,000 shares authorized, 3,000 shares issued and outstanding		$ 300,000
Common Stock, $10 par value, 100,000 shares authorized, 41,800 shares issued, 41,300 shares outstanding	$418,000	
Paid-in Capital in Excess of Par Value, Common	722,000	1,140,000
Total Contributed Capital		$1,440,000
Retained Earnings		608,400
Total Contributed Capital and Retained Earnings		$2,048,400
Less Treasury Stock, Common (500 shares, at cost)	$ 24,000	
Foreign Currency Translation Adjustment	10,000	34,000
Total Stockholders' Equity		$2,014,400

specific amount of cash or designated assets. Rather, such a balance means that assets as a whole have been increased.

Retained Earnings can carry a debit balance. Generally, this happens when a company's dividends and subsequent losses are greater than its accumulated profits from operations. In such a case, the firm is said to have a **deficit** (debit balance) in Retained Earnings. A deficit is shown in the stockholders' equity section of the balance sheet as a deduction from contributed capital.

A corporation may be required or may want to restrict all or a portion of its retained earnings. A **restriction on retained earnings** means that dividends can be declared only to the extent of the *unrestricted* retained earnings. The following are several reasons a company might restrict retained earnings:

1. *A contractual agreement.* For example, bond indentures may place a limitation on the dividends the company can pay.

2. *State law.* Many states do not allow a corporation to distribute dividends or purchase treasury stock if doing so reduces equity below a minimum level because this would impair the legal capital of the company.

3. *Voluntary action by the board of directors.* Often a board decides to retain assets in the business for future needs. For example, the company may be planning to build a new plant and may want to show that dividends will be limited to save enough money for the building. A company might also restrict retained earnings to show a possible future loss of assets resulting from a lawsuit.

A restriction on retained earnings does not change the total retained earnings or stockholders' equity of the company. It simply divides retained earnings into two parts: restricted and unrestricted. The unrestricted amount represents earnings kept in the business that the company can use for dividends and other purposes. Also, the restriction of retained earnings does not restrict cash or other assets in any way. It simply explains to the readers of the financial statements that a certain amount of assets generated by earnings will remain in the business for the purpose stated. It is still management's job to make sure enough cash or assets are on hand to fulfill the purpose. Also, the removal of a restriction does not necessarily mean that the board of directors can then declare a dividend.

Restrictions on retained earnings, called *reserves,* are much more common in some foreign countries than in the United States. In Sweden, for instance, reserves are used to respond to fluctuations in the economy. The Swedish tax code allows companies to set up contingency reserves for the purpose of maintaining financial stability. Appropriations to those reserves reduce tax-able income and income taxes. The reserves become taxable when they are reversed, but they are available to absorb losses should they occur. For example, Skandia Group, a large Swedish insurance company, reported a net income of only SK1,242 million in 1998, less than half the result of SK3,402 million in 1997. An examination of its statement of stockholders' equity shows a transfer of SK1,277 million to restricted reserves in 1997, a good year, but restricted reserves of SK588 million were transferred back to unrestricted reserves in 1998, a less successful year. Skandia also increased its dividends in 1998 to SK384 million and still had SK12.6 billion in restricted reserves.[20]

The most common way to disclose restricted retained earnings is by reference to a note to the financial statements. For example:

Retained Earnings (Note 15) $900,000

Note 15:
Because of plans to expand the capacity of the company's clothing division, the board of directors has restricted retained earnings available for dividends by $300,000.

Stock Dividends

A **stock dividend** is a proportional distribution of shares of a corporation's stock to its shareholders. A stock dividend does not change the firm's assets and liabilities because there is no distribution of assets, as there is when a cash dividend is distributed. A board of directors may declare a stock dividend for several reasons:

1. It may want to give stockholders some evidence of the company's success without paying a cash dividend, which would affect working capital.

2. It may seek to reduce the stock's market price by increasing the number of shares outstanding, although this goal is more often met by a stock split.

3. It may want to make a nontaxable distribution to stockholders. Stock dividends that meet certain conditions are not considered income, so they are not taxed.

4. It may wish to increase the company's permanent capital by transferring an amount from retained earnings to contributed capital.

The total stockholders' equity is not affected by a stock dividend. The effect of a stock dividend is to transfer a dollar amount from retained earnings to the contributed capital section on the date of declaration. The amount transferred is the fair market value (usually, the market price) of the additional shares to be issued. The laws of most states specify the minimum value of each share transferred under a stock dividend, which is normally the minimum legal capital (par or stated value). However, generally accepted accounting principles state that market value reflects the economic effect of small stock distributions (less than 20 to 25 percent of a company's outstanding common stock) better than par or stated value does. For this reason, market price should be used to account for small stock dividends.[21]

To illustrate the accounting for a stock dividend, let us assume that Caprock Corporation has the following stockholders' equity structure:

Contributed Capital
Common Stock, $5 par value, 100,000 shares
authorized, 30,000 shares issued and outstanding $ 150,000
Paid-in Capital in Excess of Par Value, Common 30,000

Total Contributed Capital $ 180,000
Retained Earnings 900,000

Total Stockholders' Equity $1,080,000

Suppose that the board of directors declares a 10 percent stock dividend on February 24, distributable on March 31 to stockholders of record on March 15, and that the market price of the stock on February 24 is $20 per share. The entries to record the declaration and distribution of the stock dividend are shown below.

Date of Declaration

A = L + OE Feb. 24 Stock Dividends Declared   60,000
  −   Common Stock Distributable   15,000
  +   Paid-in Capital in Excess of Par
  +   Value, Common   45,000
                  Declared a 10 percent stock dividend
                  on common stock, distributable on
                  March 31 to stockholders of record
                  on March 15:
                  30,000 shares × .10 = 3,000 shares
                  3,000 shares × $20/share = $60,000
                  3,000 shares × $5/share = $15,000

Date of Record

Mar. 15 No entry required.

Date of Distribution

A = L + OE Mar. 31 Common Stock Distributable   15,000
  −   Common Stock   15,000
  +   Distributed a stock dividend of
                  3,000 shares

The effect of this stock dividend is to permanently transfer the market value of the stock, $60,000, from retained earnings to contributed capital and to increase the number of shares outstanding by 3,000. The Stock Dividends Declared account is used to record the total amount of the stock dividend. Retained Earnings is reduced by the amount of the stock dividend when the Stock Dividends Declared account is closed to Retained Earnings at the end of the accounting period. Common Stock Distributable is credited for the par value of the stock to be distributed (3,000 × $5 = $15,000).

In addition, when the market value is greater than the par value of the stock, Paid-in Capital in Excess of Par Value, Common must be credited for the amount by which the market value exceeds the par value. In this case, the total market value of the stock dividend ($60,000) exceeds the total par value ($15,000) by $45,000. No entry is required on the date of record. On the distribution date, the common stock is issued by debiting Common Stock Distributable and crediting Common Stock for the par value of the stock ($15,000).

Common Stock Distributable is not a liability account because there is no obligation to distribute cash or other assets. The obligation is to distribute additional shares of capital stock. If financial statements are prepared between the date of declaration and the date of distribution, Common Stock Distributable should be reported as part of contributed capital:

Contributed Capital
    Common Stock, $5 par value, 100,000 shares
      authorized, 30,000 shares issued and outstanding $ 150,000
      Common Stock Distributable, 3,000 shares   15,000
    Paid-in Capital in Excess of Par Value, Common   75,000
      Total Contributed Capital $ 240,000
    Retained Earnings   840,000
    Total Stockholders' Equity $1,080,000

    Three points can be made from this example. First, the total stockholders' equity is the same before and after the stock dividend. Second, the assets of the corporation are not reduced as in the case of a cash dividend. Third, the proportionate ownership in the corporation of any individual stockholder is the same before and after the stock dividend. To illustrate these points, assume that a stockholder owns 1,000 shares before the stock dividend. After the 10 percent stock dividend is distributed, this stockholder would own 1,100 shares, as illustrated below.

Stockholders' Equity	Before Dividend	After Dividend
Common Stock	$ 150,000	$ 165,000
Paid-in Capital in Excess of Par Value, Common	30,000	75,000
Total Contributed Capital	$ 180,000	$ 240,000
Retained Earnings	900,000	840,000
Total Stockholders' Equity	$1,080,000	$1,080,000
Shares Outstanding	30,000	33,000
Stockholders' Equity per Share	$ 36.00	$ 32.73

Stockholders' Investment

Shares owned	1,000	1,100
Shares outstanding	30,000	33,000
Percentage of ownership	3⅓%	3⅓%
Proportionate investment ($1,080,000 × .03⅓)	$36,000	$36,000

Both before and after the stock dividend, the stockholders' equity totals $1,080,000 and the stockholder owns 3⅓ percent of the company. The proportionate investment (stockholders' equity times percentage ownership) remains at $36,000.

    All stock dividends have an effect on the market price of a company's stock. But some stock dividends are so large that they have a material effect. For example, a 50 percent stock dividend would cause the market price of the stock to drop about 33 percent because the increase is now one-third of shares outstanding. The AICPA has decided that large stock dividends, those greater than 20 to 25 percent, should be accounted for by transferring the par or stated value of the stock on the date of declaration from retained earnings to contributed capital.[22]

Stock Splits

A **stock split** occurs when a corporation increases the number of issued shares of stock and reduces the par or stated value proportionally. A company may plan a stock split when it wants to lower the stock's market value per share and increase the demand for the stock at this lower price. This action may be necessary if the market value per share has become so high that it hinders the trading of the stock or if the company wants to signal to the market its success in achieving its operating goals. For example, the action of The Gillette Company in a recent year in declaring a 2-for-1 stock split and raising its cash dividend achieved these strategic objectives. These actions were viewed positively by the market by pushing the share price to $106 from an earlier share price of $77. After the stock split, the number of shares outstanding doubled, thereby cutting the share price in half and also the dividend per share. Most important, each stockholder's total wealth is unchanged as a result of the stock split.

To illustrate a stock split, suppose that Caprock Corporation has 30,000 shares of $5.00 par value stock outstanding. The market value is $70.00 per share. The corporation plans a 2-for-1 split. This split will lower the par value to $2.50 and increase the number of shares outstanding to 60,000. A stockholder who previously owned 400 shares of the $5.00 par stock would own 800 shares of the $2.50 par stock after the split. When a stock split occurs, the market value tends to fall in proportion to the increase in outstanding shares of stock. For example, a 2-for-1 stock split would cause the price of the stock to drop by approximately 50 percent, to about $35.00. It would also halve earnings per share and cash dividends per share (if the board does not increase the dividend). The lower price and the increase in shares tend to promote the buying and selling of shares.

A stock split does not increase the number of shares authorized. Nor does it change the balances in the stockholders' equity section of the balance sheet. It simply changes the par value and the number of shares issued, both shares outstanding and shares held as treasury stock. Therefore, an entry is not necessary. However, it is appropriate to document the change by making a memorandum entry in the general journal.

July 15   The 30,000 shares of $5 par value common stock that are issued and outstanding were split 2 for 1, resulting in 60,000 shares of $2.50 par value common stock issued and outstanding.

The change for the Caprock Corporation is as follows:

Before Stock Split (from page 642)

Contributed Capital	
Common Stock, $5 par value, 100,000 shares authorized, 30,000 shares issued and outstanding	$ 150,000
Paid-in Capital in Excess of Par Value, Common	30,000
Total Contributed Capital	$ 180,000
Retained Earnings	900,000
Total Stockholders' Equity	$1,080,000

After Stock Split

Contributed Capital	
Common Stock, $2.50 par value, 100,000 shares authorized, 60,000 shares issued and outstanding	$ 150,000
Paid-in Capital in Excess of Par Value, Common	30,000
Total Contributed Capital	$ 180,000
Retained Earnings	900,000
Total Stockholders' Equity	$1,080,000

Although the amount of stockholders' equity per share would be half as much, each stockholder's proportionate interest in the company would remain the same.

If the number of split shares will exceed the number of authorized shares, the board of directors must secure state and stockholders' approval before it can issue additional shares.

Book Value

The word *value* is associated with shares of stock in several ways. Par value or stated value is set when the stock is authorized and establishes the legal capital of a company. Neither par value nor stated value has any relationship to a stock's book value or market value. The **book value** of a company's stock represents the total assets of the company less its liabilities. It is simply the stockholders' equity of the company or, to look at it another way, the company's net assets. The **book value per share**, therefore, represents the equity of the owner of one share of stock in the net assets of the corporation. That value, of course, does not necessarily equal the amount the shareholder would receive if the company were sold or liquidated. It differs in most cases because assets are usually recorded at historical cost, not at the current value at which they could be sold.

To determine the book value per share when a company has only common stock outstanding, divide the total stockholders' equity by the total common shares outstanding. In computing the shares outstanding, common stock distributable is included. Treasury stock (shares previously issued and now held by the company), however, is not included. For example, suppose that Caprock Corporation has total stockholders' equity of $1,030,000 and 29,000 shares outstanding after recording the purchase of treasury shares. The book value per share of Caprock's common stock is $35.52 ($1,030,000 ÷ 29,000 shares).

If a company has both preferred and common stock, the determination of book value per share is not so simple. The general rule is that the call value (or par value, if a call value is not specified) of the preferred stock plus any dividends in arrears is subtracted from total stockholders' equity to determine the equity pertaining to common stock. As an illustration, refer to the stockholders' equity section of Tri-State Corporation's balance sheet in Exhibit 3. Assuming that there are no dividends in arrears and that the preferred stock is callable at $105, the equity pertaining to common stock is calculated as follows:

Total stockholders' equity	$2,014,400
Less equity allocated to preferred shareholders (3,000 shares × $105)	315,000
Equity pertaining to common shareholders	$1,699,400

There are 41,300 shares of common stock outstanding (41,800 shares issued less 500 shares of treasury stock). The book values per share are computed as follows:

Preferred Stock: $315,000 ÷ 3,000 shares = $105 per share
Common Stock: $1,699,400 ÷ 41,300 shares = $41.15 per share

If we assume the same facts except that the preferred stock is 8 percent cumulative and that one year of dividends is in arrears, the stockholders' equity would be allocated as follows:

Total stockholders' equity		$2,014,400
Less: Call value of outstanding preferred shares	$315,000	
Dividends in arrears ($300,000 × .08)	24,000	
Equity allocated to preferred shareholders		339,000
Equity pertaining to common shareholders		$1,675,400

The book values per share are then as follows:

Preferred Stock: $339,000 ÷ 3,000 shares = $113 per share
Common Stock: $1,675,400 ÷ 41,300 shares = $40.57 per share

Undeclared preferred dividends fall into arrears on the last day of the fiscal year (the date shown on the financial statements). Also, dividends in arrears do not apply to unissued preferred stock.

Chapter Review

REVIEW OF LEARNING OBJECTIVES

Check out ACE, a self-quizzing program on chapter content, at http://college.hmco.com.

1. **Identify the issues related to evaluating the quality of a company's earnings.** Current and prospective net income is an important component in many ratios used to evaluate a company. The user should recognize that the quality of reported net income can be influenced by certain choices made by management. First, management exercises judgment in choosing the accounting methods and estimates that are used in computing net income. Second, discontinued operations, extraordinary gains or losses, and changes in accounting methods may affect net income positively or negatively.

2. **Prepare a corporate income statement.** The corporate income statement shows comprehensive income—all revenues, expenses, gains, and losses for the accounting period, except for prior period adjustments. The top part of the corporate income statement includes all revenues, costs and expenses, and income taxes that pertain to continuing operations. The bottom part of the statement contains any or all of the following: discontinued operations, extraordinary items, and accounting changes. Earnings per share data should be shown at the bottom of the statement, below net income.

3. **Show the relationships among income taxes expense, deferred income taxes, and net of taxes.** Income taxes expense is the taxes applicable to income from operations on an accrual basis. Income tax allocation is necessary when differences between accrual-based accounting income and taxable income cause a material difference between income taxes expense as shown on the income statement and actual income tax liability. The difference between income taxes expense and income taxes payable is debited or credited to an account called Deferred Income Taxes. *Net of taxes* is a phrase used to indicate that the effect of taxes has been considered when showing an item on the income statement.

4. **Describe the disclosure on the income statement of discontinued operations, extraordinary items, and accounting changes.** Because of their unusual nature, a gain or loss on discontinued operations and on extraordinary items, and the cumulative effect of accounting changes must be disclosed on the income statement separately from continuing operations and net of income taxes. Relevant information about any accounting change is shown in the notes to the financial statements.

5. **Compute earnings per share.** Stockholders and other readers of financial statements use earnings per share data to evaluate a company's performance and to compare it with the performance of other companies. Therefore, earnings per share data are presented on the face of the income statement. The amounts are computed by dividing the income applicable to common stock by the number of common shares outstanding for the year. If the number of shares outstanding has varied during the year, then the weighted-average number of common shares outstanding should be used in the computation. When the company has a complex capital structure, both basic and diluted earnings per share must be disclosed on the face of the income statement.

6. **Prepare a statement of stockholders' equity.** A statement of stockholders' equity shows changes over the period in each component of the stockholders' equity section of the balance sheet. This statement reveals much more about the transactions that affect stockholders' equity than does the statement of retained earnings.

7. **Account for stock dividends and stock splits.** A stock dividend is a proportional distribution of shares of a corporation's stock to the company's stockholders. Here is a summary of the key dates and accounting treatment of stock dividends.

Key Date	Stock Dividend
Date of declaration	Debit Stock Dividends Declared for the market value of the stock to be distributed (if it is a small stock dividend), and credit Common Stock Distributable for the stock's par value and Paid-in Capital in Excess of Par Value, Common for the excess of the market value over the stock's par value.
Date of record	No entry.
Date of distribution	Debit Common Stock Distributable and credit Common Stock for the par value of the stock that has been distributed.

A stock split is usually undertaken to reduce the market value of a company's stock and improve the demand for the stock. Because there is normally a decrease in the par value of the stock in proportion to the number of additional shares issued, a stock split has no effect on the dollar amounts in the stockholders' equity accounts. The split should be recorded in the general journal by a memorandum entry only.

8. **Calculate book value per share.** Book value per share is the stockholders' equity per share. It is calculated by dividing stockholders' equity by the number of common shares outstanding plus shares distributable. When a company has both preferred and common stock, the call or par value of the preferred stock plus any dividends in arrears is deducted from total stockholders' equity before dividing by the common shares outstanding.

REVIEW OF CONCEPTS AND TERMINOLOGY

The following concepts and terms were introduced in this chapter:

LO 5   **Basic earnings per share:** The net income applicable to common stock divided by the weighted-average number of common shares outstanding.

LO 8   **Book value:** The total assets of a company less its liabilities; stockholders' equity.

LO 8   **Book value per share:** The equity of the owner of one share of stock in the net assets of the corporation.

LO 5   **Complex capital structure:** A capital structure that includes convertible preferred stocks or bonds, or stock options that can be converted into common stock.

LO 2   **Comprehensive income:** The change in a company's equity during a period from sources other than owners; it includes net income, changes in unrealized investment gains and losses, and other items affecting equity.

LO 4   **Cumulative effect of an accounting change:** The effect that a different accounting principle would have had on the net income of prior periods if it had been used instead of the old principle.

LO 3   **Deferred Income Taxes:** The account used to record the difference between the Income Taxes Expense and Income Taxes Payable accounts.

LO 6   **Deficit:** A debit balance in the Retained Earnings account.

LO 5 **Diluted earnings per share:** The net income applicable to common stock divided by the sum of the weighted-average number of common shares outstanding plus potentially dilutive securities.

LO 4 **Discontinued operations:** Segments of a business that are no longer part of its ongoing operations.

LO 4 **Extraordinary items:** Events or transactions that are both unusual in nature and infrequent in occurrence.

LO 3 **Income tax allocation:** An accounting method used to accrue income taxes expense on the basis of accounting income whenever there are differences between accounting and taxable income.

LO 3 **Net of taxes:** Taking into account the effect of applicable taxes (most often, income taxes) on an item to determine the overall effect of the item on the income statement.

LO 5 **Potentially dilutive securities:** Stock options and convertible preferred stocks or bonds, which have the potential to dilute earnings per share.

LO 1 **Quality of earnings:** The substance of earnings and their sustainability into future accounting periods.

LO 6 **Restriction on retained earnings:** The required or voluntary identification of a portion of retained earnings that cannot be used to declare dividends.

LO 6 **Retained earnings:** Stockholders' claims to assets arising from the earnings of the business; the accumulated earnings of a corporation from its inception, minus any losses, dividends, or transfers to contributed capital.

LO 4 **Segments:** Distinct parts of business operations, such as lines of business or classes of customer.

LO 5 **Simple capital structure:** A capital structure in which there are no stocks, bonds, or stock options that can be converted into common stock.

LO 6 **Statement of stockholders' equity:** A financial statement that summarizes changes in the components of the stockholders' equity section of the balance sheet; also called *statement of changes in stockholders' equity.*

LO 7 **Stock dividend:** A proportional distribution of shares of a corporation's stock to its stockholders.

LO 7 **Stock split:** An increase in the number of outstanding shares of stock accompanied by a proportionate reduction in the par or stated value.

REVIEW
PROBLEM

Comprehensive Stockholders' Equity Transactions

LO 6
LO 7
LO 8

The stockholders' equity of the Szatkowski Company on June 30, 20x1, is shown below.

Contributed Capital
Common Stock, no par value, $6 stated value,
1,000,000 shares authorized, 250,000 shares
issued and outstanding ... $1,500,000
Paid-in Capital in Excess of Stated Value, Common ... 820,000

Total Contributed Capital ... $2,320,000
Retained Earnings ... 970,000

Total Stockholders' Equity ... $3,290,000

Stockholders' equity transactions for the next fiscal year were as follows:

a. The board of directors declared a 2-for-1 stock split.
b. The board of directors obtained authorization to issue 50,000 shares of $100 par value, 6 percent noncumulative preferred stock, callable at $104.
c. Issued 12,000 shares of common stock for a building appraised at $96,000.
d. Purchased 8,000 shares of the company's common stock for $64,000.

e. Issued 20,000 shares of preferred stock for $100 per share.

f. Sold 5,000 shares of treasury stock for $35,000.

g. Declared cash dividends of $6 per share on preferred stock and $.20 per share on common stock.

h. Date of record.

i. Paid the preferred and common stock cash dividends.

j. Declared a 10 percent stock dividend on common stock. The market value was $10 per share. The stock dividend is distributable after the end of the fiscal year.

k. Closed Net Income for the year, $340,000.

l. Closed the Cash Dividends Declared and Stock Dividends Declared accounts to Retained Earnings.

Because of a loan agreement, the company is not allowed to reduce retained earnings below $100,000. The board of directors determined that this restriction should be disclosed in the notes to the financial statements.

REQUIRED

1. Record the preceding transactions in journal form.

2. Prepare the stockholders' equity section of the company's balance sheet on June 30, 20x2, including appropriate disclosure of the restriction on retained earnings.

3. Compute the book values per share of common stock on June 30, 20x1 and 20x2, and of preferred stock on June 30, 20x2, using end-of-year shares outstanding.

ANSWER TO REVIEW PROBLEM

1. Prepare the entries in journal form.

a. Memorandum entry: 2-for-1 stock split, common, resulting in 500,000 shares issued and outstanding of no par value common stock with a stated value of $3

b. No entry required.

c. Building	96,000	
Common Stock		36,000
Paid-in Capital in Excess of Stated Value, Common		60,000

        Issued 12,000 shares of common stock for a building appraised at $96,000

d. Treasury Stock, Common	64,000	
Cash		64,000

        Purchased 8,000 shares of common stock for the treasury for $8 per share

e. Cash	2,000,000	
Preferred Stock		2,000,000

        Issued 20,000 shares of $100 par value preferred stock at $100 per share

f. Cash	35,000	
Retained Earnings	5,000	
Treasury Stock, Common		40,000

        Sold 5,000 shares of treasury stock for $35,000, originally purchased for $8 per share

g. Cash Dividends Declared	221,800	
Cash Dividends Payable		221,800

        Declared cash dividends of $6 per share on 20,000 shares of preferred stock and $.20 per share on 509,000 shares of common stock:

$$20,000 \times \$6 = \$120,000$$
$$509,000 \times \$.20 = \underline{101,800}$$
$$\overline{\$221,800}$$

h. No entry required.

i. Cash Dividends Payable	221,800	
Cash		221,800

        Paid cash dividends to preferred and
        common stockholders

j. Stock Dividends Declared	509,000	
Common Stock Distributable		152,700
Paid-in Capital in Excess of Stated Value, Common		356,300

        Declared a 50,900-share stock
        dividend (509,000 × .10) on $3 stated
        value common stock at a market value
        of $509,000 (50,900 × $10)

k. Income Summary	340,000	
Retained Earnings		340,000

        Closed the Income Summary account
        to Retained Earnings

l. Retained Earnings	730,800	
Cash Dividends Declared		221,800
Stock Dividends Declared		509,000

        Closed the Cash Dividends Declared
        and Stock Dividends Declared accounts
        to Retained Earnings

2. Prepare the stockholders' equity section of the balance sheet.

Szatkowski Company
Stockholders' Equity
June 30, 20x2

Contributed Capital		
Preferred Stock, $100 par value, 6 percent noncumulative, 50,000 shares authorized, 20,000 shares issued and outstanding		$2,000,000
Common Stock, no par value, $3 stated value, 1,000,000 shares authorized, 512,000 shares issued, 509,000 shares outstanding	$1,536,000	
Common Stock Distributable, 50,900 shares	152,700	
Paid-in Capital in Excess of Stated Value, Common	1,236,300	2,925,000
Total Contributed Capital		$4,925,000
Retained Earnings (Note x)		574,200
Total Contributed Capital and Retained Earnings		$5,499,200
Less Treasury Stock, Common (3,000 shares, at cost)		24,000
Total Stockholders' Equity		$5,475,200

Note x: The board of directors has restricted retained earnings available for dividends by the amount of $100,000 as required under a loan agreement.

3. Compute the book values.

  June 30, 20x1
    Common Stock: $3,290,000 ÷ 250,000 shares = $13.16 per share
  June 30, 20x2
    Preferred Stock: Call price of $104 per share equals book value per share
    Common Stock:
      ($5,475,200 − $2,080,000) ÷ (509,000 shares + 50,900 shares) =
      $3,395,200 ÷ 559,900 shares = $6.06 per share

Chapter Assignments

BUILDING YOUR
KNOWLEDGE
FOUNDATION

QUESTIONS

1. What is quality of earnings, and what are two ways in which quality of earnings may be affected?

2. Why would the reader of financial statements be interested in management's choice of accounting methods and estimates? Give an example.

3. What is comprehensive income? How does comprehensive income differ from net income?

4. In the first quarter of 1994, AT&T, the giant telecommunications company, reported a net loss because it reduced its income by $1.3 billion, or $.96 per share, as a result of changing its method of accounting for disability and severance payments. Without this charge, the company would have earned $1.15 billion, or $.85 per share. Where on the corporate income statement do you find the effects of changes in accounting principles? As an analyst, how would you treat this accounting change?

5. "Accounting income should be geared to the concept of taxable income because the public understands that concept." Comment on this statement, and tell why income tax allocation is necessary.

6. Nabisco had about $1.3 billion of deferred income taxes in 1996, equal to about 11 percent of total liabilities. This percentage has risen or remained steady for many years. Given management's desire to put off the payment of taxes as long as possible, the long-term growth of the economy and inflation, and the definition of a liability (probable future sacrifice of economic benefits arising from present obligations), make an argument for not accounting for deferred income taxes.

7. Why should a gain or loss on discontinued operations be disclosed separately on the income statement?

8. Explain the two major criteria for extraordinary items. How should extraordinary items be disclosed in the financial statements?

9. When an accounting change occurs, what disclosures must be made in the financial statements?

10. How are earnings per share disclosed in the financial statements?

11. When does a company have a simple capital structure? A complex capital structure?

12. What is the difference between basic and diluted earnings per share?

13. What is the difference between the statement of stockholders' equity and the stockholders' equity section of the balance sheet?

14. When does a company have a deficit in retained earnings?

15. What is the purpose of a restriction on retained earnings and why might a company have restrictions on its retained earnings?

16. Explain how the accounting treatment of stock dividends differs from that of cash dividends.

17. What is the difference between a stock dividend and a stock split? What is the effect of each on the capital structure of the corporation?

18. Would you expect a corporation's book value per share to equal its market value per share? Why or why not?

SHORT EXERCISES

SE 1.

LO 1   Quality of Earnings

Each of the items at the top of the next page is a quality of earnings issue. Indicate whether the item is (a) an accounting method, (b) an accounting estimate, or (c) a nonoperating item. For any item for which the answer is (a) or (b), indicate which alternative is usually the more conservative choice.

1. LIFO versus FIFO
2. Extraordinary loss
3. Ten-year useful life versus 15-year useful life
4. Effect of change in accounting principle
5. Straight-line versus accelerated method
6. Discontinued operations
7. Immediate write-off versus amortization
8. Increase in percentage of uncollectible accounts versus a decrease

SE 2.

LO 2 Corporate Income Statement

Assume that Griswold Company's chief financial officer gave you the following information: Net Sales, $720,000; Cost of Goods Sold, $350,000; Loss from Discontinued Operations (net of income tax benefit of $70,000), $200,000; Loss on Disposal of Discontinued Operations (net of income tax benefit of $16,000), $50,000; Operating Expenses, $130,000; Income Taxes Expense on Continuing Operations, $100,000. From this information, prepare the company's income statement for the year ended June 30, 20xx. (Ignore earnings per share information.)

SE 3.

LO 3 Use of Corporate Income Tax Rate Schedule

Using the corporate tax rate schedule in Table 1, compute the income tax liability for taxable income of (1) $400,000 and (2) $20,000,000.

SE 4.

LO 5 Earnings per Share

During 20x1, Jimmo Corporation reported a net income of $669,200. On January 1, Jimmo had 360,000 shares of common stock outstanding. The company issued an additional 240,000 shares of common stock on August 1. In 20x1, the company had a simple capital structure. During 20x2, there were no transactions involving common stock, and the company reported net income of $870,000. Determine the weighted-average number of common shares outstanding for 20x1 and 20x2. Also, compute earnings per share for 20x1 and 20x2.

SE 5.

LO 6 Statement of Stockholders' Equity

Refer to the statement of stockholders' equity for Tri-State Corporation in Exhibit 2 to answer the following questions: (1) At what price per share were the 5,000 shares of common stock sold? (2) What was the conversion price per share of the common stock? (3) At what price was the common stock selling on the date of the stock dividend? (4) At what price per share was the treasury stock purchased?

SE 6.

LO 6 Effects of Stockholders'
LO 7 Equity Actions

Tell whether each of the following actions will increase, decrease, or have no effect on total assets, total liabilities, and total stockholders' equity.

1. Declaration of a stock dividend
2. Declaration of a cash dividend
3. Stock split
4. Restriction of retained earnings
5. Purchase of treasury stock

SE 7.

LO 6 Restriction of Retained Earnings

Swift Company has a lawsuit filed against it. The board took action to restrict retained earnings in the amount of $2,500,000 on May 31, 20x1, pending the outcome of the suit. On May 31, the company had retained earnings of $3,725,000. Show how the restriction on retained earnings would be disclosed as a note to the financial statements.

SE 8.

LO 7 Stock Dividends

On February 15, Green Mountain Corporation's board of directors declared a 2 percent stock dividend applicable to the outstanding shares of its $10 par value common stock, of which 200,000 shares are authorized, 130,000 are issued, and 20,000 are held in the treasury. The stock dividend was distributable on March 15 to stockholders of record on March 1. On February 15, the market value of the common stock was $15 per share. On March 30, the board of directors declared a $.50 per share cash dividend. No other stock transactions have occurred. Record the necessary transactions on February 15, March 1, March 15, and March 30.

SE 9.

LO 7 Stock Split

On August 10, the board of directors of Symula International declared a 3-for-1 stock split of its $9 par value common stock, of which 800,000 shares were authorized and 250,000 were issued and outstanding. The market value on that date was $60 per share. On the same date, the balance of Paid-in Capital in Excess of Par Value, Common was $6,000,000, and the balance of Retained Earnings was $6,500,000. Prepare the stockholders' equity section of the company's balance sheet after the stock split. What journal entry, if any, is needed to record the stock split?

SE 10.
LO 8 Book Value for Preferred and Common Stock

Given the stockholders' equity section of the Talmage Corporation's balance sheet shown below, what is the book value per share for both the preferred and the common stock?

Contributed Capital		
Preferred Stock, $100 par value, 8 percent cumulative, 10,000 shares authorized, 500 shares issued and outstanding*		$ 50,000
Common Stock, $10 par value, 100,000 shares authorized, 40,000 shares issued and outstanding	$400,000	
Paid-in Capital in Excess of Par Value, Common	516,000	916,000
Total Contributed Capital		$ 966,000
Retained Earnings		275,000
Total Stockholders' Equity		$1,241,000

*The preferred stock is callable at $104 per share, and one year's dividends are in arrears.

EXERCISES

E 1.
LO 1 Effect of Alternative Accounting Methods

At the end of its first year of operations, a company calculated its ending merchandise inventory according to three different accounting methods, as follows: FIFO, $95,000; average-cost, $90,000; LIFO, $86,000. If the average-cost method is used by the company, net income for the year would be $34,000.

1. Determine net income if the FIFO method is used.

2. Determine net income if the LIFO method is used.

3. Which method is more conservative?

4. Will the consistency convention be violated if the company chooses to use the LIFO method?

5. Does the full-disclosure convention require disclosure of the inventory method selected by management in the financial statements?

E 2.
LO 2 Corporate Income Statement

Assume that the Abbey Furniture Company's chief financial officer gave you the following information: Net Sales, $1,900,000; Cost of Goods Sold, $1,050,000; Extraordinary Gain (net of income taxes of $3,500), $12,500; Loss from Discontinued Operations (net of income tax benefit of $30,000), $50,000; Loss on Disposal of Discontinued Operations (net of income tax benefit of $13,000), $35,000; Selling Expenses, $50,000; Administrative Expenses, $40,000; Income Taxes Expense on Continuing Operations, $300,000.

From this information, prepare the company's income statement for the year ended June 30, 20xx. (Ignore earnings per share information.)

E 3.
LO 2 Corporate Income
LO 3 Statement
LO 4
LO 5

The following items are components on the income statement of Burda Corporation for the year ended December 31, 20x1:

Sales	$500,000
Cost of Goods Sold	(275,000)
Operating Expenses	(112,500)
Total Income Taxes Expense for Period	(82,350)
Income from Operations of a Discontinued Segment	80,000
Gain on Disposal of Segment	70,000
Extraordinary Gain on Retirement of Bonds	36,000
Cumulative Effect of a Change in Accounting Principle	(24,000)
Net Income	$192,150
Earnings per share	$.96

Recast the 20x1 income statement in proper multistep form, including allocating income taxes to appropriate items (assume a 30 percent income tax rate) and showing earnings per share figures (200,000 shares outstanding).

E 4. Using the corporate tax rate schedule in Table 1, compute the income tax liability for the following situations:

Situation	Taxable Income
A	$ 70,000
B	85,000
C	320,000

E 5. The Cohn Corporation reported the following accounting income before income taxes, income taxes expense, and net income for 20x2 and 20x3:

	20x2	20x3
Income before income taxes	$280,000	$280,000
Income taxes expense	88,300	88,300
Net income	$191,700	$191,700

Also, on the balance sheet, deferred income taxes liability increased by $38,400 in 20x2 and decreased by $18,800 in 20x3.

1. How much did Cohn Corporation actually pay in income taxes for 20x2 and 20x3?

2. Prepare entries in journal form to record income taxes expense for 20x2 and 20x3.

E 6. During 20x1, the De La Haza Corporation reported a net income of $1,529,500. On January 1, De La Haza had 700,000 shares of common stock outstanding. The company issued an additional 420,000 shares of common stock on October 1. In 20x1, the company had a simple capital structure. During 20x2, there were no transactions involving common stock, and the company reported net income of $2,016,000.

1. Determine the weighted-average number of common shares outstanding each year.

2. Compute earnings per share for each year.

E 7. The board of directors of the Edelen Company has approved plans to acquire another company during the coming year. The acquisition should cost approximately $550,000. The board took action to restrict retained earnings of the company in the amount of $550,000 on July 17, 20x1. On July 31, the company had retained earnings of $975,000. Show how the restriction on retained earnings can be disclosed as a note to the financial statements.

E 8. The stockholders' equity section of Farhad Corporation's balance sheet on December 31, 20x2, appears as follows:

Contributed Capital	
Common Stock, $2 par value, 500,000 shares authorized, 400,000 shares issued and outstanding	$ 800,000
Paid-in Capital in Excess of Par Value, Common	1,200,000
Total Contributed Capital	$2,000,000
Retained Earnings	4,200,000
Total Stockholders' Equity	$6,200,000

Prepare a statement of stockholders' equity for the year ended December 31, 20x3, assuming the following transactions occurred in sequence during 20x3:

a. Issued 10,000 shares of $100 par value, 9 percent cumulative preferred stock at par after obtaining authorization from the state.

b. Issued 40,000 shares of common stock in connection with the conversion of bonds having a carrying value of $600,000.

c. Declared and issued a 2 percent common stock dividend. The market value on the date of declaration was $14 per share.

d. Purchased 10,000 shares of common stock for the treasury at a cost of $16 per share.

e. Earned net income of $460,000.

f. Declared and paid the full year's dividend on preferred stock and a dividend of $.40 per share on common stock outstanding at the end of the year.

E 9.

The Garonski Company has 30,000 shares of its $1 par value common stock outstanding. Record the following transactions as they relate to the company's common stock:

July 17   Declared a 10 percent stock dividend on common stock to be distributed on August 10 to stockholders of record on July 31. Market value of the stock was $5 per share on this date.

     31   Record date.

Aug. 10   Distributed the stock dividend declared on July 17.

Sept. 1   Declared a $.50 per share cash dividend on common stock to be paid on September 16 to stockholders of record on September 10.

E 10.

The Hao Company currently has 500,000 shares of $1 par value common stock authorized with 200,000 shares outstanding. The board of directors declared a 2-for-1 split on May 15, when the market value of the common stock was $2.50 per share. The Retained Earnings balance on May 15 was $700,000. Paid-in Capital in Excess of Par Value, Common on this date was $20,000.

     Prepare the stockholders' equity section of the company's balance sheet before and after the stock split. What entry, if any, would be necessary to record the stock split?

E 11.

On January 15, the board of directors of Imhoff International declared a 3-for-1 stock split of its $12 par value common stock, of which 800,000 shares were authorized and 200,000 were issued and outstanding. The market value on that date was $45 per share. On the same date, the balance of Paid-in Capital in Excess of Par Value, Common was $4,000,000, and the balance of Retained Earnings was $8,000,000.

     Prepare the stockholders' equity section of the company's balance sheet before and after the stock split. What entry, if any, is needed to record the stock split?

E 12.

Below is the stockholders' equity section of the Tri-Town Corporation's balance sheet. Determine the book value per share for both the preferred and the common stock.

Contributed Capital		
Preferred Stock, $100 per share, 6 percent cumulative, 10,000 shares authorized, 200 shares issued and outstanding*		$ 20,000
Common Stock, $5 par value, 100,000 shares authorized, 10,000 shares issued, 9,000 shares outstanding	$50,000	
Paid-in Capital in Excess of Par Value, Common	28,000	78,000
Total Contributed Capital		$ 98,000
Retained Earnings		95,000
Total Contributed Capital and Retained Earnings		$193,000
Less Treasury Stock, Common (1,000 shares at cost)		15,000
Total Stockholders' Equity		$178,000

*The preferred stock is callable at $105 per share, and one year's dividends are in arrears.

PROBLEMS

P 1.

Zalme Company began operations this year. At the beginning of 20xx, the company purchased plant assets of $900,000, with an estimated useful life of ten years and no salvage value. During the year, the company had net sales of $1,300,000, salaries expense of $200,000, and other expenses of $80,000, excluding depreciation. In addition, Zalme Company purchased inventory as follows:

Jan. 15	400 units at $400	$160,000
Mar. 20	200 units at $408	81,600
June 15	800 units at $416	332,800
Sept. 18	600 units at $412	247,200
Dec. 9	300 units at $420	126,000
Total	2,300 units	$947,600

At the end of the year, a physical inventory disclosed 500 units still on hand. The managers of Zalme Company know they have a choice of accounting methods, but are unsure how those methods will affect net income. They have heard of the FIFO and LIFO inventory methods and the straight-line and double-declining-balance depreciation methods. Ignore income taxes.

REQUIRED

1. Prepare two income statements for Zalme Company, one using the FIFO and straight-line methods, the other using the LIFO and double-declining-balance methods.

2. Prepare a schedule accounting for the difference in the two net income figures obtained in **1.**

3. What effect does the choice of accounting method have on Zalme's inventory turnover? What conclusions can you draw?

4. How does the choice of accounting methods affect Zalme's return on assets? Assume the company's only assets are cash of $80,000, inventory, and plant assets. Use year-end balances to compute the ratios. Is your evaluation of Zalme's profitability affected by the choice of accounting methods?

P 2.

LO 2 **Corporate Income**
LO 3 **Statement**
LO 4
LO 5

Information concerning operations of the Norris Weather Gear Corporation during 20xx is as follows:

a. Administrative expenses, $180,000.
b. Cost of goods sold, $840,000.
c. Cumulative effect of an accounting change in depreciation methods that increased income (net of taxes, $40,000), $84,000.
d. Extraordinary loss from an earthquake (net of taxes, $72,000), $120,000.
e. Sales (net), $1,800,000.
f. Selling expenses, $160,000.
g. Income taxes expense applicable to continuing operations, $210,000.

REQUIRED

Prepare the corporation's income statement for the year ended December 31, 20xx, including earnings per share information. Assume a weighted average of 100,000 common shares outstanding during the year.

P 3.

LO 2 **Corporate Income**
LO 3 **Statement and**
LO 4 **Evaluation of**
LO 5 **Business Operations**

During 20x3 Dasbol Corporation engaged in a number of complex transactions to restructure the business—selling off a division, retiring bonds, and changing accounting methods. The company has always issued a simple single-step income statement, and the accountant has accordingly prepared the December 31 year-end income statements for 20x2 and 20x3, as shown below.

Dasbol Corporation Income Statements For the Years Ended December 31, 20x3 and 20x2		
	20x3	20x2
Net Sales	$1,000,000	$1,200,000
Cost of Goods Sold	(550,000)	(600,000)
Operating Expenses	(225,000)	(150,000)
Income Taxes Expense	(164,700)	(135,000)
Income from Operations of a Discontinued Segment	160,000	
Gain on Disposal of Discontinued Segment	140,000	
Extraordinary Gain on Retirement of Bonds	72,000	
Cumulative Effect of a Change in Accounting Principle	(48,000)	
Net Income	$ 384,300	$ 315,000
Earnings per share	$ 1.92	$ 1.58

The president of the company, Joseph Dasbol, is pleased to see that both net income and earnings per share increased by 22 percent from 20x2 to 20x3 and intends to announce to the stockholders that the restructuring is a success.

REQUIRED

1. Recast the 20x3 and 20x2 income statements in proper multistep form, including allocating income taxes to appropriate items (assume a 30 percent income tax rate) and showing earnings per share figures (200,000 shares outstanding).

2. What is your assessment of Dasbol Corporation's restructuring plan and business operations in 20x3?

P 4.
LO 6   Stock Dividend and Stock
LO 7   Split Transactions and Stockholders' Equity

The stockholders' equity section of the balance sheet of Pittman Corporation as of December 31, 20x4, was as follows:

Contributed Capital	
Common Stock, $4 par value, 500,000 shares authorized,	
200,000 shares issued and outstanding	$ 800,000
Paid-in Capital in Excess of Par Value, Common	1,000,000
Total Contributed Capital	$1,800,000
Retained Earnings	1,200,000
Total Stockholders' Equity	$3,000,000

The following transactions occurred in 20x5 for Pittman Corporation:

Feb. 28   The board of directors declared a 10 percent stock dividend to stockholders of record on March 25 to be distributed on April 5. The market value on this date is $16.

Mar. 25   Date of record for stock dividend.

Apr. 5   Issued stock dividend.

Aug. 3   Declared a 2-for-1 stock split.

Nov. 20   Purchased 18,000 shares of the company's common stock at $8 per share for the treasury.

Dec. 31   Declared a 5 percent stock dividend to stockholders of record on January 25 to be distributed on February 5. The market value per share was $9.

REQUIRED

1. Record the transactions for Pittman Corporation in T accounts.

2. Prepare the stockholders' equity section of the company's balance sheet as of December 31, 20x5. Assume net income for 20x5 is $108,000.

P 5.
LO 6   Dividends and Stock
LO 7   Split Transactions and Stockholders' Equity

The stockholders' equity section of the Rigby Moving and Storage Company's balance sheet as of December 31, 20x2, was as follows:

Contributed Capital	
Common Stock, $2 par value, 3,000,000 shares	
authorized, 500,000 shares issued and outstanding	$1,000,000
Paid-in Capital in Excess of Par Value, Common	400,000
Total Contributed Capital	$1,400,000
Retained Earnings	1,080,000
Total Stockholders' Equity	$2,480,000

The company engaged in the following stockholders' equity transactions during 20x3:

Mar. 5   Declared a $.40 per share cash dividend to be paid on April 6 to stockholders of record on March 20.

20   Date of record.

Apr. 6   Paid the cash dividend.

June 17   Declared a 10 percent stock dividend to be distributed August 17 to stockholders of record on August 5. The market value of the stock was $14 per share.

Aug. 5   Date of record.

17   Distributed the stock dividend.

Oct. 2   Split its stock 3 for 1.

Dec. 27   Declared a cash dividend of $.20 payable January 27, 20x4, to stockholders of record on January 14, 20x4.

On December 9, the board of directors restricted retained earnings for a pending lawsuit in the amount of $200,000. The restriction should be shown in the notes to the firm's financial statements.

REQUIRED

1. Record the 20x3 transactions in journal form.

2. Prepare the stockholders' equity section of the company's balance sheet as of December 31, 20x3, with an appropriate disclosure of the restriction on retained earnings. Assume net income for the year is $400,000.

P 6.

**LO 6 Comprehensive
LO 7 Stockholders' Equity
LO 8 Transactions**

On December 31, 20x1, the stockholders' equity section of the Toczycki Company's balance sheet appeared as follows:

Contributed Capital		
Common Stock, $8 par value, 200,000 shares authorized,		
60,000 shares issued and outstanding		$ 480,000
Paid-in Capital in Excess of Par Value, Common		1,280,000
Total Contributed Capital		$1,760,000
Retained Earnings		824,000
Total Stockholders' Equity		$2,584,000

The following are selected transactions involving stockholders' equity in 20x2: On January 4, the board of directors obtained authorization for 20,000 shares of $40 par value noncumulative preferred stock that carried an indicated dividend rate of $4 per share and was callable at $42 per share. On January 14, the company sold 12,000 shares of the preferred stock at $40 per share and issued another 2,000 in exchange for a building valued at $80,000. On March 8, the board of directors declared a 2-for-1 stock split on the common stock. On April 20, after the stock split, the company purchased 3,000 shares of common stock for the treasury at an average price of $12 per share; 1,000 of these shares subsequently were sold on May 4 at an average price of $16 per share. On July 15, the board of directors declared a cash dividend of $4 per share on the preferred stock and $.40 per share on the common stock. The date of record was July 25. The dividends were paid on August 15. The board of directors declared a 15 percent stock dividend on November 28, when the common stock was selling for $20. The record date for the stock dividend was December 15, and the dividend was to be distributed on January 5. The board of directors noted that note disclosure must be made of a bank loan agreement that requires minimum retained earnings. No cash dividends can be declared or paid if retained earnings fall below $100,000.

REQUIRED

1. Record the above transactions in journal form.

2. Prepare the stockholders' equity section of the company's balance sheet as of December 31, 20x2, including an appropriate disclosure of the restrictions on retained earnings. Net loss for 20x2 was $218,000. (**Hint:** Use T accounts to keep track of transactions.)

3. Compute the book value per share for preferred and common stock (including common stock distributable) on December 31, 20x1 and 20x2, using end-of-year shares outstanding.

ALTERNATE PROBLEMS

P 7.

**LO 2 Corporate Income
LO 3 Statement
LO 4
LO 5**

Income statement information for the Sim Corporation during 20x1 is as follows:

a. Administrative expenses, $220,000.
b. Cost of goods sold, $880,000.
c. Cumulative effect of a change in inventory methods that decreased income (net of taxes, $56,000), $120,000.
d. Extraordinary loss from a storm (net of taxes, $20,000), $40,000.
e. Income taxes expense, continuing operations, $84,000.
f. Net sales, $1,780,000.
g. Selling expenses, $380,000.

REQUIRED

Prepare Sim Corporation's income statement for 20x1, including earnings per share, assuming a weighted average of 200,000 shares of common stock outstanding for 20x1.

P 8.

LO 6   **Stock Dividend and Stock**
LO 7   **Split Transactions and
        Stockholders' Equity**

The stockholders' equity section of Waterbury Linen Mills, Inc., as of December 31, 20x2, was as follows:

Contributed Capital
Common Stock, $3 par value, 500,000 shares
   authorized, 40,000 shares issued and outstanding $120,000
   Paid-in Capital in Excess of Par Value, Common 37,500

   Total Contributed Capital $157,500
Retained Earnings 120,000

Total Stockholders' Equity $277,500

A review of the stockholders' equity records of Waterbury Linen Mills, Inc., disclosed the following transactions during 20x3:

Mar. 25   The board of directors declared a 5 percent stock dividend to stockholders of record on April 20 to be distributed on May 1. The market value of the common stock was $24 per share.
Apr. 20   Date of record for the stock dividend.
May   1   Issued the stock dividend.
Sept. 10 Declared a 3-for-1 stock split.
Dec. 15   Declared a 10 percent stock dividend to stockholders of record on January 15 to be distributed on February 15. The market price on this date is $9 per share.

REQUIRED

1. Record the transactions for Waterbury Linen Mills, Inc., in T accounts.

2. Prepare the stockholders' equity section of the company's balance sheet as of December 31, 20x3. Assume net income for 20x3 is $247,000.

P 9.

LO 6   **Dividends and Stock**
LO 7   **Split Transactions and
        Stockholders' Equity**

The balance sheet of the O'Connor Woolen Company disclosed the following stockholders' equity as of September 30, 20x1:

Contributed Capital
Common Stock, $4 par value, 1,000,000 shares
   authorized, 300,000 shares issued and outstanding $1,200,000
   Paid-in Capital in Excess of Par Value, Common 740,000

   Total Contributed Capital $1,940,000
Retained Earnings 700,000

Total Stockholders' Equity $2,640,000

The following stockholders' equity transactions were completed during the next fiscal year in the order presented:

20x1
Dec. 17   Declared a 10 percent stock dividend to be distributed January 20 to stockholders of record on January 1. The market value per share on the date of declaration was $8.

20x2
Jan.   1   Date of record.
      20   Distributed the stock dividend.
Apr. 14   Declared a $.50 per share cash dividend. The cash dividend is payable May 15 to stockholders of record on May 1.
May   1   Date of record.
      15   Paid the cash dividend.
June 17   Split its stock 2 for 1.
Sept. 15 Declared a cash dividend of $.30 per share payable October 10 to stockholders of record on October 1.

On September 14, the board of directors restricted retained earnings for plant expansion in the amount of $300,000. The restriction should be shown in the notes to the financial statements.

REQUIRED

1. Record the above transactions in journal form.

2. Prepare the stockholders' equity section of the company's balance sheet as of September 30, 20x2, with an appropriate disclosure of the restriction of retained earnings. Assume net income for the year is $300,000.

EXPANDING YOUR CRITICAL THINKING, COMMUNICATION, AND INTERPERSONAL SKILLS

SKILLS DEVELOPMENT

Conceptual Analysis

SD 1.

LO 1 **Classic Quality of**
LO 4 **Earnings**

On Tuesday, January 19, 1988, *International Business Machines Corp. (IBM),* the world's largest computer manufacturer, reported greatly increased earnings for the fourth quarter of 1987. Despite this reported gain in earnings, the price of IBM's stock on the New York Stock Exchange declined by $6 per share to $111.75. In sympathy with this move, most other technology stocks also declined.[23]

IBM's fourth-quarter net earnings rose from $1.39 billion, or $2.28 a share, to $2.08 billion, or $3.47 a share, an increase of 49.6 percent and 52.2 percent over the year-earlier period. Management declared that these results demonstrated the effectiveness of IBM's efforts to become more competitive and that, despite the economic uncertainties of 1988, the company was planning for growth.

The apparent cause of the stock price decline was that the huge increase in income could be traced to nonrecurring gains. Investment analysts pointed out that IBM's high earnings stemmed primarily from factors such as a lower tax rate. Despite most analysts' expectations of a tax rate between 40 and 42 percent, IBM's was a low 36.4 percent, down from the previous year's 45.3 percent. Analysts were also disappointed in IBM's revenue growth. Revenues within the United States were down, and much of the growth in revenues came through favorable currency translations, increases that might not be repeated. In fact, some estimates of the fourth-quarter earnings attributed $.50 per share to currency translations and another $.25 to tax-rate changes.

Other factors contributing to the rise in earnings were one-time transactions, such as the sale of Intel Corporation stock and bond redemptions, along with a corporate stock buyback program that reduced the amount of stock outstanding in the fourth quarter by 7.4 million shares.

The analysts were concerned about the quality of IBM's earnings. Identify four quality of earnings issues reported in the case and the analysts' concern about each. In percentage terms, what is the impact of the currency changes on fourth-quarter earnings? Comment on management's assessment of IBM's performance. Do you agree with management? (Optional question: What has IBM's subsequent performance been?) Be prepared to discuss your answers to the questions in class.

Ethical Dilemma

SD 2.

LO 7 **Ethics and Stock Dividends**

For 20 years *Bass Products Corporation,* a public corporation, has followed the practice of paying a cash dividend every quarter and has promoted itself to investors as a stable, reliable company. Recent competition from Asian companies has negatively affected its earnings and cash flows. As a result, Sandra Bass, president of the company,

| Cash Flow | CD-ROM | Communication | Critical Thinking | Ethics | General Ledger | Group Activity | Hot Links to Real Companies | International | Internet | Key Ratio | Memo | Spreadsheet |

is proposing that the board of directors declare a stock dividend of 5 percent this year instead of a cash dividend. She says, "This will maintain our consecutive dividend record and will not require any cash outflow." What is the difference between a cash dividend and a stock dividend? Why does a corporation usually distribute either kind of dividend, and how does each affect the financial statements? Is the action proposed by Bass ethical?

SD 3.

LO 1 Effect of Alternative
LO 5 Accounting Methods on
Executive Compensation

At the beginning of 20x1, Ted Lazzerini retired as president and principal stockholder in *Tedtronics Corporation,* a successful producer of personal computer equipment. As an incentive to the new management, Lazzerini supported the board of directors' new executive compensation plan, which provides cash bonuses to key executives for years in which the company's earnings per share equal or exceed the current dividends per share of $2.00, plus a $.20 per share increase in dividends for each future year. Thus, for management to receive the bonuses, the company must earn per-share income of $2.00 the first year, $2.20 the second, $2.40 the third, and so forth. Since Lazzerini owns 500,000 of the 1,000,000 common shares outstanding, the dividend income will provide for his retirement years. He is also protected against inflation by the regular increase in dividends. Earnings and dividends per share for the first three years of operation under the new management are as follows:

	20x3	20x2	20x1
Earnings per share	$2.50	$2.50	$2.50
Dividends per share	2.40	2.20	2.00

During this time, management earned bonuses totaling more than $1 million under the compensation plan. Lazzerini, who had taken no active part on the board of directors, began to worry about the unchanging level of earnings and decided to study the company's annual report more carefully. The notes to the annual report revealed the following information:

a. Management changed from the LIFO inventory method to the FIFO method in 20x1. The effect of the change was to decrease cost of goods sold by $200,000 in 20x1, $300,000 in 20x2, and $400,000 in 20x3.

b. Management changed from the double-declining-balance accelerated depreciation method to the straight-line method in 20x2. The effect of this change was to decrease depreciation by $400,000 in 20x2 and by $500,000 in 20x3.

c. In 20x3, management increased the estimated useful life of intangible assets from five to ten years. The effect of this change was to decrease amortization expense by $100,000 in 20x3.

1. Compute earnings per share for each year according to the accounting methods in use at the beginning of 20x1. (Use common shares outstanding.)

2. Is the action of the executives ethical? Have the executives earned their bonuses? What serious effect has the compensation package apparently had on the net assets of Tedtronics Corporation? How could Lazzerini have protected himself?

Research Activity

SD 4.

LO 2 Corporate Income
LO 3 Statement, Statement of
LO 4 Stockholders' Equity, and
LO 6 Book Value
LO 7
LO 8

Select the annual reports of three corporations, using one or more of the following sources: your library, the Fingraph® Financial Analyst™ CD-ROM software that accompanies this text, or the Needles Accounting Resource Center web site at http://college.hmco.com. You may choose companies from the same industry or at random, at the direction of your instructor. (If you completed the related research activity in the chapter on contributed capital, use the same three companies.) Prepare a table with a column for each corporation. Then, for any year covered by the balance sheet, the statement of stockholders' equity, and the income statement, answer the following questions: Does the company own treasury stock? Was any treasury stock bought or retired? Did the company declare a stock dividend or a stock split? What other transactions appear in the statement of stockholders' equity? Has the company deferred any income taxes? Were there any discontinued operations, extraordinary items, or accounting changes? Compute the book value per common share for the company. In *The Wall Street Journal* or the financial section of another daily newspaper, find the current market price of each company's common stock and compare it to the book value you computed. Should there be any relationship between the two values? Be prepared to discuss your answers to these questions in class.

Decision-Making Practice

SD 5. | *Metzger Steel Corporation (MSC)* is a small specialty steel manufacturer located in northern Alabama that has been owned by the Metzger family for several generations. Arnold Metzger is a major shareholder in MSC by virtue of his having inherited 200,000 shares of common stock in the company. Metzger has not shown much interest in the business because of his enthusiasm for archaeology, which takes him to far parts of the world. However, when he received the minutes of the last board of directors meeting, he questioned a number of transactions involving stockholders' equity. He asks you, as a person with a knowledge of accounting, to help him interpret the effect of these transactions on his interest in MSC.

LO 6 **Analyzing Effects of**
LO 7 **Stockholders' Equity**
LO 8 **Transactions**

You begin by examining the stockholders' equity section of MSC's December 31, 20x1, balance sheet:

Metzger Steel Corporation Stockholders' Equity December 31, 20x1	
Contributed Capital	
Common Stock, $10 par value, 5,000,000 shares authorized, 1,000,000 shares issued and outstanding	$10,000,000
Paid-in Capital in Excess of Par Value, Common	25,000,000
Total Contributed Capital	$35,000,000
Retained Earnings	20,000,000
Total Stockholders' Equity	$55,000,000

Then you read the relevant parts of the minutes of the December 15, 20x2, meeting of the firm's board of directors:

Item A: The president reported the following transactions involving the company's stock during the last quarter.

October 15. Sold 500,000 shares of authorized common stock through the investment banking firm of T.R. Kendall at a net price of $50 per share.

November 1. Purchased 100,000 shares for the corporate treasury from Lucy Metzger at a price of $55 per share.

Item B: The board declared a 2-for-1 stock split (accomplished by halving the par value and doubling each stockholder's shares), followed by a 10 percent stock dividend. The board then declared a cash dividend of $2 per share on the resulting shares. Cash dividends are declared on outstanding shares and shares distributable. All these transactions are applicable to stockholders of record on December 20 and are payable on January 10. The market value of MSC stock on the board meeting date after the stock split was estimated to be $30.

Item C: The chief financial officer stated that he expected the company to report net income for the year of $4,000,000.

1. Prepare a stockholders' equity section of MSC's balance sheet as of December 31, 20x2, that reflects the transactions above. (**Hint:** Use T accounts to analyze the transactions. Also, use a T account in order to keep track of the shares of common stock outstanding.)

2. Write a memorandum to Arnold Metzger that shows the book value per share and Metzger's percentage of ownership at the beginning and end of the year. Explain the difference and state whether Metzger's position has improved during the year. Tell why or why not and state how Metzger may be able to maintain his percentage of ownership.

FINANCIAL REPORTING AND ANALYSIS

Interpreting Financial Reports

FRA 1.
LO 6 Interpretation of Statement of Stockholders' Equity

The consolidated statement of stockholders' equity for **Jackson Electronics, Inc.,** a manufacturer of a broad line of electrical components, appears as presented below.

Jackson Electronics, Inc.
Consolidated Statement of Stockholders' Equity
(In thousands)

	Preferred Stock	Common Stock	Paid-in Capital in Excess of Par Value, Common	Retained Earnings	Treasury Stock, Common	Total
Balance at September 30, 20x1	$2,756	$3,902	$14,149	$119,312	($ 942)	$139,177
Year Ended September 30, 20x2						
Net income	—	—	—	18,753	—	18,753
Redemption and retirement of Preferred Stock (27,560 shares)	(2,756)	—	—	—	—	(2,756)
Stock options exercised (89,000 shares)	—	89	847	—	—	936
Purchases of Common Stock for treasury (501,412 shares)	—	—	—	—	(12,552)	(12,552)
Issuance of Common Stock (148,000 shares) in exchange for convertible subordinated debentures	—	148	3,635	—	—	3,783
Issuance of Common Stock (715,000 shares) for cash	—	715	24,535	—	—	25,250
Issuance of 500,000 shares of Common Stock in exchange for investment in Electrix Company shares	—	500	17,263	—	—	17,763
Cash dividends—Common Stock ($.80 per share)	—	—	—	(3,086)	—	(3,086)
Balance at September 30, 20x2	$ —	$5,354	$60,429	$134,979	($13,494)	$187,268

REQUIRED

This statement of stockholders' equity has eight summary transactions. Show that you understand it by preparing an entry in journal form with an explanation for each. In each case, if applicable, determine the average price per common share. At times you will also have to make assumptions about an offsetting part of the entry. For example, assume debentures (long-term bonds) are recorded at face value and that employees pay cash for stock purchased under company incentive plans.

Group Activity: Assign each transaction to a different group to develop the entry and present the explanation to the class.

FRA 2.
LO 3 Analysis of Income Taxes from Annual Report

In its 1999 annual report, **The Washington Post Company,** a newspaper publishing and television broadcasting company based in Washington, D.C., provided the following data about its current and deferred income tax provisions (in millions):[24]

	1999	
	Current	Deferred
U.S. federal	$ 94.6	$30.3
Foreign	1.3	—
State	23.7	(.3)
	$119.6	$30.0

1. What was the 1999 income taxes expense? Record in journal form the overall income tax liability for 1999, using income tax allocation procedures.

2. In the long-term liability section of the balance sheet, The Washington Post Company shows deferred income taxes of $112.4 million in 1999 versus $83.7 million in 1998. This shows an increase in the amount of deferred income taxes. How do such deferred income taxes arise? What would cause deferred income taxes to increase? Give an example of this process. Given the definition of a liability, do you see a potential problem with the company's classifying deferred income taxes as a liability?

International Company

FRA 3.

LO 6 **Restriction of**
Retained Earnings

In some countries, including Japan, the availability of retained earnings for the payment of dividends is restricted. The following disclosure appeared in the annual report of *Yamaha Motor Company, Ltd.,* the Japanese motorcycle manufacturer:[25]

> The Commercial Code of Japan provides that an amount not less than 10 percent of the total of cash dividends and bonuses [paid] to directors and corporate auditors be appropriated as a legal reserve until such reserve equals 25 percent of stated capital. The legal reserve may be used to reduce a deficit or may be transferred to stated capital, but is not available as dividends.

Stated capital is equivalent to common stock. For Yamaha, this legal reserve amounted to ¥34.4 billion, or $310 million. How does this practice differ from that in the United States? Why do you think it is government policy in Japan? Do you think it is a good idea?

Toys "R" Us Annual Report

FRA 4.

LO 2 **Corporate Income**
LO 4 **Statement, Statement of**
LO 6 **Stockholders' Equity, and**
LO 8 **Book Value per Share**

Refer to the Toys "R" Us annual report to answer the following questions:

1. Does Toys "R" Us have discontinued operations, extraordinary items, or cumulative changes in accounting principles? Would you say the income statement for Toys "R" Us is relatively simple or relatively complex?

2. What transactions most commonly affect the stockholders' equity section of the balance sheet of Toys "R" Us? Examine the statement of stockholders' equity.

3. Compute the book value of Toys "R" Us stock in 2000 and 1999 and compare it to the market price. What interpretation do you place on these relationships?

Fingraph® Financial Analyst™

FRA 5.

LO 1 **Stockholders' Equity**
LO 2 **Analysis**
LO 4
LO 5
LO 6
LO 7
LO 8

Choose any two companies from the same industry in the Fingraph® Financial Analyst™ CD-ROM software.

1. In the annual reports for the companies you have selected, identify the corporate income statement and its summary of significant accounting policies, usually the first note to the financial statements. Did the companies report any discontinued operations, extraordinary items, or accounting changes? What percentage impact did these items have on earnings per share? Summarize the methods and estimates each company uses in a table. If the company changed its accounting methods, was the change the result of a new accounting standard or a voluntary choice by management? Evaluate the quality of earnings for each company.

2. Did the companies report a statement of stockholders' equity or summarize the changes in stockholders' equity in the notes only? Did the companies declare any stock dividends or stock splits? Calculate book value per common share.

3. Find in the financial section of your local paper the current market prices of the companies' common stock. Discuss the difference between market price per share and book value per share.

4. Find and read references to earnings per share in management's discussion and analysis in each annual report.

5. Write a one-page executive summary that highlights the quality of earnings for these companies, the relationship of book value and market value, and the existence or absence of stock splits or dividends, including reference to management's assessment. Include your table as an attachment to your report.

Internet Case

FRA 6.

LO 2 **Comparison of**
LO 5 **Comprehensive Income**
LO 6 **Disclosures**

Reporting comprehensive income by public companies is a recent requirement. No specific guidelines were stated for how this amount and its components are disclosed. Choose two companies in the same industry from the Needles Accounting Resource Center at http://college.hmco.com. Using companies under web links, go to the annual reports on the web sites for the two companies you have selected. In the latest annual report, look at the financial statements. How have your two companies reported comprehensive income—as a part of the income statement, a part of stockholders' equity, or a separate statement? What items cause there to be a difference between net income and comprehensive income? Is comprehensive income greater or less than net income? Is comprehensive income more volatile than net income? Which measure of income is used to compute basic earnings per share?

ENDNOTES

1. DaimlerChrysler AG, *Annual Report*, 1999.
2. Cited in *The Week in Review* (Deloitte Haskins & Sells), February 28, 1985.
3. "Up to the Minute, Down to the Wire," *Twentieth Century Mutual Funds Newsletter,* 1996.
4. Ann Davis, "SEC Case Claims Profit Management by Grace," *The Wall Street Journal,* April 7, 1999.
5. Bernard Condon, "Pick a Number, Any Number," *Forbes,* March 23, 1998.
6. Sears, Roebuck and Co., *Annual Report,* 1997.
7. *Statement of Financial Accounting Standards No. 130,* "Reporting Comprehensive Income" (Norwalk, Conn.: Financial Accounting Standards Board, 1997).
8. American Institute of Certified Public Accountants, *Accounting Trends & Techniques* (New York: American Institute of Certified Public Accountants, 1999).
9. *Statement of Financial Accounting Standards No. 109,* "Accounting for Income Taxes" (Norwalk, Conn.: Financial Accounting Standards Board, 1992).
10. American Institute of Certified Public Accountants, *Accounting Trends & Techniques* (New York: American Institute of Certified Public Accountants, 1999).
11. Accounting Principles Board, *Opinion No. 30,* "Reporting the Results of Operations" (New York: American Institute of Certified Public Accountants, 1973), par. 20.
12. Ibid.
13. American Institute of Certified Public Accountants, *Accounting Trends & Techniques* (New York: American Institute of Certified Public Accountants, 1999).
14. Accounting Principles Board, *Opinion No. 20,* "Accounting Changes" (New York: American Institute of Certified Public Accountants, 1971), par. 20.
15. American Institute of Certified Public Accountants, *Accounting Trends & Techniques* (New York: American Institute of Certified Public Accountants, 1999).
16. Accounting Principles Board, *Opinion No. 15,* "Earnings per Share" (New York: American Institute of Certified Public Accountants, 1969), par. 12.
17. Minnesota Mining and Manufacturing Company, *Annual Report,* 1999.
18. *Statement of Financial Accounting Standards No. 128,* "Earnings per Share and the Disclosure of Information About Capital Structure" (Norwalk, Conn.: Financial Accounting Standards Board, 1997).
19. Dollar General Corporation, *Annual Report,* 1999.
20. Skandia Group, *Annual Report,* 1998.
21. *Accounting Research Bulletin No. 43* (New York: American Institute of Certified Public Accountants, 1953), chap. 7, sec. B, par. 10.
22. Ibid., par. 13.
23. "Technology Firms Post Strong Earnings But Stock Prices Decline Sharply," *The Wall Street Journal,* January 21, 1988; Donald R. Seace, "Industrials Plunge 57.2 Points—Technology Stocks' Woes Cited," *The Wall Street Journal,* January 21, 1988.
24. The Washington Post Company, *Annual Report,* 1999.
25. Yamaha Motor Company, Ltd., *Annual Report,* 1999.

LEARNING OBJECTIVES

1 Identify the management issues related to issuing long-term debt.

2 Identify and contrast the major characteristics of bonds.

3 Record the issuance of bonds at face value and at a discount or premium.

4 Use present values to determine the value of bonds.

5 Use the straight-line and effective interest methods to amortize bond discounts and premiums.

6 Account for bonds issued between interest dates and make year-end adjustments.

7 Account for the retirement of bonds and the conversion of bonds into stock.

8 Explain the basic features of mortgages payable, installment notes payable, long-term leases, and pensions and other postretirement benefits as long-term liabilities.

AT&T Corporation Long-term liabilities, or long-term debt, are obligations of a business that are due to be paid after one year or beyond the operating cycle, whichever is longer. Decisions related to the issuance of long-term debt are among the most important that management has to make because, next to the success or failure of a company's operations, how the company finances its operations is the most important factor in the company's long-term viability. AT&T Corporation is a company that has a large amount of long-term debt, as shown by the figures for 1999 in the Financial Highlights.[1] Total liabilities are greater than stockholders' equity, and the debt to equity ratio is .9 ($81,762 ÷ $87,644). What factors might have influenced AT&T's management to incur such a large amount of debt?

In the past, AT&T was the nation's only long-distance telephone company. The investments in power lines, transformers, computers, and other types of property, plant, and equipment required for this business are enormous. These are mostly long-term assets, and the most sensible way to finance them is through long-term financing. When the business was protected from competition, management could reasonably predict sufficient earnings and cash flow to meet the debt and interest obligations. Also, over the years, AT&T has been very generous to employees in promising benefits that will be paid after the employees retire. Now that AT&T is facing open competition for its markets, the company must reassess not only the kind of business it is but also the amount and kinds of debt it carries. The company

Financial Highlights	
(In millions)	
Liabilities	
Total current liabilities	$ 28,207
Long-term debt	$ 21,591
Long-term benefit-related liabilities	3,964
Deferred income taxes	24,199
Other long-term liabilities and deferred credits	3,801
Total long-term liabilities	$ 53,555
Total liabilities	$ 81,762
Stockholders' equity	87,644
Total liabilities and stockholders' equity	$169,406

has expanded its data, Internet, broadband, local, and wireless networks. This expansion required increased capital spending and borrowing. The amount and type of debt a company incurs will depend on many factors, including the nature of the business, its competitive environment, the state of the financial markets, and the predictability of its earnings.

Management Issues Related to Issuing Long-Term Debt

Profitable operations and short-term credit are seldom sufficient for a growing business that must invest in long-term assets and in research and development and other activities that will produce income in future years. For such assets and activities, the company requires funds that will be available for longer periods of time. Two key sources of long-term funds are the issuance of capital stock and the issuance of long-term debt in the form of bonds, notes, mortgages, and leases. The management issues related to issuing long-term debt are (1) whether or not to have long-term debt, (2) how much long-term debt to have, and (3) what types of long-term debt to have.

The Decision to Issue Long-Term Debt

A key decision faced by management is whether to rely solely on stockholders' equity—capital stock issued and retained earnings—for long-term funds for the business or to rely partially on long-term debt for those funds.

Because long-term debts represent financial commitments that must be paid at maturity and interest or other payments that must be paid periodically, common stock would seem to have two advantages over long-term debt: Common stock does not have to be paid back, and dividends on common stock are usually paid only if the company earns sufficient income. Long-term debt does, however, have some advantages over common stock:

1. *Stockholder control* Since bondholders and other creditors do not have voting rights, common stockholders do not relinquish any control of the company.

2. *Tax effects* The interest on debt is tax deductible, whereas dividends on common stock are not. For example, if a corporation pays $100,000 in interest and the income tax rate is 30 percent, the net cost to the corporation is $70,000 because it will save $30,000 on its income taxes. To pay $100,000 in dividends, the company would have to earn $142,857 before taxes [$100,000 ÷ (1 − .30)].

3. *Financial leverage* If a corporation is able to earn more on its assets than it pays in interest on debt, all of the excess will increase its earnings for stockholders. This concept is called **financial leverage**, or *trading on the equity*. For example, if a company is able to earn 12 percent, or $120,000, on a $1,000,000 investment financed by long-term 10 percent notes, it will earn $20,000 before taxes ($120,000 − $100,000). Financial leverage makes heavily debt-financed investments in office buildings and shopping centers attractive to investors: They hope to earn a return that exceeds the cost of the interest on the underlying debt. The debt to equity ratio is considered an overall measure of the financial leverage of a company.

Despite these advantages, using debt financing is not always in a company's best interest. First, because cash is required to make periodic interest payments and to

Figure 1
Average Debt to Equity for Selected Industries

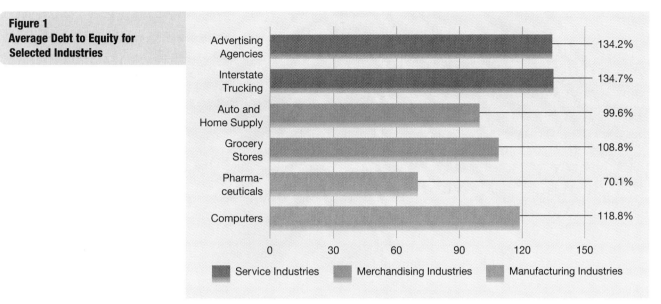

Industry	Debt to Equity
Advertising Agencies	134.2%
Interstate Trucking	134.7%
Auto and Home Supply	99.6%
Grocery Stores	108.8%
Pharma-ceuticals	70.1%
Computers	118.8%

Service Industries   Merchandising Industries   Manufacturing Industries

Source: Data from Dun & Bradstreet, *Industry Norms and Key Business Ratios,* 1999–2000.

pay back the principal amount of the debt at the maturity date, a company whose plans for earnings do not pan out, whose operations are subject to ups and downs, or whose cash flow is weak can be in danger. If the company fails to meet its obligations, it can be forced into bankruptcy by creditors. In other words, a company may become overcommitted. Consider, for example, the heavily debt-financed airline industry. Companies such as TWA and Continental Airlines became bankrupt because they could not make payments on their long-term debt and other liabilities. Second, financial leverage can work against a company if the earnings from its investments do not exceed its interest payments. This happened during the savings and loan crisis when long-term debt was used to finance the construction of office buildings that subsequently could not be leased for enough money to cover interest payments. In recent years, the good economy has enabled airlines to take advantage of their high financial leverage to improve earnings.

How Much Debt

Although some companies carry amounts of total debt that exceed 100 percent of their stockholders' equity, many companies carry less, as can be seen from Figure 1, which shows the average debt to equity for selected industries. The range is from about 70 percent to 135 percent of equity. Clearly the use of debt financing varies widely across industries. Firms that own a high percentage of long-term assets would be looking to long-term financing as an option. We saw previously that AT&T has a debt to equity ratio of .9 times. Financial leverage makes it advantageous to have long-term debt so long as the company earns a satisfactory income and is able to make interest payments and repay the debt at maturity. Because failure to make timely interest payments could possibly force a company into bankruptcy, it is important for companies to assess the risk of default or nonpayment of interest or principal.

A common measure of how much risk a company is undertaking with its debt is the **interest coverage ratio**. It measures the degree of protection a company has from default on interest payments. This measure can help to assess the safety of AT&T in light of its increasing amount of debt. This ratio for AT&T, which in 1999 had income before taxes of $6,685 million and interest expense of $1,651 million, is computed as follows:

FOCUS ON BUSINESS PRACTICE

Missing interest payments on debt is serious business for companies. On March 3, 1995, Trans World Airlines, Inc. (TWA), reached the end of a 30-day grace period on the payment of $255 million of interest on its long-term notes. Standard & Poor's lowered the company's debt rating to D, its lowest category. If TWA had not paid by the end of the day, any group representing at least 25 percent of its noteholders could have forced the company into bankruptcy by invoking an acceleration notice that would make all the loans due immediately.[2] This action would have been unfortunate because the company was recovering after many years of losses. The company was able to meet the interest payment and continue its recovery. However, intense competition within the airline industry forced TWA to file for bankruptcy again in early 2001 before being purchased by American Airlines.

$$\text{Interest Coverage Ratio} = \frac{\text{Income Before Taxes} + \text{Interest Expense}}{\text{Interest Expense}}$$

$$= \frac{\$6,685,000,000 + \$1,651,000,000}{\$1,651,000,000}$$

$$= 5.0 \text{ times}$$

This ratio shows that the interest expense for AT&T is covered 5.0 times. The coverage ratio for AT&T is in line with previous years and shows that AT&T has adequate interest coverage in spite of its large amount of debt.

What Types of Long-Term Debt

The most common type of long-term debt is long-term bonds (most of which are also called *debentures*). These can have many different characteristics, including the time until repayment, the amount of interest, whether or not the company can elect to repay early, and whether the bonds can be converted into other securities like common stock. However, there are many other types of long-term debt. Some examples are long-term notes, mortgages, and long-term leases. AT&T, for example, has a mixture of long-term obligations, as shown by the following excerpt from its 1999 annual report (in millions):

Financial Highlights: Long-Term Obligations		
(This table shows the outstanding long-term debt obligations at December 31.)		
Interest Rates (b)	Maturities	1999
Debentures and Notes		
4.38%–6.00%	2001–2014	$ 5,251
6.34%–7.50%	2000–2029	8,068
7.53%–8.50%	2000–2026	4,762
8.60%–11.13%	2000–2031	3,763
Variable rate	2000–2054	867
Total debentures and notes		22,711
Other		362
Less: Unamortized discount—net		(127)
Total long-term obligations		22,946
Less: Currently maturing long-term debt		1,355
Net long-term obligations		$21,591

It is important that managers know the characteristics of the various types of long-term liabilities so that they can structure a company's long-term financing to the best advantage of the company.

The Nature of Bonds

A **bond** is a security, usually long term, representing money borrowed from the investing public by a corporation or some other entity. (Bonds are also issued by the U.S. government, state and local governments, and foreign companies and countries to raise money.) A bond must be repaid at a specified time and requires periodic payments of interest.* Interest is usually paid semiannually (twice a year). Bonds must not be confused with stocks. Because stocks are shares of ownership, stockholders are owners. Bondholders are creditors. Bonds are promises to repay the amount borrowed, called the *principal*, and interest at a specified rate on specified future dates.

A bondholder receives a bond certificate (in past years) or a registration number (in recent years) as evidence of the organization's debt. In most cases, the face value (denomination) of the bond is $1,000 or some multiple of $1,000. A **bond issue** is the total number of bonds issued at one time. For example, a $1,000,000 bond issue could consist of 1,000 $1,000 bonds. Because a bond issue can be bought and held by many investors, the organization usually enters into a supplementary agreement called a **bond indenture**. The bond indenture defines the rights, privileges, and limitations of the bondholders. It generally describes such things as the maturity date of the bonds, interest payment dates, interest rate, and other characteristics of the bonds. Repayment plans and restrictions also may be covered.

The prices of bonds are stated in terms of a percentage of face value. A bond issue quoted at 103½ means that a $1,000 bond costs $1,035 ($1,000 × 1.035). When a bond sells at exactly 100, it is said to sell at face or par value. When it sells above 100, it is said to sell at a premium; below 100, at a discount. A $1,000 bond quoted at 87.62 would be selling at a discount and would cost the buyer $876.20.

A bond indenture can be written to fit the financing needs of an individual organization. As a result, the bonds being issued in today's financial markets have many different features. Several of the more important ones are described in the following paragraphs.

Secured or Unsecured Bonds

Bonds can be either secured or unsecured. If issued on the general credit of the organization, they are **unsecured bonds** (also called *debenture bonds*). **Secured bonds** give the bondholders a pledge of certain assets as a guarantee of repayment. The security identified by a secured bond can be any specific asset of the organization or a general category of asset, such as property, plant, or equipment.

Term or Serial Bonds

When all the bonds of an issue mature at the same time, they are called **term bonds**. For instance, an organization may decide to issue $1,000,000 worth of

---

*At the time this chapter was written, the market interest rates on corporate bonds were volatile. Therefore, the examples and problems in this chapter use a variety of interest rates to demonstrate the concepts.

bonds, all due 20 years from the date of issue. If the bonds in an issue mature on several different dates, the bonds are **serial bonds**. An example of serial bonds would be a $1,000,000 issue that calls for retiring $200,000 of the principal every five years. This arrangement means that after the first $200,000 payment is made, $800,000 of the bonds would remain outstanding for the next five years. In other words, $1,000,000 is outstanding for the first five years, $800,000 for the second five years, and so on. An organization may issue serial bonds to ease the task of retiring its debt.

Accounting for Bonds Payable

When the board of directors of a corporation decides to issue bonds, it customarily presents the proposal to the stockholders. If the stockholders agree to the issue, the company prints the certificates and draws up an appropriate legal document. The bonds are then authorized for issuance. It is not necessary to make a journal entry for the authorization, but most companies prepare a memorandum in the Bonds Payable account describing the issue. This note lists the number and value of bonds authorized, the interest rate, the interest payment dates, and the life of the bonds.

Once the bonds are issued, the corporation must pay interest to the bondholders over the life of the bonds (in most cases, semiannually) and the principal of the bonds at maturity.

Balance Sheet Disclosure of Bonds

Bonds payable and unamortized discounts or premiums (which we explain later) are typically shown on a company's balance sheet as long-term liabilities. However, if the maturity date of the bond issue is one year or less and the bonds will be retired using current assets, Bonds Payable should be listed as a current liability. If the issue is to be paid with segregated assets or replaced by another bond issue, the bonds should still be shown as a long-term liability.

Important provisions of the bond indenture are reported in the notes to the financial statements, as illustrated by the earlier excerpt from the AT&T annual report. Often reported with them is a list of all bond issues, the kinds of bonds, interest rates, any securities connected with the bonds, interest payment dates, maturity dates, and effective interest rates.

Bonds Issued at Face Value

Suppose that the Vason Corporation has authorized the issuance of $100,000 of 9 percent, five-year bonds on January 1, 20x0. According to the bond indenture, interest is to be paid on January 1 and July 1 of each year. Assume that the bonds are sold on January 1, 20x0, for their face value. The entry to record the issuance is as follows:

A = L + OE
+   +

20x0			
Jan. 1	Cash	100,000	
	Bonds Payable		100,000
	Sold $100,000 of 9 percent, five-year bonds at face value		

As stated above, interest is paid on January 1 and July 1 of each year. Therefore, the corporation would owe the bondholders $4,500 interest on July 1, 20x0:

$$\text{Interest} = \text{Principal} \times \text{Rate} \times \text{Time}$$
$$= \$100,000 \times .09 \times \frac{6}{12} \text{ year}$$
$$= \$4,500$$

The interest paid to the bondholders on each semiannual interest payment date (January 1 or July 1) would be recorded as follows:

A* = L + OE
−   −
*Assumes cash paid.

Bond Interest Expense	4,500	
Cash (or Interest Payable)		4,500
Paid (or accrued) semiannual interest to bondholders of 9 percent, five-year bonds		

Face Interest Rate and Market Interest Rate

When issuing bonds, most organizations try to set the face interest rate as close as possible to the market interest rate. The **face interest rate** is the rate of interest paid to bondholders based on the face value, or principal, of the bonds. The rate and amount are fixed over the life of the bond. An organization must decide in

FOCUS ON BUSINESS PRACTICE

The price for many bonds may be found daily in business publications like *The Wall Street Journal*. For instance, to the right are the quotations for a number of AT&T Corporation bonds.[4] The first bond is an AT&T bond with a face interest rate of 5⅛ percent that is due in 2001. The current yield is 5.2 percent based on the closing price of 97⅞. Five $1,000 bonds were traded (volume), and the last sale was up by ¼ point from the previous day's last sales.

		New York Exchange Bonds			
		Corporation Bonds (Volume) $10,063,000			
Bonds	**Cur Yld**	**Vol**	**Close**	**Net Chg**	
ATT 5⅛01	5.2	5	97⅞	+	¼
ATT 7⅛02	7.2	50	99½	...	
ATT 6¾04	6.9	34	97½	+	¼
ATT 5⅝04	6.0	10	93¼	+	⅝
ATT 7½06	7.5	55	100	−	⅛
ATT 7¾07	7.7	100	101⅛	+	¼
ATT 6s09	6.9	176	86½	+	½
ATT 8⅛22	8.4	228	96½	−	¾
ATT 8⅛24	8.5	466	96	...	
ATT 6½29	8.1	51	80½	+	⅞
ATT 8⅝31	8.8	385	98⅝	+	⅛

advance what the face interest rate will be to allow time to file with regulatory bodies, publicize the issue, and print the certificates.

The **market interest rate** is the rate of interest paid in the market on bonds of similar risk. It is also referred to as the *effective interest rate*. The market interest rate fluctuates daily. Because an organization has no control over the market interest rate, there is often a difference between the market interest rate and the face interest rate on the issue date. The result is that the issue price of the bonds does not always equal their face value. If the market interest rate is higher than the face interest rate, the issue price will be less than the face value and the bonds are said to be issued at a **discount**. The discount equals the excess of the face value over the issue price. On the other hand, if the market interest rate is lower than the face interest rate, the issue price will be more than the face value and the bonds are said to be issued at a **premium**. The premium equals the excess of the issue price over the face value.

Bonds Issued at a Discount

Suppose that the Vason Corporation issues $100,000 of 9 percent, five-year bonds at 96.149 on January 1, 20x0, when the market interest rate is 10 percent. In this case, the bonds are being issued at a discount because the market interest rate exceeds the face interest rate. The following entry records the issuance of the bonds at a discount:

20x0				
Jan. 1	Cash		96,149	
	Unamortized Bond Discount		3,851	
	Bonds Payable			100,000
	Sold $100,000 of 9 percent, five-year bonds at 96.149			
	Face amount of bonds	$100,000		
	Less purchase price of bonds ($100,000 × .96149)	96,149		
	Unamortized bond discount	$ 3,851		

A = L + OE
+ +
   −

In the entry, Cash is debited for the amount received ($96,149), Bonds Payable is credited for the face amount ($100,000) of the bond liability, and the difference ($3,851) is debited to Unamortized Bond Discount. If a balance sheet is prepared right after the bonds are issued at a discount, the liability for bonds payable is reported as follows:

Long-Term Liabilities		
9% Bonds Payable, due 1/1/x5	$100,000	
Less Unamortized Bond Discount	3,851	$96,149

Unamortized Bond Discount is a contra-liability account: Its balance is deducted from the face amount of the bonds to arrive at the carrying value, or present value, of the bonds. The bond discount is described as unamortized because it will be amortized (written off) over the life of the bonds.

Bonds Issued at a Premium

When bonds have a face interest rate above the market rate for similar investments, they are issued at a price above the face value, or at a premium. For example, assume that the Vason Corporation issues $100,000 of 9 percent, five-year bonds for $104,100 on January 1, 20x0, when the market interest rate is 8 percent. This means that investors will purchase the bonds at 104.1 percent of their face value. The issuance would be recorded as follows:

A = L + OE
\+   \+
     \+

20x0
Jan. 1   Cash   104,100
     Unamortized Bond Premium   4,100
     Bonds Payable   100,000
       Sold $100,000 of 9 percent, five-year
       bonds at 104.1 ($100,000 × 1.041)

Right after this entry is made, bonds payable would be presented on the balance sheet as follows:

Long-Term Liabilities
  9% Bonds Payable, due 1/1/x5 $100,000
  Unamortized Bond Premium   4,100 $104,100

The carrying value of the bonds payable is $104,100, which equals the face value of the bonds plus the unamortized bond premium. The cash received from the bond issue is also $104,100. This means that the purchasers were willing to pay a premium of $4,100 to buy these bonds because their face interest rate was higher than the market interest rate.

Bond Issue Costs

Most bonds are sold through underwriters, who receive a fee for taking care of the details of marketing the issue or for taking a chance on receiving the selling price. Such costs are connected with the issuance of bonds. Because bond issue costs benefit the whole life of a bond issue, it makes sense to spread the costs over that period. It is generally accepted practice to establish a separate account for bond issue costs and to amortize them over the life of the bonds. However, issue costs decrease the amount of money a company receives from a bond issue. They have the effect, then, of raising the discount or lowering the premium on the issue. As a result, bond issue costs can be spread over the life of the bonds through the amortization of a discount or premium. Because this method simplifies recordkeeping, we assume in the text and problems of this book that all bond issue costs increase the discounts or decrease the premiums of bond issues.

Using Present Value to Value a Bond

OBJECTIVE

4 Use present values to determine the value of bonds

Present value is relevant to the study of bonds because the value of a bond is based on the present value of two components of cash flow: (1) a series of fixed interest payments and (2) a single payment at maturity.* The amount of interest a bond pays is fixed over its life. However, the market interest rate varies from day to day. Thus, the amount investors are willing to pay for a bond changes as well.

Assume, for example, that a particular bond has a face value of $10,000 and pays fixed interest of $450 every six months (a 9 percent annual rate). The bond is due in five years. If the market interest rate today is 14 percent, what is the present value of the bond?

To determine the present value of the bond, we use Table 4 in the appendix on future value and present value tables to calculate the present value of the periodic interest payments of $450, and we use Table 3 in the same appendix to calculate the present value of the single payment of $10,000 at maturity. Since interest payments are made every six months, the compounding period is half a year. Because of this, it is necessary to convert the annual rate to a semiannual rate of 7 percent (14 percent divided by two six-month periods per year) and to use ten periods

*A knowledge of present value concepts, as presented in the appendix on time value of money, is necessary to an understanding of this section.

In 1993, interest rates on long-term debt were at historically low levels, which induced some companies to attempt to lock in those low costs for long periods. One of the most aggressive companies in that regard was The Walt Disney Company, which issued $150 million of 100-year bonds at a yield of only 7.5

percent. It was the first time since 1954 that 100-year bonds had been issued. Some analysts wondered if even Mickey Mouse could survive 100 years. Investors who purchase these bonds are taking a financial risk because if interest rates rise, which they are likely to do, then the market value of the bonds will decrease. Since then, other companies, including The Coca-Cola Company, Columbia HCA Healthcare, IBM, Bell South, and even the People's Republic of China, have followed suit with 100-year bonds.[5]

(five years multiplied by two six-month periods per year). Using this information, we compute the present value of the bond:

Present value of ten periodic payments at 7 percent (from Table 4 in the appendix on future value and present value tables): $450 × 7.024	$3,160.80
Present value of a single payment at the end of ten periods at 7 percent (from Table 3 in the appendix on future value and present value tables): $10,000 × .508	5,080.00
Present value of $10,000 bond	$8,240.80

The market interest rate has increased so much since the bond was issued (from 9 percent to 14 percent) that the value of the bond is only $8,240.80 today. That amount is all investors would be willing to pay at this time for a bond that provides income of $450 every six months and a return of the $10,000 principal in five years.

If the market interest rate falls below the face interest rate, say to 8 percent (4 percent semiannually), the present value of the bond will be greater than the face value of $10,000.

Present value of ten periodic payments at 4 percent (from Table 4 in the appendix on future value and present value tables): $450 × 8.111	$ 3,649.95
Present value of a single payment at the end of ten periods at 4 percent (from Table 3 in the appendix on future value and present value tables): $10,000 × .676	6,760.00
Present value of $10,000 bond	$10,409.95

Amortizing a Bond Discount

OBJECTIVE

5 Use the straight-line and effective interest methods to amortize bond discounts and premiums

In the example on page 674, Vason Corporation issued $100,000 of five-year bonds at a discount because the market interest rate of 10 percent exceeded the face interest rate of 9 percent. The bonds were sold for $96,149, resulting in an unamortized bond discount of $3,851. Because this discount affects interest expense in each year of the bond issue, the bond discount should be amortized (reduced gradually) over the life of the issue. This means that the unamortized bond discount will decrease gradually over time and that the carrying value of the bond issue (face value less unamortized discount) will increase gradually. By the maturity date of the bond, the carrying value of the issue will equal its face value, and the unamortized bond discount will be zero.

Calculation of Total Interest Cost

When bonds are issued at a discount, the effective interest rate paid by the company is greater than the face interest rate on the bonds. The reason is that the interest cost to the company is the stated interest payments *plus* the amount of the bond discount. That is, although the company does not receive the full face value of the bonds on issue, it still must pay back the full face value at maturity. The difference between the issue price and the face value must be added to the total interest payments to arrive at the actual interest expense. The full cost to the corporation of issuing the bonds at a discount is as follows:

Cash to be paid to bondholders	
Face value at maturity	$100,000
Interest payments ($100,000 × .09 × 5 years)	45,000
Total cash paid to bondholders	$145,000
Less cash received from bondholders	96,149
Total interest cost	$ 48,851

Or, alternatively:

Interest payments ($100,000 × .09 × 5 years)	$ 45,000
Bond discount	3,851
Total interest cost	$ 48,851

The total interest cost of $48,851 is made up of $45,000 in interest payments and the $3,851 bond discount, so the bond discount increases the interest paid on the bonds from the stated interest rate to the effective interest rate. The *effective interest rate* is the real interest cost of the bond over its life.

For each year's interest expense to reflect the effective interest rate, the discount must be allocated over the remaining life of the bonds as an increase in the interest expense each period. The process of allocation is called *amortization of the bond discount*. Thus, interest expense for each period will exceed the actual payment of interest by the amount of the bond discount amortized over the period.

Some companies and governmental units issue bonds that do not require periodic interest payments. These bonds, called **zero coupon bonds**, are simply a promise to pay a fixed amount at the maturity date. They are issued at a large discount because the only interest earned by the buyer or paid by the issuer is the discount. For example, a five-year, $100,000 zero coupon bond issued at a time when the market rate is 14 percent, compounded semiannually, would sell for only $50,800. That amount is the present value of a single payment of $100,000 at the end of five years. The discount of $49,200 ($100,000 − $50,800) is the total interest cost; it is amortized over the life of the bond.

Methods of Amortizing a Bond Discount

There are two ways of amortizing bond discounts or premiums: the straight-line method and the effective interest method.

STRAIGHT-LINE METHOD The **straight-line method** is the easier of the two amortization methods, with equal amortization of the discount for each interest period. Suppose that the interest payment dates for the Vason Corporation bond issue are January 1 and July 1. The amount of the bond discount amortized and the interest cost for each semiannual period are calculated in four steps.

1. Total Interest Payments = Interest Payments per Year × Life of Bonds

$$= 2 \times 5 = 10$$

2. Amortization of Bond Discount per Interest Period = $\dfrac{\text{Bond Discount}}{\text{Total Interest Payments}}$

$$= \frac{\$3,851}{10} = \$385^*$$

*Rounded.

3. Cash Interest Payment = Face Value × Face Interest Rate × Time

$$= \$100,000 \times .09 \times \frac{6}{12} = \$4,500$$

4. Interest Cost per Interest Period = Interest Payment + Amortization of Bond Discount

$$= \$4,500 + \$385 = \$4,885$$

On July 1, 20x0, the first semiannual interest date, the entry would be as follows:

A* = L + OE
− + −
Assumes cash paid.

20x0			
July 1	Bond Interest Expense	4,885	
	Unamortized Bond Discount		385
	Cash (or Interest Payable)		4,500
	Paid (or accrued) semiannual interest to bondholders and amortized the discount on 9 percent, five-year bonds		

Notice that the bond interest expense is $4,885, but the amount paid to the bondholders is the $4,500 face interest payment. The difference of $385 is the credit to Unamortized Bond Discount. This lowers the debit balance of the Unamortized Bond Discount account and raises the carrying value of the bonds payable by $385 each interest period. Assuming that no changes occur in the bond issue, this entry will be made every six months for the life of the bonds. When the bond issue matures, there will be no balance in the Unamortized Bond Discount account, and the carrying value of the bonds will be $100,000—exactly equal to the amount due the bondholders.

The straight-line method has long been used, but it has a certain weakness. Because the carrying value goes up each period and the bond interest expense stays the same, the rate of interest falls over time. Conversely, when the straight-line method is used to amortize a premium, the rate of interest rises over time. Therefore, the Accounting Principles Board has ruled that the straight-line method can be used only when it does not lead to a material difference from the effective interest method.[6]

EFFECTIVE INTEREST METHOD   To compute the interest and amortization of a bond discount for each interest period under the **effective interest method**, a constant interest rate is applied to the carrying value of the bonds at the beginning of the interest period. This constant rate equals the market rate, or effective rate, at the time the bonds are issued. The amount to be amortized each period is the difference between the interest computed by using the effective rate and the actual interest paid to bondholders.

As an example, we use the same facts presented earlier—a $100,000 bond issue at 9 percent, with a five-year maturity and interest to be paid twice a year. The market, or effective, interest rate at the time the bonds were issued was 10 percent. The bonds were sold for $96,149, a discount of $3,851. The interest and amortization of the bond discount are shown in Table 1.

Table 1. Interest and Amortization of a Bond Discount: Effective Interest Method

	A	B	C	D	E	F
Semiannual Interest Period	Carrying Value at Beginning of Period	Semiannual Interest Expense at 10% to Be Recorded* (5% × A)	Semiannual Interest to Be Paid to Bondholders (4½% × $100,000)	Amortization of Bond Discount (B − C)	Unamortized Bond Discount at End of Period (E − D)	Carrying Value at End of Period (A + D)
0					$3,851	$ 96,149
1	$96,149	$4,807	$4,500	$307	3,544	96,456
2	96,456	4,823	4,500	323	3,221	96,779
3	96,779	4,839	4,500	339	2,882	97,118
4	97,118	4,856	4,500	356	2,526	97,474
5	97,474	4,874	4,500	374	2,152	97,848
6	97,848	4,892	4,500	392	1,760	98,240
7	98,240	4,912	4,500	412	1,348	98,652
8	98,652	4,933	4,500	433	915	99,085
9	99,085	4,954	4,500	454	461	99,539
10	99,539	4,961†	4,500	461	—	100,000

*Rounded to the nearest dollar.

†Last period's interest expense equals $4,961 ($4,500 + $461); it does not equal $4,977 ($99,539 × .05) because of the cumulative effect of rounding.

The amounts in the table (using period 1) were computed as follows:

Column A   The carrying value of the bonds is their face value less the unamortized bond discount ($100,000 − $3,851 = $96,149).

Column B   The interest expense to be recorded is the effective interest. It is found by multiplying the carrying value of the bonds by the effective interest rate for one-half year ($96,149 × .10 × ½ = $4,807).

Column C   The interest paid in the period is a constant amount computed by multiplying the face value of the bonds by their face interest rate by the interest time period ($100,000 × .09 × ½ = $4,500).

Column D   The discount amortized is the difference between the effective interest expense to be recorded and the interest to be paid on the interest payment date ($4,807 − $4,500 = $307).

Column E   The unamortized bond discount is the balance of the bond discount at the beginning of the period less the current period amortization of the discount ($3,851 − $307 = $3,544). The unamortized discount decreases each interest payment period because it is amortized as a portion of interest expense.

Column F   The carrying value of the bonds at the end of the period is the carrying value at the beginning of the period plus the amortization during the period ($96,149 + $307 = $96,456). Notice that the sum of the carrying value and the unamortized discount (Column F + Column E) always equals the face value of the bonds ($96,456 + $3,544 = $100,000).

The entry to record the interest expense is exactly like the one used when the straight-line method is applied. However, the amounts debited and credited to the various accounts are different. Using the effective interest method, the entry for July 1, 20x0, would be as follows:

A* = L + OE
− + −
*Assumes cash paid.

	20x0			
	July 1	Bond Interest Expense	4,807	
		Unamortized Bond Discount		307
		Cash (or Interest Payable)		4,500
		Paid (or accrued) semiannual interest to bondholders and amortized the discount on 9 percent, five-year bonds		

Notice that it is not necessary to prepare an interest and amortization table to determine the amortization of a discount for any one interest payment period. It is necessary only to multiply the carrying value by the effective interest rate and subtract the interest payment from the result. For example, the amount of discount to be amortized in the seventh interest payment period is $412, calculated as follows: ($98,240 × .05) − $4,500.

VISUAL SUMMARY OF THE EFFECTIVE INTEREST METHOD   The effect on carrying value and interest expense of the amortization of a bond discount using the effective interest method can be seen in Figure 2 (which is based on the data from Table 1). Notice that initially the carrying value (the issue price) is less than the face value, but that it gradually increases toward the face value over the life of the bond issue.

Notice also that interest expense exceeds interest payments by the amount of the bond discount amortized. Interest expense increases gradually over the life of the bond because it is based on the gradually increasing carrying value (multiplied by the market interest rate).

Figure 2
Carrying Value and Interest Expense—Bonds Issued at a Discount

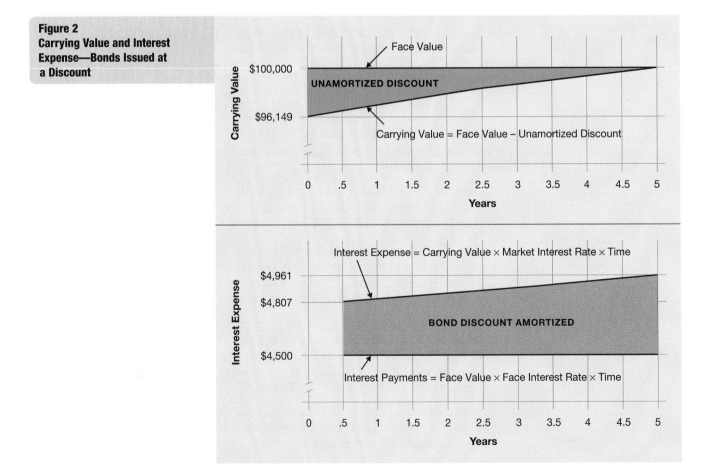

Amortizing a Bond Premium

In our example on pages 674–675, Vason Corporation issued $100,000 of five-year bonds at a premium because the market interest rate of 8 percent was less than the face interest rate of 9 percent. The bonds were sold for $104,100, which resulted in an unamortized premium of $4,100. Like a discount, a premium must be amortized over the life of the bonds so that it can be matched to its effects on interest expense during that period. In the following sections, the total interest cost is calculated and the bond premium is amortized using the straight-line and the effective interest methods.

Calculation of Total Interest Cost

Because the bondholders paid more than face value for the bonds, the premium of $4,100 ($104,100 − $100,000) represents an amount that the bondholders will not receive at maturity. The premium is in effect a reduction, in advance, of the total interest paid on the bonds over the life of the bond issue.

The total interest cost over the issue's life can be computed as follows:

Cash to be paid to bondholders	
Face value at maturity	$100,000
Interest payments ($100,000 × .09 × 5 years)	45,000
Total cash paid to bondholders	$145,000
Less cash received from bondholders	104,100
Total interest cost	$ 40,900

Or, alternatively:

Interest payments ($100,000 × .09 × 5 years)	$ 45,000
Less bond premium	4,100
Total interest cost	$ 40,900

Notice that the total interest payments of $45,000 exceed the total interest cost of $40,900 by $4,100, the amount of the bond premium.

Methods of Amortizing a Bond Premium

The two methods of amortizing a bond premium are the straight-line method and the effective interest method.

STRAIGHT-LINE METHOD   Under the straight-line method, the bond premium is spread evenly over the life of the bond issue. As with bond discounts, the amount of the bond premium amortized and the interest cost for each semiannual period are computed in four steps.

1. Total Interest Payments = Interest Payments per Year × Life of Bonds
$$= 2 \times 5 = 10$$

2. Amortization of Bond Premium per Interest Period $= \dfrac{\text{Bond Premium}}{\text{Total Interest Payments}}$
$$= \frac{\$4,100}{10} = \$410$$

3. Cash Interest Payment = Face Value × Face Interest Rate × Time
$$= \$100,000 \times .09 \times \frac{6}{12} = \$4,500$$

4. Interest Cost per Interest Period = Interest Payment − Amortization of Bond Premium

$$= \$4{,}500 - \$410 = \$4{,}090$$

On July 1, 20x0, the first semiannual interest date, the entry would be:

A* = L + OE

− − −

*Assumes cash paid.

20x0			
July 1	Bond Interest Expense	4,090	
	Unamortized Bond Premium	410	
	Cash (or Interest Payable)		4,500
	Paid (or accrued) semiannual interest to bondholders and amortized the premium on 9 percent, five-year bonds		

Notice that the bond interest expense is $4,090, but the amount received by the bondholders is the $4,500 face interest payment. The difference of $410 is the debit to Unamortized Bond Premium. This lowers the credit balance of the Unamortized Bond Premium account and the carrying value of the bonds payable by $410 each interest period. Assuming that the bond issue remains unchanged, the same entry will be made on every semiannual interest date over the life of the bond issue. When the bond issue matures, there will be no balance in the Unamortized Bond Premium account, and the carrying value of the bonds payable will be $100,000, exactly equal to the amount due the bondholders.

As noted earlier in this chapter, the straight-line method should be used only when it does not lead to a material difference from the effective interest method.

EFFECTIVE INTEREST METHOD   Under the straight-line method, the effective interest rate changes constantly, even though the interest expense is fixed, because the effective interest rate is determined by comparing the fixed interest expense with a carrying value that changes as a result of amortizing the discount or premium. To apply a fixed interest rate over the life of the bonds based on the actual market rate at the time of the bond issue requires the use of the effective interest method. Under this method, the interest expense decreases slightly each period (see Table 2, Column B) because the amount of the bond premium amortized increases slightly (Column D). This occurs because a fixed rate is applied each period to the gradually decreasing carrying value (Column A).

The first interest payment is recorded as follows:

A* = L + OE

− − −

*Assumes cash paid.

20x0			
July 1	Bond Interest Expense	4,164	
	Unamortized Bond Premium	336	
	Cash (or Interest Payable)		4,500
	Paid (or accrued) semiannual interest to bondholders and amortized the premium on 9 percent, five-year bonds		

Notice that the unamortized bond premium (Column E) decreases gradually to zero as the carrying value decreases to the face value (Column F). To find the amount of premium amortized in any one interest payment period, subtract the effective interest expense (the carrying value times the effective interest rate, Column B) from the interest payment (Column C). In semiannual interest period 5, for example, the amortization of premium is $393, calculated as follows: $4,500 − ($102,674 × .04).

VISUAL SUMMARY OF THE EFFECTIVE INTEREST METHOD   The effect of the amortization of a bond premium using the effective interest method on carrying value and interest expense can be seen in Figure 3 (based on data from Table 2).

Table 2. Interest and Amortization of a Bond Premium: Effective Interest Method

	A	B	C	D	E	F
Semiannual Interest Period	Carrying Value at Beginning of Period	Semiannual Interest Expense at 8% to Be Recorded* (4% × A)	Semiannual Interest to Be Paid to Bondholders (4½% × $100,000)	Amortization of Bond Premium (C − B)	Unamortized Bond Premium at End of Period (E − D)	Carrying Value at End of Period (A − D)
0					$4,100	$104,100
1	$104,100	$4,164	$4,500	$336	3,764	103,764
2	103,764	4,151	4,500	349	3,415	103,415
3	103,415	4,137	4,500	363	3,052	103,052
4	103,052	4,122	4,500	378	2,674	102,674
5	102,674	4,107	4,500	393	2,281	102,281
6	102,281	4,091	4,500	409	1,872	101,872
7	101,872	4,075	4,500	425	1,447	101,447
8	101,447	4,058	4,500	442	1,005	101,005
9	101,005	4,040	4,500	460	545	100,545
10	100,545	3,955†	4,500	545	—	100,000

*Rounded to the nearest dollar.
†Last period's interest expense equals $3,955 ($4,500 − $545); it does not equal $4,022 ($100,545 × .04) because of the cumulative effect of rounding.

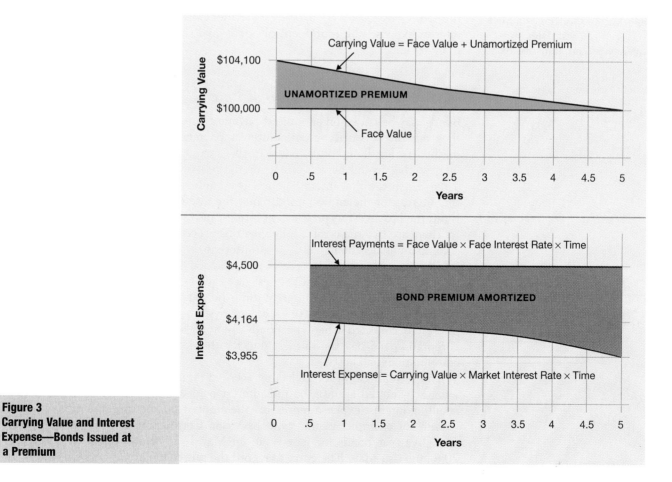

Figure 3
Carrying Value and Interest Expense—Bonds Issued at a Premium

Interest and amortization tables like those in Tables 1 and 2 are ideal applications for computer spreadsheet soft-

ware such as Lotus and Microsoft Excel. Once the tables have been constructed with the proper formula in each cell, only five variables must be entered to produce the entire table. The five variables are the face value of the bonds, the selling price, the life of the bonds, the face interest rate, and the effective interest rate.

Notice that initially the carrying value (issue price) is greater than the face value, but that it gradually decreases toward the face value over the life of the bond issue. Notice also that interest payments exceed interest expense by the amount of the premium amortized and that interest expense decreases gradually over the life of the bond because it is based on the gradually decreasing carrying value (multiplied by the market interest rate).

Other Bonds Payable Issues

OBJECTIVE

6 Account for bonds issued between interest dates and make year-end adjustments

Several other issues arise in accounting for bonds payable. Among these issues are the sale of bonds between interest payment dates, the year-end accrual of bond interest expense, the retirement of bonds, and the conversion of bonds into common stock.

Sale of Bonds Between Interest Dates

Bonds may be issued on an interest payment date, as in the previous examples, but they are often issued between interest payment dates. The generally accepted method of handling bonds issued in this manner is to collect from investors the interest that would have accrued for the partial period preceding the issue date. Then, when the first interest period is completed, the corporation pays investors the interest for the entire period. Thus, the interest collected when bonds are sold is returned to investors on the next interest payment date.

There are two reasons for following this procedure. The first is a practical one. If a company issued bonds on several different days and did not collect the accrued interest, records would have to be maintained for each bondholder and date of purchase. In such a case, the interest due each bondholder would have to be computed on the basis of a different time period. Clearly, large bookkeeping costs would be incurred under this kind of system. On the other hand, if accrued interest is collected when the bonds are sold, on the interest payment date the corporation can pay the interest due for the entire period, eliminating the extra computations and costs.

The second reason for collecting accrued interest in advance is that when that amount is netted against the full interest paid on the interest payment date, the resulting interest expense represents the amount for the time the money was borrowed. For example, assume that the Vason Corporation sold $100,000 of 9 percent, five-year bonds for face value on May 1, 20x0, rather than on January 1, 20x0, the issue date. The entry to record the sale of the bonds is as follows:

20x0

A = L + OE
+ + +

May 1	Cash	103,000	
	Bond Interest Expense		3,000
	Bonds Payable		100,000
	Sold 9 percent, five-year bonds at face value plus four months' accrued interest $100,000 \times .09 \times \frac{4}{12} = \$3,000$		

As shown, Cash is debited for the amount received, $103,000 (the face value of $100,000 plus four months' accrued interest of $3,000). Bond Interest Expense is credited for the $3,000 of accrued interest, and Bonds Payable is credited for the face value of $100,000.

When the first semiannual interest payment date arrives, the entry that follows is made:

20x0

A* = L + OE
−   −

*Assumes cash paid.

July 1	Bond Interest Expense	4,500	
	Cash (or Interest Payable)		4,500
	Paid (or accrued) semiannual interest $100,000 \times .09 \times \frac{6}{12} = \$4,500$		

Notice that the entire half-year interest is both debited to Bond Interest Expense and credited to Cash because the corporation pays bond interest only once every six months, in full six-month amounts. This process is illustrated in Figure 4. The actual interest expense for the two months that the bonds were outstanding is $1,500. This amount is the net balance of the $4,500 debit to Bond Interest Expense on July 1 less the $3,000 credit to Bond Interest Expense on May 1. You can see these steps clearly in the T account for Bond Interest Expense below:

Bond Interest Expense

Bal.	0	May 1	3,000
July 1	4,500		
Bal.	1,500		

Year-End Accrual for Bond Interest Expense

Bond interest payment dates rarely correspond with a company's fiscal year. Therefore, an adjustment must be made at the end of the accounting period to accrue the interest expense on the bonds from the last payment date to the end of the fiscal year. Further, if there is any discount or premium on the bonds, it must also be amortized for the fractional period.

Remember that in an earlier example, Vason Corporation issued $100,000 in bonds on January 1, 20x0, at 104.1 (see page 674). Suppose the company's fiscal year ends on September 30, 20x0. In the period since the interest payment and

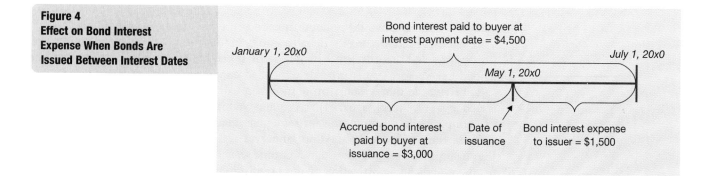

Figure 4
Effect on Bond Interest Expense When Bonds Are Issued Between Interest Dates

amortization of the premium on July 1, three months' worth of interest has accrued, and the following adjusting entry under the effective interest method must be made:

A = L + OE	20x0		
+ −	Sept. 30	Bond Interest Expense	2,075.50
−		Unamortized Bond Premium	174.50
		Interest Payable		2,250.00

To record accrual of interest on 9 percent bonds payable for three months and amortization of one-half of the premium for the second interest payment period

This entry covers one-half of the second interest period. Unamortized Bond Premium is debited for $174.50, which is one-half of $349, the amortization of the premium for the second period from Table 2. Interest Payable is credited for $2,250, three months' interest on the face value of the bonds ($100,000 × .09 × ³/₁₂). The net debit figure of $2,075.50 ($2,250.00 − $174.50) is the bond interest expense for the three-month period.

When the January 1, 20x1, payment date arrives, the entry to pay the bondholders and amortize the premium is as follows:

A = L + OE	20x1		
− − −	Jan. 1	Bond Interest Expense	2,075.50
−		Interest Payable	2,250.00
		Unamortized Bond Premium	174.50
		Cash		4,500.00

Paid semiannual interest including interest previously accrued, and amortized the premium for the period since the end of the fiscal year

As shown here, one-half ($2,250) of the amount paid ($4,500) was accrued on September 30. Unamortized Bond Premium is debited for $174.50, the remaining amount to be amortized for the period ($349.00 − $174.50). The resulting bond interest expense is the amount that applies to the three-month period from October 1 to December 31.

Bond discounts are recorded at year end in the same way as bond premiums. The difference is that the amortization of a bond discount increases interest expense instead of decreasing it, as a premium does.

Retirement of Bonds

OBJECTIVE

7 Account for the retirement of bonds and the conversion of bonds into stock

Most bond issues give the company a chance to buy back and retire the bonds at a specified **call price**, usually above face value, before maturity. Such bonds are known as **callable bonds**, and give the company flexibility in financing its operations. For example, if bond interest rates drop, the company can call its bonds and reissue debt at a lower interest rate. A company might also call its bonds if it has earned enough to pay off the debt, the reason for having the debt no longer exists, or it wants to restructure its debt to equity ratio. The bond indenture states the time period and the prices at which the bonds can be redeemed. The retirement of a bond issue before its maturity date is called **early extinguishment of debt**.

Let's assume that Vason Corporation can call or retire the $100,000 of bonds issued at a premium (page 674) at 105 and that it decides to do so on July 1, 20x3. (To simplify the example, the retirement is made on an interest payment date.) Because the bonds were issued on January 1, 20x0, the retirement takes place on the seventh interest payment date. Assume that the entry for the required interest payment and the amortization of the premium has been made. The entry to retire the bonds is as follows:

A = L + OE
− − −
  −

20x3
July 1 | Bonds Payable | 100,000 |
  | Unamortized Bond Premium | 1,447 |
  | Loss on Retirement of Bonds | 3,553 |
  | Cash | | 105,000
  | Retired 9 percent bonds at 105 | |

In this entry, the cash paid is the face value times the call price ($100,000 ×
1.05 = $105,000). The unamortized bond premium can be found in Column E of
Table 2. The loss on retirement of bonds occurs because the call price of the bonds
is greater than the carrying value ($105,000 − $101,447 = $3,553). The loss, if
material, is presented as an extraordinary item on the income statement.

Sometimes a rise in the market interest rate can cause the market value of
bonds to fall considerably below their face value. If it has the cash to do so, the
company may find it advantageous to purchase the bonds on the open market and
retire them, rather than wait and pay them off at face value. An extraordinary gain
is recognized for the difference between the purchase price of the bonds and the
carrying value of the retired bonds. For example, assume that because of a rise in
interest rates, Vason Corporation is able to purchase the $100,000 bond issue on
the open market at 85, making it unnecessary to call the bonds at the higher price
of 105. Then the entry would be as follows:

A = L + OE
− − +
  −

20x3
July 1 | Bonds Payable | 100,000 |
  | Unamortized Bond Premium | 1,447 |
  | Cash | | 85,000
  | Gain on Retirement of Bonds | | 16,447
  | Purchased and retired | |
  | 9 percent bonds at 85 | |

Conversion of Bonds into Common Stock

Bonds that can be exchanged for other securities of the corporation (in most cases,
common stock) are called **convertible bonds**. Convertibility enables an investor
to make more money if the market price of the common stock rises, because the
value of the bonds then rises. However, if the common stock price does not rise,
the investor still holds the bonds and receives both the periodic interest payments
and the principal at the maturity date.

Several factors related to the issuance of convertible bonds are favorable to the
company. First, the interest rate is usually less than the company would have to
offer if the bonds were not convertible. An investor is willing to give up some current interest for the prospect that the value of the stock will increase, and therefore
the value of the bonds will also increase. Another advantage is that management
will not have to give up any current control of the company. Unlike stockholders,
bondholders do not have voting rights. A third benefit is tax savings. Interest paid
on bonds is fully deductible for income tax purposes, whereas cash dividends on
common stock are not. Fourth, the company's income will be affected favorably if
the company earns a return that exceeds the interest cost of the bonds. Finally, the
convertible feature offers financial flexibility. If the market value of the stock rises
to a level at which the bond is worth more than face value, management can avoid
repaying the bonds by calling them for redemption, thereby forcing the bondholders to convert their bonds into common stock. The bondholders will agree to convert because the common stock they will receive will be worth more than they
would receive if the bonds were redeemed.

One major disadvantage of bonds is that interest must be paid semiannually.
Inability to make an interest payment could force the company into bankruptcy.
Common stock dividends are declared and paid only when the board of directors
decides to do so. Another disadvantage is that when the bonds are converted, they

become new outstanding common stock. These new shares give stockholders' rights to the bondholders and reduce the proportional ownership of the existing stockholders.

When a bondholder wishes to convert bonds into common stock, the common stock is recorded at the carrying value of the bonds. The bond liability and the associated unamortized discount or premium are written off the books. For this reason, no gain or loss on the transaction is recorded. For example, suppose that Vason Corporation's bonds are not called on July 1, 20x3. Instead, the corporation's bondholders decide to convert all the bonds to $8 par value common stock under a convertible provision of 40 shares of common stock for each $1,000 bond. The entry would be as follows:

A = L + OE	20x3			
− +	July 1	Bonds Payable	100,000	
− +		Unamortized Bond Premium	1,447	
		Common Stock		32,000
		Paid-in Capital in Excess of Par		
		Value, Common		69,447
		Converted 9 percent bonds payable into		
		$8 par value common stock at a rate		
		of 40 shares for each $1,000 bond		

The unamortized bond premium is found in Column E of Table 2. At a rate of 40 shares for each $1,000 bond, 4,000 shares will be issued, with a total par value of $32,000 (4,000 × $8). The Common Stock account is credited for the amount of the par value of the stock issued. In addition, Paid-in Capital in Excess of Par Value, Common is credited for the difference between the carrying value of the bonds and the par value of the stock issued ($101,447 − $32,000 = $69,447). No gain or loss is recorded.

Other Long-Term Liabilities

OBJECTIVE

8 Explain the basic features of mortgages payable, installment notes payable, long-term leases, and pensions and other postretirement benefits as long-term liabilities

A company may have other long-term liabilities besides bonds. The most common are mortgages payable, installment notes payable, long-term leases, and pensions and other postretirement benefits.

Mortgages Payable

A **mortgage** is a long-term debt secured by real property. It is usually paid in equal monthly installments. Each monthly payment includes interest on the debt and a reduction in the debt. Table 3 shows the first three monthly payments on a $50,000, 12 percent mortgage. The mortgage was obtained on June 1, and the monthly payments are $800. According to the table, the entry to record the July 1 payment would be as follows:

A = L + OE	July 1	Mortgage Payable	300	
− − −		Mortgage Interest Expense	500	
		Cash		800
		Made monthly mortgage payment		

Notice from the entry and from Table 3 that the July 1 payment represents interest expense of $500 ($50,000 × .12 × $\frac{1}{12}$) and a reduction in the debt of $300 ($800 − $500). Therefore, the unpaid balance is reduced to $49,700 by the July payment. August's interest expense is slightly less than July's because of the decrease in the debt.

Table 3. Monthly Payment Schedule on a $50,000, 12 Percent Mortgage

Payment Date	A Unpaid Balance at Beginning of Period	B Monthly Payment	C Interest for 1 Month at 1% on Unpaid Balance* (1% × A)	D Reduction in Debt (B − C)	E Unpaid Balance at End of Period (A − D)
June 1					$50,000
July 1	$50,000	$800	$500	$300	49,700
Aug. 1	49,700	800	497	303	49,397
Sept. 1	49,397	800	494	306	49,091

*Rounded to the nearest dollar.

Installment Notes Payable

A long-term note can be paid at its maturity date by making a lump-sum payment that includes the amount borrowed plus the interest. Often, however, the terms of a note will call for a series of periodic payments. Such a note is called an **installment note payable** because each payment includes the interest to date plus a repayment of part of the amount that was borrowed.

For example, let's assume that on December 31, 20x1, $100,000 is borrowed on a 15 percent installment note, to be paid annually over five years. The entry to record the note is as follows:

A = L + OE + +	20x1 Dec. 31	Cash 　Notes Payable 　　Borrowed $100,000 at 15 percent 　　on a five-year installment note	100,000

                         100,000

PAYMENTS OF ACCRUED INTEREST PLUS EQUAL AMOUNTS OF PRINCIPAL   Installment notes most often call for payments consisting of accrued interest plus equal amounts of principal repayment. The amount of each installment decreases because the amount of principal on which the accrued interest is owed decreases by the amount of the previous principal payment. Banks use installment notes to finance equipment purchases by businesses; such notes are also common for other kinds of purchases when payment is spread over several years. They can be set up on a revolving basis whereby the borrower can borrow additional funds as the installments are paid. Moreover, the interest rate charged on installment notes may be adjusted periodically as market interest rates change.

On our sample installment note for $100,000, the principal declines by an equal amount each year for five years, or by $20,000 per year ($100,000 ÷ 5 years). The interest is calculated on the balance of the note that remains each year. Because the balance of the note declines each year, the amount of interest declines as well. For example, the entries for the first two payments of the installment note would be as follows:

A = L + OE − − −	20x2 Dec. 31	Notes Payable Interest Expense 　Cash 　　Made first installment payment on note 　　$100,000 × .15 = $15,000	20,000 15,000 	 35,000

20x3
A = L + OE   Dec. 31   Notes Payable   20,000
‾ ‾ ‾   Interest Expense   12,000
                              Cash   32,000
                                 Made second installment payment on note
                                 $80,000 × .15 = $12,000

Notice that the amount of the payment decreases from $35,000 to $32,000 because the amount of interest accrued on the note has decreased from $15,000 to $12,000. The difference of $3,000 is the interest on the $20,000 that was repaid in 20x2. Each subsequent payment decreases by $3,000, as the note itself decreases by $20,000 each year until it is fully paid. This example assumes that the repayment of principal and the interest rate remain the same from year to year.

PAYMENTS OF ACCRUED INTEREST PLUS INCREASING AMOUNTS OF PRINCIPAL

Less commonly, the terms of an installment note, like those used for leasing equipment, may call for equal periodic (monthly or yearly) payments. Under this method, the interest is deducted from the equal payments to determine the amount by which the principal will be reduced each year.

This procedure, presented in Table 4, is similar to that for mortgages, shown in Table 3. Each equal payment of $29,833 is allocated between interest and principal reduction. Each year the interest is calculated on the remaining principal. As the principal decreases, the annual interest also decreases, and because the payment remains the same, the amount by which the principal decreases becomes larger each year. The entries for the first two years, with data taken from Table 4, follow:

20x2
A = L + OE   Dec. 31   Notes Payable   14,833
‾ ‾ ‾   Interest Expense   15,000
                              Cash   29,833
                                 Made first installment payment on note
20x3
A = L + OE   Dec. 31   Notes Payable   17,058
‾ ‾ ‾   Interest Expense   12,775
                              Cash   29,833
                                 Made second installment payment on note

Similar entries will be made for the next three years.

Table 4. Payment Schedule on a $100,000, 15 Percent Installment Note

	A	B	C	D	E
Payment Date	Unpaid Principal at Beginning of Period	Equal Annual Payment	Interest for 1 Year at 15% on Unpaid Principal* (15% × A)	Reduction in Principal (B − C)	Unpaid Principal at End of Period (A − D)
					$100,000
20x2	$100,000	$29,833	$15,000	$14,833	85,167
20x3	85,167	29,833	12,775	17,058	68,109
20x4	68,109	29,833	10,216	19,617	48,492
20x5	48,492	29,833	7,274	22,559	25,933
20x6	25,933	29,833	3,900†	25,933	—

*Rounded to the nearest dollar.
†The last year's interest equals $3,900 ($29,833 − $25,933); it does not exactly equal $3,890 ($25,933 × .15) because of the cumulative effect of rounding.

How is the equal annual payment calculated? Because the $100,000 borrowed is the present value of the five equal annual payments at 15 percent interest, it is possible to use present value tables to calculate the annual payments. Using Table 4 from the appendix on future value and present value tables, here is the calculation:

Periodic Payment × Factor (Table 4 in the appendix on future value and present value tables: 15%, 5 periods) = Present Value

Periodic Payment × 3.352 = $100,000

Periodic Payment = $100,000 ÷ 3.352

= $29,833

Table 4 shows that five equal annual payments of $29,833 at 15 percent will reduce the principal balance to zero (except for the discrepancy due to rounding).

Long-Term Leases

There are several ways for a company to obtain new operating assets. One way is to borrow money and buy the asset. Another is to rent the equipment on a short-term lease. A third way is to obtain the equipment on a long-term lease. The first two methods do not create accounting problems. In the first case, the asset and liability are recorded at the amount paid, and the asset is subject to periodic depreciation. In the second case, the lease is short term in relation to the useful life of the asset, and the risks of ownership remain with the owner, called the **lessor**. This type of agreement is called an **operating lease**. It is proper accounting procedure for the renter, called the **lessee**, to treat operating lease payments as an expense and to debit the amount of each monthly payment to Rent Expense.

The third alternative, a long-term lease, is one of the fastest-growing ways of financing operating equipment in the United States today. It has several advantages. For instance, a long-term lease requires no immediate cash payment, and it costs less than a short-term lease. Acquiring the use of plant assets under long-term leases does cause several accounting challenges, however. Often, such leases cannot be canceled. Also, their duration may be about the same as the useful life of the asset. Finally, they may provide for the lessee to buy the asset at a nominal price at the end of the lease. The lease is much like an installment purchase because the risks of ownership are transferred to the lessee. Both the lessee's available assets and its legal obligations (liabilities) increase because the lessee must make a number of payments over the life of the asset.

The Financial Accounting Standards Board has described this kind of long-term lease as a **capital lease**. The term reflects the provisions of such a lease, which make the transaction more like a purchase or sale on installment. The FASB has ruled that in the case of a capital lease, the lessee must record an asset and a long-term liability equal to the present value of the total lease payments during the lease term. In doing so, the lessee must use the present value at the beginning of the lease.[7] Much like a mortgage payment, each lease payment consists partly of interest expense and partly of repayment of debt. Further, depreciation expense is figured on the asset and entered on the records of the lessee.

Suppose, for example, that Isaacs Company enters into a long-term lease for a machine used in its manufacturing operations. The lease terms call for an annual payment of $4,000 for six years, which approximates the useful life of the machine (see Table 5). At the end of the lease period, the title to the machine passes to Isaacs. This lease is clearly a capital lease and should be recorded as an asset and a liability according to FASB *Statement No. 13*.

A lease is a periodic payment for the right to use an asset or assets. Present value techniques can be used to place a value on the asset and on the corresponding liability associated with a capital lease. If Isaac's interest cost is 16 percent, the present value of the lease payments can be computed as follows:

Table 5. Payment Schedule on a 16 Percent Capital Lease

	A	B	C	D
Year	Lease Payment	Interest (16%) on Unpaid Obligation* (D × 16%)	Reduction of Lease Obligation (A − B)	Balance of Lease Obligation (D − C)
Beginning				$14,740
1	$ 4,000	$2,358	$ 1,642	13,098
2	4,000	2,096	1,904	11,194
3	4,000	1,791	2,209	8,985
4	4,000	1,438	2,562	6,423
5	4,000	1,028	2,972	3,451
6	4,000	549†	3,451	—
	$24,000	$9,260	$14,740	

*Computations are rounded to the nearest dollar.
†The last year's interest equals $549 ($4,000 − $3,451); it does not exactly equal $552 ($3,451 × .16) because of the cumulative effect of rounding.

Periodic Payment × Factor (Table 4 in the appendix on future value and present value tables: 16%, 6 periods) = Present Value

$$\$4,000 \times 3.685 = \$14,740$$

The entry to record the lease contract is as follows:

A = L + OE
+ +

Equipment Under Capital Lease	14,740	
Obligations Under Capital Lease		14,740
To record capital lease on machinery		

Equipment Under Capital Lease is classified as a long-term asset; Obligations Under Capital Lease is classified as a long-term liability. Each year, Isaacs must record depreciation on the leased asset. Using straight-line depreciation, a six-year life, and no salvage value, the following entry would record the depreciation:

A = L + OE
−   −

Depreciation Expense, Equipment Under Capital Lease	2,457	
Accumulated Depreciation, Equipment Under Capital Lease		2,457
To record depreciation expense on capital lease		

The interest expense for each year is computed by multiplying the interest rate (16 percent) by the amount of the remaining lease obligation. Table 5 shows these calculations. Using the data in the table, the first lease payment would be recorded as follows:

A = L + OE
−   −   −

Interest Expense (Column B)	2,358	
Obligations Under Capital Lease (Column C)	1,642	
Cash		4,000
Made payment on capital lease		

Pensions

Most employees who work for medium- and large-sized companies are covered by some sort of pension plan. A **pension plan** is a contract between a company and its employees in which the company agrees to pay benefits to the employees after they retire. Many companies contribute the full cost of the pension, but frequently the employees also pay part of their salary or wages toward their pension. The contributions from both parties are typically paid into a **pension fund**, from which benefits are paid to retirees. In most cases, pension benefits consist of monthly payments to retired employees and other payments upon disability or death.

There are two kinds of pension plans. Under a *defined contribution plan*, the employer is required to contribute an annual amount specified by an agreement between the company and its employees or by a resolution of the board of directors. Retirement payments depend on the amount of pension payments the accumulated contributions can support. Under a *defined benefit plan*, the employer's annual contribution is the amount required to fund pension liabilities arising from employment in the current year, but the exact amount will not be determined until the retirement and death of the current employees. Under a defined benefit plan, the amount of future benefits is fixed, but the annual contributions vary depending on assumptions about how much the pension fund will earn. Under a defined contribution plan, each year's contribution is fixed, but the benefits vary depending on how much the pension fund earns.

Accounting for annual pension expense under a defined contribution plan is simple. After the required contribution is determined, Pension Expense is debited and a liability (or Cash) is credited.

Accounting for annual expense under a defined benefit plan is one of the most complex topics in accounting; thus, the intricacies are reserved for advanced courses. In concept, however, the procedure is simple. First, the amount of pension expense is determined. Then, if the amount of cash contributed to the fund is less than the pension expense, a liability results, which is reported on the balance sheet. If the amount of cash paid to the pension plan exceeds the pension expense, a prepaid expense arises and appears on the asset side of the balance sheet. For example, the annual report for Philip Morris Companies, Inc., includes among assets on the balance sheet a prepaid pension of $1,367 million.[8]

In accordance with the FASB's *Statement No. 87*, all companies should use the same actuarial method to compute pension expense.[9] However, because of the need to estimate many factors, such as the average remaining service life of active employees, the expected long-run return on pension plan assets, and expected future salary increases, the computation of pension expense is not simple. In addition, actuarial terminology further complicates pension accounting. In nontechnical terms, the pension expense for the year includes not only the cost of the benefits earned by people working during the year but interest costs on the total pension obligation (which are calculated on the present value of future benefits to be paid) and other adjustments. Those costs are reduced by the expected return on the pension fund assets.

All employers whose pension plans do not have sufficient assets to cover the present value of their pension benefit obligations (on a termination basis) must record the amount of the shortfall as a liability on their balance sheets. The investor no longer has to read the notes to the financial statements to learn whether or not the pension plan is fully funded. However, if a pension plan does have sufficient assets to cover its obligations, then no balance sheet reporting is required or permitted.

Other Postretirement Benefits

In addition to pensions, many companies provide health care and other benefits to employees after retirement. In the past, these **other postretirement benefits** were accounted for on a cash basis; that is, they were expensed when the benefits were paid, after an employee had retired. The FASB has concluded, however, that those benefits are earned by the employee, and that, in accordance with the matching rule, they should be estimated and accrued during the period of time the employee is working.[10]

The estimates must take into account assumptions about retirement age, mortality, and, most significantly, future trends in health care benefits. Like pension benefits, such future benefits should be discounted to the current period. In a field test conducted by the Financial Executives Research Foundation, it was determined that the change to accrual accounting increased postretirement benefits by two to seven times the amount recognized on a cash basis.

Chapter Review

REVIEW OF LEARNING OBJECTIVES

↑
Check out ACE, a self-quizzing program on chapter content, at http://college.hmco.com.

1. Identify the management issues related to issuing long-term debt. Long-term debt is used to finance long-term assets and business activities that have long-term earnings potential, such as property, plant, and equipment and research and development. In issuing long-term debt, management must decide (1) whether or not to have long-term debt, (2) how much long-term debt to have, and (3) what types of long-term debt to have. Among the advantages of long-term debt financing are that (1) common stockholders do not relinquish any control, (2) interest on debt is tax deductible, and (3) financial leverage may increase earnings. Disadvantages of long-term financing are that (1) interest and principal must be repaid on schedule, and (2) financial leverage can work against a company if a project is not successful.

2. Identify and contrast the major characteristics of bonds. A bond is a security that represents money borrowed from the investing public. When a corporation issues bonds, it enters into a contract, called a *bond indenture*, with the bondholders. The bond indenture identifies the major conditions of the bonds. A corporation can issue several types of bonds, each having different characteristics. For example, a bond issue may or may not require security (secured versus unsecured bonds). It may be payable at a single time (term bonds) or at several times (serial bonds).

3. Record the issuance of bonds at face value and at a discount or premium. When bonds are issued, the bondholders pay an amount equal to, less than, or greater than the bonds' face value. Bondholders pay face value for bonds when the interest rate on the bonds approximates the market rate for similar investments. The issuing corporation records the bond issue at face value as a long-term liability in the Bonds Payable account.

Bonds are issued at an amount less than face value when their face interest rate is lower than the market rate for similar investments. The difference between the face value and the issue price is called a *discount* and is debited to Unamortized Bond Discount.

When the face interest rate on bonds is greater than the market interest rate on similar investments, investors are willing to pay more than face value for the bonds. The difference between the issue price and the face value is called a *premium* and is credited to Unamortized Bond Premium.

4. Use present values to determine the value of bonds. The value of a bond is determined by summing the present values of (a) the series of fixed interest payments of the bond issue and (b) the single payment of the face value at maturity. Tables 3 and 4 in the appendix on future value and present value tables should be used in making these computations.

5. Use the straight-line and effective interest methods to amortize bond discounts and premiums. When bonds are sold at a discount or a premium, the interest rate is adjusted from the face rate to an effective rate that is close to the market rate when the bonds were issued. Therefore, bond discounts or premiums have the effect of increasing or decreasing the interest expense on the bonds over their life. Under these conditions, it is necessary to amortize the discount or premium over the life of the bonds by using either the straight-line method or the effective interest method.

The straight-line method allocates a fixed portion of the bond discount or premium each interest period to adjust the interest payment to interest expense. The effective interest method, which is used when the effects of amortization are material, results in a constant rate of interest on the carrying value of the bonds. To find interest and the amortization of discounts or premiums, the effective interest rate is applied to the carrying value of the bonds (face value minus the discount or plus the premium) at the beginning of the interest period. The amount of the discount or premium to be amortized is the difference between the interest figured by using the effective rate and that obtained by using the face rate. The results of using the effective interest method on bonds issued at a discount or a premium are summarized below and compared with issuance at face value.

	Bonds Issued At		
	Face Value	**Discount**	**Premium**
Trend in carrying value over bond term	Constant	Increasing	Decreasing
Trend in interest expense over bond term	Constant	Increasing	Decreasing
Interest expense versus interest payments	Interest expense = interest payments	Interest expense > interest payments	Interest expense < interest payments
Classification of bond discount or premium	Not applicable	Contra-liability (deducted from Bonds Payable)	Liability (added to Bonds Payable)

6. Account for bonds issued between interest dates and make year-end adjustments. When bonds are sold on dates between the interest payment dates, the issuing corporation collects from investors the interest that has accrued since the last interest payment date. When the next interest payment date arrives, the corporation pays the bondholders interest for the entire interest period.

When the end of a corporation's fiscal year does not fall on an interest payment date, the corporation must accrue bond interest expense from the last interest payment date to the end of the company's fiscal year. This accrual results in the inclusion of interest expense on the income statement in the year incurred and interest payable on the balance sheet.

7. Account for the retirement of bonds and the conversion of bonds into stock. Callable bonds can be retired before maturity at the option of the issuing corporation. The call price is usually an amount greater than the face value of the bonds, so the corporation usually recognizes a loss when the bonds are retired. An extraordinary gain can be recognized on the early extinguishment of debt when a company purchases its bonds on the open market at a price below carrying value. This happens when a rise in the market interest rate causes the market value of the bonds to fall.

Convertible bonds allow the bondholder to convert bonds to stock in the issuing corporation. In this case, the common stock issued is recorded at the carrying value of the bonds being converted. No gain or loss is recognized.

8. Explain the basic features of mortgages payable, installment notes payable, long-term leases, and pensions and other postretirement benefits as long-term liabilities. A mortgage is a long-term debt secured by real property. It usually is paid in equal monthly installments. Each payment is partly interest expense and partly debt repayment. Installment notes payable are long-term notes that are paid in a series of payments. Part of each payment is interest, and part is repayment of principal. If a long-term lease is a capital lease, the risks of ownership lie with the lessee. Like a mortgage payment, each lease payment is partly interest and partly a reduction of debt. For a capital lease, both an asset and a long-term liability should be recorded. The liability should be equal to the present value at the beginning of the lease of the total lease payments over the lease term. The recorded asset is subject to depreciation. Pension expense must be recorded in the current period. Other postretirement benefits should be estimated and accrued while the employee is still working.

REVIEW OF CONCEPTS AND TERMINOLOGY

The following concepts and terms were introduced in this chapter:

LO 2   **Bond:** A security, usually long term, representing money borrowed from the investing public by a corporation or some other entity.

LO 2   **Bond indenture:** A supplementary agreement to a bond issue that defines the rights, privileges, and limitations of bondholders.

LO 2   **Bond issue:** The total value of bonds issued at one time.

LO 7   **Callable bonds:** Bonds that an organization can buy back and retire at a call price before maturity.

LO 7   **Call price:** A specified price, usually above face value, at which a corporation may, at its option, buy back and retire bonds before maturity.

LO 8   **Capital lease:** A long-term lease in which the risk of ownership lies with the lessee and whose terms resemble a purchase or sale on installment.

LO 7   **Convertible bonds:** Bonds that can be exchanged for other securities of the corporation, usually its common stock.

LO 3   **Discount:** The amount by which the face value of a bond exceeds the issue price; occurs when the market interest rate is higher than the face interest rate.

LO 7   **Early extinguishment of debt:** The retirement of a bond issue before its maturity date.

LO 5   **Effective interest method:** A method of amortizing bond discounts or premiums that applies a constant interest rate, the market rate at the time the bonds were issued, to the carrying value of the bonds at the beginning of each interest period.

LO 3   **Face interest rate:** The rate of interest paid to bondholders based on the face value of the bonds.

LO 1   **Financial leverage:** The ability to increase earnings for stockholders by earning more on assets than is paid in interest on debt incurred to finance the assets; also called *trading on the equity*.

LO 8   **Installment note payable:** A long-term note paid off in a series of payments, of which part is interest and part is repayment of principal.

LO 1   **Interest coverage ratio:** A measure of the degree of protection a company has from default on interest payments; income before taxes and interest expense divided by interest expense.

LO 8   **Lessee:** The renter who pays rent to use a leased asset legally owned by the lessor.

LO 8   **Lessor:** The legal owner of a leased asset who receives rent for its use from the lessee.

LO 3   **Market interest rate:** The rate of interest paid in the market on bonds of similar risk; also called *effective interest rate.*

LO 8   **Mortgage:** A long-term debt secured by real property; usually paid in equal monthly installments, of which part is interest and part is repayment of principal.

LO 8   **Operating lease:** A short-term or cancelable lease in which the risks of ownership lie with the lessor, and whose payments are recorded by the lessee as a rent expense.

LO 8   **Other postretirement benefits:** Health care and other nonpension benefits paid to a worker after retirement but earned while the employee is still working.

LO 8   **Pension fund:** A fund established through contributions from an employer (and, sometimes, employees) from which payments are made to employees after retirement or on disability or death.

LO 8   **Pension plan:** A contract between a company and its employees under which the company agrees to pay benefits to the employees after they retire.

LO 3   **Premium:** The amount by which the issue price of a bond exceeds its face value; occurs when the market interest rate is lower than the face interest rate.

LO 2   **Secured bonds:** Bonds that give the bondholders a pledge of certain assets as a guarantee of repayment.

LO 2   **Serial bonds:** A bond issue with several different maturity dates.

LO 5   **Straight-line method:** A method of amortizing bond discounts or premiums that allocates the discount or premium equally over each interest period of the life of a bond.

LO 2   **Term bonds:** Bonds of a bond issue that all mature at the same time.

LO 2   **Unsecured bonds:** Bonds issued on the general credit of an organization; also called *debenture bonds.*

LO 5   **Zero coupon bonds:** Bonds that do not pay periodic interest but that promise to pay a fixed amount on the maturity date.

REVIEW PROBLEM

Interest and Amortization of a Bond Discount, Bond Retirement, and Bond Conversion

LO 3
LO 5
LO 7

When the Merrill Manufacturing Company was expanding its metal window division, it did not have enough capital to finance the expansion. So management sought and received approval from the board of directors to issue bonds. Merrill Manufacturing planned to issue $5,000,000 of 8 percent, five-year bonds in 20x1. Interest would be paid on June 30 and December 31 of each year. The bonds would be callable at 104, and each $1,000 bond would be convertible into 30 shares of $10 par value common stock.

On January 1, 20x1, the bonds were sold at 96 because the market rate of interest for similar investments was 9 percent. Merrill Manufacturing decided to amortize the bond discount by using the effective interest method. On July 1, 20x3, management called and retired half the bonds, and investors converted the other half into common stock.

REQUIRED

1. Prepare an interest and amortization schedule for the first five interest periods.
2. Prepare the journal entries to record the sale of the bonds, the first two interest payments, the bond retirement, and the bond conversion.

ANSWER TO REVIEW PROBLEM

1. Prepare a schedule for the first five interest periods.

Interest and Amortization of Bond Discount

Semiannual Interest Payment Date	Carrying Value at Beginning of Period	Semiannual Interest Expense* (9% × ½)	Semiannual Interest Paid per Period (8% × ½)	Amortiza-tion of Discount	Unamortized Bond Discount at End of Period	Carrying Value at End of Period
Jan. 1, 20x1					$200,000	$4,800,000
June 30, 20x1	$4,800,000	$216,000	$200,000	$16,000	184,000	4,816,000
Dec. 31, 20x1	4,816,000	216,720	200,000	16,720	167,280	4,832,720
June 30, 20x2	4,832,720	217,472	200,000	17,472	149,808	4,850,192
Dec. 31, 20x2	4,850,192	218,259	200,000	18,259	131,549	4,868,451
June 30, 20x3	4,868,451	219,080	200,000	19,080	112,469	4,887,531

*Rounded to the nearest dollar.

2. Prepare the journal entries.

20x1

Jan.   1   Cash — 4,800,000
Unamortized Bond Discount — 200,000
 Bonds Payable — 5,000,000
  Sold $5,000,000 of 8 percent,
  five-year bonds at 96

June 30   Bond Interest Expense — 216,000
 Unamortized Bond Discount — 16,000
 Cash — 200,000
  Paid semiannual interest and
  amortized the discount on 8 percent,
  five-year bonds

Dec. 31   Bond Interest Expense — 216,720
 Unamortized Bond Discount — 16,720
 Cash — 200,000
  Paid semiannual interest and
  amortized the discount on 8 percent,
  five-year bonds

20x3

July   1   Bonds Payable — 2,500,000
Loss on Retirement of Bonds — 156,235
 Unamortized Bond Discount — 56,235
 Cash — 2,600,000
  Called $2,500,000 of 8 percent bonds
  and retired them at 104
  $112,469 × ½ = $56,235*

*Rounded.

July	1	Bonds Payable	2,500,000		
		Unamortized Bond Discount		56,234	
		Common Stock		750,000	
		Paid-in Capital in Excess of Par			
		Value, Common		1,693,766	

Converted $2,500,000 of 8 percent
bonds into common stock:
2,500 × 30 shares = 75,000 shares
75,000 shares × $10 = $750,000
$112,469 − $56,235 = $56,234
$2,500,000 − ($56,234 + $750,000)
= $1,693,766

Chapter Assignments

QUESTIONS

1. What are the advantages and disadvantages of issuing long-term debt?

2. What are a bond issue and a bond indenture? What information is found in a bond indenture?

3. What are the essential differences between (a) secured and debenture bonds, and (b) term and serial bonds?

4. Napier Corporation sold $500,000 of 5 percent, $1,000 bonds on the interest payment date. What would the proceeds from the sale be if the bonds were issued at 95, at 100, and at 102?

5. If you were about to buy bonds on which the face interest rate was less than the market interest rate, would you expect to pay more or less than par value for the bonds?

6. Why does the amortization of a bond discount increase interest expense to an amount greater than interest paid? Why does the amortization of a premium have the opposite effect?

7. When the effective interest method of amortizing a bond discount or premium is used, why does the amount of interest expense change from period to period?

8. When bonds are issued between interest dates, why is it necessary for the issuer to collect an amount equal to accrued interest from the buyer?

9. Why would a company want to exercise the call provision of a bond when it can wait to pay off the debt?

10. What are the advantages of convertible bonds to the company issuing them and to the investor?

11. What are the two components of a uniform monthly mortgage payment?

12. What are the two methods of repaying an installment note?

13. Under what conditions is a long-term lease called a capital lease? Why should an accountant record both an asset and a liability in connection with this type of lease? What items should appear on the income statement as the result of a capital lease?

14. What is a pension plan? What is a pension fund?

15. What is the difference between a defined contribution plan and a defined benefit plan? In general, how is expense determined under each plan? What assumptions must be made to account for the expenses of such a plan?

16. What are other postretirement benefits, and how is the matching rule applied?

SHORT EXERCISES

SE 1.

LO 1 Bond Versus Common Stock Financing

Indicate whether each of the following is an advantage or a disadvantage of using long-term bond financing rather than issuing common stock.

1. Interest paid on bonds is tax deductible.
2. Sometimes projects are not as successful as planned.
3. Financial leverage can have a negative effect when investments do not earn as much as the interest payments on the related debt.
4. Bondholders do not have voting rights in a corporation.
5. Positive financial leverage may be achieved.

SE 2.

LO 3 Journal Entries for
LO 5 Interest Using the Straight-Line Method

On April 1, 20x1, Taylor Corporation issued $4,000,000 in 8.5 percent, five-year bonds at 98. The semiannual interest payment dates are April 1 and October 1. Prepare journal entries for the issue of the bonds by Taylor on April 1, 20x1, and the first two interest payments on October 1, 20x1, and April 1, 20x2. Use the straight-line method and ignore year-end accruals.

SE 3.

LO 3 Journal Entries for
LO 5 Interest Using the
LO 6 Effective Interest Method

On March 1, 20xx, River Front Freight Company sold $100,000 of its 9.5 percent, 20-year bonds at 106. The semiannual interest payment dates are March 1 and September 1. The effective interest rate is approximately 8.9 percent. The company's fiscal year ends August 31. Prepare journal entries to record the sale of the bonds on March 1, the accrual of interest and amortization of premium on August 31, and the first interest payment on September 1. Use the effective interest method to amortize the premium.

SE 4.

LO 4 Valuing Bonds Using Present Value

Mine-Mart, Inc., is considering the sale of two bond issues. Choice A is a $400,000 bond issue that pays semiannual interest of $32,000 and is due in 20 years. Choice B is a $400,000 bond issue that pays semiannual interest of $30,000 and is due in 15 years. Assume that the market rate of interest for each bond is 12 percent. Calculate the amount that Mine-Mart, Inc., will receive if both bond issues occur. (Calculate the present value of each bond issue and sum.)

SE 5.

LO 3 Journal Entries for Bond
LO 6 Issues

Macrofilm Company is authorized to issue $900,000 in bonds on June 1. The bonds carry a face interest rate of 8 percent, with interest to be paid on June 1 and December 1. Prepare journal entries for the issue of the bonds under the independent assumptions that (a) the bonds are issued on September 1 at 100 and (b) the bonds are issued on June 1 at 103.

SE 6.

LO 6 Sale of Bonds Between Interest Dates

Tripp Corporation sold $200,000 of 9 percent, ten-year bonds for face value on September 1, 20xx. The issue date of the bonds was May 1, 20xx. The company's fiscal year ends on December 31, and this is its only bond issue. Record the sale of the bonds on September 1 and the first semiannual interest payment on November 1, 20xx. What is the bond interest expense for the year ended December 31, 20xx?

SE 7.

LO 3 Year-End Accrual of
LO 5 Bond Interest
LO 6

On October 1, 20x1, Alexus Corporation issued $500,000 of 9 percent bonds at 96. The bonds are dated October 1 and pay interest semiannually. The market rate of interest is 10 percent, and the company's year end is December 31. Prepare the entries to record the issuance of the bonds, the accrual of the interest on December 31, 20x1, and the payment of the first semiannual interest on April 1, 20x2. Assume that the company does not use reversing entries and uses the effective interest method to amortize the bond discount.

SE 8.

LO 7 Journal Entry for Bond Retirement

The Falstaf Corporation has outstanding $800,000 of 8 percent bonds callable at 104. On December 1, immediately after the payment of the semiannual interest and the amortization of the bond discount were recorded, the unamortized bond discount equaled $21,000. On that date, $480,000 of the bonds were called and retired. Prepare the entry to record the retirement of the bonds on December 1.

SE 9.

LO 7 Journal Entry for Bond Conversion

The Degas Corporation has $1,000,000 of 6 percent bonds outstanding. There is $20,000 of unamortized discount remaining on the bonds after the March 1, 20x2, semiannual interest payment. The bonds are convertible at the rate of 20 shares of $10 par value common stock for each $1,000 bond. On March 1, 20x2, bondholders presented $600,000 of the bonds for conversion. Prepare the journal entry to record the conversion of the bonds.

SE 10.

LO 8   Mortgage Payable

Sternberg Corporation purchased a building by signing a $300,000 long-term mortgage with monthly payments of $2,400. The mortgage carries an interest rate of 8 percent. Prepare a monthly payment schedule showing the monthly payment, the interest for the month, the reduction in debt, and the unpaid balance for the first three months. (Round to the nearest dollar.)

EXERCISES

E 1.

LO 1   Interest Coverage Ratio

Compute the interest coverage ratios for 20x1 and 20x2 from the partial income statements of Treefarm Company:

	20x2	20x1
Income from operations	$23,890	$18,460
Interest expense	5,800	3,300
Income before income taxes	$18,090	$15,160
Income taxes	5,400	4,500
Net income	$12,690	$10,660

E 2.

LO 3   Journal Entries for
LO 5   Interest Using the Straight-
**   Line Method**

Mizray Corporation issued $4,000,000 in 10.5 percent, ten-year bonds on February 1, 20x1, at 104. The semiannual interest payment dates are February 1 and August 1.

Prepare journal entries for the issue of bonds by Mizray on February 1, 20x1, and the first two interest payments on August 1, 20x1, and February 1, 20x2. Use the straight-line method and ignore year-end accruals.

E 3.

LO 3   Journal Entries for
LO 5   Interest Using the Straight-
**   Line Method**

Collins Corporation issued $8,000,000 in 8.5 percent, five-year bonds on March 1, 20x1, at 96. The semiannual interest payment dates are March 1 and September 1.

Prepare journal entries for the issue of the bonds by Collins on March 1, 20x1, and the first two interest payments on September 1, 20x1, and March 1, 20x2. Use the straight-line method and ignore year-end accruals.

E 4.

LO 3   Journal Entries for
LO 5   Interest Using the
LO 6   Effective Interest Method

The Wooden Toy Company sold $500,000 of 9.5 percent, 20-year bonds on April 1, 20xx, at 106. The semiannual interest payment dates are April 1 and October 1. The effective interest rate is approximately 8.9 percent. The company's fiscal year ends September 30.

Prepare journal entries to record the sale of the bonds on April 1, the accrual of interest and amortization of premium on September 30, and the first interest payment on October 1. Use the effective interest method to amortize the premium.

E 5.

LO 3   Journal Entries for
LO 5   Interest Using the
LO 6   Effective Interest Method

On March 1, 20x1, the Herring Corporation issued $1,200,000 of 10 percent, five-year bonds. The semiannual interest payment dates are March 1 and September 1. Because the market rate for similar investments was 11 percent, the bonds had to be issued at a discount. The discount on the issuance of the bonds was $48,670. The company's fiscal year ends February 28.

Prepare journal entries to record the bond issue on March 1, 20x1; the payment of interest and the amortization of the discount on September 1, 20x1; the accrual of interest and the amortization of the discount on February 28, 20x2; and the payment of interest on March 1, 20x2. Use the effective interest method. (Round answers to the nearest dollar.)

E 6.

LO 4   Valuing Bonds Using
**   Present Value**

Kitchens, Inc., is considering the sale of two bond issues. Choice A is an $800,000 bond issue that pays semiannual interest of $64,000 and is due in 20 years. Choice B is an $800,000 bond issue that pays semiannual interest of $60,000 and is due in 15 years. Assume that the market interest rate for each bond is 12 percent.

Calculate the amount that Kitchens, Inc., will receive if both bond issues are made. (**Hint:** Calculate the present value of each bond issue and sum.)

E 7.

LO 4 Valuing Bonds Using Present Value

Use the present value tables in the appendix on future value and present value tables to calculate the issue price of a $1,200,000 bond issue in each of the following independent cases, assuming that interest is paid semiannually:

a. A ten-year, 8 percent bond issue; the market interest rate is 10 percent.
b. A ten-year, 8 percent bond issue; the market interest rate is 6 percent.
c. A ten-year, 10 percent bond issue; the market interest rate is 8 percent.
d. A 20-year, 10 percent bond issue; the market interest rate is 12 percent.
e. A 20-year, 10 percent bond issue; the market interest rate is 6 percent.

E 8.

LO 4 Zero Coupon Bonds

The state of Arkansas needs to raise $100,000,000 for highway repairs. Officials are considering issuing zero coupon bonds, which do not require periodic interest payments. The current market interest rate for the bonds is 10 percent. What face value of bonds must be issued to raise the needed funds, assuming the bonds will be due in 30 years and compounded annually? How would your answer change if the bonds were due in 50 years? How would both answers change if the market interest rate were 8 percent instead of 10 percent?

E 9.

**LO 5 Journal Entries for
LO 6 Interest Payments Using
the Effective Interest
Method**

The long-term debt section of the Garcia Corporation's balance sheet at the end of its fiscal year, December 31, 2001, was as follows:

Long-Term Liabilities
  Bonds Payable—8 percent, interest payable
    1/1 and 7/1, due 12/31/13 $1,000,000
    Less Unamortized Bond Discount   80,000 $920,000

Prepare the journal entries relevant to the interest payments on July 1, 2002, December 31, 2002, and January 1, 2003. Assume an effective interest rate of 10 percent.

E 10.

**LO 3 Journal Entries for Bond
LO 6 Issue**

Speaker Symphonics, Inc., is authorized to issue $1,800,000 in bonds on June 1. The bonds carry a face interest rate of 9 percent, which is to be paid on June 1 and December 1.

Prepare journal entries for the issue of the bonds by Speaker Symphonics, Inc., under the assumptions that (a) the bonds are issued on September 1 at 100 and (b) the bonds are issued on June 1 at 105.

E 11.

**LO 6 Sale of Bonds Between
Interest Dates**

Daniel Corporation sold $400,000 of 12 percent, ten-year bonds at face value on September 1, 20xx. The issue date of the bonds was May 1, 20xx.

1. Record the sale of the bonds on September 1 and the first semiannual interest payment on November 1, 20xx.

2. The company's fiscal year ends on December 31 and this is its only bond issue. What is the bond interest expense for the year ended December 31, 20xx?

E 12.

**LO 3 Year-End Accrual of
LO 5 Bond Interest
LO 6**

Sao Corporation issued $1,000,000 of 9 percent bonds on October 1, 20x1, at 96. The bonds are dated October 1 and pay interest semiannually. The market interest rate is 10 percent, and the company's fiscal year ends on December 31.

Prepare the entries to record the issuance of the bonds, the accrual of the interest on December 31, 20x1, and the first semiannual interest payment on April 1, 20x2. Assume the company does not use reversing entries and uses the effective interest method to amortize the bond discount.

E 13.

**LO 4 Time Value of Money and
LO 7 Early Extinguishment of
Debt**

Rupp, Inc., has a $1,400,000, 8 percent bond issue that was issued a number of years ago at face value. There are now ten years left on the bond issue, and the market interest rate is 16 percent. Interest is paid semiannually.

1. Using present value tables, figure the current market value of the bond issue.

2. Record the retirement of the bonds, assuming the company purchases the bonds on the open market at the calculated value.

E 14.

**LO 7 Journal Entry for Bond
Retirement**

The Berman Corporation has outstanding $1,600,000 of 8 percent bonds callable at 104. On September 1, immediately after recording the payment of the semiannual interest and the amortization of the discount, the unamortized bond discount equaled $42,000. On that date, $960,000 of the bonds were called and retired.

Prepare the entry to record the retirement of the bonds on September 1.

LO 7 Journal Entry for Bond Conversion

E 15. The Imaoka Corporation has $400,000 of 6 percent bonds outstanding. There is $20,000 of unamortized discount remaining on these bonds after the July 1, 20x8, semiannual interest payment. The bonds are convertible at the rate of 40 shares of $5 par value common stock for each $1,000 bond. On July 1, 20x8, bondholders presented $300,000 of the bonds for conversion.

Prepare the journal entry to record the conversion of the bonds.

LO 8 Mortgage Payable

E 16. Stars Corporation purchased a building by signing a $150,000 long-term mortgage with monthly payments of $2,000. The mortgage carries an interest rate of 12 percent.

1. Prepare a monthly payment schedule showing the monthly payment, the interest for the month, the reduction in debt, and the unpaid balance for the first three months. (Round to the nearest dollar.)
2. Prepare journal entries to record the purchase and the first two monthly payments.

LO 8 Recording Lease Obligations

E 17. Island Corporation has leased a piece of equipment that has a useful life of 12 years. The terms of the lease are $43,000 per year for 12 years. Island currently is able to borrow money at a long-term interest rate of 15 percent. (Round answers to the nearest dollar.)

1. Calculate the present value of the lease.
2. Prepare the entry to record the lease agreement.
3. Prepare the entry to record depreciation of the equipment for the first year using the straight-line method.
4. Prepare the entries to record the lease payments for the first two years.

LO 8 Installment Notes Payable: Unequal Payments

E 18. Assume that on December 31, 20x1, $40,000 is borrowed on a 12 percent installment note, to be paid annually over four years. Prepare the entry to record the note and the first two annual payments, assuming that the principal is paid in equal annual installments and the interest on the unpaid balance accrues annually. How would your answer change if the interest rate rose to 13 percent in 20x3?

LO 8 Installment Notes Payable: Equal Payments

E 19. Assume that on December 31, 20x1, $40,000 is borrowed on a 12 percent installment note, to be paid in equal annual payments over four years. Calculate to the nearest dollar the amount of each equal payment, using Table 4 from the appendix on future value and present value tables. Prepare a payment schedule table similar to Table 4 in the text, and record the first two annual payments.

PROBLEMS

LO 3 Bond Transactions—
LO 5 Straight-Line Method
LO 6

REQUIRED

P 1. Abel Corporation has $10,000,000 of 10.5 percent, 20-year bonds dated June 1, with interest payment dates of May 31 and November 30. The company's fiscal year ends on December 31. It uses the straight-line method to amortize bond premiums or discounts.

1. Assume the bonds are issued at 103 on June 1. Prepare journal entries for June 1, November 30, and December 31.
2. Assume the bonds are issued at 97 on June 1. Prepare journal entries for June 1, November 30, and December 31.
3. Assume the bonds are issued at face value plus accrued interest on August 1. Prepare journal entries for August 1, November 30, and December 31.

LO 3 Bond Transactions—
LO 5 Effective Interest
LO 6 Method

REQUIRED

P 2. Julio Corporation has $8,000,000 of 9.5 percent, 25-year bonds dated March 1, with interest payable on March 1 and September 1. The company's fiscal year ends on November 30. It uses the effective interest method to amortize bond premiums or discounts. (Round amounts to the nearest dollar.)

1. Assume the bonds are issued at 102.5 on March 1 to yield an effective interest rate of 9.2 percent. Prepare journal entries for March 1, September 1, and November 30.
2. Assume the bonds are issued at 97.5 on March 1 to yield an effective interest rate of 9.8 percent. Prepare journal entries for March 1, September 1, and November 30.

3. Assume the bonds are issued on June 1 at face value plus accrued interest. Prepare journal entries for June 1, September 1, and November 30.

P 3.

LO 3 **Bonds Issued at a**
LO 5 **Discount and a Premium**
LO 6

Waxman Corporation issued bonds twice during 20x2. A summary of the transactions involving the bonds follows.

20x2

Jan. 1 Issued $6,000,000 of 9.9 percent, ten-year bonds dated January 1, 20x2, with interest payable on June 30 and December 31. The bonds were sold at 102.6, resulting in an effective interest rate of 9.4 percent.

Mar. 1 Issued $4,000,000 of 9.2 percent, ten-year bonds dated March 1, 20x2, with interest payable March 1 and September 1. The bonds were sold at 98.2, resulting in an effective interest rate of 9.5 percent.

June 30 Paid semiannual interest on the January 1 issue and amortized the premium, using the effective interest method.

Sept. 1 Paid semiannual interest on the March 1 issue and amortized the discount, using the effective interest method.

Dec. 31 Paid semiannual interest on the January 1 issue and amortized the premium, using the effective interest method.

31 Made an end-of-year adjusting entry to accrue interest on the March 1 issue and to amortize two-thirds of the discount applicable to the second interest period.

20x3

Mar. 1 Paid semiannual interest on the March 1 issue and amortized the remainder of the discount applicable to the second interest period.

REQUIRED

Prepare journal entries to record the bond transactions. (Round amounts to the nearest dollar.)

P 4.

LO 3 **Bond Interest and**
LO 5 **Amortization Table**
LO 7 **and Bond Retirements**

In 20x1, the Fender Corporation was authorized to issue $60,000,000 of six-year unsecured bonds. The bonds carried a face interest rate of 9 percent, payable semiannually on June 30 and December 31. The bonds were callable at 105 any time after June 30, 20x4. All of the bonds were issued on July 1, 20x1, at 95.568, a price yielding an effective interest rate of 10 percent. On July 1, 20x4, the company called and retired half the outstanding bonds.

REQUIRED

1. Prepare a table similar to Table 1 to show the interest and amortization of the bond discount for 12 interest payment periods, using the effective interest method. (Round results to the nearest dollar.)

2. Calculate the amount of loss on early retirement of one-half of the bonds on July 1, 20x4.

P 5.

LO 3 **Comprehensive**
LO 5 **Bond Transactions**
LO 6
LO 7

The Katz Corporation, a company whose fiscal year ends on June 30, engaged in the following long-term bond transactions over a three-year period:

20x3

Nov. 1 Issued $40,000,000 of 12 percent debenture bonds at face value plus accrued interest. Interest is payable on January 31 and July 31, and the bonds are callable at 104.

20x4

Jan. 31 Made the semiannual interest payment on the 12 percent bonds.

June 30 Made the year-end accrual of interest payment on the 12 percent bonds.

July 1 Issued $20,000,000 of 10 percent, 15-year convertible bonds at 105. Interest is payable on June 30 and December 31, and each $1,000 bond is convertible into 30 shares of $10 par value common stock. The market rate of interest is 9 percent.

31 Made the semiannual interest payment on the 12 percent bonds.

Dec. 31 Made the semiannual interest payment on the 10 percent bonds and amortized the bond premium.

20x5

Jan. 31 Made the semiannual interest payment on the 12 percent bonds.

Feb. 28 Called and retired all of the 12 percent bonds, including accrued interest.

June 30 Made the semiannual interest payment on the 10 percent bonds and amortized the bond premium.

July 1 Accepted for conversion into common stock all of the 10 percent bonds.

REQUIRED

Prepare journal entries to record the bond transactions, making all necessary accruals and using the effective interest method. (Round all calculations to the nearest dollar.)

ALTERNATE PROBLEMS

P 6.

LO 3 **Bond Transactions—**
LO 5 **Straight-Line Method**
LO 6

Bassi Corporation has $8,000,000 of 9.5 percent, 25-year bonds dated March 1, with interest payable on March 1 and September 1. The company's fiscal year ends on November 30, and it uses the straight-line method to amortize bond premiums or discounts.

REQUIRED

1. Assume the bonds are issued at 103.5 on March 1. Prepare journal entries for March 1, September 1, and November 30.

2. Assume the bonds are issued at 96.5 on March 1. Prepare journal entries for March 1, September 1, and November 30.

3. Assume the bonds are issued on June 1 at face value plus accrued interest. Prepare journal entries for June 1, September 1, and November 30.

P 7.

LO 3 **Bond Transactions—**
LO 5 **Effective Interest Method**
LO 6

Khan Corporation has $20,000,000 of 10.5 percent, 20-year bonds dated June 1, with interest payment dates of May 31 and November 30. The company's fiscal year ends December 31. It uses the effective interest method to amortize bond premiums or discounts. (Round amounts to the nearest dollar.)

REQUIRED

1. Assume the bonds are issued at 103 on June 1 to yield an effective interest rate of 10.1 percent. Prepare journal entries for June 1, November 30, and December 31.

2. Assume the bonds are issued at 97 on June 1 to yield an effective interest rate of 10.9 percent. Prepare journal entries for June 1, November 30, and December 31.

3. Assume the bonds are issued at face value plus accrued interest on August 1. Prepare journal entries for August 1, November 30, and December 31.

P 8.

LO 3 **Bonds Issued at a**
LO 5 **Discount and a Premium**
LO 6

Pakesh Corporation issued bonds twice during 20x1. The transactions were as follows:

20x1

Jan. 1 Issued $2,000,000 of 9.2 percent, ten-year bonds dated January 1, 20x1, with interest payable on June 30 and December 31. The bonds were sold at 98.1, resulting in an effective interest rate of 9.5 percent.

Apr. 1 Issued $4,000,000 of 9.8 percent, ten-year bonds dated April 1, 20x1, with interest payable on March 31 and September 30. The bonds were sold at 102, resulting in an effective interest rate of 9.5 percent.

June 30 Paid semiannual interest on the January 1 issue and amortized the discount, using the effective interest method.

Sept. 30 Paid semiannual interest on the April 1 issue and amortized the premium, using the effective interest method.

Dec. 31 Paid semiannual interest on the January 1 issue and amortized the discount, using the effective interest method.

31 Made an end-of-year adjusting entry to accrue interest on the April 1 issue and to amortize half the premium applicable to the second interest period.

20x2

Mar. 31 Paid semiannual interest on the April 1 issue and amortized the premium applicable to the second half of the second interest period.

REQUIRED

Prepare journal entries to record the bond transactions. (Round amounts to the nearest dollar.)

EXPANDING YOUR CRITICAL THINKING, COMMUNICATION, AND INTERPERSONAL SKILLS

SKILLS DEVELOPMENT

Conceptual Analysis

SD 1.

LO 3 Bond Interest Rates and Market Prices

R.J. Reynolds Tobacco Holdings, Inc., is one of the largest tobacco companies. Among its long-term debts is a bond due in 2013 that carries a face interest rate of 9¼ percent. Recently this bond sold on the New York Stock Exchange at 113. Does this bond sell at a discount or a premium? Assuming the bond was originally issued at face value, have interest rates risen or declined since the date of issue? Do you expect the market rate of interest on this bond to be more or less than 9¼ percent? Does the current market price affect either the amount that the company pays in semiannual interest or the amount of interest expense for the same period? Explain your answers.

SD 2.

LO 8 Lease Financing

Federal Express Corporation, known for overnight delivery and distribution of high-priority goods and documents throughout the world, has an extensive fleet of aircraft and vehicles. In its 1999 annual report, the company stated that it "utilizes certain aircraft, land, facilities, and equipment under capital and operating leases which expire at various dates through 2025. In addition, supplemental aircraft are leased under agreements which generally provide for cancellation upon 30 days' notice." The annual report further stated that the minimum commitments for capital leases and noncancelable operating leases for 2000 were $15,023,000 and $1,011,957,000, respectively.[11] What is the difference between a capital lease and an operating lease? How do the accounting procedures for the two types of leases differ? How do you interpret management's reasoning in placing some aircraft under capital leases and others under operating leases? Why do you think the management of FedEx leases most of its aircraft instead of buying them?

Ethical Dilemma

SD 3.

LO 2 Bond Indenture and Ethical Reporting

Celltech Corporation, a biotech company, has a $24,000,000 bond issue outstanding that has several restrictive provisions in its bond indenture. Among them are requirements that current assets exceed current liabilities by a ratio of 2 to 1 and that income before income taxes exceed the annual interest on the bonds by a ratio of 3 to 1. If those requirements are not met, the bondholders can force the company into bankruptcy. The company is still awaiting Food and Drug Administration (FDA) approval of its new product CMZ-12, a cancer treatment drug. Management had been counting on sales of CMZ-12 this year to meet the provisions of the bond indenture. As the end of the fiscal year approaches, the company does not have sufficient current assets or income before taxes to meet the requirements. Roger Landon, the chief financial officer, proposes, "Since we can assume that FDA approval will occur early next year, I suggest we book sales and receivables from our major customers now in anticipation of next year's sales. This action will increase our current assets and our income before taxes. It is essential that we do this to save the company. Look at all the people who will be hurt if we don't do it." Is Landon's proposal acceptable accounting? Is it ethical? Who could be harmed by it? What steps might management take?

Cash Flow | CD-ROM | Communication | Critical Thinking | Ethics | General Ledger | Group Activity | Hot Links to Real Companies | International | Internet | Key Ratio | Memo | Spreadsheet

Research Activity

SD 4.
LO 3 **Reading the Bond Markets**

Obtain a copy of a recent issue of *The Wall Street Journal* from your school or local library. Or, if you have access to an Internet service, visit *The Wall Street Journal*'s home page. In the newspaper, find Section C, "Money & Investing," and turn to the page where the New York Exchange Bonds are listed. Notice, first, the Dow Jones Bond Averages of 20 bonds, ten utilities, and ten industrials. Are the averages above or below 100? Is this a premium or a discount? Is the market interest rate above or below the face rate of the average bond? Now, identify three bonds from those listed. Choose one that sells at a discount, one that sells at a premium, and one that sells for approximately 100. For each bond, write the name of the company, the face interest rate, the year the bond is due, the current yield, and the current closing market price. (Some bonds have the letters *cv* in the Yield column. This means the bonds are convertible into common stock and the yield may not be meaningful.) For each bond, explain the relationships between the face interest rate, the current yield, and the closing price. What other factors affect the current yield of a bond? Be prepared to discuss your findings in class.

Decision-Making Practice

SD 5.
LO 1 **Issuance of Long-Term**
LO 2 **Bonds Versus Leasing**
LO 8

The *Weiss Chemical Corporation* plans to build or lease a new plant that will produce liquid fertilizer for the agricultural market. The plant is expected to cost $800,000,000 and will be located in the southwestern United States. The company's chief financial officer, Sharon Weiss, has spent the last several weeks studying different means of financing the plant. From her talks with bankers and other financiers, she has decided that there are two basic choices: The plant can be financed through the issuance of a long-term bond or through a long-term lease. Details for the two options are as follows:

a. Issue $800,000,000 of 25-year, 16 percent bonds secured by the new plant. Interest on the bonds would be payable semiannually.
b. Sign a 25-year lease for an existing plant calling for lease payments of $65,400,000 on a semiannual basis.

Weiss wants to know what the effect of each choice will be on the company's financial statements. She estimates that the useful life of the plant is 25 years, at which time it is expected to have an estimated residual value of $80,000,000.

Weiss plans a meeting to discuss the alternatives. Prepare a short memorandum to her identifying the issues that should be considered in making this decision. (**Note:** You are not asked to make any calculations, discuss the factors, or recommend an action.)

FINANCIAL REPORTING AND ANALYSIS

Interpreting Financial Reports

FRA 1.
LO 4 **Valuing Bonds Using**
Present Value

International Paper Company has 9 percent bonds due in 2006 (in four years) and 9 percent bonds due in 2016 (in 14 years).[12]

REQUIRED

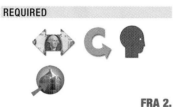

Using present value tables and assuming a current market interest rate of 8 percent, calculate the market value of $100,000,000 of each bond issue. Interest is paid semiannually. Will these bonds sell in the market at a premium or a discount? Explain. Also tell why there is a difference in the market value of the two issues.

FRA 2.
LO 7 **Characteristics of**
Convertible Debt

Amazon.com, Inc., gained renown as an online marketplace for books, records, and other products. Its stock price has risen greatly but the company has yet to earn a profit. To support its enormous growth, the company issued $1,250,000,000 in 4¾ percent convertible notes due in 2009 at face value. Interest is payable on February 1 and

August 1. The notes are convertible into common stock at a price of $156 per share, which is 27 percent above the market price of $123 for the common stock on the date of issue. The market value of Amazon.com's common stock has been quite volatile. Earlier it was $200 per share.[13]

REQUIRED

What reasons can you suggest for Amazon.com's management choosing notes that are convertible into common stock rather than simply issuing nonconvertible notes or issuing common stock directly? Are there any disadvantages to this approach? If the price of the company's common stock returns to $200 per share, what would be the total theoretical value of the notes? If the holders of the notes were to elect to convert the notes into common stock, what would be the effect on the company's debt to equity ratio and what would be the effect on the percentage ownership of the company by other stockholders?

International Company

FRA 3.
LO 1 Comparison of Interest Coverage

Japanese companies have historically relied more on debt financing and are more highly leveraged than U.S. companies. For instance, **NEC Corporation** and **Sanyo Electric Co.,** two large Japanese electronics companies, had debt to equity ratios of about 3.6 and 2.5, respectively, in 1998. From the selected data from the companies' annual reports below (in millions of yen), compute the interest coverage ratios for the two companies for the two years and comment on the riskiness of the companies and on the trends presented.[14]

	NEC		Sanyo	
	1998	1997	1998	1997
Interest Expense	61,257	60,463	33,001	31,765
Income Before Income Taxes	90,993	121,222	38,267	41,486

Group Activity: Assign the two companies to different groups to calculate the ratios and discuss the results. Debrief by discussing the advantages and disadvantages of a debt-laden capital structure.

Toys "R" Us Annual Report

FRA 4.
LO 1 Business Practice, Long-
LO 8 Term Debt, and Leases

Refer to the Financial Statements and the Notes to Consolidated Financial Statements in the Toys "R" Us annual report and answer the following questions.

1. Is it the practice of Toys "R" Us to own or lease most of its property and equipment?
2. What proportion of total assets is financed with long-term debt? Calculate Toys "R" Us's interest coverage ratios for 1999 and 2000 and comment on the trend.
3. In what countries has Toys "R" Us incurred long-term debt? Which maturity date is farthest in the future?
4. Does Toys "R" Us lease property predominantly under capital leases or under operating leases? How much was rental expense for operating leases in 2000?

Fingraph® Financial Analyst™

FRA 5.
LO 1 Long-Term Liabilities
LO 2
LO 8

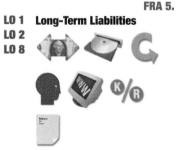

Select any two companies from the same industry on the Fingraph® Financial Analyst™ CD-ROM software.

1. In the annual reports for the companies you have selected, identify the long-term liabilities from the balance sheet and any reference to any long-term liabilities in the summary of significant accounting policies or notes to the financial statements. There is likely to be a separate note for each type of long-term liability. What are the most important current liabilities for each company? What are the most important long-term liabilities for each company?
2. Display and print in tabular and graphical form the Balance Sheet Analysis page. Prepare a table that compares the debt to equity and interest coverage ratios for both companies for two years.

3. Locate the statements of cash flows in the two companies' annual reports. Have the companies been increasing or decreasing their long-term debt? If increasing, what were each company's most important sources of long-term financing over the past two years? If decreasing, which liabilities are being decreased?

4. Find and read references to long-term liabilities in management's discussion and analysis in each annual report.

5. Write a one-page executive summary that highlights the most important types of long-term liabilities for these companies, identifies accounting policies for specific long-term liabilities, and compares the debt to equity and interest coverage trends of the two companies, including reference to management's assessment. Include the Fingraph® page and your table as an attachment to your report.

Internet Case

FRA 6.

LO 1 **Effect of Leases on**
LO 8 **Debt to Equity Ratio**

Through the Needles Accounting Resource Center at http://college.hmco.com, go to the annual report at **United Airlines'** web site. Like most airlines United Airlines leases a portion of its aircraft used in daily operations. It also leases facilities at airport terminals. Within the most recent annual report disclosures, find the note disclosure on leases. Compare the dollar amount of operating leases (which are not on the balance sheet) with the total liabilities computed from the balance sheet. Does the amount of lease payments exceed the total liabilities? Compute the debt to equity ratio from the balance sheet. Discuss the impact these operating leases would have on the debt to equity ratio if these leases were reported on the balance sheet as an asset and a corresponding liability.

ENDNOTES

1. AT&T Corporation, *Annual Report*, 1999.
2. Susan Carey, "TWA Today Faces a Key Deadline on Senior Notes," *The Wall Street Journal*, March 3, 1995.
3. Quentin Hardy, "Japanese Companies Need to Raise Cash, But First a Bond Market Must Be Built," *The Wall Street Journal*, October 20, 1992.
4. Quotations from *The Wall Street Journal*, May 26, 2000.
5. Bill Barnhart, "Bond Bellwether," *Chicago Tribune*, December 4, 1996.
6. Accounting Principles Board, *Opinion No. 21*, "Interest on Receivables and Payables" (New York: American Institute of Certified Public Accountants, 1971), par. 15.
7. *Statement of Financial Accounting Standards No. 13*, "Accounting for Leases" (Norwalk, Conn.: Financial Accounting Standards Board, 1976), par. 10.
8. Philip Morris Companies, Inc., *Annual Report*, 1999.
9. *Statement of Financial Accounting Standards No. 87*, "Employers' Accounting for Pensions" (Norwalk, Conn.: Financial Accounting Standards Board, 1985).
10. *Statement of Financial Accounting Standards No. 106*, "Employers' Accounting for Post-retirement Benefits Other Than Pensions" (Norwalk, Conn.: Financial Accounting Standards Board, 1990).
11. FedEx Corporation, *Annual Report*, 1999.
12. International Paper Company, *Annual Report*, 1998.
13. Amazon.com, *Press Release*, January 28, 1999.
14. NEC Corporation, *Annual Report*, 1998; and Sanyo Electric Co., *Annual Report*, 1998.

17

The Statement of Cash Flows

Marriott International, Inc. Marriott International, Inc., is a world leader in lodging and contract services. The balance sheet, income statement, and statement of stockholders' equity presented in the company's annual report give an excellent picture of management's philosophy and performance.

Those three financial statements are essential to the evaluation of a company, but they do not tell the entire story. Some information that they do not contain is presented in a fourth statement, the statement of cash flows, as shown in the Financial Highlights on the next page.[1] This statement shows how much cash was generated by the company's operations during the past three years and how much was used in or came from investing and financing activities. Marriott feels that maintaining adequate cash flows is important to the future of the company. In fact, Marriott's emphasis on cash flows is reflected in its executive compensation plan for its chief executive officer and senior executive officers. A review of the plan indicates that a measure of cash flows, at the firm or business group level, is the financial measure given the highest weight in determining compensation. Why would Marriott emphasize cash flows to such an extent?

Strong cash flows are essential to management's key goal of liquidity. If cash flows exceed the amount needed for operations and expansion, the company will not have to borrow additional funds. The excess cash flows will be available to reduce the company's debt and improve its financial position by lowering its debt to equity ratio. Another reason for the emphasis on cash flows may be the belief that strong cash flows from operations create shareholder value or increase the market value of the company's stock.

The statement of cash flows demonstrates management's commitments for the company in ways that are not readily apparent in the other financial statements. For example, the statement of cash flows can show whether management's focus is on the short term or the long term. This statement is required by the FASB[2] and satisfies the FASB's long-held position that a primary objective of financial statements is to provide investors and creditors with information about a company's cash flows.[3]

Financial Highlights: Consolidated Statement of Cash Flows

Marriott International, Inc., and Subsidiaries

	1999	1998	1997
		(In millions)	
Operating Activities			
Net income	$400	$ 390	$ 324
Adjustments to reconcile to cash provided by operations:			
Depreciation and amortization	162	140	126
Income taxes	87	76	64
Timeshare activity, net	(102)	28	(118)
Other	19	(22)	88
Working capital changes:			
Accounts receivable	(126)	(104)	(190)
Inventories	(17)	15	(3)
Other current assets	(38)	(16)	(15)
Accounts payable and accruals	326	98	266
Cash provided by operations	711	605	542
Investing Activities			
Capital expenditures	(929)	(937)	(520)
Acquisitions	(61)	(48)	(859)
Dispositions of property and equipment	436	332	571
Loan advances	(144)	(48)	(95)
Loan collections and sales	54	169	47
Other	(143)	(192)	(190
Cash used in investing activities	(787)	(724)	(1,046)
Financing Activities			
Issuance of long-term debt	831	1,294	16
Repayment of long-term debt	(173)	(473)	(15)
Redemption of convertible subordinated debt	(120)	—	—
Issuance of common stock	43	15	—
Dividends paid	(52)	(37)	—
Purchase of treasury stock	(354)	(398)	—
Advances (to) from Old Marriott	—	(100)	576
Cash provided by (used in) financing activities	175	301	577
Increase/(Decrease) in Cash and Equivalents	99	182	73
Cash and Equivalents, beginning of year	390	208	135
Cash and Equivalents, end of year	$489	$ 390	$ 208

Overview of the Statement of Cash Flows

OBJECTIVE

1 Describe the statement of cash flows, and define *cash* and *cash equivalents*

The **statement of cash flows** shows how a company's operating, investing, and financing activities have affected cash during an accounting period. It explains the net increase (or decrease) in cash during the accounting period. For purposes of preparing this statement, **cash** is defined to include both cash and cash equivalents. **Cash equivalents** are defined by the FASB as short-term, highly liquid investments, including money market accounts, commercial paper, and U.S. Treasury bills. A company maintains cash equivalents to earn interest on cash that would otherwise remain unused temporarily. Suppose, for example, that a company has $1,000,000 that it will not need for 30 days. To earn a return on this amount, the company may place the cash in an account that earns interest (such as a money market account), it may loan the cash to another corporation by purchasing that corporation's short-term notes (commercial paper), or it may purchase a short-term obligation of the U.S. government (Treasury bills). In this context, short-term refers to original maturities of 90 days or less. Since cash and cash

VIDEO CASE

Goodyear Tire & Rubber Company

Objectives

- To state the purposes of the statement of cash flows.
- To identify the three components of the statement of cash flows.
- To identify the reasons why cash flows from operating activities usually differs from net income.
- To understand the importance of cash flows from investing and financing activities.

Background for the Case

Goodyear was founded in 1898 by Frank Seiberling, who borrowed $3,500 to start a bicycle tire factory and subse-

quently began making tires for horseless carriages. Today Goodyear is the world's largest tire and rubber company, with factories in 28 countries and more than 100,000 employees. In a recent year, sales exceeded $14 billion.

In addition to Goodyear brand tires, the company makes Dunlop, Kelly, Fulda, Lee, Sava, and Debica tires and rubber products for the automotive and industrial markets.

Goodyear's vision is to be ranked by all measures as the best tire and rubber company in the world. It intends to accomplish this vision by achieving

- fast and profitable growth in all core businesses.

- a number 1 or 2 market position.
- strategic acquisitions and expansions.
- lowest cost producer.

To achieve these objectives, especially "fast and profitable growth" and "strategic acquisitions and expansions," Goodyear will need adequate funding. Management expects the funding to come from strong cash flows, divestiture of underperforming, nonstrategic assets, and debit issues. Within this framework, management must maintain the company's financial health and a strong balance sheet, with a debt to debt plus equity ratio of 25 to 30 percent.

Goodyear's performance in meeting the challenge of achieving adequate funding requires an ability to read and understand the statement of cash flows.

For more information about Goodyear Tire & Rubber Company, visit the company's web site through the Needles Accounting Resource Center at:
http://college.hmco.com

Required

1. What are the purposes and three main components of the statement of cash flows?

2. What is the most important amount in the statement of cash flows and why?

3. What is the relationship of cash flows from operating activities to net income for Goodyear, and how do you account for the difference?

4. What are the principal investing and financing activities for Goodyear?

equivalents are considered the same, transfers between the Cash account and cash equivalents are not treated as cash receipts or cash payments. In effect, cash equivalents are combined with the Cash account on the statement of cash flows.

Cash equivalents should not be confused with short-term investments or marketable securities, which are not combined with the Cash account on the statement of cash flows. Purchases of marketable securities are treated as cash outflows and sales of marketable securities as cash inflows on the statement of cash flows. In this chapter, cash will be assumed to include cash and cash equivalents.

Purposes of the Statement of Cash Flows

OBJECTIVE

2 State the principal purposes and uses of the statement of cash flows

The primary purpose of the statement of cash flows is to provide information about a company's cash receipts and cash payments during an accounting period. A secondary purpose of the statement is to provide information about a company's operating, investing, and financing activities during the accounting period. Some information about those activities may be inferred by examining other financial statements, but it is on the statement of cash flows that all the transactions affecting cash are summarized.

Internal and External Uses of the Statement of Cash Flows

The statement of cash flows is useful internally to management and externally to investors and creditors. Management uses the statement to assess liquidity, to determine dividend policy, and to evaluate the effects of major policy decisions involving investments and financing. In other words, management may use the statement to determine if short-term financing is needed to pay current liabilities, to decide whether to raise or lower dividends, and to plan for investing and financing needs.

Investors and creditors will find the statement useful in assessing the company's ability to manage cash flows, to generate positive future cash flows, to pay its liabilities, to pay dividends and interest, and to anticipate its need for additional financing. Also, they may use the statement to explain the differences between net income on the income statement and the net cash flows generated from operations. In addition, the statement shows both the cash and the noncash effects of investing and financing activities during the accounting period.

Classification of Cash Flows

OBJECTIVE

3 Identify the principal components of the classifications of cash flows, and state the significance of noncash investing and financing transactions

The statement of cash flows classifies cash receipts and cash payments into the categories of operating, investing, and financing activities. The components of these activities are illustrated in Figure 1 and summarized below.

1. **Operating activities** include the cash effects of transactions and other events that enter into the determination of net income. Included in this category as cash inflows are cash receipts from customers for goods and services, interest and dividends received on loans and investments, and sales of trading securities. Included as cash outflows are cash payments for wages, goods and services, expenses, interest, taxes, and purchases of trading securities. In effect, the income statement is changed from an accrual to a cash basis.

2. **Investing activities** include the acquiring and selling of long-term assets, the acquiring and selling of marketable securities other than trading securities or cash equivalents, and the making and collecting of loans. Cash inflows include the cash received from selling long-term assets and marketable securities and from collecting loans. Cash outflows include the cash expended for purchases of long-term assets and marketable securities and the cash loaned to borrowers.

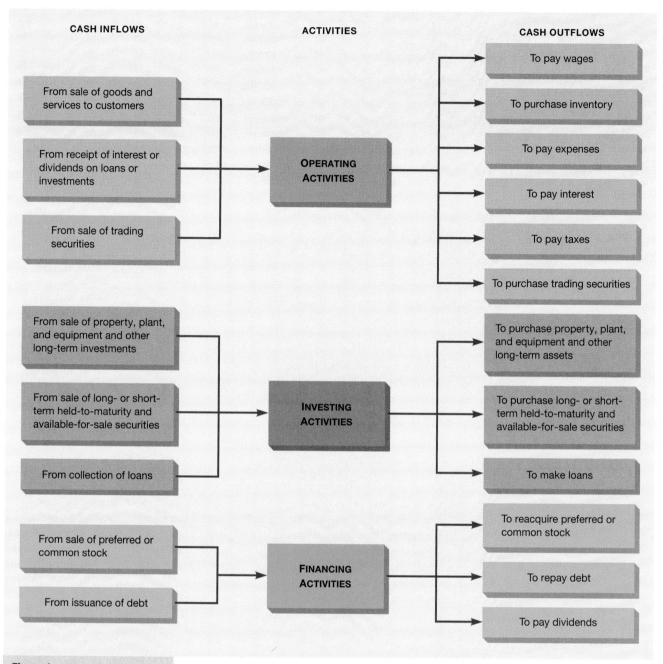

Figure 1
Classification of Cash Inflows and Cash Outflows

3. **Financing activities** include obtaining resources from or returning resources to owners and providing them with a return on their investment, and obtaining resources from creditors and repaying the amounts borrowed or otherwise settling the obligations. Cash inflows include the proceeds from issues of stocks and from short-term and long-term borrowing. Cash outflows include the repayments of loans (excluding interest) and payments to owners, including cash dividends. Treasury stock transactions are also considered financing activities. Repayments of accounts payable or accrued liabilities are not considered repayments of loans under financing activities, but are classified as cash outflows under operating activities.

A company will occasionally engage in significant **noncash investing and financing transactions** involving only long-term assets, long-term liabilities, or

stockholders' equity, such as the exchange of a long-term asset for a long-term liability or the settlement of a debt by issuing capital stock. For instance, a company might take out a long-term mortgage for the purchase of land and a building, or it might convert long-term bonds into common stock. Such transactions represent significant investing and financing activities, but they would not be reflected on the statement of cash flows because they do not involve either cash inflows or cash outflows. However, one purpose of the statement of cash flows is to show investing and financing activities, and because such transactions will affect future cash flows, the FASB has determined that they should be disclosed in a separate schedule as part of the statement of cash flows. In this way, the reader of the statement will see the company's investing and financing activities more clearly.

Format of the Statement of Cash Flows

 The statement of cash flows, as shown in the Financial Highlights for Marriott International at the beginning of this chapter, is divided into three sections. The first section, cash flows from operating activities, is presented using the indirect method. This is the most common method and is explained in learning objective 5 of this chapter. The other two sections of the statement of cash flows are the cash flows from investing activities and the cash flows from financing activities. The individual cash inflows and outflows from investing and financing activities are shown separately in their respective categories. Normally, cash outflows for the purchase of plant assets are shown separately from cash inflows from the disposal of plant assets. However, some companies follow the practice of combining these two lines in order to show the net amount of outflow, because the inflows are not usually material.

A reconciliation of the beginning and ending balances of cash is shown near the bottom of the statement. It shows that Marriott International had a net increase in cash of $99 million in 1999, which together with the beginning balance of $390 million results in $489 million of cash and cash equivalents on hand at the end of the year.

Analyzing the Statement of Cash Flows

OBJECTIVE

4 Analyze the statement of cash flows

Like the other financial statements, the statement of cash flows can be analyzed to reveal significant relationships. Two areas analysts examine when studying a company are cash-generating efficiency and free cash flow.

Cash-Generating Efficiency

Cash-generating efficiency is the ability of a company to generate cash from its current or continuing operations. Three ratios are helpful in measuring cash-generating efficiency: cash flow yield, cash flows to sales, and cash flows to assets. These ratios are computed and discussed below for Marriott International for 1999.[4] Data for the computations are obtained from the Financial Highlights for Marriott International at the beginning of this chapter and below; all dollar amounts used to compute the ratios are stated in millions.

Cash flow yield is the ratio of net cash flows from operating activities to net income, as follows:

$$\text{Cash Flow Yield} = \frac{\text{Net Cash Flows from Operating Activities}}{\text{Net Income}}$$

$$= \frac{\$711}{\$400}$$

$$= 1.8 \text{ times}$$

Marriott International provides a good cash flow yield of 1.8 times; that is, operating activities are generating about 80 percent more cash flow than net income. If special items, such as discontinued operations, appear on the income statement and are material, income from continuing operations should be used as the denominator.

Financial Highlights for Marriott International

(In millions of dollars)

	1999	1998	1997
Net Sales	$8,739	$7,968	$7,236
Total Assets	7,324	6,233	5,161

Cash flows to sales is the ratio of net cash flows from operating activities to sales.

$$\text{Cash Flows to Sales} = \frac{\text{Net Cash Flows from Operating Activities}}{\text{Net Sales}}$$

$$= \frac{\$711}{\$8,739}$$

$$= 8.1\%$$

Marriott generates cash flows to sales of 8.1 percent. The company generated a positive but relatively small percentage of net cash from sales.

Cash flows to assets is the ratio of net cash flows from operating activities to average total assets, as follows:

$$\text{Cash Flows to Assets} = \frac{\text{Net Cash Flows from Operating Activities}}{\text{Average Total Assets}}$$

$$= \frac{\$711}{(\$7,324 + \$6,233) \div 2}$$

$$= 10.5\%$$

The cash flows to assets is higher than cash flows to sales because Marriott has a good asset turnover ratio (sales ÷ average total assets) of approximately 1.3 times (10.5% ÷ 8.1%). Cash flows to sales and cash flows to assets are closely related to the profitability measures profit margin and return on assets. They exceed those measures by the amount of the cash flow yield ratio because cash flow yield is the ratio of net cash flows from operating activities to net income.

Although Marriott's cash flow yield and cash flows to assets are relatively good, its efficiency at generating cash flows from operating activities, as measured by cash flows to sales, could be improved.

Free Cash Flow

It would seem logical for the analysis to move along to investing and financing activities. For example, in 1999 Marriott has a net cash outflow of $787 million in the investing activities section, which could indicate that the company is expanding. However, that figure mixes capital expenditures for plant assets, which reflect management's expansion of operations, with the acquisition of hotel chains and loans and repayments. Also, cash flows from financing activities provided $175 million, but that figure combines financing activities associated with long-term debt and stocks with dividends paid to stockholders. While something can be learned by looking at those broad categories, many analysts find it more informative to go beyond them and focus on a computation called free cash flow.

Free cash flow is the amount of cash that remains after deducting the funds the company must commit to continue operating at its planned level. The commitments must cover current or continuing operations, interest, income taxes, dividends, and net capital expenditures. Cash requirements for current or continuing operations, interest, and income taxes must be paid or the company's creditors and the government can take legal action. Although the payment of dividends is not strictly required, dividends normally represent a commitment to stockholders. If these payments are reduced or eliminated, stockholders will be unhappy and the price of the company's stock will fall. Net capital expenditures represent management's plans for the future.

If free cash flow is positive, it means that the company has met all of its planned cash commitments and has cash available to reduce debt or expand. A negative free cash flow means that the company will have to sell investments, borrow money, or issue stock in the short term to continue at its planned levels. If free cash flow remains negative for several years, a company may not be able to raise cash by issuing stock or bonds.

Since cash commitments for current or continuing operations, interest, and income taxes are incorporated in cash flows from current operations, free cash flow for Marriott is computed as follows (in millions):

$$\text{Free Cash Flow} = \text{Net Cash Flows from Operating Activities} - \text{Dividends}$$
$$- \text{Purchases of Plant Assets} + \text{Sales of Plant Assets}$$

$$= \$711 - \$52 - \$929 + \$436$$

$$= \$166$$

Purchases and sales of plant assets appear in the investing activities section of the statement of cash flows. Marriott reports both capital expenditures and dispositions of property and equipment. Dividends are found in the financing activities section. Marriott has positive free cash flow of $166 million due primarily to its strong operating cash flow of $711 million and $436 million cash received on disposal of property and equipment. The cash provided by financing activities was the lowest in three years, only $175 million, and possible because of increasing cash provided by operations. The company repaid long-term debt of $293 million ($173 + $120) while issuing new debt of $831 million. Marriott also issued common stock in the amount of $43 million and purchased treasury stock for $354 million. The result is that financing activities were a positive $175 million.

Cash flows can vary from year to year, so it is best to look at trends in cash flow measures over several years when analyzing a company's cash flows. Marriott's cash flow yield has shown little variation over the past three years. Management sums up in the annual report:

Cash from Operations
The company's operating cash flow is stable, and typically does not fluctuate widely within an economic cycle.[8]

The Indirect Method of Preparing the Statement of Cash Flows

OBJECTIVE

5 Use the indirect method to determine cash flows from operating activities

To demonstrate the preparation of the statement of cash flows, we will work through an example step by step. The data for this example are presented in Exhibits 1 and 2. Those two exhibits present Ryan Corporation's balance sheets for December 31, 20x1 and 20x0, and its 20x1 income statement. Since the changes in the balance sheet accounts will be used for analysis, those changes are shown in Exhibit 1. Whether the change in each account is an increase or a decrease is also shown. In addition, Exhibit 2 contains data about transactions that affected non-current accounts. Those transactions would be identified by the company's accountants from the records.

There are four steps in preparing the statement of cash flows:

1. Determine cash flows from operating activities.
2. Determine cash flows from investing activities.
3. Determine cash flows from financing activities.
4. Use the information obtained in the first three steps to compile the statement of cash flows.

Determining Cash Flows from Operating Activities

The first step in preparing the statement of cash flows is to determine cash flows from operating activities. The income statement indicates a business's success or failure in earning an income from its operating activities, but it does not reflect the inflow and outflow of cash from those activities. The reason is that the income statement is prepared on an accrual basis. Revenues are recorded even though the

	20x1	20x0	Change	Increase or Decrease
Ryan Corporation **Comparative Balance Sheets** **December 31, 20x1 and 20x0**				
Assets				
Current Assets				
Cash	$ 46,000	$ 15,000	$ 31,000	Increase
Accounts Receivable (net)	47,000	55,000	(8,000)	Decrease
Inventory	144,000	110,000	34,000	Increase
Prepaid Expenses	1,000	5,000	(4,000)	Decrease
Total Current Assets	$238,000	$185,000	$ 53,000	
Investments Available for Sale	$115,000	$127,000	($ 12,000)	Decrease
Plant Assets				
Plant Assets	$715,000	$505,000	$210,000	Increase
Accumulated Depreciation	(103,000)	(68,000)	(35,000)	Increase
Total Plant Assets	$612,000	$437,000	$175,000	
Total Assets	$965,000	$749,000	$216,000	
Liabilities				
Current Liabilities				
Accounts Payable	$ 50,000	$ 43,000	$ 7,000	Increase
Accrued Liabilities	12,000	9,000	3,000	Increase
Income Taxes Payable	3,000	5,000	(2,000)	Decrease
Total Current Liabilities	$ 65,000	$ 57,000	$ 8,000	
Long-Term Liabilities				
Bonds Payable	295,000	245,000	50,000	Increase
Total Liabilities	$360,000	$302,000	$ 58,000	
Stockholders' Equity				
Common Stock, $5 par value	$276,000	$200,000	$ 76,000	Increase
Paid-in Capital in Excess of Par Value, Common	189,000	115,000	74,000	Increase
Retained Earnings	140,000	132,000	8,000	Increase
Total Stockholders' Equity	$605,000	$447,000	$158,000	
Total Liabilities and Stockholders' Equity	$965,000	$749,000	$216,000	

Exhibit 1
**Comparative Balance Sheets
with Changes in Accounts
Indicated for Ryan Corporation**

cash for them may not have been received, and expenses are recorded even though the cash for them may not have been expended. As a result, to arrive at cash flows from operations, the figures on the income statement must be converted from an accrual basis to a cash basis.

There are two methods of converting the income statement from an accrual basis to a cash basis: the direct method and the indirect method. Under the **direct method**, each item on the income statement is adjusted from the accrual basis to the cash basis. The result is a statement that begins with cash receipts from sales

Exhibit 2
Income Statement and Other Information on Noncurrent Accounts for Ryan Corporation

Ryan Corporation
Income Statement
For the Year Ended December 31, 20x1

Net Sales		$698,000
Cost of Goods Sold		520,000
Gross Margin		$178,000
Operating Expenses (including Depreciation Expense of $37,000)		147,000
Operating Income		$ 31,000
Other Income (Expenses)		
Interest Expense	($23,000)	
Interest Income	6,000	
Gain on Sale of Investments	12,000	
Loss on Sale of Plant Assets	(3,000)	(8,000)
Income Before Income Taxes		$ 23,000
Income Taxes		7,000
Net Income		$ 16,000

Other transactions affecting noncurrent accounts during 20x1:

1. Purchased investments in the amount of $78,000.
2. Sold investments for $102,000 that cost $90,000.
3. Purchased plant assets in the amount of $120,000.
4. Sold plant assets that cost $10,000 with accumulated depreciation of $2,000 for $5,000.
5. Issued $100,000 of bonds at face value in a noncash exchange for plant assets.
6. Repaid $50,000 of bonds at face value at maturity.
7. Issued 15,200 shares of $5 par value common stock for $150,000.
8. Paid cash dividends in the amount of $8,000.

and interest and deducts cash payments for purchases, operating expenses, interest payments, and income taxes to arrive at net cash flows from operating activities. The **indirect method**, on the other hand, does not require the individual adjustment of each item on the income statement, but lists only those adjustments necessary to convert net income to cash flows from operations. Because the indirect method is more common, it will be used to illustrate the conversion of the income statement to a cash basis in the sections that follow. The direct method is presented in a supplemental objective at the end of the chapter.

FOCUS ON BUSINESS PRACTICE

The direct method and the indirect method of determining cash flows from operating activities produce the same results. If the direct method is used, a reconciliation of net income to net cash flows from operating activities must be provided in a separate schedule. The FASB recommends, but does not require, the direct method, but a survey of large companies showed that an overwhelming majority, 98 percent, chose to use the indirect method.[9] The reasons for choosing the indirect method vary, but chief financial officers tend to prefer it because it is easier and less expensive to implement. Also, with the required reconciliation under the direct method, the same information is provided as under the indirect method.

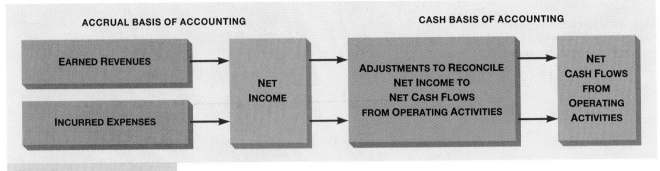

**Figure 2
Indirect Method of
Determining Net Cash Flows
from Operating Activities**

The indirect method, as illustrated in Figure 2, focuses on items from the income statement that must be adjusted to reconcile net income to net cash flows from operating activities. The items that require attention are those that affect net income but not net cash flows from operating activities, such as depreciation and amortization, gains and losses, and changes in the balances of current asset and current liability accounts. The reconciliation of Ryan Corporation's net income to net cash flows from operating activities is shown in Exhibit 3. Each adjustment is discussed in the following sections.

DEPRECIATION   Cash payments for plant assets, intangibles, and natural resources occur when the assets are purchased and are reflected as investing activities on the statement of cash flows at that time. When depreciation expense, amortization expense, and depletion expense appear on the income statement, they simply indicate allocations of the costs of the original purchases to the current accounting period; they do not affect net cash flows in the current period. The amount of such expenses can usually be found by referring to the income statement or a note to the financial statements. For Ryan Corporation, the income statement reveals depreciation expense of $37,000, which would have been recorded as follows:

A = L + OE Depreciation Expense   37,000
–   –   Accumulated Depreciation   37,000
                    To record annual depreciation on plant assets

The recording of depreciation involved no outlay of cash even though depreciation expense appears on the income statement. Thus, to derive cash flows from operations, an adjustment for depreciation is needed to increase net income by the amount of depreciation recorded.

GAINS AND LOSSES   Gains and losses that appear on the income statement also do not affect cash flows from operating activities and need to be removed from this section of the statement of cash flows. The cash receipts generated from the disposal of the assets that resulted in the gains or losses are shown in the investing section of the statement of cash flows. Thus, gains and losses are removed from net income (preventing double counting) to reconcile net income to cash flows from operating activities. For example, on the income statement, Ryan Corporation showed a $12,000 gain on the sale of investments, and this is subtracted from net income to reconcile net income to net cash flows from operating activities. The reason for this is that the $12,000 is already included (added) in the investing activities section as part of the $102,000 cash from the sale of the investment. Because the gain is included in the calculation of net income, the $12,000 gain needs to be subtracted to prevent double counting. Also, Ryan Corporation showed a $3,000 loss on the sale of plant assets. Following the same logic, the $3,000 loss is already reflected in the $5,000 sale of plant assets in the investing activities section. Thus, the $3,000 is added to net income to reconcile net income to net cash flows from operating activities.

Exhibit 3
Schedule of Cash Flows from Operating Activities: Indirect Method

Ryan Corporation
Schedule of Cash Flows from Operating Activities
For the Year Ended December 31, 20x1

Cash Flows from Operating Activities

Net Income		$16,000
Adjustments to Reconcile Net Income to Net		
Cash Flows from Operating Activities		
Depreciation	$37,000	
Gain on Sale of Investments	(12,000)	
Loss on Sale of Plant Assets	3,000	
Changes in Current Assets and Current Liabilities		
Decrease in Accounts Receivable	8,000	
Increase in Inventory	(34,000)	
Decrease in Prepaid Expenses	4,000	
Increase in Accounts Payable	7,000	
Increase in Accrued Liabilities	3,000	
Decrease in Income Taxes Payable	(2,000)	14,000
Net Cash Flows from Operating Activities		$30,000

CHANGES IN CURRENT ASSETS Decreases in current assets other than cash have positive effects on cash flows, and increases in current assets have negative effects on cash flows. For example, refer to the balance sheets and income statement for Ryan Corporation in Exhibits 1 and 2. Note that net sales in 20x1 were $698,000 and that Accounts Receivable decreased by $8,000. Thus, cash received from sales was $706,000, calculated as follows:

$$\$706,000 = \$698,000 + \$8,000$$

Collections were $8,000 more than sales recorded for the year. This relationship may be illustrated as follows:

Accounts Receivable

Sales to Customers	Beg. Bal.	55,000	706,000 →	Cash Receipts from Customers
	→ 698,000			
	End. Bal.	47,000		

Thus, to reconcile net income to net cash flows from operating activities, the $8,000 decrease in Accounts Receivable is added to net income.

Inventory may be analyzed in the same way. For example, Exhibit 1 shows that Inventory increased by $34,000 from 20x0 to 20x1. This means that Ryan Corporation expended $34,000 more in cash for purchases than was included in cost of goods sold on the income statement. As a result of this expenditure, net income is higher than the net cash flows from operating activities, so $34,000 must be deducted from net income.

Using similar logic, the decrease of $4,000 in Prepaid Expenses is added to net income to reconcile net income to net cash flows from operations.

CHANGES IN CURRENT LIABILITIES Changes in current liabilities have the opposite effects on cash flows from those of changes in current assets. Increases in current liabilities are added to net income, and decreases in current liabilities are deducted from net income to reconcile net income to net cash flows from operating activities. For example, note from Exhibit 1 that Ryan Corporation had a

$7,000 increase in Accounts Payable from 20x0 to 20x1. This means that Ryan Corporation paid $7,000 less to creditors than what appears as purchases on the income statement. This relationship may be visualized as follows:

Accounts Payable

Cash Payments to Suppliers	←—— 547,000	Beg. Bal.	43,000	
			554,000*	←— Purchases
		End. Bal.	50,000	

*Purchases = Cost of Goods Sold ($520,000) + Increase in Inventory ($34,000).

As a result, $7,000 is added to net income to reconcile net income to net cash flows from operating activities.

Using similar logic, the increase of $3,000 in Accrued Liabilities is added to net income, but the decrease of $2,000 in Income Taxes Payable is deducted from net income to reconcile net income to net cash flows from operating activities.

SCHEDULE OF CASH FLOWS FROM OPERATING ACTIVITIES   In summary, Exhibit 3 shows that by using the indirect method, net income of $16,000 has been adjusted by reconciling items totaling $14,000 to arrive at net cash flows from operating activities of $30,000. This means that although net income was $16,000, Ryan Corporation actually had net cash flows available from operating activities of $30,000 to use for purchasing assets, reducing debts, or paying dividends.

SUMMARY OF ADJUSTMENTS   The effects of items on the income statement that do not affect cash flows may be summarized as follows:

	Add to or Deduct from Net Income
Depreciation Expense	Add
Amortization Expense	Add
Depletion Expense	Add
Losses	Add
Gains	Deduct

The adjustments for increases and decreases in current assets and current liabilities may be summarized as follows.

	Add to Net Income	Deduct from Net Income
Current Assets		
Accounts Receivable (net)	Decrease	Increase
Inventory	Decrease	Increase
Prepaid Expenses	Decrease	Increase
Current Liabilities		
Accounts Payable	Increase	Decrease
Accrued Liabilities	Increase	Decrease
Income Taxes Payable	Increase	Decrease

Determining Cash Flows from Investing Activities

OBJECTIVE

6 Determine cash flows from investing activities and financing activities

The second step in preparing the statement of cash flows is to determine cash flows from investing activities. Each account involving cash receipts and cash payments from investing activities is examined individually. The objective is to explain the change in each account balance from one year to the next.

Investing activities center on the long-term assets shown on the balance sheet, but they also include transactions affecting short-term investments from the current assets section of the balance sheet and investment gains and losses from the income statement. The balance sheets in Exhibit 1 show that Ryan Corporation has long-term assets of investments and plant assets, but no short-term investments. The income statement in Exhibit 2 shows that Ryan has investment-related items in the form of a gain on the sale of investments and a loss on the sale of plant assets.

The schedule at the bottom of Exhibit 2 lists the following five items pertaining to investing activities in 20x1:

1. Purchased investments in the amount of $78,000.
2. Sold investments for $102,000 that cost $90,000.
3. Purchased plant assets in the amount of $120,000.
4. Sold plant assets that cost $10,000 with accumulated depreciation of $2,000 for $5,000.
5. Issued $100,000 of bonds at face value in a noncash exchange for plant assets.

The following paragraphs analyze the accounts related to investing activities to determine their effects on Ryan Corporation's cash flows.

INVESTMENTS   The objective here is to explain the corporation's $12,000 decrease in investments, all of which are classified as available-for-sale securities. This is accomplished by analyzing the increases and decreases in the Investments account to determine the effects on the Cash account. Purchases increase investments, and sales decrease investments. Item 1 in Ryan's list of investing activities shows purchases of $78,000 during 20x1.

This transaction is recorded as follows:

A = L + OE
+
−

Investments	78,000	
Cash		78,000
Purchase of investments		

The entry shows that the effect of this transaction is a $78,000 decrease in cash flows.

Item 2 in the list shows a sale of investments for $102,000 that cost $90,000, which results in a gain of $12,000. This transaction was recorded as follows:

A = L + OE
+   +
−

Cash	102,000	
Investments		90,000
Gain on Sale of Investments		12,000
Sale of investments for a gain		

The effect of this transaction is a $102,000 increase in cash flows. Note that the gain on sale of investments is included in the $102,000. This is the reason it was excluded earlier (see page 722) in computing cash flows from operations. If it had been included in that section, it would have been counted twice.

The $12,000 decrease in the Investments account (unrelated to the $12,000 gain above) during 20x1 has now been explained, as seen in the following T account:

Investments

Beg. Bal.	127,000	Sales	90,000
Purchases	78,000		
End. Bal.	**115,000**		

The cash flow effects from these transactions are shown in the Cash Flows from Investing Activities section on the statement of cash flows as follows:

Purchase of Investments	($ 78,000)
Sale of Investments	102,000

Notice that purchases and sales are listed separately as cash outflows and cash inflows to give readers of the statement a complete view of investing activity. Some companies prefer to combine them into a single net amount.

If Ryan Corporation had short-term investments or marketable securities, the analysis of cash flows would be the same.

PLANT ASSETS   In the case of plant assets, it is necessary to explain the changes in both the asset account and the related accumulated depreciation account. According to Exhibit 1, Plant Assets increased by $210,000 and Accumulated Depreciation increased by $35,000. Purchases increase plant assets, and sales decrease plant assets. Accumulated depreciation is increased by the amount of depreciation expense and decreased by the removal of the accumulated depreciation associated with plant assets that are sold. Three items listed in Exhibit 2 affect plant assets. Item **3** in the list on the previous page indicates that Ryan Corporation purchased plant assets totaling $120,000 during 20x1, as shown by the following entry:

A = L + OE			
+	Plant Assets	120,000	
−	Cash		120,000
	Purchase of plant assets		

This transaction results in a cash outflow of $120,000.

Item **4** states that Ryan Corporation took plant assets that had cost $10,000 and had accumulated depreciation of $2,000, and sold them for $5,000, which resulted in a loss of $3,000. The entry to record this transaction is as follows:

A = L + OE			
+	Cash	5,000	
+ −	Accumulated Depreciation	2,000	
+	Loss on Sale of Plant Assets	3,000	
−	Plant Assets		10,000
	Sale of plant assets at a loss		

Note that in this transaction the positive cash flow is equal to the amount of cash received, or $5,000. The loss on the sale of plant assets is included here and excluded from the operating activities section (see page 722) by adjusting net income for the amount of the loss. The amount of a loss or gain on the sale of an asset is determined by the amount of cash received and does not represent a cash outflow or inflow.

The disclosure of these two transactions in the investing activities section of the statement of cash flows is as follows:

Purchase of Plant Assets	($120,000)
Sale of Plant Assets	5,000

As with investments, cash outflows and cash inflows are not combined here, but are sometimes combined into a single net amount.

Item **5** on the list of Ryan's investing activities is a noncash exchange that affects two long-term accounts, Plant Assets and Bonds Payable. It was recorded as follows:

A = L + OE			
+ +	Plant Assets	100,000	
	Bonds Payable		100,000
	Issued bonds at face value for plant assets		

Although this transaction does not involve an inflow or outflow of cash, it is a significant transaction involving both an investing activity (the purchase of plant assets) and a financing activity (the issue of bonds payable). Because one purpose of the statement of cash flows is to show important investing and financing activities, the transaction is listed in a separate schedule, either at the bottom of the statement of cash flows or accompanying the statement, as follows:

Schedule of Noncash Investing and Financing Transactions

Issue of Bonds Payable for Plant Assets $100,000

Through our analysis of the preceding transactions and the depreciation expense for plant assets of $37,000, all the changes in the plant assets accounts have now been accounted for, as shown in the following T accounts:

Plant Assets

Beg. Bal.	505,000	Sale	10,000
Cash Purchase	120,000		
Noncash Purchase	100,000		
End. Bal.	715,000		

Accumulated Depreciation

Sale	2,000	Beg. Bal.	68,000
		Dep. Exp.	37,000
		End. Bal.	103,000

If the balance sheet had included specific plant asset accounts, such as Buildings and Equipment and their related accumulated depreciation accounts, or other long-term asset accounts, such as intangibles or natural resources, the analysis would have been the same.

Determining Cash Flows from Financing Activities

The third step in preparing the statement of cash flows is to determine cash flows from financing activities. The procedure is similar to the analysis of investing activities, including treatment of related gains or losses. The only difference is that the accounts to be analyzed are the short-term borrowings, long-term liabilities, and stockholders' equity accounts. Cash dividends from the statement of stockholders' equity must also be considered. Since Ryan Corporation does not have short-term borrowings, only long-term liabilities and stockholders' equity accounts are considered here. The following items from Exhibit 2 pertain to Ryan Corporation's financing activities in 20x1:

5. Issued $100,000 of bonds at face value in a noncash exchange for plant assets.
6. Repaid $50,000 of bonds at face value at maturity.
7. Issued 15,200 shares of $5 par value common stock for $150,000.
8. Paid cash dividends in the amount of $8,000.

BONDS PAYABLE Exhibit 1 shows that Bonds Payable increased by $50,000 in 20x1. This account is affected by items **5** and **6**. Item **5** was analyzed in connection with plant assets. It is reported on the schedule of noncash investing and financing transactions (see Exhibit 4), but it must be remembered here in preparing the T account for Bonds Payable. Item **6** results in a cash outflow, which can be seen in the following transaction.

A = L + OE Bonds Payable 50,000
−   −   Cash 50,000
      Repayment of bonds at face value
      at maturity

Exhibit 4
Statement of Cash Flows:
Indirect Method

Ryan Corporation
Statement of Cash Flows
For the Year Ended December 31, 20x1

Cash Flows from Operating Activities			
Net Income			$ 16,000
Adjustments to Reconcile Net Income to Net			
Cash Flows from Operating Activities			
Depreciation		$ 37,000	
Gain on Sale of Investments		(12,000)	
Loss on Sale of Plant Assets		3,000	
Changes in Current Assets and Current Liabilities			
Decrease in Accounts Receivable		8,000	
Increase in Inventory		(34,000)	
Decrease in Prepaid Expenses		4,000	
Increase in Accounts Payable		7,000	
Increase in Accrued Liabilities		3,000	
Decrease in Income Taxes Payable		(2,000)	14,000
Net Cash Flows from Operating Activities			$ 30,000
Cash Flows from Investing Activities			
Purchase of Investments		($ 78,000)	
Sale of Investments		102,000	
Purchase of Plant Assets		(120,000)	
Sale of Plant Assets		5,000	
Net Cash Flows from Investing Activities			(91,000)
Cash Flows from Financing Activities			
Repayment of Bonds		($ 50,000)	
Issue of Common Stock		150,000	
Dividends Paid		(8,000)	
Net Cash Flows from Financing Activities			92,000
Net Increase (Decrease) in Cash			$ 31,000
Cash at Beginning of Year			15,000
Cash at End of Year			$ 46,000

Schedule of Noncash Investing and Financing Transactions

Issue of Bonds Payable for Plant Assets			$100,000

This cash outflow is shown in the financing activities section of the statement of cash flows as follows:

Repayment of Bonds   ($50,000)

The change in the Bonds Payable account can be explained as follows:

Bonds Payable

Repayment	50,000	Beg. Bal.	245,000
		Noncash Issue	100,000
		End. Bal.	295,000

If Ryan Corporation had notes payable, either short-term or long-term, the analysis would be the same.

COMMON STOCK   As with plant assets, related stockholders' equity accounts should be analyzed together. For example, Paid-in Capital in Excess of Par Value, Common should be examined with Common Stock. In 20x1 Ryan Corporation's Common Stock account increased by $76,000 and Paid-in Capital in Excess of Par Value, Common increased by $74,000. Those increases are explained by item **7** in the list on page 727, which states that Ryan Corporation issued 15,200 shares of stock for $150,000.

The entry to record the cash inflow was as follows:

A = L + OE
+   +
        +

Cash	150,000	
Common Stock		76,000
Paid-in Capital in Excess of Par Value, Common		74,000
Issued 15,200 shares of $5 par value common stock		

The cash inflow is shown in the financing activities section of the statement of cash flows as follows:

Issue of Common Stock $150,000

The analysis of this transaction is all that is needed to explain the changes in the two accounts during 20x1, as follows:

Common Stock		Paid-in Capital in Excess of Par Value, Common	
Beg. Bal. 200,000		Beg. Bal. 115,000	
Issue 76,000		Issue 74,000	
End. Bal. 276,000		End. Bal. 189,000	

RETAINED EARNINGS   At this point in the analysis, several items that affect retained earnings have already been dealt with. For instance, in the case of Ryan Corporation, net income was used as part of the analysis of cash flows from operating activities. The only other item affecting the retained earnings of Ryan Corporation is the payment of $8,000 in cash dividends (item **8** in the list on page 727), as reflected by the following transaction.

A = L + OE
−   −

Retained Earnings	8,000	
Cash		8,000
Cash dividends for 20x1		

Ryan Corporation would have declared the dividend before paying it and therefore would have debited the Cash Dividends Declared account instead of Retained Earnings, but after paying the dividend and closing the Cash Dividends Declared account to Retained Earnings, the effect is as shown. Cash dividends are displayed in the financing activities section of the statement of cash flows:

Dividends Paid   ($8,000)

The following T account shows the change in the Retained Earnings account:

Retained Earnings			
Dividends 8,000	Beg. Bal.	132,000	
	Net Income	16,000	
	End. Bal.	140,000	

Compiling the Statement of Cash Flows

OBJECTIVE

7 Use the indirect method to prepare a statement of cash flows

At this point in the analysis, all income statement items have been analyzed, all balance sheet changes have been explained, and all additional information has been taken into account. The resulting information may now be assembled into a statement of cash flows for Ryan Corporation, as presented in Exhibit 4. The Schedule of Noncash Investing and Financing Transactions is presented at the bottom of the statement.

Preparing the Work Sheet

SUPPLEMENTAL OBJECTIVE

8 Prepare a work sheet for the statement of cash flows

To assist in preparing the statement of cash flows for more complex companies, accountants have developed a work sheet approach. The work sheet approach uses the indirect method of determining cash flows from operating activities because of its basis in changes in the balance sheet accounts.

Procedures in Preparing the Work Sheet

The work sheet for Ryan Corporation is presented in Exhibit 5. The work sheet has four columns, labeled as follows:

Column A: Description

Column B: Account balances for the end of the prior year (20x0)

Column C: Analysis of transactions for the current year

Column D: Account balances for the end of the current year (20x1)

Five steps are followed in preparing the work sheet. As you read each one, refer to Exhibit 5.

1. Enter the account names from the balance sheets (Exhibit 1) in column A. Note that all accounts with debit balances are listed first, followed by all accounts with credit balances.

2. Enter the account balances for 20x0 in column B and the account balances for 20x1 in column D. In each column, total the debits and the credits. The total debits should equal the total credits in each column. (This is a check of whether all accounts were correctly transferred from the balance sheets.)

3. Below the data entered in step **2,** insert the headings Cash Flows from Operating Activities, Cash Flows from Investing Activities, and Cash Flows from Financing Activities, leaving several lines of space between each one. As you do the analysis in step **4,** write the results in the appropriate categories.

4. Analyze the changes in each balance sheet account, using information from both the income statement (see Exhibit 2) and other transactions affecting noncurrent accounts during 20x1. (The procedures for this analysis are presented in the next section.) Enter the results in the debit and credit columns. Identify each item with a letter. On the first line, identify the change in cash with an (x). In a complex situation, these letters will refer to a list of explanations on another working paper.

5. When all the changes in the balance sheet accounts have been explained, add the debit and credit columns in both the top and the bottom portions of column C. The debit and credit columns in the top portion should equal each other. They should *not* be equal in the bottom portion. If no errors have been

Exhibit 5
Work Sheet for the Statement of Cash Flows

Ryan Corporation
Work Sheet for Statement of Cash Flows
For the Year Ended December 31, 20x1

(A) → Description	Account Balances 12/31/x0	Analysis of Transactions		Account Balances 12/31/x1
		Debit	Credit	
Debits				
Cash	15,000	(x) 31,000		46,000
Accounts Receivable (net)	55,000		(b) 8,000	47,000
Inventory	110,000	(c) 34,000		144,000
Prepaid Expenses	5,000		(d) 4,000	1,000
Investments Available for Sale	127,000	(h) 78,000	(i) 90,000	115,000
Plant Assets	505,000	(j) 120,000	(k) 10,000	715,000
		(l) 100,000		
Total Debits	817,000			1,068,000
Credits				
Accumulated Depreciation	68,000	(k) 2,000	(m) 37,000	103,000
Accounts Payable	43,000		(e) 7,000	50,000
Accrued Liabilities	9,000		(f) 3,000	12,000
Income Taxes Payable	5,000	(g) 2,000		3,000
Bonds Payable	245,000	(n) 50,000	(l) 100,000	295,000
Common Stock	200,000		(o) 76,000	276,000
Paid-in Capital	115,000		(o) 74,000	189,000
Retained Earnings	132,000	(p) 8,000	(a) 16,000	140,000
Total Credits	817,000	425,000	425,000	1,068,000
Cash Flows from Operating Activities				
Net Income		(a) 16,000		
Decrease in Accounts Receivable		(b) 8,000		
Increase in Inventory			(c) 34,000	
Decrease in Prepaid Expenses		(d) 4,000		
Increase in Accounts Payable		(e) 7,000		
Increase in Accrued Liabilities		(f) 3,000		
Decrease in Income Taxes Payable			(g) 2,000	
Gain on Sale of Investments			(i) 12,000	
Loss on Sale of Plant Assets		(k) 3,000		
Depreciation Expense		(m) 37,000		
Cash Flows from Investing Activities				
Purchase of Investments			(h) 78,000	
Sale of Investments		(i) 102,000		
Purchase of Plant Assets			(j) 120,000	
Sale of Plant Assets		(k) 5,000		
Cash Flows from Financing Activities				
Repayment of Bonds			(n) 50,000	
Issue of Common Stock		(o) 150,000		
Dividends Paid			(p) 8,000	
		335,000	304,000	
Net Increase in Cash			(x) 31,000	
		335,000	335,000	

made, the difference between columns in the bottom portion should equal the increase or decrease in the Cash account, identified with an (x) on the first line of the work sheet. Add this difference to the lesser of the two columns, and identify it as either an increase or a decrease in cash. Label the change with an (x) and compare it with the change in Cash on the first line of the work sheet, also labeled (x). The amounts should be equal, as they are in Exhibit 5, where the net increase in cash is $31,000. Also, the new totals from the debit and credit columns should be equal.

When the work sheet is complete, the statement of cash flows may be prepared using the information in the lower half of the work sheet.

Analyzing the Changes in Balance Sheet Accounts

The most important step in preparing the work sheet is the analysis of the changes in the balance sheet accounts (step **4**). Although a number of transactions and reclassifications must be analyzed and recorded, the overall procedure is systematic and not overly complicated. It is as follows:

1. Record net income.
2. Account for changes in current assets and current liabilities.
3. Use the information about other transactions to account for changes in non-current accounts.
4. Reclassify any other income and expense items not already dealt with.

In the following explanations, the identification letters refer to the corresponding transactions and reclassifications on the work sheet.

a. Net Income   Net income results in an increase in Retained Earnings (entry **a**). Under the indirect method, it is the starting point for determining cash flows from operating activities. Under this method, additions and deductions are made to net income to arrive at cash flows from operating activities.

b–g. Changes in Current Assets and Current Liabilities   Entries **b** to **g** record the effects on cash flows of the changes in current assets and current liabilities. In each case, there is a debit or credit to the current asset or current liability to account for the change from year to year and a corresponding debit or credit in the operating activities section of the work sheet. For example, work sheet entry **b** records the decrease in Accounts Receivable as a credit (decrease) to Accounts Receivable and as a debit in the operating activities section because the decrease has a positive effect on cash flows. Work sheet entries **c–g** reflect the effects on cash flows from operating activities of the changes in the other current assets and current liabilities. As you study these entries, note how the effects of each entry on cash flows are automatically determined by debits or credits reflecting changes in the balance sheet accounts.

h–i. Investments   Among the other transactions affecting noncurrent accounts during 20x1 (see Exhibit 2 on page 721), two pertain to investments. One is the purchase for $78,000, and the other is the sale at $102,000. The purchase (entry **h**) is recorded on the work sheet as a cash flow in the investing activities section. Note that instead of a credit to Cash, a credit entry with the appropriate designation is made in the appropriate section in the lower half of the work sheet. The sale transaction (entry **i**) is more complicated because it involves a gain that appears on the income statement and is included in net income. This entry records the cash inflow in the investing activities section, accounts for the remaining difference in the Investments account, and removes the gain on sale of investments from net income.

j–m. PLANT ASSETS AND ACCUMULATED DEPRECIATION The four transactions that affect plant assets and the related accumulated depreciation are the purchase of plant assets, the sale of plant assets at a loss, the noncash exchange of bonds for plant assets, and the depreciation expense for the year. Because these transactions may appear complicated, it is important to work through them systematically when preparing the work sheet. First, the purchase of plant assets for $120,000 is entered (entry **j**) in the same way the purchase of investments was entered in entry **h**. Second, the sale of plant assets (entry **k**) is similar to the sale of investments, except that a loss is involved. The cash inflow from this transaction is $5,000. The rest of the entry is necessary in order to add the loss back into net income in the operating activities section of the statement of cash flows (since it was deducted to arrive at net income and no cash outflow resulted) and to record the effects on plant assets and accumulated depreciation.

The third transaction (entry **l**) is the noncash issue of bonds for the acquisition of plant assets. Note that this transaction does not affect Cash. Still, it needs to be recorded because the objective is to account for all changes in the balance sheet accounts. It is listed at the end of the statement of cash flows (Exhibit 4) in the schedule of noncash investing and financing transactions.

At this point, the increase of $210,000 ($715,000 − $505,000) in plant assets has been explained by the two purchases less the sale ($120,000 + $100,000 − $10,000 = $210,000), but the change in Accumulated Depreciation has not been completely explained. The depreciation expense for the year needs to be entered (entry **m**). The debit is to the operating activities section of the work sheet because, as explained earlier in the chapter, no current cash outflow is required for depreciation expense. The effect of this debit is to add the amount for depreciation expense back into net income. The $35,000 increase in Accumulated Depreciation has now been explained by the sale transaction and the depreciation expense (−$2,000 + $37,000 = $35,000).

n. BONDS PAYABLE Part of the change in Bonds Payable was explained in entry **l** when a noncash transaction, a $100,000 issue of bonds in exchange for plant assets, was entered. All that remains to be entered is the repayment (entry **n**).

o. COMMON STOCK AND PAID-IN CAPITAL IN EXCESS OF PAR VALUE, COMMON One transaction affects both these accounts. It is an issue of 15,200 shares of $5 par value common stock for a total of $150,000 (entry **o**).

p. RETAINED EARNINGS Part of the change in Retained Earnings was recognized when net income was entered (entry **a**). The only remaining effect to be recognized is the $8,000 in cash dividends paid during the year (entry **p**).

x. CASH The final step is to total the debit and credit columns in the top and bottom portions of the work sheet and then to enter the net change in cash at the bottom of the work sheet. The columns in the upper half equal $425,000. In the lower half, the debit column totals $335,000 and the credit column totals $304,000. The credit difference of $31,000 (entry **x**) equals the debit change in cash on the first line of the work sheet.

The Direct Method of Preparing the Statement of Cash Flows

SUPPLEMENTAL OBJECTIVE

9 Use the direct method to determine cash flows from operating activities and prepare a statement of cash flows

To this point in the chapter, the indirect method of preparing the statement of cash flows has been used. In this section, the direct method is presented.

Determining Cash Flows from Operating Activities

The principal difference between the indirect and the direct methods appears in the cash flows from operating activities section of the statement of cash flows. As you have seen, the indirect method starts with net income from the income statement and converts it to net cash flows from operating activities by adding or subtracting items that do not affect net cash flows. The direct method takes a different approach. It converts each item on the income statement to its cash equivalent, as illustrated in Figure 3. For instance, sales are converted to cash receipts from sales, and purchases are converted to cash payments for purchases. Exhibit 6 shows the schedule of cash flows from operating activities under the direct method for Ryan Corporation. The conversion of the components of Ryan Corporation's income statement to those figures is explained in the following paragraphs.

CASH RECEIPTS FROM SALES Sales result in a positive cash flow for a company. Cash sales are direct cash inflows. Credit sales are not, because they are originally recorded as accounts receivable. When they are collected, they become cash inflows. You cannot, however, assume that credit sales are automatically inflows of cash, because the collections of accounts receivable in any one accounting period are not likely to equal credit sales. Receivables may be uncollectible, sales from a prior period may be collected in the current period, or sales from the current period may be collected in the next period. For example, if accounts receivable increase from one accounting period to the next, cash receipts from sales will not be as great as sales. On the other hand, if accounts receivable decrease from one accounting period to the next, cash receipts from sales will exceed sales.

The relationships among sales, changes in accounts receivable, and cash receipts from sales are reflected in the following formula:

$$\text{Cash Receipts from Sales} = \text{Sales} \begin{cases} + \text{ Decrease in Accounts Receivable} \\ \qquad\qquad\text{or} \\ - \text{ Increase in Accounts Receivable} \end{cases}$$

Refer to the balance sheets and income statement for Ryan Corporation in Exhibits 1 and 2. Note that sales were $698,000 in 20x1 and that accounts receivable

Figure 3
Direct Method of Determining Net Cash Flows from Operating Activities

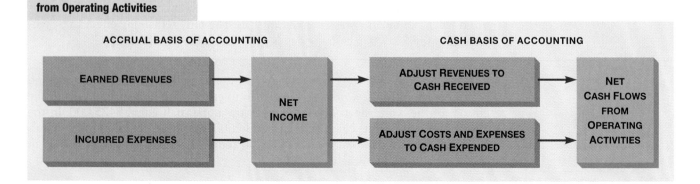

Exhibit 6
Schedule of Cash Flows from Operating Activities: Direct Method

Ryan Corporation
Schedule of Cash Flows from Operating Activities
For the Year Ended December 31, 20x1

Cash Flows from Operating Activities		
Cash Receipts from		
Sales	$706,000	
Interest Received	6,000	$712,000
Cash Payments for		
Purchases	$547,000	
Operating Expenses	103,000	
Interest	23,000	
Income Taxes	9,000	682,000
Net Cash Flows from Operating Activities		$ 30,000

decreased by $8,000. Thus, cash received from sales is $706,000:

$$\$706,000 = \$698,000 + \$8,000$$

Collections were $8,000 more than sales recorded for the year.

CASH RECEIPTS FROM INTEREST AND DIVIDENDS Although interest and dividends received are most closely associated with investment activity and are often called investment income, the FASB has decided to classify the cash received from these items as operating activities. To simplify the examples in this text, it is assumed that interest income equals interest received and that dividend income equals dividends received. Thus, based on Exhibit 2, interest received by Ryan Corporation is assumed to equal $6,000, which is the amount of interest income.

CASH PAYMENTS FOR PURCHASES Cost of goods sold (from the income statement) must be adjusted for changes in two balance sheet accounts to arrive at cash payments for purchases. First, cost of goods sold must be adjusted for changes in inventory to arrive at net purchases. Then, net purchases must be adjusted for the change in accounts payable to arrive at cash payments for purchases. If inventory has increased from one accounting period to another, net purchases will be greater than cost of goods sold because net purchases during the period have exceeded the dollar amount of the items sold during the period. If inventory has decreased, net purchases will be less than cost of goods sold. Conversely, if accounts payable have increased, cash payments for purchases will be less than net purchases; if accounts payable have decreased, cash payments for purchases will be greater than net purchases.

These relationships may be stated in equation form as follows:

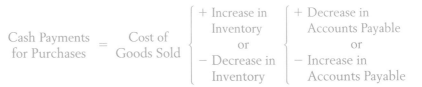

From Exhibits 1 and 2, cost of goods sold is $520,000, inventory increased by $34,000, and accounts payable increased by $7,000. Thus, cash payments for purchases is $547,000, as the following calculation shows:

$$\$547,000 = \$520,000 + \$34,000 - \$7,000$$

In this example, Ryan Corporation purchased $34,000 more inventory than it sold and paid out $7,000 less in cash than it made in purchases. The net result is that cash payments for purchases exceeded cost of goods sold by $27,000 ($547,000 − $520,000).

CASH PAYMENTS FOR OPERATING EXPENSES   Just as cost of goods sold does not represent the amount of cash paid for purchases during an accounting period, operating expenses do not match the amount of cash paid to employees, suppliers, and others for goods and services. Three adjustments must be made to operating expenses to arrive at the cash outflows. The first adjustment is for changes in prepaid expenses, such as prepaid insurance or prepaid rent. If prepaid assets increase during the accounting period, more cash will have been paid out than appears on the income statement as expenses. If prepaid assets decrease, the expenses shown on the income statement will exceed the cash spent.

The second adjustment is for changes in liabilities resulting from accrued expenses, such as wages payable and payroll taxes payable. If accrued liabilities increase during the accounting period, operating expenses on the income statement will exceed the cash spent. And if accrued liabilities decrease, operating expenses will fall short of cash spent.

The third adjustment is made because certain expenses do not require a current outlay of cash; those expenses must be subtracted from operating expenses to arrive at cash payments for operating expenses. The most common expenses in this category are depreciation expense, amortization expense, and depletion expense. For example, Ryan Corporation recorded 20x1 depreciation expense of $37,000. No cash payment was made in this transaction. Therefore, to the extent that operating expenses include depreciation and similar items, an adjustment is needed to reduce operating expenses to the amount of cash expended.

The three adjustments to operating expenses are summarized in the equations that follow.

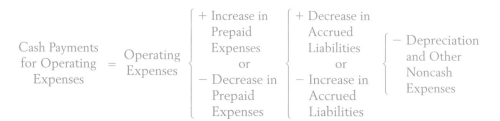

According to Exhibits 1 and 2, Ryan's operating expenses (including depreciation of $37,000) were $147,000, prepaid expenses decreased by $4,000, and accrued liabilities increased by $3,000. As a result, Ryan Corporation's cash payments for operating expenses are $103,000, computed as follows:

$$\$103,000 = \$147,000 - \$4,000 - \$3,000 - \$37,000$$

If there are prepaid expenses and accrued liabilities that are *not* related to specific operating expenses, they are not included in these computations. One example is income taxes payable, which is the accrued liability related to income taxes expense. The cash payment for income taxes will be discussed shortly.

CASH PAYMENTS FOR INTEREST   The FASB classifies cash payments for interest as operating activities, although some authorities argue that they should be considered financing activities because of their association with loans incurred to finance the business. The FASB feels that interest expense is a cost of operating a business, and this is the position followed in this text. Also, for the sake of simplicity, all examples in this text assume that interest payments are equal to interest expense on the income statement. Thus, based on Exhibit 2, Ryan Corporation's interest payments are assumed to be $23,000 in 20x1.

CASH PAYMENTS FOR INCOME TAXES The amount of income taxes expense that appears on the income statement rarely equals the amount of income taxes actually paid during the year. To determine cash payments for income taxes, income taxes (from the income statement) are adjusted by the change in Income Taxes Payable. If Income Taxes Payable increased during the accounting period, cash payments for taxes will be less than the expense shown on the income statement. If Income Taxes Payable decreased, cash payments for taxes will exceed income taxes on the income statement. In other words, the following equation is applicable:

$$\begin{matrix} \text{Cash Payments} \\ \text{for Income Taxes} \end{matrix} = \begin{matrix} \text{Income} \\ \text{Taxes} \end{matrix} \begin{cases} + \text{ Decrease in Income Taxes Payable} \\ \qquad\qquad\quad \text{or} \\ - \text{ Increase in Income Taxes Payable} \end{cases}$$

In 20x1, Ryan Corporation showed income taxes of $7,000 on its income statement and a decrease of $2,000 in Income Taxes Payable on its balance sheets (see Exhibits 1 and 2). As a result, cash payments for income taxes during 20x1 were $9,000, calculated as follows:

$$\$9,000 = \$7,000 + \$2,000$$

Compiling the Statement of Cash Flows

The Ryan Corporation's statement of cash flows under the direct method is presented in Exhibit 7. The only differences between that statement of cash flows and the one based on the indirect method shown in Exhibit 4 occur in the first and last sections. The middle sections, which present cash flows from investing activities and financing activities, net increases or decreases in cash, and the schedule of noncash investing and financing activities, are the same under both methods.

The first section of the statement in Exhibit 7 shows the net cash flows from operating activities on a direct basis, as presented in Exhibit 6. The last section is the same as the cash flows from operating activities section of the statement of cash flows under the indirect method (see Exhibit 4 on page 728). The FASB believes that when the direct method is used, a schedule must be provided that reconciles net income to net cash flows from operating activities. Thus, the statement of cash flows under the direct method includes a section that accommodates the main difference between it and the indirect method.

Exhibit 7
Statement of Cash Flows:
Direct Method

Ryan Corporation
Statement of Cash Flows
For the Year Ended December 31, 20x1

Cash Flows from Operating Activities

Cash Receipts from		
Sales	$706,000	
Interest Received	6,000	$712,000
Cash Payments for		
Purchases	$547,000	
Operating Expenses	103,000	
Interest	23,000	
Income Taxes	9,000	682,000
Net Cash Flows from Operating Activities		$ 30,000 ←

Cash Flows from Investing Activities

Purchase of Investments	($ 78,000)	
Sale of Investments	102,000	
Purchase of Plant Assets	(120,000)	
Sale of Plant Assets	5,000	
Net Cash Flows from Investing Activities		(91,000)

Cash Flows from Financing Activities

Repayment of Bonds	($ 50,000)	
Issue of Common Stock	150,000	
Dividends Paid	(8,000)	
Net Cash Flows from Financing Activities		92,000
Net Increase (Decrease) in Cash		$ 31,000
Cash at Beginning of Year		15,000
Cash at End of Year		$ 46,000

Schedule of Noncash Investing and Financing Transactions

Issue of Bonds Payable for Plant Assets	$100,000

Reconciliation of Net Income to Net Cash Flows from Operating Activities

Net Income		$ 16,000
Adjustments to Reconcile Net Income to Net		
Cash Flows from Operating Activities		
Depreciation	$ 37,000	
Gain on Sale of Investments	(12,000)	
Loss on Sale of Plant Assets	3,000	
Changes in Current Assets and Current Liabilities		
Decrease in Accounts Receivable	8,000	
Increase in Inventory	(34,000)	
Decrease in Prepaid Expenses	4,000	
Increase in Accounts Payable	7,000	
Increase in Accrued Liabilities	3,000	
Decrease in Income Taxes Payable	(2,000)	14,000
Net Cash Flows from Operating Activities		$ 30,000 ←

Chapter Review

1. Describe the statement of cash flows, and define *cash* and *cash* *equivalents*. The statement of cash flows explains the changes in cash and cash equivalents from one accounting period to the next by showing cash inflows and cash outflows from the operating, investing, and financing activities of a company for an accounting period. For purposes of preparing the statement of cash flows, *cash* is defined to include cash and cash equivalents. *Cash equivalents* are short-term (90 days or less), highly liquid investments, including money market accounts, commercial paper, and U.S. Treasury bills.

2. State the principal purposes and uses of the statement of cash flows. The primary purpose of the statement of cash flows is to provide information about a company's cash receipts and cash payments during an accounting period. Its secondary purpose is to provide information about a company's operating, investing, and financing activities. The statement is useful to management as well as to investors and creditors in assessing the liquidity of a business, including its ability to generate future cash flows and to pay debts and dividends.

3. Identify the principal components of the classifications of cash flows, and state the significance of noncash investing and financing transactions. Cash flows may be classified as stemming from (1) operating activities, which include the cash effects of transactions and other events that enter into the determination of net income; (2) investing activities, which include the acquiring and selling of long- and short-term marketable securities and property, plant, and equipment, and the making and collecting of loans, excluding interest; or (3) financing activities, which include the obtaining and returning or repaying of resources, excluding interest, to owners and creditors. Noncash investing and financing transactions are also important because they are exchanges of assets and/or liabilities that are of interest to investors and creditors when evaluating the financing and investing activities of a business.

4. Analyze the statement of cash flows. In analyzing a company's statement of cash flows, analysts tend to focus on cash-generating efficiency and free cash flow. Cash-generating efficiency is a company's ability to generate cash from its current or continuing operations. Three ratios used in measuring cash-generating efficiency are cash flow yield, cash flows to sales, and cash flows to assets. Free cash flow is the cash that remains after deducting funds a company must commit to continue operating at its planned level. Such commitments must cover current or continuing operations, interest, income taxes, dividends, and net capital expenditures.

5. Use the indirect method to determine cash flows from operating activities. Under the indirect method, net income is adjusted for all noncash effects and for items that need to be converted from an accrual to a cash basis to arrive at a cash flow basis, as follows:

Cash Flows from Operating Activities		
Net Income		xxx
Adjustments to Reconcile Net Income to Net Cash Flows from Operating Activities		
(List of individual items)	xxx	xxx
Net Cash Flows from Operating Activities		xxx

6. **Determine cash flows from investing activities and financing activities.** Cash flows from investing activities are determined by identifying the cash flow effects of the transactions that affect each account relevant to investing activities. Such accounts include all long-term assets and short-term marketable securities. The same procedure is followed for financing activities, except that the accounts involved are short-term borrowings, long-term liabilities, and stockholders' equity. The effects of gains and losses reported on the income statement must also be considered. After the changes in the balance sheet accounts from one accounting period to the next have been explained, all the cash flow effects should have been identified.

7. **Use the indirect method to prepare a statement of cash flows.** The statement of cash flows lists cash flows from operating activities, investing activities, and financing activities, in that order. The sections on investing and financing activities are prepared by examining individual accounts involving cash receipts and cash payments from investing and financing activities to explain year-to-year changes in the account balances. Significant noncash transactions are included in a schedule of noncash investing and financing transactions that accompanies the statement of cash flows.

SUPPLEMENTAL OBJECTIVES

8. **Prepare a work sheet for the statement of cash flows.** A work sheet is useful in preparing the statement of cash flows for complex companies. The basic procedures are to analyze the changes in the balance sheet accounts for their effects on cash flows (in the top portion of the work sheet) and to classify those effects according to the format of the statement of cash flows (in the lower portion of the work sheet). When all changes in the balance sheet accounts have been explained and entered on the work sheet, the change in the Cash account will also be explained, and all necessary information will be available to prepare the statement of cash flows. The work sheet approach lends itself to the indirect method of preparing the statement of cash flows.

9. **Use the direct method to determine cash flows from operating activities and prepare a statement of cash flows.** The principal difference between a statement of cash flows prepared under the direct method and one prepared under the indirect method appears in the cash flows from operating activities section. Instead of beginning with net income and making additions and subtractions, as is done with the indirect method, the direct method converts each item on the income statement to its cash equivalent by adjusting for changes in the related current asset or current liability accounts and for other items such as depreciation. The rest of the statement of cash flows is the same under the direct method, except that a schedule that reconciles net income to net cash flows from operating activities must be included.

REVIEW OF CONCEPTS AND TERMINOLOGY

The following concepts and terms were introduced in this chapter:

LO 1 **Cash:** For purposes of the statement of cash flows, both cash and cash equivalents.

LO 1 **Cash equivalents:** Short-term (90 days or less), highly liquid investments, including money market accounts, commercial paper, and U.S. Treasury bills.

LO 4 **Cash flows to assets:** The ratio of net cash flows from operating activities to average total assets.

LO 4 **Cash flows to sales:** The ratio of net cash flows from operating activities to sales.

LO 4 **Cash flow yield:** The ratio of net cash flows from operating activities to net income.

LO 4 **Cash-generating efficiency:** The ability of a company to generate cash from its current or continuing operations.

LO 5 **Direct method:** The procedure for converting the income statement from an accrual basis to a cash basis by separately adjusting each item on the income statement.

LO 3 **Financing activities:** Business activities that involve obtaining resources from or returning resources to owners and providing them with a return on their investment, and obtaining resources from creditors and repaying any amounts borrowed or otherwise settling the obligations.

LO 4 **Free cash flow:** The amount of cash that remains after deducting the funds a company must commit to continue operating at its planned level; net cash flows from operating activities minus dividends paid minus net capital expenditures.

LO 5 **Indirect method:** The procedure for converting the income statement from an accrual basis to a cash basis by adjusting net income for items that do not affect cash flows, including depreciation, amortization, depletion, gains, losses, and changes in current assets and current liabilities.

LO 3 **Investing activities:** Business activities that involve the acquiring and selling of long-term assets, the acquiring and selling of marketable securities other than trading securities or cash equivalents, and the making and collecting of loans.

LO 3 **Noncash investing and financing transactions:** Significant investing and financing transactions that do not involve an actual cash inflow or outflow but involve only long-term assets, long-term liabilities, or stockholders' equity, such as the exchange of a long-term liability for a long-term asset or the settlement of a debt by issuing capital stock.

LO 3 **Operating activities:** Business activities that involve the cash effects of transactions and other events that enter into the determination of net income.

LO 1 **Statement of cash flows:** A primary financial statement that shows how a company's operating, investing, and financing activities have affected cash during an accounting period.

REVIEW PROBLEM

LO 4
LO 5
LO 6
LO 7
SO 9

The Statement of Cash Flows

The 20x2 income statement for Northwest Corporation is presented below, and the comparative balance sheets for the years 20x2 and 20x1 are shown on the next page.

Northwest Corporation Income Statement For the Year Ended December 31, 20x2		
Net Sales		$1,650,000
Cost of Goods Sold		920,000
Gross Margin		$ 730,000
Operating Expenses (including Depreciation Expense of $12,000 on Buildings and $23,100 on Equipment, and Amortization Expense of $4,800)		470,000
Operating Income		$ 260,000
Other Income (Expenses)		
Interest Expense	($55,000)	
Dividend Income	3,400	
Gain on Sale of Investments	12,500	
Loss on Disposal of Equipment	(2,300)	(41,400)
Income Before Income Taxes		$ 218,600
Income Taxes		52,200
Net Income		$ 166,400

Northwest Corporation
Comparative Balance Sheets
December 31, 20x2 and 20x1

	20x2	20x1	Change	Increase or Decrease
Assets				
Cash	$ 115,850	$ 121,850	($ 6,000)	Decrease
Accounts Receivable (net)	296,000	314,500	(18,500)	Decrease
Inventory	322,000	301,000	21,000	Increase
Prepaid Expenses	7,800	5,800	2,000	Increase
Long-Term Investments	36,000	86,000	(50,000)	Decrease
Land	150,000	125,000	25,000	Increase
Buildings	462,000	462,000	—	—
Accumulated Depreciation, Buildings	(91,000)	(79,000)	(12,000)	Increase
Equipment	159,730	167,230	(7,500)	Decrease
Accumulated Depreciation, Equipment	(43,400)	(45,600)	2,200	Decrease
Intangible Assets	19,200	24,000	(4,800)	Decrease
Total Assets	$1,434,180	$1,482,780	($ 48,600)	
Liabilities and Stockholders' Equity				
Accounts Payable	$ 133,750	$ 233,750	($100,000)	Decrease
Notes Payable (current)	75,700	145,700	(70,000)	Decrease
Accrued Liabilities	5,000	—	5,000	Increase
Income Taxes Payable	20,000	—	20,000	Increase
Bonds Payable	210,000	310,000	(100,000)	Decrease
Mortgage Payable	330,000	350,000	(20,000)	Decrease
Common Stock, $10 par value	360,000	300,000	60,000	Increase
Paid-in Capital in Excess of Par Value	90,000	50,000	40,000	Increase
Retained Earnings	209,730	93,330	116,400	Increase
Total Liabilities and Stockholders' Equity	$1,434,180	$1,482,780	($ 48,600)	

The following additional information was taken from the company's records:

a. Long-term investments (available-for-sale securities) that cost $70,000 were sold at a gain of $12,500; additional long-term investments were made in the amount of $20,000.

b. Five acres of land were purchased for $25,000 to build a parking lot.

c. Equipment that cost $37,500 with accumulated depreciation of $25,300 was sold at a loss of $2,300; new equipment costing $30,000 was purchased.

d. Notes payable in the amount of $100,000 were repaid; an additional $30,000 was borrowed by signing notes payable.

e. Bonds payable in the amount of $100,000 were converted into 6,000 shares of common stock.

f. The Mortgage Payable account was reduced by $20,000 during the year.

g. Cash dividends declared and paid were $50,000.

REQUIRED

1. Prepare a schedule of cash flows from operating activities using the (a) indirect method and (b) direct method.

2. Prepare a statement of cash flows using the indirect method.

3. Compute cash flow yield, cash flows to sales, cash flows to assets, and free cash flow for 20x2.

1. (a) Prepare a schedule of cash flows from operating activities using the indirect method.

Northwest Corporation
Schedule of Cash Flows from Operating Activities
For the Year Ended December 31, 20x2

Cash Flows from Operating Activities		
Net Income		$166,400
Adjustments to Reconcile Net Income to		
Net Cash Flows from Operating Activities		
Depreciation Expense, Buildings	$ 12,000	
Depreciation Expense, Equipment	23,100	
Amortization Expense, Intangible Assets	4,800	
Gain on Sale of Investments	(12,500)	
Loss on Disposal of Equipment	2,300	
Changes in Current Assets		
and Current Liabilities		
Decrease in Accounts Receivable	18,500	
Increase in Inventory	(21,000)	
Increase in Prepaid Expenses	(2,000)	
Decrease in Accounts Payable	(100,000)	
Increase in Accrued Liabilities	5,000	
Increase in Income Taxes Payable	20,000	(49,800)
Net Cash Flows from Operating Activities		$116,600

1. (b) Prepare a schedule of cash flows from operating activities using the direct method.

Northwest Corporation
Schedule of Cash Flows from Operating Activities
For the Year Ended December 31, 20x2

Cash Flows from Operating Activities		
Cash Receipts from		
Sales	$1,668,500[1]	
Dividends Received	3,400	$1,671,900
Cash Payments for		
Purchases	$1,041,000[2]	
Operating Expenses	427,100[3]	
Interest	55,000	
Income Taxes	32,200[4]	1,555,300
Net Cash Flows from Operating Activities		$ 116,600

1. $1,650,000 + $18,500 = $1,668,500
2. $920,000 + $21,000 + $100,000 = $1,041,000
3. $470,000 + $2,000 − $5,000 − ($12,000 + $23,100 + $4,800) = $427,100
4. $52,200 − $20,000 = $32,200

2. Prepare a statement of cash flows using the indirect method.

Northwest Corporation
Statement of Cash Flows
For the Year Ended December 31, 20x2

Cash Flows from Operating Activities

Net Income		$166,400
Adjustments to Reconcile Net Income to		
Net Cash Flows from Operating Activities		
Depreciation Expense, Buildings	$ 12,000	
Depreciation Expense, Equipment	23,100	
Amortization Expense, Intangible Assets	4,800	
Gain on Sale of Investments	(12,500)	
Loss on Disposal of Equipment	2,300	
Changes in Current Assets and		
Current Liabilities		
Decrease in Accounts Receivable	18,500	
Increase in Inventory	(21,000)	
Increase in Prepaid Expenses	(2,000)	
Decrease in Accounts Payable	(100,000)	
Increase in Accrued Liabilities	5,000	
Increase in Income Taxes Payable	20,000	(49,800)
Net Cash Flows from Operating Activities		$116,600

Cash Flows from Investing Activities

Sale of Long-Term Investments	$ 82,500[1]	
Purchase of Long-Term Investments	(20,000)	
Purchase of Land	(25,000)	
Sale of Equipment	9,900[2]	
Purchase of Equipment	(30,000)	
Net Cash Flows from Investing Activities		17,400

Cash Flows from Financing Activities

Repayment of Notes Payable	($100,000)	
Issuance of Notes Payable	30,000	
Reduction in Mortgage	(20,000)	
Dividends Paid	(50,000)	
Net Cash Flows from Financing Activities		(140,000)

Net Increase (Decrease) in Cash	($ 6,000)
Cash at Beginning of Year	121,850
Cash at End of Year	$115,850

Schedule of Noncash Investing and Financing Transactions

Conversion of Bonds Payable into Common Stock	$100,000

1. $70,000 + $12,500 (gain) = $82,500
2. $37,500 − $25,300 = $12,200 (book value) − $2,300 (loss) = $9,900

3. Compute cash flow yield, cash flows to sales, cash flows to assets, and free cash flow for 20x2.

$$\text{Cash Flow Yield} = \frac{\$116,600}{\$166,400} = .7 \text{ times}$$

$$\text{Cash Flows to Sales} = \frac{\$116,600}{\$1,650,000} = 7.1\%$$

$$\text{Cash Flows to Assets} = \frac{\$116,600}{(\$1,434,180 + \$1,482,780) \div 2} = 8.0\%$$

$$\text{Free Cash Flow} = \$116,600 - \$50,000 - \$25,000 - \$30,000 + \$9,900$$
$$= \$21,500$$

Chapter Assignments

**BUILDING YOUR
KNOWLEDGE
FOUNDATION**

QUESTIONS

1. In the statement of cash flows, what is the term *cash* understood to include?
2. To earn a return on cash on hand during 20x3, Sallas Corporation transferred $45,000 from its checking account to a money market account, purchased a $25,000 Treasury bill, and invested $35,000 in common stocks. How will each of these transactions affect the statement of cash flows?
3. What are the purposes of the statement of cash flows?
4. Why is the statement of cash flows needed when most of the information in it is available from a company's comparative balance sheets and income statement?
5. What are the three classifications of cash flows? Give some examples of each.
6. Why is it important to disclose certain noncash transactions? How should they be disclosed?
7. Define *cash-generating efficiency* and identify three ratios that measure cash-generating efficiency.
8. Define *free cash flow* and identify its components. What does it mean to have a positive or a negative free cash flow?
9. What are the essential differences between the direct method and the indirect method of determining cash flows from operations?
10. In determining net cash flows from operating activities (assuming the indirect method is used), what are the effects on cash generated from the following items: (a) an increase in accounts receivable, (b) a decrease in inventory, (c) an increase in accounts payable, (d) a decrease in wages payable, (e) depreciation expense, and (f) amortization of patents?
11. Cell-Borne Corporation had a net loss of $12,000 in 20x1 but had positive cash flows from operations of $9,000. What conditions may have caused this situation?
12. What is the proper treatment on the statement of cash flows of a transaction in which a building that cost $50,000 with accumulated depreciation of $32,000 is sold at a loss of $5,000?
13. What is the proper treatment on the statement of cash flows of (a) a transaction in which buildings and land are purchased by the issuance of a mortgage for $234,000 and (b) a conversion of $50,000 in bonds payable into 2,500 shares of $6 par value common stock?
14. Why is the work sheet approach considered to be more compatible with the indirect method than with the direct method of determining cash flows from operations?
15. Assuming in each of the following independent cases that only one transaction occurred, what transactions would be likely to cause (a) a decrease in investments and (b) an increase in common stock? How would each case be treated on the work sheet for the statement of cash flows?

16. Glen Corporation has the following other income and expense items: interest expense, $12,000; interest income, $3,000; dividend income, $5,000; and loss on the retirement of bonds, $6,000. Where does each of these items appear on or affect the statement of cash flows, assuming the direct method is used?

Short Exercises

SE 1.

LO 3 Classification of Cash Flow Transactions

Tosca Corporation engaged in the transactions below. Identify each as (a) an operating activity, (b) an investing activity, (c) a financing activity, (d) a noncash transaction, or (e) none of the above.

1. Sold land.
2. Declared and paid a cash dividend.
3. Paid interest.

4. Issued common stock for plant assets.
5. Issued preferred stock.
6. Borrowed cash on a bank loan.

SE 2.

LO 4 Cash-Generating Efficiency Ratios and Free Cash Flow

In 20x2, Wu Corporation had year-end assets of $550,000, net sales of $790,000, net income of $90,000, net cash flows from operating activities of $180,000, purchases of plant assets of $120,000, sales of plant assets of $20,000, and paid dividends of $40,000. In 20x1, year-end assets were $500,000. Calculate the cash-generating efficiency ratios of cash flow yield, cash flows to sales, and cash flows to assets. Also calculate free cash flow.

SE 3.

LO 4 Cash Flow Efficiency and Free Cash Flow

Examine the cash flow measures in part **3** of the review problem in this chapter. Discuss the meaning of these ratios.

SE 4.

LO 5 Computing Cash Flows from Operating Activities: Indirect Method

Specialty Products Corporation had a net income of $33,000 during 20x1. During the year, the company had depreciation expense of $14,000. Accounts receivable increased by $11,000, and accounts payable increased by $5,000. Those were the company's only current assets and current liabilities. Use the indirect method to determine net cash flows from operating activities.

SE 5.

LO 5 Computing Cash Flows from Operating Activities: Indirect Method

During 20x1, Ayzarian Corporation had a net income of $72,000. Included on the income statement was depreciation expense of $8,000 and amortization expense of $900. During the year, accounts receivable decreased by $4,100, inventories increased by $2,700, prepaid expenses decreased by $500, accounts payable decreased by $7,000, and accrued liabilities decreased by $850. Use the indirect method to determine net cash flows from operating activities.

SE 6.

LO 6 Cash Flows from Investing Activities and Noncash Transactions

During 20x1, Rhode Island Company purchased land for $750,000. It paid $250,000 in cash and signed a $500,000 mortgage for the rest. The company also sold a building that had originally cost $180,000, on which it had $140,000 of accumulated depreciation, for $190,000 cash and a gain of $150,000. Prepare the cash flows from investing activities and schedule of noncash investing and financing transactions sections of the statement of cash flows.

SE 7.

LO 6 Cash Flows from Financing Activities

During 20x1, South Carolina Company issued $1,000,000 in long-term bonds at 96, repaid $150,000 of bonds at face value, paid interest of $80,000, and paid dividends of $50,000. Prepare the cash flows from the financing activities section of the statement of cash flows.

SE 8.

LO 7 Identifying Components of the Statement of Cash Flows

Assuming the indirect method is used to prepare the statement of cash flows, tell whether each of the following items would appear (a) in cash flows from operating activities, (b) in cash flows from investing activities, (c) in cash flows from financing activities, (d) in the schedule of noncash investing and financing transactions, or (e) not on the statement of cash flows at all.

1. Dividends paid
2. Cash receipts from sales
3. Decrease in accounts receivable
4. Sale of plant assets

5. Gain on sale of investment
6. Issue of stock for plant assets
7. Issue of common stock
8. Net income

SE 9.

SO 9 Cash Receipts from Sales and Cash Payments for Purchases: Direct Method

During 20x2, Nebraska Wheat Company, a marketer of whole-grain products, had sales of $426,500. The ending balance of Accounts Receivable was $127,400 in 20x1 and $96,200 in 20x2. Also, during 20x2, Nebraska Wheat Company had cost of goods sold of $294,200. The ending balance of inventory was $36,400 in 20x1 and $44,800 in 20x2. The ending balance of Accounts Payable was $28,100 in 20x1 and $25,900 in 20x2.

Using the direct method, calculate cash receipts from sales and cash payments for purchases in 20x2.

SE 10.

SO 9 Cash Payments for Operating Expenses and Income Taxes: Direct Method

During 20x2, Nebraska Wheat Company had operating expenses of $79,000 and income taxes expense of $12,500. Depreciation expense of $20,000 for 20x2 was included in operating expenses. The ending balance of Prepaid Expenses was $3,600 in 20x1 and $2,300 in 20x2. The ending balance of Accrued Liabilities (excluding Income Taxes Payable) was $3,000 in 20x1 and $2,000 in 20x2. The ending balance of Income Taxes Payable was $4,100 in 20x1 and $3,500 in 20x2.

Calculate cash payments for operating expenses and income taxes in 20x2 using the direct method.

EXERCISES

E 1.

LO 1 Classification of Cash
LO 3 Flow Transactions

Smelt Corporation engaged in the following transactions. Identify each as (a) an operating activity, (b) an investing activity, (c) a financing activity, (d) a noncash transaction, or (e) not on the statement of cash flows. (Assume the indirect method.)

1. Declared and paid a cash dividend.
2. Purchased a long-term investment.
3. Received cash from customers.
4. Paid interest.
5. Sold equipment at a loss.
6. Issued long-term bonds for plant assets.
7. Received dividends on securities held.
8. Issued common stock.
9. Declared and issued a stock dividend.
10. Repaid notes payable.
11. Paid employees their wages.
12. Purchased a 60-day Treasury bill.
13. Purchased land.

E 2.

LO 4 Cash-Generating Efficiency Ratios and Free Cash Flow

In 20x5, Wicker Corporation had year-end assets of $4,800,000, net sales of $6,600,000, net income of $560,000, net cash flows from operating activities of $780,000, dividends of $240,000, and net capital expenditures of $820,000. In 20x4, year-end assets were $4,200,000. Calculate the cash-generating efficiency ratios of cash flow yield, cash flows to sales, and cash flows to assets. Also calculate free cash flow.

E 3.

LO 5 Cash Flows from Operating Activities: Indirect Method

The condensed single-step income statement for the year ended December 31, 20x2, of Green Fields Chem Company, a distributor of farm fertilizers and herbicides, appears as follows:

Sales		$6,500,000
Less: Cost of Goods Sold	$3,800,000	
Operating Expenses (including depreciation of $410,000)	1,900,000	
Income Taxes	200,000	5,900,000
Net Income		$ 600,000

Selected accounts from the company's balance sheets for 20x2 and 20x1 are as follows:

	20x2	20x1
Accounts Receivable	$1,200,000	$850,000
Inventory	420,000	510,000
Prepaid Expenses	130,000	90,000
Accounts Payable	480,000	360,000
Accrued Liabilities	30,000	50,000
Income Taxes Payable	70,000	60,000

Present in good form a schedule of cash flows from operating activities using the indirect method.

E 4.

LO 5 Computing Cash Flows from Operating Activities: Indirect Method

During 20x1, Boulevard Corporation had a net income of $41,000. Included on the income statement was depreciation expense of $2,300 and amortization expense of $300. During the year, accounts receivable increased by $3,400, inventories decreased by $1,900, prepaid expenses decreased by $200, accounts payable increased by $5,000, and accrued liabilities decreased by $450. Determine net cash flows from operating activities using the indirect method.

E 5.

LO 5 Preparing a Schedule of Cash Flows from Operating Activities: Indirect Method

For the year ended June 30, 20xx, net income for Norris Corporation was $7,400. The following is additional information: (a) Depreciation expense was $2,000; (b) accounts receivable increased by $4,400 during the year; (c) inventories increased by $7,000, and accounts payable increased by $14,000 during the year; (d) prepaid rent decreased by $1,400, and salaries payable increased by $1,000; and (e) income taxes payable decreased by $600 during the year. Use the indirect method to prepare a schedule of cash flows from operating activities.

E 6.

LO 6 Computing Cash Flows from Investing Activities: Investments

Wix Company's T account for long-term available-for-sale investments at the end of 20x3 is as follows:

Investments			
Beg. Bal.	38,500	Sales	39,000
Purchases	58,000		
End. Bal.	57,500		

In addition, Wix's income statement shows a loss on the sale of investments of $6,500. Compute the amounts to be shown as cash flows from investing activities and show how they are to appear in the statement of cash flows.

E 7.

LO 6 Computing Cash Flows from Investing Activities: Plant Assets

The T accounts for plant assets and accumulated depreciation for Wix Company at the end of 20x3 are as follows:

Plant Assets			
Beg. Bal.	65,000	Disposals	23,000
Purchases	33,600		
End. Bal.	75,600		

Accumulated Depreciation			
Disposals	14,700	Beg. Bal.	34,500
		Depreciation	10,200
		End. Bal.	30,000

In addition, Wix Company's income statement shows a gain on sale of plant assets of $4,400. Compute the amounts to be shown as cash flows from investing activities and show how they are to appear on the statement of cash flows.

E 8.

LO 6 Determining Cash Flows from Investing and Financing Activities

All transactions involving Notes Payable and related accounts engaged in by Wix Company during 20x3 are as follows:

Cash	18,000	
Notes Payable		18,000
Bank loan		
Patent	30,000	
Notes Payable		30,000
Purchase of patent by issuing note payable		

Notes Payable	5,000	
Interest Expense	500	
Cash		5,500
Repayment of note payable at maturity		

Determine the amounts of the transactions affecting financing activities and show how they are to appear on the statement of cash flows for 20x3.

E 9.

LO 7 Preparing the Statement of Cash Flows: Indirect Method

Tham Corporation's 20x2 income statement and its comparative balance sheets for June 30, 20x2 and 20x1, are as follows:

Tham Corporation
Income Statement
For the Year Ended June 30, 20x2

Sales	$468,000
Cost of Goods Sold	312,000
Gross Margin	$156,000
Operating Expenses	90,000
Operating Income	$ 66,000
Interest Expense	5,600
Income Before Income Taxes	$ 60,400
Income Taxes	24,600
Net Income	$ 35,800

Tham Corporation
Comparative Balance Sheets
June 30, 20x2 and 20x1

	20x2	20x1
Assets		
Cash	$139,800	$ 25,000
Accounts Receivable (net)	42,000	52,000
Inventory	86,800	96,800
Prepaid Expenses	6,400	5,200
Furniture	110,000	120,000
Accumulated Depreciation, Furniture	(18,000)	(10,000)
Total Assets	$367,000	$289,000
Liabilities and Stockholders' Equity		
Accounts Payable	$ 26,000	$ 28,000
Income Taxes Payable	2,400	3,600
Notes Payable (long-term)	74,000	70,000
Common Stock, $10 par value	230,000	180,000
Retained Earnings	34,600	7,400
Total Liabilities and Stockholders' Equity	$367,000	$289,000

Additional information: (a) Issued $44,000 note payable for purchase of furniture; (b) sold furniture that cost $54,000 with accumulated depreciation of $30,600 at carrying value; (c) recorded depreciation on the furniture during the year, $38,600; (d) repaid a note in the amount of $40,000; (e) issued $50,000 of common stock at par value; and (f) declared and paid dividends of $8,600. Without using a work sheet, prepare a statement of cash flows for 20x2 using the indirect method.

E 10.

LO 7 Preparing a Work Sheet
SO 8 for the Statement of Cash Flows: Indirect Method

Using the information in **E 9,** prepare a work sheet for the statement of cash flows for Tham Corporation for 20x2. From the work sheet, prepare a statement of cash flows using the indirect method.

E 11.

SO 9 Computing Cash Flows from Operating Activities: Direct Method

Vlieg Corporation engaged in the following transactions in 20x2. Using the direct method, compute the various cash flows from operating activities as required.

a. During 20x2, Vlieg Corporation had cash sales of $41,300 and sales on credit of $123,000. During the same year, accounts receivable decreased by $18,000. Determine the cash receipts from sales during 20x2.
b. During 20x2, Vlieg Corporation's cost of goods sold was $119,000. During the same year, merchandise inventory increased by $12,500 and accounts payable decreased by $4,300. Determine the cash payments for purchases during 20x2.
c. During 20x2, Vlieg Corporation had operating expenses of $45,000, including depreciation of $15,600. Also during 20x2, related prepaid expenses decreased by $3,100 and relevant accrued liabilities increased by $1,200. Determine the cash payments for operating expenses to suppliers of goods and services during 20x2.
d. Vlieg Corporation's income taxes expense for 20x2 was $4,300. Income taxes payable decreased by $230 that year. Determine the cash payments for income taxes during 20x2.

E 12.

SO 9 Preparing a Schedule of Cash Flows from Operating Activities: Direct Method

The income statement for the Vasquez Corporation is as follows:

Vasquez Corporation Income Statement For the Year Ended June 30, 20xx		
Sales		$122,000
Cost of Goods Sold		60,000
Gross Margin		$ 62,000
Operating Expenses		
Salaries Expense	$32,000	
Rent Expense	16,800	
Depreciation Expense	2,000	50,800
Income Before Income Taxes		$ 11,200
Income Taxes		2,400
Net Income		$ 8,800

Additional information: (a) Accounts receivable increased by $4,400 during the year; (b) inventories increased by $7,000, and accounts payable increased by $14,000 during the year; (c) prepaid rent decreased by $1,400, while salaries payable increased by $1,000; and (d) income taxes payable decreased by $600 during the year. Using the direct method, prepare a schedule of cash flows from operating activities as illustrated in Exhibit 6.

PROBLEMS

LO 1   **Classification of**
LO 3   **Transactions**

P 1. Analyze each transaction below and place X's in the appropriate columns to indicate its classification and its effect on cash flows using the indirect method.

Transaction	Cash Flow Classification				Effect on Cash		
	Operating Activity	Investing Activity	Financing Activity	Noncash Trans-action	Increase	Decrease	No Effect
1. Incurred a net loss.							
2. Declared and issued a stock dividend.							
3. Paid a cash dividend.							
4. Collected accounts receivable.							
5. Purchased inventory with cash.							
6. Retired long-term debt with cash.							
7. Sold available-for-sale securities at a loss.							
8. Issued stock for equipment.							
9. Purchased a one-year insurance policy with cash.							
10. Purchased treasury stock with cash.							
11. Retired a fully depreciated truck (no gain or loss).							
12. Paid interest on note.							
13. Received cash dividend on investment.							
14. Sold treasury stock.							
15. Paid income taxes.							
16. Transferred cash to money market account.							
17. Purchased land and building with a mortgage.							

LO 4   **The Statement of Cash**
LO 7   **Flows: Indirect Method**

P 2. The comparative balance sheets for Sharma Fabrics, Inc., for December 31, 20x3 and 20x2, appear on the next page. Additional information about Sharma Fabrics' operations during 20x3 is as follows: (a) net income, $56,000; (b) building and equipment depreciation expense amounts, $30,000 and $6,000, respectively; (c) equipment that cost $27,000 with accumulated depreciation of $25,000 sold at a gain of $10,600; (d) equipment purchases, $25,000; (e) patent amortization, $6,000; purchase of patent, $2,000; (f) funds borrowed by issuing notes payable, $50,000; notes payable repaid, $30,000; (g) land and building purchased for $324,000 by signing a mortgage for the total cost; (h) 3,000 shares of $20 par value common stock issued for a total of $100,000; and (i) paid cash dividend, $18,000.

REQUIRED

1. Using the indirect method, prepare a statement of cash flows for Sharma Fabrics, Inc. (Do not use a work sheet.)

2. Why did Sharma Fabrics have an increase in cash of $134,400 when it recorded net income of $56,000? Discuss and interpret.

3. Compute and assess cash flow yield and free cash flow for 20x3.

Sharma Fabrics, Inc. Comparative Balance Sheets December 31, 20x3 and 20x2		
	20x3	**20x2**
Assets		
Cash	$189,120	$ 54,720
Accounts Receivable (net)	204,860	150,860
Inventory	225,780	275,780
Prepaid Expenses	—	40,000
Land	50,000	—
Building	274,000	—
Accumulated Depreciation, Building	(30,000)	—
Equipment	66,000	68,000
Accumulated Depreciation, Equipment	(29,000)	(48,000)
Patents	8,000	12,000
Total Assets	$958,760	$553,360
Liabilities and Stockholders' Equity		
Accounts Payable	$ 21,500	$ 73,500
Notes Payable	20,000	—
Accrued Liabilities (current)	—	24,600
Mortgage Payable	324,000	—
Common Stock, $20 par value	360,000	300,000
Paid-in Capital in Excess of Par Value	114,400	74,400
Retained Earnings	118,860	80,860
Total Liabilities and Stockholders' Equity	$958,760	$553,360

P 3.

LO 4 Statement of Cash Flows:
LO 7 Indirect Method

The comparative balance sheets for Karidis Ceramics, Inc., for December 31, 20x3 and 20x2, appear on the next page. The following is additional information about Karidis Ceramics' operations during 20x3: (a) net income was $96,000; (b) building and equipment depreciation expense amounts were $80,000 and $60,000, respectively; (c) intangible assets were amortized in the amount of $20,000; (d) investments in the amount of $116,000 were purchased; (e) investments were sold for $150,000, on which a gain of $34,000 was recorded; (f) the company issued $240,000 in long-term bonds at face value; (g) a small warehouse building with the accompanying land was purchased through the issue of a $320,000 mortgage; (h) the company paid $40,000 to reduce mortgage payable during 20x3; (i) the company borrowed funds in the amount of $60,000 by issuing notes payable and repaid notes payable in the amount of $180,000; and (j) cash dividends in the amount of $36,000 were declared and paid.

REQUIRED

1. Using the indirect method, prepare a statement of cash flows for Karidis Ceramics. (Do not use a work sheet.)

2. Why did Karidis Ceramics experience a decrease in cash in a year in which it had a net income of $96,000? Discuss and interpret.

3. Compute and assess cash flow yield and free cash flow for 20x3.

Karidis Ceramics, Inc.
Comparative Balance Sheets
December 31, 20x3 and 20x2

	20x3	20x2
Assets		
Cash	$ 277,600	$ 305,600
Accounts Receivable (net)	738,800	758,800
Inventory	960,000	800,000
Prepaid Expenses	14,800	26,800
Long-Term Investments	440,000	440,000
Land	361,200	321,200
Building	1,200,000	920,000
Accumulated Depreciation, Building	(240,000)	(160,000)
Equipment	480,000	480,000
Accumulated Depreciation, Equipment	(116,000)	(56,000)
Intangible Assets	20,000	40,000
Total Assets	$4,136,400	$3,876,400
Liabilities and Stockholders' Equity		
Accounts Payable	$ 470,800	$ 660,800
Notes Payable (current)	40,000	160,000
Accrued Liabilities	10,800	20,800
Mortgage Payable	1,080,000	800,000
Bonds Payable	1,000,000	760,000
Common Stock	1,200,000	1,200,000
Paid-in Capital in Excess of Par Value	80,000	80,000
Retained Earnings	254,800	194,800
Total Liabilities and Stockholders' Equity	$4,136,400	$3,876,400

P 4.

LO 4 The Work Sheet and the
LO 7 Statement of Cash Flows:
SO 8 Indirect Method

Use the information for Karidis Ceramics, Inc., given in **P 3,** to complete the following requirements.

REQUIRED

1. Prepare a work sheet for the statement of cash flows for Karidis Ceramics, Inc.
2. Answer requirements **1, 2,** and **3** in **P 3** if that problem was not assigned.

P 5.

SO 9 Cash Flows from Operating
Activities: Direct Method

The income statement for Tanucci Clothing Store is at the top of the next page. The following is additional information: (a) other sales and administrative expenses include depreciation expense of $104,000 and amortization expense of $36,000; (b) accrued liabilities for salaries were $24,000 less than the previous year, and prepaid expenses were $40,000 more than the previous year; and (c) during the year accounts receivable (net) increased by $288,000, accounts payable increased by $228,000, and income taxes payable decreased by $14,400.

REQUIRED

Using the direct method, prepare a schedule of cash flows from operating activities as illustrated in Exhibit 6.

Tanucci Clothing Store
Income Statement
For the Year Ended June 30, 20xx

Net Sales		$4,900,000
Cost of Goods Sold		
Beginning Inventory	$1,240,000	
Net Cost of Purchases	3,040,000	
Goods Available for Sale	$4,280,000	
Ending Inventory	1,400,000	
Cost of Goods Sold		2,880,000
Gross Margin		$2,020,000
Operating Expenses		
Sales and Administrative Salaries Expense	$1,112,000	
Other Sales and Administrative Expenses	624,000	
Total Operating Expenses		1,736,000
Income Before Income Taxes		$ 284,000
Income Taxes		78,000
Net Income		$ 206,000

P 6.

LO 4   The Statement of Cash
LO 7   Flows: Indirect Method

O'Brien Corporation's comparative balance sheets as of December 31, 20x2 and 20x1, and its income statement for the year ended December 31, 20x2, follow.

O'Brien Corporation
Comparative Balance Sheets
December 31, 20x2 and 20x1

	20x2	20x1
Assets		
Cash	$ 82,400	$ 25,000
Accounts Receivable (net)	82,600	100,000
Inventory	175,000	225,000
Prepaid Rent	1,000	1,500
Furniture and Fixtures	74,000	72,000
Accumulated Depreciation, Furniture and Fixtures	(21,000)	(12,000)
Total Assets	$394,000	$411,500
Liabilities and Stockholders' Equity		
Accounts Payable	$ 71,700	$100,200
Income Taxes Payable	700	2,200
Notes Payable (long-term)	20,000	10,000
Bonds Payable	50,000	100,000
Common Stock, $10 par value	120,000	100,000
Paid-in Capital in Excess of Par Value	90,720	60,720
Retained Earnings	40,880	38,380
Total Liabilities and Stockholders' Equity	$394,000	$411,500

O'Brien Corporation
Income Statement
For the Year Ended December 31, 20x2

Net Sales		$804,500
Cost of Goods Sold		563,900
Gross Margin		$240,600
Operating Expenses (including Depreciation Expense of $23,400)		224,700
Income from Operations		$ 15,900
Other Income (Expenses)		
Gain on Disposal of Furniture and Fixtures	$ 3,500	
Interest Expense	(11,600)	(8,100)
Income Before Income Taxes		$ 7,800
Income Taxes		2,300
Net Income		$ 5,500

The following is additional information about 20x2: (a) furniture and fixtures that cost $17,800 with accumulated depreciation of $14,400 were sold at a gain of $3,500; (b) furniture and fixtures were purchased in the amount of $19,800; (c) a $10,000 note payable was paid and $20,000 was borrowed on a new note; (d) bonds payable in the amount of $50,000 were converted into 2,000 shares of common stock; and (e) $3,000 in cash dividends were declared and paid.

REQUIRED

1. Using the indirect method, prepare a statement of cash flows. Include a supporting schedule of noncash investing and financing transactions. (Do not use a work sheet.)

2. What are the primary reasons for O'Brien Corporation's large increase in cash from 20x1 to 20x2, despite its low net income?

3. Compute and assess cash flow yield and free cash flow for 20x2.

ALTERNATE PROBLEMS

P 7. Analyze each transaction below and place X's in the appropriate columns to indicate its classification and its effect on cash flows using the indirect method.

LO 1 Classification of
LO 3 Transactions

Transaction	Cash Flow Classification				Effect on Cash		
	Operating Activity	Investing Activity	Financing Activity	Noncash Trans-action	Increase	Decrease	No Effect
1. Earned a net income.							
2. Declared and paid cash dividend.							
3. Issued stock for cash.							
4. Retired long-term debt by issuing stock.							
5. Paid accounts payable.							
6. Purchased inventory with cash.							
7. Purchased a one-year insurance policy with cash.							
8. Purchased a long-term investment with cash.							
9. Sold trading securities at a gain.							
10. Sold a machine at a loss.							
11. Retired fully depreciated equipment.							
12. Paid interest on debt.							
13. Purchased available-for-sale securities (long-term).							
14. Received dividend income.							
15. Received cash on account.							
16. Converted bonds to common stock.							
17. Purchased 90-day Treasury bill.							

P 8.

LO 4 Statement of Cash Flows:
SO 9 Direct Method

Flanders Corporation's 20x2 income statement and its comparative balance sheets as of June 30, 20x2 and 20x1, appear on the next page. The following is additional information about 20x2: (a) equipment that cost $48,000 with accumulated depreciation of $34,000 was sold at a loss of $8,000; (b) land and building were purchased in the amount of $200,000 through an increase of $200,000 in the mortgage payable; (c) a $40,000 payment was made on the mortgage; (d) the notes were repaid, but the company borrowed an additional $60,000 through the issuance of a new note payable; and (e) a $120,000 cash dividend was declared and paid.

REQUIRED

1. Use the direct method to prepare a statement of cash flows. Include a supporting schedule of noncash investing and financing transactions. Do not use a work sheet, and do not include a reconciliation of net income to net cash flows from operating activities.

2. What are the primary reasons for Flanders Corporation's large increase in cash from 20x1 to 20x2?

3. Compute and assess cash flow yield and free cash flow for 20x2.

Flanders Corporation
Income Statement
For the Year Ended June 30, 20x2

Sales		$2,081,800
Cost of Goods Sold		1,312,600
Gross Margin		$ 769,200
Operating Expenses (including Depreciation Expense of $120,000)		378,400
Income from Operations		$ 390,800
Other Income (Expenses)		
Loss on Disposal of Equipment	($ 8,000)	
Interest Expense	(75,200)	(83,200)
Income Before Income Taxes		$ 307,600
Income Taxes		68,400
Net Income		$ 239,200

Flanders Corporation
Comparative Balance Sheets
June 30, 20x2 and 20x1

	20x2	20x1
Assets		
Cash	$ 334,000	$ 40,000
Accounts Receivable (net)	200,000	240,000
Inventory	360,000	440,000
Prepaid Expenses	1,200	2,000
Property, Plant, and Equipment	1,256,000	1,104,000
Accumulated Depreciation, Property, Plant, and Equipment	(366,000)	(280,000)
Total Assets	$1,785,200	$1,546,000
Liabilities and Stockholders' Equity		
Accounts Payable	$ 128,000	$ 84,000
Notes Payable (due in 90 days)	60,000	160,000
Income Taxes Payable	52,000	36,000
Mortgage Payable	720,000	560,000
Common Stock, $5 par value	400,000	400,000
Retained Earnings	425,200	306,000
Total Liabilities and Stockholders' Equity	$1,785,200	$1,546,000

P 9.

LO 4 **The Work Sheet and the**
LO 7 **Statement of Cash Flows:**
LO 8 **Indirect Method**

Use the information for O'Brien Corporation given in **P 6** to answer the following requirements.

REQUIRED

1. Prepare a work sheet to gather information for the preparation of the statement of cash flows.
2. Answer requirements **1, 2,** and **3** in **P 6** if that problem was not assigned.

EXPANDING YOUR CRITICAL THINKING, COMMUNICATION, AND INTERPERSONAL SKILLS

SKILLS DEVELOPMENT

Conceptual Analysis

SD 1.

LO 5   **Direct Versus Indirect**
SO 9   **Method**

Collins Industries, Inc., a manufacturing company, uses the direct method of presenting cash flows from operating activities in its statement of cash flows. As noted in the text, most companies use the indirect method.[10]

Explain the difference between the direct and indirect methods of presenting cash flows from operating activities. Then choose either the direct or the indirect method and tell why it is the best way of presenting cash flows from operations. Be prepared to discuss your opinion in class.

Group Activity. Assign in-class groups. Have each group develop a position for either the direct or indirect method of presentation and defend that position in a debate.

Ethical Dilemma

SD 2.

LO 3   **Ethics and Cash Flow**
      Classifications

Chemical Waste Treatment, Inc., is a fast-growing company that disposes of chemical wastes. The company has an $800,000 line of credit at its bank. One section in the loan agreement says that the ratio of cash flows from operations to interest expense must exceed 3.0. If this ratio falls below 3.0, the company must reduce the balance outstanding on its line of credit to one-half the total line if the funds borrowed against the line of credit exceed that amount.

After the end of the fiscal year, the controller informs the president: "We will not meet the ratio requirements on our line of credit in 20x2 because interest expense was $1.2 million and cash flows from operations were $3.2 million. Also, we have borrowed 100 percent of our line of credit. We do not have the cash to reduce the credit line by $400,000." The president says, "This is a serious situation. To pay our ongoing bills, we need our bank to increase our line of credit, not decrease it. What can we do?" "Do you recall the $500,000 two-year note payable for equipment?" replied the controller. "It is now classified as 'Proceeds from Notes Payable' in cash flows provided from financing activities in the statement of cash flows. If we move it to cash flows from operations and call it 'Increase in Payables,' it would increase cash flows from operations to $3.7 million and put us over the limit." "Well, do it," ordered the president. "It surely doesn't make any difference where it is on the statement. It is an increase in both places. It would be much worse for our company in the long term if we failed to meet this ratio requirement."

What is your opinion of the president's reasoning? Is the president's order ethical? Who benefits and who is harmed if the controller follows the president's order? What are management's alternatives? What would you do?

Research Activity

SD 3.

LO 3   **Basic Research Skills**
LO 4

Select the annual reports of three corporations, using one or more of the following sources: your library or the Fingraph® Financial Analyst™ CD-ROM software that

Cash Flow

CD-ROM

Communication

Critical
Thinking

Ethics

General
Ledger

Group
Activity

Hot Links
to Real
Companies

International

Internet

Key Ratio

Memo

Spreadsheet

accompanies this text. You may choose them from the same industry or at random, at the direction of your instructor. (If you did a related exercise in a previous chapter, use the same three companies.) Prepare a table with a column for each corporation. Then, for any year covered by the statement of cash flows, answer the following questions: Does the company use the direct or the indirect approach? Is net income more or less than net cash flows from operating activities? What are the major causes of differences between net income and net cash flows from operating activities? Compute cash flow efficiency ratios and free cash flow. Does the dividend appear secure? Did the company make significant capital expenditures during the year? How were the expenditures financed? Do you notice anything unusual about the investing and financing activities of your companies? Do the investing and financing activities provide any insights into management's plan for each company? If so, what are they? Be prepared to discuss your findings in class.

Decision-Making Practice

SD 4.

LO 4 **Analysis of Cash Flow**
LO 7 **Difficulty**

May Hashimi, president of ***Hashimi Print Gallery, Inc.,*** is examining the following income statement, which has just been handed to her by her accountant, Lou Klein, CPA.

Hashimi Print Gallery, Inc. Income Statement For the Year Ended December 31, 20x2	
Net Sales	$884,000
Cost of Goods Sold	508,000
Gross Margin	$376,000
Operating Expenses (including Depreciation Expense of $20,000)	204,000
Operating Income	$172,000
Interest Expense	24,000
Income Before Income Taxes	$148,000
Income Taxes	28,000
Net Income	$120,000

After looking at the statement, Hashimi said to Klein, "Lou, the statement seems to be well done, but what I need to know is why I don't have enough cash to pay my bills this month. You show that I earned $120,000 in 20x2, but I have only $24,000 in the bank. I know I bought a building on a mortgage and paid a cash dividend of $48,000, but what else is going on?" Klein replied, "To answer your question, we have to look at comparative balance sheets and prepare another type of statement. Take a look at these balance sheets." The statement handed to Hashimi is on the next page.

1. To what statement is Klein referring? From the information given, prepare the additional statement using the indirect method.
2. Hashimi Print Gallery, Inc., has a cash problem despite profitable operations. Why?

Hashimi Print Gallery, Inc. Comparative Balance Sheets December 31, 20x2 and 20x1		
	20x2	**20x1**
Assets		
Cash	$ 24,000	$ 40,000
Accounts Receivable (net)	178,000	146,000
Inventory	240,000	180,000
Prepaid Expenses	10,000	14,000
Building	400,000	—
Accumulated Depreciation	(20,000)	—
Total Assets	$832,000	$380,000
Liabilities and Stockholders' Equity		
Accounts Payable	$ 74,000	$ 96,000
Income Taxes Payable	6,000	4,000
Mortgage Payable	400,000	—
Common Stock	200,000	200,000
Retained Earnings	152,000	80,000
Total Liabilities and Stockholders' Equity	$832,000	$380,000

FINANCIAL REPORTING AND ANALYSIS

Interpreting Financial Reports

FRA 1.

LO 4 Cash-Generating Efficiency and Free Cash Flow

The statement of cash flows for **Tandy Corporation,** the owner of Radio Shack and other retail store chains, appears on the next page. For the two years shown, compute the cash-generating efficiency ratios of cash flow yield, cash flows to sales, and cash flows to assets. Also compute free cash flow for the two years. Assume that you report to an investment analyst who has asked you to analyze Tandy's statement of cash flows for 1998 and 1999. Prepare a memorandum to the investment analyst that assesses Tandy's cash-generating efficiency and evaluates its available free cash flow in light of its financing activities. Are there any special operating circumstances that should be taken into consideration? Refer to your computations and to Tandy's Statement of Cash Flows as attachments. The following data come from Tandy's annual report (in thousands):[11]

	1999	1998	1997
Net Sales	$4,126.2	$4,787.9	$5,372.2
Total Assets	2,142.0	1,993.6	2,317.5

Tandy Corporation
Statement of Cash Flows
For the Years Ended December 31, 1999 and 1998

(In millions)	1999	1998
Cash flows from operating activities:		
Net income (loss)	$297.9	$ 61.3
Adjustments to reconcile net income (loss) to net cash provided by operating activities:		
Restricted stock awards	9.6	82.6
Provision for loss on sale of Computer City	—	108.2
Depreciation and amortization	90.2	99.0
Deferred income taxes and other items	49.0	(4.0)
Provision for credit losses and bad debts	9.9	12.5
Changes in operating assets and liabilities:		
Receivables	(38.3)	(36.7)
Inventories	52.6	85.6
Other current assets	15.1	17.7
Accounts payable, accrued expenses and income taxes	75.6	(11.4)
Net cash provided by operating activities	561.6	414.8
Investing activities:		
Additions to property, plant and equipment	(102.4)	(131.5)
Proceeds from sale of property, plant and equipment	5.6	6.7
Proceeds from sale of Computer City	—	36.5
Investment in North Point Communication	(20.0)	—
Other investing activities	(4.2)	(4.7)
Net cash used by investing activities	(121.0)	(93.0)
Financing activities:		
Purchases of treasury stock	(422.2)	(337.4)
Proceeds from sale of common stock put options	4.4	0.3
Sale of treasury stock to employee stock plans	39.5	35.4
Proceeds from exercise of stock options	42.0	22.4
Dividends paid	(42.5)	(44.8)
Changes in short-term borrowings, net	(42.3)	(44.9)
Additions to long-term borrowings	100.6	45.7
Repayments of long-term borrowings	(20.0)	(39.9)
Net cash used by financing activities	(340.5)	(363.2)
Increase (decrease) in cash and cash equivalents	100.1	(41.4)
Cash and cash equivalents, beginning of period	64.5	105.9
Cash and cash equivalents, end of period	$164.6	$ 64.5

International Company

The following data pertain to two of Japan's most well-known and successful companies[12] (numbers are in billions of yen):

	Sony Corporation		Canon, Inc.	
	1999	1998	1999	1998
Net sales	¥6,415	¥6,425	¥2,622	¥2,826
Net income	179	222	70	110
Average total assets	6,351	6,041	2,658	2,792
Net cash flows from operating activities	663	612	309	247
Dividends	25	22	15	16
Net capital expenditures	340	356	202	194

Calculate the cash flow yield, cash flows to sales, cash flows to assets, and free cash flow for the two years for each company. Which company is most efficient in generating cash flow? Which company has the best year-to-year trend? Which company most likely will need external financing?

Toys "R" Us Annual Report

Refer to the statement of cash flows in the Toys "R" Us annual report to answer the following questions:

1. Does Toys "R" Us use the direct or the indirect method of reporting cash flows from operating activities? Other than net earnings, what are the most important factors affecting cash flows from operating activities? Explain the trend of each.

2. Based on the cash flows from investing activities, would you say that Toys "R" Us is a contracting or an expanding company?

3. Calculate the cash flow yield, cash flows to sales, cash flows to assets, and free cash flow for the last three years for Toys "R" Us. How would you evaluate the company's cash-generating efficiency? Does Toys "R" Us need external financing? If so, where has it come from?

Fingraph® Financial Analyst™

Choose any two companies from the same industry in the Fingraph® Financial Analyst™ CD-ROM software.

1. In the annual reports for the companies you have selected, identify the statement of cash flows. Do the companies use the direct or indirect form of the statement?

2. Display and print in tabular and graphical form the Statement of Cash Flows: Operating Activities Analysis page. Prepare a table that compares the cash flow yield, cash flows to sales, and cash flows to assets for both companies for two years. Are the ratios moving in the same or opposite directions? Study the operating activities sections of the statements to determine the main causes of differences between the net income and cash flows from operations. How do the companies compare?

3. Display and print in tabular and graphical form the Statement of Cash Flows: Investing and Financing Activities Analysis page. Prepare a table that compares the free cash flow for both companies for two years. How do the companies compare? Are the companies growing or contracting? Study the investing and financing activities sections of the statements to determine the main causes of differences between the companies.

4. Find and read references to cash flows in the liquidity analysis section of management's discussion and analysis in each annual report.

5. Write a one-page executive summary that reports your findings from parts **1–4,** including your assessment of the companies' comparative liquidity. Include the Fingraph® pages and your tables as attachments to your report.

Internet Case

FRA 5.

LO 4   Follow-up Analysis of Cash Flows

Through the Needles Accounting Resource Center at http://college.hmco.com, go to the annual report on the web site for **Marriott International, Inc.** Find the financial statements including the statement of cash flows. Compare Marriott's cash flow performance for the most recent year with the 1999 statement at the beginning of this chapter by (1) identifying major changes in operating, investing, and financing activities, (2) reading management's financial review of cash flows, and (3) calculating the cash flow ratios (cash flow yield, cash flows to sales, cash flows to assets, and free cash flow) for the most recent year. Be prepared to discuss your conclusions in class.

ENDNOTES

1. Marriott International, Inc., *Annual Report*, 1999.
2. *Statement of Financial Accounting Standards No. 95*, "Statement of Cash Flows" (Norwalk, Conn.: Financial Accounting Standards Board, 1987).
3. *Statement of Financial Accounting Concepts No. 1*, "Objectives of Financial Reporting for Business Enterprises" (Norwalk, Conn.: Financial Accounting Standards Board, 1978), par. 37–39.
4. Marriott International, Inc., *Annual Report*, 1999.
5. Gary Slutsker, "Look at the Birdie and Say: 'Cash Flow,'" *Forbes*, October 25, 1993.
6. Jonathan Clements, "Yacktman Fund Is Bloodied but Unbowed," *The Wall Street Journal*, November 8, 1993.
7. Jeffrey Laderman, "Earnings, Schmearnings—Look at the Cash," *Business Week*, July 24, 1989.
8. Marriott International, Inc., *Annual Report*, 1999.
9. American Institute of Certified Public Accountants, *Accounting Trends & Techniques* (New York: AICPA, 1999).
10. Ibid.
11. Tandy Corporation, *Annual Report*, 1999.
12. Sony Corporation, *Annual Report*, 1999; and Canon, Inc., *Annual Report*, 1999.

Financial Performance Evaluation

DECISION POINT: A USER'S FOCUS

Material Sciences Corporation Material Sciences Corporation (MSC) is a technology-based manufacturer of continuously process-coated and specialty engineered materials and services. It makes such products as coil-plated metal, disc-brake-noise dampers, and industrial films. The company has implemented a strategic plan that focuses on long-term strategies, which include the following:[1]

- Use cash flow return on assets as the primary financial and operating measure throughout the company
- Focus on asset management, cost control, and the optimization of manufacturing and distribution facilities
- Grow the business through internal growth, partnering, and acquisitions
- Increase value through technology

How does the management of a company like MSC go about implementing such a strategic plan?

To make its strategic plan operational, MSC's management develops key financial performance measures linked to each of its strategies. Each measure should be an indicator of success or failure in meeting one or more of the strategies. This approach motivates and rewards employees for working toward corporate objectives. It provides concrete proof that the company is achieving its objectives and helps coordinate the company's business processes. Customers and potential investors perceive the company as reliable and progressive in meeting its financial targets. When MSC's management reports to stockholders, it emphasizes its annual and long-term success in achieving the key performance measures. For example, financial highlights from a recent annual report included the following:

- Net sales for the year were up 46 percent
- Working capital was reduced by 32.8 percent
- Cash provided by operating activities, net of capital expenditures (free cash flow), was $52.3 million
- Selling, general, and administrative expenses declined to 12.0 percent from 16.5 percent (of sales)
- Total debt was reduced by $48.5 million

The measurement and reporting of financial performance is a key component in successfully managing a business. For managers to implement their strategic plans using financial measures of performance, they must understand the comprehensive framework commonly employed by internal and external users to evaluate their company's results. This chapter provides that framework.

Financial Performance Evaluation by Internal and External Users

OBJECTIVE

1 Describe and discuss financial performance evaluation by internal and external users

Financial performance evaluation, also called *financial statement analysis*, comprises all the techniques users of financial statements employ to show important relationships in an organization's financial statements and to relate them to important financial objectives. Users of financial statements who perform financial performance evaluations fall into two categories: internal users and external users. Both groups have a strong interest in financial performance. Internal users include top managers, who set and strive to achieve financial performance objectives, middle-level managers of business processes, and employee stockholders. External users are creditors and investors who want to assess management's accomplishment of financial objectives, as well as customers who form cooperative agreements with the company.

Internal Users

The setting of financial performance objectives is a major function of management's plan to achieve the company's strategic goals. All strategic and operating plans established by management must eventually be stated in terms of financial objectives. One of the primary objectives of management is to increase the wealth of the owners or stockholders of the business, but this objective must be divided into components. The Decision Point listed examples of MSC's performance objectives. A complete financial plan should have balanced financial performance objectives in all of the following categories:

Business Objectives	Links to Financial Performance
Liquidity	Ability to pay bills when due and to meet unexpected needs for cash
Profitability	Ability to earn a satisfactory net income
Long-term solvency	Ability to survive for many years
Cash flow adequacy	Ability to generate sufficient cash through operating, investing, and financing activities
Market strength	Ability to increase the wealth of owners

The main responsibility of management is to put into action and to carry out the plans that are designed to achieve the financial performance objectives. Management must constantly monitor key financial performance measures, determine the cause of any deviations in the measures, and propose corrective actions. Annual measures provide data for long-term trend analysis. Reports should be formatted to highlight key performance measures. Management develops monthly, quarterly, and annual reports that compare actual performance with objectives for key financial measures in each of the above categories.

External Users

Creditors make loans in the form of trade accounts, notes, or bonds. They expect them to be repaid according to specified terms and to receive interest on the notes and bonds payable. Investors buy capital stock, from which they hope to receive dividends and an increase in value. Both groups face risks. The creditor faces the risk that the debtor will fail to pay back the loan. The investor faces the risks that dividends will be reduced or not paid and that the market price of the stock will drop. For both groups, the goal is to achieve a return that makes up for the risk. In general, the greater the risk taken, the greater the return required as compensation.

Any one loan or any one investment can turn out badly. As a result, most creditors and investors put their funds into a **portfolio**, or a group of loans or investments. The portfolio is designed to average both the returns and the risks. Nevertheless, individual decisions about the loans or stock in the portfolio must still be made. It is in making those individual decisions that financial performance evaluation is most useful. Creditors and investors use financial performance evaluation in two general ways: (1) to judge past performance and current position and (2) to judge future potential and the risk connected with that potential.

Assessment of Past Performance and Current Position

Past performance is often a good indicator of future performance. Therefore, an investor or creditor looks at the trends of past sales, expenses, net income, cash flow, and return on investment not only as means of judging management's past performance but also as possible indicators of future performance. In addition, an evaluation of current position will tell, for example, what assets the business owns and what liabilities must be paid. It will also tell what the cash position is, how much debt the company has in relation to equity, and what levels of inventories and receivables exist. Knowing a company's past performance and current position is often important in judging future potential and the related risk.

Assessment of Future Potential and Related Risk

Information about the past and present is useful only to the extent that it bears on decisions about the future. An investor judges the potential earning ability of a company because that ability will affect the market price of the company's stock and the amount of dividends the company will pay. A creditor judges the potential debt-paying ability of the company.

The riskiness of an investment or loan depends on how easy it is to predict future profitability or liquidity. If an investor can predict with confidence that a company's earnings per share will be between $2.50 and $2.60 in the next year, the investment is less risky than if the earnings per share are expected to fall between $2.00 and $3.00. For example, the potential associated with an investment in an established and stable electric utility, or a loan to it, is relatively easy to predict on the basis of the company's past performance and current position. The potential associated with investment in a small Internet firm, on the other hand, may be much harder to predict. For this reason, the investment in or loan to the electric utility carries less risk than the investment in or loan to the small Internet company.

Often, in return for taking a greater risk, an investor in the Internet company will demand a higher expected return (increase in market price plus dividends) than will an investor in the utility company. Also, a creditor of the Internet company will demand a higher interest rate and possibly more assurance of repayment (a secured loan, for instance) than a creditor of the utility company. The higher interest rate reimburses the creditor for assuming a higher risk.

Standards for Financial Performance Evaluation

When evaluating financial performance, decision makers must judge whether the relationships they have found are favorable or unfavorable. Three commonly used standards of comparison are (1) rule-of-thumb measures, (2) past performance of the company, and (3) industry norms.

Rule-of-Thumb Measures

Many financial analysts, investors, and lenders employ ideal, or rule-of-thumb, measures for key financial ratios. For example, it has long been thought that a current ratio (current assets divided by current liabilities) of 2:1 is acceptable. The credit-rating firm of Dun & Bradstreet, in its *Industry Norms and Key Business Ratios,* offers such rules of thumb as the following:

Current debt to tangible net worth   Ordinarily, a business begins to pile up trouble when this relationship exceeds 80 percent.

Inventory to net working capital   Ordinarily, this relationship should not exceed 80 percent.

Although such measures may suggest areas that need further investigation, there is no proof that the specified levels are the best for every company. A company with a current ratio higher than 2:1 may have a poor credit policy (resulting in accounts receivable being too large), too much inventory, or poor cash management. Another company may have a ratio lower than 2:1 as a result of excellent management in all three of those areas. Thus, rule-of-thumb measures must be used with great care.

Past Performance of the Company

An improvement over rule-of-thumb measures is the comparison of a company's financial measures or ratios over a period of time. Such a comparison will give the analyst at least some basis for judging whether a measure or ratio is improving or deteriorating. It may also be helpful in showing future trends. However, because trends reverse at times, such projections must be made with care. Another problem with trend analysis is that the past may not be a useful measure of adequacy. In other words, past performance may not be enough to meet present needs. For example, even if return on total investment improved from 3 percent one year to 4 percent the next, the 4 percent return may in fact not be adequate.

Industry Norms

One way of making up for the limitations of using past performance as a standard is to use industry norms. Such norms tell how a company's performance compares with the average performance of other companies in the same industry. For example, suppose that companies in an industry have an average rate of return on total investment of 8 percent. In such a case, a company whose rate of return is only 3 percent is probably not performing adequately. Industry norms can also be used to judge trends. Suppose that a company's profit margin dropped from 12 to 10 percent because of a downward turn in the economy. If other companies in the same industry experienced an average drop in profit margin from 12 to 4 percent, that norm would indicate that the first company had done relatively well. Sometimes, instead of industry averages, data for the industry leader or a specific competitor are used for evaluation.

There are three limitations to using industry norms as standards. First, two companies that seem to be in the same industry may not be strictly comparable. For example, consider two companies in the oil industry. One company may be purchasing oil products and then marketing them through service stations. The other, an international company, may discover, produce, refine, and market its own oil products. The operations of these two companies cannot be compared because they are different.

Second, most large companies today operate in more than one industry. Some of these **diversified companies**, or *conglomerates*, operate in many unrelated industries. The individual segments of a diversified company generally have different rates of profitability and different degrees of risk. In evaluating the consolidated financial statements of such companies, it is often impossible to use industry norms as standards. There are simply no other companies that are similar enough. A requirement by the Financial Accounting Standards Board, presented in *Statement No. 131*, provides a partial solution to this problem. It states that diversified companies must report segment profit or loss, certain revenue and expense items, and segment assets for each of their operating segments. Depending on how the company is organized, segment information may be reported for operations in different industries or in different geographical areas or for major customers.[2]

An example of segment reporting may be found in Exhibit 1. Goodyear Tire & Rubber Co. is a well-known tire company, but it also has significant engineered products and chemical products divisions. The selected data on sales, income, and assets for those segments shown in Exhibit 1 allow the analyst to compute important profitability performance measures, such as profit margin, asset turnover, and return on assets, for each segment and to compare them to their respective industry norm. Note that the tire business is divided into geographic segments and that separate data are reported for each segment.

The third limitation of industry norms is that companies in the same industry with similar operations may use different acceptable accounting procedures. That is, different methods may be used to value inventories, or different methods may be used to depreciate similar assets. Even so, if little information about a company's prior performance is available, industry norms probably offer the best available standards for judging current performance—as long as they are used with care.

Sources of Information

The external analyst is often limited to using publicly available information about a company. The major sources of information about publicly held corporations are reports published by the company, SEC reports, business periodicals, and credit and investment advisory services.

Reports Published by the Company

The annual report of a publicly held corporation is an important source of financial information. The main parts of an annual report are (1) management's analysis of the past year's operations, (2) the financial statements, (3) the notes to the statements, including the principal accounting procedures used by the company, (4) the auditors' report, and (5) the summary of operations for a five- or ten-year period.

(In millions)	1999	1998	1997
Sales			
North American Tire	$ 6,355.3	$ 6,235.2	$ 6,207.5
Europe Tire	2,558.6	2,061.0	2,022.5
Eastern Europe, Africa, and Middle East Tire	796.2	850.0	904.7
Latin American Tire	930.8	1,245.6	1,413.4
Asia Tire	575.9	501.8	666.9
Total Tires	**11,216.8**	**10,893.6**	**11,215.0**
Engineered Products	1,210.1	1,279.3	1,324.0
Chemical Products	928.4	970.8	1,089.1
Total Segment Sales	**13,355.3**	**13,143.7**	**13,628.1**
Income			
North American Tire	$ 19.0	$ 378.6	$ 382.5
Europe Tire	188.0	199.7	166.7
Eastern Europe, Africa, and Middle East Tire	49.8	102.4	102.4
Latin American Tire	67.7	186.1	233.5
Asia Tire	26.0	7.5	58.6
Total Tires	**350.5**	**874.3**	**943.7**
Engineered Products	71.0	111.8	130.1
Chemical Products	118.9	139.6	128.3
Total Segment Income (EBIT)	**540.4**	**1,125.7**	**1,202.1**
Assets			
North American Tire	$ 4,847.7	$ 3,944.6	$ 3,596.6
Europe Tire	3,336.1	1,690.0	1,460.4
Eastern Europe, Africa, and Middle East Tire	897.1	898.1	663.0
Latin American Tire	820.7	993.8	979.5
Asia Tire	725.5	744.0	522.3
Total Tires	**10,627.1**	**8,270.5**	**7,221.8**
Engineered Products	673.6	678.9	630.3
Chemical Products	644.5	576.5	541.0
Total Segment Assets	**11,945.2**	**9,525.9**	**8,393.1**

Source: Goodyear Tire & Rubber Co., *Annual Report*, 1999.

Most publicly held companies also publish interim financial statements. An **interim financial statement** reports data for a period of less than one year, usually a quarter or a month. Interim reports present limited information in the form of condensed financial statements, which need not be subjected to a full audit by the independent auditor. The interim statements are watched closely by the financial community for early signs of important changes in a company's earnings trend.

FOCUS ON BUSINESS TECHNOLOGY

Performance reports and other financial information, stock quotes, reference data, and news about companies and markets are available instantaneously to individuals on the Internet through such services as CompuServe, America Online, Yahoo, and Wall Street Journal Interactive Edition. The Internet is an international web of computer-driven communications systems that links tens of millions of homes and businesses through telephone, cable, and computer networks. With access to the online services of brokers like Charles Schwab & Co., Inc., which allow customers to use their own computers to buy and sell stock and other securities, individuals today have resources equivalent to those used by many professional analysts.

SEC Reports

Publicly held corporations must file annual reports, quarterly reports, and current reports with the Securities and Exchange Commission (SEC). All such reports are available to the public at a small charge. The SEC requires companies to submit their annual reports in a standard form (Form 10-K) that contains more information than their published annual reports. For that reason, Form 10-K is a valuable source of information. It is available free of charge to stockholders of the company. The SEC quarterly report (Form 10-Q) presents important facts about interim financial performance. The SEC current report (Form 8-K) must be filed within a few days of the date of certain significant events, such as the sale or purchase of a division of the company or a change in auditors. This report is often the first indicator of important changes that may affect a company's financial performance in the future. Many company reports filed with the Securities and Exchange Commission are now available on the Internet at http://www.sec.gov/edgarhp.htm.

Business Periodicals and Credit and Investment Advisory Services

Financial analysts must keep up with current events in the financial world. Probably the best source of financial news is *The Wall Street Journal*, which is published every business day and is the most complete financial newspaper in the United States. Some helpful magazines, published every week or every two weeks, are *Forbes*, *Barron's*, *Fortune*, and the *Financial Times*.

For further details about the financial history of companies, the publications of such services as Moody's Investors Service, Inc., and Standard & Poor's are useful. Data on industry norms, average ratios and relationships, and credit ratings are available from such agencies as The Dun & Bradstreet Corp. In its *Industry Norms and Key Business Ratios*, Dun & Bradstreet offers an annual analysis giving 14 ratios for each of 125 industry groups, classified as retailing, wholesaling, manufacturing, and construction. *Annual Statement Studies*, published by Robert Morris Associates, presents many facts and ratios for 223 different industries. A number of private services are also available for a yearly fee.

An example of specialized financial reporting that is readily available to the public is Mergent's *Handbook of Dividend Achievers*, which profiles companies that have increased their dividends consistently over the past ten years. A sample listing from that publication—for PepsiCo, Inc.—is shown in Exhibit 2. A wealth of information about the company is summarized on one page: the market action of its stock; summaries of its business operations, recent developments, and prospects;

Exhibit 2
Sample Listing from Mergent's *Handbook of Dividend Achievers*

NYSE SYMBOL PEP
Rec. Pr. 40 7/8 (5/31/00)

PEPSICO INC.

YIELD 1.4%
P/E RATIO 30.1

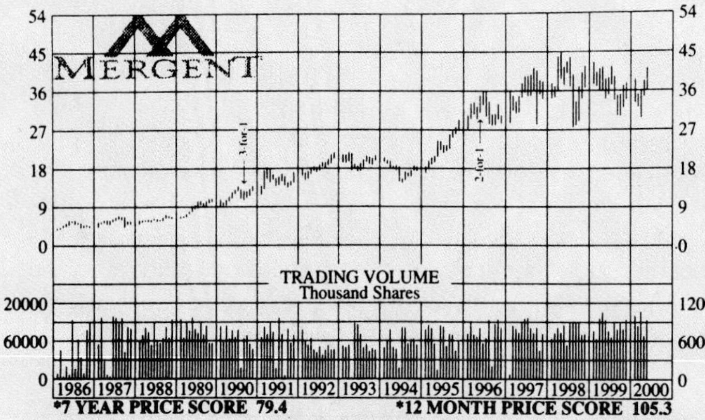

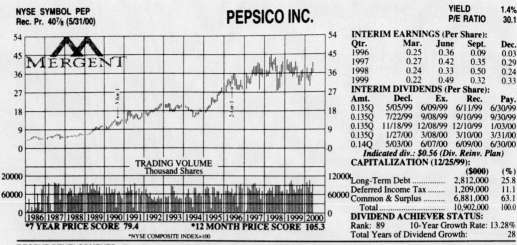

***7 YEAR PRICE SCORE 79.4** ***12 MONTH PRICE SCORE 105.3**
*NYSE COMPOSITE INDEX=100

INTERIM EARNINGS (Per Share):

Qtr.	Mar.	June	Sept.	Dec.
1996	0.25	0.36	0.09	0.03
1997	0.27	0.42	0.35	0.29
1998	0.24	0.33	0.50	0.24
1999	0.22	0.49	0.32	0.33

INTERIM DIVIDENDS (Per Share):

Amt.	Decl.	Ex.	Rec.	Pay.
0.135Q	5/05/99	6/09/99	6/11/99	6/30/99
0.135Q	7/22/99	9/08/99	9/10/99	9/30/99
0.135Q	11/18/99	12/08/99	12/10/99	1/03/00
0.135Q	1/27/00	3/08/00	3/10/00	3/31/00
0.14Q	5/03/00	6/07/00	6/09/00	6/30/00

Indicated div.: $0.56 (Div. Reinv. Plan)

CAPITALIZATION (12/25/99):

	($000)	(%)
Long-Term Debt	2,812,000	25.8
Deferred Income Tax	1,209,000	11.1
Common & Surplus	6,881,000	63.1
Total	10,902,000	100.0

DIVIDEND ACHIEVER STATUS:
Rank: 89 10-Year Growth Rate: 13.28%
Total Years of Dividend Growth: 28

RECENT DEVELOPMENTS: For the year ended 12/25/99, net income rose 2.9% to $2.05 billion from $1.99 billion in the previous year. Total net sales decreased 8.9% to $20.37 billion from $22.35 billion the year before. Net sales from Pepsi-Cola increased 46.4% to $4.38 billion, while Frito-Lay group sales climbed 5.8% to $11.62 billion. Tropicana sales amounted to $2.25 billion. Operating profit amounted to $2.81 billion compared to $2.58 billion a year earlier.

PROSPECTS: Results are benefiting from PEP's strategy of focusing on high-margin, high-return businesses that generate strong cash flow. PEP will be focusing more on its international snack segment going forward. As part of this intiative, PEP plans to expand the Frito-Lay structure from its current two divisions, Frito-Lay North America and Frito-Lay International, by establishing two new companies: Frito-Lay Europe/Middle East/Africa and Frito-Lay Latin America/Asia Pacific/Australia.

BUSINESS

PEPSICO INC. operates on a worldwide basis within the soft drinks, juice and snack-foods businesses. The beverages segment, which accounted for 21% of sales in 1999 (30% of operating profit), manufactures concentrates, and markets PEPSI, PEPSI-COLA, DIET PEPSI, PEPSI ONE, PEPSI MAX, MOUNTAIN DEW, MUG, ALL SPORT, AQUAFINA, MIRINDA, SLICE and allied brands worldwide, and 7-UP internationally. This segment also operates soft drink bottling businesses principally in the United States. The juice segment, 11% (6%), includes Tropicana Products, Inc., which manufactures and sells its products under trademarks such as TROPICANA PURE PREMIUM, and TROPICANA SEASONS BEST. Snack Foods, 57% (70%), manufactures and markets snack chips through Frito-Lay Inc. Well-known brands include: DORITOS, RUFFLES and LAYS. On 10/6/97, the Company spun off its Restaurant unit, TRICON Global Restaurants.

ANNUAL FINANCIAL DATA

	12/25/99	12/26/98	12/27/97	12/28/96	12/30/95	12/31/94	12/25/93
Earnings Per Share	[5] **1.37**	[4] **1.31**	[1] **0.95**	[2] **0.72**	[2] **1.00**	[3] **1.11**	**0.98**
Cash Flow Per Share	**2.06**	**2.12**	**1.65**	**1.79**	**2.08**	**2.09**	**1.97**
Tang. Book Val. Per Share	**1.47**	...	**0.72**	...	...	...	...
Dividends Per Share	**0.53**	**0.51**	**0.48**	**0.43**	**0.38**	**0.34**	**0.29**
Dividend Payout %	**38.7**	**38.9**	**50.5**	**59.7**	**38.0**	**30.6**	**29.6**
INCOME STATEMENT (IN MILLIONS):							
Total Revenues	20,367.0	22,348.0	20,917.0	31,645.0	30,421.0	28,472.4	25,020.7
Costs & Expenses	16,452.0	18,530.0	17,149.0	27,380.0	25,694.0	23,694.2	20,670.0
Depreciation & Amort.	1,032.0	1,234.0	1,106.0	1,719.0	1,740.0	1,577.0	1,444.2
Operating Income	2,818.0	2,584.0	2,662.0	2,546.0	2,987.0	3,201.2	2,906.5
Net Interest Inc./(Exp.)	d245.0	d321.0	d353.0	d499.0	d555.0	d554.6	d484.0
Income Before Income Taxes	3,656.0	2,263.0	2,309.0	2,047.0	2,432.0	2,664.4	2,422.5
Income Taxes	1,606.0	270.0	818.0	898.0	826.0	880.4	668.0
Equity Earnings/Minority Int.	83.0	...	...	...	...	...	...
Net Income	[5] 2,050.0	[4] 1,993.0	[1] 1,491.0	[2] 1,149.0	[2] 1,606.0	[3] 1,784.0	1,754.5
Cash Flow	3,082.0	3,227.0	2,597.0	2,868.0	3,346.0	3,361.0	3,198.7
Average Shs. Outstg. (000)	1,496,000	1,519,000	1,570,000	1,606,000	1,608,000	1,607,200	1,620,200
BALANCE SHEET (IN MILLIONS):							
Cash & Cash Equivalents	1,056.0	394.0	2,883.0	786.0	1,498.0	1,488.1	1,856.2
Total Current Assets	4,173.0	4,362.0	6,251.0	5,139.0	5,546.0	5,072.2	5,164.1
Net Property	5,266.0	7,318.0	6,261.0	10,191.0	9,870.0	9,882.8	8,855.6
Total Assets	17,551.0	22,660.0	20,101.0	24,512.0	25,432.0	24,792.0	23,705.8
Total Current Liabilities	3,788.0	7,914.0	4,257.0	5,139.0	5,230.0	5,270.4	6,574.9
Long-Term Obligations	2,812.0	4,028.0	4,946.0	8,439.0	8,509.0	8,840.5	7,442.6
Net Stockholders' Equity	6,881.0	6,401.0	6,936.0	6,623.0	7,313.0	6,856.1	6,338.7
Net Working Capital	385.0	d3,552.0	1,994.0	...	316.0	d198.2	d1,410.8
Year-end Shs. Outstg. (000)	1,455,000	1,471,000	1,502,000	1,545,000	1,576,000	1,579,800	1,597,600
STATISTICAL RECORD:							
Operating Profit Margin %	13.8	11.6	12.7	8.0	9.8	11.2	11.6
Net Profit Margin %	10.1	8.9	7.1	3.6	5.3	6.3	7.0
Return on Equity %	29.8	31.1	21.5	17.3	22.0	26.0	27.7
Return on Assets %	11.7	8.8	7.4	4.7	6.3	7.2	7.4
Debt/Total Assets %	16.0	17.8	24.6	34.4	33.5	35.7	31.4
Price Range	42 9/16-30 1/8	44 13/16-27 9/16	41 5/16-28 1/4	35 7/8-27 1/4	29 3/8-16 15/16	20 9/16-14 5/8	21 13/16-17 1/4
P/E Ratio	31.1-22.0	34.2-21.0	43.5-29.7	49.8-37.8	29.4-16.9	18.5-13.2	22.3-17.6
Average Yield %	1.5	1.4	1.4	1.4	1.6	1.9	1.5

Statistics are as originally reported. Adj. for 2-for-1 stk. split, 5/96 [1] Incls. non-recurr. chrgs. $290.0 million: bef. disc. oper. gain $651.0 mill. [2] Incls. non-recurr. chrgs. 1/31/96. $716.0 mill.: non-cash chrg. 12/31/95. $520.0 mill. [3] Bef. acctg. change chrg. 12/31/94: $32.0 mill. [4] Incl. one-time chrg. of $288.0 mill. [5] Incls. one-time chrg of $65.0 mill.

OFFICERS:
R. A. Enrico, Chmn., C.E.O.
K. M. von der Heyden, Vice-Chmn.
S. S. Reinemund, Pres., C.O.O.

INVESTOR CONTACT: M. D. Moore, (914) 253-3035

PRINCIPAL OFFICE: 700 Anderson Hill Rd., Purchase, NY 10577-1444

TELEPHONE NUMBER: (914) 253-2000
FAX: (914) 253-2070
WEB: www.pepsico.com
NO. OF EMPLOYEES: 118,000 (approx.)
SHAREHOLDERS: 220,000 (approx.)
ANNUAL MEETING: In May
INCORPORATED: DE. Sep., 1919: reincorp., NC. Dec., 1986

INSTITUTIONAL HOLDINGS:
No. of Institutions: 903
Shares Held: 859,297,794
% Held: 59.0

INDUSTRY: Bottled and canned soft drinks (SIC: 2086)

TRANSFER AGENT(S): BankBoston, N.A., Boston, MA

Source: Reprinted with permission of Mergent FIS, Inc., from *Handbook of Dividend Achievers,* 2000.

earnings and dividend data; annual financial data for the past ten years; and other information. The data in those summaries can be used to do many of the trend analyses and calculate the ratios explained in this chapter.

Tools and Techniques of Financial Performance Evaluation

OBJECTIVE

4 Apply horizontal analysis, trend analysis, and vertical analysis to financial statements

Few numbers are very significant when looked at individually. It is their relationship to other numbers or their change from one period to another that is important. The tools of financial performance evaluation are intended to show relationships and changes. Among the more widely used tools are horizontal analysis, trend analysis, vertical analysis, and ratio analysis. We will illustrate these tools with a comprehensive financial evaluation of Sun Microsystems, Inc. Sun Microsystems was formed in 1982 and has emerged as a global leader in network computing. The company developed many of the core networking technologies that today are the basis of the Internet and corporate intranets, including the widely adopted Java technology.

Horizontal Analysis

Generally accepted accounting principles require the presentation of comparative financial statements that give financial information for the current year and the previous year. A common starting point for studying such statements is **horizontal analysis**, which begins with the computation of changes from the previous year to the current year in both dollar amounts and percentages. The percentage change must be computed to relate the size of the change to the size of the dollar amounts involved. A change of $1 million in sales is not as impressive as a change of $1 million in net income, because sales is a larger amount than net income.

Exhibits 3 and 4 present the comparative balance sheets and income statements for Sun Microsystems, Inc., with the dollar and percentage changes shown. The percentage change is computed as follows:

$$\text{Percentage Change} = 100 \times \left(\frac{\text{Amount of Change}}{\text{Base Year Amount}} \right)$$

The **base year** in any set of data is always the first year to be considered. For example, when considering data from 1999 and 2000, 1999 is the base year. Between those two years, Sun Microsystems' total current assets increased by $689 million, from approximately $6,188 million to $6,877 million, or by 11.1 percent. This is computed as follows:

$$\text{Percentage Change} = 100 \times \left(\frac{\$689 \text{ million}}{\$6,188 \text{ million}} \right) = 11.1\%$$

An examination of the components of current assets in the comparative balance sheets shows the changes from 1999 to 2000. All current assets categories except short-term investments increased. It is important to consider both the dollar amount of the increase and the percentage increase. For example, cash and cash equivalents increased 67.9 percent compared with an 80.8 percent increase in inventories. However, the dollar increase in cash and cash equivalents is three times the dollar increase in inventories ($748 million versus $249 million). There was a corresponding increase in total current liabilities of $1,511 million, or 46.5 percent. Total assets increased $5,653 million, or 66.5 percent, which included an

Exhibit 3
Comparative Balance Sheets with Horizontal Analysis

Sun Microsystems, Inc.
Consolidated Balance Sheets
June 30, 2000 and 1999

(In millions, except per share amounts)	2000	1999	Increase (Decrease) Amount	Percentage
Assets				
Current Assets				
Cash and Cash Equivalents	$ 1,849	$1,101	$ 748	67.9
Short-Term Investments	626	1,591	(965)	(60.7)
Accounts Receivable, Net of Allowances of $534				
in 2000 and $340 in 1999	2,690	2,310	380	16.5
Inventories	557	308	249	80.8
Deferred Tax Assets	673	506	167	33.0
Other Current Assets	482	372	110	29.6
Total Current Assets	$ 6,877	$6,188	$ 689	11.1
Property, Plant and Equipment, Net	$ 2,095	$1,614	$ 481	29.8
Long-Term Investments	4,496	0	4,496	*
Other Assets, Net	684	697	(13)	(1.9)
Total Assets	$14,152	$8,499	$5,653	66.5
Liabilities and Stockholders' Equity				
Current Liabilities				
Short-Term Borrowings	$ 7	$ 2	$ 5	250.0
Accounts Payable	924	756	168	22.2
Accrued Payroll-Related Liabilities	751	520	231	44.4
Accrued Liabilities and Other	1,366	991	375	37.8
Deferred Revenues and Customer Deposits	1,289	576	713	123.8
Income Taxes Payable	422	403	19	4.7
Total Current Liabilities	$ 4,759	$3,248	$1,511	46.5
Deferred Income Taxes	364	192	172	89.6
Long-Term Debt and Other Obligations	1,720	192	1,528	795.8
Stockholders' Equity	7,309	4,867	2,442	50.2
Total Liabilities and Stockholders' Equity	$14,152	$8,499	$5,653	66.5

* Not meaningful.
Source: Sun Microsystems, Inc., *Annual Report*, 2000.

increase of $4,496 million in long-term investments. Total stockholders' equity increased by $2,442 million, or 50.2 percent. All of this shows Sun Microsystems to be a rapidly growing company.

The most important findings from the income statements in Exhibit 4 are that net revenues increased by $3,915 million, or 33.2 percent; operating income increased by $873 million, or 57.4 percent; and net income increased by $824 million, or 80.0 percent. These extremely positive results were achieved in part because net revenues grew faster (33.2 percent) than total operating expenses (25.2 percent).

Exhibit 4
Comparative Income Statements with Horizontal Analysis

Sun Microsystems, Inc.
Consolidated Income Statements
For the Years Ended June 30, 2000 and 1999

(In millions, except per share amounts)	2000	1999	Increase (Decrease) Amount	Increase (Decrease) Percentage
Net Revenues	$15,721	$11,806	$3,915	33.2
Costs of Sales	7,549	5,670	1,879	33.1
Gross Margin	$ 8,172	$ 6,136	$2,036	33.2
Operating Expenses:				
Research and Development	1,630	1,280	350	27.3
Selling, General and Administrative	4,137	3,215	922	28.7
Purchased In-Process Research and Development	12	121	(109)	(90.1)
Total Operating Expenses	$ 5,779	$ 4,616	$1,163	25.2
Operating Income	$ 2,393	$ 1,520	$ 873	57.4
Gain on Sale of Investment, Net	208	0	208	*
Interest Income, Net	170	85	85	100.0
Income Before Income Taxes	$ 2,771	$ 1,605	$1,166	72.6
Provision for Income Taxes	917	575	342	59.5
Net Income	$ 1,854	$ 1,030	$ 824	80.0
Net Income per Common Share—Basic	$ 1.18	$ 0.67	$ 0.51	76.1
Net Income per Common Share—Diluted	$ 1.10	$ 0.63	$ 0.47	74.6
Shares Used in the Calculation of the Net Income per Common Share—Basic	1,576	1,544	32	2.1
Shares Used in the Calculation of the Net Income per Common Share—Diluted	1,689	1,641	48	2.9

* Not meaningful.
Source: Sun Microsystems, Inc., *Annual Report,* 2000.

Trend Analysis

A variation of horizontal analysis is **trend analysis**, in which percentage changes are calculated for several successive years instead of for two years. Trend analysis, with its long-run view, is important because it may point to basic changes in the nature of a business. In addition to providing comparative financial statements, most companies present a summary of operations and data about other key indicators for five or more years. Net revenues and operating income from Sun Microsystems' summary of operations, together with a trend analysis, are presented in Exhibit 5.

Trend analysis uses an **index number** to show changes in related items over a period of time. For index numbers, the base year is equal to 100 percent. Other years are measured in relation to that amount. For example, the 2000 index for Sun Microsystems' net revenues was figured as follows (dollar amounts in millions):

$$\text{Index} = 100 \times \left(\frac{\text{Index Year Amount}}{\text{Base Year Amount}} \right) = 100 \times \left(\frac{\$15,721}{\$7,095} \right) = 221.6$$

Exhibit 5
Trend Analysis

	Sun Microsystems, Inc. Net Revenues and Operating Income Trend Analysis				
	2000	**1999**	**1998**	**1997**	**1996**
Dollar Values (in millions)					
Net Revenues	15,721	11,806	9,862	8,661	7,095
Operating Income	2,393	1,520	1,114	1,099	675
Trend Analysis (in percentages)					
Net Revenues	221.6	166.4	139.0	122.1	100.0
Operating Income	354.5	225.2	165.0	162.8	100.0

Source: Sun Microsystems, Inc., *Annual Report*, 2000.

The trend analysis presented in Exhibit 5 clearly shows that operating income has grown faster than net revenues at Sun Microsystems. However, both net revenues and operating income have increased every year. Figure 1 presents these trends in graphic form.

Vertical Analysis

In **vertical analysis**, percentages are used to show the relationship of the different parts to a total in a single statement. The analyst sets a total figure in the statement equal to 100 percent and computes each component's percentage of that total. (The total figure would be total assets or total liabilities and stockholders' equity on the balance sheet, and net revenues or net sales on the income statement.) The resulting statement of percentages is called a **common-size statement**. Common-size balance sheets and common-size income statements for Sun Microsystems are shown in financial statement form in Exhibits 6 and 7 and in pie-chart form in Figures 2 and 3.

Figure 1
Trend Analysis Presented Graphically for Sun Microsystems, Inc.

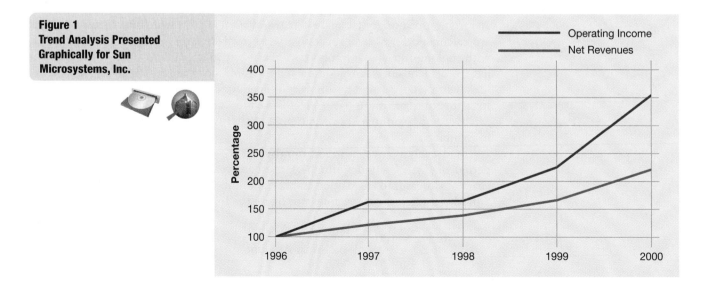

Exhibit 6
Common-Size Balance Sheets

	2000	1999
Sun Microsystems, Inc. **Common-Size Balance Sheets** **June 30, 2000 and 1999**		
Assets		
Current Assets	48.6%	72.8%
Net Property, Plant and Equipment	14.8	19.0
Long-Term Investments	31.8	
Other Assets, Net	4.8	8.2
Total Assets	100.0%	100.0%
Liabilities and Stockholders' Equity		
Current Liabilities	33.6%	38.2%
Deferred Income Taxes	2.6	2.3
Long-Term Debt and Other Obligations	12.2	2.3
Total Liabilities	48.4%	42.7%
Total Stockholders' Equity	51.6	57.3
Total Liabilities and Stockholders' Equity	100.0%	100.0%

Note: Amounts do not precisely total 100 percent in all cases due to rounding.
Source: Sun Microsystems, Inc., *Annual Report*, 2000.

Figure 2
Common-Size Balance Sheets Presented Graphically for Sun Microsystems, Inc.

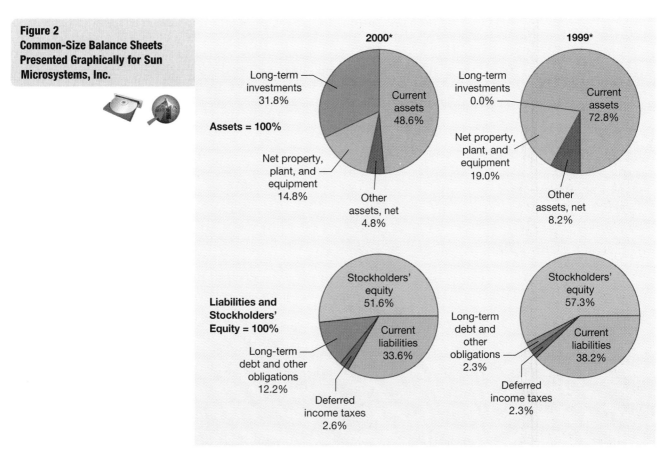

* Rounding causes some additions not to total precisely.

Exhibit 7
Common-Size Income Statements

	2000	1999
Sun Microsystems, Inc.		
Common-Size Income Statements		
For the Years Ended June 30, 2000 and 1999		
Net Revenues	100.0%	100.0%
Cost of Sales	48.0	48.0
Gross Margin	52.0%	52.0%
Operating Expenses:		
Research and Development	10.4%	10.8%
Selling, General and Administrative	26.3	27.2
Purchased In-Process R&D	0.1	1.0
Total Operating Expenses	36.8%	39.1%
Operating Income	15.2%	12.9%
Gain on Sale of Investment, Net	1.3	0.0
Interest, Net	1.1	0.7
Income Before Income Taxes	17.6%	13.6%
Provision for Income Taxes	5.8	4.9
Net Income	11.8%	8.7%

Note: Rounding causes some additions and subtractions not to total precisely.
Source: Sun Microsystems, Inc., *Annual Report*, 2000.

Vertical analysis is useful for comparing the importance of specific components in the operation of a business. Also, comparative common-size statements can be used to identify important changes in the components from one year to the next. As shown in Exhibit 6 and Figure 2, from 1999 to 2000 the composition of Sun Microsystems' assets shifted from current assets toward long-term investments, while current liabilities and stockholders' equity decreased due to new long-term

Figure 3
Common-Size Income Statements Presented Graphically for Sun Microsystems, Inc.

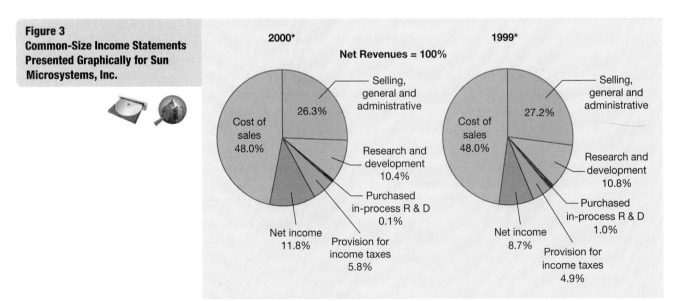

*Rounding causes some additions not to total precisely.
Note: Interest and gains are not presented.

debt. The main conclusions to be drawn from this analysis are that current assets and current liabilities make up a large portion of Sun Microsystems' financial structure and that until 2000 the company had few long-term liabilities.

The common-size income statements in Exhibit 7, illustrated in Figure 3, show that from 1999 to 2000 Sun Microsystems reduced its operating expenses by 2.3 percent of revenues (39.1% − 36.8%). This reduction contributed to an increase in operating income as a percentage of net revenues of 2.3 percent (15.2% − 12.9%).

Common-size statements are often used to make comparisons between companies. They allow an analyst to compare the operating and financing characteristics of two companies of different size in the same industry. For example, the analyst might want to compare Sun Microsystems with other companies in terms of percentage of total assets financed by debt or in terms of selling, general, and administrative expenses as a percentage of net revenues. Common-size statements would show those and other relationships.

Ratio Analysis

Ratio analysis is a technique of financial performance evaluation that identifies meaningful relationships between the components of the financial statements. To be most meaningful, the interpretation of ratios must include a study of the underlying data. Ratios are useful in evaluating a company's financial position and operations and in comparing financial data for several years or for several companies. The primary purpose of ratios is to point out areas needing further investigation. To interpret ratios correctly, an analyst must have a general understanding of the company and its environment. Ratios may be expressed in several ways. For example, a ratio of net income of $100,000 to sales of $1,000,000 may be stated as (1) net income is 1/10 or 10 percent of sales; (2) the ratio of sales to net income is 10 to 1 (10:1), or sales are 10 times net income; or (3) for every dollar of sales, the company has an average net income of 10 cents.

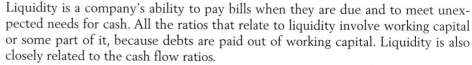

Comprehensive Illustration of Ratio Analysis

OBJECTIVE

5 Apply ratio analysis to financial statements in a comprehensive evaluation of a company's financial performance

The financial condition and operating results of any company can be evaluated through the use of comprehensive ratio analysis. Sun Microsystems' performance as reported in its annual report can be compared for the years 1999 and 2000 with regard to the following objectives: (1) liquidity, (2) profitability, (3) long-term solvency, (4) cash flow adequacy, and (5) market strength. Most data for the analyses come from the financial statements presented in Exhibits 3 and 4. Other data are presented as needed.

Evaluating Liquidity

Liquidity is a company's ability to pay bills when they are due and to meet unexpected needs for cash. All the ratios that relate to liquidity involve working capital or some part of it, because debts are paid out of working capital. Liquidity is also closely related to the cash flow ratios.

The liquidity ratios from 1999 to 2000 for Sun Microsystems are presented in Exhibit 8. The **current ratio** and the **quick ratio** are measures of short-term debt-paying ability. The principal difference between the two is that the numerator of the current ratio includes inventories and prepaid expenses. Inventories take longer to convert to cash than do the assets included in the numerator of the quick ratio.

Exhibit 8
Liquidity Ratios of Sun Microsystems, Inc.

(Dollar amounts in millions)	2000	1999

Current ratio: Measure of short-term debt-paying ability

$$\frac{\text{Current Assets}}{\text{Current Liabilities}} \qquad \frac{\$6,877}{\$4,759} = 1.4 \text{ times} \qquad \frac{\$6,188}{\$3,248} = 1.9 \text{ times}$$

Quick ratio: Measure of short-term debt-paying ability

$$\frac{\text{Cash} + \text{Marketable Securities} + \text{Receivables}}{\text{Current Liabilities}}$$

$$\frac{\$1,849 + \$626 + \$2,690}{\$4,759} \qquad \frac{\$1,101 + \$1,591 + \$2,310}{\$3,248}$$

$$= \frac{\$5,165}{\$4,759} = 1.1 \text{ times} \qquad = \frac{\$5,002}{\$3,248} = 1.5 \text{ times}$$

Receivable turnover: Measure of relative size of accounts receivable and effectiveness of credit policies

$$\frac{\text{Net Sales}}{\text{Average Accounts Receivable*}} \qquad \frac{\$15,721}{(\$2,690 + \$2,310) \div 2} \qquad \frac{\$11,806}{(\$2,310 + \$1,846) \div 2}$$

$$= \frac{\$15,721}{\$2,500} = 6.3 \text{ times} \qquad = \frac{\$11,806}{\$2,078} = 5.7 \text{ times}$$

Average days' sales uncollected: Measure of average days taken to collect receivables

$$\frac{\text{Days in Year}}{\text{Receivable Turnover}} \qquad \frac{365 \text{ days}}{6.3 \text{ times}} = 57.9 \text{ days} \qquad \frac{365 \text{ days}}{5.7 \text{ times}} = 64.0 \text{ days}$$

Inventory turnover: Measure of relative size of inventory

$$\frac{\text{Cost of Goods Sold}}{\text{Average Inventory*}} \qquad \frac{\$7,549}{(\$557 + \$308) \div 2} \qquad \frac{\$5,670}{(\$308 + \$346) \div 2}$$

$$= \frac{\$7,549}{\$433} = 17.4 \text{ times} \qquad = \frac{\$5,670}{\$327} = 17.3 \text{ times}$$

Average days' inventory on hand: Measure of average days taken to sell inventory

$$\frac{\text{Days in Year}}{\text{Inventory Turnover}} \qquad \frac{365 \text{ days}}{17.4 \text{ times}} = 21.0 \text{ days} \qquad \frac{365 \text{ days}}{17.3 \text{ times}} = 21.1 \text{ days}$$

Payables turnover: Measure of relative size of accounts payable

$$\frac{\text{Cost of Goods Sold} +/- \text{Change in Inventory*}}{\text{Average Accounts Payable*}} \qquad \frac{\$7,549 + \$249}{(\$924 + \$756) \div 2} \qquad \frac{\$5,670 - \$38}{(\$756 + \$496) \div 2}$$

$$= \frac{7,798}{840} = 9.3 \text{ times} \qquad = \frac{5,632}{626} = 9.0 \text{ times}$$

Average days' payable: Measure of average days taken to pay accounts payable

$$\frac{\text{Days in Year}}{\text{Payables Turnover}} \qquad = \frac{365 \text{ days}}{9.3 \text{ times}} = 39.3 \text{ days} \qquad = \frac{365 \text{ days}}{9.0 \text{ times}} = 40.6 \text{ days}$$

*1998 figures are from Sun Microsystems' 1999 annual report.
Source: Sun Microsystems, Inc., *Annual Report*, 2000.

At Sun Microsystems, both ratios decreased from 1999 to 2000. The current ratio was 1.9 times in 1999 and 1.4 times in 2000, and the quick ratio was 1.5 times in 1999 and 1.1 in 2000. The primary reason for the decreasing results is that current liabilities grew at a faster rate than current assets.

Analysis of two major components of current assets, receivables and inventory, shows improving trends. The major change in this category of ratios is in the receivable turnover. The relative size of accounts receivable and the effectiveness of credit policies are measured by the **receivable turnover**, which rose from 5.7 times in 1999 to 6.3 times in 2000. The related ratio of **average days' sales uncollected** decreased by about six days, from 64.0 days in 1999 to 57.9 days in 2000. The **inventory turnover**, which measures the relative size of inventories, remained stable. Inventory turnover increased from 17.3 times in 1999 to 17.4 times in 2000. This results in a stable **average days' inventory on hand** of 21.1 days in 1999 and 21 days in 2000.

Average days' sales uncollected is added to average days' inventory on hand to determine the **operating cycle**, the time it takes to sell products and collect for them. At Sun Microsystems, the operating cycle decreased from 85.1 days in 1999 (64.0 days + 21.1 days) to 78.9 days in 2000 (57.9 days + 21.0 days). Related to the operating cycle is the number of days the company takes to pay its accounts payable. The **payables turnover** increased from 9.0 times in 1999 to 9.3 times in 2000. This results in average days' payable of 40.6 days in 1999 and 39.3 days in 2000. Thus, if the **average days' payable** is subtracted from the operating cycle, the days of financing required fall from 44.5 days in 1999 to 39.6 days in 2000, a significant improvement. Overall, Sun Microsystems' liquidity remains strong.

Evaluating Profitability

Profitability reflects a company's ability to earn a satisfactory income so that investors and stockholders will continue to provide capital to the company. Profitability is also closely linked to liquidity because earnings ultimately produce cash flow. For this reason, evaluating profitability is important to both investors and creditors. The profitability ratios of Sun Microsystems, Inc., are shown in Exhibit 9.

From 1999 to 2000, **profit margin**, which measures the net income produced by each dollar of sales, increased from 8.7 to 11.8 percent, and **asset turnover**, which measures how efficiently assets are used to produce sales, decreased from 1.7 to 1.4 times. The result is an increase in overall earning power of the company, or **return on assets**, from 14.5 percent in 1999 to 16.4 percent in 2000. These relationships are illustrated in the computations that follow.

FOCUS ON BUSINESS PRACTICE

Efforts to link managers' compensation to the company's performance measures and to the creation of shareholder wealth are increasing. One such measure compares the return on assets to the company's cost of debt and equity capital. If the return on assets exceeds the cost of financing the assets with debt and equity, then management is indeed creating value for the shareholders. Coca-Cola calls this excess *economic profit*. In 1998 Coca-Cola reported economic profits of $2.48 billion, with its stock price tracking the growth and decline of these economic profits.

Exhibit 9
Profitability Ratios of Sun Microsystems, Inc.

(Dollar amounts in millions)	2000	1999

Profit margin: Measure of net income produced by each dollar of sales

$$\frac{\text{Net Income*}}{\text{Net Sales}} \qquad \frac{\$1,854}{\$15,721} = 11.8\% \qquad \frac{\$1,030}{\$11,806} = 8.7\%$$

Asset turnover: Measure of how efficiently assets are used to produce sales

$$\frac{\text{Net Sales}}{\text{Average Total Assets}^\dagger} \qquad \frac{\$15,721}{(\$14,152 + \$8,499) \div 2} \qquad \frac{\$11,806}{(\$8,499 + \$5,711) \div 2}$$

$$= \frac{\$15,721}{\$11,326} = 1.4 \text{ times} \qquad = \frac{\$11,806}{\$7,105} = 1.7 \text{ times}$$

Return on assets: Measure of overall earning power, or profitability

$$\frac{\text{Net Income}}{\text{Average Total Assets}^\dagger} \qquad \frac{\$1,854}{\$11,326} = 16.4\% \qquad \frac{\$1,030}{\$7,105} = 14.5\%$$

Return on equity: Measure of the profitability of stockholders' investments

$$\frac{\text{Net Income}}{\text{Average Stockholders' Equity}^\dagger} \qquad \frac{\$1,854}{(\$7,309 + \$4,867) \div 2} \qquad \frac{\$1,030}{(\$4,867 + \$3,514) \div 2}$$

$$= \frac{\$1,854}{\$6,088} = 30.5\% \qquad = \frac{\$1,030}{\$4,191} = 24.6\%$$

*In comparing companies in an industry, some analysts use income before income taxes as the numerator to eliminate the effect of differing tax rates among firms.
†1998 figures are from Sun Microsystems' 1999 annual report.
Source: Sun Microsystems, Inc., *Annual Report,* 2000.

	Profit Margin		Asset Turnover		Return on Assets
	$\dfrac{\text{Net Income}}{\text{Net Sales}}$	$\times$	$\dfrac{\text{Net Sales}}{\text{Average Total Assets}}$	$=$	$\dfrac{\text{Net Income}}{\text{Average Total Assets}}$
2000	11.8%	$\times$	1.4	$=$	16.5%
1999	8.7%	$\times$	1.7	$=$	14.8%

The small difference in the two sets of return on assets figures results from the rounding of the ratios used in the above computation. Finally, the profitability of stockholders' investments, or **return on equity**, was also higher at 24.6 percent in 1999 and 30.5 percent in 2000.

Evaluating Long-Term Solvency

Long-term solvency has to do with a company's ability to survive for many years. Investors and creditors evaluate long-term solvency ratios to detect early signs that a company is headed for financial difficulty. Studies have indicated that accounting ratios can show as much as five years in advance that a company may fail.[3] Declining profitability and liquidity ratios are key indicators of possible business failure. Two other ratios that analysts often consider when assessing long-term solvency are debt to equity and interest coverage. Long-term solvency ratios are shown in Exhibit 10.

Exhibit 10
Long-Term Solvency Ratios of Sun Microsystems, Inc.

(Dollar amounts in millions)	2000	1999

Debt to equity ratio: Measure of capital structure and leverage

$$\frac{\text{Total Liabilities}}{\text{Stockholders' Equity}} \qquad \frac{\$6,843}{\$7,309} = .9 \text{ times} \qquad \frac{\$3,632}{\$4,867} = .7 \text{ times}$$

Interest coverage ratio: Measure of creditors' protection from default on interest payments

$$\frac{\text{Income Before Income}}{\text{Taxes} + \text{Interest Expense}} \qquad \frac{\$2,771 + \$84}{\$84} \qquad \frac{\$1,605 + \$1}{\$1}$$
$$\text{Interest Expense} \qquad\qquad = 34.0 \text{ times} \qquad = 1,606.0 \text{ times}$$

Source: Sun Microsystems, Inc., *Annual Report*, 2000.

Increasing amounts of debt in a company's capital structure mean that the company is becoming more heavily leveraged. Increasing debts negatively affect long-term solvency because they represent increasing legal obligations to pay interest periodically and the principal at maturity. Failure to make those payments can result in bankruptcy. The **debt to equity ratio** measures capital structure and leverage by showing the amount of a company's assets provided by creditors in relation to the amount provided by stockholders. Sun Microsystems' debt to equity ratio was only .7 times in 1999 and .9 times in 2000. Recall from Exhibit 3 that the company has little short-term debt and increasing long-term debt, and that it has ample current assets as reflected by its current ratio and quick ratio. All of these factors contribute to long-term solvency. As to the future, "The Company believes the level of financial resources is a significant competitive factor in its industry, and it may choose at any time to raise additional capital through debt or equity financing to strengthen its financial position, facilitate growth, and provide the Company with additional flexibility to take advantage of business opportunities that may arise."[4]

If debt is risky, why have any? The answer is that the level of debt is a matter of balance. Despite its riskiness, debt is a flexible means of financing business operations. Sun Microsystems is using debt to help finance an increase in long-term investments. The interest paid on that debt is deductible for income tax purposes, whereas dividends paid on stock are not. Because debt usually carries a fixed interest charge, the cost of financing can be limited and leverage can be used to advantage. If the company is able to earn a return on assets greater than the cost of interest, it can make an overall profit.* However, the company runs the risk of not earning a return on assets equal to the cost of financing those assets, thereby incurring a loss.

The **interest coverage ratio** measures the degree of protection creditors have from a default on interest payments. Because of its increasing amount of long-term debt, Sun Microsystems' interest coverage ratio declined from 1,606.0 times in 1999 to 34.0 times in 2000. Interest coverage is not a problem for the company despite this decline because interest coverage of 34 is more than adequate.

Evaluating Cash Flow Adequacy

Because cash flows are needed to pay debts when they are due, cash flow measures are closely related to liquidity and long-term solvency. Sun Microsystems' cash

*In addition, there are advantages to being a debtor in periods of inflation because the debt, which is a fixed dollar amount, may be repaid in cheaper dollars.

Exhibit 11
Cash Flow Adequacy Ratios of Sun Microsystems, Inc.

(Dollar amounts in millions)	2000	1999

Cash flow yield: Measure of the ability to generate operating cash flows in relation to net income

$$\frac{\text{Net Cash Flows from Operating Activities}}{\text{Net Income}}$$

$$\frac{\$3,754}{\$1,854} = 2.0 \text{ times}$$

$$\frac{\$2,511}{\$1,030} = 2.4 \text{ times}$$

Cash flows to sales: Measure of the ability of sales to generate operating cash flows

$$\frac{\text{Net Cash Flows from Operating Activities}}{\text{Net Sales}}$$

$$\frac{\$3,754}{\$15,721} = 23.9\%$$

$$\frac{\$2,511}{\$11,806} = 21.3\%$$

Cash flows to assets: Measure of the ability of assets to generate operating cash flows

$$\frac{\text{Net Cash Flows from Operating Activities}}{\text{Average Total Assets*}}$$

$$\frac{\$3,754}{(\$14,152 + \$8,499) \div 2}$$

$$= \frac{\$3,754}{\$11,326} = 33.1\%$$

$$\frac{\$2,511}{(\$8,499 + \$5,711) \div 2}$$

$$= \frac{\$2,511}{\$7,105} = 35.3\%$$

Free cash flow: Measure of cash generated or cash deficiency after providing for commitments

Net Cash Flows from Operating Activities − Dividends − Net Capital Expenditures

$$\$3,754 - \$0 - \$982$$
$$= \$2,772$$

$$\$2,511 - \$0 - \$740$$
$$= \$1,771$$

*The 1998 figure is from Sun Microsystems' 1999 annual report.
Source: Sun Microsystems, Inc., *Annual Report*, 2000.

flow adequacy ratios are presented in Exhibit 11. By most measures, the company's ability to generate positive operating cash flows showed improvement from 1999 to 2000. Key to the improvement was that net cash flows from operating activities had a large increase, from $2,511 million in 1999 to $3,754 million in 2000, while net income, net sales, and average total assets increased by lesser amounts. **Cash flow yield**, or the relationship of cash flows from operating activities to net income, decreased from 2.4 to 2.0 times. **Cash flows to sales**, or the ability of sales to generate operating cash flows, increased from 21.3 percent to 23.9 percent. **Cash flows to assets**, or the ability of assets to generate operating cash flows, decreased from 35.3 percent to 33.1 percent.

 Free cash flow, the cash generated or the cash deficiency after providing for commitments, also increased and remains very positive, primarily because the increase in capital expenditures was smaller than the increase in net cash flows from operating activities and because the company pays no dividends. Management's comment with regard to cash flows in the future is, "The Company believes that the liquidity provided by existing cash, cash equivalents, and investments along with the borrowing arrangements . . . will provide sufficient capital to meet the Company's capital requirements through fiscal 2001."[5]

Evaluating Market Strength

 The market price of a company's stock is of interest to the analyst because it represents what investors as a whole think of the company at a point in time. Market price is the price at which the stock is bought and sold. It provides information about how investors view the potential return and risk of owning the company's

Exhibit 12
Market Strength Ratios of Sun Microsystems, Inc.

	2000	1999

Price/earnings ratio: Measure of investor confidence in a company

$$\frac{\text{Market Price per Share*}}{\text{Earnings per Share}} \qquad \frac{\$90.9375}{\$1.10} = 82.7 \text{ times} \qquad \frac{\$34.4375}{\$.63} = 54.7 \text{ times}$$

Dividends yield: Measure of the current return to an investor in a stock

$$\frac{\text{Dividends per Share}}{\text{Market Price per Share}} \qquad \text{Sun Microsystems does not pay a dividend.}$$

*Market price is from Sun Microsystems' annual report.
Source: Sun Microsystems, Inc., *Annual Report*, 2000.

stock. Market price by itself is not very informative, however. Companies differ in number of outstanding shares and amount of underlying earnings and dividends. Thus, market price must be related to earnings by considering the price/earnings ratio and the dividends yield. Those ratios for Sun Microsystems appear in Exhibit 12 and have been computed using the market price for Sun Microsystems' stock at the end of 1999 and 2000.

The **price/earnings (P/E) ratio**, which measures investor confidence in a company, is the ratio of the market price per share to earnings per share. The P/E ratio is useful in comparing the relative values placed on the earnings of different companies and in comparing the value placed on a company's shares in relation to the overall market. A stock with a lower P/E ratio gives an investor more underlying earnings per dollar invested. However, Sun Microsystems' P/E ratio increased from 54.7 times in 1999 to 82.7 times in 2000. Such an increase suggests that investors believe earnings per share will increase in future years. It signals investors' confidence in Sun Microsystems. The **dividends yield** measures a stock's current return to an investor in the form of dividends. Because Sun Microsystems pays no dividend, it may be concluded that investors expect their return from owning the company's stock to come from increases in its market value.

Summary of the Financial Performance Evaluation of Sun Microsystems, Inc.

This ratio analysis clearly shows that Sun Microsystems' financial condition is strong, as measured by its liquidity, long-term solvency, and cash flow adequacy ratios. The company's profitability is excellent and increased from 1999 to 2000, as measured by its profitability ratios. This performance has been rewarded by a higher market price per share.

Chapter Review

REVIEW OF LEARNING OBJECTIVES

1. Describe and discuss financial performance evaluation by internal and external users. Managers set financial performance objectives on which their companies are judged. Creditors and investors, as well as managers, use financial performance evaluation to judge the past performance and current

Check out ACE, a self-quizzing program on chapter content, at http://college.hmco.com.

position of a company, and also to judge its future potential and the risk associated with it. Creditors use the information gained from their evaluation to make reliable loans that will be repaid with interest. Investors use the information to make investments that will provide a return that is worth the risk.

2. Describe and discuss the standards for financial performance evaluation. Three commonly used standards for financial performance evaluation are rule-of-thumb measures, the company's past performance, and industry norms. Rule-of-thumb measures are weak because of the lack of evidence that they can be widely applied. The past performance of a company can offer a guideline for measuring improvement but is not helpful in judging performance relative to other companies. Although the use of industry norms overcomes this last problem, its disadvantage is that firms are not always comparable, even in the same industry.

3. State the sources of information for financial performance evaluation. The main sources of information about publicly held corporations are company-published reports, such as annual reports and interim financial statements; SEC reports; business periodicals; and credit and investment advisory services.

4. Apply horizontal analysis, trend analysis, and vertical analysis to financial statements. Horizontal analysis involves the computation of changes in both dollar amounts and percentages from year to year. Trend analysis is an extension of horizontal analysis in that percentage changes are calculated for several years. The changes are usually computed by setting a base year equal to 100 and calculating the results for subsequent years as percentages of that base year. Vertical analysis uses percentages to show the relationship of the component parts to a total in a single statement. The resulting financial statements, which are expressed entirely in percentages, are called common-size statements.

5. Apply ratio analysis to financial statements in a comprehensive evaluation of a company's financial performance. A comprehensive ratio analysis includes the evaluation of a company's liquidity, profitability, long-term solvency, cash flow adequacy, and market strength. The ratios for measuring these characteristics are found in Exhibits 8 to 12.

REVIEW OF CONCEPTS AND TERMINOLOGY

The following concepts and terms were introduced in this chapter:

LO 5   Asset turnover: Net sales divided by average total assets. Used to measure how efficiently assets are used to produce sales.

LO 5   Average days' inventory on hand: Days in the year divided by inventory turnover. Shows the average number of days taken to sell inventory.

LO 5   Average days' payable: Days in year divided by payables turnover. Used to measure days to pay accounts payable.

LO 5   Average days' sales uncollected: Days in the year divided by receivable turnover. Shows the speed at which receivables are turned over—literally, the number of days, on average, that a company must wait to receive payment for credit sales.

LO 4   Base year: In financial performance evaluation, the first year to be considered in any set of data.

LO 5   Cash flows to assets: Net cash flows from operating activities divided by average total assets. Used to measure the ability of assets to generate operating cash flows.

LO 5   Cash flows to sales: Net cash flows from operating activities divided by net sales. Used to measure the ability of sales to generate operating cash flows.

LO 5   Cash flow yield: Net cash flows from operating activities divided by net income. Used to measure the ability to generate operating cash flows in relation to net income.

LO 4 **Common-size statement:** A financial statement in which the components of a total figure are stated as percentages of that total.

LO 5 **Current ratio:** Current assets divided by current liabilities. Used as a measure of short-term debt-paying ability.

LO 5 **Debt to equity ratio:** Total liabilities divided by stockholders' equity. Used to measure capital structure and leverage by showing the amount of a company's assets provided by creditors in relation to the amount provided by stockholders.

LO 2 **Diversified companies:** Companies that operate in more than one industry; also called *conglomerates*.

LO 5 **Dividends yield:** Dividends per share divided by market price per share. Used as a measure of the current return to an investor in a stock.

LO 1 **Financial performance evaluation:** All the techniques users of financal statements employ to show important relationships in an organization's financial statements and to relate them to important financial objectives; also called *financial statement analysis*.

LO 5 **Free cash flow:** Net cash flows from operating activities minus dividends minus net capital expenditures. Used to measure the cash generated or the cash deficiency after providing for commitments.

LO 4 **Horizontal analysis:** A technique for evaluating financial performance that involves the computation of changes in both dollar amounts and percentages from the previous to the current year.

LO 4 **Index number:** In trend analysis, a number from which changes in related items over a period of time are measured. Calculated by setting the base year equal to 100 percent.

LO 5 **Interest coverage ratio:** Income before income taxes plus interest expense divided by interest expense. Used as a measure of the degree of protection creditors have from a default on interest payments.

LO 3 **Interim financial statement:** A financial statement that reports data for a period of less than one year, usually a quarter or a month.

LO 5 **Inventory turnover:** The cost of goods sold divided by average inventory. Used to measure the relative size of inventory.

LO 5 **Operating cycle:** Average days' sales uncollected plus average days' inventory on hand. Shows the time it takes to sell products and collect for them.

LO 5 **Payables turnover:** Cost of goods sold plus or minus change in inventory divided by average accounts payable. Used to measure relative size of accounts payable.

LO 1 **Portfolio:** A group of loans or investments designed to average the returns and risks of a creditor or investor.

LO 5 **Price/earnings (P/E) ratio:** Market price per share divided by earnings per share. Used as a measure of investor confidence in a company and as a means of comparing values among stocks.

LO 5 **Profit margin:** Net income divided by net sales. Used to measure net income produced by each dollar of sales.

LO 5 **Quick ratio:** The more liquid current assets—cash, marketable securities or short-term investments, and receivables—divided by current liabilities. Used as a measure of short-term debt-paying ability.

LO 4 **Ratio analysis:** A technique of financial performance evaluation that identifies meaningful relationships between the components of the financial statements.

LO 5 **Receivable turnover:** Net sales divided by average accounts receivable. Used as a measure of the relative size of accounts receivable and the effectiveness of credit policies.

LO 5 **Return on assets:** Net income divided by average total assets. Used to measure overall earning power, or profitability.

LO 5 **Return on equity:** Net income divided by average stockholders' equity. Used to measure the profitability of stockholders' investments.

LO 4 **Trend analysis:** A type of horizontal analysis in which percentage changes are calculated for several successive years instead of for two years.

LO 4 **Vertical analysis:** A technique for evaluating financial performance that uses percentages to show the relationships of the different parts to a total in a single financial statement.

REVIEW PROBLEM

LO 5

Comparative Evaluation of Two Companies

Maggie Washington is considering an investment in one of two fast-food restaurant chains because she believes the trend toward eating out more often will continue. Her choices have been narrowed to Quik Burger and Big Steak, whose balance sheets and income statements appear below and on the next page.

Balance Sheets December 31, 20xx (In thousands)		
	Quik Burger	**Big Steak**
Assets		
Cash	$ 2,000	$ 4,500
Accounts Receivable (net)	2,000	6,500
Inventory	2,000	5,000
Property, Plant, and Equipment (net)	20,000	35,000
Other Assets	4,000	5,000
Total Assets	$30,000	$56,000
Liabilities and Stockholders' Equity		
Accounts Payable	$ 2,500	$ 3,000
Notes Payable	1,500	4,000
Bonds Payable	10,000	30,000
Common Stock, $1 par value	1,000	3,000
Paid-in Capital in Excess of Par Value, Common	9,000	9,000
Retained Earnings	6,000	7,000
Total Liabilities and Stockholders' Equity	$30,000	$56,000

The statements of cash flows show that net cash flows from operations were $2,200,000 for Quik Burger and $3,000,000 for Big Steak. Net capital expenditures were $2,100,000 for Quik Burger and $1,800,000 for Big Steak. Dividends of $500,000 were paid by Quik Burger and $600,000 by Big Steak. The market prices of the stocks of Quik Burger and Big Steak were $30 and $20, respectively. Financial information pertaining to prior years is not readily available to Maggie Washington. Assume that all notes payable are current liabilities and that all bonds payable are long-term liabilities.

REQUIRED

Conduct a comprehensive ratio analysis of Quik Burger and Big Steak and compare the results. Perform the analysis by carrying out the steps that follow. Use end-of-year balances for averages, assume no change in inventory, and round all ratios and percentages to one decimal place.

1. Prepare an analysis of liquidity.
2. Prepare an analysis of profitability.

Income Statements **For the Year Ended December 31, 20xx** **(In thousands, except per share amounts)**		
	Quik Burger	**Big Steak**
Net Sales	$53,000	$86,000
Costs and Expenses		
Cost of Goods Sold	$37,000	$61,000
Selling Expenses	7,000	10,000
Administrative Expenses	4,000	5,000
Total Costs and Expenses	$48,000	$76,000
Income from Operations	$ 5,000	$10,000
Interest Expense	1,400	3,200
Income Before Income Taxes	$ 3,600	$ 6,800
Income Taxes	1,800	3,400
Net Income	$ 1,800	$ 3,400
Earnings per Share	$ 1.80	$ 1.13

3. Prepare an analysis of long-term solvency.

4. Prepare an analysis of cash flow adequacy.

5. Prepare an analysis of market strength.

K/R   6. Indicate in the last column the company that apparently had the more favorable ratio in each case. (Consider differences of .1 or less to be neutral.)

7. In what ways would access to prior years' information aid this analysis?

ANSWER TO REVIEW K/R PROBLEM

Ratio Name	Quik BurgerZ	Big Steak	6. Company with More Favorable Ratio*
1. Liquidity analysis			
a. Current ratio	$\dfrac{\$2,000 + \$2,000 + \$2,000}{\$2,500 + \$1,500}$	$\dfrac{\$4,500 + \$6,500 + \$5,000}{\$3,000 + \$4,000}$	
	$= \dfrac{\$6,000}{\$4,000} = 1.5$ times	$= \dfrac{\$16,000}{\$7,000} = 2.3$ times	Big Steak
b. Quick ratio	$\dfrac{\$2,000 + \$2,000}{\$2,500 + \$1,500}$	$\dfrac{\$4,500 + \$6,500}{\$3,000 + \$4,000}$	
	$= \dfrac{\$4,000}{\$4,000} = 1.0$ times	$= \dfrac{\$11,000}{\$7,000} = 1.6$ times	Big Steak
c. Receivable turnover	$\dfrac{\$53,000}{\$2,000} = 26.5$ times	$\dfrac{\$86,000}{\$6,500} = 13.2$ times	Quik Burger

*This analysis indicates the company with the apparently more favorable ratio. Class discussion may focus on conditions under which different conclusions may be drawn.

(continued)

Ratio Name	Quik Burger	Big Steak	6. Company with More Favorable Ratio
d. Average days' sales uncollected	$\dfrac{365}{26.5} = 13.8$ days	$\dfrac{365}{13.2} = 27.7$ days	Quik Burger
e. Inventory turnover	$\dfrac{\$37,000}{\$2,000} = 18.5$ times	$\dfrac{\$61,000}{\$5,000} = 12.2$ times	Quik Burger
f. Average days' inventory on hand	$\dfrac{365}{18.5} = 19.7$ days	$\dfrac{365}{12.2} = 29.9$ days	Quik Burger
g. Payables turnover	$\dfrac{\$37,000 + 0}{\$2,500} = 14.8$ times	$\dfrac{\$61,000 + 0}{\$3,000} = 20.3$ times	Big Steak
h. Average days' payable	$\dfrac{365}{14.8} = 24.7$ days	$\dfrac{365}{20.3} = 18.0$ days	Big Steak

2. **Profitability analysis**

a. Profit margin	$\dfrac{\$1,800}{\$53,000} = 3.4\%$	$\dfrac{\$3,400}{\$86,000} = 4.0\%$	Big Steak
b. Asset turnover	$\dfrac{\$53,000}{\$30,000} = 1.8$ times	$\dfrac{\$86,000}{\$56,000} = 1.5$ times	Quik Burger
c. Return on assets	$\dfrac{\$1,800}{\$30,000} = 6.0\%$	$\dfrac{\$3,400}{\$56,000} = 6.1\%$	Neutral
d. Return on equity	$\dfrac{\$1,800}{\$1,000 + \$9,000 + \$6,000}$ $= \dfrac{\$1,800}{\$16,000} = 11.3\%$	$\dfrac{\$3,400}{\$3,000 + \$9,000 + \$7,000}$ $= \dfrac{\$3,400}{\$19,000} = 17.9\%$	Big Steak

3. **Long-term solvency analysis**

a. Debt to equity ratio	$\dfrac{\$2,500 + \$1,500 + \$10,000}{\$1,000 + \$9,000 + \$6,000}$ $= \dfrac{\$14,000}{\$16,000} = .9$ times	$\dfrac{\$3,000 + \$4,000 + \$30,000}{\$3,000 + \$9,000 + \$7,000}$ $= \dfrac{\$37,000}{\$19,000} = 1.9$ times	Quik Burger
b. Interest coverage ratio	$\dfrac{\$3,600 + \$1,400}{\$1,400}$ $= \dfrac{\$5,000}{\$1,400} = 3.6$ times	$\dfrac{\$6,800 + \$3,200}{\$3,200}$ $= \dfrac{\$10,000}{\$3,200} = 3.1$ times	Quik Burger

4. **Cash flow adequacy analysis**

a. Cash flow yield	$\dfrac{\$2,200}{\$1,800} = 1.2$ times	$\dfrac{\$3,000}{\$3,400} = .9$ times	Quik Burger
b. Cash flows to sales	$\dfrac{\$2,200}{\$53,000} = 4.2\%$	$\dfrac{\$3,000}{\$86,000} = 3.5\%$	Quik Burger
c. Cash flows to assets	$\dfrac{\$2,200}{\$30,000} = 7.3\%$	$\dfrac{\$3,000}{\$56,000} = 5.4\%$	Quik Burger
d. Free cash flow	$\$2,200 - \$500 - \$2,100$ $= (400)$	$\$3,000 - \$600 - \$1,800$ $= \$600$	Big Steak

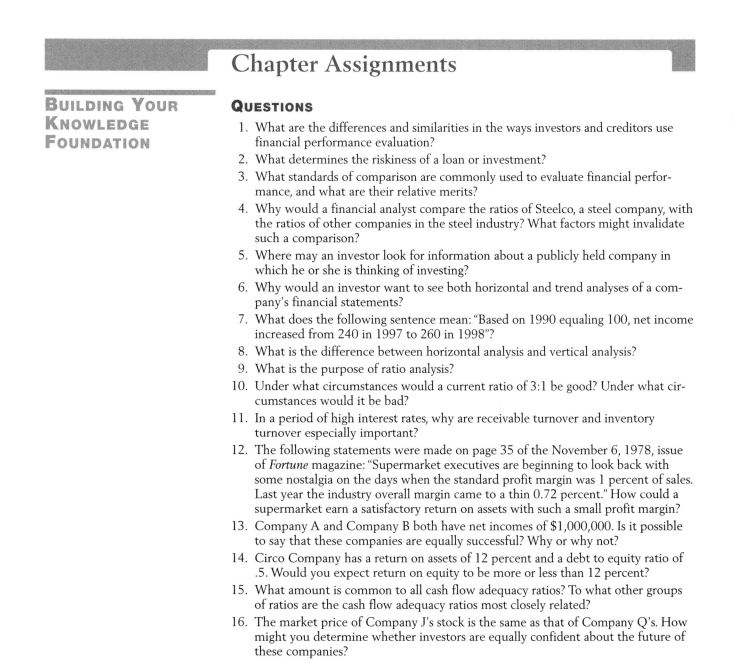

Ratio Name	Quik Burger	Big Steak	6. Company with More Favorable Ratio
5. Market strength analysis			
a. Price/earnings ratio	$\dfrac{\$30}{\$1.80} = 16.7$ times	$\dfrac{\$20}{\$1.13} = 17.7$ times	Big Steak
b. Dividends yield	$\dfrac{\$500,000/1,000,000}{\$30} = 1.7\%$	$\dfrac{\$600,000/3,000,000}{\$20} = 1.0\%$	Quik Burger

7. Usefulness of prior years' information
Prior years' information would be helpful in two ways. First, turnover, return, and cash flows to assets ratios could be based on average amounts. Second, a trend analysis could be performed for each company.

Chapter Assignments

BUILDING YOUR KNOWLEDGE FOUNDATION

QUESTIONS

1. What are the differences and similarities in the ways investors and creditors use financial performance evaluation?
2. What determines the riskiness of a loan or investment?
3. What standards of comparison are commonly used to evaluate financial performance, and what are their relative merits?
4. Why would a financial analyst compare the ratios of Steelco, a steel company, with the ratios of other companies in the steel industry? What factors might invalidate such a comparison?
5. Where may an investor look for information about a publicly held company in which he or she is thinking of investing?
6. Why would an investor want to see both horizontal and trend analyses of a company's financial statements?
7. What does the following sentence mean: "Based on 1990 equaling 100, net income increased from 240 in 1997 to 260 in 1998"?
8. What is the difference between horizontal analysis and vertical analysis?
9. What is the purpose of ratio analysis?
10. Under what circumstances would a current ratio of 3:1 be good? Under what circumstances would it be bad?
11. In a period of high interest rates, why are receivable turnover and inventory turnover especially important?
12. The following statements were made on page 35 of the November 6, 1978, issue of *Fortune* magazine: "Supermarket executives are beginning to look back with some nostalgia on the days when the standard profit margin was 1 percent of sales. Last year the industry overall margin came to a thin 0.72 percent." How could a supermarket earn a satisfactory return on assets with such a small profit margin?
13. Company A and Company B both have net incomes of $1,000,000. Is it possible to say that these companies are equally successful? Why or why not?
14. Circo Company has a return on assets of 12 percent and a debt to equity ratio of .5. Would you expect return on equity to be more or less than 12 percent?
15. What amount is common to all cash flow adequacy ratios? To what other groups of ratios are the cash flow adequacy ratios most closely related?
16. The market price of Company J's stock is the same as that of Company Q's. How might you determine whether investors are equally confident about the future of these companies?

SHORT EXERCISES

SE 1.
LO 1 Objectives and Standards
LO 2 of Financial Performance Evaluation

Indicate whether each of the following items is (a) an objective or (b) a standard of comparison of financial performance evaluation.

1. Industry norms
2. Assessment of the company's past performance
3. The company's past performance
4. Assessment of future potential and related risk
5. Rule-of-thumb measures

SE 2.
LO 3 Sources of Information

For each piece of information listed below, indicate whether the *best* source would be (a) reports published by the company, (b) SEC reports, (c) business periodicals, or (d) credit and investment advisory services.

1. Current market value of a company's stock
2. Management's analysis of the past year's operations
3. Objective assessment of a company's financial performance
4. Most complete body of financial disclosures
5. Current events affecting the company

SE 3.
LO 4 Trend Analysis

Using 20x0 as the base year, prepare a trend analysis for the following data, and tell whether the results suggest a favorable or an unfavorable trend. (Round your answers to one decimal place.)

	20x2	20x1	20x0
Net sales	$158,000	$136,000	$112,000
Accounts receivable (net)	43,000	32,000	21,000

SE 4.
LO 4 Horizontal Analysis

Compute the amount and percentage changes for the income statements that appear below, and comment on the changes from 20x0 to 20x1. (Round the percentage changes to one decimal place.)

SiteWorks, Inc.
Comparative Income Statements
For the Years Ended December 31, 20x1 and 20x0

	20x1	20x0
Net Sales	$180,000	$145,000
Cost of Goods Sold	112,000	88,000
Gross Margin	$ 68,000	$ 57,000
Operating Expenses	40,000	30,000
Operating Income	$ 28,000	$ 27,000
Interest Expense	7,000	5,000
Income Before Income Taxes	$ 21,000	$ 22,000
Income Taxes	7,000	8,000
Net Income	$ 14,000	$ 14,000
Earnings per share	$ 1.40	$ 1.40

SE 5.
LO 4 Vertical Analysis

Express the comparative balance sheets that appear at the top of the next page as common-size statements, and comment on the changes from 20x0 to 20x1. (Round computations to one decimal place.)

SE 6.
LO 5 Liquidity Analysis

Using the information for SiteWorks, Inc., in **SE 4** and **SE 5,** compute the current ratio, quick ratio, receivable turnover, average days' sales uncollected, inventory turnover, average days' inventory on hand, payables turnover, and average days' payable for 20x0

SiteWorks, Inc. Comparative Balance Sheets December 31, 20x1 and 20x0		
	20x1	**20x0**
Assets		
Current Assets	$ 24,000	$ 20,000
Property, Plant, and Equipment (net)	130,000	100,000
Total Assets	$154,000	$120,000
Liabilities and Stockholders' Equity		
Current Liabilities	$ 18,000	$ 22,000
Long-Term Liabilities	90,000	60,000
Stockholders' Equity	46,000	38,000
Total Liabilities and Stockholders' Equity	$154,000	$120,000

and 20x1. Inventories were $4,000 in 19x9, $5,000 in 20x0, and $7,000 in 20x1. Accounts Receivable were $6,000 in 19x9, $8,000 in 20x0, and $10,000 in 20x1. Accounts Payable were $9,000 in 19x9, $10,000 in 20x0, and $12,000 in 20x1. There were no marketable securities or prepaid assets. Comment on the results. (Round computations to one decimal place.)

SE 7.

LO 5 Profitability Analysis

Using the information for SiteWorks, Inc., in **SE 4** and **SE 5,** compute the profit margin, asset turnover, return on assets, and return on equity for 20x0 and 20x1. In 19x9, total assets were $100,000 and total stockholders' equity was $30,000. Comment on the results. (Round computations to one decimal place.)

SE 8.

**LO 5 Long-Term Solvency
Analysis**

Using the information for SiteWorks, Inc., in **SE 4** and **SE 5,** compute the debt to equity and interest coverage ratios for 20x0 and 20x1. Comment on the results. (Round computations to one decimal place.)

SE 9.

**LO 5 Cash Flow Adequacy
Analysis**

Using the information for SiteWorks, Inc., in **SE 4, SE 5,** and **SE 7,** compute the cash flow yield, cash flows to sales, cash flows to assets, and free cash flow for 20x0 and 20x1. Net cash flows from operating activities were $21,000 in 20x0 and $16,000 in 20x1. Net capital expenditures were $30,000 in 20x0 and $40,000 in 20x1. Cash dividends were $6,000 in both years. Comment on the results. (Round computations to one decimal place.)

SE 10.

LO 5 Market Strength Analysis

Using the information for SiteWorks, Inc., in **SE 4, SE 5,** and **SE 9,** compute the price/earnings and dividends yield ratios for 20x0 and 20x1. The company had 10,000 shares of common stock outstanding in both years. The price of SiteWorks' common stock was $30 in 20x0 and $20 in 20x1. Comment on the results. (Round computations to one decimal place.)

Exercises

E 1.

LO 1 Objectives, Standards,
LO 2 and Sources of
LO 3 Information for Financial
Performance Evaluation

Identify each of the following as (a) an objective of financial performance evaluation, (b) a standard for financial performance evaluation, or (c) a source of information for financial performance evaluation:

1. Average ratios of other companies in the same industry
2. Assessment of the future potential of an investment
3. Interim financial statements
4. Past ratios of the company
5. SEC Form 10-K
6. Assessment of risk
7. A company's annual report

E 2. Compute the amount and percentage changes for the following balance sheets, and comment on the changes from 20x1 to 20x2. (Round the percentage changes to one decimal place.)

Fodor Company
Comparative Balance Sheets
December 31, 20x2 and 20x1

	20x2	20x1
Assets		
Current Assets	$ 37,200	$ 25,600
Property, Plant, and Equipment (net)	218,928	194,400
Total Assets	$256,128	$220,000
Liabilities and Stockholders' Equity		
Current Liabilities	$ 22,400	$ 6,400
Long-Term Liabilities	70,000	80,000
Stockholders' Equity	163,728	133,600
Total Liabilities and Stockholders' Equity	$256,128	$220,000

E 3. Using 20x1 as the base year, prepare a trend analysis of the following data, and tell whether the situation shown by the trends is favorable or unfavorable. (Round your answers to one decimal place.)

	20x5	20x4	20x3	20x2	20x1
Net sales	$25,520	$23,980	$24,200	$22,880	$22,000
Cost of goods sold	17,220	15,400	15,540	14,700	14,000
General and administrative expenses	5,280	5,184	5,088	4,896	4,800
Operating income	3,020	3,396	3,572	3,284	3,200

E 4. Express the comparative income statements that follow as common-size statements, and comment on the changes from 20x1 to 20x2. (Round computations to one decimal place.)

Fodor Company
Comparative Income Statements
For the Years Ended December 31, 20x2 and 20x1

	20x2	20x1
Net Sales	$424,000	$368,000
Cost of Goods Sold	254,400	239,200
Gross Margin	$169,600	$128,800
Selling Expenses	$106,000	$ 73,600
General Expenses	50,880	36,800
Total Operating Expenses	$156,880	$110,400
Net Operating Income	$ 12,720	$ 18,400

E 5.
Partial comparative balance sheet and income statement information for Road Company follows.

	20x2	20x1
Cash	$ 6,800	$ 5,200
Marketable Securities	3,600	8,600
Accounts Receivable (net)	22,400	17,800
Inventory	27,200	24,800
Total Current Assets	$ 60,000	$ 56,400
Accounts Payable	$ 20,000	$ 14,100
Net Sales	$161,280	$110,360
Cost of Goods Sold	108,800	101,680
Gross Margin	$ 52,480	$ 8,680

The year-end balances for Accounts Receivable and Inventory were $16,200 and $25,600, respectively, in 20x0. Accounts Payable was $15,300 in 20x0 and is the only current liability.

Compute the current ratio, quick ratio, receivable turnover, average days' sales uncollected, inventory turnover, average days' inventory on hand, payables turnover, and average days' payable for each year. (Round computations to one decimal place.) Comment on the change in the company's liquidity position, including its operating cycle and required days of financing from 20x1 to 20x2.

E 6.
Davis FormalWear Shop has been in business for four years. Because the company has recently had a cash flow problem, management wonders whether there is a problem with receivables or inventories.

Here are selected figures from Davis FormalWear Shop's financial statements (in thousands):

	20x4	20x3	20x2	20x1
Net sales	$288	$224	$192	$160
Cost of goods sold	180	144	120	96
Accounts receivable (net)	48	40	32	24
Merchandise inventory	56	44	32	20
Accounts payable	25	20	15	10

Compute receivable turnover, inventory turnover, and payables turnover for each of the four years, and comment on the results relative to the cash flow problem that Davis FormalWear Shop has been experiencing. Merchandise inventory was $22,000, accounts receivable was $22,000 and accounts payable was $8,000 in 20x0. Round computations to one decimal place.

E 7.
At year end, Jareau Company had total assets of $640,000 in 20x0, $680,000 in 20x1, and $760,000 in 20x2. Its debt to equity ratio was .67 in all three years. In 20x1, the company had net income of $77,112 on revenues of $1,224,000. In 20x2, the company had net income of $98,952 on revenues of $1,596,000. Compute the profit margin, asset turnover, return on assets, and return on equity for 20x1 and 20x2. Comment on the apparent cause of the increase or decrease in profitability. (Round the percentages and other ratios to one decimal place.)

E 8.
An investor is considering investing in the long-term bonds and common stock of Companies F and G. Both companies operate in the same industry. In addition, both companies pay a dividend per share of $4 and a yield of 10 percent on their long-term bonds. Other data for the two companies appear on the next page.

	Company F	Company G
Total assets	$2,400,000	$1,080,000
Total liabilities	1,080,000	594,000
Income before income taxes	288,000	129,600
Interest expense	97,200	53,460
Earnings per share	3.20	5.00
Market price of common stock	40	47.50

Compute the debt to equity, interest coverage, price/earnings (P/E), and dividends yield ratios, and comment on the results. (Round computations to one decimal place.)

LO 5   Cash Flow Adequacy Analysis

E 9. Using the data below, taken from the financial statements of Wong, Inc., compute the cash flow yield, cash flows to sales, cash flows to assets, and free cash flow. (Round computations to one decimal place.)

Net sales	$6,400,000
Net income	704,000
Net cash flows from operating activities	912,000
Total assets, beginning of year	5,780,000
Total assets, end of year	6,240,000
Cash dividends	240,000
Net capital expenditures	596,000

PROBLEMS

LO 4   Horizontal and Vertical Analysis

P 1. The condensed comparative income statements and balance sheets of Sanborn Corporation appear below and on the next page. All figures are given in thousands of dollars.

	Sanborn Corporation Comparative Income Statements For the Years Ended December 31, 20x2 and 20x1	
	20x2	**20x1**
Net Sales	$3,276,800	$3,146,400
Cost of Goods Sold	2,088,800	2,008,400
Gross Margin	$1,188,000	$1,138,000
Operating Expenses		
Selling Expenses	$ 476,800	$ 518,000
Administrative Expenses	447,200	423,200
Total Operating Expenses	$ 924,000	$ 941,200
Income from Operations	$ 264,000	$ 196,800
Interest Expense	65,600	39,200
Income Before Income Taxes	$ 198,400	$ 157,600
Income Taxes	62,400	56,800
Net Income	$ 136,000	$ 100,800
Earnings per share	$ 3.40	$ 2.52

REQUIRED

Perform the following analyses. Round all ratios and percentages to one decimal place.

1. Prepare schedules showing the amount and percentage changes from 20x1 to 20x2 for Sanborn's comparative income statements and balance sheets.

Sanborn Corporation
Comparative Balance Sheets
December 31, 20x2 and 20x1

	20x2	20x1
Assets		
Cash	$ 81,200	$ 40,800
Accounts Receivable (net)	235,600	229,200
Inventory	574,800	594,800
Property, Plant, and Equipment (net)	750,000	720,000
Total Assets	$1,641,600	$1,584,800
Liabilities and Stockholders' Equity		
Accounts Payable	$ 267,600	$ 477,200
Notes Payable (short-term)	200,000	400,000
Bonds Payable	400,000	—
Common Stock, $10 par value	400,000	400,000
Retained Earnings	374,000	307,600
Total Liabilities and Stockholders' Equity	$1,641,600	$1,584,800

2. Prepare common-size income statements and balance sheets for 20x1 and 20x2.

3. Comment on the results in **1** and **2** by identifying favorable and unfavorable changes in the components and composition of the statements.

P 2.

LO 5 **Analyzing the Effects of Transactions on Ratios**

Koz Corporation engaged in the transactions listed in the first column of the following table. Opposite each transaction is a ratio and space to indicate the effect of each transaction on the ratio.

		Effect		
Transaction	**Ratio**	**Increase**	**Decrease**	**None**
a. Sold merchandise on account.	Current ratio			
b. Sold merchandise on account.	Inventory turnover			
c. Collected on accounts receivable.	Quick ratio			
d. Wrote off an uncollectible account.	Receivable turnover			
e. Paid on accounts payable.	Current ratio			
f. Declared cash dividend.	Return on equity			
g. Incurred advertising expense.	Profit margin			
h. Issued stock dividend.	Debt to equity ratio			
i. Issued bond payable.	Asset turnover			
j. Accrued interest expense.	Current ratio			
k. Paid previously declared cash dividend.	Dividends yield			
l. Purchased treasury stock.	Return on assets			
m. Recorded depreciation expense.	Cash flow yield			

REQUIRED

Place an X in the appropriate column to show whether the transaction increased, decreased, or had no effect on the indicated ratio.

LO 5 **Ratio Analysis**

P 3. Additional data (in thousands of dollars) for Sanborn Corporation in 20x2 and 20x1 follow. This information should be used in conjunction with the data in **P 1**.

	20x2	20x1
Net cash flows from operating activities	($196,000)	$144,000
Net capital expenditures	$40,000	$65,000
Dividends paid	$44,000	$34,400
Number of common shares	40,000,000	40,000,000
Market price per share	$18	$30

Selected balances (in thousands of dollars) at the end of 20x0 were Accounts Receivable (net), $206,800; Inventory, $547,200; Total Assets, $1,465,600; Accounts Payable, $386,600; and Stockholders' Equity, $641,200. All of Sanborn's notes payable were current liabilities; all of the bonds payable were long-term liabilities.

REQUIRED

Perform the following analyses. Round all answers to one decimal place, and consider changes of .1 or less to be neutral. After making the calculations, indicate whether each ratio improved or deteriorated from 20x1 to 20x2 by writing *F* for favorable or *U* for unfavorable.

1. Prepare a liquidity analysis by calculating for each year the (a) current ratio, (b) quick ratio, (c) receivable turnover, (d) average days' sales uncollected, (e) inventory turnover, (f) average days' inventory on hand, (g) payables turnover, and (h) average days' payable.

2. Prepare a profitability analysis by calculating for each year the (a) profit margin, (b) asset turnover, (c) return on assets, and (d) return on equity.

3. Prepare a long-term solvency analysis by calculating for each year the (a) debt to equity ratio and (b) interest coverage ratio.

4. Prepare a cash flow adequacy analysis by calculating for each year the (a) cash flow yield, (b) cash flows to sales, (c) cash flows to assets, and (d) free cash flow.

5. Prepare a market strength analysis by calculating for each year the (a) price/earnings ratio and (b) dividends yield.

LO 5 **Comprehensive Ratio Analysis of Two Companies**

P 4. Ginger Adair is considering an investment in the common stock of a chain of retail department stores. She has narrowed her choice to two retail companies, Lewis Corporation and Ramsey Corporation, whose income statements and balance sheets are shown on the next page. During the year, Lewis Corporation paid a total of $100,000 in dividends. The market price per share of its stock is currently $60. In comparison, Ramsey Corporation paid a total of $228,000 in dividends, and the current market price of its stock is $76 per share. Lewis Corporation had net cash flows from operations of $543,000 and net capital expenditures of $1,250,000. Ramsey Corporation had net cash flows from operations of $985,000 and net capital expenditures of $2,100,000. Information for prior years is not readily available. Assume that all notes payable are current liabilities and all bonds payable are long-term liabilities and that there is no change in inventory.

REQUIRED

Conduct a comprehensive ratio analysis for each company, using the available information. Compare the results. Round percentages and ratios to one decimal place, and consider changes of .1 or less to be indeterminate.

1. Prepare an analysis of liquidity by calculating for each company the (a) current ratio, (b) quick ratio, (c) receivable turnover, (d) average days' sales uncollected, (e) inventory turnover, (f) average days' inventory on hand, (g) payables turnover, and (h) average days' payable.

2. Prepare an analysis of profitability by calculating for each company the (a) profit margin, (b) asset turnover, (c) return on assets, and (d) return on equity.

3. Prepare an analysis of long-term solvency by calculating for each company the (a) debt to equity ratio and (b) interest coverage ratio.

4. Prepare an analysis of cash flow adequacy by calculating for each company the (a) cash flow yield, (b) cash flows to sales, (c) cash flows to assets, and (d) free cash flow.

	Lewis Corporation	Ramsey Corporation
Assets		
Cash	$ 160,000	$ 384,800
Marketable Securities	406,800	169,200
Accounts Receivable (net)	1,105,600	1,970,800
Inventories	1,259,600	2,506,800
Prepaid Expenses	108,800	228,000
Property, Plant, and Equipment (net)	5,827,200	13,104,000
Intangibles and Other Assets	1,106,400	289,600
Total Assets	$9,974,400	$18,653,200
Liabilities and Stockholders' Equity		
Accounts Payable	$ 688,000	$ 1,145,200
Notes Payable	300,000	800,000
Income Taxes Payable	100,400	146,800
Bonds Payable	4,000,000	4,000,000
Common Stock, $20 par value	2,000,000	1,200,000
Paid-in Capital in Excess of Par Value, Common	1,219,600	7,137,200
Retained Earnings	1,666,400	4,224,000
Total Liabilities and Stockholders' Equity	$9,974,400	$18,653,200

	Lewis Corporation	Ramsey Corporation
Net Sales	$25,120,000	$50,420,000
Costs and Expenses		
Cost of Goods Sold	$12,284,000	$29,668,000
Selling Expenses	9,645,200	14,216,400
Administrative Expenses	1,972,000	4,868,000
Total Costs and Expenses	$23,901,200	$48,752,400
Income from Operations	$ 1,218,800	$ 1,667,600
Interest Expense	388,000	456,000
Income Before Income Taxes	$ 830,800	$ 1,211,600
Income Taxes	400,000	600,000
Net Income	$ 430,800	$ 611,600
Earnings per share	$ 4.31	$ 10.19

5. Prepare an analysis of market strength by calculating for each company the (a) price/earnings ratio and (b) dividends yield.

6. Indicate in the right-hand column which company had the more favorable ratio in each case.

7. How could the analysis be improved if information from prior years were available?

ALTERNATE PROBLEMS

P 5.

LO 5 Analyzing the Effects of Transactions on Ratios

Benson Corporation, a clothing retailer, engaged in the transactions listed in the first column of the table below. Opposite each transaction is a ratio and space to mark the effect of each transaction on the ratio.

Transaction	Ratio	Effect Increase	Effect Decrease	Effect None
a. Issued common stock for cash.	Asset turnover			
b. Declared cash dividend.	Current ratio			
c. Sold treasury stock.	Return on equity			
d. Borrowed cash by issuing note payable.	Debt to equity ratio			
e. Paid salaries expense.	Inventory turnover			
f. Purchased merchandise for cash.	Current ratio			
g. Sold equipment for cash.	Receivable turnover			
h. Sold merchandise on account.	Quick ratio			
i. Paid current portion of long-term debt.	Return on assets			
j. Gave sales discount.	Profit margin			
k. Purchased marketable securities for cash.	Quick ratio			
l. Declared 5 percent stock dividend.	Current ratio			
m. Purchased a building.	Free cash flow			

REQUIRED

Place an X in the appropriate column to show whether the transaction increased, decreased, or had no effect on the indicated ratio.

P 6.

LO 5 Ratio Analysis

The condensed comparative income statements and balance sheets of Basie Corporation appear below and on the next page. All figures are given in thousands of dollars, except earnings per share.

Basie Corporation
Comparative Income Statements
For the Years Ended December 31, 20x2 and 20x1

	20x2	20x1
Net Sales	$800,400	$742,600
Cost of Goods Sold	454,100	396,200
Gross Margin	$346,300	$346,400
Operating Expenses		
Selling Expenses	$130,100	$104,600
Administrative Expenses	140,300	115,500
Total Operating Expenses	$270,400	$220,100
Income from Operations	$ 75,900	$126,300
Interest Expense	25,000	20,000
Income Before Income Taxes	$ 50,900	$106,300
Income Taxes	14,000	35,000
Net Income	$ 36,900	$ 71,300
Earnings per share	$ 1.23	$ 2.38

Basie Corporation **Comparative Balance Sheets** **December 31, 20x2 and 20x1**		
	20x2	**20x1**
Assets		
Cash	$ 31,100	$ 27,200
Accounts Receivable (net)	72,500	42,700
Inventory	122,600	107,800
Property, Plant, and Equipment (net)	577,700	507,500
Total Assets	$803,900	$685,200
Liabilities and Stockholders' Equity		
Accounts Payable	$104,700	$ 72,300
Notes Payable (due in less than one year)	50,000	50,000
Bonds Payable	200,000	110,000
Common Stock, $10 par value	300,000	300,000
Retained Earnings	149,200	152,900
Total Liabilities and Stockholders' Equity	$803,900	$685,200

Additional data for Basie Corporation in 20x2 and 20x1 are as follows:

	20x2	**20x1**
Net cash flows from operating activities	$64,000	$99,000
Net capital expenditures	$119,000	$38,000
Dividends paid	$31,400	$35,000
Number of common shares	30,000	30,000
Market price per share	$40	$60

Balances of selected accounts at the end of 20x0 were Accounts Receivable (net), $52,700; Inventory, $99,400; Accounts Payable, $64,800; Total Assets, $647,800; and Stockholders' Equity, $376,600. All of the bonds payable were long-term liabilities.

REQUIRED

Perform the following analyses. Round percentages and ratios to one decimal place, and consider changes of .1 or less to be neutral. After making the calculations, indicate whether each ratio had a favorable (*F*) or unfavorable (*U*) change from 20x1 to 20x2.

1. Conduct a liquidity analysis by calculating for each year the (a) current ratio, (b) quick ratio, (c) receivable turnover, (d) average days' sales uncollected, (e) inventory turnover, (f) average days' inventory on hand, (g) payables turnover, and (h) average days' payable.

2. Conduct a profitability analysis by calculating for each year the (a) profit margin, (b) asset turnover, (c) return on assets, and (d) return on equity.

3. Conduct a long-term solvency analysis by calculating for each year the (a) debt to equity ratio and (b) interest coverage ratio.

4. Conduct a cash flow adequacy analysis by calculating for each year the (a) cash flow yield, (b) cash flows to sales, (c) cash flows to assets, and (d) free cash flow.

5. Conduct a market strength analysis by calculating for each year the (a) price/earnings ratio and (b) dividends yield.

EXPANDING YOUR CRITICAL THINKING, COMMUNICATION, AND INTERPERSONAL SKILLS

SKILLS DEVELOPMENT

Conceptual Analysis

SD 1.

LO 2 **Standards for Financial**
LO 5 **Performance Evaluation**

Helene Curtis, a well-known, publicly owned corporation, became a takeover candidate and sold out in the 1990s after years of poor profit performance. "By almost any standard, Chicago-based Helene Curtis rates as one of America's worst-managed personal care companies. In recent years its return on equity has hovered between 10% and 13%, well below the industry average of 18% to 19%. Net profit margins of 2% to 3% are half that of competitors. . . . As a result, while leading names like Revlon and Avon are trading at three and four times book value, Curtis trades at less than two-thirds book value."[6] Considering that many companies in other industries are happy with a return on equity of 10 percent to 13 percent, why is this analysis so critical of Curtis's performance? Assuming that Curtis could double its profit margin, what other information would be necessary to project the resulting return on stockholders' investment? Why are Revlon's and Avon's stocks trading for more than Curtis's? Be prepared to discuss your answers to these questions in class.

SD 2.

LO 3 **Using Segment Information**

Refer to Exhibit 1, which shows the segment information of **Goodyear Tire & Rubber Company.** In what business segments does Goodyear operate? What is the relative size of the business segments in terms of sales and total segment income in the most recent year? Which segment is most profitable in terms of the performance measure return on assets? In the tires segment, which region of the world is largest and which is most profitable in terms of return on assets?

SD 3.

LO 3 **Use of Published Reports**

Refer to Exhibit 2, which contains the **PepsiCo, Inc.,** listing from Mergent's *Handbook of Dividend Achievers.* Assume that an investor has asked you to assess PepsiCo's recent history and prospects. Write a memorandum to the investor that addresses the following points:

1. PepsiCo's earnings history. (What generally has been the relationship between PepsiCo's return on assets and its return on equity over the years 1993 to 1999? What does this tell you about the way the company is financed? What figures back up your conclusion?)

2. The trend of PepsiCo's stock price and price/earnings ratio for the seven years shown.

3. PepsiCo's prospects, including developments that are likely to affect the future of the company.

Ethical Dilemma

SD 4.

LO 3 **Management of Earnings**

Managers of most companies are very sensitive to the fact that analysts watch key performance measures, such as whether the firm is meeting earnings targets. A slight weakening of analysts' confidence can severely affect the price of a company's stock. The Securities and Exchange Commission (SEC) has been cracking down on the management of earnings to achieve financial goals by targeting companies for review. For instance, the SEC filed a complaint against **W. R. Grace & Co.** for releasing $1.5 mil-

| Cash Flow | CD-ROM | Communication | Critical Thinking | Ethics | General Ledger | Group Activity | Hot Links to Real Companies | International | Internet | Key Ratio | Memo | Spreadsheet |

lion from reserves into earnings in order to meet earnings targets. Grace officials say that the amount is immaterial and that it is in accord with accounting rules to book an immaterial item. (It was about 1.5 percent of net income.) The SEC, on the other hand, argues that it is a matter of principle: "Does anyone think that it's acceptable to intentionally book an error for the purpose of making earnings targets?" Some think such action on the part of the SEC will harm confidence in the companies.[7] Do you think it is unethical for a company's management to increase earnings periodically through the use of one-time transactions, such as adjustments of reserves or sale of assets, on which it has a profit?

Research Activity

SD 5.

LO 3 Use of Investors' Services

Find *Moody's Investors Service* or *Standard & Poor's Industry Guide* in your library. Locate reports on three corporations. You may choose the corporations at random or choose them from the same industry, if directed to do so by your instructor. (If you did a related exercise in a previous chapter, use the same three companies.) Write a summary of what you learned about each company's financial performance, including what measures of performance were mentioned in the write-ups and the company's prospects for the future, and be prepared to discuss your findings in class.

Decision-Making Practice

SD 6.

LO 4 Effect of One-Time Item
LO 5 on Loan Decision

Apple a Day, Inc., and *Unforgettable Edibles, Inc.,* both operate food catering businesses in the metropolitan area. Their customers include *Fortune* 500 companies, regional firms, and individuals. The two firms reported similar profit margins for the current year, and both determine bonuses for managers based on reaching a target profit margin and return on equity. Each firm has submitted a loan request to you, a loan officer for City National Bank, with the following information:

	Apple a Day	Unforgettable Edibles
Net Sales	$625,348	$717,900
Cost of Goods Sold	225,125	287,080
Gross Margin	$400,223	$430,820
Operating Expenses	281,300	371,565
Operating Income	$118,923	$ 59,255
Gain on Sale of Real Estate		81,923
Interest Expense	(9,333)	(15,338)
Income Before Income Taxes	$109,590	$125,840
Income Taxes	25,990	29,525
Net Income	$ 83,600	$ 96,315
Average Stockholders' Equity	$312,700	$390,560

1. Perform a vertical analysis and prepare a common-size income statement for each firm. Compute profit margin and return on equity.

2. Discuss your results, the bonus plan for management, and loan considerations. Make a recommendation about which company is a better risk for receiving the loan.

FINANCIAL REPORTING AND ANALYSIS

Interpreting Financial Reports

FRA 1.

LO 4 Trend Analysis

H. J. Heinz Company is a global company engaged in several lines of business, including food service, infant foods, condiments, pet foods, tuna, and weight control food products. A five-year summary of operations and other related data for Heinz appears at the top of the next page.[8]

Five-Year Summary of Operations and Other Related Data H. J. Heinz Company and Subsidiaries					
	1999	1998	1997	1996	1995
	(Dollars in thousands, except per share data)				
Summary of Operations					
Sales	$9,299,610	$9,209,284	$9,397,007	$9,112,265	$8,086,794
Cost of products sold	5,944,867	5,711,213	6,385,091	5,775,357	5,119,597
Interest expense	258,815	258,616	274,746	277,411	210,585
Provision for income taxes	360,790	453,415	177,193	364,342	346,982
Net income	474,341	801,566	301,871	659,319	591,025
Other Related Data					
Dividends paid: Common	484,817	452,966	416,923	381,871	345,358
Total assets	8,053,634	8,023,421	8,437,787	8,623,691	8,247,188
Total debt	3,376,413	5,806,905	5,997,366	3,363,828	3,401,076
Shareholders' equity	1,803,004	2,216,516	2,440,921	2,706,757	2,472,869

REQUIRED

Prepare a trend analysis for Heinz with 1995 as the base year and discuss the results. Identify important trends and tell whether the trends are favorable or unfavorable. Discuss significant relationships among the trends.

International Company

FRA 2.
LO 5 Comparison of International Company Operating Cycles

Ratio analysis enables one to compare the performance of companies whose financial statements are presented in different currencies. For instance, selected 1999 data for two large pharmaceutical companies—one American, *Pfizer, Inc.,* and one Swiss, *Roche*—are presented below (in millions):[9]

	Pfizer, Inc. (U.S.)	Roche (Swiss)
Net Sales	$14,133	SFr.27,567
Cost of Goods Sold	2,528	8,734
Accounts Receivable	3,864	6,178
Inventories	1,654	6,546
Accounts Payable	951	2,378

Accounts receivable in 1998 were $2,914 for Pfizer and SFr.4,535 for Roche. Inventories in 1998 were $1,828 for Pfizer and SFr.5,389 for Roche. Accounts payable in 1998 were $971 for Pfizer and SFr.2,088 for Roche.

For each company calculate the receivable, inventory, and payables turnovers and the respective days associated with each. Then determine the operating cycle for each company and the days of financing required for current operations. Compare the results.

Group Activity: Divide the class into groups to make the calculations. Ask half of the groups to analyze Pfizer and the other half to analyze Roche. Have the entire class compare and discuss results.

Toys "R" Us Annual Report

FRA 3.
LO 5 Comprehensive Ratio Analysis

Refer to the Toys "R" Us annual report, and conduct a comprehensive ratio analysis that compares data from 2000 and 1999. If you have been computing ratios for Toys "R" Us in previous chapters, you may prepare a table that summarizes the ratios for 2000 and 1999 and show calculations only for the ratios not previously calculated. If this is the first time you are doing a ratio analysis for Toys "R" Us, show all your computations. In

either case, after each group of ratios, comment on the performance of Toys "R" Us. Round your calculations to one decimal place. Prepare and comment on the following categories of ratios:

Liquidity analysis: Current ratio, quick ratio, receivable turnover, average days' sales uncollected, inventory turnover, average days' inventory on hand, payables turnover, and average days' payable (Accounts Receivable, Inventory, and Accounts Payable were [in millions] $175, $2,464, and $1,280, respectively, in 1998.)

Profitability analysis: Profit margin, asset turnover, return on assets, and return on equity (Comment on the effect of the restructuring in 1999 on the company's profitability.)

Long-term solvency analysis: Debt to equity ratio and interest coverage ratio

Cash flow adequacy analysis: Cash flow yield, cash flows to sales, cash flows to assets, and free cash flow

Market strength analysis: Price/earnings ratio and dividends yield

Fingraph® Financial Analyst™

FRA 4.

LO 5   Comprehensive Financial Performance Evaluation

Choose any company in the Fingraph® Financial Analyst™ CD-ROM software database.

1. Display and print for the company you have selected the following pages:
   a. Balance Sheet Analysis
   b. Current Assets and Current Liabilities Analysis
   c. Liquidity and Asset Utilization Analysis
   d. Income from Operations Analysis
   e. Statement of Cash Flows: Operating Activities Analysis
   f. Statement of Cash Flows: Investing and Financing Activities Analysis
   g. Market Strength Analysis

2. Prepare an executive summary that describes the financial condition and performance of your company for the past two years. Attach the pages you printed above in support of your analysis.

Internet Case

FRA 5.

LO 2   Use of Investors' Services
LO 3

Through the Needles Accounting Resource Center at http://college.hmco.com, go to the web site for **Moody's Investors Service.** Click on Ratings, which will show revisions of debt ratings issued by Moody's in the past few days. Choose a rating that has been upgraded or downgraded and read the short press announcement related to it. What reasons does Moody's give for the change in rating? What is Moody's assessment of the future of the company or institution? What financial performance measures are mentioned in the article? Write a summary of your findings and be prepared to share it in class.

ENDNOTES

1. Adapted from Material Sciences Corporation, *Annual Report*, 1998.
2. *Statement of Financial Accounting Standards No. 131*, "Segment Disclosures" (Norwalk, Conn.: Financial Accounting Standards Board, 1997).
3. William H. Beaver, "Alternative Accounting Measures as Indicators of Failure," *Accounting Review*, January 1968; and Edward Altman, "Financial Ratios, Discriminant Analysis and the Prediction of Corporate Bankruptcy," *Journal of Finance*, September 1968.
4. Sun Microsystems, Inc., "Management's Discussion and Analysis," *Annual Report*, 2000.
5. Ibid.
6. *Forbes*, November 13, 1978, p. 154.
7. Elizabeth MacDonald, "Firms Say SEC Earnings Scrutiny Goes Too Far," *The Wall Street Journal*, February 1, 1999.
8. H. J. Heinz Company, *Annual Report*, 1999.
9. Pfizer, Inc., *Annual Report*, 1999; and Roche Group, *Annual Report*, 1999.

APPENDIX A

International Accounting

As businesses grow, they naturally look for new sources of supply and new markets in other countries. Today, it is common for businesses, called *multinational* or *transnational corporations*, to operate in more than one country, and many of them operate throughout the world. Table 1 shows the extent of the foreign business of four of the largest U.S. corporations. IBM, for example, has operations in 80 countries and receives almost 60 percent of its sales from outside the United States. Other industrial countries, such as Switzerland, France, Germany, Great Britain, the Netherlands, and Japan, have also given rise to numerous worldwide corporations. For example, 98 percent of the sales of Nestlé, the large Swiss food company, are made outside Switzerland. Examples of companies that receive more than half of their sales from outside their home countries are Michelin, the French tire maker; Unilever, the British/Netherlands consumer products company; and Sony, the Japanese electronics company. More than 500 companies are listed on at least one stock exchange outside their home country.

In addition, sophisticated investors no longer restrict their investment activities to domestic securities markets. Many Americans invest in foreign securities markets, and non-Americans invest heavily in the stock market in the United States. Figure 1 shows that from 1980 to 1997, the total value of securities traded on the world's stock markets increased over 18-fold, with the U.S. share of the pie declining from 55 to 52 percent. During the same period, emerging markets in the rest of the world increased from 16 to 26 percent.

Foreign business transactions have two major effects on accounting. First, most sales or purchases of goods and services in other countries involve different currencies. Thus, one currency needs to be translated into another, using exchange rates.[1] An *exchange rate* is the value of one currency in terms of another. For example, an English company purchasing goods from a U.S. company and paying in U.S. dollars must exchange British pounds for U.S. dollars before making payment. In effect, currencies are goods

Table 1. Extent of Foreign Revenues for Selected U.S. Companies

Company	Foreign Revenues (millions)	Total Revenues (millions)	Foreign Revenues (percentage)
Exxon	$80,708	$100,697	80.1
IBM	46,364	81,667	56.8
Ford	43,819	144,416	30.3
General Motors	40,918	132,863	30.8

Source: "The 100 Largest U.S. Multinationals," *Forbes*, July 27, 1999. Reprinted by permission of *Forbes* Magazine © 1999 Forbes.

that can be bought and sold. Table 2 lists the exchange rates of several currencies in terms of dollars. It shows the exchange rate for the British pound as $1.438 per pound on a particular date. Like the price of any good or service, these prices change daily according to supply and demand for the currencies. Accounting for these price changes in recording foreign transactions and preparing financial statements for foreign subsidiaries is discussed in the next two sections.

The second major effect of international business on accounting is that financial standards differ from country to country, which makes it difficult to compare companies from different countries. The obstacles to achieving comparability and some of the progress in solving the problem are discussed later in this chapter.

Accounting for Transactions in Foreign Currencies

Among the first activities of an expanding company in the international market are the buying and selling of goods and services. For example, a U.S. maker of precision tools may expand by selling its product to foreign customers. Or it might lower its

Figure 1
Value of Securities Traded on the World's Stock Markets

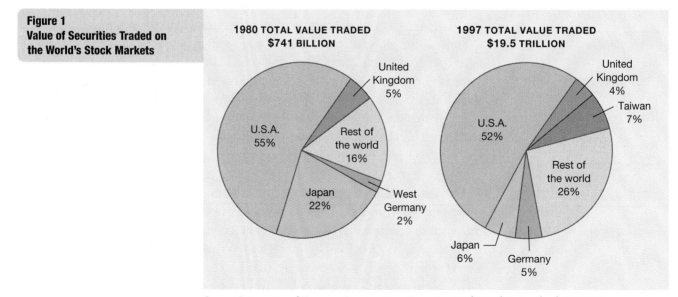

Source: International Finance Corporation, *Emerging Stock Markets Factbook*, © 1998.

Table 2. Partial Listing of Foreign Exchange Rates

Country	Price in $ U.S.	Country	Price in $ U.S.
Australia (dollar)	0.559	Hong Kong (dollar)	0.128
Brazil (real)	0.550	Japan (yen)	0.009
Britain (pound)	1.438	Mexico (peso)	0.10
Canada (dollar)	0.677	Russia (ruble)	0.359
Europe (euro)	0.871	Singapore (dollar)	0.577

Source: Data from *The Wall Street Journal,* September 7, 2000.

product cost by buying a less expensive part from a source in another country. In previous chapters, all transactions were recorded in dollars, and it was assumed that the dollar is a uniform measure in the same way that the inch and the centimeter are. But in the international marketplace, a transaction may take place in Japanese yen, British pounds, or some other currency. The values of these currencies in relation to the dollar rise and fall daily. If there is a delay between the date of sale or purchase and the date of receipt or payment of cash, the amount of cash involved may be different from that originally agreed upon due to changing exchange rates.

FOREIGN SALES   When a domestic company sells merchandise abroad, it may bill either in its own country's currency or in the foreign currency. If the billing and the subsequent payment are both in the domestic currency, no accounting problem arises. For example, assume that the precision toolmaker sells $160,000 worth of tools to a British company and bills the British company in dollars. The entry to record the sale and receipt is familiar:

Date of Sale

A = L + OE	Accounts Receivable, British company	160,000
+ +	Sales	160,000

Date of Receipt

A = L + OE	Cash	160,000
+	Accounts Receivable, British company	160,000
−		

However, if the U.S. company bills the British company in British pounds and accepts payment in pounds, the U.S. company may incur an *exchange gain or loss*. A gain or loss will occur if the exchange rate between dollars and pounds changes between the date of sale and the date of receipt. Since gains and losses tend to off-set one another, a single account is used during the year to accumulate the activity. The net exchange gain or loss is reported on the income statement. For example, assume that the sale of $160,000 above was billed as £100,000, reflecting an exchange rate of 1.60 (that is, $1.60 per pound) on the sale date. Now assume that by the date of receipt, the exchange rate has fallen to 1.50. The entries to record the transactions follow:

Date of Sale

A = L + OE	Accounts Receivable, British company	160,000
+ +	Sales	160,000
	£100,000 × $1.60 = $160,000	

Date of Receipt

A = L + OE	Cash	150,000	
+ −	Exchange Gain or Loss	10,000	
−	Accounts Receivable, British company		160,000
	£100,000 × $1.50 = $150,000		

The U.S. company has incurred an exchange loss of $10,000 because it agreed to accept a fixed number of British pounds in payment, and the value of each pound dropped before the payment was made. Had the value of the pound in relation to the dollar increased, the U.S. company would have made an exchange gain.

FOREIGN PURCHASES   Purchases are the opposite of sales. The same logic applies to them, except that the relationship of exchange gains and losses to changes in exchange rates is reversed. For example, assume that the maker of precision tools purchases $15,000 of a certain part from a Japanese supplier. If the purchase and subsequent payment are made in U.S. dollars, no accounting problem arises.

Date of Purchase

| A = L + OE | Purchases | 15,000 | |
| + − | Accounts Payable, Japanese company | | 15,000 |

Date of Payment

| A = L + OE | Accounts Payable, Japanese company | 15,000 | |
| − − | Cash | | 15,000 |

However, the Japanese company may bill the U.S. company in yen and be paid in yen. If so, the U.S. company will incur an exchange gain or loss if the exchange rate changes between the date of purchase and the date of payment. For example, assume that the transaction is for 2,500,000 yen and the exchange rates on the dates of purchase and payment are $.0090 and $.0085 per yen, respectively. The entries follow.

Date of Purchase

A = L + OE	Purchases	22,500	
+ −	Accounts Payable, Japanese company		22,500
	¥2,500,000 × $.0090 = $22,500		

Date of Payment

A = L + OE	Accounts Payable, Japanese company	22,500	
− − +	Exchange Gain or Loss		1,250
	Cash		21,250
	¥2,500,000 × $.0085 = $21,250		

In this case the U.S. company received an exchange gain of $1,250 because it agreed to pay a fixed ¥2,500,000, and between the dates of purchase and payment the exchange value of the yen decreased in relation to the dollar.

REALIZED VERSUS UNREALIZED EXCHANGE GAIN OR LOSS   The preceding illustration dealt with completed transactions (in the sense that payment was completed). In each case, the exchange gain or loss was recognized on the date of receipt or payment. If financial statements are prepared between the sale or purchase and the subsequent receipt or payment, and exchange rates have changed, there will be unrealized gains or losses. The Financial Accounting Standards Board, in its *Statement No. 52*, requires that exchange gains and losses "shall be included in determining net income for the period in which the exchange rate changes."[2] The requirement includes interim (quarterly) statements and applies whether or not a transaction is complete.

This ruling has caused much debate. Critics charge that it gives too much weight to fleeting changes in exchange rates, causing random changes in earnings that hide long-run trends. Others believe that the use of current exchange rates to value receivables and payables as of the balance sheet date is a major step toward economic reality (current values). To illustrate, we will use the preceding case, in which a U.S. company buys parts from a Japanese supplier. We will assume that the transaction has not been completed by the balance sheet date, when the exchange rate is $.0080 per yen:

	Date	Exchange Rate ($ per Yen)
Date of purchase	Dec. 1	.0090
Balance sheet date	Dec. 31	.0080
Date of payment	Feb. 1	.0085

The accounting effects of the unrealized gain are as follows:

	Dec. 1	Dec. 31	Feb. 1
Purchase recorded in U.S. dollars (billed as ¥2,500,000)	$22,500	$22,500	$22,500
Dollars to be paid to equal ¥2,500,000 (¥2,500,000 × exchange rate)	22,500	20,000	21,250
Unrealized gain (or loss)	—	$ 2,500	
Realized gain (or loss)			$ 1,250

A = L + OE + −	Dec. 1	Purchases 　　Accounts Payable, Japanese company	22,500	22,500
A = L + OE − +	Dec. 31	Accounts Payable, Japanese company 　　Exchange Gain or Loss	2,500	2,500
A = L + OE − − −	Feb. 1	Accounts Payable, Japanese company Exchange Gain or Loss 　　Cash	20,000 1,250	21,250

In this case, the original sale was billed in yen by the Japanese company. Following the rules of *Statement No. 52*, an exchange gain of $2,500 is recorded on December 31, and an exchange loss of $1,250 is recorded on February 1. Even though these large fluctuations do not affect the net exchange gain of $1,250 for the whole transaction, the effect on each year's income statements may be important.

Restatement of Foreign Subsidiary Financial Statements

Growing companies often expand by setting up or buying foreign subsidiaries. If a foreign subsidiary is more than 50 percent owned and the parent company exercises control, then the foreign subsidiary should be included in the consolidated financial statements (see the discussion of parent and subsidiary companies in Appendix B). The consolidation procedure is the same as that for domestic subsidiaries, except that the statements of the foreign subsidiary must be restated in the reporting currency before consolidation takes place. The *reporting currency* is the currency in which the consolidated financial statements are presented. Clearly, it makes no sense to combine the assets of a Mexican subsidiary stated in pesos with the assets of the U.S. parent company stated in dollars. Most U.S. companies present their financial statements in U.S. dollars, so the following discussion assumes that the U.S. dollar is the reporting currency used.[3]

Restatement is the stating of one currency in terms of another. The method of restatement depends on the foreign subsidiary's functional currency. The *functional currency* is the currency of the place where the subsidiary carries on most of its business. Generally, it is the currency in which a company earns and spends its cash. The functional currency to be used depends on the kind of foreign operation in which the subsidiary takes part.

There are two broad types of foreign operation. Type I includes operations that are fairly self-contained and integrated within a certain country or economy. Type II includes those that are mainly a direct and integral part or extension of the parent company's operations. As a general rule, Type I subsidiaries use the currency of the country in which they are located, and Type II subsidiaries use the currency of the parent company. If the parent company is a U.S. company, the functional currency of a Type I subsidiary will be the currency of the country in which the subsidiary carries on its business, and the functional currency of a Type II subsidiary will be the U.S. dollar.

Statement No. 52 makes an exception when a Type I subsidiary operates in a country in which there is hyperinflation (as a rule of thumb, more than 100 percent cumulative inflation over three years)—for example, Brazil or Argentina. In such a case, the subsidiary is treated as a Type II subsidiary, with the functional currency being the U.S. dollar. Restatements in these situations do not affect cash flows because they are done simply for the convenience of preparing consolidated statements.

PROBLEMS

P 1.

Recording International Transactions: Fluctuating Exchange Rate

Part A: Cleveland Corporation purchased a special-purpose machine from Leipzig Corporation on credit for DM 50,000. At the date of purchase, the exchange rate was $.55 per mark. On the date of the payment, which was made in marks, the value of the mark had increased to $.60.

Prepare journal entries to record the purchase and payment in Cleveland Corporation's accounting records.

Part B: U.S. Corporation made a sale on account to U.K. Company on November 15 in the amount of £300,000. Payment was to be made in British pounds on February 15. U.S. Corporation's fiscal year is the same as the calendar year. The British pound was worth $1.70 on November 15, $1.58 on December 31, and $1.78 on February 15.

Prepare journal entries to record the sale, year-end adjustment, and collection on U.S. Corporation's books.

P 2.

International Transactions

High Valley Company, whose year end is June 30, engaged in the following international transactions (exchange rates in parentheses):

May 15 Purchased goods from a Japanese firm for $110,000; terms n/10 in U.S. dollars (yen = $.0080).
    17 Sold goods to a German company for $165,000; terms n/30 in marks (mark = $.55).
    21 Purchased goods from a Mexican company for $120,000; terms n/30 in pesos (peso = $.10).
    25 Paid for the goods purchased on May 15 (yen = $.0085).
    31 Sold goods to an Italian firm for $200,000; terms n/60 in lire (lira = $.0005).

June 5 Sold goods to a British firm for $56,000; terms n/10 in U.S. dollars (pound = $1.30).

7 Purchased goods from a Japanese firm for $221,000; terms n/30 in yen (yen = $.0085).

15 Received payment for the sale made on June 5 (pound = $1.80).

16 Received payment for the sale made on May 17 (mark = $.60).

17 Purchased goods from a French firm for $66,000; terms n/30 in U.S. dollars (franc = $.16).

20 Paid for the goods purchased on May 21 (peso = $.09).

22 Sold goods to a British firm for $108,000; terms n/30 in pounds (pound = $1.80).

30 Made year-end adjusting entries for incomplete foreign exchange transactions (franc = $.17; peso = $.09; mark = $.60; lira = $.0003; pound = $1.70; yen = $.0090).

July 7 Paid for the goods purchased on June 7 (yen = $.0085).

19 Paid for the goods purchased on June 17 (franc = $.15).

22 Received payment for the goods sold on June 22 (pound = $1.60).

30 Received payment for the goods sold on May 31 (lira = $.0004).

REQUIRED

Prepare entries in journal form for these transactions.

ENDNOTES

1. At the time this chapter was written, exchange rates were fluctuating rapidly. Thus, the examples, exercises, and problems in this book use exchange rates in the general range for the countries involved.
2. *Statement of Financial Accounting Standards No. 52*, "Foreign Currency Translation" (Norwalk, Conn.: Financial Accounting Standards Board, 1981), par. 15.
3. This section is based on the requirements of *Statement of Financial Accounting Standards No. 52*, "Foreign Currency Translation" (Norwalk, Conn.: Financial Accounting Standards Board, 1981).

APPENDIX B

Long-Term Investments

One corporation may invest in another corporation by purchasing bonds or stocks. These investments may be either short term or long term. In this section, we are concerned with long-term investments.

Long-Term Investments in Bonds

Like all investments, investments in bonds are recorded at cost, which is the price of the bonds plus the broker's commission. When bonds are purchased between interest payment dates, the purchaser must also pay an amount equal to the interest that has accrued on the bonds since the last interest payment date. Then, on the next interest payment date, the purchaser receives an interest payment for the whole period. The payment for accrued interest should be recorded as a debit to Interest Income, which will be offset by a credit to Interest Income when the semiannual interest is received.

Subsequent accounting for a corporation's long-term bond investments depends on the classification of the bonds. If the company may at some point decide to sell the bonds, they are classified as *available-for-sale securities*. If the company plans to hold the bonds until they are paid off on their maturity date, they are considered *held-to-maturity securities*. Except in industries like insurance and banking, it is unusual for companies to buy the bonds of other companies with the express purpose of holding them until they mature, which can be in 10 to 30 years. Therefore, most firms classify long-term bond investments as available-for-sale securities. Such bonds are subsequently accounted for at fair value, much like equity or stock investments are. Fair value is usually the market value. When bonds are intended to be held to maturity, which is rare, they are accounted for not at fair value but at cost, adjusted for the amortization of their discount or premium. The procedure is similar to accounting for long-term bond liabilities, except that separate accounts for discounts and premiums are not used.

Long-Term Investments in Stock

All long-term investments in stocks are recorded at cost, in accordance with generally accepted accounting principles. The treatment of the investment in the accounting records after the initial purchase depends on the extent to which the investing company can exercise significant influence or control over the operating and financial policies of the other company.

The Accounting Principles Board defined the important terms *significant influence* and *control* in its *Opinion No. 18. Significant influence* is the ability to affect the operating and financial policies of the company whose shares are owned, even though the investor holds 50 percent or less of the voting stock. Ability to influence a company may be shown by representation on the board of directors, participation in policy making, material transactions between the companies, exchange of managerial personnel, and technological dependency. For the sake of uniformity, the APB decided that unless there is proof to the contrary, an investment of 20 percent or more of the voting stock should be presumed to confer significant influence. An investment of less than 20 percent of the voting stock would not confer significant influence.[1]

Control is defined as the ability of the investing company to decide the operating and financial policies of the other company. Control is said to exist when the investing company owns more than 50 percent of the voting stock of the company in which it has invested.

Thus, in the absence of information to the contrary, a noninfluential and noncontrolling investment would be less than 20 percent ownership. An influential but noncontrolling investment would be 20 to 50 percent ownership. And a controlling investment would be more than 50 percent ownership. The accounting treatment differs for each kind of investment.

NONINFLUENTIAL AND NONCONTROLLING INVESTMENT   Available-for-sale securities are debt or equity securities that are not classified as trading or held-to-maturity securities. When equity securities are involved, the further criterion is that they be noninfluential and noncontrolling investments of less than 20 percent of the voting stock. The Financial Accounting Standards Board requires a *cost adjusted to market method* for accounting for available-for-sale securities. Under this method, available-for-sale securities must be recorded initially at cost and thereafter adjusted periodically through the use of an allowance account to reflect changes in the market value.[2]

Available-for-sale securities are classified as long term if management intends to hold them for more than one year. When accounting for long-term available-for-sale securities, the unrealized gain or loss resulting from the adjustment is not reported on the income statement, but is reported as a special item in the stockholders' equity section of the balance sheet and in comprehensive income disclosure.

At the end of each accounting period, the total cost and the total market value of these long-term stock investments must be determined. If the total market value is less than the total cost, the difference must be credited to a contra-asset account called Allowance to Adjust Long-Term Investments to Market. Because of the long-term nature of the investment, the debit part of the entry, which represents a decrease in value below cost, is treated as a temporary decrease and does not appear as a loss on the income statement. It is shown in a contra-stockholders' equity account called Unrealized Loss on Long-Term Investments. Thus, both of these accounts are balance sheet accounts. If the market value exceeds the cost, the allowance account is added to Long-Term Investments and the unrealized gain appears as an addition to stockholders' equity.[3]

When long-term investments in stock are sold, the difference between the sale price and what the stock cost is recorded and reported as a realized gain or loss on the income statement. Dividend income from such investments is recorded by a debit to Cash and a credit to Dividend Income.

For example, assume the following facts about the long-term stock investments of Coleman Corporation:

June 1, 20x0 Paid cash for the following long-term investments: 10,000 shares of Durbin Corporation common stock (representing 2 percent of outstanding stock) at $25 per share; 5,000 shares of Kotes Corporation common stock (representing 3 percent of outstanding stock) at $15 per share.

Dec. 31, 20x0 Quoted market prices at year end: Durbin common stock, $21; Kotes common stock, $17.

Apr. 1, 20x1 Change in policy required sale of 2,000 shares of Durbin Corporation common stock at $23.

July 1, 20x1 Received cash dividend from Kotes Corporation equal to $.20 per share.

Dec. 31, 20x1 Quoted market prices at year end: Durbin common stock, $24; Kotes common stock, $13.

Entries to record these transactions follow.

Investment

20x0

A = L + OE
+
−

June 1	Long-Term Investments	325,000	
	Cash		325,000
	Made investments in Durbin common stock (10,000 shares × $25 = $250,000) and Kotes common stock (5,000 shares × $15 = $75,000)		

Year-End Adjustment

20x0

A = L + OE
−   −

Dec. 31	Unrealized Loss on Long-Term Investments	30,000	
	Allowance to Adjust Long-Term Investments to Market		30,000
	Recorded reduction of long-term investment to market		

Company	Shares	Market Price	Total Market	Total Cost
Durbin	10,000	$21	$210,000	$250,000
Kotes	5,000	17	85,000	75,000
			$295,000	$325,000

Total Cost − Total Market Value = $325,000 − $295,000 = $30,000

Sale

20x1

A = L + OE
+
−

Apr. 1	Cash	46,000	
	Loss on Sale of Investments	4,000	
	Long-Term Investments		50,000
	Sold 2,000 shares of Durbin common stock		

2,000 × $23 = $46,000
2,000 × $25 = 50,000

Loss $ 4,000

Dividend Received

20x1

A = L + OE
+   +

July 1   Cash   1,000
             Dividend Income   1,000
                 Received cash dividend from Kotes stock
                 5,000 × $.20 = $1,000

Year-End Adjustment

20x1

A = L + OE
+   +

Dec. 31   Allowance to Adjust Long-Term
               Investments to Market   12,000
                   Unrealized Loss on Long-Term
                   Investments   12,000
                       Recorded the adjustment in long-
                       term investment so it is reported
                       at market

The adjustment equals the previous balance ($30,000 from the December 31, 20x0, entry) minus the new balance ($18,000), or $12,000. The new balance of $18,000 is the difference at the present time between the total market value and the total cost of all investments. It is figured as follows:

Company	Shares	Market Price	Total Market	Total Cost
Durbin	8,000	$24	$192,000	$200,000
Kotes	5,000	13	65,000	75,000
			$257,000	$275,000

Total Cost − Total Market Value = $275,000 − $257,000 = $18,000

The Allowance to Adjust Long-Term Investments to Market and the Unrealized Loss on Long-Term Investments are reciprocal contra accounts, each with the same dollar balance, as can be shown by the effects of these transactions on the T accounts:

CONTRA-ASSET ACCOUNT		**CONTRA-STOCKHOLDERS' EQUITY ACCOUNT**	
Allowance to Adjust Long-Term Investments to Market		**Unrealized Loss on Long-Term Investments**	
20x1 12,000	20x0 30,000	20x0 30,000	20x1 12,000
	Bal. 20x1 18,000	Bal. 20x1 18,000	

The Allowance account reduces long-term investments by the amount by which the cost of the investments exceeds market; the Unrealized Loss account reduces stockholders' equity by a similar amount. The opposite effects will exist if market value exceeds cost, resulting in an unrealized gain.

INFLUENTIAL BUT NONCONTROLLING INVESTMENT   As we have seen, ownership of 20 percent or more of a company's voting stock is considered sufficient to influence the operations of that corporation. When this is the case, the investment in the stock of the influenced company should be accounted for using the *equity method*. The equity method presumes that an investment of 20 percent or more is more than a passive investment, and that therefore the investing company should share proportionately in the success or failure of the investee company. The three main features of this method are as follows:

1. The investor records the original purchase of the stock at cost.

2. The investor records its share of the investee's periodic net income as an increase in the Investment account, with a corresponding credit to an income account. In like manner, the investor records its share of the investee's periodic loss as a decrease in the Investment account, with a corresponding debit to a loss account.

3. When the investor receives a cash dividend, the asset account Cash is increased and the Investment account is decreased.

To illustrate the equity method of accounting, we will assume the following facts about an investment by Vassor Corporation. On January 1 of the current year, Vassor acquired 40 percent of the voting common stock of Block Corporation for $180,000. With this share of ownership, Vassor can exert significant influence over the operations of Block. During the year, Block Corporation reported net income of $80,000 and paid cash dividends of $20,000. The entries that follow are to record these transactions by Vassor Corporation.

Investment

A = L + OE	Investment in Block Corporation	180,000	
+	Cash		180,000
−	Invested in Block Corporation common stock		

Recognition of Income

A = L + OE	Investment in Block Corporation	32,000	
+ +	Income, Block Corporation Investment		32,000
	Recognized 40% of income reported		
	by Block Corporation		
	40% × $80,000 = $32,000		

Receipt of Cash Dividend

A = L + OE	Cash	8,000	
+	Investment in Block Corporation		8,000
−	Cash dividend from Block Corporation		
	40% × $20,000 = $8,000		

The balance of the Investment in Block Corporation account after these transactions is $204,000, as shown here:

Investment in Block Corporation

Investment	180,000	Dividend received	8,000
Share of income	32,000		
Bal.	204,000		

CONTROLLING INVESTMENT   In some cases, an investor who owns less than 50 percent of the voting stock of a company may exercise such powerful influence that for all practical purposes the investor controls the policies of the other company. Nevertheless, ownership of more than 50 percent of the voting stock is required for accounting recognition of control. When a controlling interest is owned, a parent-subsidiary relationship is said to exist. The investing company is known as the *parent company*, the other company as the *subsidiary*. Because the two corporations are separate legal entities, each prepares separate financial statements.

Table 1. Accounting Treatments of Long-Term Investments in Stock		
Level of Ownership	Percentage of Ownership	Accounting Treatment
Noninfluential and noncontrolling	Less than 20%	Cost initially; investment adjusted subsequent to purchase for changes in market value
Influential but noncontrolling	Between 20% and 50%	Equity method; investment valued subsequently at cost plus investor's share of income (or minus investor's share of loss) minus dividends received
Controlling	More than 50%	Financial statements consolidated

However, owing to their special relationship, they are viewed for public financial reporting purposes as a single economic entity. For this reason, they must combine their financial statements into a single set of statements called *consolidated financial statements*.

Accounting for consolidated financial statements is very complex. It is usually the subject of an advanced accounting course. However, most large public corporations have subsidiaries and must prepare consolidated financial statements. It is therefore important to have some understanding of accounting for consolidations.

The proper accounting treatments for long-term investments in stock are summarized in Table 1.

PROBLEMS

Methods of Accounting for Long-Term Investments

P 1. Diversified Corporation has the following long-term investments:

1. 60 percent of the common stock of Down Corporation
2. 13 percent of the common stock of West Lake, Inc.
3. 50 percent of the nonvoting preferred stock of Invole Corporation
4. 100 percent of the common stock of its financing subsidiary, DCF, Inc.
5. 35 percent of the common stock of the French company Maison de Boutaine
6. 70 percent of the common stock of the Canadian company Alberta Mining Company

For each of these investments, tell which of the following methods should be used for external financial reporting, and why.

a. Cost adjusted to market method
b. Equity method
c. Consolidation of parent and subsidiary financial statements

Long-Term Investment Transactions

P 2. Red Bud Corporation made the following transactions in its Long-Term Investments account over a two-year period:

20x0

Apr. 1 Purchased with cash 20,000 shares of Season Company stock for $152 per share.

June   1   Purchased with cash 15,000 shares of Abbado Corporation stock for $72 per share.

Sept.   1   Received a $1 per share dividend from Season Company.

Nov.   1   Purchased with cash 25,000 shares of Frankel Corporation stock for $110 per share.

Dec. 31   Market values per share of shares held in the Long-Term Investments account were as follows: Season Company, $140; Abbado Corporation, $32; and Frankel Corporation, $122.

20x1

Feb.   1   Because of unfavorable prospects for Abbado Corporation, Abbado stock was sold for cash at $40 per share.

May   1   Purchased with cash 10,000 shares of Schulian Corporation for $224 per share.

Sept.   1   Received $2 per share dividend from Season Company.

Dec. 31   Market values per share of shares held in the Long-Term Investments account were as follows: Season Company, $160; Frankel Corporation, $140; and Schulian Corporation, $200.

REQUIRED

Prepare entries to record these transactions in the Red Bud Corporation records. Assume that all investments represent less than 20 percent of the voting stock of the company whose stock was acquired.

P 3.

Long-Term Investments: Equity Method

The Modi Company owns 40 percent of the voting stock of the Vivanco Company. The Investment account for this company on the Modi Company's balance sheet had a balance of $600,000 on January 1, 20xx. During 20xx, the Vivanco Company reported the following quarterly earnings and dividends paid:

Quarter	Earnings	Dividends Paid
1	$ 80,000	$ 40,000
2	60,000	40,000
3	160,000	40,000
4	(40,000)	40,000
	$260,000	$160,000

The Modi Company exercises a significant influence over the operations of the Vivanco Company and therefore uses the equity method to account for its investment.

REQUIRED

1.   Prepare the entries in journal form that the Modi Company must make each quarter in accounting for its investment in the Vivanco Company.

2.   Prepare a T account for the investment in common stock of the Vivanco Company. Enter the beginning balance, relevant portions of the entries made in **1,** and the ending balance.

ENDNOTES

1.   The Financial Accounting Standards Board points out in its *Interpretation No. 35* (May 1981) that although the presumption of significant influence applies when 20 percent or more of the voting stock is held, the rule is not a rigid one. All relevant facts and circumstances should be examined in each case to find out whether or not significant influence exists. For example, the FASB notes five circumstances that may remove the element of significant influence: (1) The company files a lawsuit against the investor or complains to a government agency; (2) the investor tries and fails to become a director; (3) the investor agrees not to increase its holdings; (4) the company is operated by a small group that ignores the investor's wishes; (5) the investor tries and fails to obtain additional information from the company that is not available to other stockholders.

2.   *Statement of Financial Accounting Standards No. 115,* "Accounting for Certain Investments in Debt and Equity Securities" (Norwalk, Conn.: Financial Accounting Standards Board, 1993).

3.   If the decrease in value is deemed permanent, a different procedure is followed to record the decline in market value of the long-term investment. A loss account that appears on the income statement is debited instead of the Unrealized Loss account.

Appendix C

The Time Value of Money

Simple Interest and Compound Interest

Interest is the cost associated with the use of money for a specific period of time. Because interest is a cost associated with time, and "time is money," it is also an important consideration in any business decision. *Simple interest* is the interest cost for one or more periods, under the assumption that the amount on which the interest is computed stays the same from period to period. *Compound interest* is the interest cost for two or more periods, under the assumption that after each period the interest of that period is added to the amount on which interest is computed in future periods. In other words, compound interest is interest earned on a principal sum that is increased at the end of each period by the interest for that period.

EXAMPLE—SIMPLE INTEREST   Joe Sanchez accepts an 8 percent, $30,000 note due in ninety days. How much will he receive in total at that time? Remember that the formula for calculating simple interest is as follows:

$$\text{Interest} = \text{Principal} \times \text{Rate} \times \text{Time}$$
$$= \$30,000 \times 8/100 \times 90/360$$
$$= \$600$$

Therefore, the total that Sanchez will receive is calculated as follows:

$$\text{Total} = \text{Principal} + \text{Interest}$$
$$= \$30,000 + \$600$$
$$= \$30,600$$

EXAMPLE—COMPOUND INTEREST   Ann Clary deposits $5,000 in a savings account that pays 6 percent interest. She expects to leave the principal and accumulated interest in the account for three years. How much will her account total at the end of three years? Assume that the interest is paid at the end of the year and is added to the principal at that time, and that this total in turn earns interest. The amount at the end of three years is computed as follows:

(1) Year	(2) Principal Amount at Beginning of Year	(3) Annual Amount of Interest (Col. 2 × 6%)	(4) Accumulated Amount at End of Year (Col. 2 + Col. 3)
1	$5,000.00	$300.00	$5,300.00
2	5,300.00	318.00	5,618.00
3	5,618.00	337.08	5,955.08

At the end of three years, Clary will have $5,955.08 in her savings account. Note that the annual amount of interest increases each year by the interest rate times the interest of the previous year. For example, between year 1 and year 2, the interest increased by $18 ($318 – $300), which exactly equals 6 percent times $300.

Future Value of a Single Invested Sum at Compound Interest

Another way to ask the question in the example of compound interest above is, What is the future value of a single sum ($5,000) at compound interest (6 percent) for three years? *Future value* is the amount that an investment will be worth at a future date if invested at compound interest. A businessperson often wants to know future value, but the method of computing the future value illustrated above is too time-consuming in practice. Imagine how tedious the calculation would be if the example were ten years instead of three. Fortunately, there are tables that simplify solving problems involving compound interest. Table 1, showing the future value of $1 after a given number of time periods, is an example. It is actually part of a larger table, Table 1 in the appendix on future value and present value tables. Suppose that we want to solve the problem of Clary's savings account above. We

Table 1. Future Value of $1 after a Given Number of Time Periods

Periods	1%	2%	3%	4%	5%	6%	7%	8%	9%	10%	12%	14%	15%
1	1.010	1.020	1.030	1.040	1.050	1.060	1.070	1.080	1.090	1.100	1.120	1.140	1.150
2	1.020	1.040	1.061	1.082	1.103	1.124	1.145	1.166	1.188	1.210	1.254	1.300	1.323
3	1.030	1.061	1.093	1.125	1.158	1.191	1.225	1.260	1.295	1.331	1.405	1.482	1.521
4	1.041	1.082	1.126	1.170	1.216	1.262	1.311	1.360	1.412	1.464	1.574	1.689	1.749
5	1.051	1.104	1.159	1.217	1.276	1.338	1.403	1.469	1.539	1.611	1.762	1.925	2.011
6	1.062	1.126	1.194	1.265	1.340	1.419	1.501	1.587	1.677	1.772	1.974	2.195	2.313
7	1.072	1.149	1.230	1.316	1.407	1.504	1.606	1.714	1.828	1.949	2.211	2.502	2.660
8	1.083	1.172	1.267	1.369	1.477	1.594	1.718	1.851	1.993	2.144	2.476	2.853	3.059
9	1.094	1.195	1.305	1.423	1.551	1.689	1.838	1.999	2.172	2.358	2.773	3.252	3.518
10	1.105	1.219	1.344	1.480	1.629	1.791	1.967	2.159	2.367	2.594	3.106	3.707	4.046

Source: Excerpt from Table 1 in the appendix on future value and present value tables.

simply look down the 6 percent column in Table 1 until we reach the line for three periods and find the factor 1.191. This factor, when multiplied by $1, gives the future value of that $1 at compound interest of 6 percent for three periods (years in this case). Thus, we solve the problem as follows:

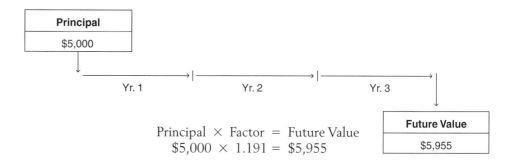

Principal × Factor = Future Value
$5,000 × 1.191 = $5,955

Except for a rounding difference of $.08, the answer is exactly the same as that calculated earlier.

Future Value of an Ordinary Annuity

Another common problem involves an *ordinary annuity*, which is a series of equal payments made at the end of equal intervals of time, with compound interest on these payments.

The following example shows how to find the future value of an ordinary annuity. Assume that Ben Katz makes a $200 payment at the end of each of the next three years into a savings account that pays 5 percent interest. How much money will he have in his account at the end of the three years? One way of computing the amount is shown in the following table.

(1) Year	(2) Beginning Balance	(3) Interest Earned (5% × Col. 2)	(4) Periodic Payment	(5) Accumulated at End of Period (Col. 2 + Col. 3 + Col. 4)
1	—	—	$200	$200.00
2	$200.00	$10.00	200	410.00
3	410.00	20.50	200	630.50

Katz would have $630.50 in his account at the end of three years, consisting of $600.00 in periodic payments and $30.50 in interest.

This calculation can also be simplified by using Table 2. We look down the 5 percent column until we reach three periods and find the factor 3.153. This factor, when multiplied by $1, gives the future value of a series of three $1 payments at compound interest of 5 percent. Thus, we solve the problem as shown on the next page.

Table 2. Future Value of an Ordinary Annuity of $1 Paid in Each Period for a Given Number of Time Periods

Periods	1%	2%	3%	4%	5%	6%	7%	8%	9%	10%	12%	14%	15%
1	1.000	1.000	1.000	1.000	1.000	1.000	1.000	1.000	1.000	1.000	1.000	1.000	1.000
2	2.010	2.020	2.030	2.040	2.050	2.060	2.070	2.080	2.090	2.100	2.120	2.140	2.150
3	3.030	3.060	3.091	3.122	3.153	3.184	3.215	3.246	3.278	3.310	3.374	3.440	3.473
4	4.060	4.122	4.184	4.246	4.310	4.375	4.440	4.506	4.573	4.641	4.779	4.921	4.993
5	5.101	5.204	5.309	5.416	5.526	5.637	5.751	5.867	5.985	6.105	6.353	6.610	6.742
6	6.152	6.308	6.468	6.633	6.802	6.975	7.153	7.336	7.523	7.716	8.115	8.536	8.754
7	7.214	7.434	7.662	7.898	8.142	8.394	8.654	8.923	9.200	9.487	10.09	10.73	11.07
8	8.286	8.583	8.892	9.214	9.549	9.897	10.26	10.64	11.03	11.44	12.30	13.23	13.73
9	9.369	9.755	10.16	10.58	11.03	11.49	11.98	12.49	13.02	13.58	14.78	16.09	16.79
10	10.46	10.95	11.46	12.01	12.58	13.18	13.82	14.49	15.19	15.94	17.55	19.34	20.30

Source: Excerpt from Table 2 in the appendix on future value and present value tables.

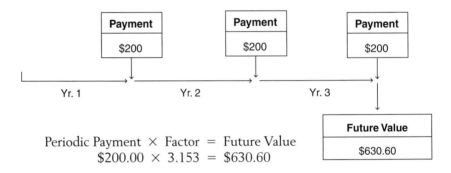

$$\text{Periodic Payment} \times \text{Factor} = \text{Future Value}$$
$$\$200.00 \times 3.153 = \$630.60$$

Except for a rounding difference of $.10, this result is the same as our earlier one.

Present Value

Suppose that you had the choice of receiving $100 today or one year from today. Intuitively, you would choose to receive the $100 today. Why? You know that if you have the $100 today, you can put it in a savings account to earn interest, so that you will have more than $100 a year from today. Therefore, we can say that an amount to be received in the future (future value) is not worth as much today as an amount to be received today (present value) because of the cost associated with the passage of time. In fact, present value and future value are closely related. *Present value* is the amount that must be invested now at a given rate of interest to produce a given future value. For example, assume that Sue Dapper needs $1,000 one year from now. How much should she invest today to achieve that goal if the interest rate is 5 percent? From earlier examples, the following equation may be established.

$$\text{Present Value} \times (1.0 + \text{Interest Rate}) = \text{Future Value}$$
$$\text{Present Value} \times 1.05 = \$1,000.00$$
$$\text{Present Value} = \$1,000.00 \div 1.05$$
$$\text{Present Value} = \$952.38$$

Thus, to achieve a future value of $1,000.00, a present value of $952.38 must be invested. Interest of 5 percent on $952.38 for one year equals $47.62, and these two amounts added together equal $1,000.00.

PRESENT VALUE OF A SINGLE SUM DUE IN THE FUTURE When more than one time period is involved, the calculation of present value is more complicated. Consider the following example. Don Riley wants to be sure of having $4,000 at the end of three years. How much must he invest today in a 5 percent savings account to achieve this goal? Adapting the above equation, we compute the present value of $4,000 at compound interest of 5 percent for three years in the future.

Year	Amount at End of Year	Divide by		Present Value at Beginning of Year
3	$4,000.00	÷	1.05	=	$3,809.52
2	3,809.52	÷	1.05	=	3,628.11
1	3,628.11	÷	1.05	=	3,455.34

Riley must invest a present value of $3,455.34 to achieve a future value of $4,000.00 in three years.

This calculation is again made much easier by using the appropriate table. In Table 3, we look down the 5 percent column until we reach three periods and find the factor .864. This factor, when multiplied by $1, gives the present value of $1 to be received three years from now at 5 percent interest. Thus, we solve the problem as shown below.

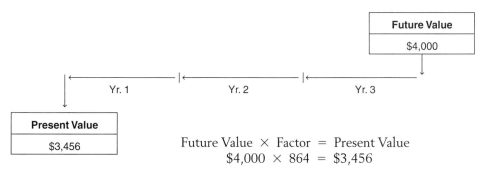

Future Value × Factor = Present Value
$4,000 × 864 = $3,456

Except for a rounding difference of $.66, this result is the same as the one above.

Table 3. Present Value of $1 to Be Received at the End of a Given Number of Time Periods

Periods	1%	2%	3%	4%	5%	6%	7%	8%	9%	10%
1	0.990	0.980	0.971	0.962	0.952	0.943	0.935	0.926	0.917	0.909
2	0.980	0.961	0.943	0.925	0.907	0.890	0.873	0.857	0.842	0.826
3	0.971	0.942	0.915	0.889	0.864	0.840	0.816	0.794	0.772	0.751
4	0.961	0.924	0.888	0.855	0.823	0.792	0.763	0.735	0.708	0.683
5	0.951	0.906	0.863	0.822	0.784	0.747	0.713	0.681	0.650	0.621
6	0.942	0.888	0.837	0.790	0.746	0.705	0.666	0.630	0.596	0.564
7	0.933	0.871	0.813	0.760	0.711	0.665	0.623	0.583	0.547	0.513
8	0.923	0.853	0.789	0.731	0.677	0.627	0.582	0.540	0.502	0.467
9	0.914	0.837	0.766	0.703	0.645	0.592	0.544	0.500	0.460	0.424
10	0.905	0.820	0.744	0.676	0.614	0.558	0.508	0.463	0.422	0.386

Source: Excerpt from Table 3 in the appendix on future value and present value tables.

PRESENT VALUE OF AN ORDINARY ANNUITY   It is often necessary to compute the present value of a series of receipts or payments. When we calculate the present value of equal amounts equally spaced over a period of time, we are computing the present value of an ordinary annuity.

For example, assume that Kathy Foster has sold a piece of property and is to receive $15,000 in three equal annual payments of $5,000, beginning one year from today. What is the present value of this sale, assuming a current interest rate of 5 percent? This present value may be computed by calculating a separate present value for each of the three payments (using Table 3) and summing the results, as shown in the table below.

Future Receipts (Annuity)			Present Value Factor at 5 Percent (from Table 3)	Present Value
Year 1	Year 2	Year 3		
$5,000			× .952 =	$ 4,760
	$5,000		× .907 =	4,535
		$5,000	× .864 =	4,320
Total Present Value				$13,615

The present value of this sale is $13,615. Thus, there is an implied interest cost (given the 5 percent rate) of $1,385 associated with the payment plan that allows the purchaser to pay in three installments.

We can make this calculation more easily by using Table 4. We look down the 5 percent column until we reach three periods and find the factor 2.723. This factor, when multiplied by $1, gives the present value of a series of three $1 payments (spaced one year apart) at compound interest of 5 percent. Thus, we solve the problem as shown below.

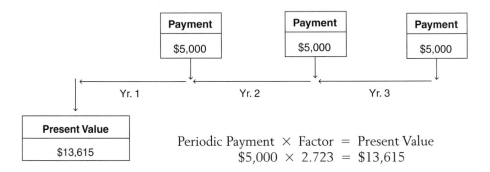

Periodic Payment × Factor = Present Value
$5,000 × 2.723 = $13,615

This result is the same as the one computed earlier.

Time Periods

In all of the previous examples, and in most other cases, the compounding period is one year, and the interest rate is stated on an annual basis. However, in each of the four tables, the left-hand column refers not to years but to periods. This wording is intended to accommodate compounding periods of less than one year. Savings accounts that record interest quarterly and bonds that pay interest semiannually are cases in which the compounding period is less than one year. To use the tables

Table 4. Present Value of an Ordinary Annuity of $1 Received Each Period for a Given Number of Time Periods

Periods	1%	2%	3%	4%	5%	6%	7%	8%	9%	10%
1	0.990	0.980	0.971	0.962	0.952	0.943	0.935	0.926	0.917	0.909
2	1.970	1.942	1.913	1.886	1.859	1.833	1.808	1.783	1.759	1.736
3	2.941	2.884	2.829	2.775	2.723	2.673	2.624	2.577	2.531	2.487
4	3.902	3.808	3.717	3.630	3.546	3.465	3.387	3.312	3.240	3.170
5	4.853	4.713	4.580	4.452	4.329	4.212	4.100	3.993	3.890	3.791
6	5.795	5.601	5.417	5.242	5.076	4.917	4.767	4.623	4.486	4.355
7	6.728	6.472	6.230	6.002	5.786	5.582	5.389	5.206	5.033	4.868
8	7.652	7.325	7.020	6.733	6.463	6.210	5.971	5.747	5.535	5.335
9	8.566	8.162	7.786	7.435	7.108	6.802	6.515	6.247	5.995	5.759
10	9.471	8.983	8.530	8.111	7.722	7.360	7.024	6.710	6.418	6.145

Source: Excerpt from Table 4 in the appendix on future value and present value tables.

in such cases, it is necessary to (1) divide the annual interest rate by the number of periods in the year, and (2) multiply the number of periods in one year by the number of years.

For example, assume that a $6,000 note is to be paid in two years and carries an annual interest rate of 8 percent. Compute the maturity (future) value of the note, assuming that the compounding period is semiannual. Before using the table, it is necessary to compute the interest rate that applies to each compounding period and the total number of compounding periods. First, the interest rate to use is 4 percent (8% annual rate ÷ 2 periods per year). Second, the total number of compounding periods is 4 (2 periods per year × 2 years). From Table 1, therefore, the maturity value of the note is computed as follows:

$$\text{Principal} \times \text{Factor} = \text{Future Value}$$
$$\$6,000 \times 1.170 = \$7,020$$

The note will be worth $7,020 in two years.

This procedure for determining the interest rate and the number of periods when the compounding period is less than one year may be used with all four tables.

Applications of Present Value to Accounting

The concept of present value is widely applicable in the discipline of accounting. Here, the purpose is to demonstrate its usefulness in some simple applications. In-depth study of present value is deferred to more advanced courses.

IMPUTING INTEREST ON NON-INTEREST-BEARING NOTES   Clearly there is no such thing as an interest-free debt, regardless of whether the interest rate is explicitly stated. The Accounting Principles Board has declared that when a long-term note does not explicitly state an interest rate (or if the interest rate is unreasonably low), a rate based on the normal interest cost of the company in question should be assigned, or imputed.[1]

The following example applies this principle. On January 1, 20x0, Gato purchased merchandise from Haines by issuing an $8,000 non-interest-bearing note due in two years. Gato can borrow money from the bank at 9 percent interest. Gato paid the note in full after two years.

Note that the $8,000 note represents partly a payment for merchandise and partly a payment of interest for two years. In recording the purchase and sale, it is necessary to use Table 3 to determine the present value of the note. The calculation follows.

$$\text{Future Payment} \times \text{Present Value Factor (9\%, 2 years)} = \text{Present Value}$$
$$\$8,000 \times .842 = \$6,736$$

The imputed interest cost is $1,264 ($8,000 − $6,736) and is recorded as a discount on notes payable in Gato's records and as a discount on notes receivable in Haines's records.

The entries necessary to record the purchase in the Gato records and the sale in the Haines records are as follows:

Gato Journal			Haines Journal		
Purchases	6,736		Notes Receivable	8,000	
Discount on			Discount on		
Notes Payable	1,264		Notes Receivable		1,264
Notes Payable		8,000	Sales		6,736

Gato: A = L + OE, − − +
Haines: A = L + OE, + + −

On December 31, 20x0, the adjustments to recognize the interest expense and interest income are as follows:

Gato Journal			Haines Journal		
Interest Expense	606.24		Discount on		
Discount on			Notes Receivable	606.24	
Notes Payable		606.24	Interest Income		606.24

Gato: A = L + OE, + −
Haines: A = L + OE, + +

The interest is calculated by multiplying the amount of the original purchase by the interest rate for one year ($6,736.00 × .09 = $606.24). When payment is made on December 31, 20x0, the following entries are made in the respective journals.

Gato Journal			Haines Journal		
Interest Expense	657.76		Discount on		
Notes Payable	8,000.00		Notes Receivable	657.76	
Discount on			Cash	8,000.00	
Notes Payable		657.76	Interest Income		657.76
Cash		8,000.00	Notes Receivable		8,000.00

Gato: A = L + OE, − + − −
Haines: A = L + OE, + + + −

The interest entries represent the remaining interest to be expensed or realized ($1,264 − $606.24 = $657.76). This amount approximates (because of rounding differences in the table) the interest for one year on the purchase plus last year's interest [($6,736 + $606.24) × .09 = $660.80].

VALUING AN ASSET   An asset is recorded because it will provide future benefits to the company that owns it. These future benefits are the basis for the definition of an asset. Usually, the purchase price of the asset represents the present value of these future benefits. It is possible to evaluate a proposed purchase price for an asset by comparing that price with the present value of the asset to the company.

For example, Sam Hurst is thinking of buying a new machine that will reduce his annual labor cost by $700 per year. The machine will last eight years. The interest rate that Hurst assumes for making managerial decisions is 10 percent. What is the maximum amount (present value) that Hurst should pay for the machine?

The present value of the machine to Hurst is equal to the present value of an ordinary annuity of $700 per year for eight years at compound interest of 10 percent. Using the factor from Table 4, we compute the value as follows:

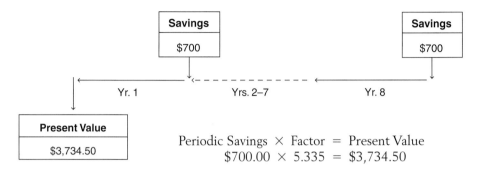

Periodic Savings × Factor = Present Value
$700.00 × 5.335 = $3,734.50

Hurst should not pay more than $3,734.50 for the new machine because this amount equals the present value of the benefits that will be received from owning the machine.

DEFERRED PAYMENT   A seller will sometimes agree to defer payment for a sale in order to encourage the buyer to make the purchase. This practice is common, for example, in the farm implement industry, where the farmer needs the equipment in the spring but cannot pay for it until the fall crop is in. Assume that Plains Implement Corporation sells a tractor to Dana Washington for $50,000 on February 1, agreeing to take payment ten months later, on December 1. When this type of agreement is made, the future payment includes not only the sales price of the tractor but also an implied (imputed) interest cost. If the prevailing annual interest rate for such transactions is 12 percent compounded monthly, the actual sale (purchase) price of the tractor would be the present value of the future payment, computed using the factor from Table 3 (10 periods, 1 percent), as follows:

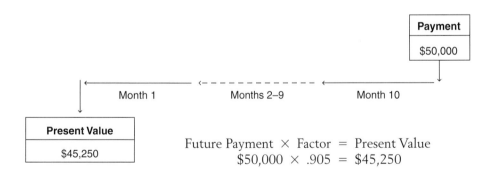

Future Payment × Factor = Present Value
$50,000 × .905 = $45,250

The purchase in Washington's records and the sale in Plains's records are recorded at the present value, $45,250. The balance consists of interest expense or interest income. The entries necessary to record the purchase in Washington's records and the sale in Plains's records are as follows:

	Washington Journal			Plains Journal			
A = L + OE	Feb. 1 Tractor	45,250		Accounts Receivable	45,250		A = L + OE
+ +	Accounts Payable		45,250	Sales		45,250	+ +
	Purchased tractor			Sold tractor			

When Washington pays for the tractor, the entries are as follows:

	Washington Journal			Plains Journal			
A = L + OE	Dec. 1	Accounts Payable	45,250		Cash	50,000		A = L + OE
− − −		Interest Expense	4,750		Accounts Receivable		45,250	− +
		Cash		50,000	Interest Income		4,750	+
		Paid on account, including imputed interest expense			Received on account from Washington, including imputed interest earned			

INVESTMENT OF IDLE CASH   Childware Corporation, a toy manufacturer, has just completed a successful fall selling season and has $10,000,000 in cash to invest for six months. The company places the cash in a money market account that is expected to pay 12 percent annual interest. Interest is compounded monthly and credited to the company's account each month. How much cash will the company have at the end of six months, and what entries will be made to record the investment and the monthly interest? The future value factor from Table 1 is based on six monthly periods of 1 percent (12 percent divided by 12 months), and the future value is computed as follows:

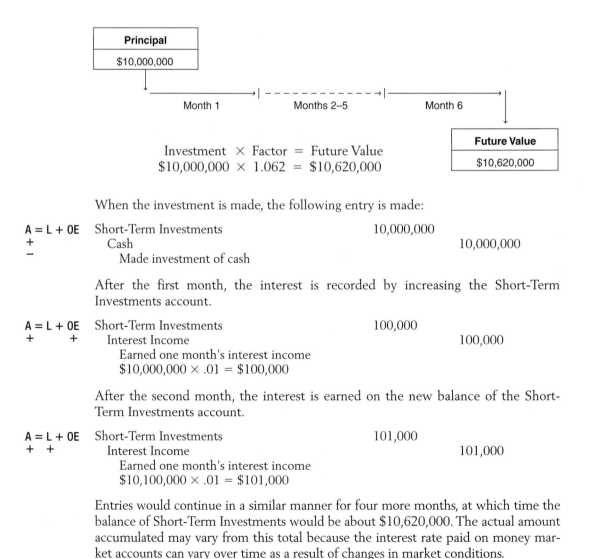

Investment × Factor = Future Value
$10,000,000 × 1.062 = $10,620,000

When the investment is made, the following entry is made:

A = L + OE	Short-Term Investments	10,000,000	
+	Cash		10,000,000
−	Made investment of cash		

After the first month, the interest is recorded by increasing the Short-Term Investments account.

A = L + OE	Short-Term Investments	100,000	
+ +	Interest Income		100,000
	Earned one month's interest income $10,000,000 × .01 = $100,000		

After the second month, the interest is earned on the new balance of the Short-Term Investments account.

A = L + OE	Short-Term Investments	101,000	
+ +	Interest Income		101,000
	Earned one month's interest income $10,100,000 × .01 = $101,000		

Entries would continue in a similar manner for four more months, at which time the balance of Short-Term Investments would be about $10,620,000. The actual amount accumulated may vary from this total because the interest rate paid on money market accounts can vary over time as a result of changes in market conditions.

ACCUMULATION OF A FUND When a company owes a large fixed amount due in several years, management would be wise to accumulate a fund with which to pay off the debt at maturity. Sometimes creditors, when they agree to provide a loan, require that such a fund be established. In establishing the fund, management must determine how much cash to set aside each period in order to pay the debt. The amount will depend on the estimated rate of interest the investments will earn. Assume that Vason Corporation agrees with a creditor to set aside cash at the end of each year to accumulate enough to pay off a $100,000 note due in five years. Since the first contribution to the fund will be made in one year, five annual contributions will be made by the time the note is due. Assume also that the fund is projected to earn 8 percent, compounded annually. The amount of each annual payment is calculated using Table 2 (5 periods, 8 percent), as follows:

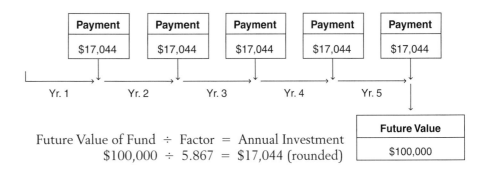

Future Value of Fund ÷ Factor = Annual Investment
$100,000 ÷ 5.867 = $17,044 (rounded)

Future Value
$100,000

Each year's contribution to the fund is $17,044, which is recorded as follows:

A = L + OE
+
−

Loan Repayment Fund	17,044	
Cash		17,044
Recorded annual contribution to loan repayment fund		

OTHER ACCOUNTING APPLICATIONS There are many other applications of present value in accounting, including accounting for installment notes, valuing a bond, and recording lease obligations. Present value is also applied in such areas as pension obligations; premium and discount on debt; depreciation of property, plant, and equipment; capital expenditure decisions; and generally any problem in which time is a factor.

EXERCISES

Tables 1 to 4 in the appendix on future value and present value tables may be used where appropriate to solve these exercises.

E 1.
Future Value Calculations

Wieland receives a one-year note for $3,000 that carries a 12 percent annual interest rate for the sale of a used car.

Compute the maturity value under each of the following assumptions: (1) The interest is simple interest. (2) The interest is compounded semiannually. (3) The interest is compounded quarterly. (4) The interest is compounded monthly.

E 2.
Future Value Calculations

Find the future value of (1) a single payment of $20,000 at 7 percent for ten years, (2) ten annual payments of $2,000 at 7 percent, (3) a single payment of $6,000 at 9 percent for seven years, and (4) seven annual payments of $6,000 at 9 percent.

E 3.
Future Value Calculations

Assume that $40,000 is invested today. Compute the amount that would accumulate at the end of seven years when the interest rate is (1) 8 percent compounded annually, (2) 8 percent compounded semiannually, and (3) 8 percent compounded quarterly.

Future Value Calculations

E 4. Calculate the accumulation of periodic payments of $1,000 made at the end of each of four years, assuming (1) 10 percent annual interest compounded annually, (2) 10 percent annual interest compounded semiannually, (3) 4 percent annual interest compounded annually, and (4) 16 percent annual interest compounded quarterly.

Future Value Applications

E 5. a. Two parents have $20,000 to invest for their child's college tuition, which they estimate will cost $40,000 when the child enters college twelve years from now.

Calculate the approximate rate of annual interest that the investment must earn to reach the $40,000 goal in twelve years. (**Hint:** Make a calculation; then use Table 1 in the appendix on future value and present value tables.)

b. Ted Pruitt is saving to purchase a summer home that will cost about $64,000. He has $40,000 now, on which he can earn 7 percent annual interest.

Calculate the approximate length of time he will have to wait to purchase the summer home. (**Hint:** Make a calculation; then use Table 1 in the appendix on future value and present value tables.)

Working Backward from a Future Value

E 6. Gloria Faraquez has a debt of $90,000 due in four years. She wants to save enough money to pay it off by making annual deposits in an investment account that earns 8 percent annual interest.

Calculate the amount she must deposit each year to reach her goal. (**Hint:** Use Table 2 in the appendix on future value and present value tables; then make a calculation.)

Determining an Advance Payment

E 7. Ellen Saber is contemplating paying five years' rent in advance. Her annual rent is $9,600.

Calculate the single sum that would have to be paid now for the advance rent, if we assume compound interest of 8 percent.

Present Value Calculations

E 8. Find the present value of (1) a single payment of $24,000 at 6 percent for twelve years, (2) twelve annual payments of $2,000 at 6 percent, (3) a single payment of $5,000 at 9 percent for five years, and (4) five annual payments of $5,000 at 9 percent.

Present Value of a Lump-Sum Contract

E 9. A contract calls for a lump-sum payment of $60,000. Find the present value of the contract, assuming that (1) the payment is due in five years, and the current interest rate is 9 percent; (2) the payment is due in ten years, and the current interest rate is 9 percent; (3) the payment is due in five years, and the current interest rate is 5 percent; and (4) the payment is due in ten years, and the current interest rate is 5 percent.

Present Value of an Annuity Contract

E 10. A contract calls for annual payments of $1,200. Find the present value of the contract, assuming that (1) the number of payments is seven, and the current interest rate is 6 percent; (2) the number of payments is fourteen, and the current interest rate is 6 percent; (3) the number of payments is seven, and the current interest rate is 8 percent; and (4) the number of payments is fourteen, and the current interest rate is 8 percent.

Non-Interest-Bearing Note

E 11. On January 1, 20x0, Pendleton purchased a machine from Leyland by signing a two-year, non-interest-bearing $32,000 note. Pendleton currently pays 12 percent interest to borrow money at the bank.

Prepare entries in Pendleton's and Leyland's journals to (1) record the purchase and the note, (2) adjust the accounts after one year, and (3) record payment of the note after two years (on December 31, 20x2).

Valuing an Asset for the Purpose of Making a Purchasing Decision

E 12. Oscaro owns a service station and has the opportunity to purchase a car wash machine for $30,000. After carefully studying projected costs and revenues, Oscaro estimates that the car wash machine will produce a net cash flow of $5,200 annually and will last for eight years. Oscaro believes that an interest rate of 14 percent is adequate for his business.

Calculate the present value of the machine to Oscaro. Does the purchase appear to be a correct business decision?

Deferred Payment

E 13. Johnson Equipment Corporation sold a precision tool machine with computer controls to Borst Corporation for $800,000 on January 1, agreeing to take payment nine months later, on October 1. Assuming that the prevailing annual interest rate for such a transaction is 16 percent compounded quarterly, what is the actual sale (purchase) price of the machine tool, and what journal entries will be made at the time of the purchase (sale) and at the time of the payment (receipt) on the records of both Borst and Johnson?

Investment of Idle Cash

E 14. Scientific Publishing Company, a publisher of college books, has just completed a successful fall selling season and has $5,000,000 in cash to invest for nine months, beginning on January 1. The company placed the cash in a money market account that is expected to pay 12 percent annual interest compounded monthly. Interest is credited to the company's account each month. How much cash will the company have at the end of nine months, and what entries are made to record the investment and the first two monthly (February 1 and March 1) interest amounts?

Accumulation of a Fund

E 15. Laferia Corporation borrowed $3,000,000 from an insurance company on a five-year note. Management agreed to set aside enough cash at the end of each year to accumulate the amount needed to pay off the note at maturity. Since the first contribution to the fund will be made in one year, four annual contributions are needed. Assuming that the fund will earn 10 percent compounded annually, how much will the annual contribution to the fund be (round to nearest dollar), and what will be the journal entry for the first contribution?

Negotiating the Sale of a Business

E 16. Horace Raftson is attempting to sell his business to Ernando Ruiz. The company has assets of $900,000, liabilities of $800,000, and owner's equity of $100,000. Both parties agree that the proper rate of return to expect is 12 percent; however, they differ on other assumptions. Raftson believes that the business will generate at least $100,000 per year of cash flows for twenty years. Ruiz thinks that $80,000 in cash flows per year is more reasonable and that only ten years in the future should be considered. Using Table 4 in the appendix on future value and present value tables, determine the range for negotiation by computing the present value of Raftson's offer to sell and of Ruiz's offer to buy.

ENDNOTE

1. Accounting Principles Board, *Opinion No. 21*, "Interest on Receivables and Payables" (New York: American Institute of Certified Public Accountants, 1971), par. 13.

APPENDIX D

Future Value and Present Value Tables

Table 1 provides the multipliers necessary to compute the future value of a *single* cash deposit made at the *beginning* of year 1. Three factors must be known before the future value can be computed: (1) the time period in years, (2) the stated annual rate of interest to be earned, and (3) the dollar amount invested or deposited.

EXAMPLE—TABLE 1   Determine the future value of $5,000 deposited now that will earn 9 percent interest compounded annually for five years. From Table 1, the necessary multiplier for five years at 9 percent is 1.539, and the answer is

$$\$5,000 \times 1.539 = \$7,695$$

Where r is the interest rate and n is the number of periods, the factor values for Table 1 are

$$\text{FV Factor} = (1 + r)^n$$

Situations requiring the use of Table 2 are similar to those requiring Table 1 except that Table 2 is used to compute the future value of a *series* of *equal* annual deposits at the end of each period.

Table 1. Future Value of $1 After a Given Number of Time Periods

Periods	1%	2%	3%	4%	5%	6%	7%	8%	9%	10%	12%	14%	15%
1	1.010	1.020	1.030	1.040	1.050	1.060	1.070	1.080	1.090	1.100	1.120	1.140	1.150
2	1.020	1.040	1.061	1.082	1.103	1.124	1.145	1.166	1.188	1.210	1.254	1.300	1.323
3	1.030	1.061	1.093	1.125	1.158	1.191	1.225	1.260	1.295	1.331	1.405	1.482	1.521
4	1.041	1.082	1.126	1.170	1.216	1.262	1.311	1.360	1.412	1.464	1.574	1.689	1.749
5	1.051	1.104	1.159	1.217	1.276	1.338	1.403	1.469	1.539	1.611	1.762	1.925	2.011
6	1.062	1.126	1.194	1.265	1.340	1.419	1.501	1.587	1.677	1.772	1.974	2.195	2.313
7	1.072	1.149	1.230	1.316	1.407	1.504	1.606	1.714	1.828	1.949	2.211	2.502	2.660
8	1.083	1.172	1.267	1.369	1.477	1.594	1.718	1.851	1.993	2.144	2.476	2.853	3.059
9	1.094	1.195	1.305	1.423	1.551	1.689	1.838	1.999	2.172	2.358	2.773	3.252	3.518
10	1.105	1.219	1.344	1.480	1.629	1.791	1.967	2.159	2.367	2.594	3.106	3.707	4.046
11	1.116	1.243	1.384	1.539	1.710	1.898	2.105	2.332	2.580	2.853	3.479	4.226	4.652
12	1.127	1.268	1.426	1.601	1.796	2.012	2.252	2.518	2.813	3.138	3.896	4.818	5.350
13	1.138	1.294	1.469	1.665	1.886	2.133	2.410	2.720	3.066	3.452	4.363	5.492	6.153
14	1.149	1.319	1.513	1.732	1.980	2.261	2.579	2.937	3.342	3.798	4.887	6.261	7.076
15	1.161	1.346	1.558	1.801	2.079	2.397	2.759	3.172	3.642	4.177	5.474	7.138	8.137
16	1.173	1.373	1.605	1.873	2.183	2.540	2.952	3.426	3.970	4.595	6.130	8.137	9.358
17	1.184	1.400	1.653	1.948	2.292	2.693	3.159	3.700	4.328	5.054	6.866	9.276	10.760
18	1.196	1.428	1.702	2.026	2.407	2.854	3.380	3.996	4.717	5.560	7.690	10.580	12.380
19	1.208	1.457	1.754	2.107	2.527	3.026	3.617	4.316	5.142	6.116	8.613	12.060	14.230
20	1.220	1.486	1.806	2.191	2.653	3.207	3.870	4.661	5.604	6.728	9.646	13.740	16.370
21	1.232	1.516	1.860	2.279	2.786	3.400	4.141	5.034	6.109	7.400	10.800	15.670	18.820
22	1.245	1.546	1.916	2.370	2.925	3.604	4.430	5.437	6.659	8.140	12.100	17.860	21.640
23	1.257	1.577	1.974	2.465	3.072	3.820	4.741	5.871	7.258	8.954	13.550	20.360	24.890
24	1.270	1.608	2.033	2.563	3.225	4.049	5.072	6.341	7.911	9.850	15.180	23.210	28.630
25	1.282	1.641	2.094	2.666	3.386	4.292	5.427	6.848	8.623	10.830	17.000	26.460	32.920
26	1.295	1.673	2.157	2.772	3.556	4.549	5.807	7.396	9.399	11.920	19.040	30.170	37.860
27	1.308	1.707	2.221	2.883	3.733	4.822	6.214	7.988	10.250	13.110	21.320	34.390	43.540
28	1.321	1.741	2.288	2.999	3.920	5.112	6.649	8.627	11.170	14.420	23.880	39.200	50.070
29	1.335	1.776	2.357	3.119	4.116	5.418	7.114	9.317	12.170	15.860	26.750	44.690	57.580
30	1.348	1.811	2.427	3.243	4.322	5.743	7.612	10.060	13.270	17.450	29.960	50.950	66.210
40	1.489	2.208	3.262	4.801	7.040	10.290	14.970	21.720	31.410	45.260	93.050	188.900	267.900
50	1.645	2.692	4.384	7.107	11.470	18.420	29.460	46.900	74.360	117.400	289.000	700.200	1,084.000

Table 2. Future Value of $1 Paid in Each Period for a Given Number of Time Periods

Periods	1%	2%	3%	4%	5%	6%	7%	8%	9%	10%	12%	14%	15%
1	1.000	1.000	1.000	1.000	1.000	1.000	1.000	1.000	1.000	1.000	1.000	1.000	1.000
2	2.010	2.020	2.030	2.040	2.050	2.060	2.070	2.080	2.090	2.100	2.120	2.140	2.150
3	3.030	3.060	3.091	3.122	3.153	3.184	3.215	3.246	3.278	3.310	3.374	3.440	3.473
4	4.060	4.122	4.184	4.246	4.310	4.375	4.440	4.506	4.573	4.641	4.779	4.921	4.993
5	5.101	5.204	5.309	5.416	5.526	5.637	5.751	5.867	5.985	6.105	6.353	6.610	6.742
6	6.152	6.308	6.468	6.633	6.802	6.975	7.153	7.336	7.523	7.716	8.115	8.536	8.754
7	7.214	7.434	7.662	7.898	8.142	8.394	8.654	8.923	9.200	9.487	10.090	10.730	11.070
8	8.286	8.583	8.892	9.214	9.549	9.897	10.260	10.640	11.030	11.440	12.300	13.230	13.730
9	9.369	9.755	10.160	10.580	11.030	11.490	11.980	12.490	13.020	13.580	14.780	16.090	16.790
10	10.460	10.950	11.460	12.010	12.580	13.180	13.820	14.490	15.190	15.940	17.550	19.340	20.300
11	11.570	12.170	12.810	13.490	14.210	14.970	15.780	16.650	17.560	18.530	20.650	23.040	24.350
12	12.680	13.410	14.190	15.030	15.920	16.870	17.890	18.980	20.140	21.380	24.130	27.270	29.000
13	13.810	14.680	15.620	16.630	17.710	18.880	20.140	21.500	22.950	24.520	28.030	32.090	34.350
14	14.950	15.970	17.090	18.290	19.600	21.020	22.550	24.210	26.020	27.980	32.390	37.580	40.500
15	16.100	17.290	18.600	20.020	21.580	23.280	25.130	27.150	29.360	31.770	37.280	43.840	47.580
16	17.260	18.640	20.160	21.820	23.660	25.670	27.890	30.320	33.000	35.950	42.750	50.980	55.720
17	18.430	20.010	21.760	23.700	25.840	28.210	30.840	33.750	36.970	40.540	48.880	59.120	65.080
18	19.610	21.410	23.410	25.650	28.130	30.910	34.000	37.450	41.300	45.600	55.750	68.390	75.840
19	20.810	22.840	25.120	27.670	30.540	33.760	37.380	41.450	46.020	51.160	63.440	78.970	88.210
20	22.020	24.300	26.870	29.780	33.070	36.790	41.000	45.760	51.160	57.280	72.050	91.020	102.400
21	23.240	25.780	28.680	31.970	35.720	39.990	44.870	50.420	56.760	64.000	81.700	104.800	118.800
22	24.470	27.300	30.540	34.250	38.510	43.390	49.010	55.460	62.870	71.400	92.500	120.400	137.600
23	25.720	28.850	32.450	36.620	41.430	47.000	53.440	60.890	69.530	79.540	104.600	138.300	159.300
24	26.970	30.420	34.430	39.080	44.500	50.820	58.180	66.760	76.790	88.500	118.200	158.700	184.200
25	28.240	32.030	36.460	41.650	47.730	54.860	63.250	73.110	84.700	98.350	133.300	181.900	212.800
26	29.530	33.670	38.550	44.310	51.110	59.160	68.680	79.950	93.320	109.200	150.300	208.300	245.700
27	30.820	35.340	40.710	47.080	54.670	63.710	74.480	87.350	102.700	121.100	169.400	238.500	283.600
28	32.130	37.050	42.930	49.970	58.400	68.530	80.700	95.340	113.000	134.200	190.700	272.900	327.100
29	33.450	38.790	45.220	52.970	62.320	73.640	87.350	104.000	124.100	148.600	214.600	312.100	377.200
30	34.780	40.570	47.580	56.080	66.440	79.060	94.460	113.300	136.300	164.500	241.300	356.800	434.700
40	48.890	60.400	75.400	95.030	120.800	154.800	199.600	259.100	337.900	442.600	767.100	1,342.000	1,779.000
50	64.460	84.580	112.800	152.700	209.300	290.300	406.500	573.800	815.100	1,164.000	2,400.000	4,995.000	7,218.000

EXAMPLE—TABLE 2   What will be the future value at the end of 30 years if $1,000 is deposited each year on January 1, beginning in one year, assuming 12 percent interest compounded annually? The required multiplier from Table 2 is 241.3, and the answer is

$$\$1,000 \times 241.3 = \$241,300$$

The factor values for Table 2 are

$$FVa\ Factor = \frac{(1 + r)^n - 1}{r}$$

Table 3. Present Value of $1 to Be Received at the End of a Given Number of Time Periods

Periods	1%	2%	3%	4%	5%	6%	7%	8%	9%	10%	12%
1	0.990	0.980	0.971	0.962	0.952	0.943	0.935	0.926	0.917	0.909	0.893
2	0.980	0.961	0.943	0.925	0.907	0.890	0.873	0.857	0.842	0.826	0.797
3	0.971	0.942	0.915	0.889	0.864	0.840	0.816	0.794	0.772	0.751	0.712
4	0.961	0.924	0.888	0.855	0.823	0.792	0.763	0.735	0.708	0.683	0.636
5	0.951	0.906	0.883	0.822	0.784	0.747	0.713	0.681	0.650	0.621	0.567
6	0.942	0.888	0.837	0.790	0.746	0.705	0.666	0.630	0.596	0.564	0.507
7	0.933	0.871	0.813	0.760	0.711	0.665	0.623	0.583	0.547	0.513	0.452
8	0.923	0.853	0.789	0.731	0.677	0.627	0.582	0.540	0.502	0.467	0.404
9	0.914	0.837	0.766	0.703	0.645	0.592	0.544	0.500	0.460	0.424	0.361
10	0.905	0.820	0.744	0.676	0.614	0.558	0.508	0.463	0.422	0.386	0.322
11	0.896	0.804	0.722	0.650	0.585	0.527	0.475	0.429	0.388	0.350	0.287
12	0.887	0.788	0.701	0.625	0.557	0.497	0.444	0.397	0.356	0.319	0.257
13	0.879	0.773	0.681	0.601	0.530	0.469	0.415	0.368	0.326	0.290	0.229
14	0.870	0.758	0.661	0.577	0.505	0.442	0.388	0.340	0.299	0.263	0.205
15	0.861	0.743	0.642	0.555	0.481	0.417	0.362	0.315	0.275	0.239	0.183
16	0.853	0.728	0.623	0.534	0.458	0.394	0.339	0.292	0.252	0.218	0.163
17	0.844	0.714	0.605	0.513	0.436	0.371	0.317	0.270	0.231	0.198	0.146
18	0.836	0.700	0.587	0.494	0.416	0.350	0.296	0.250	0.212	0.180	0.130
19	0.828	0.686	0.570	0.475	0.396	0.331	0.277	0.232	0.194	0.164	0.116
20	0.820	0.673	0.554	0.456	0.377	0.312	0.258	0.215	0.178	0.149	0.104
21	0.811	0.660	0.538	0.439	0.359	0.294	0.242	0.199	0.164	0.135	0.093
22	0.803	0.647	0.522	0.422	0.342	0.278	0.226	0.184	0.150	0.123	0.083
23	0.795	0.634	0.507	0.406	0.326	0.262	0.211	0.170	0.138	0.112	0.074
24	0.788	0.622	0.492	0.390	0.310	0.247	0.197	0.158	0.126	0.102	0.066
25	0.780	0.610	0.478	0.375	0.295	0.233	0.184	0.146	0.116	0.092	0.059
26	0.772	0.598	0.464	0.361	0.281	0.220	0.172	0.135	0.106	0.084	0.053
27	0.764	0.586	0.450	0.347	0.268	0.207	0.161	0.125	0.098	0.076	0.047
28	0.757	0.574	0.437	0.333	0.255	0.196	0.150	0.116	0.090	0.069	0.042
29	0.749	0.563	0.424	0.321	0.243	0.185	0.141	0.107	0.082	0.063	0.037
30	0.742	0.552	0.412	0.308	0.231	0.174	0.131	0.099	0.075	0.057	0.033
40	0.672	0.453	0.307	0.208	0.142	0.097	0.067	0.046	0.032	0.022	0.011
50	0.608	0.372	0.228	0.141	0.087	0.054	0.034	0.021	0.013	0.009	0.003

Table 3 is used to compute the value today of a single amount of cash to be received sometime in the future. To use Table 3, you must first know: (1) the time period in years until funds will be received, (2) the stated annual rate of interest, and (3) the dollar amount to be received at the end of the time period.

EXAMPLE—TABLE 3   What is the present value of $30,000 to be received 25 years from now, assuming a 14 percent interest rate? From Table 3, the required multiplier is .038, and the answer is

$$\$30,000 \times .038 = \$1,140$$

14%	15%	16%	18%	20%	25%	30%	35%	40%	45%	50%	Periods
0.877	0.870	0.862	0.847	0.833	0.800	0.769	0.741	0.714	0.690	0.667	1
0.769	0.756	0.743	0.718	0.694	0.640	0.592	0.549	0.510	0.476	0.444	2
0.675	0.658	0.641	0.609	0.579	0.512	0.455	0.406	0.364	0.328	0.296	3
0.592	0.572	0.552	0.516	0.482	0.410	0.350	0.301	0.260	0.226	0.198	4
0.519	0.497	0.476	0.437	0.402	0.328	0.269	0.223	0.186	0.156	0.132	5
0.456	0.432	0.410	0.370	0.335	0.262	0.207	0.165	0.133	0.108	0.088	6
0.400	0.376	0.354	0.314	0.279	0.210	0.159	0.122	0.095	0.074	0.059	7
0.351	0.327	0.305	0.266	0.233	0.168	0.123	0.091	0.068	0.051	0.039	8
0.308	0.284	0.263	0.225	0.194	0.134	0.094	0.067	0.048	0.035	0.026	9
0.270	0.247	0.227	0.191	0.162	0.107	0.073	0.050	0.035	0.024	0.017	10
0.237	0.215	0.195	0.162	0.135	0.086	0.056	0.037	0.025	0.017	0.012	11
0.208	0.187	0.168	0.137	0.112	0.069	0.043	0.027	0.018	0.012	0.008	12
0.182	0.163	0.145	0.116	0.093	0.055	0.033	0.020	0.013	0.008	0.005	13
0.160	0.141	0.125	0.099	0.078	0.044	0.025	0.015	0.009	0.006	0.003	14
0.140	0.123	0.108	0.084	0.065	0.035	0.020	0.011	0.006	0.004	0.002	15
0.123	0.107	0.093	0.071	0.054	0.028	0.015	0.008	0.005	0.003	0.002	16
0.108	0.093	0.080	0.060	0.045	0.023	0.012	0.006	0.003	0.002	0.001	17
0.095	0.081	0.069	0.051	0.038	0.018	0.009	0.005	0.002	0.001	0.001	18
0.083	0.070	0.060	0.043	0.031	0.014	0.007	0.003	0.002	0.001		19
0.073	0.061	0.051	0.037	0.026	0.012	0.005	0.002	0.001	0.001		20
0.064	0.053	0.044	0.031	0.022	0.009	0.004	0.002	0.001			21
0.056	0.046	0.038	0.026	0.018	0.007	0.003	0.001	0.001			22
0.049	0.040	0.033	0.022	0.015	0.006	0.002	0.001				23
0.043	0.035	0.028	0.019	0.013	0.005	0.002	0.001				24
0.038	0.030	0.024	0.016	0.010	0.004	0.001	0.001				25
0.033	0.026	0.021	0.014	0.009	0.003	0.001					26
0.029	0.023	0.018	0.011	0.007	0.002	0.001					27
0.026	0.020	0.016	0.010	0.006	0.002	0.001					28
0.022	0.017	0.014	0.008	0.005	0.002						29
0.020	0.015	0.012	0.007	0.004	0.001						30
0.005	0.004	0.003	0.001	0.001							40
0.001	0.001	0.001									50

The factor values for Table 3 are

$$\text{PV Factor} = (1 + r)^{-n}$$

Table 3 is the reciprocal of Table 1.

Table 4 is used to compute the present value of a *series* of *equal* annual cash flows.

EXAMPLE—TABLE 4   Arthur Howard won a contest on January 1, 2002, in which the prize was $30,000, the money was payable in 15 annual installments of $2,000 every December 31, beginning in 2002. Assuming a 9 percent interest rate, what is

Table 4. Present Value of $1 Received Each Period for a Given Number of Time Periods

Periods	1%	2%	3%	4%	5%	6%	7%	8%	9%	10%	12%
1	0.990	0.980	0.971	0.962	0.952	0.943	0.935	0.926	0.917	0.909	0.893
2	1.970	1.942	1.913	1.886	1.859	1.833	1.808	1.783	1.759	1.736	1.690
3	2.941	2.884	2.829	2.775	2.723	2.673	2.624	2.577	2.531	2.487	2.402
4	3.902	3.808	3.717	3.630	3.546	3.465	3.387	3.312	3.240	3.170	3.037
5	4.853	4.713	4.580	4.452	4.329	4.212	4.100	3.993	3.890	3.791	3.605
6	5.795	5.601	5.417	5.242	5.076	4.917	4.767	4.623	4.486	4.355	4.111
7	6.728	6.472	6.230	6.002	5.786	5.582	5.389	5.206	5.033	4.868	4.564
8	7.652	7.325	7.020	6.733	6.463	6.210	5.971	5.747	5.535	5.335	4.968
9	8.566	8.162	7.786	7.435	7.108	6.802	6.515	6.247	5.995	5.759	5.328
10	9.471	8.983	8.530	8.111	7.722	7.360	7.024	6.710	6.418	6.145	5.650
11	10.368	9.787	9.253	8.760	8.306	7.887	7.499	7.139	6.805	6.495	5.938
12	11.255	10.575	9.954	9.385	8.863	8.384	7.943	7.536	7.161	6.814	6.194
13	12.134	11.348	10.635	9.986	9.394	8.853	8.358	7.904	7.487	7.103	6.424
14	13.004	12.106	11.296	10.563	9.899	9.295	8.745	8.244	7.786	7.367	6.628
15	13.865	12.849	11.938	11.118	10.380	9.712	9.108	8.559	8.061	7.606	6.811
16	14.718	13.578	12.561	11.652	10.838	10.106	9.447	8.851	8.313	7.824	6.974
17	15.562	14.292	13.166	12.166	11.274	10.477	9.763	9.122	8.544	8.022	7.120
18	16.398	14.992	13.754	12.659	11.690	10.828	10.059	9.372	8.756	8.201	7.250
19	17.226	15.678	14.324	13.134	12.085	11.158	10.336	9.604	8.950	8.365	7.366
20	18.046	16.351	14.878	13.590	12.462	11.470	10.594	9.818	9.129	8.514	7.469
21	18.857	17.011	15.415	14.029	12.821	11.764	10.836	10.017	9.292	8.649	7.562
22	19.660	17.658	15.937	14.451	13.163	12.042	11.061	10.201	9.442	8.772	7.645
23	20.456	18.292	16.444	14.857	13.489	12.303	11.272	10.371	9.580	8.883	7.718
24	21.243	18.914	16.936	15.247	13.799	12.550	11.469	10.529	9.707	8.985	7.784
25	22.023	19.523	17.413	15.622	14.094	12.783	11.654	10.675	9.823	9.077	7.843
26	22.795	20.121	17.877	15.983	14.375	13.003	11.826	10.810	9.929	9.161	7.896
27	23.560	20.707	18.327	16.330	14.643	13.211	11.987	10.935	10.027	9.237	7.943
28	24.316	21.281	18.764	16.663	14.898	13.406	12.137	11.051	10.116	9.307	7.984
29	25.066	21.844	19.189	16.984	15.141	13.591	12.278	11.158	10.198	9.370	8.022
30	25.808	22.396	19.600	17.292	15.373	13.765	12.409	11.258	10.274	9.427	8.055
40	32.835	27.355	23.115	19.793	17.159	15.046	13.332	11.925	10.757	9.779	8.244
50	39.196	31.424	25.730	21.482	18.256	15.762	13.801	12.234	10.962	9.915	8.305

the present value of Mr. Howard's prize on January 1, 2002? From Table 4, the required multiplier is 8.061, and the answer is:

$$\$2,000 \times 8.061 = \$16,122$$

The factor values for Table 4 are

$$\text{PVa Factor} = \frac{1 - (1 + r)^{-n}}{r}$$

Table 4 is the columnar sum of Table 3. Table 4 applies to *ordinary annuities*, in which the first cash flow occurs one time period beyond the date for which the present value is to be computed.

14%	15%	16%	18%	20%	25%	30%	35%	40%	45%	50%	Periods
0.877	0.870	0.862	0.847	0.833	0.800	0.769	0.741	0.714	0.690	0.667	1
1.647	1.626	1.605	1.566	1.528	1.440	1.361	1.289	1.224	1.165	1.111	2
2.322	2.283	2.246	2.174	2.106	1.952	1.816	1.696	1.589	1.493	1.407	3
2.914	2.855	2.798	2.690	2.589	2.362	2.166	1.997	1.849	1.720	1.605	4
3.433	3.352	3.274	3.127	2.991	2.689	2.436	2.220	2.035	1.876	1.737	5
3.889	3.784	3.685	3.498	3.326	2.951	2.643	2.385	2.168	1.983	1.824	6
4.288	4.160	4.039	3.812	3.605	3.161	2.802	2.508	2.263	2.057	1.883	7
4.639	4.487	4.344	4.078	3.837	3.329	2.925	2.598	2.331	2.109	1.922	8
4.946	4.772	4.607	4.303	4.031	3.463	3.019	2.665	2.379	2.144	1.948	9
5.216	5.019	4.833	4.494	4.192	3.571	3.092	2.715	2.414	2.168	1.965	10
5.453	5.234	5.029	4.656	4.327	3.656	3.147	2.752	2.438	2.185	1.977	11
5.660	5.421	5.197	4.793	4.439	3.725	3.190	2.779	2.456	2.197	1.985	12
5.842	5.583	5.342	4.910	4.533	3.780	3.223	2.799	2.469	2.204	1.990	13
6.002	5.724	5.468	5.008	4.611	3.824	3.249	2.814	2.478	2.210	1.993	14
6.142	5.847	5.575	5.092	4.675	3.859	3.268	2.825	2.484	2.214	1.995	15
6.265	5.954	5.669	5.162	4.730	3.887	3.283	2.834	2.489	2.216	1.997	16
6.373	6.047	5.749	5.222	4.775	3.910	3.295	2.840	2.492	2.218	1.998	17
6.467	6.128	5.818	5.273	4.812	3.928	3.304	2.844	2.494	2.219	1.999	18
6.550	6.198	5.877	5.316	4.844	3.942	3.311	2.848	2.496	2.220	1.999	19
6.623	6.259	5.929	5.353	4.870	3.954	3.316	2.850	2.497	2.221	1.999	20
6.687	6.312	5.973	5.384	4.891	3.963	3.320	2.852	2.498	2.221	2.000	21
6.743	6.359	6.011	5.410	4.909	3.970	3.323	2.853	2.498	2.222	2.000	22
6.792	6.399	6.044	5.432	4.925	3.976	3.325	2.854	2.499	2.222	2.000	23
6.835	6.434	6.073	5.451	4.937	3.981	3.327	2.855	2.499	2.222	2.000	24
6.873	6.464	6.097	5.467	4.948	3.985	3.329	2.856	2.499	2.222	2.000	25
6.906	6.491	6.118	5.480	4.956	3.988	3.330	2.856	2.500	2.222	2.000	26
6.935	6.514	6.136	5.492	4.964	3.990	3.331	2.856	2.500	2.222	2.000	27
6.961	6.534	6.152	5.502	4.970	3.992	3.331	2.857	2.500	2.222	2.000	28
6.983	6.551	6.166	5.510	4.975	3.994	3.332	2.857	2.500	2.222	2.000	29
7.003	6.566	6.177	5.517	4.979	3.995	3.332	2.857	2.500	2.222	2.000	30
7.105	6.642	6.234	5.548	4.997	3.999	3.333	2.857	2.500	2.222	2.000	40
7.133	6.661	6.246	5.554	4.999	4.000	3.333	2.857	2.500	2.222	2.000	50

An *annuity due* is a series of equal cash flows for N time periods, but the first payment occurs immediately. The present value of the first payment equals the face value of the cash flow; Table 4 then is used to measure the present value of N − 1 remaining cash flows.

EXAMPLE—TABLE 4   Determine the present value on January 1, 2002, of 20 lease payments; each payment of $10,000 is due on January 1, beginning in 2002. Assume an interest rate of 8 percent.

$$\text{Present Value} = \text{Immediate Payment} + \begin{cases} \text{Present Value of 19 Subsequent} \\ \text{Payments at 8\%} \end{cases}$$

$$= \$10,000 + (\$10,000 \times 9.604) = \$106,040$$

Company Name Index

Subject Index

Note: **Boldface** type indicates key terms.

Allowance for Uncollectible Accounts account, 399, 399–400, 401, 402–405
Allowance method, 399, 399–400
Allowance to Adjust Long-Term Investments to Market account, 815
Allowance to Adjust Short-Term Investments to Market account, 396
American Institute of Certified Public Accountants (AICPA), 26
  on acquisition cost of property, plant, and equipment, 474
  on depreciation, 476
  ethical code of, 27
  on inventory pricing, 431
  on matching rule application to inventories, 428
  on start-up costs, 225
  on stock dividends, 643
Amortization
  of bond discounts, 676–680
  of bond premiums, 681–684
Annual reports, 8, 48
  components of, 268–273
  for financial performance evaluation, 769–770
  length of, 226
  summary, 226
Annual Statement Studies, 771
Annuities. *See also* Ordinary annuities
  annuities due, 841
APB. *See* Accounting Principles Board (APB)
Articles of incorporation, 589
Asset(s), 16
  cash flows to, 717–718, 784, 784(exh.)
  on classified balance sheet, 230–231
  depreciable, disposal of, 481–485
  intangible, 231
  investment in partnership, 561
  liquid. *See* Short-term liquid assets
  long-term (fixed; long-lived; operating; plant; tangible). *See* Depreciation; Property, plant, and equipment
  net, 16
  noncash, issuance of stock for, 603
  other, 231
  preference as to, 599
  purchase by incurring liabilities, 18
  purchase with cash, 18
  short-term. *See* Short-term liquid assets
  valuing using present value, 828–829
  withdrawal by removing from partnership, 564–565
Asset impairment, 469
Asset turnover, 241, 781, 782(exh.)
Audit(s), 26

Audit committee, 589
Audit trails, 362
Authorization, as control activity, 349
Authorized stock, 592
Automated fiscal year-end accounting packages, 140
Available-for-sale securities, 397, 814
Average-cost method, 434
Average days' sales uncollected, 390
Average days' inventory on hand, 430, 780(exh.), **781**
Average days' payable, 516, 516–517, 780(exh.), **781**
Average days' sales collected, 780(exh.), **781**

Bad debts. *See* Uncollectible accounts
Bad Debts Expense account, 399–400, 401, 402–405
Balance(s), 55
  compensating, 392
  normal, 64
  trial. *See* Trial balance
Balance sheet(s), 23(exh.), **24**
  classified, 228, 229(exh.), 230–235
  consolidated, 269
  disclosure of bonds on, 672
  reading and graphing, 233(exh.), 233–235, 234(fig.)
Balance sheet accounts, analyzing changes in, 732–733
Balance Sheet columns
  under periodic inventory system, 194, 195(exh.), 196
  under perpetual inventory account, 192–193
Banking, 393
Bank loans, 519
Bank reconciliation, 357, 357–358
  illustration of, 358–359, 359(exh.)
  recording transactions after, 360
Bank statements, 355(fig.)
Bar codes, 178
Barron's magazine, 771
Base year, 773
Basic earnings per share, 637
Beginning inventory, 188
Betterments, 493
Boards of directors, 589
Bond(s), 671, 671–688
  amortizing discount on, 676–680
  amortizing premium on, 681–684
  balance sheet disclosure of, 672
  callable, 686
  conversion into common stock, 687–688
  convertible, 687–688
  costs of issuing, 675
  face interest rate and market interest rate and, 673–674
  interest rates on, 676
  issued at discount, 674, 676–680
  issued at face value, 673
  issued at premium, 674–675, 681–684

  long-term investments in, 814
  present value to value, 675–676
  prices of, in business publications, 673
  retirement of, 686–687
  sale between interest dates, 684–685, 685(fig.)
  secured and unsecured, 671
  statement of cash flows and, 727–729, 728(exh.)
  term and serial, 671–672
  year-end accrual for interest expense on, 685–686
  zero coupon, 677
Bond indentures, 671
Bonding, 350
Bond Interest Expense account, sale of bonds between interest dates and, 685
Bond issues, 671
Bonds Payable account
  changes in, analyzing, 733
  sale of bonds between interest dates and, 685
Bonuses, 561
  of chief executive officers, 7
  to new partners, 562–563
  to old partners, 561–562
Bookkeeping, 8
Book of original entry. *See* Journal(s)
Book value, 469, 645, 645–646
Book value per share, 645
Brand names, 488
B-to-B (business-to-business) transactions, 362
Budget(s), operating, 176
Budgeting, capital, 470–472
Buildings. *See also* Property, plant, and equipment
  acquisition cost of, 475
Bulletin boards, 311
Business(es), 5. *See also* Corporations; Management; Merchandising businesses; Partnership(s)
  forms of, 13–15, 14(table)
  goals, activities, and performance measures of, 5–7, 6(fig.)
  service, 174
  sole proprietorships, 14, 232
Business publications
  bond prices in, 673
  for financial performance evaluation, 771, 772(exh.), 773
Business-to-business (B-to-B) transactions, 362
Business transactions, 12. *See also* Purchase(s); Sale(s)
  analyzing and processing, 55–62, 57(fig.)
  business-to-business, 362
  electronic conduction of, 176
  internal control over, 351–357
  international, valuation of, 66
  as object of measurement, 12

take-home pay computation and, 530–531, 531(fig.)

Payroll liabilities, 522, 523(fig.), 524–525

Payroll register, 531, 532(exh.)

Peachtree Complete Accounting for Windows, 307, 308(fig.)

Pension contributions, withholding for, 524

Pension expense account, 693

Pension funds, 693

Pension plans, 692, 692–693

P/E (price/earnings) ratio, 593–594, 785, 785(exh.)

Percentage of net sales method, 400, 400–401, 403(fig.), 403–404

Performance evaluation, financial. *See* Financial performance evaluation

Performance measures, 7

Periodic inventory system, 177, 177–178, 187(exh.), 187–191, 188(fig.)

average-cost method under, 434

cost of goods sold under, 188

first-in, first-out method under, 434–435

last-in, first-out method under, 435–436, 436(fig.)

merchandise in transit under, 432, 432(fig.)

merchandise on hand not included in inventory under, 432

pricing inventory under, 431–436, 439(exh.), 439–444

purchases of merchandise under, 188–190

sales of merchandise and, 190–191

specific identification method under, 433–434

work sheet under, 194–197

Periodicity, 93

Permanent accounts, 134

Perpetual inventory system, 177, 183–186

credit card sales and, 186

inventory losses and, 186

inventory valuation under, 436–444, 438(fig.), 439(exh.)

purchases of merchandise and, 183–184

sales of merchandise and, 184–186

work sheet under, 191–193, 192(exh.)

Personal account. *See* Withdrawals account

Personnel procedures, internal control and, 350

Petty Cash account, 361, 362

Petty cash funds, 360, 360–362

disbursements from, 361, 361(fig.)

establishing, 360–361

reimbursing, 361–362

Petty cash vouchers, 161(fig.), **361**

Physical controls, internal control and, 349

Physical deterioration, 476

Physical inventory, 178

Plant and equipment, depreciation of, 100–101

Plant assets. *See* Property, plant, and equipment

Portfolios, 767

Post-closing trial balance, 143, 143(exh.)

Posting, 68

of cash payments journal, 324

to ledger, 68–69, 69(exh.)

Posting Reference (Post. Ref.) column

in cash receipts journal, 320, 324

in general ledger, 68, 69

in purchases journal, 317

in sales journal, 316

Potentially dilutive securities, 638

Preferred stock, 598, 598–600

Preferred Stock account, stock issuance and, 601

Premiums, 674

on bonds, 674–675

Prepaid expenses, 98, 98(fig.), 98–100

Present value, 824–826

accumulation of a fund and, 831

deferred payments and, 829–830

imputing interest on non-interest-bearing notes and, 827–828

investment of idle cash and, 830

of ordinary annuities, 826, 827(table), 840–841(table)

of single sum due in future, 825, 825(table)

tables of, 838–841(table)

to value bonds, 675–676

valuing assets using, 828–829

Price(s), call (redemption), 600, 686

Price/earnings (P/E) ratio, 593, 593–594, **785,** 785(exh.)

Principal, of bonds, payment of, 689–691, 690(table)

Principle of duality, 54

Production method, 478, 478–479, 480(fig.), 480–481, 481(fig.)

Product warranty liability, estimated, 527–528

Professional ethics, 27, 27–28

acquisition cost of long-term assets and, 475

confidentiality and, 325

data destruction and, 357

fraudulent financial reporting and, 228

internal control limitations and, 350

inventory accounting to manipulate income and, 443

management's responsibility for ethical reporting and, 227–228

manipulation of earnings and, 94

money laundering and, 393

payroll fraud and, 533

recognition, valuation, and classification and, 50

whistle-blowers and, 631

Profit(s), 92

economic, 781

gross, 181

Profitability, 6, 240

evaluation of, 240–245, 781–782, 782(exh.)

target level of, 244

Profitability management, 176, 177(exh.)

Profitability measurement, 92–95

accounting period issue and, 93

continuity issue and, 93–94

matching issue and, 94–95

net income and, 92–93

Profit margin, 241, 781, 782(exh.)

Promissory notes, 405. *See also* Notes receivable

maker of, 405

non-interest-bearing, imputing interest on, 827–828

payee of, 405

Property, plant, and equipment, 230. *See also* Long-term assets

acquisition cost of, 473–476

changes in, analyzing, 733

on classified balance sheet, 230–231

discarded, disposal of, 482

exchanges of, 483–485

sale for cash, 482–483

statement of cash flows and, 726–727

Property tax payable, estimated liability for, 526–527

Proprietorship. *See* Owner's equity

Purchase(s)

of assets by incurring liabilities, 18

of assets with cash, 18

cash payments for, 735–736

on credit, 189

foreign, 810

of interest from partner, 560–561

internal control of, 353–355(fig.), 356–357

of merchandise, 183–184, 189

net, 188

net cost of, 188

returns and allowances and, 184, 189, 190, 194, 197, 366

transportation costs on, 189

of treasury stock, 604–605

Purchase orders, 354–355(fig.), 356

Purchase requisitions, 354–355(fig.), 356

Purchases account

under periodic inventory system, 189, 194, 197

purchases discounts and, 198

Purchases discounts, 197, 197–198

Purchases Discounts account, 198

under periodic inventory system, 194

Purchases journal, 317, 317–319, 318(exh.), 319(exh.)

Purchases Returns and Allowances account, 189

Print and Electronic Supplements for Instructors

Instructor's Solutions Manual. The manual contains answers to all text exercises, problems, and skills development cases:

Electronic Solutions. This online resource, which contains solutions from the printed Instructor's Solutions Manual, allows instructors to manipulate the numbers in the classroom or to distribute solutions electronically.

Test Bank with Achievement Test Masters and Answers. This test bank provides more than 3,000 true-false, multiple choice, short essay, and critical thinking questions, as well as exercises and problems.

NEW! HMTesting Computerized Test Bank. This Windows- and Mac-based supplement allows instructors to create tests based on any combination of questions in the Test Bank.

NEW! HMClassPrep Instructor CD-ROM. This CD includes the complete Course Manual, the Solutions Manual (also available in print), selected Video Cases from the text, and Web links to the Accounting Transaction Tutor and other Web material.

NEW! Needles Accounting Resource Center Instructor Web Site. This site includes downloadable Teaching Transparencies, Electronic Solutions, PowerPoint slides, and links to other valuable text resources.

Teaching Transparency Masters. This online resource contains figures, tables, and learning objectives from the text, as well as supplementary material from outside the text.

Solutions Transparencies. More than 1,200 transparencies provide solutions for every exercise, problem, and case in the text, including the appendixes.

NEW! Blackboard Course Cartridges. These cartridges provide flexible, efficient, and creative ways to present learning materials and manage distance learning courses. Specific resources include chapter overviews, check figures for in-text problems, practice quizzes, PowerPoint slides, and Excel Solutions. In addition to course management benefits, instructors may make use of an electronic grade book, receive papers from students enrolled in the course via the Internet, and track student use of the communication and collaboration functions.

NEW! WebCT e-Packs. These e-packs provide instructors with a flexible, Internet-based education platform. The WebCT e-Packs come with a full array of features to enrich the online learning experience, including online quizzes, bulletin board, chat tool, whiteboard, and other functionality. The e-packs contain text-specific resources, including chapter overviews, check figures, practice quizzes, PowerPoint slides, and Excel Solutions.

PowerPoint Classroom Presentation Slides. This online lecture system offers 50-60 slides per chapter. The slides contain classroom presentation materials, discussion questions, figures, exhibits, and tables.

NEW! Video Cases. These videos accompany the in-text cases and provide real-world opportunities to reinforce key terms and concepts.

Practice Set Instructor's Solutions Manual. For each student practice set, there is a solutions manual for instructors.

Participate in Teaching Accounting Online

This online training course from Faculty Development Programs provides suggestions for integrating new technologies into accounting education. Available within Blackboard.com, the course includes the following modules: Designing Course Basics; Be the Student; Common Online Tools; Designing Teaching Strategies; Designing Learning Activities; Designing Outcomes Assessment; and Delivering a Course. For more information contact your Houghton Mifflin sales representative or our faculty services center at (800) 733.1717.